Contemporary Authors®

NEW REVISION SERIES

ISSN 0275-7176

Contemporary Authors®

A Bio-Bibliographical Guide to Current Writers in Fiction, General Nonfiction, Poetry, Journalism, Drama, Motion Pictures, Television, and Other Fields

NEW REVISION SERIES
volume 161

THOMSON
™
GALE

Detroit • New York • San Francisco • New Haven, Conn. • Waterville, Maine • London

THOMSON

GALE

Contemporary Authors, New Revision Series, Vol. 161

Project Editor
Amanda D. Sams

Editorial
Amy Elisabeth Fuller, Michelle Kazensky, Lisa
Kumar, Mary Ruby, Rob Russell

Composition and Electronic Capture
Gary Oudersluys

Manufacturing
Drew Kalasky

LIBRARY OF CONGRESS CATALOG CARD NUMBER 81-640179

ISBN-13: 978-0-7876-7915-6
ISBN-10: 0-7876-7915-1
ISSN 0275-7176

This title is also available as an e-book.
ISBN-13: 978-1-4144-2913-7
ISBN-10: 1-4144-2913-4
Contact your Gale Group sales representative for ordering information.

Printed in the United States of America
10 9 8 7 6 5 4 3 2 1

Contents

Indexing note: All *Contemporary Authors* entries are indexed in the *Contemporary Authors* cumulative index, which is published separately and distributed twice a year.

As always, the most recent Contemporary Authors cumulative index continues to be the user's guide to the location of an individual author's listing.

Preface

Contemporary Authors (*CA*) provides information on approximately 120,000 writers in a wide range of media, including:

- Current writers of fiction, nonfiction, poetry, and drama whose works have been issued by commercial publishers, risk publishers, or university presses (authors whose books have been published only by known vanity or author-subsidized firms are ordinarily not included)

- Prominent print and broadcast journalists, editors, photojournalists, syndicated cartoonists, graphic novelists, screenwriters, television scriptwriters, and other media people

- Notable international authors

- Literary greats of the early twentieth century whose works are popular in today's high school and college curriculums and continue to elicit critical attention

A *CA* listing entails no charge or obligation. Authors are included on the basis of the above criteria and their interest to *CA* users. Sources of potential listees include trade periodicals, publishers' catalogs, librarians, and other users.

How to Get the Most out of *CA*: Use the Index

The key to locating an author's most recent entry is the *CA* cumulative index, which is published separately and distributed twice a year. It provides access to *all* entries in *CA* and *Contemporary Authors New Revision Series* (*CANR*). Always consult the latest index to find an author's most recent entry.

For the convenience of users, the *CA* cumulative index also includes references to all entries in these Thomson Gale literary series: *African-American Writers, African Writers, American Nature Writers, American Writers, American Writers: The Classics, American Writers Retrospective Supplement, American Writers Supplement, Ancient Writers, Asian American Literature, Authors and Artists for Young Adults, Authors in the News, Beacham's Encyclopedia of Popular Fiction: Analyses, Beacham's Encyclopedia of Popular Fiction: Biography and Resources, Beacham's Guide to Literature for Young Adults, Beat Generation: A Gale Critical Companion, Bestsellers, Black Literature Criticism, Black Literature Criticism Supplement, Black Writers, British Writers, British Writers: The Classics, British Writers Retrospective Supplement, British Writers Supplement, Children's Literature Review, Classical and Medieval Literature Criticism, Concise Dictionary of American Literary Biography, Concise Dictionary of American Literary Biography Supplement, Concise Dictionary of British Literary Biography, Concise Dictionary of World Literary Biography, Contemporary American Dramatists, Contemporary Authors Autobiography Series, Contemporary Authors Bibliographical Series, Contemporary British Dramatists, Contemporary Canadian Authors, Contemporary Dramatists, Contemporary Literary Criticism, Contemporary Novelists, Contemporary Poets, Contemporary Popular Writers, Contemporary Southern Writers, Contemporary Women Dramatists, Contemporary Women Poets, Contemporary World Writers, Dictionary of Literary Biography, Dictionary of Literary Biography Documentary Series, Dictionary of Literary Biography Yearbook, DISCovering Authors, DISCovering Authors 3.0, DISCovering Authors: British Edition, DISCovering Authors: Canadian Edition, DISCovering Authors Modules, Drama Criticism, Drama for Students, Encyclopedia of World Literature in the 20th Century, Epics for Students, European Writers, Exploring Novels, Exploring Poetry, Exploring Short Stories, Feminism in Literature, Feminist Writers, Gay & Lesbian Literature, Guide to French Literature, Harlem Renaissance: A Gale Critical Companion, Hispanic Literature Criticism, Hispanic Literature Criticism Supplement, Hispanic Writers, International Dictionary of Films and Filmmakers: Writers and Production Artists, International Dictionary of Theatre: Playwrights, Junior DISCovering Authors, Latin American Writers, Latin American Writers Supplement, Latino and Latina Writers, Literature and Its Times, Literature and Its Times Supplement, Literature Criticism from 1400-1800, Literature of Developing Nations for Students, Major Authors and Illustrators for Children and Young Adults, Major Authors and Illustrators for Children and Young Adults Supplement, Major 21st Century Writers (eBook version), Major 20th-Century Writers, Modern American Women Writers, Modern Arts Criticism, Modern Japanese Writers, Mystery and Suspense Writers, Native North American Literature, Nineteenth-Century Literature Criticism, Nonfiction Classics for Students, Novels for Students, Poetry Criticism, Poetry for Students, Poets: American and British, Reference Guide to American Literature, Reference Guide to English Literature, Reference Guide to Short Fiction, Reference Guide to World Literature, Science Fiction Writers, Shakespearean Criticism, Shakespeare for Students, Shakespeare's Characters for Students, Short Stories for Students, Short Story Criticism, Something About the Author, Something About the Author Autobiography Series, St. James Guide to Children's Writers, St. James Guide to Crime & Mystery Writers, St. James Guide to Fantasy Writers, St. James Guide to Horror, Ghost & Gothic Writers, St. James Guide to Science Fiction Writers, St. James Guide to Young Adult Writers, Supernatural Fiction*

Writers, Twayne Companion to Contemporary Literature in English, Twayne's English Authors, Twayne's United States Authors, Twayne's World Authors, Twentieth-Century Literary Criticism, Twentieth-Century Romance and Historical Writers, Twentieth-Century Western Writers, William Shakespeare, World Literature and Its Times, World Literature Criticism, World Literature Criticism Supplement, World Poets, World Writing in English, Writers for Children, Writers for Young Adults, and *Yesterday's Authors of Books for Children.*

A Sample Index Entry:

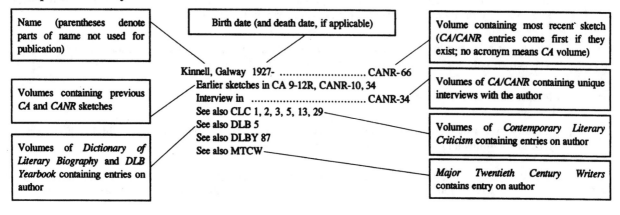

How Are Entries Compiled?

The editors make every effort to secure new information directly from the authors; listees' responses to our questionnaires and query letters provide most of the information featured in *CA*. For deceased writers, or those who fail to reply to requests for data, we consult other reliable biographical sources, such as those indexed in Thomson Gale's *Biography and Genealogy Master Index*, and bibliographical sources, including *National Union Catalog, LC MARC,* and *British National Bibliography*. Further details come from published interviews, feature stories, and book reviews, as well as information supplied by the authors' publishers and agents.

An asterisk (*) at the end of a sketch indicates that the listing has been compiled from secondary sources believed to be reliable but has not been personally verified for this edition by the author sketched.

What Kinds of Information Does An Entry Provide?

Sketches in *CA* contain the following biographical and bibliographical information:

- **Entry heading:** the most complete form of author's name, plus any pseudonyms or name variations used for writing

- **Personal information:** author's date and place of birth, family data, ethnicity, educational background, political and religious affiliations, and hobbies and leisure interests

- **Addresses:** author's home, office, or agent's addresses, plus e-mail and fax numbers, as available

- **Career summary:** name of employer, position, and dates held for each career post; resume of other vocational achievements; military service

- **Membership information:** professional, civic, and other association memberships and any official posts held

- **Awards and honors:** military and civic citations, major prizes and nominations, fellowships, grants, and honorary degrees

- **Writings:** a comprehensive, chronological list of titles, publishers, dates of original publication and revised editions, and production information for plays, television scripts, and screenplays

- **Adaptations:** a list of films, plays, and other media which have been adapted from the author's work

- **Sidelights:** a biographical portrait of the author's development; information about the critical reception of the author's works; revealing comments, often by the author, on personal interests, aspirations, motivations, and thoughts on writing

- **Interview:** a one-on-one discussion with authors conducted especially for *CA*, offering insight into authors' thoughts about their craft

- **Autobiographical essay:** an original essay written by noted authors for *CA*, a forum in which writers may present themselves, on their own terms, to their audience

- **Photographs:** portraits and personal photographs of notable authors

- **Biographical and critical sources:** a list of books and periodicals in which additional information on an author's life and/or writings appears

- **Obituary Notices** in *CA* provide date and place of birth as well as death information about authors whose full-length sketches appeared in the series before their deaths. The entries also summarize the authors' careers and writings and list other sources of biographical and death information.

Related Titles in the *CA* Series

Contemporary Authors Autobiography Series complements *CA* original and revised volumes with specially commissioned autobiographical essays by important current authors, illustrated with personal photographs they provide. Common topics include their motivations for writing, the people and experiences that shaped their careers, the rewards they derive from their work, and their impressions of the current literary scene.

Contemporary Authors Bibliographical Series surveys writings by and about important American authors since World War II. Each volume concentrates on a specific genre and features approximately ten writers; entries list works written by and about the author and contain a bibliographical essay discussing the merits and deficiencies of major critical and scholarly studies in detail.

Available in Electronic Formats

GaleNet. *CA* is available on a subscription basis through GaleNet, an online information resource that features an easy-to-use end-user interface, powerful search capabilities, and ease of access through the World-Wide Web. For more information, call 1-800-877-GALE.

Licensing. *CA* is available for licensing. The complete database is provided in a fielded format and is deliverable on such media as disk, CD-ROM, or tape. For more information, contact Thomson Gale's Business Development Group at 1-800-877-GALE, or visit us on our website at www.galegroup.com/bizdev.

Suggestions Are Welcome

The editors welcome comments and suggestions from users on any aspect of the *CA* series. If readers would like to recommend authors for inclusion in future volumes of the series, they are cordially invited to write the Editors at *Contemporary Authors*, Thomson Gale, 27500 Drake Rd., Farmington Hills, MI 48331-3535; or call at 1-248-699-4253; or fax at 1-248-699-8054.

Contemporary Authors Product Advisory Board

The editors of *Contemporary Authors* are dedicated to maintaining a high standard of excellence by publishing comprehensive, accurate, and highly readable entries on a wide array of writers. In addition to the quality of the content, the editors take pride in the graphic design of the series, which is intended to be orderly yet inviting, allowing readers to utilize the pages of *CA* easily and with efficiency. Despite the longevity of the *CA* print series, and the success of its format, we are mindful that the vitality of a literary reference product is dependent on its ability to serve its users over time. As literature, and attitudes about literature, constantly evolve, so do the reference needs of students, teachers, scholars, journalists, researchers, and book club members. To be certain that we continue to keep pace with the expectations of our customers, the editors of *CA* listen carefully to their comments regarding the value, utility, and quality of the series. Librarians, who have firsthand knowledge of the needs of library users, are a valuable resource for us. The *Contemporary Authors* Product Advisory Board, made up of school, public, and academic librarians, is a forum to promote focused feedback about *CA* on a regular basis. The seven-member advisory board includes the following individuals, whom the editors wish to thank for sharing their expertise:

- **Anne M. Christensen,** Librarian II, Phoenix Public Library, Phoenix, Arizona.

- **Barbara C. Chumard,** Reference/Adult Services Librarian, Middletown Thrall Library, Middletown, New York.

- **Eva M. Davis,** Youth Department Manager, Ann Arbor District Library, Ann Arbor, Michigan.

- **Adam Janowski, Jr.,** Library Media Specialist, Naples High School Library Media Center, Naples, Florida.

- **Robert Reginald,** Head of Technical Services and Collection Development, California State University, San Bernadino, California.

- **Stephen Weiner,** Director, Maynard Public Library, Maynard, Massachusetts.

International Advisory Board

Well-represented among the 120,000 author entries published in *Contemporary Authors* are sketches on notable writers from many non-English-speaking countries. The primary criteria for inclusion of such authors has traditionally been the publication of at least one title in English, either as an original work or as a translation. However, the editors of *Contemporary Authors* came to observe that many important international writers were being overlooked due to a strict adherence to our inclusion criteria. In addition, writers who were publishing in languages other than English were not being covered in the traditional sources we used for identifying new listees. Intent on increasing our coverage of international authors, including those who write only in their native language and have not been translated into English, the editors enlisted the aid of a board of advisors, each of whom is an expert on the literature of a particular country or region. Among the countries we focused attention on are Mexico, Puerto Rico, Spain, Italy, France, Germany, Luxembourg, Belgium, the Netherlands, Norway, Sweden, Denmark, Finland, Taiwan, Singapore, Malaysia, Thailand, South Africa, Israel, and Japan, as well as England, Scotland, Wales, Ireland, Australia, and New Zealand. The sixteen-member advisory board includes the following individuals, whom the editors wish to thank for sharing their expertise:

- **Lowell A. Bangerter,** Professor of German, University of Wyoming, Laramie, Wyoming.

- **Nancy E. Berg,** Associate Professor of Hebrew and Comparative Literature, Washington University, St. Louis, Missouri.

- **Frances Devlin-Glass,** Associate Professor, School of Literary and Communication Studies, Deakin University, Burwood, Victoria, Australia.

- **David William Foster,** Regent's Professor of Spanish, Interdisciplinary Humanities, and Women's Studies, Arizona State University, Tempe, Arizona.

- **Hosea Hirata,** Director of the Japanese Program, Associate Professor of Japanese, Tufts University, Medford, Massachusetts.

- **Jack Kolbert,** Professor Emeritus of French Literature, Susquehanna University, Selinsgrove, Pennsylvania.

- **Mark Libin,** Professor, University of Manitoba, Winnipeg, Manitoba, Canada.

- **C.S. Lim,** Professor, University of Malaya, Kuala Lumpur, Malaysia.

- **Eloy E. Merino,** Assistant Professor of Spanish, Northern Illinois University, DeKalb, Illinois.

- **Linda M. Rodríguez Guglielmoni,** Associate Professor, University of Puerto Rico—Mayagüez, Puerto Rico.

- **Sven Hakon Rossel,** Professor and Chair of Scandinavian Studies, University of Vienna, Vienna, Austria.

- **Steven R. Serafin,** Director, Writing Center, Hunter College of the City University of New York, New York City.

- **David Smyth,** Lecturer in Thai, School of Oriental and African Studies, University of London, England.

- **Ismail S. Talib,** Senior Lecturer, Department of English Language and Literature, National University of Singapore, Singapore.

- **Dionisio Viscarri,** Assistant Professor, Ohio State University, Columbus, Ohio.

- **Mark Williams,** Associate Professor, English Department, University of Canterbury, Christchurch, New Zealand.

CA Numbering System and Volume Update Chart

Occasionally questions arise about the *CA* numbering system and which volumes, if any, can be discarded. Despite numbers like "29-32R," "97-100" and "255," the entire *CA* print series consists of 340 physical volumes with the publication of *CA* Volume 255. The following charts note changes in the numbering system and cover design, and indicate which volumes are essential for the most complete, up-to-date coverage.

CA First Revision	• 1-4R through 41-44R (11 books) *Cover:* Brown with black and gold trim. There will be no further First Revision volumes because revised entries are now being handled exclusively through the more efficient *New Revision Series* mentioned below.
CA Original Volumes	• 45-48 through 97-100 (14 books) *Cover:* Brown with black and gold trim. 101 through 255 (155 books) *Cover:* Blue and black with orange bands. The same as previous *CA* original volumes but with a new, simplified numbering system and new cover design.
CA Permanent Series	• *CAP*-1 and *CAP*-2 (2 books) *Cover:* Brown with red and gold trim. There will be no further Permanent Series volumes because revised entries are now being handled exclusively through the more efficient *New Revision Series* mentioned below.
CA New Revision Series	• CANR-1 through CANR-161 (161 books) *Cover:* Blue and black with green bands. Includes only sketches requiring significant changes; **sketches are taken from any previously published CA, CAP, or CANR volume.**

If You Have:	You May Discard:
CA First Revision Volumes 1-4R through 41-44R and *CA Permanent Series* Volumes 1 and 2	*CA* Original Volumes 1, 2, 3, 4 and Volumes 5-6 through 41-44
CA Original Volumes 45-48 through 97-100 and 101 through 255	**NONE:** These volumes will not be superseded by corresponding revised volumes. Individual entries from these and all other volumes appearing in the left column of this chart may be revised and included in the various volumes of the *New Revision Series*.
CA New Revision Series Volumes *CANR*-1 through *CANR*-161	**NONE:** The *New Revision Series* does not replace any single volume of *CA*. Instead, volumes of *CANR* include entries from many previous *CA* series volumes. All *New Revision Series* volumes must be retained for full coverage.

A Sampling of Authors and Media People Featured in This Volume

Joseph Bruchac

Bruchac is a renowned Native-American storyteller who draws on his heritage to write original novels, picture books, poetry, and nonfiction. He is also an editor and publisher who has brought many other acclaimed Native-American authors into the public eye, and is nationally known as a live storyteller. His recent young-adult novel, *Wabi: A Hero's Tale,* portrays the story of a shapeshifting owl who falls in love with a local tribal girl, and who must travel on a dangerous quest to save his paramour's people.

Nora Ephron

Ephron is a novelist, journalist, and screenwriter known for her acerbic, often autobiographical style. She is best known for her numerous, successful romantic comedy screenplays, including those for *When Harry Met Sally , Sleepless in Seattle, You've Got Mail,* and *Bewitched.* She has also directed several of her own screenplays. Her most recent book, *I Feel Bad about My Neck: And Other Thoughts on Being a Woman,* is a series of essays exploring the challenges of growing old.

Laura Esquivel

Mexican author Esquivel gained international recognition with her first novel, *Como agua para chocolate (Like Water for Chocolate).* The book became a number-one best seller in Mexico, and the movie adaptation became one of the highest-grossing foreign films of the 1990s. Employing a strong sense of magical realism, Esquivel blends culinary knowledge, sensuality, and alchemy with fables and cultural lore to create her stories. Her most recent novel is titled *Malinche,* and it provides a fictional account of the legendary Mexican historical figure Malinalli, who served as the conquistador Cortez's mistress and guide.

Neal Gabler

Gabler is a historian who specializes in film and American culture. His first book, *An Empire of their Own: How the Jews Invented Hollywood,* focuses on the achievements of film moguls such as Samuel Goldwyn, Louis B. Mayer, and Jack Warner. The book won a prize from the Los Angeles Times Book Review in 1989. Gabler's most recent book is a highly-anticipated biography of Walt Disney, which closely examines Disney's powerful but often controversial impact on American culture.

Cormac McCarthy

McCarthy is often compared to other Southern-based writers such as William Faulkner, Carson McCullers, and Flannery O'Connor. Many of his novels are set in eastern Tennessee or the American Southwest, and his prose style has earned both praise for its lyricism and criticism for its ambitious construction. His 1992 novel *All the Pretty Horses* won the National Book Award, and is often considered his most accessible work. His most recent novel is titled *The Road,* and is a post-apocalyptic meditation on absolute morality and the struggle for survival. The book also won the 2007 Pulitzer Prize for fiction.

Charles Nicholl

British journalist Nicholl has written a wide range of nonfiction works that blend historical intrigue with arduous adventure. Much of Nicholl's work examines the Elizabethan era of England, including the book *The Reckoning: The Murder of Christopher Marlowe* and *The Creature in the Map: A Journey to El Dorado.* Nicholl has also traveled among drug smugglers in South America and prostitutes in Burma for his source material, and his work has earned him several awards, including the Hawthornden Prize. His most recent book is a biography titled *Leonardo da Vinci: Flights of the Mind.*

Steven D. Stark

Stark is a journalist, a well-known commentator for National Public Radio, and a frequent author of magazine articles for periodicals such as the *Atlantic Monthly* and the *New York Times.* His books explore the social impact of popular culture on society, including *Glued to the Set: The Sixty Television Shows and Events that Made Us Who We Are.* He has also profiled the effect of the Beatles on popular culture in his 2005 book *Meet the Beatles: A Cultural History of the Band that Shook Youth, Gender, and the World.*

Zhong Gui Tong

Chinese writer, editor, and novelist Tong, who writes under the pseudonym Su Tong, is probably best known in America as the author of the source material for director Zhang Yimou's film *Red Lantern.* Indeed, the movie received an Academy Award nomination in 1992. The novella "Wives and Concubines," which inspired the film, concerns a young woman who is compelled by circumstance to become the fourth concubine of an old and wealthy merchant. His most recent novel in English is titled *My Life as Emperor,* and it recounts the degeneration of a fictional Chinese prince when he ascends to the position of emperor and is corrupted by absolute power.

A

ALBAHARI, David 1948-

PERSONAL: Born March 15, 1948, in Pec, Serbia, Yugoslavia (now known as Serbia); permanent resident of Canada since October, 1994; son of Isak (a physician) and Mara Albahari; married Bojana Zivkovic (an English teacher), January 26, 1985; children: Natan, Rebeka. *Ethnicity:* "Jewish." *Education:* Studied English language and literature at the University of Belgrade, graduated in 1970; participated in the International Writing Program, University of Iowa, 1986. *Religion:* Jewish. *Hobbies and other interests:* Hiking, collecting stamps, rock and roll.

ADDRESSES: Home—Calgary, Alberta, Canada.

CAREER: Writer.

MEMBER: Serbian PEN Centre, Association of Literary Translators (Serbia).

AWARDS, HONORS: Ivo Andric Award, best collection of short stories published in Yugoslavia in 1982, 1983, for *Opis smrti;* Stanislav Vinaver Award for short stories, 1993, and Branko Copic Award for fiction, 1994, both for *Pelerina;* international writer in residence, Markin-Flanagan distinguished writers program, University of Calgary, 1994-95; Canada Council Arts grant, 1995; NIN Award, best novel published in Yugoslavia in 1996, 1997, for *Mamac.*

WRITINGS:

NOVELS

Sudija Dimitrijevic (title means "Judge Dimitrijevic"), Matica srpska (Novi Sad, Serbia), 1978.

Cink (title means "Zinc"), Filip Visnjic (Belgrade, Serbia), 1988.

Kratka knjiga (title means "Short Book"), Vreme knjige (Belgrade, Serbia), 1993.

Snezni covek, Vreme knjige (Belgrade, Serbia), 1995, translation by Ellen Elias-Bursac published as *Snow Man,* Douglas & McIntyre (Vancouver, British Columbia, Canada), 2005.

Mamac, Stubovi kulture (Belgrade, Serbia), 1996, translation by Peter Agnone published as *Bait,* Northwestern University (Evanston, IL), 2001.

Tsing, Northwestern University Press (Evanston, IL), 1997.

Gec i Majer, Stubovi Kulture (Belgrade, Serbia), 1998, translation by Ellen Elias-Bursac published as *Gotz and Meyer,* Harvill Press (London, England), 2004, Harcourt (Orlando, FL), 2005.

SHORT STORIES

Porodicno vreme (title means "Family Time"), Matica srpska (Novi Sad, Serbia) 1973.

Obicne price (title means "Ordinary Tales"), ICS (Belgrade, Serbia), 1978.

Opis smrti (title means "Description of Death"), Rad (Belgrade, Serbia), 1982.

Fras u supi (title means "Shock in the Shed"), Rad (Belgrade, Serbia), 1984.

Jednostavnost (title means "Simplicity"), Rad (Belgrade, Serbia), 1988.

Pelerina (title means "The Cloak"), KOS (Belgrade, Serbia), 1993.

Izabrane price (title means "Selected Stories"), Vreme knjige (Belgrade, Serbia), 1994.

Words Are Something Else: Writings from an Unbound Europe, translated by Ellen Elias-Bursac, edited by Tomislav Longinovic, foreword by Charles Simic, Northwestern University (Evanston, IL), 1996.

Neobicne Price, Stubovi Kulture (Belgrade, Serbia), 1999.

Drugi Jezik (title means "Second Language"), Stubovi Kulture (Belgrade, Serbia), 2003.

ESSAYS

Prepisivanje sveta (title means "Copying the World"), KOV (Vrsac, Serbia), 1996.

Teret: eseji, Forum Pisaca (Belgrade, Serbia), 2004.

NONFICTION

(With others) *Drugom stranom: Almanah novog talasa u SFRJ* (rock music history and criticism), Istrazivacko-izdavacki centar (New Belgrade, Serbia), 1983.

(Author of preface) Sabitaj Buki Finci, *Seacanja* (history), Jevrejski kulturni i humintarni fond (Belgrade, Serbia), 1995.

Contributor to periodicals, including *In Motion Magazine.* Work translated into other languages, including Hebrew, Polish, Italian, German, Slovak, and French.

EDITOR

Savremena svetska prica (title means "Contemporary World Short Stories"), Prosveta (Belgrade, Serbia), 1982.

(With Mihajlo Pantic) *Najbolje price 1989* (short stories), Decje novine (Gornji Milanovac, Serbia), 1989.

Savremena americka knjizevnost (title means "Contemporary American Literature"; fiction and poetry), Gradac (Cacak, Serbia), 1989.

Uhvati ritam: Rok I knjizevnost (title means "Catch the Rhythm: Rock and Literature"), Globus (Novi Sad, Serbia), 1990.

Najkrace price na svetu (title means "The Shortest Stories in the World"), Cicero (Belgrade, Serbia), 1993.

OTHER

Beschreibung des Todes: Erzahlungen, Wieser (Klagenfurt, Austria), 1993.

Sudija Dimitrijeviac, Narodna knj. Alfa (Belgrade, Serbia), 1996.

Mrak, Narodna knj. Alfa (Belgrade, Serbia), 1997.

Antologija Jevrejskih Pripovedaca, Srpska Knjizevna Zadruga (Belgrade, Serbia), 1998.

Svetski Putnik (fiction), Stubovi Kulture (Belgrade, Serbia), 2001.

Translator of books into Serbian, including *Him with His Foot in His Mouth,* by Saul Bellow; *Selected Stories,* by Peter Carey; *Pale Fire* and *Despair,* by Vladimir Nabokov; *In a Free State,* by V.S. Naipaul; *The Crying of Lot 49,* by Thomas Pynchon; *Fool for Love,* by Sam Shepard; *Selected Stories, In My Father's Court,* and *Selected Stories for Children,* by Isaac Bashevis Singer; and *Too Far to Go,* by John Updike.

SIDELIGHTS: Serbian writer David Albahari is among the literary lights of the former Yugoslavia. He has produced novels, short stories, and essays in addition to editing and translating other works. He won the 1983 Ivo Andric Award for the 1982 short story collection *Opis smrti,* a volume with "thought-provoking writing" that "is an amazing combination of the contemporary and the philosophical," praised Branko Mikasinovich in *World Literature Today.* Albahari writes in a postmodernist style, a style which often draws attention to the act of writing itself. "Postmodernists such as David Albahari ask whether there is a story to be told and whether one should write at all," observed Radmila Gorup in a *World Literature Today* review of Albahari's 1988 novel *Cink.*

In 1989 Albahari and Mihajlo Pantic compiled and edited a collection of short stories by Serbian and Croatian authors, *Najbolje price 1989,* a work labeled a "gallant effort" by *World Literature Today* contributor Vasa D. Mihailovich. This anthology includes pieces by writers written in traditional and experimental styles. "The overall impression gained from *Najbolje price 1989* is that the short story in Yugoslavia is very much alive and well," declared Mihailovich.

Translated into English by Ellen Elias-Bursac, Albahari's 1996 short story collection *Words Are Something Else: Writings from an Unbound Europe* consists of two parts. The first section, written in more traditional literary forms, contains stories featuring an elderly couple and their grown son and daughter, all of whom live in suburban Belgrade. The second half of the collection includes works in experimental forms and addresses aesthetic questions.

Describing the first section of *Words Are Something Else, Christian Science Monitor* contributor David Kirby observed that "there is a curious charm to this group of stories, stemming less from what the characters say than how they say it," noting that Albahari "finds the significant within the trivial." Later tales in *Words Are Something Else* include a man's recollections of childhood and a debate between a writer and his wife. In his review, Kirby wrote of both sections when he noted that "a little of this kind of thing—actually, a little of both kinds—goes a long way."

Albahari details his life in the former Yugoslavia and his immigration to Canada in the fictionalized memoir *Bait*. Written in one long paragraph, the book also deals with his mother, who became a Jewish convert just before the outbreak of World War II. *Booklist* contributor John Green felt this work presented "artful meditations on the meaning of otherness."

Albahari reached a large body of English-language readers with the publication of *Gotz and Meyer,* a novel dealing with the Holocaust in Serbia. In little less than a half year in 1942, over five thousand Serbian Jews were killed by the Nazis in mobile killing vans, trucks which ran the exhaust into the airtight compartment where the Jews were riding, supposedly being transported out of the country. *Gotz and Meyer* takes its name from two German soldiers—"embodiments of the banality of evil" according to a contributor for *Publishers Weekly*—who drove the truck in which a college professor's relations died. Now the professor is reconstructing the crime and has tracked down the names even of these drivers, obsessed with the deaths and the inability or unwillingness of others to prevent such mass crimes.

Again written in one long paragraph, the 168-page book is "simple and eloquent," as well as "stirring," according to *Booklist* contributor Hazel Rochman. Other reviewers had similar positive assessments. A *Kirkus Reviews* critic found the work a "brilliantly disturbing novel," while for *People* reviewer Francine Prose it was "haunting" and a "dazzling meditation on history, memory, identity and the nature of evil." The *Publishers Weekly* writer also commended *Gotz and Meyer,* as a "numbed but moving elegy." For Edward Cone, writing in *Library Journal,* the novel was an "impressive commentary," and for Alan Wall, writing in *European Judaism,* it was "compelling." Further praise came from *Guardian Online* critic Nicholas Lezard, who termed

the novel "unimprovable, astonishingly moving and intelligent," and from *San Francisco Chronicle Online* contributor Jason Thompson, who termed it "a masterful addition to the literature of the Holocaust and a fascinating philosophical meditation on that enormity."

Speaking with Mark Thwaite of *ReadySteadyBook.com,* Albahari explained the inspiration for the heavily-researched *Gotz and Meyer:* "I've known for years that the story about the holocaust of the Serbian Jewish community has never been told, and I was waiting for the right voice to tell it. I thought that it was, in a way, my duty to write about it, and not only about the story itself but also about how one deals with that terrible legacy today."

BIOGRAPHICAL AND CRITICAL SOURCES:

BOOKS

Albahari, David, *Bait,* translated by Peter Agnone, Northwestern University (Evanston, IL), 2001.

PERIODICALS

Booklist, February 15, 1998, Bosiljka Stevanovic, reviews of *Mamac* and *Snezni covek,* p. 992; June 1, 2001, John Green, review of *Bait,* p. 1834; September 1, 2005, Hazel Rochman, review of *Gotz and Meyer,* p. 57.
Christian Science Monitor, October 31, 1996, David Kirby, review of *Words Are Something Else: Writings from an Unbound Europe,* p. B1.
European Judaism, autumn, 2004, Alan Wall, review of *Gotz and Meyer,* p. 136.
Kirkus Reviews, June 15, 1996, review of *Words Are Something Else,* p. 858; September 15, 2005, review of *Gotz and Meyer,* p. 989.
Library Journal, November 1, 1996, review of *Words Are Something Else,* p. 109; August 1, 2005, Edward Cone, review of *Gotz and Meyer,* p. 64.
New York Times Book Review, August 25, 1996, review of *Words Are Something Else,* p. 19.
People, December 19, 2005, Francine Prose, review of *Gotz and Meyer,* p. 55.
Publishers Weekly, June 24, 1996, review of *Words Are Something Else,* pp. 55-56, September 19, 2005, review of *Gotz and Meyer,* p. 41.

Review of Contemporary Fiction, spring, 2006, Mark Axelrod, review of *Gotz and Meyer,* p. 147.

Washington Post Book World, September 8, 1996, review of *Words Are Something Else,* p. 12.

World Literature Today, autumn, 1987, Branko Mikasinovich, review of *Opis smrti,* p. 656; winter, 1990, Radmila Gorup, review of *Cink,* pp. 153-154; autumn, 1990, Vasa D. Mihailovich, review of *Najbolje price 1989,* p. 668; January-April, 2005, Marijeta Bozvic, review of *Drugi jezik,* p. 105.

ONLINE

Frugalfun.com, http://www.frugalfun.com/ (December 18, 2006), Wendy Boudling, "David Albahari."

Guardian Online, http://books.guardian.co.uk/ (January 22, 2005), Nicholas Lezard, review of *Gotz and Meyer.*

ReadySteadyBook.com, http://www.readysteadybook.com/ (October 8, 2005), Mark Thwaite, "Articles & Interviews: David Albahari."

San Francisco Chronicle Online, http://www.sfgate.com/ (December 25, 2005), Jason Thompson, "Faceless Evil Given a Name—or Names," review of *Gotz and Meyer.**

*   *   *

ALI, Tariq 1943-

PERSONAL: Born October 21, 1943, in Lahore, India (now Pakistan); son of Mazhar Ali Khan (a landowner) and Tahira Hyat. *Education:* Punjab University, B.A. (with honors), 1963; also attended Oxford University.

ADDRESSES: Home—London, England. *Office*—New Left Review, 6 Meard St., London W1F 0EG, England. *E-mail*—tariq.ali3@btinternet.com.

CAREER: Writer and political activist; leading member of Fourth International; Verso Books, London, England, editor. Fellow, Transnational Institute, Amsterdam, Netherlands.

WRITINGS:

NONFICTION; EXCEPT AS NOTED

(Compiler) *The Thoughts of Chairman Harold,* with illustrations by Ralph Steadman, Gnome Press (London, England), 1967.

(Editor) *The New Revolutionaries: A Handbook of the International Radical Left,* Morrow (New York, NY), 1969, published in England as *New Revolutionaries: Left Opposition,* Owen (London, England), 1969.

Pakistan: Military Rule or People's Power?, Morrow (New York, NY), 1970.

The Coming British Revolution, J. Cape (London, England), 1972.

(With Gerry Hedley) *Chile: Lessons of the Coup: Which Way to Workers' Power?,* International Marxist Group (London, England), 1974.

1968 and After: Inside the Revolution, Blond & Briggs (London, England), 1978.

Trotsky for Beginners, Pantheon (New York, NY), 1980.

Can Pakistan Survive?, Penguin (New York, NY), 1983.

(Editor) *What Is Stalinism?,* Penguin (New York, NY), 1984.

(Editor) *The Stalinist Legacy: Its Impact on Twentieth-Century World Politics,* Penguin (New York, NY), 1984.

An Indian Dynasty: The Story of the Nehru-Gandhi Family, Putnam (New York, NY), 1985, revised edition published as *The Nehrus and the Gandhis: an Indian Dynasty,* Picador (London, England), 2005.

Street Fighting Years: An Autobiography of the Sixties, Collins (London, England), 1987, Verso (New York, NY), 2005.

Revolution from Above: Where Is the Soviet Union Going?, Hutchinson (London, England), 1988.

(With Howard Brenton) *Moscow Gold,* Nick Hern (London, England), 1990.

Redemption (novel), Chatto & Windus (London, England), 1990.

Shadows of the Pomegranate Tree (novel), Chatto & Windus (London, England), 1992, Verso (New York, NY), 1993.

(Contributor) *21: 21 Picador Authors Celebrate 21 Years of International Writing,* Picador (London, England), 1993.

(With Susan Watkins) *1968—Marching in the Streets,* Free Press (New York, NY), 1998.

(With Howard Brenton) *Ugly Rumours,* Nick Hern (London England), 1998.

Fear of Mirrors (novel), Dufour Editions (Chester Springs, PA), 1998.

The Book of Saladin (novel), Verso (London, England), 1999.

The Stone Woman (novel), Verso (London, England), 2000.

(Editor) *Masters of the Universe? NATO's Balkan Crusade,* Verso (London, England), 2000.

The Clash of Fundamentalisms: Crusades, Jihads and Modernity, Verso (London, England), 2002.

The Illustrious Corpse (play), Oberon (London, England), 2003.

Bush in Babylon: The Recolonisation of Iraq, Verso (New York, NY), 2003.

Rough Music: Blair/Bombs/Baghdad/London/Terror/, Verso (New York, NY), 2005.

(With David Barsamian) *Speaking of Empire and Resistance: Conversations with Tariq Ali,* New Press (New York, NY), 2005.

A Sultan in Palermo (novel), Verso (New York, NY), 2005.

Pirates of the Caribbean: Axis of Hope, Verso (New York, NY), 2006.

The Leopard and the Fox, Seagull Books (London, England), 2007.

The Dictatorship of Capital: Politics and Culture in the 21st Century, Verso (New York, NY), 2008.

Author, with Howard Brenton and Andy de la Tour, of *Snogging Ken* ("disposable theater" play); contributor to *New Left Review, Inprecor, New Statesman & Society, Monthly Review,* and *Red Weekly.* Member of editorial board, *Labour Focus on Eastern Europe* and *New Left Review.*

SIDELIGHTS: Tariq Ali is well known in Great Britain as a political activist, social commentator, historian, filmmaker, and novelist. Born in what is now Pakistan, and educated in India and at Oxford University, Ali embraced leftist politics as a young man. In the late 1960s he was an active radical in London, protesting his country's involvement in the Vietnam War as well as its policies toward the Soviet Union and other socialist nations. More recently he has written books and commentary about the ongoing political struggles in India and Pakistan, while continuing his sometimes-scathing criticism of the British government and what he sees as United States imperialism throughout the world, but especially in the Middle East.

Ali's nonfiction reflects the broad range of his interests. He has published first-hand accounts of life in the Soviet Union and in post-Soviet Russia, memoirs and studies of the student movement in the 1960s, simple explana-

tory texts on Stalinism and Trotskyism, and modern political histories of India and the Balkan crisis. In a *Monthly Review* piece on Ali's *Revolution from Above: Where Is the Soviet Union Going?,* Daniel Singer noted that the author "manages to pass on to the reader the excitement of a country where serious periodicals sell like hot cakes, where books, films, plays are political events, where people simultaneously discover their past and the art of political debate." Singer added that *Revolution from Above* "deserves to be read by all Western leftists interested in the fate of the Soviet Union. . . . Whether one agrees with [Ali] or not, his chapters raise all the issues the left must tackle: the resistance of bureaucracy, market and planning in a single state, the relevance of memory, the power to be granted to the Soviets, and, finally, Russians' relations with the outside world. Besides, the book is topical despite the furious pace of events."

The 1990s ushered in a new phase in Ali's writing career. He began to publish fiction that also illustrates his views of the world as a leftist and a historian. Four of his novels, *Shadows of the Pomegranate Tree, The Book of Saladin, The Stone Woman,* and *A Sultan in Palermo* address various aspects of Muslim empire-building in different historical eras. *Shadows of the Pomegranate Tree* centers on the fall of Islam in Spain. *The Book of Saladin* is a fictitious memoir dictated by the great ruler Salah-al-Din, who wrested Jerusalem from Christian control in the twelfth century. This work seeks to dismiss the European stereotype of Saladin as a ruthless and godless conqueror; indeed, *World Literature Today* critic Bruce King emphasized the novel's postcolonial sensibilities, observing that the book is "shaped by modern sensibilities as well as facts" that depict European Crusaders in a distinctly negative light while recounting the story with all the "excitement of an old Hollywood epic." A *Kirkus Reviews* correspondent declared that, in *The Book of Saladin,* "one is carried along by the sheer gallop of the storytelling and dead-on sense of time and place." *The Stone Woman* moves ahead to the end of the nineteenth century and views the decline of the Ottoman Empire through the eyes of one jaded family. A contributor to *Kirkus Reviews* deemed the novel "a richly woven historical tapestry." James Hopkin, in *New Statesman,* praised the "grace and guile" with which Ali constructs the narrative, and commended the novel as "enchanting" and "captivating."

Set in twelfth-century Sicily, *A Sultan in Palermo* examines the final months in the reign of the Sultan

Rujari, or King Roger, last in the line of a Norman family which had taken power from the Muslim rulers of Sicily a century earlier. The bishops are angry with Roger for surrounding himself by concubines, eunuchs, and Muslim intellectuals, and long for his death so that they can regain power. Told through the eyes of the twelfth-century celebrated geographer, Muhammad al-Idrisi, the novel "explores the struggles that face people living under occupation," as Liz Winer noted in a *Tikkun* review. Winer went on to comment, "Ali asks important questions like: when is rebellion not only justified but wise, and how does one survive without collaborating?" Reviewing the same novel in *Washington Report on Middle East Affairs*, Sara Powell had further praise for Ali's fiction, noting that his "works resemble a rich tapestry in which continuous threads of various hues—religion, love, politics—reflect the human condition." Originally conceived as a series of four novels dealing with Muslim history, Ali changed the "Islam Quartet" to the "Islam Quintet" after the events of September 11, 2001. Powell concluded: "Will the eagerly awaited fifth volume be set in contemporary times? This reader can't wait to find out."

Ali's other novels include *Redemption,* a comic account of political radicals in Eastern Europe attempting to cope with social and economic changes during the 1990s, and *Fear of Mirrors,* a candid portrayal of life in Germany since the nation's reunification. A *Publishers Weekly* contributor considered *Redemption* a "hilarious trip down memory lane" for readers familiar with the radical Left, but added that Ali makes the book surprisingly moving as well as satirical. Of *Fear of Mirrors,* *Booklist* correspondent David Cline wrote that the work "reveals a keen mind and strong political insight." A *Publishers Weekly* reviewer likewise considered the book "valuable . . . especially for those interested in the current thinking of the European [L]eft."

In the new millennium, Ali has continued to offer critiques of the British government and of other Western powers, primarily the United States. Fueled by the events of 9/11, Ali changed the direction of a book he was already at work on, publishing in 2002 *The Clash of Fundamentalisms: Crusades, Jihads and Modernity,* a scathing indictment of fundamentalism in both Islam and the Christian right as well as in U.S. imperialism. Ali explores events prior to September 11, 2001, and deals with the political history of Islam, its founding myths, its origins, its culture, its riches, and its divi-

sions. At the same time, he also takes to task the Western powers for their hegemonic policies vis-a-vis Islamic states in the last hundred years. According to Abigail B. Bakan, writing in *Labour/Le Travail,* "the bulk of the manuscript traces the various periods of collusion and conflict between U.S. imperialism and the dominant classes, or sections of classes, from Jerusalem to Pakistan, from Pakistan to Kashmir, from Afghanistan to India."

In his 2003 title, *Bush in Babylon: The Recolonisation of Iraq,* Ali again focuses on what he sees as wrong-minded and failed U.S. policies in the Middle East, this time critiquing the Second Iraq War from a leftist perspective. Similarly, in *Rough Music: Blair/Bombs/Baghdad/London/Terror/,* Ali calls for a rethinking of Britain's foreign policy. In particular, Ali postulates that the pro-American policies of Prime Minister Tony Blair have led to further destabilization in global security. As Tom Nairn noted in *Arena Magazine, Rough Music* "makes many points going beyond British culture, and invites wider speculation on the world of contemporary nationalism and ideologically motivated violence."

BIOGRAPHICAL AND CRITICAL SOURCES:

PERIODICALS

Arena Magazine, February-March, 2006, Tom Nairn, "The New Furies," review of *Rough Music: Blair/ Bombs/Baghdad/London/Terror,* p. 25.
Booklist, November 15, 1998, David Cline, review of *Fear of Mirrors,* p. 564.
Economist, April 29, 1989, "1,001 Slights," p. 92; August 19, 2000, "A Fictional Clash of Civilisations—On the Edge," p. 76.
Kirkus Reviews, September 15, 1998, review of *Fear of Mirrors;* November 1, 1998, review of *The Book of Saladin,* p. 1560; August 15, 2000, review of *The Stone Woman,* p. 1144.
Labour/Le Travail, fall, 2005, Abigail B. Bakan, "Imperialism and Its Discontents," review of *The Clash of Fundamentalisms: Crusades, Jihads and Modernity,* p. 269.
Middle East Quarterly, summer, 2004, Patrick Clawson, review of *Bush in Babylon: The Recolonisation of Iraq,* p. 82.
Monthly Review, October, 1989, Daniel Singer, review of *Revolution from Above: Where Is the Soviet Union Going?,* p. 61.

Nation, June 5, 1989, Boris Kagarlitsky, review of *Revolution from Above,* p. 765.

New Republic, May 27, 1985, Shiva Naipaul, review of *An Indian Dynasty: The Story of the Nehru-Gandhi Family,* p. 26.

New Statesman, January 8, 1999, Jane Jakeman, review of *The Book of Saladin,* p. 55; April 24, 2000, Nina Raine, interview with Tariq Ali, Howard Brenton, and Andy de la Tour, p. 43; September 11, 2000, James Hopkin, review of *The Stone Woman,* p. 56.

New York Times Book Review, April 21, 1985, William Borders, review of *An Indian Dynasty,* p. 25.

Publishers Weekly, October 18, 1991, review of *Redemption,* p. 50; October 12, 1998, reviews of *Fear of Mirrors* and *The Book of Saladin,* p. 59; June 26, 2000, review of *The Stone Woman.*

Reference & Research Book News, November, 2005, review of *Street Fighting Years: An Autobiography of the Sixties.*

Tikkun, July-August, 2005, Liz Winer, review of *A Sultan in Palermo,* p. 71.

Washington Report on Middle East Affairs, December, 2005, Sara Powell, review of *A Sultan in Palermo,* p. 70.

World Literature Today, winter, 2000, Bruce King, review of *The Book of Saladin,* p. 245.

ONLINE

British Council Online, http://www.contemporary writers.com/ (December 18, 2006), "Contemporary Writers: Tariq Ali."

Tariq Ali Home Page, http://www.tariqali.org (December 18, 2006).

University of California, Berkeley Institute of International Studies Web site, http://globetrotter. berkeley.edu/ (May 8, 2003), interview with Tariq Ali.*

*   *   *

ANTRIM, Donald 1959(?)-

PERSONAL: Born c. 1959 in New York, NY; grew up in Brooklyn, NY.

ADDRESSES: Home—New York, NY.

CAREER: Novelist.

AWARDS, HONORS: Nominated for PEN/Faulkner Award for Fiction, 1998, for *The Hundred Brothers;* named one of *New Yorker*'s "Twenty Writers for the Twenty-first Century," 1999; awarded fellowships from the National Endowment for the Arts, the John Simon Guggenheim Memorial Foundation, and the Dorothy and Lewis B. Cullman Center for Scholars and Writers at the New York Public Library.

WRITINGS:

Elect Mr. Robinson for a Better World (novel), Viking (New York, NY), 1993.

The Hundred Brothers (novel), Crown (New York, NY), 1997.

The Verificationist (novel), Bloomsbury (New York, NY), 2000.

The Afterlife (memoir), Farrar, Straus and Giroux (New York, NY), 2006.

Contributor to the *New Yorker.*

SIDELIGHTS: Donald Antrim, according to Eric Wittmershaus in an online *Flak* profile, "is regularly mentioned alongside postmodern heavyweights like Thomas Pynchon, David Foster Wallace and Donald Barthelme." Speaking to Wittmershaus, Antrim offhandedly remarked that receiving such accolades is exciting, "though I would say that I don't carry around praise or approbation for very long before I forget it all and feel lost and doomed as usual." Doomed, added Wittmershaus, "would be an apt description for the narrators of his three novels," which *New York Times* critic A.O. Scott described as "exercises in unfettered fabulation, at once wildly inventive and meticulously controlled."

Antrim's books, including *Elect Mr. Robinson for a Better World* and *The Hundred Brothers,* have been described by critics as darkly satirical. *Elect Mr. Robinson* tells of the title character's attempts to pacify the hallucinatory violence of a small town. In the *New York Times Book Review* Ed Weiner called Antrim "a writer of undeniable power and sensuality" whose "suburban gothic" style of novel contains characters "experiencing a winding of a breakdown." Critic Dominick Donald commented in the *Times Literary Supplement* that Antrim's "dispassionate narrative, eye for self-mocking jargon, neatly judged irony and multi-layered construction all work well on their own, but when put together, the layered narrative is obstructive, and the humour has no bite." In contrast, the novel was praised by a writer in the *New Yorker* as "richly funny, even whimsical, and bizarrely familiar."

Antrim's second novel, *The Hundred Brothers,* is literally the story of a clan of one hundred male siblings. "For mythic and satiric purposes," commented Hal Espen in the *New York Times Book Review,* the author "has concocted a fantastically large brood whose prodigious father is dead but still uninterred." The brothers, whose personalities vary to a wide degree, then join together to put to rest their father's remains. "Antrim is a fiercely intelligent writer," Espen concluded, "who maintains rigorous control over his material."

The Verificationist is narrated by Tom, "a clinical psychologist, faculty member at the Krakower Institute, advocate of its Young Women of Strength teen counseling program," and hapless organizer of a dinner for his colleagues at the local Pancake House, as Paul Maliszewski described it in *Review of Contemporary Fiction.* Not much for Tom comes easily, even a query as to the health of his wife sends him into internal conflict: "Why was I unable to respond with a simple, perfunctory answer to this meaningless, polite question? It was because I was intuitively aware that Escobar wanted to make love to my wife."

A "comedy of bad manners," as *Time* critic R.Z. Sheppard labeled it, *The Verificationist* has Tom spitting water at his psychologist peers, propping trash cans against their office doors, and causing a scene at the Pancake House. Antrim "is a manic prose stylist," declared a *Publishers Weekly* critic, "capable of balancing lush pastoral descriptions with outrageous turbocharged riffs on sex and marriage and psychoanalysis." While Edward St. John, writing in *Library Journal,* thought the novel keeps readers "at arm's length" compared to *The Hundred Brothers,* Trevor Lewis, writing in London's *Sunday Times,* found more to recommend: "There is a method and a message here concerning the fragile emotional threads that tether us to reality and sanity." *The Verificationist,* concluded Andrew Roe in a *Salon.com* review, "goes further than Antrim's previous novels. It's more brazen, more shot through with the raw ache of relationships and the nakedness of emotional experience, with the tragedy of our inability to connect."

Antrim turns from fiction to memoir with his 2006 *The Afterlife,* the story of his controlling, alcoholic, and artistic mother who died of cancer in 2000. Antrim uses a "tone . . . of bitter, matter-of-fact comedy, or else a kind of deadpan at least as devastating as any howl of anguish," according to Scott, to recount memories of his eccentric uncle, his father who twice married Antrim's mother, his own reactions to being alternately ignored and smothered by his mother, and his efforts to come to terms with her death. Reviewers generally found that Antrim's memoir gave new life to that genre. Writing in *Newsweek,* Cathleen McGuigan found it a "stunning" as well as "heartbreaking" work, further praising Antrim as an "elegantly spare writer." Similarly, a *Kirkus Reviews* critic called *The Afterlife* an "elegant memoir" and a "luminous meditation on the past." Further praise came from *Booklist* contributor Donna Seaman, who termed *The Afterlife* "elegiac," and from Mark Alan Williams, writing in *Library Journal,* who felt the work was "poignant but also uplifting." For a *Publishers Weekly* reviewer, the same work was a "compassionate portrait of a flawed and destructive woman."

BIOGRAPHICAL AND CRITICAL SOURCES:

BOOKS

Antrim, Donald, *The Verificationist,* Bloomsbury (New York, NY), 2000.
Antrim, Donald, *The Afterlife,* Farrar, Straus and Giroux (New York, NY), 2006.

PERIODICALS

Booklist, April 15, 2006, Donna Seaman, review of *The Afterlife,* p. 20.
Hartford Courant (Hartford, CT), July 2, 2006, Carole Goldberg, review of *The Afterlife.*
Kirkus Reviews, March 1, 2006, review of *The Afterlife,* p. 215.
Library Journal, January, 2000, Edward St. John, review of *The Verificationist,* p. 154; April 15, 2006, Mark Alan Williams, review of *The Afterlife,* p. 75.
Newsweek, June 5, 2006, Cathleen McGuigan, "A Death in the Family," review of *The Afterlife,* p. 59.
New Yorker, October 25, 1993, review of *Elect Mr. Robinson for a Better World,* p. 131.

New York Times, June 18, 2006, A.O. Scott, review of *The Afterlife.*

New York Times Book Review, November 7, 1993, Ed Weiner, review of *Elect Mr. Robinson for a Better World,* p. 20; March 30, 1997, Hal Espen, review of *The Hundred Brothers;* February 20, 2000, Dwight Garner, "More Coffee? Wonder What She Meant by That?," p. 9; March 25, 2001, Scott Veale, review of *The Verificationist,* p. 28.

Publishers Weekly, January 17, 2000, review of *The Verificationist,* p. 43; March 6, 2005, review of *The Afterlife,* p. 55.

Review of Contemporary Fiction, summer, 2000, Paul Maliszewski, review of *The Verificationist,* p. 179.

Sunday Times (London, England), May 7, 2000, Trevor Lewis, review of *The Verificationist,* p. 50.

Time, February 28, 2000, R.Z. Sheppard, review of *The Verificationist,* p. 100.

Times Literary Supplement, September 24, 1993, Dominick Donald, review of *Elect Mr. Robinson for a Better World,* p. 20; April 21, 2001, Nick Laird, review of *The Verificationist,* p. 22.

Wall Street Journal, March 17, 2000, Andrew Horton, review of *The Verificationist,* p. W9.

ONLINE

Bold Type, http:// www.randomhouse.com/boldtype/ (February, 2000), Larry Weissman, "Donald Antrim."

Flak, http:// www.flakmag.com/ (April 1, 2000), Eric Wittmershaus, "Donald Antrim: An Interview."

Salon.com, http:// www.salon.com/ (February 2, 2000), Andrew Roe, "The Verificationist."*

*   *   *

AYLETT, Steve 1967-

PERSONAL: Born 1967, in Bromley, South London, England. *Education:* Left school at age seventeen.

ADDRESSES: Agent—MBA Literary Agents Ltd., 62 Grafton Way, London W1P 5LD, England.

CAREER: Writer, c. 1994—. Also worked in a book warehouse and in trade and law publishing. Also toured in the "Shroud" show, as a silent impersonator of the Shroud of Turin.

AWARDS, HONORS: Philip K. Dick Award finalist, 1998, for *Slaughtermatic;* Jack Trevor Story Prize, 2006.

WRITINGS:

FICTION

The Crime Studio (novel), Serif (London, England), 1994, Four Walls Eight Windows (New York, NY), 2001.

Bigot Hall: A Gothic Childhood (novel), Serif (London, England), 1995.

Slaughtermatic (novel), Four Walls Eight Windows (New York, NY), 1998.

Toxicology (short stories), Four Walls Eight Windows (New York, NY), 1999.

The Inflatable Volunteer (novel), Orion (London, England), 1999.

Atom (novel), Four Walls Eight Windows (New York, NY), 2000.

Only an Alligator: Accomplice 1 (novel), Orion (London, England), 2001.

Shamanspace, Codex Books (Hove, England), 2001.

The Velocity Gospel: Accomplice 2 (novel), Orion (London, England), 2002.

Dummyland: Accomplice 3 (novel), Orion (London, England), 2002.

Karloff's Circus: Accomplice 4 (novel), Orion (London, England), 2004.

Lint (novel), Thunder's Mouth Press (New York, NY), 2005.

(Editor) *And Your Point Is?,* Raw Dog Screaming Press (Hyattsville, MD), 2006.

Fain the Sorcerer, PS Publishing (Hornsea, East Yorkshire, England), 2006.

Also contributor of stories to anthologies, including *Disco Biscuits.* Aylett was recorded reading excerpts from *Toxicology, Atom, The Inflatable Volunteer, Bigot Hall,* and *Only an Alligator* for a CD titled *Staring Is Its Own Reward.* Also author of *Tao Te Jinx.* Aylett's work has been translated into Spanish, Czech, Italian, French, Japanese, German, Russian, and Greek.

SIDELIGHTS: Steve Aylett is an English writer who is known for his quirky, unsettling fiction, which includes both novels and short stories. His first book, *The Crime*

Studio, is an episodic novel that relates disturbing events in Beerlight, a dangerous, futuristic metropolis replete with unlikely criminals. *The Crime Studio* won praise from David V. Barrett, writing in *New Statesman & Society,* for its "sharpness" and "cohesion." Several years after its British publication, *The Crime Studio* was published in the United States. A *Publishers Weekly* reviewer felt that Aylett presents "a world devoid of morality and consequence" with "biting sarcasm and eloquent wit." For James Sallis, reviewing the work in the *Magazine of Fantasy and Science Fiction,* Aylett's noir futuristic glimpse was a "kind of floor plan for the ultimate America, where individualism has been taken to the limits, bulletproof underwear is openly on sale, and paranoia is regarded not as mental aberration but as standard urban equipment."

Aylett's second novel, *Bigot Hall: A Gothic Childhood,* was acknowledged by Barrett as "gloriously appalling." *Bigot Hall* exposes the tension, violence, and sexuality of seemingly mundane domestic life, and the novel's host of oddball characters include an incestuous brother and sister, a mother who cooks mysterious meals, a father who regularly dispenses banal insights, and a twisted, bothersome uncle. Speaking with Richard Marshall of *3AM Magazine,* Aylett further described the quirkiness of this novel which, though not published in the United States, has nonetheless become a minor cult classic here: "[*Bigot Hall* is] a gothic parody of this bunch of English people living in this smashed up manor house, with moose heads on the wall salivating and speaking and strange things like that. Fungal spores growing into monks. And half the building is closed off because it's full of nuns in welding masks and no one goes in there because of these nuns doing all the welding."

Aylett followed *Bigot Hall* with the novel *Slaughtermatic,* in which he returns to Beerlight, the setting of the earlier *The Crime Studio,* to chronicle a wrongheaded burglary and the chaos that ensues. In *Slaughtermatic,* bank robber Dante Cubit and his pill-popping companion, the Entropy Kid, conduct a heist in which Cubit, who masterminded the ultimately bungled caper, must resort to time travel as a means of avoiding capture. This time-travel escapade in turn leads to the duplication of Cubit, and this event results in still further complications, including the eventual necessity of destroying Cubit's second self. Plans go further awry, however, when the duplicate Cubit dodges death and

triggers a chase that involves a pair of racist police officers, a hired assassin, a conniving attorney, and Cubit's gun-wielding lover, Rosa Control. A critic at *Complete Review* claimed that *Slaughtermatic* "doesn't quite fit together as a novel," and a *Kirkus Reviews* critic described the novel as "a baffling exercise in virtual reality storytelling." The *Complete Review* critic conceded, however, that the novel is nonetheless "a hell of a ride, and worthwhile for all that," and even the *Kirkus Reviews* critic summarized the story as "droll, convoluted gamesmanship." John Mort, meanwhile, regarded *Slaughtermatic,* in his *Booklist* assessment, as "a mockery of a novel." But Michael Porter wrote in the *New York Times Book Review* that *Slaughtermatic* constitutes a "hyperkinetically violent, hilarious time-traveling crime caper." Porter added, "While the body count is high, the tone is anything but grim, thanks to Aylett's wickedly funny commentary." *Slaughtermatic* received attention as a finalist for the Philip K. Dick Award in 1998. Aylett also returns to his fictional locale of Beerlight in the novel *Atom.*

Among Aylett's other publications is *Toxicology,* a collection of short stories in a range of genres and experimental forms. The volume includes "If Armstrong Was Interesting," which lists various antics—donning Mickey Mouse ears, confessing to a crime—that astronaut Neil Armstrong might have initiated while becoming the first human being to step onto the surface of the moon, and "Gigantic," wherein mankind's heinous deeds—including the nuclear bombings of Japan—are punished by a storm in which corpses fall to earth like drops of rain. Daniel Reitz, writing in the *New York Times Book Review,* declared that Aylett showed himself guilty of "preening cleverness" with *Toxicology.* In addition, Reitz contended that "the banality of these stories defeats any points [Aylett] is trying to make."

Aylett once told *CA:* "It's less insulting to the reader to say something in a few words, like 'Progress accelerates downhill,' rather than spend an entire book saying that. I've seen *Toxicology* described as a liquid concentrate, which you're not supposed to drink without dilution, which is nice. Though I thought there were a few lighter stories in there too. I still just write the kind of books I'd like to read, that I'd like to find out there, and luckily enough people share that taste to be into them.

"Placing your head inside the reaction out there will certainly rot your brain, it's a displacement of energy.

Stay in your own body, you see? People may read one of my things and think it's all a particular way, for good or ill. But there's *Slaughtermatic,* which is fairly conventional old-time satire which nobody else does these days. Then there's *The Inflatable Volunteer,* which has no satire and is this big splurge of funny poetics. And later there's stuff that's unlike any of that because I've hardly started yet. So I have to disregard all this. My head stays here."

Aylett presents a fictional biography in his 2005 work, *Lint,* creating an antagonist reminiscent of science fiction writer Philip K. Dick. Aylett's protagonist is Jeff Lint, who, like Dick, was born in Chicago in 1928. His early career was in the pulp magazines, such as *Amazing Stories,* and then he spent much of his career manufacturing formula science fiction books and working in every genre one could think of, from short stories to comics. Carl Hays, writing in *Booklist,* concluded: "Readers with the taste for offbeat humor of the Douglas Adams, genre-spoofing variety should savor Aylett's latest." Similar praise came from a *Publishers Weekly* contributor who termed the book a "laugh-out-loud (mock) biography." Ed Parks, reviewing from *Village Voice,* was less impressed, however, feeling this faux biography fell short of being "mock comic"; instead, it merely has the "wobbly energy of a first draft." Rick Kleffel, writing for *Agony Magazine,* had a more positive assessment of *Lint,* concluding that it "is clearly the work of a mind in the advanced stages of both creative genius and insanity." For Kleffel, *Lint* "is every bit as brilliant, as hilarious, as pithy and as psychedelic as anything [Aylett] describes as being written by Lint."

Aylett further noted for *CA:* "I certainly don't think in words. I'm not sure that anyone does, really. Does anyone really think in sentences, like in films when you see someone thinking and you hear a voice-over? I don't anyway. I see stuff visually, as shapes, colours, textures and mechanisms sort of hanging there in space. If there's a hole in someone's argument I visually see a hole in it, in the armature and mass of the thing. Although it may take time to translate it all back into words and express them. And in writing I'll see the shape and colour of a sentence before I know what the words are in it. I'll see the shape of a whole book that way before it's written, and so far, the books have all ended up the way I saw them originally.

"I often feel people don't see past all the fireworks to what I'm talking about. Maybe sometime I'll do something with all the fireworks stripped out, no jokes, for the hard-of-reading—so they'll see what's always been there from the beginning.

"For postmodernist bullshit, the law is streets ahead. Anyone who's sat in on an adversarial court case, seen the mechanisms of the law, the subjectivity, the basic disengagement from fact, truth thrown to the wind, it really is like being in the mouth of madness. The person who's in the right might win the case, but not because he's in the right—just for other, quite surreally disassociated reasons. Reality gets the kiss-off at the start. The lawyer Harpoon Specter is great to write, he's a monster who operates in that totally unanchored, mutable alternate dimension. He says right at the start of *The Crime Studio,* 'The law is where reality goes to die'—he knows this."

BIOGRAPHICAL AND CRITICAL SOURCES:

PERIODICALS

Booklist, February 15, 1998, John Mort, review of *Slaughtermatic,* p. 990; June 1, 2005, Carl Hays, review of *Lint,* p. 1766.

Kirkus Reviews, February 15, 1998, review of *Slaughtermatic,* p. 208.

Library Journal, August 1, 2005, Jim Dwyer, review of *Lint,* p. 64.

Magazine of Fantasy and Science Fiction, May, 2002, James Sallis, review of *The Crime Studio,* p. 32.

New Statesman & Society, August 18, 1995, David V. Barrett, "Myths and Mirrors," p. 334.

New York Times Book Review, June 21, 1998, Michael Porter, "Pulp Fiction"; December 26, 1999, Daniel Reitz, review of *Toxicology,* p. 15.

Publishers Weekly, August 27, 2001, review of *The Crime Studio,* p. 56; May 16, 2005, review of *Lint,* p. 45.

Village Voice, March 16, 2006, Ed Park, "Dharma and Jeff," review of *Lint.*

ONLINE

3AM Magazine, http://www.3ammagazine.com/ (December 18, 2006), Richard Marshall, "An Interview with Steve Aylett."

Agony Magazine, http://trashotron.com/agony/ (April 19, 2005), Rick Kleffel, review of *Lint.*

Bookslut.com, http://www.bookslut.com/ (December 18, 2006), Justin Taylor, "An Interview with Steve Aylett."

Complete Review, http: //www.complete-review.com/ (May 9, 2001), review of *Slaughtermatic.*

Crime Time, http://www.crimetime.co.uk/ (December 18, 2006), Steve Aylett, "Atom by Atom."

FractalMatter.com, http://www.fractalmatter.com/ (December 18, 2006), Mo Ali, interview with Steve Aylett.

Goaste, http://davidguy.brinkster.net/goaste/ (December 18, 2006), "An Interview with Steve Aylett."

Steve Aylett Home Page, http://www.steveaylett.com (December 18, 2006).

Zone-SF.com, http://www.zone-sf.com/ (December 18, 2006), Steve Aylett, "Not Waiting for a Niche."

B

BANG, Mary Jo 1946-

PERSONAL: Born October 22, 1946, in Waynesville, MO; daughter of Eugene D. Ward and Helen Sergeant. *Education:* Northwestern University, B.A. (summa cum laude), 1971, M.A., 1975; Westminster University, London, B.A. (with distinction), 1989; Columbia University, M.F.A., 1998.

ADDRESSES: Home—St. Louis, MO. *Office*—Department of English, Writing Program, 1 Brookings Dr., Washington University, St. Louis, MO 63130. *E-mail*—maryjobang@aol.com.

CAREER: Poetry editor, *Boston Review,* 1995-2005; Washington University, St. Louis, MO, associate professor of English and director of the writing program.

MEMBER: PEN, National Book Critics Circle, Modern Language Association, Poetry Society of America, Academy of American Poets, Poets House.

AWARDS, HONORS: "Discovery"/*Nation* award, 1995; Katherine Bakeless Nason Prize for Poetry, Middlebury College, 1996, for *Apology for Want;* Great Lakes College Association New Writers Award, 1998; Hodder Fellowship, Princeton University, 1999; award from University of Georgia Contemporary Poets Series Competition, 2000; Alice Fay di Castagnola Award, Poetry Society of America, 2000, for *Louise in Love,* and 2005, for *Elegy;* Guggenheim Foundations fellow, 2004; also winner of the Pushcart Prize.

WRITINGS:

POETRY

Apology for Want, University Press of New England (Hanover, NH), 1997.

Louise in Love, Grove (New York, NY), 2001.
The Downstream Extremity of the Isle of Swans, University of Georgia Press (Athens, GA), 2001.
The Eye like a Strange Balloon: Poems, Grove (New York, NY), 2004.
Elegy, Graywolf Press (St. Paul, MN), 2007.

Contributor of poetry to periodicals, including the *New Republic, Yale Review, Kenyon Review, Volt, Paris Review, New Yorker,* and *New American Writing.* Bang's poetry has also been represented in several anthologies, including *Best American Poetry,* 2001, 2004, and 2007.

SIDELIGHTS: Mary Jo Bang is an acclaimed poet whose first collection, *Apology for Want,* received the Katherine Bakeless Nason Prize for first book of poetry in 1996. Her other works include *Louise in Love, The Downstream Extremity of the Isle of Swans,* and *The Eye like a Strange Balloon: Poems.*

There is a "quiet anarchy" in the poetry of *Apology for Want,* wrote Susan Conley in *Ploughshares.* Conley noted that the subject matter of the work is culturally American, the poetry's voice is "subversive and unsettling." Bang's poetry shows readers an avenue to "a new way of looking at what we've grown into," argued Frank Allen in the *American Book Review.*

Many critics were enthusiastic in their response to the collection. Allen found Bang's imagery contained "beautiful, difficult thought." Ellen Kaufman in *Library Journal* called the collection "allusive," arguing that *Apology for Want* demonstrates "occasional flashes of brilliance."

The poems in the collection *Louise in Love* focus on a woman named Louise and her family and friends, including her boyfriend Ham and her sister Lydia. The characters have not been completely fleshed out, and the adventures they embark on have a dream-like quality about them. The overall themes dealing with life and death are unraveled in verse some reviewers compared to noted writers John Keats and Virginia Woolf. "Her language is musical," observed Donna Seaman in a review for *Booklist*. Many reviewers lauded Bang's poetry in this collection, finding it fresh and surprising at every turn. Readers will "delight in Bang's unsparing . . . time-channeling," noted one *Publishers Weekly* contributor.

In 2004, Bang published the poetry collection *The Eye like a Strange Balloon*. Rather than focus on a specific set of characters like *Louise in Love,* this book consists of poems demonstrating ekphrasis, or poetry based on works of art. She describes in detail artwork by the likes of Redon Odilon, Max Ernst, Paula Rego, and more, to the point that the original subject matter is almost forgotten. Together the poems speak about the idea of art itself. Reviewers again praised Bang's efforts with this volume, citing the poetry's vividness and intricacy. This "superbly crafted work" comes alive on the page, wrote *Booklist* contributor Donna Seaman. Others carried similar sentiments in regard to the poet's deft use of language. There is "music in Bang's lines," noted E.M. Kaufman in a review for the *Library Journal.* In one review, *Antioch Review* contributor Malinda Markham simply asserted: "Read this book."

BIOGRAPHICAL AND CRITICAL SOURCES:

PERIODICALS

American Book Review, January, 1999, Frank Allen, review of *Apology for Want,* p. 28; July, 2002, review of *The Downstream Extremity of the Isle of Swans,* p. 28.

Antioch Review, summer, 2005, Malinda Markham, review of *The Eye like a Strange Balloon: Poems,* p. 600.

Booklist, January 1, 2001, Donna Seaman, review of *Louise in Love,* p. 902; November 15, 2004, Donna Seaman, review of *The Eye like a Strange Balloon,* p. 547.

Chelsea, 1998, review of *Apology for Want,* p. 128.

Kirkus Reviews, December 15, 2000, review of *Louise in Love,* p. 1728.

Library Journal, August, 1997, Ellen Kaufman, review of *Apology for Want,* p. 92; December, 2000, Ellen Kaufman, review of *Louise in Love,* p. 145; January 1, 2005, E.M. Kaufman, review of *The Eye like a Strange Balloon,* p. 116.

New York Times Book Review, March 4, 2001, David Kirby, review of *Louise in Love,* p. 23.

New Yorker, October 6, 1997, review of *Apology for Want,* p. 123.

Ploughshares, winter, 1997, Susan Conley, review of *Apology for Want,* p. 214; spring, 2003, Mary Jo Bang, "The Eye like a Strange Balloon Mounts Toward Infinity," p. 14.

Prairie Schooner, fall, 2003, Molly Bendall, review of *Louise in Love,* p. 185.

Publishers Weekly, July 28, 1997, review of *Apology for Want,* p. 71; November 6, 2000, review of *Louise in Love,* p. 84; October 18, 2004, review of *The Eye like a Strange Balloon,* p. 61.

Sewanee Review, summer, 2003, David Biespiel, "Free-verse Styles," p. 470.

ONLINE

Jacket Magazine, http://jacketmagazine.com/ (December 5, 2006), biography of Mary Jo Bang.

Powells.com, http://www.powells.com/ (December 5, 2006), Jill Owens, review of *Louise in Love.*

Washington University in St. Louis, Writing Program Web site, http://artsci.wustl.edu/ (December 5, 2006), biography of Mary Jo Bang.

*   *   *

BARNARD, F.M. 1921-
(Frederick Mechner Barnard)

PERSONAL: Born January 25, 1921, in Moravská Ostrava (now Ostrava), Czechoslovakia (now Czech Republic); naturalized British citizen; son of Albert (a merchant) and Gisela (an accountant) Mechner; married Rachel Zeisler, August, 1941 (died April 12, 1950); married Margot Auguste Martha Mann (an artist), October 27, 1951; children: Yvonne Ruth. *Ethnicity:* Czech/British. *Education:* Oxford University, B.A. (hons.), 1947, diploma of education, 1949, M.A., 1951; University of Leicester, Ph.D., 1962. *Hobbies and other interests:* Music, skating, skiing, bush walking.

ADDRESSES: Home—Miller Lake, Ontario, Canada.

CAREER: Worked at odd jobs in England, including farm worker in Tingrith, Bedfordshire, England, and shoe repairer in Oxford, England, 1939-43; lecturer in economics and department head at a grammar school in Leicester, England, 1948-59; University of Salford, Salford, England, senior lecturer in economics and political science and director of social studies, 1959-64; University of Saskatchewan, Saskatoon, Saskatchewan, Canada, associate professor, 1964-65, professor of political science, 1965-70, department chair, 1964-65; University of Western Ontario, London, Ontario, Canada, professor of politics, 1970-86, professor emeritus, 1986—. University of Leicester, England, extra-mural lecturer, 1948-59; leader of annual student tours of Europe. *Military service:* British Army, 1943-45; served in Europe; received King's Medal for loyal service.

AWARDS, HONORS: Fellow of German Academic Exchange Service, 1959, 1960, 1963-64; grant from German Federal Research Foundation, 1964; senior research fellow, Alexander von Humboldt Foundation, 1964, 1970, 1978; Canada Council, grants, 1965, 1967, fellowships, 1969-70, 1976-77; Social Sciences and Humanities Research Council of Canada, grant, 1981-82, fellowship, 1983-84; Prize for the Advancement of Herder Studies, International Herder Society, 2002.

WRITINGS:

Swischen Aufklärung und Politischer Romantik (title means "Between Enlightenment and Political Romanticism"), Erich Schmidt Verlag (Berlin, Germany), 1964.

Herder's Social and Political Thought, Clarendon Press (Oxford, England), 1965, 2nd edition, 1967.

(Translator, editor, and author of introduction) *Herder on Social and Political Culture,* Cambridge University Press (Cambridge, England), 1969.

Self-Direction and Political Legitimacy: Rousseau and Herder, Oxford University Press (New York, NY), 1988.

Pluralism, Socialism, and Political Legitimacy: Reflections on Opening Up Communism, Cambridge University Press (New York, NY), 1991.

Democratic Legitimacy, McGill-Queen's University Press (Ithaca, NY), 2001.

Herder on Nationality, Humanity, and History, McGill-Queen's University Press (Ithaca, NY), 2003.

Reason and Self-Enactment in History and Politics: Themes and Voices of Modernity, McGill-Queen's University Press (Ithaca, NY), 2006.

Contributor to books, including *Socialism with a Human Face: Slogan and Substance,* University of Saskatchewan Press (Saskatoon, Saskatchewan, Canada), 1973; *Culture and Legitimacy,* edited by Toivo Miljan, Wilfrid Laurier University (Waterloo, Ontario, Canada), 1982; *Sophia and Praxis: The Boundaries of Politics,* edited by J.M. Porter, Chatham House (Chatham, Ontario, Canada), 1984; *Modern Political Theory: From Hobbes to Marx,* Routledge (London, England), 1989; and *Czechoslovakia: Seventy Years,* Macmillan (London, England), 1991. Contributor of articles and reviews to journals in the United States, England, and Canada, including *Journal of the History of Ideas, American Political Science Review, Canadian Journal of Economics and Political Science, Political Studies, East Central Europe, History and Theory,* and *Modern Language Review.*

BIOGRAPHICAL AND CRITICAL SOURCES:

BOOKS

Porter, J.M., and Richard Vernon, editors, *Unity, Plurality, and Politics: Essays in Honour of F.M. Barnard,* Croom Helm (London, England), 1986.

*   *   *

BARNARD, Frederick Mechner
See BARNARD, F.M.

*   *   *

BEIGBEDER, Frédéric 1965-

PERSONAL: Born September 21, 1965, in Neuilly-sur-Seine, France; son of an employment counselor and a literary translator; divorced; children: Chlöe.

ADDRESSES: Agent—Editions Dargaud, 15/27 rue Moussorgski, Paris 75 018, France.

CAREER: Writer, journalist, literary critic, novelist, and actor. *Paris Première,* literary columnist, 1997—; Flammarion (publisher), literary director, beginning 2002. Formerly worked in advertising. Founder and editor of periodicals *Genereaux,* 1992—, *Deluxe,* 1993—, and

NRV, 1996—. Also founder and president of Caca's Club, 1984-93; founder and secretary-general of Prix de Flore, 1994—. Actor in films, including *Les Infortunes de la beauté,* 1999; *Restauratec* (television), 2002; *Imposture,* 2005; and *Comme t'y es belle!,* 2006. Previously worked in advertising, including for the firm Young & Rubicam.

WRITINGS:

Mémoires d'un jeune homme derange, Editions La Table Rond (Paris, France), 1990.
Vacances dans le coma, Editions Grasset (Paris, France), 1994.
L'amour dure trois ans, Editions Grasset (Paris, France), 1997.
Nouvelles sous ecstasy, Edition Gallimard (Paris France), 1999.
99 francs, Editions Grasset (Paris, France), 2000.
14,99 euros, Editions Grasset (Paris, France), 2001.
Dernier inventaire avant liquidation, Editions Grasset (Paris, France), 2001.
Barbie, Editions Assouline (Paris, France), 2001.
(With Philippe Bertrand) *Rester Normal,* Editions Dargaud (Paris, France), 2002.
Windows on the World (novel), B. Grasset (Paris, France), 2003, translated by Frank Wynne, Miramax/Hyperion (New York, NY), 2005.
Égoïste romantique: roman, B. Grasset (Paris, France), 2005.

Also cowriter and adapter for the film *Les Infortunes de la beauté;* contributor of reviews to periodicals, including *Lire, Paris Match, Elle, Le Figaro Literaire* and *Techni art.;* also contributor to *Masque et la Plume,* a literary radio program.

ADAPTATIONS: Writings have been adapted for films, including his novel *99 francs,* and his short story "The Day All Women Loved Me."

SIDELIGHTS: By the age of thirty-five, Frédéric Beigbeder had published five novels, started four magazines and become "l'enfant terrible" of the French advertising world. From a privileged upbringing in the Neuilly section of Paris, Beigbeder graduated from prestigious schools and immediately set out to become a fixture of the Paris nightclub scene. A self-proclaimed dandy and literary snob, he organized soirees at a private club, chez Castel, for the in-crowd for ten years. This led him to ten years in the advertising business and, beginning in 1997, with Thierry Ardisson, he held court on the literary and cultural goings on of France nightly on prime time television. He is the founder and editor of three magazines, *Genereux* in 1992, *Deluxe* in 1994, and *NRV,* a literary review in 1996. Beigbeder's range as a literary critic also encompasses reviews and critiques for several French magazines.

The French advertising world was a rich pool of talent in the 1980s, and the most talented players attained rock star status. Beigbeder, along with film director Jean Jacques Beineix and musician and multi-media artist Jean Paul Goude, were considered the crème de la crème. This is the world Beigbeder ruthlessly dissects in his novel *99 francs,* which is a thinly disguised roman à clef that apparently cost him his high-paying job at the multinational ad agency, Young & Rubicam. From the beginning of the book, the narrator claims that "I am writing the book to get fired." Beigbeder's premise is clear: everything and everybody is for sale. "In my profession, no one wants you to be happy, because happy people don't consume," the narrator tells us. He argues that advertising is a perversion of democracy. Bruce Crumley, reviewing the book for *Time International,* wrote: "Whether or not he wins one of the prestigious awards soon to be doled out during France's literary high season, Frédéric Beigbeder has already secured first prize for audacity with his novel, *99 francs,* a hyperbolic savaging of the author's own profession, advertising."

Beigbeder's other novels are no less controversial: in his 1997 book, *L'amour dure trois ans,* he develops his theory that love cannot exist for more than three years. His *Nouvelles sous ecstasy* is an ode to drugs, especially the nightclub drug, ecstasy.

In the tradition of the urbane and cynical cultural arbiters of the twentieth century, Beigbeder's iconoclastic novels and biting reviews have won him a cult following in France. His novel *Windows on the World* has also been translated into English and tells of the 9/11 terrorist attack on the World Trade Center, with each chapter in the book representing one minute, adding up to 105 minutes and ending with the final crumbling of the center's Twin Towers. In the novel, a young, divorced Texan father named Carthew Yorston takes his sons Jerry and David to the Windows on the World restaurant in one of the World Trade Center's Twin Towers and is soon trapped inside after one of the airplanes crashes into the building. As it becomes more and more apparent that they may not make it out alive, the father reflects on his failures in life. The novel also includes the reflections of a French writer after the event has occurred. Referring to *Windows on the World* as "a remarkable achievement." a contributor to the *Economist* went on to write that "this novel is steeped in both humility and deep affection for America." A *Publishers Weekly* contributor wrote that "Beigbeder invests his narrators with such profound humanity that the book is far more than a litany of catastrophe: it is, on all levels, a stunning read."

BIOGRAPHICAL AND CRITICAL SOURCES:

BOOKS

Beigbeder, Frédéric, *99 francs,* Editions Grasset (Paris, France), 2000.

PERIODICALS

AdAgeGlobal, December, 2000, Lawrence J. Spear, review of *99 francs,* p. 10.
Bookseller, November 29, 2002, Barbara Casassus, "Author Takes up Flammarion Role," p. 10.
Economist, June 30, 2001, review of *Dernier inventaire avant liquidation,* p. 10; May 21, 2005, review of *Windows on the World,* p. 89.
Entertainment Weekly, March 25, 2005, Jennifer Reese, review of *Windows on the World,* p. 76.
Guardian (London, England), September 11, 2004, Josh Lacey, review of *Windows on the World.*
Kirkus Reviews, December 15, 2004, review of *Windows on the World,* p. 1152.
Kliatt, July, 2006, Nola Theiss, review of *Windows on the World,* p. 17.
Library Journal, January 1, 2005, Patrick Sullivan, review of *Windows on the World,* p. 93.
National Review, June 20, 2005, Ross G. Douthat, review of *Windows on the World,* p. 48.
New York Times Book Review, April 17, 2005, Stephen Metcalf, review of *Windows on the World.*
Publishers Weekly, January 24, 2005, review of *Windows on the World,* p. 219.
San Francisco Chronicle, March 20, 2005, Sylvia Brownrigg, review of *Windows on the World.*
Time International, October 2, 2000, Bruce Crumley, review of *99 francs,* p. 86.

ONLINE

Frédéric Beigbeder Home Page, http://www.chez.com/fulham/index2.html (November 29, 2006).
Internet Movie Database, http://www.imdb.com/ (November 29, 2006), information on author's film work.
Salon.com, http://www.salon.com/ (March 20, 2005), Laura Miller, review of *Windows on the World.**

*   *   *

BIRNBAUM, Phyllis 1945-

PERSONAL: Born May 27, 1945, in Bronx, NY; daughter of Louis (in business) and Ruth (a teacher) Birnbaum; married Ashok Trimbak Modak (an engineer), September 24, 1971. *Education:* Barnard College, B.A., 1967; University of California, Berkeley, M.A., 1972.

ADDRESSES: Home—Watertown, MA. *Agent*—Fifi Oscard, 110 W. 40th St., New York, NY 10018.

CAREER: University of Tokyo Press, Tokyo, Japan, editor, 1966-69. Columbia University, fellow of Translation Center, 1979.

MEMBER: National Book Critics Circle.

AWARDS, HONORS: Japan-U.S. Friendship Commission Prize for translating *Confessions of Love.*

WRITINGS:

An Eastern Tradition (novel), Seaview Books (El Cerrito, CA), 1980.
(Translator) *Rabbits, Crabs, Etc.: Stories by Japanese Women,* University of Hawaii Press (Honolulu, HI), 1982.
Modern Girls, Shining Stars, the Skies of Tokyo: Five Japanese Women, Columbia University Press (New York, NY), 1999.
Glory in a Line: A Life of Foujita—The Artist Caught between East and West, Faber & Faber (New York, NY), 2006.

Also translator of the novel *Confessions of Love,* by Uno Chiyo. Contributor of articles, translations, and reviews to magazines.

SIDELIGHTS: In her book *Modern Girls, Shining Stars, the Skies of Tokyo: Five Japanese Women,* Phyllis Birnbaum presents the stories of five twentieth-century Japanese women who had the courage to defy their culture's deep-seated discrimination against women. Since feudal times, sexism was extreme in Japan. A woman's inferiority was considered a simple fact of life, and a wife was held in complete subordination to her husband and sons. While a man might have many mistresses without rebuke, a woman who took a lover was liable to be imprisoned. Western concepts of freedom and equality for women were first introduced during the mid-nineteenth century, causing shock waves throughout the country, even though most women were far too timid to embrace the new ideas.

In a collection of essays originally designed for publication in the *New Yorker,* Birnbaum profiles two writers, two actresses, and a painter. All led stormy lives and two came to tragic ends: actress Matsuo Sumako, who scandalized the public with both her unconventional private life and the revolutionary roles she brought to the stage, eventually took her own life; and Takamura Chieko, a progressive painter, ended her days in an insane asylum. Writers Uno Chiyo and Yanagiwara Byakuren, along with film star Takamine Hideko, had the advantage of being born a little later, when the rigid attitudes about women had loosened a little. Uno still managed to shock with her free-ranging love life and the candor with which she wrote about it. Yanagiwara left her powerful but crude husband for a younger, poorer man, shaming her spouse by printing her request for a divorce in the newspapers. Takamine, who began her career as a child star exploited by greedy relatives, went on to shape an admirable career that included hundreds of films, some with the country's top directors.

Reviewing *Modern Girls, Shining Stars, the Skies of Tokyo, Booklist* reviewer Grace Fill commented: "These portraits provide a view of Japanese women who . . . demonstrated enormous strength and helped create change for many others." Kathleen A. Shanahan, a *Library Journal* contributor, noted that Birnbaum "has a refreshing style; she points out the biases in previous biographies of these women and adds her own comments, never pretending that a biography can be completely free of bias. Highly recommended."

Birnbaum next turned her attention to the flamboyant and enigmatic Japanese artist Foujita, whose monumental ego, bizarre costumes, and stunning drawings of women and cats were the talk of Paris from his arrival there in 1913 through the 1920s. According to Birnbaum's biography, *Glory in a Line: A Life of Foujita—The Artist Caught between East and West,* Foujita's self-aggrandizing attitude and scandalous behavior may have shocked French society, but these traits also added to the artist's celebrity and boosted sales of his line drawings, woodcuts, and other artworks. Foujita's popularity in the West peaked in the early 1920s when he was finally acknowledged as the serious and hard-working artist that he truly was, but his acceptance was short-lived. Birnbaum tells Foujita's story with the empathy of a biographer who understands the Asian culture from which he came, according to *International Herald Tribune* reviewer Janet Maslin.

Foujita's heady success was cut short by a tax scandal and other personal troubles that drove him out of France and eventually back to his homeland. There, during the 1930s, Foujita was commissioned by the Japanese government to create propagandistic paintings—paintings which glorified Japanese military aggression and the cruelty of war so forcefully that he was criticized around the world. As his reputation eroded, Foujita reportedly lashed out against the West, yet he spent the last years of his life rather quietly in the French countryside. For the most part, *Glory in a Line* was well received by western critics. *New York Times* contributor Christopher Benfey called it a "briskly and stylishly written book" but one that "left me wishing for more." Maslin suggested that Birnbaum may have neglected or downplayed the more controversial facets of this colorful character, both in Paris and in his homeland, but she also called Foujita's biography "an intriguing book on the basis of its odd story . . . and its exploration of the many contradictions he embodied." A *Kirkus Reviews* contributor similarly noted Birnbaum's tendency to focus especially on Foujita's glory years in Paris but in the end called the book an "evenhanded portrait" of a "conflicted artist proud of Japanese culture and stung by Western racism."

BIOGRAPHICAL AND CRITICAL SOURCES:

PERIODICALS

Booklist, January 1, 1999, Grace Fill, review of *Modern Girls, Shining Stars, the Skies of Tokyo: Five*

Japanese Women, p. 802; November 1, 2006, Donna Seaman, review of *Glory in a Line: A Life of Foujita—The Artist Caught between East and West,* p. 19.

International Herald Tribune, December 12, 2006, Janet Maslin, review of *Glory in a Line.*

Kirkus Reviews, December 1, 1998, review of *Modern Girls, Shining Stars, the Skies of Tokyo;* September 1, 2006, review of *Glory in a Line,* p. 883.

Library Journal, October 15, 1980, review of *An Eastern Tradition,* p. 2229; January, 1999, Kathleen A. Shanahan, review of *Modern Girls, Shining Stars, the Skies of Tokyo,* p. 112.

New York Times, January 14, 2007, Christopher Benfey, review of *Glory in a Line.*

New York Times Book Review, October 12, 1980, review of *An Eastern Tradition,* p. 42.

Publishers Weekly, June 20, 1980, review of *An Eastern Tradition,* p. 73; August 6, 1982, review of *Rabbits, Crabs, Etc.: Stories by Japanese Women,* p. 67; August 7, 2006, review of *Glory in a Line,* p. 41.

Saturday Review, July, 1980, review of *An Eastern Tradition,* p. 58.

*   *   *

BLACKLOCK, Dyan 1951-

PERSONAL: Born 1951; married; husband's name David; children: two sons, one daughter.

ADDRESSES: Office—Omnibus Books, 335 Unley Rd., Malvern, South Australia 5061, Australia. *E-mail*—dyan_blacklock@scholastic.com.au.

CAREER: Omnibus Books, Malvern, South Australia, Australia, publisher, 1996—. Formerly worked as an editor, teacher, librarian, shopkeeper, and counselor.

AWARDS, HONORS: Eve Pownall Award, Australian children's book of the year, information category, Children's Book Council of Australia, 2001, for *Olympia: Warrior Athletes of Ancient Greece;* Centenary medal for services to Australia through literature, 2003.

WRITINGS:

JUVENILE

Comet Vomit and Other Surprising Stories, Allen & Unwin (St. Leonards, New South Wales, Australia), 1995.

The Lighthouse, illustrated by Steven Woolman, Era Publications (Flinders Park, South Australia, Australia), 1995.

Call It Love (short stories), Allen & Unwin (St. Leonards, New South Wales, Australia), 1996.

Crab Bait (short stories), Allen & Unwin (St. Leonards, New South Wales, Australia), 1996.

Pankration: The Ultimate Game, Allen & Unwin (St. Leonards, New South Wales, Australia), 1997, Albert Whitman (Morton Grove, IL), 1999.

Nudes and Nikes: Champions and Legends of the First Olympics, Allen & Unwin (St. Leonards, New South Wales, Australia), 1997.

I Want Earrings!, illustrated by Craig Smith, Omnibus (Norwood, South Australia, Australia), 1997.

Olympia: Warrior Athletes of Ancient Greece, illustrated by David Kennett, Omnibus Books (Malvern, South Australia, Australia), 2000, Walker and Co. (New York, NY), 2001.

Crash! The Search for the Stinson, Omnibus Books (Malvern, South Australia, Australia), 2000.

The Roman Army: The Legendary Soldiers Who Created an Empire, illustrated by David Kennett, Walker and Co. (New York, NY), 2004.

SIDELIGHTS: Dyan Blacklock is the author of several collections of short stories for young readers that have been praised for their humor and sensitivity, their realism, and their appeal to both boys and girls, avid and reluctant readers alike. In her first collection, *Comet Vomit and Other Surprising Stories,* the thirteen stories "cover fantasy, fear, and farce; some present serious moments of discovery of such matters as the brevity of human life, . . . the capacity to overcome fear, and loyalty to one's home and family," observed Alan Horsfield in *Magpies.* Horsfield noted that much of the appeal of *Comet Vomit* comes from Blacklock's use of the natural language of her target audience, her fast-paced plots, and satisfying endings. Similar qualities grace *Crab Bait,* another collection of tales for middle-grade readers. According to Russ Merrin, a reviewer for *Magpies,* the stories resonate with "sensitivity, subtlety, humour and poignancy." Individual tales depict the pros and cons of belonging to the popular group at school, family troubles, the comeuppance of a rich girl, or a science-fiction approach to handling a bully. "Dyan Blacklock captures the uncertainty, gullibility and guilelessness of children, while remaining keenly attuned to their thoughts, values, attitudes and mores," Merrin concluded. *School Librarian* contributor Sarah Reed called *Crab Bait* "great for tempting less enthusiastic readers."

Pankration: The Ultimate Game, a novel for young adults, shares with Blacklock's earlier works an ability to inspire enthusiasm in young audiences. Set in ancient Greece, the novel centers on Nic, the pampered son of wealthy parents who is sent away from his Athens home when a plague threatens the city. On board a ship, he meets and is befriended by the ship's captain, an Olympic hopeful training for the pankration event, an especially brutal form of boxing. When pirates attack the ship, young Nic is sold into slavery, escapes, and returns to Athens in time for the games, where he meets up with old enemies as well as old friends and encounters a whole new set of challenges and adventures. In *School Librarian,* critic Jonathan Weir made note of *Pankration*'s "pacy and involving story," and the author's smooth incorporation of Grecian history. Weir further observed that "the characters and their motivations are never anything short of convincing." *Bulletin of the Center for Children's Books* reviewer Elizabeth Bush commented that though "kid-pleasing adventure-story staples abound" in Blacklock's plot, the author's skill for including historical detail and her avoidance of didacticism raises "the tale beyond simple costume drama." The result is a book that is "about as satisfying as it gets," concluded Bush.

The Roman Army: The Legendary Soldiers Who Created an Empire provides another look at the classical world. This nonfiction work combines illustrations and text to depict the many aspects of military life in ancient Rome. Blacklock explains the overall organization of the Roman army, from its hierarchy and uniforms to strategies of war, fighting techniques, and deployment patterns. She describes the work behind the scenes required to mount a successful army, from training of soldiers to providing supply convoys and building the roads necessary to carry the troops and convoys. She writes, not only of the soldiers and military leaders, but also of the variety of support personnel required to supply the soldiers' needs and even of the treatment of prisoners of war. She describes the Roman military weapons and hardware, such as the catapult and other heavy field equipment. Lest such a technical work overwhelm a young reader, Blacklock uses plentiful illustrations to amplify and demystify the technical content of the book. Both Carolyn Phelan of *Booklist* and Anne Chapman Callaghan of *School Library Journal* commented on the riveting drawings and the successful blending of illustration and text, reminiscent of the style of a comic book or graphic novel. Phelan called The Roman Army a "dynamic book," while Callaghan recommended it as a "captivating" introduction to Roman military history.

For older adolescents, Blacklock produced a collection of stories about love and other intensely felt emotions in *Call It Love.* For a younger audience, the author wrote *The Lighthouse,* a picture book about death and grief in which an elderly man loses his wife of many years, grieves the loss of the person who was to him a "lighthouse," and eventually learns to enjoy life again. This "soundly-written story" is also a "sentimental reminiscence," according to Annette Meiklejohn in *Magpies,* but "is saved from becoming maudlin by the author's use of clear and very simple language."

Blacklock told *CA:* "Since becoming the publisher of Omnibus Books in 1996, my own writing has taken a back seat. I am more concerned with other people's writing, and helping to create new work is very pleasurable. I still write (there are currently three novels on the go in my computer) but I am very tough on myself these days. I see so much work that it often fills me with anxiety. There are very few original ideas out there. I still love to write—I'm just a lot pickier about what I keep and what I throw away."

BIOGRAPHICAL AND CRITICAL SOURCES:

PERIODICALS

Australian Book Review, June, 1995, review of *Comet Vomit and Other Surprising Stories,* p. 61.
Booklist, March 1, 2004, Carolyn Phelan, review of *The Roman Army: The Legendary Soldiers Who Created an Empire,* p. 1189.
Bulletin of the Center for Children's Books, June, 1999, Elizabeth Bush, review of *Pankration: The Ultimate Game,* pp. 344-345.
Children's Book Watch, May, 2004, review of *The Roman Army,* p. 8.
Kliatt, July, 1997, review of *Call It Love,* p. 20.
Library Media Connection, August-September, 2004, Sandra Lee, review of *The Roman Army,* p. 74.
Magpies, July, 1995, Alan Horsfield, review of *Comet Vomit and Other Surprising Stories,* p. 27; September, 1995, Annette Meiklejohn, review of *The Lighthouse,* p. 27; March, 1997, Russ Merrin, review of *Crab Bait,* p. 32; September, 1997, review of *Nudes and Nikes: Champions and Legends of the First Olympics,* p. 42.
School Librarian, spring, 1998, Sarah Reed, review of *Crab Bait,* p. 46; summer, 1998, Jonathan Weir, review of *Pankration,* pp. 76, 78.

School Library Journal, April, 2004, Anne Chapman Callaghan, review of *The Roman Army,* p. 165.

Washington Post Book World, April 25, 2004, Eliabeth Ward, review of *The Roman Army,* p. 11.

*   *   *

BLAKE, Robin 1948-
(Robin James Blake)

PERSONAL: Born December 12, 1948, in Preston, Lancashire, England; son of John (an engineer) and Beryl Blake; married Frances Waugh (a publisher), December 23, 1981; children: Matthew, Nicholas, Spike. *Education:* Jesus College, Cambridge, B.A., 1970, postgraduate certificate in education, 1972, M.A., 1974; Chelsea College, London, diploma, 1975. *Religion:* "Once a Catholic."

ADDRESSES: Home—London, England. *Agent*—Gill Coleridge, Rogers, Coleridge, White, 20 Powys Mews, London W.11, England. *E-mail*—robin@gosh.easynet. co.uk.

CAREER: Schoolteacher in England 1971-74; Institute for Tourism, Varna, Bulgaria, English teacher, 1975-76; English teacher at an English high school in Istanbul, Turkey, 1976-78; Capital Radio, London, England, broadcaster, producer, and writer of news, educational programs, and general features, 1979-86; freelance writer, 1986—. University of London, lecturer in radio production at Goldsmiths College, 1987-89.

MEMBER: Society of Authors, Radio Academy (member of council, 1984—), Association of Cinematograph and Television Technicians (member of executive committee, 1981-84).

WRITINGS:

Enigma (radio play), first broadcast by Capital Radio, 1984.

Mind over Medicine: Can the Mind Kill or Cure?, Pan Books (London, England), 1987.

(With Eleanor Stephens) *Compulsion: A Psychological Study,* Boxtree (London, England), 1987.

Fat Man's Shadow (novel), Penguin (London, England), 1991.

The Gwailo (novel), Penguin (London, England), 1992.

Anthony Van Dyck: A Life, 1599-1641, Ivan R. Dee (Chicago, IL), 2000.

Essential Modern Art, Parragon (Bath, England), 2000.

(With Clive Powell-Williams) *Cold Burial,* Penguin (London, England), 2001.

Saints, Collins (London, England), 2001.

(With Malcolm Warner) *Stubbs and the Horse,* Yale University Press (New Haven, CT), 2004.

George Stubbs and the Wide Creation: Animals, People, and Places in the Life of George Stubbs, 1724-1806, Chatto & Windus (London, England), 2005.

Writer of six-play series *Tales of a City,* broadcast by Capital Radio, 1983. Radio critic for *Tablet,* 1984. Contributor to periodicals, including *Independent on Sunday* and *Financial Times.*

SIDELIGHTS: Robin Blake once told *CA:* "I am motivated only by the desire to make a living by being a good writer. I will write for any medium that holds out this prospect, but I love radio particularly because of its devotion to words and to bringing them alive."

More recently Blake added: "I never write for radio now. I am still motivated by trying to write well while making a living, but this has turned out to be far from easy, and much of my time has been occupied by different forms of ghost-writing, which at least helps to pay the bills. It seems to me that, as publishers and booksellers have fallen increasingly for the allure of rapid mass sales, 'good writing' has begun to look like a niche market, comparable to cookery books or train spotters' guides. At the same time libraries hardly seem to be about 'serious' books at all any more, with pitiful acquisition budgets and absolutely no ambition to take a lead in promoting good writing. The same can be said of the education system. We await the impact of paperless publishing and the implications thereof for authors. I fear it will all make the economic position of the professional writer even more dire than it is today."

Blake wrote the "lively biography" *Anthony Van Dyck: A Life, 1599-1641,* which *Times Literary Supplement* contributor Theodore K. Rabb described as "a highly personal account" of the life of an artist who "left few letters or other private documentation," combined with Blake's "entertaining speculations, particularly about [Van Dyck's] psychology, sexual inclinations, and attitude toward the powerful figures he painted." According to Rabb, "the basic story of the career is well told, and, to make up for the penurious illustrations, Blake lists some of the Web sites where the pictures can be found."

BIOGRAPHICAL AND CRITICAL SOURCES:

PERIODICALS

Times Literary Supplement, September 17, 1999, Theodore K. Rabb, review of *Anthony Van Dyck: A Life, 1599-1641,* pp. 18-19.

*   *   *

BLAKE, Robin James
    See BLAKE, Robin

*   *   *

BREEDEN, David 1958-

PERSONAL: Born March 23, 1958, in Granite City, IL; son of Marion and Mary Breeden; children: Audrey, Jesse, Patrick. *Ethnicity:* "White." *Education:* Southeastern Illinois College, A.A., 1978; Southern Illinois University, B.A., 1981; University of Iowa, M.F.A., 1985; University of Southern Mississippi, Ph.D., 1988; student at Meadville Lombard Theological Seminary, 2005—; also attended Bread Loaf Writers' Conference, 1995, and Naropa Institute. *Religion:* Unitarian-Universalist. *Hobbies and other interests:* Travel.

ADDRESSES: Home—Chicago, IL; Broughton, IL. *E-mail*—david.breeden@sbcglobal.net; david breeden182@yahoo.com.

CAREER: Substitute teacher at public schools in Iowa City, IA, 1983-85; Arkansas State University, Jonesboro, assistant professor of English, 1988-91; Schreiner College, Kerrville, TX, professor of English, 1991-2005, department chair, 1995-2004 divisional dean, School of Liberal Arts, 1999-2002, and publisher, Press of the Guadalupe. Texas Tech University, teacher at Fredericksburg campus, 2005; conference participant; public speaker; gives readings from his works. Virtual Arts

Collective (Web site), editor; staff writer for *Circle* magazine and *Audio Books Today* Web site; judge of literary awards.

MEMBER: American Literary Translators Association, PEN Center USA West, National Writers Union, Association of Literary Scholars and Critics, Associated Writing Programs, Popular Culture Association, Unitarian Universalist Poets Cooperative, Sigma Tau Delta.

AWARDS, HONORS: Grants from Texas Commission of the Arts, 1992, 1993; Best of the Fest Award, Great Lakes Independent Film Festival, 2003, for *Off the Wall;* Bordon-Holton Award for Sermonic Excellence.

WRITINGS:

Picnics (poetry chapbook), Black Buzzard (Arlington, VA), 1985.

Hey, Schliemann (poetry), Edwin Mellen Press (Lewiston, NY), 1990.

Double Headed End Wrench (poetry), Cloverdale Press (Bristol, IN), 1992.

Building a Boat (poetry chapbook), March Street Press (Chapel Hill, NC), 1995.

The Guiltless Traveler (poetry chapbook), March Street Press (Greensboro, NC), 1996.

Another Number (novel), Silver Phoenix Press (Austin, TX), 1998.

Stack to the Moon (novel), Crossroads Press (Minneapolis, MN), 2000.

Artistas (novel), Superior Books (Indian Lake, NY), 2001.

(With William W. Woods) *Off the Wall* (short film), Vision Crew Unlimited (Hollywood, CA), 2002.

Surviving the Coup (poetry chapbook), March Street Press (Greensboro, NC), 2003.

Ice Cream and Suicide: Difficult Poems for the Masses, UKA Press (Bristol, England), 2005.

A Poet's Guide to Divorce; or, Passivity's Charms, Fine Tooth Press (Waterbury, CT), 2005.

Stigmata Is like That, March Street Press (Greensboro, NC), 2006.

Author of a novel, *Chucking the Cliffs Notes,* published in electronic form by the former Web site PulpBits. com.; film scripts include *House Whine,* British Columbia Film Commission, and *Golgotha Hanger;* plays include *Aunt Emma's Wake* and *Daddy Wasn't Right,* included in *Writer's Hood.* Author of "Ask Dr.

Poetry," a column in the *Montrose Morning Sun* and at the *Lone Star Internet Culture Cafe* Web site. Contributor of poetry, short stories, essays, articles, and reviews to magazines and Web sites, including *Poet Lore, Mid-American Review, Fine Madness, California Quarterly, Wormwood Review, Rockhurst Review, Amarillo Bay, Turnstile, Borderlands,* and *Boston Literary Review.* Contributing editor, *Inklings;* past editor, *Context South.*

Breeden's papers are archived at Southern Illinois University.

SIDELIGHTS: David Breeden told *CA:* "My primary motivation in writing is a compulsion to do so. I exist in a world of symbol and language. I can either be manipulated by them, or I can choose to do the manipulating.

"My main influences as a writer have been Emily Dickinson, William Carlos Williams, and Allen Ginsberg.

"In process I am creatively messy. That is, I like to leave the materials out on the table all the time and play with them whenever the book strikes. I carry a small notebook with me at all times.

"The themes in my writing are materiality, spirituality, and the problems the disjunctions between them create. I didn't choose the subjects, they chose me!

"My writing has changed with time from a lyric impulse to a narrative impulse. Now I've circled back to lyricism again."

*   *   *

BROCKMEIER, Kevin 1972-

PERSONAL: Born 1972.

ADDRESSES: Home and office—Little Rock, AR. *Agent*—Jennifer Carlson, Dunow & Carlson Literary Agent, 27 W. 20th St., Ste. 103, New York, NY 10011.

CAREER: Novelist and short story writer. Instructor at Iowa Writers Workshop, University of Iowa.

AWARDS, HONORS: Nelson Algren Award, *Chicago Tribune*; Italo Calvino Short Fiction Award; James Michener-Paul Engel fellowship; three O. Henry awards; National Endowment for the Arts grant.

WRITINGS:

FOR CHILDREN

City of Names (novel), Viking (New York, NY), 2002.
Grooves: A Kind of Mystery (novel), Katherine Tegen Books (New York, NY), 2006.

OTHER

Things That Fall from the Sky (short fiction), Pantheon (New York, NY), 2002.
The Truth about Celia (adult novel), Pantheon (New York, NY), 2003.
The Brief History of the Dead (adult novel), Pantheon (New York, NY), 2006.

Contributor of fiction to periodicals, including *Georgia Review, New Yorker,* and *McSweeney's.* Contributor of fiction to anthologies, including *The Oxford American, The Best American Short Stories, The Year's Best Fantasy and Horror,* and *The O. Henry Prize Stories.*

ADAPTATIONS: Warner Bros. acquired film rights to *The Brief History of the Dead.*

SIDELIGHTS: An O. Henry Prize-winning author of short fiction, Kevin Brockmeier has gained critical recognition for his lyrical prose. Though he began his career focusing on short fiction for adults, Brockmeier has also expanded his audience to teen readers with the novels *City of Names* and *Grooves: A Kind of Mystery.* "I began writing children's fiction for two reasons," the author explained to an interviewer for *Earth Goat* online. "First of all, I began to read children's fiction again . . . and I found that the best of them offered me as much aesthetic pleasure as the adult fiction I was reading. Second, when I was in college, I used to teach at a nursery school, where I would make up stories for the children in my class, and I wanted to find a way of continuing to tell stories to those particular children."

In all his works, Brockmeier's characters often find themselves in absurd situations. His fiction borders the fantastical and often draws on fairy tales for inspiration; one story in *Things That Fall from the Sky,* for example, brings Rumplestiltskin into the future—or, at least, half of him because, according to the Grimm fairy tale, the original Rumplestiltskin tore himself in half. Other tales include the story of a man who lives on a never-ending airplane, a thirty-something male babysitter who becomes obsessed with the toddler he cares for, and a man who realizes the sky is falling while he copes with his wife's extramarital affair. Reviewing *Things That Fall from the Sky, Booklist* contributor James Klise wrote that Brockmeier "demonstrates a fluid use of language, playfulness of story, and mature insight into a world" of strange choices, while in *Publishers Weekly* a critic deemed the author "a formidable young writer."

In contrast to the serious overtones in *Things That Fall from the Sky,* the plot of *City of Names* revolves around a book discovered by fifth-grader Howie that is titled *The Secret Guide to North Mellwood.* A fold-out map of Howie's home city contained within the book allows the boy to transport instantly to any point when he utters the location's "true" name. Even stranger things are happening below ground, however; town hero Larry Boone, thought to be dead for centuries, is still alive and well and keeping the magic of the city's names flowing. "There's nothing like a bit of unexpected magic to liven up a thoroughly ordinary day," Anne O'Malley wrote in her *Booklist* review of the novel, while in *Kirkus Reviews* a critic deemed *City of Names* "a giddy but enjoyable ride with a whiff of mystery . . . that may leave readers regarding their own supposedly ordinary neighborhoods with new eyes."

Also written for younger readers, *Grooves: A Kind of Mystery* is an odd-ball adventure that follows the same tone of *City of Names.* When Dwayne, a seventh grader living in a small town, runs a phonograph needle down his jeans, he discovers that the grooves of his jeans contain a hidden call for help. With two friends, Dwayne tackles the mystery head on, challenging the town's most powerful businessman, who he believes is turning factory workers into personality-less zombies. Readers who enjoy "wacky fantasies . . . will be delighted," predicted a *Kirkus Reviews* contributor in a review of *Grooves.* Debbie Carton, writing in *Booklist,* considered Brockmeier's tale "a frothy, fanciful, and entertaining blend of science fiction and mystery," and Walter Minkel wrote in *School Library Journal* that, "with its crazy deadpan humor, [*Grooves*] . . . is a hoot."

Brockmeier's adult novels include *The Truth about Celia,* which focuses on the kidnapping of a seven-year-old girl, and *The Brief History of the Dead.* Recommended to sophisticated teen readers by *School Library Journal* critic Matthew L. Moffett, *The Brief History of the Dead* follows a researcher struggling to survive in Antarctica and make her way back to a civilization that may no longer exist. Meanwhile, the still-existing dead dwell in a place known as The City, but last there only as long as someone remembers them. "The elegiac, thoughtful tone of the writing is balanced by the survivor's adventure-filled travels across the frozen landscape," wrote Moffett, and Charles de Lint complimented Brockmeier's writing, noting in the *Magazine of Science Fiction and Fantasy* that "his prose is wonderful, ranging from straightforward to elegant and luminous."

"I've found that my children's books are more conversational in tone than my adult books, and a lot more jokey," Brockmeier noted in his *Earth Goat* interviewer. "I want them to read as though you're listening to a child who's simply telling you his story as it occurs to him, along with anything else that happens to cross his mind," the writer added. In characterizing his work to Diane Baroni for *Interview,* Brockmeier dubbed his style "speculative autobiography." Regarding his inspiration, he told an interviewer for *Powells.com:* "I write out of gratitude for all the books I have loved over the years."

BIOGRAPHICAL AND CRITICAL SOURCES:

PERIODICALS

Booklist, February 15, 2002, James Klise, review of *Things That Fall from the Sky,* p. 990; June 1, 2002, Anne O'Malley, review of *City of Names,* p. 1720; July, 2003, Elsa Gaztambide, review of *The Truth about Celia,* p. 1863; January 1, 2006, Allison Block, review of *The Brief History of the Dead,* p. 52; February 1, 2006, Debbie Carton, review of *Grooves: A Kind of Mystery,* p. 47.

Bulletin of the Center for Children's Books, May, 2002, review of *City of Names,* p. 312; March, 2006, Karen Coats, review of *Grooves,* p. 303.

Guardian (London, England), April 8, 2006, Colin Greenland, "Living on Cola," p. 17.

Interview, April, 2002, Diane Baroni, "Book 'Em: Five First-Time Authors to Bookmark," p. 76.

Kirkus Reviews, February 1, 2002, review of *Things that Fall from the Sky,* p. 119; May 1, 2002, review of *City of Names,* p. 649; May 1, 2003, review of

The Truth about Celia, p. 622; December 1, 2005, review of *The Brief History of the Dead,* p. 1243; January 15, 2006, review of *Grooves,* p. 82.

Kliatt, November, 2006, Mary Purucker, review of *The Brief History of the Dead,* p. 42.

Library Journal, February 15, 2006, Barbara Hoffert, review of *The Brief History of the Dead,* p. 106.

Magazine of Science Fiction and Fantasy, April, 2006, Charles de Lint, review of *The Brief History of the Dead,* p. 33.

New Statesman, March 27, 2006, Alex Larman, "End of the World as We Know It," p. 54.

Publishers Weekly, January 14, 2002, review of *Things that Fall from the Sky,* p. 37; May 27, 2002, review of *City of Names,* p. 60; June 30, 2003, review of *The Truth about Celia,* p. 56; December 19, 2005, review of *The Brief History of the Dead,* p. 38.

School Library Journal, July, 2002, Elaine E. Knight, review of *City of Names,* p. 113; March, 2006, Walter Minkel, review of *Grooves,* p. 218; July, 2006, Matthew L. Moffett, review of *The Brief History of the Dead,* p. 132.

Washington Post Book World, April 2, 2006, Andrew Sean Greer, "Soul Survivor," p. 13.

ONLINE

Del Sol Literary Dialogues, http://www.webdelsol.com/ Literary_Dialogues/ (January 8, 2007), Mary Mc-Myne, interview with Brockmeier.

Earth Goat, http://earthgoat.blogspot.com/ (April 3, 2006), interview with Brockmeier.

Interstitial Arts Foundation Web site, http://www. interstitialarts.org/ (January 8, 2007), "Kevin Brockmeier."

Powells.com, http://www.powells.com/ (January 8, 2007), interview with Brockmeier.

Random House Web site, http://www.randomhouse.com/ (January 8, 2007), "Kevin Brockmeier."*

*   *   *

BROWN, Sandra 1948-
(Laura Jordan, Rachel Ryan, Erin St. Claire)

PERSONAL: Born March 12, 1948, in Waco, TX; daughter of Jimmie (a journalist) and Martha (a counselor) Cox; married Michael Brown (a television producer and former television anchor), August 17, 1968; children: Rachel, Ryan. *Education:* Attended Texas Christian University, Oklahoma State University, and University of Texas at Arlington. *Hobbies and other interests:* Reading, movies, travel, and hosting get-togethers.

ADDRESSES: Home—Arlington, TX. *Agent*—Maria Carvainis Agency, 1270 Avenue of the Americas, Ste. 2320, New York, NY 10020. *E-mail*—sandrab@sandra brown.net.

CAREER: Writer. Merle Norman Cosmetics Studios, Tyler, TX, manager, 1971-73; KLTV-TV, Tyler, TX, weather reporter, 1972-75; WFAA-TV, Dallas, TX, weather reporter, 1976-79; Dallas Apparel Mart, Dallas, TX, model, 1976-87.

MEMBER: Author's Guild, Mystery Writers of America, International Association of Crime Writers, Novelists, Inc., and Literacy Partners, RWA, International Thriller Writers.

AWARDS, HONORS: American Business Women's Association's Distinguished Circle of Success; B'nai B'rith's Distinguished Literary Achievement Award; A.C. Greene Award; Romance Writers of America's Lifetime Achievement Award; Texas Cultural Trust.

WRITINGS:

ROMANCE NOVELS

(Under pseudonym Laura Jordan) *Hidden Fires,* Richard Gallen (New York, NY), 1982, published under name Sandra Brown, Warner (New York, NY), 1997.

(Under pseudonym Laura Jordan) *The Silken Web,* Richard Gallen (New York, NY), 1982, published under name Sandra Brown, Warner (New York, NY), 1992.

Breakfast in Bed, Bantam (New York, NY), 1983, Wheeler (Rockland, MA), 1996.

Heaven's Price, Bantam (New York, NY), 1983.

Relentless Desire, Berkley-Jove (New York, NY), 1983.

Tempest in Eden, Berkley-Jove (New York, NY), 1983.

Temptation's Kiss, Berkley-Jove (New York, NY), 1983, Wheeler (Rockland, MA), 1998.

Tomorrow's Promise, Harlequin (Tarrytown, NY), 1983.

In a Class by Itself, Bantam (New York, NY), 1984, Random House (New York, NY), 1999.

Send No Flowers, Bantam (New York, NY), 1984, Wheeler (Rockland, MA), 1999.

Sunset Embrace, Bantam (New York, NY), 1984.

Riley in the Morning, Bantam (New York, NY), 1985, reprinted, 2001.

Thursday's Child, Bantam (New York, NY), 1985, reprinted, 2002.

Another Dawn, Bantam (New York, NY), 1985.

22 Indigo Place, Bantam (New York, NY), 1986.

The Rana Look, Bantam (New York, NY), 1986.

Demon Rumm, Bantam (New York, NY), 1987, reprinted, 2005.

Fanta C, Bantam (New York, NY), 1987.

Sunny Chandler's Return, Bantam (New York, NY), 1987, reprinted, 2004.

Adam's Fall, Bantam (New York, NY), 1988, Wheeler (Rockland, MA), 1994.

Hawk O'Toole's Hostage, Bantam (New York, NY), 1988, Wheeler (Rockland, MA), 1997.

Slow Heat in Heaven (also see below), Warner (New York, NY), 1988.

Tidings of Great Joy, Bantam (New York, NY), 1988.

Long Time Coming, Doubleday (New York, NY), 1989, reprinted, Bantam Books (New York, NY), 2006.

Temperatures Rising, Doubleday (New York, NY), 1989, reprinted, Bantam Books (New York, NY), 2006.

Best Kept Secrets (also see below), Warner (New York, NY), 1989, reprinted, 2003.

A Whole New Light, Doubleday (New York, NY), 1989.

Breath of Scandal, Warner (New York, NY), 1991.

Another Dawn, Warner (New York, NY), 1991.

Mirror Image (also see below), Severn, 1991.

French Silk, Warner (New York, NY), 1992.

A Secret Splendor, Harlequin (Tarrytown, NY), 1992.

Shadows of Yesterday, also published as *Relentless Desire,* Warner (New York, NY), 1992.

Three Complete Novels (contains *Mirror Image, Best Kept Secrets,* and *Slow Heat in Heaven*), Wings Books (New York, NY), 1992.

Where There's Smoke, Warner (New York, NY), 1993.

Charade, Warner (New York, NY), 1994.

The Witness, Warner (New York, NY), 1995.

Exclusive, Warner (New York, NY), 1996.

Fat Tuesday, Warner (New York, NY), 1997.

Unspeakable, Warner (New York, NY), 1998.

The Alibi, Random House (New York, NY), 1999.

Standoff, Warner (New York, NY), 2000.

The Switch, Warner (New York, NY), 2000.

Envy, Warner (New York, NY), 2001.

The Crush, Warner (New York, NY), 2002.

The Rana Look, Bantam Doubleday Dell (New York, NY), 2002.

Hello, Darkness, Simon & Schuster (New York, NY), 2003.

White Hot, Simon & Schuster (New York, NY), 2004.

Chill Factor, Simon & Schuster (New York, NY), 2005.

Ricochet, Simon & Schuster. (New York, NY), 2006.

Three Complete Novels in One Volume (includes *Heaven's Price, Breakfast in Bed,* and *Send No Flowers,*), Wings Books (New York, NY), 2007.

"TEXAS!" SERIES

Texas! Lucky, Doubleday (New York, NY), 1990.

Texas! Chase, Doubleday (New York, NY), 1990.

Texas! Sage, Bantam (New York, NY), 1992.

Texas! Trilogy (contains *Texas! Lucky, Texas! Sage,* and *Texas! Chase*), 1992.

NOVELS; UNDER PSEUDONYM RACHEL RYAN

Love beyond Reason, Dell (New York, NY), 1981, published under name Sandra Brown, Thorndike (Thorndike, ME), 1996.

Love's Encore, Dell (New York, NY), 1981, published under name Sandra Brown, Bantam (New York, NY), 1997.

Eloquent Silence, Dell (New York, NY), 1982, published under name Sandra Brown, Thorndike (Thorndike, ME), 1996.

A Treasure Worth Seeking, Dell (New York, NY), 1982, published under name Sandra Brown, Warner (New York, NY), 1997.

Prime Time, Dell (New York, NY), 1983, published under name Sandra Brown, Thorndike (Thorndike, ME), 1996.

NOVELS; UNDER PSEUDONYM ERIN ST. CLAIRE

Not Even for Love, Harlequin (Tarrytown, NY), 1982, reprinted, Warner Books (New York, NY), 2003.

A Kiss Remembered, Harlequin (Tarrytown, NY), 1983.

A Secret Splendor, Harlequin (Tarrytown, NY), 1983.

Seduction by Design, Harlequin (Tarrytown, NY), 1983, published under name Sandra Brown, Warner (New York, NY), 2001.

Bittersweet Rain, Harlequin (Tarrytown, NY), 1984.

Words of Silk, Harlequin (Tarrytown, NY), 1984, reprinted, Warner Books (New York, NY), 2004.

Led Astray, Harlequin (Tarrytown, NY), 1985.
Sweet Anger, Harlequin (Tarrytown, NY), 1985.
Tiger Prince, Harlequin (Tarrytown, NY), 1985.
Above and Beyond, Harlequin (Tarrytown, NY), 1986.
Honor Bound, Harlequin (Tarrytown, NY), 1986.
The Devil's Own, Harlequin (Tarrytown, NY), 1987.
Two Alone, Harlequin (Tarrytown, NY), 1987.
Thrill of Victory, Harlequin (Tarrytown, NY), 1989.

Books have been translated into thirty languages.

ADAPTATIONS: A television movie based on *French Silk* was produced in the 1990s, starring Susan Lucci; books have been adapted as sound recordings, including *The Switch* and *A Treasure Worth Seeking,* Brilliance Audio (Grand Haven, MI), 2005.

SIDELIGHTS: Sandra Brown has written more than sixty novels in a span of some twenty-five years. Although her early work falls strictly into the genre of the romance novel, her books have steadily evolved in length and complexity, successfully combining traditional romance elements with several other genres, including mystery, the political thriller, and crime fiction. In the process, her readership has grown dramatically. With more than fifty million copies of her novels in print and more than four dozen appearances on the *New York Times* bestseller list, Brown has emerged as one of the most successful commercial novelists of her generation. From her modest beginnings working as a pseudonymous writer of Harlequin romances, she is today one of the best-paid authors in America, commanding as much as four million dollars per title.

Brown was raised in Fort Worth, Texas, and grew up reading detective novels and dreaming of a career as a dancer. She married in 1968 and spent the early years of the 1970s working in television commercials and serving as a part-time television weather forecaster. When she was laid off from her weather job in 1979, she began reading and writing romance novels. A visit to a romance writers' conference helped her to understand how to enter the business, and by 1981 she was selling her work. Her first two novels, *Love's Encore* and *Love Beyond Reason,* were accepted within thirteen days of one another. Brown told *Twbookmark.com:* "It was as though all the lights came on, and I realized what I was supposed to do with my life. I was writing like a fiend." Over the next decade she penned an average of six books per year, gradually dropping the

pseudonyms in favor of using her own name. Her output eventually diminished as her books became more ambitious in scope and substance.

A typical Brown bestseller features a large cast of characters, a plot rife with secrets and intrigues (often family-based) that keep the reader guessing, a heroine in danger, and a liberal helping of what a writer in *Kirkus Reviews* referred to as "raunchy sex scenes." Brown's heroines are most often career women who are seeking not only romance but also fame and fortune. Cat Delany, the protagonist of *Charade,* is a soap-opera star who must undergo a heart transplant. She is subsequently stalked by a mysterious serial killer seeking revenge on the person who has received his dead lover's heart. The killer may even be her new romantic interest, crime novelist Alex Pierce.

Kendall Deaton, the protagonist in *The Witness,* is an ambitious public defender who becomes embroiled in the prejudices of a small Southern town. A fatal car accident, amnesia, adultery, and a terrible secret lead Kendall to a finale involving the F.B.I. and surprising revelations about the true identities of the novel's central characters. In *Exclusive,* set in Washington, DC, the president's infant son has apparently died of sudden infant death syndrome (SIDS). Reporter Barrie Travis is granted an exclusive interview with the first lady that leads her to believe the baby's death may have actually been a murder. In the course of investigating the case, she becomes romantically involved with a former presidential advisor who may have also been the first lady's former lover. Travis uncovers information about the first family that gravely contradicts its public image. *Unspeakable* pits a secretive Texas ranch hand and a deaf widow against a rapist-murderer who breaks out of prison with revenge on his mind. As the pace quickens, it becomes clear that the ranch hand, Jack Sawyer, knows a great deal more about his employers—and the killer—than he lets on.

Most reviewers have agreed that the strength of Brown's work lies in her storytelling ability. Reviewing *The Witness* for *Booklist,* Mary Frances Wilkens wrote of Brown: "Though not an elegant writer, this prolific author writes a true page-turner that is recommended for fans of graphic crime fiction." A reviewer in *Publishers Weekly* echoed this view, describing *Exclusive* as a "nimbly plotted political thriller" that "despite merely serviceable prose," provides an "intricate weave of false leads, sinister motives and long-hidden truths [that] is engrossing." Susan Clifford, reviewing *Unspeakable* in the *Library Journal,* commended Brown for weaving "a tight web that catches and holds the reader from first page to last." *Booklist* correspondent Donna Seaman noted that, "in her steamy, relentless thrillers . . . Brown writes with vehement vulgarity and extravagant bloodthirstiness."

A *Twentieth-Century Romance and Historical Writers* contributor attributed much of Brown's success to the fact "that she invites her readers into a fantasy world of passion, intrigue, and danger." The Texas-born Brown has set much of her fiction in the American South, and the contributor believed that her "steamy settings with a touch of decadence . . . contribute greatly to a brooding, oppressive atmosphere . . . [which] in turn, increases the underlying menace and tension surrounding the characters." The contributor also credited Brown with being one of the few writers to successfully break the traditional romance formula by writing books that do not have happy endings.

The author has continued to churn out widely read multiple-genre novels, such as *Standoff,* about a female television reporter who gets taken hostage along with the handsome Doc by teenagers holding up a convenience store. Vanessa Bush, writing in *Booklist,* commented that the novel "will intrigue." According to a *Publishers Weekly* contributor, in her novel *Envy,* Brown "craft[s] a novel within a novel within a novel." When a book editor, Mans Matherly-Reed, starts reading a novel from a slush pile, she becomes entranced by the highly charged, sexual writing. Throughout the book, Brown alternates between the novel sent in by a mysterious stranger, the story about a purloined novel within the stranger's novel, and the tale of Mans herself and her sociopath husband. The *Publishers Weekly* contributor noted that the author "stages one dramatic scene after another."

In her thriller titled *The Crush,* Brown presents Dr. Rennie Newton, who finds a gangster innocent while serving on a jury only to have the contract killer, Ricky Lozada, start sending her flowers and calling her. When one of Rennie's colleagues winds up murdered, the doctor becomes a suspect as Detective Wick Threadgill investigates and soon finds himself falling for the aloof Rennie. The jealous Ricky learns of Wick's intentions and makes plans to do away with him. *Booklist* contributor Kristine Huntley wrote: "This novel delivers a menacing villain and page-turning suspense." A *Kirkus Reviews* contributor called *The Crush* a "pretty good suspenser."

Chill Factor focuses on Lily Martin, a magazine publisher whose ex-husband, Dutch Burton, is police chief of Cleary, North Carolina. Lily, who has refused to make another go of it with Dutch, accidentally hits a man with her car and takes him back to a mountain cabin to escape from a storm. Before long, she finds herself attracted to Ben Tierney, even though she begins to suspect that he is a serial killer being searched for by Butch and the FBI. A *Publishers Weekly* contributor wrote: "Lust, jealousy and murder suffuse Brown's crisp thriller." Kristine Huntley, writing in *Booklist,* noted: "The suspense builds as Brown's novel chugs toward a gripping, surprising conclusion."

In *Hello, Darkness,* Brown borrows from the Clint Eastwood movie *Play Misty for Me* to write of a female disc jockey named Paris Gibson who encounters a man named Valentino. It turns out that Valentino blames Paris's on-air advice for his failure in love. Valentino calls in to Paris's radio show and announces that he already has his girlfriend held hostage, has raped her, and is going to kill her in three days before turning his vengeance on Paris. Suspecting that this is more than just a fantasy caller, Paris turns to her ex-boyfriend, a police psychologist, for help. Writing in *Booklist,* Kristine Huntley noted that the novel "is full of thrills and chills that will keep readers turning the pages."

White Hot revolves around Sayre Lynch, who left Destiny, Louisiana, and changed her name to get away from her father, the corrupt Huff Hoyle, who owns a successful iron foundry. Sarah returns when her younger brother is found dead from a shotgun blast, which authorities initially believe to be a suicide. However, the more Sarah and a young detective learn, the more her brother's death begins to look like murder. As Sayre tries to sort everything out, including whether or not her older brother is actually the murderer, she begins to find herself attracted to her father's pesky right-hand man, Beck Merchant. A *Publishers Weekly* contributor noted: "White-hot labor disputes, family conflict, murder and romance are ablaze" in Brown's novel. Kristine Huntley, writing in *Booklist,* commented that the novel "sizzles, thanks mainly to a compelling cast of characters."

The author features the case of a judge's wife who kills an intruder whom she may have known, in the novel *Richochet.* Called to the house to investigate, Detective Duncan Hatcher becomes suspicious when he sees the intruder was killed with one pinpoint shot. The judge's wife, Elsie, later claims that the judge wants her dead and Duncan finds himself attracted to her despite his growing suspicions about her truthfulness and innocence. Writing in *Kirkus Reviews,* a contributor noted that the novel contains "enough twists to keep fans guessing." "Gripping and absorbing, this is Brown's best thriller in years," wrote Kristine Huntley in *Booklist.* A *Publishers Weekly* contributor noted: "Tight plotting, a hot love story with some nice twists and a credible ending help make this a standout thriller."

In addition to producing work under her own name, Brown has published many volumes under the pseudonyms Laura Jordan, Rachel Ryan, and Erin St. Claire. She once commented in *CA:* "I can't fathom an occupation from which I could derive so much satisfaction as that of writing. It's simply something I *must* do. Being paid to do it is icing on the cake."

BIOGRAPHICAL AND CRITICAL SOURCES:

BOOKS

Contemporary Southern Writers, St. James Press (Detroit, MI), 1999.
Twentieth-Century Romance and Historical Writers, edited by Aruna Vasudevan, St. James Press (Detroit, MI), 1994.

PERIODICALS

Booklist, May 1, 1995, Mary Frances Wilkens, review of *The Witness,* p. 1530; May 15, 1996, Mary Frances Wilkens, review of *Exclusive,* pp. 1546-1547; May 1, 1998, Donna Seaman, review of *Unspeakable,* p. 1477; March 15, 2000, Vanessa Bush, review of *Standoff,* p. 1292; August, 2000, Brad Hooper, review of *The Switch,* p. 2072; September 1, 2002, Kristine Huntley, review of *The Crush,* p. 4; September 1, 2003, Kristine Huntley, review of *Hello, Darkness,* p. 5; July, 2004, Kristine Huntley, review of *White Hot,* p. 1796; August, 2005, Kristine Huntley, review of *Chill Factor,* p. 1997; July 1, 2006, Kristine Huntley, review or *Ricochet,* p. 6.
Entertainment Weekly, September 10, 2004, review of *White Hot,* p. 171; September 9, 2005, review of *Chill Factor,* p. 149; August 18, 2006, Lynette Rice, review of *Ricochet,* p. 142.

Kirkus Reviews, March 15, 1994, review of *Charade,* p. 318; April 15, 1995, review of *The Witness,* p. 486; August 15, 2002, review of *The Crush,* p. 1157; July 1, 2004, review of *White Hot,* p. 589; May 15, 2006, review of *Ricochet,* p. 479.
Library Journal, May 15, 1998, Susan Clifford, review of *Unspeakable,* p. 112; September 15, 2001, Catherine Swenson, review of *The Switch,* p. 129; August 1, 2003, review of *Hello, Darkness,* p. 993; October 15, 2003, Samantha J. Gust, review of *Hello, Darkness,* p. 95; July, 2004, Samantha J. Gust, review of *White Hot,* p. 67; August 1, 2005, Nanette Wargo Donohue, review of *Chill Factor,* p. 65.
People, September 21, 1998, Alec Foege, "Texas Tornado," p. 81.
Publishers Weekly, March 21, 1994, review of *Charade,* p. 52; May 6, 1996, review of *Exclusive,* pp. 67-68; April 24, 2000, review of *Standoff,* p. 61; July 31, 2000, review of *The Switch,* p. 73; August 7, 2000, review of *Standoff,* p. 40; July 16, 2001, review of *Envy,* p. 157; September 10, 2001, Daisy Maryles, "Envying Brown," p. 19; September 2, 2002, review of *The Crush,* p. 54; June 7, 2004, review of *White Hot,* p. 29; June 20, 2005, review of *Chill Factor,* p. 55; June 19, 2006, review of *Ricochet,* p. 40; October 2, 2006, review of *Ricochet,* p. 58.
State (Columbia, SC), September 27, 2006, review of *Ricochet.*

ONLINE

Bookreporter.com, http://www.bookreporter.com/ (December 2, 2006), "Author Talk," interviews with author dating back to 1997; Maggie Harding, reviews of *Ricochet, Chill Factor,* and *White Hot;* Joe Hartlaub, review of *Hello, Darkness;* Robert O'Hara, review of *The Crush;* Debbie Ann Weiner, reviews of *The Switch, Envy,* and *Standoff;* Sofrina Hinton, review of *The Alibi;* Susanne Trani, review of *Unspeakable.*
Sandra Brown Home Page, http://www.sandrabrown.net (December 2, 2006).
Twbookmark, http://www.twbookmark.com/ (May 19, 2001), "Sandra Brown."*

*   *   *

BRUCHAC, Joseph 1942-
(Joseph Bruchac, III)

PERSONAL: Surname pronounced *"brew*-shack"; born October 16, 1942, in Saratoga Springs, NY; son of Joseph E., Jr. (a taxidermist and publisher) and Marion (a homemaker and publisher) Bruchac; married Carol Worthen (director of a nonprofit organization), June 13, 1964; children: James Edward, Jesse Bowman. *Ethnicity:* "Native American (Abenaki)/Slovak/English." *Education:* Cornell University, A.B., 1965; Syracuse University, M.A., 1966; graduate study at State University of New York—Albany, 1971-73; Union Institute of Ohio Graduate School, Ph.D., 1975. *Politics:* Liberal Democrat. *Religion:* "Methodist and Native-American spiritual traditions." *Hobbies and other interests:* Gardening, music, martial arts.

ADDRESSES: Home and office—Greenfield Review Press, P.O. Box 308, Greenfield Center, NY 12833. *Agent*—Barbara Kouts Agency, P.O. Box 560, Bellport, NY 11713. *E-mail*—nudatlog@earthlink.net.

CAREER: Keta Secondary School, Ghana, West Africa, teacher of English and literature, 1966-69; Skidmore College, Saratoga Springs, NY, instructor in creative writing and African and black literatures, 1969-73; University without Walls, coordinator of college program at Great Meadow Correctional Facility, 1974-81; writer and storyteller, 1981—. Greenfield Review Press, Greenfield Center, NY, publisher and editor of *Greenfield Review,* beginning 1969; Greenfield Review Literary Center, director, 1981—; musician with Dawn Land Singers, recording stories and music on *Abenaki Cultural Heritage* and *Alnobak,* Good Mind Records. Member of adjunct faculty at Hamilton College, 1983, 1985, 1987, and State University of New York—Albany, 1987-88; storyteller-in-residence at CRC Institute for Arts in Education, 1989-90, and at other institutions, including Oklahoma Summer Arts Institute, St. Regis Mohawk Indian School, Seneca Nation School, Onondaga Indian School, Institute of Alaska Native Arts, and Annsville Youth Facility; featured storyteller at festivals and conferences; presents workshops, poetry readings, and storytelling programs. Print Center, member of board of directors, 1975-78; Returning the Gift, national chairperson, 1992; judge of competitions, including PEN Prison Writing Awards, 1977, National Book Award for Translation, 1983, and National Book Award for Poetry, 1995; past member of literature panels, Massachusetts Arts Council, Vermont State Arts Council, Illinois Arts Council, and Ohio Arts Council.

MEMBER: Poetry Society of America, PEN, National Storytelling Association (member of board of directors, 1992-94), Native Writers Circle of the Americas (chairperson, 1992-95), Wordcraft Circle of Native Writers and Storytellers, Hudson Valley Writers Guild, Black Crow Network.

AWARDS, HONORS: Poetry fellow, Creative Artists Public Service, 1973, 1982; fellow, National Endowment for the Arts, 1974; editors' fellow, Coordinating Council of Literary Magazines, 1980; Rockefeller fellow, 1982; PEN Syndicated Fiction Award, 1983; American Book Award, 1984, for *Breaking Silence;* Yaddo residency, 1984, 1985; Cherokee Nation Prose Award, 1986; fellow, New York State Council on the Arts, 1986; Benjamin Franklin Audio Award, Publishers Marketing Association, 1992, for *The Boy Who Lived with the Bears,* and Person of the Year Award, 1993; Hope S. Dean Memorial Award for Notable Achievement in Children's Literature, 1993; Mountains and Plains Award, 1995, for *A Boy Called Slow;* Knickerbocker Award, 1995; Paterson Children's Book Award, 1996, for *Dog People; Boston Globe/Horn Book* Honor Award, 1996, for *The Boy Who Lived with the Bears;* Writer of the Year Award, and Storyteller of the Year Award, Wordcraft Circle of Native Writers and Storytellers, both 1998; Lifetime Achievement Award, Native Writers Circle of the Americas, 1999; Independent Publishers Outstanding Book of the Year designation, 2003, for *Our Stories Remember;* Sequoyah Book Award, Oklahoma Library Association, 2004, for *Skeleton Man;* Parent's Choice Award; Skipping Stones Honor Award for Multicultural Children's Literature; Virginia Hamilton Literary Award, 2005; Young Adult Award, American Indian Library Association, 2006, for *Hidden Roots.*

WRITINGS:

RETELLER; FOLK-TALE COLLECTIONS

Turkey Brother and Other Iroquois Folk Tales, Crossing Press (Trumansburg, NY), 1975.

Stone Giants and Flying Heads: Adventure Stories of the Iroquois, Crossing Press (Trumansburg, NY), 1978.

Iroquois Stories: Heroes and Heroines, Monsters and Magic, Crossing Press (Trumansburg, NY), 1985.

The Wind Eagle, Bowman Books, 1985.

The Faithful Hunter and Other Abenaki Stories, Bowman Books, 1988.

Return of the Sun: Native American Tales from the Eastern Woodlands, Crossing Press (Trumansburg, NY), 1990.

Native American Stories, Fulcrum Press (Golden, CO), 1991.

Hoop Snakes, Hide-Behinds, and Sidehill Winders, Crossing Press (Trumansburg, NY), 1991.

(With Jonathan London) *Thirteen Moons on Turtle's Back: A Native American Year of Moons,* Philomel (New York, NY), 1992.

Flying with the Eagle, Racing the Great Bear: Stories from Native North America, Bridgewater (New York, NY), 1993.

Native American Animal Stories, Fulcrum Press (Golden, CO), 1993.

The Native American Sweat Lodge, Crossing Press (Trumansburg, NY), 1993.

(With Gayle Ross) *The Girl Who Married the Moon: Stories from Native North America,* BridgeWater (New York, NY), 1994.

Dog People: Native Dog Stories, Fulcrum Press (Golden, CO), 1995.

Native Plant Stories, Fulcrum Press (Golden, CO), 1995.

The Boy Who Lived with the Bears, and Other Iroquois Stories, HarperCollins (New York, NY), 1995.

Between Earth and Sky: Legends of Native-American Sacred Places, illustrated by Thomas Locker, Harcourt (San Diego, CA), 1996.

The Circle of Thanks, BridgeWater (New York, NY), 1996.

Four Ancestors: Stories, Songs, and Poems, BridgeWater (New York, NY), 1996.

(Reteller, with son, James Bruchac) *When the Chenoo Howls: Native-American Tales of Terror,* illustrated by William Sauts Netamu'xwe Bock, Walker (New York, NY), 1998.

(With James Bruchac) *Native American Games and Stories,* illustrated by Kayeri Akwek, Fulcrum Press (Golden, CO), 2000.

Foot of the Mountain and Other Stories, Holy Cow! Press (Duluth, MN), 2002.

PICTURE BOOKS

(Reteller) *The First Strawberries,* illustrated by Anna Vojtech, Dial (New York, NY), 1993.

Fox Song, illustrated by Paul Morin, Philomel (New York, NY), 1993.

(Reteller) *The Great Ball Game,* illustrated by Susan L. Roth, Dial (New York, NY), 1994.

A Boy Called Slow: The True Story of Sitting Bull, illustrated by Rocco Baviera, Philomel (New York, NY), 1995.

Gluskabe and the Four Wishes, illustrated by Christine Shrader, Cobblehill Books (Boston, MA), 1995.

(With Gayle Ross) *The Story of the Milky Way,* illustrated by Virginia A. Stroud, Dial (New York, NY), 1995.

The Maple Thanksgiving, illustrated by Anna Vojtech, Celebration (Nobleboro, ME), 1996.

(With Melissa Fawcett) *Makiawisug: Gift of the Little People,* Little People (Warsaw, IN), 1997.

Many Nations: An Alphabet of Native America, Troll Publications (Mahwah, NJ), 1997.

Crazy Horse's Vision, illustrated by S.D. Nelson, Lee & Low Books (New York, NY), 2000.

Squanto's Journey: The Story of the First Thanksgiving, illustrated by Greg Shed, Silver Whistle (San Diego, CA), 2000.

(Reteller, with James Bruchac) *How Chipmunk Got His Stripes,* illustrated by José Aruego and Ariane Dewey, Dial (New York, NY), 2001.

Seasons of the Circle: A Native-American Year, illustrated by Robert F. Goetzel, BridgeWater (New York, NY), 2002.

(Reteller, with James Bruchac) *Turtle's Race with Beaver: A Traditional Seneca Story,* illustrated by José Aruego and Ariane Dewey, Dial Books for Young Readers (New York, NY), 2003.

(Reteller, with James Bruchac) *Raccoon's Last Race: A Traditional Abenaki Story,* illustrated by José Aruego and Ariane Dewey, Dial Books for Young Readers (New York, NY), 2004.

FICTION; FOR CHILDREN

Children of the Longhouse, Dial (New York, NY), 1996.

Eagle Song (chapter book), Dial (New York, NY), 1997.

The Arrow over the Door (chapter book), illustrated by James Watling, Dial (New York, NY), 1998.

The Heart of a Chief, Dial (New York, NY), 1998.

Sacajawea: The Story of Bird Woman and the Lewis and Clark Expedition, Silver Whistle (San Diego, CA), 2000.

Skeleton Man, HarperCollins (New York, NY), 2001.

The Journal of Jesse Smoke: A Cherokee Boy ("My Name Is America" series), Scholastic (New York, NY), 2001.

The Winter People, Dial (New York, NY), 2002.

Pocahontas (young-adult novel), Silver Whistle (Orlando, FL), 2003.

The Warriors, Darby Creek (Plain City, OH), 2003.

Hidden Roots (novel), Scholastic (New York, NY), 2004.

Dark Pond, illustrated by Sally Wern Comport, HarperCollins (New York, NY), 2004.

Whisper in the Dark, illustrated by Sally Wern Comport, HarperCollins (New York, NY), 2005.

Code Talker: A Novel about the Navajo Marines of World War II (young-adult novel), Dial Books (New York, NY), 2005.

Wabi: A Hero's Tale (young-adult novel), Dial (New York, NY), 2006.

Geronimo (young-adult novel), Scholastic (New York, NY), 2006.

Bearwalker, HarperCollins (New York, NY), 2007.

The Way, Darby Creek (Plain City, OH), 2007.

FICTION; FOR ADULTS

The Road to Black Mountain (short stories), Thorp Springs Press (Austin, TX), 1976.

The Dreams of Jesse Brown (short stories), Cold Mountain Press, 1978.

The White Moose (short stories), Blue Cloud Quarterly, 1988.

Turtle Meat, and Other Stories (short stories), Holy Cow! Press (Minneapolis, MN), 1992.

Dawn Land (novel), Fulcrum Press (Golden, CO), 1993.

Long River (sequel to *Dawn Land*), Fulcrum Press (Golden, CO), 1995.

The Waters Between: A Novel of the Dawn Land, University Press of New England (Hanover, NH), 1998.

POETRY

Indian Mountain, Ithaca House (Ithaca, NY), 1971.

The Buffalo in the Syracuse Zoo, Greenfield Review Press (Greenfield Center, NY), 1972.

Great Meadow, Dustbooks (Paradise, CA), 1973.

The Manabozho, Blue Cloud Quarterly, 1973.

Flow, Cold Mountain Press, 1975.

This Earth Is a Drum, Cold Mountain Press, 1976.

There Are No Trees inside the Prison, Blackberry Press, 1978.

Mu'ndu Wi Go, Blue Cloud Quarterly, 1978.

Entering Onondaga, Cold Mountain Press, 1978.

The Good Message of Handsome Lake, Unicorn Press (Greensboro, NC), 1979.

Translators' Son, Cross-Cultural Communications (Merrick, NY), 1980.

Ancestry, Great Raven (Fort Kent, ME), 1981.

Remembering the Dawn, Blue Cloud Quarterly, 1983.

Walking with My Sons, Landlocked Press, 1985.

Tracking, Ion Books, 1985.

Near the Mountains, White Pine (Buffalo, NY), 1986.

Langes Gedachtnis/Long Memory, OBEMA (Osnabruck, Germany), 1988.

The Earth under Sky Bear's Feet, illustrated by Thomas Locker, Philomel (New York, NY), 1995.

No Borders, Holy Cow! Press (Duluth, MN), 1999.

Above the Line, West End Press (Albuquerque, NM), 2003.

NONFICTION

The Poetry of Pop, Dustbooks (Paradise, CA), 1973.

How to Start and Sustain a Literary Magazine, Provision (Austin, TX), 1980.

Survival This Way: Interviews with American Indian Poets, University of Arizona (Tucson, AZ), 1987.

(With Michael Caduto) *Keepers of the Earth: Native American Stories and Environmental Activities for Children,* Fulcrum Press (Golden, CO), 1989.

(With Michael Caduto) *Keepers of the Animals: Native American Stories and Wildlife Activities for Children,* Fulcrum Press (Golden, CO), 1990.

(With Michael Caduto) *Keepers of the Night: Native American Stories and Nocturnal Activities for Children,* Fulcrum Press (Golden, CO), 1994.

(With Michael Caduto) *Keepers of Life: Discovering Plants through Native American Stories and Earth Activities for Children,* Fulcrum Press (Golden, CO), 1994.

Native Wisdom, HarperSanFrancisco (San Francisco, CA), 1995.

Roots of Survival: Native American Storytelling and the Sacred, Fulcrum Press (Golden, CO), 1996.

(With Michael Caduto) *Native American Gardening,* Fulcrum Press (Golden, CO), 1996.

Bowman's Store (autobiography), Dial (New York, NY), 1997.

Lasting Echoes: An Oral History of Native American People, Harcourt (New York, NY), 1997.

Tell Me a Tale: A Book about Storytelling, Harcourt (New York, NY), 1997.

Buffalo Boy (biography), illustrated by Baviera, Silver Whistle Books (San Diego, CA), 1998.

Seeing the Circle (autobiography), photographs by John Christian Fine, R.C. Owen (Katonah, NY), 1999.

The Trail of Tears (chapter book), illustrated by Diana Magnuson, Random House (New York, NY), 1999.

Trails of Tears, Paths of Beauty, National Geographic Society (Washington, DC), 2000.

Navajo Long Walk: The Tragic Story of a Proud People's Forced March from Their Homeland, illustrated by Shonto Begay, National Geographic Society (Washington, DC), 2002.

Our Stories Remember: American Indian History, Culture, and Values through Storytelling, Fulcrum Press (Golden, CO), 2003.

Jim Thorpe's Bright Path (biography; for children), illustrated by S.D. Nelson, Lee & Low Books (New York, NY), 2004.

(With James Bruchac) *Rachel Carson: Preserving a Sense of Wonder* (biography; for children), Fulcrum Press (Golden, CO), 2004.

At the Edge of Ridge Road (memoir), Milkweed (Minneapolis, MN), 2005.

Jim Thorpe: The Original All-American (biography; for children), Dial (New York, NY), 2006.

OTHER

Pushing up the Sky: Seven Native American Plays for Children, illustrated by Teresa Flavin, Dial (New York, NY), 2000.

Also editor of anthologies, including *The Last Stop: Prison Writings from Comstock Prison,* 1973; *Words from the House of the Dead: Prison Writing from Soledad,* 1974; *Aftermath: Poetry in English from Africa, Asia, and the Caribbean,* 1977; *The Next World: Thirty-two Third World American Poets,* 1978; *Songs from Turtle Island: Thirty-two American Indian Poets,* [Yugoslavia], 1982; *Songs from This Earth on Turtle's Back: Contemporary American Indian Poetry,* 1983; *Breaking Silence: Contemporary Asian-American Poets,* 1983; *The Light from Another Country: Poetry from American Prisons,* 1984; *North Country: An Anthology of Contemporary Writing from the Adirondacks and the Upper Hudson Valley,* 1986; *New Voices from the Longhouse: Contemporary Iroquois Writing,* 1989; *Raven Tells Stories: Contemporary Alaskan Native Writing,* 1990; *Singing of Earth,* 1993; *Returning the Gift,* 1994; *Smoke Rising,* 1995; and *Native Wisdom,* 1995. Audiotapes include *Iroquois Stories, Alnobak, Adirondack Tall Tales,* and *Abenaki Cultural Heritage,* all Good Mind Records; and *Gluskabe Stories,* Yellow Moon Press. Work represented in more than a hundred anthologies, including *Carriers of the Dream Wheel; Come to Power; For Neruda, for Chile; New Worlds of Literature; Paris Review Anthology,* and *Sports Shorts: An Anthology of Short Stories,* 2005. Contributor of more than three hundred stories, poems, articles, and

reviews to magazines, including *American Poetry Review, Akwesasne Notes, Beloit Poetry Journal, Chariton Review, Kalliope, Mid-American Review, Nation, Poetry Northwest, River Styx,* and *Virginia Quarterly Review.* Editor, *Trojan Horse,* 1964, *Greenfield Review,* 1969-87, *Prison Writing Review,* 1976-85, and *Studies in American Indian Literature,* 1989—. Member of editorial board, Cross-Cultural Communications, *Parabola, Storytelling Journal, MELUS,* and *Obsidian.* Translator from Abenaki, Ewe, Iroquois, and Spanish.

ADAPTATIONS: Several of Bruchac's books have been recorded on audiocassette, including *Keepers of the Earth, Keepers of the Animals, Keepers of Life,* and *Dawn Land,* all released by Fulcrum; and *The Boy Who Lived with the Bears,* released by Caedmon/Parabola.

SIDELIGHTS: According to *Publishers Weekly* contributor Sybil Steinberg, Joseph Bruchac ranks as "perhaps the best-known contemporary Native American storyteller." Bruchac draws on his heritage for his critically acclaimed collections, including *Flying with the Eagle, Racing the Great Bear: Stories from Native North America* and *The Girl Who Married the Moon: Stories from Native North America.* These stories also influence Bruchac's novels, such as *Dawn Land* and its sequels *Long Land* and *The Waters Between: A Novel of the Dawn Land,* a series about the Abenaki living in the American northeast prior to the arrival of Columbus. "His stories," Steinberg concluded, "are often poignant, funny, ironic—and sometimes all three at once." In addition to his original novels, picture books, poetry, and nonfiction, Bruchac's work as an editor and publisher has brought many other acclaimed Native-American authors into the public eye. He published early books by Leslie Marmon Silko and Linda Hogan, whose voices have since become well known in the field of Native-American literature. He is also a nationally known live storyteller, and his performances have been recorded on audiocassette.

Dawn Land, Bruchac's first novel, introduces readers to the character of Young Hunter, and in 1995's *Long River,* Young Hunter's adventures continue as he battles a wooly mammoth and an evil giant. In *Dawn Land* and *Long River,* as well as the concluding novel *The Waters Between* Bruchac incorporates actual myths from his own Abenaki heritage. His children's stories, like his novels, entertain and educate young readers by interweaving Native-American history and myth. The biography *A Boy Called Slow,* for example, recounts the story of the Lakota boy who would grow up to become Sitting Bull. Bruchac's ability to "gently correct" stereotypes of Native-American culture was noted by Carolyn Polese in *School Library Journal.* In *The Great Ball Game* he relates the importance of ball games in Native-American tradition as a substitute for war, tying neatly together history and ethics lessons in "an entertaining tale," commented Polese. He combines several versions of a Native-American tale in *Gluskabe and the Four Wishes.*

Bruchac writes prolifically in several genres, including fiction, poetry, and nonfiction. Several of his nonfiction titles for adults explain the value of storytelling. In *Our Stories Remember: American Indian History, Culture, and Values through Storytelling* he relates stories from many different Native-American nations to illustrate their core values and culture. Writing in *School Library Journal,* S.K. Joiner noted that, "Part cultural lesson, part history, and part autobiography, the book contains a wealth of information," while *Booklist* contributor Deborah Donovan dubbed it a "thought-provoking work, enriched with valuable annotated reading lists."

Bruchac's nonfiction titles for young people include several biographies of Native Americans and pivotal figures in the environmental movement. In *Rachel Carson: Preserving a Sense of Wonder* he presents a biography of the author of *Silent Spring,* a book credited with inspiring the environmental movement in the 1960s. Writing in *Booklist,* Carolyn Phelan noted that "Bruchac writes lyrically about [Carson's] . . . love of nature, particularly the ocean, and concludes with an appreciation of her impact on the environment." The picture-book biography *Jim Thorpe's Bright Path* recounts the life of the famed Native-American athlete. *School Library Journal* contributor Liza Graybill noted that Bruchac's "theme of overcoming personal and societal obstacles to reach success is strongly expressed."

Not all of Bruchac's picture books are nonfiction; many of his books for the very young are based on traditional Native-American tales. *The First Strawberries,* his first picture book, is based on a Cherokee tale, while *Raccoon's Last Race* is a story drawn from the Abenaki tradition. The latter tale explains how Raccoon, once tall and fast, became the squat, slow creature he is today. Noting that *Raccoon's Last Race* is one of several collaborations between Bruchac, his son, James Bruchac, and husband-and-wife illustration team José Aruego and

Ariane Dewey, a *Kirkus Reviews* contributor noted: "Readers will hope this foursome keeps on rolling." *Horn Book* reviewer Kitty Flynn noted that "the Bruchacs' well-paced retelling is alive with sound, . . . making the story well suited for reading aloud."

In *The Dark Pond,* Bruchac revisits the genre he previously explored in *Skeleton Man*: thrillers for young readers. Arnie, a half-Shawnee student at an all-white prep school, is drawn to a mysterious dark pool in the woods. He senses that something is lurking there, and his fears are confirmed when he discovers that Native-American groundskeeper Mitch Sabattis believes a gigantic worm lives in the pond and is determined to kill the creature. Arnie, remembering the traditional tales of his family, decides to do what he can to help slay this monster. "This is a creepy, fast-moving tale that will appeal to fans of horror stories, with a message about self-discovery neatly tucked in as well," wrote Paula Rohrlick in *Kliatt.* B. Allison Gray noted in *School Library Journal* that Bruchac's "eerie story skillfully entwines Native American lore, suspense, and the realization that people are not always what they seem." *Whisper in the Dark* wraps Narragansett legend around an all-too-real modern danger as Maddie confronts the mystery of a seemingly supernatural stalker. "Bruchac interweaves suspense with Indian folklore endlessly," commented Claire Rosser in *Kliatt,* while Wendi Hofenberg wrote in *School Library Journal* that "Maddi's narration is swirl and spare, creating a mood of terror tempered by Narragansett words and chants of courage."

Bruchac draws on history for many of his novels. His young-adult novel *Code Talker: A Novel about the Navajo Marines of World War II,* for example, gives readers an inside perspective on the role Navajo Marines played in sending vital encoded messages during World War II. Told from the perspective of sixteen-year-old Ned Begay, who is technically too young to be in the military, the story reveals how the Navajo language, once a tongue the U.S. government attempted to eliminate, was now valued highly by the U.S. military. "The narrative pulls no punches about war's brutality and never adopts an avuncular tone," noted *Booklist* contributor Carolyn Phelan. As *Kliatt* reviewer Paula Rohrlick commented, "readers unfamiliar with the fascinating story of the code talkers will come away impressed by their achievements." In *Geronimo,* Bruchac relates the story of the famous Native-American leader through the eyes of the man's adopted grandson. "Fans of history, or of themes of survival and freedom, will find it fascinating—certainly different from other fare about the man," wrote Nina Lindsay in *School Library Journal.*

Other novels by Bruchac draw solely on legend. *Wabi: A Hero's Tale* is the story of an owl who learns a secret about his people: he can shape shift and take human form. He falls in love with a local tribal woman, but her people banish him when they discover his true identity. In order to save his love's people, he must go on a dangerous quest. "Bruchac's storytelling skills are on full display in this tale," wrote a *Publishers Weekly* contributor. Lisa Prolman, in *School Library Journal,* suggested: "Give this novel to . . . anyone who enjoys reading about journeys of self-discovery," while a critic for *Kirkus Reviews* maintained that "readers won't be able to turn the pages fast enough."

"I was born in 1942, in Saratoga Springs, New York, during October, that month the Iroquois call the Moon of Falling Leaves," Bruchac once commented "My writing and my interests reflect my mixed ancestry, Slovak on one side and Native American (Abenaki) and English on the other. Aside from attending Cornell University and Syracuse and three years of teaching in West Africa, I've lived all of my life in the small Adirondack foothills town of Greenfield Center in a house built by my grandfather.

"Much of my writing and my life relates to the problem of being an American. While in college I was active in civil rights work and in the anti-war movement. . . . I went to Africa to teach—but more than that, to be taught. It showed me many things. How much we have as Americans and take for granted. How much our eyes refuse to see because they are blinded to everything in a man's face except his color. And, most importantly, how human people are everywhere—which may be the one grace that can save us all.

"I write poetry, fiction, and some literary criticism and have been fortunate enough to receive recognition in all three areas. After returning from Ghana in 1969, my wife, Carol, and I started the *Greenfield Review* and the Greenfield Review Press. Since 1975, I've been actively involved in storytelling, focusing on northeastern Native-American tales and the songs and traditions of the Adirondack Mountains of upstate New York, and I am frequently a featured performer at storytelling gatherings. I've also done a great deal of work in teaching and helping start writing workshops in American

prisons. I believe that poetry is as much a part of human beings as is breath—and that, like breath, poetry links us to all other living things and is meant to be shared.

"My writing is informed by several key sources. One of these is nature, another is the Native-American experience (I'm part Indian). . . . I like to work outside, in the earthmother's soil, with my hands . . . but maintain my life as an academic for a couple of reasons: it gives me time to write (sometimes) and it gives me a chance to share my insights into the beautiful and all-too-fragile world of human life and living things we have been granted. Which is one of the reasons I write—not to be a man apart, but to share."

In an interview with Eliza T. Dresang on the *Cooperative Children's Book Center Web site,* Bruchac noted that he does not expect to run out of things to write about. He told Dresang: "The last thirty years of my life in particular have been blessed with so many . . . experiences and by the generosity of so many Native people who have shared their stories and their understanding of their land with me that I know I can never live long enough to share everything I've learned. But I'll try."

BIOGRAPHICAL AND CRITICAL SOURCES:

PERIODICALS

Booklist, February 15, 1993, p. 1075; July, 1993, p. 1969; October 15, 1993, p. 397; November 15, 1993, p. 632; December 15, 1993, p. 749; August, 1994, p. 2017; September, 1994, p. 55; October 15, 1994, p. 377; December 15, 1994, p. 756; September 1, 1997, p. 69; September 15, 1997, pp. 234, 237; December 5, 1997, p. 688; February 15, 1998; October 1, 2002, Heather Hepler, review of *Seasons of the Circle: A Native-American Year,* p. 316, and GraceAnne A. DeCandido, review of *The Winter People,* p. 322; April 15, 2003, Deborah Donovan, review of *Our Stories Remember: American Indian History, Culture, and Values through Storytelling,* p. 1444; September 15, 2003, John Peters, review of *Turtle's Race with Beaver,* p. 244, and Ed Sullivan, review of *Pocahontas,* p. 229; July, 2004, Carolyn Phelan, review of *Rachel Carson: Preserving a Sense of Wonder,* p. 1838; August, 2004, Todd Morning, review of *The Dark*

Pond, p. 1932, and Stephanie Zvirin, review of *Jim Thorpe's Bright Path,* p. 1938; February 15, 2005, Carolyn Phelan, review of *Code Talker:: A Novel about the Navajo Marines of World War II,* p. 1078; September 1, 2005, Holly Koelling, review of *Whisper in the Dark,* p. 131; November 15, 2005, Anna Rich, audiobook review of *Crazy Horse's Vision,* p. 64; March 15, 2006, GraceAnne A. DeCandido, review of *Geronimo,* p. 43.

Horn Book, January-February, 1994, p. 60; March-April, 1994, p. 209; November-December, 1994, p. 738; March-April, 1995, p. 203; September-October, 1995, p. 617; January-February, 2005, Kitty Flynn, review of *Raccoon's Last Race,* p. 102.

Kirkus Reviews, March 15, 1996, p. 445; May 1, 1996, p. 685; December 1, 1996, p. 1734; January 1, 2004, review of *Hidden Roots,* p. 34; October 15, 2004, review of *Raccoon's Last Race,* p. 1002; January 15, 2005, review of *Code Talker,* p. 117; July 1, 2005, review of *Whisper in the Dark,* p. 732; September, 2005, Paula Rohrlick, review of *The Dark Pond,* p. 25; February 1, 2006, review of *Wabi: A Hero's Tale,* p. 128.

Kliatt, July, 2004, Paula Rohrlick, review of *The Dark Pond,* p. 7; March, 2005, Paula Rohrlick, review of *Code Talker,* p. 8; July, 2005, Claire Rosser, review of *Whisper in the Dark,* p. 8; January, 2006, Edna Boardman, review of *Foot of the Mountain, and Other Stories,* p. 26; March, 2006, Paula Rohrlick, review of *Geronimo,* p. 6.

Publishers Weekly, March 15, 1993, p. 68; June 28, 1993, p. 76; July 19, 1993, pp. 254, 255; August 29, 1994, p. 79; January 9, 1995, p. 64; July 31, 1995, p. 68; July 14, 1997, p. 83; September 8, 1997, p. 78; November 24, 1997, p. 75; May 31, 2004, review of *Jim Thorpe's Bright Path,* p. 76; May 1, 2006, review of *Wabi,* p. 64.

School Library Journal, March, 1993, p. 161; August, 1993, p. 205; September, 1993, pp. 222, 238; February, 1994, p. 78; November, 1994, p. 112; December, 1994, p. 96; February, 1995, p. 104; October, 1995, Carolyn Polese, review of *A Boy Called Slow,* p. 145; July, 2002, Anne Chapman Callaghan, review of *Navajo Long Walk: The Tragic Story of a Proud People's Forced March from Their Homeland,* p. 131; November, 2002, Rita Soltan, review of *The Winter People,* p. 154; July, 2003, S.K. Joiner, review of *Our Stories Remember,* p. 155; February, 2004, Alison Follos, review of *Hidden Roots,* p. 141; May, 2004, Sean George, review of *Pocahontas,* p. 140; June, 2004, Liza Graybill, review of *Jim Thorpe's Bright Path,* p. 124; August, 2004, B. Allison Gray, review of *The Dark Pond,* p. 115; December, 2004, Catherine Threadgill, review of *Raccoon's Last Race,* p. 127; February, 2005, B. Allison Gray, audiobook review of *Skeleton Man,* p. 75; May, 2005, Patricia Manning, review of *Code Talker,* p. 24; August, 2005, review of *Code Talker,* p. 50, and Wendi Hoffenberg, review of *Whisper in the Dark,* p. 121; October, 2005, review of *Code Talker,* p. S67; November, 2005, Alison Follos, review of *Sports Shorts: An Anthology of Short Stories,* p. 128; April, 2006, Lisa Prolman, review of *Wabi,* and Nina Lindsay, review of *Geronimo,* both p. 134.

Teacher Librarian, February, 2005, Betty Winslow, review of *The Journal of Jesse Smoke,* p. 14.

Voice of Youth Advocates, February, 2006, Tracy Piombo, review of *At the End of Ridge Road,* p. 508.

ONLINE

Children's Literature Web site, http://www.childrenslit.com/ (June 22, 2006).

Cooperative Children's Book Center Web site, http://www.education.wisc.edu/ccbc/ (October 22, 1999), Eliza T. Dresang, interview with Bruchac.

Joseph Bruchac Home Page, http://www.josephbruchac.com (June 22, 2006).*

* * *

BRUCHAC, Joseph, III
See BRUCHAC, Joseph

C

CARTER, Steven 1956-

PERSONAL: Born October 23, 1956, in New York, NY; son of Alfred M. (in business) and Sydelle (a teacher) Carter. *Education:* Cornell University, B.S., 1978.

CAREER: Writer and lecturer. Has appeared on numerous television programs, including *Oprah, Sally Jesse Raphael, Good Morning America, CBS This Morning,* and the *Today Show.*

WRITINGS:

What Every Man Should Know About the New Woman: A Survival Guide, McGraw Hill (New York, NY), 1984.
(With Joshua Levine) *How to Make Love to a Computer,* Pocket Books (New York, NY), 1984.
(With Harold Levinson) *Phobia-Free: A Medical Breakthrough Linking Ninety Percent of All Phobia and Panic Attacks to a Hidden Physical Problem,* M. Evans (New York, NY), 1985.
(With Julia Sokol) *Men Who Can't Love: When a Man's Fear Makes Him Run from Commitment (and What a Smart Woman Can Do about It),* M. Evans (New York, NY), 1986.
(With Julia Sokol) *What Really Happens in Bed: A Demystification of Sex,* M. Evans (New York, NY), 1988.
(With Julia Sokol) *What Smart Women Know,* M. Evans (New York, NY), 1990.
Lives without Balance: When You're Giving Everything You've Got and Still Not Getting What You Hoped For, Random House (New York, NY), 1992.
(With Julia Sokol) *He's Scared, She's Scared: Understanding the Hidden Fears that Sabotage Your Relationships,* Delacorte Press (New York, NY), 1993.
(With Julia Sokol) *Men like Women Who like Themselves (and Other Secrets that the Smartest Women Know about Partnership and Power),* Delacorte Press (New York, NY), 1996.
(With Julia Sokol) *Getting to Commitment: Overcoming the Eight Greatest Obstacles to Lasting Connection (and Finding the Courage to Love),* M. Evans (New York, NY), 1998.
This Is How Love Works: Nine Essential Secrets You Need to Know, M. Evans (New York, NY), 2001.
(With Julia Sokol) *Help! I'm in Love with a Narcissist,* M. Evans (New York, NY), 2005.

Contributor to periodicals, including *Cosmopolitan, Glamour, New Woman,* and *Mademoiselle.*

SIDELIGHTS: Steven Carter and his coauthor, Julia Sokol, write about fear-of-commitment issues in relationships and have coauthored numerous books on various aspects of the topic. For example, in *What Smart Women Know,* Carter and Sokol discuss unrewarding relationships and what "smart" women look for in a man. Genevieve Stuttaford, writing in *Publishers Weekly,* noted that the book contains "some common-sense recommendations." *He's Scared, She's Scared: Understanding the Hidden Fears That Sabotage Your Relationships* focuses on fear of commitment by both men and women and delineates the differences. Case histories study specific examples of commitment fear, and the authors include quizzes to help men and women explore their commitment issues. A *Publishers Weekly* contributor wrote that the authors "uncover the more subtle ways men and women sabotage love."

In their self-help book *Men like Women Who like Themselves (and Other Secrets that the Smartest Women Know about Partnership and Power)*, Carter and Sokol provide a guideline featuring what women who are successful in relationships practice when meeting, dating, and having an intimate relationship with a man. A *Publishers Weekly* contributor commented that the authors provide "sound advice on how to recognize a potentially abusive man, [and] when to seek counseling." *Help! I'm in Love with a Narcissist* is a guide to recognizing and dealing with a mate who always puts himself or herself first. The authors discuss the causes of narcissism, how to seek outside support, and how to end the relationship if necessary. A *Publishers Weekly* contributor noted that "their advice boils down to taking care of yourself first."

BIOGRAPHICAL AND CRITICAL SOURCES:

PERIODICALS

Publishers Weekly, October 26, 1990, Genevieve Stuttaford, review of *What Smart Women Know*, p. 61; August 30, 1993, review of *He's Scared, She's Scared: Understanding the Hidden Fears That Sabotage Your Relationships*, p. 86; May 6, 1996, review of *Men like Women Who like Themselves (and Other Secrets that the Smartest Women Know about Partnership and Power)* p. 60; December 20, 2004, review of *Help! I'm in Love with a Narcissist*, p. 49.*

*   *   *

CASTELLUCCI, Cecil 1969-

PERSONAL: Born 1969, in New York, NY; daughter of scientists. *Education:* Concordia University, B.F.A.; studied theatre at École Florent (Paris, France), and Groundling's (Los Angeles, CA).

ADDRESSES: Home—Los Angeles, CA. *Home and office*—P.O. Box 29095, Los Angeles, CA 90039. *E-mail*—misscecil@earthlink.com.

CAREER: Musician and entertainer. Alpha 60 Film Club, founding member; film writer and director; MTV, field producer of *Big Urban Myth Show*; performance artist; indie rock musician.

AWARDS, HONORS: Explorations film grant, Canada Council; PAFPS grant, National Film Board of Canada; named Hero in Education, California State Lottery, 2001.

WRITINGS:

Boy Proof (young-adult novel), Candlewick Press (Cambridge, MA), 2005.
Queen of Cool (young-adult novel), Candlewick Press (Cambridge, MA), 2006.
Beige (young-adult novel), Candlewick Press (Cambridge, MA), 2007.

Also author of *The P.L.A.I.N. Janes*, a graphic novel illustrated by Jim Rugg and published by DC Comics. Screenwriter and director of *Happy Is Not Hard to Be*; writer of numerous performance pieces, including "The Shirt and Other Awkward Stories," "The Ladies' Room," and "My Heart, the Whore."

ADAPTATIONS: Boy Proof was adapted for audiobook by Recorded Books, 2006.

SIDELIGHTS: Writing is just one of Cecil Castellucci's many interests; she is also a film director, a performance artist, an indie rock musician who performs under the name Nerdy Girl, and a frequent volunteer at reading programs for children. It was as a result of her volunteer interests that Castellucci read a large number of young-adult novels. With *Boy Proof* she took the next step and produced one of her own. In her new career as a young-adult novelist, Castellucci has also produced the teen reads *The Queen of Cool* and *Beige*, as well as the text for the graphic novel *The P.L.A.I.N. Janes*, part of D.C. Comics' girl-focused Minx imprint.

At the center of *Boy Proof* is Victoria, a "brooding, smart, self-confident narrator," in the words of *Horn Book* contributor Christine H. Heppermann. With her shaved head and assorted body piercings, Egg—as Victoria is known among her friend—is pretty sure she is "boy proof." The young woman's life as the daughter of a special-effects artist and a television star working on a comeback has given her a very cynical outlook on Hollywood and the wider world that seems to focus on celebrities as if they truly mattered. Despite the exterior she has created for the world at large, Victoria is a straight-A student with a sharp mind and an affection for monster movies. Her cinematic interests, in addition to providing her with a creative outlet, gives her a chance to argue with the members of the Science-Fiction and Fantasy Club, who refuse to share the same viewpoint on Hollywood. When Max Garter transfers into Victoria's prep school, all the teen's assumptions begin to fragment. In addition to their growing love interest, Victoria has to deal with her parents' impending divorce and her mother's efforts to win the teen to her side. Jealousy and disillusionment also enter the mix in Castellucci's coming-of-age tale.

Castellucci introduces another teen heroine, sixteen-year-old Libby Brin, in *The Queen of Cool*, described by *Horn Book* contributor Christine Heppermann as an "engaging first-person narrative" that reveals the "vacuous existence of teens with no interests other than themselves." Bored with her best-of-everything life, parties, high-fashion clothes, and an endless string of shallow and interchangeable friends of both sexes, Libby acts out her frustration by disrupting the Fall Formal at her exclusive private high school. Realizing that something in her life is terribly wrong, Libby surprises even herself by volunteering at the Los Angeles zoo, where an interest in science and relationships with two unusual friends help the teen add the missing emotional pieces to her life. "Castellucci clearly knows what goes on in the lives of many teens," noted Gail E. Wellman in a *School Library Journal* appraisal of the novel, the critic adding that the writer's engaging prose and "satisfying ending" will attract even reluctant readers. In a *Kirkus Reviews* appraisal of *The Queen of Cool*, a reviewer dubbed the novel a "smart, edgy take on one adolescent's search for identity and meaning in life," while in *Kliatt* Myrna Marler wrote that the novel's "action is fast-paced with quick cuts from scene to scene a la MTV." Praising Libby's "lively, intimate" narration, Shelle Rosenfeld concluded in *Booklist* that *The Queen of Cool* provides teen readers with a "quick, engaging read."

BIOGRAPHICAL AND CRITICAL SOURCES:

PERIODICALS

Booklist, February 15, 2005, Hazel Rochman, review of *Boy Proof,* p. 1072; February 15, 2006, Shelle Rosenfeld, review of *The Queen of Cool,* p. 90.
Bulletin of the Center for Children's Books, April, 2006, review of *The Queen of Cool,* p. 346.
Horn Book, May-June, 2005, Christine H. Heppermann, review of *Boy Proof,* p. 322; March-April, 2006, Christine M. Heppermann, review of *The Queen of Cool,* p. 182.
Kirkus Reviews, February 1, 2005, review of *Boy Proof,* p. 175; February 15, 2006, p. 179.
Kliatt, March, 2005, Claire Rosser, review of *Boy Proof,* p. 8; March, 2006, Myrna Marler, review of *The Queen of Cool,* p. 8.
Publishers Weekly, February 21, 2005, review of *Boy Proof,* p. 176; June 27, 2005, "Flying Starts," p. 27; February 20, 2006, review of *The Queen of Cool,* p. 158.
School Library Journal, April, 2005, Sarah Couri, review of *Boy Proof,* p. 129; March, 2006, Gail E. Wellman, review of *The Queen of Cool,* p. 220.
Voice of Youth Advocates, February, 2006, C.J. Bott, review of *The Queen of Cool,* p. 482.

ONLINE

Cecil Castellucci Home Page, http://home.earthlink.net/~seaskull (June 3, 2005).*

*   *   *

CAYTON, Andrew R.L. 1954-
(Andrew Robert Lee Cayton)

PERSONAL: Born May 9, 1954, in Cincinnati, OH; son of Robert Frank (a librarian) and Vivian (a high school teacher) Cayton; married Mary Kupiec (a college professor), August 23, 1975; children: Elizabeth Renanne. *Education:* University of Virginia, B.A. (with high honors), 1976; Brown University, M.A., 1977, Ph.D., 1981.

ADDRESSES: Home—Oxford, OH. *Office*—Miami University, Department of History, Oxford, OH 45056-1879. *E-mail*—caytonar@muohio.edu.

CAREER: Historian, educator, and writer. Harvard University, Cambridge, MA, lecturer, 1980-81, instructor in history and literature, 1981-82; Ball State University, Muncie, IN, assistant professor, 1982-86, associate professor of history, beginning 1986; Miami University, Department of History, Miami, OH, distinguished professor. Visiting assistant professor at Wellesley College, 1981-82.

MEMBER: American Historical Association, Organization of American Historians, Society for Historians of the Early American Republic, Indiana Historical Society, Ohio Historical Society.

AWARDS, HONORS: Ohioana Book Award for History, 1987, for *The Frontier Republic.*

WRITINGS:

The Frontier Republic: Ideology and Politics in the Ohio Country, 1780-1825, Kent State University Press (Kent, OH), 1986.

(With Peter S. Onuf) *The Midwest and the Nation: Rethinking the History of an American Region,* Indiana University Press (Bloomington, IN), 1990.

(Editor, with Jeffrey P. Brown) *The Pursuit of Public Power: Political Culture in Ohio, 1787-1861,* Kent State University Press (Kent, OH), 1994.

Frontier Indiana, Indiana University Press (Bloomington, IN), 1996.

(With Elisabeth Israels Perry and Allan M. Winkler) *America: Pathways to the Present: Civil War to the Present,* Prentice Hall (Needham, MA), 1998.

(With Elisabeth Israels Perry and Allan M. Winkler) *America: Pathways to the Present: America in the Twentieth Century,* Prentice Hall (Needham, MA), 1998.

(Editor, with Fredrika J. Teute) *Contact Points: American Frontiers from the Mohawk Valley to the Mississippi, 1750-1830,* University of North Carolina Press (Chapel Hill, NC), 1998.

(Editor and contributor, with Susan E. Gray) *The American Midwest: Essays on Regional History,* Indiana University Press (Bloomington, IN), 2001.

America: Pathways to the Present: Modern American History (teacher's edition), Prentice Hall (Needham, MA), 2002.

Ohio: The History of a People, Ohio State University Press (Columbus, OH), 2002.

(With Fred Anderson) *The Dominion of War: Empire and Liberty in North America, 1500-2000,* Viking (New York, NY), 2005.

(Editor, with Stuart D. Hobbs) *The Center of a Great Empire: The Ohio Country in the Early American Republic,* Ohio University Press (Athens, OH), 2005.

(General editor, with Richard Sisson and Christian Zacher) *The American Midwest: An Interpretive Encyclopedia,* Indiana University Press (Bloomington, IN), 2007.

Contributor to books, including *Pathways to the Old Northwest: An Observance of the Bicentennial of the Northwest Ordinance: Proceedings of a Conference held at Franklin College of Indiana, July 10-11, 1987,* Indiana Historical Society, 1998; contributor to history journals. Coeditor of *Old Northwest: A Journal of Regional Life and Letters.*

SIDELIGHTS: Andrew R.L. Cayton once told *CA:* "While my writing is primarily addressed to a scholarly audience, I undertook it for personal reasons. I grew up in the Ohio Valley and have always felt both fascinated and perplexed by its culture. I decided to study the early political history of the Midwest in order to get a fuller sense of where the region's political institutions came from. More broadly, I am interested in the question of midwestern regionalism.

"My academic research and publications are really nothing more than an effort to discover my own social and cultural origins. My maternal grandfather spent much of my childhood regaling me with long stories about his ancestors and the history of northern Kentucky. What I try to do is pretty much the same thing, although within the restrictions of an academic discipline."

Cayton has written or edited several books focusing primarily on the eighteenth and nineteenth-century history of trans-Appalachian North America. In his book *Frontier Indiana,* the author writes about various frontier figures in an effort to delineate the world outlook held by people on the frontier at that time. E.J. Fabyan, writing in *History: Review of New Books,* commented that "a wide cast of . . . characters are brought to new levels of historical evaluation and interpretation that reflect not only the mechanics of their lives but, in often unique ways, the meaning as well." Fabyan also noted the author's "fine writing and powerful prose."

Clayton collaborated with Fred Anderson to write *The Dominion of War: Empire and Liberty in North America, 1500-2000.* In their book, the authors discuss their belief that the use of force to build empires has been the norm in the history of North America since 1500. A *Kirkus Reviews* contributor noted that the authors present a case "that from the start, America . . . has been augmented and empowered by . . . spasms of war fever." In addition to discussing specific wars, such as the Mexican-American War, the authors also profile leading figures in imperial ambition affecting North America, from Antonio Lopez de Santa Anna and William Penn to such well-known modern figures as Generals Douglas MacArthur and Colin Powell. Jay Freeman, writing in *Booklist,* called the *Dominion of War* "a well-written and important reinterpretation of our past." In *History: Review of New Books,* Ruud Janssens noted that "the authors have written excellent chapters on individual political and military leaders."

Cayton also served as coeditor with Susan E. Gray of *The American Midwest: Essays on Regional History,* Writing about the various contributors to the anthology, *Michigan Historical Review* contributor Ellen Nore noted: "Although the authors do not speak with a single voice, they offer consistently provocative views." The author is also coeditor with Stuart D. Hobbs of *The Center of a Great Empire: The Ohio Country in the Early American Republic.* The book presents various historians writing about the region between Lake Erie and the Ohio River around the closing years of the eighteenth century and the beginning of the nineteenth. The contributors explore issues such as Indian relocation.

BIOGRAPHICAL AND CRITICAL SOURCES:

PERIODICALS

Booklist, November 15, 2004, Jay Freeman, review of *The Dominion of War: Empire and Liberty in North America, 1500-2000,* p. 547.
Foreign Affairs, May-June, 2005, Walter Russell Mead, review of *The Dominion of War,* p. 138.
History: Review of New Books, fall, 1997, E.J. Fabyan, review of *Frontier Indiana,* p. 14; spring, 2005, Ruud Janssens, review of *The Dominion of War,* p. 92.
Kirkus Reviews, November 1, 2004, review of *The Dominion of War,* p. 1033.
Michigan Historical Review, fall, 2002, Ellen Nore, review of *The American Midwest: Essays on Regional History,* p. 189.
New Statesman, July 25, 2005, Michael Lind, review of *The Dominion of War,* p. 52.
Parameters, spring, 2006, Robert L. Bateman, review of *The Dominion of War,* p. 143.
Publishers Weekly, November 22, 2004, review of *The Dominion of War,* p. 52.
Reference & Research Book News, November, 2005, review of *The Center of a Great Empire: The Ohio Country in the Early American Republic.*

Washington Post Book World, January 30, 2005, by Andrew J. Bacevich, review of *The Dominion of War,* p. BW05.

ONLINE

Ohio University Department of History Web site, http://www.units.muohio.edu/history/ (December 3, 2006), faculty profile of author.*

*   *   *

**CAYTON, Andrew Robert Lee
See CAYTON, Andrew R.L.**

*   *   *

CLAXTON, Guy Lennox 1947-

PERSONAL: Born June 20, 1947, in London, England; son of Eric and Ruby Mary Claxton; married Vicky Anne Lewis, August 22, 1970 (divorced, 1979). *Ethnicity:* "White." *Education:* Cambridge University, B.A. (with honors), 1969, M.A., 1973; Oxford University, D.Phil., 1974.

ADDRESSES: Home—Totnes, Devon, England.

CAREER: University of London, London, England, lecturer in psychology of education at Institute of Education, 1974-79, and at Chelsea College, beginning 1979. Schumacher College, founding faculty member; University of Bristol, visiting professor.

MEMBER: British Psychological Society (fellow).

WRITINGS:

The Little Ed Book (nonfiction), Routledge & Kegan Paul (Boston, MA), 1978.
(With Anand Ageha) *Wholly Human: Western and Eastern Visions of the Self and Its Perfection,* Routledge & Kegan Paul (Boston, MA), 1981.
Live and Learn, Harper & Row (New York, NY), 1984.

Teaching to Learn: A Direction for Education, Cassell (London, England), 1990.

The Heart of Buddhism, Crucible, 1990.

Educating the Inquiring Mind: The Challenge for School Science, Harvester Wheatsheaf (New York, NY), 1991.

Noises from the Darkroom: The Science and Mystery of the Mind, Aquarian (London, England), 1994.

Wise Up: The Challenge of Lifelong Learning, St. Martin's Press (New York, NY), 1999.

Hare Brain, Tortoise Mind: Why Intelligence Increases When You Think Less, Ecco Press (Hopewell, NJ), 1999.

Building Learning Power: Helping Young People Become Better Learners, TLO (Bristol, England), 2002.

The Wayward Mind: An Intimate History of the Unconscious, Little, Brown (New York, NY), 2005.

EDITOR

(And contributor) *Cognitive Psychology: New Directions,* Routledge & Kegan Paul (Boston, MA), 1980.

Beyond Therapy: The Impact of Eastern Religions on Psychological Theory and Practice, Wisdom Publications (London, England), 1986.

Growth Points in Cognition, Routledge (New York, NY), 1988.

(Coeditor) *Liberating the Learner: Lessons for Professional Development in Education,* Routledge (New York, NY), 1996.

(With Terry Atkinson) *The Intuitive Practitioner: On the Value of Not Always Knowing What One Is Doing,* Open University Press (Philadelphia, PA), 2000.

(With Gay Watson and Stephen Batchelor) *The Psychology of Awakening: Buddhism, Science, and Human Welfare,* S. Weiser (York Beach, ME), 2000.

(With Gordon Wells) *Learning for Life in the 21st Century: Sociocultural Perspectives on the Future of Education,* Blackwell Publishers (Malden, MA), 2002.

(With Rosamund Sutherland and Andrew Pollard) *Learning and Teaching Where Worldviews Meet,* Trentham Books (Sterling, VA), 2003.

BIOGRAPHICAL AND CRITICAL SOURCES:

PERIODICALS

Booklist, February 15, 1999, Mary Carroll, review of *Hare Brain, Tortoise Mind: Why Intelligence Increases When You Think Less,* p. 1005.

Kirkus Reviews, December 15, 1998, review of *Hare Brain, Tortoise Mind,* p. 1772.

Library Journal, January, 1999, Elizabeth Goeters, review of *Hare Brain, Tortoise Mind,* p. 130.

Publishers Weekly, January 11, 1999, review of *Hare Brain, Tortoise Mind,* p. 63; November 1, 1999, review of *Wise Up: The Challenge of Lifelong Learning,* p. 65.

ONLINE

Professor Guy Claxton: Who Is Guy Claxton?, http://www.guyclaxton.com (March 6, 2007).

* * *

COLBERT, Jaimee Wriston 1951-

PERSONAL: Born October 20, 1951; U.S. citizen. *Education:* University of Washington, Seattle, B.A.; Brown University, M.A.

ADDRESSES: Home—Endicott, NY. *Office*—Department of English, State University of New York at Binghamton, P.O. Box 6000, Binghamton, NY 13902. *E-mail*—jcolbert@binghamton.edu.

CAREER: Texas Southern University, Houston, instructor in English, 1978-79; Georgetown University, Washington, DC, developer of creative writing course, 1979-80; Northeastern University, Boston, MA, began as lecturer, became senior lecturer in writing, 1980-89; Ohio State University, Columbus, lecturer in writing, 1989-91; University of Maine at Augusta, Augusta, lecturer in writing and communications, 1992-99; University of Missouri—St. Louis, St. Louis, assistant professor and distinguished visiting writer, 1999-2000; Columbia College, Chicago, IL, assistant professor and artist in residence, 2000-01; State University of New York at Binghamton, Binghamton, associate professor of creative writing, 2001—. Trinity College, teacher, 1979-80; Georgetown University, adjunct instructor, 1979-80; Stonecoast Writers' Conference, faculty associate, 1995-98; Maine Writers and Publishers Alliance, teacher of fiction writing workshops, 1995-99; Rockport College, adjunct faculty for Maine Photographic Workshops, 1996-99; Colby College, visiting assistant professor, 1998-99; University of Southern Maine, teacher of advanced fiction workshop, 1998-99;

judge of writing contests; gives readings from her works. Maine State Prison, facilitator of creative writing group and publisher of the journal *Rogue's Gallery,* 1994-98; Potato Eyes Foundation, began as board member, became vice president, 1993-98.

AWARDS, HONORS: Zephyr Literary Award, 1993; Delogu Award, outstanding woman fiction writer, University of Southern Maine, 1995; Willa Cather Fiction Prize, 1997, for *Climbing the God Tree;* fiction fellow, Wesleyan Writers' Conference, 1999; Pushcart Prize nominations, 1999, the short story for "What the Deer Know," 2003, for the short story "Haole Girl Blue," and 2006, for the short story "Just Watching for Jesus."

WRITINGS:

Final Light (poetry chapbook), Bootleg Press (North Carolina), 1993.
Sex, Salvation, and the Automobile (short stories), Zephyr Publishing (Bruce, WI), 1994.
Climbing the God Tree (novel in stories), Helicon Nine Editions (Kansas City, MO), 1998.
Dream Lives of Butterflies (novel in stories), BookMark Press (Kansas City, MO), 2007.

Work represented in anthologies, including *Ohio Short Fiction,* 1995; *Live Poets Anthology,* 1996; and *Peculiar Pilgrims,* Hourglass Press (Chicago, IL), 2006. Contributor to literary journals, including *Louisiana Literature, Prairie Schooner, Green Mountains Review, Connecticut Review, New Letters, Tampa Review, Tri-Quarterly, Pacific Coast Journal, Chaminade Literary Review,* and *Snake Nation Review.* Senior fiction editor, *Natural Bridge,* 1999.

ADAPTATIONS: Colbert's short stories have been broadcast by Maine Public Radio; some were also selected for live performances on a program titled *Maine Speaks.*

SIDELIGHTS: Jaimee Wriston Colbert once told *CA:* "*Climbing the God Tree* is a novel in stories that evolves around the repercussions of a murder, a stillbirth, a fatal accident, and a rape, most taking place before the beginning of the book. The killer is in a maximum security prison, located in the fictional town of Rock Harbor, Maine. The book examines the lives of the perpetrators and the victims. The murderer is a brilliant man, but

touched by a cavernous darkness, a 'fallen angel' who longs for forgiveness but is unable to believe in it. The rapist is a simple man who does not have the capacity to understand what he did, but whose heart can embrace what his mind cannot. *Climbing the God Tree* is an exploration of violence—personal and at the hands of another—[and] how lives around it are touched. Ultimately, Rock Harbor becomes both a haven and a prison, a place people flee to and want to escape from. The book is about loss and retribution, with characters who cling tenaciously to the possibility of forgiveness and the triumph of love.

"I am from Hawaii but lived in a small town on the coast of Maine for several years. Among the teaching hats I wore until recently is a creative writing workshop I ran at the Maine State Prison, a maximum security facility. There I sat with men who had done the worst a person could do, but who were learning to rise above these things, to discover the human in themselves. Through their tales and trials I became interested in the issues addressed in *Climbing the God Tree,* but my writing is never about 'issues.' I am interested in stories and how these can illuminate the raw edges of human experience. My work is about these edges. It explores the darkness in all of us, yet ultimately reveals the hope that is born when a person chooses to go on, no matter what. I am compelled by characters who exhibit that sort of strength, that gritty survivalism. My work is not 'uplifting.' A well known agent once told me after considering then declining to represent me: 'This is the sort of dark and intelligent work I cannot sell.' I am not interested in the problems of the rich, the angst of the well-heeled.

"That is not to say my work is always grim. Indeed, often I use humor in the way we need humor in our lives—to get us through. My characters have been described by reviewers as quirky, vivid, and gritty. I love my characters and, in their worst moments, their worst behaviors, I keep loving them—the way a parent keeps loving her wildest child. *Climbing the God Tree* was a wonderful opportunity for me to explore many characters.

"My novel manuscript *An Inordinate Love* has three point-of-view characters. It's set in Hawaii, which is the home in my blood. My family has been there for five generations, and the land—its people, its raw sensual beauty—is reflected throughout much of my writing. The novel is about a family's disintegration then regeneration, mental illness, Hawaiian mythology, and mysticism. I have been told that alternating points of view are not popular with the publishing industry, but the advice I give my own students is: write the stories you'd want to read. Another novel manuscript, *Shark Girls,* is based loosely on a real shark attach in Hawaii in 1958. Ultimately it is about our need to believe in the possibility of miracles in a random, troubled world.

"I am in the middle of my life, and it's taken me this long to start publishing books, which is okay. I'm grateful for the recognition, and I'm also grateful that I've had to work this many years to get it. I also know that I'll keep working and writing the stories I want to tell, to explore, to understand in their deepest ways, without regard to whether they are considered 'commercially viable.' John Hawkes, one of my finest teachers at Brown University, used to lament that his critically acclaimed work wasn't being picked up by a 'big' publisher, that it wasn't being reviewed in the *New York Times.* When these things happened, did that make him a better writer? I believe in giving my heart to the story that must be told, the way it needs to be told. This is what I try to teach my students: be true to your stories, and your stories will speak the truth."

*   *   *

CRESP, Gael 1954-

PERSONAL: Born April 2, 1954, in Benalla, Australia; daughter of Edward Thomas (a "fitter and turner") and Roma Carmel (a homemaker) Cresp; married Stephen John Wilbourne (a computer consultant), May 10, 1975; children: Emily Jane, Elizabeth Alice, Rebecca Elana. *Ethnicity:* "Australian." *Education:* Royal Melbourne Institute of Technology (now RMIT University), B.S., 1975; Chisholm Institute (now Monash University), graduate diploma, 1982; Frankston Technical and Further Education, certificate in writing, 1990; Holmesglen Technical and Further Education, certificate in workplace training, 1999.

ADDRESSES: Home—Malvern East, Victoria, Australia. *E-mail*—story@lantanasystems.com.au.

CAREER: Swinburne University of Technology, Hawthorn, Australia, librarian, 1994-2000; Lantana Systems Pty. Ltd., Malvern, Victoria, Australia, principal, 2000—. Professional storyteller, 1984—; presenter of storytelling workshops in Australia and elsewhere.

MEMBER: Storytelling Guild of Australia (president of Victoria branch, 1998-2000).

WRITINGS:

The Biography of Gilbert Alexander Pig (juvenile), illustrated by David Cox, Benchmark/Cygnet (Melbourne, Australia), 1999, published as *The Tale of Gilbert Alexander Pig,* Barefoot Books (Cambridge, MA), 2000.
Fish for Breakfast, illustrated by Anna Pignataro, Windy Hollow (Melbourne, Australia), 2002.

SIDELIGHTS: Gael Cresp once told *CA:* "I have been a professional storyteller since 1984, although my father says I have been telling stories all my life. I have three children and more than twenty grandchildren, nieces, and nephews. I grew up in Seaford, a bayside suburb forty kilometers south of Melbourne in Victoria, Australia. I am the second eldest of ten children, and that is why I have so many nieces and nephews!

"I use my own stories and poems in performance and undertake considerable research prior to adapting traditional stories for telling. I do not always know why I tell a particular story or adapt it in a particular way, although some years down the track I can usually come up with a good explanation (that is, story!) about what it means.

"I work four days a week at a university library in Hawthorn, near Melbourne. I go around the library reminding people that they promised to carry out certain jobs before the next meeting. When they say that someone else has to do something first, I go to that person and find out what is stopping him or her from completing the task. I am often referred to as a third person, and occasionally a fourth. Sometimes I feel like the old woman in the story of the pig who would not jump over the stile!

"Regarding *The Biography of Gilbert Alexander Pig,* I was prompted to tell the traditional story of the three little pigs from a contemporary perspective by the need to make the story relevant to people today. Once I began to use a black trumpet-playing pig, a modern setting followed logically.

"Traditional stories have information in them that will assist us in making decisions about our lives. When we are confronted with the need to make our own way in the world, we have some choices to make. The message I took from the traditional version of the story as a child was that there was no place for fun and games. I must work hard, build on strong foundations, and lock myself in (to a secure job and a proper house) if I were to be happy and successful. The story of Gilbert Alexander Pig began as a joke to poke fun at this idea and to suggest that there are, indeed, alternatives.

"I hope that every child or adult that comes to this story has heard the traditional tale of the three little pigs and notices and comments on the differences between the two tales. Any awareness or consideration of the alternatives that Gilbert Alexander Pig presents means my job has been well done. I would like people to admire Gilbert's courage, his tenacity, his athletic prowess, and his ability to negotiate. I would like them to admire the wolf because he finally listens and so actually gains friendship and a wonderful skill. I would like readers and listeners to be encouraged and empowered to make similar changes to the patterns of their lives. Most of all, I would like people to enjoy the story, to laugh at the dialogue and the illustrations, and to find the images and the story dancing in their minds long after the book is closed.

"The character of Gilbert Alexander Pig was inspired by the life of my friend, jazz trumpeter Gil Askey. To be a professional musician, even today, requires one to live differently than the majority of people. To play jazz on a trumpet is also to work on the edge of the music world (where string instruments and classical music are seen as the peak area). For Gil to do both of these things through the sixties and seventies was incredibly brave.

"The most remarkable thing about Gil is his lack of resentment and bitterness about the appalling treatment he and other black people received over the years. He has used his enormous talent to reach out to all kinds of people, to offer them a path into his joy in music and music-making. Gil has done a remarkable job of encouraging children—especially teenage boys—to undertake the difficult task of learning an instrument. The discipline to practice and the need to be cooperative in a band or orchestra are enormously valuable lessons to learn.

"I felt that Gil recognized that a lot of the resentment and violence offered to those who are different (black, 'arty') comes from fear and jealousy. His philosophy seems to be: 'Offer to share and to teach people, and they will become your friends.'"

Recently Cresp added: "I now work four days a week in a computer consultancy where I do office work and write in between phone calls.

"The story of *Fish for Breakfast* was inspired by the loss of a sun hat and the presence of a large number of eagles in a national park around an extinct volcano crater."

D

de la CRUZ, Melissa 1971-

PERSONAL: Born 1971, in Quezon City, the Philippines; married (an architect). *Education:* Columbia University, B.A., 1993.

ADDRESSES: Home—Los Angeles, CA. *Agent*—Richard Abate, International Creative Management, 40 W. 57th St., New York, NY 10019.

CAREER: Writer, novelist, and editor. Computer programmer, 1993-2001. Formerly worked as a child model.

WRITINGS:

NOVELS

Cat's Meow (novel), illustrated by Kim de Marco, Scribner's (New York, NY), 2001.
(With Karen Robinovitz) *How to Become Famous in Two Weeks or Less,* Ballantine Books (New York, NY), 2003.
(With Karen Robinovitz) *The Fashionista Files: Adventures in Four-Inch Heels and Faux Pas,* Ballantine Books (New York, NY), 2004.
Fresh off the Boat, HarperCollins (New York, NY), 2005.
Blue Bloods, Hyperion Books for Children (New York, NY), 2006.
Angels on Sunset Boulevard, Simon & Schuster Books for Young Readers (New York, NY), 2007.

Blue Bloods: Masquerade, Hyperion Books for Children (New York, NY), 2007.

"AU PAIRS" SERIES; NOVELS

The Au Pairs, Simon & Schuster (New York, NY) 2004.
Skinny-Dipping, Simon & Schuster Books for Young Readers (New York, NY), 2006.
Sun-Kissed, Simon & Schuster Books for Young Readers (New York, NY), 2006.

Contributor to periodicals, including *Allure, New York Times, San Francisco Chronicle, Feed, McSweeneys, Hamptons Country, Nerve, Marie Claire, Gotham, Hamptons, Lifetime, Glamour, New York Press,* and *Manhattan Style.*

Author of columns, "Shop Tart" and "Beauty Duty," and senior fashion editor, *Hintmag.com.*

Author's works have been translated into numerous languages.

SIDELIGHTS: Author and former computer programmer Melissa de la Cruz found material for her first novel, *Cat's Meow,* in both her own life and the lives of those she writes about as a fashion journalist. Her protagonist, Cat McAllister, was a child actress, just as de la Cruz once was; and Cat dreams of socialite celebrity, something de la Cruz remembers from her childhood as well. After moving from Manila, where her mother was a socialite and her father an investment banker, to the suburban United States, she longs for some of the trappings of her former life. Speaking to Amy Larocca in *New York Magazine,* de la Cruz recalled, "I would read books by Jay McInerney and dream of some kind of return to glamour."

Reviewing *Cat's Meow* for the *Los Angeles Times Book Review,* Mark Rozzo described de la Cruz's novel as a kind of celebrity-obsessed *Inferno,* saying that "Cat is a hilarious Virgil leading us down into New York's rings of fashion hell." In pursuit of a wealthy husband to help bolster her status among the New York social aristocracy, and to pay her mounting credit card bills, Cat starts by throwing herself her fourth twenty-fifth birthday party and quickly adopts a Chinese orphan as a status symbol. When her money runs out and she loses her apartment, she is forced to look for work. Good fortune finally strikes when she finds a job at a fashion Web site (de la Cruz is an editor at an online fashion magazine) that sends her to runway shows in Paris and other chi-chi locales.

Several reviewers noted the humor in *Cat's Meow,* as well as de la Cruz's eye for telling details. A reviewer for *Publishers Weekly,* for example, suggested that "society page addicts will no doubt enjoy its irreverent spin on the glamorous life." Tobin Levy, writing for *Look Online,* called *Cat's Meow* "a delightful quick reading satire as sick and twisted as it is funny and addictive." Rozzo wrote that while the frothy shallowness of the book and its heroine may be initially off-putting, de la Cruz makes Cat a character readers begin to care about. He concluded, de la Cruz "pinpoints the sinister vanities of this air-headed realm while making it all sound absurdly fun."

With *The Au Pairs,* de la Cruz inaugurated a popular series featuring a trio of young women hired as summer au pairs to the wealthy, Hamptons-dwelling Perry family. The culturally diverse characters come from diverse backgrounds. Eliza comes from a wealthy family whose fortunes abruptly deteriorated when her father's financial chicanery and shady accounting practices were discovered. She is desperate to fight her way back to the top of the social order, but Jeremy, a handsome gardener, causes her to reconsider her ideas of class and status. Mara, a small-town girl, takes the job to earn needed money for college, but she initially finds it difficult to fit into the brazen and luxurious life of the Hamptons. When a friendship with the Perry's eldest son, Ryan, evolves into something more, her surprise

quickly becomes delight. Gorgeous Brazilian model Jacqui has an ulterior motive for coming to the United States: she is searching for Luca, a young man she knew in Sao Paolo and with whom she wants to rekindle a relationship. Underlying de la Cruz's "over-the-top fantasy of high life in the Hamptons is a trio of fairly ordinary teen romances," commented a *Publishers Weekly* reviewer. "Strong writing and interesting characters help set this book apart from the many other books that seem similar," noted Amanda MacGregor in *Kliatt.* A *Kirkus Reviews* critic remarked that "teen girls will voyeuristically enjoy the slightly decadent escapism" of de la Cruz's first Au Pairs novel.

The three au pairs return in *Skinny-Dipping,* which finds Mara and Jacqui again working for the Perry family while Eliza has taken a job in a popular nightclub. Relationships have shifted, as Eliza takes up with Mara's old boyfriend Ryan Perry without realizing that Mara wants him back. Jacqui, temporarily swearing off men, finds herself tempted back into the game by Philippe. Her rival, however, may be undefeatable, since her employer, Mrs. Perry, also has an interest in the gorgeous young man. "The story is ultimately about the fleeting nature of popularity and how easy it is to get caught up in the game," commented *School Library Journal* reviewer Michele Capozzella. In the series' third installment, *Sun-Kissed,* Jacqui finds herself trying to keep the Perrys from splitting up (and depriving her of a job). Eliza pursues a career in fashion by taking a job with Mikael Lappin, a once-hot designer looking to make a comeback. A scheming coworker, Mikael's assistant and Eliza's boyfriend's ex, sabotages her plans. Mara wants to reunite with Ryan Perry but finds herself deprived of time by her new job as a journalist for *Hamptons* magazine. "As always, the girls' foibles are fun but trite," remarked Jane Cronkhite, writing in *School Library Journal.*

The protagonist of *Fresh off the Boat,* fourteen-year-old Vicenza, nicknamed V, is a new arrival to the United States. After growing up wealthy and privileged in the Philippines, V struggles to adjust to a much more modest and diminished lifestyle in America. Here, she has to work in a cafeteria run by her mother, and she shops for clothes at the Salvation Army. Though she attends a private girls' school on an academic scholarship, she's socially awkward and has no friends there. Perhaps worst of all, people around her in San Francisco insult her by calling her FOB—Fresh Off the Boat. When V corresponds with a friend back in the Philippines, however, she creates a dream life in which she's popular, wealthy, and romantically happy. As V progresses, however, she makes a first friend in Isobel and comes to realize that, despite her own troubles, her mother is having even greater difficulty adjusting to the family's new life. "In the end, the colorful details and the mother-daughter relationship make up for some familiar plotting," noted a *Publishers Weekly* reviewer. *Kliatt* contributor Stephanie Squicciarini called the novel a "satisfying and quietly humorous read."

De la Cruz adds an element of the fantastic to her work in *Blue Bloods,* a new approach to the traditional vampire tale suggesting that New York's social elite are, in fact, undying vampires. The vampires came to America on the Mayflower, and de la Cruz explains that they do not die; instead, their old souls simply take up residence in a new shell, or body. In modern times, Schuler Van Alen and her friend, Bliss, struggle against the social barriers put up by the group of popular kids, led by Mimi and Jack Force. When Schuyer and Bliss turn fifteen years old, however, they develop unusual symptoms, including a taste for raw meat. Soon they learn that they are part of the vampiric blue bloods. Their previous problems pale in comparison to the struggle to learn to cope with the vampire lifestyle, to adhere to the strict codes of conduct (such as never draining so much blood from a human that they die), and finding their way through an unfamiliar and frightening new society. In the background, the entire vampire population finds itself facing a new and unfamiliar danger, as someone has started murdering vampires who are supposed to be immortal. *Booklist* reviewer Jennifer Mattson observed that "many teens will savor the thrilling sense of being initiated into an exclusive secret society" as they read the novel. Sharon Rawlins, writing in *School Library Journal,* commented that the book's "intriguing plot will keep teens reading."

BIOGRAPHICAL AND CRITICAL SOURCES:

PERIODICALS

Booklist, July, 2004, Ilene Cooper, review of *The Au Pairs,* p. 1833; April 15, 2005, Debbie Carton, review of *Fresh off the Boat,* p. 1447; May 15, 2006, Jennifer Mattson, "After the First Bite," review of *Blue Bloods,* p. 56.

Kirkus Reviews, June 1, 2004, review of *The Au Pairs,* p. 535; April 1, 2006, review of *Blue Bloods,* p. 344.

Kliatt, September, 2005, Amanda MacGregor, review of *The Au Pairs,* p. 18; September, 2006, Stephanie Squicciarini, review of *Fresh off the Boat,* p. 21.

Los Angeles Times Book Review, August 12, 2001, Mark Rozzo, review of *Cat's Meow,* p. 10.

New York Magazine, July 30, 2001, Amy Larocca, "Smart Set: Melissa de la Cruz."

Publishers Weekly, July 30, 2001, review of *Cat's Meow,* p. 63; June 21, 2004, review of *The Au Pairs,* p. 64; May 9, 2005, review of *Fresh off the Boat,* p. 72; June 5, 2006, review of *Blue Bloods,* p. 64; June 26, 2006, review of *Skinny-Dipping,* p. 54.

School Library Journal, July, 2005, Michele Capozzella, review of *Skinny-Dipping,* p. 101; October, 2005, review of *Fresh off the Boat,* p. S73; June, 2006, Jane Cronkhite, review of *Sun-Kissed,* and Sharon Rawlins, review of *Blue Bloods,* p. 152.

ONLINE

Beatrice.com, http://www.Beatrice.com/ (December 5, 2006), Ron Hogan, interview with Melissa de la Cruz.

Look Online, http://www.lookonline.com/ (December 5, 2006), Tobin Levy, review of *Cat's Meow.*

Melissa de la Cruz Home Page, http://www.melissa-delacruz.com (December 5, 2006).

Melissa de la Cruz MySpace, http://www.myspace.com/melissadelacruz (December 5, 2006).

Teen Magazine, http://www.teenmag.com/ (December 5, 2006), profile of Melissa de la Cruz.

Teenreads.com, http://www.teenreads.com/ (July 20, 2005), July 20, 2005, interview with Melissa de la Cruz.

Your Look Your Life, http://www.yourlookyourlife.com/ (December 5, 2006), "Fashion Windows: Your Look, Your Life."*

*   *   *

DODD, David 1957-
(David G. Dodd)

PERSONAL: Born February 14, 1957, in Livermore, CA; son of Frank Whitney (a mechanical engineer) and Suzanne (a mechanical engineer) Dodd; married Heather MacLeod, 1982 (divorced); married Diana Bentley Spaulding (a librarian), June 10, 1995; children:

(second marriage) Rosemary Spaulding, Alexander David. *Ethnicity:* "White; of Norwegian descent primarily." *Education:* University of California, Davis, B.A., 1979; University of California, Berkeley, M.L.I. S., 1990. *Politics:* "Green." *Religion:* Unitarian-Universalist.

ADDRESSES: *Home*—Petaluma, CA. *Agent*—Sandra Choron, March Tenth Inc., 4 Myrtle St. Haworth, NJ 07641. *E-mail*—ddodd@well.com.

CAREER: University of Colorado, Colorado Springs, head of cataloging at Kraemer Family Library, 1994-97; Santa Cruz City County Library, Santa Cruz, CA, branch manager, 1997-98; Marin County Free Library, San Rafael, CA, senior librarian, branch manager, and administrative librarian, 1999-2004; San Francisco Public Library, San Francisco, CA, district manager and chief of technical services, 2004; San Rafael Public Library, San Rafael, director, 2004—.

MEMBER: American Library Association, California Library Association.

WRITINGS:

(With Robert Weiner) *The Grateful Dead and the Deadheads: An Annotated Bibliography,* Greenwood Press (Westport, CT), 1997.
(Editor, with Diana Spaulding) *The Grateful Dead Reader,* Oxford University Press (New York, NY), 2000.
(Editor, with Alan Trist, and author of annotations) *The Complete Annotated Grateful Dead Lyrics: The Collected Lyrics by Robert Hunter and John Barlow; Lyrics to All Original Songs, and Selected Traditional and Cover Songs,* foreword by Robert Hunter, illustrated by Jim Carpenter, Free Press (New York, NY), 2005.

Contributor to books, including *Perspectives on the Dead,* edited by Robert Weiner, Greenwood Press (Westport, CT), 1999. Contributor of articles and reviews to various periodicals, including *Bloomsbury Review, Library Journal,* and *College and Research Libraries News.*

SIDELIGHTS: David Dodd once told *CA:* "I'm primarily a librarian, and secondarily a big fan of The Grateful Dead, and that has led me to combine my interests into the work I've done on the Web and in print. In the future, I hope to write more fiction."

More recently Dodd commented: "As a librarian I have the privilege of being allowed to be a generalist. I can be interested in everything, and I am! My three books center on the Grateful Dead, but as anyone who pokes around in *The Complete Annotated Grateful Dead Lyrics: The Collected Lyrics by Robert Hunter and John Barlow; Lyrics to All Original Songs, and Selected Traditional and Cover Songs* will soon realize, the band and its lyrics serve as a springboard from which I can freely jump from subject to subject. I seek to explore 'interconnectedness': I believe that we are all connected and that separateness is an illusion. That's why my favorite writer is Richard Powers. He, too, is about connection."

BIOGRAPHICAL AND CRITICAL SOURCES:

ONLINE

David Dodd Home Page, http://arts.ucsc.edu/gdead/agdl/david.html (March 7, 2007).

*   *   *

DODD, David G.
  See DODD, David

*   *   *

DRUZHNIKOV, Yuri 1933-

PERSONAL: Born April 17, 1933, in Moscow, USSR (now Russia); immigrated to the United States, 1987; naturalized U.S. citizen; son of Ilya (an artist) and Alida (an archivist) Druzhnikov; married, 1983; wife's name Valerie (a physician); children: Elena, Ilya. *Ethnicity:* "Russian, Christian." *Education:* Attended University of Latvia; Moscow Pedagogical University, Ph.D. *Politics:* "Liberal, Democrat, cosmopolitan." *Religion:* Christian.

ADDRESSES: *Home*—Davis, CA. *Office*—Department of German and Russian, University of California, Davis, CA 95616. *Agent*—Natalie Gremiachkin, Bol. Brouuaya 6a RAO, Moscow 103670, Russia.

CAREER: University of California, Davis, professor of Russian literature, 1988—. *Exhibitions:* Organizer of the Moscow exhibition, "The Ten Years of a Non-Writer," 1987.

MEMBER: International PEN (vice president of a New York center for writers in exile).

AWARDS, HONORS: Named honorary academician, St. Petersburg Academy of Humanities; award from a national competition for the best Russian-American writer of the year 1998, for *Prisoner of Russia: Alexander Pushkin and Political Uses of Nationalism; Angels on the Head of a Pin* was cited among ten best Russian novels of the twentieth century, University of Warsaw, 1999.

WRITINGS:

Angels on the Head of a Pin (novel), Liberty (New York, NY), 1989.
Prisoner of Russia: Alexander Pushkin and Political Uses of Nationalism (published originally in Russian, 1992), Transaction Publishers (New Brunswick, NJ), 1998.
I Was Born in a Line (essays), Hermitage (Tenafly, NJ), 1994.
Informer 001: The Myth of Pavlik Morozov (novel), Transaction Publishers (New Brunswick, NJ), 1996.
Passport to Yesterday (novel), Hermitage (Tenafly, NJ), 1998.
Collected Works, six volumes, VIA Press (Baltimore, MD), 1998.
Contemporary Russian Myths: A Skeptical View of the Literary Past (essays), Edwin Mellen (Lewiston, NY), 1999.
Madonna from Russia (novel), Peter Owen (London, England), 2006.
The Life and Death of Pushkin (monograph), Edwin Mellen (Lewiston, NY), 2006.

Also author of other books, including *Wait till Sweet Sixteen* (novel); *Teacher in Love* (short stories); and *Father for a Day* (comedy), published in the 1970s; *Micronovels,* 1991; and *Selected Prose,* two volumes, published in St. Petersburg, Russia, 1999. Editor of literary journals.

BIOGRAPHICAL AND CRITICAL SOURCES:

BOOKS

The Phenomenon of Yuri Druzhnikov (essays), Slavica Orientale (Warsaw, Poland), 2000.

Svirsky, Vladimir, *The Prose of Yuri Druzhnikov,* Challenge (Washington, DC), 1994.

ONLINE

Yuri Druzhnikov Home Page, http://www.druzhnikov. com (March 7, 2007).

*   *   *

DUNCAN, Dave 1933-
   (Sarah B. Franklin, Ken Hood)

PERSONAL: Born June 30, 1933, in Newport-on-Tay, Scotland; immigrated to Canada, 1955; naturalized Canadian citizen, 1960; married Janet Hopwell, 1959; children: one son, two daughters. *Education:* University of St. Andrews, B.Sc., 1955.

ADDRESSES: Home—Victoria, British Columbia, Canada. *Agent*—Richard Curtis Associates, Inc., 171 E. 74th St., 2nd Fl., New York, NY, 10021.

CAREER: Writer and geologist. Worked as geologist, 1955-76; manager of geological consulting business, 1976-86.

MEMBER: Science Fiction Writers of America, Writers Guild of Alberta.

AWARDS, HONORS: Canadian Science Fiction and Fantasy Award, Canadian Science Fiction and Fantasy Association, 1990, for *West of January.*

WRITINGS:

"THE SEVENTH SWORD" FANTASY SERIES

The Reluctant Swordsman, Ballantine/Del Rey (New York, NY), 1988.
The Coming of Wisdom, Ballantine/Del Rey (New York, NY), 1988.
The Destiny of the Sword, Ballantine/Del Rey (New York, NY), 1988.

"A MAN OF HIS WORD" FANTASY SERIES

Magic Casement, Ballantine/Del Rey (New York, NY), 1990.

Faery Lands Forlorn, Ballantine/Del Rey (New York, NY), 1991.

Perilous Seas, Ballantine/Del Rey (New York, NY), 1991

Emperor and Clown, Ballantine/Del Rey (New York, NY), 1991.

"A HANDFUL OF MEN" FANTASY SERIES

The Cutting Edge, Ballantine/Del Rey (New York, NY), 1992.

Upland Outlaws, Ballantine/Del Rey (New York, NY), 1993.

The Stricken Field, Ballantine/Del Rey (New York, NY), 1993.

The Living God, Ballantine/Del Rey (New York, NY), 1994.

"OMAR" FANTASY SERIES

The Reaver Road, Ballantine/Del Rey (New York, NY), 1992.

The Hunters' Haunt, Ballantine/Del Rey (New York, NY), 1995.

"THE GREAT GAME" FANTASY SERIES

Past Imperative, Avon (New York, NY), 1995.
Present Tense, Avon (New York, NY), 1996.
Future Indefinite, Avon (New York, NY), 1997.

"KING'S BLADES" FANTASY SERIES

The Guilded Chain, Avon (New York, NY), 1998.
Lord of the Fire Lands, Avon (New York, NY), 1999.
Sky of Swords, Eos (New York, NY), 2000.
Paragon Lost, Eos (New York, NY), 2002.
Impossible Odds, Eos (New York, NY), 2003.
The Jaguar Knights, Eos (New York, NY), 2004.

"KING'S DAGGERS" FANTASY SERIES

Sir Stalwart, Avon Books (New York, NY), 1999.
Crooked House, Avon Books (New York, NY), 2000.

Silvercloak, Avon Books (New York, NY), 2001.

"DODEC" FANTASY SERIES

Children of Chaos, Tor (New York, NY), 2006.
The Mother of Lies, Tor (New York, NY), 2007.

OTHER FANTASY

A Rose-Red City, Ballantine/Del Rey (New York, NY), 1987.

The Cursed, Ballantine/Del Rey (New York, NY), 1995.

(First published under pseudonym Sarah B. Franklin) *Daughter of Troy,* Avon Books (New York, NY), 1998.

The Alchemist's Apprentice, Ace Books (New York, NY), 2007.

SCIENCE-FICTION NOVELS

Shadow, Ballantine/Del Rey (New York, NY), 1987.
West of January, Ballantine/Del Rey (New York, NY), 1989.
Strings, Ballantine/Del Rey (New York, NY), 1990.
Hero!, Ballantine/Del Rey (New York, NY), 1991.

Also author of *"Years of Longdirk"* series, writing as Ken Hood, including *Demon Sword,* 1995, *Demon Rider,* 1997, and *Demon Knight,* 1998.

SIDELIGHTS: Dave Duncan is a prolific Scottish-born Canadian writer of fantasy and science fiction novels. Creator of the fantasy series "The Seventh Sword," "A Man of His Word," and "A Handful of Men," Duncan is known as a skilled world builder and often combines humor with the classic elements of fantasy fiction, an approach that has gained him a wide readership.

Duncan's fantasy novel *The Cursed* "partakes . . . of the real skill with the basics of storytelling, world building, and deployment of classic fantasy elements that distinguish Duncan's other books," commented Roland Green in *Booklist.* With *The Cursed,* found a *Publishers Weekly* critic, Duncan "offers an amusing and well-proportioned blend of religion, prophecy and magic, as well as a touch of intellectual good humor in a lively, earthy tale."

Most of Duncan's works, however, are parts of series, including his lauded "Seventh Sword" series and the "Great Game" trilogy. *Future Indefinite* is similar to the other novels in the "Great Game" trilogy, according to Roland Green in *Booklist,* in that it is "tightly written, intelligent, and original." Though Green argued that it may not be among Duncan's most accessible works, the critic nonetheless found that the novel "provides a decisive and satisfactory end" to the series. A *Publishers Weekly* contributor noted: "The trilogy as a whole isn't likely to be the most popular work of this author of numerous classic fantasy tales . . . but it should be ranked as one of his most demanding, original and intelligent."

Duncan's "King's Blades" series was also lauded by critics as original. The series revolves around the knights trained as one of the "King's Blades" at the sword academy Ironhall. The first in the series, *The Gilded Chain,* follows Durandel as he "pursues adventure and the horrifying secrets of immortality," summarized a *Publishers Weekly* contributor. "Duncan's people are marvelously believable, his landscapes deliciously exotic, his swordplay breathtaking." The reviewer also called the book a "handsomely crafted commentary on honor and betrayal."

Lord of the Fire Lands, published in 1999, was also lauded by critics. A *Publishers Weekly* contributor praised the work's "sophisticated structure and themes" and noted: "Duncan can swashbuckle with the best, but his characters feel more deeply and think more clearly than most, making his novels, especially this one, suitable for a particularly wide readership."

Sky of Swords, the third novel in the "King's Blades" series is actually a prequel to *The Gilded Chain.* The story revolves around Princess Malinda and her efforts to protect her brother so he can one day assume the throne. Her mission is made more difficult, however, because the King's Blades are mostly in exile or hiding. In his review in *Booklist,* Roland Green noted that the novel "reads well on its own—a rare virtue in these days of interwoven googolplexologies." Susan Salpini, writing in the *School Library Journal,* called *Sky of Swords* "an entertaining, swashbuckling adventure."

In the fourth "King's Blades" series novel, titled *Paragon Lost,* Sir Beaumont, thought to be a paragon of the King's Blades, is sent on a mission to keep Princess Isabelle away from Czar Igor and to protect the secrets

of the King's Blades as well. In a review in *Booklist,* Roland Green called the novel "a tightly written, rather Dumas-like story, lighthearted at times but never frivolous or dumb." A *Kirkus Reviews* contributor deemed the novel "a rousing addition . . . to the series," adding that it is "inventive, labyrinthine, witty, and thoroughly engaging."

Impossible Odds continues Duncan's "King's Blades" series. Grand Duke Rubin seeks to enlist the aid of the King's Blades to battle a sorcerer intent on taking over his duchy. The Duke, however, is not really a duke at all but a duchess. Nevertheless, a group of Blades sets out to do battle with Rubin's enemies, who turn out to be more than just one sorcerer. In a review in *Publishers Weekly,* a contributor noted: "Canadian author Duncan explores the perils and pitfalls of dynastic politics in this swash-buckling fantasy." Roland Green, writing in *Booklist,* commented that the novel has "plenty of intrigue and action to draw new fantasy readers as well as established fans." A *Kirkus Reviews* contributor referred to *Impossible Odds* as "something like a fantasy whodunit—agreeably knotty and misleading."

Jaguar Knights finds Sir Wolf in the trail of his brother, Sir Lynx, who has taken possession of a magical talisman that is turning him into a jaguar as he searches for the king's ex-mistress, who was kidnapped by the half-human, half-animal creatures who own the talisman. *Booklist* contributor Roland Green commented that the author is "as deft as ever with the Blades' small-group politics and the convolutions of the [Blades'] world." A *Publishers Weekly* contributor referred to *Jaguar Knights* as an "energetic fantasy" and noted the author's "unadorned style."

In the first novel in the "Dodec" series, *Children of Chaos,* Duncan tells the story of four young siblings who are given up by the doge of Celebre while it was under siege by the Vigaelians. The four are eventually separated to live very different lives, from a super-talented stone mason to a member of a war cult. The novel follows the four siblings as they reach adulthood and eventually reunite many years later. "Duncan's storytelling has never been better in this superb fantasy," wrote a *Publishers Weekly* contributor. According to Regina Schroeder, writing in *Booklist:* "Webs of conspiracy and the complex relations of siblings re-meeting . . . add density to an entertaining big story." A *Kirkus Reviews* contributor wrote: "Duncan's mad plots, dark intrigues, vivid cast and lashings of magic leave many engrossing mysteries to be elucidated in volume two."

Duncan once told *CA:* "Even as a child I wanted to be a writer, but not to the exclusion of wanting to earn a decent living. In the summer of 1984 I began writing a novel, more or less on the spur of the moment, thinking it would be a fun thing to try. I rapidly became hooked to the point where I began sneaking time away from my work. I wrote a huge fantasy novel, a science fiction novel, and then a rewrite of the fantasy as a trilogy. After all that I produced *A Rose-Red City.* In the spring of 1986 the oil business collapsed. For the first time in thirty years I was out of work. Two weeks after I completed my last consulting project, Del Rey publishers offered to buy *A Rose-Red City.* I followed with *Shadow* and then another rewrite of the trilogy, 'The Seventh Sword.' It was the final version that began to attract attention from readers."

BIOGRAPHICAL AND CRITICAL SOURCES:

PERIODICALS

Booklist, May 1, 1995, Roland Green, review of *The Cursed,* p. 1555; August, 1997, Roland Green, review of *Future Indefinite,* p. 1886; October 1, 1998, Roland Green, review of *The Gilded Chain,* p. 313; September 15, 2000, Roland Green, review of *Sky of Swords,* p. 222; September 1, 2002, Roland Green, review of *Paragon Lost,* p. 70; November 15, 2003, Roland Green, review of *Impossible Odds,* p. 588; September 1, 2004, Roland Green, review of *The Jaguar Knights,* p. 74; May 15, 2006, Regina Schroeder, review of *Children of Chaos,* p. 37.

Kirkus Reviews, July 1, 2002, review of *Paragon Lost,* p. 923; July 15, 2004, review of *The Jaguar Knights,* p. 665; April 15, 2006, review of *Children of Chaos,* p. 386.

Library Journal, October 15, 2002, Jackie Cassada, review of *Paragon Lost,* p. 98; October 15, 2003, Jackie Cassada, review of *Impossible Odds,* p. 102; October 15, 2004, Jackie Cassada, review of *The Jaguar Knights,* p. 58; June 15, 2006, Jackie Cassada, review of *Children of Chaos,* p. 62.

Publishers Weekly, April 10, 1995, review of *The Cursed,* p. 57; July 14, 1997, review of *Future Indefinite,* p. 69; October 12, 1998, review of *The Gilded Chain,* p. 62; September 27, 1999, review of *Lord of the Fire Lands,* p. 78; August 26, 2002, review of *Paragon Lost,* p. 48; September 1, 2003, review of *Impossible Odds,* p. 1105; October 6, 2003, review of *Impossible Odds,* p. 66; July 12, 2004, review of *The Jaguar Knights,* p. 48; April 17, 2006, review of *Children of Chaos,* p. 169.

School Library Journal, December, 2000, Susan Salpini, review of *Sky of Swords,* p. 168.

ONLINE

Dave Duncan Home Page, http://www.daveduncan.com (December 28, 2006).

SFFWorld.com, http://www.sffworld.com/ (December 29, 2006), Arthur Bangs, review of *Children of Chaos,* and Rob Bedford, review of *Paragon Lost.*

SFReviews.net, http://www.sfreviews.net/ (December 28, 2006), review of *Children of Chaos.*

Writers Write, http://www.writerswrite.com/ (December 29, 2006), Claire E. White, "A Conversation with Dave Duncan."*

*   *   *

DUNN, Susan 1945-

PERSONAL: Born July 19, 1945; daughter of Carl and Ruth Dunn. *Education:* Smith College, A.B. (cum laude), 1966; Harvard University, Ph.D., 1973.

ADDRESSES: Home—Williamstown, MA. *Office*—Program in Leadership Studies, Stetson Hall, Williams College, Williamstown, MA 01267-2600. *E-mail*—susan.dunn@williams.edu.

CAREER: Harvard University, Cambridge, MA, teaching fellow, 1967-70, instructor, 1970-73; Wellesley College, Wellesley, MA, instructor, 1971-73; Williams College, Williamstown, MA, assistant professor, 1973-78, associate professor, 1978-88, professor of humanities, 1988—, chair of romance languages department, 1982-85. Visiting scholar at New York University, 1984-85, and Columbia University, 1985-86.

MEMBER: Organization of American Historians, Southern Historical Association, Virginia Historical Society, Phi Beta Kappa.

AWARDS, HONORS: Fellow of National Endowment for the Humanities, 1975-76, 1985, 1990, 1997, Camargo Foundation, 1991, American Philosophical Society, 1985-86, and Columbia University Seminar on Eighteenth-Century European Culture, 1991—.

WRITINGS:

Nerval et le roman historique, Editions Lettres Modernes (Paris, France), 1981.

The Deaths of Louis XVI: Regicide and the French Political Imagination, Princeton University Press (Princeton, NJ), 1994.

(Editor, with Gary Jeffrey Jacobsohn) *Diversity and Citizenship: Rediscovering American Nationhood,* Rowman & Littlefield (Lanham, MD), 1996.

Sister Revolutions: French Lightning, American Light, Faber & Faber (New York, NY), 1999.

(With James MacGregor Burns) *The Three Roosevelts: Patrician Leaders Who Transformed America,* Atlantic Monthly Press (New York, NY), 2001.

(With James MacGregor Burns) *George Washington,* Henry Holt (New York, NY), 2004.

Jefferson's Second Revolution: The Election Crisis of 1800 and the Triumph of Republicanism, Houghton Mifflin (Boston, MA), 2004.

(Editor) *Something That Will Surprise the World: The Essential Writings of the Founding Fathers,* Basic Books (New York, NY), 2006.

Dominion of Memories: Jefferson, Madison, and the Decline of Virginia, Basic Books (New York, NY), 2007.

Contributor to journals, including *Harvard, History and Theory,* and *William and Mary Quarterly.*

SIDELIGHTS: Susan Dunn's areas of interest and expertise include American and French revolutionary history and the political careers of Theodore and Franklin Roosevelt.

In *The Deaths of Louis XVI: Regicide and the French Political Imagination,* Dunn briefly discusses the trial and beheading of the king by guillotine and then considers how French writers, including Lamartine, Hugo, Michelet, Balzac, and Camus interpreted his execution and how it affected the nation. Dunn investigates whether Louis XVI was punished for his own particular crimes or as a sacrifice to cleanse France of its ills and pave the way for a rebirth. A writer for the *Virginia Quarterly Review* said that Dunn shows that "the French are highly ambivalent about both the moral and political fact of such a move two hundred years after the fact." William Doyle noted in the *Times Literary Supplement* that biographer John Hardman is of the opinion that Louis XVI had no cult following after his death, as

had Charles I. Doyle wrote that Dunn shows "how wrong this perception is." Doyle said Louis XVI's execution "marked French memory far more deeply and permanently than did that of Charles I in Britain." Christopher Smith wrote in the *Journal of European Studies* that *The Deaths of Louis XVI* "is a fascinating demonstration of the interest of historiography with an extra dimension given by treating poetry and fiction on an equal footing with writing on politics."

Dunn edited (with Gary Jeffrey Jacobsohn) *Diversity and Citizenship: Rediscovering American Nationhood,* a collection of six essays that were first presented as lectures commemorating the bicentennial of Williams College in 1993. Richard C. Sinopoli said in *American Political Science Review* that "this volume offers a good starting point for an educated general readership to begin thinking about our pluralistic democracy and the forms of civic attachments and obligations it can sustain."

In *Sister Revolutions: French Lightning, American Light* Dunn explores how the American and French Revolutions, both founded on the same Enlightenment ideals, have produced such different results. *Booklist* reviewer Mary Carroll wrote that Dunn "seeks to apply the lessons of the past to the present." The subtitle is taken from a 1790 letter written by Gouverneur Morris, a delegate to the 1787 Constitutional Convention in Philadelphia who later became the United States minister to France in 1792. He wrote that the French "have taken Genius instead of Reason for their Guide, adopted Experiment instead of Experience, and wander in the dark because they prefer Lightning to Light." The colonists made individual rights the priority of the struggles, while the French sought unity above all else, first as revolutionaries, then as subjects of Napoleon.

Library Journal reviewer Stephen Kent Shaw called the book an "insightful work." Paul Gray said in *Time* that *Sister Revolutions* "shows not only how the French and American experiments developed, but also why their differing examples have continued to beguile ambitious leaders."

In *The Three Roosevelts: Patrician Leaders Who Transformed America,* Dunn and coauthor, Pulitzer Prize-winner James MacGregor Burns, discuss the political legacies of Theodore, Franklin, and Eleanor Roosevelt, and the influences that shaped the politics of the three figures. Burns and Dunn "do an excellent job of summarizing the political theology shared by these three Knickerbocker bluebloods," commented a reviewer for *Publishers Weekly*. The contributor concluded that the authors "do great justice to three remarkable lives superbly lived."

BIOGRAPHICAL AND CRITICAL SOURCES:

PERIODICALS

American Historical Review, February, 1996, Sylvia Neely, review of *The Deaths of Louis XVI: Regicide and the French Political Imagination,* p. 190.

American Political Science Review, March, 1997, Richard C. Sinopoli, review of *Diversity and Citizenship: Rediscovering American Nationhood,,* p. 189.

Booklist, October 15, 1999, Mary Carroll, review of *Sister Revolutions: French Lightning, American Light,* p. 414.

European History Quarterly, October, 1996, Nigel Aston, review of *The Deaths of Louis XVI,* p. 603.

French Review, May, 1983, Robert T. Denomme, review of *Nerval et le roman historique,* pp. 947-948; October, 1998, Gita May, review of *The Deaths of Louis XVI,* p. 128.

French Studies, January, 1999, Ceri Crossley, review of *The Deaths of Louis XVI,* p. 70.

Journal of European Studies, June, 1995, Christopher Smith, review of *The Deaths of Louis XVI,* p. 208.

Journal of Modern History, June, 1996, A. Lloyd Moote, review of *The Deaths of Louis XVI,* p. 463.

Library Journal, October 1, 1999, Stephen Kent Shaw, review of *Sister Revolutions,* p. 108.

Political Science Quarterly, fall, 1997, Philip Gleason, review of *Diversity and Citizenship,* p. 504.

Publishers Weekly, September 20, 1999, review of *Sister Revolutions,* p. 63; January 15, 2001, review of *The Three Roosevelts: Patrician Leaders Who Transformed America,* p. 59.

Smithsonian, December, 2000, Timothy Foote, review of *Sister Revolutions,* p. 145.

Time, December 6, 1999, Paul Gray, "Power to the People: How the Americans and French Revolted," p. 112.

Times Literary Supplement, March 10, 1995, William Doyle, "Another Bloodless Revolution?," p. 34.

Virginia Quarterly Review, spring, 1995, review of *The Deaths of Louis XVI,* p. 44.

ONLINE

Williams College Web site: Susan Dunn Home Page, http://www.williams.edu/humanities/sdunn (March 7, 2007).

*   *   *

DUVALL, Aimee
See THURLO, Aimée

E

EARLEY, Pete 1951-

PERSONAL: Born September 5, 1951, in Douglas, AZ; married; children: seven. *Education:* Phillips University, Enid, OK, B.S., 1973.

ADDRESSES: Home—Herndon, VA.

CAREER: Writer, novelist, educator, and journalist. *Enid News & Eagle,* Enid, OK, reporter, 1972-73; *Emporia Gazette,* Emporia, KS, staff writer, 1973-75; *Tulsa Tribune,* Tulsa, OK, investigative reporter, 1975-78, Washington, DC correspondent, 1978-80; *Washington Post,* Washington, DC, reporter, 1980-86; freelance writer, 1986—. Visiting faculty member, Goucher College, 2006.

AWARDS, HONORS: Robert F. Kennedy Book Award for Social Justice and Edgar Fact-Crime Award winner, Mystery Writers of America, 1995, both for *Circumstantial Evidence: Death, Life, and Justice in a Southern Town.*

WRITINGS:

Family of Spies: Inside the John Walker Spy Ring, Bantam (New York, NY), 1988.
Prophet of Death: The Mormon Blood-Atonement Killings, Morrow (New York, NY), 1991.
The Hot House: Life inside Leavenworth Prison, Bantam (New York, NY), 1992.
Circumstantial Evidence: Death, Life, and Justice in a Southern Town, Bantam (New York, NY), 1995.
Confessions of a Spy: The Real Story of Aldrich Ames, Putnam (New York, NY), 1996.
Super Casino: Inside the "New" Las Vegas, Bantam (New York, NY), 2000.
(With Gerald Shur) *WITSEC: Inside the Federal Witness Protection Program,* Bantam (New York, NY), 2002.
Deep Cover, Tor Books (New York, NY), 2004.
The Big Secret, Forge (New York, NY), 2004.
Lethal Secrets (novel), Forge (New York, NY), 2005.
Crazy: A Father's Search through America's Mental Health Madness, G.P. Putnam's Sons (New York, NY), 2006.
The Apocalypse Stone (novel), Forge (New York, NY), 2006.

ADAPTATIONS: Some of Earley's writings have been adapted for audiocassette; *Family of Spies* was adapted as a TV miniseries for CBS Television.

SIDELIGHTS: Pete Earley is an investigative reporter who writes extensively on crime and espionage. He is widely respected as an "old school" reporter who covers tough stories and keeps his personal opinion to himself. Charles Bowden wrote in the *Los Angeles Times:* "Before we had schools of journalism, there was a straightforward task called reporting that took you where you had not been, and told you what you had not known. *The Hot House* is by this kind of reporter, and gives the readers reporting at its very finest."

"I want to take you places you normally wouldn't go and introduce you to people who you normally wouldn't meet," Earley said on his home page. "So far, I've written books about the two most damaging spies in recent history—John Walker, Jr. and Aldrich Ames—and taken readers 'inside' a hard-core penitentiary, a sex-crazed religious cult, a racially-charged unsolved murder in the Deep South, a billion-dollar Las Vegas casino and WIT-SEC: the Federal Witness Protection Program, which hides criminals who cooperate with prosecutors."

His first book, *Family of Spies: Inside the John Walker Spy Ring,* relates the various activities of naval officer John Walker and his relatives during a seventeen-year period in which the family relayed more than one million government secrets to Soviet authorities. During the course of his espionage work, Walker enlisted his brother and his best friend, and he even exploited his mother for delivery purposes. In addition, he assured his own security by luring his son into the spy ring, thus allowing for the maintenance of the operations—and substantial profits—after Walker personally withdrew from active spying. *New York Times Book Review* writer Lucinda Franks described the Walker operation as "one of the most damaging spy networks in American history," and she praised Earley for using the comments of financially motivated ringleader Walker "to expose his superficially slick but profoundly distorted mind." Franks wrote that *Family of Spies* is "paced and organized as seamlessly as a novel," but she also noted that it is "a thoroughly researched and unblurred work of nonfiction."

The Hot House: Life inside Leavenworth Prison is a look at the maximum-security Federal prison in Leavenworth, Kansas. The book concentrates on several inmates and follows their day-to-day activities. Earley reports on the conditions of incarceration of Thomas Silverstein. "Of all the guards and convicts in my book," said Earley, "I'm asked the most questions about Thomas Silverstein, who stabbed a guard to death in 1983 and has been kept under 'no human contact' ever since. When I met him, he was locked in a basement cell buried so deeply under the prison that the only sounds were the buzzing of the fluorescent lights in the ceiling. Those lights were kept on twenty-four hours a day. Imagine being locked up in total isolation inside four walls since 1983—your only contact is with guards who detest you—and the entire time the lights are kept burning non-stop." Occasionally, Silverstein is allowed drawing and painting supplies and his remarkable drawings are part of Earley's book.

Wilbert Rideau and Ron Wikberg, Louisiana State Penitentiary inmates who jointly assessed *The Hot*

House in the *San Francisco Review of Books,* noted that these individuals "evoke no sympathy" and added, "they will make readers wonder why they should sustain these prisoners' lives." Rideau and Wikberg related that their own warden, John P. Whitley, characterized *The Hot House* as "a damn good book." Bowden wrote in the *Los Angeles Times Book Review* that *The Hot House* provides "reporting at its very finest," and he described it as "a very convincing piece of the truth." Bowden observed: "What we get in *The Hot House* is the life, and the life is brutal, dull, and filled with the constant pursuit of power and the constant flight from fear."

Earley followed *The Hot House* with *Circumstantial Evidence: Death, Life, and Justice in a Southern Town,* a 1995 book that examines Walter McMillan's conviction and sentencing to death for murders committed in Monroeville, Alabama, in 1986. The police found McMillan, an African-American drug dealer, guilty on the basis of perjured testimony and withholding of evidence. But the intercession of lawyer Bryan Stevenson, together with a provocative report on CBS-TV's news show *Sixty Minutes,* finally prompted a new investigation that exposed questionable police practices and inconsistencies in previous testimony, whereupon McMillan was freed. *New York Times Book Review* contributor Glenna Whitley acknowledged that *Circumstantial Evidence* demonstrates "how subtle and overt racism conspired to condemn a man while giving lip service to the legal system's supposed objectivity."

Earley's next book, *Confessions of a Spy: The Real Story of Aldrich Ames,* concerns the Central Intelligence Agency (CIA) bureaucrat who spied for the Soviet Union and betrayed more than twenty U.S. agents. Ames's treasonous conduct is believed to have led to the executions of some of these American agents. Earley, who obtained access to the imprisoned Ames, quotes him as bragging about the money he made. *New York Times* reviewer Christopher Lehmann-Haupt, while writing that *Confessions of a Spy* concluded that it reveals Ames "as an example of a quintessential twentieth-century figure, the self-analytical man who doesn't understand himself at all."

In preparing his report on the new Las Vegas for *Super Casino: Inside the "New" Las Vegas,* Earley gained complete access to the billion-dollar Luxor casino. The owners of the Luxor, and of the Circus Circus casino as well, gave Earley unprecedented carte blanche to attend any and all meetings, to interview any staff members he chose, and to freely observe life inside the Luxor and Circus Circus casinos. The first half of the book explains Las Vegas's transformation from the old Vegas of the Mob and the Rat Pack to the corporate, family-oriented Las Vegas of today. The second half is a series of interviews and anecdotes from the Luxor. He introduces Vegas executives, dealers, floor managers, security personnel, hookers, and dancers, all of whom talk with surprising candor about their job and the casino.

Written with Gerald Shur, *WITSEC: Inside the Federal Witness Protection Program* examines the controversial program to protect those who testify against criminals in federal court. The program is especially used with organized crime figures who fear retribution from their former associates. This book had its beginnings in Earley's research at the Leavenworth Federal Prison for *Hot House.* Several inmates with ties to organized crime told Earley how they had been convicted by testimony of co-conspirators who were given new identities. "Unfortunately," said Earley, "I kept running into dead ends until I met Gerald Shur, the government attorney who invented WITSEC. We joined forces and Shur took me behind the scenes. He knew every top mobster who had flipped over—beginning with Joe Valachi and ending with Sammy the Bull."

Shur was a career federal prosecutor who found his calling in Robert Kennedy's Organized Crime and Racketeering Section of the 1960s Justice Department. His years in the task force taught him that only credible witnesses with important information could win convictions and that the government had to establish some way to get these witnesses to cooperate. Shur's creation, the WITSEC, is credited with gaining crucial convictions in the battle against organized crime and drug cartels in America. The program also has its detractors. Critics claim that some relocated criminals continued their criminal activities, and some non-criminal witnesses were treated like criminals themselves. Others criticize the use of government money to help criminals disappear into unsuspecting communities.

Shur began writing his memoirs about the same time Earley started researching the program for his own book. After several meetings, they decided to collaborate. Eric Wargo commented in *Book:* "This book focuses much less on WITSEC'S achievements than on its mistakes, growing pains, and critics. Firsthand stories

reveal the severe psychological toll that living a lie for the sake of justice inflicts on families (something Shur experienced when he and his wife had to use his own program's services after agents uncovered a plot against them in 1991)." After finishing the book, Earley said: "My favorite section of my book is about WITNESS X, the wife of a mobster whose entire world was turned upside down when her husband testified against his real-life Soprano's mob boss. She spent hours telling me her story. After hearing it, I came to believe that the most difficult challenge most criminals and their families ever faced was entering and surviving WITSEC."

Crazy: A Father's Search through America's Mental Health Madness chronicles Earley's earnest attempt to find help for his depressed and psychotic son within the American mental health and justice systems. During his senior year of college, Earley's son Mike experienced a mental breakdown and was diagnosed with bipolar disorder. Mike's condition leads to a psychotic episode during which he breaks into a neighbor's house to take a bubble bath, causing much damage in the process. Arrested and jailed, Mike's behavior was seen as a crime rather than a manifestation of a mental illness for which he needed help. Earley traces his son's course through the criminal justice system and relates the convoluted, frustrating, and ineffectual attempt to get Mike the help he needed. In a larger narrative, Earley examines the state of mentally ill inmates at the Miami-Date County jail, where he studied conditions for a year. He found that inmates with mental disorders were often neglected, routinely beaten, and rarely received any sort of treatment for their conditions. Loopholes in the law prevent the state from ordering treatment unless the inmate has been convicted of a crime, which resulted in inmates being jailed without conviction but denied help. In most cases the inmates were free to make their own decisions about whether or not to be treated or hospitalized; the jails could not force treatment against their will. "Earley builds a compelling case that America's legal system is distorted by its deference to the irrational wishes of people incapable of understanding their own best interests," commented Allan Luncy in the *Philadelphia Inquirer.* He concludes that jails have taken the place of the many mental hospitals and treatment centers that have closed over the years; with nowhere else to go, the mentally ill often end up incarcerated, but without treatment for their mental problems. "Society has gone backwards in its handling of the mentally ill, he argues, and we must develop modern long-term treatment facilities where they can be helped and kept safe," noted a

Kirkus Reviews critic. Earley is appalled and incensed by the "barbarous illogicality of laws that allow mentally ill people like Mike to be punished yet languish untreated," noted Lynne Maxwell in the *Library Journal.*

In addition to his investigative journalism work, Earley is also a novelist. *Lethal Secrets* opens as Soviet physicist Andrei Bobkov flees to protect his life from agents who believe he knows too much about a thermonuclear bomb the Soviets have hidden in Washington, DC. Fifty years later, Deputy U.S. Marshall Wyatt Conway takes on the task of protecting Russian mob member Sergey Pudin, a government witness endangered by Vladimir Khrenkov, an assassin who wants to kill Pudin before he testifies. Meanwhile, Movladi "The Viper" Islamov, a former student of Conway's, has become a dangerous international terrorist who is aware of the bomb hidden in the American capital. A budding romance with CIA agent Kimberly Lodge spices up Conway's life. Faced with failure, Conway must remain connected with the Russian investigation while racing the clock to thwart a plan to detonate the nuclear bomb. Early "knows his stuff" as he "seamlessly works in complex detail about everything from government bureaucracy to weapons technology," noted a *Publishers Weekly* reviewer. The author "keeps pace and paranoia effectively high," observed a contributor to *Kirkus Reviews.*

The Apocalypse Stone combines "religious magic, courtroom drama, political machinations and sexual hijinks in a potboiler that's more readable than believable," remarked a critic in *Publishers Weekly.* Virginia Circuit Court judge Evan Spencer lives a happy and fulfilling life, personally and professionally. When Spencer comes into the possession of a plain white stone, his fortunes change drastically. He accuses his beautiful wife of being unfaithful, suffers disturbing dreams and visions, and finds himself presiding over the trial of an inner-city African-American youth accused of raping and killing the daughter of one of his wealthy patrons. As the trial quickly progresses, the powers of the stone affect Spencer more and more, deepening his visions and causing him to manifest stigmata. In the background, a determined Catholic priest searches for the talismanic stone, well aware of the object's powers and hoping to secure it before much damage is done. Before the stone has finished with Spencer, he will experience changes at home and at work even as he faces the ultimate question of his salvation.

BIOGRAPHICAL AND CRITICAL SOURCES:

PERIODICALS

Barron's, February 7, 2000, Ann C. Logue, review of *Super Casino: Inside the "New" Las Vegas,* p. A36.

Book, March-April, 2002, Eric Wargo, review of *WITSEC: Inside the Federal Witness Protection Program,* p. 73.

Booklist, November 1, 1999, review of *Super Casino,* p. 482.

Corrections Today, May, 1992, Paul H. Hahn, review of *The Hot House: Life inside Leavenworth Prison,* p. 82.

Federal Bar News & Journal, July, 1992, review of *The Hot House,* p. 396.

Federal Probation, September, 1992, Stephen Loew, review of *The Hot House,* p. 85.

Kirkus Reviews, December 15, 2001, review of *WITSEC,* p. 1734; May 1, 2004, review of *The Big Secret,* p. 410; April 1, 2005, review of *Lethal Secrets,* p. 372; March 1, 2006, review of *Crazy: A Father's Search through America's Mental Health Madness,* p. 219.

Kliatt Young Adult Paperback Guide, March, 1999, review of *Confessions of a Spy,* p. 62.

Library Journal, January, 1992, Frances Sandiford, review of *The Hot House,* p. 154; July, 1995, Sandra K. Lindheimer, review of *Circumstantial Evidence: Death, Life, and Justice in a Southern Town,* p. 100; May 15, 1997, Daniel Blewett, review of *Confessions of a Spy: The Real Story of Aldrich Ames,* p. 87; August, 1999, James Dudley, review of *Confessions of a Spy,* p. 164; December 1999, review of *Super Casino,* p. 164; February 1, 2002, Diedre Root, review of *WITSEC,* p. 164; March 15, 2006, Lynne Maxwell, review of *Crazy,* p. 86.

Los Angeles Times Book Review, February 16, 1992, review of *The Hot House,* p. 3.

Moscow News, November 25, 1994, Nataliya Gevorkyan, interview with Pete Earley, p. 14.

New Statesman, March 14, 1997, Brian Cathcart, review of *Confessions of a Spy,* p. 48.

New York Law Journal, October 31, 1995, Jennifer Kleiner, review of *Circumstantial Evidence,* p. 2.

New York Times, February 24, 1997, Christopher Lehmann-Haupt, review of *Confessions of a Spy,* p. C16.

New York Times Book Review, January 8, 1989, Lucinda Franks, review of *Confessions of a Spy,* p. 9; March

29, 1992, Dennis J. Carroll, review of *The Hot House,* p. 16; October 8, 1995, Glenna Whitely, review of *Circumstantial Evidence,* p. 26.

Pacific Historical Review, November, 2001, Hal K. Rothman, review of *WITSEC,* p. 627.

Philadelphia Inquirer, May 17, 2006, Allan Luncy, "*Crazy;* How Legal System Fails the Mentally Ill," review of *Crazy.*

Psychology Today, May-June, 2006, review of *Crazy,* P. 34.

Publishers Weekly, December 20, 1991, review of *The Hot House,* p. 70; June 26, 1995, review of *Circumstantial Evidence,* p. 96; November 22, 1999, review of *Super Casino,* p. 47; November 26, 2001, review of *WITSEC,* p. 48; June 28, 2004, review of *The Big Secret,* p. 33; May 9, 2005, review of *Lethal Secrets,* p. 43; February 6, 2006, review of *Crazy,* p. 60; April 17, 2006, review of *The Apocalypse Stone,* p. 166.

San Francisco Review of Books, January, 1992, review of *Circumstantial Evidence,* p. 10.

SciTech Book News, June, 2006, review of *Crazy.*

Times Literary Supplement, July 11, 1997, L. Britt Snider, review of *Confessions of a Spy,* p. 28.

U.S. New and World Report, February 17, 1997, Harrison Rainie, review of *Confessions of a Spy,* p. 8.

Wall Street Journal, February 7, 2000, Allan T. Demaree, review of *Super Casino,* p. A36.

Washington Post, February 20, 2002, Anthan Theoharis, review of *WITSEC,* p. C03.

Washington Post Book World, March 14, 1993.

ONLINE

Goucher College Web site, http://www.goucher.com/ (April 12, 2006), "Pete Earley Publishes Book on the American Mental Health System," review of *Crazy.*

Internet Movie Database, http://www.imdb.com/ (December 5, 2006), filmography of Pete Earley.

Pete Earley Home Page, http://www.peteearley.com (December 5, 2006).*

*   *   *

ELLIS, Deborah 1960-

PERSONAL: Born August 8, 1960, in Cochrane, Ontario, Canada; daughter of Keith (an office manager) and Betty (a nurse) Ellis. *Politics:* "Feminist, anti-war." *Hobbies and other interests:* Bicycling, exploring the woods.

CAREER: Writer, mental health counselor, and civil rights activist. Margaret Frazer House, Toronto, Ontario, Canada, mental health worker, 1988—.

AWARDS, HONORS: Book of the Year for Children shortlist, Canadian Library Association, 1999, Governor General's Award, 2000, and Silver Birch Reading Award shortlist, 2001, all for *Looking for X;* Ruth Schwartz Children's Book Award for young adult/middle reader category, Rose Avenue Public School, 2003, for *Parvana's Journey;* Book of the Year Children Award, 2003, Honour Book, for *Parvana's Journey* and *Company of Fools.*

WRITINGS:

NONFICTION

Women of the Afghan War, Praeger Books (Westport, CT), 2000.

Three Wishes: Israeli and Palestinian Children Speak, Groundwood Books (Toronto, Ontario, Canada), 2004.

Our Stories, Our Songs: African Children Talk about AIDS, Fitzhenry & Whiteside (Markham, Ontario, Canada), 2005.

I Am a Taxi, Groundwood Books (Toronto, Ontario, Canada), 2006.

Jackal in the Garden: An Encounter with Bihzad, Watson-Guptill Publications (New York, NY), 2006.

NOVELS; FOR YOUNG ADULTS

Haley and Scotia, Frog-in-the-Well (San Francisco, CA), 1995.

Looking for X, Groundwood Books (Toronto, Ontario, Canada), 1999.

A Company of Fools, Fitzhenry & Whiteside Ltd. (Markham, Ontario, Canada), 2002.

The Heaven Shop, Fitzhenry & Whiteside (Markham, Ontario, Canada), 2004.

"BREADWINNER" TRILOGY

The Breadwinner, Groundwood Books (Toronto, Ontario, Canada), 2000.

Parvana's Journey, Groundwood Books (Toronto, Ontario, Canada), 2002.

Mud City, Groundwood Books (Toronto, Ontario, Canada), 2003.

SIDELIGHTS: Canadian writer Deborah Ellis's political activism has inspired her writings for young adults. In *Looking for X,* an eleven-year-old girl who calls herself Khyber, after the famous mountain pass in Afghanistan, lives with her single mother and five-year-old autistic twin brothers in a poor section of Toronto. Khyber struggles through the challenges of her days essentially friendless until she meets a mysterious homeless woman named X, whom she befriends. One day, a group of skinheads harasses X and Khyber in the park, and when the school is vandalized at the same time, Khyber is blamed. So the girl goes in search of X, to corroborate her story, and this starts an odyssey through the world of the homeless in Toronto. Anita L. Burkam, writing in the *Horn Book,* noted that while a reader may expect Khyber's life to be bleak, given all her problems, Ellis instead strives to show the joy in the poor girl's life, mainly provided by her love for her mother and brothers. "What you wouldn't expect are the marvelous characterizations and fiercely close family ties Deborah Ellis has created here," Burkam remarked. For Leslie Ann Lacika, writing in *School Library Journal,* Khyber's "quirky" life is not quite believable, but Ellis's rich characterizations make up for the lack. "Khyber is a likable protagonist and readers will appreciate how she copes with her issues," Lacika continued.

Ellis's interest in Afghanistan takes a front-and-center role in her next young adult novel, *The Breadwinner.* Published in early 2001, before the September 11th attack on the World Trade Center and the ensuing war on terrorism conducted by the United States mainly in Afghanistan, *The Breadwinner* provides a child's-eye view of life under the Taliban regime. Ellis's protagonist is Parvana, an eleven-year-old girl whose scholarly father is imprisoned by the Taliban, leaving the family to starve, since women are not allowed to work or even to leave their homes unattended by a male relative. So Parvana decides to disguise herself as a boy and go out into the streets to earn money to feed her mother and small brothers. "*The Breadwinner* is a potent portrait of life in contemporary Afghanistan," John Green wrote in *Booklist.* A contributor to *Publishers Weekly* commented that "the topical issues introduced, coupled with this strong heroine, will make this novel of interest to many conscientious teens."

Ellis donated all profits from the sale of *The Breadwinner* to a charitable organization that funds schools for Afghan girls living in Pakistani refugee camps. The author visited these refugee camps in order to collect stories of the war in Afghanistan as fought by the Soviet Union in the early 1990s. The resulting book, *Women of the Afghan War,* also contains first-person narratives of Soviet women soldiers, which Ellis traveled to Moscow in order to obtain. It was while she was recording stories among the Afghans that she heard of a young girl who cut off her hair and donned boys' clothing in order to go out onto the streets of Kabul and earn her family's living. "Something just went click in my head and I knew that I had to do a book about that person," Ellis told Debra Huron in *Herizons.*

The Breadwinner is the first book in Ellis's "Breadwinner" trilogy, which includes *Parvana's Journey* and *Mud City.* In the sequel *Parvana's Journey,* Parvana, who is now thirteen, is wandering through Afghanistan following the death of her father. As she is searching for her mother and siblings, who have disappeared in the chaos of war following the Taliban takeover, she teams up with other abandoned children in an effort to survive. In a review in *Skipping Stones,* George Ayres noted the "vivid descriptions of hunger, bombing and mine fields." Kathleen T. Isaacs, writing in the *School Library Journal,* called the novel "an unforgettable read."

Mud City switches its focus to Parvana's friend Shauzia, a fourteen year old who decides to leave the refugee camp where the children have found safety. Shauzia's decision to leave is based partly on her dislike of the demanding camp leader. Wandering the streets of Peshawar disguised as a boy, Shauzia does whatever she can to survive, only to ultimately return to the refugee camp with a new appreciation for the camp's leader Mrs. Weera. "The story is strong on message," wrote Hazel Rochman in *Booklist.* Referring to the novel as "poignant" in a review in *Resource Links,* Anne Hatcher noted: "Ellis creates a compelling and heart wrenching depiction of life in the refugee camps." *School Library Journal* contributor Kathleen Isaacs noted that "this novel conveys a distinctive sense of place."

Ellis turns to the distant past for her novel *A Company of Fools.* In 1349 France, choirboy Henri keeps a journal of the Plague Year and details his friendship with another orphan at the Abbey of St. Luc named Micah. Full of life, it is Micah who turns Henri's life around. Eventually, the two friends join with the monks in establishing a performing troupe called the Company of Fools with the purpose of providing some relief for the suffering people around them. In the process, Micah proves to be an angelic singer whose singing, according to some, can cure the plague. Micah at first becomes enamored with his own singing and supposed powers only to have Henri bring him back to earth again. Burkham, writing again in *Horn Book* noted that "the friendship between the two boys [is] a universal theme particularly well placed in Ellis's lively and historically plausible tale."

The Heaven Shop tells the story of Binti, a southern African child who is relatively well off in that she attends a private school and has a weekly radio show. Nevertheless, Binti's mother and father die of AIDS, and Binti winds up living with uncaring relatives. After running away, she eventually reunites with her prostitute sister and her brother, who was in prison. Hazel Rochman, writing in *Booklist,* noted that the author "creates a vivid sense of the place and characters that are angry, kind, brave, and real." *Kliatt* contributor Claire Rosser wrote: "By reading this gripping story, students will understand how the epidemic of AIDS in Africa has changed individuals and whole societies."

In her nonfiction book, *Three Wishes: Palestinian and Israeli Children Speak,* Ellis relays the words and messages of twenty children caught up in decades long conflict between Palestine and Israel. They talk of bombs and checkpoints and how the crisis around them has affected their lives. "The specifics and the passionate immediacy of the voices will spark discussion," wrote Hazel Rochman in *Booklist. School Library Journal* contributor Alison Follos referred to *Three Wishes* as "an excellent presentation of a confusing historic struggle, told within a palpable, perceptive and empathetic format."

Ellis continues with children's views of a difficult life with *Our Stories, Our Songs: African Children Talk about AIDS.* For the book, Ellis, interviews more than fifty children from sub-Saharan Africa and, through their stories and thoughts, provides a look at the extreme poverty that pervades this land and its economic and emotional impact on the children and others who live there. Melissa Christy Buron, writing in the *School Library Journal,* called *Our Stories, Our Songs* "an impressive offering whose chilling accounts remain with

readers long after the book is finished." Hazel Rochman wrote in *Booklist,* that "the [children's] short, simple sentences and the small photographs capture a wide variety of individual experience."

Ellis once commented: "I'm fascinated by the capacity of children to cope in a dangerous world, to live in it with joy and dignity. That is the general theme running through my books for young readers.

"Sometimes I enjoy writing, sometimes I hate it because it takes me away from more pleasurable activities, but always I am compelled to do it. There is nothing so satisfying as completing another manuscript, knowing I've gotten through it one more time. Maybe it will sell, maybe it won't—that's up to the gods—but at least I didn't quit, and that feels great."

BIOGRAPHICAL AND CRITICAL SOURCES:

PERIODICALS

American Libraries, April, 2006, "*Three Wishes: Israeli and Palestinian Children Speak* Denied in Ontario," p. 15.
Booklist, May 15, 2000, Anne O'Malley, review of *Looking for X,* p. 1739; March 1, 2001, John Green, review of *The Breadwinner,* p. 1275; November 15, 2003, Hazel Rochman, review of *Mud City,* p. 597; September 1, 2004, Hazel Rochman, review of *The Heaven Shop,* p. 120; September 1, 2004, Hazel Rochman, review of *Three Wishes,* p. 122; October 1, 2005, Hazel Rochman, review of *Our Stories, Our Songs: African Children Talk about AIDS,* p. 52.
Bookseller, February 18, 2005, review of *The Heaven Shop,* p. 38.
Chicago Tribune, December 4, 2001, Patrick D. Reardon, "Books Find Ways to Speak to Children about War," includes discussion of *The Breadwinner.*
Christian Century, December 14, 2004, review of *The Heaven Shop,* p. 24.
Financial Times, May 14, 2005, review of *The Heaven Shop,* p. 33.
Herizons, summer, 2001, Debra Huron, "Transcending Borders," p. 36.
Horn Book, July, 2000, Anita L. Burkam, review of *Looking for X,* p. 456; January-February, 2003, Anita L. Burkam, review of *A Company of Fools,* p. 70; November-December, 2005, Betty Carter, review of *Our Stories, Our Songs,* p. 733.

Kirkus Reviews, August 1, 2004, review of *The Heaven Shop,* p. 740.

Kliatt, September, 2003, Claire Rosser, review of *Mud City,* p. 7; September, 2004, Claire Rosser, review of *The Heaven Shop,* p. 8; March, 2005, Claire Rosser, review of *Mud City,* p. 18.

Maclean's, November 12, 2001, Brian Bethune, "Kabul for Kids: A Canadian Scores with a Tale of Taliban Oppression," p. 56.

Publishers Weekly, March 19, 2001, review of *The Breadwinner,* p. 100; November 17, 2003, Nathalie Atkinson, "A Timely Trilogy: Canadian Author Deborah Ellis Finds International Success Detailing the Struggles of Afghan Refuges," p. 22; December 20, 2004, review of *The Heaven Shop,* p. 60.

Resource Links, December, 2003, Anne Hatcher, review of *Mud City,* p. 14; October, 2004, Victoria Pennell, review of *The Heaven Shop,* p. 28; December, 2005, Joan Marshall, review of *Our Stories, Our Songs,* p. 41.

School Library Journal, July, 2000, Leslie Ann Lacika, review of *Looking for X,* p. 104; July, 2001, Kathleen Isaacs, review of *The Breadwinner,* p. 106; October, 2003, review of *Parvana's Journey,* p. S43; November, 2003, Kathleen Issacs, review of *Mud City,* p. 138; October, 2004, Kathleen Isaacs, review of *The Heaven Shop,* p. 161, and Alison Follos, review of *Three Wishes,* p. 190; March, 2005, Kathleen T. Isaacs, review of *Parvana's Journey,* p. 68; April, 2005, review of *Three Wishes,* p. S45; November, 2005, Melissa Christy Buron, review of *Our Stories, Our Songs,* p. 156; December, 2005, Rick Margolis, "When Children Suffer: Canadian Writer and Activist Deborah Ellis Talks about the AIDS epidemic," p. 40.

Skipping Stones, May-August, 2003, George Ayres, review of *Parvana's Journey,* p. 30.

Time International, November 26, 2001, Bryan Walsh, "Veil of Tears: A Children's Book Details Life under the Taliban," p. 66.

ONLINE

Allen & Unwin Web site, http://www.allenunwin.com/ (December 26, 2006), interview with author.

Bookreporter.com, http://www.bookreporter.com/ (December 29, 2006), brief biography of author.

Groundwood Books Web site, http://www.groundwood. com/ (February 23, 2002), biography of Deborah Ellis.

Stellar Awards Web site, http://www.stellaraward.ca/ (December 29, 2006), brief profile of author.

Writers Union Canada Web site, http://www.writers union.ca/ (December 26, 2006), brief biography of author.*

* * *

ELLISON, Robert H. 1967-

PERSONAL: Born February 13, 1967; U.S. citizen; son of Robert (an Air Force officer) and Judith (a homemaker) Ellison; married Lori Lynn Haney (a counselor), July 14, 1990; children: Hunter, Emmalee. *Ethnicity:* "Caucasian." *Education:* University of Texas at Austin, B.A., 1988; University of North Texas, M.A., 1991, Ph.D., 1995. *Religion:* Baptist. *Hobbies and other interests:* Reading, drama.

ADDRESSES: Office—Department of English, East Texas Baptist University, 1209 N. Grove St., Marshall, TX 75670. *E-mail*—rellison@etbu.edu.

CAREER: East Texas Baptist University, Marshall, assistant professor, 1995-2000, associate professor, 2000-03, professor of English, 2003—, head of department, 1998-2004.

MEMBER: American Society of Church History, Southern Conference on British Studies.

WRITINGS:

The Victorian Pulpit: Spoken and Written Sermons in Nineteenth-Century Britain, Susquehanna University Press (Selinsgrove, PA), 1998.

Contributor to books, including *John Keble in Context,* edited by Kirstie Blair, Anthem (London, England), 2004. Contributor to periodicals, including *Victorian Studies, Christian History and Biography, Victorian Literature and Culture,* and *Religion and the Arts.*

* * *

EPHRON, Nora 1941-

PERSONAL: Born May 19, 1941, in New York, NY; daughter of Henry (a writer) and Phoebe (a writer) Ephron; married Dan Greenburg (a writer), April 9, 1967 (divorced); married Carl Bernstein (a journalist), April

14, 1976 (divorced, 1980); married Nicholas Pileggi (a writer), 1987; children: (second marriage) Jacob, Max. *Education:* Wellesley College, B.A., 1962.

ADDRESSES: Agent—Lynn Nesbit, International Creative Management, 40 W. 57th St., New York, NY 10019.

CAREER: Writer, screenwriter, movie director, movie producer. *New York Post,* New York, NY, reporter, 1963-68; freelance journalist, 1968-72; *Esquire* magazine, New York, NY, columnist and contributing editor, 1972-73; *New York* magazine, New York, NY, contributing editor, 1973-74; *Esquire,* senior editor and columnist, 1974-76. Director of films, including *Lucky Numbers,* 2000; also appeared as actor in the films *Crimes and Misdemeanors,* 1989, and *Husbands and Wives,* 1992.

AWARDS, HONORS: Penney-Missouri award from University of Missouri Journalism School and J.C. Penney & Co., 1973; D.H.L. from Briarcliff College, 1974; with Alice Arlen, nomination for best original screenplay, American Academy of Motion Picture Arts and Sciences, 1984, for *Silkwood;* nomination for best original screenplay, American Academy of Motion Picture Arts and Sciences, 1989, for *When Harry Met Sally . . .;* Ian McLellan Hunter Award, Writers Guild of America East, 2003, for lifetime achievement in writing.

WRITINGS:

Wallflower at the Orgy (collection of articles), Viking (New York, NY), 1970.
Crazy Salad: Some Things about Women (collection of articles), Knopf (New York, NY), 1975, reprinted, Modern Library (New York, NY), 2000.
Scribble, Scribble: Notes on the Media (collection of columns), Knopf (New York, NY), 1979.
Heartburn (novel; also see below), Knopf (New York, NY), 1983.
Nora Ephron Collected, Avon Books (New York, NY), 1991.
Imaginary Friends (play), produced on Broadway at the Barrymore Theater, 2002.
I Feel Bad about My Neck: And Other Thoughts on Being a Woman, Knopf (New York, NY), 2006.

SCREENPLAYS

Perfect Gentleman (television movie), CBS-TV, 1978.

(With Alice Arlen) *Silkwood,* Twentieth Century-Fox, 1983.
Heartburn (adapted from her novel), Paramount Pictures, 1986.
When Harry Met Sally . . ., Castle Rock Entertainment, 1989.
(With Alice Arlen) *Cookie,* Warner Brothers, 1989.
My Blue Heaven, Warner Brothers, 1990.
(With sister, Delia Ephron; also director) *This Is My Life* (based on the novel by Meg Wolitzer), Twentieth Century-Fox, 1992.
(With David S. Ward and Jeff Arch; also director) *Sleepless in Seattle,* Tri-Star Pictures, 1993.
(With Pete Dexter, Jim Quinlan; also director and co-producer) *Michael,* New Line Cinema, 1996.
(With Delia Ephron; also director and co-producer with Lauren Shuler-Donner) *You've Got Mail,* Warner Brothers, 1998.
(With Delia Ephron; also director) *Desert Rose* (based on Larry McMurtry's novel of the same title), Columbia Pictures, 2002.
(With Delia Ephron; also director) *Bewitched,* Columbia Pictures, 2005.

Also coauthor of the screenplays *Modern Bride* and *Maggie,* both with Alice Arlen, and *Mixed Nuts,* with Delia Ephron, also director, produced in 1994. Author of screenplay for *Hanging Up,* 2000. Also wrote for television series *Adam's Rib,* 1973. Contributor of short stories, essays, and reviews to periodicals, including *O, The Oprah Magazine.*

SIDELIGHTS: Nora Ephron is no stranger to public scrutiny. In the early 1960s, her parents, writers Henry and Phoebe Ephron, based their successful play, *Take Her, She's Mine,* on their eldest daughter's letters home from Wellesley College. Later, Nora Ephron gained a reputation as an acerbic, often autobiographical reporter and columnist, regularly writing for such publications as *New York* magazine and *Esquire.* Finally, Ephron chronicled her much-publicized breakup with second husband Carl Bernstein in her novel *Heartburn,* which she later adapted for the screen.

Heartburn tells the story of Rachel Samstat, a well-known cookbook author, who discovers while she is seven months pregnant with their second child that her political columnist husband is having an affair with an elegant socialite. The plot, which mirrors the circumstances of Ephron's own divorce, has been criticized for its obviously autobiographical origins. "How could

[Ephron] publish a *roman* so shamelessly *a clef,* exposing the warts, peccadilloes and worse of family, ex-husbands and friends?" wrote Art Seidenbaum in the *Los Angeles Times Book Review.* "How awfully lucky for those who treat them badly . . . that when journalists get mad they reach for a typewriter instead of a gun," observed Grace Glueck in the *New York Times Book Review.*

Ephron defended her right to use material from her own life as inspiration for a novel. "I've always written about my life," Ephron explained to Stephanie Mansfield in a *Washington Post* interview coinciding with the release of *Heartburn.* "That's how I grew up. 'Take notes. Everything is copy.' All that stuff my mother said to us. I think it would have been impossible for me to go through the end of my marriage and not written about it, because although it was the most awful thing I've ever been through . . . it was by *far* the most interesting."

Other critics found the novel and its screenplay adaptation witty and realistic. "Long after the chatter has abated," observed *Time* magazine reviewer Stefan Kanfer, "*Heartburn* will be providing insights and laughter." Kanfer continued: "[As] Nora Ephron is about to learn, leaving well is the best revenge."

Ephron's next screenplay, *Silkwood,* tells the story of activist Karen Silkwood, a worker in a plutonium fuel rod plant who uncovers evidence of slipshod manufacturing procedures but dies shortly thereafter in a car accident that many speculated was more than accidental. Based on a true story, the film won a nomination for best original screenplay from the American Academy of Motion Picture Arts and Sciences. Some critics found the film's interpretation of the circumstances surrounding Silkwood's death disturbing. "The film cannot supply the truth because no one really knows the truth," states Sheila Benson in the *Los Angeles Times.*

Ephron's 1989 comedy *When Harry Met Sally . . .* was a success with critics and fans alike. Following the twelve-year friendship and eventual courtship of a modern New York couple, the film blends witty one-liners with startlingly accurate observations about the dating scene. Ephron made her directorial debut in 1992 with *This Is My Life,* a comedy which she wrote with her sister, Delia. *New York Times* contributor Janet Maslin found the screenplay witty, full of "small, wry touches," and a "distinctive comic style." Ephron's

directing, she added, produces a single vision of New York Life that "even at its most generous and funny manages to retain a penetrating clarity." Ephron attributes the film's accurate portrayal of family relationships, particularly sisters' bonds, to her collaboration with her own sister.

Ephron, who has seen many of the scripts she has written (or co-written) produced, acknowledges the collaborative nature of script-writing in general. "When a movie comedy works, it starts with a script, then you get a director who adds, and an actor who adds, and it gets funnier and funnier," she told Allessandra Stanley of the *New York Times.*

In her film *Sleepless in Seattle,* Ephron and cowriters David S. Ward and Jeff Arch present a story about an engaged woman in Baltimore who hears on a call-in radio talk show the young son of a widowed husband living in Seattle talking about his father's difficulties. The more she hears, the more she becomes enamored with the boy's father until they eventually meet, leading to a romance. Meredith Berkman, writing in *Entertainment Weekly* commented: "Sleepless is just the kind of happily-ever-after tale that delightfully skews our perspective on real-life love." *New Statesman & Society* contributor Jonathan Romney wrote: "The film's sob quotient depends on the knowing ingenuity with which Ephron——who here directs as well as co-writes——rings her ironic changes on our expectations. She's not afraid to ladle on knowingly shloky gestures."

Ephron turns to the stage for the first time as the author of the play *Imaginary Friends,* which focuses on the famous, real-life feud between writers Lillian Hellman and Mary McCarthy. The play examines the women's careers and their youths, as well as the famous defamation law suit brought by Hellman against McCarthy when McCarthy appeared on a television talk show and said of Hellman: "Every word she writes is a lie, including 'and' and 'the,'" as noted by Lisa D. Horowitz in *Daily Variety.* In her review of the play, Horowitz noted: "Ephron makes it clear she thinks these are writers worth reading, and worth writing about. With the inclusion of various timely issues—literary feuds, freedom of speech, political pariahs—she makes them pertinent to contemporary . . . [audiences] as well." Writing in the *Hollywood Reporter,* Frank Scheck commented that Ephron has "turned it into a series of vaudevillian sketches, complete with song-and-dance numbers." Noting "the playful and bitchy imagination of Nora Ephron," *Nation* contributor David Kaufman also wrote that "even if the comic-book tone seems, at first, to trivialize Hellman and McCarthy, it ultimately brings them down to a human scale, where their foibles are writ large, enabling us to see that on one level their war really stemmed from the clash of two outsized personalities vying for public attention."

In her 2005 movie *Bewitched,* Ephron, who also directed the film, based the screenplay (written with Delia Ephron) on the 1960' television series of the same name. In the film, Isabel, who is really a witch, falls for an egotistical, hard-luck actor named Jack, who is making an updated sitcom titled *Bewitched.* When Isabel lands a part on the series, she becomes more popular than Jack, leading at first to jealously but eventually love. Brian Lowry, writing in *Variety,* noted that "finding a fresh way to tackle such material is admirable." In a review in the *New Yorker,* Anthony Lane wrote: "The result is clever, and the narrative twistings keep you on your toes." In his review of the film in *Newsweek,* David Ansen wrote: "This pop-Pirandellian concept, written by Ephron with her sister Delia, yields some healthy laughs."

Ephron ponders growing older in her book *I Feel Bad about My Neck: And Other Thoughts on Being a Woman.* The essays focus primarily on how Ephron is coping with growing older while exploring topics such as plastic surgery and shopping for clothes to hide an aging body. A reviewer writing in *California Bookwatch,* referred to *I Feel Bad about My Neck* as a "blend of autobiography and reflection." A *Kirkus Reviews* contributor referred to the book as "a disparate assortment of sharp and funny pieces revealing the private anguishes, quirks and passions of a woman on the brink of senior citizenhood." Toni Bentley, writing in *Publishers Weekly,* commented that Ephron provides "an intelligent, alert, entertaining perspective that does not take itself too seriously."

BIOGRAPHICAL AND CRITICAL SOURCES:

BOOKS

Authors in the News, Volume 2, Thomson Gale (Detroit, MI), 1976.

Contemporary Literary Criticism, Thomson Gale (Detroit, MI), Volume 17, 1981, Volume 31, 1985.

Ephron, Nora, *Scribble, Scribble,* Knopf (New York, NY), 1979.

Ephron, Nora, *Heartburn,* Knopf (New York, NY), 1983.

Ephron, Nora, *I Feel Bad about My Neck: And Other Thoughts on Being a Woman,* Knopf (New York, NY), 2006.

Newsmakers, 1992 Cumulation, Thomson Gale (Detroit, MI), 1992.

PERIODICALS

America's Intelligence Wire, August 4, 2006, "Juggling Act; Interview with Author Nora Ephron."

Back Stage West, October 10, 2002, Gi-Gi Downs, review of *Imaginary Friends,* p. 12.

Baltimore Sun, September 17, 2006, Susan Reimer, review of *I Feel Bad about My Neck.*

California Bookwatch, October, 2006, review of *I Feel Bad about My Neck.*

Contra Costa Times (Walnut Creek, CA), September 27, 2006, Lynn Carey, review of *I Feel Bad about My Neck.*

Daily Variety, October 2, 2002, Lisa D. Horowitz, review of *Imaginary Friends,* p. 11; December 13, 2002, Charles Isherwood, review of *Imaginary Friends,* p. 6; January 30, 2003, Robert Hofler, review of *Imaginary Friends,* p. 5; February 26, 2003, Dave McNary, "Writers Guild East Taps Ephron for Hunter Kudos," p. 59; June 20, 2005, Brian Lowry, review of *Bewitched,* p. 28.

Dallas Morning News, August 30, 2006, Jerome Weeks, review of *I Feel Bad about My Neck.*

Entertainment Weekly, February 28, 1992, Owen Gleiberman, review of *This Is My Life,* p. 4; July 31, 1992, Jill Rachlin, review of *This Is My Life,* p. 66; December 10, 1993, Meredith Berkman, review of *Sleepless in Seattle,* p. 80; October 28, 2005, Timothy Gunatilaka, review of *Bewitched,* p. 67.

Fast Company, May, 2003, Anne Kreamer, "Women as Heroines of Their Own Lives," interview with author, p. 73.

Hollywood Reporter, December 13, 2002, Frank Scheck, review of *Imaginary Friends,* p. 16; February 25, 2003, Zorianna Kit, review of *Bewitched,* p. 1.

Interview, July, 2005, Sarah Cristobal, review of *Bewitched,* p. 30.

Kirkus Reviews, May 15, 2006, review of *I Feel Bad about My Neck,* p. 504.

Los Angeles Times, December 14, 1983, Sheila Benson, review of *Silkwood.*

Los Angeles Times Book Review, April 17, 1983, Art Seidenbaum, review of *Heartburn,* p. 2.

Nation, January 27, 2003, David Kaufman, review of *Imaginary Friends,* p. 32.

New Statesman & Society, September 24, 1993, Jonathan Romney, review of *Sleepless in Seattle,* p. 50.

Newsweek, June 27, 2005, David Ansen, review of *Bewitched,* p. 63; July 31, 2006, Nicki Gostin, review of *I Feel Bad about My Neck,* p. 55.

New Yorker, June 27, 2005, Anthony Lane, review of *Bewitched,* p. 105.

New York Times, January 24, 1991, Allessandra Stanley, "When Nora Met Wendy: The Subject Was Comedy," p. B4; February 21, 1992, Janet Maslin, review of *This Is My Life,* p. C8; December 13, 1998, Dinitia Smith, "FILM; She's a Director With an Edge: She's a Writer"; December 18, 1998, Janet Maslin, review of *You've Got Mail.*

New York Times Book Review, April 24, 1983, Grace Glueck, review of *Heartburn.*

People, March 2, 1992, Joanne Kaufman, review of *This Is My Life,* p. 16.

Publishers Weekly, July 4, 2005, Leah Rozen, review of *Bewitched,* p. 29; June 5, 2006, Toni Bentley, review of *I Feel Bad about My Neck,* p. 46.

State (Columbia, SC), September 27, 2006, Claudia Smith Brinson, review of *I Feel Bad about My Neck.*

Texas Monthly, November, 2006, Sarah Bird, review of *I Feel Bad about My Neck,* p. 356.

Time, April 11, 1983, Stefan Kanfer, review of *Heartburn* (film), p. 94; July 31, 1989, Richard Corliss, review of *When Harry Met Sally . . .,* p. 65; January 27, 1992, Garry Wills, "How to Repossess a Life: Nora Ephron Takes Control by Telling Her Story Her Way," profile of author, p. 62; February 24, 1992, Richard Schickel, review of *This Is My Life,* p. 68; July 4, 2005, Richard Schickel, review of *Bewitched,* p. 80.

Variety, March 25, 2002, "'Sweet Smell of Success' Composer Marvin Hamlisch and Lyricist Craig Carnelia Have Written the Score for Nora Ephron's 'Imaginary Friends,'" p. 91; October 7, 2002, Lisa D. Horowitz, review of *Imaginary Friends,* p. 32; June 17, 2005, Brian Lowry, review of *Bewitched,* p. 4.

W, December, 2002, Hilary De Vries, "Curtain Call: Writer, Director and Now Playwright Nora Ephron Enters a New Stage with *Imaginary Friends,*" p. 194.

Washington Post, April 25, 1983, Stephanie Mansfield, "Nora Ephron's Open Sock Drawer," interview with author, p. D1.

ONLINE

Internet Movie Database, http://www.imdb.com/ (December 30, 2006), information on author's film work.

New York Magazine, http://nymag.com/ (December 20, 2006), Boris Kachka, review of *I Feel Bad about My Neck.*

NNDB, http://www.nndb.com/ (December 30, 2006), information on author's film work.

Salon.com, http://www.salon.com/ (August 8, 2006), Rebecca Traister "What's So Damn Great about Aging," profile of author.*

* * *

ESQUIVEL, Laura 1950-

PERSONAL: Born September 20, 1950, in Mexico; daughter of Julio Caesar (a telegraph operator) and Josephina Esquivel; married Alfonso Arau (a film director), 1975; children: Sandra. *Education:* Attended Escuela Normal de Maestros, Mexico. *Hobbies and other interests:* Cooking.

ADDRESSES: Home—Mexico City, Mexico.

CAREER: Writer and screenwriter. Has written and directed children's theater; previously worked as a teacher for eight years. Producer of the film *La Mirada de la ausencia,* 1990.

AWARDS, HONORS: Ariel Award nomination for best screenplay, Mexican Academy of Motion Pictures, Arts and Sciences, for *Chido One.*

WRITINGS:

Chido One (screenplay), 1985.

Como agua para chocolate: novela de entregas mensuales con recetas, amores, y remedios caseros (novel), Editorial Planeta Mexicana, 1989, translation by Carol Christensen and Thomas Christensen published as *Like Water for Chocolate: A Novel in Monthly Installments, with Recipes, Romances, and Home Remedies,* Doubleday (New York, NY), 1991.

Like Water for Chocolate (screenplay; based on her novel of the same title), Miramax, 1992.

Little Ocean Star (screenplay for children), 1994.

Ley del amor (novel), translation by Margaret Sayers Peden published as *The Law of Love*, Crown Publishers (New York, NY), 1996.

Intimas suculencias: Tratado filosofico de cocina (novel), Ollero & Ramos (Madrid, Spain), 1998.

Between Two Fires: Intimate Writings on Life, Love, Food, and Flavor (novel), translation by Stephen Lytle, Crown Publishers (New York, NY), 2000.

Tan velos como el deseo (novel), Plaza y Janes Editores (Barcelona, Spain), 2001, translation by Stephen Lytle published as *Swift as Desire,* Crown Publishers (New York, NY), 2001.

Malinche (novel), translated by Ernesto Mestre-Reed, illustrations by Jordi Castells, Atria Books (New York, NY), 2006.

Also author of the story for the film *Tacos de oro,* 1985. *Like Water for Chocolate* was also published in serial format in its entirety in the *New York Times'* Metro Section, 2004.

SIDELIGHTS: Mexican author Laura Esquivel, who gained international recognition with her first novel, *Como agua para chocolate* (*Like Water for Chocolate*), began writing when she worked in a theater workshop for children and found that there was little material available for them to perform. She then moved into writing for children's public television, and then into screenwriting.

Working in partnership with her husband, Mexican director Alfonso Arau, Esquivel wrote the screenplay for the 1985 Mexican release *Chido One,* which Arau directed. The film's success prompted the couple to continue their collaboration, and Arau became the director when Esquivel adapted *Like Water for Chocolate* for the screen. Both the novel and movie were enormously popular. A number-one best-seller in Mexico in 1990, the book has been translated into numerous languages, including an English language version, which enjoyed a longstanding run on the *New York Times Book Review* best-seller list in 1993. The movie became one of the highest-grossing foreign films of the decade. Employing in this work the brand of magic realism that Gabriel García Márquez popularized, Esquivel blends culinary knowledge, sensuality, and alchemy with fables and cultural lore to capture what *Washington Post* reviewer Mary Batts Estrada called "the secrets of love and life as revealed by the kitchen."

Like Water for Chocolate is the story of Tita, the youngest of three daughters born to Mama Elena, the tyrannical owner of the De la Garza ranch. Tita is a victim of tradition: as the youngest daughter in a Mexican family she is obliged to remain unmarried and to care for her mother. Experiencing pain and frustration as she watches Pedro, the man she loves, marry her older sister Rosaura, Tita faces the added burden of having to bake the wedding cake. But because she was born in the kitchen and knows a great deal about food and its powers, Tita is able to bake her profound sense of sorrow into the cake and make the wedding guests ill. "From this point," as James Polk remarked in the *Tribune Books,* "food, sex and magic are wondrously interwoven." For the remainder of the novel, Tita uses her special culinary talents to provoke strange reactions in Mama Elena, Rosaura, Tita's other sister, Gertrudis, and many others.

Food has played a significant role in Esquivel's life since she was a child. Remembering her early cooking experiences and the aromas of foods cooked in her grandmother's house, she told *New York Times* correspondent Molly O'Neill that "I watch cooking change the cook, just as it transforms the food." The author added: "Food can change anything." For Esquivel, cooking is a reminder of the alchemy between concrete and abstract forces. Writing in the *Los Angeles Times Book Review,* Karen Stabiner remarked that Esquivel's novel "is a wondrous, romantic tale, fueled by mystery and superstition, as well as by the recipes that introduce each chapter." Polk, in his *Tribune Books* review, wrote that "*Like Water for Chocolate* (a Mexican colloquialism meaning, roughly, agitated or excited) is an inventive and mischievous romp—part cookbook, part novel."

Esquivel followed with *The Law of Love,* a highly imaginative novel that features reincarnation and cosmic retribution and attests to the primacy of love. The story opens with the sixteenth-century Spanish conquest of Tenochtitlan, the future site of Mexico City, and the rape of an Aztec princess atop a temple. Many centuries later the principal actors of this earlier drama reappear as astro-analyst Azucena, her missing soul mate Rodrigo, and planetary presidential candidate Isabel in a confrontation that finally breaks the cycle of vengeance and hatred with love and forgiveness. The text is accompanied by a compact disc with music and cartoon illustrations. This "multimedia event," as described by Lilian Pizzichini in the *Times Literary Supplement,* incorporates elements of magic realism, science fiction, and New Age philosophy. Pizzichini concluded: "Esquivel dresses her ancient story in a collision of literary styles that confirm her wit and ingenuity. She sets herself a mission to explore the redemptive powers of love and art and displays boundless enthusiasm for parody."

In *Swift as Desire,* Esquivel explores communication between people, telling the story of Jubilo, a former telegraph operator who now has Parkinson's disease and is mostly blind and mute. His daughter Lluvia, hoping to help him to communicate and also hoping to bring him back together with her mother Lucha, from whom he is estranged, installs telegraph equipment in his bedroom so that he can tap out messages in Morse code; a computer translates them into written words. Jubilo's life story is told in flashbacks, revealing how he learned of the power of communication and words when he became a telegraph operator and sent messages of love and fate over the wires. Jubilo has certain gifts: his hearing is so sensitive that he can hear the movements of a fetus in his wife's womb; he can hear people's true thoughts, which are often different from the telegraph messages they send. In the *New York Times,* William Ferguson wrote that although Esquivel's prose is occasionally "cloying," the book "has many charms." Writing in the *Knight-Ridder/Tribune News Service,* Katrinka Blicke noted that the storyline is sometimes interrupted by digressions on sunspots or World War II history. However, she wrote, "Jubilo is a fascinating character." In another *Knight-Ridder/Tribune News Service* review, Marta Barber wrote that "the love story of Jubilo and Lucha warms the heart even when it doesn't jolt the mind." In *School Library Journal,* Adriana Lopez praised the book as "a smooth, simple read for devotees of a quality romance." A *Publishers Weekly* contributor commented: "Esquivel's storytelling abilities are in top form here, and despite its unoriginality, the novel succeeds in conveying a touching message of the power of familial and romantic love."

In her novel *Malinche,* Esquival provides a fictional account of the legendary Mexican historical figure Malinalli, who served as the conquistador Cortez's mistress and guide. Although Malinalli has been considered a traitor in South American history, Esquival presents a different view of the woman as someone who loves her people and initially views Cortez as the reincarnation of the god Quetzalcoatl until she realizes the real nature of his mission. A *Kirkus Reviews* contributor commented on the novel, noting: "Esquivel is less interested in fleshing out the plot than in delineating the belief system of the pre-Aztec civilization, everything that happens to Malinalli is swathed in imagery and deep spiritual significance." In a review in the *Philadelphia Inquirer,* Tanya Barrientos noted that the author's "prose . . . sings with the rhythm of myth." Mary Margaret Benson wrote in the *Library Journal* that "the descriptions of Malinche's beliefs in the roles of the ancient gods and her observations on Christianity are fascinating and well written."

BIOGRAPHICAL AND CRITICAL SOURCES:

BOOKS

Authors and Artists for Young Adults, Volume 29, Thomson Gale (Detroit, MI), 1999.

PERIODICALS

Americas, September, 1999, Cecilia Novella, review of *Intimas suculencias: Tratago filosofico de cocina,* p. 60.

Booklist, June 1, 2001, Kathleen Hughes, review of *Swift as Desire,* p. 1798; February 15, 2006, Joanne Wilkinson, review of *Malinche,* p. 5.

Financial Times, July 8, 2006, Diana Stech, review of *Malinche,* p. 33.

Kirkus Reviews, March 1, 2006, review of *Malinche,* p. 198.

Knight-Ridder/Tribune News Service, September 26, 2001, Marta Baber, review of *Swift as Desire,* p. K7344; October 10, 2001, Katrinka Blicke, review of *Swift as Desire,* p. K5186.

Library Journal, December, 2000, Wendy Miller, review of *Between Two Fires: Intimate Writings on Life, Love, Food, and Flavor,* p. 131; July, 2001, Mary Margaret Benson, review of *Swift as Desire,* p. 122; April 15, 2006, Mary Margaret Benson, review of *Malinche,* p. 66.

Los Angeles Times Book Review, November 1, 1992, Karen Stabiner, review of *Like Water for Chocolate,* p. 6.

Milwaukee Journal Sentinel, May 3, 2006, Lori Price, review of *Malinche.*

New Statesman, August 27, 2001, Rachel Cooke, "Pleasure Zone," p. 39.

New York Times, March 31, 1993, Molly O'Neill, "Sensing the Spirit in All Things, Seen and Unseen," interview with author, pp. C1, C8; October 7, 2001, William Ferguson, review of *Swift as Desire,* p. 22.

Philadelphia Inquirer, August 16, 2006, Tanya Barrientos, review of *Malinche.*

Publishers Weekly, February 5, 1996, Paul Nathan, "Esqsuivel's Next," p. 24; July 3, 2000, John F. Baker, "Esquival Back to Family for Crown," p. 12; December 4, 2000, review of *Between Two Fires,* p. 70; July 16, 2001, review of *Swift as Desire,* p. 165; May 30, 2005, John F. Baker, "Esquivel Is Back," p. 9; February 27, 2006, review of *Malinche,* p. 31.

School Library Journal, September, 2001, Adriana Lopez, review of *Swift as Desire,* p. S33; November, 2001, Molly Connally, review of *Swift as Desire,* p. 191.

Times Literary Supplement, October 18, 1996, Lilian Pizzichini, review of *The Law of Love,* p. 23; October 5, 2001, Claudia Pugh-Thomas, review of *Swift as Desire,* p. 26.

Tribune Books (Chicago, IL), October 18, 1992, James Polk, review of *Like Water for Chocolate,* p. 8.

Washington Post, September 25, 1992, Mary Batts Estrada, review of *Like Water for Chocolate,* p. B2.

ONLINE

Internet Movie Database, http:www.imdb.com/ (December 20, 2006), information on author's film work.*

*　　*　　*

EVANIER, David

PERSONAL: Married. *Education:* Attended Cherry Lawn School, Darien, CT.

ADDRESSES: Home—New York, NY. *E-mail*—devanier@earthlink.net.

CAREER: Writer, educator, novelist, and short-story writer. University of California Los Angeles (UCLA), creative writing instructor; Douglas College, Vancouver, British Columbia, Canada, creative writing instructor. Screenwriting Fellowship, 1992-93, Chesterfield Film Company (Universal-Amblin). The Writers Community, writer-in-residence.

AWARDS, HONORS: Aga Khan Fiction Prize; McGinniss-Ritchie Short Fiction Award; MacDowell Colony Fellowship (five times); Yaddo Foundation Fellowship Wurlitzer Foundation Fellowship.

WRITINGS:

(Coeditor) *The Nonconformers: Articles of Dissent,* Ballantine Books (New York, NY), 1962.

The Swinging Headhunter, November House (Vancouver, British Columbia, Canada), 1972.

The One-Star Jew (short stories), North Point (San Francisco, CA), 1983.

Red Love (novel), Scribner's (New York, NY), 1991.

Making the Wiseguys Weep: The Jimmy Roselli Story, Farrar, Straus (New York, NY), 1998.

(With Joe Pantoliano) *Who's Sorry Now: The True Story of a Stand-Up Guy,* Dutton (New York, NY), 2002.

Roman Candle: The Life of Bobby Darin, Rodale (Emmaus, PA), 2004.

The Great Kisser (novel), Rager Media (Medina, OH), 2006.

Event (literary magazine), founding editor; *Paris Review,* former fiction editor.

Contributor to periodicals, including *New Republic, Paris Review, Antioch Review, Commentary, Southwest Review, TriQuarterly, Saint Ann's Review, New York Times Magazine, New York Times Book Review, Witness, Chelsea, Ninth Letter, Beloit Fiction Journal, Heeb, Midstream, Moment, Dissent, Nation,* and *Mister Beller's Neighborhood.*

Contributor to anthologies, including *Best American Short Stories.*

Making the Wiseguys Weep has been optioned as a film by Touchstone/Disney.

SIDELIGHTS: David Evanier's *The One-Star Jew* is a collection of stories, the longest of which bears the book's title, a reference to Luther Glick, a pony-tailed Jew in his fifties who is into "cosmic consciousness" and who belongs to a Buddhist sect that meets in a Westchester church attic. Milton Hindus wrote in the *National Review* that he first learned of Evanier through their mutual admiration of the poetry of Charles Reznikoff. Hindus noted that Evanier included Reznikoff's poem "Kaddish" in his "My Rabbi, Ray Charles, and Singing Birds." In this story a young couple about to marry asks their rabbi to include the poem, a variation on the prayer for the dead, in their ceremony. The rabbi is willing but wants to omit the last two lines, which he considers too depressing and disturbing. The couple insist that they be included, and the rabbi complies.

Evanier's stories in *The One-Star Jew* revolve around New York as it was and as it is. He paints a picture of old New York and the places his father had taken him as a child—the Automat, the Paramount Theater, and the Laffmovie, all now replaced by decadence. He writes of people like Ben Knapp, a fundraiser who dies at the foot of the stairs in the Times Square subway station. Hindus remarked that "compassion, humor, individualization—these or variations upon these qualities are characteristic of all fourteen stories. . . . The book is written in clear, hard-edged prose, and yet its innermost core is poetic. Evanier is a New Yorker in a sense in which the *New Yorker* hardly is (The *New Yorker,* I would say, is a non-New Yorker's idea of what a New Yorker is or ought to be)." Hindus noted that from his observations, anecdotes, and stories Evanier "has made an absorbing, readable, thoughtful book that, though never crudely calculating or exploitative of sentiment, arouses a real feeling of nostalgia and recognition in an old New Yorker of an earlier generation."

In 1951, Julius and Ethel Rosenberg were tried for conspiring to pass atomic secrets to the Soviet Union. Evanier's *Red Love* is a fictional account of their story. He renames the Rosenbergs Solly and Dolly Rubell. Solly, who had been a victim of the poverty and racism of rural Alabama, turned to Communism in 1930 at age eleven. Manny Block defended the Rosenbergs, and the government called Ethel's brother David Greenglass and his wife, Ruth, as witnesses. In the end Julius and Ethel chose not to reveal information about their collaborators and were sentenced to death by electric chair. A number of viewpoints are expressed in the thirty-three vignettes. "The novel evokes the dreams, often shredded by sanctimonious dogma, of Americans drawn to the Communist Party from the Depression to the McCarthy era," wrote Andy Solomon in the *New York Times Book Review.*

Evanier's fictional author and narrator, introduced in the prologue, is Gerald Lerner, who, like Evanier, has written two novels and publishes in "reactionary literary magazines" and similar publications. "Still, we can't assume that Evanier shares Gerald Lerner's views, for they so often appear to be ironic," noted Roger Draper in the *New Leader.* Other narrators enter with conflicting views, including an informer who talks of giving the FBI notes of his conversations with leftists and an FBI agent who feels that Dolly had been the driving force of their operation. Draper pointed out that President Dwight Eisenhower felt Ethel Rosenberg was the leader of the spy ring, in spite of the fact that she had only a high school education and was not likely to have been in the position of power.

Lerner reports on the stories of characters that include Sylvia Pollack. In the chapter "The Last Stalinist," Sylvia relates that her son was denied admittance to a mental hospital while she was away working as an activist. On her return she found he had hanged himself in her apartment. In another vignette, Manya Poffnick, who testified for the defense in the Rubells' trial, tells how she became disillusioned with the Communist Party and joined the Black Panther Party. Idealist Sammy Kuznekov joined the Young Communist League and fought in the Spanish Civil War to ultimately discover that the Russians were no better than Nazis. When Antonio Carelli's Communist father was deported, Antonio followed him to the Soviet Union only to find himself a prisoner in the labor camps. "Letters from Amerika," consists of notes exchanged by the Rubells written in their prison cells before their executions.

Lerner talks about his first contact with the Communist Party in the 1950s. His politics changed after a visit to Israel in 1961, but because he was still intrigued by the left he began writing *Red Love.* "Lerner's odyssey through what remains of the Rosenbergs' generation, not the fate of the two principals, is the real story of *Red Love,*" wrote Draper. "Evanier implies the men and women of this milieu were guilty only of catastrophically wishful thinking. . . . Nonetheless, I am not at all sure that I would have been as fair to the Rosenbergs' world as David Evanier has managed to be."

Chilton Williamson, Jr., commented in the *National Review* on the vignette "The Reverend Very Big Bob." He wrote that the "madcap spoof on radio evangelism, while wickedly funny in itself, comes out of nowhere to create the suspicion that its inclusion has a political rather than an artistic rational, that it is intended as a token attack on the Middle America the Rubells and their fellow 'progressives' despised—as a piddling ideological counterweight to the massively anti-progressive thrust of the novel." Williamson called *Red Love* "a social and political novel whose realism, pathos, satire, and tragedy are lightened by comic surrealism that shades in places into pure farce, much of it hilarious. . . . David Evanier's finest literary achievement to date."

Evanier's *Making the Wise Guys Weep: The Jimmy Roselli Story* follows the career of the Italian-American tenor from Frank Sinatra's hometown of Hoboken, New Jersey. Roselli was not well known outside of the New York City area, in part because Sinatra was a hard act to follow. Roselli was born in the tenements in 1925. His mother died when he was young, and his father left him in the care of his grandfather, a longshoreman who spoke no English. Roselli was in his thirties before he was noticed with songs like "Mala Femmena" and "Innamorata." Until that time he had sung in small clubs and bars. Roselli opened each performance with his grandfather's words, "Cante, guaglione, cante!" ("Sing, little one, sing!") He associated with mob figures, was friendly with Sam Giancana, and sang at the wedding of John Gotti Jr., but his resistance to mob demands for a cut of his action hampered his career. Evanier quotes Roselli and tells his story with the help of friends, family, musicians, and promoters who knew him. A *Publishers Weekly* reviewer wrote: "Evanier's depiction of Italian-American life is vivid, as is the image of Roselli."

Evanier explores the life of another popular singer in *Roman Candle: The Life of Bobby Darin.* Darin was a popular teen idol and singer in the late 1950s, known for hits such as "Mack the Knife" and "Splish Splash." A highly intelligent young man, Darin's musical career was driven by the knowledge that his health was fragile after rheumatic fever damaged his heart. Evanier recounts how, with his drive to succeed, Darin made an impact as an early rock singer, an actor, a music industry publisher and entrepreneur, and as a folk singer. "Evanier's sturdy bio quickly notes how the specter of early death spurred Bobby Darin to early fame," commented a *Publishers Weekly* reviewer. The book includes numerous interviews with people who knew and worked with Darin, providing contemporary insight from close associates. Evanier also looks at the musician's personal life, including his difficult marriage to another hugely popular entertainer, Sandra Dee. Evanier's biography, noted a reviewer on *MyShelf.com,* "will let the younger generation know who Bobby Darin was and what an important part in the music industry he played, as well as how wonderful it was to hear his voice and think that we, the listeners, knew him, for we really thought we did."

Evanier collaborated with popular actor Joe Pantoliano to producer *Who's Sorry Now: The True Story of a Stand-Up Guy,* Pantoliano's autobiography and the story of his early life, his turbulent youth, and his rise to fame in the TV and movie business. "Joey Pants," as Pantoliano calls himself, is well-known for his role as Ralph Cifaretto on the television series *The Sopranos,* a hugely popular series about mobsters and organized crime. In the book, Pantoliano offers a "jovial account of his 1950s and '60s youth in Hoboken and Fort Lee, NJ," noted a *Publishers Weekly* reviewer. Pantoliano and Evanier describe the actor's upbringing in an Italian-American family filled with eccentrics and distinctive personalities. The authors recount stories of Pantoliano's parents and their difficult relationship; his delinquent friends; his sometimes unusual relatives; and his numerous girlfriends. Pantoliano notes how the family was frequently uprooted when their luck or a landlord's patience ran out and they were evicted. Once a dyslexic, Pantoliano's academic achievements were minimal, but early experiences with acting helped him to achieve stability and balance. Notably, the actor spent time around family associates who were involved with the mob, particularly wise guy Florie, who moved in after being released from prison. The *Publishers Weekly* reviewer commented that Pantoliano "writes with energy, humor, and honesty," while *Booklist* contributor David Pitt observed that the actor writes "in a style that will be instantly familiar to his fans: tough, outspoken, but with a charming side, too."

The Great Kisser is a novel constructed from a series of eight connected short stories. Evanier "exhibits mastery in this new collection" of short fiction, commented a contributor to *Publishers Weekly.* In the book, Evanier collects a series of observations and episodes from the life of aging, unhappy writer and editor Michael Goldberg. Throughout the stories, Goldberg struggles with feelings of insecurity and inadequacy in all the important areas of his life as he searches for love, family, and success. In "The Tapes," Goldberg reconstructs the previous twenty-five years of his life when his therapist dies and leaves him access to a quarter-century of their taped sessions. After his father's death in "The Man Who Gave up Women," Goldberg reflects on the difficulty of enduring his father's constant insults. "Scraps" tells of his first girlfriend at age fourteen and his attempts to find acceptance from her family. In the title story, Goldberg's mother's death prompts him to recall the difficulties he endured with her over the years. "Evanier's stories boil with a satisfying sense of rage, stoked by sharp observation," concluded the *Publishers Weekly* reviewer.

BIOGRAPHICAL AND CRITICAL SOURCES:

PERIODICALS

Booklist, December 15, 1998, Mike Tribby, review of *Making the Wiseguys Weep: The Jimmy Roselli*

Story, p. 716; October 15, 2002, David Pitt, review of *Who's Sorry Now: The True Story of a Stand-Up Guy,* p. 374.

Kirkus Reviews, October 1, 2006, review of *The Great Kisser,* p. 977.

National Review, July 22, 1983, Milton Hindus, review of *The One-Star Jew,* p. 881; April 1, 1991, Chilton Williamson, Jr., review of *Red Love,* p. 48.

New Leader, May 20, 1991, Roger Draper, review of *Red Love,* p. 3.

New York Times, March 6, 2005, "Darin the 'Brain,' Dogs in the Garden," review of *Roman Candle: The Life of Bobby Darin,* p. 12.

New York Times Book Review, June 2, 1991, Andy Solomon, review of *Red Love,* p. 20.

Publishers Weekly, April 15, 1983, review of *The One-Star Jew,* p. 46; December 14, 1990, Sybil Steinberg, review of *Red Love,* p. 54; November 16, 1998, review of *Making the Wiseguys Weep,* p. 65; September 9, 2002, review of *Who's Sorry Now,* p. 54; October 18, 2004, review of *Roman Candle,* p. 58; September 18, 2006, review of *The Great Kisser,* p. 34.

ONLINE

BobbyDarin.net, http://www.bobbydarin.net/ (January 2, 2007), review of *Roman Candle.*

David Evanier Home Page, http://www.davidevanier.com (January 2, 2007).

MyShelf.com, http://www.myshelf.com/ (January 2, 2007), review of *Roman Candle.**

F

FADERMAN, Lillian 1940-

PERSONAL: Born July 18, 1940, in Bronx, NY; daughter of Mary Lifton; partner of Phyllis Irwin; children: Avrom. *Education:* University of California, Berkeley, A.B., 1962; University of California, Los Angeles, M.A., 1964, Ph.D., 1967.

ADDRESSES: Office—California State University, Department of English, Peters Business Bldg. 445, M/S PB98, Fresno, CA 93740. *E-mail*—lillianf@csufresno. edu.

CAREER: Writer, editor, historian, and educator. California State University, Fresno, member of faculty beginning 1967, associate professor, 1971-72, professor of English, 1973—, chair of English department, 1971-72, dean of School of Humanities, 1972-73, assistant vice president of academic affairs, 1973-76. Visiting professor, University of California, Los Angeles, 1989-91.

AWARDS, HONORS: Best Lesbian/Gay Book Award, American Library Association, 1982, for *Surpassing the Love of Men: Romantic Friendship Between Women from the Renaissance to the Present,* and 1992, for *Odd Girls and Twilight Lovers: A History of Lesbian Life in Twentieth-Century America;* Lambda Literary Awards, 1992, for *Odd Girls and Twilight Lovers,* 1995, for *Chloe Plus Olivia: Lesbian Literature from the Seventeenth Century to the Present,* and 2000, for *To Believe in Women: What Lesbians Have Done for America;* Monette/Horwitz Award for distinguished contributions to lesbian/gay scholarship, 1999; James Brudner Award for exemplary lesbian/gay scholarship, Yale University, 2001; distinguished senior scholar award, American Association of University Women, 2002; Lambda Literary Award and Judy Grahn Award for memoirs, both 2004, both for *Naked in the Promised Land;* Bill Whitehead Award, Publishers Triangle, for exemplary scholarship in lesbian/gay studies, 2006.

WRITINGS:

(With Barbara Bradshaw) *Speaking for Ourselves: American Ethnic Writing,* Scott, Foresman (Glenview, IL), 1969, 2nd edition, 1975.

(Editor, with Luis Omar Salinas) *From the Barrio: A Chicano Anthology,* Canfield Press (San Francisco, CA), 1973.

(Editor and translator, with Brigitte Eriksson) *Lesbian-Feminism in Turn-of-the-Century Germany,* Naiad Press (Tallahassee, FL), 1980, published as *Lesbians in Germany,* 1990.

Surpassing the Love of Men: Romantic Friendship and Love between Women from the Renaissance to the Present, Morrow (New York, NY), 1981.

Scotch Verdict: Miss Pirie and Miss Woods v. Dame Cumming Gordon, Morrow (New York, NY), 1983.

Odd Girls and Twilight Lovers: A History of Lesbian Life in Twentieth-Century America, Columbia University Press (New York, NY), 1991.

(Editor) *Chloe Plus Olivia: An Anthology of Lesbian Literature from the Seventeenth Century to the Present,* Viking (New York, NY), 1994.

(With Ghia Xiong) *I Begin My Life All Over: The Hmong and the American Immigrant Experience,* Beacon Press (Boston, MA), 1998.

To Believe in Women: What Lesbians Have Done for America—A History, Houghton Mifflin (Boston, MA), 1999.

Naked in the Promised Land: A Memoir, Houghton Mifflin (Boston, MA), 2003.

(With Stuart Timmons) *Gay L.A.: A History of Sexual Outlaws, Power Politics, and Lipstick Lesbians,* Basic Books (New York, NY), 2006.

Great Events from History: Gay, Lesbian, Bisexual, and Transgender Events, 1848-2006, Salem Press (Pasadena, CA), 2007.

Contributor of articles to journals, including *Massachusetts Review, New England Quarterly, Journal of Popular Culture, Conditions, Signs, Journal of Homosexuality,* and *Journal of the History of Sexuality.* Contributor to periodicals, including *Advocate.*

SIDELIGHTS: Author, educator, and historian Lillian Faderman's *Surpassing the Love of Men: Romantic Friendship and Love between Women from the Renaissance to the Present* "is a comprehensive and illuminating study of women's struggles to live and love as they please," Phyllis Grosskurth wrote in the *New York Review of Books.* Three historical periods—the sixteenth through the eighteenth centuries, the nineteenth century, and the twentieth century—are examined from both a literary and a cultural perspective in the book, summarized Benjamin DeMott in *Atlantic,* noting Faderman's focus on sexual as well as nonsexual woman-to-woman relationships.

According to Carolyn G. Heilbrun in the *New York Times Book Review, Surpassing the Love of Men* demonstrates that, "except when women preempted male power or tried to pass as men, they were usually, until quite recently, left free to love one another." Faderman's "quite thorough scholarship," noted *Washington Post Book World* reviewer Joanna Russ, indicates that "the Lesbian did not even exist in Europe until the 1880s and in the United States until 1910." She added: "Love between women, which did exist, was unlike Lesbianism in being socially honored, not secretive, and extremely common." Keith Walker wrote in the *Times Literary Supplement* that Faderman "stumbled over this not startlingly original version of events when she was reading Emily Dickinson's love poems and letters to Sue Gilbert," the woman who later became her sister-in-law, "and noticed that Dickinson showed no guilt and moreover that her niece, editing the letters early in this century, felt obliged to bowdlerize them."

Many critics have found *Surpassing the Love of Men* praiseworthy. Heilbrun described the book as "a welcome and needed history" and stated that "its ac-count of women loving women before the twentieth century is invaluable." Walker, however, objected to "the cosy glow engendered by the belief that lesbian relationships are finer, more enduring, and more satisfying than heterosexual ones." Grosskurth, similarly, believed that probably "many such relationships exist, but by investing them all with a romantic coloration, [Faderman] never considers the tensions, irritations, or jealousy engendered by most close relationships." According to Russ: "At times she seems to say that sexism and the segregation of the sexes causes love between women, a confusingly negative view that contradicts her assertion of the normality (statistical and other) of such behavior."

"Despite my deep unease at some of these implicit assumptions," Grosskurth wrote, "I think this is an important book; certainly one of the most significant contributions yet made to feminist literature." DeMott concluded that *Surpassing the Love of Men* remains "a work of genuine interest and value. Its pages are filled with vivid portraits of heroes and heroines struggling to lead their contemporaries out of delusion on sex and gender matter, and with astonishingly fresh disclosures about details of sexist feeling from age to age."

Faderman's other studies of woman-to-woman love include *To Believe in Women: What Lesbians Have Done for America—A History.* Faderman asserts that many women who have been important in social reform movements can be considered lesbian, including suffragists Susan B. Anthony and Carrie Chapman Catt, first lady Eleanor Roosevelt, settlement house founder and peace activist Jane Addams, and medical doctors Marie Zakrzewska, Mary Walker, and Emily Blackwell. In this work, Faderman expands her definition of lesbianism beyond romantic love between women to "intense woman-to-woman relating and commitment." *New York Times Book Review* commentator Karla Jay called this a "generous definition," allowing that some will consider Faderman's "tendentious claims . . . a welcome corrective to biographies that erased lesbian existence." *Advocate* contributor Ricardo Ortiz noted that "whether or not they would have called themselves lesbian, each [of the women profiled] was able to effect change thanks partly to the support of a loving, long-term female life partner." Jay found it problematic, though, that Faderman puts such emphasis on the contribution of lesbian relationships to these women's activism. "Sexual orientation was probably less of a factor for these reformers than the financial wherewithal that freed them from the tedious demands of earning a living," Jay remarked. Also, Faderman holds up these relationships as models for both same-sex and mixed-sex couples to emulate in balancing personal life and career, but these female couples, Jay pointed out, sometimes had a very traditional division of labor, with one partner handling domestic matters so the other could work for her cherished causes. "Faderman may inadvertently be broadcasting a discouraging message about the prospects for combining family life with a profession or social activism," Jay concluded. Despite these reservations, she pronounced the book "a decent starting point for learning about these pioneers and their contributions to American life" and recommended it "for those who need a dose of pride and a slice of history."

Odd Girls and Twilight Lovers is a scholarly examination of the transition of women's close relationships of the nineteenth century to the rise of lesbianism in the 1920s, a societal change made possible by women's growing economic independence. However, once women's relationships were capable of supplanting heterosexual marriage, public acceptance of them fell by the wayside. Women's once-innocuous "romantic friendships" became something more sinister as norms continued to shift throughout the century.

Odd Girls was well received as a close examination of a previously overlooked topic, and in time the book became a standard text in many women's studies courses. One of Faderman's assertions in the book is that in the nineteenth and early twentieth century, before female same-sex relationships became widely suspect as "abnormal," women were able to express their affections for other women, and even to live in female domestic partnerships, without suffering the opprobrium they would during the more restrictive decades of the mid-twentieth century. Patricia Sarles in *Library Journal* called the book "a necessity for women's studies collections." Jane Mills, reviewing the book for *New Statesman & Society,* remarked that Faderman illustrates that "even during the worst period of persecution, gay and lesbian subculture grew and defined itself more clearly than ever before." Noting that the contemporary idea of homosexuality did not exist much more than a hundred years ago, *New York Times Book Review* writer Jeffrey Escoffier complimented Faderman's "grand narrative synthesis of the cultural, social and political history of lesbian life since the late nineteenth century."

Faderman's life story takes center stage in *Naked in the Promised Land: A Memoir,* in which she examines her roots as the daughter of a poor, single immigrant

traumatized by the death of her parents at the hands of the Nazis. From the sweatshops of Brooklyn, the young Lillian saw her mother and aunt struggle. When the threesome moved to Hollywood in search of a better life, Lillian was determined to save her histrionic mother by becoming a movie star. Years of acting lessons and one nose job later, Lillian was inclined to drop out of school and use her body as a nude model and stripper while she came to grips with her sexual orientation. A vigilant career counselor steered her toward college, but the sex work continued, along with her twisted relationship with her psychologically fragile mother. During her senior year of high school, Lillian entered into a sham marriage with a gay Jewish psychologist—an ill-fated move that pleased her mother immensely. Lillian later put herself through college by posing nude and dancing under the name Mink Frost in San Francisco's Tenderloin district, a double life in the straight-laced 1950s if ever there was one.

After obtaining her Ph.D., Faderman was astounded to discover that the sexism she faced in academia, where all the tenured teaching positions went to her male classmates, mirrored the ostensibly harsher street life she thought she had left behind. Despite her academic standing, Faderman was offered only a low-prestige job at Fresno State. She took it, and as the years passed, rose through the ranks in academia, becoming a leading scholar at her university and helping to pioneer the field of women's studies. Having ended her marriage years earlier, she embarked on a life-long relationship with a colleague, Phyllis Irwin, and together they raised Faderman's son, who was conceived through artificial insemination.

Naked in the Promised Land garnered good reviews. Writing in *Publishers Weekly,* Michael Bronski noted that though Faderman's previous books "caused considerable alarm in conservative academic circles . . . uncovering the threads of past Sapphic desire was nothing compared to confessing to being a stripper decades ago." A writer for *Publishers Weekly* called the memoir "exceedingly honest, endearing and profound." Focusing largely on how Faderman's "identities as working-class, Jewish, female, lesbian, sex worker, and student did not neatly mesh," wrote Susan Freeman in the *Miami Herald,* the story is a "tale of a life stretched long, encompassing the ghosts of Nazi Germany and hope for the future, the possibility not only embodied by the child but also by an extraordinary woman whose struggles and chutzpah merit our attention." A reviewer on *PopMatters* commented that "the author's education in the fields of sociology and ethnic studies suits the groundwork well, as she is able to use integral literary devices to draw the picture of the era, the class struggles, and effects of the Holocaust climate at the time." Carolyn See, noting the similarities between Faderman's life and her own as a woman breaking new ground in the 1960s, wrote in the *Washington Post* that "Faderman is strong in her belief that all voiceless humans deserve voices, and a respectable place in our American history."

Other critics thought the memoir could have been more introspective. "Faderman's achievements are nothing short of awe-inspiring," wrote Kera Bolonik in the *San Francisco Chronicle,* but "a life as daring and rich as hers warrants a more psychologically probing memoir: Had Faderman showed less metaphoric flesh, then *Naked in the Promised Land* just may have bared a bit more soul." Similarly, Barbara Sjoholm of the *Seattle Times* called the book "fascinating," but concluded that "Faderman leaves us convinced of her success—yet still wondering, a little, who she is." But as Faderman told Bronski in an interview for *Publishers Weekly,* her previous books are about "giving public voice to people who had been silenced. This memoir is really about giving so many private parts of myself a public voice." Aside from herself, Faderman told Bronski, the book is about her mother. "From earliest childhood, I understood how difficult my mother's life was. And it fueled my desire to save her. It was my love for her—even when we fought so terribly—that allowed me to open myself up to the love of other women."

In *Gay L.A.: A History of Sexual Outlaws, Power Politics, and Lipstick Lesbians,* Faderman turns again to detailed American social history as she and coauthor Stuart Timmons examine the "social, political, and cultural history of lesbian and gay life in Los Angeles," noted a *Publishers Weekly* reviewer. Based on more than 250 interviews and on a variety of primary source materials, Faderman and Timmons explore in depth the gay and lesbian history of the southern California area from the 1800s to the present. They note that early settlers contributed to the demise of the sexually tolerant culture of the region's Native American populations. They explore the emergence of numerous gay and lesbian institutions and note that the atmosphere of Los Angeles contributed more to the growth and development of these institutions than any other location in the world. The authors report on the gay lifestyles of the silent film stars of the 1920s and other popular entertainment figures of later eras. They note more shameful

episodes in the city's history, when LAPD vice squads deliberately targeted and entrapped gays. Conversely, Faderman and Timmons observe how Los Angeles became a stronghold of gay and lesbian activism, with the development of organizations such as PRIDE and the openly gay lifestyles that proliferated during the 1960s and 1970s. The devastation wrought by AIDS in the 1980s and the reconfiguration of gay lifestyles in the wake of this dreadful disease also figure prominently in the authors' narrative. Faderman and Timmons also discuss current gay and lesbian issues in depth, including topics related to gender and identity. Despite a turbulent history, Los Angeles remains a trend-setting hub of gay and lesbian culture.

A *Kirkus Reviews* critic called *Gay L.A.* "an exceptionally literate, overstuffed chronicle of gay Tinseltown," as well as "vital intellectual fare brimming with fascinating history." Whitney Scott, writing in *Booklist,* named the work a "meticulously researched, very readable text." *Library Journal* reviewer Whitney Strub called the book "magisterial," also noting that it is "full of fascinating anecdotes . . ., wise and fair analysis, and significant and inspiring examples of courageous resistance" during time periods when gay and lesbian lifestyles were less acceptable than today. The *Publishers Weekly* reviewer concluded that Faderman and Timmons's book is "easily the subject's definitive work."

BIOGRAPHICAL AND CRITICAL SOURCES:

BOOKS

Faderman, Lillian, *Naked in the Promised Land: A Memoir,* Houghton Mifflin (Boston, MA), 2003.
Feminist Writers, St. James Press (Detroit, MI), 1995, pp. 167-168.
Gay and Lesbian Biography, St. James Press (Detroit, MI), 1997, pp. 160-163.

PERIODICALS

Advocate, June 22, 1999, Ricardo Ortiz, review of *To Believe in Women,* p. 127.
Atlantic, March, 1981, Benjamin DeMott, review of *Surpassing the Love of Men: Romantic Friendship and Love between Women from the Renaissance to the Present,* p. 86.

Booklist, September 15, 2006, Whitney Scott, review of *Gay L.A.: A History of Sexual Outlaws, Power Politics, and Lipstick Lesbians,* p. 9.

Kirkus Reviews, August 1, 2006, review of *Gay L.A.,* p. 766.

Library Journal, August, 1991, Patricia Sarles, review of *Odd Girls and Twilight Lovers,* p. 128; March 15, 1998, review of *I Begin My Life All Over: The Hmong and the American Immigrant Experience,* p. 81; September 1, 2006, Whitney Strub, review of *Gay L.A.,* p. 166.

Los Angeles Times, February 16, 2003, Wendy Smith, "Keeping Her Own Promise," review of *Naked in the Promised Land,* p. R-12.

Miami Herald, March 9, 2003, Susan Freeman, "Nazi Ghosts Shape a Life of Courage Resilience."

New Statesman & Society, July 17, 1992, Jane Mills, review of *Odd Girls and Twilight Lovers,* p. 48.

New York Review of Books, May 28, 1981, Phyllis Grosskurth, review of *Surpassing the Love of Men,* p. 12.

New York Times Book Review, April 5, 1981, Carolyn Heilbrun, review of *Surpassing the Love of Men,* p. 12; June 28, 1992, Jeffrey Escoffier, "Out of the Closet and Into History," pp. 1, 24; October 3, 1999, Karla Jay, review of *To Believe in Women: What Lesbians Have Done for America—A History,* p. 23.

Publishers Weekly, May 16, 1994, review of *Chloe Plus Olivia: An Anthology of Lesbian Literature from the Seventeenth Century to the Present,* p. 48; February 23, 1998, review of *I Begin My Life All Over,* p. 59; November 18, 2002, review of *Naked in the Promised Land,* p. 49; February 24, 2003, Michael Bronski, "Memoir and Mystery," p. 48; July 24, 2006, review of *Gay L.A.,* p. 45.

San Francisco Chronicle, March 2, 2003, Kera Bolonik, "A Scholar Laid Bare."

Seattle Times, June 29, 2003, Barbara Sjoholm, "Memoir Reveals Too Little of Inner Self."

St. Louis Post-Dispatch, February 23, 2003, Colleen Kelly Warren, review of *Naked in the Promised Land.*

Times Literary Supplement, September 4, 1981, Keith Walker, review of *Surpassing the Love of Men,* p. 1014.

Washington Post, February 21, 2003, Carolyn See, "Pleased to Meet Me," p. C4.

Washington Post Book World, May 3, 1981, Joanna Russ, review of *Surpassing the Love of Men.*

Women's Review of Books, December, 1999, Nan Alamilla Boyd, review of *To Believe in Women,* p. 6.

ONLINE

Matt and Andrej Koymansky Web site, http://andrejkoymasky.com/ (May 18, 2003), biography of Lillian Faderman.

Philadelphia City Paper, http://www.citypaper.net/ (June 24-July 1, 1999), Kristin Keith, "Twenty Questions," interview with Lillian Faderman.

PopMatters, http://www.popmatters.com/ (April 8, 2003), Natalie Hope McDonald, review of *Naked in the Promised Land.**

*   *   *

FEIFFER, Jules 1929-
(Jules Ralph Feiffer)

PERSONAL: Born January 26, 1929, in Bronx, NY; son of David (held a variety of positions, including dental technician and sales representative) and Rhoda (a fashion designer) Feiffer; married Judith Sheftel (a film production and publishing executive), September 17, 1961 (divorced, 1983); married Jennifer Allen (a journalist and stand-up comic), September 11, 1983; children: (first marriage) Kate; (second marriage) Halley, Julie. *Education:* Attended Art Students League, New York, NY, 1946, and Pratt Institute, 1947-48 and 1949-51.

ADDRESSES: Home—New York, NY. *Agent*—Royce Carlton Incorporated, 866 United Nations Plaza, New York, NY 10017. *E-mail*—info@julesfeiffer.com.

CAREER: Writer, cartoonist, playwright, editorial cartoonist, illustrator, novelist, screenwriter, and commentator. Assistant to cartoonist Will Eisner, 1946-51, and ghostwriter for Eisner's comic book *The Spirit,* 1949-51; author of syndicated cartoon strip, *Clifford,* 1949-51; held a variety of positions in the art field, 1953-56, including producer of slide films, writer for Columbia Broadcasting System's *Terry Toons,* and designer of booklets for an art firm; author of cartoon strip (originally titled *Sick, Sick, Sick,* later changed to *Feiffer*), published in *Village Voice,* 1956-97, published weekly in London *Observer,* 1958-66, and 1972-82, and regularly in *Playboy,* beginning 1959, *New Yorker,* beginning 1993, and *New Statesman & Society,* beginning 1994; syndicated cartoonist, beginning 1959, including syndication by Universal Press Syndicate,

Kansas City, MO; *New York Times,* editorial cartoonist, 1997-2000. Yale University, faculty member at Yale Drama School, 1973-74; Northwestern University, instructor; Southampton College, currently adjunct professor. Columbia University, senior fellow in National Arts Journalism Program, 1997-98. Appeared as himself in a number of films and documentaries. Exhibitions and retrospectives mounted at the U.S. Library of Congress, the JCC of Washington, DC, the New York Historical Society and the School of Visual Arts. *Military service:* U.S. Army, Signal Corps, 1951-53; worked in cartoon animation unit.

MEMBER: PEN, American Academy of Arts and Letters, Authors League of America, Authors Guild (life member), Dramatists Guild (member of council), Writers Guild of America East.

AWARDS, HONORS: Special George Polk Memorial Award, Department of Journalism, Long Island University, 1962; named most promising playwright of 1966-67 season by New York drama critics; London Theater Critics Award, 1967, and Obie Award from *Village Voice,* 1969, both for *Little Murders;* Outer Circle Critics Award, 1969, for *Little Murders,* and 1970, for *The White House Murder Case;* Antoinette Perry (Tony) Award nomination, best play, 1976, for *Knock Knock;* Pulitzer Prize for editorial cartooning, 1986; Venice Film Festival Best Screenplay, 1989, for *I Want to Go Home;* Lifetime Achievement Award, National Cartoonist Society; Lifetime Achievement Award, Writers Guild of America, for screenplays; Writers Guild of America West, animation writing award.

WRITINGS:

CARTOON COLLECTIONS

Sick, Sick, Sick, McGraw-Hill (New York, NY), 1958, published with introduction by Kenneth Tynan, Collins (New York, NY), 1959.
Passionella and Other Stories, McGraw-Hill (New York, NY), 1959.
Boy, Girl, Boy, Girl, Random House (New York, NY), 1961.
Feiffer's Album, Random House (New York, NY), 1963.
The Penguin Feiffer, Penguin (New York, NY), 1966.
Feiffer's Marriage Manual, Random House (New York, NY), 1967.

Feiffer on Civil Rights, Anti-Defamation League of B'nai B'rith (New York, NY), 1967.
Pictures at a Prosecution: Drawings and Text from the Chicago Conspiracy Trial, Grove Press (New York, NY), 1971.
Feiffer on Nixon: The Cartoon Presidency, Random House (New York, NY), 1974.
(With Israel Horovitz) *VD Blues,* Avon (New York, NY), 1974.
Tantrum: A Novel in Cartoons, Knopf (New York, NY), 1979.
Popeye: The Movie Novel (based on the screenplay by Feiffer), edited by Richard J. Anobile, Avon (New York, NY), 1980.
Jules Feiffer's America: From Eisenhower to Reagan, edited by Steve Heller, Knopf (New York, NY), 1982.
(Coauthor) *Outer Space Spirit, 1952,* Kitchen Sink Press (Princeton, WI), 1983.
Marriage Is an Invasion of Privacy and Other Dangerous Views, Andrews & McMeel (Fairway, KS), 1984.
Feiffer's Children, Andrews & McMeel (Fairway, KS), 1986.
Ronald Reagan in Movie America: A Jules Feiffer Production, Andrews & McMeel (Fairway, KS), 1988.
The Complete Color Terry and the Pirates, Remco, 1990.

PUBLISHED PLAYS

The Explainers (satirical review; produced in Chicago, IL, at Playwright's Cabaret Theater, 1961), McGraw-Hill (New York, NY), 1960.
Crawling Arnold (one act; first produced in Spoleto, Italy, at Festival of Two Worlds, 1961; first produced in United States in Cambridge, MA, at Poets' Theater, 1961), Dramatists Play Service (New York, NY), 1963.
Hold Me! (first produced off-Broadway at American Place Theater, 1977), Random House (New York, NY), 1963.
The Unexpurgated Memoirs of Bernard Mergendeiler (one-act; first produced in Los Angeles, CA, at Mark Taper Forum, 1967), Random House (New York, NY), 1965.
Little Murders (two-act comedy; first produced on Broadway at Broadhurst Theater, 1967; first American play produced on the West End, London, England, by Royal Shakespeare Company at Aldw-

ych Theater, 1967; also see below), Random House (New York, NY), 1968, reprinted, Penguin (New York, NY), 1983.

(With others) *Dick and Jane* (one act; produced in New York, NY, at Eden Theater as part of *Oh! Calcutta!,* devised by Kenneth Tynan, 1969; also see below), published in *Oh! Calcutta!,* edited by Kenneth Tynan, Grove (New York, NY), 1969.

Feiffer's People: Sketches and Observations (produced as *Feiffer's People* in Edinburgh, Scotland, at International Festival of Music and Drama, 1968), Dramatists Play Service (New York, NY), 1969.

The White House Murder Case: A Play in Two Acts [and] *Dick and Jane: A One-Act Play* (*The White House Murder Case* first produced off-Broadway at Circle in the Square Downtown, 1970), Grove (New York, NY), 1970.

Knock Knock (first produced in New York, NY, at Circle Repertory Theater, 1976), Hill & Wang (New York, NY), 1976.

Elliot Loves (first produced on Broadway, 1989), Grove (New York, NY), 1989.

Anthony Rose, Dramatists Play Service (New York, NY), 1990.

A Bad Friend (produced in New York, NY, 2003), Dramatists Play Service (New York, NY), 2005.

UNPUBLISHED PLAYS

The World of Jules Feiffer, produced in New Jersey at Hunterdon Hills Playhouse, 1962.

God Bless, first produced in New Haven, CT, at Yale University, 1968; produced on the West End by Royal Shakespeare Company at Aldwych Theater, 1968.

Munro (adapted by Feiffer from story in *Passionella, and Other Stories*), first produced in Brooklyn, NY, at Prospect Park, 1971.

(With others) *Watergate Classics,* first produced in New Haven, CT, at Yale University, 1973.

Grownups, first produced in Cambridge, MA, at Loeb Drama Center, 1981; produced on Broadway at Lyceum Theater, December, 1981.

A Think Piece, first produced in New York, NY, at Circle Repertory Theater, 1982.

Carnal Knowledge (revised version of play of same title originally written c. 1970; also see below), first produced in Houston, TX, at Stages Repertory Theater, 1988.

Also author of *Interview* and *You Should Have Caught Me at the White House,* both c. 1962.

SCREENPLAYS

Munro (animated cartoon; adapted by Feiffer from story in *Passionella, and Other Stories*), Rembrandt Films, 1961.

Carnal Knowledge (adapted from Feiffer's unpublished, unproduced play of same title written c. 1970), Avco Embassy, 1971.

Little Murders (adapted by author from play of same title), Twentieth Century-Fox, 1971.

Popeye, Paramount/Walt Disney Productions, 1980.

Grown-Ups (television screenplay), Playboy Entertainment Group, 1985.

I Want to Go Home, MK2 Productions, 1989.

I Lost My Bear, 2005.

Also author of the unproduced screenplays, *Little Brucie* and *Bernard and Huey.*

FOR CHILDREN

The Man in the Ceiling, HarperCollins (New York, NY), 1993.

A Barrel of Laughs, a Vale of Tears, HarperCollins (New York, NY), 1995.

Meanwhile, HarperCrest (New York, NY), 1997.

(With Daniel M. Pinkwater) *Five Novels: The Boy from Mars, Slaves of Spiegel, The Snarkout Boys, The Avocado of Death, The Last Gur,* Farrar, Straus & Giroux (New York, NY), 1997.

I Lost My Bear, William Morrow (New York, NY), 1998.

Bark, George, HarperCollins Juvenile Books (New York, NY), 1999.

I'm Not Bobby!, Michael di Capua Books/Hyperion Books for Children (New York, NY), 2001.

By the Side of the Road, Michael di Capua Books/ Hyperion Books for Children (New York, NY), 2002.

The House across the Street, Michael di Capua Books/ Hyperion Books for Children (New York, NY), 2002.

The Daddy Mountain, Michael di Capua Books/ Hyperion Books for Children (New York, NY), 2004.

A Room with a Zoo, Michael di Capua Books/Hyperion Books for Children (New York, NY), 2005.

Henry, the Dog with No Tail, Simon & Schuster Books for Young Readers (New York, NY), 2007.

OTHER

(Illustrator) Robert Mines, *My Mind Went All to Pieces,* Dial (New York, NY), 1959.

(Illustrator) Norton Juster, *The Phantom Tollbooth,* Random House (New York, NY), 1961.

Harry, the Rat with Women (novel), McGraw-Hill (New York, NY), 1963.

(Editor and annotator) *The Great Comic Book Heroes,* Dial (New York, NY), 1965, published with new illustrations and without original comic-book stories), Fantagraphics (Stamford, CT), 2003.

Silverlips (television play), Public Broadcasting Service, 1972.

(With Herb Gardner, Peter Stone, and Neil Simon) *Happy Endings* (television play), American Broadcasting Companies, 1975.

Akroyd (novel), Simon & Schuster (New York, NY), 1977.

(Author of introduction) Rick Marshall, editor, *The Complete E.C. Segar Popeye,* Fantagraphics (Stamford, CT), 1984.

Feiffer: The Collected Works, Volume 1: *Clifford,* Fantagraphics (Stamford, CT), 1989.

Feiffer: The Collected Works, Volume 2: *Munro,* Fantagraphics (Stamford, CT), 1989.

Feiffer: The Collected Works, Volume 3: *Sick, Sick, Sick,* Fantagraphics (Stamford, CT), 1991.

Feiffer: The Collected Works: Passionella, Fantagraphics (Stamford, CT), 1993.

(With Ted Rall) *Revenge of the Latchkey Kids: An Illustrated Guide to Surviving the '90s and Beyond,* Workman Publishing Company, 1998 (New York, NY).

(Illustrator) Florence Parry Heide, *Some Things Are Scary,* Candlewick Press (Cambridge, MA), 2000.

(Illustrator) Jenny Allen, *The Long Chalkboard and Other Stories,* Pantheon Books (New York, NY), 2006.

Writer on the television series, *The Nudnik Show,* 1991.

Vanity Fair contributing editor.

ADAPTATIONS: The Feiffer Film, based on Feiffer's cartoons, was released in 1965; *Harry, the Rat with Women* was made into a play and produced in Detroit, MI, at Detroit Institute of Arts, 1966; *Passionella, and Other Stories* was adapted by Jerry Bock and Sheldon Harnick into "Passionella," a one-act musical produced on Broadway as part of *The Apple Tree,* 1967, revived 2006; *Jules Feiffer's America: From Eisenhower to Reagan* was adapted by Russell Vandenbroucke into a play titled *Feiffer's America; What Are We Saying?,* a parody on Feiffer's cartoons, was produced in Rome, Italy.

SIDELIGHTS: On learning that *Hudson Review* contributor John Simon described Jules Feiffer's play *Little Murders* as "bloody-minded," and made reference to its "grotesque horror" and "hideous reality," those who only know Feiffer as a cartoonist and not as a playwright might be more than a little surprised. Such brutal words are unexpected when used to characterize the work of a cartoonist—whom we might imagine would only want to make us laugh.

Feiffer revealed the origins of his somewhat black humor in a *Washington Post* interview with Henry Allen: "Back then [in the 1950s], comedy was still working in a tradition that came out of World War II . . . . Comedy was mired in insults and gags. It was Bob Hope and Bing Cosby, Burns and Allen, Ozzie and Harriet. There was no such thing as comedy about relationships, nothing about the newly urban and collegiate Americans. What I was interested in was using humor as a reflection of one's own confusion, ambivalence and dilemma, dealing with sexual life as one knew it to be." His cartoons presented a mixture of social commentary and political satire previously reserved for the editorial page of the newspaper.

From the beginning of his career Feiffer avoided the silliness expected of a nonpolitical cartoonist. His characters include people who are odd enough to be humorous but who at the same time can elicit a painful, empathetic response from his readers: Passionella, who achieves movie stardom because she has the world's largest breasts; Bernard Mergeneiler, known for his romantic failures; and an inventor who creates a "Lonely Machine" that makes light conversation and delivers sympathetic remarks whenever necessary.

Feiffer's concerns as a cartoonist have followed him to the stage, but some critics have faulted Feiffer's plays for being too dependent on his cartoons for inspiration. In the *Village Voice* Carll Tucker, for example, commented: "Feiffer's genius as a cartoonist is for dramatic moments—establishing and comically concluding a situation in eight still frames. His characters have personality only for the purpose of making a point: They do not have, as breathing dramatic characters must, the freedom to develop, to grow away from their status as idea-bearers."

Other critics voiced their approval for what they have seen as the influence of Feiffer's cartoons in his work for the theater. In Alan Rich's *New York* magazine review of Feiffer's play, *Knock Knock,* for example, the critic noted: "What gives [the play] its humor—and a great deal of it is screamingly funny—is the incredible accuracy of [Feiffer's] language, and his use of it to paint the urban neurosis in exact colors. This we know from his cartoons, and we learn it anew from this endearing, congenial theater piece." Other commentators on New York's theatrical scene, such as *Dictionary of Literary Biography* contributor Thomas Edward Ruddick, have been able to separate Feiffer's dramatic work from his other creative efforts. "Feiffer's plays show considerable complexity of plot, character, and idea, and command attention," Ruddick noted, "not dependent upon Feiffer's other achievements. His plays, independently, constitute a noteworthy body of work."

Those who enjoyed Feiffer for his adults-only satire may have been surprised to see the cartoonist venture into the children's book market in the 1990s. For his part, Feiffer is the father to essentially three generations of girls; in 1993, when *The Man in the Ceiling* was published, he had thirty-one-year-old Kate, eleven-year-old Halley (to whom that book is dedicated) and fifteen-month-old Julie. "I'm glad they're girls," the author told *Publishers Weekly* writer John F. Baker. "Boys are terribly active and geared toward just the sort of sports I was never any good at."

Feiffer's attraction to the youth market arose "from a combination of his fond recollections of reading to Halley as a small child . . . and an illustrator friend's interest in doing a book," according to Baker. In *The Man in the Ceiling,* Feiffer writes and illustrates the tale of Jimmy, a little boy who dreams of being a cartoonist. His aptitude for drawing underscores the fact that the boy is "not much good at anything else, including such boyish but unFeiffer-like pastimes as sports," Baker continued.

"Yes, I did cartoons as a kid, just like Jimmy," Feiffer admitted in the *Publishers Weekly* piece. "And I rediscovered some of them while I was working on [the book]. But those drawings of Jimmy's were the toughest part; I had to get the tone just right—they mustn't be too satirical—and it terrified me for a long time. I left them right to the end."

Feiffer's caution was rewarded by the favorable reviews that greeted *The Man in the Ceiling.* Jonathan Fast, in fact, singled out Jimmy's artwork, noting in his *New York Times Book Review* piece, "the adventures of Mini-Man, Bullethead, and The Man in the Ceiling, Jimmy's *magnum opus,* are reprinted in glorious pencil and run as long as six pages." Evidently Feiffer's efforts also reached a younger audience: Nine-year-old reviewer Erin Smith told the *San Francisco Review of Books* that the work "has great pictures. The story is just as funny. The best pictures are the comics that Jimmy drew."

In 1995, Feiffer released his second children's book, *A Barrel of Laughs, a Vale of Tears.* The volume is comprised of fairy tales with a slightly acerbic air meant to appeal to children and parents alike. Featuring King Whatchamacallit, who speaks in spoonerisms: "My son, when you're around, no till gets soiled—er, no soil gets tilled; no noo gets shailed—that is, no shoe gets nailed." Another urbane character, J. Wellington Wizard, amused children's author Daniel M. Pinkwater. "Written with conviction, not to say innocence, Mr. Feiffer's ebullient story renders the reader capable of maximum suspension of disbelief—and what would be corny is touching instead," Pinkwater declared in the *New York Times Book Review.*

The young protagonist of *Meanwhile,* Raymond, is deeply engrossed in his comic book when his mother calls. Hoping to avoid having to respond, Raymond applies a longstanding comic book tradition: he uses the almost magical word "meanwhile" to change the scene he is in, putting him outside the range of his mother's call. Raymond's use of "meanwhile," however, does not work out well. First, he is transported to a pirate ship. Forced to walk the plank, he manages to invoke the scene-changing word just in the nick of time. When his next scene turns out to be the wild west, he finds himself chased by a determined posse. Saving himself at the last moment, he goes to outer space, where his ship is destroyed by marauding Martians. Things look bleak until Raymond applies a pair of even stronger magic words from storytelling: "The End." Reviewer Mary M. Burns, writing in the *Horn Book Magazine,* called Feiffer's book "great fun, action filled, and a solid invitation to create one's own series of meanwhiles." *Booklist* reviewer Stephanie Zvirin noted that younger readers would enjoy Feiffer's "funny, freewheeling, action-packed" artwork, but also observed that older readers would best be able to "spot the irony and appreciate the wit and the careful interplay between fantasy and reality" that Feiffer weaves into the story.

I Lost My Bear recounts what happens when a youngster suffers the trauma of losing her stuffed bear. "With great comic insight, Feiffer captures the high drama that ensues when a child misplaces a beloved possession," commented Lauren Adams in the *Horn Book Magazine.* Thoroughly distressed at her predicament, the young protagonist searches and searches, but is unable to locate her beloved teddy bear. Her mom is too busy to help, and advises her to think like a detective and remember where she left it. Her father tells her to find the bear herself as a lesson in responsibility. Irascible big sister at first wants nothing to do with her little sister's troubles, but later offers some sage advice, telling her to close her eyes and throw another stuffed animal, hoping that it will land in the same place. The narrator follows this advice, which leads to other happy discoveries, but still no bear. Finally, at bedtime, she locates the missing toy. "The girl's palpable concern for her bear . . . will evoke both amusement and empathy among readers of all ages," commented a reviewer in *Publishers Weekly.*

The young male narrator of *The House Across the Street,* frustrated and angry at restrictions placed on him by his parents, begins to imagine a story about the boy in the house across the street, where things are better. For that young man, life is free and easy. His parents dote on his every whim, immediately reacting to his requests and buying him anything he wants. He has a pet lion, and a shark in the swimming pool. He does not have to observe table manners, and he can boss around his big sister and babysitter. Best of all, he can come and go as he wishes, and is not restricted by his parents. Soon, the boy reveals that the house across the street is actually empty and the boy who lives there does not exist, but the mild power fantasy has its desired effect of helping him deal with his negative emotions. In the book, Feiffer "gets a child's anger about the adult authority that holds him at home exactly right," remarked Hazel Rochman in a *Booklist* review. "Children will be willing participants in this larger-than-life fantasy, even as they recognize it for what it is," commented *School Library Journal* reviewer Wendy Lukehart.

The Daddy Mountain finds a young girl facing a daunting task: climbing to the top of Daddy Mountain, her father transformed into a large and imposing hill. Beginning at his feet, the girl traverses the difficult geography of ankles, knees, belt, shirt, and more as she climbs upward. She offers running commentary on her ascent, describing the difficulties of navigating each body part. Climbing while grabbing a shirt is fine, for example; grabbing skin is not. Feiffer depicts the scene in muted grays for the father, bright colors for the daughter. Finally, she reaches the very top and perches on her

grinning father's head, even as her mother disapproves of the heights she has scaled. Adults will "nod in recognition of daddies' special fondness for roughhousing," observed Jennifer Mattson in *Booklist.* A *Publishers Weekly* critic called the book "lighthearted, affectionate fare," while a *Kirkus Reviews* contributor named it "another crowd-pleaser from Feiffer."

A Room with a Zoo is based, in part, on Feiffer's experiences when his youngest daughter started her campaign to get a puppy. In the book, young Julie is a dedicated animal lover who desperately wants a dog, but her parents tell her she is still too young to care for a canine. Her parents do their best to accommodate her wishes for a pet, however, allowing her to have a wild variety of lower-maintenance creatures. Among the pets that occupy the family's Manhattan apartment are a fish, a kitten, a turtle, a hamster, a hermit crab, and a rabbit. Julie has no trouble taking charge of her smaller pets in her quest to prove herself responsible enough to own a dog. Despite all best intentions, pet ownership comes with its downside, including vomiting cats, cannibalistic fish, and scampering hamsters. After the long travails, including a chaotic scene involving her parents, the cat, the hamster, and an injury requiring an emergency room visit and stitches, Julie finally gets the dog she has been wanting. "This is briskly written with lots of amusing moments, though some of them will be funniest to adults," wrote *Booklist* reviewer Ilene Cooper. Susan Hepler, writing in *School Library Journal,* noted that children are likely to be charmed by the "tone of the narration, the childlike logic, and the winning way she takes charge of her pets and herself by story's end." A reviewer in *Publishers Weekly* observed that "young animal lovers should have no trouble identifying with this spunky heroine's intense range of emotions, brought on by her menagerie."

As Feiffer revealed to Baker, the best part of being a children's author is the honest response from his young readers: "It's much more direct even than in the theater, so much more heartening. You create something out of love and devotion, and when you get it back, you can't believe it."

In addition to his prolific output of children's books, Feiffer has also remained active as a playwright over the years. In *The Bad Friend,* Feiffer recreates an intensely Stalinist Jewish family in the 1950s. Mother Naomi is adamantly dedicated to the cause, though father Shelly sometimes wavers in his dedication to

Stalin and communism. Their daughter, Rose, rejects the tenets of communism and rebels against both of her parents. To cope, Rose associates with a man she meets on the Brooklyn Heights esplanade: Emil, a painter and photographer, who allows Rose to air her frustrations and come to terms with her own thoughts and feelings about her parents and their communism. Rose also frequently encounters Fallon, an FBI agent who tries to coax information from her about her Uncle Morty, a suspected communist and Hollywood screenwriter. Viewers "come to see how her parents' stark worldview, dividing humanity into good guys and bad guys much the way the Westerns Uncle Morty pens do, has shaped Rose's nature almost against her will," observed Charles Isherwood in *Variety.* In the course of the play, Naomi begins to see Shelly's questioning of Stalinism as a personal betrayal; Naomi's brother gives in to pressure and names names at the anti-communist House Un-American Activities Committee's hearings; and, inadvertently, Rose betrays her own best friend. Though the play takes place in the early 1950s, "its themes continue to resonate," commented Irene Backalenick in *Back Stage.* "False illusions, true betrayals, and, most of all, threats to civil rights are not unfamiliar in today's political climate."

BIOGRAPHICAL AND CRITICAL SOURCES:

BOOKS

Anobile, Richard J., *Popeye: The Movie Novel,* Avon (New York, NY), 1980.

Cohen, Sarah Blacher, editor, *From Hester Street to Hollywood: The Jewish-American Stage and Screen,* Indiana University Press (Bloomington, IN), 1983.

Contemporary Dramatists, 4th edition, St. James Press (Detroit, MI), 1988.

Contemporary Literary Criticism, Thomson Gale (Detroit, MI), Volume 2, 1974, Volume 8, 1978, Volume 64, 1991.

Corliss, Richard, *Talking Pictures: Screenwriters in the American Cinema,* Overlook Press (New York, NY), 1974.

Dictionary of Literary Biography, Thomson Gale (Detroit, MI), Volume 7: *Twentieth-Century American Dramatists,* 1981, Volume 44: *American Screenwriters, Second Series,* 1986.

PERIODICALS

Back Stage, June 27, 2003, Irene Backalenick, review of *A Bad Friend,* p. 48.

Booklinks, May, 2006, Shutta Crum, review of *Bark, George,* p. 32.

Booklist, December 1, 1997, Stephanie Zvirin, review of *Meanwhile,* p. 636; April 1, 1998, review of *I Lost My Bear,* p. 1331; March 15, 1999, review of *I Lost My Bear,* p. 1302; August, 1999, Stephanie Zvirin, review of *Bark, George,* p. 2052; January 1, 2000, review of *Bark, George,* p. 824; December 1, 2002, Hazel Rochman, review of *The House across the Street,* p. 673; May 1, 2004, Jennifer Mattson, review of *The Daddy Mountain,* p. 1562; September 15, 2005, Ilene Cooper, review of *A Room with a Zoo,* p. 66; September 15, 2006, Carl Hays, review of *The Long Chalkboard and Other Stories,* p. 35; September 15, 2006, Gordon Flagg, review of *Passionella and Other Stories,* p. 35.

Bulletin of the Center for Children's Books, June, 1998, review of *I Lost My Bear,* p. 360; November, 1999, review of *Bark, George,* p. 91; December, 2000, review of *Some Things Are Scary,* p. 146; September, 2002, review of *By the Side of the Road,* p. 15; January, 2003, review of *The House across the Street,* p. 197; December, 2005, review of *A Room with a Zoo,* p. 179.

Chicago Tribune, August 5, 2002, "Feiffer Draws on Years of Experience," interview with Jules Feiffer.

Child, May, 2004, Julie Yates Walton, review of *The Daddy Mountain,* p. 47.

Commonweal, November 22, 2002, reviews of *Bark, George, By the Side of the Road, I Lost My Bear, I'm Not Bobby!,* and *Meanwhile,* p. 20.

Daily Variety, June 10, 2003, Charles Isherwood, review of *A Bad Friend,* p. 2.

Five Owls, Annual, 2002, review of *I'm Not Bobby!,* p. 76.

Hollywood Reporter, July 3, 2003, Frank Scheck, review of *A Bad Friend,* p. 5.

Horn Book Magazine, September-October, 1997, Mary M. Burns, review of *Meanwhile,* p. 557; March-April, 1998, Lauren Adams, review of *I Lost My Bear,* p. 212; January, 2001, review of *Some Things Are Scary,* p. 83; May-June, 2004, Joanna Rudge Long, review of *The Daddy Mountain,* p. 310; November-December, 2005, Sarah Ellis, review of *A Room with a Zoo,* p. 718.

Hudson Review, summer, 1967, John Simon, review of *Little Murders.*

Instructor, April, 1998, review of *Meanwhile,* p. 26; May, 1998, review of *Meanwhile,* p. 62; April, 1999, review of *I Lost My Bear,* p. 18; May, 1999, review of *I Lost My Bear,* p. 12; May, 2003, review of *Bark, George,* p. 56.

Kirkus Reviews, April 1, 2004, review of *The Daddy Mountain,* p. 328; December 1, 2005, "The Best

Children's Books of 2005," review of *A Room with a Zoo,* p. S1; December 1, 2005, "Q&A with Jules Feiffer," p. S10.

Library Media Connection, January, 2003, review of *By the Side of the Road,* p. 78.

Maclean's, December 11, 2000, review of *Some Things Are Scary,* p. 59.

Magpies, November, 2000, review of *Some Things Are Scary,* p. 30.

Newsweek, June 14, 1999, review of *Bark, George,* p. 77.

New York, February 2, 1976, Alan Rich, review of *Knock Knock.*

New Yorker, May 18, 1987, Edith Oliver, review of *Little Murders,* p. 87; November 30, 1998, review of *I Lost My Bear,* p. 118; December 12, 2005, "For Kids," review of *A Room with a Zoo,* p. 109.

New York Times, March 4, 2003, Mel Gussow, "Jules Feiffer, Freed of His Comic Strip Duties, Finds a New Visibility," profile of Jules Feiffer, p. E1.

New York Times Book Review, December 19, 1982, review of *Jules Feiffer's America,* p. 8; November 14, 1993, Jonathan Fast, review of *The Man in the Ceiling,* p. 57; December 31, 1995, Daniel M. Pinkwater, review of *A Barrel of Laughs, a Vale of Tears,* p. 12; November 18, 2001, Dwight Garner, "Better Not Call Me Again. I'm a Monster," review of *I'm Not Bobby!,* p. 25.

New York Times Magazine, June 15, 2003, Deborah Solomon, "Playing with History," profile of Jules Feiffer, p. 13.

Parents, December, 1997, review of *Meanwhile,* p. 204; December, 1998, review of *I Lost My Bear,* p. 234.

People, October 30, 2000, review of *Some Things Are Scary,* p. 50.

Print, May-June, 1998, Steven Heller, "Jules Feiffer, Cartoonist, Author, and Playwright," interview with Jules Feiffer, p. 40B.

Publishers Weekly, October 25, 1993, John F. Baker, review of *The Man in the Ceiling,* p. 62; July 14, 1997, review of *Meanwhile,* p. 82; January 26, 1998, review of *I Lost My Bear,* p. 91; October 16, 2000, review of *Some Things Are Scary,* p. 76; September 29, 2003, review of *Some Things Are Scary,* p. 67; April 5, 2004, review of *The Daddy Mountain,* p. 60; August 22, 2005, review of *A Room with a Zoo,* p. 64; September 18, 2006, review of *The Long Chalkboard and Other Stories,* p. 43.

Reading Teacher, October, 2001, review of *Some Things Are Scary,* p. 180.

San Francisco Review of Books, April-May, 1994, Erin Smith, review of *The Man in the Ceiling.*

School Librarian, spring, 2001, review of *Some Things Are Scary,* p. 34.

School Library Journal, September, 1997, Lisa S. Murphy, review of *Meanwhile,* p. 180; March, 1998, Julie Cummins, review of *I Lost My Bear,* p. 179; September, 1999, Barbara Scotto, review of *Bark, George,* p. 182; December, 1999, review of *Bark, George,* p. 40; January, 2001, Maryann H. Owen, review of *Some Things Are Scary,* p. 101; February, 2003, Wendy Lukehart, review of *The House across the Street,* p. 111; June, 2004, Grace Oliff, review of *The Daddy Mountain,* p. 108; October, 2004, review of *Bark, George,* p. S28; November, 2005, Susan Hepler, review of *A Room with a Zoo,* p. 90.

Variety, November 18, 2002, "Jules Feiffer Returns to the Stage with His First Play in More Than a Decade," review of *A Bad Friend,* p. 51; June 16, 2003, Charles Isherwood, review of *A Bad Friend,* p. 35.

Village Voice, February 2, 1976, Carll Tucker, profile of Jules Feiffer.

Washington Post, August 17, 1979, Henry Allen, interview with Jules Feiffer.

ONLINE

Internet Movie Database, http://www.imdb.com/ (January 2, 2007), filmography of Jules Feiffer.

Jules Feiffer Home Page, http://www.julesfeiffer.com (January 2, 2007).

Lambiek.net, http://www.lambiek.net/ (January 2, 2007), biography of Jules Feiffer.

New York State Writers Institute Web site, http://www.albany.edu/writers-inst/ (January 2, 2007), biography of Jules Feiffer.

NNDB, http://www.nndb.com/ (January 2, 2007), biography of Jules Feiffer.

Pegasos Web site, http://www.kirjasto.sci.fi/ (January 2, 2007), biography of Jules Feiffer.

Royce Carlton Incorporated Web site, http://www.roycecarlton.com/ (January 2, 2007), biography of Jules Feiffer.

*   *   *

FEIFFER, Jules Ralph
See FEIFFER, Jules

FERGUSON, Craig 1962-
(Bing Hitler)

PERSONAL: Born May 17, 1962, in Glasgow, Scotland; son of Robert and Janet Ferguson; divorced; children: Milo Hamish.

CAREER: Actor, producer, writer, musician, comic, and television show host. Host of *Late Late Show with Craig Ferguson* (a late-night comedy and variety program), CBS Television, 2005—.

Television series appearances include *The Ferguson Theory,* 1994; *Freakazoid!,* 1995; *Maybe This Time,* ABC, 1995; *The Drew Carey Show,* ABC, 1996-2000; *Hercules,* syndicated, 1998; *Buzz Lightyear of Star Command,* 2000; and *The Legend of Tarzan,* 2001.

Appearances on episodic television include "Confidence and Paranoia," *Red Dwarf,* 1988; "Peeled Grapes and Pedicures," *Chelmsford 1 2 3,* 1988; *Have I Got News for You,* 1991; *The Brain Drain,* 1993; and "Suites for the Sweet," *Almost Perfect,* CBS, 1996. Other television appearances include *Dream Baby,* PBS, 1992; *Drew's Dance Party Special,* ABC, 1998, *Life as We Know It,* 2005; and *American Dad!,* 2006.

Film appearances include *Modern Vampires,* Sterling Home Entertainment, 1998; *The Big Tease,* Warner Bros., 1999; *Saving Grace,* Fine Line Features, 2000; *Chain of Fools,* Warner Bros., 2000; *Born Romantic,* 2000; *Life without Dick,* Columbia Pictures, 2002; *I'll Be There,* Warner Bros., 2003; *Lenny the Wonder Dog,* Winslow Productions, 2004; *Lemony Snicket's A Series of Unfortunate Events,* Paramount Pictures, 2004; *Trust Me,* Quadriga Production, 2005; and *Niagara Motel,* Muse Entertainment Enterprises, 2005.

Film work includes (executive producer) *The Big Tease,* Warner Bros., 1999; (coproducer) *Saving Grace,* Fine Line Features, 2000. Stage appearances include *Bad Boy Johnny and the Prophets of Doom,* produced at the Theatre at Union Chapel, Islington, London, England, 1994.

AWARDS, HONORS: Audience Award for Best Film, Aspen, Dallas, and Valencia film festivals, for *I'll Be There;* Emmy Award nomination, 2006, for an episode of the *Late Late Show with Craig Ferguson;* Best New Director award, Napa Valley Film Festival.

WRITINGS:

(And producer) *The Big Tease* (screenplay), Warner Bros., 1999.

(And producer; with Mark Crowdy) *Saving Grace,* Fine Line Features, 2000.

(And director) *I'll Be There* (screenplay), Warner Bros., 2003.

Between the Bridge and the River (novel), Chronicle Books (San Francisco, CA), 2006.

Writer on television programs, including *The Russ Abbot Show,* 1986, *The Ferguson Theory,* 1994, *The Craig Ferguson Show,* 1990, *The Craig Ferguson Story,* 1991, *Doc Martin,* 2004-05, and *Late Late Show with Craig Ferguson.*

SIDELIGHTS: A longtime comic, stage performer, and musician, Scottish actor Craig Ferguson is perhaps best known to American television audiences for his portrayal of the obnoxious boss Nigel Wick on *The Drew Carey Show.* The versatile Ferguson is also a screenwriter, director, and producer. His film works include *The Big Tease,* in which Ferguson plays hairdresser Crawford MacKenzie. Under the impression that he has been invited to compete for the Platinum Scissors Award at the World Freestyle Championship in Los Angeles, MacKenzie flies out of Glasgow with a British documentary crew to follow his every move. As with another mock documentary about hapless Britons arriving on American shores, *This Is Spinal Tap,* things are not quite as MacKenzie expected: he has only been invited to the competition as a spectator. With the help of a Hollywood publicist played by Frances Fisher, however, "MacKenzie gets his chance to tease, comb, and mousse his way to the top," in the words of *Los Angeles Times* reviewer Susan King. Bob Campbell in the New Orleans *Times-Picayune* called *The Big Tease* "the snappiest comedy sleeper since *South Park,*" and described Ferguson's portrayal of MacKenzie as "the most endearingly outrageous U.K. export since Austin Powers."

Equally outrageous is the plot of *Saving Grace,* the title of which refers to the name of Brenda Blethyn's character. Suddenly widowed when her husband falls out of an airplane, and faced with heavy bills created by her husband's failed investments, Grace joins forces with her soon-to-be unemployed gardener (Ferguson) to start a profitable home-based business—growing marijuana. As the plot unfolds, it becomes apparent that more than a few upstanding citizens of the sleepy Cornish coastal town like to light up now and then. But the story consists of more than just a few giggles over dope, according to Joe Leydon in *Variety,* who described it as "more character-driven than plot-propelled." "Although unlikely to prove this year's *Full Monty,*" wrote Graham Fuller in *Interview,* the film "should bring a little high to the late summer box office." Striking a similar note, Richard Schickel in *Time,* while noting that it is "not as tightly wound as the best of its breed," called *Saving Grace* "a genial way to pass the time." Lisa Schwarzbaum of *Entertainment Weekly* also expressed reservations about the film, but conceded that it has "dopey good vibes." Leydon in *Variety* was more outspoken in his praise, comparing the movie to *Local Hero* and pronouncing it a "spiritedly daft and droll gem of straight-faced lunacy."

In January, 2005, Ferguson became the host of the late-night comedy and talk program on CBS Television, the *Late Late Show with Craig Ferguson,* taking over from departing host Craig Kilborn. Ferguson serves as a writer for the program in addition to being its jovial frontman. "After a disastrous first few weeks he has made the program his own, with running gags and hilarious impressions of Prince Charles, Sean Connery, Dr. Phil, and Michael Caine in space," observed a biographer on *NNDB.* "Describing himself as a cheeky giant Scotsman, he displays an innate knack not just for comedy but for interesting and energetic interviews, where—unlike most chat show hosts—he seems genuinely interested in his guests," the biographer continued.

With *Between the Bridge and the River,* Ferguson makes his initial bow as a novelist. The book is a "Jungian jaunt through evangelical extremism, terminal illness, fleeting love and Hollywood excess," observed reviewer Nick Madigan in the *Baltimore Sun.* It is, Madigan continued, "a tale of spiritual rebirth, a journey of lost souls seeking light." Ferguson "displays hyperkinetic chops in his first novel, a witty, furiously paced and frequently hysterical account of showbiz redemption," commented Jonathan Durbin in *People.* The cast includes half-brothers Saul and Leon, illegitimate sons of Peter Lawford and Frank Sinatra, respectively, and corrosive, difficult Hollywood moguls. Scotsman George is a lawyer dying of cancer, and his old friend Fraser has become a televangelist with a sex-addiction problem. The four disparate characters move toward a "cosmically intertwined awakening via the dark paths

of the collective unconscious," remarked Scott Brown in *Entertainment Weekly,* which will involve the appearances of psychoanalyst and dream analysis pioneer Carl Jung. Ferguson's "first novel may surprise those who haven't already seen past the 'cheeky wee monkey' endearments to the thoughtful, complicated guy increasingly on display in his nightly monologues, but it's likely to be welcomed by those who have—or who, like Ferguson, are more likely to spend their late nights reading," observed Ellen Gray in the *Philadelphia Daily News.* "Ferguson knows how to keep people awake," commented Bob Lunn in the *Library Journal,* "and he does just that with his lively first novel."

BIOGRAPHICAL AND CRITICAL SOURCES:

BOOKS

Contemporary Theatre, Film, and Television, Volume 33, Thomson Gale (Detroit, MI), 2001.

PERIODICALS

Atlanta Journal-Constitution, February 25, 2000, Eleanor Ringel Gillespie, review of *The Big Tease,* p. 11.
Baltimore Sun, May 10, 2006, Nick Madigan, "Funnyman Ferguson Goes Deep in New Book," review of *Between the Bridge and the River.*
Boston Globe, February 11, 2000, Jay Carr, review of *The Big Tease,* p. C6.
Broadcasting & Cable, April 10, 2006, Joel Topcik, "Flash!," review of *Between the Bridge and the River,* p. 8.
Chicago Tribune, May 26, 2006, Terry Armour, "*Late Late* Host Hitting Zanies," interview with Craig Ferguson.
Daily Variety, January 7, 2005, Brian Lowry, review of the *Late Late Show with Craig Ferguson,* p. 10; March 15, 2005, Michael Learmonth, "Scot Takes *Late* Rates to Highland," profile of Craig Ferguson, p. 28.
Entertainment Weekly, February 4, 2000, Lisa Schwarzbaum, review of *The Big Tease,* p. 48; August 11, 2000, review of *Saving Grace,* p. 52; March 31, 2006, Scott Brown, review of *Between the Bridge and the River,* p. 67.
Interview, August, 2000, Graham Fuller, review of *Saving Grace,* p. 39.

Library Journal, March 15, 2006, Bob Lunn, review of *Between the Bridge and the River,* p. 62.

Los Angeles Magazine, April, 2006, "Q&A: Questions, Answers, Dish. It's All Here," interview with Craig Ferguson, p. 168.

People, January 17, 2005, Laura J. Downey, "Craig Ferguson Sounds Off," interview with Craig Ferguson, p. 43; March 7, 2005, Terry Kelleher, review of the *Late Late Show with Craig Ferguson,* p. 40; May 1, 2006, Jonathan Durbin, review of *Between the Bridge and the River,* p. 52.

Philadelphia Daily News, April 17, 2006, Ellen Gray, "TV's Ferguson Is a Reader and a Writer," profile of Craig Ferguson; May 17, 2006, Ellen Gray, "*Late Late Show* Host Makes His Debut as a Novelist," review of the *Between the Bridge and the River.*

Pittsburgh Post-Gazette, March 16, 2000, Susan King and Mitchell Hill, "A Quest for Stardom: Craig Ferguson, Who Left Scotland for Filmdom, Writes Screenplays between 'Drew Carey' Jokes," p. B5.

Time, August 14, 2000, Richard Schickel, review of *Saving Grace,* p. 78.

Times-Picayune (New Orleans, LA), April 14, 2000, Bob Campbell, review of *The Big Tease,* p. L32.

Variety, January 31, 2000, Joe Leydon, review of *Saving Grace,* p. 33.

World Entertainment News Network, April 16, 2006, "Craig Ferguson 'At Home with Weirdos,'" interview with Craig Ferguson, and "Craig Ferguson's Novel Autobiography," review of *Between the Bridge and the River.*

ONLINE

Craig Ferguson MySpace, http://www.myspace.com (December 5, 2006).

Craig Ferguson Online, http://severed-dreams.net/craigferguson (December 5, 2006).

Internet Movie Database, http://www.imdb.com/ (December 5, 2006), filmography of Craig Ferguson.

Late Late Show Web site, http://www.cbs.com/latenight/latelate/ (December 5, 2006).

NNDB, http://www.nndb.com/ (December 5, 2006), biography of Craig Ferguson.

Reel.com, http://www.reel.com/ (December 5, 2006), Pam Grady, "The Big Teaser: Craig Ferguson Lets His Hair Down," interview with Craig Ferguson.

Scotland on Sunday, http://news.scotsman.com/ (November 20, 2005) "The Eligibles 2005—Top Fifty Men," profile of Craig Ferguson.*

FERRIGNO, Robert 1948(?)-

PERSONAL: Surname is pronounced "fur-*reen*-yo;" born c. 1948, in FL; married; wife's name Jody; children: Jake, Dani. *Education:* Holds B.A. degree; Bowling Green State University, M.F.A., 1971.

ADDRESSES: Home and office—P.O. Box 934, Kirkland, WA 98083. *Agent*—Sandra Dijkstra, 1155 Camino del Mar, No. 515, Del Mar, CA 92014. *E-mail*—rcferrigno@comcast.net.

CAREER: Writer, journalist, educator, and professional gambler. Instructor in English and literature in Seattle, WA, 1971-73; feature writer for *Orange County Register,* until 1988; instructor in journalism at California State University, Fullerton. Spent five years as a professional poker player.

AWARDS, HONORS: Shamus Award nomination, Best P.I. Novel, Private Eye Writers of America, 2005, for *The Wake-Up.*

WRITINGS:

NOVELS

The Horse Latitudes, Morrow (New York, NY), 1990.
The Cheshire Moon, Morrow (New York, NY), 1993.
Dead Man's Dance, Putnam (New York, NY), 1995.
Dead Silent, Putnam (New York, NY), 1996.
Heartbreaker, Pantheon (New York, NY), 1999.
Flinch, Pantheon (New York, NY), 2001.
Scavenger Hunt, Pantheon (New York, NY), 2003.
The Wake Up, Pantheon (New York, NY), 2004.
Prayers for the Assassin, Scribner (New York, NY), 2006.

Contributor to periodicals, including *California* and *Women's Sports and Fitness.*

The *Rocket* (a punk rock magazine), founder.

ADAPTATIONS: All of Ferrigno's novels are under option by Hollywood studios.

SIDELIGHTS: Author, educator, and journalist Robert Ferrigno drew critical attention with the 1990 publication of his first novel, *The Horse Latitudes*. The author began the book after his wife survived a difficult pregnancy and gave birth to their son, Jake. "Even though they both pulled out of it, and they're both fine, it gave me a very powerful sense that life is fleeting," Ferrigno told Dennis McLellan in the *Los Angeles Times*. "It made me realize I had been talking and thinking about writing a book for a long time, but should probably not count on having the rest of my life to finish it." Ferrigno started *The Horse Latitudes* while working as a feature writer for the *Orange County Register*, rising at four each morning to write. But after about eighteen months, his heavy schedule began to take its toll, and with his wife's encouragement, Ferrigno quit his job at the newspaper to work on his novel full time.

Ferrigno's gamble proved to be a profitable one, as William Morrow and Company bought the rights to his unfinished novel for 150,000 dollars in 1988. Set in southern California, *The Horse Latitudes* concerns Danny DiMedici, a former marijuana dealer who lost his taste for the outlaw life after killing a man. DiMedici's amoral wife Lauren, a corporate motivational psychologist, left him after he reformed, explaining that "God hates a coward." As the novel opens, DiMedici is attempting to come to terms with his recent divorce: "There were nights when Danny missed Lauren so bad that he wanted to take a fat man and throw him through a plate-glass window." He is soon visited by the police, who inform him that Lauren has disappeared and that her current lover, a scientist who has discovered a way to use fetal tissue to preserve youth, has been murdered at her beach house. A suspect in the killing, DiMedici searches for Lauren and is pursued himself by a pair of police officers and several other eccentric characters.

Some reviewers of *The Horse Latitudes* compared Ferrigno to Elmore Leonard and Raymond Chandler. Chicago *Tribune Books* contributor Gary Dretzka commented that "the chases, kidnappings, beatings, blackmail and extortion attempts that result after this crazy California salad is tossed are imaginatively rendered and make for a quick, chilling, often humorous read." Though he found *The Horse Latitudes* to be unoriginal, Michael Dirda acknowledged in the *Washington Post* that "Ferrigno does possess some genuine storytelling skills. He can make you afraid, he can make you laugh . . . and he can make you keep turning his pages." Dirda also observed that *The Horse Latitudes* reads like a film script, "which may be fine if you were expecting a movie, but not so good if you were hoping for a novel." *Time* contributor Margaret Carlson was more enthusiastic, calling *The Horse Latitudes* "a work of *noir* literature that is the most memorable fiction debut of the season. With a magic all his own, [Ferrigno] has written an illuminating novel that never fails to entertain but also, surprisingly, makes us feel."

The seamy underworld Ferrigno depicts in *The Horse Latitudes* is similar to one the author experienced firsthand. Dissatisfied with the job of teaching English and literature he had landed after graduate school, Ferrigno quit and spent the next six years playing poker for a living. He resided in a high-crime area of downtown Seattle, where one of his neighbors was a heroin dealer. Ferrigno turned to writing after taking a freelance assignment for an alternative weekly newspaper. "There is an intensity in coming home at four in the morning and throwing a couple of thousand dollars on your bed and throwing it in the air [and saying], I won all of it!," he told McLellan. "But that wasn't even close to getting 10 dollars for an article with your name on it."

Ferrigno followed *The Horse Latitudes* with *The Cheshire Moon*, published in 1993. In this novel a reporter, Quinn, and his photographer sidekick, Jen Takamura, pursue the murderer of Quinn's best friend, Andy. Andy had witnessed a killing, and the murderer found it necessary to dispose of Andy as well, making his death appear a suicide. The killer is Emory Roy Liston, a "crazed rhinoceros of a former pro football player," according to Christopher Lehmann-Haupt in the *New York Times*. Liston, who attends night school, polishes his football trophies regularly, and is a frequent cable shopping-channel customer, "provides the spice" of the novel, wrote Michael Anderson in the *New York Times Book Review*. "Despite the conventionality of its plot, Mr. Ferrigno develops the qualities he showed off with such promise in his first novel," commented Lehmann-Haupt, who particularly noted Ferrigno's "black wit embellished with images of violence." The reviewer concluded that *The Cheshire Moon* is "a lot of fun to read, and Mr. Ferrigno certainly knows how to lay contrasting colors on his canvas."

Ferrigno continued to set his novels in rich-for-exploitation southern California. His 1995 novel, *Dead Man's Dance*, features investigative reporter Quinn attempting to uncover the brutal murder of his southern

California judge stepfather and untangling a massive web of deceit in the process. "A slick, sleek story that races to a slam-bang ending" is how *Booklist* contributor Emily Melton described it. *Dead Silent* has at its lurid core the decadent world of the music business as independent music producer Nick Carbonne investigates how the naked, dead bodies of his wife and best friend ended up in his hot tub. As Joe Gores commented in the *San Francisco Chronicle,* "set in the glitter and grit of the southern California dreamtime, *Dead Silent* probes, with almost despairing violence, lives of such amorality that few of us can imagine them."

A *Publisher Weekly* contributor called Ferrigno's *Heartbreaker* "his best novel in years. . . . a cinematic thriller . . . populated by mean drug dealers, beautiful surfers, 'trust fund babies,' 'thugs on commission' and murderers for hire." Val Duran, an ex-undercover cop escaping his past, leaves Miami for a quiet life as a stuntman in Los Angeles only to find himself enmeshed in the psychodrama of his girlfriend's scheming family while attempting to avoid the vengeful drug dealer who killed his partner.

Featured in Ferrigno's next two thrillers is tabloid journalist Jimmy Gage. In *Flinch,* this cool and engaging antihero "stumbles on evidence which may link his absurdly competitive brother to a serial killer," explained Joanne Wilkinson in *Booklist.* A *Publishers Weekly* reviewer praised *Flinch* for its "expansive canvas, spot-on characterizations, excellent prose and incisive dialogue."

Gage reappears in *Scavenger Hunt,* Ferrigno's seventh novel. In this thriller, Gage is enlisted to write an article about the tell-all script of Hollywood director Garrett Walsh, recently released from prison for a murder he was falsely accused of committing. Soon Walsh is dead and Gage risks his life against a cast of crooked and powerful Hollywood characters in order to set the record straight about Walsh's innocence. J. Kingston Pierce of *January Magazine* reflected that Ferrigno's "tale of ambition and guilt is driven by what for him is particularly dense, circuitous plotting, buttressed by clever dialogue."

The Wake Up is "another hugely entertaining thriller from the underappreciated Ferrigno," remarked Joanne Wilkinson in *Booklist.* In the wake of a botched sting operation that left many dead, special operations agent Frank Thorpe has been fired by his longtime employer,

a clandestine group that takes on cases the U.S. government could not or would not handle itself. Stunned by his current situation, depressed and unemployed, Thorpe spends most of his time aimlessly wandering around Los Angeles. During an interlude at the airport, Thorpe sees an arrogant businessman slap a ten-year-old Mexican vendor. His sense of justice outraged, he determines to track down the man and give him a wake-up, teaching him a valuable lesson in civility. Calling on some contacts, Thorpe identifies the man as Douglas Meacham, a dealer in antique art. Thorpe concocts a scheme to call into question the authenticity of a Mayan artifact recently sold by Meacham, which quickly escalates into a chaotic bloodbath that he has no hope of controlling. In the book, "characters are believable, the dialogue crackles, and the plot moves briskly. The author wastes not one word as he smoothly snaps the plot into place," commented Oline H. Cogdill in the *South Florida Sun-Sentinel.*

Ferrigno takes a step away from his usual hardboiled adventures to tell a futuristic story of terrorism and revenge in *Prayers for the Assassin.* In the year 2040, civil war has devastated the United States and fractured the country into two antagonistic sections, the Islamic States of America, occupying the northern territories, and the Bible Belt, located in the southern areas. In the course of the story, historian and researcher Sarah Dougin, a young, moderate Muslim, discovers that the nuclear attacks that leveled Washington, DC, and New York were not the doing of Israel, as has been popularly believed. Instead, the attacks were orchestrated by a fanatical, remorseless Islamic billionaire intent on attacking the Christian South. Intent on confirming her findings, Sarah goes underground, accompanied by her ex-lover, Muslim fighter Rakkim Epps. Along the way, they risk constant discovery and must dodge the lethal intentions of a hired assassin named Darwin. Ferrigno "deserves props for his imaginative portrayal of a futuristic America, which is often highlighted through startling details," observed Wilkinson in another *Booklist* review.

BIOGRAPHICAL AND CRITICAL SOURCES:

BOOKS

Contemporary Literary Criticism, Volume 65, Thomson Gale (Detroit, MI), 1991, pp. 47-50.

Ferrigno, Robert, *The Horse Latitudes,* Morrow (New York, NY), 1990.

PERIODICALS

Booklist, April 15, 1995, Emily Melton, review of *Dead Man's Dance,* p. 1452; October 15, 2001, Joanne Wilkinson, review of *Flinch,* p. 386; May 1, 2002; August, 2004, Joanne Wilkinson, review of *The Wake-Up,* p. 1905; December 1, 2005, Joanne Wilkinson, review of *Prayers for the Assassin,* p. 6.

Guardian (London, England), March 19, 2006, James Flint, "Jihad Cola," review of *Prayers for the Assassin.*

Kirkus Reviews, August 15, 2001, review of *Flinch,* p. 1166; July 1, 2004, review of *The Wake-Up,* p. 593; November 1, 2005, review of *Prayers for the Assassin,* p. 1157.

Library Journal, May 1, 1995, Stacie Browne Chandler, review of *Dead Man's Dance,* p. 130; October 1, 2001, Emily Doro, review of *Flinch,* p. 140; December, 2002, Susan Clifford Braun, review of *Scavenger Hunt,* p. 177; July, 2004, Bob Lunn, review of *The Wake-Up,* p. 69; August 1, 2005, Rex E. Klett, "2005 Shamus Award Nominees," p. 59.

Los Angeles Times, March 2, 1990, Dennis McLellan, "Author Gambles, Hits the Jackpot," profile of Robert Ferrigno, p. E1.

Los Angeles Times Book Review, November 13, 2001, Michael Harris, review of *Flinch,* p. E1.

New Yorker, February 22, 1993, review of *The Cheshire Moon,* p. 183.

New York Times, March 19, 1990, Christopher Lehmann-Haupt, review of *The Horse Latitudes,* p. C20; February 25, 1993, Christopher Lehmann-Haupt, review of *The Cheshire Moon,* p. B2.

New York Times Book Review, February 7, 1993, Michael P. Anderson, review of *The Cheshire Moon,* p. 22; July 15, 1995, Marilyn Stasio, review of *Dead Man's Dance,* p. 16; September 8, 1996, Marilyn Stasio, review of *Dead Silent,* p. 26.

Publishers Weekly, January 5, 1990, Sybil Steinberg, review of *The Horse Latitudes,* p. 62; August 2, 1993, review of *Cheshire Moon,* p. 30; June 17, 1996, review of *Dead Silent,* p. 45; March 15, 1999, review of *Heartbreaker,* p. 44; August 13, 2001, review of *Flinch,* p. 282; December 16, 2002, review of *Scavenger Hunt,* p. 47; November 14, 2005, review of *Prayers for the Assassin,* p. 42.

San Francisco Chronicle, August 27, 1996, Joe Gores, review of *Dead Silent,* p. B3.

South Florida Sun-Sentinel, Oline H. Cogdill, "The Best of Villains," review of *The Wake-Up.*

Time, March 26, 1990, Margaret Carlson, review of *The Horse Latitudes,* p. 78; March 15, 1993, review of *The Cheshire Moon,* p. 75.

Tribune Books (Chicago, IL), March 11, 1990, Gary Dretzka, review of *The Horse Latitudes,* p. 6.

Village Voice, April 3, 1990, review of *The Horse Latitudes,* p. 76.

Wall Street Journal, March 9, 1990, Tom Nolan, review of *The Horse Latitudes,* p. A11.

Washington Post, March 16, 1990, Michael Dirda, "Fast Ride of Familiar Turf," review of *The Horse Latitudes,* p. B3; February 18, 1993, Tom Nolan, review of *The Cheshire Moon,* p. A16.

ONLINE

January Magazine, http://www.januarymagazine.com/ (February 15, 2003), J. Kingston Pierce, review of *Scavenger Hunt;* (January 25, 2007), J. Kingston Pierce, interview with Robert Ferrigno.

Robert Ferrigno Home Page, http://www.robertferrigno. com (January 2, 2007).*

*   *   *

FRANKLIN, Sarah B.
See DUNCAN, Dave

*   *   *

FRY, Michael G. 1934-
(Michael Graham Fry)

PERSONAL: Born November 5, 1934, in Brierley, England; son of Cyril Victor (a surveyor) and Margaret Mary Fry; married Anna Maria Fulgoni, May, 1957; children: Michael Gareth, Gabriella, Margaret Louise. *Education:* University of London, B.Sc. (with honors), 1956, Ph.D., 1963. *Religion:* Roman Catholic.

ADDRESSES: Home—Manhattan Beach, CA. *Office*—School of International Relations, University of Southern California, Los Angeles, CA 90089.

CAREER: Writer, editor, and educator. University of Toronto, Toronto, Ontario, Canada, lecturer in history, 1961-62; University of Saskatchewan, Saskatoon, lecturer, 1962-63, assistant professor of history, 1963-65; Carleton University, Ottawa, Ontario, Canada, assistant professor, 1965-66, associate professor, 1966-72, professor of history, 1972-78, associate director of School of International Affairs, 1973-76, director, 1976-77; School of International Affairs, University of Denver, Denver, CO, dean and professor, 1978-81; School of International Relations, University of Southern California, Los Angeles, director and professor, 1981—, currently professor emeritus of international relations. Visiting professor, University of Leningrad, 1976, University of Cairo, and Middle East Center, University of Utah, 1979. *Military service:* British Army, 1956-58.

MEMBER: International Studies Association (vice-president, 1977), Society for Historians of American Foreign Relations, Royal Historical Society (fellow, 1992—).

AWARDS, HONORS: Canada Council Fellowships, 1966, 1967, 1968, 1973, and 1976; North Atlantic Treaty Organization research fellowship, 1969-70; Faculty Lifetime Achievement Award, University of Southern California, 2006.

WRITINGS:

Illusions of Security: North Atlantic Diplomacy, 1918-1922, University of Toronto Press (Toronto, Ontario, Canada), 1972.

(Editor) *"Freedom and Change": Essays in Honour of Lester B. Pearson,* McClelland & Stewart (Toronto, Ontario, Canada), 1975.

Lloyd George and Foreign Policy, Volume I: *The Education of a Statesman, 1890-1916,* McGill-Queen's University Press (Montreal, Quebec, Canada), 1977.

(With Itamar Rabinovich) *Despatches from Damascus: Gilbert Mackereth and British Policy in the Levant, 1933-39,* Tel Aviv University Press (Tel Aviv, Israel), 1986.

History, the White House, and the Kremlin: Statesmen as Historians, Pinter (New York, NY), 1991.

Power, Personalities and Policies, F. Cass (Portland, OR), 1992.

The North Pacific Triangle: The United States, Japan, and Canada at Century's End, University of Toronto Press (Toronto, Ontario, Canada), 1998.

(Editor, with Erik Goldstein and Richard Langhorne) *Guide to International Relations and Diplomacy,* Continuum (New York, NY), 2002.

Contributor to history and international relations journals, including *Canadian Journal of History, Journal of Modern History, Royal United States Institution Journal, Diplomatic History, Historical Journal, International Studies Quarterly, Review of International Studies, Albion,* and *International History Review.*

SIDELIGHTS: Michael G. Fry once told *CA:* "I am a student of international history, the international relations of the great powers in the 20th century, and the functioning of the international system. I am a historian who is attempting to cross disciplinary boundaries and relate to other scholars in the field of international relations. I am also concerned with dissent about foreign and defence policies."

BIOGRAPHICAL AND CRITICAL SOURCES:

ONLINE

University of Southern California Web site, http://www.usc.edu/ (summer, 2006), "Faculty News."*

*   *   *

FRY, Michael Graham
See FRY, Michael G.

G

GABALDON, Diana 1952-

PERSONAL: Surname pronounced "*GAB*-uhl-dohn"; born January 11, 1952, in Williams, AZ; daughter of Antonio (Tony) and Jacqueline Gabaldon; married Douglas Watkins (in construction and real estate), c. 1977; children: Laura Juliet, Samuel Gordon, Jennifer Rose. *Education:* Arizona State University, B.S., 1973, Ph.D., 1978; University of California, San Diego, M.S., 1975.

ADDRESSES: Home and office—Phoenix, AZ. *E-mail*—dgabaldon@aol.com.

CAREER: Writer, novelist, and educator. Northern Arizona University, laboratory technician, 1972-73; University of Pennsylvania, researcher, 1978-79; University of California, Los Angeles, researcher, 1979-80; Arizona State University, Center for Environmental Studies, Tempe, AZ, 1980-92, began as field ecologist, became assistant professor of research; full-time freelance writer, 1992—.

AWARDS, HONORS: Best First Novel Award from B. Dalton Bookstores, and Best Book of the Year Award from the Romance Writers of America, both 1991, both for *Outlander;* Quill Award, 2006, for *A Breath of Snow and Ashes.*

WRITINGS:

"OUTLANDER" SERIES; HISTORICAL NOVELS

Outlander, Delacorte (New York, NY), 1991.
Dragonfly in Amber, Delacorte (New York, NY), 1992.
Voyager, Delacorte (New York, NY), 1994.
Drums of Autumn, Delacorte (New York, NY), 1997.
The Outlandish Companion: In Which Much Is Revealed Regarding Claire and Jamie Fraser, Their Lives and Times, Antecedents, Adventures, Companions, and Progeny, with Learned Commentary (and Many Footnotes), Delacorte (New York, NY), 1999.
The Fiery Cross, Delacorte (New York, NY), 2001.
Lord John and the Private Matter, Doubleday Canada, 2003.
A Breath of Snow and Ashes, Delacorte Press (New York, NY), 2005.

OTHER

(Author of introduction) Thomas Paine, *Common Sense,* Bantam Dell (New York, NY), 2004.

Also author of comic book scripts for Walt Disney Productions, 1979-80. Contributor of software reviews to *Byte* magazine. Contributor of articles to scholarly journals and periodicals, including *Infoworld, BYTE,* and *PC Magazine. Science Software* (a scholarly journal on scientific computation), founder and editor, 1980s and 1990s. Author's works have been translated into several languages.

SIDELIGHTS: Diana Gabaldon is a former biologist and university professor who has become the bestselling writer of the "Outlander" series of historical fantasy novels. Gabaldon's writing career began with two unlikely endeavors, considering the eventual direction of her career. While she was an assistant professor at

Arizona State University in the 1980s, she became an expert in the use of software programs for scientific research. This led to her founding the scholarly journal *Science Software,* which she ran and edited. While this experience gave her a good deal of writing experience, she credits her freelance work writing comics about Mickey Mouse, Donald Duck, and Uncle Scrooge for Walt Disney Productions from 1979 to 1980 for teaching her "most of what I know about the mechanics of storytelling," as she states on her home page.

The Disney work and other freelance assignments provided Gabaldon with additional income for her family, and she began to believe that she could succeed as a full-time writer. "From the late 70's to the early 90's, I wrote anything anybody would pay me for," she said. "This ranged from articles on how to clean a longhorn cow's skull for living-room decoration to manuals on elementary math instruction on the Apple II . . . to a slew of software reviews and application articles done for the computer press." When her contract expired at the university in 1992, Gabaldon decided she was ready to take the plunge and become a full-time writer. But instead of continuing to write nonfiction, she started to write a historical novel set in eighteenth-century Scotland. Using her knowledge of computers, she joined discussion forums, where she eventually found an encouraging audience for her forays into fiction. She also made contacts online that helped her finish her first novel, *Outlander,* and find an agent and publisher.

Outlander was published in 1991. Its protagonist, English nurse Claire Randall, visits Scotland in 1945, hoping to rekindle a marriage stressed by separation during World War II. Occupying herself by collecting plant samples while her husband studies history, she accidentally touches a stone in an ancient circle similar to Stonehenge, and she is transported to the year 1743. The novel then recounts events leading to the Second Jacobite Rising through her modern eyes. While in the 1700s, Claire marries outlaw Scotsman Jamie Fraser, and she eventually must choose between returning to her husband in the twentieth century and remaining with Jamie. *Outlander* garnered awards from both the Romance Writers of America and B. Dalton Bookstores in the year of its publication. A *Publishers Weekly* reviewer hailed *Outlander* as "absorbing and heartwarming"; and Cynthia Johnson of the *Library Journal* lauded the book as "a richly textured historical novel with an unusual and compelling love story."

Gabaldon followed *Outlander* with *Dragonfly in Amber.* This novel recounts Claire and Jamie's desperate at-tempt to alter history by preventing Charles Stuart from instigating the Jacobite uprising that led to the slaughter of the Scots at the battle of Culloden. When they fail at this, they use Claire's knowledge of history to prepare Jamie's family and clan for this disaster as best they can. However, *Dragonfly in Amber* also deals with a second story in a different timeline—Claire's trip to Scotland with her daughter Brianna in 1968 to tell her about her real father, Jamie Fraser. A *Publishers Weekly* critic commended Gabaldon's "fresh and offbeat historical view" and asserted that *Dragonfly in Amber* is "compulsively readable."

The third volume in the saga, *Voyager,* appeared on the *Publishers Weekly* hardcover bestsellers list in January 1994. In this installment, having discovered that Jamie did not die at the battle of Culloden, Claire returns to the eighteenth century to be with him. The years spent apart are recounted, and adventures lead the couple to America in pursuit of Jamie's kidnapped nephew. Roland Green, reviewing *Voyager* in *Booklist,* praised its "highly appealing characters" and "authentic feel." *Locus* contributor Carolyn Cushman felt that Gabaldon "masterfully interweaves" plot elements separated by two centuries, "crossing time periods with abandon but never losing track of the story."

Though a *Publishers Weekly* reviewer labeled *Voyager* a "triumphant conclusion" to the story of Claire and Jamie, Gabaldon was preparing a fourth book that would carry the characters through the American Revolution. *Drums of Autumn* leapt onto the bestseller lists as soon as it appeared in 1997. Set in the New World, the novel finds the two lovers building a life as the Americans set about building a nation. Jamie and Claire first arrive at Charleston, South Carolina, then join other Scottish exiles along the Cape Fear River in North Carolina. Troubled by events there, the couple moves inland to the mountains in search of tranquility. The couple's attempts at avoiding conflict and an impending war give the book an epic quality. In the view of one *Booklist* contributor, "Gabaldon is clearly trying to write on the same scale as Margaret Mitchell, and in terms of length and of thoroughness of research, largely succeeds." A reviewer for *Maclean's* noted that "the meticulous period detail is in contrast to the serendipitous development of the central premise: the love story of a modern woman somehow flung into the past."

This quality of *Drums of Autumn* reflects its author's approach to all of the books in the series. In an interview published in *Heart to Heart,* Gabaldon discussed some of her feelings about the series she began with *Outlander:* "Part of my purpose in my books has been to tell the complete story of a relationship and a marriage; not just to end with 'happily ever after,' leaving the protagonists at the altar or in bed. . . . I wanted to show some of the complicated business of actually living a successful marriage." Concerning the history depicted in the first four novels, Gabaldon revealed that she "wanted to show the changing face of the world at that time, moving from the ancient feudal system of Highland clans to the violent upheavals of democracy in the New World." She further noted that with "Claire's perspective as a time-traveler, we see the events of that time through a modern eye, and can fully appreciate their significance to the future that will come."

Four years after *Drums of Autumn,* Gabaldon completed the next installment of Claire and Jamie's adventures in colonial America with *The Fiery Cross.* Taking place in the years 1771 and 1772, the novel tells how Jamie, who is now a landowner, is asked by the governor of North Carolina to form a militia in preparation for what looks like the upcoming war against the British. Reluctant at first to comply, Jamie is convinced by Claire, who knows the Revolution is inevitable, that this is the right thing to do. Although the initial crisis is averted and the militia is dispersed, Claire and readers know that war still lies ahead. *People* contributor Bella Stander claimed that new readers to the series will not know "who the characters are, how they got to the colonies, and why we should care." On the other hand, Johnson praised the novel in the *Library Journal,* asserting that the writing "is superb—lush, evocative, and sensual, with a wealth of historic detail and a good deal of humor."

A Breath of Snow and Ashes returns to Claire and Jamie's world in 1772 as the American Revolution is about to unfold. Jamie has been asked to assist England suppress the revolution, but he is reluctant because Claire knows the eventual outcome of the revolution. Jamie is additionally stunned when he discovers an obituary dated 1776—his own obituary—suggesting that he will die at the culmination of the revolution. Against the tumult of the formation of the United States, Jamie and Claire struggle against the implacable force of history that has yet to happen and the inevitability of events they cannot change. Gabaldon makes her time-traveling themes convincing and her plotting "plausible because her research is so meticulous and her characters so sympathetic: heroic, yet attractively flawed,"

observed Kathy Weissman, reviewing the novel for *Bookreporter.com.* Weissman commented that "there is something so honest, rich, and complete about the alternative worlds Gabaldon creates that I think she is a kind of genius."

"From the moment she penned her very first novel in her best-selling Outlander series back in 1991, it was clear that Diana Gabaldon wrote her own rules," observed Bron Sibree in an *Asia Africa Intelligence Wire* review. In addition to building a vast and appreciative audience, Gabaldon also tested her abilities and stretched the definitions of overlapping genres, creating stories that effectively combine elements of science fiction, fantasy, romance, and historical fiction. Gabaldon "rankles at the categorisation of her novels as women's fiction by some booksellers and bristles at the merest mention of the word 'romance' in conjunction with her novels," Sibree noted. This is a principle that Gabaldon adheres to steadfastly; in 2003, for example, she declined to conduct any book signings in Barnes and Noble stores until the chain agreed to move her books from the romance section to general fiction. In addition to her determination to reach both male and female audiences with her work, what Gabaldon "very consciously brings to her fiction is a scientist's penchant for observation, and the ability to draw patterns out of chaos," Sibree concluded.

Because her series has grown into quite a complex tale, Gabaldon has written *The Outlandish Companion: In Which Much Is Revealed Regarding Claire and Jamie Fraser, Their Lives and Times, Antecedents, Adventures, Companions, and Progeny, with Learned Commentary (and Many Footnotes),* which explains the "Outlander" series for fans, including plot synopses, character backgrounds, how time travel works in her stories, and even provides information about her personal life.

BIOGRAPHICAL AND CRITICAL SOURCES:

PERIODICALS

Arizona Daily Star, October 24, 2006, "*Outlander* Author to Talk Here," profile of Diana Gabaldon.

Asia Africa Intelligence Wire, November 12, 2005, Bron Sibree, "Breath of Fresh Air in Fiction Stakes," interview with Diana Gabaldon.

Booklist, November 15, 1993, Roland Green, review of *Voyager;* November 15, 1996, review of *Drums of Autumn;* February 1, 2006, Neal Wyatt, review of *A Breath of Snow and Ashes,* p. 74.

Heart to Heart, September-October, 1994, review of *Voyager,* pp. 3, 8-9.

Library Journal, July, 1991, Cynthia Johnson, review of *Outlander,* p. 134; January, 2002, Cynthia Johnson, review of *The Fiery Cross,* p. 152.

Locus, January, 1994, Carolyn Cushman, review of *Voyager,* p. 29.

Maclean's, February 17, 1997, review of *Drums of Autumn,* p. 71; August 9, 1999, "Tying Up Loose Ends: A Best-selling Novelist Pens a Reference Book to Answer Her Fans' Queries," p. 21; January 14, 2002, "Over and Under Achievers: Teaching the Ropes of the Rock," p. 6.

People, April 14, 1997, review of *Drums of Autumn,* p. 64; December 24, 2001, Bella Stander, review of *The Fiery Cross,* p. 39.

Publishers Weekly, May 31, 1991, review of *Outlander,* p. 59; June 22, 1992, review of *Dragonfly in Amber,* p. 49; December 20, 1993, p. 52; January 17, 1994, p. 2; January 6, 1997, p. 50; January 13, 1997, p. 18; November 19, 2001.

Swiss News, November, 2005, review of *A Breath of Snow and Ashes,* p. 61.

ONLINE

Bookreporter.com, http://www.bookreporter.com/ (August 22, 2001), transcript of online chat with Diana Gabaldon; (December 5, 2006), Roz Shea, review of *The Fiery Cross,* and Kathy Weissman, review of *A Breath of Snow and Ashes.*

Diana Gabaldon Home Page, http://www.cco.caltech. edu/~gatti/gabaldon (November 11, 2002).

Ladies of Lallybroch Web site, http://www.lallybroch. com/ (December 5, 2006).

Writing-World.com, http://www.writing-world.com/ (December 5, 2006), Susan Perry, interview with Diana Gabaldon.*

*   *   *

GABLER, Neal 1950(?)-

PERSONAL: Born c. 1950. *Education:* Attended University of Michigan.

CAREER: Writer. Cohost of *Sneak Previews,* PBS-TV.

AWARDS, HONORS: Prize from *Los Angeles Times Book Review,* 1989, for *An Empire of Their Own: How the Jews Invented Hollywood.*

WRITINGS:

An Empire of Their Own: How the Jews Invented Hollywood, Crown (New York, NY), 1988.

Winchell: Gossip, Power, and the Culture of Celebrity, Knopf (New York, NY), 1994.

Life, the Movie: How Entertainment Conquered Reality, Knopf (New York, NY), 1998.

(With Frank Rich and Joyce Antler) *Television's Changing Image of American Jews,* American Jewish Committee (New York, NY), 2000.

Walt Disney: The Triumph of the American Imagination, Knopf (New York, NY), 2006.

Contributor to periodicals, including *American Film, New York Times Book Review,* and *Video Review.*

SIDELIGHTS: Neal Gabler is a historian who specializes in film and American culture. His first book, *An Empire of Their Own: How the Jews Invented Hollywood,* relates the achievements of such film moguls as Samuel Goldwyn, Louis B. Mayer, Jack Warner, and Harry Cohn. In so doing, it traces the development of Hollywood from its origins to the McCarthy era. In *An Empire of Their Own* Gabler maintains that these pioneering Jewish movie producers, most of whom hailed from Eastern Europe, recreated themselves as American businessmen. They did so in an industry that fosters such pursuits. Many films produced under these moguls perpetuated the image of America as what Ron Grossman, writing in the *Chicago Tribune,* described as "a land of miracles and a place where hard work and talent make dreams come true." Men like Goldwyn and Cohn, because of their Jewish heritage, might ordinarily have found themselves cast as outsiders in America, Gabler contended, but in their films they sought to fashion an endearing image of America—one particularly evident in Frank Capra's films and the equally popular Andy Hardy series—as a nearly magical land of seemingly limitless riches and fairness.

An Empire of Their Own was well received upon publication in 1988. Molly Haskell, a noted author of film criticism, wrote in the *New York Times Book Review* that Gabler had produced an "enthralling book of social history," while another film authority, *Los Angeles Times Book Review* contributor Charles Champlin, hailed *An Empire of Their Own* as a "lively and scholarly history." Lindsay Anderson, noted as both a filmmaker and critic, wrote in the *Times Literary Supplement* that *An*

Empire of Their Own, along with A. Scott Berg's *Goldwyn,* provides a "comprehensive and graphic account of Hollywood's dream factories."

Gabler followed *An Empire of Their Own* with *Winchell: Gossip, Power, and the Culture of Celebrity,* a biography of the influential newspaper and radio journalist Walter Winchell, who enjoyed particular popularity in the 1930s. Winchell became famous for his syndicated gossip column, originating in the *New York Graphic* during the 1920s, in which he emphasized the hardships, both personal and professional, of famous contemporaries. A nationwide radio show increased Winchell's fame in the 1930s and 1940s, when he served as a staunch advocate of America's war effort. Winchell's fortunes declined in the 1950s, when he supported Senator Joseph McCarthy's anticommunist investigations, and by the 1960s he was futilely attempting to find a distributor for his column.

For Gabler, Winchell is a key figure in the shift in emphasis in America from high culture to mass-market entertainment. Winchell, according to Gabler, fostered interest in celebrities and elevated celebrity behavior to the level of actual news. Gabler's rendering of Winchell's life, in turn, results in a history of these developments in American culture. "Writing that Winchell was 'arguably one of the principal architects' of modern American culture, Mr. Gabler turns the columnist's life into the springboard for a fascinating social history," observed Michiko Kakutani in her *New York Times* review of *Winchell.* She added that Gabler's "novelistic approach [gives] the reader a vivid, psychologically acute portrait of Winchell himself."

Likewise impressed with Gabler's achievement in *Winchell* was Frank Rich, who wrote in the *New York Times Book Review* that "Gabler captures the magnetism of Winchell's demonic energy." Rich described *Winchell* as "imaginatively written and authoritatively reported." Murray Kempton, writing in the *Los Angeles Times Book Review,* noted: "Gabler is not to be envied the labors of his exhumations; but he has worked at them wonderfully and surprised us with the revelation that [Winchell's] bones do indeed live and are almost as vividly deplorable as when they were flesh."

Walt Disney: The Triumph of the American Imagination is Gabler's ambitious biography of Walt Disney, who revolutionized animated films and created the Disneyland and Disney World theme parks. Gabler maintains

that Disney exerted a tremendous influence not only on American culture and values, but on the global culture as well. Yet Disney's reputation, as well as the critical assessment of his work, "has gone through more violent swings than that of nearly any other popular artist," according to Michiko Kakutani in the *New York Times.* While some hold him up as a visionary, others deride him as someone who pandered to the masses and sentimentalized everything to make it more palatable. At more than 800 pages, Gabler's book makes a thorough investigation into Walt Disney's motivations and achievements. Kakutani recommended the book as "a thoughtful, incisive and largely straightforward account" of a "lonely, eccentric, immensely gifted man: an ambitious workaholic, driven more by perfectionism than by dreams of entrepreneurial power." John Hartl, reviewing the biography for the *Seattle Times,* called *Walt Disney* "delightfully addictive."

BIOGRAPHICAL AND CRITICAL SOURCES:

PERIODICALS

Bookpage, September 15, 2006, Gordon Flagg, review of *Walt Disney: The Triumph of the American Imagination,* p. 4.

Chicago Tribune, December 26, 1988, Ron Grossman, review of *An Empire of Their Own: How the Jews Invented Hollywood.*

Kirkus Reviews, October 15, 2006, review of *Walt Disney,* p. 1054.

Los Angeles Times Book Review, September 25, 1988, Charles Champlin, review of *An Empire of Their Own,* pp. 2, 11-12; November 13, 1994, Murray Kempton, review of *Winchell: Gossip, Power and the Culture of Celebrity,* pp. 1, 10-11.

New York, October 24, 1994, Walter Kim, review of *Winchell,* pp. 73-74.

New York Review of Books, May 18, 1989, review of *An Empire of Their Own,* pp. 28-33.

New York Times, October 20, 1988, Christopher Lehmann-Haupt, review of *An Empire of Their Own,* p. C24; October 18, 1994, Michiko Kakutani, review of *Winchell,* p. B3; November 14, 2006, Michiko Kakutani, review of *Walt Disney.*

New York Times Book Review, October 23, 1988, Molly Haskell, review of *An Empire of Their Own,* pp. 1, 57-9; October 23, 1994, Frank Rich, review of *Winchell,* pp. 1, 31-33.

Times Literary Supplement, December 15, 1989, Lindsay Anderson, review of *An Empire of Their Own,* p. 1387.

ONLINE

Bookpage, http://www.bookpage.com/ (December 8, 2006), Pat H. Broeske, review of *Walt Disney.*

Seattle Times Online, http://seattletimes.nwsource.com/ (November 3, 2006), John Hartl, review of *Walt Disney.**

*   *   *

GIBLIN, James Cross 1933-

PERSONAL: Surname is pronounced with a hard "g"; born July 8, 1933, in Cleveland, OH; son of Edward Kelley (a lawyer) and Anna (a teacher) Giblin. *Education:* Attended Northwestern University, 1951; Western Reserve University (now Case Western Reserve University), B.A., 1954; Columbia University, M.F.A., 1955.

ADDRESSES: Home—New York, NY. *Office*—Clarion Books, 215 Park Ave. S., New York, NY 10003.

CAREER: Freelance writer, 1955—. Worked as a temporary typist and at the British Book Centre, 1955-59; Criterion Books, Inc., New York, NY, assistant editor, 1959-62; Lothrop, Lee & Shepard Co., New York, associate editor, 1962-65, editor, 1965-67; Seabury Press, Inc., New York, editor-in-chief of Clarion Books (for children), 1967-79, vice president, 1975-79; Houghton Mifflin Company, New York, editor and publisher of Clarion Books, 1979-89, contributing editor, 1989—. Adjunct professor at Graduate Center of the City University of New York, 1979-83.

MEMBER: Society of Children's Book Writers and Illustrators (member of board of directors), Authors Guild, Children's Book Council (president, 1976).

AWARDS, HONORS: American Library Association notable children's book citations, 1980, for *The Scarecrow Book,* 1981, for *The Skyscraper Book,* 1982, for *Chimney Sweeps: Yesterday and Today,* 1985, for *The Truth about Santa Claus,* 1986, for *Milk: The Fight for Purity,* 1987, for *From Hand to Mouth,* 1988, for *Let There Be Light: A Book about Windows,* 1990, for *The Riddle of the Rosetta Stone: Key to Ancient Egypt,* 1991, for *The Truth about Unicorns,* 1993, for *Be Seated: A Book about Chairs,* 1995, for *When Plague*

Strikes: The Black Death, Smallpox, and AIDS, 1997, for *Charles A. Lindbergh: A Human Hero,* and 2000, for *The Amazing Life of Benjamin Franklin;* Golden Kite Award for nonfiction, Society of Children's Book Writers and Illustrators (SCBWI), 1982, and National Book Award for children's nonfiction, 1983, both for *Chimney Sweeps: Yesterday and Today;* Golden Kite Award for nonfiction, SCBWI, 1984, for *Walls: Defenses throughout History,* and 1989, for *Let There Be Light: A Book about Windows; Boston Globe-Horn Book* Nonfiction Honor Book, 1986, for *The Truth about Santa Claus; Washington Post*-Children's Book Guild Award for Nonfiction, 1996, for body of work; Honor Book, Orbis Pictus Award for nonfiction, National Council of Teachers of English, 1998, for *Charles A. Lindbergh: A Human Hero,* and 2001, for *The Amazing Life of Benjamin Franklin;* Robert F. Sibert Informational Book Award, American Library Association, for *The Life and Death of Adolf Hitler,* 2003.

WRITINGS:

My Bus Is Always Late (one-act play; produced in Cleveland, OH, at Western Reserve University, 1953), Dramatic Publishing, 1954.

(With Dale Ferguson) *The Scarecrow Book,* Crown (New York, NY), 1980.

The Skyscraper Book, illustrated by Anthony Kramer, photographs by David Anderson, Crowell (New York, NY), 1981.

Chimney Sweeps: Yesterday and Today, illustrated by Margot Tomes, Crowell (New York, NY), 1981.

Fireworks, Picnics, and Flags: The Story of the Fourth of July Symbols, illustrated by Ursula Arndt, Clarion Books (New York, NY), 1983.

Walls: Defenses throughout History, Little, Brown (Boston, MA), 1984.

The Truth about Santa Claus, Crowell (New York, NY), 1985.

Milk: The Fight for Purity, Crowell (New York, NY), 1986.

From Hand to Mouth; or, How We Invented Knives, Forks, Spoons, and Chopsticks & the Table Manners to Go with Them, Crowell (New York, NY), 1987.

Let There Be Light: A Book about Windows, Crowell (New York, NY), 1988.

The Riddle of the Rosetta Stone: Key to Ancient Egypt, Crowell (New York, NY), 1990.

Writing Books for Young People (adult nonfiction), The Writer, Inc. (Boston, MA), 1990.

The Truth about Unicorns, illustrated by Michael Mc-Dermott, Harper (New York, NY), 1991.

Edith Wilson: The Woman Who Ran the United States, illustrated by Michele Laporte, Viking (New York, NY), 1992.

George Washington: A Picture Book Biography, illustrated by Michael Dooling, Scholastic Press (New York, NY), 1992.

Be Seated: A Book about Chairs, HarperCollins (New York, NY), 1993.

Thomas Jefferson: A Picture Book Biography, illustrated by Michael Dooling, Scholastic Press (New York, NY), 1994.

When Plague Strikes: The Black Death, Smallpox, and AIDS, illustrated by David Frampton, HarperCollins (New York, NY), 1995.

(Reteller) *The Dwarf, the Giant, and the Unicorn: A Tale of King Arthur* (children's fiction), illustrated by Claire Ewart, Clarion Books (New York, NY), 1996.

Charles A. Lindbergh: A Human Hero, Clarion Books (New York, NY), 1997.

The Mystery of the Mammoth Bones: And How It Was Solved, HarperCollins (New York, NY), 1999.

The Amazing Life of Benjamin Franklin, illustrated by Michael Dooling, Scholastic Press (New York, NY), 2000.

(Editor and author of introduction) *The Century That Was: Reflections on the Last One Hundred Years,* Atheneum (New York, NY), 2000.

The Life and Death of Adolf Hitler, Clarion Books (New York, NY), 2002.

Secrets of the Sphinx, illustrated by Bagram Ibatoulline, Scholastic Press (New York, NY), 2004.

Good Brother, Bad Brother: The Story of Edwin Booth and John Wilkes Booth, Clarion Books (New York, NY), 2005.

The Boy Who Saved Cleveland: Based on A True Story (children's fiction), Henry Holt (New York, NY), 2006.

The Many Rides of Paul Revere, Scholastic Press (New York, NY), 2007.

Also author of a play based on William Styron's novel *Lie Down in Darkness.* Contributor of original short stories to anthologies, including *Am I Blue? Coming out of the Silence,* edited by Marion Dane Bauer, HarperCollins (New York, NY), 1994, and *Tomorrowland: Stories about the Future,* edited by Michael Cart, Scholastic Press (New York, NY), 1999. Contributor of articles and stories for children to *Cobblestone, Cricket,* and *Highlights for Children,* and of articles for adults to *Children's Literature in Education, Horn Book, Publishers Weekly, School Library Journal, Washington Post, Writer,* and *Writer's Digest.*

SIDELIGHTS: James Cross Giblin has been a major figure in the field of children's book publishing since the 1970s. Not only has he edited the work of many important authors during his years at Clarion Books, but Giblin himself has written many books for young readers. He has won awards and critical acclaim for his children's books, including *Chimney Sweeps: Yesterday and Today, The Truth about Santa Claus, Let There Be Light: A Book about Windows,* and *Charles A. Lindbergh: A Human Hero. Chimney Sweeps* won the National Book Award for children's nonfiction in 1983.

As Giblin once explained: "Nonfiction books for children aged eight to twelve [give] me the opportunity to pursue my research interests, meet interesting and stimulating experts in various fields, and share my enthusiasms with a young audience. I try to write books that I would have enjoyed reading when I was the age of my readers." Giblin was born July 8, 1933, in Cleveland, Ohio. A shy, bookish child, he grew up in nearby Painesville. As a boy, he enjoyed the comic strip "Blondie," and, with his mother's help, he began drawing his own strips. Giblin once recalled: "I filled sketchbook after sketchbook with action-filled pictures drawn in boxes like those of the comics. Mother helped me to print the words I wanted to put in the balloons, and later I learned how to print them myself." Giblin also enjoyed going to the movies as a youngster, and he once noted: "My favorites weren't films made for children but spy movies set in Germany and Nazi-occupied areas such as *Casablanca.* I also liked melodramas starring emotional actresses like Bette Davis and Greer Garson, especially if they took place in exotic settings . . . or had to do with World War II."

In junior high, Giblin worked on the school paper, which helped him overcome some of his shyness. He reminisced in his autobiographical essay in *Sixth Book of Junior Authors:* "Robert K. Payne, my ninth-grade English teacher, did more than anyone to draw me out of my isolation. Mr. Payne encouraged his classes to try new things, including a mimeographed class newspaper. And he was determined that I should not only contribute pieces to the paper but also edit it." Giblin continued: "I backed away from the responsibility at first, as I backed away from so many things then. But Mr. Payne was persistent, and at last I allowed myself to become involved. Once I did, I discovered that I loved working with my classmates on the paper and thinking up ideas for each new issue."

Giblin discovered a new interest when he got to high school. He answered a notice in the local paper about auditions for a community theater production of the play *Outward Bound,* and, as he once recalled: "My parents drove me to the barn theatre on the outskirts of town, and I nervously entered the rustic auditorium. When I arrived home three hours later—one of the actors had given me a ride—I couldn't restrain my excitement. 'I got a part! I got a part!' I shouted as I raced through the darkened house to the back porch, where my parents were sitting. The director had cast me as the idealistic young Reverend Duke in the play, which tells the story of a group of English people traveling on an ocean liner who gradually realize that they have died and are on their way to Heaven . . . or to Hell." Giblin added: "As a shy youth of sixteen I might be reluctant to reveal my feelings, but I found I had no trouble expressing them through the character of the Reverend Duke. When the play was over and I walked to the center of the stage to take my bow, the applause seemed like an endorsement not just of my acting but of me personally. I felt a surge of confidence that I had never known before. . . . After *Outward Bound* I was hooked on the theatre. I tried out for and got parts in all of the Le Masque Club productions . . . at Harvey High School, and the following summer I was cast in the small but funny role of the Lost Private in a professional production of the comedy *At War with the Army* at Rabbit Run Theatre in nearby North Madison."

After graduating from high school, Giblin studied drama at Northwestern University. However, he was unhappy there, and after one semester he transferred to Western Reserve University (now Case Western Reserve University) near his parents's home. He did well; in addition to starring in many stage productions at Western Reserve, he won a contest to costar in a radio drama in New York City with actress Nina Foch. As Giblin gained experience on the stage, his ambitions changed. He once noted: "The actor has very little control over his situation, and I now knew that I wanted control. So I turned my attention to directing and playwriting." An experience with an old woman on a bus inspired him to write his first play, *My Bus Is Always Late,* which was produced locally and published by the Dramatic Publishing Company in 1954.

Soon after, Giblin began studying for a Master of Fine Arts degree in playwriting at Columbia University in New York. Upon earning it, he remained in New York City to write, supporting himself by working as a temporary office worker. He became involved in efforts to adapt William Styron's novel *Lie Down in Darkness* for the stage, but the project fell through for various reasons. This failure deeply affected Giblin. He once explained: "I'd put almost a year of hard work and anticipation into *Lie Down in Darkness.* I'd drawn on my deepest feelings in order to write it, and in the process it had become my personal statement as much as Styron's. I tried to start a new play in that late spring of 1957, but I discovered, painfully, that I'd already expressed most of what I had to say in *Lie Down in Darkness.*"

After a recuperative visit home to Painesville, Giblin returned to New York in hopes of finding a more dependable career. He started out as a special order clerk at the British Book Centre, then joined the staff of Criterion Books in 1959, first as a publicity director, and later as an editor. He enjoyed the work, especially when given the opportunity to edit books for young readers. Deciding to concentrate solely on works for children, he moved on to Lothrop, Lee and Shepard in 1962.

While working at Lothrop, Giblin started to think about writing his own books. He once recalled: "In 1964, after editing J.J. McCoy's career book, *The World of the Veterinarian,* I decided to try writing a similar book about publishing, and drafted an outline for it and several sample chapters." Though a publisher expressed initial interest in the book, in the end, it was rejected since the potential market was felt to be too small. Giblin had ambivalent feelings, as he noted in his autobiographical essay in *Sixth Book of Junior Authors:* "I really wasn't sorry. While part of me wanted to resume my writing career, another part—remembering the *Lie Down in Darkness* experience—hung back from making the necessary commitment to it."

In the late 1960s, Giblin went to work for Seabury Press, where he was instrumental in developing the company's children's division, Clarion Books. In the 1970s, a trip to China inspired him to try another book project of his own—"an anthology of Chinese writings about the doings of Chinese young people in the years since the Communist Revolution of 1949," as he once described it. But this time the project did not go through because it was considered "too political." However, by this time Giblin was writing again, contributing articles about children's books to periodicals and lecturing at conferences of children's book writers and librarians.

In 1980, Giblin collaborated with Dale Ferguson on his first children's title, *The Scarecrow Book.* Since then, he has written many more children's nonfiction titles on a wide range of subjects, among them *The Skyscraper Book, Walls: Defenses throughout History,* and *Let There Be Light,* In 1989, Giblin decided he was tired of juggling his role as editor-in-chief of Clarion Books with his expanding career as a writer, so he retired to contributing editor status.

The author's children's books have continued to range far afield. Giblin has explored such topics as milk pasteurization, Fourth of July celebrations, eating utensils, chairs, plagues, and mammoth bones, among many others. Many reviewers have praised Giblin's ability to tell complex stories in a way that is simple, understandable, and entertaining. Elizabeth S. Watson, writing in a *Horn Book* review of *The Riddle of the Rosetta Stone: Key to Ancient Egypt,* stated that "the author has done a masterful job of distilling information, citing the highlights, and fitting it all together." *New York Times Book Review* contributor Philip M. Isaacson lauded Giblin's writing skills in *Let There Be Light,* noting that the author "has condensed a daunting body of material to provide young readers with a great deal of information about the evolution and technology of windows."

Some critics have also pointed out that Giblin's accounts, while easy to understand, are loaded with valuable detail. Giblin's "relaxed, affable manner belies the amount of information he offers," wrote Amy L. Cohn in a *School Library Journal* review of *Chimney Sweeps.* Other critics have observed that this wealth of information is derived from the author's painstaking research. "Giblin has such a flair for historic detail and research that he translates hordes of tales into a singular creation of Santa Claus," proclaimed a *School Library Journal* reviewer about *The Truth about Santa Claus.* An evaluation of the same book by a writer for the *Bulletin of the Center for Children's Books* lauded Giblin's command of his subject, stating that the author had done "his usual good job of research and well-organized presentation." Reviewing Giblin's *The Mystery of the Mammoth Bones: And How It Was Solved,* a *Publishers Weekly* critic praised the author for having "the pacing of an ace detective [as he] unveils the painstaking steps in artist and naturalist Charles Willson Peale's 1801 discovery of mammoth bones."

In addition to his books about interesting subjects and events, Giblin has written biographies of such historical figures as founding fathers George Washington, Thomas Jefferson, and Benjamin Franklin, and aviator Charles Lindbergh. Like his earlier works, Giblin's nonfiction books continue to find favor with reviewers and young readers alike. For example, assessing Giblin's *The Amazing Life of Benjamin Franklin,* Ilene Cooper wrote in *Booklist:* "[His] writing is lively, and he wisely uses the story of Franklin's estrangement from his only living son, a Royalist, to heighten dramatic tension." *Horn Book* reviewer Mary M. Burns wrote of the same biography: "Giblin demonstrates his mastery of the historical-biographical genre—he knows how to define a theme, develop a narrative, and maintain his focus to the last sentence." Giblin's initial foray into fiction, *The Dwarf, the Giant, and the Unicorn: A Tale of King Arthur,* met with mixed reviews. Carolyn Phelan, writing for *Booklist,* praised it as a "good read-aloud," while a *Publishers Weekly* reviewer stated that Giblin's efforts were "without memorable results."

Giblin's *The Century That Was: Reflections on the Last One Hundred Years* is something of a departure for him, although it is a natural extension of his former work as an editor. He compiled and edited a collection of thematic essays by eleven noted children's writers, each one looking at a different aspect of life in America in the twentieth century. Hazel Rochman, writing in *Booklist,* pointed out that while editor Giblin made no effort to produce a "comprehensive" history, "the individual approaches, both personal and historical, will stimulate young people to look back and also forward to where we're going next." A *Horn Book* reviewer voiced a similar opinion, stating: "One of the older formulas of outstanding nonfiction . . . is the essay. It's back, and in fine fettle for a new generation of readers."

In *The Life and Death of Adolf Hitler,* Giblin questions what sort of man could design and carry out the horrific plans of the leader of "the thousand year Reich," how he was able to gain support for his crimes and genocide, and why he was not stopped. Giblin studies Hitler's middle-class childhood, his relationships, vegetarianism, rise to power and fall, as well as commenting on contemporary neo-Nazis, including members of the Aryan Nations organization, white power groups, and skinheads. A *Kirkus Reviews* contributor wrote that the volume "is so readable that it should hold younger readers and educate older ones who may need their brains refilled with the facts of history." *School Library Journal* reviewer Andrew Medlar described this volume as "a biography in the truest sense, this is a terrifying must for all libraries."

Giblin studies two famous brothers in *Good Brother, Bad Brother: The Story of Edwin Booth and John Wilkes*

Booth. Both brothers were actors, and Edwin was considered the most accomplished of his time, but although he is considered the "good" brother, he also suffered from severe alcoholism. John Wilkes, the "bad" brother, assassinated President Abraham Lincoln, but before that had been known as the happier and smarter of the brothers. Giblin follows the lives of the brothers through playbills, diaries, and photographs, as well as the writings of John Wilkes, penned before his capture. He notes the events that led to the assassination and John Wilkes's plans for aiding the Southern cause, an issue that divided the family. In reviewing *Good Brother, Bad Brother* for the *School Library Journal,* Jennifer Ralston wrote: "The writing is engaging and eminently readable, and presents history in a manner that is, in essence, consummate storytelling."

The Boy Who Saved Cleveland: Based on A True Story is a work of historical fiction that recounts how, in 1798, ten-year-old Seth Doan saved the tiny town of Cleveland, Ohio, consisting of just three log cabins, corn fields, and forest. The Doans had lost their other three sons, and they and their daughter, along with the other two families, were stricken with a form of malaria. By necessity, Seth handled all the chores without benefit of horse or mule and walked two miles each way to the mill, where he ground corn to keep his feverish family alive. He also did the same for the other families, in spite of the fact that he was also ill. *Booklist* reviewer Kay Weisman wrote that "this story feels like a natural extension of [Giblin's] highly respected nonfiction work."

Giblin has commented on the enjoyment that he derives from investigating the factual details of his subjects and how important this task is to his work. "I love research," the author told *Publishers Weekly* interviewer Wendy Smith. "I love going down to Washington on a vacation week and using the Library of Congress. I enjoy making things clear for readers—maybe 'clear' is a unifying word in my work as an author and editor."

BIOGRAPHICAL AND CRITICAL SOURCES:

BOOKS

Children's Literature Review, Volume 29, Thomson Gale (Detroit, MI), 1993.
Sixth Book of Junior Authors and Illustrators, H.W. Wilson (Bronx, NY), 1989.

Something about the Author Autobiography Series, Volume 12, Thomson Gale (Detroit, MI), 1991.

PERIODICALS

Booklist, December 1, 1996, Carolyn Phelan, review of *The Dwarf, The Giant, and the Unicorn: A Tale of King Arthur,* pp. 666-667; February 15, 2000, Ilene Cooper, review of *The Amazing Life of Benjamin Franklin,* p. 1105; March 1, 2000, Hazel Rochman, review of *The Century That Was: Reflections on the Last One Hundred Years,* p. 1235; April 1, 2002, Todd Morning, review of *The Life and Death of Adolph Hitler,* p. 1336; May 1, 2005, GraceAnne A. DeCandido, review of *Good Brother, Bad Brother: The Story of Edwin Booth and John Wilkes Booth,* p. 1586; April 15, 2006, Kay Weisman, review of *The Boy Who Saved Cleveland: Based on a True Story,* p. 58.

Bulletin of the Center for Children's Books, September, 1985, review of *The Truth about Santa Claus.*

Horn Book, November-December, 1990, Elizabeth S. Watson, review of *The Riddle of the Rosetta Stone: Key to Ancient Egypt,* p. 758; March, 2000, review of *The Century That Was,* p. 211, May-June, 2000, Mary M. Burns, review of *The Amazing Life of Benjamin Franklin,* p. 333; May-June, 2002, Peter D. Sieruta, review of *The Life and Death of Adolph Hitler,* p. 346; May-June, 2005, Betty Carter, review of *Good Brother, Bad Brother,* p. 349.

Kirkus Reviews, March 15, 2002, review of *The Life and Death of Adolph Hitler,* p. 411; May 1, 2005, review of *Good Brother, Bad Brother,* p. 539; March 1, 2006, review of *The Boy Who Saved Cleveland,* p. 229.

New York Times Book Review, March 12, 1989, Philip M. Isaacson, review of *Let There Be Light: A Book about Windows;* January 16, 1994, p. 20.

Publishers Weekly, July 26, 1985, Wendy Smith, "PW Interviews James Giblin," p. 169; November 11, 1996, review of *The Dwarf, the Giant, and the Unicorn,* p. 75; January 25, 1999, review of *The Mystery of the Mammoth Bones; And How It Was Solved,* p. 97; April 17, 2006, review of *The Boy Who Saved Cleveland,* p. 187.

School Library Journal, January, 1983, Amy L. Cohn, review of *Chimney Sweeps: Yesterday and Today,* p. 75; October, 1985, review of *The Truth about Santa Claus,* p. 192; May, 2002, Andrew Medlar, review of *The Life and Death of Adolph Hitler,* p. 170; April, 2005, review of *Secrets of the Sphinx,*

p. 42; May, 2005, Jennifer Ralston, review of *Good Brother, Bad Brother,* p. 150; May, 2006, Pat Peach, review of *The Boy Who Saved Cleveland,* p. 88.

Voice of Youth Advocates, October, 2000, Leah J. Sparks, review of *The Century That Was,* p. 285.*

*   *   *

GOODE, Diane 1949-
(Diane Capuozzo Goode)

PERSONAL: Born September 14, 1949, in Brooklyn, NY; daughter of Armand R. (a dentist) and Paule Capuozzo; married David A. Goode (an author and professor), May 26, 1973; children: Peter. *Education:* Attended École des Beaux Arts, Aix-en-Provence, France, 1971-72; Queens College of the City University of New York, B.F.A., 1972.

ADDRESSES: Home and office—Watchung, NJ. *E-mail*—goodedog@mac.com.

CAREER: Substitute teacher at public schools in New York, NY, 1972-73; children's book illustrator and writer, 1975—. University of California, Los Angeles, teacher of a studio workshop on children's book illustration, 1976-79; juror of competitions. *Exhibitions:* Work shown at Master Eagle Gallery, New York, NY, and represented in permanent collection of Kerlan Collection; exhibitor at museums, colleges, and libraries, including Metropolitan Museum of Art, 1982, Denver Public Library, 1985, Krasl Art Center, 1987, Mount Holyoke College Art Museum, 1991-92, and Cedar Rapids Museum of Art, 1998-2001.

AWARDS, HONORS: Award for illustration, Southern California Council on Literature for Children and Young People, 1976, for *The Selchie's Seed* and *Little Pieces of the West Wind,* and 1979, for *Dream Eater;* Caldecott honor book award, American Library Association, 1983, for *When I Was Young in the Mountains;* Parents' Choice Award, 1985, for *Watch the Stars Come Out,* and 1986, for *I Go with My Family to Grandma's;* included in *Redbook* list of top ten children's picture books and named *Reading Rainbow* feature selection, both 1985, for *Watch the Stars Come Out;* included among best children's books of the year, Child Study Children's Book Committee, 1987, for *I Go with My*

Family to Grandma's, and 1989, for *I Hear a Noise; Storytelling World* Award, 1998, for *Diane Goode's Book of Giants and Little People;* cited in picks of the list, *American Bookseller,* for *Where's Our Mama?, Diane Goode's American Christmas, The Diane Goode Book of American Folk Tales and Songs, Watch the Stars Come Out,* and *I Go with My Family to Grandma's;* included among notable children's trade books in the field of social studies, National Council of Social Studies and Children's Book Council, for *The Diane Goode Book of American Folk Tales and Songs, Watch the Stars Come Out, I Go with My Family to Grandma's,* and *When I Was Young in the Mountains;* notable book citation, American Library Association, for *Tattercoats: An Old English Tale, Watch the Stars Come Out,* and *When I Was Young in the Mountains;* Teachers' Choice award, National Council of Teachers of English, for *Watch the Stars Come Out* and *When I Was Young in the Mountains;* book of the year citation, Library of Congress, for *When I Was Young in the Mountains;* children's choice citation, International Reading Association and Children's Book Council, for *The Unicorn and the Plow.*

WRITINGS:

SELF-ILLUSTRATED

Diane Goode's Little Library of Christmas Classics (contains *The Nutcracker, Christmas Carols, The Fir Tree,* and *The Night before Christmas*), Random House (New York, NY), 1983.

I Hear a Noise, Dutton (New York, NY), 1988.

The Diane Goode Book of American Folk Tales and Songs, compiled by Ann Durell, Dutton (New York, NY), 1989.

Diane Goode's American Christmas, Dutton (New York, NY), 1990.

Where's Our Mama?, Dutton (New York, NY), 1991.

Diane Goode's Book of Silly Stories and Songs, Dutton (New York, NY), 1992.

Diane Goode's Christmas Magic: Poems and Carols, Random House (New York, NY), 1992.

The Little Books of Nursery Animals (contains *The Little Book of Cats, The Little Book of Farm Friends, The Little Book of Mice,* and *The Little Book of Pigs*), Dutton (New York, NY), 1993.

Diane Goode's Book of Scary Stories and Songs, Dutton (New York, NY), 1994.

Mama's Perfect Present, Dutton (New York, NY), 1996.

Diane Goode's Book of Giants and Little People, Dutton (New York, NY), 1997.

The Dinosaur's New Clothes, Blue Sky (New York, NY), 1999.

Cinderella, the Dog, and Her Little Glass Slipper, Blue Sky (New York, NY), 2000.

Tiger Trouble!, Blue Sky (New York, NY), 2001.

Monkey Mo Goes to Sea, Blue Sky (New York, NY), 2002.

Thanksgiving Is Here!, HarperCollins (New York, NY), 2003.

Mind Your Manners!, Farrar, Straus & Giroux (New York, NY), 2005.

The Most Perfect Spot, HarperCollins (New York, NY), 2006.

ILLUSTRATOR:

Christian Garrison, *Little Pieces of the West Wind,* Bradbury (Scarsdale, NY), 1975.

Shulamith Levey Oppenheim, *The Selchie's Seed,* Bradbury (Scarsdale, NY), 1975, revised edition, Harcourt (New York, NY), 1996.

Christian Garrison, *Flim and Flam and the Big Cheese,* Bradbury (Scarsdale, NY), 1976.

Flora Annie Steele, *Tattercoats: An Old English Tale,* Bradbury (Scarsdale, NY), 1976.

(And translator) Madame de Beaumont, *Beauty and the Beast,* Bradbury (Scarsdale, NY), 1978.

Christian Garrison, *The Dream Eater,* Bradbury (Scarsdale, NY), 1978.

Emoeke de Papp Severo, translator, *The Good-Hearted Youngest Brother,* Bradbury (Scarsdale, NY), 1981.

Louise Moeri, *The Unicorn and the Plow,* Dutton (New York, NY), 1982.

Cynthia Rylant, *When I Was Young in the Mountains,* Dutton (New York, NY), 1982.

J.M. Barrie, *Peter Pan,* edited by Josette Frank, Random House (New York, NY), 1983.

Carlo Collodi, *The Adventures of Pinocchio,* Random House (New York, NY), 1983.

Amy Ehrlich, adaptor, *The Random House Book of Fairy Tales,* Random House (New York, NY), 1985.

Riki Levinson, *Watch the Stars Come Out,* Dutton (New York, NY), 1985.

Deborah Hautzig, *The Story of the Nutcracker Ballet,* Random House (New York, NY), 1986.

Riki Levinson, *I Go with My Family to Grandma's,* Dutton (New York, NY), 1986.

Julian Hawthorne, reteller, *Rumpty-Dudget's Tower,* Knopf (New York, NY), 1987.

(And translator) Charles Perrault, *Cinderella,* Knopf (New York, NY), 1988.

Noel Streatfeild, *Ballet Shoes,* Random House (New York, NY), 1991.

Noel Streatfeild, *Theater Shoes,* Random House (New York, NY), 1994.

Lloyd Alexander, *The House Gobbaleen,* Dutton (New York, NY), 1995.

Robert Louis Stevenson, *A Child's Garden of Verses,* Morrow (New York, NY), 1998.

Cynthia Rylant, *Christmas in the Country,* Blue Sky (New York, NY), 2002.

Margaret Wise Brown, *Christmas in the Barn,* HarperCollins (New York, NY), 2004.

Cynthia Ryland, *Alligator Boy,* Harcourt (New York, NY), 2007.

Also illustrator of many record album covers and book covers.

Watch the Stars Come Out was translated into Spanish.

SIDELIGHTS: Diane Goode is an award-winning author-illustrator of children's books best known for her anthologies of folktales and songs. She has also paired her illustrations with the writings of other authors.

"When I was a child I loved books and art," Goode once told *CA.* "Reading allowed me to escape into the reality of others, and drawing let me create my own. My father was of Italian descent, and my mother was French. My brother and I enjoyed the richness of both cultures. We traveled to Europe every summer from the time we were infants, visiting family and the great cathedrals and museums of the world. These early impressions helped shape my appreciation for life and art. I was bedazzled by Michelangelo's 'Descent from the Cross.' Could marble be warm and luminous? Could monumental forms be at once tender and powerful? Man's creative ability seemed staggering. I saw the works of Da Vinci, Rembrandt, Botticelli, Lautrec, Monet, Manet, Cézanne, and all the great artists. I was awestruck. I was in love with art!

"I have been drawing ever since I can remember, but my formal education began at Queens College in art history. I soon switched to fine arts, where I tried my hand at everything: drawing, painting, sculpture, etching, and color theory. I took a year off to study in France. It was an artist's dream.

"After graduating, I taught high school for a year, putting together a portfolio at night. In my blissful ignorance of publishing, I had decided to illustrate children's books. It was just as well that I was so naive, or else I would have been too afraid to try. As luck would have it, I was contracted to illustrate my first picture book in 1973. I was twenty-four then and knew nothing at all about commercial art. Since I was living in California, my New York publisher taught me color separation over the phone!"

An early award-winner for Goode was *The Selchie's Seed,* by Shulamith Oppenheim. The success of that work acted as an encouragement to Goode in her craft and an entry to future illustrating for other authors and publishers. With the boxed set *Diane Goode's Little Library of Christmas Classics,* Goode lends her artist's vision to some of the most popular Christmas tales. "This small, gaily decorated slipcase holds four books that Goode has illustrated in extremely pretty, full-color, animated holiday scenes," noted a reviewer for *Publishers Weekly.* George A. Woods observed in the *New York Times* that the "star of this package . . . is Diane Goode, whose illustrations lend just the right accompanying note to each book."

Goode delights in retelling and illustrating oft-told tales and verses, and many critics delight in her resulting efforts. Her adaptation of Julian Hawthorne's *Rumpty Dudget's Tower* brought praise from Jeanne Marie Clancy in *School Library Journal:* "Goode's colorful cross-hatched illustrations for her adaptation enhance the story and capture the spirit of the characters, especially the mischievous Rumpty-Dudget." A *Booklist* reviewer commented that the "beauty and wit of Goode's well-composed artwork will draw readers into the rather old-fashioned tale." *Horn Book* contributor Margaret A. Bush concluded that Goode's "fine execution of both text and illustration breathes new life into the old story, making it freshly accessible as an old-fashioned fairy tale, eminently suited for reading aloud." Goode's illustrations have also been credited with attractively interpreting Robert Louis Stevenson's collection *A Child's Garden of Verses. School Library Journal* critic Robin L. Gibson observed that the artist "applies her characteristically charming illustrations to Stevenson's poems with appealing results." Gibson also noted that Goode "captures the exuberance of childhood in many pictures."

"All of my work is done on opaline parchment," Goode told *CA.* "I sketch lightly in pencil and use watercolors applied with very fine sable brushes. Sometimes I use color pencil with the paint to soften the atmosphere. I always begin with several rough dummies and then work on the individual pages, sketching very loosely and fast to establish movement and composition. I do these dozens of times, repositioning, enlarging, reducing, adding, and omitting. There are always hundreds of sketches for each book. It sounds tedious, but it is the most exciting part of creating the book."

Goode began creating her own self-illustrated books in 1988 with the publication of *I Hear a Noise.* A reviewer for *Junior Bookshelf* deemed the debut "a joyously funny book," summarizing: "In its high spirits, its high humour, the book is entirely original." Goode tells the story without narrative, employing only dialogue and artwork to address the familiar fear of bedtime fiends. Like many little boys, the hero, lying in bed, complains that he hears a noise. While his mother tries to comfort him, a green dragon swoops in, snatches them, and flies off with both in tow. Back at its castle, the monster's siblings argue over these human trophies. Until, that is, their mother steps in, insisting that the captives be returned to their home. "Goode . . . puts an amusing new twist on the well-worn subject of monsters at bedtime," noted a *Kirkus Reviews* contributor. A reviewer for *Booklist* called Goode's first book a "gloriously spine-tingling thriller." "Goode's engagingly expressive creatures . . .," concluded the critic, "will leave youngsters clamoring for yet one more read of this soft-edged, bedtime chiller."

After launching her writing career, Goode began focusing much of her creative energy on anthologies. She wrote and illustrated volumes of folktales and silly stories, and in *Diane Goode's Book of Scary Stories and Songs* she tackles tales featuring ghosts and goblins from around the world. *Horn Book* correspondent Nancy Vasilakis dubbed the book a "welcome addition to the Halloween or storytelling shelves." A *Publishers Weekly* reviewer, noting that the funny stories "are rather tame," assured readers that the book "will be appreciated more for its rich multicultural flavor than for its fright value." In *Diane Goode's Book of Giants and Little People,* the author-illustrator deals with the theme of the "triumph of a small but clever hero over a gigantic adversary," according to *Booklist* reviewer Julie Corsaro. Working once again with tall tales and folktales from around the world, Goode puts together a smorgasbord of stories. Corsaro noted that "Goode's elegant watercolors bring it all together, her appealing cartoon-style art displaying a penchant for the compelling contrast between big and small." A *Publishers Weekly* contributor felt that her stories of giants and little people added to Goode's "stable of stellar collections." "With this blithely spirited book," concluded the reviewer, "Goode has done it again . . . and that's no exaggeration."

Goode's French heritage and travels proved essential to the creation of two further books, *Where's Our Mama* and *Mama's Perfect Present.* In the first title, two children have become separated from their mother at the Gare d'Orsay train station in Paris. Aided by a kindly French *gendarme,* the brother and sister set out to find their beautiful mother, treking from one place to the next. The reader all the while sees the mother in one corner of a crowded page, and finally the children see her as well. Set earlier in the century, *Where's Our Mama* was written in tribute to Goode's own mother. A writer for *Kirkus Reviews* observed that the book is reminiscent of a Russian folktale and called it "a charming transformation of a story that deftly dramatizes the child's-eye view of a most important person." *Horn Book* contributor Mary M. Burns concluded her review by stating that "the book is as gallic as a shrug, as logical as Pascal, and as winning as a song by Maurice Chevalier. A witty, wonderful production. *C'est magnifique!*"

"Mayhem? Mais Oui! The rosy-cheeked children who searched Paris high and low in *Where's Our Mama?* are back," celebrated a *Publishers Weekly* review of *Mama's Perfect Present.* Now accompanied by their dachshund, Zaza, who leaves destruction in its wake, the siblings are searching for the perfect birthday gift for their beloved mother. Not surprisingly, each place they visit is also visited with chaos as a result of their rambunctious dog. A *Publishers Weekly* reviewer promised that this sequel "will leave young readers chuckling at Zaza's exploits and everyone else chuckling an appreciative ooh-la-la." Mary M. Burns observed in *Horn Book:* "This is a true picture story, with the understated text serving as a straight-faced, innocent commentary on the action, which is visualized through careful manipulation of line, deft shading, and delicate hatching." In a *Booklist* starred review, Ilene Cooper commented that "the story is clever and full of fun, but it is really the pictures that make this come alive."

In *The Dinosaur's New Clothes,* Goode gave a Hans Christian Andersen classic "a prehistoric makeover," according to a *Publishers Weekly* contributor. Goode parodies the original royals with a gaggle of pompadoured dinosaurs holding court at Versailles. In this palace, a Tyrannosaurus rex—*king* of all dinosaurs—stars as the clothes-horse emperor of Andersen's original. "It's all good silly fun," concluded the reviewer, "a light parody of Andersen's send-up of gullibility and greed."

Goode's often humorous work is grounded in a private life that provides the author with the necessary stability and lightness. "I've been married since 1973," Goode once told *CA.* "Our son Peter was born in 1978 and is a fine artist already. I often rely on him to read manuscripts for an opinion and critique of my work. He has helped me see the world through a child's eyes.

"We have lived in four states and have had many small pets along the way: parrots, love birds, hamsters, cats, and mice. We've settled in Watchung, New Jersey, and each day we are visited by wild deer, raccoons, rabbits, hedgehogs, a pheasant, and an owl. We now have a Welsh Corgi named Katie and a big yellow Lab named Jack. We love to travel in France, and we love to cook. I still read as much as I can. I listen to books on tape as I paint.

"Working in the field of children's literature has been a great joy. How lucky to be able to do the work I love and also contribute in some small way to the lives of our children. How lucky to find in my work the two things I've cherished since childhood: art and books."

More recently Goode told *CA:* "My books are usually characterized by delicate, detailed paintings. A few years ago my art director told me that she loved the rough preliminary drawings from my dummies and suggested that I use them as the final art for *Monkey Mo Goes to Sea.* I loved the idea. I always felt pure line captures energy and emotion like nothing else.

"Regardless of technique, I do intensive background research, at least six dummies, and countless preliminary drawings for every book. The trick is to keep the freshness of the original drawings as I work through revision after revision.

"I begin by laying out the text, quickly and roughly sketching the story from start to finish in one sitting. I then go back and work on individual pages, always relating each to the one before, the one following, and to the story as a whole. I do this on architect's tissue, and I tape the rough sketches to layout spreads that are painted on my studio walls. I can see the entire book at a glance, and I can easily play with the pagination by moving the taped pieces around.

"Still on the wall, I work the composition by tearing up and taping sections of the sketches to get the best balance between text and illustration. The text is also printed, cut out, and can be easily moved around the pages with tape. The play between text and illustration is critical. I try numerous layouts until I come to what I think gives me the best possible pacing for the story. Every time I think I have a viable dummy, I print out the version in dummy-book form to get a sense of turning the pages.

"After choosing the best dummy, I develop and finalize the individual illustrations in either pen and ink or pencil. I then print out the final line drawings on a heavy-stock watercolor paper. After experimenting with various color palettes, I hand-paint each one with gouache and watercolor.

"When you depend on pure line for expression, the slightest variation in length or thickness of the line of the mouth, the angle of an eyebrow, the sweep of a tail, the pose of a foot, changes the mood of the entire illustration. I often do the same small character over and over until the line is right, until I can just dash it off and it seems to come alive. My theme for this style is 'less is more.'

"In a successful picture book, illustration and text should move together like perfectly attuned partners in a dance. The illustrations not only support, but can serve as a counterpoint to the text. If I've done it right, the effort should not be evident; it should look easy and natural. It's an exciting process."

BIOGRAPHICAL AND CRITICAL SOURCES:

PERIODICALS

Booklist, January 15, 1988, review of *Rumpty Dudget's Tower,* p. 862; December 1, 1988, review of *I Hear a Noise,* pp. 647-648; October 1, 1994, p. 321; July, 1996, Ilene Cooper, review of *Mama's Perfect Present,* p. 1824; September 15, 1997, Julie Corsaro, review of *Diane Goode's Book of Giants and Little People,* p. 237.

Bulletin of the Center for Children's Books, September, 1991, review of *Where's Our Mama?,* p. 10; December, 1996, review of *Mama's Perfect Present,* p. 136.

Five Owls, September-October, 1991, review of *Where's Our Mama?,* p. 9.

Horn Book, March-April, 1988, Margaret A. Bush, review of *Rumpty Dudget's Tower,* pp. 199-200; September-October, 1988, Margaret A. Bush, review of *I Hear a Noise,* p. 615; November-December, 1991, Mary M. Burns, review of *Where's Our Mama?,* pp. 727-728; September-October, 1992, Nancy Vasilakis, review of *Diane Goode's Book of Silly Stories and Songs,* p. 592; January-February, 1995, Nancy Vasilakis, review of *Diane Goode's Book of Scary Stories and Songs,* p. 75; November-December, 1996, Mary M. Burns, review of *Mama's Perfect Present,* pp. 723-724.

Junior Bookshelf, April, 1989, review of *I Hear a Noise,* p. 61; June, 1992, review of *Where's Our Mama?,* p. 102.

Kirkus Reviews, July 1, 1988, review of *I Hear a Noise,* p. 973; August 1, 1991, review of *Where's Our Mama?,* p. 1010.

New York Times, December 4, 1983, George A. Woods, review of *Diane Goode's Little Library of Christmas Classics,* pp. 77-79.

New York Times Book Review, April 19, 1992, review of *Where's Our Mama?,* p. 16; January 19, 1997, review of *Mama's Perfect Present,* p. 24.

Publishers Weekly, September 2, 1983, review of *Diane Goode's Little Library of Christmas Classics,* p. 80; July 29, 1988, Kimberly Olson Fakih and Diane Roback, review of *I Hear a Noise,* p. 230; June 29, 1992, review of *Diane Goode's Book of Silly Stories and Songs,* p. 61; September 7, 1992, Elizabeth Devereaux, review of *Diane Goode's Christmas Magic,* p. 67; July 4, 1994, review of *Diane Goode's Book of Scary Stories and Songs,* p. 60; September 2, 1996, review of *Mama's Perfect Present,* p. 129; July 28, 1997, review of *Diane Goode's Book of Giants and Little People,* p. 73; June 28, 1999, review of *The Dinosaur's New Clothes,* p. 78.

School Library Journal, January, 1988, Jeanne Marie Clancy, review of *Rumpty Dudget's Tower,* p. 66; February, 1989, Trev Jones, review of *I Hear a Noise,* p. 69; September, 1992, Heide Piehler, review of *Diane Goode's Book of Silly Stories and Songs,* p. 215; September, 1994, Beth Tegart, review of *Diane Goode's Book of Scary Stories and Songs,* p. 207; September, 1996, Wendy Lukeheart, review of *Mama's Perfect Present,* p. 178; November, 1997, Jeanne Clancy Watkins, review of *Diane Goode's Book of Giants and Little People,* p. 107; January, 1999, Robin L. Gibson, review of *A Child's Garden of Verses,* p. 121.

Washington Post Book World, February 9, 1992, review of *Where's Our Mama?,* p. 11.

*   *   *

GOODE, Diane Capuozzo
    See GOODE, Diane

*   *   *

GREENHOUSE, Linda 1947-

PERSONAL: Born January 9, 1947, in New York, NY; daughter of H. Robert (a physician) and Dorothy Greenhouse; married Eugene R. Fidell (an attorney). *Education:* Radcliffe College, B.A., 1968; Yale University, M.S.L., 1978.

CAREER: Writer, journalist, educator, and lecturer. *New York Times,* New York, NY, assistant to James Reston, 1968-69, local staff member, 1969-73, local political staff member, 1974—, state legislative bureau chief, 1976-77, U.S. Supreme Court correspondent, 1978—. State University of New York at Albany, Phi Beta Kappa Visiting Scholar, 2006. Practicing Law Institute, faculty member. Frequent lecturer at colleges, universities, and law schools throughout the United States. Guest on television programs, including PBS's *Washington Week in Review,* the *Charlie Rose Show,* and *Dennis Miller.*

MEMBER: American Academy of Arts and Sciences (fellow, 1994—), American Philosophical Society, Yale Law Association (member of executive committee), American Law Institute (honorary member).

AWARDS, HONORS: Ford Foundation fellowship for journalists at Yale Law School, 1977-78; John Peter Zenger Special Media Award, New York State Bar Association, 1993; Pulitzer Prize, 1998, for excellence in reporting on the Supreme Court beat; Goldsmith Career Award for Excellence in Journalism, Shorenstein Center on the Press, Politics, and Public Policy at the John F. Kennedy School of Government at Harvard University, 2004, for her work as the *New York Times*'s Supreme Court correspondent; Radcliffe Institute Medal, Radcliffe Institute for Advanced Study, Harvard University, 2006; Henry Friendly Medal, American Law Institute; John Chancellor Award for Excellence in Journalism, Annenberg School, University of Pennsylvania.

WRITINGS:

Becoming Justice Blackmun: Harry Blackmun's Supreme Court Journey, Time Books/Henry Holt (New York, NY), 2005.

SIDELIGHTS: Writer and journalist Linda Greenhouse is a *New York Times* reporter who won the Pulitzer Prize in 1998 for her coverage of the U.S. Supreme Court. She is the author of *Becoming Justice Blackmun: Harry Blackmun's Supreme Court Journey,* an in-depth biography of U.S. Supreme Court Justice Harry Blackmun, a noted jurist whose work left a strong legacy in the Supreme Court and had profound effects on U.S. society as well. Blackmun was appointed to the Supreme Court in 1970 by President Richard M. Nixon. When he took his position on the court, Blackmun was expected to vote along conservative lines, in tandem with his lifelong friend, Chief Justice Warren Berger. At first, Blackmun and Berger's judicial opinions and philosophies did coincide. However, over the years Blackmun's attitudes evolved until he became one of the court's more liberal justices. For example, Blackmun once supported the death penalty. Greenhouse notes that he became more disdainful of capital punishment with each term, until he was able to completely denounce it as unconstitutional by the time of his retirement in 1994. Blackmun was personally chosen by Berger to write the majority opinion in the landmark abortion case Roe v. Wade. Greenhouse notes that this judicial opinion marked the beginning of an ideological rift between the two lifelong friends. Blackmun's evolving ideology, staunch support of Roe v. Wade, and changing opinions on everything from poverty to women's rights eventually caused irreversible damage to his six-decade friendship with Berger. Greenhouse delves deeply into archival records, vast collections of personal papers, a lengthy oral history recorded by the justice, and other primary documents to assemble a detailed portrait of Blackmun's personal and professional life. Blackmun's "judicial trek is simply and gracefully told" by Greenhouse, commented Gordon Turiff in the *Advocate.*

Greenhouse portrays Blackmun as a "self-effacing and scholarly judge, devoid of partisanship, willing to follow his ideas wherever they led him," commented a *Publishers Weekly* reviewer. A *Kirkus Reviews* critic described the book as being "detailed and well considered: a welcome study of Blackmun's contributions to the law." Turiff called Greenhouse's work "an important book, important for the lesson it teaches us that we are all capable of change and for the reminder that we resist change at the risk of intellectual dishonesty and emotional turmoil."

BIOGRAPHICAL AND CRITICAL SOURCES:

PERIODICALS

Advocate, September, 2005, Gordon Turiff, review of *Becoming Justice Blackmun: Harry Blackmun's Supreme Court Journey,* p. 765.

America, October 17, 2005, Mary Meehan, "One of Nine," review of *Becoming Justice Blackmun,* p. 24.

American Prospect, September, 2005, Stanley I. Kutler, "The Conservative as Liberal," review of *Becoming Justice Blackmun,* p. 38.

Booklist, May 15, 2005, Vernon Ford, review of *Becoming Justice Blackmun,* p. 1619.

Commentary, July-August, 2005, Ken I. Kersch, "Wild about Harry," review of *Becoming Justice Blackmun,* p. 69.

Florida Bar Journal, February, 2006, C.D. Rogers, review of *Becoming Justice Blackmun,* p. 44.

Kirkus Reviews, March 15, 2005, review of *Becoming Justice Blackmun,* p. 333.

National Review, August 8, 2005, Robert P. George, "Wild about Harry," review of *Becoming Justice Blackmun,* p. 47.

Publishers Weekly, April 11, 2005, review of *Becoming Justice Blackmun,* p. 45.

Trial, February, 2006, Robert S. Peck, review of *Becoming Justice Blackmun,* p. 71.

Washington Monthly, July-August, 2005, Stephen Pomper, "Blackmun's Drift: Linda Greenhouse Charts, but Doesn't Explain, How a Conservative Judge Came to Write Roe v. Wade," review of *Becoming Justice Blackmun,* p. 58.

ONLINE

American Law Institute Web site, http://www.ali.org/ (January 2, 2007), "Anthony Lewis and Linda Greenhouse Become First Nonlawyers to Receive Institute's Henry Friendly Medal."

Bookreporter.com, http://www.bookreporter.com/ (January 2, 2007), Stuart Shiffman, review of *Becoming Justice Blackmun.*

Harvard University Radcliffe Institute for Advanced Study Web site, http://www.radcliffe.edu/ (June 8, 2006), "Linda Greenhouse '68 Wins 2006 Radcliffe Institute Medal."

Internet Movie Database, http://www.imdb.com/ (January 2, 2007), filmography of Linda Greenhouse.

Pulitzer Prize Web site, http://www.pulitzer.org/ (January 2, 2007).

State University of New York at Albany Web site, http://www.albany.edu/ (January 2, 2007), "Linda Greenhouse, Pulitzer Prize-winning *New York Times* Supreme Court Journalist, to Speak on 'Court, Country, and Culture.'"

Timeswatch.org, http://www.timeswatch.org/ (September 27, 2006), Clay Waters, "NPR Reporter Stunned at Linda Greenhouse Speech."*

*   *   *

GURA, Philip F. 1950-
(Philip Francis Gura)

PERSONAL: Born June 14, 1950, in Ware, MA; son of Oswald Eugene and Stephanie R. Gura; married Leslie Ann Cohig, August 4, 1979; children: David Austin, Katherine Blair, Daniel Alden. *Ethnicity:* "Caucasian." *Education:* Harvard University, A.B. (magna cum laude), 1972, Ph.D., 1977.

ADDRESSES: Home—Chapel Hill, NC. *Office*—Department of English, University of North Carolina, Chapel Hill, NC 27599-3520. *E-mail*—gura@email.unc.edu.

CAREER: Writer, historian, and educator. Middlebury College, Middlebury, VT, instructor in American literature, 1974-76; University of Colorado, Boulder, assistant professor, 1976-80, associate professor of English, 1980-85, director of American studies, 1978-80, director of graduate studies, 1981-85, professor of English and American Studies, 1985-87; University of North Carolina, Chapel Hill, professor of English and Adjunct Professor of American studies, 1987-98, professor of English and American Studies and Adjunct Professor of Religious Studies, 1998-2000, William S. Newman Distinguished Professor of American Literature and Culture, 2000—, adjunct professor of religious studies. Fellow, Charles Warren Center for Studies in American History, Harvard University, 1980-81; senior fellow, National Endowment for the Humanities, Institute of Early American History and Culture, Williamsburg, VA, 1985-86, member of national council, 1991-94; Peterson fellow, American Antiquarian Society, 1989, 1998, 2002-03.

MEMBER: Modern Language Association of America, Colonial Society of Massachusetts, American Antiquarian Society, Massachusetts Historical Society (corresponding member, 1996).

AWARDS, HONORS: Norman Foerster Prize in American Literature, Modern Language Association of America, 1977, for "Thoreau's Maine Woods Indians: More Representative Men"; Chancellor's Writing Award, University of Colorado, 1985; Faculty Fellowship, Council on Research and Creative Work, University of Colorado, 1985-86; Kate B. and Hall J. Peterson Fellowships, American Antiquarian Society, 1989, 1998, and 2002-03; Frances Densmore Prize, American Musical Instrument Society, 1996; Award of Merit, Society of Early Americanists, 2000; ASCAP-Deems Taylor Special Citation, 2000, for *America's Instrument;* University Post-Baccalaureate Distinguished Teaching Award, University of North Carolina at Chapel Hill, 2004; James Russell Wiggins Lecturer, American Antiquarian Society, 2004; Andrew W. Mellon Distinguished Scholar in Residence, American Antiquarian Society, 2006-07.

WRITINGS:

The Wisdom of Words: Language, Theology, and Literature in the New England Renaissance, Wesleyan University Press (Middletown, CT), 1981.
(Editor, with Joel Myerson) *Critical Essays on American Transcendentalism,* G.K. Hall (Boston, MA), 1982.
A Glimpse of Sion's Glory: Puritan Radicalism in New England, 1620-1660, Wesleyan University Press (Middletown, CT), 1983.
(Editor) *Memoirs of Stephen Burroughs,* Northeastern University Press (Boston, MA), 1988.
Early Nineteenth-Century Painting in Rural Massachusetts: John Howe of Greenwich and Enfield, c. 1803-1845, with a Transcription of His "Printer's Book," c. 1832, American Antiquarian Society (Worcester, MA), 1991.

The Crossroads of American History and Literature, Penn State University Press (University Park, PA), 1996.
(With James F. Bollman) *America's Instrument: The Banjo in the Nineteenth Century,* University of North Carolina Press (Chapel Hill, NC), 1999.
(Editor) *Buried from the World: Inside the Massachusetts State Prison, 1829-31, The Memorandum Books of the Rev. Jared Curtis,* Massachusetts Historical Society (Boston, MA), 2001.
(Editor, with others) *The Norton Anthology of American Literature, Sixth Edition,* W.W. Norton (New York, NY), 2002, 7th edition, 2007.
C.F. Martin and His Guitars, 1796-1873, University of North Carolina Press (Chapel Hill, NC), 2003.
Jonathan Edwards: America's Evangelical, Hill and Wang (New York, NY), 2005.

English Language Notes, member of editorial board, 1977-85; *Early American Literature,* member of editorial board, 1984-87, associate editor, 1987-89, editor, 1989-99, advisory editor, 1999—; *American Literature,* member of editorial board, 1989-93; *William and Mary Quarterly,* member of editorial board, 1991-94; *American Periodicals,* member of advisory board, 1992—; *A History of the Book in America,* member of editorial board, 1992—; *Book History,* member of advisory board, 1997—; *Reencounters with Colonialism: New Perspectives on the Americas,* advisory editor, 1997-2002.

Contributor to literature and history journals, including *American Literature, Virginia Quarterly, Yale Review,* and *Sewanee Review.*

Contributor to books, including *American Writers before 1800: A Biographical and Critical Dictionary,* edited by James A. Levernier and Douglas Wilmes, Greenwood Press (Westport, CT), 1983; and *Henry David Thoreau: Modern Critical Views,* edited by Harold Bloom, Chelsea House (New York, NY), 1987. Associate editor, 1987-89, editor, 1989-99, *Early American Literature.*

SIDELIGHTS: In *The Wisdom of Words: Language, Theology, and Literature in the New England Renaissance,* Philip F. Gura examines the cultural context out of which American literary symbolism emerged in the decades before the Civil War. Gura focuses on religion and language theory in the first section of the book, while in the latter chapters he discusses the works of such writers as Ralph Waldo Emerson, Henry David

Thoreau, and Herman Melville. In the *Journal of American History,* Robert D. Richardson, Jr., wrote that "the integrity of [Gura's] study lies in its fidelity to the issues and judgments of the period about which he is writing. Thus his work is solid and will last, and his readers are free to make their own connections with the present."

Gura continues his examination of New England history in *A Glimpse of Sion's Glory: Puritan Radicalism in New England, 1620-1660.* In this work, Gura asserts that the Puritans were not as ideologically homogeneous as some historians have suggested and that there were, in fact, numerous acts of dissent committed by Puritan radicals. Divided into three sections, *A Glimpse of Sion's Glory* catalogs the various types of Puritan dissent, discusses the response of the Puritan establishment to radical thinkers, and provides case studies of three radicals: Anne Hutchinson, Samuel Gorton, and William Pynchon. In the *American Historical Review,* Theodore Dwight Bozeman stated that "Gura displays the most thorough and integrated knowledge of New England dissent from 1620 to 1660 yet attained by any historian." Pauline Maier, writing in the *New York Times Book Review,* also offered praise for *A Glimpse of Sion's Glory:* "[Gura's] book is an evocative account of the 17th century; so sustained a work of intelligence and human sensitivity is always a rare achievement."

A practicing musician who plays clawhammer banjo in fiddle contests around the southeastern United States, Gura dedicates a pair of books to the history and development of two ubiquitous American stringed instruments, the banjo and the guitar. In *America's Instrument: The Banjo in the Nineteenth Century,* Gura and collaborator James F. Bollman, a prominent banjo collector, produce a work that "is and will remain the definitive history of the production, advertisement, and distribution of the banjo in nineteenth-century America," commented Chris Goertzen in *Notes.* Gura provides an overview of existing scholarship on the origins of the banjo, particularly its origins in long-necked stringed instruments from Africa. He looks at how the production of the banjo evolved and how access to and innovation on the instrument expanded with mass production and greater availability. The author profiles some early entrepreneurs who helped broaden banjo usage, availability, and respectability, including S.S. Stewart. Gura also explores how innovations in design and materials led to great improvements in the instrument's quality in the latter part of the nineteenth century. "The book is so dense in its documentation and technological

detail that few apart from banjo lovers will read it from cover to cover," Goertzen noted, but he also concluded: "This study, while groundbreaking in its coverage of manufacturing, decoration, and advertising, is also so thorough that I cannot imagine it ever making sense to redo it."

Gura charts the history of another popular stringed instrument in *C.F. Martin and His Guitars, 1796-1873.* Martin is one of the most stable and sturdy brands of guitar, and various types of Martins are used and cherished by specialists in music genres ranging from folk to bluegrass to modern rock. With his book, Gura "has written the early history of the company from correspondence, invoices, company records and letters from performers and simple customers alike," noted *Sing Out!* reviewer Tom Druckenmiller. "Gura has interpreted the sources and drawn them together into a fascinating narrative that will inform anyone interested not just in the guitar or guitar making, but in nineteenth-century American musical life and commerce in general," observed Gary R. Boye in *Notes.* The history also contains a great deal of biographical and business information on the company's founder, Christian Frederick Martin. Gura "delves into a side of American musical history and of the guitar that is almost totally unexplored, and gives us a portrait of a master craftsman and businessman," commented Boye. Gura "has truly created a book, which can be enjoyed on a number of different levels," Druckenmiller remarked, from aficionados seeking photographs of early guitars, to historians interested in musical life during the mid-1800s, to students of business and marketing looking for insights into how the Martin company has remained strong and competitive for almost two centuries. Gura's "presentation and observations, based on his research of the materials loaned to him by Martin as well as other historical records, present a picture and put Martin in a context which cannot be achieved simply by observation and study of the instruments themselves," noted George Gruhn in the *Folk Music Journal.* Boye concluded that Gura's book is a "model of archival research and is finely written and thoroughly documented."

Jonathan Edwards: America's Evangelical is Gura's biography of Edwards, considered by many to be America's most influential theologian. As a pastor, writer, philosopher, and revivalist, Edwards also espoused many ideas that were controversial during the time of his career during the middle 1700s. Edwards was a devout Calvinist, a preacher who delivered sermons declaring everyone guilty of original sin, that the only virtue man can aspire to is love of God, and that whether or not someone goes to Hell is not based on good deeds or even salvation, but on a predestined fate already determined by God at the individual's creation. Conversely, Edwards also preached a softer, more emotional approach to God and religion, stressing the emotional aspects of experiencing God and the personal experience of loving God. Gura looks carefully at some of Edwards's more famous sermons, including the well-known "Sinners in the Hands of an Angry God" sermon. He recounts Edwards's early years, his studies at Yale University, his conflict with the Northampton church (that dismissed him as pastor) and with the Williams family (relatives all), his fiery career as a preacher and theologian, and his final position as Princeton University's third president. The author delineates Edwards's position within the Great Awakening, a period of intense religious revival in 1734-35, and sees Edwards's convincing preaching and religious dedication as the "beginning of the great tradition of American evangelicalism," commented a *Kirkus Reviews* critic. Edwards, stated Daniel Sullivan in the *Weekly Standard,* was "uniquely attuned to the psychology of [religious] conversion, and his endless revolution against spiritual complacency, with its anxiety as well as its hope, still agitates the American psyche." Gura "helpfully explains Edwards's special place in American literary history," noted Gerald R. McDermott in *History: Review of New Books.* A *Publishers Weekly* critic concluded that "Gura's brilliant cultural history of Edwards and his times splendidly reveals a side of the evangelist that has often been overlooked."

BIOGRAPHICAL AND CRITICAL SOURCES:

PERIODICALS

American Historical Review, April, 1985, Theodore Dwight Bozeman, review of *A Glimpse of Sion's Glory,* p. 478.

Booklist, February 15, 2005, Gilbert Taylor, review of *Jonathan Edwards: America's Evangelical,* p. 1038.

Books & Culture, September-October, 2005, Allen Guelzo, "Unpalatable to Modern Sensibilities," review of *Jonathan Edwards,* p. 16.

Christianity and Literature, summer, 2006, Michael G. Ditmore, review of *Jonathan Edwards,* p. 595.

Folk Music Journal, annual 2005, George Gruhn, review of *C.F. Martin & His Guitars, 1796-1873,* p. 651.

History: Review of New Books, winter, 2006, Gerald R. McDermott, review of *Jonathan Edwards,* p. 45.

Journal of American History, June, 1982, Robert D. Richardson, Jr., review of *The Wisdom of Words.*

Kirkus Reviews, December 15, 2004, review of *Jonathan Edwards,* p. 1182.

Library Journal, August, 2003, Eric C. Shoaf, review of *C.F. Martin & His Guitars, 1796-1873,* p. 86; March 1, 2005, George Westerlund, review of *Jonathan Edwards,* p. 90.

New York Times Book Review, April 1, 1984, Pauline Maier, review of *A Glimpse of Sion's Glory,* p. 21.

Notes, March, 2001, Chris Goertzen, review of *America's Instrument,* p. 604; September, 2004, Gary R. Boye, review of *C.F. Martin & His Guitars, 1796-1873,* p. 147.

Philadelphia Inquirer, March 30, 2005, Carlin Romano, "In Jonathan Edwards' Footsteps Right to Terri Schiavo's Hospice," review of *Jonathan Edwards: America's Evangelical.*

Publishers Weekly, January 24, 2005, review of *Jonathan Edwards,* p. 237.

Sing Out!, spring, 2004, Tom Druckenmiller, review of *C.F. Martin and His Guitars, 1796-1873,* p. 104.

Weekly Standard, March 21, 2005, Daniel Sullivan, "The Heart Specialist: The American Mind Owes a Lot to Jonathan Edwards," review of *Jonathan Edwards,* p. 35.

ONLINE

University of North Carolina, Chapel Hill, http://english.unc.edu/ (January 2, 2007), biography of Philip F. Gura.*

*   *   *

GURA, Philip Francis
   See GURA, Philip F.

H

HAGER, Alan 1940-

PERSONAL: Born February 18, 1940, in New York, NY; son of Read (a banker) and Louisa (a journalist and publicity director) Hager; married Laura Stortoni (a poet and professor of Italian), April 19, 1965 (divorced May 8, 1976); married Carol A. Burke (a financial and investment executive), August 6, 1977 (divorced March 8, 1999); children: (second marriage) Stephen Read, Louisa Wilson. *Ethnicity:* "Caucasian." *Education:* Harvard University, B.A., 1962; attended Sorbonne, University of Paris, 1962-63; University of California, Berkeley, M.A., 1970, Ph.D., 1978. *Politics:* "Wishy-washy Democrat." *Religion:* Episcopalian. *Hobbies and other interests:* All racket sports, jazz music, drums, classical piano.

ADDRESSES: Home—Chicago, IL. *Office*—Department of English, State University of New York College at Cortland, P.O. Box 2000, Cortland, NY 13045. *E-mail*—hagera@snycorva.cortland.edu.

CAREER: University of Oklahoma, Norman, instructor in English, 1977-79; Loyola University of Chicago, Chicago, IL, assistant professor of English, 1979-88; University of Illinois at Chicago Circle, Chicago, visiting lecturer in English, 1989-93; State University of New York College at Cortland, assistant professor, 1993-96, associate professor, 1996-2000, professor of English, 2000—. Dominican College of San Rafael, visiting assistant professor, 1973; lecturer at educational institutions, including University of Chicago, 1989, Purdue University, 1990, Cornell University, 1994, State University of New York at Binghamton, 1994, and Arizona State University, 1996; public speaker on literary topics; guest on media programs. Also jazz and rock drummer. *Military service:* U.S. Army, Artillery, 1964-68; served in Germany; became lieutenant.

MEMBER: Modern Language Association of America, Boccaccio Society, Sidney Society, Marlowe Society, Milton Society, Renaissance Society of America, Sixteenth Century Studies Association, French Colonial Historical Society, Mystery Writers of America, Midwest Modern Language Association.

AWARDS, HONORS: Fellow, Newberry Library, 1988-89; other academic honors.

WRITINGS:

FICTION

The Tollbooth, Looking Glass Press (Kansas City, KS), 2004.
Bedtime Confidential, Looking Glass Press (Kansas City, KS), 2006.

NONFICTION

Shakespeare's Political Animal: Schema and Schemata in the Canon, University of Delaware Press (Newark, DE), 1990.
Dazzling Images: The Masks of Sir Philip Sidney, University of Delaware Press (Newark, DE), 1991.
(Editor and contributor) *Major Tudor Authors: A Bio-Bibliographical Critical Sourcebook,* Greenwood Press (Westport, CT), 1997.

(Editor) *Understanding Romeo and Juliet: A Student Casebook to Issues, Sources, and Historic Documents,* Greenwood Press (Westport, CT), 1999.

(Editor) *The Age of Milton: Major 17-Century British and American Authors: A Bio-Bibliographical Critical Sourcebook,* Greenwood Press (Westport, CT), 2004.

(Editor) *Encyclopedia of British Writers: 16th, 17th, and 18th Centuries,* 2 volumes, Facts on File (New York, NY), 2005.

Contributor to books, including Dennis C. Kay, editor, *Sir Philip Sidney: An Anthology of Modern Criticism,* Oxford University Press (Oxford, England), 1987. Contributor of articles and reviews to academic journals and literary magazines, including *Annals of Scholarship, Canadian Journal of Italian Studies, English Literature History, Journal of English and Germanic Philology, Machiavelli Studies, Renaissance Quarterly, Studies in English Literature,* and *Upstart Crow.*

SIDELIGHTS: Educator and author Alan Hager once commented: "I have been something of a gypsy scholar, having taught jazz appreciation at the Lycée d'Ivry in the suburbs of Paris, 1962; everything from driver safety, and survey, to the infiltration course while serving in the U.S. Army from 1964-68, and writing and literature—mostly Renaissance and modernist—at Berkeley; Dominican College, San Rafael; Oklahoma University; Loyola University; University of Illinois, Chicago; Robert Morris College, and now at the State University of New York at Cortland, where I am a professor of English.

"I have also visited and given lectures at Cornell University, St. Anselm College, and at the Tompkins County Community College Honors Colloquium, but also, as part of personal outreach interests, at high schools such as New Trier in Winnetka, Francis Parker, Chicago Latin, and Lincoln Park in Chicago. With teaching loads always moderately heavy, I think I have had more students than anyone I know.

"Both of my parents were born in the Far East, one an Episcopal missionary's daughter, the other the son of a mining engineer and entrepreneur based in Manila, and met at the Lycée Français in Shanghai, which they both attended," Hagar once noted. "They met again at a dinner party in New York designed to match that couple of Caucasians with a peculiar common origin. From both sides of my family I think I have inherited an interest in

reading and writing, in racquet sports from table tennis to badminton and paolta, but mainly tennis and squash. Jazz and Baroque music have also been passions, as well as boating from sweep oar to sailing to water-skiing.

"Some of my scholarly writing, such as *Understanding Romeo and Juliet: A Student Casebook to Issues, Sources and Historic Documents,* and my work for encyclopedias, have been aimed at large audiences, from high school at least on. Also my fiction would want universal appeal. I believe one learns how to write well only with models. In criticism, I look to the style if not the content of C.S. Lewis and Stephen Greenblatt; for my fiction, Raymond Chandler and J.D. Salinger and my friends, Mike Mewshaw and Pat Conroy. For content, my idol is Richard Wilbur.

"Authors write, I feel, out of a desire to convert readers to life and that makes them priestly in the largest sense. I teach, I hope, ideas options, attitudes, and curiosity. I write from full titles and cryptic notes on the backs of an abundance of unused deposit slips in my checkbooks. I won't lose those too easily. I think our greatest natural resource is the education of our inhabitants and it makes me sad if and when American grade schools, high schools, colleges, and universities, as great as they are, do not promote creativity."

BIOGRAPHICAL AND CRITICAL SOURCES:

PERIODICALS

Booklist, October 1, 1997, review of *Major Tudor Authors: A Bio-Bibliographical Critical Sourcebook* p. 354; August, 2004, Mary Ellen Quinn, review of *The Age of Milton: An Encyclopedia of Major 17th-Century British and American Authors,* p. 1972; July, 2005, Craig Bunch, review of *Encyclopedia of British Writers: 16th, 17th, and 18th Centuries,* p. 1938.

Genre, Volume XXV, number 1, p. 220.

Journal of English and Germanic Philology, April, 1993, Arthur F. Kinney, review of *Dazzling Images: The Masks of Sir Philip Sidney,* p. 226.

Library Journal, September 1, 2004, Lee Ehlers, review of *The Age of Milton,* p. 186; April 15, 2005, Mirela Roncevic, review of *Encyclopedia of British Writers,* p. 126.

Modern Philology, Richard C. McCoy, review of *Dazzling Images: The Masks of Sir Philip Sidney,* p. 351.

Notes and Queries, March, 1992.

Review of English Studies, February, 1993, review of *Shakespeare's Political Animal: Schema and Schemata in the Canon,* pp. 103-104.

School Library Journal, March, 2000, Sally Margolis, review of *Understanding Romeo and Juliet: A Student Casebook to Issues, Sources, and Historical Documents,* p. 253; June, 2005, Pat Bender, review of *Encyclopedia of British Writers: 16th, 17th, and 18th Centuries,* p. 90.

Times Literary Supplement, August 13, 2004, Kevin de Ornellas, review of *The Age of Milton,* p. 29.*

* * *

HALLS, Kelly Milner 1957-
(Kelly Milner)

PERSONAL: Born December 6, 1957, in Amarillo, TX; daughter of Gene and Georgia Milner; divorced; children: Kerry, Vanessa. *Education:* Attended Brigham Young University. *Politics:* Democrat. *Religion:* "Do no harm." *Hobbies and other interests:* Tennis, skiing, painting, paleontology, animals, free speech and anti-censorship efforts.

ADDRESSES: Home—Spokane, WA. *Agent*—Ken Wright, Writers House, 21 W. 26th St., New York, NY 10010. *E-mail*—KellyMilnerH@yahoo.com.

CAREER: Author and freelance journalist. *Book Report/Kids Reads,* former executive editor. Personal assistant to author Chris Crutcher.

MEMBER: Society of Children's Book Writers and Illustrators, American Library Association, Young Adult Library Services Association, Freedom to Read Foundation, National Coalition Against Censorship.

AWARDS, HONORS: American Bookseller "Pick of the List" science book, 1995, for *Dino-Trekking: The Ultimate Dinosaur Lover's Travel Guide; Highlights* Award for best science feature, 1995; Top Ten Science Books designation, *Booklist,* 2003, for *Dinosaur Mummies;* Benjamin Franklin Award, 2005, for *Albino Animals,* and 2006, for *Wild Dogs: Past and Present;* Conservation Book of the Year, 2005, for *Wild Dogs: Past and Present;* Children's Choice Award, 2006, for *Wild Dogs: Past and Present.*

WRITINGS:

Dino-Trekking: The Ultimate Dinosaur Lover's Travel Guide, illustrated by Rick Spears, Wiley (New York, NY), 1996.

Baby Chick, Boyds Mills Press (Honesdale, PA), 1999.

Kids Go! Denver: A Fun-Filled, Fact-Packed Travel and Activity Book, John Muir Publications (Santa Fe, NM), 1999.

(With others) *365 Outdoor Activities,* illustrated by Anne Kennedy, Publications International (Lincolnwood, IL), 2000.

I Bought a Baby Chicken, illustrated by Karen Stormer Brooks, Boyds Mills Press (Honesdale, PA), 2000.

(With others) *School Projects for Pennies,* illustrated by George Ulrich, Publications International (Lincolnwood, IL), 2001.

(With others) *365 Things To Do on a Saturday,* illustrated by George Ulrich, Publications International (Lincolnwood, IL), 2001.

Look What You Can Make with Craft Sticks: Over 80 Pictured Crafts and Dozens of Other Ideas, Boyds Mills Press (Honesdale, PA), 2002.

Look What You Can Make with Plastic-Foam Trays: Over 90 Pictured Crafts and Dozens of Other Ideas, Boyds Mills Press (Honesdale, PA), 2003.

Dinosaur Mummies: Beyond Bare-Bone Fossils, illustrated by Rick Spears, Darby Creek Publishing. (Plain City, OH), 2003.

Albino Animals, Darby Creek Publishing (Plain City, OH), 2004.

Wild Dogs: Past and Present, Darby Creek Publishing (Plain City, OH), 2005.

The Random House Dinosaur Travel Guide, illustrated by Luis V. Rey, Random House (New York, NY), 2006.

(With others) *Tales of the Cryptids: Mysterious Creatures That May or May Not Exist,* illustrated by Rick Spears, Darby Creek Publishing (Plain City, OH), 2006.

Mysteries of the Mummy Kids, Darby Creek Publishing (Plain City, OH), 2007.

Cells and Systems ("Science Fair Projects" series), Heinemann Library (Chicago, IL), 2007.

Forces and Motion ("Science Fair Projects" series), Heinemann Library (Chicago, IL), 2007.

Astronomy and Space ("Science Fair Projects" series), Heinemann Library (Chicago, IL), 2007.

Rocks and Minerals ("Science Fair Projects" series), Heinemann Library (Chicago, IL), 2007.

Contributor to *Children's Writer's and Illustrator's Market,* edited by Alice Pope, F&W Publications (Cincinnati, OH) 1997-2008; *Stress Fractures,* edited by Terry Trueman, HarperCollins (New York, NY), 2003; *Essential Guide to Children's Books and Their Creators,* edited by Anita Silvey, 2003; and *The Continuum Encyclopedia of Young Adult Literature,* edited by Bernice Cullinan and Bonnie Kunzel, revised edition, 2004. Contributor to periodicals, including *Teen People, Writer's Digest, Highlights for Children, Guidepost for Kids, Guidepost for Teens, Parenting Teens, Boy's Life, Fox Kids, Booklist, Book Magazine, Book Links, Dinosaurus, Kid City, Child Life, Humpty Dumpty, Children' Digest, Voice of Youth Advocates, Family Fun, U.S. Kids, Child Life, Dig, Ask, Hullabaloo, New Jersey Monthly, Wyoming, Chicago Tribune, Denver Post, Washington Post, Atlanta Journal Constitution, Fort Worth Star-Telegram,* and *Jurassic Park Institute.* Contributing editor, *Dino Times, Dinosaurus,* and *Archaeology's Dig.*

SIDELIGHTS: Kelly Milner Halls is the author of both fiction and nonfiction books for children and a frequent contributor to periodicals for and about children. One of her early, and favorite, books is *I Bought a Baby Chicken,* which was inspired by a baby chick given to her oldest daughter when she suffered a severe case of chicken pox while in the second grade. The family built a coop and filled it with chicks. By the time Kerry began third grade, their coop contained more than two dozen fully-grown chickens. The book for young children is a counting book, in which a little girl and her family buy baby chicks at the general store. As in real life, other members of the family add to the total until there are more than fifty head. A *Publishers Weekly* contributor wrote: "This country tale is chipper and sunny from beginning to end."

Halls is coauthor of a number of craft books for children, including *Look What You Can Make with Craft Sticks: Over 80 Pictured Crafts and Dozens of Other Ideas.* The sticks of the title are craft sticks, but also tongue depressors and ice cream sticks, all of which are part of projects that incorporate glue, paint, paper, fabric, and odds and ends to create games, toys, doll furniture, and decorative items. Other projects involve

the making of boxes, signs, mobiles, and other unusual items from newspaper, using papier-mache techniques. This theme continues with *Look What You Can Make with Plastic-Foam Trays: Over 90 Pictured Crafts and Dozens of Other Ideas,* in which projects ranging from quite easy to more difficult utilize the common plastic foam tray, glue, markers, paint, glitter, and other craft items. Projects include a macaroni collage and a mosaic sailboat. *School Library Journal* reviewer Genevieve Gallagher was impressed with the book, "both for its craft ideas and its environmentally friendly use for those foam trays."

In *Dinosaur Mummies: Beyond Bare-Bone Fossils,* Halls goes beyond the study of dinosaur bones and includes feathers and the "skin, hearts, and muscles and goop-filled stomachs." She concentrates on six finds and includes cartoons along with actual photographs. A *Kirkus Reviews* contributor commented that "young dinosaur fans will latch onto this heavily illustrated report like starving velociraptors at a picnic."

In *Albino Animals,* Milner covers albinism among mammals, amphibians, reptiles, and humans. She considers albinos to be "beautiful examples of nature's diversity." She notes that their stark whiteness makes them more easily identified in the wild by predators and that their skin and eyes are particularly sensitive to the sun. Because of these challenges, albinos must often make serious adjustments in their behavior to survive. In reviewing *Albino Animals* in *Booklist,* Gillian Engberg wrote: "The wild facts and eye-popping visuals will encourage children to learn more about the underlying basic science."

The ancestors of the contemporary dog are studied in *Wild Dogs: Past and Present,* with explanations of how fossils and DNA determine what dog ancestors looked like. Halls includes a variety of sidebars, charts, and maps, notes how conservation and the reintroduction of species can impact other species, and concludes with an overview of today's domesticated dogs. Susan Oliver wrote in *Children's Review:* "Halls conveys complex scientific information as she explains why some species die out while others survive and evolve."

Halls once commented: "Though I work full-time as a freelance writer, I am fast becoming a YA literature advocate, determined to broaden the reach of these outstanding coming-of-age stories and authors."

Halls once told *CA:* "I had a teacher in third grade tell me I was a good writer, that I should consider being a writer when I grew up. I was intrigued and realized as a journalism student in high school that might actually be possible. Reporters like Linda Ellerbee inspired me to study journalism in college. My children inspired me to write nonfiction for young readers.

"My writing process for young readers is no different than my process for adult readers. I hold my work for children to the same three-source standard I use for any adult publication. If anyone deserves accuracy, it's children.

"The most surprising thing I've learned is that when I say I get paid for being weird, they all think they are weird, as individuals. Every kid feels a little uneasy in their skin, and my owning my 'weird' seems to help them learn to herald it too. I've had the most positive response from kids and adults on Albino Animals, and I love that book too. But Tales of the Cryptids was also great fun to write and research.

"I was a reluctant reader in school. I only read books about vampires, reptiles, and Abraham Lincoln for the longest time. So I write the books I would have liked to find when I was a kid. I hope my books will help inspire reluctant readers to explore new worlds in books—not just mine, but across the board. I hope they'll help kids find a sense of connection, to know they are never truly alone in this universe. I hope they learn to wear their weird with pride, like I do."

BIOGRAPHICAL AND CRITICAL SOURCES:

PERIODICALS

Booklist, April 1, 2000, Lauren Peterson, review of *I Bought a Baby Chicken,* p. 1468; June 1, 2004, Gillian Engberg, review of *Albino Animals,* p. 1722; December 1, 2005, Gillian Engberg, review of *Wild Dogs: Past and Present,* p. 59.

Children's Digest, January-February, 2006, Tyler Zipes, review of *Dinosaur Mummies: Beyond Bare-Bone Fossils,* p. 14.

Kirkus Reviews, August 1, 2003, review of *Dinosaur Mummies,* p. 1017.

Publishers Weekly, January 17, 2000, review of *I Bought a Baby Chicken,* p. 55.

School Library Journal, July, 2000, Karen James, review of *I Bought a Baby Chicken,* p. 79; April, 2002, Lynda Ritterman, review of *Look What You Can Make with Craft Sticks: Over 80 Pictured*

Crafts and Dozens of Other Ideas, p. 132; February, 2003, Genevieve Gallagher, review of *Look What You Can Make with Plastic-Foam Trays: Over 90 Pictured Crafts and Dozens of Other Ideas,* p. 131; December, 2003, Steven Engelfried, review of *Dinosaur Mummies,* p. 168; August, 2004, Jenna Miller, review of *Albino Animals,* p. 137; November, 2005, Susan Oliver, review of *Wild Dogs,* p. 160.

Teacher Librarian, February, 2005, Teri Lesesne, "Wild Dogs, Dinosaurs, and Baby Chicks: An Interview with Kelly Milner Halls," p. 46.

ONLINE

Boyds Mills Press Web site, http://www.boydsmills press.com/ (November 28, 2006), biography.

Kelly Milner Halls Home Page, http://www.kellymilner halls.com (November 28, 2006).

*   *   *

HARTNETT, Sonya 1968-

PERSONAL: Born March 23, 1968, in Melbourne, Victoria, Australia; daughter of Philip Joseph (a proofreader) and Virginia Mary (a nurse) Hartnett. *Education:* Royal Melbourne Institute of Technology, B.A., 1988.

ADDRESSES: Home—Northcote, Victoria, Australia.

CAREER: Writer. Member of board, St. Martin's Theatre, Melbourne, Victoria, Australia.

AWARDS, HONORS: Ena Noël Award, International Board on Books for Youth, 1996, for *Wilful Blue;* Shaeffer Pen Prize, Victoria Premier's Literary Awards, Miles Franklin Inaugural Kathleen Mitchell Award, Book of the Year honor book designation, Children's Book Council of Australia (CBCA), and New South Wales State Literary Award shortlist, all 1996, all for *Sleeping Dogs;* CBCA Book of the Year shortlist, 1999, for *All My Dangerous Friends,* and 2000, for *Stripes of the Sidestep Wolf;* Aurealis Award for Best Young-Adult Novel, and Australian Publishers Association (APA) Award shortlist, both 2000, CBCA Book of the Year

Award for Older Readers shortlist, and New South Wales State Literary Award shortlist, both 2001, and *Guardian* Children's Fiction Prize and *Mail on Sunday/John Llewellyn Rhys* Prize shortlist, both 2002, all for *Thursday's Child;* Australian Children's Book of the Year for Older Readers, 2002, for *Forest;* Commonwealth Writers Prize (South East Asia/South Pacific Region), *Age* Book of the Year designation, Miles Franklin Award shortlist, New South Wales State Literary Award shortlist, Victorian Premier's Literary Award shortlist, and Orange Prize for Fiction longlist, all 2003, and Dublin Literary Award nomination, 2004, all for *Of a Boy;* APA Book Design Award shortlist, 2004, for *The Silver Donkey;* Victorian Premier's Literary Award shortlist, Queensland Premier's Literary Award shortlist, *Courier Mail* Young Reader Book of the Year designation, CBC Young Reader Book of the Year designation, and *Age* Book of the Year shortlist, all 2005, all for *Surrender.*

WRITINGS:

NOVELS; FOR CHILDREN AND YOUNG ADULTS

Trouble All the Way, Rigby (Adelaide, South Australia, Australia), 1984.

Sparkle and Nightflower, Rigby (Adelaide, South Australia, Australia), 1986.

The Glass House, Pan Macmillan (Sydney, New South Wales, Australia), 1990

Wilful Blue, Viking (Ringwood, Victoria, Australia), 1994.

Sleeping Dogs, Viking (New York, NY), 1995.

The Devil Latch, Viking (Ringwood, Victoria, Australia), 1996.

Black Foxes, Viking (Ringwood, Victoria, Australia), 1996.

Princes, Viking (Ringwood, Victoria, Australia), 1997, Viking (New York, NY), 1998.

All My Dangerous Friends, Viking (New York, NY), 1998.

Stripes of the Sidestep Wolf, Viking (Ringwood, Victoria, Australia), 1999, Candlewick Press (Cambridge, MA), 2005.

Thursday's Child, Penguin (New York, NY), 2000.

Forest, Penguin (Ringwood, Victoria, Australia), 2001.

Of a Boy, Viking (Camberwell, Victoria, Australia), 2002, published as *What the Birds See,* Candlewick Press (Cambridge, MA), 2003.

The Silver Donkey (for children), illustrated by Don Powers, Viking (New York, NY), 2004.

Surrender, Viking (Camberwell, Victoria, Australia), 2005, Candlewick Press (Cambridge, MA), 2006.

The Ghost's Child, Penguin (Camberwell, Victoria, Australia), 2007.

Also contributor to *There Must Be Lions: Stories about Mental Illness,* Ginninderra Press, 1998.

Author's work has been translated into Chinese, Dutch, and Swedish.

SIDELIGHTS: The novels of award-winning Australian writer Sonya Hartnett, although often classified for a young-adult readership, transcend the genre due to their psychological depth and sophistication. Called intense, and often devastating, her works, which include *Sleeping Dogs, Surrender, What the Birds See,* and *Thursday's Child,* explore human character and the differences in the way in which individuals perceive the world around them. Noting that the marketing of her novels has been a constant frustration, Hartnett explained to *Bookseller* contributor Benedicte Page that "I'm conscious that whatever book I'm working on will probably come out as a teenage novel, but I never pull any punches on account of that. I never make an idea less complicated. I think, 'If this comes out for teenagers and they don't understand it, it's not my concern.'"

"I was the second eldest of six very boisterous, outgoing children," Hartnett once explained, "but was shy and fairly withdrawn myself. I think I started writing because, in a make-believe world, I was no longer so friendless—to the characters, at least, I was someone very important." Her own shyness would shape Hartnett's focus as a writer; as she explained to Margot Hillel in *Reading Time,* "I guess the major influence on me has been my own personality given that I am intrinsically shy, which has enabled me to look and listen a lot of the time and I learnt a lot from that. My characters are not based on people I know, but all the knowledge you have in your head comes into your writing."

Hartnett's novels are most influenced by what she calls her "strong romantic streak" and her "taste for the bizarre." "I'm always amazed and delighted," Hartnett once stated, "by the very strange, factual stories that pop up in newspapers—'Girl lives in cupboard for sixteen years'—things like that. What goes on behind closed doors intrigues me. I like the idea that everyone has their own view of 'reality' and crave to know what this view is, and how it differs from mine." Hartnett is also very interested in her character's perceptions of time, and how each person relates to the other—"the very subtle aspects of our daily lives with others, the words that we emphasise, the glances from the corners of the eyes. If I hope to examine anything in the novels I write, it is how amazingly different we are from each other, that what is astonishing to one may be mundane to another, that there is an infinite number of ways to live a life. My own life seems incredibly mundane to me, and I love to write about lives lived at the other end of the spectrum—lives that, to the characters, must by necessity also seem mundane and 'normal.'"

Indeed, the characters in Hartnett's *Sleeping Dogs* could be said to be living "at the other end of the spectrum." Taking place in a rundown trailer park in the dusty Australian outback, the story concerns the reclusive Willow family: Griffin Willow, an alcoholic, patriarchal bully; his unstable wife, Grace; and their five children, including sons Jordan and Oliver and twenty-three-year-old daughter Michelle. Living an isolated existence save for the few people who stop at their run-down campground (no one ever comes for a second stay), Michelle and Jordan eventually develop an incestuous relationship as a way to survive. When a curious camper—a painter by the name of Bow Fox, who is attracted to Michelle—learns of this secret from youngest son Oliver, he decides to interfere in the family's delicate emotional balance by breaking through their walls of secrecy. "Reminiscent of William Faulkner or Tennessee Williams in its examination of a convoluted and incestuous family, the story moves with hideous inevitability to a devastating climax," noted Patty Campbell in *Horn Book*. Novelist Jonathan Harlen commented in a *Magpies* article that *Sleeping Dogs* is "so beautifully written that even hopelessness becomes a pleasure."

Wilful Blue is similar to *Sleeping Dogs* in its focus on despair and tragedy. Jesse McGee and Guy DeFoe are part of a group of young artists who have been commissioned by a wealthy patroness to create works of art for Sanquedeet, a newly formed Australian artist's retreat. While Jesse thrives in the austere, creative environment and socializes with the other artists, Guy emotionally withdraws and ultimately takes his own life, leaving his friend obsessed by his seemingly pointless actions. Praising Hartnett for her "fluid, lyrical prose and deft characterizations," *School Library Journal* contributor Alice Casey Smith added that young-adult readers of *Wilful Blue* will share, with Jesse, "the guilty helplessness of survivors of suicide."

Paralleling the tale of a pair of twins imprisoned by King Richard III in the Tower of London, *Princes* tells the story of Indigo and Ravel, identical twins dwelling together in a rat-infested mansion. After their parents mysteriously disappear, Ravel wonders if he should enter the outside world and look for a job. Indigo, tottering on the brink of insanity, finds the loss of his brother too much to consider, and so begins playing mind-games with his twin, games Ravel is equally skilled to play. As the story progresses, Ravel realizes the extent of his brother's madness, understanding that Indigo may have caused the disappearance of their parents, and begins to fear for his own safety. While several critics warned that the book contains horrific stories that might be unsuitable for younger adolescents, *Kliatt* reviewer Paula Rohrlick suggested that *Princes* "might appeal to fans of horror stories who can appreciate an unusual narrative." Noting that Hartnett's "cool bravado could attract a type of cult following," a *Publishers Weekly* critic found that the book's "cruelties escalate and finally explode in a climax that's a little too easily achieved but fitting nonetheless."

Again the author tackles serious themes in *All My Dangerous Friends,* a work about a group of young adults caught up in a cycle of drug and alcohol abuse, sexual promiscuity, and shoplifting. Told from the viewpoint of two main characters, "Hartnett is able to maintain an intriguing and intertwined plot," according to *Journal of Adolescent & Adult Literacy* contributor Thomas McPherson. Some reviewers questioned whether the subjects dealt with in the book were suitable for a young adult audience. However, McPherson found that "the issues, although quite stark and brutal at times, are dealt with reflectively in a way that could be used as a model for our students." Writing in *Magpies*, critic Kerry Nealy came to a similar conclusion about Hartnett's characters in general, most of whom tend to be amoral, self-centered, shallow, and cruel. "They are often not meant to be liked, that is the point of their existence in her stories," wrote Nealy, suggesting that Hartnett does not create characters to emulate, but rather to show readers another side, however unpleasant, of human behavior.

Hartnett explores the complex relationship that develops when abnormalities intersect in her psychological thriller *Surrender.* A lonely, repressed boy who is haunted by his role in the death of a mentally disabled older brother years before, Anwell lives in a small town where little disrupts the dullness of his life. When he meets wild, uncivilized Finnegan, the limitations on his life are suddenly challenged and deeper impulses released. Recognizing their bond and uniting in their devotion to Gabriel's dog, Surrender, the boys evolve into mirror images, one "good" and one "bad," and gain a psychological wholeness by living vicariously through each other. Told in the boys' dual narratives, as one of the boys—now aged twenty—lies close to death, *Surrender* serves up what Francisca Goldsmith described in *School Library Journal* as a "stew of unhappiness, mischief, and outright criminality." Calling the novel "potent and disquieting," *Booklist* contributor Holly Koelling recommended *Surrender* for more mature teen readers "willing to experience some of humanity's bleaker aspects." A *Kirkus Reviews* writer maintained that Hartnett's "grim, beautifully written tale of adolescent yearnings gone awry" is enriched by the author's "delicate, measured, heartbreaking portrait" of a complex tale of "love, guilt, revenge and sorrow."

Life in rural areas is the focus of the novels *Stripes of the Sidestep Wolf* and *Thursday's Child,* both of which feature families struggling to survive in the Australian countryside. In the first story, twenty-something Satchel O'Rye lives with his parents in a dying town, hoping that one day he will find employment. Emotionally tied to his mother and mentally ill father, Satchel looks for work locally, hoping to avoid the fate of his friend, Leroy, who had to move to the city to find employment. Torn between the need to establish an independent life and the draw of his roots in a rural, run-down town, Satchel stumbles upon a solution when he sights a strange wolf-like creature that might be a rare survivor of marsupial believed to be extinct: Should he capitalize on the creature by promoting the animal's existence, or leave the animal—as well as his backwater community—in peace? The young man's decision becomes more pressing when tragedy strikes. Describing *Stripes of the Sidestep Wolf* as "a serious but not a depressing novel," *Magpies* critic Lyn Linning praised Hartnett for creating characters "whom one can like and feel compassion for." Linning concluded of the novel that "Hartnett has indeed created a moving image of truth," while in *School Library Journal* Janet Hilbun described *Stripes of the Sidestep Wolf* "hauntingly beautiful" and "a complex, introspective novel with vivid characters."

Dubbed as a "unique and fascinating [reading] experience" by *School Library Journal* contributor Bruce Ann Shook, *Thursday's Child* follows the life of another young resident of the Australian countryside, this time during the Great Depression. Harper Flute tells her story as she grows from a child of six to a young woman of twenty-one, revealing all of the family hardships and poverty she endured along the way. Much of the book revolves around the actions of Harper's younger brother Tin, an intelligent, but overly sensitive boy who prefers to live under the family's small house in a series of tunnels he dug. As the years go by, Tin's asocial behavior intensifies, with the young child eventually living alone as a feral boy in the wilderness. Again, Hartnett was noted for her ability to not turn *Thursday's Child* into a heavy-hearted read. Remarked *Magpies* contributor Lyn Linning, "Harper's strength, endurance and way of looking at the world as she struggles to make meaning of her life ensure that *Thursday's Child* is neither pessimistic or depressing to read." Linning went on to call *Thursday's Child* a "significant extension" of the author's works, as well as "a valuable addition to Australian literature for both young people and adults of any age." Noting the author's use of humor, as well as her "clever choice of language," *Kliatt* reviewer Phyllis LaMontagne described *Thursday's Child* "a story about independence and the need that we all have to shape our own lives without interference from others."

In the opening scene of *What the Birds See*—published in Australia as *Of a Boy*—Hartnett describes the disappearance of three Australian children on their way to an ice cream shop. The book's focus then shifts to Adrian, an unhappy nine year old who lives with his grandmother because his mother is unfit and his father wants nothing to do with him. Adrian is an outcast in his school, desperately longing for friendship with other children. He thinks he may have found it when three mysterious children move into the house across the street. Adrian befriends the oldest girl, Nicole, who seems quite intrigued by the case of the missing children. Together, Adrian and Nicole begin to search for the children, but only disastrous consequences await them.

Reviewing *What the Birds See,* a *Kirkus Reviews* writer described the work as "bleakly haunting," a "novel [that] focuses its lens on a child struggling to survive in a family of emotional cripples." In *Horn Book,* Christine M. Heppermann maintained that "Hartnett excels at letting her characters' secret pain color everything they see and touch," and noted that her young protagonist "fairly oozes unhappiness." Gillian Engberg, reviewing *What the Birds See* for *Booklist,* called the story's ending "shocking, and the telling, unusually honest and haunting," while in *School Library Journal* Daniel L. Darigan concluded that "rarely is a sentence turned so well, a setting so remarkably established, and a plot so evenly polished as in this book."

Taking place in rural western France during World War I, Hartnett's award-winning illustrated novel *The Silver Donkey* features a framing narrative about two young sisters who discover a British lieutenant and deserter hiding in the forest outside their village. Suffering from temporary blindness and traumatized by the horrors of a recent battle, Lieutenant Shepherd repays the sisters' kindness in bringing him food; during each of their visits, he tells a story that begins with the silver donkey charm he carries in his pocket. One story follows the donkey that carried the virgin Mary to Bethlehem; another finds a donkey rescuing injured soldiers on the battlefront. As the war winds to a close, the girls gain help to plan the soldier's escape across the English Channel, and Hartnett's tale winds to a gentle ending. Reviewing the novel for *Kliatt,* Janis Flint-Ferguson praised *The Silver Donkey* as "a war story that shows the courage and goodwill of humanity," and in *Horn Book* Joanna Rudge Long described Hartnett's story as "provocative, timely, and elegantly honed." Praising Don Powers' pencil illustrations, a *Kirkus Reviews* writer concluded that "Hartnett's powerful imagery and her inimitable deftness with language" enrich a book that can be read as "an old-fashioned children's story," while a *Publishers Weekly* critic described it as both "delicately told and deeply resonant."

Hartnett, who shares her home with her dog and cat and works part time as a bookseller, finds that the life of a writer makes loneliness impossible. "My life feels cluttered with the characters I've created over the years—none of them really ever leave, probably because of their origins in my head," she once explained. She counts among her strongest influences authors like Robert Cormier, Robertson Davies, Feodor Dostoevsky, Anne Tyler, and Mervyn Peake, all of whom she describes as being "writers with a strong eye for detail, for the bizarre, for blackness, for the minute intricacies of human relationships and the human condition." These authors have inspired her "never to be afraid to write exactly as I choose, to never hesitate in saying and doing as I please. There is still a lot of timid literature being written for the young, and I refuse to be timid, especially in a world where television and movies may freely show material that an author, having written similar things, must defend again and again. I read Cormier's *After the First Death* in my teens and knew that was the sort of book I wanted to write: brave, fierce, realistic, unshrinking, shocking. If my books stay in the reader's mind as clearly as *After the First Death* has stayed in mine, I shall have achieved the best a writer can hope to achieve: to write words that live."

BIOGRAPHICAL AND CRITICAL SOURCES:

BOOKS

Authors and Artists for Young Adults, Volume 35, Thomson Gale (Detroit, MI), 2000.
St. James Guide to Young Adult Writers, 2nd edition, St. James Press (Detroit, MI), 1999.

PERIODICALS

Booklist, October 15, 1994, p. 418; February 15, 1996, p. 1004; July, 2002, John Green, review of *Thursday's Child,* p. 1847; April 15, 2003, Gillian Engberg, review of *What the Birds See,* p. 1462; March 1, 2005, Carolyn Phelan, review of *Stripes of the Sidestep Wolf,* p. 1181; February 1, 2006, Holly Koelling, review of *Surrender,* p. 44; November 15, 2006, GraceAnne A. DeCandido, review of *The Silver Donkey,* p. 48.

Bookseller, October 25, 2002, Benedicte Page, "A Chronicler of Lost Children," p. 23.

Bulletin of the Center for Children's Books, April, 1998, review of *Princes,* p. 281; May, 2002, review of *Thursday's Child,* p. 325; March, 2003, review of *What the Birds See,* p. 275; March, 2005, Deborah Stevenson, review of *Stripes of the Sidestep Wolf,* p. 294; April, 2006, Deborah Stevenson, review of *Surrender,* p. 356.

Horn Book, March-April, 1996, Patty Campbell, "The Sand in the Oyster," pp. 240-243; July-August, 2002, Christine M. Heppermann, review of *Thursday's Child,* p. 460; May-June, 2003, Christine M. Heppermann, review of *What the Birds See,* p. 347; May-June, 2004, Tim Wynne-Jones, "Tigers and Poodles and Birds, Oh My!," p. 265; March-April, 2006, Caitlin J. Berry, review of *Surrender,* p. 188; September-October, 2006, Joanna Rudge Long, review of *The Silver Donkey,* p. 584.

Journal of Adolescent & Adult Literacy, November, 2000, Thomas McPherson, review of *All My Dangerous Friends,* pp. 301-302.

Kirkus Reviews, April 15, 2002, review of *Thursday's Child,* p. 89; February 1, 2003, review of *What the Birds See,* p. 230; January 1, 2005, review of *Stripes of the Sidestep Wolf,* p. 52; March 1, 2006, review of *Surrender,* p. 230; October 1, 2006, review of *The Silver Donkey,* p. 1015.

Kliatt, May, 1998, Paula Rohrlick, review of *Princes,* p. 6; September, 2003, Phyllis LaMontagne, review of *Thursday's Child,* p. 17; September, 2006, Janis Flint-Ferguson, review of *The Silver Donkey,* p. 13.

Magpies, September, 1995, p. 34; May, 1997, Jonathan Harlen, "A Writer's Perspective," pp. 10-13; March 30, 1998, review of *Princes,* p. 83; September, 1998, Kerry Neary, review of *All My Dangerous Friends,* p. 38; May, 1999, Lyn Linning, review of *Stripes of the Sidestep Wolf,* p. 36; September, 2000, Lyn Linning, review of *Thursday's Child,* p. 36.

Publishers Weekly, August 29, 1994, p. 80; September 4, 1995, p. 70; March 30, 1998, review of *Princes,* p. 83; June 3, 2002, Sonya Hartnett, review of *Thursday's Child,* p. 89; January 27, 2003, review of *What the Birds See,* p. 261; October 13, 2003, review of *Thursday's Child,* p. 82; January 10, 2005, review of *Stripes of the Sidestep Wolf,* p. 57; March 6, 2006, review of *Surrender,* p. 76; November 13, 2006, review of *The Silver Donkey,* p. 58.

Reading Time, May, 1996, interview with Margot Hillel, pp. 3-5; February, 1997, p. 28.

School Library Journal, December, 1994, Alice Casey Smith, review of *Wilful Blue,* p. 130; November, 1995, p. 119; June, 1998, Molly S. Kinney, review of *Princes,* p. 146; May, 2002, Bruce Ann Shook, review of *Thursday's Child,* p. 153; May, 2003, Daniel L. Darigan, review of *What the Birds See,* p. 153; March, 2005, Janet Hilbun, review of *Stripes of the Sidestep Wolf,* p. 212; March, 2006, Francisca Goldsmith, review of *Surrender,* p. 222; December, 2006, Jane G. Connor, review of *The Silver Donkey,* p. 144.

Times Educational Supplement, October 11, 2002, review of *Thursday's Child,* p. 13; January 3, 2003, Geraldine Brennan, review of *What the Birds See,* p. 23.

Tribune Books (Chicago, IL), May 25, 2003, review of *What the Birds See,* p. 5.

Voice of Youth Advocates, April, 1996, review of *Sleeping Dogs,* p. 26; June, 2002, review of *Thursday's Child,* p. 118; June, 2003, review of *What the Birds See,* p. 130; June, 2005, Ed Goldberg, review of *Stripes of the Sidestep Wolf,* p. 130; April, 2006, Patrick Jones, review of *Surrender,* p. 46.

ONLINE

Age Online, http://www.theage.com.au/ (October 31, 2004), "Children, Adults, Anything."

Contemporary Writers Web site, http://www.contemporarywriters.com/ (January 25, 2007), "Sonya Hartnett."

Penguin Books Australia Web site, http://www.penguin.com.au/ (January 25, 2007), "Sonya Hartnett."*

*   *   *

HASSLER, Jon 1933-
(Jon Francis Hassler)

PERSONAL: Born March 30, 1933, in Minneapolis, MN; son of Leo Blaise (a grocer) and Ellen (a teacher) Hassler; married Marie Schmitt, August 18, 1956; children: Michael, Elizabeth, David. *Education:* St. John's University, B.A., 1955; University of North Dakota, M.A., 1960. *Religion:* Roman Catholic. *Hobbies and other interests:* "Landscapes (gazing at them, walking through them, and painting pictures of them)."

ADDRESSES: Home—Sauk Rapids, MN. *Office*—Department of English, St. John's University, Collegeville, MN 56321. *E-mail*—johassl@aol.com.

CAREER: High school English teacher in Melrose, MN, 1955-56, Fosston, MN, 1956-69, and Park Rapids, MN, 1959-65; Bemidji State University, Bemidji, MN, instructor in English, 1965-68; Brainerd Community College, Brainerd, MN, instructor in English, 1968-80; St. John's University, Collegeville, MN, 1980—, began as writer-in-residence, became Regent's Professor.

AWARDS, HONORS: Novel of the Year designation, Friends of American Writers, 1978, for *Staggerford;* Guggenheim Foundation fellowship, 1980; Best Fiction of 1987 award, Society of Midland Authors, for *Grand Opening;* Colman Barry Award for Distinguished Contributions to Religion and Society, Saint John's University, 2003; Minnesota State Arts Board fellowship; honorary degrees from Assumption College, University of North Dakota, and the University of Notre Dame; the Jon Hassler Theater in Plainview, MN, was named in honor of Hassler.

WRITINGS:

The Red Oak and Other Poems, privately printed, 1968.
Four Miles to Pinecone (young adult), F. Warne (New York, NY), 1977.
Staggerford, Atheneum (New York, NY), 1977.
Simon's Night, Atheneum (New York, NY), 1979.

Jemmy (young adult), Atheneum (New York, NY), 1980.

The Love Hunter, Morrow (New York, NY), 1981.

A Green Journey, Morrow (New York, NY), 1985, reprinted, Ballantine Books (New York, NY), 1996.

Grand Opening, Morrow (New York, NY), 1987.

North of Hope, Ballantine Books (New York, NY), 1990, reprinted, Loyola Press (Chicago, IL), 2006.

Dear James, Ballantine Books (New York, NY, 1993, reprinted with new introduction by Joan Wester Anderson, Loyola Press (Chicago, IL), 2006.

Rookery Blues, Ballantine Books (New York, NY), 1995.

The Dean's List, Ballantine Books (New York, NY), 1997.

Underground Christmas, Afton Historical Society Press (Afton, MN), 1998.

Keepsakes & Other Stories, with wood engravings by Gaylord Schanilec, Afton Historical Society Pres (Afton, MN), 1999.

My Staggerford Journal, Ballantine Books (New York, NY), 1999.

Rufus at the Door and Other Stories, with wood engravings by Gaylord Schanilec, Afton Historical Society Press (Afton, MN), 2000.

Good People—from an Author's Life (essays), Loyola Press (Chicago, IL), 2001.

The Staggerford Flood, Viking (New York, NY), 2002.

The Staggerford Murders [and] *The Life and Death of Nancy Clancy's Nephew* (two novellas), Plume (New York, NY), 2004.

The New Woman, Viking (New York, NY), 2005.

Churches of Minnesota, photographs by Doug Ohman, Minnesota Historical Society Press (St. Paul, MN), 2006.

Also author of play adaptation of *Simon's Night,* produced in a drama workshop in Minnesota. Contributor of short stories to literary journals, including *Prairie Schooner* and *Blue Cloud Quarterly.* Manuscript collection held at St. Cloud State University, St. Cloud, MN.

ADAPTATIONS: A Green Journey was adapted as a television movie by the National Broadcasting Company, 1988.

SIDELIGHTS: "[Jon] Hassler is a very traditional writer with exciting, real, complex, and intriguing subject matter," writes *Contemporary Novelists* essayist C.W. Truesdale. "But," adds Truesdale, "[Hassler's] strengths are quiet and (on the surface) unremarkable. . . . He is

not bold and audacious. . . . [His] presence is subtle, quiet, and apparently unobtrusive." "Hassler is a writer good enough to restore your faith in fiction," proclaimed Randolph Hogan in the *New York Times Book Review,* noting: "His subjects are life, love and death—what the best novels have always been about—and he writes with wisdom and grace." In his novels, Hassler explores the relationships, thoughts, and feelings of ordinary people in the small towns of midwestern America. John H. Hafner declared in an *America* review of *Dear James:* "Hassler does for his Catholic, upper-midwest world what John Cheever did for his WASP New England one, though Hassler seems to have more affection for his characters than Cheever had for his." This comparison is not surprising given what the Hassler once commented in an interview with *CA:* "[John Cheever] was my teacher. I never knew him, but when I decided I wanted to write, he was the one I centered on. I read him for style, not particularly for plot and obviously not for setting. He taught me a lot." Commenting on his choice of locale, Hassler once told *CA:* "Since I was a year old I have lived in Minnesota small towns, so it's no wonder that most of my fiction focuses on small-town culture, particularly the various gaps and bridges between the young and the old."

"As a mark of his traditional practice, Hassler never uses stream of consciousness . . . nor does he use first person singular narrative," declares Truesdale. "What Hassler does use with increasing mastery and fluidity are three other mnemonic techniques: flashbacks, journal entries, and letters," summarizes Truesdale. "Hassler's concentration on church themes has earned him a reputation as a Catholic novelist," reported Gerald M. Costello in a *U.S. Catholic* review of *Dear James.* "Hassler tackles church topics . . . soberly and thoughtfully . . . and his writing skills are . . . first-rate. . . . Hassler generally gets it just right when he's writing about the church and church people," wrote Costello, lauding *Dear James* as "a refreshing treat: a contemporary work of fiction that manages to handle church matters intelligently and without condescension." "[Hassler] takes no overt political position. . . even though he sometimes seems obsessed with Church politics and the behaviors of the priests, sisters, and laypersons who people may of his novels. . . . He is more fascinated with the political infighting and machinations of a huge and powerful Church that is in a state of transition than he is in the spiritual or mystical character of its clergy and laypeople," remarks Truesdale, noting: "In some cases, he defuses potentially explosive conflicts by turning them into high comedy." "Hassler is fascinated by richly compelling individuals who have sacrificed themselves to principle of one sort or another," adds Truesdale.

Hassler's first adult novel, *Staggerford*, concerns Miles Pruitt, a Minnesota high school English teacher. Miles's life is staid and boring; he spends his time regretting lost opportunities and old loves. His story is "a series of astoundingly vacuous conversations, journal entries that seek to clarify what went wrong with his plans, and classes that consist, for the most part, of students to whom the love poems of Rod McKuen would be too challenging," Joyce Carol Oates wrote in the *New York Times Book Review*. Although Oates felt that "Hassler's characters are rather close to being two-dimensional," she admitted that there is "something likable about the novel." *Best Sellers* reviewer R.C. Anderson found "too many stock characters" in *Staggerford*, but he believed that Hassler "succeeds in fleshing them out in witty detail." Anderson concluded that *Staggerford* compares favorably with *Main Street*, Sinclair Lewis's novel of small-town Minnesota life. "One cannot avoid comparing" the two books, Anderson wrote. "Hassler's passive, unevaluative tone softens considerably the heavy-handed ridicule to which Lewis subjects his characters, and if his work is less vivid, it lacks also Lewis's cloying self-righteousness."

Hassler fictionalizes some of the problems facing the elderly in *Simon's Night*. The title character, Simon Peter Shea, is a retired professor who, after accidentally setting his house on fire, decides to enter the Norman Home, a home for the elderly. "After a stay of only a few days," wrote Richard Bradford in the *New York Times Book Review*, "Simon realizes that the place will be the death of him—first intellectually and eventually in the clinical sense." With the help and advice of a young doctor, Simon finds the strength to leave the home and live in his cabin in the woods. Bradford praised the novel, indicating that Hassler's themes "are mature and important—the tenacity of mind and love, the unforgivable waste of good brains and useful people simply because they are no longer young, the unarguable fact that there is truly no half-way station, like the Norman House, between life and death. Yet the novel's style is colloquial and modest, full of anecdote, rich with scenes and characters of tremendous comic vitality." Bradford claimed that *Simon's Night* is "one of the most delightful novels I have read in years, a work of manifold virtues, felicitous, intelligent and very funny."

In *The Love Hunter*, Hassler explores the friendship between two colleagues, Chris MacKensie and Larry Quinn, at a small Minnesota college. Larry is dying from multiple sclerosis, and he and Chris go on a hunting trip to help him forget his pain. Chris has decided

to kill Larry during the trip, to end his pain and in order to marry Larry's wife, with whom he is secretly in love. Hogan commented that this story "is always plausible, and [Hassler] never allows it to lapse into melodrama—which a less talented writer might have done." "You know you're in good hands immediately, from Hassler's masterly handling of exposition," praised Bruce Allen in the *Chicago Tribune Book World*, lauding: "The first five pages of this novel should be required reading for aspiring writers."

In *A Green Journey*, Hassler returns to the character Agatha McGee, who appeared in *Staggerford* and in previous short stories. Hassler explained in his interview with *CA* that "[by the time of *A Green Journey*] I knew [Agatha McGee] so well, I decided to . . . put her up against something she couldn't control, and I think it worked; I think it made her more interesting than ever." Agatha is an elderly Catholic school teacher with strong traditional religious beliefs. Her beliefs are challenged by a new bishop with modern ideas and by an unmarried pregnant woman Agatha befriends. During a church-sponsored trip to Dublin, Agatha's moral values are tested by these companions. The strength of the book, according to *Chicago Tribune* contributor Clarence Peterson, is in the "believable characters carefully observed." Victoria K. Musmann commented in the *Los Angeles Times Book Review*: "Hassler's characters have old-fashioned values and typical human failings; they make this a novel to restore your faith in humanity."

A Green Journey's "Miss Agatha McGee of Staggerford, Minnesota, and Father James O'Hannon of Ballybergs, north of Dublin . . . [became] soulmates through their correspondence over several years" and later resurface in the novel *Dear James*, stated *Commonweal* contributor Joseph Hynes. "In *Dear James* (as the title suggests), [Hassler] makes extensive and highly dramatic use of some of the letters that Agatha McGee writes to James O'Hannon (but only mails to him much later) and the letters that she has saved from him," recounts Truesdale. "In her correspondence with O'Hannon," noted Bill Peatman in the *National Catholic Reporter*, "Agatha reveals how confined she feels in her town and how bored she is with her friends [telling James] all the latest gossip." In this "popular and important" novel, wrote Hynes, the two protagonists "meet again . . . during Agatha's pilgrimage to Italy with American students [and an] intensely chaste love for each other . . . grows . . . most movingly, and Hassler is expert in persuading us that such love is possible and healing, spiritually and physically, even as he refuses to wax sentimental or soft-pedal the difficulties of any kind of attachment."

Dear James is "a contemporary love story with a ring of truth to it," summarized Costello. "The theme of *Dear James* is 'forgiveness,'" according to Peatman, who believed that despite a flaw "with the redemption of Agatha," the novel "provided a collection of characters whose relationships succeed in bringing out critical issues of human life: friendship, love, faithfulness, conflict and reconciliation." "Characters often have to balance conflicting values, conflicting moods," stated Hafner, adding that "balancing tradition and change is a major theme of *Dear James*." Hafner contended that readers will overlook the "few unconvincing contrivances [of the novel's complex plot]" and maintained that the story's few, almost-stereotypical characters "have a quirk or two that makes them emerge as individuals." Also remarking on some of the novel's "loose ends" and noting that at times "Hassler leans in the direction of caricature," Costello positively concluded: "Hassler's warm and absorbing novel *Dear James* . . . adds up to: a good tale, well told, and a story peopled with multidimensional characters. . . . The dialogue sparkles."

Rookery Blues and its sequel *The Dean's List* follow Leland Edwards, a "journeyman professor of English, accomplished pianist and organizer of the short-lived but splendid Icejam Quintet," described Loren F. Schmidtberger in an *America* review of *The Dean's List*. A *Publishers Weekly* critic claimed that both novels are equally "droll and charming" presentations of "campus life" and "advancing middleage [concerns]," and in the critic's assessment of *The Dean's List,* the latter's characters are judged to be "a bit predictable and stuck in the 1960s . . . [yet] endearing." *Rookery Blues* portrays Rookery State College around the time of Vietnam. In it, claimed *Christian Century* contributor W. Dale Brown, "Hassler satirizes the pretensions and foibles of the academic community with uproarious humor and incisive accuracy." *The Dean's List* portrays Leland, now the Rookery State College dean, a quarter century later. "[It] is structured more like a journal than a traditional novel, and much of the material in it is not integrated into a unified plot, yet for the most part it coheres as the responses of a well-intentioned, mid-Western intellectual to the griefs, joys and routines that life grants him," indicated Schmidtberger, who believed that "Hassler's best scenes outweigh having to push through a labored chapter." With "humor . . . affection . . . [and] quirky, eccentric, but believable characters," commented *Library Journal* reviewer Barbara E. Kemp, Hassler writes of "the small gains and losses that make up daily life for most people."

Hassler published several volumes of stories and essays and then *The Staggerford Flood,* which brings together Agatha McGee, now eighty, and a number of old friends. The elderly schoolteacher's home is threatened when the worst spring flood in a century threatens to engulf it. In reviewing the novel in *America,* Ed Block wrote: "Few readers or reviewers have noticed the archetypal dimension in a number of Mr. Hassler's novels. His first, *Staggerford,* for instance, involves the 'resurrection' of a town and some of its citizens after the death of a random victim of violence. In *The Staggerford Flood* the archetypal dimension is even more subtly suggested. Only careful attention reveals that the flood takes place during the last week of Lent. Of course the pervasiveness of water is a further clue to a possible ethic pattern."

The Staggerford Murders [and] *The Life and Death of Nancy Clancy's Nephew* consists of two novellas, the first of which is set in Staggerford and involves a murder and a disappearance, and which is narrated by five characters, one of whom is Grover, the elderly desk clerk of a dingy hotel. The second story, described as "much more dour" by a *Kirkus Reviews* contributor, is a reflection on life by turkey farmer W.D. Nestor, nephew of Nancy Clancy.

In *The New Woman,* Agatha, now eighty-seven, is living in an apartment building for seniors when she finds herself confronting a murder, a missing child, and a mysterious box. In reviewing the novel in the *Detroit Free Press,* Susan Hall-Balduf commented that her favorite Hassler story is *North of Hope,* which is about a priest who comes back to his hometown after being away for two decades to find that his former sweetheart has had a sad life without him. Hall-Balduf recommended the reading of *The New Woman* "if your heart needs lifting . . . *The New Woman* is very amusing. Agatha is funnier than she realizes, and yet she's so formidable in the way of old school teachers that the reader hardly dares to snicker."

Because of his realistic and compelling portraits of ordinary characters, some critics suggest that Hassler is a rising talent in American fiction. "Unlike so many contemporary writers," Hogan wrote, "[Hassler] creates characters you come to care about and believe in. He added that [perhaps what's] most striking about Mr. Hassler's writing is the voice. It makes you want to keep on reading just to remain in the company of such a wise man." Allen praised the "richness of the character portrayal" in Hassler's work and "his ability to make decent people both complicated and interesting." He concluded that Hassler is "one of our very best novelists." "What makes Hassler such an interesting and engaging novelist—and what will probably make him outlast all or almost all of his flashier contemporaries," assesses Truesdale, "is not just that he is unashamedly a traditional novelist but that he does so well what he does, that he involves the reader so deeply in his characters that no matter who we might be we really care about them, talk about them as if they were very real and interesting people. . . . I suspect that Jon Hassler will come to be recognized as a major 20th-century novelist."

BIOGRAPHICAL AND CRITICAL SOURCES:

BOOKS

An Interview with Jon Hassler, Dinkytown Antiquarian Bookstore (Minneapolis, MN), 1990.

Contemporary Novelists, 6th edition, St. James Press (Detroit, MI), 1996.

PERIODICALS

America, September 25, 1993, John H. Hafner, review of *Dear James,* p. 20; October 18, 1997, Loren F. Schmidtberger, review of *The Dean's List,* p. 26; December 9, 2002, Ed Block, review of *The Staggerford Flood,* p. 21.

Best Sellers, September, 1977, R.C. Anderson, review of *Staggerford,* p. 166.

Chicago Tribune, June 23, 1985, Clarence Peterson, review of *A Green Journey.*

Chicago Tribune Book World, December 13, 1981, Bruce Allen, review of *The Love Hunter.*

Christian Century, August 28, 1996, W. Dale Brown, review of *Rookery Blues,* p. 822.

Commonweal, July 16, 1993, Joseph Hynes, review of *Dear James.*

Detroit Free Press, December 14, 2005, Susan Hall-Balduf, review of *The New Woman.*

Kirkus Reviews, July 15, 2002, review of *The Staggerford Flood,* p. 979; October 1, 2004, review of *The Staggerford Murders* [and] *The Life and Death of Nancy Clancy's Nephew* p. 931.

Library Journal, May 1, 1997, Barbara E. Kemp, review of *The Dean's List;* December, 1999, Mary Paumier Jones, review of *My Staggerford Journal,* p. 132.

Los Angeles Times Book Review, February 3, 1985, Victoria K. Musmann, review of *A Green Journey,* p. 9.

National Catholic Reporter, May 28, 1993, Bill Peatman, review of *Dear James,* p. 33.

New York Times Book Review, July 24, 1977, Joyce Carol Oates, review of *Staggerford,* p. 14; October 28, 1979, Richard Bradford, review of *Simon's Night,* p. 79; August 16, 1981, Randolph Hogan, review of *The Love Hunter,* p. 9.

Publishers Weekly, April 14, 1997, review of *The Dean's List,* p. 54; August 23, 1999, review of *Keepsakes & Other Stories,* p. 48; July 29, 2002, review of *The Staggerford Flood,* p. 50; December 20, 2004, review of *The Staggerford Murders* [and] *The Life and Death of Nancy Clancy's Nephew,* p. 38.

Renascence: Essays on Values in Literature, winter, 2003, Joseph Plut, "Conversation with Jon Hassler: *North of Hope,*" p. 145.

U.S. Catholic, January, 1994, Gerald M. Costello, review of *Dear James,* p. 48.

ONLINE

BookPage Online, http://www.bookpage.com/ (November 28, 2006), Alden Mudge, "Finding Balance between the Ridiculous and Sublime: A Talk with Jon Hassler."

Jon Hassler Home Page, http://home.comcast.net/~ktebo (November 29, 2006).*

*   *   *

HASSLER, Jon Francis
See HASSLER, Jon

*   *   *

HAYTER, Sparkle 1958-
(Sparkle Lynnette Hayter)

PERSONAL: Born March, 1958, in Pouce Coupe, British Columbia, Canada; daughter of Ron (a journalist and local politician) and Jac'y (an English teacher and poet) Hayter; divorced, 1993. *Education:* Attended the University of Alberta; studied film at New York University.

ADDRESSES: E-mail—holmes222@hotmail.com.

CAREER: Cable News Network (CNN), New York, NY, and Atlanta, GA, began as intern, became assignment editor, producer, field producer, and writer, early 1980s-86; freelance television correspondent, 1986-94; writer, 1994—. Affiliated with Global Television, Toronto, Ontario, Canada.

AWARDS, HONORS: Arthur Ellis Award for best first mystery novel, Crime Writers of Canada, 1994, for *What's a Girl Gotta Do?*

WRITINGS:

"ROBIN HUDSON" DETECTIVE SERIES

What's a Girl Gotta Do? Soho (New York, NY), 1994.
Nice Girls Finish Last, Viking (New York, NY), 1996.
Revenge of the Cootie Girls, Viking (New York, NY), 1997.
The Last Manly Man, William Morrow (New York, NY), 1998.
The Chelsea Girl Murders, William Morrow (New York, NY), 2000.

OTHER

Naked Brunch, Three Rivers Press (New York, NY), 2003.
Bandit Queen Boogie: A Madcap Caper of Two Accidental Criminals, Three Rivers Press (New York, NY), 2004.

Contributor of poetry to literary journals, including *Fiddlehead* and *Quarry,* and of articles and opinion pieces to the *New York Times, Nation,* and *Globe and Mail.*

SIDELIGHTS: Sparkle Hayter is the author of a series of humorous detective novels featuring an attractive, confident, wisecracking amateur detective—a character that Hayter freely admits to using as an alter ego. Her "Robin Hudson" mysteries have won a devoted following of readers and earned enthusiastic reviews for their deft plotting and engaging characters.

Hayter was born in Pouce Coupe, British Columbia, but grew up in Edmonton, Alberta, where her journalist father also became a local politician. Her mother, Jac'y, was a poet and teacher who passed on her love of literature to her daughter. Her parents named her "Sparkle" because of an exuberant personality that made itself known to them even before she emerged into the world. Such a name was considered rather eccentric, to say the least, in the staid Canadian prairie city where she was raised, and Hayter sometimes resorted to using her more conventional middle name, Lynnette, to escape teasing.

An avid reader, Hayter also wrote from an early age, and had her poetry published in Canadian literary journals when she was still in high school. She enrolled in the University of Alberta, but on a jaunt with a friend to New York City in 1979, decided to transfer to New York University for its prestigious film studies course. Within a few years, she found work with the fledgling Cable News Network (CNN), and eventually rose to become a producer and news writer there. Her experiences with the network would provide much of the comic fodder for Robin Hudson and her exasperating bosses and coworkers inside the news business.

It was an actual life-threatening event that spurred the creation of Hayter's appealing heroine. While working in Atlanta one night in 1983, Hayter was accosted on a dark, empty street by a man who attempted to sexually assault her. She fought back with an umbrella, but the trauma triggered an almost transcendent experience in which she conceived an alter ego in contrast to what she calls her standard "nice Canadian girl" persona.

Hayter took a preliminary stab at detective fiction starring a prototype of the Hudson character while traveling through India. On the trip, she ran out of reading material, so she penned a story about the slaying of a large number of characters with comically obnoxious personalities—based on people that Hayter actually knew and disliked. It went unpublished, but after an arduous time spent working as a freelance journalist in war-torn Afghanistan, she returned to New York and ventured into stand-up comedy to defeat her innate fear of public performance. Writing and gleaning responses to her jokes sharpened Hayter's comic timing, which she found translated quite well into scripting characters and plots on the page. She retooled that first story as a Robin Hudson mystery, sent it out to publishers and agents, and endured several dozen rejections before *What's a Girl Gotta Do?* was published by Soho Press.

What's a Girl Gotta Do? won Hayter the Arthur Ellis Award for best first mystery novel from Crime Writers of Canada that same year. Halter's alter ego, Robin Hudson, is introduced as an All News Network on-air journalist, a vivacious, smart, funny redhead whose marriage to a colleague is on the rocks. She spots her husband romancing a younger female colleague at a holiday work party, and Hudson's ego is already a bit shattered due to a recent demotion after she infamously burped into a live microphone at a White House press conference. At the fancy hotel party, someone slips her a note that hints about the findings of a private investigator, and if interested, she can find out more at Room 13D. Hudson arrives at the door, but no one answers; when the man inside is later found murdered, she becomes the prime suspect.

Hudson is forced to solve her way out of this predicament, and the plot spins around her estranged husband's new love, a break-in at her apartment, and several other coworkers with secrets to hide. *What's a Girl Gotta Do?* was reviewed enthusiastically by *Washington Post Book World* writer Stephen Stark. "This is a mystery where you wait on the edge of your seat not for the next murder, but for the next thing Robin is going to say," Stark declared. Other critiques commended the indomitable, endearing heroine, as well as the behind-the-scenes glimpse of a powerful television news network. "Not only has Hayter created a good screwball plot, with loads of characters you love to hate, but she has a genuine gift for the odd turn of phrase," declared *Belles Lettres* reviewer Bettina Berch. A *Booklist* critic faulted the first-time author's style, but conceded that the novel had other attributes. "This is not the most literate mystery," remarked Emily Melton, "but it's cute and funny and gutsy and entertaining."

Hayter won a contract with Viking to write several more Robin Hudson mysteries. Her quirky telejournalist heroine returned with *Nice Girls Finish Last.* Freshly divorced and cautiously dating, Hudson is perplexed by mounting evidence that someone seems to be trying to kill the men with whom she has had dates. Inter-office troubles at the All News Network conspire to make her workday traumatic as well. When her gynecologist is found dead and evidence links him to an S&M club in the city, Hudson is assigned to the story, though she is disheartened by the sensationalist angle that her boss demands. Meanwhile, Hudson's religious aunt is visiting her in the city, and Hudson is forced to maintain a certain demure appearance while investigating the New York area's sexual underworld. The mishap-filled man-

ner in which the murder mystery and her personal life intersect brings the plot to a close. The book is "sassy and bright, with real laughs at the end of the funny lines," remarked a *Kirkus Reviews* reviewer of *Nice Girls Finish Last.* A *Publishers Weekly* reviewer stated that the author "has a splendid time spoofing egos on both sides of the camera."

Revenge of the Cootie Girls is Hayter's third Robin Hudson mystery. Once again, she sets the work in her adopted home, New York City, and peoples Robin's life with an eccentric secondary cast of coworkers and friends. The plot starts off with an invitation to a Halloween scavenger hunt, and the news correspondent brings along several of her equally iconoclastic female friends to help; mixed into the night's festivities is their search for Hudson's suddenly missing intern. The clues to her whereabouts, naturally, merge with those of the scavenger hunt—but as Hudson and her friends take part, she realizes that she is revisiting all of the same places that she so memorably encountered on her very first visit to Manhattan in 1979 with her old friend Julie. Here, Hudson draws upon her own comic mishaps from her first visit, when she and her Edmonton friend met two men who turned out to be involved in organized crime. Hudson's character is also drawn back into her problematic adolescence in Minnesota, during which she suffered the taunts of her classmates as a "cootie girl"—as did all her friends. In the end, Hudson and her posse solve the mystery and break up a money laundering racket in the process. Commenting upon its memory-laden subplot, a *Publishers Weekly* reviewer called it a "bittersweet but lively romp."

The complex plot of *The Last Manly Man* includes a drug that enhances sexual potency, radical vegan activists, Hudson's most recent assignment for a "Man of the Future" news report, and chimpanzee research. Hudson's personal life—especially her dating travails—also figure comically into the plot, especially when she discovers that someone in New York is impersonating her. Again, Hayter earned positive reviews for the depiction of her memorable alter ego and the quick-paced plot. Reviewing *The Last Manly Man* for *Quill & Quire,* Lynn Crosbie called it "a smooth and enjoyable read, densely plotted, and highly eventful. . . . The book is amusing, if graspingly so at times, and endearingly sex-centered." A *New York Times Book Review* assessment from crime reviewer Marilyn Stasio faulted what she termed Hayter's excessive use of humor, though she found in her characterization of modern New York life "just the right dash of caustic wit."

Hayter branched out with *Naked Brunch,* a stand-alone horror novel with a comic touch. Secretary Annie Engel does not remember tearing out the throats of businessmen until confronted by Marco Potenza, who tells her she is a werewolf. Meanwhile, Annie has fallen in love with Jim, another werewolf, who warns her about Marco, as Marco does about Jim. *Booklist* contributor Kristine Huntley wrote: "Hayter mixes chick lit . . . and mystery . . . with dark fantasy for a jolly good romp."

Hayter's next novel, *Bandit Queen Boogie: A Madcap Caper of Two Accidental Criminals,* is a comic mystery in which blonde Chloe Bowen and Blackie Maher, a tattooed brunette, finish college and head out on a road trip to Italy. As they travel they attract an ongoing number of married men who proposition them. Chloe and Blackie subsequently rip them off after drugging them when they return to their hotel rooms. They go too far, however, when they steal a statue of the Hindu god Ganesh. Other characters include a coke-snorting heiress, depressed newspaperman, and an Indian mob family. In a *Booklist* review, Jenny McLarin commented that Hayter's stories work well not only because of the plots and characters she creates "but because she does so in a dry, straight-faced prose style that makes it all the funnier."

BIOGRAPHICAL AND CRITICAL SOURCES:

BOOKS

Heising, Wilmetta L., *Detecting Women 2: A Reader's Guide and Checklist for Mystery Series Written by Women,* Purple Moon Press (Dearborn, MI), 1996.

PERIODICALS

Belles Lettres, spring, 1994, Bettina Berch, review of *What's a Girl Gotta Do?,* p. 70.
Booklist, May 1, 2003, Kristine Huntley, review of *Naked Brunch,* p. 1585; June 1, 2004, Jenny McLarin, review of *Bandit Queen Boogie: A Madcap Caper of Two Accidental Criminals,* p. 1707.
Kirkus Reviews, January 1, 1996, review of *Nice Girls Finish Last,* p. 26; February 1, 1997, review of *Revenge of the Cootie Girls,* p. 175; June 1, 2004, review of *Bandit Queen Boogie,* p. 509.
Library Journal, January, 1996, Rex E. Klett, review of *Nice Girls Finish Last,* p. 148; July, 2004, Karen Core, review of *Bandit Queen Boogie,* p. 70.
New York Times Book Review, August 2, 1998, Marilyn Stasio, review of *The Last Manly Man,* p. 24.
Publishers Weekly, January 15, 1996, review of *Nice Girls Finish Last,* p. 449; January 20, 1997, review of *Revenge of the Cootie Girls,* p. 396.
Quill & Quire, July, 1998, Lynn Crosbie, review of *The Last Manly Man,* p. 37.
Washington Post Book World, February 6, 1994, Stephen Stark, review of *What's a Girl Gotta Do?,* p. 4.

ONLINE

Beatrice.com, http://www.beatrice.com/ (December 29, 2006), Ron Hogan, interview.
January Online, http://www.januarymagazine.com/ (December 29, 2006), Newton Love and Delphine Cingal, "Sparkle Hayter Finishes First" (interview).
Mystery One Bookstore, http://www.mysteryone.com/ (December 29, 2006), Jon Jordan, "Interview with Sparkle Hayter."
No Exit Press, http://www.noexit.co.uk/ (December 29, 2006), biography.
Richmond Review, http://www.richmondreview.co.uk/ (December 29, 2006), Victoria Williams, review of *Nice Girls Finish Last.*
Sparkle Hayter Home Page, http://www.sparklehayter.com (December 29, 2006).*

*   *   *

HAYTER, Sparkle Lynnette
See HAYTER, Sparkle

*   *   *

HERMAN, Michelle 1955-

PERSONAL: Born March 9, 1955, in Brooklyn, NY; daughter of Morton and Sheila Herman; married Glen Holland (a painter); children: Grace. *Education:* Brooklyn College, City University of New York, B.S., 1976; University of Iowa, M.F.A., 1986. *Religion:* Jewish.

*ADDRESSES: Home—*Clintonville, OH. *Office—* Department of English, Ohio State University, 165 Denney Hall, 164 West 17th Ave., Columbus, OH 43210; fax: 614-292-7816. *E-mail*—herman.2@osu.edu.

CAREER: Associated Press, reporter, 1976; freelance editor, 1976-84; M.F.A. Program in Creative Writing, Ohio State University, Columbus, director and associate professor of English, 1988—, now professor of English.

AWARDS, HONORS: Teaching-writing fellow, University of Iowa, 1985-86; creative writing fellow, National Endowment for the Arts, 1986; Syndicated Fiction Award, PEN, 1986, for "All I Want to Know"; James Michener fellow, 1987; individual artist's grants, Ohio Arts Council, 1989 and 1998; Lilly Foundation fellow, 1990; Ohio State University research awards, 1990 and 1991, and University Alumni Distinguished Teaching Award; Harold U. Ribalow Award, Hadassah, 1991, for *Missing;* Copernicus Foundation grant.

WRITINGS:

Missing (novel), Ohio State University Press (Columbus, OH), 1990.
A New and Glorious Life (novellas), Carnegie Mellon University Press (Pittsburgh, PA), 1998.
Dog: A Short Novel, MacAdam/Cage (San Francisco, CA), 2005.
The Middle of Everything: Memoirs of Motherhood (essays), University of Nebraska Press (Lincoln, NE), 2005.

Work represented in anthologies, including *Twenty under Thirty: Best Stories by America's New Young Writers.* Contributor to periodicals, including *North American Review, Story, Southern Review,* and *American Scholar.* Fiction editor of *Journal.*

SIDELIGHTS: Michelle Herman has won significant acclaim for her novel *Missing* and her collection of three novellas, *A New and Glorious Life. Missing* concerns an elderly Jewish woman, Rivke Vasilevsky, who lives alone in her small apartment in Brooklyn. Vasilevsky's ties to the rest of the world are somewhat tenuous. Although her children and grandchildren visit and phone regularly, the old woman lives in relative isolation, napping most days and lying awake most evenings. Among her few consolations are visits from her granddaughter Rachel, a photographer. While sharing her own photographs with Rachel, Vasilevsky determines to salvage the beads from a dress she is wearing in one of the pictures. When she is unable to find the dress, she immediately springs into action, even drawing up a list of possible suspects who may have stolen the dress. Gradually, she becomes unhinged by the incident, which serves as a catalyst for the old woman's recollections of her long, rather depressing life. This flood of memories, in turn, leads to greater realization of life's often sad ways.

Missing won praise as a profound and refreshing literary debut. "What a relief," exclaimed Eve Shelnutt in the *Columbus Dispatch,* "to observe a young writer forgoing youth-culture portrayals for a searing investigation into the mind of an 89-year-old Jewish widow." Frances A. Koestler in the *New York Times Book Review* believed that Herman "has managed an impressive feat of transgenerational empathy by penetrating the psyche of an old woman, [but] her book lacks structure." Reviewing the work in *Ohio Writer,* Abby Frucht found *Missing* "beautiful" and added that the novel "is an act of devotion, and its final sad moments are deeply satisfying." Kathryn Ruth Bloom wrote in *Hadassah* that the novel "demonstrates [Herman's] talents as a novelist." Bloom declared that "Herman's is a name to look for in the future." Similarly, Shelnutt concluded by affirming that Herman is a writer whose "gaze is unflinching and whose characters in future novels will doubtlessly compel." *Publishers Weekly* critic Sybil Steinberg called *Missing* "a small triumph: the creation of a character, and a way of life, in all their poignant human complexity."

A New and Glorious Life contains three novellas focusing on artists and academics trying to find themselves. "Filled with warm, eccentric characters," wrote a critic in *Publishers Weekly,* "each novella explores the difficulties faced by an assortment of individuals intellectually rich but emotionally uncertain." In "Auslander," a translator is drawn into the lives of a Romanian poet and her husband when the poet refuses to have her work published. "Hope among Men" tells of a woman suffering from two broken romances. The title novella, "Herman's strongest work," as Patrick Giles noted in the *New York Times Book Review,* is a love story between a composer and a poet who meet at a writers' colony. Giles called their relationship "an unexpectedly moving experience," while the *Publishers Weekly* critic felt that "Herman explores the full length of this friendship, slowly guiding the story toward a bright, charged conclusion."

Dog: A Short Novel is the story of Jill Rosen, originally from Queens, New York, and now a poet and professor at a Midwestern college. Jill, who lives alone and is distrustful of people in general, finds a beagle puppy on a foster care Web site and names him Phil, after a first failed relationship and the Phils whose books she keeps by her bed, including Roth, Larkin, Levine, and Lopate. Phil is an intelligent dog and extremely devoted to Jill, and Jill's life is made happier as she learns from Phil about loyalty, trust, and love. *Booklist* contributor Elizabeth Dickie concluded by saying that "this novel is as thought-provoking as it is charming."

Booklist reviewer Margaret Flanagan described *The Middle of Everything: Memoirs of Motherhood* as being "a unique primer on the pitfalls of striving for parental perfection." Herman writes about her childhood and her mother who suffered from depression and mental illness. She reveals how she tried to be the perfect mother to her own daughter, Grace, who suffered a breakdown at age six because she was so closely tied to Herman. Grace recovered with therapy, and Herman's memoir is an enlightening warning about attempting to reach the goal of perfection when parenting a child. "Herman writes about the multifaceted experience of parenting with elegance and hard-earned humility," commented a *Publishers Weekly* contributor.

BIOGRAPHICAL AND CRITICAL SOURCES:

BOOKS

Herman, Michelle, *The Middle of Everything: Memoirs of Motherhood,* University of Nebraska Press (Lincoln, NE), 2005.

PERIODICALS

Booklist, February 15, 2005, Margaret Flanagan, review of *The Middle of Everything: Memoir of Motherhood,* p. 1051; March 1, 2005, Elizabeth Dickie, review of *Dog: A Short Novel,* p. 1137.
Columbus Dispatch, March 25, 1990, Eve Shelnutt, review of *Missing.*
Entertainment Weekly, March 25, 2005, Leah Greenblatt, review of *Dog,* p. 79.
Hadassah, August-September, 1990, Kathryn Ruth Bloom, review of *Missing.*
Kirkus Reviews, January 1, 2005, review of *Dog,* p. 10.
Library Journal, February 1, 2005, Lisa Nussbaum, review of *Dog,* p. 68.

New York Times Book Review, February 17, 1991, Frances A. Koestler, review of *Missing,* p. 14; December 20, 1998, Patrick Giles, review of *A New and Glorious Life,* p. 18.
Ohio Writer, July-August, 1990, Abby Frucht, review of *Missing,* p. 7.
Publishers Weekly, February 9, 1990, Sybil Steinberg, review of *Missing,* p. 47; June 1, 1998, review of *A New and Glorious Life,* p. 47; January 31, 2005, review of *Dog,* p. 49, review of *Memoirs of Motherhood,* p. 57.

ONLINE

Collected Miscellany, http://kevinholtsberry.com/blog.html (June 8, 2005), Kevin Holtsberry, "A Conversation with Michelle Herman: Part I;" (June 9, 2005), Kevin Holtsberry, "A Conversation with Michelle Herman: Part II."
Conversations with Famous Writers, http://conversationswithfamouswriters.com/ (January 12, 2006), interview.
Michelle Herman Home Page, http://people.cohums.ohio-state.edu/herman2 (November 30, 2006).

*   *   *

HIGH, Philip E. 1914-
(Philip Empson High)

PERSONAL: Born April 28, 1914, in Biggleswade, England; son of William (a bank clerk) and Muriel High; married Pamela Baker, August 17, 1950 (died, September, 1997); children: Jacqueline, Beverly. *Education:* Attended high school in Canterbury, England. *Politics:* "Tory." *Religion:* "Raised Church of England, now unorthodox believer."

ADDRESSES: Home—Canterbury, Kent, England. *Agent*—Philip Harbottle, 32 Tynedale Ave., Wallsend, Tyne and Wear N28 9LS, England.

CAREER: Worked as insurance agent, realtor, shop assistant, psychic medium, and journalist, 1935-50; East Kent Road Car Co. Ltd., Kent, England, bus driver, 1950-79; writer, 1955—. *Military service:* Royal Navy; served during World War II.

WRITINGS:

SCIENCE FICTION NOVELS, EXCEPT WHERE NOTED

No Truce with Terra, Ace Books (New York, NY), 1964.

The Prodigal Sun, Ace Books (New York, NY), 1964.

The Mad Metropolis, Ace Books (New York, NY), 1966, published as *Double Illusion,* Dobson (London, England), 1970.

Reality Forbidden, Ace Books (New York, NY), 1967.

These Savage Futurians, Ace Books (New York, NY), 1967.

Twin Planets, Paperback Library (New York, NY), 1967.

The Time Mercenaries, Ace Books (New York, NY), 1968.

Invader on My Back, Robert Hale (London, England), 1968.

Butterfly Planet, Robert Hale (London, England), 1968, reprinted, Wildside Press (Rockville, MD), 2002.

Come, Hunt an Earthman, Robert Hale (London, England), 1973.

Sold—for a Spaceship, Robert Hale (London, England), 1973.

Speaking of Dinosaurs, Robert Hale (London, England), 1974.

Fugitive from Time, Robert Hale (London, England), 1978.

Blindfold from the Stars, Dennis Dobson (London, England), 1979.

The Best of Philip E. High, edited by Philip Harbottle, Wildside Press (Rockville, MD), 2002.

A Step to the Stars, edited by Philip Harbottle, Wildside Press (Rockville, MD), 2004.

Contributor to magazines and newspapers, including *Authentic Science Fiction.*

SIDELIGHTS: Philip High once told *CA:* "I write because I have to write. Once an idea is formed, it prods and nags until I begin. Once started, I keep hours that no work union would tolerate. My wife keeps calling me for meals, my friends write and ask if I am dead because I don't answer letters. I am hooked on the damn thing and my Muse stands over me with a whip.

"I have never claimed to be a great literary figure. I am a storyteller and a square one to boot. I like all the loose ends tied up by the last page and I am psychologically incapable of writing anything but a happy ending. I suppose, deep down, I write as an off-beat do-gooder, hence the happy ending solution.

"My advice to young writers is to write the type of yarn you like reading the best. If you like reading Westerns more than anything else, don't try to write a detective story. Soak yourself in Westerns, then try your hand. I papered an entire wall with rejection slips until I tried the form of literature I like most, science fiction. My first short story in this field was accepted at first attempt. Note: I don't think this rule applies to poetry. I love verse, but have written only nine poems (never considered for publication) which I can read without shuddering."

High's novels are characterized by well-constructed story lines and bizarre settings without stylistic flamboyance. In *Twin Planets,* alien invaders wreak havoc on a future alternate Earth, and the humans are compelled to try to help this Earth avoid the same fate. Aliens are the antagonists in *Invader on My Back,* as well. In this book, the aliens have separated people into groups by personality type, but they all have one thing in common—a fear of looking up as the result of their subservient status. In *Reality Forbidden,* dream machines exist that are capable of lulling humans into conformity. Don D'Ammassa observed in *Twentieth-Century Science-Fiction Writers,* "Indeed, one of the many recurring themes in High's novels is a dread of conformity and the value of the individual."

BIOGRAPHICAL AND CRITICAL SOURCES:

BOOKS

Twentieth-Century Science-Fiction Writers, 3rd edition, St. James Press (Detroit, MI), 1991.

PERIODICALS

Books and Bookmen, April, 1970, review of *The Time Mercenaries,* p. 26.

Times Literary Supplement, November 28, 1968, review of *Reality Forbidden,* p. 1346.

*   *   *

HIGH, Philip Empson
See HIGH, Philip E.

HITLER, Bing
    See FERGUSON, Craig

*   *   *

HOOD, Ken
    See DUNCAN, Dave

*   *   *

HUNTER, Allan G. 1955-

PERSONAL: Born May 7, 1955, in Beckford, Gloucestershire, England; naturalized U.S. citizen; son of William James (an air force officer) and Elsa (a homemaker) Hunter. *Ethnicity:* "White Cisalpine Celt." *Education:* St. John's College, Oxford, B.A., 1976, M.A., 1979, D.Phil., 1983. *Politics:* "Liberal/Democrat." *Religion:* Church of England. *Hobbies and other interests:* Writing novels, restoring motorcycles.

ADDRESSES: Home—Watertown, MA. *Office*—English Area, Curry College, Milton, MA 02186. *E-mail*—aghunter@curry.edu.

CAREER: Teacher of English and French at a school in England, 1976-77; Fairleigh Dickinson University, Oxford Campus, Oxford, England, senior lecturer in English, 1979-83; Peper Harow Therapeutic Community, Surrey, England, staff member, 1983-86; Curry College, Milton, MA, professor of English, 1986—, head of English area, 1987-90, 1993-95. Coordinator of justice program at Cedar Junction maximum security prison in Walpole, 1988-90; University of Massachusetts at Boston, teacher of British and American fiction courses, 1991-93; Cambridge Center for Adult Education, writing teacher, 1997—; private practice as a therapist, using writing for self-exploration; teaches private writing classes; *The Essential Indian Motorcycle Resource Book,* publisher; guest on media programs. Massachusetts Council on Prison Education, corporation member. Rugby coach and part-time referee.

MEMBER: Association for Psychological Type.

WRITINGS:

Joseph Conrad and the Ethics of Darwinism, Croom Helm (London, England), 1983.

The Therapeutic Uses of Writing, Nova Science (New York, NY), 1996, published as *The Sanity Manual,* 1999.
Life Passages: Writing Exercises for Self-Exploration, Nova Science (New York, NY), 2000.
How They Met, Xlibris (Philadelphia, PA), 2000.
(Editor) *From Coastal Command to Captivity: The Memoir of a Second World War Airman,* Pen and Sword (Barnsley, South Yorkshire, England), 2003.

Contributor to books, including *A Closer Look,* edited by Adelizzi and Goss, CC Press (Milton, MA), 1995. Staff columnist, *Shared Visions on Teaching and Learning,* 1997—. Contributor of about thirty articles and reviews to academic journals, including *Conradiana* and *Notes and Queries.*

SIDELIGHTS: Allan G. Hunter once told *CA:* "My self-help books are designed as a series of writing exercises that will allow the reader to be an active participant in the process of self-discovery. The books provide the exercises and the possible ways of assessing the writing the reader may produce. As such they provide the necessary context that allows readers to 'place' themselves and to begin further reflections upon who they may be.

"I chose to write self-help volumes when it became clear to me that many people were spending a lot of time writing, and that in very little of this writing were they allowing themselves to emerge—at all. Writing was a chore for them. Rarely were they able to use the activity of writing as a way to access their own wisdom, or to uncover what they already knew but had forgotten to ask for. My aim is to allow writers to acknowledge their own wisdom and their own vision."

Hunter also mentioned his research interests in "Shakespeare's tragic pairings" and in the later fiction of Joseph Conrad. In regard to the former, he commented: "Romeo and Juliet are perfectly paired—they have their own language and sphere of reference. Yet their equality becomes a *folie a deux.* This tragic inversion of the marriage pairing sheds light on other pairs, or twins, who identify each other throughout the plays. A detailed examination reveals exciting new readings of *As You Like It, Twelfth Night, Macbeth, King Lear,* and the last plays." In regard to the latter, Hunter wrote: "The visual element and the ironic use of cliche in Conrad's later novels works against the narrators, with all their linguistic foibles. A picture emerges of Conrad as a visually stimulated author, a character within the work, a provider of information trapped in the limitation of his own language—an act of which he allows his narrators to be only partially aware."

More recently Hunter added: *"From Coastal Command to Captivity: The Memoir of a Second World War Airman* is a memoir of my father's wartime experiences in the Royal Air Force, his time as a prisoner of war, and his release in 1945 after nearly four years of captivity in such places as Stalag Luft III. When he died, after we had been working on his memoir together for a decade, my father left the papers to me to complete. This explains why the finished memoir is attributed to me as author. Working on his life story allowed my father to reach a place of peace about events that had traumatized him for fifty years. It was, one could say, therapeutic writing at its most useful. It's also a valuable tale for any reader."

BIOGRAPHICAL AND CRITICAL SOURCES:

ONLINE

Writing for Self-Exploration, http://www.therapeutic writing.com (March 7, 2007).

J

JACKSON, Shelley 1963-

PERSONAL: Born 1963, in the Philippines; immigrated to the United States; naturalized U.S. citizen. *Education:* Stanford University, A.B.; Brown University, M.F.A.

ADDRESSES: Home—Brooklyn, NY. *E-mail*—shelley@drizzle.com.

CAREER: Writer and illustrator.

AWARDS, HONORS: Electronic Literature Award, 2001, for *Patchwork Girl.*

WRITINGS:

Patchwork Girl, by Mary/Shelley & herself (hypertext novel), Eastgate Systems, 1995.
(And illustrator) *The Old Woman and the Wave* (juvenile), DK Ink (New York, NY), 1998.
(And illustrator) *Sophia, the Alchemist's Dog* (juvenile), DK Ink (New York, NY), 2000, Atheneum Books for Young Readers (New York, NY), 2002.
The Melancholy of Anatomy (stories), Anchor (New York, NY), 2002.
Half Life: A Novel, HarperCollins (New York, NY), 2006.

ILLUSTRATOR:

Nancy Farmer, *Do You Know Me?* (juvenile), Orchard Books (New York, NY), 1993.

Rebecca C. Jones, *Great Aunt Martha* (juvenile), Dutton Children's Books (New York, NY), 1995.
Cynthia DeFelice, *Willy's Silly Grandma* (juvenile), Orchard Books (New York, NY), 1997.
Kim Siegelson, *Escape South* (juvenile), Golden Books (New York, NY), 2000, Random House (New York, NY), 2004.
Kelly Link, *Magic for Beginners,* Small Beer Press (Northhampton, MA), 2005.
Janice N. Harrington, *The Chicken-Chasing Queen of Lamar County* (juvenile), Farrar, Straus and Giroux (New York, NY), 2008.

Contributor to periodicals, including *Grand Street, Paris Review, Conjunctions, Fence,* and *Kenyon Review.*

SIDELIGHTS: Shelley Jackson creates fiction rife with base imagery and characters exhibiting disturbing behavior. Her works include *Patchwork Girl, by Mary/Shelley & herself,* a hypertext novel that has drawn comparisons to Mary Shelley's *Frankenstein.* In Jackson's novel, Mary Shelley has actually fashioned a female creature similar to the gruesome male monstrosity featured in her own novel. Shelley's female creation, fashioned like the creature in *Frankenstein* from various body parts, becomes obsessed with her creator and tracks her to America. During one notable episode in Jackson's tale, the ungainly female creation loses control of her various parts and is compelled to reassemble herself.

The Melancholy of Anatomy is a collection of short stories that Judith Rosen, writing in *Publishers Weekly,* deemed to be full of "corporeal fantasies." The collection includes "Eggs," wherein a middle-aged woman secretes from one of her tear ducts an egg that grows as large as a boulder, and "Nerve," in which a deranged individual reaps nerve fibers and fashions them into hats. Susan Salter Reynolds, writing in the *Los Angeles Times Book Review,* proclaimed *The Melancholy of Anatomy* "subversive." A *Publishers Weekly* reviewer conceded that they are also "cleverly imagined."

Half Life: A Novel is Jackson's story of Nora Olney, a twenty-eight-year-old conjoined twin, whose twin, Blanche, has been comatose for fifteen years. The story takes place in an America where so-called "twofers" are common, possibly because of radioactive fallout. Nora travels to London, where through the help of the Unity Foundation, she will have Blanche surgically separated from her body, which will result in Blanche's death. When Nora arrives, however, unexplainable events, including the fact that her own body seems to act out on its own, lead her to suspect that Blanche is trying to communicate with her. *Booklist* contributor John Green called the novel "a clever and surprisingly moving exploration of identity and connectedness." "Jackson has imagination to burn," commented Tania Barnes in the *Library Journal,* "and her writing, strange as it is, stuns."

Jackson is also an illustrator and writer of children's books. In 1998 she produced *The Old Woman and the Wave,* in which an irritable old woman discovers the magical properties of a huge wave that has hovered over her home for some time. Lisa Shea, writing in the *New York Times Book Review,* proclaimed the tale "wistful, wishful." A reviewer in the *Bulletin of the Center for Children's Books* described Jackson's book as being a "modern fable." The latter critic acknowledged Jackson's illustrations as "surrealistic collage paintings . . . with splashes of color and myriads of shapes and viewpoints."

Jackson is also the illustrator and author of *Sophia, the Alchemist's Dog.* When a royal alchemist fails to meet the expectations of the king, who pays him to turn lead into gold, his dog, Sophia, who has been feeling neglected, takes on the task and succeeds, with the help of an angel and an imp. Meanwhile, the alchemist searches for the key to making gold by painting and sketching his nightmares and visions, which the king then recognizes as being the work of a talented artist. Since gold no longer seems to be important, Sophie hides her secret in a mouse hole to be forgotten, and the alchemist becomes the royal painter, mixing egg yolks

with pigment to create his gold. Jackson uses acrylics and pen-and-ink drawings and what *Booklist* contributor Karin Snelson called "Leonardo da Vinci-style sketches and scribbles." Snelson wrote: "Jackson's artwork shines."

In addition to both illustrating and writing children's books, Jackson has provided artwork for books by other storytellers. She served as illustrator of Nancy Farmer's *Do You Know Me?,* which recounts the culture clash that ensues when a family in Zimbabwe hosts an uncle from Mozambique. "Universal themes . . . are central to this novel," declared Lyn Miller-Lachmann in the *School Library Journal.* Lois F. Anderson reported in *Horn Book* that *Do You Know Me?* "manages to deal with serious issues and . . . provoke laughter." A *Publishers Weekly* reviewer affirmed that "Jackson's spirited . . . illustrations exhibit a distinctive personality."

Jackson also supplied illustrations for Rebecca C. Jones's *Great Aunt Martha,* wherein a girl sees her playtime options limited as a consequence of a relative's visit. Jody McCoy, writing in *School Library Journal,* noted Jackson's "lively illustrations," and Martha V. Parravano, in her *Horn Book* analysis, remarked on the "strong, stylized illustrations that successfully play with perspective." Further praise came from a *Publishers Weekly* critic who declared that "Jackson's illustrations are marked by vibrant colors and varied perspectives."

Cynthia DeFelice's *Willy's Silly Grandma* impressed Nancy Vasilakis, who wrote in *Horn Book* about Jackson's "bold ink and crayon vignettes." A *Publishers Weekly* critic stated that Jackson's artwork "impressively manages to both scare and comfort." Jackson also illustrated Kelly Link's *Magic for Beginners,* a collection of surreal tales that feature zombies, ghost dogs, rabbits that camp out on a lawn and haunt a house, and a convenience store clerk who wears "experimental C.I.A. pajamas."

Jackson is developing a project she calls *Skin,* which she describes on her Home Page as being "a mortal work of art: a story tattooed on readers' bodies, one word at a time." More than two thousand tattooed participants are expected to be part of Jackson's project.

BIOGRAPHICAL AND CRITICAL SOURCES:

PERIODICALS

Booklist, April 1, 1993, Janice Del Negro, review of *Do You Know Me?,* p. 143; May 15, 1998, Susan Dove Lempke, review of *The Old Woman and the Wave,*

p. 1633; February 15, 2001, Hazel Rochman, review of *Escape South,* p. 1153; October 1, 2002, Karin Snelson, review of *Sophia, the Alchemist's Dog,* p. 336; June 1, 2005, Ray Olson, review of *Magic for Beginners,* p. 1768; July 1, 2006, John Green, review of *Half Life: A Novel,* p. 30.

Bulletin of the Center for Children's Books, March, 1998, review of *The Old Woman and the Wave,* p. 247.

Horn Book, September-October, 1993, Lois F. Anderson, review of *Do You Know Me?;* September-October, 1995, Martha V. Parravano, review of *Great Aunt Martha;* May-June, 1997, Nancy Vasilakis, review of *Willy's Silly Grandma.*

Kirkus Reviews, August 15, 2002, review of *The Alchemist's Dog,* p. 1226.

Library Journal, July 1, 2006, Tania Barnes, review of *Half Life,* p. 66.

Los Angeles Times Book Review, April 28, 2002, Susan Salter Reynolds, review of *The Melancholy of Anatomy.*

New York Times Book Review, September 20, 1998, Lisa Shea, review of *The Old Woman and the Wave,* p. 33.

Publishers Weekly, March 15, 1993, review of *Do You Know Me?;* June 26, 1995, review of *Great Aunt Martha;* February 24, 1997, review of *Willy's Silly Grandma,* p. 89; January 19, 1998, review of *The Old Woman and the Wave,* p. 377; February 4, 2002, Judith Rosen, review of *The Melancholy of Anatomy;* February 18, 2002, review of *The Melancholy of Anatomy,* p. 71; August 5, 2002, review of *Sophia, the Alchemist's Dog,* p. 72; June 6, 2005, review of *Magic for Beginners* p. 45; May 22, 2006, review of *Half Life,* p. 31.

School Library Journal, April, 1993, Lyn Miller-Lachmann, review of *Do You Know Me,?* p. 118; July, 1995, Jody McCoy, review of *Great Aunt Martha,* p. 64; October, 2002, Catherine Threadgill, review of *Sophia, the Alchemist's Dog,* p. 166.

ONLINE

Shelley Jackson Home Page, http://www.ineradicable stain.com (December 26, 2006).*

*   *   *

JACQUES, Brian 1939-

PERSONAL: Surname is pronounced "Jakes"; born June 15, 1939, in Liverpool, England; son of James (a truck driver) and Ellen Jacques; children: David, Marc. *Education:* Attended St. John's School, Liverpool, England.

Politics: "Humanitarian/socialist." *Religion:* Roman Catholic. *Hobbies and other interests:* Opera, walking the dog, crossword puzzles.

*ADDRESSES: Home—*Liverpool, England. *Office—* BBC-Radio Merseyside, 55 Paradise St., Liverpool L1 3BP, England.

CAREER: Writer and broadcaster. Formerly worked variously as a seaman, 1954-57, railway fireman, 1957-60, longshoreman, 1960-65, long-distance truck driver, 1965-75, docks representative, 1975-80, and logger, bus driver, and policeman. Freelance radio broadcaster, including for BBC-Radio and BBC-Radio 2, 1980—, including programs *Jakestown, Saturday with Brian Jacques, Schools Quiz, Flixquiz, We All Went down the Docks, Gangland Anthology, The Eternal Christmas, Centenary of Liverpool, An Eyefool of Easter, A Lifetime Habit,* and *The Hollywood Musicals,* for BBC-Radio Merseyside, retiring 2006; former contributor to *Alan Jackson Show.* Member, BBC Northwest Television advisory council. Patron of Royal Wavertree School for the Blind. Former stand-up comic; former member of folk-singing group The Liverpool Fisherman; speaker at schools and universities.

AWARDS, HONORS: National Light Entertainment Award for Radio, Sony Company, 1982, for BBC-Radio Merseyside's *Jakestown;* Rediffusion Award for Best Light Entertainment Program on Local Radio, 1982, and Commendation, 1983; Parents' Choice Honor Book for Literature and *Booklist* Editor's Choice designation, both 1987, American Library Association Best Book for Young Adults designation, and *School Library Journal* Best Book designation, all for *Redwall;* Children's Book of the Year Award, Lancashire County (England) Library, 1988, for *Redwall,* 1991, for *Mattimeo,* and for *Mossflower* and *Salamandastron;* Western Australian Young Readers' Award (Secondary), 1990, for *Redwall,* 1992, for *Mattimeo,* and for *Mossflower;* Carnegie Medal nominations, for *Redwall, Mossflower, Mattimeo,* and *Salamandastron.*

WRITINGS:

"REDWALL" NOVEL SERIES; FOR CHILDREN

Redwall (also see below), illustrated by Gary Chalk, Hutchinson (London, England), 1986, Philomel (New York, NY), 1987.

Mossflower (also see below), illustrated by Gary Chalk, Philomel (New York, NY), 1988, collector's edition, 2004.

Mattimeo (also see below), illustrated by Gary Chalk, Avon (New York, NY), 1989, reprinted, Firebird (New York, NY), 2003.

The Redwall Trilogy (contains *Redwall, Mossflower,* and *Mattimeo*), three volumes, Red Fox (London, England), 1991.

Mariel of Redwall, illustrated by Gary Chalk, Philomel (New York, NY), 1991.

Salamandastron, illustrated by Gary Chalk, Philomel (New York, NY), 1992.

Martin the Warrior, illustrated by Gary Chalk, Philomel (New York, NY), 1993.

The Bellmaker, illustrated by Allan Curless, Hutchinson (London, England), 1994, Philomel (New York, NY), 1995.

Outcast of Redwall, illustrated by Allan Curless, Philomel (New York, NY), 1995.

The Pearls of Lutra, illustrated by Allan Curless, Philomel (New York, NY), 1996.

The Long Patrol, illustrated by Allan Curless, Philomel (New York, NY), 1997.

Marlfox, Philomel (New York, NY), 1998.

The Legend of Luke, illustrated by Fangorn, Philomel (New York, NY), 1999.

Lord Brocktree, illustrated by Fangorn, Philomel (New York, NY), 2000.

Taggerung, illustrated by Peter Standley, Philomel (New York, NY), 2001.

Triss, illustrated by David Elliot, Philomel (New York, NY), 2002.

Loamhedge, illustrated by David Elliot, Philomel (New York, NY), 2003.

Rakkety Tam, illustrated by David Elliot, Philomel (New York, NY), 2004.

High Rhulain, illustrated by David Elliot, Philomel (New York, NY), 2005.

Eulalia, illustrated by David Elliot, Philomel (New York, NY), 2007.

"TRIBES OF REDWALL" SERIES; PICTURE BOOKS

Badgers, illustrated by Peter Standley, Philomel (New York, NY), 2001.

Otters, illustrated by Peter Standley, Philomel (New York, NY), 2001.

Mice, Red Fox (London, England), 2003.

Squirrels, Red Fox (London, England), 2003.

"CASTAWAYS OF THE FLYING DUTCHMAN" NOVEL SERIES; FOR CHILDREN

Castaways of the Flying Dutchman, illustrated by Ian Schoenherr, Philomel (New York, NY), 2001.

The Angel's Command, illustrated by David Elliot, Philomel (New York, NY), 2003.

Voyage of Slaves, illustrated by David Elliot, Philomel (New York, NY), 2006.

OTHER

Seven Strange and Ghostly Tales, Philomel (New York, NY), 1991.

The Great Redwall Feast (picture book), illustrated by Christopher Denise, Philomel (New York, NY), 1995.

Redwall Map and Riddler, illustrated by Chris Baker, Philomel (New York, NY), 1997.

Redwall Friend and Foe, illustrated by Chris Baker, Philomel (New York, NY), 2000.

A Redwall Winter's Tale (picture book), illustrated by Christopher Denise, Philomel (New York, NY), 2001.

The Tale of Urso Bruno: Little Father of All Bears (picture book), illustrated by Alexi Natchev, Philomel (New York, NY), 2003.

The Ribbajack, and Other Curious Yarns, Philomel (New York, NY), 2004.

The Redwall Cookbook, illustrated by Christopher Denise, Philomel (New York, NY), 2005.

Author of documentaries and plays for television and radio; author of stage play *Brown Bitter, Wet Nellies, and Scouse,* produced in Liverpool, England. Columnist for *Catholic Pictorial.*

ADAPTATIONS: Seven Strange and Ghostly Tales, was adapted for audiocassette, narrated by Jacques, Listening Library, 1996. The "Redwall" novels were adapted for audiocassette by Recorded Books. Listening Library adapted many of the "Redwall" titles, with narration by Jacques, for audiocassette. An animated television series, *Redwall,* aired on British television in 2001. The musical *Redwall: The Legend of Redwall Abbey,* featuring a libretto by Evelyn Swensson and orchestration by Vince Leonard, was published by Dramatic Publishing, 2004.

SIDELIGHTS: Known for his multi-volume "Redwall" saga, Brian Jacques is acclaimed as a "master of the animal fantasy genre," according to *Booklist* critic Sally

Estes. In his "Redwall" novels, which include *Moss-flower, Outcast of Redwall, Marlfox,* and *Taggerung,* he draws readers into a "world of woodland and meadow . . . populated with the creatures of the forest, and not a human among them," as an essayist explained in the *St. James Guide to Young-Adult Writers.* Jacques takes as his heroes the small, gentle animals of nature and pits them against rapacious predators in epic fantasy tales of battle and quest in vivid prose that has made his fantasy world seem almost real to his young fans. As a correspondent for *Time* magazine noted, "even before J.K. Rowling's Harry Potter [novels], . . . Jacques . . . was selling millions of 400-page books to spellbound children and parents." First planned as a trilogy—and initially not intended for publication at all—the "Redwall" books have blossomed into a multi-novel phenomenon with a secure and growing fandom on both sides of the Atlantic.

The plot of the "Redwall" novels, which are set in and around England's Redwall Abbey and feature a cast of anthropomorphized "gentlebeasts," features a good-versus-evil formula that appeals to both young and old. Jacques' heroes and heroines—mice, moles, hares, badgers, otters, squirrels, hawks, and the like—can be counted on to be brave, true, and kind, while villainous rats, foxes, ferrets, snakes, weasels, and stoats are consistently wicked, violent, and depraved. Such villainous creatures are dutifully defeated by the end of each novel, much to the reader's satisfaction. Interestingly, these adventurous yet comforting tales might never have seen print if it had not been for one of Jacques' former teachers.

Both Jacques' parents were Irish-Catholic immigrants to Liverpool, England, and he grew up in humble but loving surroundings, finding boyhood adventure while playing around the ocean docks near his home. Fortunately for the young Jacques, his father, a truck driver, had a healthy appreciation for literature and passed this along to his son. Through his father, Jacques learned to love books by such authors as Sir Arthur Conan Doyle, Robert Louis Stevenson, and Edgar Rice Burroughs.

Jacques wrote his first story at age ten as a school an assignment, but was immediately discouraged; believing that the tale about a crocodile and the bird who cleaned its teeth was too sophisticated to be the work of a child, Jacques' teacher called the boy a liar when Jacques insisted that he had written the story on his own. Although the event was unfortunate, because of it

Jacques realized that he had some talent. Another teacher, Austin Thomas, proved to be a less-severe critic, and encouraged the boy to read Greek literature and poetry. Higher education was not the destiny for most children growing up in Liverpool's working-class families, however. Like his friends, Jacques left school at age fifteen and started working a string of jobs that ranged from longshoreman and logger to policeman and postmaster, to stand-up comic and folk singer in a musical group called The Liverpool Fisherman.

Jacques eventually began a career as a radio personality, playwright, poet, and storyteller, and by the time he reached his early forties he had established a career as an entertainer. His well-known radio show *Jakestown,* which featured selections from Jacques' favorite operas and aired every Sunday on BBC Radio-Merseyside, was a staple for many years, until Jacques' retirement from broadcasting in the fall of 2006. It was his love of performing and giving humorous talks to children and adults, in fact, that inspired the "Redwall" saga. "I did not write my first novel, *Redwall,* with publication in mind," the author once commented. "It was mainly written as a story for [the Royal Wavertree School for the Blind in Liverpool,] where I am a patron. Luckily it was picked up by a reputable author and sent to Hutchinson." That author, Alan Durband, was one Jacques' former English teachers. He sent out the manuscript without Jacques' knowledge, and thus the "Redwall" series was born.

Redwall opens at peaceful Redwall Abbey, where a young mouse named Matthias is living as a novice among the abbots and lay creatures in a medieval-esque setting. Life at the abbey involves a lot of work, but the mice and other creatures enjoy a prosperous, comfortable existence, which Jacques describes in detail, beginning with a long description of a splendid and sumptuous feast. However, trouble is soon afoot in the form of an evil rat named Cluny the Scourge who, with his barbarous horde of followers, spends his time wreaking havoc upon the countryside. Cluny's path leads him eventually to Redwall Abbey, clearly a plum of prosperity fit for plunder. Upon hearing of Cluny's imminent approach, the Redwallers at first consider fleeing their abbey, but Matthias convinces them to stay and defend themselves.

Having stumbled upon a mysterious riddle written long ago by Martin the Warrior, the legendary mouse who founded the abbey, Matthias now hopes that by solving the riddle he will be able to locate Martin's legendary sword and defeat Cluny's army. After successfully deciphering the puzzle, the young mouse learns that he is actually Martin's descendant. He also realizes that the sword has been taken by the warlike sparrows who live in the abbey's tower. Risking his life, Matthias manages to retrieve the sword. Meanwhile, Cluny is busy besieging Redwall, where the well-fortified, well-supplied abbey is putting up a strong defense. The dastardly rat devises several plans of attack that are defeated one by one, but ultimately he manages, through trickery, to enter the abbey confines and take the gentle-beasts prisoner. The fight is not over yet, however, and Matthias leads an attack that ends in a final, lethal confrontation between the young hero and Cluny.

Jacques has continued to expand the "Redwall" saga in novels such as *Mattimeo, Salamandastron, The Pearls of Lutra,* and *Loamhedge,* which have appeared every few years since *Redwall*'s initial publication in 1986. In these volumes, Jacques go back and forth in time in the saga rather than following a strict chronological development. The story of Redwall actually begins in *Martin the Warrior,* which takes place before the abbey is actually built. A mouse named Martin—ancestor of the brave Matthias—has been enslaved by the sinister stoat Badrang, who tortures the poor mouse and forces him to work long hours without rest. Finally, Martin can take no more; he attacks one of Badrang's captains and it takes six stoat soldiers to subdue him. Tying the upstart rodent to a pole atop a hill, Badrang sentences Martin to death by leaving him exposed to roaming birds of prey. Fortunately, a mouse named Rose and Rose's friend Grumm the mole come to his rescue. After his rescue, Rose asks Martin whether he has seen her brother, who was also imprisoned by Badrang. Martin now has a mission: enlisting the help of other brave animals, he plans an attack against Badrang to defeat the stoat and free all the creature's slaves.

As readers delve into *Mossflower,* they discover Martin once again in dire circumstances. Having wandered into Mossflower Country, he imprisoned by the wildcat Verdauga, king of Kotir and ruler of the Mossflower woods. The mouse soon becomes a point of dispute between the aging and sickly Verdauga's two potential heirs: his son, Gingivere, and his daughter, Tsarmina. Gingivere is sympathetic to Martin, who insists that he did not intentionally trespass on their land. The willful and ruthless Tsarmina, however, uses the conflict in her bid for power: she manages to have her brother thrown in prison and poisons her father the king. Assuming the

throne, Tsarmina then throws Martin into the dungeon, where the mouse meets a thief named Gonff and, with the help of Gonff's talent for getting out of tight fixes, escapes. Not one to forget an injustice, Martin masses an army and causes Tsarmina's downfall. With the tyrant wildcat defeated, Martin founds Redwall Abbey in the heart of Mossflower. In this new order, members are sworn to be kind to their fellow creatures and offer aid to those in need.

Jacques's twelfth "Redwall" novel, *The Legend of Luke* is the third book in the timeline: it takes readers from the construction of the abbey and follows Martin's search for Luke, his father. The book also details the heroic deeds of Luke, and concludes Martin's part in the unfolding saga by describing his return to the abbey, where he hides the sword that will later be found by Matthias. Reviewing *The Legend of Luke* for *Booklist,* Sally Estes called the novel "another winner for the series' many fans."

In *Outcast of Redwall* Jacques focuses on a new cast of characters, although this tale also begins with its hero held prisoner by an evil carnivore. Instead of a mouse, though, this time the hero is the badger Sunflash. Sunflash, the son of Bella of Brockhall, is heir to the badgers' mountain stronghold of Salamandastron. Swartt Sixclaw, a ferret who leads a band of outlaws, is his captor until the badger escapes with the help of his friend Skarlath the hawk. Attacking Swartt with a stick, Sunflash cripples the ferret's hand, after which Swartt swears lifelong revenge. Sunflash and Skarlath each raise an army and soon begin skirmishing with the ferrets. Swartt follows his enemies to Redwall Abbey and lays siege to it. During the battle, his own infant son is lost in the confusion, and one of the abbey mice, Byrony, adopts the young ferret. Unfortunately, Veil, as the ferret is later named, is predestined by his blood to become wicked, and, despite the kindness of the Redwall creatures, he unsuccessfully tries to poison the abbey's friar. Chased away, Veil goes off in pursuit of the father who abandoned him. Meanwhile, Sunflash finds himself called to Salamandastron in dreams. At the head of a band of warrior hares and other beasts, the badger now sets off to find his true mountain home, and upon his arrival at Salamandastron, events come to a head in a final battle.

In *Mariel of Redwall* and *The Bellmaker,* Jacques introduces a brave mouse named Mariel, whose adventures reveal the history of the great bell hanging in the Redwall Abbey tower. As *Mariel of Redwall* opens, a young mouse who has been washed ashore from the sea, fends off a band of hungry seagulls with a hank of rope. With no memory of her past, the mouse draws on this event in naming herself Storm Gullwhacker. Finding her way to Redwall Abbey, Storm is befriended by another young mouse, Dandin. During a Redwall feast, one of the mice sings an ancient rhyme that sparks some of Storm's memories: knowing her name to be Mariel, she also recalls being thrown off a ship by Gabool the Wild, wicked king of the searats. Realizing her mission, Mariel joins with Dandin (who has Martin the Warrior's sword) and other friends to seek out Gabool and rescue her father. In *The Bellmaker* Mariel and Dandin unite once again, this time in a mission to defeat Foxwolf Urgan Nagru, who has usurped the throne of Southsward from good Gael Squirrelking. Joining forces with the woodland creatures still loyal to the king, the mice set about their dangerous task. Meanwhile, at the abbey, Mariel's father has visions that his daughter is in danger and sends out additional Redwallers to help.

Like *Outcast of Redwall, Salamandastron* combines characters and plotlines involving both Redwallers and the badger lords. Mara, a badger who is Lord Urthstripe's adopted daughter, together with her hare friend Pikkle Ffolger, become friends with Klitch and Goffa, a weasel and his ferret companion. The friendship leads to trouble, however, for unbeknownst to Mara and Pikkle, Klitch is the son of Ferahgo the Assassin, who is planning to lay siege to Salamandastron. Meanwhile, at Redwall Abbey the resident mice have made a similar error by befriending Dingeye and Thura, two stoats who are Ferahgo's followers. Murdering the abbey's records keeper, Dingeye and Thura steal the sword of Martin the Warrior and flee Redwall, prompting Samkin the squirrel and Arula the mole to set off in pursuit of the stoats. A third plotline involves Thrugg the otter and Dumble the dormouse, who are on a quest to find the Flowers of Icetor, the only cure for the Dryditch Fever currently plaguing Redwall.

Jacques shares more tales of Salamandastron in *Lord Brocktree,* which introduces the villainous wildcat Ungatt Trunn and the Blue Hordes. The badger Lord Brocktree meets beautiful young haremaid Dotti in the forest, and together they gather an army of moles, otters, squirrels, and hedgehogs to battle Ungatt in response to the wildcat's invasion of Salamandastron. Reviewing *Lord Brocktree* for *Horn Book,* Anne St. John lauded the author's talent for "creating memorable

characters and weaving several plot strands into one cohesive story," further noting that such talents "are at their best in this exciting adventure." Patricia A. Dollisch, reviewing the novel in *School Library Journal,* also found that the numerous characters are "easily defined and identified by their accents, a Jacques specialty."

With the events of *Redwall* as a starting point, both *Mattimeo* and *The Pearls of Lutra* focus on the descendants of Matthias. In the first-named novel, the title character is the son of Matthias. Now serving as the abbey's protector, Matthias take charge when Mattimeo and the other Redwall children are kidnaped by the fox Slagar the Cruel, who tricks the Redwallers by posing as a harmless magician during one of the abbey's feasts. Matthias assembles a band of warriors and pursues Slagar across a forbidding desert to the fox's slave kingdom. Matthias must use all his wits and courage to save his son from his wicked captor. In *The Pearls of Lutra* Martin, son of Mattimeo, son of Matthias, is faced with a challenge: to find the Pearls of Lutra, which were lost after a band of searats slaughtered the otter Lutra and his tribe. The pearls are needed as ransom for the Abbess of Redwall, whom the searats have now taken prisoner. There is one complication in the conflict that neither the searats nor Martin are aware of: Lutra's daughter, the otter Grath Longfletch, is still alive and seeking revenge for her father's death.

Taking place several years after the action in *The Pearls of Lutra, The Long Patrol* focuses on an adolescent hare named Tammo who desires to join the band of hare soldiers known as the Long Patrol, who battle the evil rat Rapscallion to defend Redwall Abbey. In *Booklist* Estes praised the manner in which Jacques "masterfully makes his familiar plot fresh, leavening it with both humor and confrontation," while *Horn Book* contributor Anne Deifendeifer dubbed the author a "master storyteller [who] spins out the plot through dialogue and the characters' interactions."

Marlfox once again finds Redwall Abbey under siege, this time by the villainous Marlfoxes and their vermin partners the river rats. Led by Queen Silth, the Marlfoxes are able to change the color of their fur and blend in with their surroundings, making them a challenging foe. In the midst of battle several valiant youngsters escape from the abbey to try and track down the tapestry of Martin the Warrior, which has been stolen by the power-hungry Marlfox Mokkan, leaving their elders behind to defend the abbey.

With *Taggerung* and *Triss* Jacques focuses on the younger generation at Redwall Abbey. Kidnaped at youth, the otter Tagg, hero of *Taggerung,* has been raised by the vermin clan of Juskarath and trained as a warrior. Once he reaches young-adulthood, however, Tagg rebels against his adopted tribe and runs away in search of his true home. During his search for Redwall Abbey, the otter takes up with a plucky mouse named Nimbalo and arrives home just in time to help his sister, Mhera, defeat the vermin who are once again attacking the abbey. *Triss* finds a young squirrel at the center of the action. One of three slaves to escape from the island of Riftgard, Triss makes her way to Redwall at the same time that members of the Long Patrol take off in search of adventure. Once again, the sword of Martin the Warrior comes into play, as Triss wields it in a face off against the persistent Ratguard army. Writing in *Horn Book,* St. John found Tagg to be "an appealing hero," while fellow *Horn Book* reviewer Barbara Scotto deemed *Triss* "another satisfying read" featuring Jacques' characteristic formula: "contentment, good cheer, plentiful food, and fine companions" balanced by "adventure, mayhem, and death, but in the end the goodness of the Abbey world."

In *Loamhedge* the spirit of Martin the Warrior inspires the brash young hare Horty Braebuck, together with two equally impulsive friends to tail two travelers, Bragoon and Sarobando, as they make their way from Redwall to Loamhedge Abbey, where they discover a cure for Horty's sister Martha Baebuck, who has been unable to walk since childhood. In another plot thread, Lonna a giant badger and a fierce warrior, sets off after Raga Bol, a pirate who, captaining his evil band of marauding searats, had attacked Lonna and left him for dead. After exacting his revenge, Lonna becomes ruler of Salamandastron.

Like most "Redwall" novels, vermin are a persistent threat in *Racketty Tam.* Led by Gulo the Savage, a wolverine from the cold northern reaches, a flood of white carnivorous foxes and ermine descends upon the innocent residents of the Mossflower woods when he learns that his traitorous brother, Askor, is hiding there, a powerful amulet in his possession. When the hoards overrun the squirrel kingdom on their way south, Racketty Tam and Doogy, two squirrel friends, go in pursuit of the savage wolverine king. After teaming up with the forces of the Long Patrol, Tam is eventually armed with the sword of Martin the Warrior. After finding his quarry, rescuing two damsels in distress, and battling Gulo to the death, Tam returns to Redwall with his new

friends, his reward true love with the beautiful squirrel Sister Armel. A smaller but no less threatening band of vermin confront the otter Tiria Wildlough in *High Rhulain,* and when she and her friends successfully fight them off, the vermin vow to avenge their disgrace. Tragically, shortly after Tiria leaves Redwall to follow a quest assigned her in a dream, Redwall is overrun by the vermin and Tiria's friend killed. Armed with a special breastplate and sling, Tiria makes her way to the Green Isle, where she helps the enslaved otter clans fight off the wildcat king Riggu Felis and finds her destiny. In *Horn Book* Anita Burkham praised the author's "trademark blend of folksy good humor and high-spirited action," adding that in *High Rhulain* the series characters exhibit a "joie de vivre that earns them the loyalty of their many fans."

With his first "Redwall" novel, Jacques created a flavorful recipe with all the right ingredients, and his portrayal of admirable heroes and contemptible villains engaged in classic battles between good and evil quickly prompted inevitable comparisons. *Redwall* was grouped by critics with other English books featuring anthropomorphized animal characters, such as Richard Adams' *Watership Down* and Kenneth Grahame's *The Wind in the Willows,* although one of the few common features is that they each feature animal protagonists exhibiting some degree of human-like behavior. Citing the comparison with *Watership Down,* however, Margery Fisher perceptively noted in her *Growing Point* assessment that, for "all the similarities of idiom, alert sophisticated narrative and neat humanisation, *Redwall* has an intriguing and unusual flavour of its own." Looking deeper into the nature of the first book in the series, *School Library Journal* contributor Susan M. Harding deemed *Redwall* more than merely a classic story of good versus evil; it is also a study of the *nature* of the two sides of this coin. Jacques, Harding continued, does not create characters who are merely "personifications of attributes," for the heroes do have flaws, and even the reprehensible Cluny has his admirable points. The "rich cast of characters, the detailed accounts of medieval warfare, and Jacques' ability to tell a good story *and* make readers think" each combine to make *Redwall* an exemplary start to the fantasy series, the critic concluded.

While settings vary and characters are legion in Jacques' series, a number of critics have remarked that readers can enter the series at any point and require little backstory to fully enjoy each novel. One reason for this is that each of the "Redwall" titles conforms, more or less, to a time-honored formula that has been summarized by *Voice of Youth Advocates* contributor Katharine L. Kan as: "Goodbeast sanctuary threatened by nogoodnik vermin and/or natural disaster, young untested heroes to the rescue." While this repeating plotline can be reassuring to fans, who know what to expect when they pick up a "Redwall" fantasy, it also has a downside. As Ruth S. Vose pointed out in her *School Library Journal* review of *Mossflower,* "suspense does not arise from the situation itself, for the end is never really in doubt." Marcus Crouch, also writing about *Mossflower* in *Junior Bookshelf,* felt that, although Jacques demonstrates narrative skill in the way he weaves different subplots together, he includes too much unnecessary detail, his style is filled with "narrative clichés," and his characters "are mostly stereotypes." Those considerations aside, Mara Alpert reflected the view of most "Redwall" fans when she wrote in her *School Library Journal* review of *Triss* that Jacques' "wonderfully imaginative and beautifully realized universe [is] . . . filled to the brim with amazing and amusing characters."

Viewed from another perspective, however, readers consistently find much to enjoy about the "Redwall" saga. In addition to the swashbuckling action, accent-filled dialogue, and bounteous feasts Jacques revels in creating, there is the enjoyment of the plotline itself. While admitting that the stories are "formulaic," Katherine Bouton asserted in her *New York Times Book Review* appraisal that they are also "wonderfully imaginative in their variety of plot and character." Jacques approaches his subject not with a heavy hand in an attempt to suggest some epic struggle, but rather with an eye toward levity. As Andy Sawyer remarked in a *School Librarian* review of *Outcast of Redwall,* not only is there much jollity in the regular feasts in which the gentlebeasts partake, but there is also plenty of "hearty japes, slapstick humour and swashbuckling action [that is] pitched perfectly at the intended readership." Much of the humor comes from the antics of the mischievous young dibbuns, but also from Jacques' satirical jibes at English upper-crust military types who in his books take the form of hares.

Another feature of Jacques' books that critics have admired is his complete lack of chauvinism: there are just as many brave and daring heroines in the series as there are heroes; likewise, the villains are often vixens or female wildcats who are just as treacherous as their male counterparts. "The author must be commended for creating a world of equal-opportunity adventuring," commented a *Publishers Weekly* reviewer. "For once,"

Carolyn Cushman wrote in her *Locus* assessment of *Mariel of Redwall,* "it's not just the boys who get to hear the spirit of Martin the Warrior—the ladies really get their chance this outing. Having a valiant female protagonist is a nice touch." Similarly, Jacques does not discriminate with regard to the age of his characters; as Tash Saecker wrote of *High Rhulain* in her *School Library Journal* review, intertwined with the book's "action, poetry, songs, courage, and vivid descriptions," he weaves "characterizations [that] are complex and show multiple sides of both adult and younger personalities."

There is something else in the books that many readers find appealing: the satisfaction of a story about good fighting evil in which both can be easily distinguished and the victor is always in the right. While some critics might see this as a drawback, others cite its benefits, one of which is encouraging young readers to keep reading. As Selma Lanes wrote in the *New York Times Book Review,* the world of Redwall is "a credible and ingratiating place . . . to which many young readers will doubtless cheerfully return." "Jacques," Sawyer concluded, "is writing for an audience who want—even need—clearly identifiable labels for their moral signposts."

While best known for his "Redwall" saga, Jacques has ventured from his fantasy series with story collections such as *Seven Strange and Ghostly Tales* and *The Ribbajack, and Other Curious Yarns,* the latter a story collection in which the author's "sly humor and suspenseful plotting will keep readers' interest engaged," according to a *Kirkus Reviews* writer. In addition, the author has on occasion also courted a younger audience, penning two "Redwall" picture books as well as *The Tale of Urso Brunov: Little Father of All Bears.* Featuring illustrations by Alexi Natchev, *The Tale of Urso Brunov* is an original tale about a miniature bear who must prove his superior strength when four younger bears in his clan are kidnaped and taken to a zoo while attempting to avoid hibernation. Describing the title character, *School Library Journal* contributor Lisa Dennis praised the repetitive phrases used in the text and characterized Urso Brunov as "a typical folktale hero, plucky, brave, self-confident, and successful." In *Booklist,* Julie Cummins noted that, in *The Tale of Urso Brunov* "Jacques displays his usual flare for animal characters and clever details."

A more substantial break from his "Redwall" universe have been his adventure novels featuring a seventeenth-century ghost ship, the *Flying Dutchman.* In the series opener, *Castaways of the Flying Dutchman,* Jacques uses the myth of the seventeenth-century ghost ship, the *Flying Dutchman,* to fashion a tale with a "spirited boy and his dog at the center," as *Horn Book* critic Peter D. Sieruta noted. In the novel, young Ben, a mute boy, and his Labrador pup Ned are saved by an angel when the ship they are on is condemned to sail on for eternity under the captaincy of the brutal Captain Vanderdecken. Because of their innocence, Ben and his dog are granted a different kind of immortality: Ben can now speak and is fluent in any language he hears, their bodies will never age, they can communicate with each other telepathically, and their task will now be to travel the world and help those in need. As they travel backward and forward through time on their mission, Ben and Ned eventually find themselves in a small English village in 1896, where they help residents save the community from a group of rapacious businessmen. GraceAnne A. DeCandido, writing in *Booklist,* described *Castaways of the Flying Dutchman* as a literary departure for Jacques and noting that the book's "swashbuckling language brims with color and melodrama." While Sieruta maintained that the different sections of the novel do not "quite mesh,"; the critic added that the story "remains involving" and that Jacques brings to life the small nineteenth-century English town with "great panache." A reviewer for *Publishers Weekly* also lauded the author's portrayal of the "bumbling thugs" who threaten the town, noting that fans of Jacques' work "will be tickled by the characters' goofy slapstick regardless of their genus."

Gaining Jacques new fans, *Castaways of the Flying Dutchman* has also sparked several sequels. In *The Angel's Command,* Ben and his loyal Labrador Ned go back in time to 1628 and return to the sea when they befriend a French pirate captain and set sail on the *Petite Marie.* After a series of seagoing adventures ends in the pirate captain's death, the duo go ashore in France, climb the Spanish Pyrenees, and become caught up in the search for a young man kidnaped by a group of black-art practitioners led by Maguda Razan. *Voyage of Slaves* finds the immortal boy and dog parting company in 1703, when Ben is captured by a slave trader and Ned becomes a performing dog with the Rizolli troupe, a caravan of traveling entertainers. Reunited when the Rizollis are also captured by the Barbary slavers, Ben and Ned must now find a way to both save themselves and the innocent actors. Noting the series' appeal to boys, Sieruta wrote in *Horn Book* that *The Angel's Command* "delivers nonstop action, pithy dialogue," and a wealth of fascinating but little-known "sea lore," and *Booklist* contributor Todd Morning deemed the book

"another page turner" which "readers who enjoyed the first book will find . . . even more exciting." Jacques' use of "vivid language, larger-than-life characters, and multiple story lines yield a sprawling, epic tale," asserted a *Kirkus Reviews* writer, while in *Publishers Weekly* a contributor wrote that, as with the "Redwall" novels, readers of *The Angel's Command* "can once again take satisfaction in the fact that virtue is rewarded, evil-doers get their comeuppance and good triumphs over evil in Jacques's universe."

Asked by a *Time* writer about the future of the "Redwall" series, Jacques was emphatic. "I love Redwall," the author explained. "Redwall is a world that I can retreat to." Speaking with Stephanie Loer in the *Writer,* Jacques explained that he planned to continue expanding the fantasy books "because there is no place I'd rather be than within the world that I've been lucky enough to create." As he admitted to Heather Frederick for *Publishers Weekly,* authoring the series has made his own life something of a fantasy. "It's a wonderful life," he explained. "I still wake up and pinch myself sometimes in the morning."

BIOGRAPHICAL AND CRITICAL SOURCES:

BOOKS

Children's Literature Review, Volume 21, Thomson Gale (Detroit, MI), 1990.
Science Fiction and Fantasy Literature, 1975-1991, Thomson Gale (Detroit, MI), 1991.
St. James Guide to Fantasy Writers, St. James Press (Detroit, MI), 1996.
St. James Guide to Young-Adult Writers, second edition, St. James Press (Detroit, MI), 1999.

PERIODICALS

Booklist, March 1, 1996, p. 1182; October 15, 1996, p. 424; February 15, 1997, Sally Estes, review of *The Pearls of Lutra,* p. 1023; December 15, 1997, Sally Estes, review of *The Long Patrol,* p. 694; December 15, 1998, Sally Estes, review of *Marlfox,* p. 750; December 15, 1999, Sally Estes, review of *The Legend of Luke,* p. 784; September 1, 2000, Sally Estes, review of *Lord Brocktree,* p. 113; March 1, 2001, GraceAnne A. DeCandido, review of *Castaways of the Flying Dutchman,* p. 1271;

August, 2001, Sally Estes, review of *Taggerung*, p. 2120; September 1, 2001, Kay Weisman, review of *A Redwall Winter's Tale*, p. 106; September 1, 2002, Sally Estes, review of *Triss*, p. 124; February 1, 2003, Todd Morning, review of *The Angel's Command*, p. 982; September 1, 2003, Julie Cummins, review of *The Tale of Urso Brunov: Little Father to All Bears*, p. 128; September 15, 2003, Chris Sherman, review of *Loamhedge*, p. 236; August, 2004, Michael Cart, review of *The Ribbajack, and Other Curious Yarns*, p. 1935; September 1, 2005, Kay Weisman, review of *High Rhulain*, p. 134; December 15, 2006, Sally Estes, review of *Voyage of Slaves*, p. 48.

Books for Your Children, spring, 1988, Jane Inglis, review of *Redwall*, p. 31.

Bulletin of the Center for Children's Books, January, 1994, p. 157; March, 1996, pp. 30-31; June, 2004, Krista Hutley, review of *The Ribbajack and Other Curious Yarns*, p. 422.

Growing Point, March, 1987, Margery Fisher, review of *Redwall*, pp. 4756-4757.

Horn Book, May-June, 1992, p. 340; January-February, 1997, pp. 85-89; March-April, 1998, Anne Deifendeifer, review of *The Long Patrol*, p. 222; May-June, 1998, p. 372; January-February, 1999, Anne St. John, review of *Marlfox*, p. 65; September-October, 2000, Anne St. John, review of *Lord Brocktree*, p. 571; March-April, 2001, Peter D. Sieruta, review of *Castaways of the Flying Dutchman*, p. 208; November-December, 2001, Anne St. John, review of *Taggerung*, pp. 750-751; January, 2003, Barbara Scotto, review of *Triss*, p. 75; March-April, 2003, Peter D. Sieruta, review of *The Angel's Command*, p. 212; January-February, 2006, Anita L. Burkam, review of *High Rhulain*, p. 82.

Junior Bookshelf, December, 1988, Marcus Crouch, review of *Mossflower*, pp. 304-305.

Kirkus Reviews, February 1, 1994, p. 144; August 1, 2001, review of *Taggerung*, p. 1125; January 1, 2003, review of *The Angel's Command*, p. 61; April 15, 2004, review of *The Ribbajack, and Other Curious Yarns*, p. 395.

Kliatt, May, 2002, Donna L. Scanlon, review of *Castaways of the Flying Dutchman*, p. 28; September, 2002, Paula Rohrlick, review of *Triss*, p. 10; November, 2002, Paula Rohrlick, review of *Taggerung*, p. 24; September, 2003, Paula Rohrlick, review of *Loamhedge*, p. 8; September, 2006, Deirdre Root, review of *Voyage of Slaves*, p. 13.

Locus, March, 1992, Carolyn Cushman, review of *Mariel of Redwall*, p. 64.

New York Times Book Review, August 23, 1987, Selma Lanes, review of *Redwall*, p. 27; February 27, 1994, Katherine Bouton, review of *Martin the Warrior*, p. 24.

Publishers Weekly, August 16, 1991, review of *Seven Strange and Ghostly Tales*, p. 58; February 20, 1995, review of *The Bellmaker*, p. 206; January 15, 1996, review of *Outcast of Redwall*, pp. 462-463; April 15, 1996, p. 34; August 19, 1996; December 30, 1996, p. 67; December 1, 1997, review of *The Long Patrol*, p. 54; January 8, 2001, review of *Castaways of the Flying Dutchman*, p. 67; March 26, 2001, Heather Frederick, "Charting a New Course," p. 34; August 27, 2001, review of *A Redwall Winter's Tale*, p. 86; December 16, 2002, review of *The Angel's Command*, p. 68; October 6, 2003, review of *The Tale of Urso Brunov*, p. 83; April 12, 2004, review of *The Ribbajack, and Other Curious Yarns*, p. 67.

School Librarian, November, 1994, Peter Andrews, review of *Redwall*, p. 151; February, 1996, Andy Sawyer, review of *Outcast of Redwall*.

School Library Journal, August, 1987, Susan M. Harding, review of *Redwall*, p. 96; November, 1988, Ruth S. Vose, review of *Mossflower*, pp. 125-126; March, 1993, p. 198; May, 1996, p. 113; January, 1998, Bruce Anne Shook, review of *The Long Patrol*, p. 112; April, 1999, Jennifer A. Fakolt, review of *Marlfox*, p. 136; February, 2000, Valerie Diamond, review of *The Legend of Luke*, p. 120; September, 2000, Patricia A. Dollisch, review of *Lord Brocktree*, p. 232; March, 2001, Eva Mitnick, review of *Castaways of the Flying Dutchman*, p. 250; September, 2001, Susan L. Rogers, review of *A Redwall Winter's Tale*, p. 190; October, 2001, Patricia A. Dollisch, review of *Taggerung*, p. 162; September, 2003, Lisa Dennis, review of *The Tale of Urso Brunov*, p. 180; October, 2003, Mara Alpert, review of *Loamhedge*, p. 168; May, 2004, Farida S. Dowler, review of *The Ribbajack and Other Curious Yarns*, p. 150; August, 2004, Francisca Goldsmith, review of *Mattimeo*, p. 76; September, 2004, Christine McGinty, review of *Rakkety Tam*, p. 208; September, 2005, Tasha Saecker, review of *High Rhulain*, p. 205; December, 2006, Tim Wadham, review of *Voyage of Slaves*, p. 146.

Time, April 16, 2001, "Riding the Waves," p. F8.

Voice of Youth Advocates, June, 1993, Katharine L. Kan, review of *Salamandastron*, p. 102.

Writer, April, 2000, Stephanie Loer, "An Interview with Brian Jacques," p. 15; February, 2005, "Brian Jacques on Writing," p. 8.

ONLINE

Official Redwall Web site, http://www.redwall.org (January 15, 2007).

Penguin Putnam Web site, http://www.penguin.co/uk/ (January 27, 2007), "Brian Jacques."*

*   *   *

JAMISON, Bill 1942-

PERSONAL: Born March 7, 1942, in Oklahoma; son of Braxton and Lois Jamison; married Cheryl Alters (a writer), 1985; children: Heather Jamison Neale. *Education:* University of North Texas, B.A., 1964; doctoral study at University of Kansas, 1967.

ADDRESSES: Home—Tesuque, NM.

CAREER: Southwest Texas State University, professor of American history. Worked in arts management, as a lecturer for the National Humanities Series, and as a consultant in London, England to British Airways and Honeywell.

AWARDS, HONORS: James Beard Award, 1994, for *Smoke and Spice: The Joy of Real Backyard Barbecue,* and 1995, for *The Border Cookbook: Authentic Home Cooking from the American Southwest and Northern Mexico.*

WRITINGS:

WITH WIFE, CHERYL ALTERS JAMISON

The Rancho de Chimayo Cookbook: The Traditional Cooking of New Mexico, Harvard Common Press (Boston, MA), 1991.

Texas Home Cooking, Harvard Common Press (Boston, MA), 1993.

Smoke and Spice: The Joy of Real Backyard Barbecue, Harvard Common Press (Boston, MA), 1994, revised edition published as *Smoke and Spice: Cooking with Smoke, the Real Way to Barbecue,* 2003.

The Border Cookbook: Authentic Home Cooking from the American Southwest and Northern Mexico, Harvard Common Press (Boston, MA), 1995.

Best Places to Stay in Mexico, 3rd edition, Houghton Mifflin (Boston, MA), 1995.

Best Places to Stay in Hawaii, 3rd edition, Houghton Mifflin (Boston, MA), 1995.

Sublime Smoke: Bold New Flavors Inspired by the Old Art of Barbecue, Harvard Common Press (Boston, MA), 1996.

The Insider's Guide to Santa Fe, Taos, and Albuquerque, 4th edition, Harvard Common Press (Boston, MA), 1996.

Best Places to Stay in the Caribbean, 4th edition, Houghton Mifflin (Boston, MA), 1996.

Born to Grill: An American Celebration, illustrations by Sara Love, Harvard Common Press (Boston, MA), 1998.

American Home Cooking: 400 Spirited Recipes Celebrating Our Rich Traditions of Home Cooking, Broadway Books (New York, NY), 1999.

A Real American Breakfast: The Best Meal of the Day, Anytime of the Day, William Morrow (New York, NY), 2002.

Chicken on the Grill: 100 Surefire Ways to Grill Perfect Chicken Every Time, William Morrow (New York, NY), 2004.

The Big Book of Outdoor Cooking and Entertaining: Spirited Recipes and Expert Tips for Barbecuing, Charcoal and Gas Grilling, Rotisserie Roasting, Smoking, Deep-Frying, and Making Merry, William Morrow (New York, NY), 2006.

Grilling for Friends: Surefire, Fun Food for Great Grill Parties, William Morrow (New York, NY), 2006.

SIDELIGHTS: Bill Jamison, with his wife, Cheryl, is the author of a number of cookbooks. The Jamisons first wrote travel guides, which led to their culinary writing. They now concentrate on food writing and have published books that reflect their tastes and backgrounds. Bill, for example, hails from the Texas Hill Country, where barbeque and grill cooking is a way of life. Neither of the Jamisons have had professional culinary training or restaurant experience, but instead have used trial and error to perfect their recipes and tips. The Jamisons were approached to write their first cookbook, *The Rancho de Chimayo Cookbook: The Traditional Cooking of New Mexico,* by the management of the Rancho de Chimayo restaurant in commemoration of their twenty-fifth anniversary. The cookbook includes recipes and a history of the restaurant and the village in which it is located.

They next published *Smoke and Spice: The Joy of Real Backyard Barbecue,* a half million copies of which were sold before it was reprinted nearly a decade later as *Smoke and Spice: Cooking with Smoke, the Real Way to Barbecue.* In this volume, the Jamisons perfect everything from the hot dog to country ribs, jerked salmon, and the traditional steak, include appropriate accompaniments, and finish with cool desserts to top off the meal. They offer instructions on building smokers and creating distinctive pastes, dry rubs, marinades, and mops. The second edition of the cookbook updates some of the old recipes and includes approximately 100 new ones.

The Border Cookbook: Authentic Home Cooking from the American Southwest and Northern Mexico contains more than 300 Western, Native American, and Spanish and Mexican-style recipes that are accompanied by histories of their origins and the cultures that created them. Patricia Sharpe noted in *Texas Monthly* that this cookbook "includes many classics that Texans know and love, such as pico de gallo and cumin-laced chili, but the most fascinating recipes may well be the ones that are least familiar."

Born to Grill: An American Celebration is a big book that includes recipes for every conceivable grill dish, including vegetarian and fish offerings. Meat dishes include nine kinds of beef burgers, plus others made of tuna, shellfish, lamb, venison, and turkey. In addition to burgers, the list of meat dishes includes chops, steaks, and kebobs, and there is a chapter devoted to grilling pizza. Other chapters discuss marinades and rubs. The Jamisons also instruct the reader on the various techniques of grilling, favoring their high-heat, open-air method. They discuss hot spots, flare ups, and other problems that can affect food quality. A *Forbes* reviewer wrote: "This could very well be the perfect summer cookbook for the backyard Prometheus."

American Home Cooking: 400 Spirited Recipes Celebrating Our Rich Traditions of Home Cooking contains dishes that are familiar and others, like conyo (roasted rabbit), that are not. Familiar meals include tuna casserole and pizza, and regional favorites, such as New England clam chowder, fried green tomatoes, and seafood salad. "Culinary trivia . . . and technique tips lend nuance and context to America's rich culinary tapestry," commented a *Publishers Weekly* contributor.

A Real American Breakfast: The Best Meal of the Day, Anytime of the Day includes 275 recipes that feature traditional offerings, such as eggs, pancakes, breads, and cereals, as well as original and international recipes, including Swedish pancakes and Asian rice porridge. Others that can be taken along are smoothies and egg sandwiches. Breakfast trivia is offered, as well as techniques. A *Publishers Weekly* contributor concluded: "Our country's breakfast traditions are wildly diverse, and the Jamisons' enthusiasm for their subject is a great incentive to get out of bed and try them all."

Chicken on the Grill: 100 Surefire Ways to Grill Perfect Chicken Every Time offers every imaginable chicken dish, from appetizers and wings to recipes that use the whole chicken. *The Big Book of Outdoor Cooking and Entertaining: Spirited Recipes and Expert Tips for Barbecuing, Charcoal and Gas Grilling, Rotisserie Roasting, Smoking, Deep-Frying, and Making Merry* covers every aspect of cooking referred to in the title, with 200 recipes for seasonings, rubs, and sauces and instructions on how to use them with various types of meat and fish, as well as vegetarian, salad, pasta, and dessert recipes, all of which can be cooked and/or eaten outdoors.

BIOGRAPHICAL AND CRITICAL SOURCES:

PERIODICALS

Booklist, March 15, 1994, Barbara Jacobs, review of *Smoke and Spice: The Joy of Real Backyard Barbecue,* p. 1314; October 15, 1995, Barbara Jacobs, review of *The Border Cookbook: Authentic Home Cooking from the American Southwest and Northern Mexico,* p. 375; April 15, 1998, Mark Koblauch, review of *Born to Grill: An American Celebration,* p. 1408; October 15, 1999, Barbara Jacobs, review of *American Home Cooking: 400 Spirited Recipes Celebrating Our Rich Traditions of Home Cooking,* p. 404.

Forbes, May 4, 1998, review of *Born to Grill,* p. S140.

Kansas City Star, June 26, 2006, Lauren Chapin, review of *The Big Book of Outdoor Cooking and Entertaining: Spirited Recipes and Expert Tips for Barbecuing, Charcoal and Gas Grilling, Rotisserie Roasting, Smoking, Deep-Frying, and Making Merry.*

Library Journal, April 15, 1998, Judith C. Sutton, review of *Born to Grill,* p. 109; October 15, 1999, Judith C. Sutton, review of *American Home Cooking,* p. 98; February 15, 2002, Judith C. Sutton, review of *A Real American Breakfast: The Best*

Meal of the Day, Anytime of the Day, p. 173; March 15, 2003, Judith C. Sutton, review of *Smoke and Spice,* p. 110; May 15, 2004, Susan Hurst, review of *Chicken on the Grill: 100 Surefire Ways to Grill Perfect Chicken Every Time,* p. 107; April 15, 2006, Judith C. Sutton, review of *The Big Book of Outdoor Cooking and Entertaining,* p. 104.

Publishers Weekly, August 21, 1995, review of *The Border Cookbook,* p. 62; March 2, 1998, review of *Born to Grill,* p. 63; August 2, 1999, review of *American Home Cooking,* p. 77; January 21, 2002, review of *A Real American Breakfast,* p. 83; February 3, 2003, review of *Smoke & Spice: Cooking With Smoke, the Real Way to Barbecue,* p. 72; February 13, 2006, review of *The Big Book of Outdoor Cooking and Entertaining,* p. 82.

Texas Monthly, October, 1995, Patricia Sharpe, review of *The Border Cookbook,* p. 130.

ONLINE

Bill Jamison Home Page, http://www.cookingwiththe jamisons.com (December 26, 2006).*

*　　*　　*

JENNINGS, Kevin 1963-

PERSONAL: Born May 8, 1963, in Fort Lauderdale, FL (various sources list birthplace as Raleigh, NC, and Winston-Salem, NC); son of Chester Henry (a Baptist preacher) and Alice Verna Jennings; partner of Jeffrey Gerard Davis. *Education:* Harvard University, B.A. (magna cum laude), 1985; Columbia University, M.A., 1994; New York University, Stern School of Business, M.B.A., 1999. *Politics:* Democrat. *Religion:* Christian. *Hobbies and other interests:* Ice hockey.

ADDRESSES: Home—New York, NY. *Office*—Gay, Lesbian, and Straight Education Network, 121 West 27th St., Ste. 804, New York, NY 10001-6207.

CAREER: Educator and author. Moses Brown School, Providence, RI, history teacher, 1985-87; Concord Academy, Concord, MA, history teacher, 1987-94; Gay, Lesbian, and Straight Education Network (GLSTEN), New York, NY, founder and executive director, 1994—. Point Foundation, trustee; Appalachian Community Fund, fundraising chair; lecturer and commentator on radio and television; editor; producer.

AWARDS, HONORS: Joseph Klingenstein fellow, 1993; Lambda Literary Award, 1998, for *Telling Tales out of School: Gays, Lesbians, and Bisexuals Revisit Their School Days;* Sundance Film Festival Audience Award for Best Documentary, 1998, for *Out of the Past.*

WRITINGS:

NONFICTION

(Editor) *Becoming Visible: A Reader in Gay and Lesbian History for High School and College Students,* Alyson Publications (Boston, MA), 1994.

(Editor) *One Teacher in Ten: Gay and Lesbian Educators Tell Their Stories,* Alyson Publications (Boston, MA), 1994, 2nd edition, Alyson Books (Los Angeles, CA), 2005.

(Editor) *Telling Tales out of School: Gays, Lesbians, and Bisexuals Revisit Their School Days,* Alyson Books (Los Angeles, CA), 1998.

(With Pat Shapiro) *Always My Child: A Parent's Guide to Understanding Your Gay, Lesbian, Bisexual, Transgendered, or Questioning Son or Daughter,* Simon & Schuster (New York, NY), 2003.

Mama's Boy, Preacher's Son: A Memoir, Beacon Press (Boston, MA), 2006.

Author and producer of documentary film *Out of the Past,* 1998.

SIDELIGHTS: Since founding the Gay, Lesbian, and Straight Education Network (GLSEN) in 1994, Kevin Jennings has been among the ranks of the leading gay rights advocates in the United States. As a speaker, writer, and commentator, he has promoted understanding and respect for people of all sexual orientations, particularly within the educational sphere. As Randal C. Archibold explained in the *New York Times,* GLSEN is staffed by fewer than twenty people, its offices located in New York's Chelsea district. With a budget comprised of foundation grants and donations, Jennings and his organization work to "raise awareness of the mistreatment of gay students as well as fight it." As Archibold reported, a 1999 GLSEN survey of almost 500 gay teens around the United States "found that 69 percent had received verbal, sexual, or physical harassment in school, and 42 percent reported having been physically harassed or assaulted." Having experienced such treatment while growing up, Jennings has dedicated much of his adulthood to fighting it. His 2006 book, *Mama's Boy, Preacher's Son: A Memoir,* documents his struggles growing up gay in an inhospitable environment, as well as other life experiences that got him to where he is today.

Jennings began his publishing career in 1994, the same year he founded and became executive director of GLSEN, by editing *Becoming Visible: A Reader in Gay and Lesbian History for High School and College Students.* Covering two millennia of human history, the book's thirty-nine readings describe the contributions of gays and lesbians to cultures around the world. Organized in a textbook-like format with each selection prefaced with notes by Jennings, the book allows readers "a chance to examine important events in the history of gays and lesbians," according to *Voice of Youth Advocates* reviewer Lynn Evarts, adding that it is "a chance that many of us need to take full advantage of." In the *Harvard Educational Review* Edward J. Miech praised Jennings's introductions as "succinct and informative," and the essays selected "engaging and insightful." Noting that because it is geared for a younger readership *Becoming Visible* avoids sexually explicit material, Heather Stephenson added in the *Lambda Book Report* that in this "groundbreaking" text, Jennings "strives to combat homophobia by building empathy, focusing from the start on prejudice and oppression," and in the process "chooses apt analogies for a teen audience."

Other edited collections by Jennings include *One Teacher in Ten: Gay and Lesbian Educators Tell Their Stories* and the Lambda Literary Award-winning *Telling Tales out of School: Gays, Lesbians, and Bisexuals Revisit Their School Days.* Recounting the experiences of homosexual teachers from a variety of educational systems in locations ranging from small towns to large cities, *One Teacher in Ten* describes dealing with "homophobic parents, the cruelty of kids, unsupportive administrators, [and] concern about exacerbating cultural differences" between teacher and student as hurdles common to many of its thirty-seven contributors, according to a *Kirkus Reviews* contributor. In *Lambda Book Report* William J. Mann commended the volume as "a proud, compelling affirmation of the power of honesty, and the value of a truly honest education," while *Harvard Educational Review* critic Karen L. Mapp dubbed it "gripping, poignant, powerful, [and]

emotionally charged." Reviewing, *Telling Tales out of School, Library Journal* contributor Debra Moore maintained that the book will "resonate with gay and bisexual readers."

Together with coauthor Pat Shapiro, Jennings has also authored one of the first books to focus on the day-to-day relationship between gay or sexually questioning teens and their parents. *Always My Child: A Parent's Guide to Understanding Your Gay, Lesbian, Bisexual, Transgendered, or Questioning Son or Daughter* counsels confused parents attempting to understand and support children who have claimed or may claim an alternative sexual orientation. Suggestions regarding appropriate lines of communication, ways of recognizing and dealing with drug abuse or depression, and situations in which a parent's advocacy can aid a child in the world at large are all discussed. Praising the book in *Library Journal,* Linda Beck commended in particular Jennings' closing essay, in which he relates his personal story of reconciling with his mother as an adult, an essay Beck cited as being written with "the most fervor."

After being told for years that he should write a book about his life, Jennings finally decided to do so. It wasn't until he suffered a near fatal heart attack in 2005, however, that he was driven to actually finish his memoir. In 2006, *Mama's Boy, Preacher's Son* was finally published. Commended by reviewer Scott Whitney in *Booklist* as a "refreshingly readable memoir," it focuses on the events in Jennings' life that were crucial to his development. *Mama's Boy, Preacher's Son* "is Jennings' memoir of coming of age, coming out and moving on, told without self-pity" said Priya Jain in a review of the book on *Salon.com.* The book documents Jennings's struggles growing up gay in a strict Baptist household in the South. It continues on through his later years in college (where he was finally able to come out) up to his experiences as an openly gay educator and activist. David R. Gillespie criticized the style in which the book was written in *Gay & Lesbian Review Worldwide,* remarking that "the book becomes a recitation of events, in more or less chronological order, which may not have been the best choice of structure given the often pedestrian nature of these events." He went on to say that "perhaps a thematic approach would have worked better, one that brought out the larger themes of Jennings' genuinely important life's work." In an interview with Matthew Robinson for *EDGE Boston,* Jennings said the book is "a tribute to my mother." The tribute was apparently a success, as a *Kirkus Reviews* contributor observed: "This memoir, which ends with

Jennings delivering the eulogy at his mom's funeral, would make any mother proud."

BIOGRAPHICAL AND CRITICAL SOURCES:

BOOKS

Jennings, Kevin, *Mama's Boy, Preacher's Son: A Memoir,* Beacon Press (Boston, MA), 2006.

PERIODICALS

Booklist, September 15, 1994, Whitney Scott, review of *One Teacher in Ten: Gay and Lesbian Educators Tell Their Stories,* p. 89; August 1, 2006, Scott Whitney, review of *Mama's Boy, Preacher's Son,* p. 17.

Gay & Lesbian Review Worldwide, November-December 2006, David R. Gillespie, "One Gay Youth," review of *Mama's Boy, Preacher's Son,* p. 42.

Harvard Educational Review, summer, 1996, Edward J. Miech, review of *Becoming Visible: A Reader in Gay and Lesbian History for High School and College Students,* pp. 408-410, and Karen L. Mapp, review of *One Teacher in Ten,* pp. 412-413.

Kirkus Reviews, July 1, 1994, review of *One Teacher in Ten,* p. 905; June 1, 2006, review of *Mama's Boy, Preacher's Son,* p. 557.

Lambda Book Report, July-August, 1994, Heather Stephenson, review of *Becoming Visible,* p. 38; March-April, 1995, William J. Mann, review of *One Teacher in Ten,* p. 47; fall, 2006, Jim Van Buskirk, review of *Mama's Boy, Preacher's Son,* p. 9.

Library Journal, May 1, 1998, David S. Azzolina, *Becoming Visible,* p. 121; November 15, 1998, Debra Moore, review of *Telling Tales out of School: Gays, Lesbians, and Bisexuals Revisit Their School Days,* p. 82; January, 2003, Linda Beck, review of *Always My Child: A Parent's Guide to Understanding Your Gay, Lesbian, Bisexual, Transgendered, or Questioning Son or Daughter,* p. 146.

New York Times, October 27, 1999, Randal C. Archibold, "A Gay Crusader Sees History on His Side," p. B2.

Voice of Youth Advocates, June, 1996, Lynn Evarts, review of *Becoming Visible,* p. 114.

ONLINE

EDGE Boston, http://www.edgeboston.com/ (September 20, 2006), Matthew Robinson, "Mama's Boy," interview with author.

Kevin Jennings Home Page, http://www.kevinjennings.com (April 5, 2007).

Salon.com, http://www.salon.com/ (August 21, 2006), Priya Jain, "Son of a Preacher Man."*

*   *   *

JEWELL, Lisa 1968-

PERSONAL: Born July 19, 1968, in London, England; daughter of Anthony (a textile agent) and Kay (a secretary) Jewell; married; children: Amelie. *Education:* Attended Barnet College and Epsom School of Art and Design.

ADDRESSES: Home—Swiss Cottage, London, England. *Agent*—Casarotto Ramsay & Associates Ltd., Waverley House, 7-12 Noel St., London W1F 8GQ, England. *E-mail*—author@lisa-jewell.co.uk.

CAREER: Novelist. Worked in the fashion industry in London, England, for five years. Has also worked as a secretary.

WRITINGS:

Ralph's Party, Plume (New York, NY), 2000.
Thirtynothing, Plume (New York, NY), 2001.
One-Hit Wonder, Dutton (New York, NY), 2002.
A Friend of the Family, Dutton (New York, NY), 2003.
Vince & Joy, Penguin (London, England), 2005, Harper (New York, NY), 2006.

SIDELIGHTS: After attending college to pursue a career in art, design, and fashion, British writer Lisa Jewell became disillusioned with the "cut-throat" world of fashion and eventually began taking evening classes in creative writing at her local adult education college in London. It was here that she discovered her talent and passion for writing, and she has since published a number of critically acclaimed novels, including *Thirtynothing* and *Vince & Joy.*

Although Barbara Sutton, writing in the *New York Times Book Review,* referred to Jewell's debut novel, *Ralph's Party* as a "sitcom novel," it gained international success as a best seller. A contributor to *Kirkus Reviews* described *Ralph's Party* as "a shameless flirt of a first novel that traces the roller-coaster lives of six people sharing the same London brownstone." The reviewer commented that "the author casts a perceptive eye on the difficulty of relationships." A reviewer in *Publishers Weekly* called the book a "light delight" that comes to "an amusing denouement."

Jewell followed *Ralph's Party* with *Thirtynothing,* "another hip and happening comic love story," wrote a contributor to *Kirkus Reviews,* complete with "endearing characters and fine comic timing." Two friends, Digby and Nadine, are thirty-year-old Londoners whose relationships with others have all been casual. When an old love comes back into Digby's life, Nadine begins to realize that her friend is the man she has loved all along. Jennifer Wulff, reviewing the novel in *People,* described *Thirtynothing* as a "witty British import" that tells the story of Digby and Nadine in a way that "is not in the least predictable" and includes "dozens of laugh-out-loud moments." A reviewer in *Publishers Weekly* stated that the book's best attribute might be "Jewell's keen observation of British pop culture." Whitney Scott, writing in *Booklist,* wrote that "Jewell's latest saucy and slangy love story should entertain audiences beyond the U.K."

In 2002 Jewell followed up *Thirtynothing,* with *One-Hit Wonder,* which *Library Journal* contributor May Brozio-Andrews called "an engaging coming-of-age tale skillfully told by interweaving the past and present." *Booklist* contributor Kathleen Hughes labeled it "part mystery, part Brit-pop fiction," noting Jewell's "masterful way of unraveling a story bit by bit to pique the reader's interest."

After publishing *A Friend of the Family,* in 2003, Jewell released the 2005 novel *Vince & Joy,* "a deliciously addictive read filled with London oddballs, horrid husbands and romantic destiny," noted a critic in *Kirkus Reviews.* Vince Mellon and Joy Downer, a pair of misfit teenagers, meet at a seaside resort while vacationing with their families. They fall in love but, through a series of misunderstandings, lose touch with one another. As the years pass, they both endure a series of failed relationships until fate brings them together again. *Entertainment Weekly* reviewer Clarissa Cruz praised the novel, calling it a "realistic, often dark portrayal of modern love," and a critic in *Publishers Weekly* remarked, "Jewell's lively prose and amusing observations . . . effortlessly guide the story toward a satisfying ending."

BIOGRAPHICAL AND CRITICAL SOURCES:

PERIODICALS

Booklist, December 1, 2000, Whitney Scott, review of *Thirtynothing,* p. 694; May 1, 2002, Kathleen Hughes, review of *One-Hit Wonder,* p. 1507.

Entertainment Weekly, October 6, 2006, Clarissa Cruz, review of *Vince & Joy,* p. 73.

Kirkus Reviews, November 1, 1999, review of *Ralph's Party,* p. 1667; November 1, 2000, review of *Thirtynothing,* p. 1507; August 1, 2006, review of *Vince & Joy,* p. 744.

Library Journal, May 1, 2002, May Brozio-Andrews, review of *One-Hit Wonder,* p. 133; July 1, 2003, Elizabeth Mellet, review of *A Friend of the Family,* p. 123; September 15, 2006, Rebecca Vnuk, review of *Vince & Joy,* p. 48.

New York Times Book Review, January 9, 2000, Barbara Sutton, review of *Ralph's Party,* p. 20.

People, February 12, 2001, Jennifer Wulff, review of *Thirtynothing,* p. 41.

Publishers Weekly, October 18, 1999, review of *Ralph's Party,* p. 68; November 6, 2000, review of *Thirtynothing,* p. 69; May 27, 2002, review of *One-Hit Wonder,* p. 38; August 7, 2006, review of *Vince & Joy,* p. 31.

ONLINE

All about Romance, http://www.likesbooks.com/ (September 15, 2001), Maria K., review of *Thirtynothing.*

Girl Posse, http://www.girlposse.com/ (January 30, 2007), "The Fifteen Question E-Mail Interview with Lisa Jewell."

Lisa Jewell Home Page, http://www.lisa-jewell.co.uk (January 30, 2007).

Telegraph Online, http://www.telegraph.co.uk/ (August 8, 2005), Alex Clark, "Lisa Jewell."

Trashionista, http://www.trashionista.com/ (March 5, 2007), review of *Vince & Joy;* (March 5, 2007), reviews of *Ralph's Party* and *A Friend of the Family.**

*　　*　　*

JORDAN, Laura
See BROWN, Sandra

JOSEPH, Sheri 1967-

PERSONAL: Born November 8, 1967, in Silver Spring, MD; daughter of Leroy and Kathleen Joseph. *Education:* University of the South, B.A., 1989; University of Georgia, Ph.D., 1997.

ADDRESSES: Home—Atlanta, GA. *Office*—Department of English, Georgia State University, 33 Gilmer St. SE, Unit 8, Atlanta, GA 30303. *E-mail*—sherijos@aol.com; engslj@langate.gsu.edu.

CAREER: Writer. University of Georgia, Athens, instructor and editorial and teaching assistant for *Georgia Review,* 1994-2000; Morehead State University, Morehead, KY, assistant professor of creative writing, 2000-02; Georgia State University, Atlanta, assistant professor of English and creative writing, 2002-06, associate professor, 2006—. Member, board of directors, AIDS Coalition of NE Georgia, 1998-2000. *Five Points* literary magazine, fiction editor, 2004—.

MEMBER: Associated Writing Programs.

AWARDS, HONORS: National Magazine Award finalist, for "The Elixir"; Bread Loaf Writers' Conference fellow; MacDowell Colony fellow; Tennessee Williams Scholar, Sewanee Writers' Conference, 2001; Walter E. Dakin fellow, 2003; Peter Taylor fellow, Kenyon Writers' Workshop, 2004; Yaddo fellow, 2006; Grub Street Book Prize, 2007, for *Stray.*

WRITINGS:

Bear Me Safely Over, Atlantic Monthly Press (New York, NY), 2002.
Stray, MacAdam/Cage (San Francisco, CA), 2007.

Contributor to anthologies, including *Birds in the Hand,* Farrar, Straus, and *After O'Connor: Stories from Contemporary Georgia,* University of Georgia Press. Contributor of short fiction to literary journals, including *Georgia Review, Kenyon Review, Shenandoah, Virginia Quarterly Review,* and *Other Voices.*

SIDELIGHTS: Sheri Joseph's first book of fiction, *Bear Me Safely Over,* is a cycle of short stories that can be read as a novel, the stories all involving the same characters and a continuing plot. In what a *Publishers Weekly* reviewer called "a gutsy, realistic, and lyrical portrait of country people struggling to find meaning in their constricted lives," Joseph introduces the reader to her three main characters. Paul is a gay teenager who has been arrested for prostitution and is verbally abused and humiliated by his stepbrother, Curtis. Curtis plays in a band and is engaged to Sidra, a sympathetic young woman whose sister died of AIDS. She is drawn to Paul for complex reasons and ends up taking him in after he fights with his family, much to the disgust of her fiancée. More trouble develops when Paul begins to develop a romantic relationship with Kent, a member of Curtis's band. Pam Kingsbury of *Southern Scribe* observed: "Joseph handles the book's themes—loss, homophobia, families reinventing themselves, and religious fundamentalism—with subtlety and assurance. Her characters, no longer religious but deeply spiritual, reach a kind of salvation by the book's end."

In *Stray,* a 2007 novel, Joseph continues to examine the relationship between Paul and Kent from *Bear Me Safely Over.* A strange love triangle develops after Kent, now married, renews his affair with Paul. Overwhelmed by feelings of guilt, Kent decides to end the relationship; in turn, Paul insinuates himself into Kent's life by making friends with Maggie, Kent's wife, who works as a public defender. Kent reveals the affair to Bernard Falk, a college professor with whom Paul lives, prompting a violent fight between Paul and Bernard. When the older man is found dead the next day, Paul is charged with murder, and Maggie, who has grown attracted to Paul, agrees to take his case. Joanne Wilkinson, writing in *Booklist,* called *Stray* a "compelling tale of reconciliation and redemption as the lovers are forced to face their flawed perceptions head-on."

Joseph once told *CA:* "*Bear Me Safely Over,* my first book, has been read by many as a novel, but it's actually a cycle of short stories. The idea was important to me in composing the book, which is multivocal and alinear, circling around various members of two Georgia families about to be joined by marriage. As I write, I try to let my characters tell me their stories and to let one story or voice rise out of another, so that they answer one another and the book builds naturally with a sort of balance of dissent like that of human communities.

"I seem to write a lot about family in various forms, especially about people who feel excluded or unsatisfied by traditional family structures, yet cannot deny a need for connection on that level, who therefore seek substitutes. And I also write about the religious impulse, again of the sort thwarted by traditional religion that nonetheless can't stop seeking something authentic to replace it."

BIOGRAPHICAL AND CRITICAL SOURCES:

PERIODICALS

Advocate, July 23, 2002, David Bahr, "Family Feud."
Booklist, April 15, 2002, John Green, review of *Bear Me Safely Over,* p. 1382; December 1, 2006, Joanne Wilkinson, review of *Stray,* p. 22.
Cincinatti CityBeat, May 5, 2002, Brandon Brady, "Writer's Block: What a Kick!"

Kirkus Reviews, March 1, 2002, review of *Bear Me Safely Over,* p. 279.
Lambda Book Report, May, 2002, Andrew Beierle, "Handsome, Headstrong, and Sexually Precocious," p. 17.
New York Times Book Review, November 25, 2002, Ann Powers, "Sex, Death, and Rock 'n' Roll."
Publishers Weekly, March 18, 2002, review of *Bear Me Safely Over,* p. 75; October 16, 2006, review of *Stray,* p. 29.
Southern Scribe, September, 2002, Pam Kingsbury, interview with Sheri Joseph.

ONLINE

Daily Texan Online, http://media.www.dailytexanonline.com/ (March 10, 2006), Nicole Taylor, "Let Talk about Sex."

K

KAHN, David 1930-

PERSONAL: Born February 7, 1930, in New York, NY; son of Jesse (a lawyer) and Florence (a glass manufacturer) Kahn; married Susanne Fiedler, October 22, 1969 (divorced); children: Oliver, Michael. *Education:* Bucknell University, A.B., 1951; Oxford University, Ph.D., 1974. *Politics:* Democrat. *Religion:* Jewish.

ADDRESSES: Home—Great Neck, NY. *E-mail*—Davidkahn1@aol.com.

CAREER: Freelance writer. *Newsday* (Long Island daily), Garden City, NY, reporter, 1955-63; *Herald Tribune,* Paris, France, desk editor, 1965-67; New York University, New York, NY, associate professor of journalism, 1975-79; *Newsday,* Melville, NY, assistant op-ed editor, 1979-98. National Security Agency scholar in residence, 1995; *Cryptologia,* founding coeditor; *Intelligence and National Security, International Journal of Intelligence and Counterintelligence,* and *Journal of Intelligence History,* member, boards of editors. Great Neck Library, member of board of trustees, 2002—, president, 2006-07.

MEMBER: American Cryptogram Association (president, 1965-67), International Association for Cryptologic Research (former board member), American Historical Association, American Committee for the History of the Second World War, New York Cipher Society (president, 1955-62), World War II Studies Association, International Intelligence History Association.

WRITINGS:

Two Soviet Spy Ciphers, privately printed, 1960, later published by Central Intelligence Agency (Langley, VA).

Plaintext in the New Unabridged, Crypto Press (New York, NY), 1963.

The Codebreakers: The Story of Secret Writing, Scribner (New York, NY), 1967.

Hitler's Spies: German Military Intelligence in World War II, Macmillan (New York, NY), 1978.

Kahn on Codes, Macmillan (New York, NY), 1983.

(Adapter) Pierre Lorain, *Clandestine Operations: The Arms and Techniques of the Resistance, 1941-44,* Macmillan (New York, NY), 1983.

Seizing the Enigma: The Race to Break the German U-Boat Codes, 1939-1943, Houghton Mifflin (Boston, MA), 1991.

The Reader of Gentleman's Mail: Herbert O. Yardley and the Birth of American Codebreaking, Yale University Press (New Haven, CT), 2004.

Contributor to *Encyclopedia Americana, Dictionary of American History, Encyclopedia of U.S. Foreign Relations,* and to *Atlantic, Scientific American, Foreign Affairs, Military Affairs, Military History Quarterly, New York Times Magazine, Cryptologia, Intelligence and National Security, Journal of Strategic Studies, IEEE Spectrum, Playboy, Penthouse, Neue Deutsche Biographie,* and *Cryptogram.* Author of introductions and forewords to books, including *The Final Solution of the Abwehr,* Garland (Camden, CT), 1989; *The Story of MAGIC: Memoirs of an American Cryptologic Pioneer,* Frank B. Rowlett, Aegean Park Press (Laguna Hills, CA), 1998; *The Secret Front,* Wilhelm Höttl, Enigma Books (New York, NY), 2003; and *La Cryptographie Militaire avant la Guerre de 1914,* Alexandre Ollier, Lavauzelle (Paris, France), 2002. Contributor to anthologies, including *Knowing One's Enemies: Intelligence Assessment before the Two World Wars,* Ernest R. May (editor), Princeton University Press (Princeton,

NJ), 1984; *In the Name of Intelligence: Essays in Honor of Walter Pforzheimer,* Hayden B. Peake and Samuel Halpern (editors), NIBC Press (Washington, DC), 1994; and *What If? 2: Eminent Historians Imagine What Might Have Been,* Robert Cowley (editor), Putnam (New York, NY), 2001. Editor and founder of *Cryptologia.*

SIDELIGHTS: David Kahn's works are the stuff of which spy thrillers are made: international intrigue, codes, and military intelligence. Kahn, however, has chosen to chronicle actual events and real personalities, writing history rather than fiction. Among his works concerned with things convert and enigmatic is *The Codebreakers: The Story of Secret Writings*, called "a classic history of cryptography," by Joseph E. Persico in the *Washington Post Book World.* The book traces the course of code making and breaking from ancient times to the present, and while such a topic might not seem a likely subject for popular success, the book in fact sold well. Myra McPherson, writing in the *Washington Post,* offered this explanation: "[Kahn] laced the heavy material in 'The Codebreakers' with fascinating asides—from Plutarch to pig latin. . . . [His] spoon-feeding of fact after fact produced the nearly impossible—a thousand-page tome on a subject hardly destined to titillate, became a best seller (100,000 in hardback)." David Hunt called *The Codebreakers* a "brilliant book" in the *Times Literary Supplement,* and to Jack Beatty in *Newsweek* it is a "much-admired study." The book grew out of Kahn's long-standing interest in cryptography. McPherson pointed out that "when [the author] was 12, he was walking past the public library in Great Neck, L.I., and 'stopped in my tracks when I saw this book about codes with this terrific title, *Secret and Urgent.* It hooked me—and I never grew up.'"

In the view of a number of critics, the appeal of Kahn's works is partly the product of his ability to combine erudition and enthusiasm. McPherson described him as "both a serious historian and purveyor, at times, of glib but interesting generalizations. . . . His books [are] a mix of the anecdotal, massive research and impressive analysis." In his *Times Literary Supplement* review of Kahn's *Hitler's Spies: German Military Intelligence in World War II*, Hunt expressed a similar opinion regarding the author's effective blend of scholarship and storytelling: "He pays proper attention to the really essential weapons of military intelligence: prisoners and captured documents . . . and intercepted enemy communications. Nevertheless, he knows what the public wants . . . and makes sure that he prints plenty of spy stories."

As the reader makes his or her way through the stories and scholarly details contained in *Hitler's Spies*, a pattern gradually emerges. In *Washington Post Book World* critic Persico's words, Kahn "has provided fare for the spy-thriller buff and a clear verdict on Germany's secret warfare: 'At every one of the strategic turning points of World War II, her intelligence failed.'" Those failures range from the comical pair of German agents who were landed on the Maine coast and spent their money on themselves rather than on gathering intelligence, to the disastrous situation that Persico described in his review: "German agents reporting from Britain were actually a serious liability. They had all come under British control and were feeding their presumed masters deliciously misleading information." As Kahn asserts however, even successful and accurate intelligence was of little use to the German war effort. Beatty described why in *Newsweek:* "There was one overwhelming flaw in the German totalitarian order: all of the information from the various services came together in one place only—the turbid mind of Adolf Hitler—and 'no facts,' writes Kahn, 'could ever have convinced Hitler that he was wrong.'"

Describing Kahn's characteristic approach to his subjects, a *New Yorker* critic stated that "[he] teaches the layman everything he can possibly grasp about an arcane speciality." That Kahn is both a respected historian and best-selling author at the same time is acknowledged by a number of writers. Leonard Bushkoff, in his *New York Times Book Review* article on *Hitler's Spies,* summarizes those qualities that contribute to the appeal and value of Kahn's works: "His judgments are balanced, authoritative, without either the banality or the sensationalism that often marks popularizing writers. The bibliography is ample, carefully subdivided, meant for use and not merely display. A serious book, clearly: handcrafted, meant to last."

Kahn continues his studies of codebreaking and espionage in his 2004 title, *The Reader of Gentleman's Mail: Herbert O. Yardley and the Birth of American Codebreaking,* which details the life of a pioneering codebreaker and intelligence officer. Yardley became persona non grata in intelligence circles for his tell-all 1931 book, *The American Black Chamber,* an insider's look at the State Department's Cipher Bureau, which was an early attempt at creating an American interception and codebreaking bureau. Kahn is the first to write a biography of Yardley, and according to *Booklist* contributor Gilbert Taylor, "Kahn tells Yardley's story with a cool eye for his reputation as a codebreaker" in this "balanced and meticulous" study. As David Alvarez noted in *History,* Yardley "is one of the most colorful and important figures in the history of intelligence and espionage," and "Kahn gives us a clear and crisp image (warts and all) of . . . [this] remarkable individual." More praise came from *Library Journal* critic Daniel K. Blewett, who called *The Reader of Gentlemen's Mail* "a revealing and well-researched book." Blewett also termed Kahn "the nation's premier historian of military intelligence."

BIOGRAPHICAL AND CRITICAL SOURCES:

PERIODICALS

American Historical Review, July, 1968, review of *The Codebreakers: The Story of Secret Writings;* April, 2006, Louis R. Sadler, review of *The Reader of Gentlemen's Mail: Herbert O. Yardley and the Birth of American Codebreaking,* pp. 501-502.

Booklist, March 15, 2004, Gilbert Taylor, review of *The Reader of Gentlemen's Mail,* p. 1260.

Christian Science Monitor, October 5, 1967, review of *The Codebreakers.*

History, summer, 2004, David Alvarez, review of *The Reader of Gentlemen's Mail,* p. 134.

Library Journal, March 15, 2004, Daniel K. Blewett, review of *The Reader of Gentlemen's Mail,* p. 88.

New Republic, February 10, 1968, review of *The Codebreakers.*

Newsweek, June 26, 1978, Jack Beatty, review of *Hitler's Spies: German Military Intelligence in World War II.*

New Yorker, July 10, 1978, review of *Hitler's Spies.*

New York Times Book Review, January 7, 1968, review of *The Codebreakers;* June 18, 1978, Leonard Bushkoff, review of *Hitler's Spies.*

Time, February 16, 1968, review of *The Codebreakers;* July 10, 1978, review of *Hitler's Spies.*

Times Literary Supplement, October 10, 1978, David Hunt, review of *Hitler's Spies.*

Washington Post, July 9, 1978, Myra McPherson, review of *Hitler's Spies.*

Washington Post Book World, August 13, 1978, Joseph E. Persico, review of *Hitler's Spies;* March 28, 2004, Jonathan Yardley, review of *The Reader of Gentlemen's Mail,* p. 2.

ONLINE

Chelsea Forum, http://www.chelseaforum.com/ (November 20, 2006), "David Kahn."

David Kahn Home Page, http://www.david-kahn.com (November 20, 2006).*

*   *   *

KAMINSKY, Stuart M. 1934-
(Stuart Melvin Kaminsky)

PERSONAL: Born September 29, 1934, in Chicago, IL; son of Leo and Dorothy Kaminsky; married Merle Gordon, August 30, 1959 (marriage ended); married Enid Lisa Perll, January 7, 1986; children: (first marriage) Peter Michael, Toby Arthur, Lucy Irene; (second marriage) Natasha Melisa Perll. *Education:* University of Illinois, B.S., 1957, M.A., 1959; Northwestern University, Ph.D., 1972. *Hobbies and other interests:* Athletics (especially basketball and football), reading detective fiction and media history/criticism.

ADDRESSES: Agent—Dominick Abel Literary Agency, Inc., 498 West End Ave., New York, NY 10024.

CAREER: Novelist and screenwriter. University of Illinois—Urbana-Champaign, Champaign, IL, science writer, 1962-64; University of Illinois—Chicago, medical writer, 1965-68; University of Michigan, Ann Arbor, MI, editor of news service, 1968-69; University of Chicago, director of public relations and assistant to the vice-president for public affairs, 1969-72; Northwestern University, Evanston, IL, assistant professor, 1973-75, associate professor of speech, 1975-79, professor of radio, television and film and head of Film Division, 1979-89; Florida State University, Sarasota, FL, founding director of Graduate Film Conservatory, 1989-94. Chicago Film Festival, chair, 1972-74, board member, 1974-75; member of film and creative arts panel, Illinois Arts Council, beginning 1978; consultant, National Endowment for the Humanities. Contributor, *Nero Wolfe* series, A&E Network. *Military service:* U.S. Army, 1957-59.

MEMBER: International Crime Writers Association, Writers Guild of America, Private Eye Writers of America, Mystery Writers of America, Popular Culture Association of America, Society for Cinema Studies.

AWARDS, HONORS: Edgar Award nomination, Mystery Writers of America, 1984, for *Black Knight in Red Square;* Edgar Award, Mystery Writers of America,

1989, for *A Cold Red Sunrise;* International Prix de Roman for crime fiction, 1990; Grand Master Award, Mystery Writers of America, 2006.

WRITINGS:

MYSTERY NOVELS

Bullet for a Star, St. Martin's (New York, NY), 1977.

Murder on the Yellow Brick Road, St. Martin's (New York, NY), 1977.

You Bet Your Life, St. Martin's (New York, NY), 1979.

The Howard Hughes Affair, St. Martin's (New York, NY), 1980.

Never Cross a Vampire, St. Martin's (New York, NY), 1980.

Death of a Dissident, Ace Books/Charter Books (New York, NY), 1981.

High Midnight, St. Martin's (New York, NY), 1981.

Catch a Falling Clown, St. Martin's (New York, NY), 1982.

He Done Her Wrong: A Toby Peters Mystery, St. Martin's (New York, NY), 1983.

When the Dark Man Calls (also see below), St. Martin's (New York, NY), 1983.

The Fala Factor, St. Martin's (New York, NY), 1984.

Black Knight in Red Square, Charter Books (New York, NY), 1984.

Down for the Count, G.K. Hall (Boston, MA), 1985.

Red Chameleon, Scribner (New York, NY), 1985.

Exercise in Terror, St. Martin's (New York, NY), 1985.

Smart Moves, St. Martin's (New York, NY), 1986.

The Man Who Shot Lewis Vance, St. Martin's (New York, NY), 1986.

Think Fast, Mr. Peters, St. Martin's (New York, NY), 1987.

A Fine, Red Rain, Scribner (New York, NY), 1987.

A Cold, Red Sunrise, Scribner (New York, NY), 1988.

Buried Caesars, Mysterious Press (New York, NY), 1989.

Poor Butterfly, Mysterious Press (New York, NY), 1990.

The Man Who Walked like a Bear: A Porfiry Rostnikov Novel, Scribner (New York, NY), 1990.

Lieberman's Folly, St. Martin's (New York, NY), 1991.

The Melting Clock, Mysterious Press (New York, NY), 1991.

Rostnikov's Vacation: An Inspector Porfiry Rostnikov Novel, Scribner (New York, NY), 1991.

Death of a Russian Priest, Fawcett Columbine (New York, NY), 1992.

The Devil Met a Lady, Mysterious Press (New York, NY), 1993.

Lieberman's Choice, St. Martin's (New York, NY), 1993.

Lieberman's Day, Holt (New York, NY), 1994.

Hard Currency, Fawcett Columbine (New York, NY), 1995.

Lieberman's Thief, Holt (New York, NY), 1995.

Tomorrow Is Another Day, Mysterious Press (New York, NY), 1995.

Dancing in the Dark, Mysterious Press (New York, NY), 1996.

Blood and Rubles, Fawcett Columbine (New York, NY), 1996.

The Green Bottle, Forge (New York, NY), 1996.

A Fatal Glass of Beer, Mysterious Press (New York, NY), 1997.

The Dog Who Bit a Policeman, Mysterious Press (New York, NY), 1998.

Devil on My Doorstep, Forge (New York, NY), 1998.

Vengeance: A Lew Fonesca Mystery, Forge (New York, NY), 1999.

Fall of a Cosmonaut, Mysterious Press/Warner (New York, NY), 2000.

The Big Silence: An Abe Lieberman Mystery, Forge (New York, NY), 2000.

A Few Minutes Past Midnight: A Toby Peters Mystery, Carroll & Graf Publishers (New York, NY), 2001.

Murder on the Trans-Siberian Express, Mysterious Press (New York, NY), 2001.

Retribution: A Lew Fonesca Novel, Forge (New York, NY), 2001.

Not Quite Kosher: An Abe Lieberman Mystery, Forge (New York, NY), 2002.

To Catch a Spy: A Toby Peters Mystery, Carroll & Graf Publishers (New York, NY), 2002.

Midnight Pass: A Lew Fonesca Mystery, Forge (New York, NY), 2003.

Mildred Pierced: A Toby Peters Mystery, Carroll & Graf Publishers (New York, NY), 2003.

The Last Dark Place: An Abe Lieberman Mystery, Forge (New York, NY), 2004.

Now You See It: A Toby Peters Mystery, Carroll & Graf Publishers (New York, NY), 2004.

Dead of Winter, Pocket Books (New York, NY), 2005.

Denial: A Lew Fonesca Mystery, Forge (New York, NY), 2005.

Always Say Goodbye: A Lew Fonesca Mystery, Forge (New York, NY), 2006.

Terror Town: An Abe Lieberman Mystery, Forge (New York, NY), 2006.

OTHER

Here Comes the Interesting Part (one-act play), first produced in New York, NY, at New York Academy of Arts and Sciences, 1968.

Don Siegel, Director (biography), Curtis Books (New York, NY), 1974.

American Film Genres: Approaches to a Critical Theory of Popular Film (textbook), Pflaum/Standard (Fairfield, NJ), 1974, 2nd revised edition, Nelson-Hall (Chicago, IL), 1984.

Clint Eastwood (biography), New American Library (New York, NY), 1975.

(Editor, with Joseph F. Hill) *Ingmar Bergman: Essays in Criticism,* Oxford University Press (Oxford, England), 1976.

John Huston: Maker of Magic (biography), Houghton Mifflin (Boston, MA), 1978.

Coop: The Life and Legend of Gary Cooper (biography), St. Martin's (New York, NY), 1980.

(With Dana Hodgdon) *Basic Filmmaking* (textbook), Arco (New York, NY), 1981.

(With Jeffrey Mahan) *American Television Genres* (textbook), Nelson-Hall (Chicago, IL), 1985.

Writing for Television, Dell (New York, NY), 1988.

(Editor) *Mystery in the Sunshine State: Florida Short Stories,* Pineapple Press (Sarasota, FL), 1999.

Hidden and Other Stories, Five Star (Unity, ME), 1999.

(Editor) *Mystery Writers of America Presents Show Business Is Murder,* Berkley Prime Crime (New York, NY), 2004.

Behind the Mystery: Top Mystery Writers Interviewed, Hot House Press (Cohasset, MA), 2005.

Also author of dialogue for the film *Once upon a Time in America,* 1984; author of story and screenplay for the film *Enemy Territory,* 1987; author of screenplay for the film *A Woman in the Wind,* 1988. Contributor to books, including *Hal in the Classroom,* edited by Ralph Amelio, Pflaum/Standard (Fairfield, NJ), 1976; *Graphic Violence on the Screen,* edited by Thomas Atkins, Simon & Schuster (New York, NY), 1976; and *Science Fiction Film,* edited by Thomas Atkins, Simon & Schuster (New York, NY), 1976. Contributor to cinema journals and other magazines, including *Man from U.N.C.L.E. Magazine, Positif, Take One, Journal of Popular Film, Journal of the Literary Imagination, Wooster Review,* and *New Mexico Quarterly.*

ADAPTATIONS: When the Dark Man Calls was adapted as a film titled *Frequence Meurtre* for Geuville Pictures in 1988; numerous novels have been adapted as audio books.

SIDELIGHTS: Stuart M. Kaminsky is an author of numerous mysteries and the creator of four distinct series sleuths: World War II-era Toby Peters, Chicago-based Abraham Lieberman, Russian police inspector Porfiry Rostnikov, and Florida private investigator Lew Fonesca. Additionally, Kaminsky has penned novels based on the popular *Rockford Files* television show. A former film scholar who helped found Florida State University's Graduate Film Conservatory, Kaminsky has devoted himself to mystery writing full time for many years—and with unqualified success. A *Publishers Weekly* reviewer commented: "One of the most prolific mystery writers working today, Kaminsky is also one of the best." The recipient of the 2006 Grand Master Award from the Mystery Writers of America, Kaminsky has also been dubbed "the pre-eminent living writer of police procedurals," by a *Kirkus Reviews* critic.

Kaminsky's Toby Peters books, including *Murder on the Yellow Brick Road, Catch a Falling Clown, Think Fast, Mr. Peters, To Catch a Spy, Mildred Pierced,* and *Now You See It* involve famous real-life characters (often of Hollywood renown) in fictional situations during the 1930s and 1940s. Kaminsky uses his vast knowledge of the time period to fill his books with nostalgic references to things past, such as Beechnut Gum and the *Dagwood and Blondie* radio show. Concerning his interest in radio, television, and film history, the author once told *CA:* "I am interested in fostering a concern for serious study of those aspects of our cultural life which are seldom considered seriously. I think our objects of nostalgia and entertainment merit serious attention."

In a review of *Catch a Falling Clown, Los Angeles Times* book editor Art Seidenbaum remarked that "the fun of Kaminsky comes in dollops of nostalgia and sometimes drops of literary insights." *Catch a Falling Clown* concerns a series of murders at a circus. The famous clown Emmett Kelley is portrayed as Toby Peters's client, while one of the suspects is none other than Alfred Hitchcock. Other novels by Kaminsky feature film stars such as Mae West, in *He Done Her Wrong,* and Judy Garland, in *Murder on the Yellow Brick Road.* Well-known names like Howard Hughes, Joe Louis, Albert Einstein, and Salvador Dali also become victims of plots against their lives or reputations in the Peters novels.

Remarking on the author's characters in *Catch a Falling Clown,* Seidenbaum observed that Kaminsky "creates people who perform a nice balancing act, between sympathy and cynicism," adding that the author's portrayal of Emmett Kelly is "credible and engaging." While some critics have complained about the over-abundance of humor and period in-jokes in the series, in a review of *Poor Butterfly* for *Publishers Weekly,* a critic concluded that the "frightful, madly comic and nostalgic incidents [are] made believable and entertaining in Kaminsky's artful handling."

Charlie Chaplin is at the center of the 2001 Toby Peters title, *A Few Minutes Past Midnight.* Peters is brought in to protect the actor, no longer quite so popular with the American public, a fact made painfully obvious when a man with a knife appears at Chaplin's wedding. Reviewing the novel in *Booklist,* Wes Lukowsky called Kaminsky's retro private eye "a good guy with a sense of humor, and every appearance he makes is a welcome one." Reviewing the same book, a *Publishers Weekly* contributor found it "an amusing story full of suitable heroics." Peters next comes to the aid of Cary Grant in *To Catch a Spy,* "a mild-mannered thriller," according to a *Kirkus Reviews* critic. Kaminsky posits the notion that Grant was a British spy during World War II, ferreting out Nazi sympathizers in Hollywood, and Peters is hired to assist in the star's efforts. A *Publishers Weekly* contributor noted: "The series may be tissue thin by this point, but fans are in for a merry ride."

In 1944, just before she begins filming *Mildred Pierce,* Joan Crawford witnesses the murder of a woman named Mildred in a public park. The woman is shot—pierced—with the bolt from a crossbow. Peters becomes involved to prove the innocence of his dentist who accidentally shot the bolt that killed his wife, Mildred. Soon, however, Peters is in over his head in this "page-turning romp," as *Booklist* contributor Connie Fletcher described the book. A critic for *Kirkus Reviews* thought *Mildred Pierced* was "more somber than Toby's usual antic fare," but a *Publishers Weekly* reviewer felt differently, noting that this twenty-third installment in the series offered the "usual amiable blend of nostalgia, humor, eccentricity and a mystery built around a celebrity." In the 2004 *Now You See It,* Peters comes to the aid of magician Harry Blackstone in the final days of World War II. A *Publishers Weekly* reviewer thought Peters's "footwork is as nimble as ever," while stronger praise came from *Booklist* contributor Fletcher, who called it a "marvelous magic trick of a mystery." Similarly, a critic for *Kirkus Reviews* concluded: "The Peters entourage, barreling ahead full tilt, provides just enough insanity to enliven a routine whodunit."

Equally popular are Kaminsky's novels about Russian inspector Porfiry Rostnikov, including *Death of a Dis-* *sident, Red Chameleon, A Cold Red Sunrise, The Dog Who Bit a Policeman,* Fall of a Cosmonaut, and *Murder on the Trans-Siberian Express* to name only a few. It is the Rostnikov series that has established Kaminsky's literary reputation, winning him a coveted Edgar Award for best mystery novel in 1989 for *A Cold Red Sunrise.* Reviewers have been particularly praiseworthy of Kaminsky's depiction of the vagaries of police work in a Russia that has changed its political stripes over the past decades. Rostnikov not only has to solve baffling murders in such far-flung locales as Moscow and Siberia, he also has to answer to bureaucratic bosses, sidestep the KGB, and struggle to get a broken toilet repaired. A wounded veteran of World War II, he likes American mystery novels and weightlifting, and he is an apolitical pragmatist. According to a *Virginia Quarterly Review* contributor, "the murky and constantly shifting moral ground of contemporary Russia is a perfect background for Kaminsky's detective Porfiry Rostnikov." Likewise, *Washington Post Book World* correspondent Jean M. White noted that the author "has staked a claim to a piece of the Russian turf. His stories are laced with fascinating tidbits of Russian history. He captures the Russian scene and character in rich detail."

Chicago's *Tribune Books* correspondent Anthony Olcott cited Kaminsky's Rostnikov books for staking a claim "on a rich virgin territory for mysteries, a kind of 87th Precinct crammed with maniacs, cowards, heroes and just plain oddities." The critic added: "Kaminsky draws his Soviet police force as the sort of place where Rostnikov can use virtually any sleuthing tricks he wishes to, provided it will help to solve his case; yet when his tactics succeed and justice is done, jail yawns as wide for him as for the bad guys. Even by itself this marriage of the hard-boiled genre and the police procedural would be a clever stroke, because of the fresh and funny possibilities it presents." In a *Booklist* review of *Death of a Russian Priest,* Peter Robertson concluded: "Kaminsky's pacing never falters, but it is his richly layered characterizations and surprising twists of plot that have been the shining jewels in this justly acclaimed series."

The end of the Cold War has provided Kaminsky with more creative opportunities, as his beleaguered Rostnikov finds himself under more stress than ever. In *The Dog Who Bit a Policeman,* Rostnikov faces wars between rival gangs, packs of man-killing dogs, and rampant corruption as "Moscow's mean streets have gone way beyond mean," to quote reviewer Thomas Gaughan in *Booklist.* Gaughan went on to comment that Kaminsky "surpasses himself in feeding readers small, telling details of the sadness of life in contemporary Moscow. . . . This is a strange, sad, and altogether wonderful novel." *Library Journal* correspondent Rex E. Klett likewise declared: "Rostnikov and his quirky team rank among the best the genre offers."

In the year 2000 *Fall of a Cosmonaut,* Rostnikov faces three cases at once: the disappearance of a former cosmonaut, the ransoming of a stolen film, and the murder of a science researcher. Initially seen as separate incidents, the three mysteries ultimately intersect. Reviewing the novel in *Book,* Jennifer Braunschweiger noted that Kaminsky "follows the strategy of a police procedural . . . and infuses his story with rich characters and settings." Fletcher, writing in *Booklist,* thought the author set a good tempo to the story, "giving his characters believable quirks, and, especially, bringing a complex society to life." A *Publishers Weekly* contributor felt that even though the separate cases "turn out to be less absorbing than they seem at first, . . . Rostnikov and his team are so vivid and palpable that it almost doesn't matter."

Rostnikov is once again in action in the 2001 *Murder on the Trans-Siberian Express,* a book which "displays Kaminsky at his deft, stage-manager best," according to *Booklist* contributor Fletcher. Once again juggling several plot lines, Kaminsky sends his Russian inspector to Vladivostock seeking to solve a hundred-year-old murder. Meanwhile, he also has a series of murders in the Moscow subway and the kidnapping of a rock star to investigate. For Fletcher, "Kaminsky never fails to craft superlative mysteries." Similar praise came from a *Kirkus Reviews* critic who felt the novel was "deftly plotted and, as usual, superbly written."

Chicago policeman Abe Lieberman was introduced in the 1991 *Lieberman's Folly,* and a new title in the series has appeared about every two years since then. As Fletcher noted in a *Booklist* review of *The Big Silence,* the novels in this series are "as much about solving moral problems as they are about solving crimes." Typically, several different story lines are going at once, as Lieberman works his way through life's quandaries to find truth and justice, often accompanied by his partner, Bill Hanrahan. For a *Publishers Weekly* critic reviewing *The Big Silence,* "the partnerships Lieberman has forged with his compatriots . . . make the resolutions and the process of achieving them a joy to follow."

In the 2002 title, *Not Quite Kosher,* for example, Lieberman is involved in the hunt for thieves, a search for a man who has said he is going to die, and in the prepara-

tions for the bar mitzvah of his grandson. His partner, meanwhile, is battling an Asian crime gang. For *Booklist* contributor Fletcher, this was "the kind of complex, diverting puzzle for which Kaminsky is famous." Similar praise was offered by a *Publishers Weekly* contributor who felt the author "delivers the goods in this seventh Lieberman novel," a "witty, entertaining read."

In *The Last Dark Place,* Lieberman hunts for the person who killed a professional assassin, and also attempts to prevent an Asian and Latino gang war. A *Publishers Weekly* contributor thought "Kaminsky's sympathetic hero and his believable family relationships make this an entertaining crime novel." A critic for *Kirkus Reviews* noted that Kaminsky has almost too many subplots in *The Last Dark Place,* but that the author "provides most of them a teasing, sometimes heartrending extra kick before calling it a day."

Kaminsky's ninth Abe Lieberman novel, *Terror Town,* was "terrific," according to a *Publishers Weekly* reviewer, who further believed that this title would gain the series more notoriety. Lieberman and Hanrahan are investigating the brutal murder of a young mother, an attack on a one-time Chicago Cubs player, and an extortion racket run by a religions fanatic. Fletcher, once again writing in *Booklist,* called this "another top-notch effort from Kaminsky."

In the late 1990s, Kaminsky introduced yet another series sleuth, the pitiable Lew Fonesca. In his debut mystery, *Vengeance,* Fonesca has come to roost in Sarasota, Florida, where he keeps a small private investigator's office behind a Dairy Queen. Asked to find two missing persons—one a rich man's trophy wife, one a kidnapped teenager—Fonesca finds solace in his personal sorrows by helping his clients. "The first episode in a new series by Edgar-winner Kaminsky is a very satisfying, exciting read," declared Lukowsky in *Booklist.* "Fonesca is a decent, troubled man hoping to recover his emotional focus. . . . Readers will be demanding the sequel before they've finished the debut." A *Publishers Weekly* contributor wrote of the same title: "As always, Kaminsky's sense of place is faultless, and he skillfully captures a parade of lively, credible characters. . . . With an early hook, he grabs readers and takes them on a memorably tumultuous ride."

Fonesca's adventures continue in *Retribution,* in which Kaminsky creates a "nail-biting missing-persons case," according to Fletcher in a *Booklist* review. A *Publishers*

Weekly writer likewise called this second installment "engrossing." In *Midnight Pass* the perennially depressed Fonesca is on the trail of a missing wife and kids, as well as on the lookout for a politician whose vote is needed in a highly charged environmental bill. Fletcher called this work a "wryly written parable set in an old-time detective context," in her *Booklist* review. Further praise came from a *Kirkus Reviews* contributor who concluded, "Kaminsky strikes a nice balance between dark and light in this fast-moving adventure."

The 2005 *Denial* finds Fonesca once again on the trail of two cases: one involves a nursing home resident who claims to have witnessed a murder, and the second is a hit-and-run case. A *Publishers Weekly* writer commented that readers "cannot help cheering for" Lew, while a *Kirkus Reviews* critic found the same work "compelling in Lew's unobtrusively sensitive way." With the fifth book in the series, *Always Say Goodbye,* Lew is on the trail of the person who killed his wife in Chicago.

Comfortable in many genres, Kaminsky has also written screenplays, textbooks, and biographies. He once discussed his aims in *CA:* "In my fiction writing, I am particularly interested in avoiding pretension. In my nonfiction, I am particularly concerned with being provocative and readable." Speaking with *Publishers Weekly* writer Leonard Picker, Kaminsky voiced his own sense of wonder at his long and prolific career: "When I started writing mystery fiction, I had no idea that I'd have as long and as successful a run as I've had."

BIOGRAPHICAL AND CRITICAL SOURCES:

PERIODICALS

Armchair Detective, spring, 1990, review of *A Cold Red Sunrise,* p. 192.

Book, November, 2000, Jennifer Braunschweiger, review of *Fall of a Cosmonaut,* p. 79.

Booklist, November 15, 1988, review of *A Cold Red Sunrise,* p. 542; May 15, 1990, review of *Poor Butterfly,* p. 1783; July, 1992, Peter Robertson, review of *Death of a Russian Priest,* p. 1923; April 15, 1997, Wes Lukowsky, review of *A Fatal Glass of Beer,* p. 1406; January 1, 1998, Wes Lukowsky, review of *Devil on My Doorstep,* p. 783; June 1, 1998, Thomas Gaughan, review of *The Dog Who Bit a Policeman,* p. 1732; November 15, 1998, Ellie Barta-Moran, review of *Never Cross a Vampire,* p. 604; August, 1999, Karen Harris, review of *The Dog Who Bit a Policeman,* p. 2075; September 15, 1999, Wes Lukowsky, review of *Vengeance: A Lew Fonesca Mystery,* p. 237; July 31, 2000, Connie Fletcher, review of *Fall of a Cosmonaut,* p. 2120; September 15, 2000, Connie Fletcher, review of *The Big Silence: An Abe Lieberman Mystery,* p. 221; May 1, 2001, Wes Lukowsky, review of *A Few Minutes Past Midnight: A Toby Peters Mystery,* p. 1635; September 1, 2001, Connie Fletcher, review of *Murder on the Trans-Siberian Express,* p. 57; September 15, 2001, Connie Fletcher, review of *Retribution: A Lew Fonesca Novel,* p. 199; November 1, 2002, Connie Fletcher, review of *Not Quite Kosher: An Abe Lieberman Mystery,* p. 452; June 1, 2003, Connie Fletcher, review of *Mildred Pierced: A Toby Peters Mystery,* p. 1750; December 15, 2003, Connie Fletcher, review of *Midnight Pass: A Lew Fonesca Mystery,* p. 731; October 1, 2004, Connie Fletcher, review of *Now You See It: A Toby Peters Mystery,* p. 313; November 1, 2004, review of *The Last Dark Place: An Abe Lieberman Mystery,* p. 468; May 1, 2005, Connie Fletcher, review of *Denial: A Lew Fonesca Mystery,* p. 1524; November 1, 2005, Bill Ott, review of *Behind the Mystery: Top Mystery Writers Interviewed,* p. 14; December 15, 2005, Connie Fletcher, review of *Terror Town: An Abe Lieberman Mystery,* p. 27.

Christian Science Monitor, August 4, 1989, B.J. Rahn, review of *A Cold Red Sunrise,* pp. 12-13.

Kirkus Reviews, August 15, 2001, review of *Murder on the Trans-Siberian Express,* p. 1168; October 1, 2002, review of *No Quite Kosher,* p. 1430; May 1, 2002, review of *To Catch a Spy,* p. 619; May 1, 2003, review of *Mildred Pierced,* p. 646; October 1, 2003, review of *Midnight Pass,* p. 1202; October 1, 2004, review of *The Last Dark Place,* p. 942; October 15, 2004, review of *Now You See It,* p. 987; April 15, 2005, review of *Denial,* p. 454; December 1, 2005, review of *Terror Town,* p. 1257.

Library Journal, May 1, 1997, Rex E. Klett, review of *A Fatal Glass of Beer,* pp. 144, 153; February 1, 1998, review of *Devil on My Doorstep,* p. 116; May 1, 1998, Rex E. Klett, review of *The Dog Who Bit a Policeman,* p. 143; October 1, 2001, Rex E. Klett, review of *Murder on the Trans-Siberian Express,* p. 146; December, 2002, Rex E. Klett, review of *Not Quite Kosher,* p. 184.

Los Angeles Times, January 20, 1982, Art Seidenbaum, review of *Catch a Falling Clown.*

New Yorker, October 12, 1987, review of *A Fine Red Rain,* p. 146.

New York Times Book Review, April 22, 1979, Newgate Callendar, review of *You Bet Your Life,* p. 20; December 22, 1991, Marilyn Stasio, review of *The Melting Clock,* p. 21; August 16, 1998, Marilyn Stasio, review of *The Dog Who Bit a Policeman,* p. 12.

Publishers Weekly, October 4, 1985, review of *Red Chameleon,* p. 70; October 28, 1988, review of *A Cold, Red Sunrise,* p. 64; April 13, 1990, Sybil Steinberg, review of *The Man Who Walked Like a Bear,* p. 57; April 27, 1990, review of *Poor Butterfly,* p. 55; May 5, 1997, review of *A Fatal Glass of Beer,* p. 202; December 15, 1997, review of *Devil on My Doorstep,* p. 51; June 1, 1998, review of *The Dog Who Bit a Policeman,* p. 48A; August 2, 1999, review of *Vengeance,* p. 76; July 31, 2000, review of *Fall of a Cosmonaut,* p. 74; October 2, 2000, review of *The Big Silence,* p. 61; June 11, 2001, review of *A Few Minutes Past Midnight,* p. 64; September 3, 2001, review of *Murder on the Trans-Siberian Express,* p. 66; October 22, 2001, review of *Retribution,* p. 51; May 27, 2002, review of *To Catch a Spy: A Toby Peters Mystery,* p. 39; November 11, 2002, review of *Not Quite Kosher,* p. 43; May 19, 2003, review of *Mildred Pierced,* p. 55; September 13, 2004, review of *Now You See It,* p. 61; October 11, 2004, review of *The Last Dark Place,* p. 59; May 9, 2005, review of *Denial,* p. 49; December 5, 2005, review of *Terror Town,* p. 34; December 19, 2005, Leonard Picker, "A New MWA Grand Master," p. 44.

Sarasota Herald Tribune (Sarasota, FL), August 6, 2002, Marjorie North, "Kaminsky Story to Air on *Nero Wolfe* Series," p. E3; June 5, 2005, Bob Morrison, "Murder Most Local," review of *Denial,* p. E4.

Tribune Books (Chicago, IL), June 24, 1990, Anthony Olcott, review of *The Man Who Walked Like a Bear,* p. 5.

Virginia Quarterly Review, spring, 1992, review of *Death of a Russian Priest,* p. 60.

Washington Post Book World, December 18, 1988, Jean M. White, review of *A Cold, Red Sunrise,* p. 8.

ONLINE

Internet Movie Database, http://www.imdb.com/ (November 20, 2006), "Stuart Kaminsky."

MysteryOne.com, http://www.mysteryone.com/ (August 28, 2002), "Stuart Kaminsky Interview."

Stuart Kaminsky Home Page, http://www.stuart kaminsky.com (November 20, 2006).

Whodunnit.com, http://www.who-dunnit.com/ (November 20, 2006), "Stuart Kaminsky," and Alan Paul Curtis, review of *Midnight Pass.**

*   *   *

KAMINSKY, Stuart Melvin
See KAMINSKY, Stuart M.

*   *   *

KERET, Etgar 1967-

PERSONAL: Born 1967, in Tel Aviv, Israel.

ADDRESSES: Home—Israel.

CAREER: Author, journalist, and filmmaker. Columnist for a weekly newspaper in Jerusalem; comic strip writer for a Tel Aviv, Israel, newspaper; comedy writer for Israeli television; lecturer at Tel Aviv University School of Film. Writer-in-residence, University of Iowa International Writing Program, 2001; participant in Sundance Institute Feature Film Program Screenwriters Lab, 2001. Director and actor, *Meduzot,* 2007. *Military service:* Served in the Israeli Army.

AWARDS, HONORS: Israeli Motion Picture Academy Award for movie *Skin Deep;* first prize, Alternative Theatre Festival, Acre, Israel, for musical *Entebbe; Yediot-Acharonot* (Israeli newspaper) selection for the fifty most important books written in Hebrew, for *Ga'gu'ai le-Kising'er;* prize winner at several international film festivals, including first prize at the Korto Festival in Italy for *The Queen of Red Hearts;* received the (Israel) Book Publishers Association's Platinum Prize several times; Prime Minister's Prize; Cinema Prize, Israeli Ministry of Culture.

WRITINGS:

IN ENGLISH TRANSLATION

Ga'gu'ai le-Kising'er, Zemorah-Bitan (Tel Aviv, Israel), 1994, translated as *Missing Kissinger,* Chatto & Windus (London, England), 2007.

How to Make a Good Script Great, Actus Tragicus (Tel Aviv, Israel), 1996.

Jetlag, Actus Tragicus (Tel Aviv, Israel), 1998.

Selected Stories, Actus Tragicus (Tel Aviv, Israel), 1998.

The Bus Driver Who Wanted to Be God and Other Stories (includes *Ha-Kaitanah shel Kneler* and selections from *Tsinorot* and *Ga'gu'ai le-Kising'er;* also see below), translation by Dalya Bilu and Miriam Shlesinger, Thomas Dunne Books (New York, NY), 2001.

Anihu (short stories), Zemorah-Bitan (Lod, Israel), 2002, translated by Miriam Shlesinger and Sondra Silverston as *The Nimrod Flip-Out,* Chatto and Windus (London, England), 2005, published as *The Nimrod Flipout,* Farrar, Straus and Giroux (New York, NY), 2006.

Dad Runs Away with the Circus (children's fiction), illustrated by Rutu Modan, Candlewick Press (Cambridge, MA), 2004.

(With Samir El-Youssef) *Gaza Blues: Different Stories,* David Paul (London, England), 2004.

One Last Story and That's It (short stories), translated by Miriam Shlesinger and others, Katha (New Delhi, India), 2005.

Jetlag: Five Graphic Novellas, translated by Dan Ofri, illustrated by Actus Tragicus (Batia Kolton and others), Toby Press (New Milford, CT), 2006.

IN HEBREW

Tsinorot (short stories; title means "Pipelines"), Am Oved (Tel Aviv, Israel), 1992.

(With Rutu Modan) *Lo banu le-henot* (comics; title means "Nobody Said It Was Going to Be Fun"), Keter (Jerusalem, Israel), 1996.

(With Assaf Hanuka) *Simta'ot ha-za'am* (comics; title means "Streets of Rage"), Zemorah-Bitan (Tel Aviv, Israel), 1997.

Ha-Kaitanah shel Kneler (novella; title means "Kneller's Happy Campers"), Zemorah-Bitan (Tel Aviv, Israel), 1998.

Pizzeria Kamikaze (graphic novel), illustrated by Asaf Hanuka, Kineret, Zemorah-Bitan, Devir (Or Yehudah, Israel), 2004.

Contributor to *Tselaliyot: 11 sipurim* (stories; title means "Silhouettes: Anthology"), Kineret, Zemorah-Bitan, Devir (Or Yehudah, Israel), 2005. Coauthor, with Jonathan Bar Giora, of *Entebbe,* a musical play produced in Acre, Israel. Also author of numerous teleplays; writer and director, with Ron Tal, of short movie *Skin Deep* (also called *Malka Red-Heart* and *Queen of Red Hearts*). Screenwriter of *$9.99,* a stop-motion animated film. Keret's writings have been translated into twenty-two languages.

ADAPTATIONS: Keret's short stories have been adapted as more than forty short films, including one that received an MTV Prize for best animated film in 1998; *Kneller's Happy Campers* was adapted for a film, *Wristcutters: A Love Story,* Halcyon Pictures, 2006.

SIDELIGHTS: Etgar Keret is a best-selling author and filmmaker who is especially popular among Israeli young people and often regarded as a spokesman for their generation. Well known for his sardonic and irreverent stories, Keret also pens a newspaper column, comic books, television scripts, and screenplays. Although he has been called "Israel's hippest best-selling young writer today," some Israeli critics have faulted Keret for avoiding political and ideological themes in his work. As Emily Gitter noted in a *Forward* magazine interview with the author, Keret "disputes the criticism that his stories are simply frivolous." Keret told Gitter: "I think my writing is ideological. But in Israel, when people talk about ideology or morals, they're always talking about politics. And I think there's a lot more to ideology and morals than politics." Keret admitted that he found it difficult to identify with the characters in Israeli literature. "They always seemed better than me—stronger and more charismatic," he told Gitter. The American writers John Cheever, Raymond Carver, and Kurt Vonnegut eventually became the strongest influences on Keret's writing.

The first collection of Keret's stories to be published in the United States is *The Bus Driver Who Wanted to Be God and Other Stories,* which includes selections from his *Tsinorot* and *Ga'gu'ai le-Kising'er* and his novella *Ha-Kaitanah shel Kneler.* The title story of the collection concerns a bus driver who refuses to open the door to latecomers on the grounds that it delays the schedules of other passengers already on the bus. One man is able to chase the bus down to a stoplight and change the driver's outlook. Benjamin Anastas, writing in the *New York Times Book Review,* noted that Keret's "impromptu, comic-monologue style works best when he engages larger subjects, as in the title story. . . . Keret serves us plenty of good laughs, particularly when he targets a monolith." In his assessment for the *Book Reporter,* Rob Cline observed that Keret "has a razor-sharp voice barbed with sarcastic wit, surprising turns of phrase . . . [and] a tremendous imagination that allows him to rethink cultural markers and myths." *Booklist*'s John Green commented, "Keret's stories are brief and powerful linguistic downpours, usually punctuated by uproarious climaxes. . . . smart, insightful, and delightfully hip." Keret's stories "juxtapose a casual realism with regular flashes of unabashed absurdity," wrote a *Publishers Weekly* reviewer, "portraying characters on the brink of adulthood forced to confront life's chaotic forces—death, justice, love, betrayal—for the first time." André Alexis, reviewing the book for Toronto's *Globe & Mail,* took exception to "the overly American idiom" of much of the writing, but found it "a work of fiction in which humour, horror, play and irony are as important as ethical concerns. . . . Keret's characters must deal with the nightmares of the past and the present."

Keret has also turned his hand to writing for children, as in the 2004 title *Dad Runs Away with the Circus,* a "fresh and beguiling domestic fantasy," according to a reviewer for *Publishers Weekly,* in which a father becomes so beguiled with the Big Top, that he joins it, leaving his family behind. However, he sends his wife and children postcards from all over the world and then has a most memorable homecoming. The *Publishers Weekly* reviewer concluded that this was a picture book for all ages: "Even those decades away from a mid-life crisis will likely declare this one a winner." Scott La Counte, writing in *School Library Journal,* described the same work as "imaginative," while for a *Kirkus Reviews* critic, "the tale has an offhand charm that suits the offbeat premise."

Also from 2004 is a collaborative effort between Keret and Palestinian author Samir El-Youssef. *Gaza Blues: Different Stories* is, as Peter Whittaker noted in the *New Internationalist,* "motivated by a desire to show that literature can bridge political divides." Keret supplied fifteen of his short-short stories for this collection, each of which provides a "glimpse into a surreal world of extreme stress and anxiety," as Whittaker further noted.

With the collection *The Nimrod Flipout,* Keret received wider recognition in the United States. Writing in *People,* Kyle Smith called the thirty tales in this book "freaky fables," and went on to observe that the author "can do more with six strange and funny paragraphs than most writers can with 600 pages." These stories continue in the author's minimalist pattern: each one is only several pages long. *Forward* magazine reviewer

Stephen Marche described the tales as "simple, startling conceits executed with diamond-cutting precision." *Tikkun* reviewer Michael Lukas also noted, "In short, uncanny, and often hilarious bursts, Etgar Keret taps into the profound existential absurdity of being Israeli." The title story concerns three friends who have become obsessed and even haunted with the suicide death of their common friend, Nimrod, from whom they receive an unexpected message via a Ouija board. Other tales blend the quotidian with the surreal. "Baby" is "a haunting tale of love and fidelity," according to *Hartford Courant* writer Helen Ubinas. "Fatso" was written as a valentine to Keret's girlfriend, but is about a lover who turns into a man. Ubinas found many of these tales "precise, raw and at times, poetic," further calling them stories that "stay with you." Similarly, Hephzibah Anderson, writing in the London *Observer,* felt the collection "perfectly captures the craziness of life in Israel today." However, Ray Olson, writing in *Booklist,* was less impressed: "These aren't stories, they're routines!" Olson went on to term the stories "vulgar, sad-sacky stuff, but amusing." Other reviewers had more favorable assessments of *The Nimrod Flipout.* A *Kirkus Reviews* critic, for example, called the work a "kaleidoscopic assortment of exact, affecting and richly comic stories," and praised Keret for his "raw, confident and direct" insights and observations. *Entertainment Weekly* reviewer Anat Rosenberg termed the tales "strangely compelling—or compelling in their strangeness," while a *Publishers Weekly* contributor found the work "brainteasing," and one that "peels away the borderlines of normalcy."

With *Jetlag: Five Graphic Novellas,* Keret adapts some of his tales to the graphic novel format, working with artists from an Israeli comics collective. Ranging from a story of a man who goes to the circus and falls in love with a monkey to the tale of a passenger on a jet who is involved in an in-flight flirtation and a prearranged crash landing, the pieces in this collection are "brief, surreal fables that set up a witty premise and then end fairly abruptly," according to a *Publishers Weekly* contributor. Olson, writing in *Booklist,* noted that Keret "writes about mundane reality invaded by the fantastic" in this collection. Similarly, Rosie Blau writing in the *Financial Times* felt that *Jetlag* "adds to the Israeli author's reputation for turning the mundane into a surreal storyline."

BIOGRAPHICAL AND CRITICAL SOURCES:

PERIODICALS

Booklist, October 15, 2001, John Green, review of *The Bus Driver Who Wanted to Be God and Other*

Stories, p. 382; December 15, 2005, Ray Olson, review of *Jetlag: Five Graphic Novellas,* p. 32; March 1, 2006, Ray Olson, review of *The Nimrod Flipout,* p. 65.

Entertainment Weekly, February 10, 2006, review of *Jetlag,* p. 139; April 7, 2006, Anat Rosenberg, review of *The Nimrod Flipout,* p. 66.

Financial Times (London, England), February 4, 2006, Rosie Blau, review of *Jetlag,* p. 33.

Forward, October 26, 2001, Emily Gitter, "Carving a 'Hip' Niche in an Epic Land;" May 5, 2006, Stephen Marche, review of *The Nimrod Flip Out.*

Globe & Mail (Toronto, Canada), June 15, 2002, André Alexis, "Israel Meets America: The Mythic and the Modern."

Guardian (London, England), March 26, 2005, review of *The Nimrod Flip Out,* p. 26.

Hartford Courant (Hartford, CT), June 25, 2006, Helen Ubinas, review of *The Nimrod Flipout.*

Kirkus Reviews, August 1, 2001, review of *The Bus Driver Who Wanted to Be God and Other Stories,* p. 1053; September 1, 2004, review of *Dad Runs Away with the Circus,* p. 868; January 1, 2006, review of *The Nimrod Flipout,* p. 11.

Metro Times (Detroit, MI), March 6, 2002, Sean Bieri, "When Words Collide."

New Internationalist, November, 2004, Peter Whittaker, review of *Gaza Blues: Different Stories,* p. 30.

New York Times Book Review, October 28, 2001, Benjamin Anastas, "No Moral, Please," p. 33.

Observer (London, England), February 13, 2005, Hephzibah Anderson, "Parables of Anarchy," p. 16.

People, April 10, 2006, Kyle Smith, review of *The Nimrod Flipout,* p. 45.

Publishers Weekly, September 17, 2001, review of *The Bus Driver Who Wanted to Be God and Other Stories,* p. 53; October 25, 2004, review of *Dad Runs Away with the Circus,* p. 47; December 12, 2005, review of *Jetlag,* p. 44; January 30, 2006, review of *The Nimrod Flipout,* p. 38.

School Library Journal, December, 2004, Scott La Counte, review of *Dad Runs Away with the Circus,* p. 112.

Shofar, summer, 2003, Stacy N. Beckwith, review of *The Bus Driver Who Wanted to Be God and Other Stories,* p. 166.

Tikkun, September-October, 2005, Ben Naparstek, "Interview with Etgar Keret," p. 70; September-October, 2006, Michael Lukas, review of *The Nimrod Flipout,* p. 74.

Times Literary Supplement, July 16, 2004, Eleanor Birne, review of *Gaza Blues: Different Stories,* p. 22; March 25, 2005, Tom Chatfield, "The Clash of Possibilities," p. 22.

Washington Post Book World, June 25, 2006, Alana Newhouse, review of *The Nimrod Flipout,* p. 15.

World Literature Today, spring, 1999, Yair Mazor, review of *Ha-Kaitanah shel Kneler,* p. 383; spring, 2002, Leslie Cohen, review of *The Bus Driver Who Wanted to Be God and Other Stories,* p. 245.

ONLINE

Believer Magazine, http://www.believermag.com/ (November 20, 2006), Ben Ehrenreich, "Etgar Keret."

Book Reporter, http://www.bookreporter.com/ (November 30, 2006), Rob Cline, review of *The Bus Driver Who Wanted to Be God and Other Stories.*

Etgar Keret Home Page, http://www.etgarkeret.com (November 20, 2006).

Eye, http://www.eye.net/ (October 18, 2001), Jason Anderson, "Keret Tops."

Institute for the Translation of Hebrew Literature, http://www.ithl.org.il/ (November 20, 2006), "Etgar Keret."

Nextbook.org, http://www.nextbook.org/ (November 20, 2006), Sara Ivry, "Beach Reading."

OpenDemocracy.net, http://www.opendemocracy.net/ (November 20, 2006), "Etgar Keret."

PEN American Center Web site, http://www.pen.org/ (November 20, 2006), "Etgar Keret."*

*   *   *

KIMMEL, Eric A. 1946-

PERSONAL: Born October 30, 1946, in Brooklyn, NY; son of Morris N. (a certified public accountant) and Anne (an elementary school teacher) Kimmel; married Elizabeth Marcia Sheridan (a professor of education), April 7, 1968 (divorced, 1975); married Doris Ann Blake, June 16, 1978; children: Bridgett (stepdaughter). *Education:* Lafayette College, A.B., 1967; New York University, M.A., 1969; University of Illinois, Ph.D., 1973. *Politics:* Democrat. *Religion:* Jewish.

ADDRESSES: Home and office—Portland, OR. *E-mail*—kimmels@earthlink.net.

CAREER: Writer. Indiana University at South Bend, assistant professor of education, 1973-78; Portland State University, Portland, OR, professor of education, 1978-94. Full-time writer, 1994—.

MEMBER: International Reading Association, Authors Guild, Authors League of America, PEN Northwest, Society of Children's Book Writers and Illustrators, Phi Beta Kappa, Phi Delta Kappa, Kappa Delta Pi.

AWARDS, HONORS: Juvenile Book Merit Award, Friends of American Writers, 1975, for *The Tartar's Sword;* Ten Best Books of 1989, Association of Booksellers for Children, for *Anansi and the Moss-covered Rock;* Present Tense—Joel A. Cavior Award for Notable Children's Book, National Council of Teachers of English, 1990, for *Hershel and the Hanukkah Goblins;* Sydney Taylor Picture Book Award, Association of Jewish Libraries (AJL), 1990, and National Jewish Book Award nomination, both for *The Chanukkah Guest;* Notable Children's Trade Book in the Field of Social Studies, Children's Book Council/National Council for the Social Studies (CBC/NCSS), 1992, for *The Greatest of All;* Notable Children's Trade Book in the Field of Social Studies, CBC/NCSS, 1992, and Aesop Prize, Children's Folklore Section of the American Folklore Society, 1993, both for *Days of Awe;* Parents' Choice Award, 1994, for *The Three Princes;* Paul A. Witty Short Story Award, International Reading Association, for *Four Dollars and Fifty Cents;* Anne Izard Storytellers' Choice Award, for *The Spotted Pony;* Irma and James H. Black Award, Bank Street College of Education, for *Three Sacks of Truth;* Sydney Taylor Award, AJL, National Jewish Picture Book Award finalist, Zena Sutherland Award, University of Chicago Lab School, Notable Children's Book selection, American Library Association, Best Children's Books of 2000, *Publishers Weekly,* and One Hundred Titles for Reading and Sharing, New York Public Library, 2000, all for *Gershon's Monster;* Best Children's Books of 2001, Bank Street College of Education, for *The Runaway Tortilla;* Notable Book selection, AJL, for *The Jar of Fools;* White House Easter Egg Roll featured book, 2001, for *The Birds' Gift: A Ukrainian Easter Story;* Sydney Taylor Award honor book, AJL, 2001, for *A Cloak for the Moon.* Several of Kimmel's books have been nominated or won state awards from organizations in Colorado, Georgia, Nebraska, Nevada, Oregon, Utah, Kentucky, Pennsylvania, and Washington, and have been named to numerous "best books," "children's choice," and "teachers' choice" lists from organizations, including the New York Public Library, the American Booksellers Association, and the Children's Book Council/International Reading Association.

WRITINGS:

FOR CHILDREN

The Tartar's Sword (novel), Coward, 1974.

(Reteller) *Mishka, Pishka, and Fishka, and Other Galician Tales,* illustrated by Christopher J. Spollen, Coward, 1976.

Why Worry?, illustrated by Elizabeth Cannon, Pantheon (New York, NY), 1979.

Nicanor's Gate, illustrated by Jerry Joyner, Jewish Publication Society, 1979.

Hershel of Ostropol, illustrated by Arthur Friedman, Jewish Publication Society, 1981.

(With Rose Zar) *In the Mouth of the Wolf,* Jewish Publication Society, 1983.

(Reteller) *Anansi and the Moss-covered Rock,* illustrated by Janet Stevens, Holiday House (New York, NY), 1988.

The Chanukkah Tree, illustrated by Giora Carmi, Holiday House (New York, NY), 1988.

Charlie Drives the Stage, illustrated by Glen Rounds, Holiday House (New York, NY), 1989.

Hershel and the Hanukkah Goblins, illustrated by Trina Schart Hyman, Holiday House (New York, NY), 1989.

The Chanukkah Guest, illustrated by Giora Carmi, Holiday House (New York, NY), 1990.

Four Dollars and Fifty Cents, illustrated by Glen Rounds, Holiday House (New York, NY), 1990.

(Reteller) *Nanny Goat and the Seven Little Kids,* illustrated by Janet Stevens, Holiday House (New York, NY), 1990.

I Took My Frog to the Library, illustrated by Blanche Sims, Viking (New York, NY), 1990.

(Reteller) *Baba Yaga: A Russian Folktale,* illustrated by Megan Lloyd, Holiday House (New York, NY), 1991.

(Adapter) *Bearhead: A Russian Folktale,* illustrated by Charles Mikolaycak, Holiday House (New York, NY), 1991.

(Reteller) *The Greatest of All: A Japanese Folktale,* illustrated by Giora Carmi, Holiday House (New York, NY), 1991.

(Adapter) *Days of Awe: Stories for Rosh Hashanah and Yom Kippur,* illustrated by Erika Weihs, Viking (New York, NY), 1991.

(Reteller) *Anansi Goes Fishing,* illustrated by Janet Stevens, Holiday House (New York, NY), 1992.

(Reteller) *Boots and His Brothers: A Norwegian Tale,* illustrated by Kimberly Bulcken Root, Holiday House (New York, NY), 1992.

(Adapter) *The Four Gallant Sisters,* illustrated by Tatiana Yuditskaya, Holt (New York, NY), 1992.

(Adapter) *The Old Woman and Her Pig,* illustrated by Giora Carmi, Holiday House (New York, NY), 1992.

(Reteller) *The Spotted Pony: A Collection of Hanukkah Stories,* illustrated by Leonard Everett Fisher, Holiday House (New York, NY), 1992.

(Reteller) *The Tale of Aladdin and the Wonderful Lamp,* illustrated by Ju-Hong Chen, Holiday House (New York, NY), 1992.

(Adapter) *Three Sacks of Truth: A Story from France,* illustrated by Robert Rayevsky, Holiday House (New York, NY), 1993.

(Adapter) *The Witch's Face: A Mexican Tale,* illustrated by Fabricio Vanden Broeck, Holiday House (New York, NY), 1993.

Asher and the Capmakers: A Hanukkah Story, illustrated by Will Hillenbrand, Holiday House (New York, NY), 1993.

(Reteller) *The Gingerbread Man,* illustrated by Megan Lloyd, Holiday House (New York, NY), 1993.

(Reteller) *Anansi and the Talking Melon,* illustrated by Janet Stevens, Holiday House (New York, NY), 1994.

One Good Tern Deserves Another (novel), Holiday House (New York, NY), 1994.

(Adapter) *I-Know-Not-What, I-Know-Not-Where: A Russian Tale,* illustrated by Robert Sauber, Holiday House (New York, NY), 1994.

(Adapter) *Iron John: A Tale from the Brothers Grimm,* illustrated by Trina Schart Hyman, Holiday House (New York, NY), 1994.

Bernal and Florinda: A Spanish Tale, illustrated by Robert Rayevsky, Holiday House (New York, NY), 1994.

(Reteller) *The Three Princes: A Tale from the Middle East,* illustrated by Leonard Everett Fisher, Holiday House (New York, NY), 1994.

(Reteller) *The Valiant Red Rooster: A Story from Hungary,* illustrated by Katya Arnold, Holt (New York, NY), 1994.

(Reteller) *The Goose Girl: A Story from the Brothers Grimm,* illustrated by Robert Sauber, Holiday House (New York, NY), 1995.

(Adapter) *Rimonah of the Flashing Sword: A North African Tale,* illustrated by Omar Rayyan, Holiday House (New York, NY), 1995.

Bar Mitzvah: A Jewish Boy's Coming of Age, Viking (New York, NY), 1995.

(Reteller) *The Adventures of Hershel of Ostropol,* illustrated by Trina Schart Hyman, Holiday House (New York, NY), 1995.

Billy Lazroe and the King of the Sea: A Tale of the Northwest, illustrated by Michael Steirnagle, Harcourt (San Diego, CA), 1996.

(Reteller) *Count Silvernose: A Story from Italy,* illustrated by Omar Rayyan, Holiday House (New York, NY), 1996.

The Magic Dreidels: A Hanukkah Story, illustrated by Katya Krenina, Holiday House (New York, NY), 1996.

One Eye, Two Eyes, Three Eyes, illustrated by Dirk Zimmer, Holiday House (New York, NY), 1996.

The Tale of Ali Baba and the Forty Thieves: A Story from the Arabian Nights, illustrated by Will Hillenbrand, Holiday House (New York, NY), 1996.

Onions and Garlic: An Old Tale, illustrated by Katya Arnold, Holiday House (New York, NY), 1996.

(Adapter) *Sirko and the Wolf: A Ukrainian Tale,* illustrated by Robert Sauber, Holiday House (New York, NY), 1997.

(Adapter) *Squash It!: A True and Ridiculous Tale,* illustrated by Robert Rayevsky, Holiday House (New York, NY), 1997.

(Reteller) *Ten Suns: A Chinese Legend,* illustrated by YongSheng Xuan, Holiday House (New York, NY), 1998.

(Reteller) *Seven at One Blow: A Tale from the Brothers Grimm,* illustrated by Megan Lloyd, Holiday House (New York, NY), 1998.

When Mindy Saved Hanukkah, pictures by Barbara McClintock, Scholastic (New York, NY), 1998.

Be Not far from Me: The Oldest Love Story: Legends from the Bible, illustrated by David Diaz, Simon & Schuster (New York, NY), 1998.

(Editor) *A Hanukkah Treasury,* illustrated by Emily Lisker, Holt (New York, NY), 1998.

(Reteller) *Easy Work!: An Old Tale,* illustrated by Andrew Glass, Holiday House (New York, NY), 1998.

(Reteller) *The Birds' Gift: A Ukrainian Easter Story,* illustrated by Katya Krenina, Holiday House (New York, NY), 1999.

(Reteller) *The Rooster's Antlers: A Story of the Chinese Zodiac,* illustrated by Yong Sheng Xuan, Holiday House (New York, NY), 1999.

Sword of the Samurai: Adventure Stories from Japan, Harcourt (New York, NY), 1999.

The Runaway Tortilla, illustrated by Randy Cecil, Winslow (Delray Beach, FL), 2000.

(Reteller) *Gershon's Monster: A Story for the Jewish New Year,* illustrated by Jon J. Muth, Scholastic (New York, NY), 2000.

The Jar of Fools: Eight Hanukkah Stories from Chelm, illustrated by Mordecai Gerstein, Holiday House (New York, NY), 2000.

Grizz!, illustrated by Andrew Glass, Holiday House (New York, NY), 2000.

Montezuma and the Fall of the Aztecs, illustrated by Daniel San Souci, Holiday House (New York, NY), 2000.

(Reteller) *The Two Mountains: An Aztec Legend,* illustrated by Leonard Everett Fisher, Holiday House (New York, NY), 2000.

Zigazak: A Hanukkah Story, illustrated by Jon Goodell, Random House (New York, NY), 2001.

A Cloak for the Moon, illustrated by Katya Krenina, Holiday House (New York, NY), 2001.

Website of the Warped Wizard (chapter book), illustrated by Jeff Shelly, Dutton (New York, NY), 2001.

(Reteller) *Anansi and the Magic Stick,* illustrated by Janet Stevens, Holiday House (New York, NY), 2001.

Robin Hook, Pirate Hunter!, illustrated by Michael Dooling, Scholastic (New York, NY), 2001.

Pumpkinhead, illustrated by Steve Haskamp, Winslow Press (Delray Beach, FL), 2001.

Website of the Cracked Cookies (chapter book), illustrated by Jeff Shelly, Dutton (New York, NY), 2001.

Why the Snake Crawls on Its Belly, illustrated by Allen Davis, Pitspopany Press (New York, NY), 2001.

(Reteller) *The Erie Canal Pirates,* illustrated by Andrew Glass, Holiday House (New York, NY), 2002.

(Reteller) *Three Samurai Cats: A Story from Japan,* illustrated by Mordicai Gerstein, Holiday House (New York, NY), 2003.

The Brass Serpent, illustrated by Joanna Miller, Pitspopany Press (New York, NY), 2002.

Brother Wolf, Sister Sparrow: Stories about Saints and Animals, illustrated by John Winch, Holiday House (New York, NY), 2003.

(And compiler) *Wonders and Miracles: A Passover Companion,* Scholastic (New York, NY), 2004.

(Reteller) *Hayyim's Ghost* (based on a story by Beatrice Silverman Weinreich), illustrated by Ari Binus, Pitspopany Press (New York, NY), 2004.

(Reteller and adaptor) *Don Quixote and the Windmills* (based on the novel by Miguel de Cervantes Saavedra), illustrated by Leonard Everett Fisher, Farrar, Straus (New York, NY), 2004.

(Reteller) *The Castle of the Cats,* illustrated by Katya Krenina, Holiday House (New York, NY), 2004.

Cactus Soup, illustrated by Phil Huling, Marshall Cavendish (New York, NY), 2004.

(Reteller) *The Spider's Gift: A Ukranian Christmas Story,* illustrated by Katya Krenina, Holiday House (New York, NY), 2005.

A Horn for Louis, illustrated by James Bernardin, Random House (New York, NY), 2005.

(Reteller and adaptor) *The Hero Beowulf,* illustrated by Leonard Everett Fisher, Farrar, Strauss (New York, NY), 2005.

(Reteller) *The Lady in the Blue Cloak: Legends from the Texas Missions,* illustrated by Susan Guevara, Holiday House (New York, NY), 2006.

(Reteller) *The Frog Princess: A Tlingit Legend from Alaska,* illustrated by Rosanne Litzinger, Holiday House (New York, NY), 2006.

(Adaptor) *Blackbeard's Last Fight,* illustrated by Leonard Everett Fisher, Farrar, Strauss (New York, NY), 2006.

(Adaptor) *The Three Cabritos* (based on the story by Peter Asbjärnsen), illustrated by Stephen Gilpin, Marshall Cavendish (New York, NY), 2007.

Stormy's Hat, illustrated by Andrea U'Ren, Farrar, Strauss (New York, NY), 2007.

(Adaptor) *Rip Van Winkle's Return* (based on the story by Washington Irving), Farrar, Strauss (New York, NY), 2007.

A Picture for Marc, illustrated by Matthew True, Random House (New York, NY), 2007.

The McElderry Book of Greek Myths, illustrated by Pep Monserrat, Margaret K. McElderry Books (New York, NY), 2007.

The Great Texas Hamster Drive: An Original Tale, illustrated by Bruce Whatley, Marshall Cavendish (New York, NY), 2007.

OTHER

Contributor to periodicals, including *Ladybug* and *Cricket.*

SIDELIGHTS: The award-winning author of dozens of picture books and novels, Eric A. Kimmel is well known for his adaptations or retellings of folktales from around the world, especially Yiddish tales. Kimmel blends a sardonic wit with traditional storyteller motifs such as mistaken identities, tests of courage and intelligence, wise fools, and tricksters. The result, a collection of tales that both entertain and teach, include *Hershel and* the Hanukkah Goblins, *The Greatest of All: A Japanese Folktale, Anansi and the Talking Melon, Baba Yaga, Bearhead: A Russian Folktale, The Four Gallant Sisters, Gershon's Monster: A Story for the Jewish New Year,* and *Cactus Soup,* the last an adaptation of the well-known folktale "Stone Soup" that is given new life through Kimmel's decision to set the story amid the Mexican Revolution. In addition to such retellings, Kimmel has also penned contemporary novels for young readers, such as *One Good Tern Deserves Another,* and chapter books such as *Website of the Warped Wizard.*

"I've been a storyteller for [more than] twenty years," Kimmel once noted. "When you stand in front of an audience of a hundred people or more, you learn very quickly what works and what doesn't. Folktales are oral stories, so it's important for the writer to be firmly rooted in oral traditions." In addition to being rooted in the oral tradition, Kimmel is also rooted in a multicultural one. Born in 1946, he was raised in an immigrant neighborhood in Brooklyn, New York, where, as he once commented, "our neighbors were Armenian, Italian, Chinese, Puerto Rican, Irish, and German. You could hear five different languages in a walk around the block." He spoke Yiddish as a child, thanks in part to the influence of his grandmother, an European immigrant and an important influence on his writing. Coming from western Ukraine and speaking five languages, she was full of stories.

More reader than athlete, as a child Kimmel was drawn to the books of Dr. Seuss, and his illustrated copy of the collected stories of the Brothers Grimm was read over and over "until it fell to pieces." "That's how I came to be a storyteller," he added, "telling other kids stories that I remembered from Grimm and from my grandmother."

In college, Kimmel majored in education and taught at the college level for many years, leaving his writing and story-telling to his spare time. In 1974 he published his first book, the children's novel *The Tartar's Sword,* and two decades later he left teaching to write full time. Working as a storyteller in schools, parks, and libraries, Kimmel adapted his narration skills to his written tales. "When I write a story," he explained for Scholastic's *Author's Online Library,* "I'm very aware of [spoken] rhythms, and I try to capture in my writing the experience of telling. And that's also important because a picture book, which most of my books are, is usually read aloud to an audience. . . . So, when I write a

story, I read it aloud over and over again many times, trying to capture the music and rhythm of the words. So you might say that what I'm trying to do is capture in written words the experience of listening to the spoken word."

Kimmel's first picture books include *Why Worry?,* a humorous tale about a neurotic cricket and a carefree grasshopper, and *Nicanor's Gate,* a legend about the building of the Second Temple. However, as Kimmel once noted, most of his early titles seemed to "sink without a trace." His big break came in the form of a request to stand in for Nobel Prize-winner Isaac Bashevis Singer and write a Hanukkah story. Searching in his pile of rejections, Kimmel selected a tale based on a folkloric character, the storyteller and wanderer Hershel Ostropoler, and produced *Hershel and the Hanukkah Goblins.* Relating how Hershel gets rid of goblins who are haunting a synagogue and keeping the locals from celebrating Hanukkah, the picture book "is welcome both as a Hanukkah story and as a trickster tale," noted *Horn Book* critic Hanna B. Zeiger.

Although he had only published a handful of books in the eight years prior to *Hershel and the Hanukkah Goblins,* since that book appeared it has been joined on library shelves by numerous other volumes by Kimmel that explore folklore from around the world. Hershel was reprised in one of these titles, *The Adventures of Hershel of Ostropol,* which includes ten adventures of the wandering storyteller, a man described as the "Jewish first cousin of tricksters like Brer Rabbit and Till Eulenspiegel" by Rodger Kamenetz in the *New York Times Book Review.* "Kimmel has a good ear, makes clever use of repetition and knows how to structure a story that has a good joke, with a hearty punch line," Kamenetz concluded.

The Chanukkah Guest, one of several holiday books by Kimmel, features a story of mistaken identity in which a bear is taken for a rabbi by a nearsighted woman. "Festivity, generosity and cooperation are all celebrated in this wintry holiday tale that children of all religions will enjoy," wrote a *Publishers Weekly* reviewer. A more unusual Hannukah story is the focus of *A Horn for Louis,* which melds the childhood of noted jazz musician Louis Armstrong with the Jewish holiday to create what a *Kirkus Reviews* writer deemed a "warm Hanukkah tale with a whiff of old New Orleans." In *A Hanukkah Treasury,* Kimmel brings together a potpourri of holiday information and tales and poems that a contributor for *Publishers Weekly* praised for including "more than enough material to keep a family going for eight days and nights." *Wonders and Miracles: A Passover Companion* contains songs, poems, and stories compiled by Kimmel that "gloriously celebrates the Passover Seder, an evening of observances, history, remembrances, and family sharing," according to *School Library Journal* contributor Susan Pine.

In *Jar of Fools* Kimmel shares eight Hanukkah stories from Chelm, the legendary Yiddish town of fools, resulting in a "true gem," according to a reviewer for *School Library Journal.* A kindhearted fool is also the focus of *Onions and Garlic,* adapted from a Jewish folktale about the poor merchant Getzel, who ultimately makes good while his acquisitive older brothers are left short. A contributor for *Kirkus Reviews* observed that Kimmel "retells the Jewish folktale . . . with lively dialogue and a comic twist at the end." Less comic is *Gershon's Monster,* a story celebrating the Jewish New Year that is based on a Hasidic legend concerning Rosh Hashanah. In this tale, Gershon the baker finally repents his wicked ways when his sins threaten the lives of his beloved twin children. "The story will achieve its full impact when children, with adult help, begin to understand why it is so important to recognize the wrongs they've committed and try to right them," wrote *Booklist* critic Ilene Cooper.

Inspired by his grandmother's stories, many of Kimmel's retellings take place in Russia and Eastern Europe. In *Baba Yaga* he retells a well-known Russian folktale replete with an evil stepmother and the sweet stepdaughter who outwits her and the local witch, Baba Yaga. "This engrossing story is both fanciful and suspenseful," wrote a *Publishers Weekly* reviewer. Kimmel presents another Russian folktale in *Bearhead,* about a half man/half bear who is raised by a human and grows into the wise fool of popular folk legend. "Kimmel's lively text plays up the broad, almost slapstick humor of the story," remarked Denise Anton Wright in a review of *Bearhead* for *School Library Journal.* *The Castle of the Cats,* a story from Latvia, brings its story of the youngest son of a farmer gives up his contest for the family lands in favor of true love. Reviewing the picture book in *School Library Journal,* Grace Oliff noted that, due to his "true storyteller's voice," Kimmel "keeps the action moving at an energetic pace without sacrificing images or details." In *Billy Lazroe and the King of the Sea* he transplants a Russian folktale to his own part of the world, setting his retelling in Oregon at the turn of the twentieth

century. "Kimmel's lyrical text . . . has a strong sense of frontier adventure," noted *Booklist* contributor Hazel Rochman, while a *Publishers Weekly* reviewer wrote that Kimmel "lets the creative juices flow in his Oregonian version of an old Russian seafaring tale."

One Eye, Two Eyes, Three Eyes was originally told to Kimmel by his grandmother; it is the story of a young girl, cast into slavery, who, with the help of a magic goat, is finally freed to marry a prince. Further Ukrainian influences are found in *The Birds' Gift,* an Easter story that deals with the origin of the intricate process of decorating eggs for the spring holiday. "Filled with warmth, the story is illustrated with charming folk-art paintings," commented Patricia Pearl Dole in *School Library Journal.* "Kimmel reserves the full force of his storytelling for folkloric rather than religious elements," noted a reviewer for *Publishers Weekly.*

Kimmel's beloved Brothers Grimm have provide him with a deep well of potential retellings. In *The Four Gallant Sisters* he adapts "The Four Artful Brothers" into a story that is "real reading pleasure," according to Linda Boyles in *School Library Journal,* the critic adding that Kimmel "couches his adaptation in the strong direct language of a master storyteller." His retelling of another Grimm story in *The Goose Girl* is "polished," according to *Booklist* reviewer Janice Del Negro. Similarly, his *Iron John* is a "seamless" retelling, as a reviewer for *Publishers Weekly* described the picture book. According to another reviewer from that magazine, Kimmel's dramatic retelling "flows from scene to scene with a clear sense of adventure and romance and an underlying sense of mystery." In *School Library Journal,* Grace Oliff dubbed Kimmel's *Seven at One Blow* a "thoroughly enjoyable retelling of a traditional tale" that includes "only minor deviations from the original Grimm story."

Three Sacks of Truth travels to France for inspiration, employing the familiar motif of a suitor who must pass tests to win the hand of the fair princess. "In this crisp and sprightly interpretation, storyteller Kimmel takes full advantage of the plot's sly humor," wrote Penny Kaganoff in *Publishers Weekly.* Other European tales retold by Kimmel include the Hungarian folktale *The Valiant Red Rooster, Count Silvernose,* a tale from Italy, *Squash It!,* from Spain, and *Easy Work,* a Norwegian folktale transplanted to America. In *Count Silvernose,* ugly Assunta comes to the rescue of her beautiful sisters, using her skill of cleverness in a story that *Booklist* reviewer Susan Dove Lempke noted "combines humor and suspense, pitting good against evil and delivering a magnificently satisfying conclusion." Reviewing *Squash It!*, Kimmel's adaptation of a Spanish tale of a flea and a royal louse, a contributor for *Kirkus Reviews* wrote that the story is peppered with "judiciously chosen details" and "is good for reading aloud to kids who relish a bit of grossness in their story-hour diet." In addition to European folktales, Kimmel mines literature in *Don Quixote and the Windmills*, which is based on Miguel Cervantes' famous novel, and *The Hero Beowulf*, his retelling of the ancient Anglo-Saxon epic.

Other published books by Kimmel range ever farther a-field, drawing from Middle Eastern, African, Asian, Mexican, and South American folklore. Teaming up with illustrator Will Hillenbrand, his retelling of *The Tale of Ali Baba and the Forty Thieves: A Story from the Arabian Nights* "captures the flavor" of the well-known original, according to *Booklist* critic Carolyn Phelan. Turning to Asia, Kimmel features a mouse living in Japan's imperial palace in *The Greatest of All* and presents tales of Japanese derring-do in *Sword of the Samurai: Adventure Stories from Japan* and *Three Samurai Cats: A Story from Japan*. "Reluctant readers looking for a short book of high adventures will be especially pleased," noted Karen Morgan in a *Booklist* review of *Sword of the Samurai*, while Barbara Scotto wrote in *School Library Journal* that readers "who delight in stories of knights will be happy to discover" Kimmel's Asian tales. Enhanced by anime-style illustrations by Mordicai Gerstein, *Three Samurai Cats* brings to life a Zen-inspired tale about a rapacious rodent and three warriors. "Humor, wisdom and excitement make this offbeat tale a winner," wrote a *Publishers Weekly* contributor of Kimmel's entertaining story. Kimmel presents a Chinese legend in *Ten Suns*, in which "narrative and the dramatic illustrations . . . work wonderfully together to create a beautiful tale of Chinese gods, misuse of power, and heroism that restores the faith of a people," according to *Booklist* contributor Helen Rosenberg. A story from the Chinese zodiac is featured in *The Rooster's Antlers*, which follows the Jade Emperor as he selects twelve animals to represent the years in his calendar.

Closer to home, Kimmel adapts an Aztec legend in *Two Mountains* to explain the formation of two mountains overlooking the Valley of Mexico. "Youngsters are likely to find the connection between the story and the geological formations intriguing," wrote a contributor for *Publishers Weekly*, "and its parallels with Adam and Eve may make for some lively discussion." More Aztec lore is served up in *Montezuma and the Fall of the Aztecs*. Cooper, reviewing the title in *Booklist*, called the book a "good introduction to a pivotal event in the Americas."

U.S. history and folklore is also a rich resource for the storyteller. In the title tale from *The Lady in the Blue Cloak: Legends of the Texas Missions* he focuses on a female figure known to appear to the Tejas Indians living near the location of the Mission of San Francisco de los Tejas in the late seventeenth century; other stories recount the origins of other Catholic missions established by Spanish colonists in the region that is now Texas. Although Kimmel's stories feature what some might perceive as "a mostly uncritical picture of the Christian mission experience," Gillian Engberg concluded in *Booklist* that Kimmel's stories in *The Lady in the Blue Cloak* "flow easily" and focus on a topic rarely covered in children's literature. Moving to safer terrain, Kimmel presents what a *Kirkus Reviews* critic characterized as a "rousing original tale of battle between canal pirates and a crew of mail carriers" in *The Erie Canal Pirates*. Based on a ballad dating from the early 1800s, the story finds a band of river pirates vanquished by Captain Flynn beneath the rushing waters of Niagara Falls. Kimmel recasts the ballad as a "joyous and good-hearted folktale, according to *Booklist* contributor Roger Leslie, the critic noting that in an author's note the storyteller clarifies his geographical distortions for more map-smart young readers. A band of scraggly pirates also makes little headway in *Blackbeard's Last Fight*, which is based on a true story from North Carolina. Kimmel's version takes place in 1718 and, as narrated by a young cabin boy, follows Lieutenant Maynard's successful efforts to vanquish the troublesome Blackbeard. Amid sword fights, musket-fire, and a chorus of hearty "arggh"s, the story was praised as "an exciting and satisfying read" by *School Library Journal* contributor Kara Schaff Dean and "exciting fare for pirate fans—as well as a discussion-provoking case study in international relations" by a *Kirkus Reviews* writer.

"I'm always looking for good stories," Kimmel once commented. "But I have no hesitation about making changes if I feel for some reason the original doesn't work, or if I can think of a way to make it better. There is no 'authentic' version. Stories evolve over centuries as tellers add and subtract. I think of myself as one link in a long, long chain."

BIOGRAPHICAL AND CRITICAL SOURCES:

BOOKS

Children's Books and Their Creators, edited by Anita Silvey, Houghton, Mifflin (Boston, MA), 1995.

Tuning Up: A Visit with Eric Kimmel, Richard C. Owen (New York, NY), 2005.

PERIODICALS

Booklist, November 15, 1992, pp. 596, 598; January 15, 1995, review of *Iron John,* p. 863; March 1, 1995, p. 1245; October 15, 1995, Janice Del Negro, review of *The Goose Girl,* pp. 398, 400; December 15, 1995, p. 715; March 15, 1996, Susan Dove Lempke, review of *Count Silvernose,* p. 1263; November 1, 1996, p. 503; December 1, 1996, Carolyn Phelan, review of *The Tale of Ali Baba and the Forty Thieves,* p. 667; December 15, 1996, Hazel Rochman, review of *Billy Lazroe and the King of the Sea,* p. 730; May 1, 1997, Helen Rosenberg, review of *Ten Suns,* p. 1520; September 15, 1997, p. 238; April 15, 1998, pp. 1448-1449; September 1, 1998, p. 133; March 15, 1999, Karen Morgan, review of *Sword of the Samurai,* p. 329; April 15, 1999, p. 1533; December 15, 1999, p. 787; January 1, 2000, Ilene Cooper, review of *Montezuma and the Fall of the Aztecs,* pp. 910, 914; May 1, 2000, p. 1678; September 1, 2000; p. 133; October 1, 2000, Ilene Cooper, review of *Gershon's Monster,* p. 362; October 15, 2002, Roger Leslie, review of *The Erie Canal Pirates,* p. 412; April 1, 2003, Ilene Cooper, review of *Brother Wolf, Sister Sparrow: Stories about Saints and Animals,* p. 1392; February 15, 2004, Ilene Cooper, review of *Wonders and Miracles: A Passover Companion,* p. 1056; April 15, 2004, Ilene Cooper, review of *Don Quixote and the Windmills,* p. 1446; September 15, 2004, Jennifer Mattson, review of *Cactus Soup,* p. 241; October 15, 2004, Julie Cummins, review of *The Castle of the Cats,* p. 410; February 1, 2006, Nancy Kim, review of *A Horn for Louis,* p. 68; March 1, 2006, Hazel Rochman, review of *Blackbeard's Last Fight,* p. 100; May 1, 2006, Gillian Engberg, review of *The Frog Princess: A Tlingit Legend from Alaska,* p. 86; October 1, 2006, Gillian Engberg, review of *The Lady in the Blue Cloak: Legends from the Texas Missions,* p. 65.

Bulletin of the Center for Children's Books, January, 1995, Roger Sutton, review of *One Good Tern Deserves Another,* p. 169; March, 2004, Betsy Hearne, review of *Wonders and Miracles,* p. 282; July-August, 2004, Karen Coats, review of *Don Quixote and the Windmills,* p. 472; April 15, 2005, Jennifer Mattson, review of *The Hero Beowulf,* p. 1452; June, 2006, Elizabeth Bush, review of *Blackbeard's Last Fight,* p. 459; September, 2006, Maggie Hommel, review of *The Frog Princess: A Tlingit Legend from Alaska,* p. 20; January, 2007, Elizabeth Bush, review of *The Lady in the Blue Cloak,* p. 219.

Horn Book, January-February, 1990, Hanna B. Zeiger, review of *Hershel and the Hanukkah Goblins,* pp. 52-53; January-February, 1991, p. 57; November-December, 1991, p. 721; September-October, 1995, p. 620; January-February, 1996, p. 83; January-February, 1997, p. 72; July-August, 1997, p. 467; September-October, 2000, p. 587; July-August, 2003, review of *Three Samurai Cats,* p. 470; January-February, 2005, Betty Carter, review of *Cactus Soup,* p. 103.

Kirkus Reviews, March 15, 1996, review of *Onions and Garlic,* p. 449; May 15, 1997, review of *Squash It!,* p. 801; November 1, 1998, p. 1600; September 1, 2002, review of *The Erie Canal Pirates,* p. 1312; April 15, 2003, review of *Brother Wolf, Sister Sparrow,* p. 608; January 15, 2004, review of *Wonders and Miracles,* p. 85; March 15, 2004, review of *Don Quixote and the Windmills,* p. 272; September 1, 2004, review of *Cactus Soup,* p. 868; October 15, 2004, review of *The Castle of the Cats,* p. 1008; May 1, 2005, review of *The Hero Beowulf,* p. 540; November 15, 2005, review of *A Horn for Louis,* p. 1234; March 1, 2006, review of *Blackbeard's Last Fight,* p. 232; May 1, 2006, review of *The Frog Princess,* p. 461; October 1, 2006, review of *The Lady in the Blue Cloak,* p 1017.

Los Angeles Times Book Review, October 25, 1998, p. 7; December 6, 1998, Anne Connor, review of *A Hanukkah Treasury,* p. 4.

New York Times Book Review, April 12, 1992, p. 28; October 22, 1995, p. 41; December 17, 1995, Rodger Kamenetz, review of *The Adventures of Hershel of Ostropol,* p. 28; June 16, 1996, p. 33; October 13, 1996, p. 26; December 8, 1996, p. 78; May 17, 1998, p. 26; December 3, 2000, p. 85.

Publishers Weekly, November 9, 1990, review of *The Chanukkah Guest,* p. 57; May 3, 1991, review of *Baba Yaga,* p. 71; August 2, 1991, p. 73; April 19, 1993, Peggy Kaganoff, review of *Three Sacks of*

Truth, p. 60; March 4, 1996, review of *Iron John,* p. 67; September 16, 1996, review of *The Tale of Ali Baba and the Forty Thieves,* p. 82; November 4, 1996, review of *Billy Lazroe and the King of the Sea,* p. 75; March 10, 1997, p. 69; October 6, 1997, p. 53; March 23, 1998, p. 95; September 28, 1998, review of *A Hanukkah Treasury,* p. 52; February 22, 1999, review of *The Birds' Gift,* p. 94; October 4, 1999, p. 75; February 7, 2000, reviews of *Two Mountains,* p. 84, and *Montezuma and the Fall of the Aztecs,* p. 86; August 28, 2000, p. 35; January 22, 2001, review of *Website of the Warped Wizard,* p. 324; February 19, 2001, review of *Robin Hook, Pirate Hunter!,* p. 90; February 26, 2001, p. 85; March 17, 2003, review of *Three Samurai Cats,* p. 76; November 8, 2004, review of *Cactus Soup,* p. 54; August 28, 2006, review of *The Lady in the Blue Cloak,* p. 58.

School Library Journal, November, 1990, p. 94; October, 1991, Denise Anton Wright, review of *Bearhead,* p. 110; May, 1992, Linda Boyles, review of *The Four Gallant Sisters,* p. 105; March, 1995, p. 198; May, 1995, p. 100; May, 1998, p. 134; June, 1998, p. 130; December, 1998, Grace Oliff, review of *Seven at One Blow,* p. 106; June, 1999, Barbara Scotto, review of *Sword of the Samurai,* p. 132; July, 1999, Patricia Pearl Dole, review of *The Birds' Gift,* p. 86; October, 1999, p. 138; March, 2000, pp. 209, 228; April, 2000, p. 121; October, 2000, review of *Jar of Fools,* pp. 64-65, 148; May, 2003, Harriett Fargnoli, review of *Brother Wolf, Sister Sparrow,* p. 137; February, 2004, Susan Pine, review of *Wonders and Miracles,* p. 166; April, 2004, Ann Welton, review of *Don Quixote and the Windmills,* p. 116; October, 2004, John Sigwald, review of *Cactus Soup,* p. 144; November, 2004, Grace Oliff, review of *The Castle of the Cats,* p. 126; April, 2005, Patricia Lothrop, review of *The Hero Beowulf,* p. 154; February, 2006, Mary Elam, review of *A Horn for Louis,* p. 120; May, 2006, Kara Schaff Dean, review of *Blackbeard's Last Fight,* p. 91; June, 2006, Kirsten Cutler, review of *The Frog Princess,* p. 136; October, 2006, S.K. Joiner, review of *The Lady in the Blue Cloak,* p. 114.

Voice of Youth Advocates, April, 1995, Marian Rafal, review of *One Good Tern Deserves Another,* p. 24.

ONLINE

Author's Online Library, http://teacher.scholastic.com/ (June 12, 2001).

Meet Authors and Illustrators, http://www.childrenslit. com/ (February 7, 2007), "Eric A. Kimmel."*

*   *   *

KIMMELMAN, Michael 1958-
(Michael Simon Kimmelman)

PERSONAL: Born May 8, 1958, in New York, NY, son of David Brown and Edythe Miriam Kimmelman; married Maria Kathleen Simson, September 10, 1988. *Education:* Yale University, B.A. (summa cum laude), 1980; Harvard University, M.A., 1982.

ADDRESSES: Office—New York Times, 229 W. 43rd St., New York, NY 10036.

CAREER: Writer, journalist. Harvard University, Cambridge, MA, teaching fellow, 1982-84; *Atlanta Journal-Constitution,* Atlanta, GA, art critic, 1984; *Philadelphia Inquirer,* Philadelphia, PA, art critic, 1985-87; *U.S. News and World Report,* Washington, DC, culture editor, 1987; *New York Times,* New York, NY, art critic, 1988-90, chief art critic, 1990—.

MEMBER: Phi Beta Kappa.

WRITINGS:

Portraits: Talking with Artists at the Met, the Modern, the Louvre, and Elsewhere, Random House (New York, NY), 1998.
The Accidental Masterpiece: On the Art of Life, and Vice Versa, Penguin Press (New York, NY), 2005.

SIDELIGHTS: Long-time chief art critic for the *New York Times* Michael Kimmelman revised a series of interviews with contemporary artists and compiled them into *Portraits: Talking with Artists at the Met, the Modern, the Louvre, and Elsewhere.* The rationale behind this collection of portraits, which were first published individually in the *New York Times,* was to meet an artist at a famous museum and let the artist talk about artworks of his or her choice. Thus readers would no longer believe the false stereotype that artists are inarticulate about art and can only express themselves through their own media. Kimmelman interviewed painters, sculptors, and photographers, such as Roy Lichtenstein, Wayne Thiebaud, Jacob Lawrence, Francis Bacon, Lucian Freud, Elizabeth Murray, Cindy Sherman, Richard Serra, Leon Golub, Nancy Spero, Brice Marden, Hans Haacke, and Chuck Close. Sometimes an artist chose a work to discuss or made comments that were unexpected given the public image of that artist. For example, Roy Lichtenstein, the father of pop art whose work is linear and boldly colored, admitted that he liked fussy and romantic paintings by eighteenth-century French painter Jean-Honore Fragonard. In preparing the articles for *Portraits,* Kimmelman added more background information on each artist, but overall the author put the reader in his place, as if the reader was with each artist in the museum.

The work met with critical approval. Martin R. Kalfatovic, writing in *Library Journal,* applauded Kimmelman's "fresh slant" on interviewing artists. Kimmelman provided "immensely satisfying object lessons" in art appreciation, declared a *Publishers Weekly* commentator. Likewise, a *Kirkus Reviews* critic described the work as "lively" and "revealing," calling the best of the interviews "surprisingly affecting." The interviews render "engaging profiles," added Donna Seaman in *Booklist.* Kimmelman has "expanded his original articles, deftly weaving lengthier information on the artists' own lives and work into his narrative. As a result, the pieces read less like idiosyncratic tours than, as the title indicates, portraits or profiles. This approach should prove useful for the general reader unfamiliar with many of the personalities involved, and Mr. Kimmelman does a good job of bringing both the artists and the art to life on the page," explained Robin Cembalest in the *New York Times.*

Several commentators had a few reservations, however. Cembalest noted that the format Kimmelman employed did not allow him to make comments by the artists understandable, if these comments were unclear. "In choosing to erase his own voice from the interviews . . . he has lost the ability to challenge or clarify. His deference can be frustrating," criticized Cembalest. "If there is a flaw in *Portraits,* it is that the pictures that illustrate each interview are in black and white and generally small," remarked *Detroit Free Press* book editor Linnea Lannon. "Obviously, the book would have been costlier with color, but in most cases it would have made the artists' observations even clearer to the reader." Cembalest concluded: "Though *Portraits* may not send readers scurrying to the galleries, there is enough here to keep them informed, entertained and more disposed to look at art in new ways."

Kimmelman presents more thoughts on art in his 2005 title, *The Accidental Masterpiece: On the Art of Life, and Vice Versa,* "an amiable, even breezy discussion . . . about the ways various artists transform their circumstances into works," as a *Kirkus Reviews* critic noted. In the course of ten chapters, Kimmelman discusses, among many other things, the work of the artist Pierre Bonnard, some of it inspired by his model, Marthe; a dentist with a penchant for collecting light bulbs; a little-known painter who reworked his work so often on the same canvas that in the end it weighed a ton; and a photographer who documented a 1914 expedition to the Antarctic. A *Publishers Weekly* contributor thought the author "delivers an uplifting art-is-good-for-you message," while the *Kirkus Reviews* critic similarly concluded, "ebullient brightness permeates these pages." Writing in *Newsweek International,* Peter Plagens felt Kimmelman "engagingly examines art matters." More praise came from *Library Journal* contributor Cheryl Ann Lajos, who called the collection of essays "thought-provoking and uniquely awesome." Trey Popp, reviewing *The Accidental Masterpiece* in the *San Francisco Chronicle,* found it "consistently enlightening, often humorous and an occasionally exhilarating adventure."

BIOGRAPHICAL AND CRITICAL SOURCES:

PERIODICALS

Artnews, September, 1998, Rex Weil, review of *Portraits: Talking with Artists at the Met, the Modern, the Louvre, and Elsewhere,* p. 132; September, 2005, David Ayers, review of *The Accidental Masterpiece: On the Art of Life and Vice Versa,* p. 92.

Booklist, August 19, 1998, Donna Seaman, review of *Portraits,* p. 1950; August, 2004, Donna Seaman, review of *The Accidental Masterpiece,* p. 1980.

Boston Globe, August 7, 2005, Barbara Fisher, review of *The Accidental Masterpiece.*

Detroit Free Press, August 16, 1998, Linnea Lannon, review of *Portraits,* p. 7H.

Kirkus Reviews, June 15, 1998, review of *Portraits,* p. 873; May 15, 2005, review of *The Accidental Masterpiece,* p. 576.

Library Journal, July, 1998, Martin R. Kalfatovic, review of *Portraits,* pp. 86-88; June 1, 2005, Cheryl Ann Lajos, review of *The Accidental Masterpiece,* p. 126.

Nation, November 7, 2005, Hal Foster, "How Art Can Save Your Life," review of *The Accidental Masterpiece,* p. 38.

Newsweek International, September 26, 2005, Peter Plagens, "Ways of Looking," review of *The Accidental Masterpiece,* p. 101.

New York Review of Books, September 2, 2005, Adam Phillips, "Art Ahead: Linger for a While, Look and Tell the Story"; December 1, 2005, Richard Dorment, "What Art Does," review of *The Accidental Masterpiece,* p. 21.

New York Times, August 24, 1998, Robin Cembalest, review of *Portraits,* p. E6.

New York Times Book Review, October 4, 1998, David Cohen, review of *Portraits,* p. 38; September 4, 2005, Adrian Searle, review of *The Accidental Masterpiece,* p. 13.

Publishers Weekly, June 15, 1998, review of *Portraits,* p. 48; May 16, 2005, review of *The Accidental Masterpiece,* p. 49.

San Francisco Chronicle, August 21, 2005, Trey Popp, review of *The Accidental Masterpiece.*

Washington Post Book World, September 25, 2005, Jonathan Keats, "On Beauty," review of *The Accidental Masterpiece,* p. 8.

ONLINE

Indiana Conversations, http://www.indiana.edu/ (November 20, 2006), "Michael Kimmelman and Betsy Stirratt."

New York Review of Books Online, http://www.nybooks.com/ (November 26, 2006), "Michael Kimmelman."

New York Times Web site, http://topics.nytimes.com/ (November 20, 2006), "Recent and Archived News Articles by Michael Kimmelman."*

*   *   *

KIMMELMAN, Michael Simon
   See KIMMELMAN, Michael

*   *   *

KINGSBURY, Donald 1929-
   (Donald MacDonald Kingsbury)

PERSONAL: Born February 12, 1929, in San Francisco, CA; immigrated to Canada, 1948, naturalized citizen, 1955; son of Hector Macdonald (a mining engineer) and Laura Kingsbury; married Mireille Fortier, 1950 (divorced, 1960); children: Dani Hector, Joel Fortier. *Education:* McGill University, B.Sc., 1956, M.Sc., 1960.

ADDRESSES: Home—Montreal, Quebec, Canada. *Agent*—Eleanor Wood, 432 Park Ave. S., Ste. 1205, New York, NY 10016.

CAREER: McGill University, Montreal, Quebec, Canada, lecturer in mathematics, 1956-86; writer, 1986—.

MEMBER: Science Fiction Writers of America.

AWARDS, HONORS: Hugo Award nominations, World Science Fiction Society, best novella, 1980, for "The Moon Goddess and the Son," and best novel, 1982, for *Courtship Rite;* Compton Crook Award, Balticon (science fiction convention), and Locus Award, *Locus* magazine, both best first novel, 1983, for *Courtship Rite;* Prometheus Award, Libertarian Futurist Society, 2002, for *Psychohistorical Crisis.*

WRITINGS:

Courtship Rite (science-fiction novel), Timescape (New York, NY), 1982, published as *Geta,* Panther (London, England), 1984.

The Moon Goddess and the Son (science-fiction novel; first published as a novella in *Analog Science Fiction/Science Fact,* 1979), Baen Books (New York, NY), 1986.

(With Larry Niven, Mark O. Martin, and Gregory Benford) *Man-Kzin Wars VI,* Baen Books (New York, NY), 1994.

Psychohistorical Crisis, Tor Books (New York, NY), 2001.

Work represented in anthologies, including *The Best Science Fiction of the Year 8* and *The Best Science Fiction Novellas of the Year 1,* both edited by Terry Carr, Ballantine Books (New York, NY), 1979; and *The Best Science Fiction Novellas of the Year 2,* edited by Terry Carr, Ballantine Books (New York, NY), 1980. Contributor to periodicals, including *Analog Science Fiction/Science Fact* and *Astounding Science Fiction.*

SIDELIGHTS: Donald Kingsbury began publishing short stories in the 1950s and produced his first full-length work in 1982. The novel *Courtship Rite* depicts the harsh planet Geta on which most native life forms are poisonous to human colonists; the people rely on eight imported "sacred" staples, genetic engineering of local "profane" plants and insects, and cannibalism during famine, evolving a complex system of rituals and customs. The formal eating of enemies, friends and relatives, criminals, and the genetically inferior has become part of their society. Group marriage within a strong clan culture developed as a response to the harsh environment. Observed H. Bruce Franklin in the *Washington Post Book World,* "Some of this is obviously meant to shock our sensibilities." Kingsbury's plot centers on the intrigues that ensue when one ruling family is advised to court an influential heretic for political reasons, ultimately deciding to test her worthiness by a challenge likely to cause her death. According to Franklin, this "society of tyrants and cannibals is offered to us as a charming fantasy of elegance and sexual freedom in which we may indulge as an alternative to our own history." Other critics have commended the author's handling of a complex plot and compared *Courtship Rite* favorably to the long visionary writings of Frank Herbert, author of the popular "Dune" series.

Kingsbury once told *CA:* "*Courtship Rite* is the first of a series of novels in which I examine the thesis of what might happen when a human culture arises that does not consider the human form as we know it to be sacred. The species of *Homo sapiens* is only a transitional form. There are many stories to be told about the transformation.

"In many ways I consider myself to be a visionary. I don't claim to predict the future, but I am not interested in worlds that are not possible. I like my science to be accurate and that includes my sociology. My stories do not include such pseudo-sciences as mental telepathy, which I consider to have no relevance to human destiny. Designing new kinds of humans, new governments, and odd cultures is my favorite sport. In *The Moon Goddess and the Son* I've tried to give historical roots to my future. Man's destiny is in space, but his roots are in the earth. History fascinates me because it says so much about what we will become."

BIOGRAPHICAL AND CRITICAL SOURCES:

PERIODICALS

Washington Post Book World, July 25, 1982, H. Bruce Franklin, review of *Courtship Rite.*

KINGSBURY, Donald MacDonald
   See KINGSBURY, Donald

*   *   *

KNOX, Elizabeth 1959-
   (Elizabeth Fiona Knox)

PERSONAL: Born February 15, 1959, in Wellington, New Zealand; daughter of Ray (a journalist) and Heather (a librarian) Knox; married Fergus Barrowman (a publisher), 1989; children: Jack. *Education:* Victoria University, B.A., 1986.

ADDRESSES: Home—Wellington, New Zealand. *Agent*—Natasha Fairweather, A.P. Watt, Ltd., 20 John St., London WC1N 2DR, England.

CAREER: Writer. *Sport* (magazine), assistant editor, 1988-93; Victoria University, Wellington, New Zealand, tutor in film studies, 1989-95; worked variously as a clerk, printer, insurance underwriter, computer operator, editor, Web page editor, publicity officer, and shop assistant. Writer-in-residence at Victoria University of Wellington, 1997.

AWARDS, HONORS: PEN award, 1988, for *After Z-Hour;* PEN fellowship, 1991; New Zealand Book Award nomination for *Treasure;* Queen Elizabeth II scholarship in letters, 1993; writing fellowship, Victoria University, 1997; Montana New Zealand Book Awards' Deutz Medal for Fiction, Readers' Choice award, Booksellers' Choice Award, and Orange Prize shortlist, all 1999, and Tasmania Pacific Region Prize, 2001, and Prix Ville de Saumur shortlist, all for *The Vintner's Luck;* Katherine Mansfield writing fellowship, 1999; Arts Foundation of New Zealand Laureate Award, 2000, 2002; named officer, New Zealand Order of Merit, 2002; ICI young writers bursary; Deutz Medal for Fiction shortlist, 2002, for *Billie's Kiss;* Commonwealth Writers Prize for Best Book in the South Pacific and South East Asian Region shortlist, 2004, for *Daylight.*

WRITINGS:

After Z-Hour, Victoria University Press (Wellington, New Zealand), 1987.

Paremata (first novel in "High Jump" trilogy; also see below), Victoria University Press (Wellington, New Zealand), 1989.

Treasure, Victoria University Press (Wellington, New Zealand), 1992.

Pomare (second novel in "High Jump" trilogy; also see below), Victoria University Press (Wellington, New Zealand), 1994.

Glamour and the Sea, Victoria University Press (Wellington, New Zealand), 1996.

Tawa (third novel in "High Jump" trilogy; also see below), Victoria University Press (Wellington, New Zealand), 1998.

The Vintner's Luck, Farrar, Straus (New York, NY), 1998.

The High Jump: A New Zealand Childhood (contains *Paremata, Pomare,* and *Tawa*), Victoria University Press (Wellington, New Zealand), 2000.

Black Oxen, Farrar, Straus (New York, NY), 2001.

Billie's Kiss, Ballantine (New York, NY), 2002.

Daylight, Ballantine (New York, NY), 2003.

Dreamhunter (first volume in "Dreamhunter Duet"), HarperCollins (Wellington, NZ), 2005, Farrar, Straus (New York, NY), 2006.

Dreamquake (second volume in "Dreamhunter Duet"), Farrar, Straus (New York, NY), 2007.

Contributor to *Privacy: The Art of Julia Morrison* (Jonathan Jensen Gallery), 1994; and *Cherries on a Plate: New Zealand Writers Talk about Their Sisters,* edited by Marilyn Duckworth, Random House, 1996. Short stories represented in anthologies, including *Now See Hear!,* edited by Ian Wedde and Gregory Burke, Victoria University Press, 1990; *Soho Square 4,* edited by Bill Manhire, Bloomsbury, 1991; *Pleasures and Dangers,* edited by Wystan Curnow and Trish Clark, Moet & Chandon/Longman Paul, 1992; *Into the Field of Play,* edited by Lloyd Jones, Tandem, 1992; and *The Picador Anthology of Contemporary New Zealand Fiction,* edited by Fergus Barrowman, Picador, 1996. Author of screenplay *The Dig,* 1994. Contributor to periodicals, including *Landfall, Metro, New Zealand Listener, Sport,* and *Stout Centre Review.*

ADAPTATIONS: The Vintner's Luck was adapted for film by Nicky Caro.

SIDELIGHTS: New Zealand writer Elizabeth Knox is known for creating novels and stories that feature intricate plots, detailed settings, and elements of mystery and the supernatural. While she first became known for adult novels such as *After Z-Hour, Black Oxen,* and *The Vintner's Luck,* more recent novels such as *Billie's Kiss* and her "Dreamhunter Duet" fantasy sequence, have proved popular with more sophisticated teen readers. Critics have referred to Knox's prose as intense and poetic, while her themes, according to a *Contemporary Novelists* essayist, reflect "the human groping for understanding in a world that often defies comprehension . . . and the eventual connections between people that ultimately give meaning to life despite the distances between them."

In *After Z-Hour* an abandoned house becomes the central location from which six characters experience hauntings of both a supernatural and psychological nature. In examining the house guests' memories, as well as the memories of a dead soldier who haunts the house, Knox illustrates "how the horrors of the past, whether personal or national, both inform and allow passage into the future."

The first of Knox's novels to be published in the United States, *The Vintner's Luck* takes place in nineteenth-century France, as winemaker Sobran Jodeau is visited by the angel Xas and the two develop an intense friendship. Arranging for their annual reunion, Sobran hopes that Xas will become his guardian angel. For his part, however, the powerful yet sensual Xas is no guide; instead the angel takes over the roles of friend, lover, and storyteller, causing Sobran's earthly relationships to diminish in value. In the *New York Times,* Richard Bernstein deemed *The Vintner's Luck* a "sophisticated, supernaturally tinged mystery," and Megan Harlan wrote in *Entertainment Weekly* that Knox's "imagistic" novel explores "the spiritual worth of sensual pleasure."

Dubbed "magic realism noir," *Daylight* draws readers to southern France, where the vacation of an Australian cop is disrupted by an unusual discovery. The body of a drowned woman discovered nearby reminds Brian Phelan of a woman he met years earlier, and sets him on a search that involved a soon-to-be sainted member of the Italian Resistance, a literary scholar, and a 200-year-old vampire. Praised as an "illuminating tour-de-force" by a *Publishers Weekly* contributor, *Daylight* also drew comparisons to *The Vintner's Luck* due to Knox's quirky mix. As a *Kirkus Reviews* writer noted, the author's "bizarre narrative impasto" is "at times as entertaining as it is certifiably insane."

More realistic in focus, *Black Oxen* is set in the near future, as Carme Risk seeks therapy to overcome a strained relationship with her absent father. Carme's treatment includes keeping a journal about her errant parent, and much of the novel concerns these journal entries and her therapist's responses to them. Knox's story veers into the supernatural, particularly in scenes set in the fictional Latin-American country of Lequama, a land of black magic and revolution. Carme's father, whom she dubs Abra Cadaver, is a healer whose body contains excess phosphorus which he uses for fuel. Ann B. Stephenson wrote in *Book* that *Black Oxen* is "brimming with intense, poetic language" and "leaves readers with the feeling that they've lived through a dense and, at times, magical history." A *Publishers Weekly* critic wrote that "Knox's lush, hyperinventive story telling is anything but traditional, and this time-traveling tale is as exuberantly unorthodox as its predecessor," while *Library Journal* contributor David W. Henderson described the novel's plot as a "fascinating, albeit tangled, web . . . for those who enjoy both the unusual and the intelligent."

Recalling the work of British novelists Emily Brontë and Jane Austen, Knox's historical novel *Billie's Kiss* is a tale of romance and mystery set in a Scottish castle in the year 1903. The central character, Billie Paxton, is one of only a few survivors after an explosion at a Scottish port sinks the Swedish steamer *Gustav Edda*. The accident killed her pregnant sister, Edith, and seriously injured her brother-in-law, Henry, a tutor whose new job at Kiss Castle was the reason for the voyage. Murdo Hesketh, the cousin of the lord of the castle, suspects that Billie might have been behind the explosion, but as he investigates the accident he finds himself falling in love with her. In addition to this central story, Knox examines the lives of the island's residents from Billie's perspective and explores the many meanings of the word "kiss." In a review of the novel, a *Publishers Weekly* critic commented that, while it falls short of Brontë's classics, *Billie's Kiss* will leave "many romance fiction fans . . . well satisfied." Praising Knox's "vibrant comic imagination," a *Kirkus Reviews* writer noted that, despite its melodramatic plot, *Billie's Kiss* "reward[s] . . . the bedazzled reader with a stunning climactic confrontation."

Written for a teen audience and compared to the books of well-known Australian writer Margaret Mahy, *Dreamhunter* is the first novel in Knox's "Dreamhunter Duet." Taking place in the early twentieth century, the novel introduces Rose Tiebold and Laura Hame, two fifteen year olds who live in Southland, a remote island nation wherein dreaming is considered dangerous. Both girls have inherited the lucrative skill that enable them to

train to become a Dreamhunter: one who ventures into The Place, a dry, arid, invisible otherworld that is "eerily suffused with atmosphere and powerfully portrayed," according to *School Library Journal* reviewer Sue Giffard. Searching The Place, where dreams are born, Dreamcatchers acquire visions, then bring them back to share with wealthy audiences at the island's Rainbow Opera. Like films, some dreams are inspiring and others are illuminating. Still others exist only to terrify. Charged with retrieving their first dreams, Laura succeeds, while cousin Rose fails. When Tziga Hame, Laura's dreamhunter father, disappears shortly thereafter, the teen receives a letter that sets her on an perilous journey. The second novel of the series, *Dreamquake*, finds Laura joined by others in her efforts to uncover the mystery underlying The Other, a mystery that involves a secret government plot, a regulator army known as the Rangers, and a series of mysterious disappearances. In *Publishers Weekly,* a critic wrote of *Dreamhunter* that Knox's "fully imagined world will surely lure readers back for multiple readings," while *Horn Book* contributor Deirdre F. Baker praised the novel as an "engrossing blend of Edwardian civility, family love, and powerfully imagined dreamscape." Noting Knox's sophisticated use of metaphor and vocabulary, Baker added that her "writing is rich and interesting," while in *Kliatt* Michele Winship called Knox's storyline "intriguing and thought provoking, a perfect blend of fantasy and suspense." Citing the novel's "nightmare climax," a *Kirkus Reviews* contributor described *Dreamhunter* as "a lyrical, intricate and ferociously intelligent fantasy."

Discussing her creative process in an interview for the New Zealand Book Club online, Knox noted: "I don't know that I can describe a typical process of my imagination. My novels creep up on me. Often I turn my back and refuse to acknowledge them. They're too 'vulgar' or preposterous. Usually I know a novel is ultimately unavoidable once I start going into fugues and seeing whole scenes. That's how they come to me-in scenes, drama, dramatic encounter, incident." Her move to young-adult fantasy with her "Dreamcatcher Duet" novels was broached by Kimberly Rothwell in an interview for *Stuff* online. "One of the really attractive things about really good young adult fiction is that sense of something about to happen, or how you can be responsible for something," Knox explained. "They are often saving the world, these young people. It also reflects when you're a teenager, you're teetering between being a hero and being lost in the crowd. It moves all the time."

BIOGRAPHICAL AND CRITICAL SOURCES:

BOOKS

Contemporary Novelists, 7th edition, St. James Press (Detroit, MI), 2001.

PERIODICALS

Book, July, 2001, Ann B. Stephenson, review of *Black Oxen,* p. 78.

Booklist, December 1, 1998, Mary Ellen Quinn, review of *The Vintner's Luck,* p. 651; January 1, 2002, Kristine Huntley, review of *Billie's Kiss,* p. 810; April 1, 2006, Jennifer Mattson, review of *Dreamhunter,* p. 43.

Bulletin of the Center for Children's Books, April, 2006, April Spisak, review of *Dreamhunter,* p. 361.

Economist, May 15, 1999, review of *The Vintner's Luck,* p. 14.

Entertainment Weekly, January 8, 1999, Megan Harlan, review of *The Vintner's Luck,* p. 63.

Horn Book, May-June, 2006, Deirdre F. Baker, review of *Dreamhunter,* p. 321.

Kirkus Reviews, January 1, 2002, review of *Billie's Kiss,* p. 11; January 15, 2003, review of *Daylight,* p. 106; Marcy 1, 2006, review of *Dreamhunter,* p. 232.

Kliatt, March, 2006, Michele Winship, review of *Dreamhunter,* p. 13.

Library Journal, November 15, 1998, Francisca Goldsmith, review of *The Vintner's Luck,* p. 91; June 15, 2001, David W. Henderson, review of *Black Oxen,* p. 104.

Los Angeles Times Book Review, December 27, 1998, review of *The Vintner's Luck,* p. 2; August 28, 2001, Michael Harris, review of *Black Oxen,* p. E10.

New York Times, December 23, 1998, Richard Bernstein, "A Randy Angel Meddles, Literally, in Earthly Affairs," p. E10.

New York Times Book Review, February 21, 1999, Nina Auerbach, "He's No Clarence," p. 15.

New Zealand Books, November, 1996.

Publishers Weekly, October 26, 1998, review of *The Vintner's Luck,* p. 43; June 25, 2001, review of *Black Oxen,* p. 46; February 11, 2002, review of *Billie's Kiss,* p. 165; March 17, 2003, review of *Daylight,* p. 59; April 3, 2006, review of *Dreamhunter,* p. 75.

Resource Links, October, 2006, Angela Thompson, review of *Dreamhunter,* p. 35.

School Library Journal, March, 2006, Sue Giffard, review of *Dreamhunter,* p. 225.

Voice of Youth Advocates, February, 2006, Laura Woodruff, review of *Dreamhunter,* p. 499.

ONLINE

Arts Foundation of New Zealand Web site, http://www.artsfoundation.org.nz/ (February 19, 2007).

New Zealand Book Club Web site, http://www.bookclub.co/nz/ (September, 2003), interview with Knox.

Stuff Web site, http://www.stuff.co.nz/ (February 21, 2007), Kimberly Rothwell, "Opportunity Knox for Elizabeth."*

*   *   *

KNOX, Elizabeth Fiona
   See KNOX, Elizabeth

*   *   *

KURLAND, Michael 1938-
   (Michael Joseph Kurland, Jennifer Plum)

PERSONAL: Born March 1, 1938, in New York, NY; son of Jack (a manufacturer) and Stephanie (a dress designer) Kurland; married three times (divorced three times). *Education:* Attended Hiram College, 1955-56, University of Maryland, 1959-60, foreign study in Germany, 1960-61, and Columbia University, 1963-64. *Politics:* Whig. *Religion:* Secular Humanist. *Hobbies and other interests:* Politics, bear baiting, barn storming, lighter-than-air craft, carnivals, vaudeville, science fiction incunabula.

ADDRESSES: Home—Petaluma, CA. *E-mail*—michael@michaelkurland.com.

CAREER: Full-time writer, 1963—. News editor, KPFK-Radio, Los Angeles, CA, 1966; High school English teacher in Ojai, CA, 1968; managing editor, *Crawdaddy Magazine,* 1969; editor, Pennyfarthing Press, San Francisco and Berkley, CA, beginning 1976.

Occasional director of plays for Squirrel Hill Theatre, beginning 1972. *Military service:* U.S. Army, Intelligence, 1958-62.

MEMBER: Authors Guild, Authors League of America, Mystery Writers of America, Science Fiction Writers of America, Institute for Twenty-First-Century Studies, Baker Street Irregulars, Computer Press Association.

AWARDS, HONORS: Edgar scroll from Mystery Writers of America, 1971, for *A Plague of Spies,* and 1979, for *The Infernal Device;* American Book Award nomination, 1979, for *The Infernal Device.*

WRITINGS:

FICTION

(With Chester Anderson) *Ten Years to Doomsday,* Pyramid Publications (New York, NY), 1964.
Mission: Third Force, Pyramid Publications (New York, NY), 1967.
Mission: Tank War, Pyramid Publications (New York, NY), 1968.
Mission: Police Action, Pyramid Publications (New York, NY), 1969.
A Plague of Spies, Pyramid Publications (New York, NY), 1969.
The Unicorn Girl, Pyramid Publications (New York, NY), 1969.
Transmission Error, Pyramid Publications (New York, NY), 1971.
(Under pseudonym Jennifer Plum) *The Secret of Benjamin Square,* Lancer Books (New York, NY), 1972.
The Whenabouts of Burr, DAW Books (New York, NY), 1975.
Pluribus, Doubleday (Garden City, NY), 1975.
Tomorrow Knight, DAW Books (New York, NY), 1976.
The Princes of Earth, Thomas Nelson (Nashville, TN), 1978.
The Infernal Device (also see below), New American Library (New York, NY), 1979.
(With Barton Whaley) *The Last President,* William Morrow (New York, NY), 1980.
Psi Hunt, Berkley (New York, NY), 1980.
(With H. Beam Piper) *Death by Gaslight* (also see below), New American Library (New York, NY), 1982.
Gashopper, Doubleday (Garden City, NY), 1987.

Ten Little Wizards (for young adults), Berkley (New York, NY), 1987.
Star Griffin, Doubleday (Garden City, NY), 1987.
Perchance, New American Library (New York, NY), 1988.
A Study in Sorcery, Ace (New York, NY), 1989.
Button Bright, Berkley (New York, NY), 1990.
Too Soon Dead, St. Martin's Press (New York, NY), 1997.
The Girls in the High-Heeled Shoes, St. Martin's Press (New York, NY), 1998.
The Infernal Device & Others: A Professor Moriarty Omnibus (contains *The Infernal Device,* the previously unpublished *The Paradol Paradox,* and *Death by Gaslight*), St. Martin's Minotaur (New York, NY), 2001.
The Great Game, St. Martin's Minotaur (New York, NY), 2001.
The Empress of India, St. Martin's Minotaur (New York, NY), 2006.

Author of editorials for *National Examiner,* 1966, and of "Impropa-Ganda" column in *Berkeley Barb,* 1967. Contributor to *Worlds of Tomorrow.*

NONFICTION

The Spymaster's Handbook, Facts on File (New York, NY), 1988.
World Espionage: A Historical Encyclopedia, Facts on File (New York, NY), 1993.
A Gallery of Rogues: Portraits in True Crime, Prentice-Hall General Reference (New York, NY), 1994.
How to Solve a Murder: The Forensic Handbook, Macmillan (New York, NY), 1995.
How to Try a Murder: The Armchair Lawyer's Handbook, Macmillan (New York, NY), 1997.
The Complete Idiot's Guide to Unsolved Mysteries, Alpha Books (Indianapolis, IN), 2000.

Also contributor of other titles to the "Complete Idiot's Guide" series.

EDITOR

Avram Davidson, *The Redward Edward Papers,* Doubleday (Garden City, NY), 1978.
The Best of Avram Davidson, Doubleday (Garden City, NY), 1979.

(From H. Beam Piper's unfinished manuscript) *First Cycle,* Ace Books (New York, NY), 1982.

My Sherlock Holmes: Untold Stories of the Great Detective, St. Martin's Minotaur (New York, NY), 2003.

Sherlock Holmes: The Hidden Years, St. Martin's Minotaur (New York, NY), 2004.

SIDELIGHTS: Michael Kurland is a prolific author of both fiction and nonfiction. With over thirty novels to his credit, he has published in genres from mainstream fiction to mystery. His first novels dealt with science fiction themes, and he built a notable career in that genre. However, by the 1980s he had moved to mystery and has become best known for his novels featuring the fictional nemesis of Sherlock Holmes, Professor Moriarty. These include *The Infernal Device, Death by Gaslight, The Great Game,* and the 2005 title *Empress of India.* Kurland has also edited and contributed stories to two Sherlock Holmes anthologies: *My Sherlock Holmes: Untold Stories of the Great Detective* and *Sherlock Holmes: The Hidden Years.*

As a science fiction author, Kurland is, as Richard A. Lupoff noted in *Twentieth-Century Science-Fiction Writers,* "highly adept at creating societies which are compellingly believable and populating them with vivid and sympathetic characters. His style is lively, warm, and highly informal. His stories are told with rapidity of pace and great variety of setting and incident." Kurland's first novel was a collaborative effort with Chester Anderson. *Ten Years to Doomsday* concerns a planet with only a decade to prepare for a planned invasion. In order to defend themselves from the attack, the people determine that they must change their feudal state to an industrial and technological one. Kurland says that this novel is intended as a parody of the works of Poul Anderson. Lupoff commented: "Either as a parody or in its own right, the book is fairly successful."

Kurland once told *CA:* "*The Unicorn Girl* is part of a unique trilogy, the middle work of a linked three-book opus with three different authors. The first [is] *The Butterfly Kid* by Chester Anderson, and the third [is] *The Probability Pad* by T.A. Waters." *The Butterfly Kid* includes the three authors as characters in a comical plot involving an alien invasion of a bohemian community in the 1960s. *The Unicorn Girl* continues with the same themes and characters, although it was less successful than the first part of the trilogy.

The protagonist of *Transmission Error* is considered likable, resourceful, and witty by critics but constantly finds himself in difficult situations. For example, he is inadvertently taken to an alien planet where he faces a potential life of slavery. Although he escapes this threat, he soon finds himself facing other challenges. Lupoff pointed to *Transmission Error* as an illustration of the weakness of many of Kurland's novels. He explained: "Their major flaw is a failure—whether by the author or his protagonist—to grapple with and satisfactorily resolve problems. The 'solutions' offered are almost invariably flight rather than confrontation."

Pluribus is regarded as Kurland's most successful science-fiction novel. Set in a future barbaric United States, the novel is replete with vivid imagery such as the horse-drawn Highway Patrol cruiser that carries the protagonist away after his arrest. *The Princes of Earth,* which Lupoff deemed "favorably comparable to standard [Robert] Heinlein juveniles," contains typical Kurland elements—future societies, characters, and movement from problem to problem. The author also uses satire, as in his parody of the Church of Scientology.

Kurland's writing career changed direction in 1979 when he was commissioned to write a Sherlock Holmes pastiche by a paperback publisher, but not from the point of view of the great detective. Thus he chose Holmes's archrival, Professor Moriarty. But in Kurland's interpretation, Moriarty is not the "Napoleon of Crime" that Holmes makes him out to be. Rather he is a highly intelligent and resourceful man who happens to steal from the rich; otherwise he attempts to do good. The first Moriarty title, *The Infernal Device,* led to a contract for further titles. *Death by Gaslight* appeared in 1982, *The Great Game* in 2001, and five years later came *Empress of India.* Allen O. Pierleoni described the Moriarty books in the *Sacramento Bee* as "fascinating, historically accurate reads in which Moriarty is shown not as some deranged genius with no regard for human life, but as a calm, sophisticated adventurer who happens to be a criminal. At the same time, Holmes is rather humorously depicted as obsessive in his suspicions that Moriarty is behind every crime committed in London."

The Great Game finds Moriarty joining forces with Holmes to prevent the assassinations of Queen Victoria of England and Emperor Franz Joseph of Austro-Hungary. A *Publishers Weekly* reviewer praised this work as a "deliciously complex and abundantly rewarding novel," and further commended the dialogue, which "sparkle[s] with wit, erudition and unerring diction." Writing in *Booklist*, Connie Fletcher noted the Moriarty novels were "acclaimed for their historical accuracy and adept plotting," going on to comment that in the *Great Game*, Kurland succeeded in bringing "fin de siecle Europe to brilliant life."

In *Empress of India*, Moriarty is unjustly accused of stealing a shipment of gold from the eponymous cargo ship and decides to catch the real villain and thus clear his name. A *Kirkus Reviews* critic felt that this title "carries forward the never-ending franchise with authentic flavor." Similarly, *Booklist* contributor David Pitt concluded: "This one's ideal for Holmes experts and novices alike."

Additionally, Kurland has served as editor for anthologies of Sherlock Holmes tales. Margaret Flanagan, reviewing *My Sherlock Holmes* in *Booklist*, found the collection "extremely entertaining." Kurland's second Holmes anthology, *Sherlock Holmes*, fills in the missing months in the great detective's life from when he seemingly fell to his death on the Reichenbach Falls in 1891 until he returned to 221 Baker Street in 1894. A *Publishers Weekly* reviewer felt Kurland "scores again in this lively all-original anthology."

BIOGRAPHICAL AND CRITICAL SOURCES:

BOOKS

Twentieth-Century Science-Fiction Writers, 3rd edition, St. James Press (Detroit, MI), 1991.

PERIODICALS

Booklist, July 1, 1975, review of *Pluribus,* p. 1109; April 1, 1978, review of *The Princes of Earth,* p. 1249; March 1, 1987, review of *Star Griffin,* p. 983; July, 2001, Connie Fletcher, review of *The Great Game,* p. 1988; December 15, 2002, Margaret Flanagan, review of *My Sherlock Holmes: Untold Stories of the Great Detective,* p. 737; December 15, 2005, David Pitt, review of *Empress of India,* p. 28.

Kirkus Reviews, March 15, 1975, review of *Pluribus,* p. 333; February 15, 1978, review of *The Princes of Earth,* p. 205; April 1, 1980, review of *The Last President,* p. 465; February 1, 1987, review of *Star Griffin,* p. 178; January 15, 1997, review of *Too Soon Dead,* p. 99; July 1, 1998, review of *The Girls in High-Heeled Shoes,* p. 934; June 1, 2001, review of *The Great Game,* p. 775; December 15, 2002, review of *My Sherlock Holmes,* p. 1809; December 1, 2005, review of *Empress of India,* p. 1258.

New York Times Book Review, August 31, 1980, review of *The Last President,* p. 17.

Publishers Weekly, March 21, 1980, review of *The Last President,* p. 54; February 6, 1987, Sybil Steinberg, review of *Star Griffin,* p. 88; January 27, 1997, review of *Too Soon Dead,* p. 80; July 30, 2001, review of *The Great Game,* p. 65; January 6, 2003, review of *My Sherlock Holmes,* p. 42; October 11, 2004, review of *Sherlock Holmes: The Hidden Years,* p. 59; November 14, 2005, review of *Empress of India,* p. 46.

Sacramento Bee (Sacramento, CA), August 21, 2006, Allen O. Pierleoni, "Elementary, My Dear Kurland."

Washington Post Book World, June 1, 1980, review of *The Last President,* p. 10.

ONLINE

Best Reviews, http://www.thebestreviews.com/ (July 6, 2001), Harriet Klausner, review of *The Great Game;* (January 26, 2003), Harriet Klausner, review of *My Sherlock Holmes;* (November 29, 2004), Harriet Klausner, review of *Sherlock Holmes: The Hidden Years;* (January 14, 2006), Harriet Klausner, review of *Empress of India.*

BookLoons.com, http://www.bookloons.com/ (November 20, 2006), Tim Davis, review of *Empress of India.*

Michael Kurland Home Page, http://www.michaelkurland.com (November 20, 2006).*

*   *   *

KURLAND, Michael Joseph
See KURLAND, Michael

L

LAMBRECHT, Bill 1950(?)-

PERSONAL: Born c. 1950; married Sandra Martin (a newspaper publisher). *Education:* Illinois Wesleyan University, B.A., 1972; University of Illinois—Springfield, M.A., 1973. *Hobbies and other interests:* Fishing.

ADDRESSES: Home—Fairhaven, MD. *E-mail*—blambrecht@post-dispatch.com.

CAREER: St. Louis Post-Dispatch, St. Louis, MO, began as Washington correspondent, became bureau chief, 1984—. Cofounder, *Bay Weekly* (newspaper).

AWARDS, HONORS: Society of Professional Journalists Award, 1989, for "Trashing the Earth"; Raymond Clapper Award, 1989, for "Trashing the Earth," 1993, for "Broken Trust," and 1999, for a series on genetic engineering; Outstanding Alumni Award, University of Illinois—Springfield, 1996; charter inductee, Bill Miller Public Affairs Reporting Hall of Fame, University of Illinois—Springfield, 2006.

WRITINGS:

Dinner at the New Gene Café: How Genetic Engineering Is Changing What We Eat, How We Live, and the Global Politics of Food, St. Martin's Press (New York, NY), 2001.

Big Muddy Blues: True Tales and Twisted Politics along Lewis and Clark's Missouri River, Thomas Dunne Books (New York, NY), 2005.

SIDELIGHTS: Bill Lambrecht is a journalist who has long specialized in both political and environmental reportage. In his first book, he demonstrates how these issues are related. *Dinner at the New Gene Café: How Genetic Engineering Is Changing What We Eat, How We Live, and the Global Politics of Food* brings Lambrecht's years of researching and reporting on science, technology, business, agriculture, politics, and the environment to bear on the controversy over genetically modified organisms (GMOs).

Lambrecht's primary career has been as the Washington, DC, correspondent for the *St. Louis Post-Dispatch.* St. Louis is the home of the Monsanto Company, a leading biotechnology corporation that has found itself at the center of the debate over GMOs. Lambrecht's research, however, took him to thirteen different countries over a period of several years. Lambrecht strives to present all sides of the story. Included in the book are interviews with Monsanto chairman Robert B. Shapiro, farmers who hope GMOs will rescue a faltering agricultural sector, and anti-GMO activists. Speaking to the *Pew Initiative on Food and Biotechnology Web site,* Lambrecht recalled: "You find people on both sides of the debate that wanted me to write more about their issues, but I had to be balanced and objective. . . . I write from the intersection of science and politics. I'm a journalist, not an advocate. I wrote this book to give people what they need to make choices about a transforming technology."

One of the major themes of Lambrecht's book is how little information the public currently has about GMOs, which do not have to be labeled as such under current U.S. government regulations. Lambrecht suggests that U.S. consumers lack the awareness of the sources of their food that other countries have developed, in part because they have not experienced the famines and scares familiar to Europe and other nations. A reviewer for *Publishers Weekly* called *Dinner at the New Gene Café* an "indispensable history" of the GMO debate, remarking on the extensive testimony from major players in the GMO controversy and Lambrecht's balanced approach to the topic.

In an interview with Katherine Mieszkowski for *Salon.com,* Lambrecht said that his research has not led him to worry unduly about GMOs. "I have more concerns about pesticides and chemicals than I do about GMOs," he explained, "and if I'm hungry late some night and somebody sticks a bag of chips in front of me, I'm not about to pull my hand away at the prospect of there being a trace of modified ingredients in the bag." Instead, Lambrecht hopes that increased public awareness will lead to better uses of GMOs. He told Mieszkowski: "It sometimes seems that American consumers think their food grows in the back room of a grocery store. There's a disconnect between eating and where food comes from in this country that is not found in Europe and many parts of the world. In the U.S., we've become almost an island, and the sooner that companies realize that they're going to have to accede to labeling, the quicker they will be able to get on to the types of genetic applications that they're promising, such as healthier food, even food that wards off disease."

In his second book, *Big Muddy Blues: True Tales and Twisted Politics along Lewis and Clark's Missouri River,* Lambrecht recounts the history of man's manipulation of the Missouri River. Stretching across eight states and 5,761 miles, the Missouri is a key waterway. Unfortunately, it has been not only neglected, but abused. Lambrecht relates how the source of the river is tainted by dangerous *E. coli* bacteria, while the mouth of it is situated next to a Superfund toxic waste cleanup site. The author traces the historic journey of explorers Meriwether Lewis and William Clark as they charted the course of the river, and uses their voyage as a means of illustrating later changes in the river. According to a *Kirkus Reviews* writer, *Big Muddy Blues* is "a strong if somewhat depressing account of the losses sustained" by the river, the environmentalists who have tried to protect it, and future generations who will face battles over water control. It is "a lucid, welcome work of environmental investigation," concluded the *Kirkus Reviews* commentator.

BIOGRAPHICAL AND CRITICAL SOURCES:

PERIODICALS

Booklist, March 15, 2005, Donna Seaman, review of *Big Muddy Blues: True Tales and Twisted Politics along Lewis and Clark's Missouri River,* p. 1250.

Kirkus Reviews, February 15, 2005, review of *Big Muddy Blues,* p. 214.

Library Journal, August, 2001, Irwin Weintraub, review of *Dinner at the New Gene Café: How Genetic Engineering Is Changing What We Eat, How We Live, and the Global Politics of Food,* p. 146; April 1, 2005, Margaret Atwater Singer, review of *Big Muddy Blues,* p. 109.

Publishers Weekly, July 30, 2001, review of *Dinner at the New Gene Café,* p. 70; February 21, 2005, review of *Big Muddy Blues,* p. 170.

ONLINE

Pew Initiative on Food and Biotechnology Web Site, http://pewagbiotech.org/ (March 19, 2002), "Bill Lambrecht: Documenting the Development of Technology," profile of Bill Lambrecht.

Salon.com, http:// www.salon.com/ (October 19, 2001), Katherine Mieszkowski, "The Genetically Engineered Pause That Refreshes."*

*   *   *

LEATHERWOOD, James Stephen
See LEATHERWOOD, Stephen

*   *   *

LEATHERWOOD, Stephen 1943-1997
(James Stephen Leatherwood, Steve Leatherwood)

PERSONAL: Born October 12, 1943, in Ozark, AL; died January, 1997; son of Aubrey Leon (an insurance executive) and Lillian Kathleen (a real estate broker) Leatherwood; married Melinda Weishaar, March 20, 1965 (divorced, 1974); children: Stephen Keith, Shannon Kathleen. *Education:* California State University—

Northridge, B.S., 1966; graduate study at San Diego State University, 1969-76; Texas A&M University, Ph.D., 1994. *Politics:* Democrat. *Religion:* Protestant.

CAREER: Writer, scientist, marine biologist, researcher, and educator. Teacher of mathematics and English and coach of football, soccer, and track at a military academy in Miami, FL, 1967; U.S. Navy marine mammal research unit, San Diego, CA, began as administrative assistant, became administrative officer in San Diego and at Point Mugu, 1968-70; Naval Oceans Systems Center, San Diego, research biologist in biomedical division, 1970-78; National Marine Fisheries Service, National Marine Mammal Laboratory, Seattle, WA, coordinator of Arctic Whale Research Task, 1978; Hubbs Sea World Research Institute, San Diego, research scientist in San Diego and institute manager in Orlando, FL, 1979-81; Hubbs Marine Research Center, San Diego, senior staff scientist at Sea World Research Institute, 1982-88; United Nations Environment Program, Nairobi, Kenya, acting secretary of Marine Mammal Action Plan, 1989; International Union for the Conservation of Nature, cetacean specialist group, La Jolla, CA, deputy chairperson, 1990, chairperson in Hong Kong, 1991-97. Oceans Unlimited, director, 1989; Ocean Park Conservation Foundation, director, 1993-97; Ocean Park Corp., director of veterinary and education department, 1994-97; Center for Research on Indian Ocean Marine Mammals (Colombo, Sri Lanka), director of cetacean research group; Whale Center (Oakland, CA), member of board of advisers; Terra Marine Research and Education, Inc., member of scientific advisory council; Marine Mammal Center (Sausalito, CA), member of scientific advisory board; Kid Lab, honorary member of board of directors; Mirage Dolphin Program, member of scientific advisory board for marine operations. Lecturer in oceanography and marine biology for expeditions aboard the ships *World Discoverer* and *Society Explorer,* in South America, the South Pacific, the Indian Ocean, IndoAustralia, and Antarctica; Oceanic Society, field instructor in the Bahamas, Baja California, Sri Lanka, Argentina, Brazil, Peru, the Seychelles, and East Africa; instructor at Laverne College and University of California extension. Consultant for the production of films and television documentaries, including *A Whale Called Sunshine,* Disney, 1972; *The Great Whales,* National Geographic Society, 1978; *A Whale for the Killing,* American Broadcasting Company, 1982; *Where Have All the Dolphins Gone?,* Public Broadcasting Service, 1989; and *Dolphins, Whales, and Us,* Columbia Broadcasting System, 1990; consultant to U.S. Marine Mammal Commission, National Fish and Wildlife Service, and International Whaling Commission. San Diego Natural History Museum, research associate.

MEMBER: Cetacean Society International (member of scientific advisory board and chairman of Cetacean Specialist Group), Society for Marine Mammalogy (charter member), American Society of Mammalogists, Alliance of Marine Mammal Parks and Aquariums (institutional member), American Association of Zoological Parks and Aquariums, American Cetacean Society, San Diego Society of Natural History (fellow), Southeast Association of Zoos and Aquariums (chair, membership and standards committee).

WRITINGS:

(With Randall R. Reeves) *The Sierra Club Handbook of Whales and Dolphins,* illustrated by Larry and Valerie Foster, Sierra Books (San Francisco, CA), 1983.

(Editor, with M.L. Jones and S.L. Swartz) *The Gray Whale, Eschrichtius robustus,* Academic Press (Orlando, FL), 1983.

(With Randall R. Reeves) *The Sea World Book of Dolphins,* Harcourt (San Diego, CA), 1987.

(Editor, with Randall R. Reeves) *The Bottlenose Dolphin: Recent Progress in Research,* Academic Press (San Diego, CA), 1990.

(With Randall R. Reeves and B.S. Stewart) *The Sierra Club Handbook of Seals and Sirenians,* Sierra Books (San Francisco, CA), 1992.

(With T.A. Jefferson and M. Webber) *Marine Mammals of the World,* United Nations Food and Agriculture Organization, 1994.

Contributor to anthologies, including *Marine Mammals of Eastern North Pacific and Arctic Waters,* edited by D. Haley, Pacific Search Press (Seattle, WA), 1986; *Research on Dolphins,* edited by M.M. Bryden and R. Harrison, Oxford University Press (New York, NY), 1986; and *Handbook of Marine Mammals,* Volume V: *The First Book of Dolphins,* edited by S.H. Ridgway and R.J. Harrison, Academic Press (London, England), 1994. Contributor to scientific journals and popular magazines.

SIDELIGHTS: Stephen Leatherwood was a marine biologist, scientist, educator, and conservation advocate who focused his work and research on cetaceans, or marine mammals such as whales, porpoises, and dolphins. *The Sierra Club Handbook of Whales and Dolphins,* by Leatherwood and Randall R. Reeves, covers more than seventy-five species of dolphins, whales, and porpoises. The book provides detailed information on topics such as physical characteristics and distinctive features, history, population distribution, and current status. Profusely illustrated with photographs and paintings, "what sets this book apart is its clear design as an identification guide," commented Susan Klimley in *Library Journal.* Many of the photographs show the animals in natural situations, Klimley noted, and the text helps clarify characteristics of animals that could easily be confused with others or misidentified. *School Library Journal* reviewer John Offen called the book a "fine introduction to the subject" of large marine mammals.

The Gray Whale, Eschrichtius robustus, edited by Leatherwood, M.L. Jones, and S.L. Swartz, collects diverse research results from twenty-five scientific studies of gray whales conducted by nearly forty researchers from around the world. The gray whale is now seen only in the waters of the North Pacific, but its fossilized remains have been found in Europe and along the eastern coast of the United States. The first section of the book, "Evolution, Fossils, and Subfossil Remains," reports on findings of gray whale bones on western North Atlantic beaches between Long Island and Florida. In the second section, "Historical Relationships and Exploitation," the researchers present studies of aboriginal, old-style, and modern fisheries that rely on harvesting the gray whale. Two reports, covering aboriginal whaling in Siberia and early Japanese whaling, "summarize information from published and unpublished sources that are otherwise practically inaccessible to Western researchers," noted Dale W. Rice in *Science.* Section three, "Demography, Distribution, and Migration," addresses these topics in terms of the known gray whale population in the North Pacific. The last section of the book, "Biology and Behavior," includes "studies on age, growth, reproduction, stomach contents, and parasites of gray whales killed in the Siberian subsistence fishery," Rice reported, as well as material on new field study techniques and associated technologies. "The phenomenal upsurge in marine mammal research during the past decade is well exemplified by this volume that treats one of the most intensively studied species of great whale," observed Rice.

BIOGRAPHICAL AND CRITICAL SOURCES:

PERIODICALS

Library Journal, November 15, 1983, Susan Klimley, review of *The Sierra Club Handbook of Whales and Dolphins,* p. 2152.

School Library Journal, March, 1984, John Offen, review of *The Sierra Club Handbook of Whales and Dolphins,* p. 180.
Science, March 8, 1985, Dale W. Rice, review of *The Gray Whale, Eschrichtius robustus,* p. 1219.
Sunset, December, 1983, review of *The Sierra Club Handbook of Whales and Dolphins,* p. 20.

ONLINE

Whales Alive!, http://csiwhalesalive.org/ (April, 1997), Alison Smith, profile of Stephen Leatherwood.*

*   *   *

LEATHERWOOD, Steve
  See LEATHERWOOD, Stephen

*   *   *

LESCROART, John
  See LESCROART, John T.

*   *   *

LESCROART, John T. 1948-
  (John Lescroart, John Thomas Lescroart)

PERSONAL: Surname is pronounced "*Les*-qua"; born January 14, 1948, in Houston, TX; son of Maurice E. and Loretta (a homemaker) Lescroart; married Leslee Ann Miller, June 13, 1976 (divorced July, 1979); married Lisa M. Sawyer (an architect), September 2, 1984; children: (second marriage) Justine Rose, John Jack Sawyer. *Education:* Attended the University of California—Santa Cruz, 1966, College of San Mateo, 1967, University of San Francisco, 1967-68; University of California—Berkeley, B.A. (with honors), 1970. *Hobbies and other interests:* Baseball, food and wine, fishing.

ADDRESSES: Home—El Macero, CA. *Office*—426 D St., Davis, CA 95616-4131. *Agent*—Barney Karpfinger, The Karpfinger Agency, 357 W. 20th St., New York, NY 10011.

CAREER: Writer, novelist, music producer, and musician. Computer room supervisor, 1970-72; professional singer and guitarist in Los Angeles and San Francisco,

CA, 1972-77; *Guitar Player,* Cupertino, CA, editor and advertising director, 1977-79; Guardians of the Jewish Homes for the Aging, Los Angeles, CA, associate director, 1979-83; A.T. Kearney, Inc. (consulting firm), Alexandria, VA, technical writer and associate consultant, 1982-85; Pettit & Martin (law firm), Los Angeles, CA, word processor and legal administrator, 1985-91. Writer, 1991—. CrowArt Records (an independent music label), founder and owner.

MEMBER: Mystery Writers of America, El Macero Country Club, Authors Guild, PEN, International Association of Crime Writers.

AWARDS, HONORS: Joseph Henry Jackson Award, San Francisco Foundation, 1978, for novel *Sunburn.*

WRITINGS:

(Editor) Craig Anderton, *Home Recording for Musicians,* GPI Publications (Saratoga, CA), 1975.
(Editor) Rusty Young, *The Pedal Steel Handbook,* GPI Publications (Saratoga, CA), 1976.
Sunburn (novel), Pinnacle Books (New York, NY) 1981.
Son of Holmes ("Auguste Lupa" series), Donald I. Fine (New York, NY), 1986.
Rasputin's Revenge: The Further Startling Adventures of Auguste Lupa—Son of Holmes ("Auguste Lupa" series), Donald I. Fine (New York, NY), 1987.
Son of Holmes and Rasputin's Revenge: The Early Works of John T. Lescroart, Donald I. Fine (New York, NY), 1995.
A Certain Justice ("Abe Glitsky" mystery series), Donald I. Fine (New York, NY), 1995.
(As John Lescroart) *Guilt* ("Abe Glitsky" mystery series), Delacorte Press (New York, NY), 1997.

Writer of more than 500 songs; recorded (with Amy Tan and Norman Mailer) *Lit Rock Sampler #1,* "Don't Quit Your Day Job" Records, San Francisco, CA.

"DISMAS HARDY" MYSTERY SERIES

Dead Irish, Donald I. Fine (New York, NY), 1989.
The Vig, Donald I. Fine, (New York, NY), 1990.
Hard Evidence, Donald I. Fine (New York, NY), 1993.
The 13th Juror, Donald I. Fine (New York, NY), 1994.

"DISMAS HARDY" MYSTERY SERIES; AS JOHN LESCROART

A Certain Justice, Donald I. Fine (New York, NY), 1996.
The Mercy Rule, Delacorte Press (New York, NY), 1998.
Nothing but the Truth, Dutton (New York, NY), 2000.
The Hearing, Dutton (New York, NY), 2001.
The Oath, Dutton (New York, NY), 2002.
The First Law, Dutton (New York, NY), 2003.
The Second Chair, Dutton (New York, NY), 2004.
The Motive, Dutton (New York, NY), 2005.
The Hunt Club, Dutton (New York, NY), 2006.
The Suspect, Dutton (New York, NY), 2007.

Contributor of short stories to anthologies, including *Best American Mystery Stories,* Houghton Mifflin, 1998; *Murderers' Row,* Otto Penzler (editor), New Millennium Press (Beverely Hills, CA), 2001; and *Thriller,* James Patterson (editor), Mira Books (Ontario, Canada), 2006).

ADAPTATIONS: The "Dismas Hardy" is available in its entirety on audio book.

SIDELIGHTS: John T. Lescroart worked at a variety of jobs, his last at a law firm, before he quit to become a full-time writer. The event that changed his life was a near-death experience when he contracted spinal meningitis from contaminated sea water and lay in a coma for eleven days before making an unexpected recovery. Since that time, his list of novels has grown, notably his popular mystery series featuring the evolving character Dismas Hardy.

Richard G. La Porte, writing in the *St. James Guide to Crime and Mystery Writers,* noted: "After a Joseph Henry Jackson Award-winning and veiled autobiographical *Sunburn . . .* Lescroart went on to a two-step experiment in the creation of a literary linkage between the Sherlock Holmes/Irene Adler liaison and Nero Wolfe called John Hamish Adler-Holmes who appears in *Son of Holmes* and *Rasputin's Revenge: The Further Startling Adventures of Auguste Lupa—Son of Holmes* as Auguste Lupa. Lupa, a British Secret Service agent with a penchant for Roman Imperial aliases, works for Mycroft Holmes, the original 'M' of the Service, but carries an American passport. After The Great War, Lupa retired to New York City and apparently took up orchid culture. Both of these relatively brief novels are well planned and researched and are believable pastiches. Lescroart is not, of course, the first to determine Nero Wolfe's parentage."

Lescroart's second series features the wayward Dismas Hardy of San Francisco's corporate culture. "In *Dead Irish,*" stated La Porte, Dismas Hardy is "a failed cop, husband, lawyer, and parent. He [is] a part-time barkeep, nursing his Guinness and darts in the Little Shamrock, catty-cornered across 9th and Lincoln from the Hall of Flowers in Golden Gate Park." *Library Journal* reviewer Rex E. Klett deemed the book "a full-bodied, substantive, and stylistic effort of the first order [with] full attention to character . . . a sympathetic protagonist, and a satisfying conclusion." Peter Robertson, writing in *Booklist,* called it "an unusual and powerful mystery."

In a *Publishers Weekly* review of *The 13th Juror* the critic stated that "the story gets off to a slow start . . . and [Lescroart] . . . comes close to telegraphing the solution to the mystery, and much of his writing about characters' personal lives is hamfisted. Despite these flaws, however, an intricate story and satisfying courtroom scenes carry the day." Dan Bogey, writing in *Booklist,* called the novel "very readable . . . with engaging characters and a riveting plot that fans of Scott Turow and John Grisham will love."

Regarding the protagonist of Lescroart's "Abe Glitsky" novels *A Certain Justice* and *Guilt,* La Porte summarized: "Back before *Dead Irish* when Hardy was a cop, his partner was Abe Glitsky. Abe stayed in the SFPD and is on his way up the promotional ladder with its treacherous snakes of political reform. Affirmative action policies posed a double-ended problem to Abe. Glitsky senior is an orthodox Jew and Abe's mother was black. Although his appearance is strongly African-American, his commitments are not."

Dawn L. Anderson, writing in *Library Journal,* called *A Certain Justice* a "heart-stopping thriller" that "will keep readers riveted to their chairs." *Chicago Tribune* reviewer Chris Petrakos made similar remarks, noting that "Lescroart does a masterly job juggling politics and justice, demonstrating along the way that the two rarely mix." A *Kirkus Reviews* critic surmised that it is not as humorous as Tom Wolfe's *Bonfire of the Vanities,* but it is "just as mordant and electric." Steve Brewer, writing in *Mostly Murder,* called *Guilt* "a blockbuster of a trial. . . . [Lescroart] establishes the main characters carefully."

La Porte stated: "Although the Hardy/Glitsky books are part of the mystery/detection genre, they are far more fully developed than most of the earlier series character studies. For one thing, the greater length gives Lescroart more time for detailing the fauna and flora of the mean streets of San Francisco and their effects on the people in the story. For another, they are primarily plot-driven, character-development studies. They are not stories of how the protagonist, The Master Detective, brings his acute powers to bear on a single problem but more the reverse. The crime and its manifestations are brought to bear on the protagonist forcing him to rise, change, and challenge himself to prove his beliefs."

La Porte summarized: "All of this [writing] is done with a smooth literary style with a padding of truth and a verisimilitude that makes you feel that you are right there where it is happening. There may not be an old bar with its dartboard on that corner of 9th and Lincoln but it seems as if there should be one. This is one of the strongest points in Lescroart's writing; the believability, not only the places, but also the people."

In *The Mercy Rule,* called a "satisfying legal thriller" by Melissa Kuzma Rokicki in *Library Journal,* Graham Russo asks defense attorney Dismas to represent him when Graham is accused of murdering his father, Sal, who had been suffering from Alzheimer's disease and a brain tumor. Graham admits to Dismas that had assisted his father with his morphine injections, but denies that he ended his father's life. Homicide detective Sarah Evans and Dismas believe that Sal was murdered, but not by Graham. A *Publishers Weekly* reviewer called the courtroom scenes "little masterpieces of battlefield maneuvering," but added that "because the book's only overarching concerns are plot-related . . . the added level of depth and concern that would create a truly great courtroom thriller are absent." *Booklist* contributor Gilbert Taylor said Lescroart "has the technical clues of the plot perfectly arranged . . . but it's his credible characters who cement this entertaining, front-rank whodunit."

Nothing but the Truth finds Dismas and his wife, Frannie, drifting apart, which explains why Dismas did not know that Frannie had been subpoenaed to appear before the grand jury to testify when her friend, Ron Beaumont, is suspected in the death of his wife, Bree, who had been a political advisor and the possible lover of a gubernatorial candidate. Ron has shared a secret with Frannie, which she refuses to relate, and now Frannie faces contempt charges and jail time. Dismas steps in to help Frannie and vows to find the actual murderer, but the first officer assigned to the case has already been murdered, and trouble comes at Dismas from all directions. A *Publishers Weekly* contributor wrote that "it's the close-to-home secrets affecting Hardy and his marriage that resonate most," and concluded by calling the novel a "winning thriller." *Booklist* reviewer Emily Melton commented on the many elements of the plot, but said that Lescroart "keeps his potboiler under control, and the result is a riveting if over-the-top thriller." Thea Davis reviewed *Nothing but the Truth* for the *Mystery Reader* online, saying that "scenes shift swiftly, although the pace is slowed by an extraordinary amount of detail."

A *Kirkus Reviews* contributor wrote that in *The Hearing,* Lescroart "lays on the political intrigue as fearlessly as if he were writing exposé journalism." Junkie Cole Burgess is found beside the body of Elaine Wager, a former assistant district attorney and the daughter of a deceased female senator. Cole, who was holding the murder weapon and whose pockets were filled with Elaine's jewelry, is coerced into making a full confession with the promise of a fix, and a friend asks Dismas to defend Cole, who has obviously been railroaded. Cole is swiftly prosecuted by a district attorney who wants the death penalty, and also by Abe Glitsky, who was actually Elaine's unacknowledged father. Abe is suspended for leaking Cole's confession and changes sides, opposing the district attorney when he sees holes in the case against Cole. The cast of *The Hearing* is large, but a *Publishers Weekly* reviewer said that its "richness and diversity . . . neither slows the pace nor confuses the narrative, as even minor characters take on memorable presence and depth." *Library Journal* reviewer Nancy McNicol called the plot "tightly constructed."

In Joe Hartlaub's review of *The Hearing* for *Book reporter.com,* he commented that Lescroart's descriptions of San Francisco are "just right." Hartlaub called the plot "intriguing, complex. . . . Lescroart's unrushed and thoughtful narrative expertly and meticulously begins to paint each piece of the puzzle and slowly put them together, one-by-one. While he does this, we really get to know and care about the people involved." Hartlaub concluded by calling *The Hearing* "an all encompassing feast for the senses with enough mystery, drama, and characterization to fill three books."

As the "Dismas Hardy" series progressed, Hardy and Glitsky began appearing together regularly. *The First*

Law finds Dismas and Abe teamed up against the head of a rogue security company. The Patrol Special has long served as a private security force for downtown merchants in San Francisco. Their connection to the police department is tenuous, but they have always worked with approval from law enforcement. Now, Wade Panos, head of the Patrol Special, has started using his power and influence to dodge complaints, misdirect a homicide investigation, and falsely accuse an innocent man whose business Panos wanted to acquire. Worse, Panos manages to smear the otherwise sterling reputations of Abe and Dismas. When they attempt to fight back, threats are made against their families. Incensed at this violation of the "first law"—to protect their own lives and the lives of their loved ones—Abe and Dismas elect to seek a solution outside the boundaries of the law. Reviewing the novel in *Publishers Weekly,* a contributor noted that "with his latest, Lescroart again lands in the top tier of crime fiction."

In *The Second Chair,* Abe and Dismas are still reeling from the bloody aftereffects of *First Law.* Both, however, have advanced in their careers, with Dismas well established as the head of his successful law firm and Abe promoted to deputy chief of investigations. Both men chafe under the low-key executive requirements of their positions, however, and both are eager to put their skills to use in the field again. When Amy Wu, an up-and-coming attorney in Dismas's firm, makes a critical error in defending a young man accused of murder, Hardy must step in as "second chair" in the trial to ensure that the high-profile case is salvaged. In the process, he rekindles his faith in the legal system. "Under Lescroart's assured hand," commented Keir Graff in *Booklist,* "this perfectly paced tale of legal procedure and big-city politics keeps us turning pages even when it's time to turn in at night." A *Publishers Weekly* reviewer commented, "old fans and those who persevere will be rewarded with a compassionate look at life's vicissitudes and a thorny multiple murder."

The Motive brings Abe to the scene of a double homicide when a wealthy businessman, Paul Hanover, and his mysterious fiance Missy D'Amiens are discovered dead in the remnants of a townhouse fire. Abe's position as deputy chief of inspectors initially keeps him away, and the investigation begins with Sergeant Dan Cuneo. However, the mayor becomes dissatisfied with Cuneo's approach and assigns Abe to the case, sparking resentment in Cuneo. Elsewhere, Dismas is hired by Hanover's daughter-in-law, who also happens to have been his serious girlfriend in college. She has been accused of murder, and with no alibi and solid motive to kill, the case seems strongly stacked against her. As Abe and Dismas investigate, contradictory evidence emerges, as does questions about Hanover's recent eligibility for a federal appointment and his girlfriend's shadowy past. Personal tragedy also intervenes, as Abe's joy at the birth of his son is tempered with the knowledge of the child's potentially fatal health problems. Lescroart's "authentic voice, methodical presentation, and ability to juggle red herrings until all pieces fall into place will keep fans following wherever his cop-lawyer friends-heroes lead," remarked a *Publishers Weekly* contributor. The easy friendship and good-natured banter between Abe and Dismas seems "as comfortable as slipping into an old gumshoe," observed Paul Katz in *Entertainment Weekly.*

The Hunt Club introduces a new pair of San Francisco-based crime-fighting characters to Lescroart's oeuvre: private investigator Wyatt Hunt and homicide detective Devin Juhle. "Longtime Lescroart fans can relax: these pals are at least as interesting and enterprising as Hardy/Glitsky," observed a *Publishers Weekly* reviewer. Both Hunt and Juhle are struggling against checkered pasts. Hunts once worked for Child Protective Services, a job he loved, but was forced out after a troubling incident. Juhle works to distance himself from a violent shoot-out that killed a former partner. Now, Hunt is affiliated with the expanding Dismas Hardy law firm, and has gathered around him an eccentric but effective group of investigators nicknamed the Hunt Club. In the book, Hunt and his team become involved with investigating the baffling murder of a federal judge and his much-younger girlfriend. As the case unfolds, the Hunt Club discovers disturbing connections to the power elite of San Francisco. When Hunt's lover, who had connections to the judge, disappears, the streetwise detective becomes determined to solve the case no matter where it leads him. Lescroart presents "an uncommonly detailed story of his hero's origins and a much smaller case of double murder," noted a *Kirkus Reviews* critic.

Lescroart once told *CA:* "I have always been intrigued with the written word. I viewed my creative writing assignments as early as the sixth grade as great fun, and I continue to feel pretty much the same way. After experimenting with short stories, poetry, and song lyrics (and continuing to do so), when I was twenty-two I took the plunge and began my first novel, which no one will ever see.

"Six years later, my novel *Sunburn* won the Joseph Henry Jackson Award from the San Francisco Founda-

tion. That award gave me the confidence to continue my pursuit of novel-writing as a career. . . . I am blessed with my wife Lisa, who is incredibly and consistently supportive of my pursuit of my dreams and my art.

"My heroes, disparate though they may be, are Ernest Hemingway, Lawrence Durrell, and John Fowles. I like Larry McMurtry and James Clavell. I am also a big fan of several mystery writers, including Arthur Conan Doyle, Rex Stout, John D. MacDonald, P.D. James, and Elmore Leonard. And I continue to believe, naively I'm sure, that if more people would read quality fiction, it would do more good for them and for the world than all the how-to and self-help books ever published."

BIOGRAPHICAL AND CRITICAL SOURCES:

BOOKS

St. James Guide to Crime and Mystery Writers, 4th edition, Thomson Gale (Detroit, MI), 1996.

PERIODICALS

Booklist, January 15, 1990, Peter Robertson, review of *Dead Irish,* p. 976; September 1, 1994, Dan Bogey, review of *The 13th Juror,* p. 27; July, 1998, Gilbert Taylor, review of *The Mercy Rule,* p. 1830; November 15, 1999, Emily Melton, review of *Nothing but the Truth,* p. 580; December 1, 2003, Keir Graff, review of *The Second Chair,* p. 626; November 1, 2005, Connie Fletcher, review of *The Hunt Club,* p. 5.

Books, summer, 1999, review of *Nothing but the Truth,* p. 20.

Chicago Tribune, July 16, 1995, Chris Petrakos, review of *A Certain Justice,* p. 6.

Entertainment Weekly, December 24, 2004, Paul Katz, review of *The Motive,* p. 73.

Kirkus Reviews, June 1, 1995, review of *A Certain Justice,* p. 731; August 1, 1998, review of *The Mercy Rule,* p. 132; November 15, 1999, review of *Nothing but the Truth,* p. 1764; February 1, 2001, review of *The Hearing,* p. 132; November 15, 2002, review of *The First Law,* p. 1647; November 15, 2003, review of *The Second Chair,* p. 1332; November 1, 2005, review of *The Hunt Club,* p. 1160.

Library Journal, January 1, 1990, Rex E. Klett, review of *Dead Irish,* p. 151; July, 1994, Dan Bogey, review of *The 13th Juror,* p. 127; July, 1995, Dawn L. Anderson, review of *A Certain Justice,* p. 121; January, 1998, review of *Guilt,* p. 176; August, 1998, Melissa Kuzma Rokicki, review of *The Mercy Rule,* p. 132; November 15, 1999, Nancy McNicol, review of *Nothing but the Truth,* p. 100; January 1, 2001, Nancy McNicol, review of *The Hearing,* p. 155; November 1, 2002, Kristen L. Smith, review of *The Oath,* p. 143; July 15, 2003, Kristen L. Smith, audiobook review of *The First Law,* p. 145; May 15, 2004, Kristen L. Smith, audiobook review of *The Second Chair,* p. 130; June 15, 2005, Kristen L. Smith, review of *The Motive,* p. 113; November 15, 2005, Nancy McNicol, review of *The Hunt Club,* p. 63.

Mostly Murder, May-June, 1997, Steve Brewer, review of *Guilt.*

New York Law Journal, January 5, 2001, Pamela Aucoin, review of *The Hearing,* p. 2

People, March 18, 2002, Sean Gannon, review of *The Oath,* p. 47; March 3, 2003, Edward Karam, review of *The First Law,* p. 41; March 1, 2004, Edward Karam, review of *The Second Chair,* p. 56.

Publishers Weekly, November 23, 1992, review of *Hard Evidence,* p. 52; June 20, 1994, review of *The 13th Juror,* pp. 93-94; August 17, 1998, review of *The Mercy Rule,* p. 48; December 13, 1999, review of *Nothing but the Truth,* p. 64; March 12, 2001, review of *The Hearing,* p. 60; November 19, 2001, review of *The Oath,* p. 46; January 13, 2003, review of *The First Law,* p. 41; December 15, 2003, review of *The Second Chair,* p. 54; November 29, 2004, review of *The Motive,* p. 22; February 7, 2005, review of *The Motive,* p. 34; October 31, 2005, review of *The Hunt Club,* p. 31; October 16, 2006, review of *The Suspect,* p. 30.

ONLINE

Bookreporter.com, http://www.bookreporter.com/ (September 12, 2001), Joe Hartlaub, review of *The Hearing.*

John Lescroart Home Page, http://www.johnlescroart. com (December 17, 2006).

Mystery Reader, http://www.themysteryreader.com/ (September 12, 2001), Thea Davis, review of *Nothing but the Truth.**

*   *   *

LESCROART, John Thomas
    See LESCROART, John T.

LIFTON, Robert Jay 1926-

PERSONAL: Born May 16, 1926, in Brooklyn, NY; son of Harold A. (a businessman) and Ciel Lifton; married Betty Jean Kirschner (a writer), March 1, 1952; children: Kenneth Jay, Karen, Natasha. *Education:* Attended Cornell University, 1942-44; New York Medical College, M.D., 1948. *Hobbies and other interests:* Tennis, films, and cartooning.

CAREER: Writer, psychiatrist, researcher, and educator. Washington School of Psychiatry, Washington, DC, and Hong Kong, member of faculty, 1954-55; Harvard University, Cambridge, MA, research associate in psychiatry, 1956-61; Yale University, New Haven, CT, associate professor, 1961-67, Foundations' Fund Research Professor in Psychiatry, 1967-84; John Jay College, City University of New York, distinguished professor of psychiatry and psychology, Graduate School University Center, and founder and director of Center for the Study of Human Violence; Harvard Medical School, visiting professor of psychiatry. Harvard Medical School, Gay Lecturer, 1976; Cornell University, Messenger Lecturer, 1980. Research psychiatrist, Walker Reed Army Institute of Research, 1956; research associate in psychiatry, Massachusetts General Hospital, 1956-61, Tokyo University, 1960-61; candidate, Boston Psychoanalytic Institute, 1957-60; affiliated with Mt. Sinai Medical Center. Organizer of redress group opposing Vietnam War, International Atomic Energy Agency, Vienna, Austria, 1975. Member, Council on East Asian Studies, Yale University, beginning 1964. Consultant to behavioral studies study section, National Institute of Mental Health, 1962-64, to New York Bar Association committee on the invasion of privacy, 1963-64, to Columbia seminars on modern Japan and Oriental thought and religion, beginning 1965, to Arnold and Porter concerning 1972 Buffalo Flood Creek disaster, 1973-74, and to Harmon and Weiss and David Berger, P.A., on psychological effects of 1979 Three Mile Island nuclear accident. *Military service:* U.S. Air Force, 1951-53; became captain.

MEMBER: American Psychiatric Association (fellow), Group for the Advancement of Psychiatry, Association for Asian Studies, American Anthropological Association, American Association for the Advancement of Science, American Academy of Arts and Sciences (fellow), Group for the Study of Psychohistorical Process (coordinator), American Academy of Psychoanalysis, Physicians for Social Responsibility, Medical Committee for Human Rights.

AWARDS, HONORS: American Academy of Arts and Sciences sponsorship, 1965, to establish psychohistory as a separate field of academic study; National Book Award for sciences, and Van Wyck Brooks Award for nonfiction, both 1969, both for *Death in Life: Survivors of Hiroshima;* public service award, New York Society of Clinical Psychologists, and Alumni Medal, New York Medical College, both 1970; Karen Horney Lecture Award, Association for the Advancement of Psychoanalysis, 1972; distinguished service award, Society for Adolescent Psychology, 1972; Mount Airy Foundation Gold Medal for excellence in psychiatry, 1973; National Book Award nomination, 1974, for *Home from the War: Vietnam Veterans—Neither Victims nor Executioners;* Hiroshima Gold Medal, 1975; Guggenheim fellowship, 1983; Gandhi Peace Award, 1984; Bertrand Russell Society award, 1985; *Los Angeles Times* Book Prize for history, 1987, for *The Nazi Doctors: Medical Killing and the Psychology of Genocide;* honorary degrees include D.Sc., Lawrence University, 1971, and Merrimack College, 1973; and D.H.L., Wilmington College, 1975, New York Medical College, 1977, Marlboro College, 1983, and Maryville College, 1983.

WRITINGS:

NONFICTION

Thought Reform and the Psychology of Totalism: A Study of "Brainwashing" in China, Norton (New York, NY), 1961.

Death in Life: Survivors of Hiroshima, Random House (New York, NY), 1968.

Revolutionary Immortality: Mao Tse-Tung and the Chinese Cultural Revolution, Random House (New York, NY), 1968.

Birds, Words, and Birds (cartoons), Random House (New York, NY), 1969.

Boundaries, Canadian Broadcasting Corp. (Toronto, Ontario, Canada), 1969, published as *Boundaries: Psychological Man in Revolution,* Random House (New York, NY), 1970.

History and Human Survival: Essays on the Young and the Old, Survivors and the Dead, Peace and War, and on Contemporary Psychohistory, Random House (New York, NY), 1970.

Home from the War: Vietnam Veterans—Neither Victims nor Executioners, Simon & Schuster (New York, NY), 1973, with a new preface and epilogue on the First Gulf War, Beacon Press (Boston, MA), 1992, with a new preface on the Second Gulf War, Other Press (New York, NY), 2005.

(With Eric Olson) *Living and Dying,* Praeger (New York, NY), 1974.

The Life of the Self: Toward a New Psychology, Simon & Schuster (New York, NY), 1976.

(With Shuichi Kato and Michael Reich) *Six Lives/Six Deaths: Portraits from Modern Japan* (originally published in Japanese as *Nihonjin no shiseikan,* 1977), Yale University Press (New Haven, CT), 1979.

Psychobirds, Countryman Press (Taftsville, VT), 1978.

The Broken Connection: On Death and the Continuity of Life, Simon & Schuster (New York, NY), 1979.

(With Richard A. Falk) *Indefensible Weapons: The Political and Psychological Case against Nuclearism,* Basic Books (New York, NY), 1982.

The Nazi Doctors: Medical Killing and the Psychology of Genocide, Basic Books (New York, NY), 1986, with a new preface by the author, Basic Books (New York, NY), 2000.

The Future of Immortality and Other Essays for a Nuclear Age, Basic Books (New York, NY), 1987.

(With Eric Markusen) *The Genocidal Mentality: Nazi Holocaust and Nuclear Threat,* Basic Books (New York, NY), 1990.

The Protean Self: Human Resilience in an Age of Fragmentation, Basic Books (New York, NY), 1993.

(With Greg Mitchell) *Hiroshima in America: Fifty Years of Denial,* Putnam (New York, NY), 1995.

Destroying the World to Save It: Aum Shinrikyo, Apocalyptic Violence, and the New Global Terrorism, Henry Holt (New York, NY), 1999.

(With Greg Mitchell) *Who Owns Death? Capital Punishment, the American Conscience, and the End of Executions,* Morrow (New York, NY), 2000, with a new afterword by the authors, Perennial (New York, NY), 2002.

Superpower Syndrome: America's Apocalyptic Confrontation with the World, Thunder's Mouth Press/Nation Books (New York, NY), 2003.

EDITOR

The Woman in America, Houghton (Boston, MA), 1965.

America and the Asian Revolutions, Trans-Action Books/Aldine (Chicago, IL), 1970, second edition, 1973.

(With Richard A. Falk and Gabriel Kolko) *Crimes of War: A Legal, Political-Documentary, and Psychological Inquiry into the Responsibilities of Leaders, Citizens, and Soldiers for Criminal Acts of War,* Random House (New York, NY), 1971.

(With Eric Olson) *Explorations in Psychohistory: The Wellfleet Papers,* Simon & Schuster (New York, NY), 1975.

(With Eric Chivian, Susanna Chivian, and John E. Mack) *Last Aid: The Medical Dimensions of Nuclear War,* W.H. Freeman (New York, NY), 1982.

(With Nicholas Humphrey) *In a Dark Time: Images for Survival,* Harvard University Press (Cambridge, MA), 1984.

(Editor, with Jacob D. Lindy) *Beyond Invisible Walls: The Psychological Legacy of Soviet Trauma, East European Therapists, and Their Patients,* Brunner-Routledge (Philadelphia, PA), 2001.

(Editor, with Richard Falk and Irene Gendzier) *Crimes of War: Iraq,* Nation Books (New York, NY), 2006.

OTHER

Contributor of articles and reviews to periodicals, including *New York Times Book Review, New York Times Magazine, New York Review of Books, Atlantic Monthly, Daedalus, Trans-Action/Society, American Scholar, New Republic, Partisan Review,* and to *American Journal of Psychiatry, Psychiatry,* and other professional journals in the fields of psychiatry, psychology, history, and Asian studies.

ADAPTATIONS: Death in Life: Survivors of Hiroshima was adapted for BBC-TV by Richard Voss in 1975.

SIDELIGHTS: Robert Jay Lifton "is an indefatigable author with a lively sense of history and a considerable capacity for assimilating and reordering huge amounts of information," declared Anthony Storr in the *Washington Post Book World.* "What chiefly interests him," Storr continued, "is the reaction of human beings to extreme situations." Outstanding among Lifton's interests is the question of how people come to terms with mortality—how they face death individually and collectively. "Whether grappling with the experience of mass destruction suffered by the survivors of Hiroshima, with nuclear weapons' potential for genocide, or with the adverse emotional sequelae in American veterans of the Vietnamese war," wrote Sidney Bloch in the *Times Literary Supplement,* "Lifton has steadfastly striven to comprehend the seemingly incomprehensible."

Lifton studies these questions using the techniques of psychohistory, a discipline that *New York Times* contributor Christopher Lehmann-Haupt defines as an "endeavor to define how individual human behavior interacts with the historical currents of a given age." This discipline found its modern form in the work of psychologist Erik Erikson, whose biographies *Young Man Luther: A Study in Psychoanalysis and History* and *Gandhi's Truth: On the Origins of Militant Nonviolence* broke new ground by integrating history and psychology in order to understand historical figures in the context of their times. Although Lifton's own work also attempts to understand history through the application of psychoanalysis, it differs from that of Erikson because it concentrates not on influential individuals who affect history, but rather on the historical processes that impact on the individual.

Psychohistory is not universally accepted by historians as a discipline in its own right. Lehmann-Haupt stated in a review of Lifton's psychohistorical *History and Human Survival: Essays on the Young and the Old, Survivors and the Dead, Peace and War, and on Contemporary Psychohistory* that "as Lifton points out, the two [areas of study] have been traditionally opposed to the degree 'that psychoanalysis seeks to eliminate history, and history seeks to eliminate psychological man.'" This is not reasonable, Lehmann-Haupt claims; after all, "no individual is free of history and no history is free of individuals." Instead, Lifton suggests that history and psychology complement each other. In a different review—of *Home from the War: Vietnam Veterans—Neither Victims nor Executioners*—Lehmann-Haupt stated: "What is provocative about Dr. Lifton's long, complex study [are] . . . the conclusions he draws that even in contemporary situations, history and psychology cannot be separated, and that therefore psychiatrists must henceforth take history into account when treating their patients—not only history as it relates to the patient, but also as it relates to the therapist."

Death in Life: Survivors of Hiroshima, Lifton's 1969 National Book award-winning study of the psychoses and behavior patterns of the more than ninety thousand survivors of the atom bomb dropped on the city at the close of World War II, uses psychohistorical methods to understand the impact the bomb had on the people who survived it—called *hibakusha,* or "explosion-affected persons," in Japanese. All survivors, Lifton found, share feelings of a close association with catastrophe and a feeling of guilt at having survived, coupled with a profound death-wish. In a *New York Times* article titled "On the Nuclear Altar," Lifton explained the *hibakusha*'s reactions more fully: "But their basic feeling was that they had been made into historical guinea pigs—had been victimized by a weapon so new, powerful, and mysterious that its effects could not be known until it had been 'tried' on a particular population. One survivor put the matter bitterly: 'There exist no words in any human language that can comfort guinea pigs who do not know the cause of their death.'" Jerome D. Frank, writing in the *New York Times Book Review,* observed that "Perhaps [*Death in Life*'s] most significant message is that the long-term psychological crippling of survivors, and the profound societal disruption caused by a nuclear attack, are at least as severe a threat to the continued existence of organized society as the extent of biological and physical destruction."

Lifton sees the possibility of nuclear holocaust as a significant factor in modern concepts of life and death. Emile Capouya wrote in *Saturday Review* of *Boundaries,* a series of essays focusing on this theme: "The possibility that civilization and life itself may be ended, deliberately or accidentally, through the exercise of our scientific and technical powers, has been present to us all through the modern period and has given rise at last to a real crisis of morale, of the animal faith that we must have if we are to carry on." Although people have always had to face their own mortality, Capouya stated, "even those persons who had had no revelation about a universal resurrection . . . might hope to survive biologically, through their children, or spiritually, through their contribution to human culture and history." Now, they may no longer have that option. David Gates, writing in *Newsweek* about a later Lifton book, *The Future of Immortality and Other Essays for a Nuclear Age,* had a parallel view; Lifton's theory, he wrote, is "that we all yearn for immortality, whether in an afterlife or in the idea that we live on through our children—or simply humankind. The threat of nuclear holocaust, therefore, has done unique psychic damage." One symptom of this damage, Gates stated, is the behavior of many young adults who are preparing for marriage and children yet doubting that they will live that long. "Traditional apocalyptic visions, said Lifton, at least saw the end of the world as redemptive," declared Gates; "nuclear self-immolation doesn't even offer that cold comfort."

One way people deal with a profound psychic disturbance such as nuclear devastation, Lifton has found, is through the device he calls "psychic numbing" or "psychic closing-off." "Human beings, Lifton observes, 'are unable to remain open to emotional experience of this intensity for any length of time, and very quickly—

sometimes within minutes—there began to occur what we may term psychic closing-off; that is, people simply ceased to feel,'" explained Henry S. Resnik in *Saturday Review.* Many of the Hiroshima *hibakusha* exhibit psychic numbing, and Lifton observed similar symptoms in Jewish survivors of Nazi Germany, in the veterans of the Vietnam War, and in student rebels in the West—all victims of an emotional overload.

Doctors in the Nazi concentration camps, Lifton has found, underwent a similar process. Lifton's study *The Nazi Doctors: Medical Killing and the Psychology of Genocide* asks the question, "How did doctors, devoted to relieving human suffering, justify the treatment of the Jews incarcerated in the camps?" The book shows that there were several factors responsible. In Germany at the time the Nazi party came to power, there was already a concept of "racial purity" that, combined with radical concepts of "euthanasia," helped lead to an organized extermination of the Jews. Doctors, stated Neal Ascherson in the *New York Review of Books,* were envisioned as "biological soldiers," fighting to preserve the purity of the state. They "were invited to see their task as a supreme expression of medical responsibility, its value only emphasized by the fact that most doctors initially found it difficult to carry out—and some found it impossible." Another attitude, used to justify experimentation on living bodies, was that the prisoners were "in practice already dead by virtue of their presence in camp"; they could therefore be regarded simply as very fresh cadavers. When actually faced with the horrors of giving injections and choosing people for experimentation, the doctors resorted to "psychic numbing," usually accomplished by means of heavy drinking, and a technique that Lifton calls "doubling"—the temporary formation of another self in order to adapt to the extreme conditions of the camp.

In his 1990 work, *The Genocidal Mentality: Nazi Holocaust and Nuclear Threat,* which Lifton coauthored with sociologist Eric Markusen, the mindset borne of the holocaust combines with the constant fear of nuclear destruction to produce what Lifton calls "nuclearism": a passive acceptance of such weapons as "normal," coupled with a heightened reliance on those same elements of destruction for safety and protection from outside enemies. Critical of the scientists who developed such weaponry, the authors also have criticism for those individuals who have "passionately embraced" nuclear weaponry as personal "solutions to death anxiety and the threat of extinction." They contrast the Nazi model, "where the habit of killing led, more or less, piecemeal, to a genocidal point of no return," by noting that the choice to use nuclear weaponry "is likely to be sudden and total. . . . The 'vicious cycle' in the nuclear sense—the unending quest for 'security' and 'stable deterrence'—can be 'broken' only in one or two ways: by setting the weapons off, or else by getting rid of all or most of them." One of the most controversial aspects of Lifton and Markusen's thesis, according to *New York Times Book Review* contributor Sheila Tobias, is the "fundamental sameness between Nazism and nuclear genocide. . . . the 'disciplined professionals' in the service of both . . . [who] are able to put their humanity on hold through psychological 'doubling' when they indulge their working selves and both [who are] are convinced of the rightness and urgency of their mission."

Criticizing the authors' argument as "repetitive and deeply flawed," Adam Roberts maintained in a review of *The Genocidal Mentality* for *New Statesman* that while Lifton and Markusen urge "a growing global consciousness" and present several schemes to diminish the existence and reliance upon nuclear weapons worldwide, the "strengths and weaknesses" of these solutions "are not explored in any detail. Instead, they are declared to be on the side of the angels." However, Lifton continues to reiterate the themes praised in his previous books, and maintains that U.S. strategists are trapped by the mentality borne of their role in a nuclear age: they developed such frightening and potentially annihilistic policies as "mutual assured destruction" as a consequence of what Lifton terms collective "disassociation," or large-scale "doubling."

Such means of adapting to the thought of ultimate destruction has resulted in the emergence of a psychological type that Lifton calls Protean Man. "In 'Protean Man' Lifton advances, with admirable conciseness, the idea that various conditions of contemporary life are contributing to the emergence of a new kind of man," explains Resnik. "The two principal historical developments Lifton cites are 'historical . . . dislocation, the break in the sense of connection which men have long felt with the vital and nourishing symbols of their cultural tradition,' and 'the flooding of imagery produced by the extraordinary flow of post-modern cultural influences over mass-communication networks.'" He concludes: "It is simply impossible, in short, to hold on to an identity or a world these days—youngsters who grew up with television scarcely know

how to try—and the only acceptable alternative, not necessarily an evil one, is to live life as 'an interminable series of experiments and explorations.'"

Lifton's strongly expressed opinions and analyses of these processes have aroused controversy among critics. Gates saw Lifton's work as "supercritical when he starts exhorting." And Richard Locke, writing in the *New York Times Book Review* about *Home from the War,* declared: "The book lacks the sensitive precision that gave tragic power to much of his first work, *Totalism and the Psychology of Thought Reform,* where he was scrupulously attentive to individual experience and moved from the particular to the general with great care." However, other critics offered different opinions. Resnik, writing about *History and Human Survival,* maintained: "Whatever his method or its inconsistencies, Lifton has superb talent as a journalist; there is virtually no psychohistorical content in his description of a week's visit to Vietnam, but the essay, which stands somewhat apart from the rest, is a bitingly understated indictment of the American presence in Southeast Asia, and is worthwhile reading in any context." Frank called *Death in Life* "an impressive, trail-breaking contribution in describing and conceptualizing the experience of surviving a taste of man's nuclear war on his own species—an experience which may fall to the lot of everyone alive today."

While Lifton's arguments may prove controversial to some readers, others see justification in his stance. Lifton "is trying to persuade us that we are living in mortal sin. Some of us may not feel the guilt, but that is because we have been numbed," contended Locke. The author, stated the reviewer, feels he must cure us out of our moral numbness. "Lifton argues that what we have to feel . . . is what he calls 'animating guilt,'" says Locke, "a sense that one has violated ultimate moral boundaries; that one must analyze the personal and social forces that led one into sin; that one must come to terms with these facts and then not merely go and sin no more but expose to all mankind the falsity of guiltlessness, the hypocrisy and deathliness of the current social order; and finally that one must exhort one's fellow man to confess his sins and convert to 'Protean' nonviolence."

Lifton expands further on his concepts of the protean in *The Protean Self: Human Resilience in an Age of Fragmentation.* The book "is a clear, concise, and affirmative look at how humans adapt to a constantly changing world," remarked Brian McCombie in *Booklist.* In what a *Publishers Weekly* contributor called a "highly stimulating, original synthesis," Lifton describes how the Protean Self assembles bits of experience and constantly seeks to reinvent itself. Those most in tune with their Protean Selves are achievers interested in personal development and growth, who are not content with the traditional patterns and paths of life, and who devise new ways to make their way in the world while seeking alternatives to narrow career options and life paths. Lifton includes biographical profiles of individuals he considers protean, including Vaclav Havel, novelist Gordon Parks, author Kurt Vonnegut, and a variety of activists and advocates. With such a focus on improvement and transformation, Lifton offers the optimistic suggestion that humans are living more hopeful, positive, and focused lives than previously thought possible in a postmodern world.

With *Hiroshima in America: Fifty Years of Denial,* Lifton once again turns his attention to the subject of Hiroshima, this time in terms of how the impact of the Hiroshima bombing has been downplayed and sometimes outright ignored in American historical contexts. Lifton and coauthor Greg Mitchell document how a documentary film of the effects of the bombings of Hiroshima and Nagasaki, created by a collaboration between American and Japanese filmmakers, was suppressed for more than two decades after the war until it was released by the Japanese government. Lifton finds the fate of that film illustrative of the American approach to the bombing, which amounts to, he asserts, a massive and systemic coverup. The United States, according to Lifton, has routinely engaged in the "suppression of information that might put a human face on what happened to the men, women, and children of Hiroshima and Nagasaki," commented Mike Moore in the *Bulletin of the Atomic Scientists.* The authors seek to disprove the commonly held belief that the dropping of the atomic bomb helped to speed the end of World War II. They argue that, even six decades later, there is a "lasting, harmful impact of Hiroshima on American society" in the form of acceptance of the presence and use of nuclear weapons, arms buildups, governmental secrecy, and denial and suppression of information on radiation's influence on health, remarked a *Publishers Weekly* reviewer. "*Hiroshima in America* is an evocative book that ought to be read by anyone who believes that the people of the United States have never faced up to horror that was committed in their name 50 years ago," Moore concluded. "Only by acknowledging that an essentially decent nation committed a grossly im-

moral act can we Americans renew ourselves and take command of our 'lethal technology'"

In *Destroying the World to Save It: Aum Shinrikyo, Apocalyptic Violence, and the New Global Terrorism,* Lifton deeply profiles the Japanese doomsday cult notorious for releasing deadly sarin gas on the Tokyo subway, killing eleven and injuring thousands. He explores the "psychological traits of the mostly educated followers of Aum's guru," Shoiko Asahara, noted a *Publishers Weekly* reviewer. In addition, Lifton considers the psychological aspects of the group's aims and motives. He describes the characteristics of Aum's belief system as a combination of New Age religion, Buddhism, and apocalyptic thinking. Lifton offers insight into the daily life of Aum members and into the rationalizations that Aum members use to justify their beliefs and behaviors. Lifton also looks at some other well-known cults in the United States, including Heaven's Gate, the Jim Jones and Charles Manson cults, and the various white supremacist groups at large in America, comparing their characteristics to those of Aum Shinrikyo. Stephen L. Hupp, writing in *Library Journal,* called the book a "gripping work," while *Booklist* reviewer David Pitt declared it to be "an intelligent, ambitious exploration of the power of cults and a definite eye-opener."

In *Who Owns Death? Capital Punishment, the American Conscience, and the End of Executions,* Lifton and coauthor Greg Mitchell look carefully at the historical, social, and ethical aspects of the death penalty in America, "highlighting the faulty logic behind it as well as its inherent conflict with the nation's moral conscience," noted Philip Y. Blue in *Library Journal.* The authors provide a history of executions in America, with information on the various methods used and data on patterns of conviction. Lifton and Mitchell assign culpability to every person involved in the lengthy bureaucratic process of establishing, applying, and carrying out a death sentence, from judges and juries to defense attorneys and state legislators. The authors seek to demonstrate the weaknesses and flaws of the death penalty system by shifting the blame from a nameless, monolithic, and conscienceless "state" to the individuals whose actions and attitudes contribute directly to moving a human being closer toward legally sanctioned death. In the book, the authors look at a number of dreadfully mishandled executions, including a case in which the convicted person's head caught on fire during electrocution. They stress the arbitrary nature of the death penalty and how it has not been applied consistently. They also make it clear that the common perception that the public at large favors the death penalty is false. Lifton and Mitchell assert that recent concerns over death penalty issues, including such factors as DNA-based exonerations and wrongful convictions, will eventually lead to the abolishment of the death penalty in the United States. An *Economist* reviewer called the book "an impassioned and informative piece of writing on a melancholy subject," while David Pitt, writing in *Booklist,* named it "an intelligent, rigorous, thought-provoking book." Reviewer Chris Byrd, writing in *Sojourners,* concluded: "In helping readers understand that people like themselves kill in their name and revealing their doubts about death's ownership, *Who Owns Death?* should, nonetheless, compel the ambivalent to reconsider their positions on capital punishment."

In *Superpower Syndrome: America's Apocalyptic Confrontation with the World,* Lifton sounds a caution on the United States's seeming determination to engage aggressively with those nations that it feels threatens its existence as a global superpower. Worse, Lifton suggests, America as a superpower now feels as though it must control history, not merely make it along with its allies. The current mindset of the American superpower, according to Lifton, is characterized by a deep sense of entitlement and complete freedom to pursue its goals. This sense was sharpened by the terrorist attacks of 9/11, which hardened American resolve to recover from the blow and vigorously reassert itself as a superpower that cannot be trifled with and belittled. Lifton expresses his belief that "American and Islamist forces are on an apocalyptic crash course" in their determination to wipe out what each perceives as evil, and in their rush to rebuild global civilization in a manner consistent with their own beliefs and worldview, noted a reviewer in the *Middle East Journal.* The author suggests that the United States would benefit from removing itself from this self-perpetuating cycle of belligerence and aggrandizement, easing away from its constant attempts to maintain its status as global superpower. He also sees the War on Terror as a manifestation of apocalyptic thinking because of its ill-defined parameters but also because of its stated goal of eradicating an equally ill-defined and amorphous "evil" at large in the world. Such a war can never come to an end, claims Lifton; apart from seeking justice against those who attacked American home soil in September, 2001, a war on "evil" can never end because evil as a concept can never be eradicated. Still, Lifton believes that the United States can remove itself from the pattern of increasing violence and confrontation. "With guarded hope, Lifton provides a complex yet clearly articulated roadmap to national self-reflection rather than international destruction," commented a *Publishers Weekly* reviewer. Jack Forman, writing in *Library Journal,* found Lifton's book to be a "clearly and forcefully written manifesto."

BIOGRAPHICAL AND CRITICAL SOURCES:

BOOKS

Erikson, Erik, *Young Man Luther: A Study in Psychoanalysis and History,* Norton (New York, NY), 1958.

Erikson, Erik, *Gandhi's Truth: On the Origins of Militant Nonviolence,* Norton (New York, NY), 1968.

Lifton, Robert Jay, *The Nazi Doctors: Medical Killing and the Psychology of Genocide,* Basic Books (New York, NY), 1986, with a new preface by the author, Basic Books (New York, NY), 2000.

Lifton, Robert Jay, and Eric Markusen, *The Genocidal Mentality: Nazi Holocaust and Nuclear Threat,* Basic Books, 1990.

Rank, Otto, *Der Doppelgaenger: Eine Psychoanalytische Studie,* Internationaler Psychoanalytischer Verlag, 1925, translation by Harry Tucker, Jr., published as *The Double: A Psychoanalytic Study,* University of North Carolina Press (Chapel Hill), 1971.

PERIODICALS

American Prospect, June 4, 2001, Gara Lamarche, review of *Who Owns Death? Capital Punishment, the American Conscience, and the End of Executions,* p. 40.

Booklist, October 15, 1993, Brian McCombie, review of *The Protean Self: Human Resilience in an Age of Fragmentation,* p. 397; September 15, 1999, David Pitt, review of *Destroying the World to Save It: Aum Shinrikyo, Apocalyptic Violence, and the New Global Terrorism,* p. 1999; November 15, 2000, David Pitt, review of *Who Owns Death?,* p. 592.

Bulletin of the Atomic Scientists, July-August, 1995, Mike Moore, review of *Hiroshima in America: Fifty Years of Denial,* p. 73.

Economist, December 16, 2000, "On Death Row; Capital Punishment in America," review of *Who Owns Death?,* p. 5.

Journal of the History of the Behavioral Sciences, spring, 2003, Christine Leuenberger, review of *Beyond Invisible Walls: The Psychological Legacy of Soviet Trauma, East European Therapists, and Their Patients,* p. 183.

Library Journal, September 1, 1999, Stephen L. Hupp, review of *Destroying the World to Save It,* p. 216; December, 2000, Philip Y. Blue, review of *Who Owns Death?,* p. 162; December, 2003, Jack Forman, review of *Superpower Syndrome,* p. 143; April 15, 2004, review of *Home from the War.*

Middle East Journal, winter, 2004, review of *Superpower Syndrome,* p. 168.

Nation, May 6, 1968, review of *Death in Life,* p. 604; November 9, 1970, review of *Boundaries,* p. 470.

New Statesman, March 29, 1991, Adam Roberts, review of *The Genocidal Mentality,* p. 31.

Newsweek, February 19, 1968, review of *Death in Life,* p. 20; October 7, 1968, review of *Revolutionary Immortality,* p. 108; June 18, 1973, review of *Home from the War,* p. 1569; March 2, 1987, David Gates, review of *The Future of Immortality,* p. 76.

New York Review of Books, March 28, 1968, review of *Death in Life,* p. 15; January 16, 1969, review of *Revolutionary Immortality,* p. 5; June 28, 1973, review of *Home from the War,* p. 22; October 31, 1974, review of *Living and Dying,* p. 6; May 28, 1987, Neal Ascherson, review of *The Nazi Doctors,* p. 29; October 25, 1990, Ian Buruma, review of *The Genocidal Mentality,* p. 15.

New York Times, September 30, 1968, review of *Revolutionary Immortality,* p. 45; February 6, 1970, Christopher Lehmann-Haupt, review of *History and Human Survival,* p. 35; August 6, 1973, Christopher Lehmann-Haupt, review of *Home from the War,* p. 29; July 26, 1979, Robert Jay Lifton, "On the Nuclear Altar"; November 4, 1979, Terrence Des Pres, review of *The Broken Connection,* p. 9; March 1, 1981, review of *The Broken Connection,* p. 31; September 25, 1986, Christopher Lehmann-Haupt, review of *The Nazi Doctors,* p. C29.

New York Times Book Review, March 31, 1968, Jerome D. Frank, review of *Death in Life,* p. 10; August 2, 1970, review of *History and Human Survival,* p. 2; December 6, 1970, review of *History and Human Survival,* p. 104; June 24, 1973, Richard Locke, review of *Home from the War,* p. 23; December 2, 1973, review of *Home from the War,* p. 74; March 10, 1974, review of *Home from the War;* July 21,

1974, review of *Living and Dying,* p. 6; November 4, 1979, review of *The Broken Connection,* p. 9; November 25, 1979, review of *The Broken Connection,* p. 74; March 1, 1981, review of *The Broken Connection,* p. 31; October 10, 1982, review of *Death in Life,* p. 35; January 16, 1983, John Woodcock, review of *Indefensible Weapons,* p. 18; December 18, 1983, review of *The Broken Connection,* p. 31; October 5, 1986, Bruno Bettelheim, review of *The Nazi Doctors,* p. 1; April 5, 1987, Thomas DePietro, review of *The Future of Immortality,* p. 34; May 27, 1990, Sheila Tobias, review of *The Genocidal Mentality,* p. 19; February 20, 1994, Richard A. Shweder, review of *The Protean Self,* p. 16; July 30, 1995, Michael Sherry, review of *Hiroshima in America,* p. 11.

Progressive, February, 2004, Amitabh Pal, review of *Superpower Syndrome,* p. 40.

Publishers Weekly, September 20, 1993, review of *The Protean Self,* p. 55; May 29, 1995, review of *Hiroshima in America,* p. 74; August 30, 1999, review of *Destroying the World to Save It,* p. 60; November 6, 2000, review of *Who Owns Death?,* p. 84; October 13, 2003, review of *Superpower Syndrome,* p. 65.

Saturday Review, February 3, 1968, review of *Death in Life,* p. 26; March 15, 1969, review of *Revolutionary Immortality,* p. 24; February 21, 1970, Henry S. Resnik, review of *History and Human Survival,* p. 35; February 20, 1971, Emile Capouya, review of *Boundaries,* p. 28; September 25, 1971, reviews of *History and Human Survival* and *Boundaries,* p. 43.

Social Analysis, spring, 2003, Michael Humphrey and Andrew Davidson, "Political Violence and Terrorism," review of *Destroying the World to Save It,* p. 152.

Sojourners, July, 2001, Chris Byrd, review of *Who Owns Death?,* p. 53.

Times Literary Supplement, April 10, 1969, review of *Revolutionary Immortality,* p. 385; July 18, 1975, review of *Living and Dying,* p. 790; June 12, 1978, Sidney Bloch, "Lethal Practice," review of *The Nazi Doctors,* p. 625; December 7, 1979, review of *Six Lives, Six Deaths,* p. 100.

Village Voice, August 15, 1974, review of *Living and Dying,* p. 26; October 14, 1986, review of *The Nazi Doctors,* p. 52.

Washington Post Book World, March 24, 1968, review of *Death in Life,* p. 6; October 20, 1968, review of *Revolutionary Immortality,* p. 5; January 25, 1970, Anthony Storr, review of *History and Human Survival,* p. 5; June 24, 1973, review of *Home from*

the War, p. 3; May 16, 1976, review of *The Life of the Self,* p. 579; April 1, 1979, review of *Six Lives, Six Deaths,* p. E4; December 23, 1979, Anthony Storr, review of *The Broken Connection,* p. 9; February 20, 1983, review of *Indefensible Weapons,* p. 9.

ONLINE

Democracy NOW!, http://www.democracynow.org/ (June 12, 2006), Amy Goodman, transcript of radio interview with Robert Jay Lifton.

NOW Web site, http://www.pbs.org/now/ (October 18, 2002), Bill Moyers, transcript of radio interview with Robert Jay Lifton.

Trauma, Culture, & the Brain Conference Web site, http://www.ptsdconference.org/ (December 17, 2006), biography of Robert Jay Lifton.

Yes!, http://www.yesmagazine.org/ (summer, 2003), Sarah Ruth van Gelder, "Finding Courage," interview with Robert Jay Lifton.*

*   *   *

LOVELL, Mary S. 1941-
(Mary Sybilla Lovell)

PERSONAL: Born October 23, 1941, in Prestatyn, Wales; daughter of William G. and Mary Catherine Shelton; married Clifford C. Lovell, October 22, 1960 (divorced, 1974); married Geoffrey A.H. Watts, July 11, 1992; children: Graeme, Robert. *Politics:* Conservative. *Religion:* Church of England. *Hobbies and other interests:* Flying, sailing, foxhunting, history, travel.

ADDRESSES: Home and office—Stroat, Gloucestershire, England. *Agent*—Robert Ducas, The Barn House, 244 Westside Rd., Norfolk, CT 06058. *E-mail*—mary@lovellbiographies.com.

CAREER: Writer, novelist, lecturer, and accountant. Worked as an accountant and business director, 1963-83, and as a technical writer and documentation manager, 1983-86; writer, 1986—; lecturer on writing and associated topics.

MEMBER: Society of Authors, Royal Overseas League, New Forest Hunt Club, R.S. Surtees Society, Master of Foxhounds Association, Royal Geographical Society (fellow).

WRITINGS:

A Hunting Pageant, Saiga Publishing (Hindhead, Surrey, England), 1981.

Cats as Pets, Saiga Publishing (Hindhead, Surrey, England), 1982.

Straight on till Morning: The Biography of Beryl Markham, St. Martin's Press (New York, NY), 1987.

(Editor) Beryl Markham, *The Splendid Outcast* (stories), North Point Press (Berkeley, CA), 1987.

The Sound of Wings: The Life of Amelia Earhart, St. Martin's Press (New York, NY), 1989.

Cast No Shadow: The Life of the American Spy Who Changed the Course of World War II, Pantheon (New York, NY), 1992.

Rebel Heart: The Scandalous Life of Jane Digby, Norton (New York, NY), 1995, published as *A Scandalous Life: The Biography of Jane Digby el Mezrab,* Richard Cohen Books (London, England), 1995.

A Rage to Live: A Biography of Richard and Isabel Burton, Norton (New York, NY), 1998.

The Mitford Girls: The Biography of an Extraordinary Family, Little, Brown (London, England), 2001, published as *The Sisters: The Saga of the Mitford Family,* Norton (New York, NY), 2002.

Bess of Hardwick: First Lady of Chatsworth, 1527-1608, Little, Brown (London, England), 2005, published as *Bess of Hardwick: Empire Builder,* Norton (New York, NY), 2006.

Contributor to periodicals, including *Cosmopolitan* and *Marie Claire.* Author of introduction to *The Perfumed Garden of Cheikh Nefzaoui: A Manual of Arabian Erotology,* Signet (New York, NY), 1999.

Some of Lovell's works have been translated into French, German, and Danish.

SIDELIGHTS: British writer Mary S. Lovell has received acclaim for her biographical portraits of adventurous people who challenged the mores of their times. The first of her books, *Straight on till Morning: The Biography of Beryl Markham,* documents the life of the colorful, tempestuous pilot who in 1936 became the first person to fly solo from England to North America. Markham grew up in Africa, was married three times, knew how to repair an airplane engine, and had trained several successful racehorses. She was, according to Lovell, a beautiful, strong, eccentric woman with a magnetic personality. Jonathan Yardley wrote in the *Washington Post Book World* that Markham "seems, in fact, to have been a character rarely encountered in life or in art: the female equivalent of a rogue."

Lovell penned the biography after meeting Markham in 1986 and becoming her friend. Lovell helped care for the aging woman during the final months of her life. The author described Markham as "highly intelligent and totally single-minded" in an interview with London *Times* reviewer Sally Brompton. *New York Times Book Review* contributor Diane Ackerman observed that *Straight on till Morning* "is the story of a phenomenal life told convincingly by someone fascinated by her subject. . . . Every page is filled with revelations, gossip, and fascinating details about Markham and the people she knew." Ackerman further commented that "Lovell's superbly researched biography is likely to be definitive."

Lovell followed *Straight on till Morning* with *The Sound of Wings: The Life of Amelia Earhart.* The biography recounts the exploits of Earhart, the aviator who gained fame by becoming the first woman to complete a solo flight across the Atlantic Ocean in 1932. Earhart's unexplained disappearance while flying over the Pacific in 1937 has long been a source of mystery, but as Lovell once told *CA, The Sound of Wings* is "*not* a theory on her disappearance." The book is, instead, a biography that follows Earhart from her quiet childhood to her years of celebrity in the 1930s. Rhoda Koenig described the story of Earhart's life as "extraordinary," in her *New York* review, and declared that Lovell writes about Earhart with "expertise and understanding." Similarly, *New York Times Book Review* contributor David M. Kennedy noted that Earhart's "life and death were the stuff of tragedy" and reported that Lovell manages to "vividly evoke that tragic aspect." *The Sound of Wings,* the critic added, provides "fascinating detail both on Earhart's relationship with her husband . . . and on technical aspects of her final flight."

Lovell also penned *Cast No Shadow: The Life of the American Spy Who Changed the Course of World War II,* which was published in 1992. *Cast No Shadow* chronicles the life of Amy Elizabeth Thorpe Pack, who spied for the Allies during World War II, often getting privileged information by seducing enemy officers. The American wife of a British diplomat, Pack was able to produce Italian and French Vichy code books for the Allies. Brooke Kroeger, reviewing *Cast No Shadow* in the *New York Times Book Review,* commended Lovell's "fast-paced narrative" and vivid descriptions.

Lovell's 1995 publication, *Rebel Heart: The Scandalous Life of Jane Digby,* explores the highly unconventional life of a Victorian era beauty whose 1830 divorce made the front page of the London *Times.* Jane Digby, an English aristocrat, defied the morals of her times by engaging in multiple marriages and infidelities; in midlife she married a bedouin sheik many years her junior. In *Booklist,* Brad Hooper noted that Digby's "incredible existence is told respectfully and authentically in all its full color" in Lovell's book. A *Publishers Weekly* reviewer felt that Lovell "brings her unconventional subject to life in this outstanding portrait."

A Rage to Live: A Biography of Richard and Isabel Burton is a dual biography of the notorious British explorer and linguist Richard Burton, and his equally adventurous wife, Isabel. Burton's travels in Africa, the Middle East, and India are documented in his own memoirs, but in this work Lovell deepens readers' understandings of the Burton marriage and the role Isabel played in popularizing and publishing her husband's works. In the *New York Times Book Review,* James R. Kincaid described the book as "an extraordinary biography" that offers proof that previous biographers of the couple "have made a set of serious blunders in understanding Isabel, the marriage, Burton and the accomplishment of both people." *New Republic* correspondent Fouad Ajami wrote of *A Rage to Live:* "Meticulously researched, it overwhelms the other accounts and it has a fuller treatment of [Burton's] wife Isabel than anything attempted in earlier books." John Reader commented in the *National Review,* "It is not often that a book comes along which inspires a serious reconsideration of all that had previously been written on its subject. But *A Rage to Live* is just such a book." Kincaid concluded that Lovell "writes with a zeal that seems to ring right out of Isabel herself. This biography is both admirably scholarly and, now and then, engagingly reckless. Lovell has transformed our view of the Burtons and their accomplishments."

Few aristocratic families have come under greater scrutiny than the Mitfords, an eccentric clan of six sisters and a brother who came of age in the early-to mid-twentieth century. Born into a slightly impoverished household, the six Mitford sisters—Nancy, Diana, Unity, Pamela, Jessica, and Deborah—all managed to court controversy in one manner or another. Lovell's biography gives equal time to the exploits of all six women, although their paths verged widely during the Second World War and afterwards. Robert Gottlieb, writing in the *New York Times Book Review,* found *The Sisters: The Saga of the Mitford Family* "fascinating the way all great family stories are fascinating." The critic added: "In her tapestry of the sisters' lives, Lovell has handled some of the big things very well. It's not easy to keep six narratives going at once, particularly when the lives of your subjects start to diverge. Yet *The Sisters* keeps track of everyone with a minimum of confusion; things are revealed in a straightforward and sensible order, so that we always know where we are. Even more important, she has managed to present everyone both clearly and with sympathy." A *Publishers Weekly* contributor felt that the book "rises with aplomb to the challenges of a group biography, deftly weaving together the narrative threads . . . to create a fascinating account of a fascinating family." In *Library Journal,* Amy Strong complimented the book as "an engrossing narrative" and "a captivating read." Gottlieb concluded: "This is a book that will educate those who hope to understand the Mitfords' hold on the imagination of an entire era and entertain those who enjoy an upper-class family saga. It's Upstairs without the Downstairs."

In *Bess of Hardwick: Empire Builder,* first published in England as *Bess of Hardwick: First Lady of Chatsworth, 1527-1608,* Lovell profiles one of the most powerful and formidable women of Tudor and Elizabethan-era England. She uses Bess's successful and eventful life as an example of how "education, connections, marriage and property management shaped the life of women in the sixteenth century," noted a *Publishers Weekly* reviewer. Bess was born in 1527, the fifth daughter of a nobleman in Derbyshire whose fortunes were on the wane. At the age of fifteen, Bess entered into the first of a series of four prosperous, fortuitous marriages that left her increasingly wealthy and schooled in the methods of acquiring land and capital. Her first marriage ended with her widowed after only two years. Her second marriage, to Sir William Cavendish, Henry VIII's treasurer, involved her deeply in land purchasing and speculation. After Cavendish's death, Bess married Sir William St. Loe, the man Lovell believes was her one true love in life. After St. Loe died suddenly and mysteriously in 1564, Bess made her fourth, final, and probably most important marriage, to the Earl of Shrewsbury, considered the richest man in England at the time. Through these marriages, Bess rose to become the second richest woman in England, outclassed in wealth only by Queen Elizabeth herself. In addition to

her financial success, Bess was also involved with some of the most notable characters of her day. She served in royal households during the reign of the notorious King Henry VIII. In her later years, along with the Earl of Shrewsbury, she helped guard the unfortunate Mary, Queen of Scots. Bess also secretly arranged a marriage between her daughter and Margaret Lennox's younger son, and (unsuccessfully) groomed the child of that union, Lady Arbella, to succeed Elizabeth on the throne of England. The biographer "has synthesized admirably a staggering amount of information here (in lineage alone), and she presents it with verve," creating "a fascinating life within an endlessly fascinating era," commented a *Kirkus Reviews* critic. Alexander Waugh, writing in the *Independent* about the English edition, remarked that Lovell "has written one of those biographies in which the reader really doesn't want the subject to die." A reviewer in *Bookseller* described Lovell's work as "a remarkable biography," while *Library Journal* contributor Tessa L.H. Minchew declared it a "meticulously researched and riveting tale."

Lovell once told *CA:* "Writing a biography is writing history. One is therefore obliged to stick ruthlessly to the facts, so it is not surprising that two-thirds of my work on any book consists of research. If I find a piece of information that I cannot substantiate elsewhere— hearsay, for example—I will only use it if it seems absolutely vital to the story and in those cases I quote that source and stress that I have been unable to substantiate it. My books contain thousands of facts relating to my subjects and the times in which they lived, and I receive hundreds of letters from readers, but I get very few letters suggesting corrections, though I do get offered additional information for which I am always grateful. I enjoy writing about adventurous women, especially those who managed to break out of the conventional mold allotted to them, before women enjoyed today's freedoms."

BIOGRAPHICAL AND CRITICAL SOURCES:

PERIODICALS

African Business, December, 1998, Stephen Williams, review of *A Rage to Live: A Biography of Richard and Isabel Burton,* p. 25.

Biography, summer, 2006, Adam Goodheart, review of *Bess of Hardwick: Empire Builder,* p. 509.

Booklist, October 15, 1995, Brad Hooper, review of *Rebel Heart: The Scandalous Life of Jane Digby,* p. 382; December 1, 2001, Allen Weakland, review of

The Sisters: The Saga of the Mitford Family, p. 626; February 15, 2006, Brad Hooper, review of *Bess of Hardwick: Empire Builder*, p. 37.

Bookseller, June 17, 2005, review of *Bess of Hardwick: Empire Builder*, p. 38.

Economist, November 3, 2001, "Blame the Governess: English Lives."

Independent (London, England), October 9, 2005, Alexander Waugh, review of *Bess of Hardwick: First Lady of Chatsworth, 1527-1608.*

Kirkus Reviews, February 1, 2006, review of *Bess of Hardwick: Empire Builder*, p. 123.

Library Journal, October 1, 1998, Julie Still, review of *A Rage to Live*, p. 103; November 1, 2001, Amy Strong, review of *The Sisters*, p. 102; March 1, 2006, Tessa L.H. Minchew, review of *Bess of Hardwick: Empire Builder*, p. 100.

National Review, December 7, 1998, John Reader, "Two for the Road," p. 67.

New Republic, January 18, 1999, Fouad Ajami, "The Fire of Great Designs," p. 27.

New York, December 4, 1989, Rhoda Koenig, review of *The Sound of Wings*, p. 148.

New York Times, June 25, 2006, Adam Goodheart, "Elizabeth 1.5," review of *Bess of Hardwick: Empire Builder.*

New York Times Book Review, August 23, 1987, Diane Ackerman, "The Splendid Cast," review of *Straight on till Morning*, p. 1; November 26, 1989, David M. Kennedy, review of *The Sound of Wings*, p. 1; June 21, 1992, Brooke Kroeger, review of *Cast No Shadow*, p. 16; January 17, 1999, James R. Kincaid, "A Wild, Roving, Vagabond Life," p. 14; February 17, 2002, Robert Gottlieb, "The Might of the Mitfords," p. 12.

Publishers Weekly, September 4, 1995, review of *Rebel Heart*, p. 60; November 12, 2001, review of *The Sisters*, p. 46; February 13, 2006, review of *Bess of Hardwick: Empire Builder*, p. 75.

Reference & Research Book News, August, 2006, review of *Bess of Hardwick: Empire Builder.*

Spectator, August 20, 2005, Anne Somerset, "House-Building and Husbandry," review of *Bess of Hardwick: First Lady of Chatsworth, 1527-1608*, p. 39.

Time, October 5, 1987, John Skow, review of *Straight on till Morning*, p. 83; January 21, 2002, Laura Miller, "Mad about the Mitfords," p. 142.

Times (London, England), July 15, 1987, Sally Brompton, interview with Mary S. Lovell.

Washington Post Book World, August 30, 1987, Jonathan Yardley, "Beryl Markham: Flying High," review of *Straight on till Morning*, p. 3; June 26, 1988, review of *Straight on till Morning*, p. 12.

ONLINE

Mary S. Lovell Home Page, http://www.lovell biographies.com (December 17, 2006).

WGBH Forum Network, http://www.forum-network.org/ (December 17, 2006), biography of Mary S. Lovell.*

*   *   *

LOVELL, Mary Sybilla
See LOVELL, Mary S.

M

MacQUEEN, John 1929-

PERSONAL: Born February 13, 1929, in Glasgow, Scotland; son of William Lochhead (a medical technician) and Grace Palmer (a nurse) MacQueen; married Winifred Wallace McWalter (a teacher), June 22, 1953; children: Hector, Angus, Donald. *Ethnicity:* "Caucasian." *Education:* University of Glasgow, M.A., 1950; Christ's College, Cambridge, B.A., 1952, M.A., 1954. *Politics:* "None." *Religion:* Christian. *Hobbies and other interests:* Poetry, walking, listening to music (mainly classical), archaeology, some forms of mathematics and philosophy, astronomy and physics (especially relativity and quantum physics), reading science fiction.

ADDRESSES: Home—Stranraer, Scotland. *E-mail*—jackmacqueen@aol.com.

CAREER: Washington University, St. Louis, MO, assistant professor of English, 1956-59; University of Edinburgh, Edinburgh, Scotland, lecturer, 1959-63, Masson Professor of Medieval and Renaissance Literature, 1963-71, professor of Scottish literature and oral tradition, 1971-88, endowment fellow, 1988-92, director of School of Scottish Studies, 1969-88. *Military service:* Royal Air Force, flying officer, 1954-56.

MEMBER: Royal Astronomical Society (fellow), Folklore Society (honorary member), Royal Society of Edinburgh (fellow).

AWARDS, HONORS: D.Litt., National University of Ireland, 1985; Fletcher of Saltoun Award for services to Scotland, Saltire Society, 1990.

WRITINGS:

St. Nynia, Oliver & Boyd (Edinburgh, Scotland), 1961, 3rd edition with supplement, John Donald (Edinburgh, Scotland), 1990.

(Editor, with T. Scott) *The Oxford Book of Scottish Verse,* Oxford University Press (Oxford, England), 1966.

Robert Henryson, Oxford University Press (Oxford, England), 1967.

Ballattis of Luve, Edinburgh University Press (Edinburgh, Scotland), 1970.

Allegory, Methuen (London, England), 1970.

(Editor, with wife Winifred MacQueen) *A Choice of Scottish Verse, 1470-1570,* Faber & Faber (London, England), 1972.

The Enlightenment and Scottish Literature, Scottish Academic Press (Edinburgh, Scotland), 1982–89.

Progress and Poetry, Scottish Academic Press (Edinburgh, Scotland), 1982.

Numerology, Edinburgh University Press (Edinburgh, Scotland), 1985

The Rise of the Historical Novel, Scottish Academic Press (Edinburgh, Scotland), 1989.

(Editor, with Winifred MacQueen) *"The Scotichronicon" in Latin and English,* Aberdeen University Press (Aberdeen, Scotland), Books 3-4, 1989, Books 1-2, 1993, Book 5, 1995.

(Editor) *Humanism in Renaissance Scotland,* Edinburgh University Press (Edinburgh, Scotland), 1990.

Place-Names in the Rhinns of Galloway and Luce Valley, Stranroes and District Local History Trust (Stranroes, Scotland), 2002.

Complete and Full with Numbers, Rodopi (New York, NY), 2006.

Contributor to scholarly journals. Editor of *Scottish Studies,* 1969-83.

SIDELIGHTS: John MacQueen once told *CA:* "I am interested in continuity and change between historical periods up to and including the present. I was trained as a classicist and find the period from Plato to Plotinus particularly interesting, both in itself and its effect on later generations. The interaction between philosophy and early Christianity goes far to produce the culture which dominated the Middle Ages and Renaissance until it was challenged by the concept of progress and the rise of science, particularly astronomy. The dominant voice of the earlier period is poetry, of the latter the novel. Additional insight may be found (oddly enough) in the study of the historical sequence and relations to be found in place-names. My writing is an attempt to investigate aspects of the situation.

"Strong influences have been the writings of H.M. and N.K. Chadwick (the teaching also of the latter), Gilbert Murray, E.R. Curtius, E.R. Dodds, John Bryce, and Alastair Fowler."

BIOGRAPHICAL AND CRITICAL SOURCES:

PERIODICALS

Times Literary Supplement, April 20, 1990, G.W.S. Barrow, review of *"The Scotichronicon" in Latin and English,* Books 3-4.

*   *   *

MANTEL, Hilary 1952-
(Hilary Mary Mantel)

PERSONAL: Born July 6, 1952, in Derbyshire, England; married Gerald McEwen (a geologist), September 23, 1972. *Education:* Attended London School of Economics and Political Science, 1970; University of Sheffield, Jur.B., 1973.

ADDRESSES: Agent—A.M. Heath & Co Ltd., 6 Warwick Court, Holborn, London WC1R 5DJ, England.

CAREER: Novelist. Worked in a variety of jobs, including salesperson and social worker in a geriatric hospital. and Lived and worked in Botswana as a secondary school teacher, 1977-82; lived and worked in Jeddah, Saudi Arabia, 1983-86.

MEMBER: British Society of Authors.

AWARDS, HONORS: Shiva Naipaul Memorial Prize for travel writing, 1987; fellow, Royal Society of Literature, 1990; Cheltenham Festival Prize, Southern Arts Literary Prize, and Winifred Holtby Award, all 1990, all for *Fludd; Sunday Express* Book of the Year award, 1992, for *A Place of Greater Safety;* Hawthornden Prize, 1999, for *The Giant, O'Brien;* Mind Book of the Year Award, 2005, for *Giving up the Ghost;* Commander of the Order of the British Empire, 2006.

WRITINGS:

NOVELS

Every Day Is Mother's Day, Chatto & Windus (London, England), 1985, Holt (New York, NY), 2000.
Vacant Possession, Chatto & Windus (London, England), 1986, Holt (New York, NY), 2000.
Eight Months on Ghazzah Street, Viking (London, England), 1988, Holt (New York, NY), 1997.
Fludd, Viking (London, England), 1989, Viking (New York, NY), 2000.
A Place of Greater Safety, Atheneum (New York, NY), 1993.
A Change of Climate, Atheneum (New York, NY), 1994.
An Experiment in Love, Holt (New York, NY), 1996.
The Giant, O'Brien, Holt (New York, NY), 1998.
Beyond Black, Holt (New York, NY), 2005.

OTHER

Learning to Talk: Short Stories, Fourth Estate (London, England), 2003.
Giving Up the Ghost (memoir), Holt (New York, NY), 2003.

Contributor to *Best Short Stories of 1987,* Heinemann (London, England), 1987, *The Best of Best Short Stories 1986-95,* Minerva, 1995, and *The Daily Telegraph Book of Contemporary Short Stories,* 1995. Film critic for *Spectator,* 1987-91. Contributor of short stories and reviews to periodicals, including *London Magazine, London Review of Books, Literary Review, New York Review of Books, New York Times, Los Angeles Times,* and *Encounter.*

SIDELIGHTS: A favorite of many readers in Great Britain since 1985, Hilary Mantel was relatively unknown in North America until the publication of her 1998 novel, *The Giant, O'Brien,* and the release, in the United States, of such acclaimed earlier works as *Every Day Is Mother's Day, Fludd,* and *Vacant Possession.* Reviewing Mantel's 2000 novel, *Fludd,* Sally E. Parry noted in *Review of Contemporary Fiction* that Mantel's prose is striking and witty, especially when the out of the ordinary happens. Her vision of the world is bleakly humorous and allows for the possibility, however remote, of a kind of grace. Mantel became the third woman to win the coveted Hawthornden Prize in eighty years when she was awarded it in 1999 for *The Giant, O'Brien.*

Born in a small town in the north of England, Mantel did not set out to be a writer; indeed, "I was the first person in my family to go to university," she explained to *Publishers Weekly* interviewer Jean Richardson. "And in my teens I believed I could do anything." Mantel studied law at the London School of Economics, but eschewed a career in politics to take a job as a social worker. When she realized she wanted to pursue writing, Mantel began to seek out quiet places to contemplate and create. One favorite spot was in a department store where she worked. Mantel would bunker down in "the sheepskin department in August," as she related to Richardson. "I was left alone for hours and hours and I could form up my sentences and marshal my thoughts." The budding author set a big goal for herself: an epic novel set in Revolutionary France.

Mantel's marriage to geologist Gerald McEwen took her to Botswana, where she taught in an elementary school and treasured the isolation as an environment for writing. With the French Revolution story stalled, Mantel decided to try something more contemporary in theme, and eventually found a publisher for her debut novel, *Every Day Is Mother's Day.*

Every Day Is Mother's Day was greeted enthusiastically by British critics, *London Magazine* contributor John Mellors providing a typical assessment in calling Mantel's literary debut "an accomplished novel of striking originality." Based loosely on the author's experiences, *Every Day Is Mother's Day* follows Isabel, a young social worker who takes on the case of a mentally retarded girl who lives with her emotionally disturbed mother. At once a "simple black comedy" and "a savage satire on social services" in the view of *Daily Mail*

reviewer Auberon Waugh, *Every Day Is Mother's Day* depicts "one of the bleakest commentaries on contemporary English life I have every read." The *Daily Mail* columnist went on to herald the author as a major new talent.

Mantel followed *Every Day Is Mother's Day* with a sequel, *Vacant Possession.* The 1986 novel takes place ten years later as the now-grown daughter, Muriel, is released from a mental institution and bent on wreaking revenge on a variety of victims, including social worker Isabel. The novel, stated Danise Hoover in *Booklist,* "will make you laugh, but you won't feel comfortable about it."

Mantel increased her literary stature with several more novels, including *A Place of Greater Safety,* a French Revolution tale that took "book of the year" honors in England. 1994's *A Change of Climate* focuses on an altrusitic couple who pick up the lost causes of a myriad of urban down-and-outers. As James Barron explained in his *New Statesman & Society* review, "Mantel takes as her theme the opposing forces of free will and fate wondering if we do have any control over our destiny or whether it is set down by some malicious divinity." Calling the novel "ambitious," Barron added that the work contained structural problems that made its outcome predictable. A critic for *Publishers Weekly* had a different take, calling the novel "beautifully written but high-strung," and praising Mantel for her "subtle foreshadowings" and "suspense to spare."

An Experiment in Love follows a young woman from her modest Lancashire upbringing to her student years at London University, where she rejects her working-class background. Dubbing Mantel's style "dry" and "ironical," *Booklist* reviewer Joanne Wilkinson added that *An Experiment in Love* "captures the pressure-cooker atmosphere of an elite university and the indelible bonds imposed by social class." "Irony prevails stoutly over sentimentality," added a *Publishers Weekly* critic of the 1996 novel, "while the finale delivers a surprising twist of horror that will shake readers to the core.

Mantel's 1998 historical novel, *The Giant, O'Brien,* is set in eighteenth-century London and based on actual events. Charles O'Brien, a man of extraordinary height and great ambition, arrives from Ireland to seek his fortune as a showman. The public is initially entranced by "the Giant," but as the novelty wears off, O'Brien's prospects dwindle and his health begins to fail. Into the picture comes physician John Hunter. Hunter, "obsessed with anatomical dissection and experimentation," according to a *Booklist* review, recognizes a fatal condition in O'Brien, and sets his own agenda to possess O'Brien's remains after the Giant dies.

More than one critic saw a deeper theme in *The Giant, O'Brien:* The author, said Richardson, "makes no concessions to the reader, who is asked to accompany the giant—a metaphor for the Irish body politic—on a journey through the squalor of Georgian London. He is a storyteller, a touching, childlike freak who finds that his immense height is only a five-minute wonder, and that he is worth more dead than alive. Underlying the story is the conflict between England and Ireland, between poetry and materialism."

The Giant, O'Brien "demands to be read . . . like a fable," remarked an *Economist* critic, "for while it roots around in the stench and swill of life, it is at the same time a highly figurative tale about truth versus fact, about meaning, and the power of language both to carry and destroy it." Mantel, the article concluded, "is herself a demonstration of her novel's theme, with an ear worthy of her giant."

In her 2003 memoir, *Giving Up the Ghost,* Mantel details her childhood in Britain during the 1950s and 1960s and documents her decade-long struggle with undiagnosed endometriosis, which left her unable to have children. Calling the book "extraordinary," an *Economist* reviewer remarked that Mantel "catches the very essence of the growing child, the small sharp-eyed observer in the corner of the room who is herself ignored and not explained to, and carries that persona through—as we all do—to her years of ostensible maturity." *New Statesman* contributor Carmen Calill concurred, labelling the memoir a "masterpiece" and adding, "commenting on a book as good as this requires firm control over superlatives."

In her 2005 novel, *Beyond Black,* Mantel extends the imagery of the "ghosts" in her memoir by exploring the world of psychics. Recently divorced Colette meets a clairvoyant, Alison, and gradually becomes an integral part of her life and her work. The two women negotiate a tricky line between the personal and professional, with Alison attempting to help Colette rid herself of a pesky ghost. Critics remarked on the humor and intelligence on display in Mantel's writing. A *Publishers*

Weekly reviewer noted that "this witty, matter-of-fact look at the psychic milieu reveals a supernatural world that can be as mundane as the world of carpet salesmen and shopkeepers," while a *Kirkus Reviews* contributor called the novel "superbly odd, but still superb." *New Statesman* reviewer Amanda Craig, while agreeing that the novel is "densely written, with confidence and wit," felt that the characters were too unlikable and the portrayal too depressing. But D.J. Taylor, writing in the *Spectator,* praised *Beyond Black* as "relentless and at the same time wonderfully funny."

BIOGRAPHICAL AND CRITICAL SOURCES:

PERIODICALS

Booklist, May 1, 1996, Joanne Wilkinson, review of *An Experiment in Love,* p. 1488; October 15, 1998, Margaret Flanagan, review of *The Giant, O'Brien,* p. 404; February 15, 2000, p. 1081; April 15, 2000, James Klise, review of *Fludd,* p. 1524.

Daily Mail, March 28, 1985, Auberon Waugh, review of *Every Day Is Mother's Day.*

Economist, October 10, 1998, review of *The Giant, O'Brien,* p. 89; December 12, 1998, review of *The Giant, O'Brien;* September 27, 2003, review of *Giving Up the Ghost,* p. 84.

Kirkus Reviews, March 1, 2005, review of *Beyond Black,* p. 251.

Library Journal, April 15, 1996, Debbie Bogenschutz, review of *An Experiment in Love,* p. 123; July, 1997, Ann H. Fisher, review of *A Change of Climate,* p. 126; February 15, 2000, Barbara Love, review of *Vacant Possession,* p. 197.

London Magazine, March, 1985, John Mellors, review of *Every Day Is Mother's Day.*

New Statesman, May 30, 1986, Bill Greenwell, review of *Vacant Possession,* p. 27; September 15, 1989, review of *Fludd,* p. 34; September 4, 1992, Brian Morton, review of *A Place of Greater Safety,* p. 38; March 18, 1994, James Barron, review of *A Change of Climate,* p. 56; May 19, 2003, Carmen Calill, review of *Giving Up the Ghost* p. 48; May 16, 2005, Amanda Craig, review of *Beyond Black,* p. 55.

New York Review of Books, October 8, 1998, John Baylor, review of *The Giant, O'Brien,* p. 12.

New York Times Book Review, July 20, 1997, review of *Eight Months on Ghazzah Street,* p. 9; October 11, 1998, Walter Kendrick, review of *The Giant, O'Brien,* p. 9.

Publishers Weekly, April 1, 1996, review of *An Experiment in Love,* p. 55; June 23, 1997, review of *A Change of Climate,* p. 69; July 14, 1997, review of *Eight Months on Ghazzah Street,* p. 64; July 13, 1998, review of *The Giant, O'Brien,* p. 60; October 5, 1998, Jean Richardson, "Hilary Mantel: The Novelist in Action," p. 60; January 31, 2000, review of *Every Day Is Mother's Day,* p. 81; April 3, 2000, review of *Fludd,* p. 60; April 11, 2005, review of *Beyond Black,* p. 34.

Review of Contemporary Fiction, spring, 2001, Sally E. Parry, review of *Fludd,* p. 207.

Spectator, September 5, 1992, Nigel Spivey, review of *A Place of Greater Safety,* p. 30; March 26, 1994, Anita Brookner, review of *A Change of Climate,* p. 34; March 4, 1995, Anita Brookner, review of *An Experiment in Love,* p. 36; May 7, 2005, D.J. Taylor, review of *Beyond Black,* p. 52.

Times Literary Supplement, June 20, 1986, review of *Vacant Possession,* p. 682; August 28, 1992, David Coward, review of *A Place of Greater Safety,* p. 17; March 25, 1994, Peter Kemp, review of *A Change of Climate,* p. 19; February 24, 1995, Julia O'Faolain, review of *An Experiment in Love,* p. 22; September 4, 1998, David Nokes, review of *The Giant, O'Brien,* p. 10.

World Literature in Review, fall, 1999, Mary Kaiser, review of *The Giant, O'Brien,* p. 737.*

*   *   *

MANTEL, Hilary Mary
   See MANTEL, Hilary

*   *   *

MARTEL, Aimee
   See THURLO, Aimée

*   *   *

MASLOWSKI, Peter 1944-

PERSONAL: Born August 28, 1944, in Cincinnati, OH; son of Karl H. (a naturalist) and Edna H. Maslowski; married Linda A. Pernack, September 16, 1968; children: Jeremy Jed, Laurel Leigh. *Education:* Miami University, Oxford, OH, A.B., 1966; Ohio State University, M.A., 1968, Ph.D., 1972. *Hobbies and other interests:* Tennis, basketball, fishing, birdwatching.

ADDRESSES: Home—Lincoln, NE. *Office*—Department of History, University of Nebraska, Oldfather Hall, Lincoln, NE 68588. *E-mail*—pmaslowski1@unl.edu.

CAREER: University of Nebraska, Lincoln, assistant professor, 1974-78, associate professor of U.S. history, 1978—. Executive board member, *War in History;* member of board of trustees, Society for Military History.

MEMBER: Organization of American Historians, American Military Institute, Southern Historical Association.

AWARDS, HONORS: Teaching award from Amoco Foundation, 1978; College of Arts and Sciences Award for Outstanding Teaching, University of Nebraska, 1986; University-Wide Outstanding Teaching and Instructional Creativity Award, University of Nebraska, 2002.

WRITINGS:

Treason Must Be Made Odious: Military Occupation and Wartime Reconstruction in Nashville, Tennessee, 1862-1865, K.T.O. Press, 1978.

(With Allan R. Millett) *For the Common Defense: A Military History of the United States of America,* Free Press (New York, NY), 1984, 2nd edition, 1994.

Armed with Cameras: The American Military Photographers of World War II, Free Press (New York, NY), 1993.

Looking for a Hero: Staff Sergeant Joe Ronnie Hooper and the Vietnam War, University of Nebraska Press (Lincoln, NE), 2004.

Contributor to history and military journals. Coeditor (with Mark Grimsley) of the "War, Society, and the Military" series, University of Nebraska Press.

SIDELIGHTS: Peter Maslowski, a professor of history, has written several books on the topic of U.S. military history and military figures. His first book, *Treason Must Be Made Odious: Military Occupation and*

Wartime Reconstruction in Nashville, Tennessee, 1862-1865, focuses on a specific aspect of post-Civil War history, while his second book, *For the Common Defense: A Military History of the United States of America,* is much a broader exploration. Maslowski next returned to a more contained topic with his third book, *Armed with Cameras: The American Military Photographers of World War II.* The volume seeks to explain how military photography was first used as a tool for intelligence training. Maslowski, whose father was a combat photographer during World War II, wrote the book based on his research of archival material and interviews he conducted over a twenty-year period.

Critical response to *Armed with Cameras* was predominantly positive. A *Publishers Weekly* contributor applauded the book's "comprehensive detail," while Bradley Jay Buchner, writing in *Armed Forces & Society,* called it "a good read." Although *Oral History Review* contributor Sylvia Danovitch felt that Maslowski's attempts to give life to the personalities of individual military photographers were "less [than] successful," she nevertheless felt that his "ability to convey the magnitude of the photographers' accomplishment is remarkable."

Maslowski next published the biography *Looking for a Hero: Staff Sergeant Joe Ronnie Hooper and the Vietnam War.* He once told *CA:* "I have a strong concern for environmental issues. In the past I worked as a professional wildlife photographer and traveled on the 'Audubon Wildlife Film Series' circuit, showing and narrating films on Arctic and U.S. wildlife."

BIOGRAPHICAL AND CRITICAL SOURCES:

PERIODICALS

Armed Forces & Society, summer, 1996, Bradley Jay Buchner, review of *Armed with Cameras: The American Military Photographers of World War II.*

Booklist, February 15, 2005, review of *Looking for a Hero: Staff Sergeant Joe Ronnie Hooper and the Vietnam War,* p. 10566.

Oral History Review, winter, 1996, Sylvia Danovitch, review of *Armed with Cameras,* p. 116.

Publishers Weekly, September 6, 1993, review of *Armed with Cameras,* p. 76.*

*   *   *

McCARTHY, Charles, Jr.
See McCARTHY, Cormac

McCARTHY, Cormac 1933-
  (Charles Mccarthy, Jr.)

PERSONAL: Born July 20, 1933, in Providence, RI; son of Charles Joseph and Gladys McCarthy; married Lee Holleman, 1961 (divorced); married Anne de Lisle, 1967 (divorced); married Jennifer Winkley, 1998; children: (first marriage) Cullen. *Education:* Attended University of Tennessee, four years.

ADDRESSES: Home—El Paso, TX. *Agent*—Amanda Urban, International Creative Management, 40 W. 57th St., New York, NY 10019.

CAREER: Writer. *Military service:* U.S. Air Force, 1953-56.

AWARDS, HONORS: Ingram-Merrill Foundation grant for creative writing, 1960; American Academy of Arts and Letters traveling fellowship to Europe, 1965-66; William Faulkner Foundation award, 1965, for *The Orchard Keeper;* Rockefeller Foundation grant, 1966; Guggenheim fellowship, 1976; MacArthur Foundation grant, 1981; Jean Stein Award, American Academy and Institution of Arts and Letters, 1991; National Book Award for fiction, 1992, and National Book Critics Award for fiction, both for *All the Pretty Horses;* Lyndhurst Foundation grant; Institute of Arts and Letters award.

WRITINGS:

The Orchard Keeper, Random House (New York, NY), 1965.

Outer Dark, Random House (New York, NY), 1968.

Child of God, Random House (New York, NY), 1974.

The Gardener's Son (teleplay; produced as part of *Visions* series, Public Broadcasting System, 1977), published as *The Gardener's Son: A Screenplay,* Ecco Press (Hopewell, NJ), 1996.

Suttree, Random House (New York, NY), 1979, reprinted, Modern Library (New York, NY), 2002.

Blood Meridian; or, The Evening Redness in the West, Random House (New York, NY), 1985, reprinted with an introduction by Harold Bloom, Modern Library (New York, NY), 2001.

All the Pretty Horses (book one in the "Border Trilogy"), Random House (New York, NY), 1992.

The Crossing (book two in the "Border Trilogy"), Random House (New York, NY), 1994.

Cities of the Plain (book three in the "Border Trilogy"), Random House (New York, NY), 1998.

The Border Trilogy (contains *All the Pretty Horses, The Crossing,* and *Cities of the Plain*), Knopf (New York, NY), 1999.

No Country for Old Men, Knopf (New York, NY), 2005.

The Sunset Limited: A Play in One Act, Vintage International (New York, NY), 2006.

The Road, Knopf (New York, NY), 2006.

Also author of the play *The Stonemason.* Contributor to *Yale Review* and *Sewanee Review.*

ADAPTATIONS: All the Pretty Horses was adapted as a film, 2002; *No Country for Old Men* was adapted as a film; *Blood Meridien* and *The Road* have been optioned for film.

SIDELIGHTS: Charles McCarthy, Jr., better known to readers as Cormac McCarthy, is frequently compared with such Southern-based writers as William Faulkner, Carson McCullers, and Flannery O'Connor. In a *Dictionary of Literary Biography* essay, Dianne L. Cox stated that McCarthy's work has in common with that of the others "a rustic and sometimes dark humor, intense characters, and violent plots; [he] shares as well their development of universal themes within a highly particularized fictional world, their seriousness of vision, and their vigorous exploration of the English language."

McCarthy's early novels were often set in eastern Tennessee, while his later work focuses on the American Southwest. He has often been singled out for his individual prose style—beautifully lyrical yet spare, eschewing commas and totally stripped of quotation marks. This style has been a source of complaint for some reviewers; in a *New York Times* review of McCarthy's *All the Pretty Horses,* for example, critic Herbert Mitgang lamented: "This reader was put off at first by the author's all too writerly writing. His joined words, without hyphenation, and his unpunctuated, breathless sentences, call too much attention to themselves." Kurt Tidmore contended in the *Washington Post Book World,* however, that "the reader is never confused. Sentences punctuate themselves by the natural rhythm of their words. Everything is perfectly clear. The poetic never overwhelms the realistic." In addition,

wrote Madison Smartt Bell in the *New York Times Book Review,* McCarthy's "elaborate and elevated" prose is "used effectively to frame realistic dialogue, for which his ear is deadly accurate." Bell continued: "Difficult as [McCarthy's writing] may sometimes be, it is also overwhelmingly seductive."

Throughout his career, McCarthy has actively avoided public attention, refusing to participate in lecture tours and seldom granting interviews. "Until very recently," observed Bell, "he shunned publicity so effectively that he wasn't even famous for it." Instead, he has concentrated upon crafting his unique and powerful fictions, unaffected by the critical acclaim that is heaped upon him with each new book.

In keeping with McCarthy's reclusive nature, little is known about his early life. He was born Charles McCarthy, Jr., in Providence, Rhode Island, on July 20, 1933, the third of six children in an Irish Catholic family. "Sometime later, he or his family—no one seems to know which—changed his name to Cormac after Cormac MacCarthy, the Irish chieftain who built Blarney Castle," explained *Texas Monthly* contributor Michael Hall. When Cormac was four, he and his family moved to Knoxville, Tennessee, where his father got a job as an attorney for the powerful Tennessee Valley Authority. "After high school, McCarthy studied engineering at the University of Tennessee, then entered the U.S. Air Force. He served in Alaska for a couple of years before returning to Tennessee and reentering the university. He married twice, having a son, Cullen, with his first wife, and living for a period in a renovated barn on a pig farm with his second wife. In 1976, he moved to Texas, the source of much of his inspiration for his most famous works." "In El Paso McCarthy has become a ghost celebrity, an urban legend," Hall wrote. In 1996, the *Texas Monthly* writer continued, several fans spent some time "going through McCarthy's trash and cataloging it . . . to prove that he was not some mythic desert hermit but just as urban as everyone else in the city of more than half a million." "Contrary to popular wisdom, McCarthy is not a recluse," Hall stated. "But he is and always has been an intensely private man and a reluctant public one."

McCarthy's first novel, *The Orchard Keeper,* deals with three people—a young man who is coming of age in the Tennessee mountains, a bootlegger, and an aged orchard keeper—whose lives are intertwined, even though they do not meet until the end of the story.

"Through these characters," wrote Cox, "the novel explores the relationship between individual integrity and independence achievable in the remote natural world of the mountains and the social obligations and strictures imposed by the community of men." J.G. Murray, reviewing *The Orchard Keeper* in *America,* felt that the book is interesting "because it does not seem to be autobiographical and [it] rejects the influence, more bad than good, of the Southern mystique." Murray finds McCarthy's view of adulthood "even more precise and sympathetic than his treatment of youth. And, as everyone knows, it is quite exceptional for young writers to be so objective."

Outer Dark, McCarthy's next novel, is "so centered on guilt and retribution that it is largely structured around scenes of judgment," according to Cox. *Outer Dark* tells the story of Culla and Rinthy, a brother and sister who suffer the consequences of their incest in very different ways. Many critics, such as Guy Davenport, compared McCarthy's style in this book to that of William Faulkner. In a *New York Times Book Review* article, Davenport wrote that *Outer Dark* "pays its homage to Faulkner," but went on to note that McCarthy's personal writing style "compels admiration, [being] compounded of Appalachian phrases as plain and as functional as an ax. In elegant counterpoint to this bare-bones English is a second diction taken from that rich store of English which is there in the dictionary to be used by those who can." A *Time* reviewer found that McCarthy's command of local dialect "is surpassed by his poetic descriptions of the land and its people. His is an Irish singing voice imbued with Southern Biblical intonations. The result is an antiphony of speech and verse played against a landscape of penance."

Lester Ballard, the title character of McCarthy's *Child of God,* is a demented backwoodsman, a murderer and necrophiliac. In this 1974 novel the author depicts the spiritual demise of Ballard and at the same time makes him a sympathetic figure. But Richard P. Brickner, writing in the *New York Times Book Review,* described *Child of God* as "an essentially sentimental novel that no matter how sternly it strives to be tragic is never more than morose." Similarly, in a review for *Commonweal,* contributor Robert Leiter called the book "thinner [and] less full-bodied than either *The Orchard Keeper* or *Outer Dark . . . Child of God* is a swift exciting read, but we are left with only incisive images strung along a thin plot line, the why and wherefore unexplained." Leiter surmised that the book "will perhaps be looked upon as a bad novel written by a good writer" and

concluded that "this would be regrettable, for *Child of God* marks a progression in McCarthy's career. He has learned restraint. The 'old themes' live on in him, but his South is not rendered with the precision of a realist. He has taken realism to the province of folk myth."

Child of God is "a reading experience so impressive, so 'new', so clearly made well that it seems almost to defy the easy esthetic categories and at the same time cause me to thrash about for some help with the necessary description of my enthusiasm," stated Doris Grumbach in *New Republic,* adding, "Cormac McCarthy is a Southerner, a born storyteller, . . . a writer of natural, impeccable dialogue, a literary child of Faulkner." Grumbach went on to say that in McCarthy's style, "the journey from death-in-life to death-in-death, from the hunted to the discovery of the hunting . . . is accomplished in rare, spare, precise yet poetic prose." The reviewer felt the author "has allowed us direct communion with his special kind of chaos; every sentence he writes illuminates, if only for a moment, the great dark of madness and violence and inevitable death that surrounds us all."

In a *New Yorker* review of *Child of God,* Robert Coles compared McCarthy to ancient Greek dramatists, saying that he "simply writes novels that tell us we cannot comprehend the riddles of human idiosyncrasy, the influence of the merely contingent or incidental upon our lives. He is a novelist of religious feeling who appears to subscribe to no creed but who cannot stop wondering in the most passionate and honest way what gives life meaning. . . . From the isolated highlands of Tennessee he sends us original stories that show how mysterious or confusing the world is. Moreover, his mordant wit, his stubborn refusal to bend his writing to the literary and intellectual demands of our era, conspire at times to make him seem mysterious and confusing—a writer whose fate is to be relatively unknown and often misinterpreted. But both Greek playwrights and Christian theologians have been aware that such may be the fate of anyone, of even the most talented and sensitive of human beings."

McCarthy's fourth novel, *Suttree,* again focuses on a misfit character, Cornelius Suttree, and the undesirable society he inhabits. In this book, the author describes Suttree as a man who has spent years in "the company of thieves, derelicts, miscreants, pariahs, poltroons, spalpeens, curmudgeons, clotpolls, murderers, gamblers, bawds, whores, trulls, brigands, topers, tosspots, sots and archsots, lobcocks, smellsmocks, runagates, rakes, and other assorted and felonious debauchees." Reviewing the book in *Spectator,* Frank Rudman called McCarthy "a magnificent writer with a resonant style that moves easily and naturally into a grand register without losing truthfulness. His ear for dialogue is as funny and authentic as that of Mark Twain." Davenport pointed out possible autobiographical elements in the novel and wondered if McCarthy "had asked what part of himself bears the imprint of the world in which he was raised, and answered himself by witnessing what these traits look like exemplified by a gallery of characters ranging from near-idiotic to noble." Writing in *National Review,* Davenport noted further that the reader is "won over . . . to Cormac McCarthy's radically original way with tone and his sense of the aloneness of people in their individuality. At the heart of *Suttree* there is a strange sense of transformation and rebirth in which the protagonist wanders in a forest, sees visions, and emerges as a stranger to all that was before familiar. This is a scene no one else could have written."

Anatole Broyard wrote of the author in a *New York Times* review of *Suttree:* "His people are so vivid that they seem exotic, but this is just another way of saying that we tend to forget the range of human differences. Mr. McCarthy's hyperbole is not Southern rhetoric, but flesh and blood. Every tale is tall, if you look at it closely enough." In *Washington Post Book World,* Edward Rothstein added another dollop of praise: "It is a measure . . . of McCarthy's skills that the reader becomes engaged with those of [Suttree's] world, even intoxicated by the miasmatic language. For every image that is tiresomely weighty, there is one which illuminates dark crevices. For every horror, there is a sensitive observation. For every violent dislocation, there is a subtly touching dialogue or gesture." Nelson Algren compared *Suttree* with McCarthy's earlier work, noting in the Chicago *Tribune Books:* "There were no telephones, indoor plumbing, electricity, or TV in [his] previous novels. . . . The language of his people was closer to the time of Shakespeare than to our own time. Here he has brought them all to town and into today—without losing the sense of old, old America. And without losing the freshness and the magic of the old wilderness. Although his new wilderness is an industrial wasteland, the magic remains."

In his next novel, 1985's *Blood Meridian; or, The Evening Redness in the West,* McCarthy leaves his home territory of Tennessee for the dusty plains of the Old West, a change possibly the result of the author's own relocation to El Paso, Texas, in 1974. *Blood Meridian* is by far McCarthy's bloodiest novel to date, detailing the adventures of a fourteen-year-old boy referred to only as "the kid" as he travels with a band of bounty hunters, paid by a Mexican governor to collect Indian scalps. The hunters, however, are not picky about their victims, leaving a long, bloody trail behind them as they go. "*Blood Meridian* comes at the reader like a slap in the face," wrote Caryn James in the *New York Times Book Review.* "While [it] is hard to get through, it is harder to ignore."

Though *Blood Meridian* is based loosely upon actual events of the 1840s and 1850s, it bears little resemblance to the historical westerns written by Louis L'Amour and others; instead it concentrates on the barren, hellish landscape and near-surreal characters that make up the band of mercenaries. Most prominent among them is a huge, hairless man named Judge Holden. Though he is not the group's leader, "the Judge" commands the respect of the others as he pontificates by the fire each night. It is against the background of Judge Holden that the kid is placed, allowing the reader to evaluate for himself the morality of each character. "*Blood Meridian* stands the world of Louis L'Amour on its head (indeed, heaps hot coals upon it)," claimed *Los Angeles Times Book Review* contributor Tom Nolan.

It is important to note, however, that the brutality depicted in McCarthy's writing has not reduced its power; rather, according to James, he "has asked us to witness evil not in order to understand it but to affirm its inexplicable reality; his elaborate language invents a world hinged between the real and surreal, jolting us out of complacency."

Winner of the National Book Award, *All the Pretty Horses* is the first installment in a three-book epic titled "The Border Trilogy." Set in 1949, it tells the story of John Grady Cole, a sixteen-year-old Texan who, along with his friend, Lacey Rawlins, sets off on horseback for Mexico. It becomes a coming-of-age tale, with Cole learning the skills of survival, facing adversity, and finding romance, all set against the backdrop of a land that has not lost the magic of the old West. "In the hands of some other writer," noted Bell, "this material might make for a combination of *Lonesome Dove* and *Huckleberry Finn,* but Mr. McCarthy's vision is deeper than Larry McMurtry's and, in its own way, darker than Mark Twain's." "What he has given us is a book of remarkable beauty and strength," wrote Tidmore, "the work of a master in perfect command of his medium."

While *All the Pretty Horses* is almost universally considered one of McCarthy's most accessible novels, it did not receive universally favorable reviews. This is due, in part, to the popularity of the novel, which opened it to criticism by reviewers previously unfamiliar with McCarthy's work. While Richard Eder, writing in the *Los Angeles Times Book Review,* admitted that "McCarthy's elevated prose does wonders for deserts, mountains, freezing winds, night landscapes and the tangibility of food, a bath and clean clothes," he warned that "loftiness gusts like a capsizing high wind, and the writing can choke on its own ornateness." Still, the strength of *All the Pretty Horses* seems to lie in the integrity of its central character, Cole, who was described by Bruce Allen in the *World & I* as "both a credible and admirable character; he is a perfect vehicle for the expression of the novel's themes." In addition to winning the National Book Award and garnering its author much greater critical attention, *All the Pretty Horses* also proved to be a tremendous commercial success.

The second installment in McCarthy's "Border Trilogy," 1994's *The Crossing* covers much of the same geographical and emotional terrain as *All the Pretty Horses. The Crossing* is divided into three sections. In the first, Billy Parham attempts to trap a wolf that has been killing cattle on his family's New Mexico ranch. After he successfully catches the animal, Billy decides to return it to its original territory in Mexico rather than kill it. Billy thus crosses the border into Mexico for the first time in the novel; unfortunately, the wolf is stolen for use in a dog-fighting arena, and Billy has to kill it to end its painful circumstance. After burying the wolf, Billy returns home to find that horse thieves have murdered his parents. The novel's second section finds Billy and his brother, Boyd, again crossing the border into Mexico in search of their parents' killers and their stolen horses. The brothers find and reclaim some of the horses, battle bandits, and have other picaresque adventures. At the close of the section, Boyd falls in love and returns home with a Mexican woman. In the third section, Billy decides after two years to journey back into Mexico to find Boyd. After hearing a song in which Boyd's death is described, Billy locates his brother's body and returns to New Mexico to bury it on his family's ranch.

As happened with *All the Pretty Horses,* critical reaction to *The Crossing* was starkly divided, with some reviewers terming the book an American masterpiece and others criticizing it as overwritten and pretentious.

Writing in the Chicago *Tribune Books,* Allen dubbed it an "ambitious novel" that "offers a masterly display of tonal control and some of the most pitch-perfect rapturous prose being written these days." In particular, Allen praised the "dozens of breathtakingly imaginative descriptive passages" in the book. In contrast, *Los Angeles Times Book Review* contributor Eder echoed his comments about *All the Pretty Horses.* Admitting that "McCarthy is a strong writer and he can be a magical one," Eder stated: "There are splendid passages in *The Crossing.*" However, the critic also criticized the author's portrayal of Mexico and disapproved of his frequent use of untranslated passages in Spanish. "What is painfully weak," averred Eder, "is much of McCarthy's portrayal and use of Mexico; and it is a very serious weakness." Michiko Kakutani, writing in the *New York Times,* also disliked the novel, commenting that "the overall result is not a mythic, post-modernist masterpiece, but a hodge-podge of a book that is derivative, sentimental and pretentious all at once." At the other end of the critical divide, *New York Times Book Review* contributor Robert Hass declared *The Crossing* to be "a miracle in prose, an American original. It deserves to sit on the same shelf certainly with [Toni Morrison's] *Beloved* and [William Faulkner's] *As I Lay Dying.*" Commending the novel's "violent and stunningly beautiful, inconsolable landscapes," Hass called *The Crossing* "a masterwork."

The trilogy concluded with 1998's *Cities of the Plain.* The last installment in the series unites John Grady Cole, the protagonist of *All the Pretty Horses,* with *The Crossing's* Billy Parham. Set in New Mexico in the 1950s, the novel finds both men working as horse wranglers at the Cross Fours Ranch. Like the previous books in the trilogy, *Cities of the Plain* contains plenty of tight dialogue, cowboy philosophy, extreme violence, and carefully rendered descriptions of the Western landscape. As in *All the Pretty Horses,* the plot comes to focus on romance—in this case, Cole's doomed love for Magdalena, an epileptic Mexican prostitute whose affections are also coveted by her pimp, Eduardo. When Cole's attempt to purchase Magdalena from her boss fails, he plots instead to smuggle her across the Mexican border. After Eduardo learns of the planned escape, however, he arranges to have Magdalena kidnapped and killed. Despite Billy's efforts to keep Cole out of trouble, the younger man returns to the brothel, seeking retribution for Magdalena's death. He enters into a knife fight with Eduardo, a battle which results in the deaths of both men.

Critics responded to the concluding volume of the "Border Trilogy" with mixed reactions. *Review of*

Contemporary Fiction critic Brian Evenson found that despite "some exceptional manipulations of prose," the novel "fails to measure up to either of the two previous volumes." Chilton Williamson, Jr., writing in the *National Review* concurred that "*Cities of the Plain* in some ways makes a less than fitting conclusion to the trilogistic narrative"—although the critic noted that "over three volumes [McCarthy's] writing has lost none of its eloquence nor the description its particularist power." In his assessment of the narrative for *World Literature Today,* William Riggan unfavorably compared its "leisurely, measured, elegiac . . . and dull" pacing and tone with the "action-rich, dialogue-filled, character-driven *Horses*" and *The Crossing.* By contrast, *Time* reviewer R.Z. Sheppard applauded McCarthy's efforts "to do for cowpunching what Melville did for whaling: describe in documentary detail how the job is done," and called the author "a virtuoso of the lyric description and the free-range sentence."

Seven years after completing the "Border Trilogy," McCarthy published *No Country for Old Men.* A year later, his book *The Road* was also released. Although *No Country for Old Men.* was met with decidedly mixed reviews, *The Road* received nearly universal praise. The latter book is the story of an unnamed man and his unnamed young son. Set in a post-apocalyptic nuclear winter, the two protagonists struggle to find food and attempt to avoid their fellow survivors, most of whom have become violent and cannibalistic. As the climate becomes colder, the protagonists begin to head south, hoping to make it to a warmer place before they freeze to death. Amidst this framework, the father and son bond is portrayed through the familiar—yet entirely skewed—road trip milieu, serving as an illustration of that which makes humanity human, and that which makes it inhuman as well. Though the father and son call themselves 'good guys' because they are not cannibals, they are unable to help others in need—they are barely able to survive themselves. This conundrum plays out in the boy's youthful and absolute sense of morality; his struggle to come to terms with this and other such contradictions is one of the book's major themes. According to *Booklist* contributor Keir Graff, the story is "rich with other explorations, too: hope in the face of hopelessness, the ephemeral nature of our existence, the vanishing worlds we all carry within us."

The book was called a masterpiece by several critics, including *Entertainment Weekly* reviewer Jennifer Reese. As did many critics, Reese remarked upon the story's conclusion, which simultaneously indicates the end of all mankind and hints at the prospect of a new age. Indeed, "the extraordinarily lovely and sad final pages . . . embrace both terrible possibilities," she stated. Norm Pattis, writing in the *Connecticut Law Tribune,* expressed dismayed surprise at the novel's somewhat hopeful ending. Nevertheless, Pattis acknowledged "perhaps that is McCarthy's point: To be is to hope, even when hope is pointless and there is nothing for which to hope." *New York Times* critic Janet Maslin also sought to explain *The Road*'s powerful ending, calling it "an embrace of faith in the face of no hope whatsoever." Maslin noted that this "leap" "adds immeasurably to the staying power of a book that is simple yet mysterious, simultaneously cryptic and crystal clear." After calling McCarthy "the elemental prose stylist of our time," *Esquire* contributor Tom Chiarella went on to state: "you shouldn't read this book for the metaphoric possibilities of change in the life of mankind. . . . You should read this book because it is exactly what a book about our future ought to be: the knife wound of our inconvenient truths."

Despite his groundbreaking success, McCarthy remains elusive. Summarizing his work, Cox stressed: "McCarthy is in no way a commercial writer. He is a novelist by profession, and he has not supplemented his income by turning his hand to more lucrative kinds of work such as Hollywood screenwriting. . . . His most perceptive reviewers have consistently predicted more of the same solid work from McCarthy, and he has fulfilled these predictions. He deserves, now, serious attention from students of literature."

BIOGRAPHICAL AND CRITICAL SOURCES:

BOOKS

Bell, Vereen, *The Achievement of Cormac McCarthy,* Louisiana State University Press (Baton Rouge, LA), 1988.

Contemporary Literary Criticism, Thomson Gale (Detroit, MI), Volume 4, 1975, Volume 57, 1990, Volume 59, 1990, Volume 101, 1997.

Dictionary of Literary Biography, Thomson Gale (Detroit, MI), Volume 6: *American Novelists since World War II, Second Series,* 1980, Volume 143: *American Novelists since World War II, Third Series,* 1994.

Hall, Wade H., and Rick Wallach, editors, *Sacred Violence: A Reader's Companion to Cormac McCarthy: Selected Essays from the First McCarthy Conference,* University of Texas at El Paso (El Paso, TX), 1995.

McCarthy, Cormac, *Suttree,* Random House (New York, NY), 1979.

PERIODICALS

America, June 12, 1965, J.G. Murray, review of *The Orchard Keeper;* October 31, 2005, Chris Byrd, review of *No Country for Old Men.*

Booklist, January 1, 1999, review of *Cities of the Plain,* p. 779; August 1, 2006, Keir Graff, review of *The Road,* p. 9.

Commonweal, March 29, 1974, Robert Leiter, review of *Child of God.*

Connecticut Law Tribune, October 23, 2006, Norm Pattis, review of *The Road.*

Entertainment Weekly, July 22, 2005, Jennifer Reese, review of *No Country for Old Men,* p. 82; September 29, 2006, Jennifer Reese, review of *The Road,* p. 85.

Esquire, September, 2006, Tom Chiarella, review of *The Road,* p. 94.

Los Angeles Times Book Review, June 9 1985, Tom Nolan, review of *Blood Meridian; or, The Evening Redness in the West;* May 17, 1992, Richard Eder, review of *All the Pretty Horses;* June 12, 1994, Richard Eder, review of *The Crossing,* p. 3.

Nation, July 6, 1998, Dagoberto Glib, review of *Cities of the Plain,* p. 38.

National Review, March 16, 1979, Gut Davenport, review of *Suttree;* October 12, 1998, Chilton Williamson, Jr., review of *Cities of the Plain,* p. 61.

New Republic, February 9, 1974, Doris Grumbach, review of *Child of God.*

New Statesman, November 14, 2005, Ruaridh Nicoll, review of *No Country for Old Men,* p. 54.

New Yorker, August 26, 1974, Robert Coles, review of *Child of God.*

New York Times, January 20, 1979, Anatole Broyard, review of *Suttree;* November 19, 1992, Herbert Mitgang, review of *All the Pretty Horses;* June 21, 1994, Michiko Kakutani, review of *The Crossing,* p. C21; September 25, 2006, Janet Maslin, review of *The Road,* p. E1.

New York Times Book Review, September 29, 1968, Guy Davenport, review of *Outer Dark;* January 13, 1974, Richard P. Brickner, review of *Child of God;* April 28, 1985, Caryn James, review of *Blood Meridian;* May 17, 1992, Madison Smartt Bell, review of *All the Pretty Horses;* June 12, 1994, Robert Hass, review of *The Crossing,* p. 1.

Newsweek, July 25, 2005, Malcolm Jones, review of *No Country for Old Men,* p. 58; September 25, 2006, review of *The Road,* p. 68.

Review of Contemporary Fiction, fall, 1998, Brian Evenson, review of *Cities of the Plain,* p. 250.

Spectator, May 24, 1980, Frank Rudman, review of *Suttree.*

Texas Monthly, July, 1998, Michael Hall, "Desperately Seeking Cormac," pp. 76-79.

Time, September 17, 1968, review of *Outer Dark;* May 18, 1998, R.Z. Sheppard, "Thar She Moos," review of *Cities of the Plain,* p. 95; July 18, 2005, Lev Grossman, review of *No Country for Old Men,* p. 73.

Tribune Books (Chicago, IL), January 28, 1979, Nelson Algren, review of *Suttree;* June 26, 1994, Bruce Allen, review of *The Crossing,* p. 5.

Vanity Fair, August, 2005, Richard B. Woodward, "Cormac McCarthy Would Rather Hang Out with Physicists than Other Writers," author interview and profile, p. 98.

Vogue, August, 2005, Taylor Antrim, review of *No Country for Old Men,* p. 164.

Washington Post, November 19, 1992, Kurt Tidmore, review of *All the Pretty Horses.*

Washington Post Book World, March 19, 1979, Edward Rothstein, review of *Suttree.*

World & I, September, 1992, Bruce Allen, review of *All the Pretty Horses;* October, 1998, Edwin T. Arnold, review of *Cities of the Plain,* p. 258.

World Literature Today, winter, 2000, William Riggan, review of *Cities of the Plain,* p. 173.*

*   *   *

McWHORTER, Kathleen T. 1944-

PERSONAL: Born October 10, 1944, in Buffalo, NY; daughter of Harry and Ruth E. Thompson; married Thomas R. McWhorter. *Education:* State University of New York at Buffalo, B.A., 1965, Ed.M., 1968, Ph.D., 1974.

ADDRESSES: Home—Akron, NY. *Office*—Niagara County Community College, 3111 Saunders Settlement Rd., Sanborn, NY 14132. *E-mail*—ktmcw@aol.com.

CAREER: Reading teacher and department head at public schools in West Seneca, NY, 1965-68; State University of New York at Buffalo, Buffalo, instructor, 1969-71; Niagara County Community College, Sanborn, NY, professor of humanities, 1971—. Consultant to Carborundum Corp., Niagara County Manpower Training Program, and Niagara County Youth Employment Training Program.

MEMBER: National Association of Developmental Educators, National Council of Teachers of English, College Reading and Learning Association, College Reading Association, Textbook Authors Association, New York State Learning Skills Association.

WRITINGS:

College Reading and Study Skills, Longman (New York, NY), 1980, 10th edition, 2007.

Efficient and Flexible Reading, Longman (New York, NY), 1983, 7th edition, 2005.

Guide to College Reading, Longman (New York, NY), 1986, 7th edition, 2007.

Study and Thinking Skills in College, Longman (New York, NY), 1988, 6th edition published as *Study and Critical Thinking Skills in College,* 2006.

Academic Reading, Longman (New York, NY), 1990, 6th edition, 2007.

The Writer's Selections, Houghton-Mifflin (Boston, MA), 1997, 3rd edition, 2006.

Successful College Writing, St. Martin's Press (New York, NY), 2000, 3rd edition, 2006.

Essential Reading Skills, Longman (New York, NY), 2002, 3rd edition, 2007.

Reading across the Disciplines, Longman (New York, NY), 2005, 3rd edition, 2007.

Seeing the Pattern: Readings for Successful Writers, Bedford (New York, NY), 2006.

Vocabulary Simplified, 2nd edition, Longman (New York, NY), 2006.

Active Reading Skills, Longman (New York, NY), 2007.

Pathways for Writing Scenarios: From Sentences to Paragraphs, Longman (New York, NY), 2007.

Expressways for Writing Scenarios: From Paragraph to Essay, Longman (New York, NY), 2007.

Contributor to *Journal of Reading* and *Reading Instruction Journal.*

*   *   *

MILNER, Kelly
   See HALLS, Kelly Milner

*   *   *

MITCHELL, John Hanson 1940-

PERSONAL: Born April 25, 1940, in Englewood, NJ; son of James A. Mitchell (an Episcopalian minister) and Virginia P. Mitchell (a school teacher); married Margaret Street (divorced, September, 1992), married Jill S.G. Brown, June, 1996; children: (first marriage) Clayton, Lelia. *Education:* Columbia University, B.S., 1967.

ADDRESSES: Home—Littleton, MA. *Office*—Massachusetts Audubon Society, South Great Rd., Lincoln, MA 01773. *Agent*—William Reiss, John Hawkins & Associates, Inc., 71 W. 23rd St., Ste. 1600, New York, NY 10010.

CAREER: Environmental Centers of Hartford, Hartford, CT, director, 1967-70; freelance writer, 1970-73; Massachusetts Audubon Society, Lincoln, MA, assistant editor, 1973-80; editor of *Sanctuary,* 1980—.

AWARDS, HONORS: Honorary Ph.D., Fitchburg State University, 1988; John Burroughs Essay Award, 1994; New England Booksellers' Award, 2000, for body of work.

WRITINGS:

Hiking Cape Cod, Eastwoods Press (New York, NY), 1975.

The Curious Naturalist, illustrated by Gordon Morrison, Prentice-Hall (Englewood Cliffs, NJ), 1980.

(Editor, with Wayne Hanley) *The Energy Book,* illustrated by Gordon Morrison, Greene (Lexington, MA), 1980.

Ceremonial Time: Fifteen Thousand Years on One Square Mile, illustrated by Gordon Morrison, Anchor Press (New York, NY), 1984.

A Field Guide to Your Own Back Yard, illustrated by Laurel Molk, Norton (New York, NY), 1985.

Living at the End of Time, Houghton (Boston, MA), 1990.

Walking towards Walden: A Pilgrimage in Search of John Hanson Mitchell, illustrated by Robert Leverett, Addison-Wesley (Reading, MA), 1995.

(With Christopher Leahy and Thomas Conuel) *The Nature of Massachusetts,* illustrated by Lars Jonsson, Addison-Wesley (Reading, MA), 1996.

Trespassing: An Inquiry into the Private Ownership of Land, Addison-Wesley (Reading, MA), 1998.

The Wildest Place on Earth: Italian Gardens and the Invention of Wilderness, illustrated by James A. Mitchell, Counterpoint (Washington, DC), 2001.

Following the Sun: From Spain to the Hebrides, Counterpoint (Washington, DC), 2002.

Looking for Mr. Gilbert: The Reimagined Life of an African American, Shoemaker & Hoard (Emeryville, CA), 2005.

The Rose Café: Love and War in Corsica, Shoemaker & Hoard (Emeryville, CA), 2007.

SIDELIGHTS: Author John Hanson Mitchell has been writing about nature, especially man's relation to it, for more than twenty years. In the books *Ceremonial Time: Fifteen Thousand Years on One Square Mile* and *Living at the End of Time,* Mitchell uses his experience and knowledge of a few scant acres of New England woodland to arrive at far-reaching notions concerning humanity's relationship with the earth. Both volumes, written as essays, rely as much on Mitchell's own life and personal vision as on the natural history of the region.

The one square mile of land known as "Scratch Flat," thirty-five miles outside Boston, Massachusetts, served as Mitchell's study ground for *Ceremonial Time.* In the *New York Times Book Review,* critic John Anthony West observed that Mitchell scrutinized the area "from every imaginable angle. He . . . consulted geologists, archaeologists, local characters, environmentalists, romantics, computer experts, Indian shamans, anyone and everyone who might provide some fresh insight into the past or present or future of Scratch Flat." Indeed, the notion of time—specifically, time as perceived by the Native Americans who originally inhabited the land—is central to the author's relationship with Scratch Flat. "The title proper, *Ceremonial Time,* is an Indian concept that makes an ocean of time, an all-encompassing sea that humanity shares eternally with the spirits of yesterday and tomorrow, free of the temporal linear constructions—minutes, months, centuries, millennia—that white men brought to this continent in 1620," commented John N. Cole in the *Washington Post Book World.* According to Cole, Mitchell portrays the events of the ice age by applying "Indian theology . . . to his graceful prose." Two Native Americans, Nompenekit and Tonupasqua (who are both ultimately descended from the Paleo-Indians that populated the region fourteen thousand years ago), aided the author with their knowledge of the ancient religion and rites practiced by their tribe well before the advent of white Europeans. Mitchell looks to the years ahead, also, even as road and home construction impinge on his one square mile of undeveloped land. After considering various fates, which could spell the demise of Scratch Flat, he opts for an optimistic alternative—the return to the values of the land's original settlers, the

Native American. West appreciated the author's use of Scratch Flat as a microcosm, remarking: "By concentrating on the particular, he has illuminated the universal. I can think of no book that provides so personal and yet so comprehensive a view of America, past, present and, potentially, future."

Mitchell wrote *Living at the End of Time* after a divorce prompted him to build a cottage in the forest behind his former home; the book itself is a meditation on humanity's interaction with nature, written in the spirit of Henry David Thoreau's *Walden* (a treatise on the appreciation of nature as well as a wide-ranging critique of morals and customs in mid-nineteenth century New England). Walden Pond, the secluded site near Concord, Massachusetts, where Thoreau lived and wrote in a small cabin, is only a short distance from Mitchell's own cottage. Like Thoreau, Mitchell used his solitude in the woods to examine issues that surpass mere surveys of flora and fauna. In *Living at the End of Time,* he tracks the legacy left behind by people who formerly occupied the territory. According to John R. Stilgoe, writing in the *New York Times Book Review,* the book "probes at land that has been touched and then abandoned—at holes left by long-gone cellars, at toppled stone walls and at rusted farm equipment smothered in ordinary forest." The author also portrays the various people he met while roaming the countryside and describes their unique link to the land. In the words of Stilgoe, Mitchell tells of "the local drunkard who camps out in the undergrowth of the interstate highway cloverleaf" to the European couple who had escaped Nazism and wish to farm self-sufficiently, free from any government interference. Michael Harris, a critic in the *Los Angeles Times Book Review,* stated that these "portraits" are "the best parts of *Living at the End of Time.*" Stilgoe praised the author's depth of perception in the *New York Times Book Review,* remarking that "Mr. Mitchell offers a penetrating assessment of the usefulness of ordinary woods."

Walking towards Walden is another Thoreau-esque work, of which was described as "a combination guide book and memoir peppered with morsels of mythology, folklore, nature, literature, art, and history" by Patricia Hassler in *Booklist.* Mitchell and two friends set out on Columbus Day to walk the fifteen miles to the Sleepy Hollow Cemetery in Concord, where Thoreau, Emerson, Hawthorne, and the Alcotts are buried. As they walked along an overgrown trail that was once taken by Revolutionary soldiers, they talked about people's devotion to a particular place, about quests and pilgrimages, and about a variety of other philosophical topics.

In *Trespassing: An Inquiry into the Private Ownership of Land,* Mitchell uses the history of a plot of land near his home to question the Western concept of land ownership. In 1654, the Puritans granted sixteen square miles of northeastern Massachusetts to some Pawtucket Indians who had become Christians. Twenty years later, the Puritans removed the tribe to an island in Boston Harbor during a war between the settlers and other Native American tribes; many of them died. The survivors eventually returned, but the tribe soon died out: the last survivor, Sarah Doublet, passed away in 1736. The land was then held by a variety of private, corporate, and governmental owners for over two hundred years, until activists seeking to block a new housing development convinced the town to purchase the part of it that was to be developed and to turn it into communal open space. From the history of this one piece of land, Mitchell expands to look at other ways of bringing privately held land into the public domain—devices such as land trusts, conservation easements, and greenbelts, for example—as well as trespassing, which Mitchell justifies by calling it "the only way to get to know a place."

Reviewers were generally positive about *Trespassing.* *Audubon* contributor Verlyn Klinkenborg said: "The beauty of *Trespassing* lies partly in the subtlety Mitchell brings to these questions [of ownership], his willingness to weigh the common need against the private right," as well as "in Mitchell's intimacy with the tract of land . . . and with its occupants, human and wild." A *Publishers Weekly* reviewer was pleased by the fact that "Mitchell neither scolds nor soothes, offering instead anecdote, history, law and keen naturalist observations."

In *The Wildest Place on Earth: Italian Gardens and the Invention of Wilderness,* Mitchell moves beyond his New England home to discuss the invention of the concept of wilderness in the gardens of ancient Egypt, medieval England, and of course Renaissance Italy. Like all of Mitchell's texts, "this poetic little book," as a *Publishers Weekly* reviewer described it, is full of anecdotes, personal recollections, and philosophical musings.

Following the Sun: From Spain to the Hebrides chronicles a three-month, 1,500-mile bicycle journey that took the author from the Spanish port town of Cadiz to the island of Lewis in the Outer Hebrides of Scotland, where he witnessed the summer solstice. In the work, Mitchell "follows the lengthening days, the blessings of the sun after the winter months, and approaches the

pilgrimage in the spirit of a pagan ablate," noted a *Kirkus Reviews* contributor. Along the way, remarked *Library Journal* critic Linda M. Kaufmann, "he meets friends old and new and explores the lore, natural history, science, and culture of the sun." Other reviewers also added favorable comments. "The text is most evocative in the indolent stretches of the sun-washed south," wrote a reviewer in *Publishers Weekly,* further noting that the author's "penchant for reported speech offers a fascinating picture of Europe."

The inspiration for Mitchell's 2005 work *Looking for Mr. Gilbert: The Reimagined Life of an African American* came to the author some thirty years earlier, when he discovered a series of antique glass plate negatives in the attic of an Massachusetts farmhouse. Although Mitchell believed the photographs had been taken by esteemed nineteenth-century ornithologist William Brewster, he later suspected that they were the work of Brewster's assistant, Robert A. Gilbert. "In prose as smoothly cadenced as the Concord River so frequently depicted in those images," remarked a critic in *Kirkus Reviews,* "Mitchell takes readers along . . . to learn more about the man who was Brewster's inseparable amanuensis." According to Vanessa Bush, writing in *Booklist,* "Mitchell renders astonishingly detailed descriptions, giving flesh to the sparse historical record of Gilbert's achievements." *Black Issues Book Review* contributor Eric Addison suggested: "Photography is the book's main motif, and it works beautifully, capturing the author's passionate yearning to . . . learn more about his subject and the world he lived in."

BIOGRAPHICAL AND CRITICAL SOURCES:

PERIODICALS

American Book Review, December, 1996, review of *Walking towards Walden: A Pilgrimage in Search of John Hanson Mitchell,* p. 1166.

Audubon, May-June, 1998, Verlyn Klinkenborg, review of *Trespassing: An Inquiry into the Private Ownership of Land,* pp. 106-108.

Black Issues Book Review, March-April, 2005, Eric Addison, review of *Looking for Mr. Gilbert: The Reimagined Life of an African American,* p. 54.

Booklist, November 1, 1995, Patricia Hassler, review of *Walking towards Walden,* p. 450; March 15, 2001, Donna Seaman, review of *The Wildest Place on Earth: Italian Gardens and the Invention of Wilderness,* p. 1343; February 1, 2005, Vanessa Bush, review of *Looking for Mr. Gilbert,* p. 935.

Kirkus Reviews, April 1, 1998, review of *Trespassing,* p. 475; February 15, 2001, review of *The Wildest Place on Earth,* p. 240; April 1, 2002, review of *Following the Sun: A Bicycle Pilgrimage from Spain to the Herbides,* p. 473; December 15, 2004, review of *Looking for Mr. Gilbert,* p. 1187.

Library Journal, October 15, 1995, Tim Markus, review of *Walking towards Walden,* p. 85; May 15, 2002, Linda M. Kaufmann, review of *Following the Sun,* p. 116.

Los Angeles Times Book Review, April 22, 1990, Michael Harris, review of *Living at the End of Time,* p. 6.

New York Times Book Review, August 12, 1984, John Anthony West, review of *Ceremonial Time: Fifteen Thousand Years on One Square Mile,* p. 27; May 13, 1990, John R. Stilgoe, "Thoreau with Bottled Gas," p. 33.

Publishers Weekly, June 22, 1998, review of *Trespassing,* p. 78; September 18, 1995, review of *Walking towards Walden,* p. 119; March 19, 2001, review of *The Wildest Place on Earth,* p. 91; April 15, 2002, review of *Following the Sun,* p. 56.

Smithsonian, February, 1999, Paul Trachtman, "Book Reviews," p. 148.

Virginia Quarterly Review, winter, 1999, review of *Trespassing,* p. 26.

Washington Post Book World, July 16, 1984, John N. Cole, review of *Ceremonial Time.*

Yankee, October, 1996, Geoffrey Elan, review of *Walking towards Walden,* p. 450.

* * *

MORGAN, Rosemarie
(Rosemarie Anne Louise Morgan)

PERSONAL: Born in London, England; immigrated to United States, 1983; U.S. citizen; daughter of Barton T. (a financier) and Patricia G. Morgan; married Ben Alexander, 1956 (died, 1996); married Russell Graves (an employment coordinator; marriage ended); children: (first marriage) Adam T., Ruth E., Miriam C.; (with Guy Streatfeild) Alice V. Morgan. *Ethnicity:* "Caucasian." *Education:* Open University, diploma, 1977; Council for National Academic Awards, B.A. (with honors), 1979; University of St. Andrews, Ph.D., 1982; postdoctoral study at Yale University, 1983-85. *Politics:* Green Party.

ADDRESSES: Home—New Haven, CT. *Office*—Department of English, Yale University, High St., New Haven,

CT 06545; fax: 203-865-7718. *E-mail*—rosemarie.morgan@yale.edu.

CAREER: Teacher of English as a second language at a secondary school in Dorset, England, 1980; Yale University, New Haven, CT, lecturer in English, 1985-2002, research fellow, 2003—. Post College, Waterbury, CT, adjunct professor, 1986-88; distinguished visiting professor, University of British Columbia, 1989, and Kansai University, Osaka, Japan, 1994. Web site designer for Hardy Association Literary Web site and Berkshire Bach Society.

MEMBER: Modern Language Association of America, Thomas Hardy Association (president, 1998), Thomas Hardy Society (vice president, 1998), Berkshire Bach Society (member of board of directors), St. Andrews Literary Society (president), University Women's Club (London, England).

AWARDS, HONORS: Award from Royal Academy of Arts, 1977-78; research grant from Russell Trust, 1983; Literary Web site Award, British Broadcasting Corp., 1999-2002.

WRITINGS:

The Man from Tekoa: A Play, Galliard (London, England), 1974.
Women and Sexuality in the Novels of Thomas Hardy, Routledge & Kegan Paul (New York, NY), 1988.
Cancelled Words: Rediscovering Thomas Hardy, Routledge & Kegan Paul (New York, NY), 1992.
(Editor) Thomas Hardy, *Far from the Madding Crowd,* Penguin World Classics (New York, NY), 1999.
(Editor) *Editing Hardy,* Thomas Hardy Association Press (New Haven, CT), 1999.
(Editor, with Richard Nemesvari) *Human Shows: Essays in Honour of Michael Millgate,* Thomas Hardy Association Press (New Haven, CT), 2000.
(Editor) *Days to Recollect: Essays Dedicated to Robert Schweik,* Thomas Hardy Association Press (New Haven, CT), 2000.
(Editor, with William W. Morgan) *The Emma Poems,* Thomas Hardy Association Press (New Haven, CT), 2001.
Student Companion to Thomas Hardy, Greenwood Press (Westport, CT), 2006.

Work represented in anthologies, including *The Feminist Companion to Literature in English,* Yale University Press (New Haven, CT), 1990; *The Literature of Place,*

Macmillan (New York, NY), 1993; *Essays from Cambridge,* Macmillan (New York, NY), 1995; *Nineteenth-Century Autobiography: Mortal Pages, Literary Lives,* Scolar Press, 1995; and *From Novel to Screen,* edited by Terry Wright, Cambridge University Press (New York, NY), 2005. Contributor of articles and reviews to periodicals.

SIDELIGHTS: Rosemarie Morgan once told *CA:* "An important goal of my writing is to challenge received interpretations of women in literature and historical views of women in Victorian society. I am also interested in the relationships between children and literature and society."

BIOGRAPHICAL AND CRITICAL SOURCES:

PERIODICALS

Times Literary Supplement, December 23, 1988, review of *Women and Sexuality in the Novels of Thomas Hardy,* p. 1414.

*   *   *

MORGAN, Rosemarie Anne Louise
    See MORGAN, Rosemarie

*   *   *

MOSER, Nancy 1955(?)-

PERSONAL: Born c. 1955; married, 1975; husband's name, Mark; children: Emily, Carson, Laurel. *Education:* College graduate. *Hobbies and other interests:* Music, needlepoint, antiques.

ADDRESSES: Home—Kansas. *Agent*—Janet Kobobel Grant, 4788 Carissa Ave., Santa Rosa, CA 95405. *E-mail*—nancy@nancymoser.com.

CAREER: Writer, inspirational speaker.

AWARDS, HONORS: Christy Award, for *Time Lottery.*

WRITINGS:

Save Me, I Fell in the Carpool, Vine Books/Servant Publications (Ann Arbor, MI), 1997.
Motherhood: A Celebration of Blessing and Blunders, Harold Shaw Publishers (Wheaton, IL), 1997.
Expecting: A Celebration of Waiting and the Wonder, Harold Shaw Publishers (Wheaton, IL), 1998.
The Seat beside Me (novel), Multnomah Publishers (Sisters, OR), 2002.
Time Lottery, Promise Press (Uhrichsville, OH), 2002.
A Steadfast Surrender (novel), Multnomah Publishers (Sisters, OR), 2003.
The Ultimatum: A Novel (novel), Multnomah Publishers (Sisters, OR), 2004.
Second Time Around, Barbour (Uhrichsville, OH), 2004.
Mozart's Sister, Bethany House (Minneapolis, MN), 2006.
The Good Nearby, Tyndale House Publishers (Carol Stream, IL), 2006.
Crossroads, Tyndale House Publishers (Carol Stream, IL), 2006.

Contributor to periodicals, including *Christianity Today.*

"MUSTARD SEED" SERIES

The Invitation, Multnomah Publishers (Sisters, OR), 1998.
The Quest, Multnomah Publishers (Sisters, OR), 1999.
The Temptation, Multnomah Publishers (Sisters, OR), 2000.

"SISTER CIRCLE" SERIES

(With Vonette Bright) *The Sister Circle,* Tyndale House Publishers (Wheaton, IL), 2003.
(With Vonette Bright) *'Round the Corner,* Tyndale House Publishers (Wheaton, IL), 2003.
(With Vonette Bright) *An Undivided Heart,* Tyndale House Publishers (Wheaton, IL), 2004.
(With Vonette Bright) *A Place to Belong,* Tyndale House Publishers (Wheaton, IL), 2005.

SIDELIGHTS: Nancy Moser is the author of several books with faith-based plots, as well as books of nonfiction and humor. Moser explains her entry into Christian writing on her Web site, saying that after receiving "a scathing rejection" from an agent for one of her secular novels, she felt her days as a writer were over before they had begun. While shopping, she went into a Christian book store, bought three novels, and soon knew that this would be her genre. Moser also said that in buying the books, "I dedicated my writing to God— even though I didn't know much about Him." Moser notes that her faith was strengthened as she made the decision to write for God and speaks of the waiting period during which she learned more about her faith, read the Bible, learned to trust, and at the end of which, began to write again.

Moser tried unsuccessfully to rewrite finished novels, but instead found publication with *The Invitation,* the first book of her "Mustard Seed" series. The work features four people who are anonymously invited to Haven, Nebraska, where they face temptation and ultimately confront Satan. *Booklist*'s John Mort described the series as "a spiritual warfare trilogy."

The Seat beside Me is Moser's novel about a plane crash into a bridge and then a frigid river that leaves all but five passengers dead. The survivors make decisions based on their faith and reflect on why they were spared when nearly 100 others were not, and a journalist covering the crash struggles in deciding whether or not to exploit the situation in writing her story. A *Publishers Weekly* contributor felt the novel to be "too long" and noted that a seven-page dialogue between two of the characters "mostly functions to present the plan for salvation," but concluded by saying that Moser "admirably demonstrates that tragedy is a life-changing opportunity, in which reassessments and changes for the better are possible." In a *Library Journal* review, Melanie C. Duncan described the novel as being "particularly powerful."

Moser has also collaborated with Vonette Bright to write novels in the "Sister Circle" series. In the first book in the series, *The Sister Circle,* Evelyn Peerbaugh is a widow in her fifties who takes borders into her home and soon finds herself trying to cope with an old hippie, a single mom and her daughter, and an elderly widow with a tarnished past. Before long, the women, although very different from each other, form a strong bond and a fellowship in Christ. In a review of *The Sister Circle* in *Publishers Weekly,* a contributor wrote: "The novel's strength is in its multifaceted and sometimes unexpected characterizations."

Second Time Around is a sequel to an earlier novel by Moser titled *Time Lottery.* In the sequel, three people win the time lottery, which allows them to go back in time and attempt to change events in their pasts. However, if they choose to stay and live in the past, they will die in the current real time. The winners include an actress who left her small-town sweetheart, a woman who had an abortion, and a bachelor CEO whose one time fiancée died in an accident. A *Publishers Weekly* contributor called the novel "a compelling read that faith fiction fans will enjoy."

In the novel *Mozart's Sister,* Moser tells the fictionalized story of the famous composer Wolfgang Amadeus Mozart's real-life older sister. Although immensely talented, Nannerl has little opportunity to develop or display her talents largely because she is a woman. The story is told by Nannerl herself as she recounts how her father focused on Amadeus even though Nannerl also performs with her brother as they are taken on tours around Europe. "Moser's writing is smooth, and there are some fascinating historical details," wrote a *Publishers Weekly* contributor. Violet Nesdoly, writing on the *BC Books* Blog site, commented that "this book delivers an authentic and moving visit to another time and place."

Changing time periods and continents in the novel *Crossroads,* a woman buys a small town in Kansas and then plans on giving it away to contest winners. The people who ultimately win the right to live in the town and start their lives anew are a diverse group—including a banker, artist, cop, and a Jewish couple—who end up changing each other's lives.

BIOGRAPHICAL AND CRITICAL SOURCES:

PERIODICALS

Booklist, January 1, 2002, John Mort, review of *The Seat beside Me,* p. 804.

Library Journal, February 1, 2002, Melanie C. Duncan, review of *The Seat beside Me,* p. 80; February 1, 2003, Shawna Saavedra Thorup, review of *The Sister Circle,* p. 68; February 1, 2006, Tamara Butler, review of *Crossroads,* p. 64.

Publishers Weekly, November 19, 2001, review of *The Seat beside Me,* p. 48; November 25, 2002, review of *The Sister Circle,* p. 40; October 18, 2004, review of *The Second Time Around,* p. 48; June 5, 2006, review of *Mozart's Sister,* p. 31.

ONLINE

BC Books Blog site, http://blogcritics.org/ (December 7, 2006), Violet Nesdoly, review of *Mozart's Sister.*

Nancy Moser Home Page, http://www.nancymoser.com (December 7, 2006).

Notes in the Key of Life Blog site, http://cindyswanslife. blogspot.com/ (January 23, 2004), Cindy Swanson, "My Interview with Christian Author Nancy Moser."

Novel Journey Blog site, http://noveljourney.blogspot. com/ (June 28, 2006), "Author Interview: Nancy Moser."

Novel Reviews Blog site, http://novelreviews.blogspot. com/ (December 7, 2006), Michelle Sutton, review of *Mozart's Sister.**

* * *

MUSSULMAN, Joseph A. 1928-
(Joseph Agee Mussulman)

PERSONAL: Born November 20, 1928, in East St. Louis, IL; son of Boyd (a merchant) and Susan Mussulman; married E. Jo-Anne Stafford (a States Arts Council administrative assistant), June 16, 1950; children: Eleanor, Claudia. *Education:* Northwestern University, B.Mus., 1950, M.Mus., 1951; Syracuse University, Ph. D., 1966.

ADDRESSES: Home—Missoula, MT. *E-mail*—jmuss@ lewis-clark.org.

CAREER: Educator, choral conductor, cartographer, writer, editor. St. Cloud Teachers College (now St. Cloud State College), St. Cloud, MN, instructor in music, 1951-52; Northwestern University, Evanston, IL, assistant to dean of music, 1952-54; Ripon College, Ripon, WI, assistant professor of music, 1954-57; University of Montana, Missoula, assistant professor, 1957-66, associate professor, 1966-71, professor of music, 1971-88. Author of interpretation programs and audio tours for museums and national parks. Designer, writer and co-producer of floaters' maps of 16 Montana rivers. Conductor, various church choirs and Missoula Symphony Chorale. Program annotator, Missoula Symphony Orchestra. Seasonal wilderness ranger, Lolo National Forest, 1981-93. Producer for the Web site *Discovering Lewis & Clark,* 1993—.

MEMBER: Pi Kappa Lambda, Phi Kappa Phi.

AWARDS, HONORS: Danforth grant, 1961, 1963, 1965; National Endowment for the Humanities grant, 1967; Montana Governor's Arts Award, 1999; award of meritorious achievement, Lewis and Clark Trail Heritage Foundation; Montana Governor's Humanities Award, 2005.

WRITINGS:

Music in the Cultured Generation: A Social History of Music in America, 1870-1900, Northwestern University Press (Evanston, IL), 1971.

The Uses of Music: An Introduction to Music in Contemporary American Life, Prentice-Hall (Englewood Cliffs, NJ), 1974.

Dear People . . . Robert Shaw: A Biography, Indiana University Press (Bloomington, IN), 1979, revised and updated edition, Hinshaw Music (Chapel Hill, NC), 1996.

(Illustrator and creator of maps) Barbara Fifer and Vicky Soderberg, *Along the Trail with Lewis & Clark,* Farcountry Press (Helena, MT), 1998.

Discovering Lewis & Clark from the Air, photography by Jim Wark, Mountain Press Publishing Company (Missoula, MT), 2004.

Contributor of articles to academic journals, including *Musical Quarterly, Centennial Review* and to the historical journal about the Lewis and Clark expedition, *We Proceeded On.*

SIDELIGHTS: An educator and scholar of music history and criticism, Joseph A. Mussulman has written books about music and also about his interest in the Lewis and Clark expedition. In his book *Music in the Cultured Generation: A Social History of Music in America, 1870-1900,* the author focuses on writings about music that appeared in four American periodicals: *Atlantic, Harper's, Scribner's,* and *Century Illustrated.* Mussulman chose these periodicals because they focused on writings for the general population, thus giving insights into the social aspects of serious music, such as opera and classical music. Barbara Hampton, writing in *Notes,* referred to the book as "eminently readable." Hampton added: "Mussulman marshalls an impressive array of evidence to convince us that the mainstream of musical life was not dominated by the conventional and the superficial." A contributor to *Musi-*

cal Quarterly wrote: "Mussulman gives a systematic exposition to the views set forth by this circle of writers and a valuable running commentary that puts it all in perspective."

In another volume titled *The Uses of Music: An Introduction to Music in Contemporary American Life,* the author discusses both the technical aspects of music and various musical genres, or types of music, from background and mood music to ceremonial, theatre, and pop music. Charles H. Kaufman, writing in *Notes,* commented: "With great agility and surprising grace [Mussulman] dances lightly across the entire musical landscape and manages to get his feet in the right place most of the time." Mussulman is also author of a biography of musician and conductor Robert Shaw.

In addition to his primary academic expertise in music, Mussulman is also a history buff, an interest he has pursued more vigorously since he retired from academia. As a result, he has contributed to two books about the Lewis and Clark expedition and created a Web site devoted to the pair's journey. In *Discovering Lewis & Clark from the Air,* the author and photographer Jim Wark follow the famous western exploratory expedition via airplane. The book includes numerous photos that are accompanied by quotes from the diaries of Lewis and Clark. In a review of *Discovering Lewis & Clark from the Air* in the periodical *Kliatt,* Raymond Puffer called the book "just too beautiful to pass up." Diane Donovan, writing in *MBR Bookwatch,* referred to the work as "a fascinating, visually pleasing survey."

BIOGRAPHICAL AND CRITICAL SOURCES:

PERIODICALS

Kliatt, September, 2004, Raymond Puffer, review of *Discovering Lewis & Clark from the Air,* p. 50.

MBR Bookwatch, May, 2005, Diane Donovan, review of *Discovering Lewis & Clark from the Air.*

Music & Letters, July, 1972, review of *Music in the Cultured Generation: A Social History of Music in America, 1870-1900,* pp. 321-322.

Musical Quarterly, April, 1972, review of *Music in the Cultured Generation,* pp. 322-329.

Notes, December, 1972, Barbara Hampton, review of *Music in the Cultured Generation,* pp. 243-244; December, 1975, Charles H. Kaufman, review of *The Uses of Music: An Introduction to Music in Contemporary American Life,* pp. 275-278.

Oregon History Quarterly, winter, 2004, Ken DuBois, review of *Discovering Lewis & Clark from the Air,* p. 659.

ONLINE

Atlanta Symphony Orchestra Web site, http://www. atlantasymphony.org/ (December 7, 2006), Nick Jones, "The Legacy of Robert Shaw."

Discovering Lewis & Clark, http://www.lewis-clark.org/ (December 23, 2006), "Joseph A. Mussulman."*

* * *

MUSSULMAN, Joseph Agee
See MUSSULMAN, Joseph A.

* * *

MYERS, Tim 1953-
(Timothy Joseph Myers)

PERSONAL: Born August 14, 1953, in Portland, OR; son of James M. (a doctor) and Tedde (a homemaker) Myers; married M. Priscilla Myers (a university professor and reading specialist), 1973; children: Seth, Nick, Cassie. *Ethnicity:* "White—with a big streak of Irish." *Education:* Colorado College, B.A., 1975; University of Wisconsin—Madison, M.A., 1976; University of Colorado—Colorado Springs, teaching credential, 1981. *Politics:* "American." *Hobbies and other interests:* Music, sports, outdoor activities science, religion, philosophy, history, art, film, parenting, traveling, children.

ADDRESSES: Home—Santa Clara, CA; Colorado Springs, CO. *Office*—753 Fremont St., Santa Clara, CA 95050. *E-mail*—tmyers@scu.edu.

CAREER: Writer, songwriter, and professional storyteller. Classroom teacher, 1977-91; university lecturer in English and education at California State— Bakersfield, State University of New York system, and Santa Clara University.

MEMBER: Society of Children's Book Writers and Illustrators, Science-Fiction and Fantasy Writers of America, National Storytelling Network, West Coast Songwriters.

AWARDS, HONORS: Winner of national poetry contest judged by John Updike; Writers of the Future contest third-place winner, for science-fiction/fantasy manuscript; Paul A. Whittey Short-Story Award nomination, International Reading Association; Notable Book for Children citation, *Smithsonian* magazine, 2000, Irma Simonton Black and James H. Black Honor Award for Excellence in Children's Literature, Bank Street College of Education, and Honor Title, *Storytelling World,* both 2001, all for *Basho and the Fox;* Storyteller's Choice award, and Asian Pacific American Honor for Literature, both 2004, both for *Tanuki's Gift;* National Council for the Social Studies/Children's Book Council Notable Social Studies Trade Book designation, 2005, and California Young Reader Medal nomination, 2007-08, both for *Basho and the River Stones.*

WRITINGS:

FOR CHILDREN

Let's Call Him Lau-Wili-Wili-Humu-Humu-Nukunuku-Nukunuku-Apuaa-Oioi, illustrated by Daryl Arakaki, Bess Press (Honolulu, HI), 1993.

Basho and the Fox, illustrated by Oki S. Han, Marshall Cavendish (Tarrytown, NY), 2000.

The Priest and the Badger, Marshall Cavendish (New York, NY), 2002.

(Reteller) *Tanuki's Gift: A Japanese Tale,* illustrated by Robert Roth, Marshall Cavendish (Tarrytown, NY), 2002.

Basho and the River Stones, illustrated by Oki S. Han, Marshall Cavendish (New York, NY), 2004.

Good Babies: A Tale of Trolls, Humans, a Witch, and a Switch, illustrated by Kelly Murphy, Candlewick Press (Cambridge, MA), 2005.

Dark-Sparkle Tea, and Other Bedtime Poems, illustrated by Kelley Cunningham, Boyds Mills Press (Honesdale, PA), 2006.

The Furry-legged Teapot, illustrated by Robert McGuire, Marshall Cavendish (New York, NY), 2007.

Out-Foxed Fox, illustrated by Ariel Ya-wen Pang, Marshall Cavendish (New York, NY), 2007.

If You Give a T-Rex a Bone, Dawn Publications, 2007.

OTHER

That Mass at Which the Tongue Is Celebrant (adult poetry chapbook), Pecan Grove Press, 2005.

Contributor of poetry, fiction, and nonfiction to various publications for children and adults, including *Cricket, Cicada, Spider, Faces, Odyssey, Cobblestone, Appleseeds, Storyworks,* and *Highlights for Children.*

ADAPTATIONS: Basho and the Fox was adapted as a dance program performed at the University of Utah, 2002, and adapted by Pat Turner as a play produced in San Rafael, CA, 2006. *Basho and the River Stones* was adapted as a play produced in Burbank, CA, 2006.

SIDELIGHTS: In his picture books for children, Tim Myers explores the literature and folklore of several cultures, while also creating original works that feature imaginative flights of fancy. Reflecting the author's interest in Japanese culture, *Basho and the Fox* and *Basho and the River Stones* feature renowned seventeenth-century Japanese poet Matsuo Basho, a man who lives a solitary life of writing and study. A sense of whimsy comes to the fore in *Good Babies: A Tale of Trolls, Humans, a Witch, and a Switch,,* while in *Dark Sparkle Tea, and Other Bedtime Poems* Myers presents poems that entertain soon-to-be-tucked-in children with all manner of "nonsense, nursery-rhyme wordplay," according to *Booklist* reviewer Gillian Engberg.

One of Basho's main pleasures was sitting under a cherry tree on the banks of a peaceful river, contemplating the world and enjoying the cherries, and this is what occupies the poet's time in *Basho and the Fox.* When the poet comes upon a fox eating the cherries from his tree, he tries to chase the creature away. The crafty fox knows who Basho is, however, and it claims that foxes also have superior poetic ability. The beast makes a bargain with Basho: If the human poet can write a fine haiku, he can claim the cherries, but if not, the fruit will belong to the fox. Basho works hard all winter, creating two haiku to offer to the fox—one of which is the poem that becomes his most famous work. When the fox rejects the poems, Basho loses confidence in his abilities. However, because showing up empty-handed means he will forfeit the cherries, Basho dashes off a last-minute haiku before his third meeting with the fox. This time the creature is actually pleased—because Basho's new haiku mentions foxes—and when the vain fox concedes defeat, Basho wins the cherries but decides to share them with the foxes anyway. The battle of wits between man and fox continues in *Basho and the River Stones,* and the cherry harvest is once again the prize. This time the greedy fox tries to trick the poet out of his fruit. While the poet offers to share the tree's yield with the fox, the bushy-tailed creatures wants more. Dressed in a monk's garb, the fox tricks Basho by offering to buy the poet's share of the cherries with three fake gold coins. When the coins are revealed to be flat, round river stones, Basho turns his setback into inspiration, writes a haiku extolling the stones' beauty, and impresses the fox with his honorable attitude. There is one more trick to be played out before the story's end.

In *School Library Journal* Barbara Scotto praised *Basho and the Fox* as a "lively tale [that] has good pacing, convincing characters, and a clever ending." "Delivered with a light touch, in a lyrical narrative benefiting its poetic hero, Myers's cunning caper offers a sage lesson," a *Publishers Weekly* reviewer noted of the same story, while in *Horn Book* a critic remarked that Myers' "gently humorous story provides a palatable introduction to a centuries-old form of poetry and one of its great masters." Praising Myers' "exotic" retelling in *Basho and the River Stones,* Carol Ann Wilson wrote in *School Library Journal* that the author's "story-telling background is apparent in the pacing of the tale and in the carefully selected, descriptive narrative," and *Booklist* reviewer Karin Snelson deemed it "a clever original fable."

In *Tanuki's Gift: A Japanese Tale,* Myers offers an adaptation of a traditional folktale about a friendship between a Buddhist priest and a tanuki, a mystical "raccoon-dog" with a reputation for mischief. During a freezing winter storm, the tanuki appears at the priest's door, begging for shelter. Despite the tanuki's dubious reputation, the priest gladly agrees to let the creature weather the storm in his house. When the tanuki returns each evening for ten winters, the two develop a deep friendship. When the tanuki asks what it can do to repay the priest for his kindness, the man asks for three pieces of gold, hoping to use the coins to hire prayers to be said after his death as a way to ensure his entrance into Paradise. When the tanuki disappears, the priest despairs that he will never see his friend again. When the tanuki returns, months later, it honorably discharges its debt to the priest, but the man realizes that the coins are is irrelevant: the tanuki's friendship is the true gift. Kay Weisman, writing in *Booklist,* called *Tanuki's Gift* "a gentle fable, suitable for both story hours and lap-sharing." A *Publishers Weekly* critic predicted that the tanuki "will win readers' hearts," and Nancy A. Gifford noted in *School Library Journal* that, "although both the story and the art are understated, the book has a strong and lasting message."

Described by a *Kirkus Reviews* writer as a "warm-hearted twist on the 'changeling child' motif," *Good Babies* draws from the folklore of Norway. Myers' retelling focuses on young parents who are suffering because their infant sleeps the day away, then cries and whimpers all night. Hearing of the family's plight, a mischievous witch decides to cause the family even more trouble; she secretly substitutes the couple's human baby for a young troll whose troll parents are suffering through the opposite problem: an infant that sleeps all night and fusses all day! When the substitution pleases both families, the witch grows frustrated: although each set of parents is concerned that their child is growing up to be much uglier than they are, they continue to love it. Ultimately, the frustrated witch performs a second switch: she places each child with its original family in what *School Library Journal* reviewer Linda Staskus described as an "enjoyable story" that will find certain fans among "children who would like to trade in their noisy younger siblings."

"As a child, I didn't have much interest in 'school stuff,'" Myers once stated. "But in sixth grade, when our teacher told us to write an essay, I decided to write a poem instead. This was totally unlike me; the idea came straight out of the blue. The day after I handed the poem in, my teacher, Sister Mary Boniface, told me to stay behind when the other kids went out to recess. I was scared to death, certain I'd get in trouble. But to my amazement, she liked the poem and asked me to write more. I've been writing ever since.

"I love to write—it gives me the same kind of joy as my other great loves, like basketball and playing rock and roll. I love the work of it, the feel of typing, the thinking and planning, the re-writing. But mostly I love words and their flavors, and the beauty and power of stories. I love nonfiction too.

"I'm the oldest of eleven children, and I grew up in Colorado, in the shadow of Pikes Peak. These circumstances have shaped me in profound ways. I love noise and fun and craziness and crowds—not surprising, is it? I'm also the kind of person who has a deep relationship with land. And I've lived in England, Norway, and Japan, and traveled to many other countries, which also comes out in some of my writing.

"As a writer, my first goal is simply to write. I think an artist does art the way a tree or flower grows: something just keeps pushing to get out from inside, from 'underground,' as it were. To me it's a completely sacred thing. I'm deeply unhappy if I can't do it. But I aim for more too—I want my writing to give pleasure, to teach, to illuminate, to comfort, and to show new ways of looking at things or remind people of old ways that still work. Of course I don't achieve these goals all the time, but I try. I also want my writing to be filled with the joy of language, and that's true even about the sad and/or serious writing I do. And I write to express joy itself. I also think fun is a very serious and powerful thing!

"Although I love serious writing for adults (and non-serious too), I love to write for kids just as much. Mainly because I just love kids. I can't resist them. And writing for kids lets me use my imagination in unique ways. That's something else at the heart of my love for writing: the unspeakable deliciousness of being able to play in the vast fields of imagination. I've written about sailors in despair because their cook accidentally dropped his muffin tins overboard, about an Olympics-style race between snails, about talking foxes and troll babies living with humans, and ocean-crossing hummingbirds and rock-star hamsters. I'm constantly amazed, and grateful, at the infinite possibilities of imagination.

"My writing is also strongly influenced by my work as a storyteller, and many of my picture books are retellings of traditional tales or original stories in a folktale style. Because I know a lot of old stories, and am constantly learning more, a lot of the feel of folktales creeps into what I write. And I love poetry, so I have a strong tendency toward rhythm and rhyme.

"There's no set time when I write; it's basically any time I can. I get up in the morning and work out at the gym, then come home and write for as long as possible. But a writer is always writing, actually, and I get ideas, or words or phrases, or other information, all the time. Even in bed at night, or while I'm taking a shower, or riding my bike. One of my favorite things is to keep a journal, where I write down anything that comes to me: an idea for a poem, a thought, a reaction to a movie I've seen, something I heard someone say, all kinds of things. Oh, and lots of doodles.

"It seems to me that God (or Allah or Nirvana or whatever name you may use) gives each of us something unutterably precious: ourselves. Each of us is completely unique. And that means each of us has a special path in life that belongs to us alone. No one but you can walk your path, and no one but you is meant to. To be the best person you can be, the best possible version of yourself: that's the heart of life. Sometimes your path can be very difficult, but it's still your path, and it's still worth all you do to walk it the best way you know how. Writing is right there at the center of my path. I love it more than words can say."

BIOGRAPHICAL AND CRITICAL SOURCES:

PERIODICALS

Booklist, September 15, 2000, Connie Fletcher, review of *Basho and the Fox,* p. 249; March 15, 2003, Kay Weisman, review of *Tanuki's Gift: A Japanese Tale,* pp. 1328; November 1, 2004, Karin Snelson, review of *Basho and the River Stones,* p. 490; March 15, 2006, Gillian Engberg, review of *Dark Sparkle Tea, and Other Bedtime Poems,* p. 49.

Bulletin of the Center for Children's Books, November, 2004, Hope Morrison, review of *Basho and the River Stones,* p. 135.

Horn Book, September, 2000, review of *Basho and the Fox,* p. 553.

Kirkus Reviews, March 15, 2003, review of *Tanuki's Gift,* pp. 474-475; August 1, 2004, review of *Basho and the River Stones,* p. 746; October 1, 2005, review of *Good Babies: A Tale of Trolls, Humans, a Witch, and a Switch,* p. 1085.

Publishers Weekly, September 25, 2000, review of *Basho and the Fox,* p. 117; February 10, 2003, review of *Tanuki's Gift,* p. 186.

School Library Journal, October, 2000, Barbara Scotto, review of *Basho and the Fox,* p. 131; July, 2003, Nancy A. Gifford, review of *Tanuki's Gift,* p. 115; October, 2004, Carol Ann Wilson, review of *Basho and the River Stones,* p. 125; December, 2005, Linda Staskus, review of *Good Babies,* p. 199; June, 2006, Lee Bock, review of *Dark Sparkle Tea, and Other Bedtime Poems,* p. 139.

ONLINE

Tim Myers Home Page, http://epl/scu.edu/~timmyers (February 7, 2007).

*   *   *

MYERS, Timothy Joseph
See MYERS, Tim

N

NADELSON, Reggie

PERSONAL: Born in New York, NY.

CAREER: Writer, journalist, and documentary filmmaker.

WRITINGS:

"ARTIE COHEN" MYSTERY SERIES

Red Mercury Blues, Faber, 1995, published as *Red Hot Blues,* St. Martin's Press (New York, NY), 1998.

Hot Poppies, Faber (London, England), 1997, St. Martin's Press (New York, NY), 1999.

Bloody London, Thomas Dunne Books (New York, NY), 1999.

Sex Dolls, Faber (London, England), 2002.

Disturbed Earth, William Heinemann (London, England), 2004, Walker & Co. (New York, NY), 2005.

Red Hook, William Heinemann (London, England), 2005, Walker & Co. (New York, NY), 2006.

Fresh Kills, William Heinemann (London, England), 2006.

Skin Trade, Arrow (London, England), 2006.

OTHER

Who Is Angela Davis? The Biography of a Revolutionary, P.H. Wyden (New York, NY), 1972.

Comrade Rockstar: The Search for Dean Reed, Chatto & Windus (London, England), 1991, revised edition, 2004, published as *Comrade Rockstar: The Life and Mystery of Dean Reed, the All-American Boy Who Brought Rock 'n' Roll to the Soviet Union,* Walker & Co. (New York, NY), 2006.

Somebody Else, Faber (London, England), 2003.

SIDELIGHTS: Reggie Nadelson has gained recognition for her mystery series featuring protagonist Artie Cohen, a Russian-American police officer in New York City. The first book in the series, *Red Mercury Blues,* was published in America as *Red Hot Blues.* The book introduces Artie Cohen who, having emigrated from Russia to the United States some twenty-five years earlier, vows never to return. But General Gennadi Ustinov, a former member of the KGB and Artie's godfather, contacts Artie and asks to meet with him. Ustinov, however, is killed on a television show before they can meet. Artie's investigation into Ustinov's death and his pursuit of the killer leads him to the Russian Mafia in New York and Moscow. Artie learns about a plot involving the smuggling of atomic weapons and a dangerous substance called red mercury. In a *Booklist* review, Bill Ott suggested that this volume can be perceived "as a suspense-filled thriller; as an atmosphere-drenched look at Russian noir; and as an introduction to a captivating new hard-boiled hero." London *Observer* critic John Snow called the book "a ripping yarn" and "a compulsive read."

Hot Poppies, Nadelson's second book in the series, finds Artie retired from the New York Police Department. He is called out of retirement when a friend, Ricky Tae, finds a dead pregnant Chinese girl in his shop and asks Artie to investigate the murder. Ricky was badly wounded in saving Artie's life during Artie's earlier Russian Mafia investigation. Ricky also asks the former police officer to find the drug dealer who has been supplying his daughter with a irradiated heroin known as Hot Poppy. In addition, Artie helps his lover, Lily Hanes, who is facing trouble in trying to adopt a girl from mainland China. Artie's investigation into these matters leads him into the underworld of New York's Chinatown with its illegal sweatshops and forced prostitution. Artie then travels to Hong Kong and eventually into China, where he uncovers the practice of selling and buying babies and young girls and where unattractive girls and weak babies are dispensable while pretty girls are forced into prostitution and healthy babies are fattened for adoption in the West. Artie eventually tracks down and confronts the ringleader, Mr. Big. As noted by a reviewer for *Publishers Weekly:* "Nadelson makes [New York's Chinatown] her own by creating fresh characters with unexpected insights that make their travails both entertaining and real."

In *Bloody London,* the Russian mob is taking control of the London real estate market. Ott felt that with this installment, the series seems to be abandoning Russian noir in favor of "a kind of surrealistic, almost-cartoonish melding of hard-boiled style and James Bondish content." Artie is now a private investigator working for his federal prosecutor mentor Sonny Lippert. Lily, now the mother of an adopted Chinese baby girl, worries that his current case will cause her past to come to the surface. Tolya Sverdloff, Artie's Russian friend from Moscow and Brighton Beach, who is now involved in high finance, has had a safe room constructed within his apartment. A *Publishers Weekly* contributor commented that "the novel really takes off . . . when Artie follows Lily to a London ready to burst from catastrophic rains and the accumulated poisons of decades of official greed and neglect."

Disturbed Earth is set in post-9/11 2002. Artie is back in New York and worried about the safety of his twelve-year-old godson, Billy Farone, when it is suspected that a serial killer is stalking New York children. Billy is missing, and a pile of bloody clothing, including a shirt given to Billy by his friend, May Luca, is found under a Brooklyn boardwalk. A young girl is found dead, and Artie calls on the Brighton Beach community of Russian emigres and mobsters to help solve the case. A *Publishers Weekly* reviewer wrote that Nadelson "pulls few punches, and the final revelation is a genuine shocker—a rare accomplishment in crime fiction these days."

Sadness pervades *Red Hook,* with Artie now married to Maxine Crabbe, who lost her firefighter husband during the terrorist attack on the World Trade Center. Artie

does not love her as he did Lily, and voices no opposition when Maxine leaves for the Jersey shore with her twin daughters, Maria and Millie. Artie will join them, but first he makes a trip to Red Hook, which is in the process of being gentrified, to meet with his old friend, retired journalist Sid McKay. Sid, who is gay and black, is upset with the state of the news media and the greed of the real estate players who are taking over, and is ultimately murdered. Other plot threads include the fear of a terrorist attack during the Republican convention and Lily' reappearance to explain why she left Artie. *New York Observer* reviewer Max Abelson wrote: "Nothing can match that vibrant real-estate map of New York, but what comes closest is the novel's central threesome—the cynical mogul, the doomed old man, the restless investigator. They've got more nervousness than nerve, which fills the novel with twitchy, wobbly energy." "Everything comes together on the waterfront in a finale so involving you won't sleep until you turn the last page," wrote Helena Kennedy for the *Guardian Online.* Marilyn Stasio, who described Nadelson as being "a regional writer to the core," noted in the *New York Times Book Review* that Nadelson views the old, abandoned neighborhoods "through those twinkling lights that make everything look beautiful at night."

Before Nadelson wrote her first mystery, she produced a book that examines the life and death of musician Dean Reed. *Comrade Rockstar: The Search for Dean Reed* follows Reed's rise to mediocre success in the United States in the early 1960s and his association with the Soviet Youth Organization, which helped him achieve true fame and notoriety. In researching his life, Nadelson interviewed those who knew him, including girlfriends and wives, his mother, and other celebrities of the time. Reed, a Colorado native, was an extra in Hollywood, a South American political activist, and a great success as a Soviet Union film and pop star during the 1970s and 1980s. Russian teens thronged to see him, and he was favored by Russian leaders because he promoted official political positions. In 1986 Reed's body was found in a lake near his home in East Germany. Nadelson discusses the mysterious circumstances surrounding his death, which may have been related to his desire to return to America. Nadelson, like many Russian women of the time, was enthralled by the handsome, charismatic singer and, after his death, she sought to discover the truth of his life and death. Following the collapse of the Soviet Union, previously secret documents became available. Much information about Reed was revealed and Nadelson included these details in the revised edition of her book, published in the United States as *Comrade Rockstar: The Life and*

Mystery of Dean Reed, the All-American Boy Who Brought Rock 'n' Roll to the Soviet Union. New Statesman writer Dave Hill found that "Nadelson conveys this bizarre narrative with wit and pathos."

BIOGRAPHICAL AND CRITICAL SOURCES:

PERIODICALS

Booklist, February 15, 1998, Bill Ott, review of *Red Hot Blues,* p. 989; January 1, 1999, Bill Ott, review of *Hot Poppies,* p. 838; November 15, 1999, Bill Ott, review of *Bloody London,* p. 607; April 15, 2006, Joanne Wilkinson, review of *Comrade Rockstar: The Life and Mystery of Dean Reed, the All-American Boy Who Brought Rock 'n' Roll to the Soviet Union,* p. 17.

Kirkus Reviews, February 1, 1998, review of *Red Hot Blues,* p. 157; April 15, 2005, review of *Disturbed Earth,* p. 454; April 15, 2006, review of *Comrade Rockstar,* p. 395; August 1, 2006, review of *Red Hook,* p. 758.

Library Journal, April 15, 2005, Roland Person, review of *Disturbed Earth,* p. 80.

New Statesman, March 22, 1991, Dave Hill, review of *Comrade Rockstar,* pp. 44-45.

New York Observer, December 11, 2006, Max Abelson, review of *Red Hook.*

New York Times Book Review, July 9, 2006, Thomas Mallon, review of *Comrade Rockstar,* p. 11; November 26, 2006, Marilyn Stasio, review of *Red Hook,* p. 21.

Observer (London, England), December 10, 1995, John Snow, review of *Red Mercury Blues,* p. 15.

Publishers Weekly, January 18, 1999, review of *Hot Poppies,* p. 331; November 22, 1999, review of *Bloody London,* p. 45; May 2, 2005, Leonard Picker, *"PW* Talks with Reggie Nadelson: 9/11 Changed Everything" (interview), p. 180, review of *Disturbed Earth,* p. 181; April 10, 2006, review of *Comrade Rockstar,* p. 61; August 14, 2006, review of *Red Hook,* p. 183.

ONLINE

Guardian Online, http://books.guardian.co.uk/ (October 29, 2005), Helena Kennedy, review of *Red Hook.**

NASAW, David 1945-

PERSONAL: Born July 18, 1945, in Cortland, NY; son of Joshua J. (a lawyer) and Beatrice (a teacher) Nasaw; married Dinita E.R. Smith (a writer), June 10, 1978; children: twins, Peter and Daniel. *Education:* Bucknell University, B.A., 1967; Columbia University, Ph.D., 1972. *Religion:* Jewish.

ADDRESSES: Home—New York, NY. *Office*—History Program, City University of New York Graduate Center, 365 5th Ave., New York, NY 10016. *Agent*—Andrew Wylie, 250 W. 57th St., Ste. 2114, New York, NY 10017. *E-mail*—dnasaw@gc.cuny.edu.

CAREER: Historian, educator, and writer. City University of New York (C.U.N.Y.), 1973—, began as associate professor of history at the College of Staten Island, became Arthur M. Schlesinger Professor of American History at The Graduate Center and chair of the C.U.N.Y. history department, executive officer of Ph.D. program, and director of the Center for the Humanities at the Graduate Center. Has appeared as himself in documentaries, including *The American Experience,* 1996, and *Ten Days That Unexpectedly Changed America: The Homestead Strike,* and *Ten Days That Unexpectedly Changed America: The Assassination of President McKinley,* both 2006.

MEMBER: American Historical Association, Organization of American Historians.

AWARDS, HONORS: National Endowment for the Humanities fellowship for college teaching, 1981-82; National Book Critics Circle Award nomination, 2001, Bancroft Prize, 2001, Sperber Prize for Biography and J. Anthony Lukas Book Prize, all for *The Chief: The Life of William Randolph Hearst.*

WRITINGS:

NONFICTION

(Editor) *Starting Your Own High School,* Random House (New York, NY), 1972.

Schooled to Order: A Social History of Public Schooling in the United States, Oxford University Press (New York, NY), 1979.

Children of the City: At Work and at Play, Doubleday (New York, NY), 1985.

(Editor) *The Course of United States History,* Dorsey Press (Chicago, IL), 1987.

Going Out: The Rise and Fall of Public Amusements, BasicBooks (New York, NY), 1993.

The Chief: The Life of William Randolph Hearst, Houghton Mifflin (Boston, MA), 2000.

(Selector and author of introduction) Andrew Carnegie, *The "Gospel of Wealth" Essays and Other Writings,* Penguin Books (New York, NY), 2006.

Andrew Carnegie, Penguin Press (New York, NY), 2006.

Contributor of articles to periodicals, including *American Heritage, Harvard Education Review, New York Times, Los Angeles Times, Wall Street Journal, Boston Globe, London Review of Books,* and *Nation.*

SIDELIGHTS: Historian and professor David Nasaw has written numerous books on history and education, including *Schooled to Order: A Social History of Public Schooling in the United States, Children of the City: At Work and at Play,* and *Going Out: The Rise and Fall of Public Amusements.* His *The Chief: The Life of William Randolph Hearst,* was nominated for a National Book Critics Circle Award in 2001.

In *Schooled to Order,* Nasaw analyzes the social function of public education. Nasaw once told *CA:* "*Schooled to Order* was written to demonstrate how the schools function not simply as 'educational' agencies, but as social and cultural agencies as well. Their task is not only or primarily to 'educate' society. The history of public schools demonstrates the ways in which elementary schools in the 1830s through the 1850s, high schools at the turn of the twentieth century, and colleges and universities in the post-World War II era were transformed in 'mission' as they were expanded to include the 'plain' people of working-class origins who had previously been excluded."

Nasaw's *Children of the City* examines the lives of turn-of-the-century children and disputes the common belief that 1900 to 1920 was an extremely unpleasant and dangerous period for city children. The book concentrates on "children born to working-class parents who owned little or no property, had received little or no formal education, and worked for wages or piece rates at skilled or unskilled jobs," commented Nasaw. In *Children of the City,* "Nasaw is up to a bit of historical revisionism and he makes a most persuasive job of it," wrote Jonathan Yardley in *Washington Post Book World,* "his research has convinced him that while life for city children in these years was far from easy, on the whole it was educational, productive and enjoyable." According to Nasaw, life in the streets was "an active, organized community with its own structures of authority, law and order. The streets were not jungles and the children were not savages."

In Nasaw's 1994 *Going Out,* he turns his attention to the ways in which public recreation has grown and changed over the course of the last hundred years. Nasaw notes that the increasing availability of electric lighting at the turn of the twentieth century altered public spaces after dark. Where before only 'sporting' men frequented dank, rank barrooms, better lit streets and public places lured unmarried working men and women as well as families to after-dark entertainments, including amusement parks, vaudeville stages, penny arcades, and baseball games. Within these public spaces, new immigrants who were otherwise segregated by neighborhood and jobs, could "submerge themselves in a corporate body, an 'American' public, that transcended these divisions," wrote Warren Goldstein in *Nation.* Where ethnic differences might be a source of jokes on vaudeville stages, immigrants used boycotts and protests if the jokes got ugly; the power of their purses kept show business entrepreneurs in line. For African-Americans, however, another dynamic prevailed.

Vaudeville shows and other forms of popular entertainment maintained the racial stereotypes found in minstrel shows from before the Civil War; while white actors donned black-face to perform such stereotypes, African-American actors were forced to perform the same insulting roles. According to Goldstein, Nasaw argues that "what enabled members of a heterogeneous white audience to come together, to forge a newly American identity, was its simultaneous ability to laugh generously at its own members (thereby enacting anew the experience of white solidarity inside every performance) while building and reinforcing—through humor, insult, song and caricature—the unbreachable wall separating whites from African Americans."

From the twenties onward, movie houses began to dominate public entertainment, and, along with the advent of television and a growing middle-class fear of urban spaces, have contributed to the demise of the great demotic public attractions. As an example, Nasaw tells us that "over twenty million men, women, and children visited Coney Island alone during the 1909 season," a number, according to Goldstein, that even today's Disneyland does not attract.

Critics were uniformly impressed with Nasaw's scholarship and argumentation. *Arts Education Policy Review* writer Samuel Hope commented that the book "helps us to face the dangers of cultural fragmentation with useful historical information and to deal thoughtfully with questions about the viability of public presentation in our own turn-of-the-century world." In his lengthy review Warren Goldstein commented: "No other book brings together so much material about so many different urban entertainment forms—and connects their history with a few simple and powerful overarching themes." *Entertainment Weekly* contributor D.A. Ball called the book "superb."

In *The Chief,* Nasaw sought to challenge the myth of William Randolph Hearst that Orson Welles so convincingly created in his film *Citizen Kane,* and substitute a more informed understanding of the influential newspaper publisher and multimillionaire.

Hearst was born in San Francisco in 1863, the son of a panhandler, George Hearst, who made an amazing fortune first in gold and then in mining. Hearst's mother set her son up to be an American aristocrat as befitted his wealth, organizing "a European tour, then prep school for the boy in New Hampshire, followed by admission to Harvard College," according to a *Business Week* contributor. After being expelled from Harvard for his poor academic performance and decadent lifestyle, Hearst began to study newspaper production. In 1887, he took over the *San Francisco Examiner,* a daily owned by his father. He spent lavishly on equipment and writers, and his pro-labor, anti-railroad paper doubled its circulation in a year. Based on his success in San Francisco, Hearst decided to try his hand in New York in the mid-1890s with the *New York Journal.* "Its prototypical story featured corrupt officialdom, a victimized public, and the newspaper as rescuing hero. And it was unflinchingly Democratic," wrote a *Business Week* contributor.

Soon Hearst began to use his newspaper influence to garner political power; Nasaw writes that Hearst was "the first publisher to understand that the communications media was potentially more powerful than the parties and their politicians." He used this insight to get

himself elected to represent New York in Congress in 1902. He later pursued the Democratic nomination for the presidency. Failed bids for the New York governor's office and the New York City mayor's office finally convinced Hearst to end his political aspirations. Instead, he turned his energies back into media, purchasing newspapers nationwide and eventually setting up a movie studio to feature the talents of his girlfriend Marion Davies, a chorus girl he had met when she was eighteen. (Hearst remained married to Millicent Willson, another former chorus girl, whom he set up in a Long Island mansion but almost never saw once he met Davies.)

As time went on, Hearst's politics shifted rightward, and his newspapers began to support Republican candidates. Although he supported Franklin Delano Roosevelt's election as president, he later began a virulent anti-communism crusade that went to the point of calling Roosevelt a "red." He solicited newspaper columns from Benito Mussolini and Adolf Hitler. His extreme anti-communism led liberals and leftists to boycott Hearst's newspapers, and eventually to the temporary demise of his empire; "in the late 1930s, as millions in debt came due, creditors seized control of Hearst's media properties," wrote the *Business Week* contributor. America's involvement in World War II boosted the public's interest in newspapers, and Hearst's papers rebounded. But he never again achieved the political and financial stature he possessed in the first twenty years of the century.

Nasaw's biography was hailed by critics as a major work on a major figure, and reviewed widely and in great depth. Reviewers were generally impressed with the detail of Nasaw's research, but differed on his presentation of the facts of Hearst's life. The reviewer from *Business Week* wrote that *The Chief* is "rigorously impartial, to the point of avoiding Judgments." The reviewer added: "Nasaw all but says, here are the facts in all of their voluptuous complexity—you decide what to make of them." Whereas *Booklist* reviewer Gilbert Taylor was grateful that "Nasaw, blessedly, eschews psychobiography," other critics wanted more analysis. An *Economist* reviewer stated that "[Hearst's] life, as told by Mr Nasaw, is a cautionary tale of how a young idealist can degenerate into a rancid reactionary." Harold Evans, who reviewed the book for the *New York Times Book Review,* was enthusiastic about Nasaw's work, noting that "he is a meticulous researcher and a cool analyst." Evans added: "At the end of his examination of all the material, Nasaw confesses that Hearst's confidence in Hitler remains 'baffling.' The conclusion is symptomatic of the scrupulous honesty that distinguishes this biography." Orville Schell, who also reviewed the book for the *New York Times Book Review,* wrote: "Even to open 'The Chief,' David Nasaw's wonderful new biography of William Randolph Hearst, is to be swept away by the narrative flowing through its pages."

In *Andrew Carnegie,* Nasaw's biography of the Scotland native turned Pittsburgh steel tycoon, the author recounts Carnegie's rise to success and his inner drive to take his wealth and impact the society at large around him, which encompassed not only his philanthropic efforts—including the endowment of more than 2,000 libraries throughout the country—but also his writings about philosophy and politics and his philanthropic efforts. Although the author writes about Carnegie's famous battles with his workers, including the violent and deadly Homestead Strike of 1892 that critically damaged Carnegie's reputation, Nasaw also delves into Carnegie's efforts as a peace activist and his fight against American imperialism. "Nasaw . . . understands narrative well, making the Carnegie biography a lively reading experience as well as a rewarding scholarly mission," wrote Steve Weinberg in the *Houston Chronicle.* A contributor to the *Economist* pointed out: "Mr Nasaw . . . seeks to humanise Carnegie by giving more attention than other biographers have to the steelman's private life, drawing extensively on unpublished bits of his autobiography, love letters and the diaries of his relatives and close friends." T.J. Stiles, writing on the *Salon.com* Web site, commented that the author "has produced the most thorough, accurate and authoritative biography of Carnegie to date." Stiles went on to note: "Carnegie has been the subject of a number of studies, and authored an autobiography of lasting influence. It speaks highly of Nasaw's prowess as a researcher, then, that he has uncovered entire episodes previously unknown to historians." Frederick J. Augustyn, Jr., writing in the *Library Journal,* noted that Nasaw "adds a new century's insight into a figure whom we all thought we knew so well."

BIOGRAPHICAL AND CRITICAL SOURCES:

BOOKS

Nasaw, David, *Children of the City: At Work and at Play,* Doubleday (New York, NY), 1985.

Nasaw, David, *Going Out: The Rise and Fall of Public Amusements,* BasicBooks (New York, NY), 1993.

Nasaw, David, *The Chief: The Life of William Randolph Hearst,* Houghton Mifflin (Boston, MA), 2000.

PERIODICALS

American Spectator, September, 2000, John Corry, review of *The Chief,* pp. 70-72.

Arts Education Policy Review, September-October, 1994, Samuel Hope, review of *Going Out,* pp. 37-38.

Booklist, April 15, 2000, Gilbert Taylor, review of *The Chief,* p. 1498; August 1, 2006, Jay Freeman, review of *Andrew Carnegie,* p. 4.

Business Week, June 12, 2000, "Publishing Magnate, Political Chameleon," p. 26.

Chronicle of Philanthropy, October 26, 2006, Anne W. Howard, review of *Andrew Carnegie.*

Economist, June 17, 2000, "Media Mogul—Better Dead than Ready," p. 6; November 4, 2006, review of *Andrew Carnegie,* p. 93.

Entertainment Weekly, December 3, 1993, D.A. Ball, review of *Going Out,* p. 66; June 16, 2000, Suzanne Ruta, review of *The Chief,* p. 84.

Fortune, October 16, 2006, Anne Fisher, review of *Andrew Carnegie,* p. 224.

Houston Chronicle, November 17, 2006, Steve Weinberg, review of *Andrew Carnegie.*

Kirkus Reviews, May 15, 2006, review of *Andrew Carnegie,* p. S18; August 1, 2006, review of *Andrew Carnegie,* p. 770.

Library Journal, September 1, 2006, Frederick J. Augustyn, Jr., review of *Andrew Carnegie,* p. 157.

Nation, September 5, 1994, Warren Goldstein, review of *Going Out,* pp. 244-247; July 10, 2000, Dana Frank, "The Devil and Mr. Hearst," p. 33.

New York Review of Books, August 10, 2000, Russell Baker, review of *The Chief,* pp. 4-6.

New York Times Book Review, June 28, 2000, Orville Schell, "Hearst, Man and Mogul: Going beyond the Myths;" July 2, 2000, Harold Evans, "Press Baron's Progress"; November 5, 2006, Richard Parker, review of *Andrew Carnegie,* p. 10.

Pittsburgh City Paper, October 19, 2006, Chris Potter, "A Conversation with David Nasaw."

Publishers Weekly, May 22, 2000, review of *The Chief,* p. 84; August 7, 2006, review of *Andrew Carnegie,* p. 44.

Time, August 7, 2000, John F. Stacks, "For Better or Hearst," p. 86.

Washington Post Book World, March 27, 1985, Jonathan Yardley, review of *Children of the City.*

World and I, November, 2000, Lloyd Eby, "Life and Times of a Press Lord," p. 228.

ONLINE

Bookreporter.com, http://www.bookreporter.com/ (February 9, 2007), Robert Finn, review of *Andrew Carnegie.*

City University of New York Web site, http://www.cuny.edu/ (October 16, 2003).

Internet Movie Database, http://www.imdb.com/ (February 9, 2007), information on author's film work.

Salon.com, http://www.salon.com/ (October 25, 2006), T.J. Stiles, review of *Andrew Carnegie.*

*   *   *

NESTLE, Marion 1936-

PERSONAL: Born 1936; children: Charles, Rebecca. *Education:* University of California, Berkeley, B.A., 1959, Ph.D., 1968, M.P.H., 1986.

ADDRESSES: Office—Department of Nutrition, Food Studies, and Public Health, New York University, 35 W. 4th St., 12th Fl., New York, NY 10012-1172. *E-mail*—marion.nestle@nyu.edu.

CAREER: Nutritionist, molecular biologist, educator, and writer. Brandeis University, Waltham, MA, lecturer in biology, 1971-73, assistant professor of biology, 1974-76; University of California, San Francisco, School of Medicine, San Francisco, CA, lecturer in biochemistry and biophysics, 1976-84, associate dean, school of medicine, human biology programs administrative director, medical scientist training program, 1976-86, lecturer in medicine, 1979-84, acting director, medical scientist training program 1983-84, lecturer in family and community medicine, 1984-85, director, John Tung/American Cancer Society clinical nutrition education center, 1984-86, adjunct associate professor, family and community medicine, 1985-86, associated faculty, Institute for Health Policy Studies and Institute for Aging Health Policy, 1983-86; Office of Disease Prevention and Health Promotion, Department of Health and Human Services, Washington, DC, staff director for nutrition policy, senior nutrition policy advisor, managing editor, *Surgeon General's Report on Nutrition and Health* (1988), 1986-88; New York University, New York, NY, School of Education, professor and chair, nutrition and food studies, 1998-2003, professor and director of Public Health Initiatives, 2003-04; Paulette Goddard Professor of Nutrition, Food Studies, and Public Health, c. 2004—, honorary professor in the Department of Sociology, 2006. Visiting professorships include Cornell University, College of Agriculture, Division of Nutritional Sciences, 2006; University of California, Berkeley, Schools of Public Policy, Public Health, and Journalism, 2006; and University of California Berkeley, Graduate School of Journalism, 2007. Also a member of numerous federal, state, city, professional, community, editorial, and advisory committees and boards, including the FDA Science Advisory Board, 1998-2001; Research!America National Advisory Committee on Prevention Research, 2000—; Harvard Business School, Private and Public, Scientific, Academic and Consumer Food Policy Committee, 1995—; *Journal of Public Health Policy,* 1999—; *Nutrition Week,* 2001—; Chez Panisse Foundation advisory board, 2005; Slow Food, USA, advisory board, 2005, and Pew Commission on Industrial Animal Production and Public Health, 2006.

MEMBER: American Association for the Advancement of Science, American Public Health Association, American Society for Clinical Nutrition, American Society for Nutrition Science, Association for the Study of Food and Society, Center for Science in the Public Interest, International Association of Culinary Professionals, James Beard Foundation, Les Dames d'Escoffier, National Association for Public Health Policy, Public Health Association of New York City, Women Chefs and Restaurateurs, Phi Beta Kappa.

AWARDS, HONORS: Recipient of numerous awards, honors, and appointments, including American Public Health Association, Food and Nutrition Section Award, 1994, for Excellence in Dietary Guidance; *Eating Well* magazine, Nutrition Educator of the Year, 1997; Roundtable for Women in Food Service, Pacesetter Award, 1999, for Educator of the Year; James Beard Foundation, Literary Award, 2003, for *Food Politics: How the Food Industry Influences Nutrition and Health; Who's Who in Food and Beverage in America,* Association of American Publisher's Award for *Food Politics* (best public health book); and World Hunger Year Harry Chapin Book Award, for *Food Politics;* UCLA Center for Society, the Individual, and Genetics distinguished fellow, 2004; Daniel E. Griffiths Research Award, New York University, 2004; Alumna of the Year, University of California Berkeley, School of Public Health, 2004; David P. Rall Award for Advocacy in Public Health, American Public Health Association, 2004; American Association for the Advancement of Science fellow, 2005; Health Quality Award, national Committee for Quality Assurance, 2005; American Society for Nutritional Sciences fellow, 2005; American Association for the Advancement of Science fellow, California Public Health Association, 2006.

WRITINGS:

NONFICTION

Nutrition in Clinical Practice, Jones Medical Publications (Greenbrae, CA), 1985.
Food Politics: How the Food Industry Influences Nutrition and Health, University of California Press (Berkeley, CA), 2002.
Safe Food: Bacteria, Biotechnology, and Bioterrorism, University of California Press (Berkeley, CA), 2003.
What to Eat, North Point Press (New York, NY), 2006.

Contributor of articles to journals and periodicals, including *American Journal of Public Health, Journal of the American Dietetic Association,* and *Muscle & Fitness/Hers.* Contributor to books, including *Encyclopedia of Ethical, Legal, and Policy Issues in Biotechnology,* edited by T.J. Murray and M.J. Mehlman, John Wiley & Sons (New York, NY), 2000, and *The Cambridge World History of Food and Nutrition,* Cambridge University Press (New York, NY), 2000.

SIDELIGHTS: Marion Nestle is a food and nutrition expert. As editor of the U.S. government's *Surgeon General's Report on Diet and Health,* she is well aware of the politics—governmental and big business—involved in food production and its not-so-safe marketing to the American consumer. Her extensive experience as an academic nutritionist, membership on a plethora of governmental and secular boards associated with the food and nutrition industry, and reviewer of articles for research and medical journals focusing on that subject, all support her credentials as author of numerous articles and her three books.

Food Politics: How the Food Industry Influences Nutrition and Health was described by David Maloof in *Natural Health* as a "devastating analysis" of the food industry in America. A reviewer for *Social Policy* called it a "carefully considered, calmly stated, devastating criticism of the nation's food industry and its efforts to get people to eat excessive amounts of unhealthy food." When asked by Mary Duenwald in an interview for the *New York Times* exactly how the food industry promotes overeating, Nestle replied: "Just by promoting eating. By spending 10 billion dollars a year in direct media advertising. That is so much more than is spent on health and nutrition education, you can't even put them in the same stratosphere."

In her book, Nestle compares America's food industry to the tobacco industry, accusing food companies of misleading consumers; obstructing regulations that would help people lead healthier lives; and marketing unhealthy food such as Coca Cola to schoolchildren. She also noted in her interview with Duenwald that the reason the 1988 *Surgeon General's Report on Nutrition and Health* was never updated as planned is because it is "too controversial. If you tell people what to eat, you have to tell them to eat less of what? The sugar industry people were in our office all the time. They most emphatically did not want us to say eat less sugar. The meat industry was really worried, since fat was a big issue, and meat is where the saturated fat is." She indicates in her book that she was told "point blank" that the report could not suggest people eat less meat, less sugar—or any other food. If it did, big business could have pulled a financial plug that would sink the entire governmental study.

Yet Nestle points out that good nutritional advice has remained constant for more than fifty years: Simply put, eat a diet rich in fruits, vegetables, and grains. Regardless, consumers seem to grow more confused by the day about what constitutes a healthy diet. She states that food industry lobbyists invested more than 52 million dollars in 1998 alone, and cited specific instances where government was "persuaded" to abandon straight talk and use increasingly sophisticated language when advising consumers. A reviewer of her book noted in the *Economist:* "A revised version of *Dietary Goals,* for example, struck out its initial recommendation to 'decrease consumption of meat' and replaced it with the harder-to-follow suggestion that Americans should 'choose meats, poultry, and fish which will reduce saturated fat intake.'"

Nestle also attacks the food industry for spiking highly processed, nutritionally empty foods, like many breakfast cereals, with supplements. The manufacturers can then market what is really junk food with mislead-ing claims of health benefits. Conversely, wholesome foods are infused with sugars, salts, and oils to make them tastier while making them a serious health risk. The reason for such highly processed food, she states, is profit. Food companies can charge much higher prices for processed food. In her interview with Duenwald, she gave an example: "Potatoes are cheap. Potato chips aren't." Nestle added: "The objective is to process foods as much as possible. But many of these highly processed foods are junk foods—relatively high in calories and low in nutrients."

Stephen H. Webb commented for the *Christian Century:* "As long as we want more than carrot sticks, brown rice, and tofu, according to Marion Nestle's new book, food companies will continue to be as deceptive as big tobacco and as cozy with the government as the military industry. Food does not really kill, then. Only people do—the people who trade on confusion and affluence to market food that tastes so good people will risk their health for it."

Webb stated, however, that "Nestle never quite answers the question of how taste buds could be so vulnerable to systematic manipulation and deception." He declared what is missing is an understanding of the basic human tendency toward gluttony and the symbolic role of certain foods in our society. As an example, he noted that most people believe a meal without meat is just not a meal. In contrast, he observed that people in poorer countries whose diets consist primarily of vegetables and grains suffer far less from "diseases that plague af-fluent Americans." Webb also commented: "As Nestle points out, most of us think that we choose food based on taste, cost and convenience; we resist thinking of ourselves as easy targets of marketing strategies. Consequently, we overestimate our own rationality and underestimate the power of advertising. Just try taking some kids to a McDonald's and forcing them to order salad. We are much less in control of our lives than we would like to think."

Stephen Clapp closed his review of the book for *Food Chemical News* by commenting: "Regardless of who is to blame for the obesity epidemic, Nestle has laid down a challenge that won't easily go away. It will be interest-ing to see how the food industry responds."

Nestle's third book, *Safe Food: Bacteria, Biotechnol-ogy, and Bioterrorism,* poses the question "who decides when food is safe?" Conservatively, more than seventy-

six million cases of food poisoning occur in this nation every year, not just from food prepared at restaurants, but also food purchased at supermarkets. In his review of the book for the *Washington Monthly,* Chris Mooney pointed out that Nestle believes food safety is not just a matter of science but a matter of politics. "In most respects, the campaign to bring safety to food produc-tion is a classic Washington tale, with big corporations energetically lobbying Congress, generating pseudo-science, gaming the regulatory process, and subverting the public good to preserve profits," commented Mooney.

In her book *What to Eat,* Nestle provides an aisle-by-aisle guide to buying food in a the supermarket. The author writes about the marketing strategies that lead consumers to buy food semi-consciously and then delves into how to shop for healthy foods in the various sections of the supermarket—from produce and diary to packaged foods and bottled water. In the process she discusses various issues such as additives and nutrition and how food production impacts the environment. Nestle also reasserts eating essential guidelines and rules that have proven over many years of study to be healthy, including consuming fewer calories, exercising more, and eating more fruits and vegetables and less unhealthy food such as candy and other junk food. Susan Male Smith, writing in *Environmental Nutrition,* noted that the author provides "insider information on corporate motivation, labeling secrets and other culinary contro-versies." In his review in *Booklist,* Mark Knoblauch wrote that the author "does present very helpful shop-ping guidelines for consumers determined to be vigilant about their food." A *Publishers Weekly* contributor wrote that the author's "prose is informative and entertaining" and noted "her intelligent and reassuring approach." Dorothy Kalins, writing in the *New York Times Book Review,* commented that Nestle "shoots straight though food industry hype," adding: "She pulls no punches."

BIOGRAPHICAL AND CRITICAL SOURCES:

PERIODICALS

Booklist, April 15, 2006, Mark Knoblauch, review of *What to Eat,* p. 16.
Business Week, May 22, 2006, "'The Rules' For Eating Smarter," interview with author, p. 92.
Christian Century, April 10, 2002, Stephen H. Webb, review of *Food Politics: How the Food Industry Influences Nutrition and Health,* p. 35.

Chronicle of Higher Education, October 13, 2006, Amy Bentley, review of *What to Eat.*

Economist, May 11, 2002, "Lean on Me; America's Food Industry," review of *Food Politics.*

Environmental Nutrition, June, 2006, Susan Male Smith, review of *What to Eat,* p. 2.

Food Chemical News, May 20, 2002, Stephen Clapp, "*Food Politics* Blames Industry for Obesity Epidemic," p. 18, and Stephen Clapp, "*Food Politics* Raises Provocative Questions," interview with Marion Nestle, p. 19.

Fortune, February 18, 2002, Julie Creswell, "Chewing Out the Food Industry," interview with Marion Nestle, p. 36.

Gourmet Retailer, February, 2006, James Mellgren, review of *What to Eat,* p. 106.

Lancet, May 18, 2002, Kathleen Nelson, "Food in the USA: Something to Chew Over," review of *Food Politics,* p. 1785.

Library Journal, March 1, 2006, Margaret K. Norden, review of *What to Eat,* p. 111.

Nation, May 6, 2002, Ian Williams, "Big Food's Real Appetites," review of *Food Politics,* p. 37.

Natural Health, July, 2002, David Maloof, review of *Food Politics,* p. 86.

New York Times, February 19, 2002, Mary Duenwald, "An 'Eat More' Message for a Fattened America," interview with Marion Nestle, p. 66.

New York Times Book Review, May 28, 2006, Dorothy Kalins, review of *What to Eat,* p. 21.

O, the Oprah Magazine, April, 2006, Patricia Volk, "My Dinner with Marion," p. 159.

People, May 22, 2006, Ericka Souter, "Eat, Drink & Be Wary," interview with author, p. 155.

Progressive Grocer, June 1, 2006, Jenny McTaggart "Healthy Skepticism," interview with author, p. 32.

Publishers Weekly, March 13, 2006, review of *What to Eat,* p. 59.

San Francisco Chronicle, March 15, 2006, Carol Ness, "Down to a Science," profile of author and review of *What to Eat.*

Saturday Evening Post, March-April, 2006, review of *What to Eat,* and "A Food Shopping Guide," brief discussion of *What to Eat,* p. 20.

Science News, May 13, 2006, review of *What to Eat,* p. 303.

Social Policy, summer, 2002, review of *Food Politics,* p. 66.

Time, June 12, 2006, Claudia Wallis, "Decoding the Grocery Store," interview with author, p. 63.

World Watch, September-October, 2002, Erik Assadourian, "Hunger for Profit," review of *Food Politics,* p. 34.

ONLINE

Atlantic, http://www.theatlantic.com/ (June 25, 2002), Ben Geman, review of *Food Politics.*

Marion Nestle Home Page, http://www.foodpolitics. com (February 9, 2007).

New York University Web site, http://www.nyu.edu/ (April 7, 2003), biography and full curriculum vitae of author.

PBS Frontline Web site, http://www.pbs.org/wgbh/ pages/frontline/ (February 9, 2007), "Interview Marion Nestle."

UC Berkeley News Web site, http://www.berkeley.edu/ news/ (April 13, 2006), Wendy Edelstein "Attention, Shoppers: Avoid the Center Aisles," profile of author and *What to Eat.*

USA Today, http://www.usatoday.com/ (April 3, 2003), Elizabeth Weise, review of *Safe Food: Bacteria, Biotechnology, and Bioterrorism.*

Washington Monthly, http://www.washingtonmonthly. com/ (February 9, 2007), Chris Mooney, "Food Fight," review of *Safe Food.*

*　　*　　*

NEW, William H. 1938-
(William Herbert New)

PERSONAL: Born March 28, 1938, in Vancouver, British Columbia, Canada; son of John (a mechanic) and Edith Annie (a homemaker) New; married Margaret Ebbs-Canavan (a teacher), 1967; children: two. *Education:* University of British Columbia, B.Ed., 1961, M.A., 1963; University of Leeds, Ph.D., 1966.

ADDRESSES: Office—Department of English, University of British Columbia, 1873 E. Mall, Vancouver, British Columbia, Canada V6T 1Z1. *E-mail*—wnew@ interchange.ubc.ca.

CAREER: University of British Columbia, Vancouver, British Columbia, Canada, professor of English, 1975-2003, Brenda and David McLean Professor of Canadian Studies, 1995-97, University Killam Professor, 2001-03, professor emeritus, 2003—. History of the Book Project, member of advisory board, 2001—; McClelland & Stewart (publisher), member of editorial board of "New Canadian Library;" Vancouver Institute, member of council.

MEMBER: Royal Society of Canada.

AWARDS, HONORS: Maxwell Cameron Medal, 1961; Killam research prize, 1988; Gabrielle Roy Medal, 1989; Jacob Biely Prize, 1994; Killam teaching prize, 1996; award of merit, Association of Canadian Studies, 2000; career achievement award, British Columbia chapter, College and University Faculty Assembly, 2001; Governor General's Award for International Canadian Studies, 2004; Lorne Pierce Medal, 2004; nominated for Governor General's Award for Poetry, 2005, for *Underwood Log;* officer of the Order of Canada, 2006.

WRITINGS:

Malcolm Lowry, McClelland & Stewart (Toronto, Ontario, Canada), 1971.

Articulating West: Essays on Purpose and Form in Modern Canadian Literature, New Press (Toronto, Ontario, Canada), 1972.

Among Worlds: An Introduction to Modern Commonwealth and South African Fiction, Press Porcepic (Erin, Ontario, Canada), 1975.

Malcolm Lowry: A Reference Guide, G.K. Hall (Boston, MA), 1978.

Dreams of Speech and Violence: The Art of the Short Story in Canada and New Zealand, University of Toronto Press (Toronto, Ontario, Canada), 1987.

A History of Canadian Literature, Macmillan (London, England), 1991, 2nd edition, McGill-Queen's University Press (Montreal, Quebec, Canada), 2003.

Land Sliding: Imagining Space, Presence, and Power in Canadian Writing, University of Toronto Press (Toronto, Ontario, Canada), 1997.

Reading Mansfield and Metaphors of Form, McGill-Queen's University Press (Montreal, Quebec, Canada), 1999.

Borderlands: How We Talk about Canada, University of British Columbia Press (Vancouver, British Columbia, Canada), 1999.

Grandchild of Empire: About Irony, Mainly in the Commonwealth, Ronsdale Press (Vancouver, British Columbia, Canada), 2003.

Some of New's writings have been translated into Chinese.

POETRY

Science Lessons, Oolichan Press (Lantzville, British Columbia, Canada), 1996.

Vanilla Gorilla (for children), illustrated by Vivian Bevis, Ronsdale Press (Vancouver, British Columbia, Canada), 1998.

Raucous, Oolichan Press, 1999.

Stone Rain: Poems, Oolichan Press (Lantzville, British Columbia, Canada), 2001.

Riverbook & Ocean, Oolichan Press (Lantzville, British Columbia, Canada), 2002.

Llamas in the Laundry: Poems (for children), illustrated by Vivian Bevis, Ronsdale Press (Vancouver, British Columbia, Canada), 2002.

Night Room, Oolichan Press (Lantzville, British Columbia, Canada), 2003.

Underwood Log, Oolichan Press (Lantzville, British Columbia, Canada), 2004.

Dream Helmet (for children), illustrated by Vivian Bevis, Ronsdale Press (Vancouver, British Columbia, Canada), 2005.

Touching Ecuador, Oolichan Press (Lantzville, British Columbia, Canada), 2006.

Along a Snake Fence Riding, Oolichan Press (Lantzville, British Columbia, Canada), 2007.

EDITOR

Four Hemispheres: An Anthology of English Short Stories from around the World, Copp Clark (Toronto, Ontario, Canada), 1971.

(With Jack Hodgins) *Voice and Vision,* McClelland & Stewart (Toronto, Ontario, Canada, 1972.

Dramatists in Canada: Selected Essays, University of British Columbia Press (Vancouver, British Columbia, Canada), 1972.

Critical Writings on Commonwealth Literatures: A Selective Bibliography to 1970, with a List of Theses and Dissertations, Pennsylvania State University Press (University Park, PA), 1975.

(With H.J. Rosengarten) *Modern Stories in English,* Crowell (New York, NY), 1975, 4th edition, Addison-Wesley (Boston, MA), 2001.

Modern Canadian Essays, Macmillan (Toronto, Ontario, Canada), 1976.

Margaret Laurence, McGraw-Hill (New York, NY), 1977.

A Political Art: Essays and Images in Honour of George Woodcock, University of British Columbia Press (Vancouver, British Columbia, Canada), 1978.

(With W.E. Messenger) *Active Voice,* Prentice-Hall Canada (Scarborough, Ontario, Canada), 1980, 3rd edition, 1991.

(With W.E. Messenger) *The Active Stylist: An Anthology of Canadian, American, and Commonwealth Prose,* Prentice-Hall (Scarborough, Ontario, Canada), 1981.

Canadian Writers in 1984: The Twenty-fifth Anniversary Issue of Canadian Literature, University of British Columbia Press (Vancouver, British Columbia, Canada), 1984.

(With W.E. Messenger) *A Twentieth-Century Anthology: Essays, Stories, and Poems,* Prentice-Hall Canada (Scarborough, Ontario, Canada), 1984, revised edition (with Kevin McNeilly and Noel Elizabeth Carrie) published as *Currents,* 2000.

Dictionary of Literary Biography, Gale (Detroit, MI), Volume 53: *Canadian Writers since 1960, First Series,* 1986, Volume 60: *Canadian Writers since 1960, Second Series,* 1987, Volume 68: *Canadian Writers, 1920-1959, First Series,* 1988, Volume 88: *Canadian Writers, 1920-1959, Second Series,* 1989, Volume 92: *Canadian Writers, 1890-1920,* 1990, Volume 99: *Canadian Writers before 1890,* 1990.

Canadian Short Fiction: From Myth to Modern, Prentice-Hall Canada (Scarborough, Ontario, Canada), 1986, 2nd edition, 1996.

Literary History of Canada: Canadian Literature in English, Volume 4, University of Toronto Press (Toronto, Ontario, Canada, 1990.

Native Writers and Canadian Writing, University of British Columbia Press (Vancouver, British Columbia, Canada), 1990.

Inside the Poem: Essays and Poems in Honour of Donald Stephens, Oxford University Press (Toronto, Ontario, Canada), 1992.

(With W.E. Messenger) *Literature in English,* Prentice-Hall Canada (Scarborough, Ontario, Canada), 1993.

Encyclopedia of Literature in Canada, University of Toronto Press (Toronto, Ontario, Canada, 2002.

(With Marta Dvorak) *Tropes and Territories,* McGill-Queen's University Press (Montreal, Quebec, Canada), 2007.

Associate editor, *World Literature Written in English,* 1971-90; editor, *Canadian Literature,* 1977-95. Member of editorial board of the periodicals *Twentieth-Century Literature,* 1970-2002, *Commonwealth,* 1970-2005, *Short Story,* 1988-2003, and *Journal of Caribbean Literatures,* 1995—; *Canadian Encyclopedia,* member of advisory board.

SIDELIGHTS: Critical reviews of William H. New's *Dictionary of Literary Biography* volumes, which profile various authors and their literary achievements, have credited the editor with presenting information on both major and lesser-known Canadian writers to achieve a complete picture of his country's literary contributions. In a review of Volume 88, *Canadian Writers, 1920-1959, Second Series,* a *Canadian Literature* critic cited New's inclusion of best-selling authors and "unorthodox" and "experimental" writers alike, summarizing: "The book not only yields information that is difficult to come by in comparable handbooks but also sketches a broad cultural profile of the years under scrutiny." The critic similarly reviewed Volume 92, *Canadian Writers, 1890-1920,* praising New for "recovering authors who, for one reason or another, have been excluded from, or distorted for the sake of inclusion in, the canon," and for "restoring such writers to their proper place."

New also edited *Literary History of Canada,* Volume 4, *Canadian Literature in English.* A collection of essays with an emphasis on the literary arts, criticism, commentary, memoirs, and biography, *Literary History of Canada* is, according to John Moss, writing in the Toronto *Globe and Mail,* "crucial to an understanding of literary history in Canada, the country. Limited as either reference or resource, it is nevertheless a good starting point in any attempt to comprehend what we have written about ourselves. It has become an institution in its own right." Further approval for *Literary History of Canada* was issued by Stephen Regan in *Canadian Literature.* Regan noted that in a country where Canadian books make up only a fraction of the country's book sales, the *Literary History of Canada* "will, in its own special way, encourage and inform the climate of change."

A History of Canadian Literature is an exhaustive work that discusses the history of Canadian literature in light of social change and European influence, categorizes contemporary styles, and suggests ways to perceive and appreciate modern Canadian writing. (The second edition also deals with ethnic minorities and multicultural influences as well.) In his *Canadian Literature* review, Arnold Davidson noted New's "thorough understanding of the historical, social, and technological groundings of literature and his ability to draw illuminating connections and/or parallels between cultural facts and texts as cultural productions." Commenting on New's "history in progress," Davidson concluded: "with *A History of Canadian Literature,* [New] has brought the nation's oeuvre to life."

BIOGRAPHICAL AND CRITICAL SOURCES:

PERIODICALS

Books in Canada, February, 1999, review of *Vanilla Gorilla,* p. 31.
Canadian Book Review Annual, 1998, review of *Vanilla Gorilla,* p. 533.
Canadian Literature, summer, 1989, Helen Tiffin, review of *Dreams of Speech and Violence: The Art of the Short Story in Canada and New Zealand,* pp. 131-133; winter, 1990, reviews of *Dictionary of Literary Biography,* Volume 88: *Canadian Writers, 1920-1959, Second Series,* and Volume 92: *Canadian Writers, 1890-1920,* pp. 202-203; autumn, 1991, Stephen Regan, review of *Literary History of Canada,* Volume 4: *Canadian Literature in English,* pp. 208-209; winter, 1991, Arnold Davidson, review of *A History of Canadian Literature,* pp. 179-183; spring, 2000, Elizabeth Hodgson, review of *Vanilla Gorilla,* p. 148.
Canadian Materials, September 3, 1999, review of *Vanilla Gorilla.*
Globe and Mail (Toronto, Ontario, Canada), May 12, 1990, John Moss, review of *Literary History of Canada;* February 22, 2003, review of *Riverbook & Ocean,* p. D4.
Quill and Quire, August, 1998, review of *Vanilla Gorilla,* p. 36; December, 2002, review of *Llamas in the Laundry: Poems,* p. 26.
Resource Links, February, 1999, review of *Vanilla Gorilla,* p. 5; June, 2005, Anne Burke, review of *Dream Helmet,* p. 22.

*   *   *

NEW, William Herbert
See NEW, William H.

*   *   *

NICHOLL, Charles 1950-

PERSONAL: Born 1950, in London, England; married; children. *Education:* Attended Cambridge University.

ADDRESSES: Home—Italy.

CAREER: Journalist and writer. Worked as a correspondent for *Rolling Stone* and appeared as himself in the films *Much Ado about Something,* 2001, and *The Real Da Vinci Code,* 2005.

AWARDS, HONORS: Young Writer of the Year Award, *Telegraph Magazine,* 1972; Nonfiction Gold Dagger Award, Crime Writers' Association, and James Tait Black Memorial Prize, University of Edinburgh, 1992, both for *The Reckoning: The Murder of Christopher Marlowe;* Hawthornden Prize, and shortlisted for W.H. Smith Literary Award, both 1998, both for *Somebody Else: Arthur Rimbaud in Africa, 1880-91;* Gulbenkian Award for Best Museum Publication, for *Elizabethan Writers.*

WRITINGS:

NONFICTION

The Chemical Theatre (literary criticism), Routledge & Kegan Paul (Boston, MA), 1980.
A Cup of News: The Life of Thomas Nashe (biography), Routledge & Kegan Paul (Boston, MA), 1984.
The Fruit Palace, St. Martin's Press (New York, NY), 1985.
Borderlines: A Journey in Thailand and Burma, Secker & Warburg (London, England), 1988, Viking (New York, NY), 1989.
The Reckoning: The Murder of Christopher Marlowe, Harcourt Brace (New York, NY), 1992.
The Creature in the Map: A Journey to El Dorado, Morrow (New York, NY), 1996.
Elizabethan Writers, National Portrait Gallery Publications (London, England), 1997.
Somebody Else: Arthur Rimbaud in Africa, 1880-91, University of Chicago Press (Chicago, IL), 1997.
Screaming in the Castle, Trafalgar Square (VT), 2000.
Leonardo da Vinci: Flights of the Mind, Viking (New York, NY), 2004.

Contributor to periodicals.

SIDELIGHTS: British journalist Charles Nicholl has written a wide range of nonfiction works that blend historical intrigue with arduous adventure. A one-time correspondent for *Rolling Stone,* the author has admitted to undertaking his quests for nebulous investigations from the most spurious of sources, including a television program and the perusal of a centuries-old map. Much of Nicholl's work has examined the Elizabethan era in England and its acts of treason and treachery among its more tarnished names, but he has also entered South America to interview drug lords and traversed Southeast Asia in search of personal enlightenment.

Nicholl's first work to attract attention was 1980's *The Chemical Theatre,* an exploration of the relationship between the medieval pseudo-science of alchemy and Elizabethan-era drama. Alchemy, as he explains, was the quest to turn base metals such as lead into more valuable ones like gold. Culling research from books written around 1600 on the craft, Nicholl explores the significant works produced for the stage around the same time and attempts to correlate their elements of plot and character with the principles and nuances of alchemy. The centerpiece of *The Chemical Theatre* is an examination of the text of William Shakespeare's *King Lear,* but the works of Ben Jonson and John Donne are also analyzed in a book D.J. Enright of the *Listener* termed "cogent, comprehensive and relatively readable."

Nicholl's next work, *A Cup of News: The Life of Thomas Nashe,* was published in 1984. This biography of the Elizabethan literary figure and contemporary of Shakespeare was the first comprehensive look at its subject, largely because of the scarcity of material Nashe left behind when he died. Nicholl profiles the sometimes-maligned figure, one of a group of educated writers known as the University Wits and author of plays, pamphlets, pornography, and anonymous attacks on the Anglican church and its leading figures of the day; Nashe also is credited with having been the author of the first-ever reference guide to Shakespeare. Nicholl's biography analyzes the writer's tumultuous career and contentious personal life before his death at the age of thirty-four, and places Nashe as a likely member of an underground group of Catholic sympathizers of the day. Nicholl, according to *Times Literary Supplement* contributor Emrys Jones, "brings to Nashe a strong sympathy for one who has often been called the first English journalist; he has done, moreover, a great deal of scholarly preparation." Nevertheless, Jones faulted the author for making what the critic felt were too many conjectures and suppositions about a life that left behind little source material. Sarah Lawson, writing for the *New Statesman,* asserted that *A Cup of News* "is not just the definitive biography of Thomas Nashe, but a very readable and highly competent guide to this whole stratum of late Elizabethan literary life."

In the early 1970s Nicholl spent time in Colombia, and later drew upon the experience to write his 1985 treatise on the South American nation's illegal cocaine industry, *The Fruit Palace,* which was described by *London Review of Books* contributor Karl Miller as "a triumphant piece of travel writing which is also a comic extravaganza." Nicholl travelled undercover in Colombia, visiting Indian encampments in the mountains where the coca leaves are picked, meeting the chemist who processed the leaves and resulting paste into a more narcotic form, fleeing—when the owner's bodyguard becomes suspicious—from a slaughterhouse where the drug is hidden inside cattle carcasses, and finally alighting at the seaside hideaway of traffickers who eventually realize he is a writer, not the potential buyer from abroad he presented himself to be. In return for his life, the drug lords enlisted Nicholl with the task of smuggling a briefcase full of cocaine onto a Swedish ship. It was one of many perilous situations during Nicholl's 1983 journey through the country chronicled in *The Fruit Palace*—he also happened to be in the ornate colonial city of Popayan on the day an earthquake leveled it.

In *The Fruit Palace,* Nicholl is frank about the dangerous situations in which he often found himself, and as *New Statesman* contributor David Montrose asserted that he "occasionally . . . appears completely unable to keep other people's business out of his nose." A *New Yorker* contributor termed the book "a tense adventure in darkness and danger," while *New York Times Book Review* writer John Hemming called Nicholl's work "one of the most absorbing travel books I have read." Hemming, author of several works on South America, declared that while reading *The Fruit Palace* "again and again I found myself reminded of sights and smells, heat, boredom, inefficiencies and pretensions of that continent." Hemming added: "This is a brilliant book, informative, well written, and fun to read."

Nicholl again undertook an arduous journey for the writing of *Borderlines: A Journey in Thailand and Burma,* first published in England in 1988 and the following year in the United States. The trek was inspired by Nicholl's viewing of a program about Buddhist monks on British television, and in 1986 he left for Southeast Asia in a quest to spend time at the Temple of Tupu's Cave, a remote Buddhist sanctum. *Borderlines* begins with Nicholl's arrival in Bangkok and his impressions of the thriving prostitution and pornography industry there; some of his information was culled from accompanying a German tourist on one of his annual forays.

Other characters in *Borderlines,* include Katai, a young Thai woman, and Harry, her supposedly gem-smuggling boyfriend. In return for "guarding" Katai when Harry is away on business, this adventurer with a penchant for quoting literature takes Nicholl to the "borderlines" of the title, where Thailand meets Burma and rebel guerrilla groups rule over the poppy fields, the harvest of which is processed into opium. Nicholl does eventually arrive at the Temple of Tupu's Cave for his spiritual rebirth, but the book's strong suit, according to *London Review of Books* contributor Mark Ford, is the way the author "drifts around purposelessly like any stunned tourist." Ford observed that Nicholl "writes up these rather bleak nonadventures with plenty of snap, crackle and pop, lacing his prose with borrowings from the Beatles, Van Morrison and Bob Dylan."

In 1992 Nicholl again examined unusual events of Elizabethan times in *The Reckoning: The Murder of Christopher Marlowe*. According to accepted lore, the famed playwright, atheist, raconteur, and possible counterfeiter was murdered in a tavern brawl in 1593. In a book that won both the James Tait Black Award for biography and a Gold Dagger Award from the Crime Writers' Association, Nicholl sets out to prove a more complex theory; specifically, that Marlowe was killed because of his underworld activities. The author posits that the playwright was recruited as an anti-Catholic spy during his student days at Cambridge University, and the argument and scuffle over the bill (the "reckoning" of the title) might not have even occurred at the tavern in question. Through investigations of the men involved, Nicholl reveals the dangerous rivalries between Catholic and Protestant factions in Reformation-era Europe that may have ultimately felled Marlowe.

The Reckoning, in addition to the prestigious awards bestowed upon it, also received extensive coverage and laudatory reviews. Reviewing it for the *New York Review of Books,* Michael Neill declared that "it would be difficult, even in the lengthiest review, to do justice to the skill with which Nicholl pieces together the fantastically complex jigsaw upon which" his book's final judgment rests. *London Review of Books* writer Hilary Mantel remarked that "Nicholl writes vividly, without the academic's compulsion to cover his back; but where he is speculating he says so clearly." Michiko Kakutani of the *New York Times* described *The Reckoning* as "an adroitly reasoned historical hypothesis . . . and, in the process, a minutely detailed portrait of the dark side of Elizabethan politics." *Los Angeles Times Book Review* contributor Christopher Hitchens advised readers that "even if you have no desperate need to re-examine the truth of Marlowe's death in light of a murder mystery, you will discover in these pages a truly Shakespearean cast of pickpockets, boasters, boozers, posturing aristos, false priests and phony judges, official torturers and charming rogues." Hitchens added: "Nicholl's accomplishment is to have wiped away some of the smears and cobwebs, and restored a portrait that has been disfigured for too long."

In his 1996 book *The Creature in the Map: A Journey to El Dorado,* Nicholl blends the travel chronicles and Elizabethan dramas found behind his past titles into an investigation of the mysterious journey of another adventurer, Sir Walter Raleigh. Raleigh was a confidant, then enemy of Queen Elizabeth I, and an explorer who navigated much of the shores of the New World and in 1595 set out to discover a famed city of gold called El Dorado that was rumored to be located the region now known as Venezuela. The aging Raleigh never found the city, but claimed to have come close in his travelogue of the journey, *The Discoverie of the Large, Rich, and Bewtiful Empyre of Guiana.*

Inspired by looking at Raleigh's map of the region to retrace the quest, Nicholl set out with a British television crew to re-enact the voyage, and presents his theories of what actually happened in *The Creature in the Map.* Raleigh, Nicholl asserts, engaged in some treacherous activity on the way, including raiding foreign ships and slaughtering a garrison of Spanish soldiers he and his crew had plied with drink. When he returned to England, he had obtained enough loot to satisfy his expedition's backers, but was executed within a short time anyway. *The Creature in the Map* also serves as a chronicle of the modern-day adventures Nicholl and his crew encountered in the South American jungle, and, as Stephen Greenblatt professed in his *Times Literary Supplement* review, the author "has combined his formidable gifts as a travel-writer with his fascination with Elizabethan overreachers to produce an extraordinary, gripping study." Greenblatt went on to note that "with a fine sense of Raleigh's predicament, a healthy scepticism, and an impressive measure of learning and patience, Nicholl untangles the rhetorical web that *The Discoverie of Guiana* weaves." Writing in the *Observer,* Patrick French termed Nicholl's tome "a wonderful book," adding: "Like an Elizabethan alchemist, Nicholl takes a trail of phrases, omissions, hints [and] subtleties and distills them into an extraordinarily convincing picture. *The Creature in the Map* is history at its most creative and beguiling."

In 1997's *Elizabethan Writers,* Nicholl explores the lives and time period of several authors who wrote during England's rule by Queen Elizabeth I, such as Ben Jonson and William Shakespeare, to give readers a more comprehensive view of their lives. *Elizabethan Writers* earned Nicholl the Gulbenkian Award for Best Museum Publication. Also appearing in 1997 was Nicholl's *Somebody Else: Arthur Rimbaud in Africa, 1880-1891.* The book focuses on the life of Rimbaud, who, as a young French poet penned at age sixteen *Une Saison en enfer* (known to English-speaking readers as *A Season in Hell*). Rimbaud would later escape a troubled life in Europe and his disastrous relationship with lover and fellow poet Paul Verlaine, who was married, for a life in Africa. Rimbaud's life in Africa began in 1880, where he worked as a gun runner and a trader, and where he would eventually cease to write poetry. A reviewer for *Publishers Weekly* maintained that with *Somebody Else* "Nicholl creates a minor classic of biography and travel," vividly portraying Rimbaud's African surroundings and showing his aim "to use himself up," as he would die in 1891 at the age of thirty-seven. Michael Mewshaw, in a *New Statesman* review, called the work "an amusing, stylish literary excursion that palls only when Nicholl strains to infuse scenes with bogus significance by tagging on allusions to Cavafy (did the 'eccentric homosexual' cross paths with Rimbaud in Alexandria?) and to Van Gogh." Acknowledging the merits of the author's ideas, Mewshaw asserted that Nicholl portrays Rimbaud's true "masterpiece" as being the poet's African travels and experiences rather than his poetry, even though information known on Rimbaud's years in Africa is limited and his poetry writing while there would eventually cease. Mewshaw explained that Nicholl's sources include the author's observations from his own experiences in Africa; information on Rimbaud from other compositions such as letters, business ledgers, and diaries; and the knowledge of Rimbaud's sister Isabelle regarding her brother's life in Africa.

In the biography *Leonardo da Vinci: Flights of the Mind*, Nicholl tells the life story of the illegitimate child of a peasant girl and a notary who went on to become perhaps the most noted figure of the Renaissance art period. The author writes not only about da Vinci's iconic paintings but also about the times in which the artist lived. He also presents numerous writings from da Vinci's notebooks. "The author's goal is to show not the genius but rather the man, and he does his best to drag Leonardo down to earth," wrote a contributor to the *Economist*. In his review in the *New Statesman*, Waldemar Januszczak noted: "Nicholl takes everything seriously—every snippet, every tradition, every speculation—examining and re-examining Leonardo's life in a

prodigious display of scholarship. His aim is obviously to provide the definitive modern biography: not an art history book as such, but a resonant uber-life in which not just Leonardo comes to life, but also his contemporaries, his times and his places."

A *Publishers Weekly* contributor referred to Nicholl's biography of da Vinci as a "penetrating, highly detailed biography, which recognizes da Vinci's 'mysterious greatness as an artist, scientist and philosopher' but avoids hagiography." Donna Seaman, writing in *Booklist*, commented that the author "takes a marvelously fresh and human approach to the fascinating life of Leonardo." A *Kirkus Reviews* contributor wrote: "Details are compelling in a long book that defies skimming."

BIOGRAPHICAL AND CRITICAL SOURCES:

PERIODICALS

Booklist, November 1, 2004, Donna Seaman, review of *Leonardo da Vinci: Flights of the Mind*, p. 461.

Christian Science Monitor, December 21, 2004, Christopher Andreae, review of *Leonardo da Vinci*.

Economist, December 9, 2004, review of *Leonardo da Vinci*; December 11, 2004, review of *Leonardo da Vinci*, p. 81.

Kirkus Reviews, October 1, 2004, review of *Leonardo da Vinci*, p. 950.

Listener, November 20, 1980, D.J. Enright, review of *The Chemical Theatre*, p. 698.

London Review of Books, June 25, 1987, Karl Miller, review of *The Fruit Palace*, p. 25; December 7, 1989, Mark Ford, review of *Borderlines: A Journey in Thailand and Burma*, p. 21; June 25, 1992, Hilary Mantel, review of *The Reckoning: The Murder of Christopher Marlowe*, p. 14.

Los Angeles Times Book Review, June 5, 1994, Christopher Hitchens, review of *The Reckoning*, p. 8.

New Statesman, May 18, 1984, Sarah Lawson, review of *A Cup of News: The Life of Thomas Nashe*, p. 26; September 6, 1985, David Montrose, review of *The Fruit Palace*, p. 26; July 18, 1997, Michael Mewshaw, review of *Somebody Else: Arthur Rimbaud in Africa, 1880-91*, p. 48; October 4, 2004, Waldemar Januszczak, review of *Leonardo da Vinci*, p. 50.

New York Review of Books, October 5, 1995, Michael Neill, review of *The Reckoning*, p. 47.

New York Times, March 4, 1994, Michiko Kakutani, review of *The Reckoning,* p. C27.

New York Times Book Review, July 6, 1986, John Hemming, review of *The Fruit Palace,* p. 11; December 5, 2004, David Gelernter, review of *Leonardo da Vinci,* p. 9.

New Yorker, September 15, 1986, review of *The Fruit Palace,* p. 120.

Observer, June 18, 1995, Patrick French, review of *The Creature in the Map: A Journey to El Dorado,* p. 16.

Publishers Weekly, April 26, 1999, review of *Somebody Else,* p. 63; October 11, 2004, review of *Leonardo da Vinci,* p. 65.

Spectator, December 4, 2004, David Ekserdjian, review of *Leonardo da Vinci,* p. 38.

Times Literary Supplement, May 18, 1984, Emrys Jones, review of *A Cup of News,* p. 540; June 12, 1992, John Bossy, review of *The Reckoning,* p. 654; August 18, 1995, Stephen Greenblatt, review of *The Creature in the Map,* p. 3.

Washington Post, November 28, 2004, Alexander Nagel, review of *Leonardo da Vinci,* p. BW10.

ONLINE

Internet Movie Database, http://www.imdb.com/ (February 9, 2007), information on author's film appearances.

Penguin Web site, http://www.penguin.co.uk/ (February 9, 2007), brief profile of author.*

*   *   *

NIETO, Sonia 1943-

PERSONAL: Born September 25, 1943, in Brooklyn, NY; daughter of Federico (a co-owner of a Caribbean grocery store) and Esther (a homemaker and co-owner of the grocery store) Cortes; married Angel Nieto, January 4, 1967; children: Alicia Nieto Lopez, Marisa Nieto McKnight. *Ethnicity:* "Puerto Rican." *Education:* St. John's University, Brooklyn, NY, B.S., 1965; New York University, M.A., 1966; University of Massachusetts at Amherst, Ed.D., 1979.

ADDRESSES: E-mail—snieto@educ.umass.edu.

CAREER: Teacher of English, Spanish, and French and coordinator of English-as-a-second-language program at a junior high school in Brooklyn, NY, 1966-68; bilingual teacher at a public bilingual school, Bronx, NY, 1968-70, curriculum specialist, 1970-72, and supervisor of summer day elementary school, 1971; Brooklyn College of the City University of New York, Brooklyn, instructor in Puerto Rican studies and deputy head of department, 1972-75; Massachusetts Department of Education, Springfield, coordinator in Bureau of Equal Educational Opportunity, 1979-80; University of Massachusetts at Amherst, Amherst, assistant professor, 1980-88, associate professor, 1988-93, professor of language, literacy, and culture, beginning 1993, currently retired, parent/teacher trainer at Bilingual Education Service Center, 1980-83, board member of University without Walls, beginning 1983, director of Cultural Diversity and Curriculum Reform Program, 1989-92. Spanish-American Institute, teacher of English as a second language to adults, 1968; Hampshire College, adjunct assistant professor, 1977; School for International Training, Brattleboro, VT, instructor, 1979; Beijing Teachers College, member of China Scholars Program, 1988; University of Pennsylvania, Gordon S. Bodek Lecturer, 1995; University of Santiago de Compostela, visiting professor, 1997; University of Massachusetts at Lowell, Virginia Biggy Lecturer, 1999; Emory University, Dora Helen Skypek Lecturer, 2001; University of Washington, Seattle, Corbally Lecturer, 2001; Keene State College, Sidore Lecturer, 2002; Washington State University, Sherry Vaughn Distinguished Lecturer in Education, 2003; Wells College, Beckman Lecturer, 2003; State University of New York at Binghamton, Couper Lecturer, 2004; Indiana University at Bloomington, Miller Lecturer, 2004; University of Rhode Island, Robert and Augusta Finkelstein Memorial Lecturer, 2004; Trinity University, Carter Lecturer, 2005; Lingo Lecturer, Washburn University, 2006; Sarah Lawrence College, Longfellow Lecturer, 2006; guest lecturer at many other institutions, including Harvard University, University of Arizona, Queens College of the City University of New York, University of Alabama, and Brown University. Massachusetts Advisory Council on Bilingual Education, member, 1990-91; Council of Chief State School Officers, member of equity review panel of Interstate New Teacher Assessment and Support Consortium, 1996. Massachusetts Advocacy Center, member of board of directors, 1983-88; National Writing Project, member of national advisory board for Project Outreach, 1995-99; Educators for Social Responsibility, member of national advisory board, 1996—; Family Diversity Projects, Amherst, member of national advisory board, 1997—; Center for Teaching and Policy, member of core advisory group, 1997—; Community Foundation of Western Massachusetts, trustee, 2003—; Center for Applied Linguistics, Washington, DC, trustee, 2006—;

advisor to many other organizations. University of Massachusetts Press, member of editorial board, 1994-96; member of editorial board of periodicals, including *Review of Educational Research*, 1997-2000, *Race, Ethnicity, and Education*, 1997—, *Excellence and Equity in Education*, 1998—, *Current Issues in Education*, 1998—, *Multicultural Perspectives*, 1999—, *Journal of School Leadership*, 1999-2003, *Qualitative Studies in Education*, 2000—, *Centro Journal*, 2000—, *Education for Urban Minorities*, 2000—, *Journal of Latinos and Education*, 2000—, *Critical Inquiry in Language Studies: An International Journal*, 2002-05, and *Teaching Education*, 2004—.

MEMBER: National Association for Bilingual Education, American Educational Research Association, National Council of Teachers of English, National Congress of Research on Language and Literacy, Phi Delta Kappa.

AWARDS, HONORS: Award from Parents United in Education and the Development of Others, 1984; Human and Civil Rights Award, Massachusetts Teachers Association, 1988; award for outstanding accomplishment in higher education, Hispanic Caucus, American Association of Higher Education, 1991; Point of Excellence Award, Kappa Delta Pi, 1994; Drylongso Award for Anti-Racist Activists, Community Change, 1995; award for service to the Latino community, Latino Scholarship Fund, 1995; Teacher of the Year Award, Hispanic Educators of Massachusetts, 1996; National Association for Multicultural Education, Multicultural Educator of the Year Award, 1997, New England Educator of the Year Award, 1998; senior fellow in urban education, Annenberg Institute, 1998-2000; meritorious service citation, city of Paterson, NJ, 1998; "critics' choice" selection, American Educational Studies Association, 1999, for *The Light in Their Eyes: Creating Multicultural Learning Communities;* D.H.L., Lesley College, 1999; resident at Bellagio Study and Conference Center in Italy, 2000; Chancellor's Medal University of Massachusetts, 2000; honorary doctorate, Bridgewater State College, 2004; named outstanding educator in the language arts, National Council of Teachers of English, 2005; Enrique T. Trueba Lifetime Achievement Award, *Journal of Latinos and Education*, 2006; senior scholar award and distinguished career award, both American Educational Research Association, 2006.

WRITINGS:

Affirming Diversity: The Sociopolitical Context of Multicultural Education, Longman (New York, NY), 1992, 4th edition, Allyn & Bacon (Boston, MA), 2004.

(Editor, with Ralph Rivera, and contributor) *The Education of Latino Students in Massachusetts: Issues, Research, and Policy Implications*, Gaston Institute for Latino Public Policy and Community (Boston, MA), 1993.

The Light in Their Eyes: Creating Multicultural Learning Communities, Teachers College Press (New York, NY), 1999.

(Editor and contributor) *Puerto Rican Students in U.S. Schools*, Lawrence Erlbaum Associates (Mahwah, NJ), 2000.

Language, Culture, and Teaching: Critical Perspectives for a New Century, Lawrence Erlbaum Associates (Mahwah, NJ), 2002.

What Keeps Teachers Going?, Teachers College Press (New York, NY), 2003.

(Editor) *Why We Teach*, Teachers College Press (New York, NY), 2005.

Contributor to books, including *Images and Identities: The Puerto Rican in Two World Contexts*, edited by Asela Rodriguez de Laguna, Transaction Books (New Brunswick, NJ), 1987; *Teaching Multicultural Literature in Grades K-8*, edited by Violet J. Harris, Christopher-Gordon (Norwood, MA), 1992; *Shifting Histories: Transforming Schools for Social Change*, edited by Capella Noya, Kathryn Geismar, and Guitele Nicoleau, Harvard Educational Review (Cambridge, MA), 1996; *Learning as a Political Act: Struggles for Learning and Learning from Struggles*, edited by J.A. Segarra and R. Dobles, Harvard Educational Review, 1999; and *Lifting Every Voice: Pedagogy and Politics of Bilingual Education*, edited by Zeynep Beykont, Harvard Education Publishing Group (Cambridge, MA), 2000. Editor of the book series "Culture, Language, and Teaching," Lawrence Erlbaum Associates. Contributor of articles and reviews to periodicals, including *Journal of Teacher Education, International Journal of Qualitative Studies in Education, School Administrator, Harvard Educational Review, Multicultural Review*, and *Theory into Practice*. Editor of special issues, *Bulletin of the Council on Interracial Books for Children*, 1983 and 1986, and *Educational Forum*, 1994.

What Keeps Teachers Going? has also been published in Spanish.

SIDELIGHTS: Sonia Nieto once told *CA:* "I write on the issues about which I am most passionate: the education of children and young adults, especially those who have been historically neglected by our schools; that is, young people of culturally and linguistically diverse backgrounds and those who live in poverty. The reasons for my steadfast interest in these issues are many, including my own experiences as a child, my education and training, and my life as a teacher, mother, and grandmother.

"I believe, and I know through my own experience, that negative beliefs about cultural, linguistic, gender, social class, and other kinds of diversity leave their imprint on students, teachers, and schools. Even well-meaning teachers who care about their students may have stereotypic beliefs and hold low expectations for them. At the same time, and equally injurious to the life chances of poor students and students from culturally and linguistically diverse families, are the conditions in the schools they attend. These conditions include disgracefully inadequate levels of funding, rigid ability tracking, unmotivated pedagogy, and irrelevant curriculum. My purpose in writing is to use my research and that of others to broaden the perspectives of educators, and indeed of citizens in general, about diversity. I am convinced that differences are not the problem; the problem resides in the negative perceptions concerning culture, race, gender, and language that are deeply embedded in our history. In my writing, I address this problem and focus my attention on the positive role that teachers and schools can play in teaching students of all backgrounds to high levels of achievement."

BIOGRAPHICAL AND CRITICAL SOURCES:

ONLINE

Welcome to Sonia Nieto's Web Page, http://www-unix. oit.umass.edu/~snieto (February 10, 2007).

*   *   *

NOLL, Mark A. 1946-
(Mark Allan Noll)

PERSONAL: Born July 18, 1946, in Iowa City, IA; son of Francis Arthur (an engineer) and Evelyn Jean Noll; married Ruth Margaret Packer, 1969; children: Mary Constance, David Luther, Robert Francis. *Education:* Wheaton College, B.A., 1968; University of Iowa, M.A., 1970; Trinity Evangelical Divinity School, M.A., 1972; Vanderbilt University, M.A., 1974, Ph.D., 1975. *Religion:* Reformed Protestant.

ADDRESSES: Office—Department of History, 219 O'Shaugnessy, University of Notre Dame, Notre Dame, IN 46556. *E-mail*—mark.noll8@nd.edu.

CAREER: Historian, educator, and author. Trinity College, Deerfield, IL, assistant professor of history, 1975-78; Wheaton College, Wheaton, IL, associate professor, 1978-84, professor of history, beginning 1984, became McManis Professor of Christian Thought, Institute for the Study of American Evangelicals, cofounder; University of Notre Dame, Francis A. McAnaney Professor of History, 2006—. Visiting professor at universities and colleges, including Harvard Divinity School, University of Chicago Divinity School, Regent College, Vancouver, and Westminister Theological Seminary; Jonathan Edwards Center, Yale University, board member.

MEMBER: American Historical Association, Organization of American Historians, American Society of Church History, Conference on Faith and History.

AWARDS, HONORS: National Humanities Medal, awarded by President George W. Bush and the National Endowment for the Humanities; named one of America's twenty-five most influential evangelicals, *Time,* 2005.

WRITINGS:

Christians in the American Revolution, Eerdmans (Grand Rapids, MI), 1977.
(With Nathan Hatch and John Woodbridge) *The Gospel in America: Themes in the Story of American Evangelicals,* Zondervan (Grand Rapids, MI), 1979.
(Editor, with Nathan Hatch, and contributor) *The Bible in America,* Oxford University Press (New York, NY), 1982.
(Editor, with others, and contributor) *Eerdmans Handbook to Christianity in America,* Eerdmans (Grand Rapids, MI), 1983.
(Editor) *The Princeton Theology, 1812-1921,* Baker Books (Ada, MI), 1983.
Between Faith and Criticism: Evangelicals, Scholarship, and the Bible in America, Harper (New York, NY), 1986, expanded edition, Baker Books (Ada, MI), 1991.
(Editor, with Roger Lundin) *Voices from the Heart: Four Centuries of American Piety,* Eerdmans (Grand Rapids, MI), 1987.

One Nation under God? Christian Faith and Political Action in America, Harper (New York, NY), 1988.

(Editor, with David Wells) *Christian Faith and Practice in the Modern World: Theology from an Evangelical Point of View,* Eerdmans (Grand Rapids, MI), 1988.

Princeton and the Republic, 1768-1822: The Search for a Christian Enlightenment in the Era of Samuel Stanhope Smith, Princeton University Press (Princeton, NJ), 1989.

(With Nathan Hatch and George Marsden) *The Search for Christian America,* Crossway (Wheaton, IL), 1983, revised edition, Helmers & Howard (Colorado Springs, CO), 1989.

(Editor) *Religion and American Politics: From the Colonial Period to the 1980s,* Oxford University Press (New York, NY), 1989.

(With Howard Kee and others) *Christianity: A Social and Cultural History,* Macmillan (New York, NY), 1991.

(Editor) *Confessions and Catechisms of the Reformation,* Baker Books (Ada, MI), 1991.

A History of Christianity in the United States and Canada, Eerdmans (Grand Rapids, MI), 1992.

(Editor, with George A. Rawlyk) *Amazing Grace: Evangelicalism in Australia, Britain, Canada, and the United States,* Baker Books (Ada, MI), 1993.

(Editor) *Evangelicalism: Comparative Studies of Popular Protestantism in North America, the British Isles, and Beyond, 1700-1990,* Oxford University Press (New York, NY), 1994.

(Editor, with David N. Livingstone) *What Is Darwinism?, and Other Writings on Science and Religion,* Baker Books (Ada, MI), 1994.

The Scandal of the Evangelical Mind, Eerdmans (Grand Rapids, MI), 1994.

Adding Cross to Crown: The Political Significance of Christ's Passion, Baker Books (Ada, MI), 1996.

Seasons of Grace, Baker Books (Ada, MI), 1997.

(Editor, with others) *Evangelicals and Science in Historical Perspective,* Oxford University Press (New York, NY), 1999.

(Editor, with D.G. Hart) *Dictionary of the Presbyterian and Reformed Tradition in America,* InterVarsity Press (Downers Grove, IL), 1999.

(Editor, with Larry Eskridge) *More Money, More Ministry: Money and Evangelicals in Recent North American History,* Eerdmans (Grand Rapids, MI), 2000.

(Editor, with Ronald F. Thiemann) *Where Shall My Wond'ring Soul Begin? The Landscape of Evangelical Piety and Thought,* Eerdmans (Grand Rapids, MI), 2000.

American Evangelical Christianity: An Introduction, Blackwell (Oxford, England), 2000.

Turning Points: Decisive Moments in the History of Christianity, Baker Books (Ada, MI), 2000.

(Editor, with David N. Livingstone) *Evolution, Scripture, and Science,* Baker Books (Ada, MI), 2000.

Protestants in America, Oxford University Press (New York, NY), 2000.

The Old Religion in a New World: The History of North American Christianity, Eerdmans (Grand Rapids, MI), 2002.

The Work We Have to Do: A History of Protestants in America, Oxford University Press (New York, NY), 2002.

(Editor) *God and Mammon: Protestants, Money, and the Market, 1790-1860,* Oxford University Press (New York, NY), 2002.

America's God: From Jonathan Edwards to Abraham Lincoln, Oxford University Press (New York, NY), 2002.

The Rise of Evangelicalism: The Age of Edwards, Whitefield, and the Wesleys, InterVarsity Press (Downers Grove, IL), 2003.

(Consulting editor, with others) *Biographical Dictionary of Evangelicals* InterVarsity Press (Downers Grove, IL), 2003.

(Editor, with Richard J. Mouw) *Wonderful Words of Life: Hymns in American Protestant History and Theology,* Eerdmans (Grand Rapids, MI), 2004.

(Editor, with Edith L. Blumhofer) *Singing the Lord's Song in a Strange Land: Hymody in the History of North American Protestantism,* University of Alabama Press (Tuscaloosa, AL), 2004.

(With Carolyn Nystrom) *Is the Reformation Over? An Evangelicalism Assessment of Contemporary Roman Catholicism,* Baker Academic (Grand Rapids, MI), 2005.

The Civil War as a Theological Crisis, University of North Carolina Press (Chapel Hill, NC), 2006.

(With Edith L. Blumhofer) *Sing Them Over Again To Me,* University of Alabama Press (Tuscaloosa, AL), 2006.

Contributor to works by others and to history and theology journals. Associate editor, *Christian Scholar's Review,* 1978-83; member of editorial committee, *Reformed Journal,* 1983-90.

SIDELIGHTS: Mark A. Noll is a leading religious scholar. He has been recognized by *Time* magazine as one of America's twenty-five most influential evangelicals and was awarded a National Humanities Medal by President George W. Bush and the National Endowment for the Humanities.

Noll has written or edited many books about the history of Christianity, and in particular American evangelicalism, and is the author of the encyclopedic *A History of Christianity in the United States and Canada.* Kevin A. Miller wrote of this book in *Christianity Today:* "Noll has given us a fine narrative history, probably the best available of Christianity in North America." Many scholars have since come to consider *A History of Christianity* to be the authoritative text on the subject. In addition, "Noll has surely become our leading teacher-historian of American Christianity," Ralph C. Wood declared in *First Things.*

Also notable among Noll's books is *The Scandal of the Evangelical Mind,* about which the author succinctly noted: "There is not much of an evangelical mind." Noll, an evangelical himself, traces the development of evangelical thought from its roots in the teachings of Catholic intellectuals St. Augustine and St. Thomas Aquinas through John Calvin and the New England Puritan theologian Jonathan Edwards. In what Noll calls the Evangelical Enlightenment, Edwards and others encouraged Christians to bring rationality, critical thought, and other Enlightenment values to bear on their religion. However, in the late nineteenth century, under increasing pressure from proponents of evolution and the new critical Biblical scholarship emanating from Germany, many evangelical Christians reverted to dogmatic assertions of faith. This anti-intellectual position, which came to be known as fundamentalism, remains a powerful strain in American evangelical thought and continues to hamper evangelical scholarship. Noll's "breathtaking panorama of evangelical history," as a *Publishers Weekly* contributor described it, "is a brilliant study by . . . a first-rate Evangelical mind."

Turning Points: Decisive Moments in the History of Christianity, the most sweeping of Noll's histories, stretches from the fall of Jerusalem in 70 A.D. to the Edinburgh Missionary Conference of 1910. *Journal of Church and State* contributor James A. Patterson noted the "considerable analytical skills" and "acute sensibility to cultural, political and social history" which Noll brings to his subject. Noll ranges far beyond mere doctrinal study, examining church-state relations and the impact secular events such as the coronation of Charlemagne and the French Revolution had on Christianity.

Noll has also written the critically praised historical overviews *The Old Religion in the New World: The History of North American Christianity* and *American Evangelical History.* "Noll upholds his reputation for clear, accessible prose and admirably organizing mountains of historical material" in *The Old Religion in a New World,* Steven Schroeder noted in a review for *Booklist,* while C. Robert Nixon praised the same book as a "clear overview of a complex subject."

In *American Evangelical Christianity,* Noll studies the position of Evangelical faiths in U.S. culture, politics, and religious life. He offers readers "not only an attractive portrayal of evangelical beliefs and practices but an accurate one as well," commented P.C. Kemeny in a review for *Journal of Religion.* Praising the work for helping to dispel some generally held assumptions about evangelical Christians, Kemeny added that Noll also "provides a much-needed historical corrective to the fictions that certain Evangelicals propagate with regard to modern science and the founding of the United States." "In the volume's most provocative chapter, 'Evangelical Politics: A Better Way,' Noll challenges the 'Religious Right' to reconsider the significance of the cross of Christ for political action. Too often, he argues, Evangelicals demonize their political opponents and forget that Christ died for them too."

America's God: From Jonathan Edwards to Abraham Lincoln, described as a "magisterial work" by a *Publishers Weekly* contributor, is a social history of Christian theology in America from colonial times to the Civil War, in which Noll notes the impact of progress, such as the printing press, on theology and theology's impact on the politics of the time. *Church History* reviewer Laurie F. Maffly-Kipp described the volume as being "a virtual tour de force, and it will be an indispensable reference tool for the study of American theology for many years to come. Noll has read—and has even had time to think about—nearly everything, and his erudition shines. His clear and succinct exposition of the organizational development of American evangelicalism after the Revolution is a wonderful piece of work, and that section only sets the context for his real interest in intellectual change. When he does reach the theology itself, he illuminates both the obscure and the downright tedious, along with the gems."

The Rise of Evangelicalism: The Age of Edwards, Whitefield, and the Wesleys is a study of the period from 1734 to 1738, during which time Jonathan Edwards led his followers in Northampton, Massachusetts, George Whitefield spoke to more Americans than any other speaker, and evangelicals, including John Wesley, formed the evangelical movement in London, England, which produced a large number of publishing houses. *Books and Culture* contributor David Hempton wrote: "One of the most engaging aspects of *The Rise of Evangelicalism* is Noll's shrewd identification of the roots of some of evangelicalism's most enduring features. These include the 'revolutionary development' of a lasting evangelical presence among African Americans pioneered by Moravians, Baptists, and Methodists; the process of globalization facilitated by the formation of the great evangelical missionary societies at the end of the 18th century (once again Moravians were the trailblazers); and evangelicalism's emphasis on individual religious experience, often to the neglect of any coherent social or corporate vision."

Noll wrote *Is the Reformation Over? An Evangelicalism Assessment of Contemporary Roman Catholicism* with journalist Carolyn Nystrom. It is a study of the changes in the Roman Catholic Church since Vatican II and an assessment of relations between evangelicalism and the Catholic Church. The study also examines how the former has taken on many of the qualities of the latter that it had found objectionable only decades earlier, including "the formalism, the anthropocentric worship, the power mongering, and the egotism" of the Church. A *Publishers Weekly* reviewer commented: "This willingness to see the proverbial beam in one's own eye is one of the great strengths of this book."

In an interview with Judy Valente for the PBS series *Religion and Ethics*, Noll defined Evangelical Protestant Christians: "Evangelicals usually stress conversion to Jesus Christ. Evangelicals stress the authority of the Bible as their chief religious authority. Evangelicals are activist in some areas of life, principally in trying to share the good news about Jesus. And evangelicals usually stress the death of Christ and his resurrection as the key, central Christian teaching." Noll explained that there is no one group of evangelicals, noting that black evangelicals, which make up a substantial percentage of the community, are usually not counted with white, Asian, and Hispanic evangelicals. He also said the evangelicals are not as political as is sometimes assumed. When asked by Valente about the difference between evangelicals and fundamentalists, he replied: "Fundamentalists historically have been defined as those who are especially influenced by the revival traditions of the nineteenth century, especially influenced by the turn

toward dispensational premillennialism as a theology in the late 19th century, and sometimes by their attitudes of separation and militancy toward the rest of the religious world and the rest of the world. Evangelical Christianity as a whole would include some fundamentalist tendencies, some fundamentalist groups, but probably most evangelicals would not want to be called fundamentalists themselves."

In projecting the future of evangelicalism, Noll told Valente: "For the years ahead, the greatest strengths of American evangelical Christianity have to be the bedrock qualities of Christian faith. The ways in which evangelicals adjust to society may be good, may be bad, may be indifferent, may be questionable in some ways, but to be a Christian of any sort, and certainly to be an evangelical Christian, is to remain confident in the work of God and Jesus Christ. So long as evangelicals are secure in that confidence, then whatever happens, they will be secure in the future."

Noll once told *CA:* "My writing arises out of my 'callings' as a historian and a Christian. Sometimes the vocations seem to get in the way of each other, but mostly it is a fruitful combination. The danger of moralizing in historical work and relativizing religion is always present. These are acceptable risks, given the intrinsic satisfaction of the task."

BIOGRAPHICAL AND CRITICAL SOURCES:

PERIODICALS

America, June 9, 1990, Christopher F. Mooney, review of *Religion and American Politics: From the Colonial Period to the 1980s,* pp. 589-590.

American Historical Review, October, 2000, Winton U. Solberg, review of *Evangelicals and Science in Historical Perspective,* pp. 1267-1268.

Atlantic Monthly, December, 2002, Benjamin Schwarz, review of *America's God: From Jonathan Edwards to Abraham Lincoln,* p. 126.

Baptist History and Heritage, summer-fall, 2003, Pamela Durso, review of *The Old Religion in a New World: The History of North American Christianity,* p. 110; winter, 2005, David W. Music, review of *Wonderful Words of Life: Hymns in American Protestant History and Theology,* p. 119.

Booklist, July, 1994, Ray Olson, review of *The Scandal of the Evangelical Mind,* pp. 1898-1899; October 1, 1996, Ray Olson, review of *Adding Cross to*

Crown: The Political Significance of Christ's Passion, p. 305; December 1, 2001, Steven Schroeder, review of *The Old Religion in a New World,* p. 608.

Books and Culture, January-February, 2003, Martin E. Marty, review of *America's God,* p. 16; July-August, 2004, David Hempton, review of *The Rise of Evangelicalism: The Age of Edwards, Whitefield, and the Wesleys,* p. 29.

Canadian Historical Review, June, 1995, review of *Amazing Grace: Evangelicalism in Australia, Britain, Canada, and the United States,* pp. 258-290.

Catholic Historical Review, April, 1990, Patrick N. Allitt, review of *Religion and American Politics: From the Colonial Period to the 1980s,* pp. 403-404; July, 1993, Edwin S. Gaustad, review of *A History of Christianity in the United States and Canada,* pp. 565-567; July, 1995, C. Allyn Russell, review of *Amazing Grace,* pp. 405-406; October, 2006, Jennifer Petrafesa McLaughlin, review of *The Rise of Evangelicalism,* p. 638.

Catholic Insight, June, 2006, James Hanrahan, review of *Is the Reformation Over? An Evangelicalism Assessment of Contemporary Roman Catholicism,* p. 44.

Choice, January, 1995, D. Jacobsen, review of *The Scandal of the Evangelical Mind,* p. 806; December, 1999, D. Jacobsen, review of *Evangelicals and Science in Historical Perspective,* p. 738; May, 2001, D.W. Germ, review of *American Evangelical Christianity: An Introduction,* p. 1644.

Christian Century, September 28, 1988, Richard Quebedeaux, review of *One Nation under God? Christian Faith and Political Action in America,* pp. 848-849; December 13, 1989, Theodore Dwight Bozeman, review of *Princeton and the Republic, 1768-1822,* pp. 1178-1179; June 13, 1990, Charles K. Piehl, review of *Religion and American Politics,* pp. 609-610; November 18, 1992, Robert T. Handy, review of *A History of Christianity in the United States and Canada,* pp. 1067-1069; December 4, 2002, Clark Gilpin, review of *America's God,* p. 40; February 1, 2006, Stephen M. Marini, review of *Wonderful Words of Life,* p. 53; May 30, 2006, Todd Shy, review of *The Civil War as a Theological Crisis,* p. 34.

Christianity Today, May 23, 1980, Richard L. Troutman, review of *The Gospel in America: Themes in the Story of American Evangelicals,* pp. 36-37; February 6, 1987, Donald K. McKim, review of *Between Faith and Criticism: Evangelicals, Scholarship, and the Bible in America,* pp. 50-51;

*April 3, 1987, review of *Voices from the Heart: Four Centuries of American Piety,* p. 32; May 12, 1989, Richard V. Pierard, review of *One Nation under God?,* pp. 62-63; June 18, 1990, John G. Stackhouse, Jr., review of *Princeton and the Republic, 1768-1822,* pp. 48-49; June 21, 1993, Kevin A. Miller, review of *A History of Christianity in the United States and Canada,* pp. 38-39; December 6, 1999, review of *Dictionary of the Presbyterian and Reformed Tradition in America,* p. 91; August, 2006, Elesha Coffman, review of *The Civil War as a Theological Crisis,* p. 66.

Church History, December, 1990, Marvin Bergman, review of *Princeton and the Republic, 1768-1822,* pp. 569-570; September, 1995, Phyllis D. Airhart, review of *Evangelicalism: Comparative Studies of Popular Protestantism in North America, the British Isles, and Beyond, 1700-1990,* pp. 535-536; December, 1998, Richard V. Pierard, review of *Turning Points: Decisive Moments in the History of Christianity,* p. 844; September, 2003, Christine Leigh Heyrman, review of *America's God,* p. 617, Grant Wacker, review of *America's God,* p. 620, E. Brooks Holifield, review of *America's God,* p. 624, and Laurie F. Maffly-Kipp, review of *America's God,* p. 634; June, 2005, John Ogasapian, review of *Wonderful Words of Life,* p. 414; March, 2004, Stuart B. Jennings, review of *God and Mammon: Protestants, Money, and the Market, 1790-1860,* p. 226; December, 2006, E. Brooks Holifield, review of *The Civil War as a Theological Crisis,* p. 939.

Commonweal, November 4, 1994, Martin E. Marty, review of *The Scandal of the Evangelical Mind,* pp. 22-25; January 13, 2006, Brad S. Gregory, review of *Is the Reformation Over?,* p. 26.

Comparative Studies in Society and History, January, 1998, Jon H. Roberts, review of *Evangelicalism,* pp. 187-188.

First Things, October, 2001, Ralph C. Wood, review of *American Evangelical Christianity,* pp. 43-46; June-July, 2002, Philip Gleason, review of *The Old Religion in a New World,* p. 57; October, 2005, Geoffrey Wainwright, review of *Is the Reformation Over?,* 40.

Historian, autumn, 1990, Larry G. Bowman, review of *Princeton and the Republic, 1768-1822,* pp. 138-139.

Interpretation, April, 2005, Dewey D. Wallace, Jr., review of *America's God,* p. 204.

Journal for the Scientific Study of Religion, December, 1989, Frank J. Lechner, review of *One Nation under God?,* p. 546; March, 1995, F. Maurice Ethridge, review of *Evangelicalism,* p. 130.

Journal of American History, December, 1990, Robert Booth Fowler, review of *Religion and American Politics,* pp. 987-988; September, 1994, Jay P. Dolan, review of *A History of Christianity in the United States and Canada,* pp. 628-629; June, 1995, Frank Lambert, review of *Evangelicalism,* pp. 199-200; June, 1996, Clyde Binfield, review of *Amazing Grace,* pp. 204-205.

Journal of Church and State, autumn, 1989, Michael Johnston, review of *One Nation under God?,* pp. 547-548; spring, 1990, David B. Calhoun, review of *Princeton and the Republic, 1768-1822,* pp. 418-420; autumn, 1990, David L. Salvaterra, review of *Religion and American Politics,* pp. 871-872; autumn, 1998, James A. Patterson, review of *Turning Points,* p. 901; spring, 2002, Lee Canipe, review of *Protestants in America,* p. 375; autumn, 2002, Charles McDaniel, review of *God and Mammon,* p. 834; winter, 2002, Marshall R. Johnston, review of *American Evangelical Christianity,* pp. 168-169; winter, 2003, Preston Jones, review of *The Old Religion in a New World,* p. 182; autumn, 2004, Don M. Shipley, Jr., review of *The Rise of Evangelicalism,* p. 897.

Journal of Ecclesiastical History, July, 1997, Bradley Longfield, review of *The Scandal of the Evangelical Mind,* pp. 498-507; July, 2002, Richard Carwardine, review of *American Evangelical Christianity,* p. 643.

Journal of Interdisciplinary Studies, September, 1997, Patrick Rist, review of *The Scandal of the Evangelical Mind,* pp. 191-192; January, 2005, Henry D. Rack, review of *The Rise of Evangelicalism,* p. 183.

Journal of Law and Religion, winter-summer, 1990, Timothy Sherrat, review of *One Nation under God?* and *Religion and American Politics,* pp. 585-595; April, 2003, Albert Zambone, review of *The Old Religion in a New World,* p. 373.

Journal of Religion, April, 2002, P.C. Kemeny, review of *American Evangelical Christianity;* April, 2003, Peter W. Williams, review of *The Old Religion in a New World,* p. 266; April, 2005, Thomas S. Kidd, review of *America's God,* p. 293, and Jonathan R. Bear, review of *Wonderful Words of Life,* p. 322; October, 2005, Dee E. Andrews, review of *The Rise of Evangelicalism,* p. 660.

Journal of Religious History, October, 1997, review of *Amazing Grace,* pp. 361-363.

Journal of Southern History, November, 1991, G. Howard Miller, review of *Princeton and the Republic, 1768-1822,* pp. 725-726; May, 1995, Martin E. Marty, review of *Evangelicalism,* pp. 363-365.

Journal of the Early Republic, spring, 1990, Mary R. Murrin, review of *Princeton and the Republic, 1768-1822,* pp. 80-81; summer, 1990, Anne M. Boylan, review of *Religion and American Politics,* pp. 259-260; May, 2005, David Stricklin, review of *Wonderful Words of Life,* p. 508.

Library Journal, April 1, 1987, Elise Chase, review of *Voices from the Heart,* p. 154; November 1, 1992, C. Robert Nixon, review of *A History of Christianity in the United States and Canada,* p. 91; October 15, 1997, George Westerlund, review of *Turning Points,* p. 66; December, 2001, C. Robert Nixon, review of *The Old Religion in a New World,* p. 133; November 1, 2002, C. Robert Nixon, review of *America's God,* p. 96; July, 2005, David I. Fulton, review of *Is the Reformation Over?,* p. 138.

National Catholic Reporter, March 18, 1983, Jack Dick, review of *The Bible in America,* p. 13; February 10, 2006, Charlene Spretnak, review of *Is the Reformation Over?,* p. 1.

National Review, July 18, 2005, Michael Potemra, review of *Is the Reformation Over?,* p. 44.

Presidential Studies Quarterly, fall, 1990, E. Brooks Holifield, review of *Religion and American Politics,* pp. 850-852.

Publishers Weekly, December 18, 1987; June 13, 1994, review of *The Scandal of the Evangelical Mind,* p. 33; October 14, 1996, review of *Adding Cross to Crown,* p. 76; October 27, 1997, review of *Turning Points,* p. 69; May 15, 2000, review of *Where Shall My Wond'ring Soul Begin? The Landscape of Evangelical Piety and Thought,* p. 110; October 16, 2000, review of *More Money, More Ministry: Money and Evangelicals in Recent North American History,* p. 69; November 26, 2001, review of *The Old Religion in a New World,* p. 58; October 21, 2002, review of *America's God,* p. 71; May 16, 2005, review of *Is the Reformation Over?,* p. 57; February 27, 2006, review of *The Civil War as a Theological Crisis,* p. 57.

School Library Journal, February, 2001, Elizabeth M. Reardon, review of *Protestants in America,* p. 137.

Theology, September-October, 2000, John Wolffe, review of *Evangelicals and Science in Historical Perspective,* pp. 389-390; May-June, 2001, D.W. Bebbington, review of *Where Shall My Wond'ring Soul Begin?,* pp. 227-228.

Theological Studies, December, 2003, Dolores Liptak, review of *The Old Religion in a New World,* p. 880; September, 2006, Thomas P. Rausch, review of *Is the Reformation Over?,* p. 684.

Theology Today, April, 1989, William Johnson Everett, review of *One Nation under God?,* pp. 87-88; July,

1990, James H. Moorhead, review of *Princeton and the Republic, 1768-1822,* pp. 188-189.

U.S. Catholic, October, 1988, Gerald M. Costello, review of *One Nation under God?,* pp. 48-51.

William & Mary Quarterly, July, 1990, review of *Princeton and the Republic, 1768-1822,* pp. 422-444.

ONLINE

Religion and Ethics Online, http://www.pbs.org/ (April 16, 2004), transcript of Judy Valente interview.

Wheaton College Web site, http://www.wheaton.edu/ (February 23, 2007), biography.

University of Notre Dame Department of History Web site, http://history.nd.edu/ (February 23, 2007), brief biography

*　　*　　*

NOLL, Mark Allan
　　See NOLL, Mark A.

O

O'CONNELL, Carol 1947-

PERSONAL: Born May 26, 1947, in New York, NY; daughter of Norman and Berta O'Connell. *Education:* Arizona State University, B.F.A.; also attended the California Institute (or Arts/Chouinard). *Hobbies and other interests:* "No time."

ADDRESSES: Home—New York, NY.

CAREER: Writer. "Writer, failed painter. Rent-money jobs: proofreader, copyeditor."

WRITINGS:

"KATHLEEN MALLORY" MYSTERIES

Mallory's Oracle, Putnam (New York, NY), 1994.
The Man Who Cast Two Shadows, Putnam (New York, NY), 1995.
Killing Critics, Putnam (New York, NY), 1996.
Stone Angel, Putnam (New York, NY), 1997.
Shell Game, Putnam (New York, NY), 1999.
Crime School, Putnam (New York, NY), 2002.
Dead Famous, Putnam (New York, NY), 2003.
Winter House, Putnam (New York, NY), 2004.
Find Me, Putnam (New York, NY), 2006.

OTHER MYSTERIES

Judas Child, Putnam (New York, NY), 1998.

ADAPTATIONS: Stone Angel and *Shell Game* have been made into sound recordings.

SIDELIGHTS: Until the early 1990s, Carol O'Connell lived in a one-room apartment in New York's Greenwich Village, "struggling to earn enough for rent money by proofreading, editing and churning out any kind of copy she'd be paid to write," in the words of *Publishers Weekly* contributor Suzanne Mantell. Once a painter, O'Connell switched to writing when she discovered that "mysteries are fascinating," as she once revealed to *CA.* After attempting to market a manuscript in New York, she came to the conclusion that publishers in that city were no longer reading their "slush piles"—large quantities of unsolicited, unagented manuscripts. Thus, for her second try, O'Connell went at it from a different angle. She sent a manuscript titled "Whistling Dogs" to Hutchinson, a British publisher, figuring that an unpublished author had a better chance with firms in the United Kingdom. She reported to Mantell that Hutchinson editor Paul Sidey's response "was so complimentary that I didn't understand at first that it was a rejection." Encouraged by British kindness, O'Connell offered Hutchinson another manuscript in 1993. They accepted it, sold the U.S. rights to Putnam for 800,000 dollars, and the result became *Mallory's Oracle.*

Mallory's Oracle is the story of police sergeant Kathleen Mallory. A street thief as a child, she is taken in by a New York police inspector and his wife. She eventually becomes a computer expert and joins the police force, though her past still affects her deeply. When her adoptive father is murdered while investigating a series of killings, she uses her grief leave to track down the killer. Andrew Vachss in the *New York Times Book*

Review had high praise for *Mallory's Oracle,* and observed that "O'Connell is either very well read or possessed of uncanny marketing instincts—no one genre will hold her book." He went on to explain that the novel is "part cozy whodunit, part police procedural, the book also contains generous dashes of surrealism, hints of the occult and a touch of horror." A *Kirkus Reviews* contributor was similarly impressed, hailing *Mallory's Oracle* as "a break-the-mold detective story, an incredible debut . . . and a blessing to female detective fans everywhere."

O'Connell followed up the success of her first published novel with three more Mallory books within three years. Not bad for a character who, as O'Connell told Emily Melton for an interview in *Booklist,* "started out as a peripheral character in a book that never worked." In *The Man Who Cast Two Shadows,* Mallory is fascinated by a corpse that appears to be her. The detective ends up adopting the murder victim's cat, and the reader sometimes sees Mallory through the cat's eyes as Mallory tracks down the killer. *Killing Critics* focuses on the murder of a performance artist that leads Mallory to revisit an old case once investigated by her father. In an article about O'Connell for the *At Wanderer's Well* Web site, a contributor noted that the ending was "surprising, touching, and vintage O'Connell." The writer also commented: "I will confidently predict that anyone who reads to page 50 will not put *Killing Critics* down."

In 1997, *Stone Angel* hit the bookstores with a tale of murders in Louisiana, complicated by the story of Mallory's own secret past and her mother's death twenty years earlier by stoning. "Here is a novel that grabs hold early and draws you all the way into a world of secrets, mysteries, murder, revenge and innocence lost," wrote a contributor to *Publishers Weekly.* Melton, writing in *Booklist,* observed that O'Connell is "now at the height of her considerable literary powers," and noted that the book is a "brilliant, not-to-be-missed performance. Wow!"

Despite the critical success of her books featuring Mallory, O'Connell set aside her troubled heroine and created Rouge Kendall for her book *Judas Child.* Assigned to investigate a kidnapping of two ten-year-old girls, Rouge is faced with a disturbing pattern resembling the disappearance and murder of his own twin sister fifteen years earlier. Melton of *Booklist* called it O'Connell's "most stunning novel yet." Melton further noted: "Few readers will be able to resist the charms of her lyrical

prose or her daringly original plot." A reviewer writing in *Publishers Weekly* commented on O'Connell's "vivid minor characters" but was not fond of the novel's "supernatural twist." Nevertheless, the reviewer noted that the "subtle characterization of people who face tragedy with resilience and spirit makes for a moving novel."

O'Connell brings Mallory back for *Shell Game,* a story in which the recurring characters of Charles, Coffey, Slope, and Riker are further revealed as Mallory investigates the death of Oliver Tree, an aging magician. Tree dies while performing an escape trick in New York's Central Park, and other magicians become the primary suspects in what Mallory believes to be his murder. Intertwined with the investigation is a tragic love story dating back to World War II France. "The Story of Kathleen Mallory concluded with *Stone Angel,*" wrote a contributor to the *At Wanderer's Well* Web site. "One can only go into the fifth novel" with "some apprehension: is there really anything more we need to know about Mallory, her friends, the continuing characters? Surprisingly, the answer is yes." Writing in the *Library Journal,* Karen Anderson called *Shell Game* "one of the best" Mallory novels. A *Publishers Weekly* contributor commented: "Her tough realism and hypnotic prose will leave readers eager for more."

In the sixth Mallory novel, *Crime School,* the heroine is helping to track down a serial killer who stalks and hangs his victims. Mallory's past is again involved when the detective learns that one of the victims was once a prostitute who read bedtime stories to Mallory when she was a street urchin. As with most of the Mallory novels, there is also a secondary puzzle, in this case involving a series of pulp Westerns that Mallory loved as a girl. "This novel is gritty, streetwise, funny—and sure to bring in more fans for the still-enigmatic Mallory," wrote a reviewer in *Publishers Weekly.* A contributor to *Kirkus Reviews* noted: "O'Connell's character-driven procedural transcends genre pigeonholing."

In *Dead Famous* Mallory is on the trail of The Reaper, the person who has killed eight jurors after shock jock Ian Zachary bolsters public outrage over the jury letting a supposed killer go free. Also on hand is crime-scene cleaner Johanna Apollo, who works for Mallory's partner Riker and has plenty of secrets of her own to keep hidden, including the fact that she may have killed an FBI agent. A *Kirkus Reviews* contributor noted that the novel contains "memorable characters and blazingly original prose." The reviewer added; "Once again, O'Connell transcends the genre." A *Publishers Weekly* contributor wrote that the author's "prose—sharp, gritty and streetwise—is in top form."

Find Me features Mallory on leave but nevertheless becoming involved in the hunt for "Mack the Knife," a serial killer who has murdered more than 100 innocent children along historic Route 66. In the process, she finds herself part of a burgeoning caravan in which parents are traveling together in search of their missing children. Mallory is also under suspicion for the murder of a woman shot in the heart and found in Mallory's apartment with a note saying "Love is the Death of Me." A *Kirkus Reviews* contributor wrote: "She gets all the genre stuff right: the cops' jaded inside jokes, the forensics jargon, the violence. Mainly, though, she's masterful at revealing the detective mind." Joe Hartlaub writing on the *BookReporter.com* Web site, commented that "fans will find their long infatuation with Mallory rewarded, and then some."

In an interview with Melton for *Booklist*, O'Connell explained how she has kept up her high output of novels. "I just write all the time," she said. "I don't really have a life." She went on to comment, "When I'm working on a novel, I just don't have time for anything but writing. That's kind of hard on friends and relatives. The contracts are murderous, but when you're in the crime genre, publishers and readers really expect you to keep on producing."

BIOGRAPHICAL AND CRITICAL SOURCES:

PERIODICALS

Booklist, June 1, 1997, Emily Melton, review of *Stone Angel,* p. 1620; April 15, 1998, Emily Melton, "Booklist Interview," p. 1370, and Emily Melton, review of *Judas Child,* p. 1390; April 15, 1999, Emily Melton, review of *Shell Game,* p. 1483; August, 2003, Connie Fletcher, review of *Dead Famous,* p. 1962.
Entertainment Weekly, December 22, 2006, Adam B. Vary, review of *Find Me,* p. 87.
Kirkus Reviews, May 15, 1994, review of *Mallory's Oracle,* p. 655; June 15, 2002, review of *Crime School,* p. 843; July 15, 2003, review of *Dead Famous,* p. 941; October 15, 2006, review of *Find Me,* p. 1040.

Library Journal, April 15, 1998, Devon Thomas, review of *Judas Child,* p. 115; June 15, 1999, Karen Anderson, review of *Shell Game,* p. 109; July, 2002, Devon Thomas, review of *Crime School,* p. 122; October 1, 2003, Lelsie Madden, review of *Dead Famous,* p. 122.
New York Times Book Review, October 2, 1994, Andrew Vachss, review of *Mallory's Oracle,* p. 33.
People, August 4, 1997, Pam Lambert, review of *Stone Angel,* p. 32.
Publishers Weekly, January 31, 1994, Suzanne Mantell, "*Mallory's Oracle* predicts Megabucks for First Novelist," interview with author, pp. 24-25; June 9, 1997, review of *Stone Angel,* p. 41; April 27, 1998, review of *Judas Child,* p. 42; June 14, 1999, review of *Shell Game,* p. 53; August 19, 2002, review of *Crime School,* p. 67; August 4, 2003, review of *Dead Famous,* p. 55; October 16, 2006, review of *Find Me,* p. 30.

ONLINE

At Wanderer's Well, http://www.dancingbadger.com/ (October 8, 2002), "Carol O'Connell, Watching Mallory Grow a Soul."
BookBrowser, http://www.bookbrowser.com/ (October 8, 2002), review of *Crime School.*
Bookreporter.com, http://www.bookreporter.com/ (February 12, 2007), Joe Hartlaub, review of *Find Me.*
Triviana, http://triviana.com/ (February 12, 2007), John Orr, "Carol O'Connell Rises to the Task," interview with author.
Who Dunnit, http://www.who-dunnit.com/ (February 12, 2007), brief profile of author.*

* * *

O'KEEFE, Susan Heyboer

PERSONAL: Born in NJ; married; husband a mental-health counselor; children: one son. *Education:* Ramapo College, B.A. (with honors); City College of New York, M.A. *Hobbies and other interests:* Reading.

ADDRESSES: Home—Edgewater, NJ. *E-mail*—susan heyboerokeefe@hotmail.com.

CAREER: Children's book author. Works for a publishing company.

AWARDS, HONORS: Goodman Award; Bank Street College Best Book of the Year designation, c. 1999, for *Good Night, God Bless.*

WRITINGS:

PICTURE BOOKS

One Hungry Monster: A Counting Book in Rhyme, illustrated by Lynn Munsinger, Joy Street Books (Boston, MA), 1989.

A Season for Giving, illustrated by Pamela T. Keating, Paulist Press (New York, NY), 1990.

A Bug from Aunt Tillie illustrated by Pamela T. Keating, Paulist Press (New York, NY), 1991.

Who Will Miss Me If I Don't Go to Church?, illustrated by Pamela T. Keating, Paulist Press (New York, NY), 1992.

Countdown to Christmas: Advent Thoughts, Prayers, and Activities, illustrated by Christopher Fey, Paulist Press (New York, NY), 1995.

(With Tara Egan Malanga) *Sleepy Angel's First Bedtime Story,* illustrated by Dennis Rockhill, Paulist Press (New York, NY), 1999.

Angel Prayers: Prayers for All Children, illustrated by Sofia Suzán, Boyds Mills Press (Honesdale, PA), 1999.

Good Night, God Bless, illustrated by Hideko Takahashi, Holt (New York, NY), 1999.

It's Great to Be Catholic!, illustrated by Patrick Kelley, Paulist Press (New York, NY), 2001.

Love Me, Love You, illustrated by Robin Spowart, Boyds Mills Press (Honesdale, PA), 2001.

What Does a Priest Do?: What Does a Nun Do?, illustrated by H.M. Alan, Paulist Press (New York, NY), 2002.

Christmas Gifts, illustrated by Jennifer Emery, Boyds Mills Press (Honesdale, PA), 2004.

Baby Day, illustrated by Robin Spowart, Boyds Mills Press (Honesdale, PA), 2006.

Hungry Monster ABC, illustrated by Lynn Munsinger, Little, Brown (New York, NY), 2007.

OTHER

(Editor) J. Stroman and K. Wilson, *Administrative Assistant's and Secretary's Handbook,* AMACOM (New York, NY), 1995.

(Editor) *Master the ACT,* Macmillan USA (New York, NY), 1999.

My Life and Death, by Alexandra Canarsie (young-adult novel), Peachtree (Atlanta, GA), 2001.

Death by Eggplant (children's novel), Roaring Brook Press (Brookfield, CT), 2004.

Be the Star That You Are!: A Book for Kids Who Feel Different ("Elf-Help Books for Kids" series), illustrated by R.W. Alley, Once Caring Place (St. Meinrad, IN), 2005.

SIDELIGHTS: Susan Heyboer O'Keefe sold her first children's book, *One Hungry Monster: A Counting Book in Rhyme,* in the late 1980s, beginning a successful writing career that has expanded from picture-book texts into teen novels such as *My Life and Death, by Alexandra Canarsie,* and children's nonfiction, such as *Be the Star That You Are!: A Book for Kids Who Feel Different,* part of the "Elf-Help" series. As a freelance writer, O'Keefe has also developed an ongoing association with Paulist Press, which produces books targeting a Roman Catholic readership.

Featuring illustrations by Lynn Munsigner, *One Hungry Monster* finds the titular creature hiding under a bed. As the counting progresses, two monsters chew on sneakers, and so on up to ten. In the process, a young boy tries to control the monsters' antics, but to no avail. Popular with readers, *One Hungry Monster* has also inspired author and coauthor to collaborate on a sequel of sorts: *Hungry Monster ABC.* Another picture book, *Good Night, God Bless,* relates a gentle story about a young boy, his family, his town, and the nearby animals as each creature prepares for bed. Writing in *Booklist,* Gilbert Taylor called the work a "simple yet pleasing" tale.

O'Keefe's *Love Me, Love You* follows a rabbit mom and her bunny as they spend the day together doing fun things, such as dressing up, playing games, and hugging each other. Similar in theme, and also featuring pastel-hued illustrations by Robin Spowart, *Baby Day* also focuses on family routine, this time watching a young cub awake to spend a cheerful day in a loving home. According to a *Publishers Weekly* contributor, in *Love Me, Love You* "the utter inseparability and synchronicity of the bunny pair shine through on every page," while in *School Library Journal,* Lisa Dennis commented that "O'Keefe's brief text bounces along in a convincingly childlike way, and the rhyming refrain will encourage even the youngest listeners to chime in." Calling *Baby Day* "a good read-aloud choice for toddlers," Carolyn Phelan added in *Booklist* that O'Keefe's picture book focuses reassuringly on "simple, familiar activities," and a *Kirkus Reviews* contributor cited the work as "a genuine book for babies" that will not suffer from repeated readings.

"I never actually set out to be a picture book writer and always thought of myself as a novelist," O'Keefe wrote on her home page. "It just took the rest of the world a while to agree with me." The author's first novel, *My Life and Death, by Alexandra Canarsie,* follows fourteen-year-old Allie, whose father's abandonment has left the girl moving from town to town with her mother. By the time she reaches the end of middle school, Allie and her mom are living in a beat-up house trailer, a situation the teen hates. During the summer before she starts high school, Allie finds a way to connect with other families by attending the funerals of strangers, and when she attends the funeral of a boy named Jimmy, she becomes convinced that he was murdered. As she delves into Jimmy's death, Allie learns the truth, not only about the dead boy but about herself as well. Dubbing the novel "part mystery and part coming-of-age story," a *Publishers Weekly* contributor found portions of *My Life and Death, By Alexandra Canarsie* somewhat "contrived." While noting that O'Keefe's "plot . . . might stretch credulity," *Kliatt* critic Paula Rohrlick nonetheless added that an encounter with the novel's protagonist is well worth it: "Alexandra, a fierce, bright, smart-mouthed girl who skips classes blithely and goes after the truth regardless of the consequences, is worth meeting," Rohrlick maintained. Calling *My Life and Death, by Alexandra Canarsie* "a good effort," James Blasingame added in his review for the *Journal of Adolescent & Adult Literacy* that, "although most of Allie's own problems appear to be approaching resolution as the novel ends, the conclusion is not saccharine or improbable," and Janet Hilbun concluded in *School Library Journal* that the young-adult novel ranks as "a strong first offering."

Geared toward middle-grade readers, *Death by Eggplant* tells the story of Bertie Hooks, an eighth grader who wants to be a master chef but keeps his dreams a secret, especially from his nemesis, class bully Nick Dekker. Everything in Bertie's life seems to be an obstacle toward reaching his goal, including Nick, Bertie's slightly wacky mom, and his dad, an actuary who wants Bertie to follow in his own footsteps. When Bertie's grades prove less than stellar, the boy ends up taking on a project for extra credit that involves carrying around a flour sack for a week and caring for it as though it is a baby. A *Publishers Weekly* contributor called *Death by*

Eggplant "appealingly outlandish" and noted that, with its "soupçon of silliness and hefty helpings of genuine humor," O'Keefe's story "will whet the appetites of young readers." A writer for *Kirkus Reviews* described the novel as "enjoyable zaniness, well-punctuated with Bertie's appetizing meal plans."

BIOGRAPHICAL AND CRITICAL SOURCES:

PERIODICALS

Booklist, October 1, 1999, Gilbert Taylor, review of *Good Night, God Bless,* p. 374; March 1, 2001, Shelley Townsend-Hudson, review of *One Hungry Monster: A Counting Book in Rhyme,* p. 1288; April 15, 2001, Lauren Peterson, review of *Love Me, Love You,* p. 1566; March 1, 2006, Carolyn Phelan, review of *Baby Day,* p. 100.

Book Report, September-October, 2002, Dian Boysen, review of *My Life and Death, by Alexandra Canarsie,* p. 56.

Journal of Adolescent & Adult Literacy, November, 2002, James Blasingame, review of *My Life and Death, by Alexandra Canarsie,* p. 270.

Kirkus Reviews, September 1, 2004, review of *Death by Eggplant,* p. 872; March 1, 2006, review of *Baby Day,* p. 237.

Kliatt, May, 2002, Paula Rohrlick, review of *My Life and Death, by Alexandra Canarsie,* p. 13.

Publishers Weekly, February 5, 2001, review of *Love Me, Love You,* p. 87; April 23, 2001, review of *One Hungry Monster,* p. 80; May 13, 2002, review of *My Life and Death, by Alexandra Canarsie,* p. 71; September 20, 2004, review of *Death by Eggplant,* p. 62.

St. Louis Post-Dispatch, July 28, 2002, Sue Bradford, review of *My Life and Death, by Alexandra Canarsie,* p. F11.

School Library Journal, April, 2001, Lisa Dennis, review of *Love Me, Love You,* p. 119; September, 2002, Janet Hilbun, review of *My Life and Death, by Alexandra Canarsie,* p. 231; February, 2005, Joyce Adams Burner, review of *Death by Eggplant,* p. 58; March, 2006, Gary Lynn Van Vleck, review of *Baby Day,* p. 200.

ONLINE

ChildrensLit.com, http://www.childrenslit.com/ (September 27, 2002), "Susan Heyboer O'Keefe."

Susan Heyboer O'Keefe Home Page, http://www.susan heyboerokeefe.com (February 7, 2007).

WritersWeekly.com, http://www.writersweekly.com/ (December 11, 2002), Susan Heyboer O'Keefe, "The Accidental Children's Writer."*

*   *   *

O'SHAUGHNESSY, Mary
(Perri O'Shaughnessy, a joint pseudonym)

PERSONAL: Born in CA; married; children: three. *Education:* University of California, Santa Barbara, B.A. (magna cum laude).

ADDRESSES: Home—CA. *E-mail*—perri@perrio.com.

CAREER: Writer.

WRITINGS:

"NINA REILLY" SERIES; WITH SISTER, PAMELA O'SHAUGH-NESSY, UNDER PSEUDONYM PERRI O'SHAUGHNESSY

Motion to Suppress, Delacorte Press (New York, NY), 1995.

Invasion of Privacy, Delacorte Press (New York, NY), 1997.

Obstruction of Justice, Delacorte Press (New York, NY), 1997.

Breach of Promise, Delacorte Press (New York, NY), 1998.

Acts of Malice, Delacorte Press (New York, NY), 1999.

Move to Strike, Delacorte Press (New York, NY), 2000.

Writ of Execution, Delacorte Press (New York, NY), 2001.

Unfit to Practice, Delacorte Press (New York, NY), 2002.

Presumption of Death, Delacorte Press (New York, NY), 2003.

Unlucky in Law, Delacorte Press (New York, NY), 2004.

Case of Lies, Delacorte Press (New York, NY), 2005.

OTHER; WITH SISTER, PAMELA O'SHAUGHNESSY, UNDER PSEUDONYM PERRI O'SHAUGHNESSY

Sinister Shorts (stories), Delacorte Press (New York, NY), 2006.

Keeper of the Keys (novel), Delacorte Press (New York, NY), 2006.

Contributor to *Ellery Queen's Mystery Magazine.*

ADAPTATIONS: A number of books have been adapted for audio.

SIDELIGHTS: See Pamela O'Shaughnessy for Sidelights.

BIOGRAPHICAL AND CRITICAL SOURCES:

PERIODICALS

Booklist May 15, 1998, Emily Melton, review of *Breach of Promise,* p. 1565; April 15, 1999, Jenny McLarin, review of *Acts of Malice,* p. 1483; May 15, 2000, Mary Frances Wilkens, review of *Move to Strike,* p. 1702; May 15, 2001, Mary Frances Wilkens, review of *Writ of Execution,* p. 1708; June 1, 2002, Mary Frances Wilkens, review of *Unfit to Practice,* p. 1646; May 15, 2004, Mary Frances Wilkens, review of *Unlucky in Law,* p. 1580; June 1, 2005, Mary Frances Wilkens, review of *Case of Lies,* p. 1713; January 1, 2006, Stephanie Zvirin, review of *Sinister Shorts,* p. 68; October 1, 2006, David Pitt, review of *Keeper of the Keys,* p. 6.

Entertainment Weekly, August 1, 2003, Karyn L. Barr, review of *Presumption of Death,* p. 82.

Kirkus Reviews, July 1, 1996, review of *Invasion of Privacy,* p. 923; July 1, 1997, review of *Obstruction of Justice,* p. 978; May 1, 1998, review of *Breach of Promise,* p. 610; May 1, 1999, review of *Acts of Malice,* p. 659; June 15, 2000, review of *Move to Strike,* p. 825; May 1, 2001, review of *Writ of Execution,* p. 615; July 15, 2002, review of *Unfit to Practice,* p. 985; June 1, 2003, review of *Presumption of Death,* p. 776; May 1, 2004, review of *Unlucky in Law,* p. 418; December 1, 2005, review of *Sinister Shorts,* p. 1258; August 15, 2006, review of *Keeper of the Keys,* p. 813.

Library Journal, September 1, 1997, Susan Gene Clifford, review of *Obstruction of Justice,* p. 220; June 1, 1998, Cecilia R. Cygnar, review of *Breach of Promise,* p. 156; June 15, 2000, Nancy McNicol, review of *Move to Strike,* p. 117; July, 2003, Nancy McNicol, review of *Presumption of Death,* p. 124; October 15, 2006, Nancy McNicol, review of *Keeper of the Keys,* p. 56.

New York Times Book Review, August 6, 1995, Marilyn Stasio, review of *Motion to Suppress,* p. 23.

Publishers Weekly, May 8, 1995, review of *Motion to Suppress,* p. 285; July 8, 1996, review of *Invasion of Privacy,* p. 75; July 7, 1997, review of *Obstruction of Justice,* p. 50; May 4, 1998, review of *Breach of Promise,* p. 202; May 24, 1999, review of *Acts of Malice,* p. 63; July 10, 2000, review of *Move to Strike,* p. 43; June 11, 2001, review of *Writ of Execution,* p. 57; June 10, 2002, review of *Unfit to Practice,* p. 40; June 14, 2004, review of *Unlucky in Law,* p. 43; June 13, 2005, review of *Case of Lies,* p. 32; November 21, 2005, review of *Sinister Shorts,* p. 29; September 18, 2006, review of *Keeper of the Keys,* p. 35.

ONLINE

Bookreporter.com, http://www.bookreporter.com/ (July 16, 2004), interview; (July 8, 2005), interview.

Decatur Daily Online, http://www.decaturdaily.com/ (March 26, 2006), Judy Counts, review of *Sinister Shorts;* (November 19, 2006), Judy Counts, review of *Keeper of the Keys.*

Perri O'Shaughnessy Home Page, http://www.perrio.com (December 31, 2006).

Readers Read, http://www.readersread.com/ (December 31, 2006), "Interview with Perri O'Schaughnessy."

ReadersRoom Coffee Chats, http://www.readersroom.com/coffee.html/ (December 31, 2006), "Bestselling Author Perri O'Shaughnessy" (interview).*

*   *   *

O'SHAUGHNESSY, Pamela
(Perri O'Shaughnessy, a joint pseudonym)

PERSONAL: Born in MO; children: one son. *Education:* Long Beach State University, B.S.; Harvard University, J.D.

ADDRESSES: Home—Hawaii. *E-mail*—perri@perrio.com.

CAREER: Writer, attorney. Practiced law in Lake Tahoe, NV.

WRITINGS:

"NINA REILLY" SERIES; WITH SISTER, MARY O'SHAUGNESSY, UNDER PSEUDONYM PERRI O'SHAUGHNESSY

Motion to Suppress, Delacorte Press (New York, NY), 1995.

Invasion of Privacy, Delacorte Press (New York, NY), 1997.

Obstruction of Justice, Delacorte Press (New York, NY), 1997.

Breach of Promise, Delacorte Press (New York, NY), 1998.

Acts of Malice, Delacorte Press (New York, NY), 1999.

Move to Strike, Delacorte Press (New York, NY), 2000.

Writ of Execution, Delacorte Press (New York, NY), 2001.

Unfit to Practice, Delacorte Press (New York, NY), 2002.

Presumption of Death, Delacorte Press (New York, NY), 2003.

Unlucky in Law, Delacorte Press (New York, NY), 2004.

Case of Lies, Delacorte Press (New York, NY), 2005.

OTHER; WITH SISTER, MARY O'SHAUGHNESSY, UNDER PSEUDONYM PERRI O'SHAUGHNESSY

Sinister Shorts (stories), Delacorte Press (New York, NY), 2006.

Keeper of the Keys, Delacorte Press (New York, NY), 2006.

Contributor to *Ellery Queen's Mystery Magazine.*

ADAPTATIONS: A number of books have been adapted for audio.

SIDELIGHTS: Pamela O'Shaughnessy and Mary O'Shaughnessy write together under the pseudonym Perri O'Shaughnessy, a combination of their own names and a tribute to Perry Mason, the character created by Erle Stanley Gardner. The sisters have turned out a series featuring attorney Nina Reilly, a Lake Tahoe lawyer who practices in the same town where Pamela once had a solo practice.

In the first book of the series, *Motion to Suppress,* Nina, also the single mother of Bob, moves from San Francisco to Tahoe after her husband betrays her. Her first client is Misty Patterson, a cocktail waitress accused of killing her husband. Marilyn Stasio, writing in the *New York Times Book Review,* assessed the novel, noting that trial lawyers who turn to writing "can usually crank up some verisimilitude for their courtroom scenes," but added that Perri O'Shaughnessy, the lawyer-writer combo, "accomplishes much more."

Invasion of Privacy features characters who include murdered filmmaker Terry London. The suspect is Bob's father, Kurt Scott, and Nina must create his defense. A *Publishers Weekly* contributor called this book a "deft, multileveled tale of legal and criminal treachery."

Nina's adventures, both in and out of the courtroom, and including her romantic alliances, continue in further installments. *Unfit to Practice* follows the action put into motion by the theft of Nina's truck, which contained sensitive case files, and leads to her possible disbarment. A *Kirkus Reviews* contributor summed up the book, writing: "An idealistic lawyer staggers under the weight of legal and ethical charges you can be certain will never stand up in court. Nina's eighth may be her most irresistible to date." Writing in *Booklist*, Mary Frances Wilkens opined: "What really gives this legal thriller its appeal is the genuinely unusual premise."

In *Presumption of Death*, Nina finds herself searching for a deadly arsonist and defending an accused young man whose defense is nonexistent. A critic for *Kirkus Reviews* deemed the story "great fun." Reviewing it for *Entertainment Weekly*, Karyn L. Barr wrote that the book "offers enough steamy sexual tension, curiously bewitching characters . . . and head-spinning plot twists to make for a fiery read."

Unlucky in Law finds Nina in California with her son and her private investigator lover, Paul van Wagoner, and becomes Paul's romantic target when he offers her his grandmother's diamond and asks her to marry him. Nina is more focused, however, on helping her former mentor, aging trial lawyer Klaus Pholmann, with a murder case, for which he has asked her to be second chair. The defendant is Stefan Wyatt, who is accused of grave robbing and murder. He admits to the robbing but says that he found two bodies in the grave rather than one. Stefan seems to be the killer, however, since his blood is found at the scene. "O'Shaughnessy comes up with the neatest solution to that classic puzzle in recent thriller memory," commented a *Publishers Weekly* reviewer.

A *Publishers Weekly* contributor described *Case of Lies* as being "the most intriguing yet." Nina returns from California to reopen her Lake Tahoe law practice. She agrees to take a case on behalf of her massage therapist, whose aunt was killed in the Ace High Lodge during a robbery, but time is running short, as none of the wit-nesses have been located. Nina would rather not ask for help from Paul, now her former lover, and instead hires his son. The novel offers insight into advanced number theory through the subplot, in which three Massachusetts Institute of Technology students gamble by counting cards. The authors have "a knack for plotting and for combining suspenseful action with a light and playful tone," concluded Wilkens in *Booklist*.

Sinister Shorts is a collection in which all of the stories, except one, were written individually. They range from detective stories to psychological thrillers to classic suspense. Stephanie Zvirin reviewed the volume in *Booklist*, naming "Gertrude Stein Solves a Mystery," which is based on a true account, as being "among the most memorable." Zvirin also favorably compared "The Furnace Man" to an Alfred Hitchcock-type thriller. Many of the stories involve bad marriages. In "To Still the Beating of Her Heart," the question is whether the husband or wife will be the one to commit murder. A *Kirkus Reviews* contributor wrote: "'His Master's Hand' is in the grand tradition of campfire horror stories, as chilling as it is slick."

Keeper of the Keys is another title outside the "Nina Reilly" series and is set in the Topanga Canyon, near Los Angeles. Architect Ray Jackson and his wife Leigh, a furniture maker, live in a house they designed. Ray creates models of all the houses he has lived in and keeps a key for each of the actual houses. When Leigh, who has found escape from their crumbling marriage with another, disappears, her policeman father suspects Ray. Kat, a friend who works in real estate and who was close to Leigh when they were younger, is also suspicious, but she helps Ray look for her friend. The keys figure in the plot because Ray uses them to delve into his past to see if he may have committed a misdeed. *Booklist* contributor David Pitt considered *Keeper of the Keys* to be "a well-paced, smartly written thriller."

The O'Shaughnessy sisters talk about what it is like to share plotting and writing tasks on their Web site: "We sometimes juggle the writing back and forth, scene by scene. . . . We are chronic tinkers, who even went so far as to change the murderer in the fourth draft during the writing of our first published novel. . . . The main thing that works about our collaboration is that we have come to trust and respect each other as writers. We like to think Perri takes what's best in both of us and puts it into the finished draft."

BIOGRAPHICAL AND CRITICAL SOURCES:

PERIODICALS

Booklist May 15, 1998, Emily Melton, review of *Breach of Promise,* p. 1565; April 15, 1999, Jenny McLarin, review of *Acts of Malice,* p. 1483; May 15, 2000, Mary Frances Wilkens, review of *Move to Strike,* p. 1702; May 15, 2001, Mary Frances Wilkens, review of *Writ of Execution,* p. 1708; June 1, 2002, Mary Frances Wilkens, review of *Unfit to Practice,* p. 1646; May 15, 2004, Mary Frances Wilkins, review of *Unlucky in Law,* p. 1580; June 1, 2005, Mary Frances Wilkens, review of *Case of Lies,* p. 1713; January 1, 2006, Stephanie Zvirin, review of *Sinister Shorts,* p. 68; October 1, 2006, David Pitt, review of *Keeper of the Keys,* p. 6.

Entertainment Weekly, August 1, 2003, Karyn L. Barr, review of *Presumption of Death,* p. 82.

Kirkus Reviews, July 1, 1996, review of *Invasion of Privacy,* p. 923; July 1, 1997, review of *Obstruction of Justice,* p. 978; May 1, 1998, review of *Breach of Promise,* p. 610; May 1, 1999, review of *Acts of Malice,* p. 659; June 15, 2000, review of *Move to Strike,* p. 825; May 1, 2001, review of *Writ of Execution,* p. 615; July 15, 2002, review of *Unfit to Practice,* p. 985; June 1, 2003, review of *Presumption of Death,* p. 776; May 1, 2004, review of *Unlucky in Law,* p. 418; December 1, 2005, review of *Sinister Shorts,* p. 1258; August 15, 2006, review of *Keeper of the Keys,* p. 813.

Library Journal, September 1, 1997, Susan Gene Clifford, review of *Obstruction of Justice,* p. 220; June 1, 1998, Cecilia R. Cygnar, review of *Breach of Promise,* p. 156; June 15, 2000, Nancy McNicol, review of *Move to Strike,* p. 117; July, 2003, Nancy McNicol, review of *Presumption of Death,* p. 124; October 15, 2006, Nancy McNicol, review of *Keeper of the Keys,* p. 56.

New York Times Book Review, August 6, 1995, Marilyn Stasio, review of *Motion to Suppress,* p. 23.

Publishers Weekly, May 8, 1995, review of *Motion to Suppress,* p. 285; July 8, 1996, review of *Invasion of Privacy,* p. 75; July 7, 1997, review of *Obstruction of Justice,* p. 50; May 4, 1998, review of *Breach of Promise,* p. 202; May 24, 1999, review of *Acts of Malice,* p. 63; July 10, 2000, review of *Move to Strike,* p. 43; June 11, 2001, review of *Writ of Execution,* p. 57; June 10, 2002, review of *Unfit to Practice,* p. 40; June 14, 2004, review of *Unlucky in Law,* p. 43; June 13, 2005, review of *Case of Lies,* p. 32; November 21, 2005, review of *Sinister Shorts,* p. 29; September 18, 2006, review of *Keeper of the Keys,* p. 35.

ONLINE

Bookreporter.com, http://www.bookreporter.com/ (July 16, 2004), interview with Pamela and Mary O'Shaughnessy; (July 8, 2005), interview with Pamela and Mary O'Shaughnessy.

Decatur Daily Online, http://www.decaturdaily.com/ (March 26, 2006), Judy Counts, review of *Sinister Shorts;* (November 19, 2006), Judy Counts, review of *Keeper of the Keys.*

Perri O'Shaughnessy Home Page, http://www.perrio. com (December 31, 2006).

Readers Read, http://www.readersread.com/ (August, 2003), "Interview with Perri O'Shaughnessy."

ReadersRoom Coffee Chats, http://www.readersroom. com/coffee.html/ (December 31, 2006), "Bestselling Author Perri O'Shaughnessy" (interview).*

*   *   *

O'SHAUGHNESSY, Perri
    See O'SHAUGHNESSY, Mary

*   *   *

O'SHAUGHNESSY, Perri
    See O'SHAUGHNESSY, Pamela

*   *   *

OWEN, Howard 1949-
    (Howard Wayne Owen)

PERSONAL: Born March 1, 1949, in Fayetteville, NC; son of E.F. and Roxie Owen; married Karen Van Neste (an editor), August 18, 1973. *Education:* University of North Carolina at Chapel Hill, A.B., 1971; Virginia Commonwealth University, M.A., 1981. *Politics:* Liberal. *Hobbies and other interests:* Travel, cooking, jogging, reading, sports.

ADDRESSES: Home—Richmond, VA. *Office*—Richmond Times-Dispatch, P.O. Box 85333, Richmond, VA 23293. *Agent*—Max Gartenberg, 521 Fifth Ave., Ste. 1700, New York, NY 10175.

CAREER: *Martinsville Bulletin,* Martinsville, VA, sports writer, 1971-73; *Gastonia Gazette,* Gastonia, NC, sports editor, 1973-74; sports editor in Chapel Hill, NC, 1974-77; *Tallahassee Democrat,* Tallahassee, FL, executive sports editor, 1977-78; *Richmond Times-Dispatch,* Richmond, VA, assistant sports editor, 1978-83, sports news editor, 1983-92, sports editor, 1992-95, deputy managing editor, 1995—. *Military service:* National Guard, 1971-77.

MEMBER: Associated Press Sports Editors Association (regional chairman, 1986-87), PEN, Virginia Writers Club (board of governors, 1997), Virginia Press Association.

AWARDS, HONORS: Virginia Press Association, writing awards, 1972 and 1973, certificates of merit, 1988 and 1991; North Carolina Press Association writing awards, 1975 and 1976.

WRITINGS:

Littlejohn (novel), Permanent Press (Sag Harbor, NY), 1992.

Fat Lightning: A Novel, Permanent Press (Sag Harbor, NY), 1994.

Answers to Lucky (novel), HarperCollins (New York, NY), 1996.

The Measured Man: A Novel, HarperCollins (New York, NY), 1997.

Harry and Ruth (novel), Permanent Press (Sag Harbor, NY), 2000.

The Rail (novel), Permanent Press (Sag Harbor, NY), 2002.

Turn Signal: A Novel, Permanent Press (Sag Harbor, NY), 2004.

Rock of Ages (sequel to *Littlejohn*), Permanent Press (Sag Harbor, NY), 2006.

SIDELIGHTS: Howard Owen is a career newspaper editor who has also distinguished himself as the author of novels that focus on the lives of ordinary characters in small Southern towns. Owen's first work, *Littlejohn,* concerns the long, often-hard life of a North Carolina farmer. Much of the narrative is composed of recollections as the hero, Littlejohn McCain, ponders his past. Additional narration is supplied by McCain's daughter, who is a professor, and his grandson, an unproductive malcontent. Robert P. Hilldrup, writing in the *Fredericksburg Free Lance-Star,* noted that Owen "sets a good

scene and carries it off without beating it to death," and he praised *Littlejohn* as "a good first novel." Another positive response was posted by Ron Carter, who declared in the *Richmond Times-Dispatch* that with *Littlejohn,* Owen had managed to produce "a sensitive, finely wrought tale filled with fully imagined characters and rich with the music of Southern speech." *New York Times Book Review* contributor Harry Middleton judged the book "quietly enchanting . . . a heartfelt celebration of the endurance of the human spirit."

In *Fat Lightning: A Novel,* Nancy Chastain is adjusting to life in her husband's hometown of Monacan, Virginia, and trying to deal with his eccentric family. Uncle Lot, for example, believes he has seen a vision of Jesus Christ on the side of his barn; a local black preacher wants to start a new church around his vision. Brian McCombie, reviewing the novel for *Booklist,* found that "heavy-handed symbols intrude, but a good read overall." A *Kirkus Reviews* contributor described *Fat Lightning* as "loopy and darkly comic, if sporadically out of control." Erik Esckilsen of *Entertainment Weekly* felt that Owen's "craftsmanship ignites interest in a place at once hospitable and unwelcoming." A critic for *Publishers Weekly* found the novel to be a "wise, warm and deeply satisfying story."

Answers to Lucky features a reconciliation between twin brothers who have been alienated. Lucky Sweatt contracts polio as a youth, moving his ambitious father to ignore the boy in favor of his healthy brother Tom Ed. When Tom Ed runs for governor years later, the brothers reunite. "The novel's strength," noted Linda Barrett Osborne in the *New York Times Book Review,* "lies in its moving portrait of Lucky and Tom Ed." The story of Lucky, according to a *Publishers Weekly* critic, "gains emotional resonance in Owen's sure evocation of Southern life." According to a critic for *Kirkus Reviews, Answers to Lucky* is "a completely engaging story about the family ties that bind—tight—and the ego-pricking legacy of growing up poor."

Owen's *The Measured Man: A Novel* is the story of Walker Fann, an editor at his father's small town newspaper. When local blacks propose construction of a slavery museum, Walker supports the idea while his father opposes it. But Walker is too weak to stand by his beliefs. Robin Nesbitt in *Library Journal* called *The Measured Man* a "well-plotted tale [about] race, family, and small-town dynamics." A critic for *Publishers Weekly* concluded that in this novel Owen "invites readers to hold up a yardstick to their own lives to calculate how far their adult behavior has strayed from the idealism of their youth."

An elderly couple is the focus of *Harry and Ruth*. Harry and Ruth fell in love in 1942, but Harry was unable to marry her because of their religious differences. He marries a Jewish girl instead, leaving Ruth pregnant with their daughter. Late in life, the couple try to tie up the loose ends of their lives and reconcile with their emotionally damaged daughter. A *Kirkus Reviews* critic found *Harry and Ruth* to be "a complicated drama, told with compassion and humor." A reviewer for *Publishers Weekly* explained that "Owen succeeds in capturing the yearnings of two people who are always aware that they belong together" and praised "Owen's old-fashioned storytelling skills."

Owen draws on his experience as a sport editor for *The Rail*, the story of a successful baseball player who is brought down by a lack of business sense and a love of alcohol. Neil Beauchamp has just been released from prison after serving two years for a drunk-driving accident in which a policeman was killed. Meeting him is his son, David, a journalist who has just lost his job and whose marriage is in crisis. Neil came from a wealthy family, but when he was young, his mother left his father, and Neil never experienced the life of leisure he might have. David is now taking him home to the family manor, which Neil has inherited along with his eccentric half-sister, Blanchard. "The pace is leisurely, the revelations apt and unexpected and the coverage of professional baseball rings absolutely true," observed a *Publishers Weekly* contributor.

Jack Stone of *Turn Signal: A Novel* is a long-haul truck driver who leaves his wife, Gina, and daughter, Shannon, for weeks at a time in Speakeasy, Virginia, while delivering his loads. One day, Jack picks up a hitch-hiker who leaves behind a manuscript about the life of a serial killer. Inspired, Jack quits his job, takes another with a local parcel delivery service, and works on the story, expanding it to become his own novel. At his thirtieth high school class reunion, he engages in conversation with Jerry Prince, a classmate and former nerd who has become a New York editor and who has his own imprint. Jerry takes the manuscript, promising to read it, but he never does. In desperation Jack travels to New York to confront Jerry and ensure that his novel is published. A *Publishers Weekly* contributor wrote that Owen's "portrayal of the agonies an aspiring writer faces are definitely nerve-wracking."

Rock of Ages, the sequel to *Littlejohn,* begins a decade after the death of the protagonist of Owen's first novel. Georgia, still a professor and in her fifties, is now once widowed and twice divorced. Georgia returns to East Geddie, North Carolina, to help her son, Justin, now engaged and a Peace Corps volunteer, with the sale of her father's house. Georgia's elderly aunt, Jenny, has been living in the house she formerly owned. Georgia suspects that the house was taken over by the threatening Blackwell family by underhanded means. Also living in the house is Pooh, the scary Blackwell son. Soon after Georgia arrives, Jenny is found dead in a pond, and Georgia realizes that her diamond ring is missing. A *Publishers Weekly* reviewer wrote that "this murder mystery is also a haunting odyssey toward redemption and repatriation." *Booklist* critic David Pitt described *Rock of Ages* as being "beautifully written, driven by its lush characterizations."

Owen once told *CA* that his strengths as a writer are "a good imagination, the discipline and training of twenty-one years of newspapering, and a thorough knowledge of the settings and characters" he writes about. He also told *CA* that he hopes to impart to readers "a feeling that there is something mystical about my characters, even though those characters often have lived what seem to be 'ordinary' lives." In his writing Owen "seeks to celebrate the often-heroic, sometimes-tragic existence of these ordinary people."

BIOGRAPHICAL AND CRITICAL SOURCES:

PERIODICALS

American Journal of Psychology, December, 1995, review of *Littlejohn,* p. 1822.

Booklist, June 1, 1994, Brian McCombie, review of *Fat Lightning: A Novel,* p. 1772; March 1, 1996, Gilbert Taylor, review of *Answers to Lucky,* p. 1123; February 15, 1997, Jennifer Henderson, review of *The Measured Man: A Novel,* p. 1005; May 1, 2006, David Pitt, review of *Rock of Ages,* p. 37.

Entertainment Weekly, September 24, 1993, review of *Littlejohn,* p. 87; November 18, 1994, Erik Esckilsen, review of *Fat Lightning,* p. 101.

Fredericksburg Free Lance-Star, October 24, 1992, Robert P. Hilldrup, review of *Littlejohn.*

Kirkus Reviews, July 15, 1992, review of *Littlejohn;* July 1, 1994, review of *Fat Lightning,* p. 877; January 1, 1996, review of *Answers to Lucky,* p. 19;

December 1, 1996, review of *The Measured Man*, p. 1697; June 15, 2000, review of *Harry and Ruth*, p. 825; February 1, 2002, review of *The Rail*, p. 134; June 1, 2004, review of *Turn Signal: A Novel*, p. 512; March 15, 2006, review of *Rock of Ages*, p. 258.

Library Journal, March 15, 1993, review of *Littlejohn*, p. 50; July 1, 1994, Thomas L. Kilpatrick, review of *Fat Lightning*, p. 129; February 1, 1997, Robin Nesbitt, review of *The Measured Man*, p. 107.

Los Angeles Times Book Review, October 9, 1994, review of *Littlejohn*, p. 10.

New York Times Book Review, January 17, 1993, Harry Middleton, review of *Littlejohn*, p. 24; September 4, 1994, Mason Buck, review of *Fat Lightning*, p. 16; May 5, 1996, Linda Barrett Osborne, review of *Answers to Lucky*, p. 22; April 27, 1997, David Murray, review of *The Measured Man*, p. 25.

Publishers Weekly, May 30, 1994, review of *Fat Lightning*, p. 34; July 11, 1994, review of *Littlejohn*, p. 76; January 1, 1996, review of *Answers to Lucky*, p. 56; December 9, 1996, review of *The Measured Man*, p. 59; June 26, 2000, review of *Harry and Ruth*, p. 50; April 1, 2002, review of *The Rail*, p. 54; May 24, 2004, review of *Turn Signal*, p. 45; May 15, 2006, review of *Rock of Ages*, p. 53.

Richmond Times-Dispatch, October 4, 1992, Ron Carter, review of *Littlejohn*.

School Library Journal, August, 1997, Dottie Kraft, review of *The Measured Man*, p. 188.

Virginia Quarterly Review, summer, 1997, review of *The Measured Man*, p. 95.

Washington Post Book World, November 7, 1993, review of *Littlejohn*, p. 11.*

*   *   *

OWEN, Howard Wayne
See OWEN, Howard

P

PARKER, Thomas Jefferson
See PARKER, T. Jefferson

*   *   *

PARKER, T. Jefferson 1954-
(Thomas Jefferson Parker)

PERSONAL: Born 1954, in Los Angeles, CA; married (wife deceased, 1992); remarried; children: two. *Education:* University of California—Irvine, B.A., 1976.

ADDRESSES: E-mail—www@tjeffersonparker.com.

CAREER: Writer. Worked as a reporter for newspapers, including the *Newport Ensign* and *Daily Pilot.*

AWARDS, HONORS: Los Angeles Times Book Award in mystery/thriller category, Edgar Allan Poe Award for Best Novel, Mystery Writers of America, and Dashiell Hammett Award nomination, all 2002, all for *Silent Joe;* Southern California Booksellers Association Book Award, 2003, for *Cold Pursuit;* Edgar Allan Poe Award for Best Novel, 2005, for *California Girl.*

WRITINGS:

MYSTERY NOVELS

Laguna Heat, St. Martin's Press (New York, NY), 1985.

Little Saigon, St. Martin's Press (New York, NY), 1988.
Pacific Beat, St. Martin's Press (New York, NY), 1991.
Summer of Fear, St. Martin's Press (New York, NY), 1993.
The Triggerman's Dance, Hyperion (New York, NY), 1996.
Where Serpents Lie, Hyperion (New York, NY), 1998.
The Blue Hour, Hyperion (New York, NY), 1999.
Red Light, Hyperion (New York, NY), 2000.
Silent Joe, Hyperion (New York, NY), 2001.
Black Water, Hyperion (New York, NY), 2002.
Cold Pursuit, Hyperion (New York, NY), 2003.
California Girl, Harcourt (New York, NY), 2004.
The Fallen, William Morrow (New York, NY), 2006.
Storm Runners, William Morrow (New York, NY), 2007.

Also contributor to *My California,* 2004.

ADAPTATIONS: Several of Parker's books have been adapted as recordings, including *The Fallen,* Brilliance Audio (Grand Haven, MI), 2006.

SIDELIGHTS: Mystery novelist T. Jefferson Parker has earned critical respect for his contributions to the genre of the California crime story first established by Dashiell Hammett and Raymond Chandler. Though some reviewers have considered elements of Parker's novels overdone or too conventional, many critics have admired his suspenseful plotting and complex characterizations.

His first novel, *Laguna Heat,* tells the story of a Los Angeles cop, Tom Shephard, who resigned from the department after he shot a boy in the line of duty and who now works as a homicide detective. Shephard finds himself tracking down a psychopath who murders by stuffing money in his victims' throats, smashing their heads in with a rock, and setting the bodies on fire. *Newsweek* contributor Peter S. Prescott admired the way Parker balanced conventional thriller elements with variations on thriller themes. Though Prescott noted that Parker weakened his novel by giving his protagonist a sex scene—thereby violating the conventions of the chaste hero's contempt for the decadence and corruption around him—and by writing in the third person, the reviewer otherwise thought *Laguna Heat* "all works smoothly."

Parker followed *Laguna Heat* with *Little Saigon,* set in Orange County's Vietnamese community. The plot involves rival brothers, one of whom is married to a popular Vietnamese singer who is kidnapped during a performance. The crime touches on elements of political strife, gang activity, and personal revenge. A critic writing in *Publishers Weekly* considered *Little Saigon* a "workmanlike suspense thriller" that "permits few surprises."

Parker's next novel, *Pacific Beat,* elicited more enthusiasm from critics. It tells the story of brothers-in-law who confront police corruption, sleazy developers, and a known sex offender while investigating the murder of their sister. *Library Journal* contributor Rex E. Klett called the novel "an outstanding, memorable, and magnetic work" enhanced by sharp detail, impressive language, and sensitive characterizations. *Kliatt* contributor Paula Rohrlick also appreciated the novel's carefully observed detail, and noted that Parker "writes passionately and convincingly." *New York Times Book Review* contributor Marilyn Stasio, however, commented that although Parker is a "powerhouse writer," he crammed too many disparate plot elements together to make *Pacific Beat* wholly believable.

Stasio had only a slightly higher opinion of Parker's *Summer of Fear,* about a California serial killer. Though she admitted that the author created some "neat twists on the conventions" of the genre, she commented that Parker is "a heavy-handed writer . . . [whose] genre ingredients are routine." A *Publishers Weekly* contributor however, commended the novel's "taut pacing and plot twists," and *Booklist* contributor Wes Lukowsky deemed the book "unforgettable."

Parker's fifth novel, *The Triggerman's Dance,* tells the story of an undercover investigation. A *Publishers Weekly* contributor found the novel intelligent, well plot-

ted, and exciting. Richard Bernstein, writing in the *New York Times,* praised *The Triggerman's Dance* for its complex characterizations and "vernacular eloquence." Pointing out some flaws in the novel, Bernstein commented that Parker did not delve as deeply as he might have done into the book's unsettling issues, but concluded that "*The Triggerman's Dance* has the psychological and moral complexity of a good novel of the American dark." *Los Angeles Times Book Review* contributor Bob Sipchen, though, considered the novel unconvincing and cliched. "The tone and details seem not so much imagined as implanted by distant memories of old TV," wrote Sipchen. He also cited evidence of "lazy craftsmanship" and "wobbly plot transitions."

Where Serpents Lie, Parker's 1998 novel, concerns the hunt for "The Horridus," a kidnapper who snatches a snake-loving child. A *Publishers Weekly* contributor hinted at some Melville-esque elements in the book, including the hero's "Ahab-like pursuit" of the madman and a prime suspect named Ishmael. The reviewer found some of Parker's material familiar, but enjoyed the novel's psychological complexity and thrilling pace.

More bizarre is Parker's 1999 novel, *The Blue Hour,* in which a chemically castrated rapist has set about killing women "and preserving their bodies for future use," as Stasio related in the *New York Times Book Review.* Stasio enjoyed the "wondrously weird characters" in the novel—a Parker trademark—and deemed the work "another insanely imaginative thriller."

In *Red Light,* police sergeant Merci Rayborn, also a character in *The Blue Hour* searches for the killer of a call girl. The investigation leads her to further study a thirty-year-old murder of a prostitute that implicates her fellow officers. The novel takes place in a gritty Southern California that does not have a future. Like most of Parker's books, dark and contemplative characters search for answers. A *Publishers Weekly* contributor observed that the story, "sizzles along, an infectious blend of atmosphere, action, and passion" but also noted that readers familiar with Parker's books might notice "formulaic twists."

A contributor to *Publishers Weekly* described *Silent Joe* as "Parker's most ambitious work to date." Lead character Joe has a disfigured face, the result of his father throwing acid on him when he was a baby. After being sent to an orphanage, he is adopted by a corrupt Orange County supervisor, who is later killed. Now a prison guard who wants to work for the sheriff's department, Joe kills the men who murdered his adoptive father and then sets out to discover an explanation for why he was killed. During his investigation, he realizes Will was not the honest man he thought. As in most of his books, reviewers praised Parker's abilities to string along a complex plot that comes together in the end. *Library Journal* contributor Rebecca House Stankowski explained: "Seemingly unconnected plotlines, vivid characterization, and real mystery merge to form a truly satisfying thriller." *Silent Joe* won the 2002 Edgar Award for Best Novel.

Black Water introduces readers to the Wildcrafts, a married couple who seem too happy to be true. After a brutal attack, Mrs. Wildcraft is dead and Archie, an officer with the Orange County Sheriff's department is nearly dead. Detectives suspect Archie of attempting a murder-suicide and failing. Merci Rayborn suspects differently. Under the pressure of a district attorney who wants a fast conviction, Merci relentlessly searches for the real killer. *Booklist* contributor Wes Lukowsky called this "a thoughtful, multilayered tale." However, not all reviewers found this to be exemplary of Parker's work. A *Publishers Weekly* contributor found *Black Water* was "lacking the kind of explosive finale that marks most of Parker's novels."

In *Cold Pursuit,* Detective Tom MacMichael leads a murder investigation during a rainy San Diego winter. Pete Braga, the victim, was the suspected murderer of MacMichael's grandfather, and a rich bigwig in the San Diego scene. Determined to perform a fair investigation, MacMichael follows the trail of evidence as it leads right back to himself. A *Kirkus Reviews* contributor called this book an "engrossing tale of a flawed hero redeemed by suffering," a description that would fit many of Parker's tales. Parker did receive some criticism on the conclusion of the novel. A *Publishers Weekly* contributor called it "rather improbable."

California Girl takes place in the 1960s, when Janelle Vonn witnesses her older brother beaten by a group of boys in an abandoned warehouse. Several years later, Janelle becomes a victim at the same location, and the men who did the beating when she was a child are determined to catch her killer. As the case is investigated, Parker introduces readers to a series of interesting characters, many of whom could be the killer, all of whom exhibit the usual characteristics of 50s and 60s stereotypes. Connie Fletcher, writing in *Booklist*, sug-

gested that Parker might have made the times too much of a force in this novel when she commented that the book was written in an "extremely heavy-handed, lugubrious fashion, hitting readers over the head with ways in which the times touched the family." Some reviewers remarked that the book was a jewel of the genre. *Entertainment Weekly* critic Chris Nashawaty compared the writing to Raymond Chandler's and Dennis Lehane's and noted its "drum-tight prose and richly layered characters."

In *The Fallen,* Parker tells of Robbie Brownlaw, a San Diego cop who develops synesthesia, a neurological disorder in which the senses get jumbled. As a result of his problem, Brownlaw can see colored shapes when he hears people speaking, which can help him detect when someone is lying. He uses his new ability as he investigates the death of an ex-cop who had joined a watchdog group. His discoveries lead him to city hall and prostitution. Meanwhile, Brownlaw's wife has left him, leading him to ponder whether or not he really wants her. "His dialogue crackles and pops in an intricate and well-paced tale set in a city where shadowy characters lurk," wrote Allison Block in *Booklist*. A *Kirkus Reviews* contributor noted: "Deftly plotted, gracefully written and, as usual with this savvy veteran . . ., it's the lead character you pay your money for." Gillian Flynn, writing in *Entertainment Weekly,* called the novel "a brainy, seriously entertaining piece."

BIOGRAPHICAL AND CRITICAL SOURCES:

PERIODICALS

Booklist, May 15, 1993, Wes Lukowsky, review of *Summer of Fear,* p. 1652; November 15, 1993, review of *Summer of Fear,* p. 640; June 1, 1996, Thomas Gaughan, review of *The Triggerman's Dance,* p. 1680; December 15, 1997, Wes Lukowsky, review of *Where Serpents Lie,* p. 667; February 1, 2000, Wes Lukowsky, review of *Red Light,* p. 996; February 15, 2001, Wes Lukowsky, review of *Silent Joe,* p. 1085; February 1, 2002, Wes Lukowsky, review of *Black Water,* p. 49; September 15, 2004, Connie Fletcher, review of *California Girl,* p. 180; February 1, 2006, Allison Brock, review of *The Fallen,* p. 6.

Entertainment Weekly, October 1, 2004, Chris Nashawaty, review of *California Girl,* p. 78; March 3, 2006, Gillian Flynn, review of *The Fallen,* p. 107.

Kirkus Reviews, February 1, 2002, review of *Black Water,* p. 146; April 2, 2003, review of *Cold Pursuit,* p. 191; September 1, 2004, review of *California Girl,* p. 840; January 15, 2006, review of *The Fallen,* p. 59.

Kliatt, September, 1992, Paula Rohrlick, review of *Pacific Beat,* p. 15.

Library Journal, June 1, 1991, Rex E. Klett, review of *Pacific Beat,* p. 200; June 15, 1992, review of *Pacific Beat,* p. 119; July, 1993, Rex E. Klett, review of *Summer of Fear,* p. 126; January, 1998, Rebecca House Stankowski, review of *Where Serpents Lie,* p. 143; March 1, 2001, Rebecca House Stankowski, review of *Silent Joe,* p. 132; February 15, 2002, Rebecca House Stankowski, review of *Black Water,* p. 179; February 15, 2003, Jo Ann Vicarel, review of *Cold Pursuit,* p. 170; June 1, 2004, Ann Kim, review of *California Girl,* p. 109; October 15, 2004, Rebecca House, review of *California Girl,* p. 55; February 1, 2006, Ken Bolton, review of *The Fallen,* p. 73.

Los Angeles Times Book Review, August 22, 1993, review of *Summer of Fear,* p. 6; June 23, 1996, Bob Sipchen, review of *The Triggerman's Dance,* p. 6.

Newsweek, September 23, 1985, Peter S. Prescott, review of *Laguna Heat,* p. 72.

New York, July 3, 1989, Rhoda Koenig, review of *Little Saigon,* p. 142.

New York Times, August 2, 1996, Richard Bernstein, review of *The Triggerman's Dance,* p. B16, C28.

New York Times Book Review, July 7, 1991, Marilyn Stasio, review of *Pacific Beat,* p. 19; July 18, 1993, Marilyn Stasio, review of *Summer of Fear,* p. 17; July 21, 1996, Marilyn Stasio, review of *The Triggerman's Dance,* p. 25; August 2, 1996; May 23, 1999, Marilyn Stasio, review of *The Blue Hour,* p. 33; April 16, 2000, Marilyn Stasio, review of *Red Light,* p. 32; February 6, 2006, Timothy Peters, "T. Jefferson Parker: The Dark Side of the California Dream," author profile, p. 20; March 26, 2006, Marilyn Stasio, review of *The Madman in the Attic.*

Publishers Weekly, July 1, 1988, Sybil Steinberg, review of *Little Saigon,* p. 67; May 24, 1993, review of *Summer of Fear,* p. 66; May 20, 1996, review of *The Triggerman's Dance,* p. 237; December 22, 1997, review of *Where Serpents Lie,* p. 38; February 7, 2000, review of *Red Light,* p. 60; March 19, 2001, review of *Silent Joe,* p. 78; February 4, 2002, review of *Black Water,* p. 49; February 10, 2003, review of *Cold Pursuit,* pp. 160-161; September 15, 2004, review of *California Girl,* p. 56; January 16, 2006, review of *The Fallen,* p. 37.

ONLINE

T. Jefferson Parker Home Page, http://www.tjefferson parker.com (December 11, 2006).*

*　　*　　*

PATENT, Dorothy Hinshaw 1940-

PERSONAL: Born April 30, 1940, in Rochester, MN; daughter of Horton Corwin (a physician) and Dorothy Kate Hinshaw; married Gregory Joseph Patent (a professor of zoology), March 21, 1964; children: David, Jason. *Education:* Stanford University, B.A., 1962; University of California, Berkeley, M.A., 1965, Ph.D., 1968; also studied at Friday Harbor Laboratories, University of Washington, 1965-67. *Hobbies and other interests:* Gardening, cooking, hiking.

ADDRESSES: Home—Missoula, MT.

CAREER: Writer, zoologist, and educator. Sinai Hospital, Detroit, MI, post-doctoral fellow, 1968-69; Stazione Zoologica, Naples, Italy, post-doctoral researcher, 1970-71; University of Montana, Missoula, faculty affiliate in department of zoology, 1975-90, acting assistant professor, 1977, faculty affiliate in environmental studies, 1995—.

MEMBER: American Institute of Biological Sciences, Authors Guild, Society of Children's Book Writers and Illustrators.

AWARDS, HONORS: The National Science Teachers Association has cited more than forty of Patent's books as outstanding science trade books; Golden Kite Honor Book, Society of Children's Book Writers, 1977, for *Evolution Goes on Every Day,* and Golden Kite Award, 1980, for *The Lives of Spiders;* Notable Book citation, American Library Association, 1982, for *Spider Magic;* Children's Books of the Year list, Library of Congress, 1985, for *Where the Bald Eagles Gather;* Best Books of the Year list, *School Library Journal,* 1986, for *Buffalo: The American Bison Today,* Best Book for Young Adults citation, American Library Association, 1986, for *The Quest for Artificial Intelligence;* Eva L. Gordon Award, American Nature Study Society, 1987, for the body of her work; Books for the Teenage citation, New York

Public Library, 1990, for *How Smart Are Animals?;* Best Books of the Year list, *School Library Journal,* and Pick of the Lists, *American Bookseller,* both 1992, and both for *Feathers;* Children's Choice Award, 1994, for *Hugger to the Rescue;* Books for the Teenage citation, New York Public Library, 1994, for *The Vanishing Feast;* AAAS Best Science Books of 1996, for *Biodiversity;* Lud Browman Award for Science Writing, Friends of the Mansfield Library, University of Montana, 1994; Best Children's Books of the Year citations, Bank Street College of Education, 1997, for *Prairies, Children Save the Rainforests,* and *Biodiversity;* Books for Young People Award, *Scientific American,* 1997, for *Pigeons;* AAAS Best Science Books of 1998, for *Apple Trees;* Best Children's Books of the Year, Bank Street College of Education, 1998, for *Back to the Wild* and *Flashy Fantastic Rain Forest Frogs,* and 1999, for *Apple Trees* and *Fire: Friend or Foe;* CBC-IRA Children's Choices selection, 1999, for *Alex and Friends: Animal Talk, Animal Thinking;* National Science Teachers Association Outstanding Science Trade Book for Children, 2002, for *Charles Darwin,* 2003, for *Life in a Grassland* and *Animals on the Trail with Lewis and Clark,* 2004, *Fabulous Fluttering Tropical Butterflies* and *Plants on the Trail with Lewis and Clark; Washington Post/* Children's Book Guild Award, 2004, for body of work. Many of Patent's books have also received state nominations and awards and have been chosen as Outstanding Science Trade Books for Children by the National Science Teachers Association.

WRITINGS:

FOR CHILDREN

Weasels, Otters, Skunks, and Their Family, illustrations by Matthew Kalmenoff, Holiday House (New York, NY), 1973.

Microscopic Animals and Plants, Holiday House (New York, NY), 1974.

Frogs, Toads, Salamanders, and How They Reproduce, illustrations by Matthew Kalmenoff, Holiday House (New York, NY), 1975.

How Insects Communicate, Holiday House (New York, NY), 1975.

Fish and How They Reproduce, illustrations by Matthew Kalmenoff, Holiday House (New York, NY), 1976.

Plants and Insects Together, illustrations by Matthew Kalmenoff, Holiday House (New York, NY), 1976.

Evolution Goes on Every Day, illustrations by Matthew Kalmenoff, Holiday House (New York, NY), 1977.

Reptiles and How They Reproduce, illustrations by Matthew Kalmenoff, Holiday House (New York, NY), 1977.

The World of Worms, Holiday House (New York, NY), 1978.

Animal and Plant Mimicry, Holiday House (New York, NY), 1978.

(With Paul C. Schroeder) *Beetles and How They Live,* Holiday House (New York, NY), 1978.

Butterflies and Moths: How They Function, Holiday House (New York, NY), 1979.

Sizes and Shapes in Nature: What They Mean, Holiday House (New York, NY), 1979.

Raccoons, Coatimundis, and Their Family, Holiday House (New York, NY), 1979.

Bacteria: How They Affect Other Living Things, Holiday House (New York, NY), 1980.

The Lives of Spiders, Holiday House (New York, NY), 1980.

Bears of the World, Holiday House (New York, NY), 1980.

Horses and Their Wild Relatives, Holiday House (New York, NY), 1981.

Horses of America, Holiday House (New York, NY), 1981.

Hunters and the Hunted: Surviving in the Animal World, Holiday House (New York, NY), 1981.

Spider Magic, Holiday House (New York, NY), 1982.

A Picture Book of Cows, photographs by William Munoz, Holiday House (New York, NY), 1982.

Arabian Horses, Holiday House (New York, NY), 1982.

Germs!, Holiday House (New York, NY), 1983.

A Picture Book of Ponies, photographs by William Munoz, Holiday House (New York, NY), 1983.

Whales: Giants of the Deep, Holiday House (New York, NY), 1984.

Farm Animals, photographs by William Munoz, Holiday House (New York, NY), 1984.

Where the Bald Eagles Gather, photographs by William Munoz, Clarion (New York, NY), 1984.

Baby Horses, photographs by William Munoz, Dodd (New York, NY), 1985.

Quarter Horses, photographs by William Munoz, Holiday House (New York, NY), 1985.

The Sheep Book, photographs by William Munoz, Dodd (New York, NY), 1985.

Thoroughbred Horses, Holiday House (New York, NY), 1985.

Draft Horses, photographs by William Munoz, Holiday House (New York, NY), 1986.

Buffalo: The American Bison Today, photographs by William Munoz, Clarion (New York, NY), 1986.

Mosquitoes, Holiday House (New York, NY), 1986.

Maggie: A Sheep Dog, photographs by William Munoz, Dodd (New York, NY), 1986.

The Quest for Artificial Intelligence, Harcourt (San Diego, CA), 1986.

Christmas Trees, Dodd (New York, NY), 1987.

All about Whales, Holiday House (New York, NY), 1987.

Dolphins and Porpoises, Holiday House (New York, NY), 1987.

The Way of the Grizzly, photographs by William Munoz, Clarion (New York, NY), 1987.

Wheat: The Golden Harvest, photographs by William Munoz, Dodd (New York, NY), 1987.

Appaloosa Horses, photographs by William Munoz, Holiday House (New York, NY), 1988.

Babies!, Holiday House (New York, NY), 1988.

A Horse of a Different Color, photographs by William Munoz, Dodd (New York, NY), 1988.

The Whooping Crane: A Comeback Story, photographs by William Munoz, Clarion (New York, NY), 1988.

Humpback Whales, photographs by Mark J. Ferrari and Deborah A. Glockner-Ferrari, Holiday House (New York, NY), 1989.

Grandfather's Nose: Why We Look Alike or Different, illustrations by Diane Palmisciano, F. Watts (New York, NY), 1989.

Singing Birds and Flashing Fireflies: How Animals Talk to Each Other, illustrations by Mary Morgan, F. Watts (New York, NY), 1989.

Where the Wild Horses Roam, photographs by William Munoz, Clarion (New York, NY), 1989.

Wild Turkey, Tame Turkey, photographs by William Munoz, Clarion (New York, NY), 1989.

Looking at Dolphins and Porpoises, Holiday House (New York, NY), 1989.

Looking at Ants, Holiday House (New York, NY), 1989.

Seals, Sea Lions, and Walruses, Holiday House (New York, NY), 1990.

Yellowstone Fires: Flames and Rebirth, photographs by William Munoz, Holiday House (New York, NY), 1990.

An Apple a Day: From Orchard to You, photographs by William Munoz, Cobblehill (New York, NY), 1990.

Flowers for Everyone, photographs by William Munoz, Cobblehill (New York, NY), 1990.

Gray Wolf, Red Wolf, photographs by William Munoz, Clarion (New York, NY), 1990.

How Smart Are Animals?, Harcourt (San Diego, CA), 1990.

A Family Goes Hunting, photographs by William Munoz, Clarion (New York, NY), 1991.

Miniature Horses, photographs by William Munoz, Cobblehill (New York, NY), 1991.

The Challenge of Extinction, Enslow (Hillside, NJ), 1991.

Where Food Comes From, photographs by William Munoz, Holiday House (New York, NY), 1991.

African Elephants: Giants of the Land, photographs by Oria Douglas-Hamilton, Holiday House, 1991.

Feathers, photographs by William Munoz, Cobblehill (New York, NY), 1992.

Places of Refuge: Our National Wildlife Refuge System, photographs by William Munoz, Clarion (New York, NY), 1992.

Nutrition: What's in the Food We Eat, photographs by William Munoz, Holiday House (New York, NY), 1992.

Pelicans, photographs by William Munoz, Clarion (New York, NY), 1992.

Cattle: Understanding Animals, photographs by William Munoz, Carolrhoda (Minneapolis, MN), 1993.

Ospreys, photographs by William Munoz, Clarion (New York, NY), 1993.

Prairie Dogs, photographs by William Munoz, Clarion (New York, NY), 1993.

Habitats: Saving Wild Places, Enslow (Hillside, NJ), 1993.

Killer Whales, photographs by John K.B. Ford, Holiday House (New York, NY), 1993.

Dogs: The Wolf Within, photographs by William Munoz, Carolrhoda Books (Minneapolis, MN), 1993.

Looking at Penguins, photographs by Graham Robertson, Holiday House (New York, NY), 1993.

Looking at Bears, photographs by William Munoz, Holiday House (New York, NY), 1994.

Horses: Understanding Animals, photographs by William Munoz, Carolrhoda (Minneapolis, MN), 1994.

Deer and Elk, photographs by William Munoz, Clarion (New York, NY), 1994.

Hugger to the Rescue, photographs by William Munoz, Cobblehill (New York, NY), 1994.

The American Alligator, photographs by William Munoz, Clarion (New York, NY), 1994.

The Vanishing Feast: How Dwindling Genetic Diversity Threatens the World's Food Supply, Harcourt Brace (San Diego, CA), 1994.

What Good Is a Tail?, photographs by William Munoz, Cobblehill (New York, NY), 1994.

West by Covered Wagon: Retracing Pioneer Trails, photographs by William Munoz, Walker (New York, NY), 1995.

Eagles of America, photographs by William Munoz, Holiday House (New York, NY), 1995.

Return of the Wolf, illustrated by Hared T. Williams, Clarion (New York, NY), 1995.

Why Mammals Have Fur, photographs by William Munoz, Cobblehill (New York, NY), 1995.

Prairies, photographs by William Munoz, Holiday House (New York, NY), 1996.

Quetzal: Sacred Bird of the Cloud Forest, illustrated by Neil Waldman, Morrow (New York, NY), 1996.

Biodiversity, photographs by William Munoz, Clarion (New York, NY), 1996.

Children Save the Rain Forest, photographs by Dan L. Perlman, Cobblehill Books, 1996.

Back to the Wild, photographs by William Munoz, Harcourt Brace (San Diego, CA), 1997.

Pigeons, photographs by William Munoz, Clarion (New York, NY), 1997.

Apple Trees, photographs by William Munoz, Lerner (Minneapolis, MN), 1997.

Flashy Fantastic Rain Forest Frogs, illustrated by Kendahl Jan Jubb, Walker (New York, NY), 1997.

Homesteading: Settling America's Heartland, photographs by William Munoz, Walker (New York, NY), 1998.

Fire: Friend or Foe, photographs by William Munoz, Clarion (New York, NY), 1998.

Alex and Friends: Animal Talk, Animal Thinking, photographs by William Munoz, Lerner (Minneapolis, MN), 1998.

Bold and Bright, Black-and-White Animals, illustrated by Kendahl Jan Jubb, Walker (New York, NY), 1998.

Mystery of the Lascaux Cave, Benchmark Books (New York, NY), 1998.

Secrets of the Ice Man, Benchmark Books (New York, NY), 1998.

Great Ice Bear: The Polar Bear and the Eskimo, illustrated by Anne Wertheim, Morrow (New York, NY), 1998.

Polar Bear: Sacred Bear of the Ice, illustrated by Anne Wertheim, Morrow (New York, NY), 1998.

In Search of Maiasaurs, Benchmark Books (New York, NY), 1999.

The Incredible Story of China's Buried Warriors, Benchmark Books (New York, NY), 1999.

Lost City of Pompeii, Benchmark Books (New York, NY), 1999.

Treasures of the Spanish Main, Benchmark Books (New York, NY), 1999.

Wild Turkeys, photographs by William Munoz, Lerner (Minneapolis, MN), 1999.

Shaping the Earth, photographs by William Munoz, Clarion (New York, NY), 2000.

The Bald Eagle Returns, photographs by William Munoz, Clarion (New York, NY), 2000.

Polar Bears, photographs by William Munoz, Carolrhoda (Minneapolis, MN), 2000.

Slinky, Scaly, Slithery Snakes, illustrated by Kendahl Jan Jubb, Walker (New York, NY), 2000.

Horses, photographs by William Munoz, Lerner (Minneapolis, MN), 2001.

Charles Darwin: The Life of a Revolutionary Thinker, Holiday House (New York, NY), 2001.

A Polar Bear Biologist at Work, F. Watts (New York, NY), 2001.

Rescuing the Prairie Bandit, F. Watts (New York, NY), 2001.

Rainforest Animals, illustrated by Ilya Spirin, Winslow House (New York, NY), 2001.

Animals on the Trail with Lewis and Clark, photographs by William Munoz, Clarion Books (New York, NY), 2002.

The Lewis and Clark Trail: Then and Now, photographs by William Munoz, Clarion Books (New York, NY), 2002.

Llamas, photographs by William Munoz, Lerner (Minneapolis, MN), 2002.

Colorful Captivating Coral Reefs, illustrations by Kendahl Jan Jubb, Walker (New York, NY), 2003.

Fabulous Fluttering Tropical Butterflies, illustrations by Kendahl Jan Jubb, Walker (New York, NY), 2003.

Life in a Dessert, photographs by William Munoz, Lerner (Minneapolis, MN), 2003.

Life in a Grassland, photographs by William Munoz, Lerner (Minneapolis, MN), 2003.

Plants on the Trail with Lewis and Clark, photographs by William Munoz, Clarion Books (New York, NY), 2003.

Garden of the Spirit Bear: Life in the Great Northern Rainforest, illustrated by Deborah Milton, Clarion Books (New York, NY), 2004.

The Right Dog for the Job: Ira's Path from Service Dog to Guide Dog, photographs by William Munoz, Walker (New York, NY), 2004.

Big Cats, illustrations by Kendahl Jan Jubb, Walker (New York, NY), 2005.

Brown Pelicans, photographs by William Munoz, Lerner (Minneapolis, MN), 2005.

White-Tailed Deer, photographs by William Munoz, Lerner (Minneapolis, MN), 2005.

The Buffalo and the Indians: A Shared Destiny, photographs by William Munoz, Clarion Books (New York, NY), 2006.

FOR ADULTS

(With Diane E. Bilderback) *Garden Secrets,* Rodale Press (Emmaus, PA), 1982, revised and expanded edition published as *The Harrowsmith Country Life Book of Garden Secrets: A Down-to-Earth Guide to the Art and Science of Growing Better Vegetables,* Camden House (Charlotte, VA), 1991.

(With Diane E. Bilderback) *Backyard Fruits and Berries,* Rodale Press (Emmaus, PA), 1984.

(With Greg Patent), *A Is for Apple: More than 200 Recipes for Eating, Munching, and Cooking America's Favorite Fruit,* Broadway Books (New York, NY), 1999.

Contributor to gardening and farming magazines. Has also written for *Arizoo, Camas, Falcon, Spider, Storyworks, Horn Book, Writer, Cricket,* and *Missoulian* newspaper. Patent's photographs have appeared in *National Gardening Magazine, Missoulian,* and in many of her children's books.

SIDELIGHTS: Dorothy Hinshaw Patent is a highly acclaimed author of over one hundred science books for young readers. A trained zoologist, Patent has written books in the biological sciences about animals from the horse to the pelican, and has examined ecological challenges in such books as *Biodiversity, Back to the Wild,* and *The Vanishing Feast.* Patent's books are geared at readers from the elementary grades through high school, and are noted for their interpretation of complex topics in concise, spirited, and informal presentations. As Zena Sutherland and May Hill Arbuthnot noted in their *Children and Books,* "Dorothy Patent has become established as an author whose books are distinguished for their combination of authoritative knowledge, detached and objective attitude, and an ability to write for the lay person with fluency and clarity," adding that "she communicates a sense of wonder at the complexity and beauty of animal life by her zest for her subject."

"Many writers have known for as long as they can remember that they wanted to write. Not me," Patent noted in *CA.* "I knew that I loved animals, the woods, and exploring, and I always wanted to learn everything possible about something that interested me. But I never yearned to be a writer." Patent remarked that she grew up a tomboy, exploring the terrain around her family's homes in Minnesota and later California with her older brother. She was always more interested in catching tadpoles, playing with toads, and collecting insects than in the more conventional interests shared by girls her age. In fact, Patent remembered having trouble making girl friends in school: "To this day I'm not sure why, but maybe it was because I'd never spent much time with girls and didn't know how to act around them."

When she was in elementary school, Patent received a gift from her mother that turned her general interest in nature into a firm resolve to know all that she could of a specific subject. As a reward for practicing the piano, her mother bought her a pair of golden guppies and she recalled: "The morning after we bought the fish, I peered into the bowl to check on my new pets. To my surprise, the adult fish weren't alone—three new pairs of eyes stared out at me from among the plants. I couldn't believe this miracle—the female fish had given birth during the night, and now I had five fish instead of two!" Patent's enthusiasm led her to read every book she could about tropical fish and to frequent a special Japanese fish store to learn even more.

Patent's curiosity helped her to excel in school, as did the encouragement of her family. "Learning was highly valued in my family," she commented in *CA.* Despite her success academically, she felt like a misfit socially. "I wanted to be like the 'in' crowd . . .," she recalled. "I admired the girls who became prom queens and cheerleaders. At the time, there was no way I could understand that some of them were living the best part of their lives during high school while the best parts of my life were yet to come and would last much longer." After high school Patent went to nearby Stanford University, one of the few highly rated schools in the nation that was coeducational at the time and had a strong science program. Patent blossomed in college, where her intelligence and intellectual curiosity were valued. Despite a tragedy during her freshman year—the suicide of her roommate—which put her "into a dark emotional frame of mind that lasted the entire four years," she wrote in her autobiographical sketch that she became involved with international folk dancing, made good friends, and had interesting, challenging classes. Many of her classes emphasized writing, and "by the end of my freshman year," she recollected, "I could set an internal switch for a paper of a certain length and write it. I'm sure this discipline and training has helped me in my writing career." After a trip to Europe with a friend, Patent enrolled in graduate school at the University of California at Berkeley, where she met the man she would marry, Greg Patent, a teaching assistant in her endocrinology class.

Patent and her new husband continued their graduate work and post-doctoral research in Friday Harbor, Washington; Detroit, Michigan; and Naples, Italy; settling for a while in North Carolina before moving to Montana. Searching for a job that would allow her to spend time with her two young boys, Patent decided to try writing and, following that age-old advice to write about what one knows best, she picked biology as her subject matter. Though her first two books were not published, one of them piqued the interest of an editor at Holiday House who eventually approached Patent with an idea for a book about the weasel family. Although she knew next to nothing about weasels, Patent agreed to write the book, *Weasels, Otters, Skunks and Their Family.* She spent hours doing research at the University of Montana library in Missoula, and received help from a professor at the university who happened to be one of the world's experts on weasels. Reviewing this debut volume in *Appraisal,* Heddie Kent found the book to be "fascinating and comprehensive." "[Patent's] style of writing is relaxed and enjoyable," noted a critic for *Science Books,* who also found *Weasels, Otters, Skunks, and Their Family* to be a "highly interesting, readable and informative book."

Patent soon developed a pattern of careful research and organization that allowed her to write first one, then two, then three books a year. "Each book was a review," she explained in *CA,* "in simple language, of everything known up to that time about the subject. I chose most of the subjects myself, and they were the things that had interested me as a child—frogs, tropical fish, reptiles, butterflies." Her 1977 title, *Evolution Goes on Every Day,* and her 1980 book, *The Lives of Spiders,* were both honored by the Society of Children's Book Writers; the former title received recognition as a Golden Kite Honor Book, and the latter won the Golden Kite Award. Reviewing *The Lives of Spiders* in *Science Books and Films,* Roy T. Cunningham called it "remarkable" for "retaining a high level of scholarship and breadth of coverage" with a "minimum of esoteric vocabulary."

In the early 1980s Patent began to work with photographer William Munoz, whose name she found in a Missoula newspaper. The two would travel together to photograph the animals for a book, and became a successful team. The first few books that Patent wrote with the help of Munoz allowed her to stay in Montana, but her desire to write books on grizzly bears, whooping cranes, and wolves soon took them to Alaska, New Mexico, Texas, and other states. *Pelicans,* a 1992 addi-tion to Patent and Munoz's collaborative efforts, is exemplary of the tone and format of much of their work together. "The book has a well-organized text with clear, crisp, full-color photos and a thorough index," noted Susan Oliver in a *School Library Journal* review. Oliver called *Pelicans* a "high-quality nature-book on an endearing clown of a bird."

Dogs of all sorts get a similar treatment in several further titles. In *Dogs: The Wolf Within,* Patent "explores selective breeding," according to *Booklist*'s Deborah Abbott, "explaining how various types of dogs have been developed to accommodate people." From Grey-hounds to Border collies, Patent explores a wide variety of such breeds in a "must" book for "dog lovers and science enthusiasts," Abbott wrote. Betsy Hearne, writing in *Bulletin of the Center for Children's Books,* commented that this "author-artist team's experience with books on various species makes for a smooth production as they coordinate appealing full-color photographs with facts on the origin, domestication, behavioral characteristics, and training potential of dogs." The Newfoundland breed came into focus in *Hugger to the Rescue,* another collaborative effort with Munoz that looks at the training of Newfoundlands as rescue dogs, and at one dog in particular, Hugger. Carol Kolb Phillips, reviewing the book in *School Library Journal,* paid special attention to Patent's "conversational, anecdote-filled narrative," and to Munoz's "attractive and informative" full-color photographs. A distant relative of dogs inspired Patent to create a work of fiction in *Return of the Wolf,* which tells the story of one lone wolf, Sedra, who is forced to leave her pack, then finds a mate, and has pups to begin to form a pack of her own. "Patent entirely resists anthropomorphism," commented Roger Sutton in *Bulletin of the Center for Children's Books,* "finding drama in the instinctive drives . . . that shape a wolf's life rather than in New Age sentimentality."

Horses are also dear to Patent's heart, and she has written about them in several volumes, including *Where the Wild Horses Roam* and *Horses.* Reviewing *Horses,* a contributor to *Appraisal* noted that "Patent has written a horse book that is a good read for pleasure or a source of information for reports." Deer, elk, eagles, bears, even pigeons and apples have received the collaborative treatment of Patent and Munoz. In *Looking at Bears* "Patent and Munoz have once again combined their talents to produce a stunning book about animals," wrote a reviewer for *Appraisal.* "The text is clear and straightforward, the format uncluttered, and on almost every page is a striking photograph of bears."

Reviewing *Pigeons* in *Booklist,* Carolyn Phelan noted, "This informative book offers a well-researched and readable text illustrated with clear, full-color photographs." Phelan found that the "most surprising chapter" dealt with studies of pigeon intelligence in which trained birds have been able to tell the difference between a Monet and a Picasso painting. "This excellent addition to science collections will make readers come away with a new respect for this common bird," Phelan concluded. Turning her skills to the plant kingdom, Patent has also written about America's most popular fruit in *Apple Trees,* a description of the life cycle of the apple from seed to fruit. A writer for *Kirkus Reviews* noted: "Crisp, full-color photographs highlight all phases of tree and apple growth, coupled with clear, detailed drawings that explain more difficult concepts and processes."

Working with Munoz and other illustrators, Patent has produced many books dealing with individual topics of evolutionary change and adaptation in animals. *Feathers* looks at the role of those quilled projections in flight, insulation, and camouflage in a "captivating volume" with "fact-filled pages" that is a "nonfiction bonanza," according to *Booklist* reviewer Abbott. Luvada Kuhn commented in *Voice of Youth Advocates:* "This small book with its handy little index will be a useful tool for the student in natural history or anyone with an interest in birds." In *What Good Is a Tail?,* Patent and Munoz teamed up "on another winning book . . . with a lively text, appealing color photographs, and intriguing science facts showing just how useful a tail can be," according to a writer for *Kirkus Reviews.* The two also worked together to determine *Why Mammals Have Fur,* an "eye-catching book . . . well designed with clear color photographs," according to a reviewer for *Appraisal.* Working with Kendahl Jan Jubb as illustrator, Patent has taken a look at animal adaptation in *Flashy Fantastic Rain Forest Frogs* and at coloration in *Bold and Bright, Black-and-White Animals.* Reviewing the former title, a writer for *Kirkus Reviews* called it a "beautiful concise look at a surprisingly varied subject." In the latter title, Patent turns her attention to fourteen animals, such as the skunk and zebra, that come in black and white and explains why. Reviewing *Bold and Bright* in *Booklist,* Shelley Townsend-Hudson noted: "There is so much to enjoy and learn in this beautiful book." The reviewer added: "It's a standout and an outstanding book." And animal intelligence is explored in *Alex and Friends,* "a fascinating discussion," according to Elizabeth S. Watson writing in *Horn Book Guide.*

Becoming increasingly concerned with the plight of wildlife, Patent remarked in her autobiographical sketch that "wild things always seem to lose out in today's world." Patent went on to note: "We need to realize that we are part of nature, that without nature, we are not whole." To aid in such a realization, Patent has written a number of books dealing with issues of preservation, endangered species, and ecology. In *Places of Refuge* she takes a look at the National Wildlife Refuge System, while in *The Challenges of Extinction* she examines the impact of plant and animal extinction. Habitat preservation and restoration is the theme of *Habitats: Saving Wild Places,* a "brief but effective introduction," as a contributor to *Kirkus Reviews* noted, and in *The Vanishing Feast* Patent tackles the threat to the world's food supplies caused by the reduction of genetic diversity. This issue is further explored in her *Biodiversity,* a science book that is "both illuminating and inspiring," according to *Horn Book* reviewer Margaret A. Bush.

With *Back to the Wild,* Patent relates the successful return of animals to the wild, and in *Children Save the Rain Forest* she tells of the efforts of children around the world to raise enough money to buy a 42,000-acre tract of rain forest in Costa Rica.

Patent has also ventured into more historical and archaeological realms in such books as *West by Covered Wagon* and *Homesteading,* and also a group of books for the "Frozen in Time" series, including *In Search of Maiasaurs, Mystery of the Lascaux Cave, Secrets of the Ice Man, The Lost City of Pompeii,* and *The Incredible Story of China's Buried Warriors.* Reviewing the last two titles in *Booklist,* Hazel Rochman noted that the books "combine dramatic history with fascinating information." Such information comes in the form of text, time-lines, and a magazine-style design that "will encourage browsing," Rochman also remarked.

The majority of Patent's books, however, explain the history, breeding, growth, and habits of various groups of animals, and have been widely praised for their clarity, thoroughness, and readability. Whether she is describing worms or whales, Patent's works appeal to students of all ages, from the bright eight-year-old to the curious high school student. She may use difficult vocabulary, but she explains the words used and often supplies a helpful glossary. Also, humorous examples of strange animal behavior and vivid pictures frequently combine to make her books more interesting than the ordinary textbook.

Patent has continued to write a wide range of children's books about both animals and numerous other topics. For example, in *Fire: Friend or Foe,* the author focuses on forest fires, with an emphasis on how people battle them and how the fires ultimately effect nature. A *Horn Book* contributor wrote: "The thoughtful discussion covers evolving policies, practices, and disagreements regarding fire fighting and controlled burning." Writing in *Booklist,* Randy Meyer commented: "The text offers rich science support." In the realm of animals, Patent focuses on the physical characteristics, habits, and habitats of polar bears in the fully illustrated book *Great Ice Bear: The Polar Bear and the Eskimo.* Carolyn Phelan, writing in *Booklist,* called *Great Ice Bear* "appealing and informative."

Patent turns to biography for her book *Charles Darwin: The Life of a Revolutionary Thinker.* The author covers Darwin's entire life, from his time as a boy on through his famous voyage on the *Beagle* and his subsequent writings. In a review in *Booklist,* Randy Meyer wrote that "the author balances the man as scientist with the man as devoted husband and father." A *Horn Book* contributor noted: "The strength of this work lies in the considerable attention given to Darwin's scientific process of observing, questioning, collecting, hypothesizing, testing, concluding, and writing." In *A Polar Bear Biologist at Work,* Patent includes numerous quotes and information gathered from Chuck Jonkel, who has studied bears for more than four decades and is especially interested in polar bears. "Patent's lucid text is brimming with . . . data," wrote Patricia Manning in the *School Library Journal.*

Animals on the Trail with Lewis and Clark is one of three books by Patent focusing on the Corps of Discovery expedition. It features the numerous wildlife species that the explorers and their crew came across during their historic exploration of the American West. In addition to photographs by William Munoz, the author includes sources and Web sites for readers to investigate further. Nancy Collins-Warner, writing in the *School Library Journal,* noted: "This competent and attractive title presents a unique approach to the Lewis and Clark Expedition." A *Kirkus Reviews* contributor wrote that the author's "easy approach to the subject helps to draw the reader in." In *The Lewis and Clark Trail: Then and Now,* the author "provides a succinct narrative account of the Lewis and Clark Expedition," as noted by Carolyn Phelan in *Booklist. Plants on the Trail with Lewis and Clark,* describes the plethora new plant life that the explorers encountered. Carolyn Phelan, writing in *Booklist,* commented that of all the recent books about the expedition, which celebrated it's 200th anniversary in 2004, "this is one of the most tightly focused, most interesting, and most beautiful."

The author has also collaborated with illustrator Kendahl Jan Jubb for a number of highly illustrated books featuring exotic animals and locales. In *Fabulous Fluttering Tropical Butterflies,* the author writes about the butterfly life cycle and mimicry in nature, as well as their eating habits and other information. A *Kirkus Reviews* contributor noted that "casual browsers as well as budding lepidopterists will be riveted." *Colorful Captivating Coral Reefs* focuses on both coral reef and the broad expanse of ocean life that it helps sustain. *Booklist* contributor Ed Sullivan called the book a "beautifully illustrated, informative title." In another collaboration with Jubb, *Big Cats,* Patent describes features common to all big cats and then describes the individual species, such as the lion, leopard, cheetah, snow leopard, tiger, and cougar. Cindy Suite, writing in *School Library Journal,* commented that young readers will enjoy "the compelling facts about these magnificent creatures."

Patent teams up with photographer William Munoz again in *The Right Dog for the Job: Ira's Path from Service Dog to Guide Dog,* which provides a close-up look at the complete training process of a service dog. *Booklist* contributor Carolyn Phelan wrote: "The informative text tells the dog's story in a straightforward way." *White-Tailed Deer* is also a collaboration between Patent and Munoz and was called "a solid offering"by Jennifer Mattson in *Booklist.*

Garden of The Spirit Bear: Life in The Great Northern Rainforest focuses on British Columbia's coastal rainforest and the animals and trees populate it. "The author clearly and artfully describes the natural processes" involved in life in the rainforest, pointed out Molly Cooney-Mesker in *Skipping Stones.* Kathy Piehl, writing in the *School Library Journal,* noted that the author "helps readers see the interrelationships that form a delicate balance for all of the inhabitants." In *The Buffalo and the Indians: A Shared Destiny,* Patent focuses on the longstanding relationship between the buffalo and Native Americans, how the destruction of the buffalo by white settlers negatively effected Native Americans, and how buffalo are making a comeback. "The lucid narrative and spacious book design . . . will draw readers into the history and prompt discussion of the connection between human and animal rights," wrote Hazel Rochman in *Booklist.*

Patent concluded: "I hope that my writing can help children get in touch with the world of living things and realize how dependent we are on them, not just on the wild world but on domesticated plants and animals as well. We owe our existence to the earth, and it is the balance of nature that sustains all life; we upset that balance at our peril. I believe that well-informed children can grow up into responsible citizens capable of making the wise but difficult decisions necessary for the survival of a livable world. I plan to continue to write for those children, helping to provide them with the information they will need in the difficult but exciting times ahead."

BIOGRAPHICAL AND CRITICAL SOURCES:

BOOKS

Authors of Books for Young People, 3rd edition, edited by Martha Ward and others, Scarecrow Press (Lanham, MD), 1990.

Children's Literature Review, Volume 19, Thomson Gale (Detroit, MI), 1990, pp. 147-166.

Major Authors and Illustrators for Children and Young Adults, 2nd edition, Thomson Gale (Detroit, MI), 2002.

Something about the Author Autobiography Series, Volume 13, Thomson Gale (Detroit, MI), 1991, pp. 137-154.

Sutherland, Zena, and May Hill Arbuthnot, *Children and Books,* 7th edition, Scott, Foresman (Chicago, IL), 1986.

PERIODICALS

Appraisal: Science Books for Young People, fall, 1974, Heddie Kent, review of *Weasels, Otters, Skunks, and Their Family,* p. 33; spring, 1994, review of *Horses,* pp. 76-77; spring, 1995, review of *Looking at Bears,* p. 46; autumn, 1995, review of *Why Mammals Have Fur,* p. 36.

Booklist, May 15, 1992, Deborah Abbott, review of *Feathers,* p. 1680; June 1, 1993, Deborah Abbott, review of *Dogs: The Wolf Within,* p. 1826; January 15, 1994, Ellen Mandel, review of *Cattle,* p. 927; May 1, 1994, Mary Harris Veeder, review of *Deer and Elk,* p. 1597; December 15, 1994, April Judge, review of *The American Alligator,* p. 749; November 1, 1995, Kay Weisman, Review of *West by Covered Wagon: Retracing the Pioneer Trails,* p. 468; March 1, 1996, Kay Weisman, review of *Eagles of America,* p. 1180; August 1996, Carolyn Phelan, review of *Quetzal: Sacred Bird of the*

Cloud Forest, p. 1899; November 1, 1996, Carolyn Phelan, review of *Prairies,* p. 494; September 1, 1997, Carolyn Phelan, review of *Pigeons,* p. 120; September 1, 1998, Shelley Townsend-Hudson, review of *Bold and Bright, Black-and-White Animals,* pp. 122-23; November 1, 1998, Carolyn Phelan, review of *Homesteading: Settling America's Heartland,* p. 488; November 15, 1998, Randy Meyer, review of *Fire: Friend or Foe,* pp. 488, 584; December 1, 1999, Carolyn Phelan, review of *Great Ice Bear: The Polar Bear and the Eskimo,* p. 699; February 1, 2000, Hazel Rochman, reviews of *The Incredible Story of China's Buried Warriors* and *Lost City of Pompeii;* March 15, 2000, Gillian Engberg, review of *Shaping the Earth,* p. 1373; October 15, 2000, Randy Meyer, review of *The Bald Eagle Returns,* p. 433; December 1, 2000, Carolyn Phelan, review of *Slinky, Scaly, Slithery Snakes,* p. 716; August, 2001, Randy Meyer, review of *Charles Darwin: The Life of a Revolutionary Thinker,* p. 2105; April 15, 2002, Carolyn Phelan, review of *Animals on the Trail with Lewis and Clark,* p. 1399; January 1, 2003, Carolyn Phelan, review of *The Lewis and Clark Trail: Then and Now,* p. 885; March 1, 2003, Carolyn Phelan, review of *Plants on the Trail with Lewis and Clark,* p. 1195; May 1, 2003, GraceAnne A. DeCandido, review of *Fabulous Fluttering Tropical Butterflies,* p. 1603; January 1, 2004, Ed Sullivan, review of *Colorful Captivating Coral Reefs,* p. 868; June 1, 2004, Carolyn Phelan, review of *The Right Dog for the Job: Ira's Path from Service Dog to Guide Dog,* p. 1723; December 15, 2004, Jennifer Mattson, review of *White-Tailed Deer,* p. 740; November 15, 2005, Carolyn Phelan, review of *Big Cats,* p. 50; June 1, 2006, Hazel Rochman, review of *The Buffalo and the Indians: A Shared Destiny,* p. 75.

Bulletin of the Center for Children's Books, July-August, 1993, Betsy Hearne, review of *Dogs: The Wolf Within,* pp. 355-356; July, 1995, Roger Sutton, review of *Return of the Wolf,* p. 394; October, 1996, p. 71; September, 1997, p. 23; December, 1998, p. 141.

Faces: People, Places, and Cultures, January, 2005, review of *The Great Ice Bear,* p. 46.

Horn Book, October, 1981, Sarah Gagne, review of *Horses and Their Wild Relatives,* pp. 558-559; September-October, 1993, Ellen Fader, review of *Ospreys,* and Maeve Visser Knoth, review of *Killer Whales,* p. 634; January 1, 1994, Christie Sylvester, review of *Looking at Penguins,* p. 825; January-February, 1995, Margaret A. Bush, review of *The*

American Alligator, p. 70; July-August, 1995, p. 481; January-February, 1997, Margaret A. Bush, reviews of *Biodiversity* and *Quetzal,* p. 78; January, 1999, review of *Fire: Friend or Foe,* p. 84; September, 2001, review of *Charles Darwin,* p. 613.

Horn Book Guide, spring, 1999, Elizabeth S. Watson, review of *Alex and Friends,* p. 107.

Kirkus Reviews, February 15, 1993, review of *Habitats,* p. 233; January 1, 1994, review of *What Good Is a Tail?,* p. 73; January 15, 1997, review of *Flashy Fantastic Rain Forest Frogs,* p. 144; February 1, 1998, review of *Apple Trees,* pp. 199-200; March 15, 2002, review of *Animals on the Trail with Lewis and Clark,* p. 423; February 15, 2003, review of *Fabulous Fluttering Tropical Butterflies,* p. 314; October 1, 2003, review of *Colorful Captivating Coral Reefs,* p. 1229; May 1, 2004, review of *The Right Dog for the Job,* p. 446; July 15, 2004, review of *Garden of the Spirit Bear: Life in the Great Northern Rainforest,* p. 692; October 1, 2005, review of *Big Cats,* p. 1086.

Publishers Weekly, July 30, 2001, review of *Charles Darwin,* p. 86.

Quarterly Review of Biology, June, 2002, Jonathan Smith, review of *Charles Darwin: The Life of a Revolutionary Thinker,* p. 175.

School Library Journal, December, 1992, Susan Oliver, review of *Pelicans,* p. 126; July, 1994, Carol Kolb Phillips, review of *Hugger to the Rescue,* p. 97; March, 2000, Andrew Medlar, review of *The Incredible Story of China's Buried Warriors,* p. 260; April, 2000, John Peters, review of *Shaping the Earth,* p. 154; July, 2000, Michele Snyder, review of *Polar Bears,* p. 96; November, 2000, Ellen Heath, review of *The Bald Eagle Returns,* p. 174; March, 2001, Karey Wehner, review of *Slinky, Scaly, Slithery Snakes,* p. 240; November, 2001, Patricia Manning, review of *A Polar Bear Biologist at Work,* p. 182; December, 2001, Arwen. Marshall, review of *Saving the Prairie Bandit,* p. 154; April, 2002, Nancy Collins-Warner, review of *Animals on the Trail with Lewis and Clark,* p. 180; March, 2003, Renee Steinberg, review of *Animals on the Trail with Lewis and Clark,* p. 172; May, 2003, Louise L. Sherman, review of *Fabulous Fluttering Tropical Butterflies,* p. 140, and Susan Scheps, review of *Plants on the Trail with Lewis and Clark,* p. 176; November, 2003, Susan Oliver, review of *Colorful Captivating Coral Reefs,* p. 129; June, 2004, Kathleen Kelly MacMillan, review of *The Right Dog for the Job,* p. 131; October, 2004, Kathy Piehl, review of *Garden of the Spirit Bear,* p.

147; April, 2005, review of *The Right Dog for the Job,* p. S29; December, 2005, Cindy Suite, review of *Big Cats,* p. 132.

Science Books: A Quarterly Review, May, 1974, review of *Weasels, Otters, Skunks, and Their Family,* p. 76.

Science Books and Films, September-October, 1981, Roy T. Cunningham, review of *The Lives of Spiders,* p. 21.

Skipping Stones, May-August, 2005, Molly Cooney-Mesker, Review of *Garden of The Spirit Bear:* p. 28.

Voice of Youth Advocates, June, 1992, Luvada Kuhn, review of *Feathers,* pp. 131-32.

ONLINE

Dorothy Hinshaw Patent Home Page, http://www. dorothyhinshawpatent.com (May 24, 2001).

Global Gourmet, http://www.globalgourmet.com/ (December 11, 2006), review of *A Is for Apple.**

*   *   *

PELAN, John

PERSONAL: Born in Richmond, VA; married; wife's name Kathy (a publisher).

ADDRESSES: Home—Seattle, WA. *Office*—Darkside Press, 13320 27th Ave. NE, Seattle, WA 98125. *E-mail*—darksidepress@qwest.net.

CAREER: Author, editor, and publisher. Silver Salamander/Midnight House/Darkside Press, Seattle, WA, owner. Taught English in Japan.

AWARDS, HONORS: International Horror Guild Award, 1996; Bram Stoker Award in anthology category, Horror Writers Association, 2002, for *The Darker Side.*

WRITINGS:

FICTION

Axolotl special 1, Axolotl Press (Eugene, OR), 1989.

(Editor) *Darkside: Horror for the New Millenium,* Roc (New York, NY), 1995.

(With Edward Lee) *Goon,* Necro Publications (Orlando, FL), 1996.

(With Edward Lee) *Shifters,* 1998.

(With Edward Lee) *Splatterspunk: The Micah Hayes Stories,* 1998.

(Editor and contributor) *The Last Continent: New Tales of Zothique,* Shadowlands Press (Centreville, VA), 1999.

An Antique Vintage, Gargadillo Publishing (Corsicana, TX), 1999.

(Editor) Manly Wade Wellman, *Fearful Rock and Other Precarious Locales,* Night Shade Books (San Francisco, CA), 2001.

(Editor, with Benjamin Adams) *The Children of Cthulhu: Chilling New Tales Inspired by H.P. Lovecraft,* Ballantine Books (New York, NY), 2002.

(Editor) *The Devil Is Not Mocked and Other Warnings: The Selected Stories of Manly Wade Wellman, Volume 2,* Night Shade Books (San Francisco, CA), 2002.

(Editor) Keith Fleming, *Can Such Things Be?; or, The Weird of the Beresfords,* Sarob Press (Wales), 2002.

(Editor) *The Darker Side,* Roc (New York, NY), 2002.

(Editor) Louisa Baldwin, *The Shadow on the Blind,* Ash-Tree Press (Ashcroft, British Columbia, Canada), 2002.

Darkness, My Old Friend (stories), Shadowlands Press (Centreville, VA), 2002.

(Editor) Manly Wade Wellman, *Sin's Doorway and Other Ominous Entrances,* Night Shade Books (San Francisco, CA), 2003.

(Editor) Manly Wade Wellman, *Owls Hoot in the Daytime and Other Omens,* Night Shade Books (San Francisco, CA), 2003.

(Editor, with Michael Reaves) *Shadows Over Baker Street: New Tales of Terror,* Ballantine Books (New York, NY), 2003.

(Editor, with Russell Kirk) *What Shadows We Pursue: Ghost Stories Volume Two,* Ash-Tree Press (Ashcroft, British Columbia, Canada), 2003.

(Editor) *A Walk on the Darkside: Visions of Horror,* Roc (New York, NY), 2004.

(Editor) *Lost on the Darkside: Voices from the Edge of Horror,* Roc (New York, NY), 2005.

(Editor) *Alone on the Darkside: Echoes from Shadows of Horror,* Roc, 2006.

(Editor) *Century's Best Horror Fiction,* Cemetery Dance (Forest Hill, MD), 2006.

(Editor) *Dark Arts,* Cemetery Dance (Forest Hill, MD), 2006.

Colour Out of Darkness, Cemetery Dance (Forest Hill, MD), 2006.

Also author of *Girl's Night Out,* 1998; author, with Edward Lee of *Cotter's Field; or, The Scene That Started It All,* 1996, *The Case of the Police Officer's Cock Ring and the Piano Player Who Had No Fingers,* 1997, *Refrigerator Full of Sperm,* 1998, *Sideshow,* 1998, *Prologue,* 1998, and *Shifters,* 2005. Contributor of short fiction to *Triptych, Urbanite, Gothic.net, Enigmatic Tales, Carpe Noctem,* and *Horrorfind.com.*

SIDELIGHTS: John Pelan is one of the foremost historians of horror, an expertise he has put to use as editor of numerous anthologies. Pelan grew up in Richmond, Virginia, raised by his mother and grandmother who, he has said gave him a Southern Gothic upbringing. He cites authors Dennis Lehane, Michael Connelly, John Sandford, Eckhart Tolle, Ken Wilbur, Joel Goldsmith, and Father Thomas Keating as having influenced his own work.

Pelan edited and contributed a story to *The Last Continent: New Tales of Zothique,* an anthology of nineteen new stories about Zothique, a super-continent rotting under the light of a dying sun, that was first created by dark fantasy master Clark Ashton Smith. Smith, who died in 1961, was known for his irony and his obvious eroticism, which his contemporary editors often felt compelled to trim.

Pelan recruited several writers to craft stories in Smith's style, allowing for flexible parameters. Edward Bryant noted in *Locus* that most of the writers grasped the necessary irony and erotic. Pelan chose many new writers to go with some of his old standbys, and, according to Bryant, they fared well.

The stories are filled with doomed relationships and dying cities. Gerald Houarner's "To Wake the Dead in Nympholos" is about the guardian of a city of ghouls who meets a woman and tries to reconcile his gloomy job with his attraction for her. Mark Chadbourn's "Love and Death at the End of the World" is a crime fiction in which five criminals who abduct a young woman meet nasty ends. Pelan's own contribution is "The Scarlet Succubus," which he wrote with Edward Lee. Other authors include David B. Silva, Jessica Amanda Salmonson, Charlee Jacob, and Lucy Taylor. Bryant summarized in his review: "Be wary of gifting your love with this book on Valentine's Day; but otherwise it's a keeper."

Among Pelan's other anthologies is *Fearful Rock and Other Precarious Locales,* a collection of short stories by Manly Wade Wellman of *Weird Tales.* Wellman died in 1986, and *Fearful Rock* is the third volume of a projected five. It contains stories written in the mid-twentieth century that still frighten. Several feature Sergeant Jaeger, a former Union soldier turned minister, in the wilds of Missouri and Arkansas during the Civil War. Four tales involve the occult detective, Keith Hilary Pursuivant. Wellman's work blends elements of Southern Gothic, folklore, classic supernatural fiction, and heroic masculinity to create a spooky atmosphere.

The Children of Cthulhu: Chilling New Tales Inspired by H.P. Lovecraft, which Pelan coedited with Benjamin Adams, is an anthology of twenty-one short stories, and like the writings of Lovecraft are dark and sinister. Poppy Z. Brite's "Are You Loathesome Tonight" brings Elvis and his peanut-butter-and-banana sandwiches to the horror genre. In "Details," by China Mieville, an elderly woman sees something looking at her from behind walls and trees, and finds it lurking in her own memories. Richard Laymon's "The Cabin in the Woods" tells of a horrible thing trying to get into a cabin at night. Other notable stories include Caitlin R. Kiernan's "Nor the Demons down under the Sea" and "A Victorian Pot Dresser" by L.H. Maynard and M.P.N. Sims. Regina Schroeder, in *Booklist,* praised the stories for doing what they intended—to titillate, horrify, and confront, just as Lovecraft did. "Altogether they constitute a fitting sacrifice to the appetites of the cult of Lovecraft and his monstrous elder gods," she wrote.

Pelan and Michael Reaves edited *Shadows Over Baker Street: New Tales of Terror,* a collection of eighteen original Sherlock Holmes tales that find the sleuth encountering Lovecraft-type horrors. A *Publishers Weekly* contributor considered Phelan's "The Mystery of the Worm" and Reaves's "The Adventure of the Arab's Manuscript" to be two of "the more successful tales."

Dark Arts is a collection for which Pelan sought contributors to write about artists, sculptors, and others whose stories reveal the dark side of their art. The opening story, Steve Rasnic Tem's "Disease Artist" is set in an antiseptic future and features a performance artist who infects himself with deadly diseases to demonstrate to his audience that we are all mortal. A twelve-year-old pianist calls on the dead in Patricia Lee Macomber's "Chained Melody." A *Publishers Weekly* contributor

wrote that Lucy Taylor's "I Hear You Quietly Singing" and Brian Hodge's "With Acknowledgments to Sun Tzu" are examples of stories of "artists whose dark visions expose the grim reality of existence" The final story is "Nightmares, Imported and Domestic," by Matt Cardin and Mark McLaughlin, who write about an artist whose dreams become more real than his actual life. Carl Hays concluded in *Booklist* that this collection is "consistently first rate."

Colour Out of Darkness is Pelan's novel featuring a tentacled alien that is spreading a contagious infection in order to take over the world. A *Publishers Weekly* reviewer noted that this story comes "replete with explicit sex and gore."

BIOGRAPHICAL AND CRITICAL SOURCES:

BOOKS

Science Fiction and Fantasy Literature 1975-1991, Thomson Gale (Detroit, MI), 1992.

PERIODICALS

Booklist, December 15, 2001, Regina Schroeder, review of *The Children of Cthulhu: Chilling New Tales Inspired by H.P. Lovecraft,* p. 709; May 15, 2006, Carl Hays, review of *Dark Arts,* p. 33.

Kirkus Reviews, October 15, 2001, review of *The Children of Cthulhu,* p. 1461; August 1, 2003, review of *Shadows Over Baker Street: New Tales of Terror,* p. 988.

Library Journal, January, 2002, Jackie Cassada, review of *The Children of Cthulhu,* p. 159.

Locus, January, 2000, Edward Bryant, review of *The Last Continent: New Tales of Zothique,* p. 31.

Publishers Weekly, February 4, 2002, review of *Fearful Rock and Other Precarious Locales,* p. 59; September 15, 2003, review of *Shadows Over Baker Street,* p. 49; January 30, 2006, review of *The Colour Out of Darkness,* p. 45; April 10, 2006, review of *Dark Arts,* p. 50.

ONLINE

Darkside Press Web site, http://www.darksidepress.com/ (January 2, 2006).*

PERSICO, Joseph E. 1930-
(Joseph Edward Persico)

PERSONAL: Born July 19, 1930, in Gloversville, NY; son of Thomas L. (a glove maker) and Blanche (a glove maker) Persico; married Sylvia Lavista (an administrator), May 23, 1959; children: Vanya, Andrea. *Education:* State University of New York at Albany, B.A., 1952; also attended Columbia University, 1955. *Hobbies and other interests:* Cooking, hiking, tennis, baroque music.

ADDRESSES: Agent—Clyde Taylor, Curtis Brown Ltd., 10 Astor Pl., New York, NY 10003.

CAREER: Writer. Consumer advocate for governor of New York, in Albany, 1956-59; U.S. Information Agency, Washington, DC, foreign service officer in Rio de Janeiro, Brazil, and Buenos Aires, Argentina, 1959-62; speechwriter for Nelson A. Rockefeller, 1966-77; writer, 1977—. Also served on the commission that oversaw the design of the National World War II Memorial in Washington, DC. *Military service:* U.S. Navy, 1952-55; became lieutenant junior grade.

MEMBER: Authors Guild, Authors League of America, American Film Institute.

AWARDS, HONORS: Book award from National Intelligence Study Center, 1979, for *Piercing the Reich;* distinguished alumnus award from State University of New York.

WRITINGS:

My Enemy, My Brother: Men and Days of Gettysburg, Viking (New York, NY), 1977, De Capo Press (New York, NY), 1996.
Piercing the Reich: The Penetration of Nazi Germany by American Secret Agents during World War II, Viking (New York, NY), 1979.
The Spiderweb (novel), Crown (New York, NY), 1979.
The Imperial Rockefeller: A Biography of Nelson A. Rockefeller, Simon & Schuster (New York, NY), 1982.
Murrow: An American Original, McGraw (New York, NY), 1988, reprinted as *Edward R. Murrow: An American Original,* De Capo Press (New York, NY), 1997.

Casey: From the OSS to the CIA, Viking (New York, NY), 1990.
Nuremberg: Infamy on Trial, Viking (New York, NY), 1994.
(With Colin Powell) *My American Journey,* Random House (New York, NY), 1995, published as *A Soldier's Way: An Autobiography,* Hutchinson (London, England), 1995, revised edition, Ballantine Books (New York, NY), 2003.
Roosevelt's Secret War: FDR and World War II Espionage, Random House (New York, NY), 2001.
Eleventh Month, Eleventh Day, Eleventh Hour: Armistice Day, 1918, World War I and Its Violent Climax, Random House (New York, NY), 2004.

Contributor to *American Heritage.*

ADAPTATIONS: Nuremberg: Infamy on Trial was adapted as a television Drama; books have been adapted as audio recordings, including *My American Journey,* Random House (New York, NY), 1995, and *Eleventh Month, Eleventh Day, Eleventh Hour,* Books on Tape, 2004.

SIDELIGHTS: Joseph E. Persico worked as a speechwriter for politician Nelson A. Rockefeller for eleven years before becoming a freelance author in 1977. Persico called upon his experiences in the political realm to write *The Imperial Rockefeller: A Biography of Nelson A. Rockefeller,* an insider's portrait of the former governor of New York who became vice president in 1973. He has also written several books about World War II, including *Piercing the Reich: The Penetration of Nazi Germany by American Secret Agents during World War II, Roosevelt's Secret War: FDR and World War II Espionage,* and *The Spiderweb,* the last a novel of suspense about the fall of Nazi Germany through the eyes of a liberated concentration camp victim.

Critics such as *New York Times Book Review* contributor Maurice Carroll found *The Imperial Rockefeller* an important contribution to an understanding of the powerful Republican politician. "Mr. Persico's account confirms what some of us always suspected," claimed Carroll. "Our outsider's impression of the inside events was accurate. Working for Nelson Rockefeller *was* like being in a royal court." Though *Newsweek* contributor Charles Kaiser noted that *The Imperial Rockefeller* is "hardly a comprehensive biography," he nonetheless admitted: "It is the most personal portrait to date of the late governor and Vice President, full of useful insights and punctuated by very funny anecdotes." *Chicago Tribune Book World* contributor Alden Whitman likewise praised the "finely nuanced and insightful biography," concluding that Persico "is an observant, admiring, critical, thoughtful deviser of a fair, often devastatingly acidic portrait of a powerful, ambitious and often thoughtless person." Whitman added: "Persico's biography is a book of substance. His keen etching of Rockefeller's appeal, his contradictions, is the work of a sensitive observer—and a compassionate one."

Persico's *Roosevelt's Secret War: FDR and World War II Espionage* examines how President Franklin D. Roosevelt dealt with his intelligence service during World War II. Roosevelt is credited with creating America's first intelligence agency, the OSS, and running it closely. "This book," wrote William D. Pederson in *Library Journal*, "keys in on the Machiavellian side of his personality, meshing it with his interest in secrecy." According to Margaret Flanagan in *Booklist*, Persico's book is "the first comprehensive account of the definitive role that espionage played in FDR's wartime agenda." Philip Bobbitt, writing for the *New York Times*, found the work to be "entertaining and even inspiring."

Persico's first book, *My Enemy, My Brother: Men and Days of Gettysburg*, was published in 1977 and reprinted in 1996. The author, using a combination historical narrative and fictionalized approach, looks at the war from the perspective of the common soldiers who did the actual fighting and the common people who experienced the tragedies of the war. Writing in *Armed Forces & Society*, Michael T. Meier, commented: "Persico's desire to 'humanize' the battle is a worthy one." *Casey: From the OSS to the CIA* follows the life of William Casey, who had a diverse career from private business and banking to the upper echelons of government, including serving as head the CIA in the 1980's. In a review in *Publishers Weekly* Genevieve Stuttaford noted that the author "writes a detailed, firmly three-dimensional biography covering each phase of a controversial life." *Hollins Critic* contributor Wayne G. Reilly, commented that Persico "has written a friendly, but I think generally fair biography."

In *Nuremberg: Infamy on Trial*, Persico delves into the Nazi war crimes trials held in Nuremberg in 1945 and 1946, with a special emphasis on the trials' ethical and legal questions, which the author believes can be applied to modern war crimes trials. "The conflicts for Mr. Persico go far beyond good and evil, justice and punishment: not only does he imagine himself into the hearts and minds of the defendants, but he insinuates himself into the complex relations between prosecutors and judges as well," wrote James E. Young in a review in the *New York Times*. Young went on to write that the author's "novelistic re-creation of the Nuremberg trials is a well-wrought example of literary nonfiction." An *American Heritage* contributor noted that the author "brings to life the trials and the terrible characters who sat in the dock."

Persico collaborated with Colin E. Powell to write the autobiography of the former U.S. Army general and later Secretary of State. Ronald Steel, writing in the *New York Times*, referred to *My American Journey* as "an endearing and well-written book." Steel added: "Reading this skillful narrative . . . you will cheer Mr. Powell on as he shoots up the Army's career pole, accumulating medals and stars all along the way." Thomas L. Dumm, writing in *America*, commented: "This book is a book for our times, but to learn its deepest lessons we must read it against its mythical intentions. To do otherwise is to take Powell at his word, and to take him at his word means to mismeasure the man himself." *Insight on the News* contributor Richard N. Perle called the book "a warm, funny, often gripping account of an extraordinary life."

In *Eleventh Month, Eleventh Day, Eleventh Hour: Armistice Day, 1918, World War I and Its Violent Climax*, Persico looks at the final days of World War I based on numerous written accounts, including official dispatches and letters written by many of the soldiers. The author focuses particularly on the final hours of the war and the mysterious decision by generals on both sides to keep their forces fighting despite their knowledge that a peace agreement was going to be signed. Gilbert Taylor, writing in *Booklist*, noted that the author "illustrates the struggle by treating its last day as typifying the war." A *Kirkus Reviews* contributor wrote that Persico "ably encapsulates the whole conflict in a highly readable narrative." Writing in *History: Review of New Books*, John Daley commented: "As a popularized introduction to life in the trenches, . . . Persico's book is an engaging read."

Persico once told *CA*: "The creative process remains to me the holiest mystery. The capacity to leave something where nothing existed before is the ultimate glory of the human mind. I write out of no such conscious awareness, but out of unreasoned compulsion. When I do not write, I experience actual mental and emotional anguish. The obsession is chronic and seemingly incurable, a disease, benign, one hopes."

BIOGRAPHICAL AND CRITICAL SOURCES:

PERIODICALS

America, January 27, 1996, Thomas L. Dumm, review of *My American Journey,* p. 26.

American Heritage, July-August, 1994, review of *Nuremberg: Infamy on Trial,* p. 107.

Armed Forces & Society, winter, 1990, Michael T. Meier, review of *My Enemy My Brother: Men and Days of Gettysburg,* p. 318.

Booklist, August, 2001, Margaret Flanagan, review of *Roosevelt's Secret War: FDR and World War II Espionage,* p. 2082; September 1, 2004, Gilbert Taylor, review of *Eleventh Month, Eleventh Day, Eleventh Hour: Armistice Day, 1918, World War I and Its Violent Climax,* p. 43.

Chicago Tribune Book World, February 7, 1982, Alden Whitman, review of *The Imperial Rockefeller: A Biography of Nelson A. Rockefeller.*

Commonweal, January 12, 1996, Don Wycliff, review of *My American Journey,* p. 20.

Contemporary Review, February, 1996, Esmond Wright, review of *A Soldier's Way: An Autobiography,* p. 106.

Entertainment Weekly, September 29, 1995, Gene Lyons, review of *My American Journey,* p. 53; November 5, 2004, Wook Kim, review of *Eleventh Month, Eleventh Day, Eleventh Hour,* p. 88.

History: Review of New Books, spring, 2005, John Daley, review of *Eleventh Month, Eleventh Day, Eleventh Hour,* p. 112.

History Teacher, May, 1996, Janet D. Stone, review of *Nuremberg,* pp. 407-408.

Hollins Critic, October, 1991, Wayne G. Reilly, review of *Casey: From the OSS to the CIA,* p. 12.

Insight on the News, November 13, 1995, Richard N. Perle, review of *My American Journey,* p. 25.

Kirkus Reviews, August 15, 2004, review of *Eleventh Month, Eleventh Day, Eleventh Hour,* p. 794.

Library Journal, December 1, 1976, Herman Hattaway, review of *My Enemy, My Brother,* p. 2486; October 15, 1978, George H. Siehl, review of *Piercing the Reich: The Penetration of Nazi Germany by American Secret Agents during World War II,* p. 2526; October 15, 1979, Barbara Conaty, review of

The Spiderweb, p. 2239; August, 2001, William D. Pederson, review of *Roosevelt's Secret War,* p. 132; October 15, 2004, Dale Farris, review of *Eleventh Month, Eleventh Day, Eleventh Hour,* p. 75.

National Review, November 6, 1995, A.J. Bacevich, review of *My American Journey,* p. 56.

Newsweek, March 15, 1982, Charles Kaiser, review of *The Imperial Rockefeller,* p. 74.

New York Times, May 29, 1994, James E. Young, review of *Neuremberg*; September 17, 1995, Ronald Steel, review of *My American Journey;* October 19, 2001, Philip Bobbitt, "A Detailed Look at Roosevelt, the Intelligence Consumer," p. E32.

New York Times Book Review, March 14, 1982, Maurice Carroll, review of *The Imperial Rockefeller,* p. 7; October 21, 2001, Thomas Powers, "Who Knew What, and When?"

Publishers Weekly, August 17, 1990, review of *Casey,* p. 58; October 4, 2004, review of *Eleventh Month, Eleventh Day, Eleventh Hour,* p. 78.

Time, March 1, 1982, R.Z. Sheppard, review of *The Imperial Rockefeller,* p. 82; November 5, 1990, Stefan Kanfer, review of *Casey,* p. 93.

ONLINE

Beliefnet, http://www.beliefnet.com/ (December 12, 2006), Paul O'Donnell, "The Greatest Generation Goes to the Mall," interview with author.*

* * *

PERSICO, Joseph Edward
    See PERSICO, Joseph E.

* * *

PIETRZYK, Leslie 1961-
    (Leslie Jeanne Pietrzyk)

PERSONAL: Born June 24, 1961, in Boston, MA; married Robert K. Rauth Jr., August 23, 1986 (deceased). *Education:* Northwestern University, B.A., 1983; American University, M.F.A., 1985.

ADDRESSES: Agent—Gail Hochman, Brandt & Hochman, 1501 Broadway, New York, NY, 10036. *E-mail*—lpietr@aol.com.

CAREER: Writer and editor.

MEMBER: Poets and Writers, Women's National Book Association.

AWARDS, HONORS: First place award, University of Alaska Southeast Fiction Contest, 1995; Chris O'Malley Fiction Prize, *Madison Review,* 1995; scholarship, Bread Loaf Writers' Conference, scholar, 1996, fellow, 1999; Frank O'Connor Memorial Award, *Descant,* 1996; Whetstone Prize, *Whetstone,* 1996; Jeanne Charpiot Goodheart Prize for Fiction, *Shenandoah,* 1996; Walter E. Dakin Fellow, Sewanee Writers' Conference, 1998; Editor's Choice Award, *Columbia,* 1999; Julia Peterkin Award, Converse College, 2003.

WRITINGS:

Pears on a Willow Tree (novel), Avon/Bard (New York, NY), 1998.
A Year and a Day (novel), William Morrow (New York, NY), 2004.

Contributor to periodicals, including *Epoch, Gettysburg Review, Iowa Review, Nebraska Review, New England Review, TriQuarterly, Shenandoah,* and *Massachusetts Review.*

SIDELIGHTS: Leslie Pietrzyk's book *Pears on a Willow Tree* is the fictional story of four generations of Polish American women. The novel traces the lives of these women from 1919 into the 1990s, from the family's original emigration from Poland to the United States, life in Michigan and Arizona, and another migration, this time to Thailand. Of Pietrzyk's characters, the older women easily hang onto ethnic tradition, while the younger women struggle over disregarding such customs. The title is taken from a Polish saying that means you are looking for something you can never find. Pietrzyk's characters include strong matriarch Rose; Helen, Rose's depressed daughter; Helen's rebellious daughter, Ginger, an alcoholic; and Ginger's responsible daughter Amy.

According to Ann Harleman in the *New York Times Book Review, Pears on a Willow Tree* depicts the feminine strength within one family. Harleman pointed out that the book's style—linked monologue chapters in the voices of the different characters—captures interest but leads to "a sketchy rendering of character and setting, the compression of insights into formulas that seen at once too pithy and pat." Harleman added that Pietrzyk's prose occasionally "opens up, rendering the everyday world in fresh ways," concluding that "this novel, heartfelt and game, augers well."

Reba Leiding, reviewing *Pears on a Willow Tree* in the *Library Journal,* noted Pietrzyk's "stereotyped" descriptions of the family's older women, but wrote that the author's observations of Ginger's tumultuous life accurately depict "the edginess and black humor of a not-quite-recovered alcoholic." In a starred *Publishers Weekly* review of the book, a contributor called the author's language "as plain and four-square as her protagonists," noting that Pietrzyk skillfully captures the different voices of her characters. This reviewer warned that "once you pick up this book, it's hard to put it down." *Washington Post* reviewer Roland Merullo concluded "*Pears on a Willow Tree* marks the debut of a genuine and fully developed talent with a most promising future. It is a rich, intricate, heartfelt novel that moves with a smoothness and sureness many experienced novelists will envy."

Pietrzyk once told CA: "My first novel *Pears on a Willow Tree* actually started as a short story about four generation of Polish-American women making pierogi (Polish dumplings). I came up with the idea of the four women in the kitchen after a visit to my grandmother's house in Detroit. I'd recently attempted to make pierogi and failed miserably, so my grandmother and I spent a lot of time talking about cooking, the two of us connecting in a way we never had before. I discovered that my grandmother was the one in the family who made the best pierogi—it was an accepted fact among her sisters, and I suddenly saw my grandmother in a whole new way.

"After finishing the story (which is now the book's first chapter). I wanted to know more about the four characters I'd created. So I wrote another story, then another. I quickly realized I was interested enough to write a whole novel about these women and their tangled relationships.

"While I consulted a lot of books to learn more about immigration to the United States, Polish customs, cooking, alcoholism, and other related topics, the most interesting research I did was sitting around the dinner table with my Polish-American grandmother, her two sisters, and a second cousin. I asked them questions about their lives and about my great-grandmother who had come to this country from Poland (I knew her—she lived to be 103—but I didn't know much about her early life). The discussions became so lively that I didn't even have to talk-the sisters just went on and on and on, getting into bitter fights about the most trivial details (like whether in was 1945 or 1946 when they got rid of the Ford car)! Again, these conversations connected me to my family in a new and different way.

"People always say to writers, write about what you know. But I prefer Eudora Welty's advice: Write about what you don't know about what you do know."

BIOGRAPHICAL AND CRITICAL SOURCES:

PERIODICALS

Library Journal, October 15, 1998, Reba Leiding, review of *Pears on a Willow Tree,* p. 101.
New York Times Book Review, October 18, 1998, Ann Harleman, review of *Pears on a Willow Tree,* p. 21.
Publishers Weekly, August 24, 1998, review of *Pears on a Willow Tree,* p. 46.
Washington Post, October 19, 1998, Roland Merullo, review of *Pears on a Willow Tree,* p. D9.

ONLINE

Leslie Pietrzyk Home Page, http://www.lesliepietrzyk. com (March 9, 2007).

*   *   *

PIETRZYK, Leslie Jeanne
See PIETRZYK, Leslie

*   *   *

PLUM, Jennifer
See KURLAND, Michael

*   *   *

PRUNTY, Morag 1964-

PERSONAL: Born April 14, 1964, in Scotland; married; children: one son.

ADDRESSES: Home—Ireland.

CAREER: Editor for magazines *Looks, More,* and *Just Seventeen,* London, England, and *Irish Tatler,* Dublin, Ireland.

WRITINGS:

Boys: A User's Guide, illustrated by Alison Everitt, Piccadilly (London, England), 1993.

NOVELS

Dancing with Mules, Pan (London, England), 2001, published as *Wild Cats and Colleens,* HarperCollins (New York, NY), 2001.
Disco Daddy, Pan (London, England), 2002.
Poison Arrows, Pan (London, England), 2003.
Superstar Lovers, Tivoli (Dublin, Ireland), 2004.
Recipes for a Perfect Marriage, Hyperion (New York, NY), 2006.

SIDELIGHTS: Morag Prunty, born in Scotland of Irish parents, has been a magazine editor since the age of nineteen. After working in England at *Looks* (where she was the magazine's youngest editor), *More,* and *Just Seventeen,* she relocated to Ireland, where she worked as editor of *Irish Tatler.*

Her first book, *Boys: A User's Guide,* is aimed at helping teenage girls understand the opposite sex. Prunty writes about the fears that go along with the first date and first kiss and about crushes, rejection, and other emotional issues. *School Librarian* reviewer Alison Hurst observed that all of these "are dealt with in a lighthearted but helpful way" and praised the accompanying cartoons by Alison Everitt, which Hurst felt help when addressing "such a sensitive subject."

Prunty's debut novel, *Dancing with Mules,* was published in the United States as *Wild Cats and Colleens.* A *Publishers Weekly* contributor wrote that one function of the book is "to blow away those blarney cobwebs from the Irish image and to show that the country is as up-to-date, materialistic and obsessed with glamour and trivia as much of the rest of the Western world." Prunty offers three heroines: Lorna, a publicist who plays too hard; Gloria, whose life began in the slums but who now does Lorna's hair in her very successful salon; and Sandy, a journalist yet to get her first big story. *New York Times Book Review* contributor

Fionn Meade felt that the Dublin-based characters "seem to be culled" from the HBO award-winning comedy *Sex and the City,* set in New York. Meade wrote that the book "is more like a polished sitcom than a searching work of fiction."

Xavier Power is an American billionaire, proud of his Irish heritage, who is looking for an Irish wife. What he has in mind is a sweet, preferably redheaded colleen, not the three wild women he meets when he travels to Ireland on his quest. He hires Lorna to plan the party at which he will meet prospects, and Lorna enlists Gloria's help. Sandy is hoping that her coverage of the event will result in her big story. *Booklist* reviewer Danise Hoover wrote: "The madcap situations that follow result in storybook-happy matchmakings for all concerned." "None of them marries the billionaire," noted Monica Collins in the *Boston Herald.* "Yet all three women find their pots of gold at the end of the rainbow." A *Kirkus Reviews* writer called *Wild Cats and Colleens* "an exuberantly absurd and intermittently amusing farce about three women looking for love and money in pop-culture-saturated contemporary Ireland."

Recipes for a Perfect Marriage contains the parallel stories of a contemporary woman and her Irish grandmother. Tressa Nolan, a New York food writer, is approaching forty and afraid that she will never marry. When her building superintendent, blue collar Dan Mullins, asks her to marry him, she accepts. She soon discovers, however, that they have nothing in common, and she wishes she could talk about her problems with her grandmother, Bernadine, who taught her to cook,

and who seemed to have the perfect marriage to her grandfather, James. Flashing back to the 1930s and 1940s, Bernadine's arranged marriage to James has been stable, but she has never forgotten her first and passionate love. "This is a clever and heartfelt take on the challenges of creating a 'happily ever after'" concluded Karen Core in *Library Journal.* The story includes Bernadine's recipes for such Irish delectables as clove-studded ham, rhubarb tart, and honey cake.

BIOGRAPHICAL AND CRITICAL SOURCES:

PERIODICALS

Booklist, October 15, 2001, Danise Hoover, review of *Wild Cats and Colleens,* p. 383; April 15, 2006, Joanne Wilkinson, review of *Recipes for a Perfect Marriage,* p. 30.

Boston Herald, December 2, 2001, Monica Collins, review of *Wild Cats and Colleens,* p. 50.

Kirkus Reviews, September 1, 2001, review of *Wild Cats and Colleens,* p. 1240.

Library Journal, May 15, 2006, Karen Core, review of *Recipes for a Perfect Marriage,* p. 91.

New York Times Book Review, December 23, 2001, Fionn Meade, review of *Wild Cats and Colleens,* p. 17.

Publishers Weekly, September 10, 2001, review of *Wild Cats and Colleens,* p. 56; February 13, 2006, review of *Recipes for a Perfect Marriage,* p. 61.

School Librarian, August, 1993, Alison Hurst, review of *Boys: A User's Guide,* p. 127.*

Q

QUAMMEN, David 1948-

PERSONAL: Born February 24, 1948, in Cincinnati, OH; son of W.A. and Mary Quammen; married Kris Ellingsen; married second wife, wife's name Betsy (a conservation activist). *Education:* Yale University, B.A., 1970; Merton College, Oxford University, B.Litt., 1973.

ADDRESSES: Home—Bozeman, MT. *Agent*—Renee Wayne Golden, 9601 Wilshire Blvd., Ste. 506, Beverly Hills, CA 90210.

CAREER: Writer.

AWARDS, HONORS: Rhodes scholar, 1970; National Magazine Award for essays and criticism, 1987; Guggenheim fellow, 1988; National Magazine Award, American Society of Magazine Editors and the Columbia University Graduate School of Journalism, 2005, for *National Geographic* essay "Was Darwin Wrong?"; John Burroughs Medal for natural-history writing, for *The Song of the Dodo.*

WRITINGS:

FICTION

To Walk the Line (novel), Knopf (New York, NY), 1970.

The Zolta Configuration (novel), Doubleday (New York, NY), 1983.

The Soul of Viktor Tronko (novel), Doubleday (New York, NY), 1987.

Blood Line: Stories of Fathers and Sons, Graywolf (St. Paul, MN), 1988.

NONFICTION

Natural Acts: A Sidelong View of Science and Nature, Schocken (New York, NY), 1985.

The Flight of the Iguana: A Sidelong View of Science and Nature, Delacorte (New York, NY), 1988.

The Song of the Dodo: Island Biogeography in an Age of Extinctions, with maps by wife, Kris Ellingsen, Scribner (New York, NY), 1996.

Wild Thoughts from Wild Places, Scribner (New York, NY), 1998.

The Boilerplate Rhino: Nature in the Eye of the Beholder, Scribner (New York, NY), 2000.

Monster of God: The Man-Eating Predator in the Jungles of History and the Mind, W.W. Norton (New York, NY), 2003.

The Reluctant Mr. Darwin: An Intimate Portrait of Charles Darwin and the Making of His Theory of Evolution, Atlas Books/Norton (New York, NY), 2006.

Contributor to periodicals, including *Rolling Stone* and *Powder.*

Contributor to books, including *Alexis Rockman,* Monacelli Press (New York, NY), 2003.

Author of monthly column, "Natural Acts," for *Outside,* 1981-96.

SIDELIGHTS: Author and naturalist David Quammen contributed a nature column to *Outside* magazine for fifteen years. He has written several books on nature and is also the author of noted fiction works. His first novel was published when he was twenty-two and is based on his experiences working in a Chicago ghetto. *To Walk the Line,* as Quammen described to *CA,* deals with "the birth, growth, and death of a friendship between a white ivy leaguer and a black militant, and is intended to map the gradual convergence of two radically different consciousnesses." *New York Times Book Review* contributor Martin Levin called the doomed relationship between these two characters an "intriguing social paradox;" nevertheless, he believed the portrayal of these characters falls flat. In contrast, John Leonard observed in the *New York Times* that "what distinguishes Mr. Quammen's book is its humor, its lack of self-pity, the electric quality of its prose and a sense of the energy that flows between people, often to destructive effect." The result, concluded Leonard, "rings as true as a knife bounced off steel."

A drastic shift in topic and style marks Quammen's next novel, *The Zolta Configuration,* a political thriller involving the development of the first hydrogen bomb. Quammen includes historical facts and characters, indicating that he "has put in a good deal of research on this book," commented T.J. Binyon in the *Times Literary Supplement.* Even though it "makes use of precise historical details," noted Stanley Ellin in the *New York Times Book Review,* "never for an instant does it give off the musty whiff of scientific treatise. Mr. Quammen's portrayal of actual people involved in making the bomb brings each to life at a touch, so we have a profound emotional stake in them and in their experiences." The critic added that Quammen "is so informed on [the history] and so adept in his presentation of it that the narrative never loses a beat in its drive to an ironic and wholly believable climax."

With his next novel, *The Soul of Viktor Tronko,* Quammen "has leaped to the head of the pack of American thriller writers," asserted *Tribune Books* contributor Alan Cheuse. The novel uses another historical idea for its premise, detailing the CIA's search for a possible Soviet "mole," or infiltrator, within its midst. Although the idea is not new, "Quammen traverses this established terrain with skill, deftly interweaving plots, achingly conveying the ordeal of a 'hostile debriefing,'" commented *Time* reviewer William A. Henry III. *Washington Post* contributor Dennis Drabelle, however, found the author's exposition somewhat confusing: "The novel proceeds via long conversation with retired agents, each of whom insists on depositing an arabesque of background and only then going on to answer [the investiga-

tor's] questions." This technique, wrote Drabelle, "frequently leaves multiple skeins of narrative dangling." Nevertheless, the critic thought *The Soul of Viktor Tronko* is a worthwhile book, for Quammen "writes posh prose" and "depicts violent action . . . with a freshness that old hands might emulate." "Finally," concluded Drabelle, "he solves the riddle of Dmitri [the 'mole'] deftly and surprisingly." William Hood echoed this praise, writing in the *New York Times Book Review* that the novel "is enhanced by [Quammen's] vivid prose, strong characters, and welcome wry humor. Readers will be well advised to pay strict attention—there are clues aplenty, but as in the real, upside-down, secret world of counter-intelligence, there is a certain amount of dissembling; things aren't always what they seem."

Also a writer of short fiction, Quammen has collected some of his work in *Blood Line: Stories of Fathers and Sons;* the three novellas have invited comparisons with Nobel-winning authors Ernest Hemingway and William Faulkner. Explained *Tribune Books* contributor James Idema: "They're old-fashioned yarns, the kind that grab the reader, make him listen to the voices, hold him to the end and then linger in his consciousness. Perhaps even more remarkable is that fact that they are . . . unabashedly derivative." Reviewer Elaine Kendall elaborated in the *Los Angeles Times:* "In style, form and subject matter, [two of the] stories recall the Hemingway of 'In Our Time' and 'My Old Man.' Quammen's prose is not as stark and his imagery is more sensuous, but the bells toll loud and clear in homage." In a third novella, wrote Kendall, "Quammen takes all the celebrated Faulkner mannerisms just one step further. The effect is eerie, as if Faulkner had bequeathed his locale, his characters, and his structure to this contemporary Montana writer, with instructions to continue the work." Even though the stories in *Blood Line* are reminiscent of these authors, the work is "too compelling to dismiss" as imitation, commented Idema. "One is obliged to praise him for the faithfulness with which he has rendered" his stories in the styles of Hemingway and Faulkner. Concluded the critic: "These are at the same time first-rate stories and tours de force of literary assimilation."

While Quammen has garnered praise for his fiction, he is perhaps best known for his writings on nature. Several of his essays on this subject were collected in *Natural Acts: A Sidelong View of Science and Nature.* Quammen is not a professional scientist, yet his work "is sound science since it raises substantive issues about why things are as they are—the nature of nature," stated Bil Gilbert in the *Washington Post Book World.* "*Natural Acts* is much superior to, in fact is not even in the genre of, earnest 'nature' books simply because Quammen is a man of scientific curiosity as well as a writer who does not need nor is inclined to substitute pious . . . cliches for real words or thoughts," added Gilbert. *Christian Science Monitor* reviewer James Kaufmann had a similar take, writing that the author "typically recasts tired scientific phrasings or ideas in funky New Journalistic fashion."

As he does in his fiction, Quammen uses his writing skills to bring his observations of nature to life; *Commonweal* contributor Tom O'Brien remarked that the author "writes in a style at once incisive and graceful, with a sure sense of the ring of English sentences and the value of stunning images." Continued the critic: "Often his essays begin with an anecdote that quickly delivers the feel of nature, or a provocative one-liner that drags a reader into the center of an issue." And these issues need not be earth-shaking to be entertaining, noted *Chicago Tribune* columnist John Husar. "Quammen flames on and on through arcane yet relevant subjects," wrote Husar, "he breathes importance into the little-known nitty-gritty of biology. He describes wondrous places, people, and situations that range from the vitality of rivers to the awesome mysteries of cold." In other words, asserted the critic, "this guy is a great, great outdoors writer."

The Flight of the Iguana: A Sidelong View of Science and Nature, Quammen's second collection of natural history essays, "is even better" than his first, asserted Harry Middleton in the *New York Times Book Review.* Like *Natural Acts,* the essays in *The Flight of the Iguana* are "very funny and very offbeat," remarked *Los Angeles Times* reviewer Lee Dembart; nevertheless, "part way through, the tone and focus shift. The articles become serious," added Dembart, "and Quammen uses science as a way to reflect on other subjects, some political, some philosophical, some just wise ruminations on this and that." Although the author ranges over a variety of subjects, "he writes with effortless control over his material and a quiet passion about it," noted Dembart. Quammen's unorthodox style and personal approach, wrote Middleton, results in "a prose loaded with ideas and emotion that is as thrilling and upsetting as a wild ride on a slightly unsettled roller coaster." Dembart stated that "Quammen likes science for its own sake, but he also likes it for the larger truths it suggests. He works the fringes of science and draws conclusions that are universal."

In another work on science and nature, *The Song of the Dodo: Island Biogeography in an Age of Extinctions,* Quammen describes the creatures he observed in his travels to various islands and discusses the global implications of island biogeography—the science that focuses on where living things live. Quammen asserts that the extinctions of some island species and the adaptations of others provide clues that will aid in understanding what is happening to nature on the planet as a whole, as the spread of industrial and residential development has caused wildlife on the mainlands to live in isolated, island-like enclaves that are unable to support a diverse population of plants and animals. Humanity is dividing up the world, he says, likening this process to cutting a Persian rug into thirty-six pieces: "What does it amount to? Have we got thirty-six nice Persian throw rugs? No. All we're left with is three dozen ragged fragments, each one worthless and commencing to come apart."

Some critics praised Quammen for mixing his ecological warnings with anecdote and travelogue, making the book accessible to a wide audience. "Quammen . . . is one of those writers who can make an academic subject fascinating," wrote James M. Glover in the *Journal of Leisure Research.* "There are profiles of eccentric personalities, conflicts between strong-headed scientists, a murder mystery, and animal stories galore, all built around the central theme." *Christian Century* contributor Debra Bendis noted that Quammen "never forgets to acknowledge his readers . . . . [He] stealthily weaves instruction around and through his travel stories, then adds maps (by wife, Kris Ellingsen) and a glossary. The author respects the reader's limits." In *BioScience,* Sahotra Sarkar lauded *The Song of the Dodo* as "a work in the finest tradition of autobiographical natural history, a tradition largely created in the last century by the great naturalist-travelers," a group that includes Charles Darwin. *New Statesman* reviewer Colin Tudge, though, thought Quammen's liberal use of anecdote is so much sugarcoating: "Quammen has succumbed to the fashionable conceit that 'popular' science has to be diluted with travelogue and soap biography." The book "would be much better without such stuff," Tudge contended.

Tudge did think highly of Quammen's scientific ideas. "In the study of islands lies half of modern biology, and David Quammen captures it all with clarity and excellent scholarship," the critic declared. In *Newsweek,* Sharon Begley applauded Quammen's "lucid explanations of evolutionary biology . . . and of the relationship between the size of an island and the number of species it can support." The latter, she stated, "is now crucial to understanding why wildlife reserves cannot support a replica of the original ecosystem and why extinctions are rolling through even America's national parks." *Nation* contributor Douglas Boucher, however, considered island biogeography less than cutting-edge science, calling it instead "a great idea whose time has passed" and that has not proved particularly valuable in resolving controversies about conservation. "The island concept is not a workable model for continental nature, either biologically or politically," he contended. "It ignores the fact that land outside parks and reserves is not like water around islands, but can be a viable habitat for millions of species. It doesn't distinguish between forms of agriculture and industry that destroy biodiversity and those that offer the possibility of living in harmony with it . . . . The planet is not a string of islands in an inhospitable sea but one biosphere, one civilization, one world. And sooner or later, all its people and pandas and penguins and protozoans will have to be able to live together on it." Sarkar pointed out that there are disagreements among scientists about the usefulness of island biogeography theory in conservation work, and expressed disappointment that Quammen "seems to deliberately avoid taking sides" and "also seems to view biodiversity conservation as a purely scientific problem," ignoring political and economic concerns.

Sarkar concluded, though, that "one book cannot do everything. Meanwhile, what this book does do (i.e., thoughtful popular science with a historical twist), it does very well indeed." Bill McKibben, writing in *Audubon,* called *The Song of the Dodo* "maybe the masterpiece of scientific journalism" and "a heroic achievement." Quammen, McKibben stated, "has given us the information we need to understand the most profound physical forces under way on the face of the earth." He and several other reviewers asserted that in this book Quammen has done an excellent job of underlining the significance of extinctions. *Newsweek* reviewer Begley observed that "it makes us care." And caring need not make one pessimistic, some critics noted. "In Mr. Quammen's hands," wrote Robert Kanigel in the *New York Times Book Review,* "the bad news of species extinction unaccountably uplifts. For it reminds us of nature's sheer, ornery diversity, and why it needs to be preserved. We share in the excitement of a new scientific discipline aborning. By book's end, we glean hints of hope that the future may not be entirely bleak."

Wild Thoughts from Wild Places contains twenty-eight of Quammen's essays culled from his columns and other pieces for *Outside* magazine. His subjects range over a wide variety of topics of note to naturalists, outdoors enthusiasts, sports buffs, and others whose lives regularly intersect with nature and the outdoors. He looks at several newly emerging viruses and the effects they are likely to have on human and animal populations; he considers the malady of cancer; he describes outrageously dangerous kayaking and skiing trips; he covers efforts to create conservation corridors throughout the United States; and he analyzes adaptive characteristics of pigeons that live in urban environments. He is "an often perceptive viewer of the landscape and a persistent interviewer," observed Randy Dykhuis in *Library Journal.* "Quammen's writing is energetic in the extreme, stuffed with information, but also with brash, provoking, indeed wild thoughts," remarked *Commonweal* reviewer Clare Collins, who further noted that "Quammen himself has a rare ability to write with broad appeal on topics ranging from whitewater kayaking to trout fishing to Telemark skiing." Quammen, Collins noted, "uses his exotic subjects as a framework for explaining everything from biodiversity to the physics of fluid dynamics to evolution."

The Boilerplate Rhino: Nature in the Eye of the Beholder, another collection derived from Quammen's *Outside* columns, provides a varied group of reports detailing encounters between humans and animals, "revealing all the gray matter and in-your-face complexities of human and non-human lives," remarked a reviewer in *Whole Earth.* Among his subjects are rattlesnake hunters; devotees of the theory that birds evolved from dinosaurs, and who want to make Tyrannosaurus Rex the official Montana state bird; the complexity and diversity of beetles; and more. Quammen is even willing to address his own shortcomings as a naturalist, admitting that he is afraid of spiders but particularly fond of snakes. The collection of essays "displays yet again how dexterously he fulfilled his monthly mandate" in *Outside* magazine, observed a writer for *Publishers Weekly.*

In *Monster of God: The Man-Eating Predator in the Jungles of History and the Mind* Quammen considers the ecological balance between humans and the existing large predators that can, and sometimes do, kill and eat people. His subjects include Asiatic lions, African and Australian crocodiles, Siberian tigers, and European brown bears. To further understand the place where humans and predators of humans coexist, he traveled to areas of the globe where these animals still live among the farmers, shepherds, hunters, and villagers. There, he talked directly to those who coexist with large predators and who regularly see their majestic beauty as well as their deadly ferocity. "The author recounts these adventures in the wonderfully exuberant, often colloquial yet basically erudite manner that marked his previous books," commented Joseph Losos in the *St. Louis Post-Dispatch.* "He switches from vulgar slang to recondite language easily; he also moves from precise description to abstract philosophizing with the same facility." In addition to the practical aspects of living in the midst of unpredictable meat-eating predators, Quammen also looks at the psychological, mythological, artistic, and spiritual aspects of mankind's long association with creatures that often see humans as just another source of food. He "incisively analyzes tales of our species' encounters with the monstrous from Gilgamesh to the Bible's leviathan to the Alien movies," noted Donna Seaman in *Booklist.*

Quammen's predictions for the future of the big predators is a dim one. By the year 2150, if the human population increases from six billion to eleven billion as expected by that time, Quammen believes that all of the big predators will have been driven extinct, except perhaps for specimens retained in zoos and other types of nature preserves. "We'll have them in zoos, and we'll have them in test tubes," he remarked to interviewer Katharine Mieszkowski on *Salon.com.* "But there will be no place where you can have the experience of walking out through forest and subjecting yourself to the wonderful, terrible, titillating sense that you're a potential prey item for a creature that's bigger and scarier and more majestic than you are." "Earth," Quammen continued, "will be more convenient and safer in the most basic, reductionist sense. It will also be uglier, more boring, and more lonely."

In her review of *Monster of God, Christian Science Monitor* reviewer Pamela S. Turner declared, simply: "Quammen is a superb science writer." A *Kirkus Reviews* critic called the book "Another good and provocative work from Quammen, sure to engage past admirers and earn new ones." His "crisp reportorial immediacy and sobering analysis make for a book that is as powerful and frightening as the animals it chronicles," stated a reviewer in *Publishers Weekly. Monster of God,* commented *American Scientist* reviewer James Sanderson, "should push us all into action, not simply to prevent the impoverishment of the world we are safeguarding for future generations, but to enrich our own world while there's still time."

In *The Reluctant Mr. Darwin: An Intimate Portrait of Charles Darwin and the Making of His Theory of Evolu-*

tion, Quammen focuses on the life of the famed naturalist following his prodigious voyage of discovery on the Beagle, and after he had married his cousin Emma Wedgwood and settled down near London. Quammen delves into Darwin's voluminous correspondence from this time period, noting that the great naturalist was averse to socializing but was eager to communicate with fellow scientists. He describes Darwin's reluctance to publish his theory of evolution, and notes how Darwin plunged into detailed scientific work of classifying barnacles, rigorous natural science designed to bolster his credibility when the time did come to present his ideas on evolution. Critically, Quammen relates how Darwin received correspondence from a young colleague, Alfred Russell Wallace, who had independently managed to derive many of the key points of Darwin's evolutionary theory. With the capable Wallace so close to unwittingly snatching away his treasured scientific work, Darwin was compelled to publish his theory in order to retain priority on its discovery. In addition, Quammen recounts Darwin's final years and explores the status of the theory of evolution since it was initially conceived. A *Kirkus Reviews* writer named the biography "A first-rate look at the English naturalist's career after the Beagle," and also concluded that Quammen's "portrait of the great man and his magnum opus is affectionate and well-paced." Quammen, remarked *Booklist* reviewer Gilbert Taylor, "proves an informative, often wry guide to Darwin's life and continuing influence."

BIOGRAPHICAL AND CRITICAL SOURCES:

BOOKS

Quammen, David, *The Song of the Dodo: Island Biogeography in an Age of Extinctions,* Scribner (New York, NY), 1996.

PERIODICALS

American Scholar, autumn, 2003, Jonathan Cook, review of *Monster of God: The Man-Eating Predator in the Jungles of History and the Mind,* p. 144.
American Scientist, January-February, 2004, James Sanderson, "Something to Chew On," review of *Monster of God,* p. 88; November-December, 2006, Bettyann Holtzmann Kevles, "On the Perils of Publishing," review of *The Reluctant Mr. Darwin: An Intimate Portrait of Charles Darwin and the Making of His Theory of Evolution,* p. 564.

Audubon, March-April, 1996, Bill McKibben, review of *The Song of the Dodo,* p. 123.

BioScience, February, 1997, Sahotra Sarkar, review of *The Song of the Dodo,* p. 124.

Booklist, July, 2003, Donna Seaman, review of *Monster of God,* p. 1853; December 1, 2003, Donna Seaman, "Top Ten Sci-Tech Books," review of *Monster of God,* p. 641; January 1, 2004, review of *Monster of God,* p. 775; June 1, 2006, Gilbert Taylor, review of *The Reluctant Mr. Darwin,* p. 29.

Chicago Tribune, November 6, 1985, John Husar, "*Natural Acts* Offers Delightful New Insights," p. 7.

Christian Century, September 24, 1997, Debra Bendis, review of *The Song of the Dodo,* p. 845.

Christian Science Monitor, May 29, 1985, James Kaufmann, review of *Natural Acts: A Sidelong View of Science and Nature,* p. 21; September 18, 2003, Pamela S. Turner, "In the Forest of the Night," review of *Monster of God.*

Commonweal, June 5, 1987, Tom O'Brien, review of *Natural Acts,* p. 364; May 22, 1998, Clare Collins, review of *Wild Thoughts from Wild Places,* p. 22.

Entertainment Weekly, July 28, 2006, Wook Kim, review of *The Reluctant Mr. Darwin,* p. 69.

Field & Stream, December 1, 2003, "Now Read This," David E. Petzal, review of *Monster of God,* p. 57.

Hollywood Reporter, September 8, 2003, Gregory McNamee, review of *Monster of God,* p. 13.

Houston Chronicle, July 28, 2006, Fritz Lanham, review of *The Reluctant Mr. Darwin.*

Journal of Leisure Research, fall, 1997, James M. Glover, review of *The Song of the Dodo,* p. 476.

Kirkus Reviews, June 15, 2003, review of *Monster of God,* p. 849; May 15, 2006, review of *The Reluctant Mr. Darwin,* p. 510.

Library Journal, January, 1998, Randy Dykhuis, review of *Wild Thoughts from Wild Places,* p. 136; August, 2003, Edell Schaefer, review of *Monster of God,* p. 126; July 1, 2006, Gloria Maxwell, review of *The Reluctant Mr. Darwin,* p. 105.

Los Angeles Times, March 1, 1988, Elaine Kendall, "Fathers and Sons: Rites of Inheritance," p. 6; June 24, 1988, Lee Dembart, review of *The Flight of the Iguana,* p. 8.

Nation, May 20, 1996, Douglas Boucher, review of *The Song of the Dodo,* p. 30.

Natural History, September, 2003, Laurence A. Marschall, review of *Monster of God,* p. 60.

New Statesman, August 30, 1996, Colin Tudge, review of *The Song of the Dodo,* p. 45.

Newsweek, May 6, 1996, Sharon Begley, review of *The Song of the Dodo,* p. 80.

New York Times, November 13, 1970, John Leonard, review of *To Walk the Line,* p. 35.

New York Times Book Review, November 15, 1970, Martin Levin, review of *To Walk the Line,* p. 68; July 3, 1983, Stanley Ellin, review of *The Zolta Configuration,* p. 8; April 21, 1985, Tom Ferrell, review of *Natural Acts,* p. 39; September 14, 1986, Patricia T. O'Conner, review of *Natural Acts;* July 12, 1987, William Hood, review of *The Soul of Viktor Tronko,* p. 12; June 26, 1988, Harry Middleton, review of *The Flight of the Iguana,* p. 39; April 21, 1996, Robert Kanigel, review of *The Song of the Dodo,* p. 11; August 27, 2006, Adrian Desmond, "The Cautious Evolutionist," review of *The Reluctant Mr. Darwin.*

OnEarth, fall, 2003, Tim Folger, "Where the Wild Things Are: As the World's Big Predators Slip toward Extinction, We're Learning That It's Lonely at the Top," review of *Monster of God,* p. 38.

Publishers Weekly, March 27, 2000, review of *The Boilerplate Rhino: Nature in the Eye of the Beholder,* p. 58; June 23, 2003, review of *Monster of God,* p. 57; September 1, 2003, Ann Geracimos, "David Quammen: In Praise of Man-Eaters," interview with David Quammen, p. 58; April 17, 2006, review of *The Reluctant Mr. Darwin,* p. 175.

SciTech Book News, September, 2006, review of *The Reluctant Mr. Darwin.*

Seattle Post-Intelligencer, October 27, 2003, John Marshall, "A Moment With . . . David Quammen, Author."

Smithsonian, April, 1996, John P. Wiley, Jr., review of *The Song of the Dodo,* p. 130.

St. Louis Post Dispatch, October 19, 2003, Joseph Losos, review of *Monster of God.*

Time, August 17, 1987, William A. Henry, III, review of *The Soul of Viktor Tronko,* p. 64.

Times Literary Supplement, February 15, 1985, T.J. Binyon, review of *The Zolta Configuration,* p. 179.

Tribune Books (Chicago, IL), July 5, 1987, Alan Cheuse, review of *The Soul of Victor Tronko,* p. 9; January 17, 1988, James Idema, review of *Blood Line: Stories of Fathers and Sons,* p. 7.

Washington Post, August 4, 1987, Dennis Drabelle, review of *The Soul of Viktor Tronko,* p. D03.

Washington Post Book World, March 31, 1985, Bil Gilbert, review of *Natural Acts,* p. 9.

Whole Earth, fall, 2000, review of *The Boilerplate Rhino,* p. 24.

ONLINE

Salon.com, http://www.salon.com/ (September 24, 2003), Katharine Mieszkowski, "Just Another Flavor of Meat," interview with David Quammen.*

R

REES, Nigel 1944-
  (Nigel Thomas Rees)

PERSONAL: Born June 5, 1944, in Liverpool, England; son of Stewart and Adeline Rees; married Susan Bates, May 6, 1978. *Education:* New College, Oxford, B.A. (with honors), 1967, M.A., 1970.

ADDRESSES: Home and office—Banbury, Oxfordshire, England. *E-mail*—nigel.rees@btinternet.com.

CAREER: Freelance television and radio reporter and producer, 1966-71; British Broadcasting Corp., London, England, actor in radio comedy shows *Week Ending,* 1971-76, and *The Burkiss Way,* 1976-80, presenter of radio programs *Twenty-Four Hours,* 1972-79, *Kaleidoscope,* 1973-75, *Today* and *Between the Lines,* both 1976-78, *Quote . . . Unquote,* 1976—, *Where Were You in '62?,* 1983-84, and *Stop Press,* 1984-86, presenter of television series *Cabbages and Kings,* 1979, *Amoebas to Zebras,* 1985-87, and *Challenge of the South,* 1987-88; *"Quote . . . Unquote" Newsletter,* publisher and editor, 1992—. Lecturer and public speaker.

WRITINGS:

Quote . . . Unquote, Allen & Unwin (London, England), 1978, St. Martin's Press (New York, NY), 1979.

Graffiti 1, Allen & Unwin (London, England), 1979.

Graffiti Lives O.K., Allen & Unwin (London, England), 1979.

Quote . . . Unquote 2, Allen & Unwin (London, England), 1980.

Graffiti 2, Allen & Unwin (London, England), 1980.

Very Interesting . . . but Stupid! A Book of Catchphrases from the World of Entertainment, Allen & Unwin (London, England), 1980.

Graffiti 3, Allen & Unwin (London, England), 1981.

Eavesdroppings, Allen & Unwin (London, England), 1981.

The Graffiti File, Allen & Unwin (London, England), 1981.

Graffiti 4, Allen & Unwin (London, England), 1982.

Slogans, Allen & Unwin (London, England), 1982.

Quote . . . Unquote 3, Allen & Unwin (London, England), 1983.

Word of Mouth, Allen & Unwin (London, England), 1983.

The Nigel Rees Book of Slogans and Catchphrases, Allen & Unwin (London, England), 1984.

The Joy of Cliches, Macdonald and Co. (London, England), 1984.

Sayings of the Century, Allen & Unwin (London, England), 1984.

The Gift of the Gab, Macdonald and Co. (London, England), 1985.

(With Vernon Noble) *A Who's Who of Nicknames,* Allen & Unwin (London, England), 1985.

Graffiti 5, Allen & Unwin (London, England), 1986.

Nudge, Nudge, Wink, Wink: A Quotebook of Love and Sex, Javelin (New York, NY), 1986.

A Dictionary of Twentieth-Century Quotations, Fontana (London, England), 1987.

Why Do We Say . . .?, Blandford (London, England), 1987, published as *The Cassell Dictionary of Word and Phrase Origins,* Cassell (London, England), 1992, published as *Cassell's Dictionary of Word and Phrase Origins,* Cassell (London, England), 2002.

The Newsmakers (fiction), Headline (London, England), 1987.

Talent (fiction), Headline (London, England), 1988.

A Family Matter (fiction), Headline (London, England), 1989.

Why Do We Quote . . .?, Blandford (London, England), 1989.

A Dictionary of Popular Phrases, Bloomsbury (London, England), 1990, published as *The Phrase that Launched 1,000 Ships,* Dell (New York, NY), 1991.

Dictionary of Phrase and Allusion, Bloomsbury (London, England), 1991, published as *Dictionary of Phrase and Fable,* Paragon (New York, NY), 1993.

Best Behaviour: A Complete Guide to Manners in the 1990s, Bloomsbury (London, England), 1992, published as *Guide to Good Manners,* 1993, published as *Good Manners,* Bloomsbury (London, England), 1994.

Politically Correct Phrasebook, Bloomsbury (London, England), 1993.

Epitaphs: Dictionary of Grave Epigrams and Memorial Eloquence, Bloomsbury (London, England), 1993.

Dictionary of Modern Quotations, Chambers, 1993.

Letter Writing: A Guide to Personal and Professional Correspondence, Bloomsbury (London, England), 1994.

Book of Humorous Anecdotes, Guinness (Glasgow, Scotland), 1994.

Brewer's Quotations: A Phrase and Fable Dictionary, Cassell (London, England), 1994.

As We Say in Our House: A Book of Family Sayings, Robson (London, England), 1994.

Dictionary of Jokes, Guinness (Glasgow, Scotland), 1995.

Dictionary of Catchphrases, Cassell (London, England), 1995.

Phrases and Sayings, Bloomsbury (London, England), 1995.

Dictionary of Cliches, Cassell (London, England), 1996.

Dictionary of Slogans, HarperCollins (New York, NY), 1997.

Companion to Quotations, Cassell (London, England), 1997, published as *Mark My Words,* Barnes & Noble (New York, NY), 2002.

Dictionary of Humorous Quotations, Cassell (London, England), 1998.

The Cassell Dictionary of Anecdotes, Cassell (London, England), 1999.

Cassell's Movie Quotations, Cassell (London, England), 2000.

Cassell's Humorous Quotations, Cassell (London, England), 2001.

Oops, Pardon, Mrs Arden! An Embarrassment of Domestic Catchphrases, Robson (London, England), 2001.

A Word in Your Shell-Like Ear: 6,000 Curious and Everyday Phrases Explained, Collins (Glasgow, Scotland), 2004.

Cassell's Dictionary of Catchphrases, Cassell (London, England), 2005.

I Told You I Was Sick: A Grave Book of Curious Epitaphs, Weidenfeld & Nicolson (London, England), 2005.

Brewer's Famous Quotations: 5,000 Quotations and the Stories behind Them, Weidenfeld & Nicolson (London, England), 2006.

A Man about a Dog: 3,000 Figleaves of Speech, Collins (Glasgow, Scotland), 2006.

Contributor to magazines and newspapers.

BIOGRAPHICAL AND CRITICAL SOURCES:

PERIODICALS

Times Literary Supplement, February 1, 1985, Geoffrey Marshall, review of *Sayings of the Century,* p. 114.

ONLINE

Welcome to the Quote . . . Unquote Website, http://btwebworld.com/quote-unquote (February 10, 2007).

*   *   *

REES, Nigel Thomas
See REES, Nigel

*   *   *

REES-JONES, Deryn

PERSONAL: Female. Education: University of Wales, University College of North Wales, Bangor, 1986-90, B.A. (with honors), M.A.; Birkbeck College, London, Ph.D., 1995.

ADDRESSES: Office—School of English, Modern Languages Bldg., University of Liverpool, Chatham St., Liverpool L69 England.

CAREER: Liverpool Hope University College, Liverpool, England, former reader in poetry; University of Liverpool, Liverpool, lecturer in English.

AWARDS, HONORS: Eric Gregory Award, 1993; writers' award, Arts Council of England, 1996; named Next Generation Poet, 2004.

WRITINGS:

The Memory Tray (poetry), Seren (Bridgend, Wales), 1993, Dufour (Chester Springs, PA), 1994.
Signs round a Dead Body (poetry), Seren (Bridgend, Wales), 1998.
Carol Ann Duffy, Northcote House (Plymouth, England), 1998, 2nd edition, 2001.
(Editor, with Alison Mark) *Contemporary Women Poets: Reading/Writing/Practice,* St. Martin's Press (New York, NY), 2000.
Quiver (poetry), Seren (Bridgend, Wales), 2004.
(Editor) *Consorting with Angels: Essays on Modern Women Poets,* Bloodaxe Books (Tarset, England), 2005.

Poetry represented in anthologies, including *Seven Poets and a City,* edited by Peter Robinson, Liverpool University, 1996.

BIOGRAPHICAL AND CRITICAL SOURCES:

PERIODICALS

Times Literary Supplement, April 23, 1999, Richard Tyrrell, review of *Signs round a Dead Body,* p. 26.

*   *   *

REICH, Christopher 1961-

PERSONAL: Born November 12, 1961, in Tokyo, Japan; son of Willie Wolfgang and Mildred Reich; married Susanne Wohlwend, July, 1994; children: Noelle. *Education:* Georgetown University, B.S.F.S; University of Texas at Austin, M.B.A.

ADDRESSES: Home—Austin, TX.

CAREER: Writer and novelist. Union Bank of Switzerland, Geneva and Zurich, portfolio manager, then Mergers and Acquisitions staff member, until 1991; Giorgio Beverly Hills Timepieces, Neuchatel, Switzerland, chief executive officer, 1992-95; writer, 1995—.

WRITINGS:

NOVELS

Numbered Account, Delacorte (New York, NY), 1998.
The Runner, Delacorte (New York, NY), 2000.
The First Billion, Delacorte (New York, NY), 2002.
The Devil's Banker, Delacorte (New York, NY), 2003.
The Patriot's Club, Delacorte (New York, NY), 2005.

SIDELIGHTS: Christopher Reich, who was born in Tokyo, Japan, and raised in Los Angeles, worked in banking before he committed himself to a writing career. Working for Union Bank of Switzerland, Reich started as a portfolio manager in Zurich and worked his way up the ladder to the bank's department of mergers and acquisitions in Geneva before leaving the business in 1991.

Reich's experience in high-level, sophisticated banking provided him with the background for his debut novel, *Numbered Account.* In this thriller Nick Neumann, a twenty-eight-year-old ex-Marine, leaves his beautiful fiancé and a budding career at Morgan Stanley on Wall Street in favor of a job at the United Swiss Bank in Zurich, Switzerland. The job gives Nick a chance to solve the mysterious murder of his father, Alexander Neumann. The murder of Nick's father occurred seventeen years before in Los Angeles, while Alexander was working for the United Swiss Bank.

Tracking down his father's killer proves complicated for Nick. Things begin to unravel when the managers of a large, numbered bank account in the name of one "the Pasha" begin to leave the company: one experiences a nervous breakdown, one defects to a rival company, and another suffers an untimely death. Eventually the U.S. Drug Enforcement Agency visits Nick to discuss the account, and Nick finds himself sucked into a swirl of Middle East terrorism, nuclear weapons, and narcotics trafficking.

Reich uses the secretive, cut-throat world of Swiss banking to create what *Denver Post* contributor Howard M. Kaplan called "a taut, interesting story." According to Kaplan, *Numbered Account* is "presented tautly, intricately and intensely with intelligence, chilling detail, suspense and intrigue."

In his third novel, *The First Billion,* Reich tells the story of John "Jett" Gallavan, a broker who seeks to reestablish his firm after the technology crash has nearly destroyed it. A former fighter pilot, Jett soon finds himself in the former Soviet bloc looking to find out what happened to his partner who disappeared after going there to investigate a promising company for investment. Jett soon runs afoul of gangsters and the FBI. Mary Frances Wilkens, writing in *Booklist,* commented: "If you want high-concept espionage, it doesn't get much better than this." A *Publishers Weekly* contributor noted the novel's "rather intriguing setup." Jeff Ayers, writing in the *Library Journal,* wrote that the novel "has its compelling moments."

Reich's next novel, *The Devil's Banker,* features forensic accountant Adam Chapel and his partner Sarah Churchill as they investigate a bombing in Paris that killed four government agents and a militant who was known to be carrying 500,000 dollars for a jihadist group. Alynda Wheat, writing in *Entertainment Weekly,* called *The Devil's Banker* a "smart, fast-paced read." A *Publishers Weekly* contributor wrote: "Reich has a lot of fascinating financial lore to pass along" and also noted the novel's "fast-paced plotting and relentless action." Ronnie H. Terpening commented in the *Library Journal:* "Reich's forte, describing the world of high finance, is amply demonstrated in this . . . international thriller."

Former tough guy Thomas Bolden, once known as "Tommy B," has come a long way as a Wall Street businessman in Reich's novel *The Patriot's Club.* When Bolden is kidnapped, he ends up being released after his kidnappers discover that he has no knowledge about certain information that they are seeking, although Bolden still has no idea what they wanted. Before long, despite his freedom, Bolden is being hunted down and has to turn to his roots on the mean streets to survive as he uncovers a diabolical secret that goes back two centuries and is leading him to a political scandal. *Booklist* contributor Mary Frances Wilkens called the novel "a first-rate, high-concept thriller that will leave readers breathless and cheering for Bolden to pull

through." A *Kirkus Reviews* contributor referred to the novel as "one part *North by Northwest,* one part *The Da Vinci Code* and one part *American Treasure.*"

BIOGRAPHICAL AND CRITICAL SOURCES:

PERIODICALS

Booklist, July, 2002, Mary Frances Wilkens, review of *The First Billion,* p. 1798; June 1, 2005, Mary Frances Wilkens, review of *The Patriot's Club,* p. 1713.

Denver Post, March 8, 1998, Howard M. Kaplan, review of *Numbered Account.*

Entertainment Weekly, August 22, 2003, Alynda Wheat, review of *The Devil's Banker,* p. 135.

Kirkus Reviews, June 15, 2005, review of *The Patriot's Club,* p. 662.

Library Journal, August, 2002, Jeff Ayers, review of *The First Billion,* p. 145; August, 2003, Ronnie H. Terpening, review of *The Devil's Banker,* p. 135.

Publishers Weekly, July 8, 2002, review of *The First Billion,* p. 30; July 28, 2003, review of *The Devil's Banker,* p. 79; June 13, 2005, review of *The Patriot's Club,* p. 32.*

* * *

REICH, Susanna 1954-

PERSONAL: Born April 10, 1954, in New York, NY; daughter of Haskell A. (a physicist) and Nancy B. (a musicologist) Reich; married Gary Golio (an artist, children's book author, and social worker), May 26, 1980; children: Laurel. *Education:* Attended Bennington College, 1971-73; New York University, B.F.A., 1976; Laban/Bartenieff Institute of Movement Studies, certificate, 1981; studied at American Ballet Theatre School and Royal Academy of Dancing, London; also attended University of Hawaii at Manoa. *Hobbies and other interests:* Hiking, swimming, gardening, travel, art.

ADDRESSES: Home and office—Ossining, NY.

CAREER: Dancer, choreographer, and teacher of modern dance at Laban/Bartenieff Institute for Movement Studies and Dance Notation Bureau, between 1977 and 1986; floral designer, 1986-88; Flowers by Susanna, owner and floral designer, 1988-98; children's book author, 1994—. Ossining Schools Arts Advocates, member of executive board, 1996-98; Westchester Dance Council, president, 1981-83; former dance teacher in Westchester County, NY; former member of modern dance companies.

MEMBER: Society of Children's Book Writers and Illustrators (member of New York regional committee), PEN.

AWARDS, HONORS: Notices for *Clara Schumann: Piano Virtuoso* include Orbis Pictus Honor Book of National Council of Teacher of English, Nonfiction Honor List, *Voice of Youth Advocates,* Washington Irving Children's Choice Honor Book, and citations among "notable books" and "best books for young adults," American Library Association, "best books of the year," *School Library Journal,* "100 titles for reading and sharing" and "best books for the teen age," New York Public Library, "best children's books of the year," Bank Street College, and "notable social studies trade book," Children's Book Council and National Council of Social Studies Teachers; International Latino Book Award and citations among "top ten arts books for youth," *Booklist,* and "100 titles for reading and sharing," New York Public Library, all for *José! Born to Dance: The Story of José Limón.*

WRITINGS:

Clara Schumann: Piano Virtuoso (juvenile), Clarion Books (New York, NY), 1999.
José! Born to Dance: The Story of José Limón (juvenile), illustrated by Raúl Colón, Simon & Schuster (New York, NY), 2005.
Penelope Bailey Takes the Stage (juvenile novel), Marshall Cavendish (Tarrytown, NY), 2006.

Contributor to periodicals, including *Bride's* and *American Dance Guild Newsletter.*

SIDELIGHTS: Susanna Reich once told *CA:* "Writing children's books is my third career in the arts. I was born in New York and raised in Hastings-on-Hudson. I grew up surrounded by music, but my response to music was different from Clara Schumann's: when I heard music, I wanted to dance!

"My passion from an early age was ballet, which I began to study at the age of seven. After stints at the American Ballet Theatre School and the Royal Academy of Dancing in London, England, my focus shifted to modern dance. I received a Bachelor of Fine Arts degree from Tisch School of the Arts at New York University and, after graduation, I danced with several modern dance companies. Later I did graduate work in dance ethnology at the University of Hawaii and studied and taught Laban Movement Analysis.

"In 1986 I stopped dancing, and for the next twelve years I worked as a floral designer, specializing in weddings. My business, Flowers by Susanna, was the official florist for Lyndhurst, the historic estate in Tarrytown that is a property of the National Trust for Historic Preservation. Among the special occasions I designed were Julia Child's eightieth birthday party and dinners for five prime ministers and for the emperor and empress of Japan.

"My writing career began in the early nineties with articles on floral design, which were published in national magazines. Later I began experimenting with picture book texts. I learned from librarians, teachers, and editors of the need for biographies of women for children. My mother, a musicologist, suggested Clara Schumann, and I began to work on a book.

"As I learned more about Clara, I became convinced that her story would appeal to children. She was an extraordinary woman, one of the great musicians of the nineteenth century. This was a time when very few women had public lives. Clara was a child prodigy, but her importance went way beyond that. She stood up to her father to marry the man she loved (the composer Robert Schumann), championed Robert's work when he was unknown, and continued her career after his mental illness and death. Imagine being a world-class pianist *and* a single mother to seven children!

"I believe that dance, floral design, and writing have much in common. The principles of all art forms are the same. If you are creative in one art form, you can use that creativity in other art forms. The same principles of balance and structure, form, and composition apply, and I use the discipline I learned as a dancer every day.

"I am happiest, though, with my latest career. Writing for kids presents a particular kind of challenge. First you have to see with the eyes of a child, to capture a child's sense of discovery, with its wonders, terrors, and excitement. Then you have to find the right word, the perfect sentence structure, the simplest way to express complex thoughts. I love the challenge of it.

"I am interested in writing biographies about artists of all kinds. I am especially drawn to exploring the relationship between an artist's life and his or her creative work."

More recently, Reich added: "I returned to my first love in my picture book, *José! Born to Dance: The Story of José Limón.* It is a biography (for readers aged five to nine) of the Mexican-American modern dancer and choreographer. In compressing José's story into a picture-book-length manuscript, my aim was to show how the sights and sounds of his childhood in Mexico and his experiences as an immigrant child were shaped into art.

"My first novel is *Penelope Bailey Takes the Stage.* In taking the leap to fiction, I combined my love of research and interest in nineteenth-century women's history and dance history with an understanding of what it feels like to be a child who yearns for the spotlight. In this book, for kids aged nine to fourteen, set in 1889 San Francisco, Penelope's strait-laced aunt will do everything in her power to thwart the girl's ambition to become an actress. But when Penelope is befriended by Isabelle Grey—a character based on the famous dancer Isadora Duncan—the young actress must decide how far she is willing to go to follow her dream.

"My next book will be a biography of the artist George Catlin. The paintings he did of American Indians in the 1830s are well known; his dramatic life story is not. It will be a tale full of travel and adventure. I call it my 'boy book,' but I hope both boys *and* girls will enjoy it."

BIOGRAPHICAL AND CRITICAL SOURCES:

PERIODICALS

Booklist, August, 1999, GraceAnne A. DeCandido, review of *Clara Schumann: Piano Virtuoso,* p. 2042; March 15, 2000, review of *Clara Schumann,* p. 1359; August, 2005, Carolyn Phelan, review of

José! Born to Dance: The Story of José Limón, p. 1965; May 15, 2006, Anne O'Malley, review of *Penelope Bailey Takes the Stage,* p. 45.
Bulletin of the Center for Children's Books, May, 1999, review of *Clara Schumann,* p. 326; September, 2005, Maggie Hommel, review of *José! Born to Dance,* p. 39.
El Paso Times, May 9, 1999, review of *Clara Schumann,* p. 5F.
Horn Book, March-April, 1999, Susan P. Bloom, review of *Clara Schumann,* p. 229.
Hungry Mind Review, summer, 1999, review of *Clara Schumann,* p. 43.
Kirkus Reviews, March 15, 1999, review of *Clara Schumann,* p. 455; July 1, 2005, review of *José! Born to Dance,* p. 742; April 1, 2006, review of *Penelope Bailey Takes the Stage,* p. 355.
Riverbank Review, fall, 1999, review of *Clara Schumann,* p. 42.
School Library Journal, April, 1999, Carol Fazioli, review of *Clara Schumann,* p. 154; October, 2005, Susan Oliver, review of *José! Born to Dance,* p. 144.
Voice of Youth Advocates, April, 2000, review of *Clara Schumann,* p. 64; August, 2000, review of *Clara Schumann,* p. 166; April, 2006, Debbie Clifford, review of *Penelope Bailey Takes the Stage,* p. 50.
Washington Post Book World, July 9, 2006, Elizabeth Ward, review of *Penelope Bailey Takes the Stage,* p. 11.

ONLINE

Susanna Reich: Children's Book Author, http://www.susannareich.com (March 9, 2007).

*   *   *

RESTON, James Barrett, Jr.
    See RESTON, James B., Jr.

*   *   *

RESTON, James B., Jr. 1941-
    (James Barrett Reston, Jr.)

PERSONAL: Born March 8, 1941, in New York, NY; son of James Barrett (a journalist) and Sarah Jane (a journalist) Reston; married Denise Brender Leary, June 12, 1971; children: three. *Education:* Attended Oxford

University, 1961-62; University of North Carolina at Chapel Hill, B.A., 1963. *Hobbies and other interests:* Woodcrafting on a lathe.

ADDRESSES: *Home*—Chevy Chase, MD. *Agent*—Timothy Seldes, Russell & Volkening, 50 W. 29th St., New York, NY 10001.

CAREER: Writer and journalist. U.S. Department of the Interior, Washington, DC, speech writer for Secretary of the Interior Morris Udall, 1964-65; *Chicago Daily News,* Chicago, IL, reporter, 1964-65; University of North Carolina at Chapel Hill, lecturer in creative writing, 1971-81; Woodrow Wilson International Center for Scholars, Washington, DC, senior fellow. Also served as a fellow at the American Academy in Rome and a scholar in residence at the Library of Congress. *Military service:* U.S. Army, Military Intelligence, 1965-68; became sergeant.

MEMBER: Authors Guild, Authors League of America, PEN, Dramatists Guild.

AWARDS, HONORS: Dupont-Columbia Award, and Prix Italia (Venice), both 1982, both for *Father Cares: The Last of Jonestown;* National Endowment for the Arts grant, 1982; Valley Forge Award, 1985, for *Sherman's March and Vietnam.*

WRITINGS:

FICTION

To Defend, to Destroy (novel), Norton (New York, NY), 1971.
The Knock at Midnight (novel), Norton (New York, NY), 1975.

NONFICTION

The Amnesty of John David Herndon, McGraw (New York, NY), 1973.
(With Frank Mankiewicz) *Perfectly Clear: Nixon from Whittier to Watergate,* Quadrangle (New York, NY), 1973.
The Innocence of Joan Little: A Southern Mystery, Quadrangle (New York, NY), 1977.

Sherman, the Peacemaker (play), first produced in Chapel Hill, NC, by the Playmakers Repertory, 1979.
Our Father Who Art in Hell: The Life and Death of Jim Jones, Quadrangle (New York, NY), 1981.
Father Cares: The Last of Jonestown (radio documentary), first aired on National Public Radio, May, 1981.
Eighty-eight Seconds in Greensboro (documentary; first aired on PBS-TV's *Frontline* series, 1983), WGBH Transcripts, 1983.
Jonestown Express (play), first produced in Providence, RI, by Trinity Square Repertory Company, May 22, 1984.
Sherman's March and Vietnam, Macmillan (New York, NY), 1985.
The Real Stuff (documentary), first aired on PBS-TV's *Frontline,* 1987.
The Mission of Discovery (documentary), first aired on PBS-TV, 1988.
The Lone Star: The Life of John Connally, Harper (New York, NY), 1989.
Collision at Home Plate: The Lives of Pete Rose and Bart Giamatti, Edward Burlingame (New York, NY), 1991.
Galileo: A Life, HarperCollins (New York, NY), 1994.
The Last Apocalypse: Europe at the Year 1000 A.D., Doubleday (New York, NY), 1998.
Warriors of God: Richard the Lionheart and Saladin in the Third Crusade, Doubleday (New York, NY), 2001.
Dogs of God: Columbus, the Inquisition, and the Defeat of the Moors, Doubleday, (New York, NY), 2005.
Fragile Innocence: A Father's Memoir of His Daughter's Courageous Journey, Harmony Books (New York, NY), 2006.

Scriptwriter for David Frost, *The Nixon Interviews,* 1976-77. Contributor of articles to *New Yorker, National Geographic, Saturday Review, New York Times Magazine, Washington Post Magazine, Omni, Esquire, New York Times Book Review, Time,* and other periodicals. Regular fiction reviewer, *Chronicle of Higher Education,* 1976-77. Books have been translated into twelve foreign languages.

ADAPTATIONS: *Father Cares: The Last of Jonestown* was adapted as a sound recording by National Public Radio (Washington, DC), 1981; *Collision at Home Plate* has been optioned for film.

SIDELIGHTS: American author and journalist James B. Reston, Jr., writes both fiction and nonfiction, sometimes combining both. Plays, novels, biographies, and television documentaries are among the various formats categorizing his larger works. For his subjects, Reston often draws from history's major socio-political events and figures, from President Richard Nixon to the crusading leaders of the first millennium. He commonly addresses destructive or warring elements of society and has repeatedly presented history as a vivid story. Reviewing Reston's book *Warriors of God: Richard the Lionheart and Saladin in the Third Crusade,* an *Economist* contributor stated: "Well aware that war makes for a rattling story, he devotes his gift for words to the construction of a thrill narrative, unashamedly infused with what he calls 'elemental romance.' His heroes are caricatures whose personality traits transcend the facts." While critics have found this style riveting, not all have appreciated his interpretation of facts and infusion of fictional elements.

Winning access to a series of recordings of the Jonestown colony's proceedings, Reston explores the Jonestown mass suicide-murder of 1978 in three different forms: as a documentary on public radio; in a book-length study of Jim Jones's commune; and in a semi-fictionalized play. While Peter Schrag faulted the book as "flawed both by uncertain purpose and by an excessive tendency to . . . speculations of various obvious sorts," he admitted in the *Nation* that the tape transcriptions are invaluable and the "book makes clear how much of a tall tale Jonestown really was." Reston's play *Jonestown Express* conveys this same idea, as Richard Zoglin suggested in *Newsweek:* "At a time when dramatists are shying away from 'big' social issues . . ., [in *Jonestown Express*] the message comes through with clarity and power: it could happen again; it could happen here."

In *Sherman's March and Vietnam,* Reston "unearths unusual and thoughtful metaphorical parallels between William Tecumseh Sherman's way of war [during the U.S. Civil War] and the conduct of the war in Vietnam," wrote Brian Burns in the *Los Angeles Times Book Review. Washington Post Book World* contributor Russell F. Weigley related: "By breaking down one of the major limits restraining the violence of war, Reston contends, Sherman accustomed American soldiers to regarding such limits lightly. [Sherman's march] pointed the way to subsequent, larger violations, destroying lives as well as property." In pursuing this theory, the author "traces Sherman's march, seeking to find out what the man was like and to measure his impact on the ethics of modern war," noted Stephen W. Sears in the *New York Times Book Review.*

In addition, Reston contrasts the resolutions of the two wars, pointing out that while dissenters in the Civil War were given amnesty, neither side involved in the Vietnam debate was given a substantial resolution. Sears found this portion of Reston's account, which "examines why a dozen years after the Paris peace accords . . . the wounds of the Vietnam era are still unhealed," convincing. Weigley likewise noted that "some of the most eloquent passages of Reston's book return to searching the Civil War for possible guidance toward escaping the divisive emotional legacy of Vietnam." While the critic faulted the author for "indulg[ing] in ambivalence and complexity," he noted that *Sherman's March and Vietnam* is "stimulating," for "the lasting damage that Sherman perpetrated against restraint in war is a theme worth emphasizing."

Reston looks further back in history for *The Last Apocalypse: Europe at the Year 1000 A.D.,* which portrays major factors in Europe's transition into a ruling Christian civilization. Various factions, among them individual kingdoms, Vikings, barbarians, and Moors, were at large in Europe; and in the years leading into the second millennium, they were being destroyed or conquered and converted to Christianity. The mass social changes occurring, rather than any one cataclysmic event, created an apocalypse, according to Reston, who openly used elements of fiction to give readers his history lesson. "Clearly, while Reston is chronicling the overall Christian triumph, he also is mourning many of the cultures that were lost," wrote David Crumm in a *Knight-Ridder/Tribune New Service* review. "It's often difficult to determine whether Reston is giving us verifiable facts or a slice of literary lore. In either case, he has an eye for unforgettable detail." Reston uses "a breezy magazine style that hits the highlights of history," assessed Crumm. "He lays out scores of colorful anecdotes and sprinkles them with a dry wit." Although *Atlanta Journal-Constitution* reviewer Steven Harvey also found the book to be a page-turner, the critic felt Reston's book was too heavily weighted in gory details and overly depended on fiction for his sources. "What we get are the exaggerations of literature in a lively paraphrase," contended Harvey. However, other reviewers, such as *Europe* contributor Robert J. Guttman, assessed Reston's style of presentation more positively, more simply recognizing the work as "a lively and engaging book."

Focusing on two principal characters, Richard the Lionheart and Saladin, Reston again explores the crusades in his next book, *Warriors of God: Richard the Lion-*

heart and Saladin in the Third Crusade. When writing this work Reston set out to "knock away the barnacles that have encrusted both of the characters," the author told Ray Suarez in an *Online NewsHour* discussion, referring to the typical Arab approach to Saladin "as a demagogue," Richard the Lionheart's persistent association with "Robin Hood lore," and the general dominance of the Cambridge school of history in the documentation of the Crusades. *Washington Post Book Review* contributor Tariq Ali recommended Reston's book as "a refreshingly unbiased popular history of the Third Crusade (1187-92)." Reviewers of *Warriors of God* again praised Reston for his exciting and vivid presentation of history, noting his flare for presenting drama, sometimes in a somewhat fictitious manner. Geoffrey Moorhouse noted Reston's skill at telling a story and "illuminating detail," but in the critic's *Guardian* review he wrote that "*Warriors of God* sometimes reads like a campfire yarn told in the American Midwest." In a more positive review, *Library Journal* contributor Jim Doyle maintained that Reston "offers the reader a captivating story in a lucid and often humorous style." "The varied landscapes of the Holy Land are described with the visual awareness of a topographical painter, and both the ecstasy and the horror of medieval warfare are tellingly evoked," stated Julian Rathbone in the *Sunday Telegraph.*

Reston is taking legal action against 20th Century Fox and director Ridley Scott for alleged copyright violations. Reston claims that *Warriors of God* was plagiarized by screenwriter William Monahan, who was hired by Scott to write the script for the film *Kingdom of Heaven,* released in 2005.

Dogs of God: Columbus, the Inquisition, and the Defeat of the Moors outlines Reston's belief that Columbus's voyage to the New World was inextricably tied to Christianity's victory over Islam in the Iberian peninsula. In the process, the author examines such figures as King Ferdinand and Queen Isabella of Spain, as well as many lesser-known historical figures. A *Publishers Weekly* contributor wrote that the author mostly "does justice to the complexities of his subject, examining the worlds of Christians, Muslims and Jews with sympathy and irony." A *Kirkus Reviews* contributor referred to the book as "a riveting portrait of 15th-century Spain."

In *Fragile Innocence: A Father's Memoir of His Daughter's Courageous Journey,* Reston writes of his daughter Hillary's struggle with a neurological problem that she developed when she was only eighteen months old after suffering from a high fever. Never diagnosed as to the cause, the attack has left her susceptible to seizures and numerous other health problems. "Much of *Fragile Innocence* is given over to the mundane but bewilderingly complex and demanding task of caring for (and keeping safe) a severely cognitively damaged young child, on the one hand, and what borders on an obsession with discovering what 'caused' all this, on the other," wrote a contributor to the *National Right to Life News.* Ted Westervelt, writing in the *School Library Journal,* noted that the author "tells a . . . nuanced and enjoyable story."

BIOGRAPHICAL AND CRITICAL SOURCES:

BOOKS

Reston, James B., Jr., *Fragile Innocence: A Father's Memoir of His Daughter's Courageous Journey,* Harmony Books (New York, NY), 2006.

PERIODICALS

Atlanta Journal-Constitution (Atlanta, GA), March 15, 1998, Steven Harvey, "Atrocities Committed en Route to Culture," p. L11.
Biography, spring, 2006, review of *Fragile Innocence,* p. 407.
Booklist, January 1, 1998, Ilene Cooper, review of *The Last Apocalypse: Europe at the Year 1000 A.D.,* p. 742; June 1, 2001, Margaret Flanagan, review of *Warriors of God: Richard the Lionheart and Saladin in the Third Crusade,* p. 1832.
California Bookwatch, April, 2006, review of *Fragile Innocence.*
Daily Variety, April 21, 2005, Gabriel Snyder, "Litigious Scholar on a 'Crusade,'" p. 6.
Economist, October 20, 2001, "Stirring Stuff; The Medieval Crusades."
Entertainment Weekly, February 24, 2006, Tina Jordan, review of *Fragile Innocence,* p. 68.
Europe, December, 1999, Robert J. Guttman, review of *The Last Apocalypse,* p. 47.
Guardian (London, England), October 20, 2001, Geoffrey Moorhouse, review of *Warriors of God,* p. 8.
Houston Chronicle (Houston, TX), July 15, 2001, Lee Cearnal, "Novel Muslim vs. Heartless Lionheart," p. 18.

Kirkus Reviews, February 15, 1998, review of *The Last Apocalypse,* p. 251; August 15, 2005, review of *Dogs of God: Columbus, the Inquisition, and the Defeat of the Moors,* p. 903; December 1, 2005, review of *Fragile Innocence,* p. 1269.

Kliatt Young Adult Paperback Book Guide, July, 1999, review of *The Last Apocalypse,* p. 34.

Knight-Ridder/Tribune News Service, March 4, 1998, David Crumm, review of *The Last Apocalypse,* p. 304K6295.

Library Journal, March 15, 1998, Norman Malwitz, review of *The Last Apocalypse,* p. 82; May 1, 2001, Jim Doyle, review of *Warriors of God,* p. 108; December 1, 2005, Martha E. Stone, review of *Fragile Innocence,* p. 155.

Los Angeles Times Book Review, March 17, 1985, Brian Burns, review of *Sherman's March and Vietnam,* p. 3.

Nation, May 2, 1981, Peter Schrag, review of *Our Father Who Art in Hell: The Life and Death of Jim Jones.*

National Right to Life News, April, 2006, review of *Fragile Innocence,* p. 14.

Newsweek, June 4, 1984, Richard Zoglin, review of *Jonestown Express.*

New York Times Book Review, February 17, 1985, Stephen W. Sears, review of *Sherman's March and Vietnam,* p. 13; April 5, 1998, David Walton, review of *The Last Apocalypse,* p. 25; June 24, 2001, John D. Thomas, review of *Warriors of God,* p. 24.

Publishers Weekly, February 16, 1998, review of *The Last Apocalypse,* p. 192; March 12, 2001, review of *Warriors of God,* p. 79; August 15, 2005, review of *Dogs of War,* p. 52.

School Library Journal, June, 2006, Ted Westervelt, review of *Fragile Innocence,* p. 194.

South Carolina Review, spring, 1998, review of *The Last Apocalypse,* p. 172.

Sunday Telegraph (London, England), October 14, 2001, Julian Rathbone, "A Just, Right, and Holy War?," p. 14.

Variety, April 4, 2005, "Angry author attacks 'Kingdom,'" p. 4.

Washington Post Book World, February 10, 1985, Russell F. Weigley, review of *Sherman's March and Vietnam,* p. BW11; September 12, 1999, review of *The Last Apocalypse,* p. 10; June 4, 2001, Tariq Ali, "The King and the Sultan," p. C4.

Washington Times, May 4, 1998, Julia Duin, "America Not Ready to Greet Millennium," p. 2.

Wilson Quarterly, spring, 1998, Toby Lester, review of *The Last Apocalypse,* p. 102.

ONLINE

James Reston, Jr., Home Page, http://restonbooks.com (December 12, 2006).

Online NewsHour, http://www.pbs.org/newshour/ (August 3, 2001), Ray Suarez, discussion with Reston about *Warriors of God.**

*   *   *

REUBEN, Shelly 1945-

PERSONAL: Born August 5, 1945, in Chicago, IL; daughter of Samuel (an inventor and real estate developer) and Ghita (a homemaker and husband's business partner) Reuben; married Charles G. King (a fire and arson consultant), May 31, 1980.

ADDRESSES: Office—401 Broadway, Ste. 703, New York, NY 10013. *Agent*—Christine Tomasino, RLR Associates, 7 W. 51st St., New York, NY 10019. *E-mail*—ShellyReuben@aol.com.

CAREER: Charles G. King Associates, New York, NY, partner, fire and arson investigator and licensed private investigator, 1980—.

MEMBER: International Association of Arson Investigators, Mystery Writers of America.

WRITINGS:

Julian Solo, Dodd (New York, NY), 1988.
Origin and Cause, Scribner's (New York, NY), 1994.
Spent Matches, Scribner's (New York, NY), 1996.
Come Home. Love, Dad, Bernard Street Books (New York, NY), 2000.
Weeping: A Fritillary Quilter Mystery, Kate's Mystery Books (Lanham, MD), 2004.
Tabula Rasa, Harcourt (Orlando, FL), 2005.
The Skirt Man, Harcourt (Orlando, FL), 2006.

Contributor to magazines, including *Fire Engineering, Law Enforcement Communications, National Underwriter,* and *Police Times.*

ADAPTATIONS: Weeping: A Fritillary Quilter Mystery was adapted for audiobook.

SIDELIGHTS: Shelly Reuben told *CA* that her novel *Julian Solo* "explores the issues of life being created out of dead matter, introducing the hero, Julian Solo, as a brilliant scientist in love with a woman diagnosed as having an incurable illness. Solo has devised a serum with which he can enter and leave the death state at will, and his goal is to save the woman he loves. He will have to kill her to save her. His adversary is a woman obsessively in love with him, a woman who tampers with his experiments and his life.

"It is my goal to bring back the emphasis on values, heroism, and moral conflict which so characterized the great novels of the nineteenth century. I would, however, like to see the scope and scale of such grandeur updated to reflect and include the issues, settings, and circumstances of our time."

In *Weeping: A Fritillary Quilter Mystery,* Reuben features a young arson expert named Fritillary Quilter, known as "Tilly." Tilly is eventually paired with her mentor, Ike Blessing, a renowned detective, and the two are charged with investigating a case Blessing believes smells of foul play. A reviewer for *Kirkus Reviews* concluded that "Reuben . . . writes unevenly, and there's scant mystery, but the tale catches fire whenever Ike and Tilly launch into one of their animated discussions of forensic evidence." A *Publishers Weekly* reviewer commented: "Tilly has an engaging voice that will appeal particularly to younger readers who care more about character than crime."

Reed's sixth mystery novel, *The Skirt Man,* is set in a small town where a bizarre fire and resulting death are under investigation. Critics noted that Reed builds a realistic rural mystery with full, well-rounded, and eccentric characters. The thriller's protagonists are the Bly family, introduced in the 2005 *Tabula Rasa.* Merry Bly, a ballerina; her mother, Annie Bly, a journalist; her father, Sebastian Bly, a state trooper; her uncle, Fire Marshal Billy Nightingale; and her admirers, the twin brothers Moe and Sonny Dillenbeck, all work together to solve the murder. Although a *Publishers Weekly* reviewer criticized the novelist for not writing what she knows about—"capable, professional women," *Library Journal* contributor Jo Ann Vicarel called the novel "several levels above the ordinary." A *Kirkus Reviews* critic was also impressed, describing the book as "a lively whodunit."

BIOGRAPHICAL AND CRITICAL SOURCES:

PERIODICALS

Booklist May 1, 2006, Frank Sennett, review of *The Skirt Man,* p. 39.

Forensic Examiner fall, 2006, review of *The Skirt Man,* p. 68.

Huntington News June 5, 2006, review of *The Skirt Man.*

Kirkus Reviews, January 1, 2004, review of *Weeping: A Fritillary Quilter Mystery,* p. 17; April 15, 2006, review of *The Skirt Man,* p. 384.

Library Journal, April 1, 2005, Barbara Hoffert, review of *Tabula Rasa,* p. 72; June 1, 2006, Jo Ann Vicarel, review of *The Skirt Man,* p. 92.

Publishers Weekly, February 9, 2004, review of *Weeping,* p. 61; April 17, 2006 review of *The Skirt Man,* p. 168.

ONLINE

Shelly Reuben Home Page, http://www.shellyreuben. com (January 30, 2007).*

*   *   *

REYNOLDS, Clay 1949-
(Richard Clay Reynolds)

PERSONAL: Born September 28, 1949, in Quanah, TX; son of Jessie Wrex (a railroad brake operator) and Pauline (a teacher's aide) Reynolds; married Julia Ann Kavanagh (a medical technologist), January 22, 1972; children: Wesley Eliot, Virginia Anne. *Ethnicity:* "White." *Education:* University of Texas at Austin, B.A., 1971; Trinity University, M.A., 1974; University of Tulsa, Ph.D., 1979. *Religion:* Protestant. *Hobbies and other interests:* Baseball, golf.

ADDRESSES: Home—McKinney, TX. *Agent*—Ethan Ellenberg, 548 Broadway St., New York, NY 10022. *E-mail*—rclayr@aol.com; clayr@info.net.

CAREER: Tulsa Junior College, Tulsa, OK, instructor in English, 1977-78; Claremore College, Claremore, OK, instructor in English, 1977-78; Lamar University,

Beaumont, TX, associate professor of English, 1978-88; University of North Texas, Denton, professor and novelist in residence, 1988-92; freelance writer and editor, 1992-98; University of Texas at Dallas, Dallas, began as associate professor, became professor of arts and humanities, 1998—, associate dean for undergraduate studies, 2001-06. Center for Texas Studies, associate director, 1990-92; Poly Karp Kusch Lecturer, 2004; also taught briefly at Villanova University, West Texas A&M University, Texas Woman's University, and University of South Dakota. Member of editorial board, *Texas Goes to War,* 1991, and *Amarillo Bay On-Line Journal of Literature.* Denton Area Little League, vice president of board of directors; active in community theater in Tulsa and Beaumont.

MEMBER: Modern Language Association of America, Authors Guild, Authors League of America, Western Writers of America, Western American Literature Association, Texas Institute of Letters, Texas Association of Creative Writing Teachers (state officer, 1989-92).

AWARDS, HONORS: Pulitzer Prize nomination for fiction, Columbia University, and Violet Crown Award, Austin Writers' League and University Co-operative, both 1992, for *Franklin's Crossing;* ALE Award for short fiction, 1993; fellow, National Endowment for the Arts, 1994; PEN Texas Awards for essay and fiction, 1997; grant, Texas Council for the Arts and Austin Writers' League, 1997; fiction award, Council on National Literature, 1998; Violet Crown Award for fiction, 2001, for *Monuments;* award for best paper, American Studies Association of Texas, 2005.

WRITINGS:

Stage Left: The Development of the American Social Drama in the Thirties, Whitston Press (Troy, NY), 1986.
The Vigil (fiction), St. Martin's Press (New York, NY), 1986.
Agatite (novel), St. Martin's Press (New York, NY), 1986.
Taking Stock: A Larry McMurtry Casebook, Southern Methodist University Press (Dallas, TX), 1989.
Franklin's Crossing (fiction), Dutton (New York, NY), 1992.
(With Marie-Madeleine Schein) *A Hundred Years of Heroes: A History of the Southwestern Exposition and Livestock Show,* Texas Christian University Press (Fort Worth, TX), 1995.

Players (novel), Carroll & Graf (New York, NY), 1997.
Twenty Questions: Answers for the Aspiring Writer, Browder Springs Press (Dallas, TX), 1998.
(With Hunter Lundy) *Let Us Prey,* Genesis Press (Columbus, MS), 1999.
Monuments (novel), Texas Tech University Press (Lubbock, TX), 2000.
The Tentmaker (fiction), Berkley (New York, NY), 2002.
Arts Poetica: A Post-Modern Parable (novel), Texas Review Press (Huntsville, TX), 2003.
Threading the Needle (novel), Texas Tech University Press (Lubbock, TX), 2003.
A Cow Can Moo: The Irony of the Artistic Lie, University of Texas at Dallas (Dallas, TX), 2004.
Of Snakes and Sex and Playing in the Rain: Random Thoughts on Harmful Things (essays), Stone River Press (Conroe, TX), 2006.
Sandhill County Lines (short stories), Texas Tech University Press (Lubbock, TX), 2007.

Contributor to many anthologies, including *Range Wars: Heated Debates, Sober Reflections, and Other Assessments of Texas Writing,* edited by Craig Clifford and Tom Pilkington, Southern Methodist University Press (Dallas, TX), 1989; *This Place of Memory: A Texas Perspective,* edited by Joyce Gibson Roach, University of North Texas Press (Denton, TX), 1992; *The Waltz He Was Born For,* edited by Janice Whittington and Andrew Hudgins, Texas Tech University Press (Lubbock, TX), 2002; *Falling from Grace: A Literary Response to the Demise of Paradise,* edited by Rick Bass and Paul Christensen, Wings Press (San Antonio, TX), 2004; and *Vittles Champagne,* edited by Jackie Pelham, Stone River Press (Conroe, TX), 2005. Contributor to periodicals, including *Chronicles of Higher Education, Publishers Weekly, Kirkus Reviews, Chronicles, Western American Literature, Dallas Morning News, Fort Worth Star Telegram, Texas Books in Review, Ploughshares, Linguistics in Literature, Bloomsbury Review, American Way, Texas Observer,* and *New York Times Book Review.* Associate editor, *Lamar Journal of the Humanities,* 1986-88, and *New Texas,* 1991-92; editor, *Texas Writers' Newsletter,* 1989-92; fiction editor, *American Literary Review,* 1990-92; contributing editor, *Descant 2000.*

SIDELIGHTS: Clay Reynolds was trained as an academic with a specialty in twentieth-century American literature. Although he published widely in literary criticism throughout the first five years of his scholastic career, he began producing fiction—a move that changed both his personal and professional direction. Since 1986, Reynolds has been an active writer of fiction and personal essays.

Reynolds's novels and many of his short stories are set in the rural American West, particularly north central Texas where he grew up. While he admits that he had no particular love of the region while he resided there, he developed a thirst to know more about the area's history, particularly its frontier past, once he moved from the region. Even though he has used contemporary settings in the bulk of his writings, he has also worked with historical backgrounds and characters. With such efforts, he is "attempting to chronicle a part of the country which has been more or less lost since the first pioneers came there to settle," he once explained to *CA*. "This was Indian Country," Reynolds added. "It was inhospitable because of climate, as well as because of the Comanche and Kiowa tribes who defended it so staunchly for nearly a hundred years. Today, it's still not very appealing as a place, but it's rich in the stuff of the frontier, and that makes for good fiction, regardless of when it was set."

Some critics have described Reynolds's writing as neo-naturalistic and "anti-revisionistic," but the author rejects such labels. "I don't think calling a novel 'realistic' or 'romantic' or anything else says very much about it, unless we're trying to pin it down to a historical period," he once told *CA*. "Essentially, I try to show people being people. Most of them are disappointed in life, regardless of how successful they may be. Very little turns out the way it's supposed to. Most of us concentrate on the good things that happen, try to ignore the bad, and just make it through another day. But in the end, it's the bad stuff that gets us, whether it's disease, old age, an accident, victimization by crime or chicanery, or something else." Refuting that such an outlook is cynical, he added, "In a sense, that's what separates a human being from the other inhabitants of this planet—we see all that's bad around us, and we go on. We try to do good, even when it's easier to be bad. That's what my novels are really about—people trying to do and be good when nothing around them seems to make any sense."

Reynolds disputes the anti-revisionist label as well. "I like to think of what I write as being more 'corrective' than anti-revisionary," he wrote. "There are a lot of attendant myths associated with the American West that were the product of laziness on the part of writers and

filmmakers in the first three decades of the motion picture industry. That was also the heyday of pulp western fiction. It's not so much that such writers deliberately obscured or ignored factual history and mixed up actuality with anachronism. It's more that they just didn't tell the whole story or that they didn't think the details completely through. That, I think, is my job as a novelist—to tell the whole story."

"Publishing is a tough business," he once told *CA*. "So much bad writing gets printed these days, and so many people do so well with it, anyone might think that it's the easiest thing in the world to write a good book, tell a good story, and then sit back and wait for the offers to roll in. But, if you think New York publishing is tough, take a look at Hollywood. There's nothing worse. Making a movie is the hardest thing in the world to do; making a good movie is harder; making a movie that actually reflects a writer's vision is nearly impossible."

Reynolds once told *CA* that the novel *Franklin's Crossing* began as "something of an accident. I was finally persuaded that a modern writer would have to learn to use a word processor or computer, and Lamar University had just obtained one for the department. A friend of mine in the computer science department suggested that the best way to learn to use a word processor was to have a project developing. I didn't have anything on the front burner just then, so I began writing what I thought would be a prologue for a novel called *Country Matters*. The novel was set in contemporary times and centered on a murder that took place at a remote ghost town called Franklin's Crossing, which I made up. It was a racially motivated murder, and my intention was to use the prologue, wherein a black scout was killed by Indians at the same site some hundred years earlier, as an ironic foil to the contemporary plot.

"I began working on the story right away, playing with and learning the word processor as I went, and before I knew it, I had more than 100 pages of plot working. But I hadn't yet reached the end of the supposed prologue. I put it aside and worried about my next novel project.

"My agent asked me to submit what I might have for a new contract, and I sent in a scenario for *Country Matters* and, as an afterthought, the prologue, which was untitled. He showed it to my present editor, who was initially pleased with it. Unfortunately, she resigned shortly afterward, and her replacement rejected the novel out of hand. We had fairly serious discussions, but he wouldn't budge. My second novel, *Agatite,* was published, and finally my editor officially 'passed' on what I had come to call *Franklin's Crossing.* I took the scenario to Dick Marek at Dutton, and he bought the idea and offered a contract on the book.

"I began work right away and worked through the winter until I hit a snag. I found out quickly that I knew very little about the West or about the people who settled it. I mean, I grew up there, thought I knew all about it, but I didn't know a thing about the details or personalities that made up the settlers in the region from which I hailed. I quit writing and started doing research. I found that through reading, library work, and archival investigation, I was able to fill in a number of gaps, but I was still short on a number of points that would be required for a believable and convincing story. For one thing, I had no idea how large a Conestoga wagon was, how long it took to saddle a horse with period tack, and what it felt like to fire a period rifle or shotgun, how long it took to load a period six-shooter, what people ate, how they repaired their clothing, and a thousand other things. I started going to historical sites and visiting museums, monuments, and restorations. I attended re-creations of battles, talked extensively with historians and preservationists. I persuaded one curator to help me load and fire a whole array of nineteenth-century weaponry, to show me how to use nineteenth-century tools and tack, and how to prepare a meal of salted meat and hard bread over a campfire.

"I found out the wealth of what I didn't know was overwhelming. I also learned that I knew almost nothing about Indians. I visited a number of Indian museums, interviewed several Native American reservations, and talked with experts of all sorts. I discovered that the 'revisionists' had almost ruined the true portrait of the Native American on the nineteenth-century plains, had done more damage, truly, than the romanticists had ever considered with their B westerns and television horse operas. I began collecting and absorbing as much data on the Comanche, Kiowa, and other plains tribes as I could.

"While I was engaged in all of this, *Lonesome Dove* was published and won the Pulitzer Prize. Pressure on me to finish my novel was intense. As completed, *Franklin's Crossing* tells only part of the story I wanted to relate. Length requirements forbade a full treatment in one book. I am hopeful that in subsequent novels I can

expand and fill the gaps left by *Franklin's Crossing.* The story of the American West is our only real history, and often it's not a pretty one. Nevertheless, it's one that needs to be remembered accurately and truly, and I hope that through my fiction, I can help readers understand much of what it was like to be alive in a time that was more bewildering that satisfying, more conscious of its destiny than of its arrival."

Reynolds crossed genres with his crime novel *Players.* The author presents the story of Eddy Lovell, a former college football player at Southern Methodist University, as a black farce. Lovell's efforts to become a major player in the Texas underworld are foiled when he is shot in an armed robbery attempt. He serves time in prison, is released, and finds a job working in a Dallas gambling den. Then his former partner turns up with two compact disks—the only loot that remains from the robbery—and Eddy becomes the center of a wheel of violence that involves a bungled attempted kidnapping of Eddy's daughter Barbara (the kidnapers seize instead an actress named Vicki) and "sophisticated computer programs that can find out any information about anyone in the world," explained *Library Journal* contributor David Dodd. "What Eddy, Vicki, the cops, and the thugs all learn," commented Wes Lukowsky in *Booklist,* "is that none of them is really a player, just pawns in a much larger game where the stake isn't easy money but life itself."

Overall the book received positive reviews from critics. "The plot is ingenious, the resolution a forehead-slapper, and every character as real as the book in hand," stated Lukowsky. "If there's justice in the publishing world, this will be Reynolds' breakout novel. Prepare for significant demand." "Despite repetitious exposition and a penchant for the burlesque," commented a *Publishers Weekly* contributor, "Reynolds' hard-edged prose is well calculated to captivate the reader right up to the final trigger squeeze."

Reynolds's novel *Monuments* returns directly to that part of West Texas he most enjoys writing about. It is the story of an unlikely partnership between a fairly typical teenaged boy and an old, old man as they ostensibly try to preserve a town landmark from destruction by a greedy railroad. More than a coming-of-age story, though, the novel deals with the more important monuments of American society: family, friendship, parent and child relationships, young love, as well as the monumental questions of integrity, honor, and the destructive elements that exist in the equally significant structures of lies, rumors, and gossip. It "attracted the interest of Judyth Keeling at Texas Tech University Press," reported Reynolds. "She immediately saw the value of the book and the marvelous reviews it's received validate both my belief in the book and her faith in it."

BIOGRAPHICAL AND CRITICAL SOURCES:

BOOKS

Twentieth-Century Western Writers, 2nd edition, St. James Press (Detroit, MI), 1991.

PERIODICALS

Booklist, July, 1997, Wes Lukowsky, review of *Players,* p. 1802.
Choice, April, 1987, review of *Stage Left: The Development of the American Social Drama in the Thirties,* p. 1230.
Kliatt, July, 1993, review of *Franklin's Crossing,* p. 14.
Library Journal, May 15, 1997, David Dodd, review of *Players,* p. 104.
New York Times Book Review, February 16, 1986, Gary Krist, review of *The Vigil,* p. 16.
Publishers Weekly, March 16, 1992, review of *Franklin's Crossing,* p. 65; May 19, 1997, review of *Players,* p. 64.
Rapport, Volume 17, number 2, 1992, review of *Franklin's Crossing,* p. 28.
Western American Literature, spring, 1993, review of *Franklin's Crossing,* p. 89.

*　　*　　*

REYNOLDS, Richard Clay
    See REYNOLDS, Clay

*　　*　　*

RINGGOLD, Faith 1930-

PERSONAL: Born October 8, 1930, in New York, NY; daughter of Andrew Louis (a sanitation worker) and Willi (a dressmaker and designer) Jones; married Robert Earl Wallace (a jazz pianist), November 1, 1950 (divorced, 1956); married Burdette Ringgold (an automobile company employee), May 19, 1962; children: (first marriage) Barbara, Michele. *Ethnicity:* "African American." *Education:* City College of the City University of New York, B.S., 1955, M.S., 1959. *Religion:* Protestant.

ADDRESSES: Agent—Marie Brown Associates, 625 Broadway, Room 902, New York, NY 10012. *E-mail*—any1canfly@aol.com.

CAREER: Teacher of art in public schools in New York City, 1955-73; University of California, San Diego, La Jolla, professor of art, 1984—. Painter, mixed media sculptor, performance artist, and writer; lecturer or performance artist at universities, and museums, including Purdue University, 1977, University of Massachusetts, 1980, Rutgers University, 1981, Occidental College, 1984, Long Island University, 1986, Mills College, 1987, Museum of Modern Art, 1988, Baltimore Museum of Art, 1988, De Pauw University, 1989, University of West Florida, 1989, San Diego Museum, 1990, Washington and Lee University, 1991, Museum of African American Art, 1991, and Atlantic Center for the Arts, 1992. *Exhibitions:* Art work featured in solo shows at Spectrum Gallery, New York, NY, 1967, 1970, Bernice Steinbaum Gallery, 1987, 1989, 1992, in touring exhibition "Faith Ringgold: A Twenty-Five-Year Survey," curated by Fine Arts Museum of Long Island, 1990-93, and elsewhere; art work represented in museums and galleries, including Boston Museum of Fine Art, Chase Manhattan Bank Collection, Clark Museum, High Museum of Atlanta, Newark Museum, Philip Morris collection, Guggenheim Museum, Metropolitan Museum of Art, Museum of Modern Art, Studio Museum of Harlem, and various locations in Europe, Asia, South America, and Africa.

AWARDS, HONORS: Travel grant for Africa, American Association of University Women, 1976; grants from National Endowment for the Arts, 1978, for sculpture, and 1989, for painting; honorary D.F.A., Moore College of Art, 1986, College of Wooster, 1987, Massachusetts College of Art, 1991, City College of the City University of New York, 1991, and Brockport State University, 1992; Guggenheim fellowship, 1987; grants from New York Foundation for the Arts, 1988, and Henry Clews Foundation (for France), 1990; Coretta Scott King Illustrator Award, Social Responsibilities Round Table, American Library Association, and Caldecott Honor Book Award, American Library Association, both 1992, for *Tar Beach;* Jane Addams Children's Book Award, 1993, *for Aunt Harriet's Underground Railroad in the Sky.*

WRITINGS:

SELF-ILLUSTRATED CHILDREN'S BOOKS

Tar Beach, Crown (New York, NY), 1991.

Aunt Harriet's Underground Railroad in the Sky, Crown (New York, NY), 1992.

Dinner at Aunt Connie's House, Hyperion (New York, NY), 1993.

My Dream of Martin Luther King, Crown (New York, NY), 1996.

Bonjour, Lonnie, Hyperion (New York, NY), 1996.

The Invisible Princess, Crown (New York, NY), 1998.

Counting to Tar Beach, Crown (New York, NY), 1999.

If a Bus Could Talk: The Story of Rosa Parks, Simon & Schuster Books for Young People, (New York, NY), 1999.

Cassie's Colorful Day, Crown (New York, NY), 1999.

Cassie's Word Quilt, Knopf (New York, NY), 2002.

OTHER

(With Linda Freeman and Nancy Roucher) *Talking to Faith Ringgold,* Crown (New York, NY), 1995.

We Flew over the Bridge: The Memoirs of Faith Ringgold, Little, Brown (Boston, MA), 1995.

Dancing at the Louvre: Faith Ringgold's French Collection and Other Story Quilts, introduction by Richard J. Powell, University of California Press (Berkeley, CA), 1998.

(With Curlee Raven Holton) *Faith Ringgold: A View from the Studio,* Bunker Hill Pub (Boston, MA), 2004.

(Illustrator) *O Holy Night: Christmas with the Boys Choir of Harlem,* HarperCollins (New York, NY), 2004.

(Illustrator) Zora Neale Hurston, *The Three Witches,* HarperCollins (New York, NY), 2006.

(Illustrator) Gwendolyn Brooks, *Bronzeville Boys and Girls,* HarperCollins (New York, NY), 2007.

Art work represented in catalogues, including *Faith Ringgold: Twenty Years of Painting, Sculpture, and Performance, 1963-1983,* Studio Museum in Harlem, 1984; *Faith Ringgold: Painting, Sculpture, Performance,* Art Museum, College of Wooster, 1985; and *Faith Ringgold: A Twenty-Five-Year Survey,* Fine Arts Museum of Long Island, 1990. Contributor to *Confirmation: An Anthology of African American Women,* edited by Amiri Baraka and Amina Baraka, Morrow (New York, NY), 1983. Contributor to periodicals, including *Artpaper, Arts, Heresies: Feminist Publication on Arts and Politics, Feminist Art Journal, Women's Art Journal,* and *Women's Artists News.*

SIDELIGHTS: Faith Ringgold is an artist and author whose works reflect her African-American heritage and often promote the importance of dreams. She creates in a variety of media, ranging from painting and sculpture to performance art. Yet she is probably best known for her "story quilts," intricately designed pieces that combine elements of her past, present, and future. More recently, Ringgold has emerged as a storyteller of note with the publication of several self-illustrated books for children. Janice M. Alberghene observed in *Twentieth-Century Children's Writers:* "Few artists combine painting, quiltmaking, and storytelling to create their works of art. When such an artist then adapts her work to create picture books for children, the result is both visually arresting and thematically nuanced. Faith Ringgold's books in this genre, *Tar Beach* and *Dinner at Aunt Connie's House,* together with *Aunt Harriet's Underground Railroad in the Sky,* an original work for children, draw upon family tradition, autobiography, and history to portray inspiring African-American heroines, both real and imagined."

Ringgold attributes her artistic leanings to her somewhat unconventional childhood. Born in New York City during the Depression, she suffered from asthma as a child and often had to stay home from school. While convalescing, Ringgold listened to jazz bands on the radio and indulged her interest in drawing. In addition, her mother regularly took her to museums, and her father entertained her with social outings and stories.

After graduating from high school, Ringgold studied art at the City College of the City University of New York. There she was taught to copy the works of artists such as Paul Cezanne and Edgar Degas. Eager for more knowledge of and contact with African American art and artists, she undertook her own studies and developed a deep appreciation for the field.

Before she could begin her own career as an artist, however, Ringgold married a jazz pianist and had two children. The marriage soon collapsed, and Ringgold continued with her education. After graduating in 1955, she began teaching in New York City's public schools. She taught for several years, then took her family to Europe to see the great works of art that she had once studied. Upon returning to the United States, Ringgold began promoting her own work across the country. These works—mostly paintings on African-American themes—reflected European techniques. But as the civil rights movement gained momentum during the 1960s, Ringgold began adopting African and African-American styles. In addition, she devoted herself increasingly to African-American causes.

Although she has worked in sculpture and in painting on canvas, Ringgold has won her greatest acclaim as an artist with her painted "story quilts" on which she relates her experiences as an African-American woman. She began framing her paintings on fabric in the early 1970s after discovering that Tibetans had practiced such artwork since the fourteenth century. In 1980, Ringgold made her first quilt and added writing to the borders of these paintings, which then became known as "story quilts." Such works as "Flag Story Quilt," "Slave Rape Story," and "Street Story Quilt" brought Ringgold greater recognition as an important and innovative artist. Her work is now part of the permanent collections at institutions such as the Metropolitan Museum of Art, the Museum of Modern Art, the Guggenheim Museum, the Boston Museum of Fine Art, and the Philadelphia Museum of Art.

Among Ringgold's works is the "Women on the Bridge" series of story quilts. Included in this series is the 1988 quilt "Tar Beach," which features a child, Cassie, talking and fantasizing while lying on the tarpaper roof of a building in Harlem during the 1930s. An editor at Crown Books saw a poster of "Tar Beach" and contracted with Ringgold for a children's book based on the quilt. Ringgold then created a series of paintings depicting scenes such as the heroine of *Tar Beach* flying over the George Washington Bridge. Upon its publication in 1991, *Tar Beach* won praise as an impressive and inspiring children's book. Rosellen Brown, writing in the *New York Times Book Review*, described Ringgold's art as "richly colored, sophisticated versions of what a child herself might paint" and concluded that "there's an air of triumph . . . in Ms. Ringgold's vision."

Ringgold followed *Tar Beach* with *Aunt Harriet's Underground Railroad in the Sky*. It features Cassie, the heroine of *Tar Beach,* and her brother, Be Be, as they magically encounter Harriet Tubman and trace their ancestors' flight from slavery via the Underground Railroad. Enola G. Aird observed in the *New York Times Book Review* that "Ringgold's illustrations here are rich with meaning."

In her subsequent children's books, Ringgold has continued to focus on African-American history. In *Dinner at Aunt Connie's House,* a young girl visits her aunt, an artist whose walls are lined with her paintings of important African American women. Ringgold's vivid illustrations depict these women recalling their struggles and triumphs. The Harlem Renaissance and the relocation of many African Americans to Paris are the subjects of the "highly unconventional story" of *Bonjour, Lonnie,* according to Susan Dove Lempke in *Booklist.* When the protagonist of this "fantastical, sweeping picture book" embarks on a quest to find loved ones, he roams throughout Paris and speaks to spirits who teach him about his "mixed racial heritage and, more broadly, black Americans' contributions to the arts," recounted a writer for *Publishers Weekly.*

In *My Dream of Martin Luther King,* Ringgold tells the story of the civil rights activist's life. The "innovative and stirring" story, said a *Publishers Weekly* reviewer, uses the framework of the narrator's own dreams, in which a young and old Dr. King appears, to "share . . . a powerful message: 'EVERY GOOD THING STARTS WITH A DREAM.'" According to *Horn Book* contributor Ellen Fader, the "message becomes more powerful and accessible with repeated readings." *Booklist* contributor Ilene Cooper thought "the fantasy framework overshadows the soul-stirring facts" but nevertheless concluded that the book's "intensity . . . will affect readers."

In *The Invisible Princess,* Ringgold again mixes fantasy with historical fact, creating what a writer for *Publishers Weekly* referred to as "an evocative, if mystifying, picture book." Once again, however, the "great presence and mythic proportions" of Ringgold's paintings prove especially striking.

BIOGRAPHICAL AND CRITICAL SOURCES:

BOOKS

Authors and Artists for Young Adults, Volume 19, Thomson Gale (Detroit, MI), 1996.

Children's Literature Review, Volume 30, Thomson Gale (Detroit, MI), 1993.

Gouma-Peterson, Thalia, *Faith Ringgold Change: Printed Story Quilts,* Bernice Steinbaum Gallery, 1989.

Ringgold, Faith, *We Flew over the Bridge: The Memoirs of Faith Ringgold,* Little, Brown (Boston, MA), 1995.

Ringgold, Faith, Linda Freeman, and Nancy Roucher, *Talking to Faith Ringgold,* Crown (New York, NY), 1995.

Turner, Robyn Montana, *Faith Ringgold,* Little, Brown (Boston, MA), 1993.

Twentieth-Century Children's Writers, 4th edition, St. James Press (Detroit, MI), 1995.

PERIODICALS

American Visions, February, 1999, Terrance Pitts, review of *Dancing at the Louvre: Faith Ringgold's French Collection and Other Story Quilts,* p. 30.

Booklist, September 1, 1995, Hazel Rochman, review of *We Flew over the Bridge: The Memoirs of Faith Ringgold,* p. 26; February 15, 1996, Ilene Cooper, review of *My Dream of Martin Luther King,* p. 1024; October 1, 1996, Susan Dove Lempke, review of *Bonjour, Lonnie,* p. 359; December 15, 1996, review of *We Flew over the Bridge,* p. 717.

Bulletin of the Center for Children's Books, March, 1991, review of *Tar Beach,* pp. 175-176; December, 1992, review of *Aunt Harriet's Underground Railroad in the Sky,* p. 121.

Five Owls, March, 1991, review of *Tar Beach,* p. 75; November, 1994, review of *Tar Beach,* p. 31; September, 1995, review of *Tar Beach,* p. 21.

Horn Book, May-June, 1991, Nancy Vasilakis, review of *Tar Beach,* p. 322; May-June, 1996, Ellen Fader, review of *My Dream of Martin Luther King,* p. 351.

Kirkus Reviews, September 1, 1995, review of *We Flew over the Bridge,* p. 1261; August 1, 1996, review of *Bonjour, Lonnie,* p. 1158.

Library Journal, September 1, 1995, Margarete Gross, review of *We Flew over the Bridge,* p. 173; November 1, 1995, review of *We Flew over the Bridge,* p. 78.

Los Angeles Times Book Review, February 25, 1996, review of *My Dream of Martin Luther King,* p. 11.

Newsweek, September 9, 1991, review of *Tar Beach,* pp. 64-65.

New York Times Book Review, February 24, 1991, Rosellen Brown, review of *Tar Beach,* p. 30; February 21, 1993, Enola G. Aird, review of *Aunt Harriet's Underground Railroad in the Sky,* p. 22; February 11, 1996, review of *My Dream of Martin Luther King,* p. 25; February 2, 1997, review of *Bonjour, Lonnie,* p. 18.

Publishers Weekly, February 15, 1991, review of *Tar Beach,* pp. 61-62; August 16, 1993, review of *Dinner at Aunt Connie's House,* p. 104; October 16, 1995, review of *We Flew over the Bridge,* p. 51; November 13, 1995, review of *Aunt Harriet's Underground Railroad in the Sky,* p. 63; January 1, 1996, review of *My Dream of Martin Luther King,* p. 70; September 2, 1996, review of *Bonjour, Lonnie,* p. 129; January 13, 1997, review of *Tar Beach,* p. 77; November 23, 1998, review of *The Invisible Princess,* p. 67.

School Arts, May, 1989, Pamela Bray, "Faith Ringgold: Artist-Storyteller," pp. 23-26.

School Library Journal, December, 1991, review of *Tar Beach,* p. 31; October, 1993, Carol Jones Collins, review of *Dinner at Aunt Connie's House,* p. 110; February, 1996, Martha Rosen, review of *My Dream of Martin Luther King,* p. 97; July, 1996, review of *Tar Beach,* p. 31; January, 1997, Louise L. Sherman, review of *Bonjour, Lonnie,* p. 89.

Village Voice Literary Supplement, April 1, 1991, review of *Tar Beach,* p. 25.

ONLINE

Faith Ringgold.com Web site, http://www.faithringgold. com (February 10, 2007).

*   *   *

ROPER, Mark 1951-

PERSONAL: Born 1951, in Swanwick, Derbyshire, England; son of Lewis and Betty Roper; *Ethnicity:* "English." *Education:* University of Reading, B.A., 1975; Oxford University, M.Phil., 1978.

ADDRESSES: Home—Piltown, County Kilkenny, Ireland. *Office*—c/o Poetry Ireland Review, 2 Proud's Ln. off St. Stephen's Green, Dublin 2, Ireland.

CAREER: Poet. Adult education teacher in Waterford and Kilkenny, Ireland; gives readings from his work.

AWARDS, HONORS: Prize from Aldeburgh Poetry Festival, 1990, for *The Hen Ark.*

WRITINGS:

The Hen Ark (poetry), Peterloo Poets (Calstock, Cornwall, England), 1991.

Catching the Light (poetry), Lagan Press (Belfast, Northern Ireland), 1996.

The Home Fire (poetry), Abbey Press (Newry, Northern Ireland), 1998.

Whereabouts (poetry), Peterloo Poets (Calstock, Cornwall, England), 2005.

Editor, *Poetry Ireland Review.*

BIOGRAPHICAL AND CRITICAL SOURCES:

PERIODICALS

Fortnight, January, 1997, Carol Rumens, review of *Catching the Light.*

Irish Literary Supplement, fall, 1997, review of *Catching the Light,* p. 11; fall, 1999, Bill Tinley, review of *The Home Fire,* p. 18.

Irish Times, January, 1999, Catriona O'Reilly, review of *The Home Fire;* August, 2005, Eamon Brennan, review of *Whereabouts.*

Metre, autumn, 1997, Tim Kendall, review of *Catching the Light.*

Poetry Ireland, spring, 1999, Mark Granier, review of *The Home Fire;* spring, 2006, Siobhan Campbell, review of *Whereabouts.*

School Librarian, summer, 1998, Colin Walter, review of *Catching the Light,* p. 98.

Stroan, 1997, Catriona Clutterbuck, "The Poetry of Mark Roper."

ONLINE

Munster Express Online, http://www.munster-express.ie/ (August 14, 1998).

*　　*　　*

ROSS, Tony 1938-

PERSONAL: Born August 10, 1938, in London, England; son of Eric Turle Lee (a businessman and magician) and Effie Ross; married Carole Jean D'Arcy (divorced); married; second wife's name Joan (divorced); married 1979; third wife's name Zoe; children: (first marriage) Philippa (adopted); (second marriage) George (stepson), Alexandra; (third marriage) Katherine.

Education: Liverpool College of Art, diplomas, 1960, 1961. *Religion:* Methodist. *Hobbies and other interests:* Sailing small boats, cats, the monarchy, collecting toy soldiers, lamb cutlets.

ADDRESSES: Home—Macclesfield, Cheshire, England.

CAREER: Smith Kline & French Laboratories, graphic designer, 1962-64; Brunnings Advertising, art director, 1964-65; Manchester Polytechnic, Manchester, England, lecturer, 1965-72, senior lecturer in illustration, 1972-85; full-time writer and illustrator, 1985—. Consultant in graphic design.

MEMBER: Society of Industrial Artists and Designers.

AWARDS, HONORS: Children's Choice selection, International Reading Association/Children's Book Center, and Best Children's Picture Book of the Year designation, *Redbook,* both 1985, both for *I'm Coming to Get You!;* Kate Greenaway Medal commended designation, 1986, for *I Want My Potty,* and shortlist, for *Dr Xargle's Book of Earth Tiggers;* Deutscher Jugendliteratur Preis (West Germany), 1986; National Art Library Illustration Award shortlis, 1998, for *Sloth's Shoes,* 1999, for *Why?,* 2000, for *The Boy Who Lost;* Nestlé Smarties Book Prize Silver Award, 2003, for *Tadpole's Promise;* two Silver Pencil awards and two Silver Paintbrush awards (Netherlands); Schonste Bucher aus Aller Welt award (East Germany).

WRITINGS:

SELF-ILLUSTRATED CHILDREN'S BOOKS

Tales from Mr. Toffy's Circus, six volumes, W.J. Thurman (London, England), 1973.

(Reteller) *Goldilocks and the Three Bears,* Andersen Press (London, England), 1976, Overlook Press (Woodstock, NY), 1992.

Hugo and the Wicked Winter, Sidgwick & Jackson (London, England), 1977.

Hugo and the Man Who Stole Colors, Follett (New York, NY), 1977.

(Reteller) *The Pied Piper of Hamelin,* Andersen Press (London, England), 1977.

Norman and Flop Meet the Toy Bandit, W.J. Thurman (London, England), 1977.

(Reteller) *Little Red Riding Hood,* Andersen Press (London, England), 1978.

Hugo and Oddsock, Andersen Press (London, England), 1978.

(Reteller) *The True Story of Mother Goose and Her Son Jack,* Andersen Press (London, England), 1979, Rourke (Windermere, FL), 1982.

The Greedy Little Cobbler, Andersen Press (London, England), 1979, Barrons (Woodbury, NY), 1980.

Hugo and the Ministry of Holidays, Andersen Press (London, England), 1980, David & Charles (North Pomfret, VT), 1987.

Jack and the Beanstalk, Andersen Press (London, England), 1980, Delacorte (New York, NY), 1981.

Puss in Boots: The Story of a Sneaky Cat, Delacorte (New York, NY), 1981.

Naughty Nigel, Andersen Press (London, England), 1982, published as *Naughty Nicky,* Holt (New York, NY), 1983.

(Reteller) *The Enchanted Pig: An Old Rumanian Tale,* Andersen Press (London, England), 1982.

The Three Pigs, Pantheon (New York, NY), 1983.

(Reteller) *Jack the Giantkiller,* Andersen Press (London, England), 1983, Dial (New York, NY), 1987.

I'm Coming to Get You! ("Towser" series), Dial (New York, NY), 1984.

Towser and Sadie's Birthday, Pantheon (New York, NY), 1984.

Towser and the Terrible Thing, Pantheon (New York, NY), 1984.

Towser and the Water Rats, Pantheon (New York, NY), 1984.

Towser and the Haunted House, Andersen Press (London, England), 1985, David & Charles (North Pomfret, VT), 1987.

The Boy Who Cried Wolf, Dial (New York, NY), 1985.

Lazy Jack, Andersen Press (London, England), 1985, Dial (New York, NY), 1986.

(Reteller) *Foxy Fables,* Dial (New York, NY), 1986.

I Want My Potty ("Little Princess" series), Kane/Miller (Brooklyn, NY), 1986, new edition, Andersen Press (London, England), 2005.

Towser and the Funny Face, David & Charles (North Pomfret, VT), 1987.

Towser and the Magic Apple, David & Charles (North Pomfret, VT), 1987.

(Reteller) *Stone Soup,* Dial (New York, NY), 1987.

Oscar Got the Blame, Andersen Press (London, England), 1987, Dial (New York, NY), 1988.

Super Dooper Jezebel, Farrar, Straus (New York, NY), 1988.

Hansel and Gretel, Andersen (London, England), 1989, Overlook Press (New York, NY), 1994.

I Want a Cat, Farrar, Straus (New York, NY), 1989.

Treasure of Cozy Cove, Andersen Press (London, England), 1989, Farrar, Straus (New York, NY), 1990.

Mrs Goat and Her Seven Little Kids, Atheneum Press (London, England), 1990.

Hansel and Gretel, David & Charles (North Pomfret, VT), 1990.

This Old Man: A Musical Counting Book, Aladdin (New York, NY), 1990, published as *This Old Man: A Musical Counting Book,* Collins (London, England), 1990.

Going Green: A Kid's Handbook to Saving the Planet, Puffin Books (New York, NY), 1990.

Happy Blanket, Farrar, Straus (New York, NY), 1990.

(Reteller) *Five Favorite Tales,* Andersen Press (London, England), 1990.

A Fairy Tale, Little, Brown (Boston, MA), 1991.

Don't Do That!, Crown (New York, NY), 1991.

Big, Bad Barney Bear, Andersen Press (London, England), 1992.

(Abridger) Lewis Carroll, *Alice's Adventures in Wonderland,* Andersen Press (London, England), 1992.

I Want to Be, Kane/Miller (Brooklyn, NY), 1993.

Eventful Years: A Tribute to the Royal Air Force, 1918-1993, Wingham Aviation Books (Elmstone, Kent, England), 1993.

(Abridger) Lewis Carroll, *Through the Looking-Glass and What Alice Found There,* Maxwell Macmillan (New York, NY), 1993.

Weather, Harcourt Brace (New York, NY), 1994.

Pets, Harcourt Brace (New York, NY), 1994.

Bedtime, Harcourt (New York, NY), 1995.

I Want My Dinner ("Little Princess" series), Andersen Press (London, England), 1995.

Shapes, Red Wagon Books (New York, NY), 1995.

Furry Tales: A Bumper Book of Ten Favourite Animal Tales, Andersen Press (London, England), 1999.

I Want a Sister ("Little Princess" series), Andersen Press (London, England), 1999.

I Don't Want to Go to Hospital ("Little Princess" series), Andersen Press (London, England), 2000.

Wash Your Hands! ("Little Princess" series), Kane/Miller (New York, NY), 2001, published as *I Don't Want to Wash My Hands,* Collins (London, England), 2003.

I Want My Dummy ("Little Princess" series), Andersen Press (London, England), 2001.

I Want My Tooth ("Little Princess" series), Andersen Press (London, England), 2002, Kane/Miller (La Jolla, CA), 2005.

Centipede's 100 Shoes, Andersen Press (London, England), 2002.

Centipede's One Hundred Shoes, Henry Holt (New York, NY), 2003.

I Don't Want to Go to Bed!, Andersen Press (London, England), 2003, Kane/Miller (La Jolla, CA), 2004.

I Want My Pacifier ("Little Princess" series), Kane/Miller (La Jolla, CA), 2004.

I Want My Mum! ("Little Princess" series), Andersen Press (London, England), 2004.

I Want a Friend ("Little Princess" series), Andersen Press (London, England), 2005.

I Want My Present ("Little Princess" series), Andersen Press (London, England), 2005.

Is It Because?, Andersen Press (London, England), 2004, Barrons Educational Series (Hauppauge, NY), 2005.

Say Please! ("Little Princess" series), Andersen Press (London, England), 2005.

I Want to Go Home! ("Little Princess" series), Andersen Press (London, England), 2006.

ILLUSTRATOR:

Iris Grender, *Did I Ever Tell You . . . ?,* Hutchinson (London, England), 1977.

Iris Grender, *The Second Did I Ever Tell You . . . ? Book,* Hutchinson (London, England), 1978.

Patricia Gray and David Mackay, *Two Monkey Tales,* Longman (London, England), 1979.

Bernard Stone, *The Charge of the Mouse Brigade,* Andersen Press (London, England), 1979.

Jean Russell, editor, *The Magnet Book of Strange Tales,* Methuen (London, England), 1980.

Philip Curtis, *Mr Browser Meets the Burrowers,* Andersen Press (London, England), 1980.

Bernard Stone, *The Tale of Admiral Mouse,* Andersen Press (London, England), 1981.

Philip Curtis, *Invasion from below the Earth,* Knopf (New York, NY), 1981.

Iris Grender, *Did I Ever Tell You about My Irish Great Grandmother?,* Hutchinson (London, England), 1981.

Naomi Lewis, *Hare and Badger Go to Town,* Andersen Press (London, England), 1981.

Iris Grender, *But That's Another Story,* Knight, 1982.

Eric Morecambe, *The Reluctant Vampire,* Methuen (London, England), 1982.

Philip Curtis, *The Revenge of the Brain Sharpeners,* Andersen (London, England), 1982.

J.K. Hooper, *Kaspar and the Iron Poodle,* Andersen Press (London, England), 1982.

Jean Russell, editor, *The Methuen Book of Sinister Stories,* Methuen (London, England), 1982.

Philip Curtis, *Mr Browser and the Mini-Meteorites,* Andersen Press (London, England), 1983.

Philip Curtis, *Invasion of the Comet People,* Knopf (New York, NY), 1983.

Philip Curtis, *Mr Browser and the Brain Sharpeners,* Andersen Press (London, England), 1983.

Hazel Townson, *The Shrieking Face,* Andersen Press (London, England), 1984.

Alan Sillitoe, *Marmalade Jim and the Fox,* Robson (London, England), 1984.

Roger Collinson, *Paper Flags and Penny Ices,* Andersen Press (London, England), 1984.

Michael Palin, *Limericks,* Red Fox (London, England), 1985.

W.J. Corbett, *The End of the Tale,* Methuen (London, England), 1985.

Philip Curtis, *Mr Browser in the Space Museum,* Andersen Press (London, England), 1985.

Hazel Townson, *Terrible Tuesday,* Andersen Press (London, England), 1985, Morrow (New York, NY), 1986.

Philip Curtis, *The Quest of the Quidnuncs,* Andersen Press (London, England), 1986.

Andrew Davies, *Alfonzo Bonzo,* Methuen (London, England), 1986.

Hiayam Oram, *Jenna and the Troublemaker,* Holt (New York, NY), 1986.

Adrian Henri, *The Phantom Lollipop Lady, and Other Poems,* Methuen (London, England), 1986.

Andrew Matthews, *Dixie's Demon,* Methuen (London, England), 1987.

Songs from Play School, A. & C. Black (London, England), 1987.

Iris Grender, *The Third Did I Ever Tell You . . . ?,* David & Charles (North Pomfret, VT), 1987.

Grender, *Did I Ever Tell You . . . What the Children Told Me?,* David & Charles (North Pomfret, VT), 1987.

Pat Thomson, *The Treasure Sock,* Delacorte (New York, NY), 1987.

Trinka H. Noble, *Meanwhile Back at the Ranch,* Dial Books for the Young (New York, NY), 1987.

Heather Eyles, *Well I Never!,* Stoddart (London, England), 1988.

Hywin Oram, *Anyone Seen Harry Lately?,* Andersen Press (London, England), 1988, David & Charles (North Pomfret, VT), 1989.

Naughty Stories, Arrow, 1989.

Ian Whybrow, *Sniff,* Bodley Head (London, England), 1989.

Adrian Henri, *Rhinestone Rhino, and Other Poems,* Methuen (London, England), 1989.

Jeanne Willis, *Earthlets, as Explained by Professor Xargle,* Dutton (New York, NY), 1989, published as *Dr Xargle's Book of Earthlets,* Andersen Press (London, England), 1989.

Barbara S. Hazen, *The Knight Who Was Afraid of the Dark,* Dial Books for Young Readers (New York, NY), 1989.

The Pop-up Book of Nonsense Verse, Random House (New York, NY), 1989.

Jack Elkington and Julia Heiles, *The Young Green Consumer Guide,* Victor Gollancz (London, England), 1990.

Andrew Matthews, *Dr Monsoon Taggart's Amazing Finishing Academy,* Mammoth (London, England), 1990.

Hazel Townson, *Victor's Party,* Andersen Press (London, England), 1990.

Vernon Scannell, *Love Shouts and Whispers,* Trafalgar (London, England), 1990.

Adèle Geras, *The Fantora Family Files,* Collins (London, England), 1990.

Alexander McCall Smith, *The Joke Machine,* Piccolo (London, England), 1990.

W.J. Corbett, *Toby's Iceberg,* Methuen (London, England), 1990.

Terrence Blacker, *In Control, Ms Wiz?,* Piccadilly (London, England), 1990.

Andrew Matthews, *Mistress Moonwater,* Mammoth (London, England), 1990.

Terrence Blacker, *Ms Wiz Banned!,* Piccadilly (London, England), 1990.

Philip Curtis, *Pen Friend from Another Planet,* Andersen Press (London, England), 1990.

Jeanne Willis, *Dr Xargle's Book of Earth Tiggers,* Andersen Press (London, England), 1990, published as *Earth Tigerlets, as Explained by Professor Xargle,* Dutton (New York, NY), 1991.

Jeanne Willis, *Dr Xargle's Book of Earth Mobiles,* Andersen Press (London, England), 1991.

Margaret Mahy, *Bubble Trouble,* Hamish Hamilton (London, England), 1991.

Hazel Townson, *Snakes Alive!, and Other Stories,* Andersen Press (London, England), 1991.

Even Naughtier Stories, Red Fox (London, England), 1991.

Vernon Scannell, *Travelling Light: Poems,* Bodley Head (London, England), 1991.

Simon Brett, *How to Be a Little Sod,* Gollancz (London, England), 1992.

Michael Rosen, *Reckless Ruby,* Andersen Press (London, England), 1992.

Michael Rosen, *Burping Bertha,* Andersen Press (London, England), 1993.

Roald Dahl, *Fantastic Mr Fox,* Viking (London, England), 1993.

Tim Healey, *It Came through the Wall,* Hutchinson (London, England), 1993, Mondo-Tronics (San Rafael, CA), 1996.

Terrence Blacker, *Ms Wiz Loves Dracula,* Macmillan (London, England), 1993.

Roald Dahl, *The Magic Finger,* Viking (London, England), 1993.

Claude Delafosse, *Animals,* Moonlight (London, England), 1994, Scholastic, Inc. (New York, NY), 1995.

Francesca Simon, *Horrid Henry,* Orion Children's Books (London, England), 1994.

Silly Stories, Orion (London, England), 1994.

Willis Hall, *The Vampire's Christmas,* Red Fox (London, England), 1994.

Hywin Oram, *The Second Princess,* Artists & Writers Guild, 1994.

Claude Delafosse, *Paintings,* Moonlight (London, England), 1994, published as *Portraits,* Scholastic, Inc. (New York, NY), 1995.

Francesca Simon, *Horrid Henry and the Secret Club,* Orion Children's (London, England), 1995.

Sally Pomme Clayton, *Tales of Amazing Maidens,* Orchard (London, England), 1995, published as *The Girl Who Went to the Underworld; The Girl Who Loved Food,* 1998.

Karen Wallace, *Ace Ghosts: A Spooky Tale from Creakie Hall,* Hamish Hamilton (London, England), 1996.

Karen Wallace, *Ghouls Rule: A Spooky Tale from Creakie Hall,* Hamish Hamilton (London, England), 1996.

Lynne Reid Banks, *Harry the Poisonous Centipede's Big Adventure: Another Story to Make You Squirm,* Collins (London, England), 1996, HarperCollins (New York, NY), 2001.

Francesca Simon, *Horrid Henry Tricks the Tooth Fairy,* Orion Children's (London, England), 1996.

Allan Ahlberg, *Miss Dirt the Dustman's Daughter,* Viking (London, England), 1996.

Lindsay Camp, *The Midnight Feast,* Andersen Press (London, England), 1996.

Willis Hall, *Vampire Park,* Bodley Head (London, England), 1996.

Michael Rosen, *Norma's Notebook,* Sundance Publishing (Littleton, MA), 1997.

Francesca Simon, *Horrid Henry's Nits,* Orion (London, England), 1997, published as *Horrid Henry's Head Lice,* Hyperion Books for Children (New York, NY), 2000.

Polly, the Most Poetic Person, Orchard (London, England), 1997.

Adrian Mitchell, *Balloon Lagoon and the Magic Islands of Poetry,* Orchard (London, England), 1997.

Geraldine McCaughrean, *The Wooden Horse; Pandora's Box,* Orchard (London, England), 1997.

Geraldine McCaughrean, *Theseus and the Minotaur; Orpheus and Eurydice; Apollo and Daphne,* Orchard (London, England), 1997.

Jeanne Willis, *Sloth's Shoes,* Andersen Press (London, England), 1997, Kane/Miller (La Jolla, CA), 1998.

Red Eyes at Night, Hodder (London, England), 1998.

The Wind in the Wallows, Andersen Press (London, England), 1998.

Lindsay Camp, *Why?,* Putnam (New York, NY), 1998.

Ian Whybrow, *Little Wolf's Haunted Hall for Small Horrors,* Collins (London, England), 1998, Carolrhoda Books (Minneapolis, MN), 2000.

Francesca Simon, *Horrid Henry Strikes It Rich,* Orion Children's (London, England), 1998, published as *Horrid Henry Gets Rich Quick,* Hyperion Books for Children (New York, NY), 2000.

Tony Bradman, selector, *The Kingfisher Treasury of Pirate Stories,* Kingfisher (Boston, MA), 1999.

Ian Whybrow, *Little Wolf's Book of Badness,* Carolrhoda Books (Minneapolis, MN), 1999.

Tony Robinson, *Tony Robinson's Kings and Queens,* Red Fox (London, England), 1999.

Francesca Simon, *Horrid Henry's Haunted House,* Orion (London, England), 1999.

Terrence Blacker, *Ms Wiz and the Sister of Doom,* Macmillan (London, England), 1999.

Jeanne Willis, *The Boy Who Lost His Bellybutton,* Andersen Press (London, England), 1999, Dorling Kindersley (New York, NY), 2000.

June Crebbin, *Tarquin, the Wonder Horse,* Walker (London, England), 2000.

Jeanne Willis, *Susan Laughs,* Andersen Press (London, England), 1999, Henry Holt (New York, NY), 2000.

Terrence Blacker, *Ms Wiz Goes to Hollywood,* Macmillan (London, England), 2000.

Ian Whybrow, *Little Wolf's Diary of Daring Deeds,* Carolrhoda Books (Minneapolis, MN), 2000.

Ian Whybrow, *Little Wolf, Forest Detective,* Andersen Press (London, England), 2000, Carolrhoda Books (Minneapolis, MN), 2001.

Jeanne Willis, *What Did I Look Like When I Was a Baby?,* G.P. Putnam (New York, NY), 2000.

Laurence Anholt, *Micky the Muckiest Boy,* Orchard (London, England), 2000.

Ian Whybrow, *There's a Spell up My Nose,* Hodder (London, England), 2000.

Ian Whybrow, *Little Wolf's Big Book of Spooks and Clues,* Omnibus (London, England), 2000.

Ian Whybrow, *Robin Hood's Best Shot,* Hodder (London, England), 2000.

Adélè Geras, *The Cats of Cuckoo Square: Two Stories,* Delacorte Press (New York, NY), 2001.

Barbara Eupan Todd, *Worzel Gummidge,* new edition, Oxford University Press (Oxford, England), 2001.

Francesca Simon, *Horrid Henry's Revenge,* Hyperion Books for Children (New York, NY), 2001.

Anna Perera, *Skew Whiff,* Oxford University Press (Oxford, England), 2001.

Jan Page, *It's Not Funny,* Corgi Pups (London, England), 2001.

Astrid Lindgren, *Pippi Goes Aboard,* new edition, Oxford University Press (Oxford, England), 2001.

Astrid Lindgren, *Pippi in the South Seas,* new edition, Oxford University Press (Oxford, England), 2001.

Oscar Wilde, *The Picture of Dorian Gray,* Viking (New York, NY), 2001.

Martin Jarvis, adaptor, Richmal Crompton, *William and the Bomb, and Other Stories,* Macmillan (London, England), 2001.

Martin Jarvis, adaptor, Richmal Crompton, *William the Great Actor, and Other Stories,* Macmillan (London, England), 2001.

Jon Blake, *One Girl School,* Oxford University Press (Oxford, England), 2001.

Martyn Beardsley, *Sir Gadabout Does His Best,* Dolphin (London, England), 2001.

Terence Blacker, *The Great Denture Adventure,* Macmillan (London, England), 2001.

Terence Blacker, *Ms Wiz, Millionaire,* Macmillan (London, England), 2001.

Andrew Matthews, reteller, *The Orchard Book of Shakespeare Stories,* Orchard (London, England), 2001, published eight volumes, 2002–03.

Jeanne Willis, *Don't Let Go!,* Andersen Press (London, England), 2002, G.P. Putnam (New York, NY), 2003.

Jeanne Willis, *Mark Two,* Andersen Press (London, England), 2002.

Ian Whybrow, *Dear Little Wolf,* First Avenue Editions (Minneapolis, MN), 2002.

Hazel Townson, *The Invisible Boy,* Andersen Press (London, England), 2002.

Paul Stewart, *The Were-Pig,* Corgi Pups (London, England), 2002.

Francesca Simon, *Horrid Henry and the Bogey Babysitter,* Dolphin (London, England), 2002.

Anne Fine, *How to Cross the Road and Not Turn into a Pizza,* Walker (London, England), 2002.

Charles Causley, *Jack the Treacle-Eater, and Other Poems,* Macmillan (London, England), 2002.

Charles Causley, *Figgie Hobbin, and Other Poems,* Macmillan (London, England), 2002.

Tony Bradman, *The Two Jacks,* Barrington Stoke (Edinburgh, Scotland), 2002.

Terence Blacker, *The Secret Life of Ms Wiz,* Macmillan (London, England), 2002.

Martyn Beardsley, *Sir Gadabout and the Little Horror,* Dolphin (London, England), 2002.

Jeanne Willis, *I Want to Be a Cowgirl,* Henry Holt (New York, NY), 2002.

Ian Whybrow, *Little Wolf's Handy Book of Poems,* First Avenue Editions (Minneapolis, MN), 2002.

Ian Whybrow, *Young Robin's Hood,* Mondo (New York, NY), 2002.

Ian Whybrow, *Little Wolf, Pack Leader,* Carolrhoda Books (Minneapolis, MN), 2002.

Barbara Mitchelhill, *The Case of the Popstar's Wedding,* Andersen Press (London, England), 2002.

Francesca Simon, *Horrid Henry's Stinkbomb,* Dolphin (London, England), 2002.

Jeanne Willis, *Mankey Monkey,* Andersen Press (London, England), 2002.

Francesca Simon, *A Triple Treat of Horrid Henry,* Dolphin (London, England), 2003.

Berlie Doherty, *Tilly Mint Tales,* new edition, Young Corgi (London, England), 2003.

Berlie Doherty, *Tricky Nelly's Birthday Treat,* Walker (London, England), 2003.

Margaret Mahy, *The Gargling Gorilla, and Other Stories,* Collins (London, England), 2003.

Jeanne Willis, *Tadpole's Promise,* Andersen Press (London, England), 2003.

Charles Causley, *The Young Man of Cury, and Other Poems,* new edition, Macmillan (London, England), 2003.

Helen Cresswell, *Lizzie Dripping,* new edition, Oxford University Press (Oxford, England), 2003.

Charles Causley, *All Day Saturday, and Other Poems,* new edition, Macmillan (London, England), 2003.

Terence Blacker, *Ms Wiz Magic,* Macmillan (London, England), 2003.

Terence Blacker, *Time Flies for Ms Wiz; Power-Crazy Ms Wiz; Ms Wiz Loves Dracula,* Macmillan (London, England), 2003.

Adèlè Geras, *The Cats of Cuckoo Square: Callie's Kitten,* Dell Yearling Books (New York, NY), 2003.

Adèlè Geras, *The Fabulous Fantora Photographs,* Oxford University Press (Oxford, England), 2003.

Adèlè Geras, *The Fabulous Fantora Files,* Oxford University Press (Oxford, England), 2003.

Astrid Lindgren, *The Best of Pippi Longstocking,* new edition, Oxford University Press (Oxford, England), 2003.

Tony Bradman, *Ali Baba and the Stolen Treasure,* Orchard (London, England), 2003.

Adèlè Geras, *The Cats of Cuckoo Square: Geejay the Hero,* Dell Yearling Books (New York, NY), 2003.

Francesca Simon, *Helping Hercules,* Dolphin (London, England), 2003.

Francesca Simon, *Horrid Henry and the Mummy's Curse,* Dolphin (London, England), 2003.

Jeanne Willis, *I Hate School,* Andersen Press (London, England), 2003, Atheneum Books for Young Readers (New York, NY), 2004.

Martyn Beardsley, *Sir Gadabout Goes Overboard,* Dolphin (London, England), 2004.

Terence Blacker, *Ms Wiz Superstar,* Macmillan (London, England), 2004.

Terence Blacker, *The Crazy World of Ms Wiz,* Macmillan (London, England), 2004.

Carol Diggory Shields, *English Fresh Squeezed!: Forty Thirst-for-Knowledge-Quenching Poems,* Handprint Books (New York, NY), 2004.

Francesca Simon, *Horrid Henry's Joke Book,* Orion Children's (London, England), 2004.

Francesca Simon, *Horrid Henry Meets the Queen* (includes audiotape), Dolphin (London, England), 2004.

Adrian Mitchell, *Daft as a Doughnut,* Orchard (London, England), 2004.

Barbara Mitchelhill, *How to Be a Detective,* Andersen Press (London, England), 2004.

John Foster, compiler, *The Flying Trapeze, and Other Puzzle Poems,* Oxford University Press (Oxford, England), 2004.

Eoin Colfer, *The Legend of Spud Murphy,* Puffin (London, England), 2004.

D.J. Lucas (pen name of Sally Grindley), *Dear Max,* Orchard (London, England), 2004, Margaret K. McElderry Books (New York, NY), 2006.

Tony Bradman, *Robin Hood and the Silver Arrow,* Orchard (London, England), 2004.

Tony Bradman, *William Tell and the Apple for Freedom,* Orchard (London, England), 2004.

Tony Bradman, *Aladdin and the Fabulous Genie,* Orchard (London, England), 2004.

Ian Whybrow, *Little Wolf, Terror of the Shivery Sea,* Carolrhoda Books (Minneapolis, MN), 2004.

Tony Bradman, *Arthur and the King's Sword,* Orchard (London, England), 2004.

Tony Bradman, *Jason and the Voyage to the Edge of the World,* Orchard (London, England), 2004.

Francesca Simon, *Horrid Henry's Big Bad Book,* Dolphin (London, England), 2004.

Jeanne Willis, *Shhh!,* Hyperion Books for Children (New York, NY), 2004.

Ian Whybrow, *Badness for Beginners: A Little Wolf and Smellybreff Adventure,* Carolrhoda Books (Minneapolis, MN), 2005.

Francesca Simon, *Horrid Henry's Wicked Ways,* Dolphin (London, England), 2005.

Francesca Simon, *Horrid Henry and the Mega-Mean Time Machine,* Dolphin (London, England), 2005.

Jeanne Willis, *Tadpole's Promise,* Atheneum Books for Young Readers (New York, NY), 2005.

Francesca Simon, *Don't Cook Cinderella,* Dolphin (London, England), 2005.

Eric Brown, *Space Ace,* Barington Stoke (Edinburgh, Scotland), 2005.

John Foster, *The Universal Vacuum Cleaner, and Other Riddle Poems,* Oxford University Press (Oxford, England), 2005.

Sally Grindley), *Bravo Max,* Orchard (London, England), 2005.

Jan Mark, *Robin Hood All at Sea,* Barrington Stoke (Edinburgh, Scotland), 2005.

Jeanne Willis, *Misery Moo,* Henry Holt (New York, NY), 2005.

Martyn Beardsley, *Sir Gadabout Goes Barking Mad,* Dolphin (London, England), 2005.

Lynne Reid Banks, *Harry the Poisonous Centipede Goes to Sea,* Collins (London, England), 2006.

Andrew Matthews, reteller, *Much Ado about Nothing: A Shakespeare Story,* Orchard (London, England), 2006.

Sammy and the Starman, Barrington Stoke (Edinburgh, Scotland), 2006.

Franscesca Simon, *Horrid Henry and the Football Fiend,* Orion (London, England), 2006.

Ian Whybrow, *Through the Cat-flap,* Hodder (London, England), 2006.

Ian Whybrow, *Alex, the Walking Accident,* Hodder (London, England), 2006.

Anne Fine, *Notso Hotso,* Farrar, Straus (New York, NY), 2006.

Paul Steward, *Dogbird, and Other Mixed-up Tales,* Corgi Pups (London, England), 2006.

Jeanne Willis, *Gorilla! Gorilla!,* Atheneum (New York, NY), 2006.

ILLUSTRATOR; "AMBER BROWN" SERIES

Paula Danziger, *Amber Brown Is Not a Crayon,* Putnam (New York, NY), 1994.

Paula Danziger, *Forever Amber Brown,* Putnam (New York, NY), 1996.

Paula Danziger, *You Can't Eat Your Chicken Pox, Amber Brown,* Putnam (New York, NY), 1996.

Paula Danziger, *Amber Brown Sees Red,* Putnam (New York, NY), 1997.

Paula Danziger, *Amber Brown Goes Fourth,* Putnam (New York, NY), 1997.

Paula Danziger, *Amber Brown Wants Extra Credit,* Putnam (New York, NY), 1997.

Paula Danziger, *Amber Brown Is Feeling Blue,* Putnam (New York, NY), 1998.

Paula Danziger, *I, Amber Brown,* Putnam (New York, NY), 1999.

Paula Danziger, *It's Justin Time, Amber Brown,* Putnam (New York, NY), 2001.

Paula Danziger, *What a Trip, Amber Brown,* Putnam (New York, NY), 2001.

Paula Danziger, *Get Ready for Second Grade, Amber Brown,* Putnam (New York, NY), 2002.

Paula Danziger, *It's a Fair Day, Amber Brown,* Putnam (New York, NY), 2002.

Paula Danziger, *Amber Brown Is Green with Envy,* Putnam (New York, NY), 2003.

Paula Danziger, *Second Grade Rules, Amber Brown,* Putnam (New York, NY), 2004.

Paula Danziger, *Orange You Glad It's Halloween, Amber Brown?,* Putnam (New York, NY), 2005.

OTHER

Author of animated television films, including *What's in a Name?, King of All The Birds, Oscar Buys the Biscuits, Muddy Milly,* and *Spacemare.* Contributor of cartoons to magazines, including *Punch* and *Town.*

ADAPTATIONS: I'm Coming to Get You! was adapted as a filmstrip. Several of Ross's books have been adapted for television. Ross's "Little Princess" books were adapted as an animated television series, broadcast on England's Channel 5 beginning 2006.

SIDELIGHTS: British author and illustrator Tony Ross is well known to both young children and their parents. Featured in dozens upon dozens of books, Ross's whimsical watercolor and pen-and-ink artwork appeals to bookworms from infancy to pre-teen, and his original self-illustrated "Little Princess" stories have even inspired an animated television series broadcast in his native England. "My training as an etcher, and my liking of graphic, rather than fine, artists, gave me a love of black line on white paper," Ross once commented. "To me, a children's illustrator is a creator of worlds for kids, and so I prefer to write my own texts. I like telling stories, I like to see children laugh, I like to draw."

In titles such such as *I'm Coming to Get You!, Super Dooper Jezebel,* and *Centipede's 100 Shoes,* Ross pairs his humorous text with his unique drawing style to both original and traditional stories. This unique approach quickly boosted Ross's reputation as an author and illustrator; in 1986, a year after he earned his first major awards for *I'm Coming to Get You,* he earned a prestigious Kate Greenaway Medal commendation. "Ross's literary tale-telling favours a deadpan humour and aims to establish intimacy with the reader," observed Jane Doonan in *Twentieth-Century Children's Writers.* "His visual style varies considerably, but whatever he does, he always displays a strong sense of page design, and a masterly control of his media. Deceptively sketchy at times, his pen romps along, in the tradition of English narrative illustration. However whiskery fine, feathery light, frothy, bold, or meticulously incised, the line has unquenchable vitality."

Ross was born in London but grew up near Liverpool. He more or less drifted into art school at age eighteen, later admitting to an interviewer that "My parents didn't really have any ambitions for me and I had none for myself and it was really a case of the only thing I could do." While in college, he sold drawings to magazines such as *New Statesman* and *Punch,* but rather than pursuing art after graduation he found more lucrative work in advertising and publicity firms. As Ross once explained how he made entree into the world of illustration, while teaching advertising part time at Manchester Polytechnic, the school "decided that there was nobody to look after the illustration group, there were illustration students and no member of staff. So they said, 'Well, you've drawn cartoons, you do it.' I said, 'I can't. I'm a designer, not an illustrator.' They said, 'You're the only one who's drawn things, so you'd better look after them.' So I took over the illustration group and thought, 'Well, if I'm doing illustration I'd better do some. I'd better find out what all this nonsense is about.'" In fact, Ross's first self-illustrated picture book, the six-volume *Tales from Mr. Toffy's Circus,* came about "simply because I felt I'd better become an illustrator."

After publishing his first books during the early 1970s, Ross soon found his work in great demand, and within a decade he was able to support himself and his family

by writing and drawing. As he was quoted as saying in *Twentieth-Century Children's Writers,* "the motivation, of course, is the enjoyment a pen and a sheet of blank paper brings—certainly to me, every time, hopefully to others."

Since beginning his career, Ross has developed a distinctive drawing style which involves the black lines and transparent blocks of vivid color characteristic of graphic art. In *I'm Coming to Get You!,* for instance, "the illustrations are in colors as loud as a yell, rendered in a scratchy fashion that intensifies the speedy effects," a *Publishers Weekly* reviewer commented. "There is a dynamic quality to Tony Ross's illustrations," a *Wilson Library Bulletin* critic similarly observed of *Hugo and Oddsock,* "a quality created with raw hues of blue, green, and red and with strong contrasts between light and dark areas. But more important are the slashing, diagonal shapes and lines." The net effect of his animated line and "strong contrasts of light and dark and big and little," is, according to Donnarae MacCann and Olga Richard in the *Wilson Library Bulletin,* a "sly, ebullient humor."

Ross shares his unique sense of humor with readers through both original stories and retellings or adaptations of traditional tales. *Super Dooper Jezebel,* for instance, "is typical Ross from the zany cartoon-style watercolors to the ironic biting humor," as Heide Pilcher declared in *School Library Journal.* In *Lazy Jack,* the illustrator's "spacious watercolors add narrative twists of their own to this traditional tale," as a critic noted in the *Bulletin of the Center for Children's Books. Lazy Jack* "is tongue-in-cheek, the art absurd, [and] the overall effect a super-silly read aloud," the critic added, while Ross's "Little Princess" books—which find a impatient but lovable young girl dealing with common childhood experiences in books such as *I Want My Mum!, I Want My Dinner,* and *Say Please!*—earned plaudits from Linda Staskus, who wrote in her *School Library Journal* review of *I Want My Tooth* that Ross's "lighthearted text" and softly colored pen-and-ink drawings present youngsters with "a good-humored and different take on a common childhood experience."

Ross's willingness to sometimes break with tradition gives his work a uniquely funny viewpoint. However, it is the combination of pictures and words that makes his books so enjoyable, according to a *Horn Book* reviewer. The artist's illustrations "add much to the humor, interacting with the text in a lively interchange that enriches and extends both." Ross's work is distinguished by his "comic imagination and a superb sense of theater," MacCann and Richard stated. As a result, they concluded, "it is hard to think of many cartoonists in recent years who have developed as rapidly as Ross with both a comic touch and a serious design interest."

His particular strengths as an illustrator have allowed Ross to develop winning collaborations with a number of popular children's-book writers, among them Paula Danziger, Lynne Reid Banks, Francesca Simon, Jeanne Willis, and Ian Whybrow. Perhaps most well known to American readers is his work for Danziger's popular "Amber Brown" series. Amber Brown is a typical third grader whose joys and troubles reflect the issues pertinent to contemporary youngsters. Ross's illustrations reveal a freckled, gangly, and sometimes scruffy Amber, as well as her pals and her surroundings. *Horn Book* correspondent Maeve Visser Knoth observed that both the text and drawings in *Amber Brown Is Not a Crayon* are "well suited to the audience," while in *Booklist* review of the same title Hazel Rochman concluded: "Ross's cartoon-style illustrations capture Amber's vital classroom—the fun and the fights, as well as the empty place when a friend moves away." As Amber makes the move to fourth grade in *Amber Brown Is Green with Envy,* Michele Shaw wrote in *School Library Journal* that Ross intrigues readers with the girl's attempts to deal with changes in her life. His "black-and-white drawings show Amber's humorous facial expressions" as she grapples with her mother's upcoming remarriage, the possibility of moving to a new house, and the frustration of being left behind when her mom and aunt take a trip to Disneyland.

Simon's "Horrid Henry" books, Reid Banks's multi-volume "Harry the Poisonous Centipede" saga, and Whybrow's "Little Wolf" stories top many a young child's "favorite series" book list because of the perfect pairing between author and illustrator. Ross's "imaginative drawings" featuring the adventures of the teen-aged centipede that stars in Reid Banks's books "enhance" the author's verbal hijinks, including her ability to tell her tale from a "limited, centipede linguistic perspective," as Kay Weisman noted in *Booklist*. A child "whose general meanness goes entirely unchecked" in Simon's series installment *Horrid Henry's Head Lice* is given a suitable verbal comeuppance courtesy of the illustrator's "droll line drawings" of the antihero's discomfort, according to *School Library Journal* critic Pat Leach. And in such books as *Little Wolf's Book of Badness* and *Little Wolf's Diary of Daring Deeds*

"Ross's colorful line drawings are hysterically appealing, adding to the humor" of Whybrow's "lively and irreverent" storyline, according to Robyn Walker' *School Library Journal* appraisal of the former title.

In an interview posted on the HarperCollins Children's Book Web site, Ross discussed the philosophy that guides his illustration work. "I'm aware of the fact that with a picture book, a simple book, once the child has read it, I like them to be able to read it again and find something else that wasn't evident the first time. I think it's important that a book can be read over and over again, and not give up everything on the first reading. So in a child-like attempt to make this happen I put little sub-plots, little bits of detail and little things that are really quite obscure, which may emerge in time. Sometimes they're so obscure they don't emerge at all!"

BIOGRAPHICAL AND CRITICAL SOURCES:

BOOKS

Twentieth-Century Children's Writers, 4th edition, St. James (Detroit, MI), 1995, pp. 827-829.

PERIODICALS

Booklist, April 15, 1994, Hazel Rochman, review of *Amber Brown Is Not a Crayon,* p. 1533; October 15, 1994, Ilene Cooper, review of *The Second Princess,* p. 438; March 15, 1995, p. 1330; January 1, 1996, Carolyn Phelan, review of *Animals,* p. 838; November 15, 1996, p. 587; June 1, 1998, Annie Ayres, review of *Sloth's Shoes,* p. 1785; May 15, 2001, Roger Leslie, review of *The Picture of Dorian Gray,* p. 1746; August 1, 2006, Kay Weisman, review of *Dear Max,* p. 86; October 15, 2006, Kay Weisman, review of *Harry the Poisonous Centipede Goes to Sea,* p. 44.

Bulletin of the Center for Children's Books, July-August, 1986, review of *Lazy Jack,* p. 217.

Horn Book, September-October, 1986, p. 604; July-August, 1994, Maeve Visser Knoth, review of *Amber Brown Is Not a Crayon,* p. 447; May-June, 1995, p. 348; September-October, 2006, Susan Dove Lempke, review of *Gorilla! Gorilla!,* p. 573.

Kirkus Reviews, March 1, 2003, review of *Centipede's 100 Shoes,* p. 397; June 15, 2004, review of *I Hate School,* p. 583.

New York Times Book Review, November 13, 1983.

Publishers Weekly, October 26, 1984, review of *I'm Coming to Get You!,* p. 104; February 21, 1994, p. 254; February 23, 1998, p. 76; February 24, 2003, review of *Centipede's 100 Shoes,* p. 70; August 7, 2006, review of *Dear Max,* p. 59; November 27, 2006, review of *Dogbird, and Other Mixed-up Tales,* p. 51.

School Library Journal, April, 1981, p. 117; September, 1986, p. 127; December, 1988, Heide Pieler, review of *Super Dooper Jezebel,* p. 92; July, 1989; March, 2001, Pat Leach, review of *Horrid Henry's Head Lice,* p. 220; May, 2001, Carrie Schadle, review of *Harry the Poisonous Centipede's Big Adventure,* p. 108; July, 2002, Ruth Semrau, review of *I Want to Be a Cowgirl,* p. 102; May, 2003, Pat Leach, review of *Little Wolf, Pack Leader,* p. 132; September, 2003, Michele Shaw, review of *Amber Brown Is Green with Envy,* p. 176; August, 2004, Marian Creamer, review of *I Hate School,* p. 104; September, 2005, Robyn Walker, review of *Badness for Beginners: A Little Wolf and Smellybreff Adventure,* p. 188; October, 2005, Linda Staskus, review of *I Want My Tooth,* p. 127; March, 2006, Catherine Threadgill, review of *Notso Hotso,* p. 187; July, 2006, Kathleen Kelly MacMillan, review of *Gorilla! Gorilla!,* p. 90; September, 2006, Alison Grant, review of *Harry the Poisonous Centipede Goes to Sea,* p. 158.

Wilson Library Bulletin, January, 1979, Donnarae MacCann and Olga Richard, review of *Hugo and Oddsock,* p. 378; March, 1985, pp. 482-83; November, 1986, pp. 47-48; June, 1989, pp. 96-97.

ONLINE

Contemporary Writers Web site, http://www.contemporarywriter.com/ (January 27, 2007), "Tony Ross."

HarperCollins Web site, http://www.harpercollins childrensbooks.co.uk/ (January 27, 2007), "Tony Ross."*

*   *   *

RUBENSTEIN, Richard E. 1938-
(Richard Edward Rubenstein)

PERSONAL: Born February 24, 1938, in New York, NY; son of Harold S. (in textiles) and Jo Rubenstein; married Elizabeth Marsh, August 26, 1962 (divorced); married Brenda Libman, September 21, 1975; children:

Alec Louis, Matthew Robert, Hannah, Shana. *Education:* Harvard University, B.A., 1959, J.D., 1963; Oxford University, M.A.Juris., 1961. *Politics:* "Leftist." *Religion:* Jewish. *Hobbies and other interests:* Playing jazz piano, cooking.

ADDRESSES: Home—Washington, DC. *Office*—Institute for Conflict Analysis and Resolution, 3300 Washington Blvd., Arlington, VA, 22201. *E-mail*—richruben@aol.com; rrubenst@gmu.edu.

CAREER: Steptoe & Johnson (law firm), Washington, DC, attorney, 1963-67; Adlai Stevenson Institute, Chicago, IL, assistant director, 1967-70; Roosevelt University, Chicago, associate professor of political science, 1970-79; Antioch University, Washington, member of law faculty, also professor of conflict resolution, professor of law, 1979-87; George Mason University, Fairfax, VA, professor of conflict resolution and public affairs, 1987—; George Mason University, Institute for Conflict Analysis and Resolution, director, 1988-1991. Malcolm X Community College, Chicago, professorial lecturer, 1969-70; University of Provence, Fulbright visiting professor, 1976-77. Consultant to National Advisory Commission on Causes and Prevention of Violence, 1968-69.

MEMBER: Phi Beta Kappa.

AWARDS, HONORS: Rhodes Scholar at Oxford University, 1959-61. Appointed University Professor, George Mason University, 2007.

WRITINGS:

(Editor, with Robert M. Fogelson) *Mass Violence in America,* Arno, 1969.

Rebels in Eden: Mass Political Violence in the United States, Little, Brown (Boston, MA), 1970.

Left Turn: Origins of the Next American Revolution, Little, Brown (Boston, MA), 1973.

(Editor) *Great Courtroom Battles,* Playboy Press (New York, NY), 1973.

Alchemists of Revolution: Terrorism in the Modern World, Basic Books (New York, NY), 1987.

Group Violence in America, Center for Conflict Analysis and Resolution, George Mason University (Fairfax, VA), 1993.

Frameworks for Interpreting Conflict: A Handbook for Journalists, Institute for Conflict Analysis and Resolution, George Mason University (Fairfax, VA), 1994.

Comrade Valentine, Harcourt (Orlando, FL), 1994.

When Jesus became God: The Epic Fight over Christ's Divinity in the Last Days of Rome, Harcourt (Orlando, FL), 1999.

Aristotle's Children: How Muslims, Christians, and Jews Rediscovered Ancient Wisdom and Illuminated the Dark Ages, Harcourt (Orlando, FL), 2003.

Thus Saith the Lord: The Revolutionary Moral Vision of Isaiah and Jeremiah, Harcourt (Orlando, FL), 2006.

Contributor to books, including *The Politics of Protest,* edited by Jerome H. Skolnick, Ballantine (New York, NY), 1969; *The Conscience of the City,* edited by Martin Meyerson, George Braziller (New York, NY), 1970; *The New American Revolution,* edited by R. Aya and N. Miller, Free Press (New York, NY), 1971; *Human Rights and Our Responsibility to Future Generations,* edited by Emmanuel Agius, University of Malta, 2002; and *The New Global Terrorism,* edited by Charles Kegley, Prentice-Hall, 2003. Series editor, with Dan C. Mc-Curry, *"American Farmers and the Rise of Agribusiness,"* Ayer (Salem, NY), 1975; and *Conflict: From Analysis to Intervention,* 2nd edition, edited by Sandra Cheldelin et al., Millenium Books (New York, NY), 2007.

Also contributor to periodicals and scholarly journals, including *Negotiation Journal, Foreign Policy,* and *Journal of Peace and Conflict Studies.*

SIDELIGHTS: Richard E. Rubenstein, having graduated from Oxford University and Harvard law school, has been a longtime professor in the field of political science and law. He has worked at several educational institutions throughout his career, including George Mason University. Rubenstein is also the author of several books on violence in politics and, more recently, of books concerning the history of Judaic and Christian theology and religion. In *Thus Saith the Lord: The Revolutionary Moral Vision of Isaiah and Jeremiah,* Rubenstein examines the biblical prophets, focusing especially on Jeremiah and Isaiah, their role in the history of Judaism, and how they changed the Jewish perception of God from a local to a universal entity. While a *Kirkus Reviews* contributor felt that the book did not meet its goal of creating "fresh insights into the world's present conflicts," other reviewers bestowed

unreserved praise. Extolling Rubenstein's research and writing, *Booklist* critic George Cohen called *Thus Saith the Lord* "a lucid and meticulously argued book."

BIOGRAPHICAL AND CRITICAL SOURCES:

PERIODICALS

Booklist, October 1, 2006, George Cohen, review of *Thus Saith the Lord: The Revolutionary Moral Vision of Isaiah and Jeremiah,* p. 30.

Kirkus Reviews, September 11, 2006, review of *Thus Saith the Lord,* p. 50.

Publishers Weekly, August 1, 2006, review of *Thus Saith the Lord,* p. 772.

ONLINE

Richard E. Rubenstein Home Page http://www.rich rubenstein.com (January 30, 2006).

*   *   *

**RUBENSTEIN, Richard Edward
See RUBENSTEIN, Richard E.**

*   *   *

**RUCKA, Greg
  (Gregory Rucka)**

PERSONAL: Born in San Francisco, CA; married Jennifer Van Meter (a writer); children: two. *Education:* Vassar College, A.B.; University of Southern California, M.F.A.

ADDRESSES: Home—Portland, OR.

CAREER: Writer. Formerly worked as a house painter, waiter, EMT, security guard, technical writer, beta tester, and fight choreographer.

AWARDS, HONORS: Eisner Award, Best Limited Series, 2000, for *Whiteout,* 2004, for *Gotham Central;* Eisner Award nomination, 2002, for *Queen & Country: Operation Broken Ground.*

WRITINGS:

NOVELS

Keeper, Bantam (New York, NY), 1996.
Finder, Bantam (New York, NY), 1997.
Shooting at Midnight, Bantam (New York, NY), 1999.
Smoker, Bantam (New York, NY), 1998.
Critical Space, Bantam (New York, NY), 2001.
Fistful of Rain, Bantam (New York, NY), 2003.
A Gentleman's Game: A Queen & Country Novel, Bantam (New York, NY), 2004.
Private Wars, Bantam (New York, NY), 2005.
Perfect Dark: Initial Vector, Tor (New York, NY), 2005.
Perfect Dark: Second Front, Tor (New York, NY), 2007.

GRAPHIC NOVELS

Whiteout, Oni Press (Portland, OR), 1999.
Batman: No Man's Land, DC Comics (New York, NY), Volume 2, 1999, Volume 5, 2001.
Grendel: Past Prime, Dark Horse (Milwaukie, OR), 2000.
Batman: Evolution, DC Comics (New York, NY), 2001.
Wonder Woman: The Hiketeia, DC Comics (New York, NY), 2002.
Queen & Country: Operation Broken Ground, Oni Press (Portland, OR), 2002.
Batman: Bruce Wayne, Fugitive, DC Comics (New York, NY), 2002.
Batman/Huntress: Cry for Blood, DC Comics (New York, NY), 2002.
Queen & Country: Volume 3: Operation Crystal Ball, Oni Press (Portland, OR), 2003.
Queen & Country: Operation Storm Front, Oni Press (Portland, OR), 2004.
Gotham Central (two volumes), DC Comics (New York, NY), 2004.
In the Line of Duty, DC Comics (New York, NY), 2004.
Batman, Death and the Maidens, DC Comics (New York, NY), 2004.
Wonder Woman, Down to Earth, DC Comics (New York, NY), 2004.
(With Mark Verheiden and Gail Simone,) *Superman, Sacrifice,* DC Comics (New York, NY), 2005.
Wonder Woman: Bitter Rivals, DC Comics (New York, NY), 2005.
Half a Life, illustrated by Michael Lark, DC Comics (New York, NY), 2005.

Wonder Woman: Eyes of the Gorgon, DC Comics (New York, NY), 2005.
(With Geoff Johns and Jeremy Johns) *Superman, the Healing Touch,* DC Comics (New York, NY), 2005.
(With Geoff Johns and Judd Winick) *The OMAC Project,* DC Comics (New York, NY), 2005.
(With Geoff Johns) *Wonder Woman: The Land of the Dead,* DC Comics (New York, NY), 2006.

Writer of comic books.

SIDELIGHTS: Greg Rucka is a novelist and a writer of comic books and graphic novels. Most of his novels feature the protagonist Atticus Kodiak, a tough, smart bodyguard who follows his heart rather than his pocketbook when it comes to taking on assignments.

Keeper takes up the abortion controversy in all its violence and pathos. Early on in the novel, Kodiak accompanies his pregnant girlfriend to a Manhattan abortion clinic that is being targeted by a militant right-to-life group, Sword of the Silent. That difficult and frightening experience causes him to sympathize with the clinic's director, Felice Romero, who is herself a target of violent threats from the group and its fanatical leader, Jonathan Crowell. As the battle between the pro-life and pro-choice contingents heats up and threatens to become increasingly violent, some concerned parties initiate a forum called "Common Ground" to try to help clear the air. When Romero makes her intention to attend Common Ground known, she receives letters from Sword of the Silent that threaten not only her life but that of her Down's Syndrome-afflicted daughter. Kodiak takes on the arduous task of keeping both safe from their would-be assassins.

Critics were impressed by a number of the novel's elements, from its even handling of the abortion controversy to how the author orchestrates the scenes of violence. A *Publishers Weekly* contributor stated that the "pros and cons of abortion are intelligently presented." The reviewer also admired Rucka's storytelling for its fast, smooth pace, interesting characters, and "clean and visual" prose. Dawn L. Anderson, writing in the *Library Journal,* called *Keeper* a "story as timely as today's headlines" and a "tense and exciting novel." *Booklist* contributor Thomas Gaughan appreciated its "characterizations of people twisted enough to murder to protect life."

Finder followed *Keeper* the next year. The novel finds Atticus Kodiak not far from where *Keeper* left him—still in New York but now working as a bouncer for a swank "bondage-and-discipline" club. The book presents the tale of Erika Wyatt, a fifteen-year-old on the run, whose father, Colonel Wyatt, is a promiscuous military intelligence agent for whom Kodiak used to work, and whose mother, when still the colonel's wife, was briefly Kodiak's lover. When Erika shows up at the sex club and is threatened at knife-point, Kodiak helps her escape, little knowing that she is the target of not just one menacing male but a whole crew of British S.A.S. officers (a group that operates with the same stealth as the U.S. Navy SEALS). Unfortunately, the intensity of Erika's dislike at being protected is only equaled by the S.A.S. officers' fervor for kidnapping her. Heavy suspense and regular eruptions of violence are the result.

A *Publishers Weekly* contributor was guarded in responding to *Finder,* noting that "if Rucka . . . ever finds a subject big enough for his tough-guy talents, he'll be a writer to watch." Robert C. Moore wrote in his *Library Journal* review that if the reader can deal with the violence "*Finder* pulls you to a satisfying conclusion." A *Kirkus Reviews* contributor appreciated the book's "fine cliff-hangers, well-executed violence, and skillfully sketched characters"; the reviewer ultimately deemed it "flawed, but still superior to most lone-wolf genre tales."

In *Smoker,* Kodiak is hired to protect a biomedical research scientist who is going to testify against the tobacco industry, accusing them of putting additives in their cigarettes to make them more addicting. *Booklist* contributor Wes Lukowsky called *Smoker* an "exciting action adventure."

Critical Space finds Kodiak protecting a woman who is, in fact, a professional killer. Kodiak finds himself up against the FBI, his own best friends, and possibly the woman herself. *Booklist* reviewer David Pitt called *Critical Space* "a first-rate thriller."

Rucker is also the author of numerous graphic novels, including *Whiteout,* which won the Eisner Award for Best Limited Series in 2000, and *Queen & Country: Operation Broken Ground,* which was nominated for an Eisner Award.

Rucka has continued to turn out novels and graphic novels or comics. For example, he has penned both graphic novels and standard novels focusing on his "Queen & Country" series. In the graphic novel *Queen & Country: Volume 3: Operation Crystal Ball,* readers find British intelligence battling terrorists across the globe in an effort to stop the unleashing of poison gas at an international soccer game. A *Publishers Weekly* contributor noted that "this book's pleasure lies in following the chase's twists and turns." *Queen & Country: Operation Storm Front* features British secret agent Tara Chace looking for the kidnappers of a Russian national. Marc Bernardin of *Entertainment Weekly* noted that readers would be "hard-pressed to find an espionage thriller as gritty."

In *A Gentleman's Game: A Queen & Country Novel,* Rucka borrows from his award-winning comics series to present a standard novel featuring British intelligence agent Chace on the trail of Muslim extremists who bombed the London Underground. Referring to the book as Rucka's "finest novel yet," *Entertainment Weekly* contributor Marc Bernardin noted that the "action . . . feels earned, not forced." A *Publishers Weekly* contributor commented on the author's "superb pacing, offbeat characters, wry plot twists and damning insight into oily schizoid Middle Eastern diplomacy." David Pitt, writing in *Booklist,* wrote that the author "does an excellent job of building the tension and suspense."

British agent Chace returns in *Private Wars,* this time coming out of retirement to rescue the son of the Uzbekistani president, whose own daughter is holding her brother captive and threatening to kill him. Marc Bernardin, once again writing in *Entertainment Weekly,* referred to the novel *Private Wars* as "a Swiss watch of a thriller: well-machined, precise, and inexorable." *Booklist* contributor David Pitt wrote: "Rucka injects the novel with a hard contemporary edge and a heavy dose of sensuality." In a review in *Publishers Weekly,* a contributor noted that this novel and its predecessor *A Gentleman's Game* "are well-researched, intriguingly complicated, exciting spy novels."

In addition to his "Queen & Country" books, Rucka continues to contribute stories about classic comic heroes, such as Wonder Woman and Batman. *Wonder Woman: Land of the Dead,* for example, which Rucka cowrote with Geoff Johns, features a blind Wonder Woman traveling to Hades to rescue Hermes. Philip Charles Crawford, writing in the *School Library Journal,* noted that as the story progresses the authors' "pacing and the art mesh to create a . . . story that provides insight into the psychology of Wonder Woman's heroism." Another Womder Woman comic, *Wonder Woman: Bitter Rivals*, finds the superhero caught up in the world of politics and underhanded dealings when she acts as an ambassador from the Amazon island of Themyscria. *Booklist* contributor Gordon Flagg wrote that the author "moves smoothly between multiple plotlines." Writing a review of *Wonder Woman: Eyes of the Gorgon*, and *Wonder Woman: The Land of the Dead*, Tina Coleman noted in *Booklist* that the comics provide "an exhilarating adventure while still allowing us to see the classic superheroine's softer side."

Rucka has also received widespread praise for the "Gotham Central" series of comics featuring both Batman, who battles the super villains, and the hardworking detectives of Gotham who go after their minions and other criminals. For example, *Half a Life* focuses on homosexual detective Renee Montoya, who is treated with disdain by her fellow officers when they discover her sexual orientation. Gordon Flagg, writing in *Booklist*, noted that the story highlights "the tense atmosphere of the squad room and the morally ambiguous world of cops."*In the Line of Duty*, another entry in the series, was called "outstanding addition to the Batman universe." by Flagg in *Booklist*.

Rucka creates a storyline involving numerous superheroes in the comic *The OMAC Project*, which features the members of the Justice League of America battling the Blue Beetle, who has learned the secret identity of all the superheroes. John Leighton, writing in the *School Library Journal*, commented: "It is interesting to see DC update its characters into contemporary personas."

BIOGRAPHICAL AND CRITICAL SOURCES:

PERIODICALS

Booklist, May 1, 1996, Thomas Gaughan, review of *Keeper*, p. 1491; October 1, 1998, Wes Lukowsky, review of *Smoker*, p. 312; September 1, 1999, George Needham, review of *Shooting at Midnight*, p. 73; December 15, 1999, Roland Green, review of *Batman: No Man's Land*, p. 761; August, 2001, David Pitt, review of *Critical Space*, p. 2099; July, 2004, Gordon Flagg, review of *In the Line of Duty*, p. 1831; September 1, 2004, David Pitt, review of *A Gentleman's Game*, p. 7; October 15, 2004, Gordon Flagg, review of *Wonder Woman: Down to Earth*, p. 396; March 15, 2005, Gordon Flagg,
review of *Wonder Woman: Bitter Rivals*, p. 1308; August, 2005, Gordon Flagg, review of *Half a Life*, p. 2012; September 15, 2005, David Pitt, review of *Private Wars*, p. 37; March 15, 2006, Tina Coleman, review of *Wonder Woman: Eyes of the Gorgon*, and *Wonder Woman: Land of the Dead*, p. 42.

Entertainment Weekly, May 14, 2004, Marc Bernardin, review of *Queen & Country: Operation Storm Front*, p. L2T26; October 1, 2004, Marc Bernardin, review of *A Gentleman's Game*, p. 77; October 28, 2005, Marc Bernardin, review of *Private Wars*, p. 95.

Kirkus Reviews, May 15, 1997, review of *Finder*, p. 750; August 15, 2004, review of *A Gentleman's Game*, p. 772; August 15, 2005, review of *Private Wars*, p. 878.

Library Journal, May 1, 1996, Dawn L. Anderson, review of *Keeper*, p. 134; June 1, 1997, Robert C. Moore, review of *Finder*, p. 150; November 1, 1998, Dawn L. Anderson, review of *Smoker*, p. 126; January, 2000, Jackie Cassada, review of *Batman: No Man's Land*, p. 168; September 15, 2001, Ronnie H. Terpening, review of *Critical Space*, p. 114; June 1, 2004, Barbara Hoffert, review of *A Gentleman's Game*, p. 102; November 1, 2004, Steve Raiteri, review of *Gotham Central*, p. 64; September 15, 2005, Ronnie H. Terpening, review of *Private Wars*, p. 57.

Library Media Connection, April-May, 2005, Catherine M. Andronik, review of *Wonder Woman: Down to Earth*, p. 82.

Publishers Weekly, April 29, 1996, review of *Keeper*, p. 53; May 26, 1997, review of *Finder*, p. 66; September 21, 1998, review of *Smoker*, p. 72; September 27, 1999, review of *Shooting at Midnight*, p. 75; December 13, 1999, review of *Batman: No Man's Land*, p. 64; July 30, 2001, review of *Critical Space*, p. 55; June 3, 2002, review of *Queen & Country: Operation Broken Ground*, p. 66; June 16, 2003, review of *Queen & Country: Volume 3: Operation Crystal Ball*, p. 53; December 15, 2003, review of *Wonder Woman: The Hiketeia*, p. 56; September 6, 2004, review of *A Gentleman's Game*, p. 45; August 29, 2005, review of *Private Wars*, p. 33.

School Library Journal, November, 2005, Steve Baker, review of *Half a Life*, p. 179; May, 2006, John Leighton, review of *The OMAC Project*, p. 160, and Andrea Lipinski, review of *Wonder Woman: Eyes of the Gorgon*, p. 160; July, 2006, Philip Charles Crawford, review of *Wonder Woman: Land of the Dead*, p. 128.

Voice of Youth Advocates, February, 2006, Rayna Patton, review of *Perfect Dark: Initial Vector*, p. 504.

ONLINE

Greg Rucka Home Page, http://www.gregrucka.com (December 12, 2006).*

*   *   *

RUCKA, Gregory
   See RUCKA, Greg

*   *   *

RUTKOWSKI, Thaddeus 1954-

PERSONAL: Born October 23, 1954, in Kingston, PA; son of B. Richard and Chia-In Rutkowski; married Randi Hoffman, February 7, 1999; children: Shay. *Ethnicity:* "Asian American." *Education:* Cornell University, B.F.A., B.A., 1976; Johns Hopkins University, M.A., 1977; attended Hunter College of the City University of New York, 1992-94.

ADDRESSES: Home—New York, NY 10002. *E-mail*—thad@thaddeusrutkowski.com.

CAREER: Writer's Voice of the West Side YMCA, New York, NY, instructor, 1999—. Asian American Writers' Workshop, instructor, 2001-03; Pace University, New York, NY, instructor, 2003-04; Hudson Valley Writers Center, Sleepy Hollow, NY, instructor, 2004-05; also works as newspaper copy editor; gives readings from his works at reading spaces and on media programs; spoken-word pieces appear on the compact discs *Family Affairs, Nuyorican Symphony,* and *Owen Wister Review.*

MEMBER: PEN, Authors Guild, National Book Critics Circle.

AWARDS, HONORS: Selected for New York Poets Live Festival at Literatur Werkstatt, Berlin, Germany, 1995; editor's choice award, *Jabberwock,* 1997; Pushcart Prize nominations, 1998, 2004, 2005; writing fellow at Yaddo, Dorset Colony, MacDowell Colony, Cummington Community of the Arts, Ragdale Foundation, and Virginia Center for the Creative Arts.

WRITINGS:

Beautiful Youth (poetry chapbook), Talent House Press (Talent, OR), 1994.
Basic Training (poetry chapbook), March Street Press (Greensboro, NC), 1996.
Journey to the Center of My Id (poetry chapbook), Linear Arts (Siaconset, MA), 1997.
Roughhouse (novel), Kaya Production (New York, NY), 1999.
Tetched (novel), Behler Publications (Lake Forest, CA), 2005.

Contributor to *How Did They Do That?,* Morrow (New York, NY), and other collections, including *Up Is Up but So Is Down: The New York Downtown Literary Scene 1974-1992,* New York University Press (New York, NY); *The Outlaw Bible of American Poetry,* Thunder's Mouth Press (New York, NY); *Unbearables,* Autonomedia (Williamsburg, NY), *The Naughty Brits: Columns from Nerve.com,* Crown (New York, NY), and *Screaming Monkeys: Critiques of Asian American Images,* Coffee House (Minneapolis, MN). Contributor to periodicals, including *American Letters & Commentary, Crowd, Fiction, Fiction International, Hayden's Ferry Review, Rattapallax, Gathering of the Tribes, Spinning Jenny, Phantasmagoria, CutBank, Faultline, Pleiades, MacGuffin, Mudfish, Cafe Review,* and *Columbia Review.*

BIOGRAPHICAL AND CRITICAL SOURCES:

PERIODICALS

American Book Review, March, 2000, review of *Roughhouse,* p. 36.
Publishers Weekly, April 5, 1999, review of *Roughhouse,* p. 224.
Small Press Bookwatch, November-December, 2005, Steven T. Karris, review of *Tetched.*

ONLINE

Thaddeus Rutkowski, Fiction Writer, http://www.thaddeusrutkowski.com (February 11, 2007).

*   *   *

RYAN, Rachel
   See BROWN, Sandra

S

SALMEN, Walter 1926-
(Walter Heinrich Salmen)

PERSONAL: Born September 20, 1926, in Paderborn, Germany; son of Joseph and Elisabeth Salmen; married January 5, 1981; wife's name Gabriele (a musician and educator). *Education:* Attended University of Heidelberg, 1944-48; University of Münster, D.Phil., 1949; University of Saarbrücken, Habilitation, 1959.

ADDRESSES: Home—Kirchzarten, Burg am Wald, Germany; fax: 076611 981066.

CAREER: University of Saarbrücken, Saarbrücken, West Germany (now Germany), dozent, 1949-66; University of Kiel, Kiel, West Germany, director of institute for musicology, 1966-74; University of Innsbruck, Innsbruck, Austria, director of institute for musicology, 1974-92, director emeritus, 1992—. Visiting professor at University of Illinois at Urbana-Champaign, 1968, City University of New York, 1974, University of Minnesota—Twin Cities, 1985, Bar Ilan University, 1989, and University of Fribourg, 1996. Deutsches Volksliedarchiv Freiburg, assistant, 1950-55.

WRITINGS:

(General editor) *Der Sozialstatus des Berufsmusikers vom 17. bis 19. Jahrhundert,* Bärenreiter (Kassel, West Germany), 1971, translation by Herbert Kaufman and Barbara Reisner published as *The Social Status of the Professional Musician from the Middle Ages to the Nineteenth Century,* Pendragon Press (New York, NY), 1983.

IN GERMAN

Das Lochamer Liederbuch: Eine musikgeschichtliche Studie (title means "The Songbook of Lochamer: A Musicohistorical Study"), Breitkopf & Härtel (Wiesbaden, West Germany), 1951.

Die Schichtung der mittelalterlichen Musikkultur in der östdeutschen Grenzlage (title means "The Social Stratas of the Medieval Musical Culture in East Germany"), Bärenreiter (Kassel, West Germany), 1954.

(With Johannes Köpp) *Liederbuch der Anna von Köln (um 1500)* (title means "The Songbook of Anna von Köln"), Schwann (Düsseldorf, West Germany), 1954.

Das Erbe des ostdeutschen Volksgesanges: Geschichte und Verzeichnis seiner Quellen und Sammlungen (title means "The Heritage of the East German Folksong"), Holzner (Würzburg, Germany), 1956.

(With Margarete Lang) *Ostdeutscher Minnesang* (title means "The East German Minnesang"), Thorbecke (Stuttgart, West Germany), 1958.

Der fahrende Musiker im europäischen Mittelalter (title means "The Traveling Minstrel in the European Middle Ages"), Bärenreiter (Kassel, West Germany), 1960.

(Editor) *Festgabe für Joseph Müller-Blattau* (title means "Homage for Joseph Müller-Blattau"), University of Saarbrücken (Saarbrücken, West Germany), 1960, 2nd edition, 1962.

(With Karl Kurt Klein) *Die Lieder Oswalds von Wolkenstein* (title means "The Songs of Oswald von Wolkenstein"), Niemeyer (Tübingen, West Germany), 1962, 2nd edition, 1975.

Johann Friedrich Reichardt, Atlantis (Freiburg, West Germany), 1963, Olms (New York, NY), 2002.

Geschichte der Musik in Westfalen (title means "A History of the Music in Westfalen"), Bärenreiter (Kassel, West Germany), Volume 1, 1963, Volume 2, 1967.

Bartold Capp (gest. 1636): Die Werke des Werler Komponisten (title means "The Works of Bartold Capp"), Aschendorff (Münster, West Germany), 1964.

Johann Friedrich Reichardt: Goethes Lieder, Oden, Balladen und Romanzen mit Musik (title means "The Songs of Johann Friedrich Reichardt with Texts of Goethe"), Henle (Munich, West Germany), Volume 1, Parts 1 and 2, 1964, Volume 2, Parts 3 and 4, 1970.

(Editor) *Beiträge zur Musikanschauung im 19. Jahrhundert* (title means "Collected Articles to the Musikanschauung in the Nineteenth Century"), Bosse (Regensburg, West Germany), 1965.

Geschichte der Rhapsodie (title means "A History of the Rhapsody"), Atlantis (Freiburg, West Germany), 1966.

Haus-und Kammermusik: Privates Musizieren im gesellschaftlichen Wandel zwischen 1600 und 1900 (title means "Domestic and Chamber Music, 1600-1900"), Deutscher Verlag für Musik (Leipzig, East Germany), 1969.

(With Heinrich W. Schwab) *Musikgeschichte Schleswig-Holsteins in Bildern* (title means "A History of Music in Schleswig-Holstein in Pictures"), Wachholz (Neumünster, West Germany), 1971.

Musikgeschichte Schleswig-Holsteins von der Frühzeit bis zur Reformation (title means "A History of Music in Schleswig-Holstein from the Earliest Times up to the Reformation"), Wachholz (Neumünster, West Germany), 1972.

(With Christoph Petzsch) *Das Lochamer Liederbuch* (title means "The Songbook of Lochamer"), Breitkopf & Härtel (Wiesbaden, West Germany), 1973.

(Editor) *Faksimile-Nachdruck von J.F. Reichardt: Über die Deutsche comische Oper, Hamburg, 1774* (title means "The German Comic Opera"), Katzbichler (Munich, Germany), 1974.

Musikleben im 16. Jahrhundert (title means "Musical Life during the Sixteenth Century"), Deutscher Verlag für Musik (Leipzig, East Germany), 1976.

(Editor) *Innsbruck Contributions to Musicology*, Helbling (Innsbruck, Austria), Volume 2: *Orgel und Orgelspiel im 16. Jahrhundert* (title means "Organ and Organ-Playing during the Sixteenth Century"), Volume 3: *Bilder zur Geschichte der Musik in Österreich* (title means "Pictures to the History of Music in Austria"), Volume 4: *Katalog der Bilder zur Musikgeschichte in Öesterreich* (title means "A Catalog of Pictures to the History of Music in Austria up to 1600"), 1980, Volume 6: *Die süddeutsch-¨esterreichische Orgelmusik im 17. und 18. Jahrhundert* (title means "The South German-Austrian Organ Music during the Seventeenth and Eighteenth Centuries"), 1980, Volume 8: *Der Spielmann im Mittelalter* (title means "The Minstrelsy during the Middle Ages"), 1983, Volume 9: *Zur Orgelmusik im 19. Jahrhundert* (title means "Organ Music during the Nineteenth Century"), 1983, Volume 10: *Jakob Stainer und seine Zeit* (title means "Jakob Stainer and His Time"), 1984, Volume 12: *Kontrabass und Bassfunktion*, 1986, Volume 15: *Musik und Tanz zur Zeit Kaiser Maximilian I*, 1992, Volume 16: *Heinrich Issac und Paul Hofhaimer im Umfeld Kaiser Maximilian I*, 1997.

Musiker im Porträt (title means "Musicians in Portraits"), C.H. Beck (Munich, West Germany), Volume 1: *Von der Spätantike bis 1600* (title means "From Late Antiquity Up to 1600"), 1982, Volume 2: *Das 17. Jahrhundert* (title means "The Seventeenth Century"), 1982, Volume 3 (with wife, Gabriele Salmen): *Das 18. Jahrhundert* (title means "The Eighteenth Century"), 1983.

Das Konzert: Eine Kulturgeschichte (title means "The Concert: A Cultural History"), C.H. Beck (Munich, West Germany), 1988.

Tanz im 17. und 18. Jahrhundert (title means "The Dance during the Seventeenth and Eighteenth Centuries"), Deutscher Verlag für Musik (Leipzig, East Germany), 1988.

Das Kousert, C.H. Beck (Munich, West Germany), 1988.

Tanz im 19. Jahrhundert (title means "The Dance during the Nineteenth Century"), Deutscher Verlag für Musik (Leipzig, East Germany), 1989.

Mozart in der Tanzkultur seiner Zeit (title means "Mozart in the Dance Culture of His Time"), Helbling (Innsbruck, Austria), 1990.

. . . Denn die Fiedel macht das Fest: Jüdische Musikanten und Tänzer vom 13. bis 20. Jahrhundert (title means ". . . The Fiddle Makes the Feast: Jewish Musicians and Dancers from the Thirteenth to the Twentieth Centuries"), Helbling (Innsbruck, Austria), 1991.

Imperiale Musik von Schloss Ambras aus der Regierungszeit Karls V und Ferdinands I, Helbling (Innsbruck, Austria), 1992.

Bilder zur Musikgeschichte Östmitteleuropas, Bärenreiter (Kassel, Germany), 1992.

Critiques musicaux d'artiste: Künstler und Gelehrte schreiben über Musik, Rombach (Freiburg, Germany), 1993.

Ongakuka-no-tanjo (title means "The Birth of the Musician"), Yosen-sha (Tokyo, Japan), 1994.

König David—eine Symbolfigur in der Musik, Universitätsverlag (Fribourg, Switzerland), 1995.

(Editor) *Terpsichore: Tanzhistorische Studien,* Olms (Hildesheim, Germany), 1997.

Beruf: Musiker; Verachtet, vergöttert, vermarktet; Eine Sozialgeschichte in Bildern, Bärenreiter (Kassel, Germany), 1997.

Der Tanzmeister: Geschichte und Profile eines Berufes vom 14. bis zum 19. Jahrhundert, Olms (Hildesheim, Germany), 1997.

Der Weimarer Musenhof, Metzler (Stuttgart, Germany), 1998.

Tanz und Tanzen im Mittelalter und in der Renaissance, Olms (Hildesheim, Germany), 1999.

Spielfrauen im Mittelalter, Olms (New York, NY), 2000.

(Editor) Johann Friedrich Reichardt, *Der Lustige Passagier: Erinnerungen Eines Musikers und Literaten,* Aufbau-Verlag (Berlin, Germany), 2002.

(Editor, with Volkmar Braunbehrens and Gabriele Busch-Salmen) *J.F. Reichardt, J.W. Goethe Briefwechsel,* Hermann Böhlaus Nachfolger (Weimar, Germany), 2002.

(Editor) *Johann Friedrich Reichardt und die Literatur: Komponieren, Korrespondieren, Publizieren,* Olms (New York, NY), 2003.

Goethe und der Tanz: Tänze-Bälle-Redouten-Ballette im Leben und Werk (on Goethe and the dance), Olms (Hildesheim, Germany), 2006.

Gartenmusik (title means "Garden Music"), Olms (Hildesheim, Germany), 2006.

Editor of *Kieler Schriften zur Musikwissenschaft,* 1967-74, and *Innsbrucker Beiträge zur Musikwissenschaft,* Helbling, 1977-98; coeditor of *Ngoma: Studien zur Volksmusik und aussereuropäischen Kunstmusik,* 1976—. Contributor of about 300 articles to musicology journals.

* * *

SALMEN, Walter Heinrich
See SALMEN, Walter

SARRIS, Greg 1952-
(Gregory M. Sarris)

PERSONAL: Born February 12, 1952, in Santa Rosa, CA; son of Emilio Arthur Hilario and Mary Bernadette Hartman; adopted son of George and Mary Sarris. *Ethnicity:* "American Indian/Filipino/Irish/Jewish." *Education:* University of California, Los Angeles, B.A., 1978; Stanford University, M.A., 1981, 1988, Ph.D., 1989.

ADDRESSES: Home—Los Angeles, CA. *Office*—Fax: 707-578-2299.

CAREER: University of California, Los Angeles, professor of English, beginning 1989; Loyola Marymount University, Los Angeles, Fletcher Jones Professor of English, 2000-05; Sonoma State University, Rohnert Park, CA, holder of Graton Rancheria Chair, 2005—. Word for Word Theater Company, chair, 1995—. Federated Indians of Graton Rancheria, chief, 1993-94, 1994-95. Turner Broadcasting System, consultant on California Indians.

MEMBER: First Americans in the Arts, Screenwriters Guild, PEN, Authors Guild, Authors League of America.

AWARDS, HONORS: Santa Fe Film Festival Award, best screenplay, and American Indian Film Festival Award, both 1996, for *Grand Avenue;* Best Reads Award, California Indian Booksellers, 1996; Bay Area Theater Critics Award, best play, 2002, for *Mission Indians.*

WRITINGS:

Keeping Slug Woman Alive: A Holistic Approach to American Indian Texts, University of California Press (Berkeley, CA), 1993.

Mabel McKay: Weaving the Dream, University of California Press (Berkeley, CA), 1994.

(Editor and contributor) *The Sound of Rattles and Clappers: A Collection of New California Indian Writing,* University of Arizona Press (Tucson, AZ), 1994.

Grand Avenue (short stories), Hyperion (New York, NY), 1994.

Grand Avenue (television miniseries; based on his short story collection), Home Box Office, 1996.

Watermelon Nights: A Novel, Hyperion (New York, NY), 1998.

(Editor, with Connie A. Jacobs and James R. Giles) *Approaches to Teaching the Works of Louise Erdrich,* Modern Language Association of America (New York, NY), 2004.

The Last Human Bear (novel), Viking (New York, NY), 2007.

SIDELIGHTS: Greg Sarris, who has both Miwok and Pomo blood, has become a recognizable figure in the fight of California Native Americans to reclaim lost land and obtain federal recognition, and also to forge a voice in which they can tell their own story. Rising from a childhood that was spent roaming from household to household, running with gangs, and held back by poverty, Sarris overcame challenges to become a scholar and an award-winning author.

In addition, Sarris has served several terms as the elected chair (or chief) of the Federated Indians of the Graton Rancheria. This group of tribes, which includes more than 1,000 California Indians of Miwok and southern Pomo ancestry, was restored as a recognized American Indian tribe in 2000. The Miwok and other California tribes endured years of problems after Europeans became the dominant force in California, including depression, unemployment, and substance abuse. However, in recent years, led by the example of Sarris and others and with improved organizational skills, these tribes have begun to empower themselves. Sarris is apt to point out, both in the classroom and in his books, that it is staggering to contemplate how the California tribes have been decimated. According to many anthropologists and historians, the area that is now the state of California was once the most heavily populated land north of the Rio Grande River. From the southern deserts to the northern forests, tribes such as the Yokuts, Wappo, Yuki, and Konkow thrived. However, after European contact, the Native American population in California plummeted by over ninety-five percent, and in the process, many cultural traits, including language and customs, were almost completely lost as well.

In his first books, *Keeping Slug Woman Alive: A Holistic Approach to American Indian Texts* and *Mabel McKay: Weaving the Dream,* Sarris sheds light on this plight, noting that the struggle has largely remained out of the consciousness of the American public. Sarris has also written fictional works, notably *Grand Avenue,* a collection of related short stories about reservation life in the northern California city of Santa Rosa. He also adapted the book for a highly rated television miniseries by the same name. The adaptation earned him several awards, including one from the American Indian Film Festival in 1996.

Like most other California Indians, Sarris's blood is an amalgamation of different ethnicities. Today, there are few remaining full-blooded Native Americans left in California. Born in Santa Rosa in 1952, Sarris would never know his real parents. While his mother, the Jewish/Irish Bunny Hartman, died during childbirth, Sarris's biological father, the Miwok/Pomo/Filipino Emilio Hilario, walked away and began a life of heavy drinking that eventually killed him. A white couple, Mary and George Sarris, adopted the boy shortly after his birth. However, as Greg grew older, the situation with his adoptive family became less than ideal. According to Sarris, his new father was also a heavy drinker and was often abusive to him and his mother. As a result, Sarris left the family and began a life of wandering, living wherever he could find shelter.

Sarris lived with several Santa Rosa families, as well as on a horse ranch and a dairy farm. By the time he was in junior high school, he was running with gangs composed of Hispanic and Indian thugs whose main pastime was seeking out white children to fight. "It was a way of saying, 'I'm here and I'm somebody,'" Sarris recalled to Alison Schneider in an interview for the *Chronicles of Higher Education.* However, Sarris's life turned around at age twelve when he met the extraordinary Mabel McKay, a Pomo elder, who gave the young man some guidance and a sense of purpose. A basket maker, McKay also taught him the importance of Indian customs and traditions that would instill in Sarris a sense of Indian pride that he had never before felt. Largely instrumental in Sarris's interest in becoming a writer, McKay, who was the last surviving member of her tribe (the Cache Creek Pomo), would be the main focus of his first two books.

Sarris attended the University of California, Los Angeles, where he played football. After a stint working as a model and an actor in Hollywood, he enrolled at Stanford University, earning his M.A., and Ph.D. in modern thought and literature. In 1989 Sarris began teaching, and soon he also began to concentrate on his writing, which for him was a healing process as well. "Many of us have inherited a very dark history. We need to light that darkness. We need to light the room we find ourselves in with stories. The only medicine we have is words," Sarris told Schneider.

In *Keeping Slug Woman Alive,* Sarris addresses the issue of Indian autobiography, as well as others topics. The book is composed of eight essays, some of which had been previously published. Inspired by the stories of McKay, Sarris mixes storytelling, ethnography, autobiography, and literary criticism in examining his chosen areas of concern. One of his main points is that of the more than 600 Indian "autobiographies" published, over eighty percent have been written by whites who have conducted interviews with the subjects, rather than by the Indians themselves. In Sarris's opinion, when a non-Indian relates these stories, the recital becomes clouded by a non-Indian worldview, and is thus tarnished. In his prologue, which is titled "Peeling Potatoes," Sarris writes of his experience sitting with several Pomo women, including McKay, as they peel potatoes and relate their stories to him. In other essays, Sarris's addresses the term "Indianness" and also his belief that Native American art should not be seen as artifact, but as art.

Critical response to the book was positive. "This text is as close to a hands-on discussion on Native American narratives as can be achieved," wrote *Choice* reviewer R. Welburn. A contributor for *Publishers Weekly* called *Keeping Slug Woman Alive* "interesting," and explained that it could "best be seen as a study in the encounter and clash between cultures." *American Quarterly* contributor Kenneth M. Roemer made special note of Sarris's narrative powers. "Sarris can construct engaging dialogue and narrative action as he weaves in and out of academic and personal discourses," Roemer wrote.

The Sound of Rattles and Clappers: A Collection of New California Indian Writing contains mostly poetry, but also some fiction and essays. Sarris contributed two short stories, "Slaughterhouse" and "Strawberry Festival," as well as the introduction. "From this place called California, then, you have the voices of many California Indians. They are singing, telling stories, their voices echoing on the pages so you will know. Listen. This place, these rolling, oak-dotted hills, redwood forests, deserts and ocean shores are sounding," Sarris wrote in the introduction. The book also contains Janice Gould's "We Exist" and Wendy Rose's "For the Scholar Who Wrote about the 'American Indian Literary Renaissance.'" A reviewer for *Native California* called the book "beautiful, lively, and fresh, rich and generous in literary style and scope."

Grand Avenue contains ten short stories, which all revolve around one clan of Pomo. Most of the stories, including "Slaughterhouse," "Joy Ride" and "How I Got to Be Queen," deal in some way with tribal divisions, often based on ethnic differences. The stories cover three generations of the clan. While the younger individuals get caught up in petty disagreements, the elders try to instill tribal traditions, such as healing songs and basketry, in an attempt to bring everyone together. In the end, each story is about cultural survival. Typically, the stories are told in first-person narrative, each one with a different speaker. Critics welcomed Sarris's first major work of fiction. *World Literature Today* contributor Greg Sanchez felt *Grand Avenue* was "well-honed and incisively crafted." A writer in the *Los Angeles Times Book Review,* called the book a "bleak, moving portrait."

Although it is a novel, *Watermelon Nights* is similar in some ways to *Grand Avenue*. Rather than focusing on a whole clan, however, the story concentrates on three generations of one Pomo family. Accordingly, the book is divided into three sections, each with a different narrator. The first section is told by Johnny Severe, a twenty-year-old used-clothing store owner. While Johnny struggles with his own sexuality, his store suffers as he lends his services to the Pomo attempt to get federal recognition. Johnny's grandmother, Elba, narrates the second section, and his mother, Iris (Elba's daughter), is the third speaker. Being the elder, Elba tells of the family's long battle with both poverty and racial prejudice, while also conferring upon everybody the story of Rosa, a family ancestor whose raping and subsequent forced marriage to a Mexican general was the beginning of the family's ethnic breakdown.

Johnny's mother, Iris, is half white and searching for her real identity. All that binds the family together is tribal tradition, and their common familial bond. "The essence of it is that despite all else, love and kindness can get us through," Sarris said, explaining the book's premise to Robert Dahlin in *Publishers Weekly*. "An ambitious debut novel," wrote Vanessa Bush in *Booklist,* adding that she felt *Watermelon Nights* was "compelling." A contributor for *Publishers Weekly* commented: "This is a rich, satisfying tale of plain folks trying to survive in an unfriendly social milieu," the contributor wrote.

BIOGRAPHICAL AND CRITICAL SOURCES:

BOOKS

Dictionary of Literary Biography, Volume 175: *Native American Writers of the United States,* Thomson Gale (Detroit, MI), 1997.
Sarris, Greg, editor, *The Sound of Rattles and Clappers: A Collection of New California Indian Writing,* University of Arizona Press (Tucson, AZ), 1994.

PERIODICALS

American Literature, June, 1994, Gail Reitenbach, review of *Keeping Slug Woman Alive: A Holistic Approach to American Indian Texts,* pp. 408-409.
American Quarterly, March, 1994, Kenneth Roemer, review of *Keeping Slug Woman Alive,* pp. 81-91.
Booklist, September 1, 1998, Vanessa Bush, review of *Watermelon Nights,* p. 68.
Choice, November, 1993, R. Welburn, review of *Keeping Slug Woman Alive,* p. 463.
Chronicle of Higher Education, July 19, 1996, interview by Alison Schneider, pp. B4-B5.
Library Journal, August, 1994, Vicki L. Toy Smith, review of *Mabel McKay: Weaving the Dream,* p. 96;
Los Angeles Times Book Review, September 4, 1994, review of *Grand Avenue,* p. 2; January 14, 1996, review of *Grand Avenue,* p. 11.
Native California, spring-summer, 1994, review of *The Sound of Rattles and Clappers: A Collection of New California Writing.*
Publishers Weekly, July 19, 1993, review of *Keeping Slug Woman Alive,* p. 247; February 28, 1994, review of *The Sound of Rattles and Clappers,* p. 78; August 3, 1998, Robert Dahlin, review of *Watermelon Nights,* pp. 55, 73.
Western American Literature, May, 1995, review of *The Sound of Rattles and Clappers,* p. 125.
Whole Earth Review, summer, 1995, Carmen Hermosillo, review of *Mabel McKay,* pp. 74-75.
World Literature Today, winter, 1996, Greg Sanchez, review of *Grand Avenue,* pp. 219-220.

SARRIS, Gregory M.
See SARRIS, Greg

*   *   *

SCANZONI, Letha Dawson 1935-

PERSONAL: Born October 9, 1935, in Pittsburgh, PA; daughter of James Jackson (a businessman) and Hilda Dawson; married John H. Scanzoni (a professor of sociology), July 7, 1956 (divorced, November 2, 1983); children: Stephen, David. *Education:* Attended Eastman School of Music, 1952-54, and Moody Bible Institute, 1954-56; Indiana University, A.B. (with high distinction), 1972. *Politics:* Democrat. *Religion:* Presbyterian. *Hobbies and other interests:* Movies, theater, music (trombonist), pet Persian cat, aerobic exercise.

ADDRESSES: Home and office—Greensboro, NC.

CAREER: Writer. Village Missions, Lookingglass, OR, rural church, music, and youth worker, 1958-61; writer, 1962—. Speaker at universities and conferences.

MEMBER: Evangelical Women's Caucus (member of executive council, 1978-82), SIECUS Associates, National Organization for Women, National Council on Family Relations, Phi Beta Kappa.

WRITINGS:

NONFICTION

Youth Looks at Love, Revell (Westwood, NJ), 1964.
Why Am I Here? Where Am I Going?, Revell (Westwood, NJ), 1966.
Sex and the Single Eye, Zondervan (Grand Rapids, MI), 1968, published as *Why Wait?,* Baker Book (Grand Rapids, MI), 1975.
Sex Is a Parent Affair: Sex Education for the Christian Home, Regal Books (St. Louis, MO), 1973, revised edition, Bantam (New York, NY), 1982.
(With Nancy Hardesty) *All We're Meant to Be: A Biblical Approach to Women's Liberation,* Word Books (Waco TX), 1974, 3rd revised edition, W.B. Eerdmans (Grand Rapids, MI), 1992.

(With John H. Scanzoni) *Men, Women, and Change: A Sociology of Marriage and Family,* McGraw (New York, NY), 1976, revised edition, 1981.

(With Virginia Ramey Mollenkott) *Is the Homosexual My Neighbor? Another Christian View,* Harper (San Francisco, CA), 1978, revised and updated (with Virginia Ramey Mollenkott) edition published as *Is the Homosexual My Neighbor? A Positive Christian Response,* HarperSanFrancisco (San Francisco, CA), 1994.

Sexuality, Westminster (Louisville, KY), 1984.

(With David G. Myers) *What God Has Joined Together? A Christian Case for Gay Marriage,* HarperSanFrancisco (San Francisco, CA), 2005.

CONTRIBUTOR

Gary Collins, editor, *The Secrets of Our Sexuality,* Word Books (Waco, TX), 1976.

Harold Twiss, editor, *Homosexuality and the Christian Faith: A Symposium,* Judson (Valley Forge, PA), 1978.

Family Factbook, Marquis (Chicago, IL), 1978.

Perry Catham, editor, *Christian Social Ethics,* Baker Book (Grand Rapids, MI), 1979.

Lina Mainiero, editor, *American Women Writers,* Volume I, Ungar (New York, NY), 1979, Volume III, 1981.

John M. Holland, editor, *Religion and Sexuality,* Association of Sexologists (San Francisco, CA), 1981.

Janet Kalven and Mary I. Buckley, editors, *Women's Spirit Bonding,* Pilgrim Press (New York, NY), 1984.

Contributor to *Christian Century, Faith at Work, Daughters of Sarah, SIECUS Report, Medical Aspects of Human Sexuality, Utne Reader,* and other periodicals. Contributing editor, *Radix;* former editorial associate, *Other Side.* Editor of *Christian Feminism Today* (formerly titled *EEWC Update*); also the content provider for the EEWC Web site.

SIDELIGHTS: Letha Dawson Scanzoni once told *CA:* "As a Christian and a feminist, I am interested in writing about religion and social issues—particularly with regard to changes in male-female roles and relationships. I also do quite a bit of travel and speaking on these subjects. Other areas of interest in my writing and speaking are biblical interpretation, marriage and family, domestic violence, friendship, sex ethics, and sex education. Sociology is of equal interest and is an area in which I try to keep current and plan to do further writing."

Scanzoni's book *All We're Meant to Be: A Biblical Approach to Women's Liberation,* written with Nancy Hardesty, was first published in 1972 and has undergone two revised editions. The authors focus on the roles of women in society, especially in the home and church. The third revised edition includes a new preface outlining the book's history and new discussions into issues such as feminism backlash and caring for older parents. It also includes a study guide. "This new edition is designed to meet the sensitivities and needs that have come into view in recent years," wrote Claire Mamola in *Women and Language.*

Scanzoni collaborated with David G. Myers to write *What God Has Joined Together? A Christian Case for Gay Marriage.* The book was called "a nice intro to progressive Christian perspectives" by Peter Meredith writing in *Mother Jones.* The authors delve into issues such as being a gay Christian and the idea of Christians accepting gays. They also present a case for establishing the validity of gay marriages. Craig L. Nessan, writing in the *Christian Century,* noted: "They honor opponents of gay marriage by taking very seriously the chief objections to greater inclusiveness for homosexual persons in the life of congregations." Sheila Peiffer wrote in *Library Journal* that the book is a "concise and compelling compilation of sociological, biological, and scriptural theses." Noting that the authors' "tone is calm, respectful and balanced," a *Publishers Weekly* contributor added that "this book cannot be pigeonholed, and that in itself is refreshing."

BIOGRAPHICAL AND CRITICAL SOURCES:

PERIODICALS

Advocate, July 5, 2005, Patrick Letellier, "David Myers," interview, includes discussion of *What God Has Joined Together? A Christian Case for Gay Marriage,* p. 4.

Christian Century, June 28, 2005, "Reformed Church Author OKs Gay Marriage," interview with author, p. 13; December 13, 2005, Craig L. Nessan, review of *What God Has Joined Together?,* p. 48.

Library Journal, August 1, 2005, Sheila Peiffer, review of *What God Has Joined Together?,* p. 93.

Mother Jones, December, 2005, Peter Meredith, review of *What God Has Joined Together?,* p. 73.

Publishers Weekly, July 12, 2004, John F. Baker, "Another Optimistic Notion Is that of a Book Making the Case for Same-Sex Marriage Aimed at Religiously Inclined Readers," p. 8; May 2, 2005, review of *What God Has Joined Together?,* p. 192.

Women and Language, spring, 1993, Claire Mamola, review of *All We're Meant to Be: A Biblical Approach to Women's Liberation,* p. 61.

ONLINE

Letha Dawson Scanzoni Home Page, http://www.lethadawsonscanzoni.com (December 14, 2006).*

* * *

SEIDEL, Kathleen G. 1951-
(Kathleen Gilles Seidel)

PERSONAL: Born October 20, 1951, in Lawrence, KS; daughter of Paul W. (a professor of chemistry) and Helen M. (a pediatrician) Gilles; married Larry R. Seidel (a management consultant), April 14, 1973; children: two. *Education:* University of Chicago, A.B., 1973; Johns Hopkins University, M.A., 1975, Ph.D., 1978. *Politics:* Democrat. *Religion:* Unitarian-Universalist.

ADDRESSES: Home—Arlington, VA. *Agent*—Adele Leone Agency, 26 Nantucket Pl., Scarsdale, NY 10583.

CAREER: Writer and educator. Northern Virginia Community College, Manassas, lecturer in English, 1977-82; full-time writer, 1982—.

MEMBER: Modern Language Association of America, Romance Writers of America, Washington Romance Writers (chairman, 1983-85).

WRITINGS:

ROMANCE NOVELS

The Same Last Name, Harlequin (New York, NY), 1983.
A Risk Worth Taking, Harlequin (New York, NY), 1983.
Mirrors and Mistakes, Harlequin (New York, NY), 1984.
After All These Years, Harlequin (New York, NY), 1984.

When Love Isn't Enough, Harlequin (New York, NY), 1984.
Don't Forget to Smile, Worldwide (Toronto, Ontario, Canada), 1986.
Maybe This Time, Pocket Books (New York, NY), 1990.
More Than You Dreamed, Pocket Books (New York, NY), 1991.
Please Remember This, Avon (New York, NY), 2002.
A Most Uncommon Degree of Popularity, St. Martin's Press (New York, NY), 2006.

SIDELIGHTS: Kathleen G. Seidel began writing romance novels for Harlequin in the 1980s, when the publisher sought American writers for a series of novels in contemporary American settings. Commenting on Seidel's impressive academic background, a *Twentieth-Century Romance and Historical Writers* contributor noted: "As a specialist in the British novel, she brings to her novels an ability to adapt formal literary structures to traditional romance conventions, such as the marriage-of-convenience plot. More than many of her contemporaries, whose work is frequently loose and episodic, Seidel structures plots built on complex models of development."

The American settings of Seidel's novels play an important role in the plots and in the characters' development. In *Don't Forget to Smile* the heroine opens a bar in a logging town in rural Oregon to try to escape her past as a beauty contestant in the South. *The Same Last Name* features a successful lawyer in New York who is better understood in the context of his Virginia childhood. This novel is also an example of Seidel's ongoing portrayal of conflicted urban professionals whose careers demand family sacrifices, a choice that clashes with their traditional backgrounds.

The characters in Seidel's novels are open and honest with one another without being verbose. Seidel prefers a spare narrative style to the highly descriptive and dramatic styles of many romance writers. Conflicts generally arise from profound differences in characters' values or personalities rather than from accidents or misunderstandings. Commenting on Seidel's divergence from most conventional romance novel styles, the *Twentieth-Century Romance and Historical Writers* contributor wrote that she is "one of several talented romance writers who emerged in the early 1980s to redefine the traditional formula."

Seidel once told *CA:* "When people find out that I have a Ph.D. in the theory of the novel, they ask, 'Why aren't you writing the Great American Novel?' 'I tried that,' I answer, 'but no one would read it.'

"In 1981, when I was engaged in the delightful chore of trying to sell my first novel, I realized that, as much as I wanted to be published, it was even more important to me to be read, and thirteen-dollar first novels do not get all that many readers.

"If you have something to say, you need to go where people are listening, and the 'brand name' category romance lines are where the readers are. My first book, as one of the launch titles for Harlequin's 'American Romance' line, had a press run of three hundred thousand.

"Perhaps the prevailing theme in my work is the notion that happiness is very often a choice. Some people make choices that nearly guarantee unhappiness. One of my heroines so wants people to like her that she is unable to act in her own interest; she must do what she thinks others want her to. In another book, the hero, a Vietnam veteran, thinks of himself as a failure and therefore structures situations so that he is certain to fail.

"What interests me is how such people change, and my plots usually show people going from making a set of choices that make them unhappy to making a set of choices that will make them happy. It is their success at doing this that makes my books compatible with the romance market.

"While it is true that there is a fair amount of mediocrity in the romance market, some of us writing for Harlequin today take our writing very seriously. We are writing books that we are proud of. We are well paid, our books have excellent distribution, and we have interested, loyal readers. Being ignored by the literary establishment is a small price to pay for that."

In her novel *A Most Uncommon Degree of Popularity,* the author goes beyond the romance genre in a story about women taking on the boorish behavior of their teenage daughters. Lydia Meadows, an ex-lawyer now raising her daughter Erin, is shocked when her popular daughter's fall from grace in the social clique leads to her own fall from grace with the mothers of Erin's friends. A *Publishers Weekly* contributor wrote that the author "catalogues the trials of upper-middle-class family life," adding that it "will appeal primarily to the sort

of people it aims to (gently) critique." Joy St. John, writing in the *Library Journal,* commented that the author writes a novel "that bridges the difficult transition from childhood to young adulthood." A *Kirkus Reviews* contributor called the novel "fun and well-told, with a personable and familiar narrator."

BIOGRAPHICAL AND CRITICAL SOURCES:

BOOKS

Twentieth-Century Romance and Historical Writers, 3rd edition, St. James Press (Detroit, MI), 1994.

PERIODICALS

Kirkus Reviews, December 1, 2005, review of *A Most Uncommon Degree of Popularity,* p. 1254.
Library Journal, January 1, 2006, Joy St. John, review of *A Most Uncommon Degree of Popularity,* p. 102.
Publishers Weekly, November 14, 2005, review of *A Most Uncommon Degree of Popularity,* p. 41.*

*   *   *

SEIDEL, Kathleen Gilles
    See SEIDEL, Kathleen G.

*   *   *

SHELTON, Napier 1931-

PERSONAL: Born December 2, 1931, in Washington, DC; son of Frederick D. (a lawyer, journalist, and economist) and Charline (a homemaker) Shelton; married Elizabeth Worth (a diplomat), June 6, 1964; children: Eleanor Shelton Loikits, Elizabeth Shelton Dawson, Martha. *Ethnicity:* "Caucasian." *Education:* Amherst College, B.A., 1955; Duke University, M.A., 1963; University of Michigan, Ph.D., 1974. *Politics:* Democrat. *Religion:* Episcopal. *Hobbies and other interests:* Birdwatching.

ADDRESSES: Home—Washington, DC. *E-mail*—ewshelton@aol.com.

CAREER: U.S. News & World Report, Washington, DC, editorial assistant, 1957-60; National Park Service, Washington, DC, writer and editor, 1963-64, editor of scientific publications, 1978-81, technical writer and editor, 1985-94. *Military service:* U.S. Marine Corps Reserve, 1949-51.

MEMBER: Audubon Naturalist Society (vice president for publications during the 1970s; member of board of directors, 1991-94), Cosmos Club (Washington, DC).

AWARDS, HONORS: Blue Pencil Award, Association of Government Communicators, 1975, for *The Nature of Shenandoah.*

WRITINGS:

Saguaro National Monument, National Park Service (Washington, DC), 1970.

The Nature of Shenandoah, National Park Service (Washington, DC), 1971.

The Life of Isle Royale, National Park Service (Washington, DC), 1975.

(Coauthor) *Great Smoky Mountains National Park,* National Park Service (Washington, DC), 1978.

Superior Wilderness: Isle Royale National Park, Isle Royale Natural History Association (Houghton, MI), 1996.

Huron: The Seasons of a Great Lake, Wayne State University Press (Detroit, MI), 1999.

Where to Watch Birds in Azerbaijan, privately printed, 2004.

Natural Missouri: Working with the Land, University of Missouri Press (Columbia, MO), 2005.

SIDELIGHTS: Napier Shelton told *CA:* "I write about my primary interests—nature and the environment—to share my knowledge and concerns. In recent years conservation and environmental issues increasingly occupy me, because the nature/earth I love is under growing attack.

"I've been interested in nature since I was six years old, and I was encouraged to write about it by my journalist father, Frederick Shelton.

"In the past, writing nonfiction books, I usually worked on them from about nine to five. Nowadays, at age seventy-four, I work shorter, more irregular hours. I

also decided to try a novel, with a rough idea about what will happen, but I am letting it develop the way it seems to want to develop."

*   *   *

SHORT, Philip 1945-

PERSONAL: Born April 17, 1945, in Bristol, England; son of Wilfred (a teacher) and Marion Short; married Christine Victoria Baring-Gould, August 9, 1968; children: Sengan (son). *Education:* Queen's College, Cambridge, B.A., 1966, M.A., 1968.

ADDRESSES: Home—Provence, France. *Office*—c/o Lloyds Bank, 20 Badminton Rd., Dowend, Bristol, England. *Agent*—David Higham Associates Ltd., 5/8 Lower John St., Golden Sq., London W1R 4HA, England.

CAREER: Journalist and writer. Freelance correspondent from Malawi, 1967-70, and Uganda, 1971-73; British Broadcasting Corp. (BBC), London, England, correspondent from Moscow, Soviet Union, 1974-76, and Peking, China, beginning in 1977, held various other positions leading to Washington bureau correspondent, retired 1997; University of Iowa, Iowa City, IA, journalism professor, c. 1978.

WRITINGS:

NONFICTION

Banda, Routledge & Kegan Paul (London, England), 1974.

The Dragon, the Bear, and the Future of the West, Hodder & Stoughton (London, England), 1981, published as *The Dragon and the Bear: Inside China and Russia Today,* 1982, published as *The Dragon and the Bear: China and Russia in the Eighties,* Morrow (New York, NY), 1982.

Mao, a Life, Hodder & Stoughton (London, England), 1999, Holt (New York, NY), 2000.

Pol Pot: Anatomy of a Nightmare, H. Holt (New York, NY), 2005.

SIDELIGHTS: Journalist Philip Short's books have focused primarily on some of the most despotic rulers of the twentieth century, including his first book *Banda,* about an eccentric Malawi dictator. Short writes about the founder of Communist China in his book *Mao, a Life.* The author recounts how Mao began at the young age of nineteen to foment rebellion against oppression and the political infighting among Mao's communist comrades, which led to his vicious takeover and subsequent totalitarian regime. *History: Review of New Books* contributor Norma Corigliano Noonan wrote: "Short analyzes Mao from his earliest youth until his death in minute detail." Noonan went on to comment that the author "vividly portrays the young Mao, alienated from his father, seeking a purpose in life through his studies and pragmatic experience, as well as the aging 'emperor,' isolated, lonely, and sad."

In a review of *Mao, a Life* in the *Economist,* a contributor wrote that the author's "journalistic style, by contrast, makes for a more complete and colourful account." Writing in the *National Review,* Christopher Caldwell wrote that the "book is a masterpiece: encyclopedic in its scope, drawing from primary sources in Chinese, Russian, and English, and riveting in its narrative." Mary Carroll commented in *Booklist* that the author's "advantage in writing a biography of [Mao] . . . is that he can tell a story." A *Publishers Weekly* contributor wrote that the biography "sheds valuable light on Mao's character but also serves as an illuminating and sweeping history of modern China." Clive Foss wrote in *History Today:* "Philip Short's massive biography is an impressive history." Foss continued: "It is also highly readable and lays the foundation for understanding Mao from his earliest years." *Library Journal* contributor Peggy Spitzer Christoff noted: "In sum, Short . . . soberly posits that Mao and his cohorts came to disregard human suffering."

Pol Pot: Anatomy of a Nightmare tells of the ruthless dictator of Cambodia whose four-year rule in the 1970s resulted in the deaths of one-fifth to one-quarter of the Cambodian population. In a review of *Pol Pot* in the *Economist,* a reviewer noted that the author "has . . . done a spectacularly efficient job of describing what happened, and how." Noting that the Short talked to both the survivors of Pot's notorious "killing fields" and perpetrators of the horrors committed there, the *Economist* contributor added: "The result is a chillingly clear portrait of Saloth Sar, the man who became Pol Pot." Outlining Pot's rise to power, the author then delves into the atrocities as Pot establishes a bizarre state in which the dictator orders all cities and towns to be evacuated so that people can work in an idealistic rural life with no wages. When the plan fails and people

revolt, Pot takes a stranglehold on power by conducting mass murders. John Leonard, writing in *Harper's,* commented: "Short wants to explain why Pol Pot's 'government by incantation' would declare war on private property and free will and spend the next forty months killing 1.5 million Cambodians."

In his review of *Pol Pot* in *Booklist,* Bryce Christensen wrote: "Deeply unsettling, Short's probing analysis reveals how the loftiest of political ideals can become the justification for the cruelest brutality. A chilling portrait." A *Kirkus Reviews* contributor referred to the biography as "a superbly wrought, richly nuanced study in evil." Michael O'Donnell noted in *Artforum International:* "The riveting chapter on the fall of Phnom Penh alone makes Philip Short's biography of Pol Pot . . . worth reading." O'Donnell went on to write: "Short is at his best when describing the historic meeting between Pol and Mao in 1975, in which the chairman's elliptical way of speaking and implied meanings were all but lost on Pol in the translation from Mao's halting English into Khmer." A *Contemporary Review* contributor reflected: "By describing Pol Pot's life one describes the background to and horrors of twentieth-century Cambodia."

BIOGRAPHICAL AND CRITICAL SOURCES:

PERIODICALS

Artforum International, April, 2005, Michael O'Donnell, review of *Pol Pot: Anatomy of a Nightmare,* p. S26.

Biography, winter, 2006, Lucien Bianco, review of *Mao, a Life,* p. 233.

Booklist, December 15, 1999, Mary Carroll, review of *Mao, a Life,* p. 755; December 15, 2004, Bryce Christensen, review of *Pol Pot,* p. 703.

Contemporary Review, March, 2005, review of *Pol Pot,* p. 189.

Economist, March 18, 2000, review of *Mao, a Life,* p. 3; November 6, 2004, review of *Pol Pot,* p. 90.

Harper's February, 2005, John Leonard, review of *Pol Pot,* p. 83.

History: Review of New Books, spring, 2000, Norma Corigliano Noonan, review of *Mao, a Life,* p. 135.

History Today, March, 2001, Clive Foss, review of *Mao, a Life,* p. 56.

Kirkus Reviews, November 15, 2004, review of *Pol Pot,* p. 1084.

Library Journal, November 15, 1999, Peggy Spitzer Christoff, review of *Mao, a Life,* p. 78; December 1, 2004, John F. Riddick, review of *Pol Pot,* p. 138.

National Review, February 21, 2000, Christopher Caldwell, review of *Mao, a Life,* p. 46; March 28, 2005, review of *Pol Pot,* p. 10.

ORBIS, fall, 2000, Arthur Waldron, review of *Mao, a Life,* p. 637.

Publishers Weekly, November 15, 1999, review of *Mao, a Life,* p. 49.

ONLINE

David Higham Associates Web site, http://www. davidhigham.co.uk/ (December 14, 2006), brief profile of author.*

*   *   *

SMITH, D. James 1955-

PERSONAL: Born June 6, 1955, in Fresno, CA; married; wife's name Kimberly. *Education:* California State University, Fresno, M.A. *Hobbies and other interests:* Motorcycling, German shepherds.

ADDRESSES: Home—Fresno, CA. *Agent*—Barbara Markowitz, PO Box 41709, Los Angeles, CA 90041.

CAREER: Writer and educator. Teacher in Selma, CA, 1979—.

MEMBER: Fresno Poets' Association.

AWARDS, HONORS: National Endowment for the Arts fellowship in poetry, 1999; New York Public Library 100 Titles for Reading and Sharing selection, 2005, and Edgar Allan Poe Award, Mystery Writers of America, 2006, both for *The Boys of San Joaquin.*

WRITINGS:

FOR CHILDREN

Fast Company, Dorling Kindersly (New York, NY), 1999.

The Boys of San Joaquin, Atheneum (New York, NY), 2005.

Probably the World's Best Story about a Dog and the Girl Who Loved Me, Atheneum (New York, NY), 2006.

Color Us All, Atheneum (New York, NY), 2007.

FOR ADULTS

Prayers for the Dead Ventriloquist (poetry), Ahsahta Press (Boise, ID), 1995.

My Brother's Passion (adult novel), Permanent Press, 2004.

Sounds the Living Make, Lewis & Clark Press, 2007.

Contributor of poetry to periodicals, including *Blackbird, Malahat Review, Notre Dame Review,* and *Stand.* Contributor to anthologies, including *Poetry of the American West,* Boise State University, 1996; and *How Much Earth,* Heyday Books, 2001.

SIDELIGHTS: A published poet as well as a novelist, D. James Smith's verse collection *Prayers for the Dead Ventriloquist,* was praised by *Choice* contributor L. Smith for containing "poems of terrible beauty, bold and real paintings in available light." A teacher in his native California, Smith is better known to younger readers through his young-adult novels, which include *Fast Company* and the Edgar Award-winning *The Boys of San Joaquin.*

As a high-school teacher, Smith is familiar with the problems and worries plaguing young people during their growing-up years, and this insight comes through in his novels for young adults. *Fast Company,* which used a dual narrative to profile a destructive young man's downward spiral, inspired *Horn Book* contributor Nancy Vasilakis to dub the book "a promising first novel." Written for a slightly younger audience, *The Boys of San Joaquin* transports readers back to early 1950s California and spins what a *Kirkus Reviews* writer deemed an "upbeat tale [that] offers a strong sense of place, plenty of growing-up and . . . spirited characters." In Smith's book, Irish-Italian-American preteen narrator Paolo O'Neil sets about tracking down a missing collection offering at his rural, small-town Catholic church. The twelve-year-old boy is helped by his clever-but-deaf, nine-year-old cousin Billy, and the two boys encounter a host of interesting experiences while solving their mystery. In a sequel to *The Boys of San*

Joaquin, Probably the World's Best Story about a Dog and the Girl Who Loved Me, Paolo tackles the world of work via a paper route he shares with Billy and six-year-old brother Georgie. When Paolo's dog Rufus is dognapped, Paolo joins friend Theresa Mueller in tracing the pup's whereabouts, but worries about Rufus soon take a back seat to confusion over his feelings for his attentive his co-sleuth.

Comparing Smith to young-adult writers Richard Peck and Bruce Clements, Elizabeth Ward wrote in her *Washington Post Book World* review of *The Boys of San Joaquin* that the novel's "very funny" plot contains "a moral sting in its tail but not an ounce of piety." In *School Library Journal* Carol A. Edwards described Paolo as a "keen narrator" and concluded that Smith's "mastery of language makes [*The Boys of San Joaquin*] a read-aloud, laugh-out-loud hit." Also commending the boy's narrative voice, Kathleen Kelly MacMillan wrote in the same periodical that in *Probably the World's Best Story about a Dog and the Girl Who Loved Me* "the real treat . . . is Paolo's first-person, present-tense narration, brimming with sly humor and lovely turns of phrase." Also remarking on Smith's likeable main character, a *Kirkus Reviews* writer noted that Paolo's "engaging" sequel "is notable for the underlying message that all kids need encouragement."

"I came to writing in my mid-thirties, when I was formally trained as a poet, and I continue as one today," Smith told *CA*. "But I was looking for a way to get the humor I enjoy with my students into my work. So began *The Boys of San Joaquin* I wanted something of the irreverence of Tom Sawyer, the dignity of Charlie Chaplin, and the ridiculousness of W.C. Fields. I found a little of each in the books' plucky narrator, Paolo.

"Paolo is so much fun because he walks around with a completely inaccurate map of the world in his head. He's been fed a ton of misinformation by his older brothers. He passes this on to his little brother, Georgie, and to his deaf cousin, Billy, along with some extra misinformation of his own. (Paolo is known to stretch the truth whenever possible, most especially if he sees some advantage in it.) Along the way, he continually wrestles with his conscience and, yes, he always ends up doing the right thing, but not without a struggle.

"Paulo continues to interest me because he is bi-cultural: his mother is Italian and his dad hails from Appalachia. His large, extended family and his home town provide a host of characters that demand that Paolo struggle to reconcile alternate viewpoints, just as so many of my own students do. This gives my students a depth that comes from their participation in a rich and varied America, and I wanted that in my fictional kids, too.

"Anyway, I like these young characters, their honesty, the way they make me laugh, which I do, unashamedly, as I sit at my computer happily banging away at the keys. What I want in these books is to present rather serious ideas with a gentle, unrelenting humor. So far, it has worked. And it's fun knowing these little guys aren't done with me yet."

BIOGRAPHICAL AND CRITICAL SOURCES:

PERIODICALS

Booklist, November 1, 1999, Hazel Rochman, review of *Fast Company,* p. 518; February 15, 2005, Mary Frances Wilkens, review of *My Brother's Passion,* p. 1062; September 1, 2006, Lynn Rutan, review of *Probably the World's Best Story about a Dog and the Girl Who Loved Me,* p. 130.

Bulletin of the Center for Children's Books, October, 1999, review of *Fast Company,* p. 69; February, 2005, Timnah Card, review of *The Boys of San Joaquin,* p. 266; October, 2006, Cindy Welch, review of *Probably the World's Best Story about a Dog and the Girl Who Loved Me,* p. 96.

Choice, November, 1995, L. Smith, review of *Prayers for the Dead Ventriloquist* p. 467.

Horn Book, September, 1999, Nancy Vasilakis, review of *Fast Company,* p. 618.

Kirkus Reviews, August 15, 2004, review of *My Brother's Passion,* p. 774; February 1, 2005, review of *The Boys of San Joaquin,* p. 182; July 1, 2006, review of *Probably the World's Best Story about a Dog and the Girl Who Loved Me,* p. 682.

Publishers Weekly, November 15, 1999, review of *Fast Company,* p. 68.

School Library Journal, October, 1999, Alison Follow, review of *Fast Company,* p. 158; January, 2005, Carol A. Edwards, review of *The Boys of San Joaquin,* p. 136; July, 2005, Erin Dennington, review of *My Brother's Passion,* p. 132; August, 2006, Kathleen Kelly MacMillan, review of *Probably the World's Best Story about a Dog and the Girl Who Loved Me,* p. 129.

Voice of Youth Advocates, February, 2000, review of *Fast Company,* p. 410.

Washington Post Book World, February 20, 2005, Elizabeth Ward, review of *The Boys of San Joaquin.*

Western American Literature, fall, 1996, pp. 272-273.

*　　*　　*

SOTO, Shirlene A. 1947-
(Shirlene Ann Soto)

PERSONAL: Born January 22, 1947, in San Luis Obispo, CA. *Ethnicity:* "Latina." *Education:* Attended University of Santa Clara; San Francisco State University, B.A., 1969; University of New Mexico, M.A., 1971, Ph.D., 1977.

ADDRESSES: Office—Chicano Studies Department, California State University, Northridge, CA 91330. *E-mail*—shirlene.soto@scun.edu.

CAREER: California Polytechnic State University, San Luis Obispo, assistant professor of history, 1977-80; California State University System, administrative fellow, c. 1980-81; California State University, Northridge, assistant vice president for academic affairs, c. 1981-85, professor of Chicano history, 1985—. University of California, Los Angeles, postdoctoral fellow, 1985-86.

MEMBER: American Studies Association, Latin American Studies Association, National Association for Chicana and Chicano Studies, Mujeres Activas en Letras y Cambio Social, Western Association of Women Historians.

AWARDS, HONORS: Ford Foundation fellow, 1972-76.

WRITINGS:

The Mexican Woman: A Study of Her Participation in the Revolution, 1910-1940, R & E Research Associates (Palo Alto, CA), 1979, revised edition published as *The Emergence of the Modern Mexican Woman: Her Participation in the Revolution and Her Struggle for Equality, 1910-1940,* Arden Press (Denver, CO), 1990.

Contributor to professional journals.

BIOGRAPHICAL AND CRITICAL SOURCES:

PERIODICALS

Hispanic American Historical Review, November, 1991, review of *The Emergence of the Modern Mexican Woman: Her Participation in the Revolution and Her Struggle for Equality, 1910-1940,* pp. 903-904.

Journal of Latin American Studies, February, 1992, review of *The Emergence of the Modern Mexican Woman,* pp. 210-211.

*　　*　　*

SOTO, Shirlene Ann
See SOTO, Shirlene A.

*　　*　　*

STARK, Steven D. 1951-

PERSONAL: Born November 21, 1951, in Washington, DC. *Education:* Harvard University, B.A., 1973; Yale University, J.D., 1979.

ADDRESSES: Agent—Writers Representatives, Inc., 116 W. 14th St., 11th Fl., New York, NY 10011.

CAREER: Journalist and writer. Harvard Law School, Cambridge, MA, lecturer on law, 1983-95; *Boston Phoenix,* Boston, MA, columnist, 1985-90; *Boston Globe,* Boston, columnist, 1990-94. Commentator for National Public Radio, 1992—, and for Voice of America, 1995—.

WRITINGS:

Glued to the Set: The Sixty Television Shows and Events That Made Us Who We Are, Free Press (New York, NY), 1997.

Writing to Win: The Legal Writer: The Complete Guide to Writing Strategies in Court and in the Office that will Make Your Case and Win It, Main Street Books (New York, NY), 1999.

Meet the Beatles: A Cultural History of the Band that Shook Youth, Gender, and the World, HarperEntertainment (New York, NY), 2005.

Contributor to periodicals, including *Atlantic Monthly* and *New York Times.*

SIDELIGHTS: Journalist Steven D. Stark, a well-known commentator for National Public Radio and a frequent author of magazine articles, published his first book, *Glued to the Set: The Sixty Television Shows and Events That Made Us Who We Are,* in 1997. Given the national attention focused on the book, including extensive excerpts in periodicals such as *USA Today* and *American Heritage,* Stark's perceptive understanding of the communications media drew praise from critics and readers alike.

The basic premise of *Glued to the Set* is best explained by its subtitle. Through discussion of sixty seminal television broadcasts, including regular weekly series and special events such as the telecast of President John F. Kennedy's funeral, Stark argues that television is more than just a reflection of the society by whom it is viewed. On the contrary, he argues, television itself often wields the power to shape its viewers. Seemingly benign programming like *The Dating Game* and *The Gong Show,* for example, actually taught their audiences that gawking at others' fumbles was acceptable. This, in turn, plowed the ground for the sensationalist tabloid shows that proliferated during the 1990s. The fast-moving *Rowan and Martin's Laugh-In,* which aired between 1968 and 1973, conditioned an entire generation of TV viewers to respond to the short vignettes that compose much of adult prime time and children's programming of today, reducing society's collective attention span in the bargain.

Michiko Kakutani, reviewing the work in the *New York Times Book Review,* hailed *Glued to the Set* for its serious look at a potentially lightweight topic, calling it "a tough, perceptive and highly entertaining cultural history." Praising Stark's thorough yet accessible style, the critic noted that although several of the book's points had been made by others: "Stark . . . has pulled them together in this volume to give the lay reader an appreciation of the myriad ways in which television reflects our changing world." However, Kakutani did take issue with what he perceived as Stark's oversimplification of some serious charges, such as the author's suggestion that the popular situation comedy *All in the*

Family spawned a nationwide wave of restlessness in the 1970s. Still, the critic continued, writing that "the reader may quibble with Mr. Stark's selection of shows in this volume," but Kakutani added that "*Glued to the Set* could well prove to be one of the best television surveys around."

Stark's next book, *Writing to Win: The Legal Writer: The Complete Guide to Writing Strategies in Court and in the Office that will Make Your Case and Win It,* focuses more on the process of legal writing than on grammatical and style issues. "The strength of *Writing to Win* lies in the perspective the reader gains both on the process of legal writing and its various genres," wrote C. Edward Good in *Trial.* Good went on to note: "This is not the stuff of law school training in the art of legal writing. And that's what makes it so good." In a review in the *Scribes Journal of Legal Writing,* Beverly Ray Burlingame called the writing guide "practical and thought-provoking." Burlingame also wrote that the author's "own comments are generally original and provocative—sometimes even controversial. Instead of focusing single-mindedly on legal writing, Stark provides related insights into lawyers, law practice, ethics, and popular culture."

Much like he did in his book *Glued to the Set,* Stark looks at the impact of a cultural phenomenon with *Meet the Beatles: A Cultural History of the Band that Shook Youth, Gender, and the World.* Instead of a standard biography, the book looks not only at the history of the four Beatles but also at both the cultural trends that led to the Beatles becoming a success and how the rock band from Liverpool, England, influenced society. "Money, anger, culture shock, generational conflict—these are some of the themes Stark addresses, though always against the context of the band's music," wrote Gregory McNamee, in the *Hollywood Reporter.* McNamee also noted: "Improbably, given the amount of ink already devoted to the subject, Stark finds fresh things to say about some of their best-known songs." Noting that Stark "provides a thorough biography of the band," a *Publishers Weekly* contributor added: "Throughout, Stark is sharp and insightful." Lloyd Jansen wrote in the *School Library Journal* that the author's "work explores the whys, an avenue of approach that has been sorely lacking in the vast Beatles literature.

BIOGRAPHICAL AND CRITICAL SOURCES:

PERIODICALS

Booklist, May 1, 2005, Gordon Flagg, review of *Meet the Beatles: A Cultural History of the Band that Shook Youth, Gender, and the World,* p. 1558.

Hollywood Reporter, June 30, 2005, Gregory McNamee, review of *Meet the Beatles,* p. 8.

Kirkus Reviews, April 1, 2005, review of *Meet the Beatles,* p. 409.

Library Journal, May 15, 2005, Lloyd Jansen, review of *Meet the Beatles,* p. 120.

New York Times Book Review, June 6, 1997, Michiko Kakutani, review of *Glued to the Set: The Sixty Television Shows and Events That Made Us Who We Are,* p. B31.

Publishers Weekly, April 25, 2005, review of *Meet the Beatles,* p. 48.

Scribes Journal of Legal Writing, January 1, 1998, Beverly Ray Burlingame, review of *Writing to Win: The Legal Writer: The Complete Guide to Writing Strategies in Court and in the Office That Will Make Your Case and Win It,* p. 78.

Trial, August, 2000, C. Edward Good, review of *Writing to Win,* p. 72.

ONLINE

OldSpeak, http://www.rutherford.org/Oldspeak/ (November 30, 2005), John W. Whitehead, "How the Beatles Changed the World: An Interview with Steven D. Stark."*

*   *   *

STARKS, Richard 1947-

PERSONAL: Born March 30, 1947, in Portsmouth, England; son of John (a naval architect) and Margaret (a writer) Starks; married Miriam Murcutt (a marketing director), October 5, 1978. *Education:* University of Aberdeen, B.Sc., 1968, M.Sc., 1969.

ADDRESSES: Office—CommuniCorp, Inc., 41 North Rd., London N7 9DP, England. *E-mail*—starksrichard@ hotmail.com.

CAREER: Canadian Pulp and Paper Industry, Toronto, Ontario, technical editor, 1970-73; *Financial Post,* Toronto, assistant editor, 1973-76; *Money Letter,* Toronto, founder and editor, 1976-83; CommuniCorp, Inc., London, England, editorial director, beginning 1978.

AWARDS, HONORS: Award of merit for distinguished financial reporting, Royal Bank of Canada, 1975, for series of articles on forest-based industries.

WRITINGS:

War of Nerves (fiction), PaperJacks (Markham, Ontario, Canada), 1977.

The Brood (fiction), Virgo Press (Toronto, Ontario, Canada), 1979.

Industry in Decline, James Lorimer and Co. (Toronto, Ontario, Canada), 1978.

(Editor) *The How to Beat Inflation Book,* Financial Education Services (Willowdale, Ontario, Canada), 1980.

The Broker (fiction), McClelland & Stewart (Toronto, Ontario, Canada), 1981.

(With wife, Miriam Murcutt) *Lost in Tibet: The Untold Story of Five American Airmen, a Doomed Plane, and the Will to Survive,* Lyon's Press (Guilford, CT), 2004.

SIDELIGHTS: Richard Starks once told *CA:* "Most writers talk about sales, advances, and royalties. It's agents who talk about art, literature, and culture. I have earned more money writing a 1,000-word article in a week than I have made writing a 100,000-word novel in a year. There must be a way of earning a living by writing fiction, but I haven't found it—at least, not yet. I'm just glad I don't write poetry."

*   *   *

ST. CLAIRE, Erin
See BROWN, Sandra

*   *   *

STERRITT, David 1944-

PERSONAL: Born September 11, 1944, in Bay Shore, NY; married Virginia Grubb, September 14, 1968; divorced; children: Jeremy, Craig. *Ethnicity:* "Caucasian." *Education:* Boston University, B.A., 1967; New York University, M.A., 1992, Ph.D., 1994.

ADDRESSES: Home and office—Baltimore, MD. *E-mail*—djsterritt@aol.com.

CAREER: Christian Science Monitor, Boston, MA, film critic and special correspondent, 1968-2005. Long Island University, C.W. Post Campus, Brookville, NY, adjunct professor, 1985-89, associate professor, 1993-99, professor of theater and film, 1999-2005, professor emeritus, 2005—. Columbia University, adjunct film professor, 1989-2005; College of Staten Island of the City University of New York, adjunct assistant professor, 1992; New York University, adjunct assistant professor, 1993; National Critics Institute, member of faculty at Eugene O'Neill Theater Center, 1994-2002; Maryland Institute College of Art, adjunct professor, 2005—; Syracuse University, member of visiting faculty, 2006—; lecturer and public speaker on film, culture, and criticism. National Public Radio, film critic for *All Things Considered,* 1979-80; film critic and commentator for several television and radio networks; New York Film Festival, member of selection committee, 1988-92; juror at other film festivals in the United States and abroad.

MEMBER: Film Critics International Federation, National Society of Film Critics (vice chair, 2004; chair, 2005—), Online Film Critics Society, New York Film Critics Circle (vice chair, 1986, 1999; chair, 1987, 2000), Columbia University Seminar on Cinema and Interdisciplinary Interpretation (cochair, 1999-2005).

AWARDS, HONORS: Grants from C.W. Post Research Committee, Long Island University, 1993-94, 1995-97, 1997-98, and Columbia University Seminars, 2005.

WRITINGS:

The Films of Alfred Hitchcock, Cambridge University Press (New York, NY), 1993.
Mad to Be Saved: The Beats, the '50s, and Film, Southern Illinois University Press (Carbondale, IL), 1998.
(Editor) *Jean-Luc Godard: Interviews,* University Press of Mississippi (Jackson, MS), 1998.
The Films of Jean-Luc Godard: Seeing the Invisible, Cambridge University Press (New York, NY), 1999.
(Editor) *Robert Altman: Interviews,* University Press of Mississippi (Jackson, MS), 2000.
(Editor) *Screening the Beats: Media Culture and the Beat Sensibility,* Southern Illinois University Press (Carbondale, IL), 2004.
(Editor, with Lucille Rhodes) *Terry Gilliam: Interviews,* University Press of Mississippi (Jackson, MS), 2004.
Guiltless Pleasures: A David Sterritt Film Reader, University Press of Mississippi (Jackson, MS), 2005.

Contributor to periodicals, *New York Times, Cahiers du cinema, Washington Post, Boston Globe, Denver Post, American Film, Film Comment, Chronicle of Higher Education, Cineaste, Mosaic, Hitchcock Annual,* and *Cinema Scope.* Editor in chief, *Boston after Dark,* 1969-70.

Author's works have been translated into Greek, Chinese and Korean.

Sterritt's collected film criticism is housed in the Harvard Film Archive, Harvard University, Cambridge, MA.

*   *   *

STURROCK, Peter A. 1924-
(Peter Andrew Sturrock)

PERSONAL: Born March 20, 1924, in South Stifford, Essex, England; immigrated to the United States, 1949; naturalized U.S. citizen, 1963; son of Albert Edward and Mabel Minnie Sturrock; married Marilyn Fern Stenson, June 23, 1963; children: (first marriage) Myra, (second marriage) Deirdre, Colin. *Ethnicity:* "English/Scottish." *Education:* Cambridge University, B.A., 1945, M.A., 1948, Ph.D., 1951.

ADDRESSES: Office—c/o Center for Space Science and Astrophysics, Varian 302, Stanford University, Stanford, CA 94035. *E-mail*—sturrock@.stanford.edu.

CAREER: Telecommunications Research Establishment, Malvern, England, scientist, 1943-46; National Bureau of Standards, Washington, DC, scientist, 1949-50; Atomic Energy Research Establishment, Harwell, England, scientist, 1951-53; Cambridge University, Cambridge, England, fellow of St. John's College,, 1952-55; Stanford University, Stanford, CA, research associate, 1955-61, professor of applied physics and engineering science 1961-66, professor of space science and astrophysics, 1966-98, director of plasma research, 1964-74 and 1980-83, and deputy director of Center for Space Science and Astrophysics, 1983-92, director, 1992-98. Varian Associates, consultant, 1957-64; National Aeronautics and Space Administration, consultant, 1962-64, member of Physical Science Committee, and director of solar flare division of Skylab Workshop, 1976-77; Enrico Fermi Summer School for Plasma-Astrophysics, director, 1966.

MEMBER: International Astronomical Union (fellow), American Astronomical Society (chair of Solar Physics Division, 1974-75), American Physics Society (fellow; chair of Plasma Physics division, 1965-66), Society for Scientific Exploration (founder; president, 1981-2001), American Association for the Advancement of Science (fellow), Royal Astronomy Society (fellow).

AWARDS, HONORS: Ford Fellow in plasma physics, European Center for Nuclear Research, 1957-58; Gravity Prize, Gravity Foundation, 1967; George Ellery Hale Prize, American Astronomical Society, 1986; Henryk Arctowski Medal, National Academy of Sciences, 1990; Space Science Award, American Institute of Aeronautics and Astronautics, 1992; Dinsdale Prize, Society for Scientific Exploration, 2006.

WRITINGS:

Static and Dynamic Electron Optics: An Account of Focusing in Lens, Deflector and Accelerator, Cambridge University Press (Cambridge, England), 1955.

(Editor) *Plasma Astrophysics,* Academic Press (New York, NY), 1967.

(Editor) *Solar Flares: A Monograph from Skylab Solar Workshop II,* Colorado Associated University Press (Boulder, CO), 1980.

(Coeditor) *Physics of the Sun,* Kluwer Academic Publishers (Hingham, MA), 1986.

Plasma Physics: An Introduction to the Theory of Astrophysical, Geophysical, and Laboratory Plasmas, Cambridge University Press (New York, NY), 1994.

The UFO Enigma: A New Review of the Physical Evidence, Warner Books (New York, NY), 1999.

SIDELIGHTS: An expert in plasma physics, Peter A. Sturrock is the author of a number of highly technical books aimed at an academic readership. Yet Sturrock is also the founder of a rather unusual group known as the Society for Scientific Exploration, whose members convene regularly to discuss unexplained phenomena, such as unidentified flying objects and psychokinesis. As is the case with Sturrock himself—a professor of space science and astrophysics—Society for Scientific Exploration members include some of the most prominent scientists and researchers in North America.

In the mid-1970s, Sturrock served as director of the solar flare division for the Skylab Workshop. The first Skylab project, launched in 1973, was a staffed space station that orbited the earth for several weeks. His work on the project led to his edited work, *Solar Flares: A Monograph from Skylab Solar Workshop II.* Plasma physics and solar flares are related topics in astrophysics. Plasma—an interstellar gas found inside stars that contains positive and negative ions—serves as conductor of electric charges. It is affected by magnetic forces, and in the age of nuclear physics has emerged as a vital element in controlled fusion experiments. Correspondingly, the solar system to which the Earth belongs is powered by the sun, a star whose temperature is so intense that scientists believe it is powered by its own cycle of nuclear reactions. Measuring solar flares, to which Sturrock has devoted much of his career research, provides a way for scientists to explore the potential of solar energy for the purposes of developing alternative energy sources and facilitating space travel.

Sturrock was also the primary editor for *Physics of the Sun.* Commissioned by the National Academy of Sciences, the three-volume work was designed to present the most current scientific knowledge and theories about the star up to 1986. Its twenty-two chapters touch upon all aspects of solar science, from conjectures about its formation, discussions of the sun's interior structures, the significance of magnetic fields surrounding it, and the aforementioned solar flares and their relevance. Reviews of Sturrock's project were positive. Robert F. Howard, evaluating it for *Science,* called it "a fundamental, authoritative reference and review for the broad field of solar physics. It was an ambitious project and it has been successful."

Sturrock has also engaged in more informal professional activities with his Society for Scientific Exploration. "If scientists are going to accept the task of trying to find responsible answers to anomalous phenomena, it is essential that these claims be subjected to the normal processes of science and scholarship, including open debate, publication and criticism," Sturrock told *Science Digest* writer Patrick Huyghe. "That's what this society hopes to provide—a forum through which research on these questions may be presented to the community of scientists and scholars."

Sturrock penned *The UFO Enigma: A New Review of the Physical Evidence.* Its contents were his distillation of proceedings from a Society for Scientific Exploration conference held in New York in 1997. The academic writings were condensed into 120 pages for a lay readership. As its title implies, the papers presented at the gathering discussed numerous phenomena in the sky believed by many ordinary citizens to be spacecraft from other galaxies. Some of the findings theorize that the lights in the night sky or large, glowing airborne objects are simply weather-related phenomena. But some sections of the book do give credence to the idea that modern science may simply not yet know enough about the universe to discredit the existence of other life forms elsewhere. A *Publishers Weekly* review commented about the somewhat dry language of *The UFO Enigma*, but noted that the findings abridged by Sturrock here "represent a hoard of raw information, and some admirably cautious reasoning, from which any reader who already cares about UFOs might be glad to learn."

BIOGRAPHICAL AND CRITICAL SOURCES:

PERIODICALS

American Scientist, September-October, 1987, George L. Withbroe, review of *Physics of the Sun, Vol. 2,* pp. 526-527; May-June 1988, George L. Withbroe, review of *Physics of the Sun, Vol. 3,* pp. 296-297.

Nature, September 18, 1986, review of *Physics of the Sun,* pp. 210-211.

Publishers Weekly, October 11, 1999, review of *The UFO Enigma: A New Review of the Physical Evidence,* p. 62.

Science, August 23, 1968, review of *Plasma Astrophysics,* p. 776; May 2, 1980, Charles L. Hyder, review of *Solar Flares: A Monograph from Skylab Solar Workshop II,* p. 491; July 25, 1986, review of *Physics of the Sun,* p. 483; January 19, 1996, David Montgomery, review of *Plasma Physics: An Introduction to the Theory of Astrophysical, Geophysical, and Laboratory Plasmas,* p. 309.

Science Digest, December, 1983, article by Patrick Huyghe, p. 68.

Sky and Telescope, June, 1986, review of *Physics of the Sun,* p. 620.

Times Higher Education Supplement, November 11, 1994, Roger Blandford, review of *Plasma Physics,* p. 30.

*   *   *

STURROCK, Peter Andrew
See STURROCK, Peter A.

T

TANENBAUM, Robert K.

PERSONAL: Born in Brooklyn, NY; son of a lawyer and teacher; married Patti Tyre; children: three. *Education:* University of California, Berkeley, B.A., 1965, law degree, 1968.

ADDRESSES: Home—Beverly Hills, CA.

CAREER: Writer, novelist, attorney, and educator. New York District Attorney's Office, New York, NY, assistant district attorney, 1968-73, chief of homicide division, 1973-76; Congressional Committee on Investigations, Washington, DC, deputy chief counsel, 1976-78; private law practice in Beverly Hills, CA, 1978-81; California State Attorney General's Office, special counsel, 1981; Beverly Hills, CA, member of city council, 1986-88, mayor, 1988-96. Deputy chief counsel for the Congressional committee investigating the assassinations of President John F. Kennedy and Dr. Martin Luther King, Jr.; special prosecution consultant in the Hillside Strangler case, 1981; guest lecturer, Boalt Hall School of Law, University of California, Berkeley, 1999.

WRITINGS:

NOVELS

No Lesser Plea, F. Watts (New York, NY), 1987.
Depraved Indifference, New American Library (New York, NY), 1989.
Immoral Certainty, Dutton (New York, NY), 1991.
Reversible Error, Dutton (New York, NY), 1992.
Material Witness, Dutton (New York, NY), 1993.
Justice Denied, Dutton (New York, NY), 1994.
Corruption of Blood, Dutton (New York, NY), 1995.
Falsely Accused, Dutton (New York, NY), 1996.
Irresistible Impulse, Dutton (New York, NY), 1997.
Act of Revenge, HarperCollins (New York, NY), 1999.
Reckless Endangerment, Signet (New York, NY), 1999.
True Justice, Pocket Books (New York, NY), 2000.
Enemy Within, Pocket Books (New York, NY), 2001.
Absolute Rage, Atria Books (New York, NY), 2002.
Resolved, Atria Books (New York, NY), 2003.
Hoax, Atria Books (New York, NY), 2004.
Fury, Atria Books (New York, NY), 2005.
Counterplay, Simon & Schuster (New York, NY), 2006.

OTHER

(With Philip Rosenberg) *Badge of the Assassin,* Dutton (New York, NY), 1979.
(With Peter S. Greenberg) *The Piano Teacher: The True Story of a Psychotic Killer,* New American Library (New York, NY), 1988.

ADAPTATIONS: Badge of the Assassin was adapted as a television movie.

SIDELIGHTS: A writer of courtroom dramas whose work has gone from mass-market paperback to hardcover bestseller, Robert K. Tanenbaum draws on his own experience as a lawyer and New York assistant district attorney to create tales of moral justice. "Of the lawyers who turned novelist in the 1980s and 1990s," wrote Jon L. Breen in the *St. James Guide to Crime and Mystery Writers,* "Robert K. Tanenbaum is among the most professionally accomplished as well as the most fictionally capable." Tanenbaum's novels have sold more than seven million copies worldwide.

Tanenbaum's books feature New York City district attorney Butch Karp who is, explained Lisa See in *Publishers Weekly,* "a fictionalized version of [Tanenbaum]. . . . Like Tanenbaum, Karp is a former college basketball player whose career was sidetracked by a serious knee injury. Working in the New York District Attorney's Office, he's surrounded by attorneys, cops, and killers who talk and act as they do in real life." Besides Karp himself, lawyer Marlene Ciampi plays an important role in the series, first as Karp's friend, then lover, and finally his wife. The relationship between the two—both career-driven—is often stormy. When Marlene gives birth to the couple's first child, it is when killers are storming the door of her apartment. In another adventure, the child is almost killed. Breen noted that the marriage between Karp and Marlene is "one of the most exasperatingly rocky, sporadically communicative marriages in mystery fiction annals." The early books are set in the 1970s, but move forward in time as the series progresses. As time goes on, Butch and Marlene's daughter Lucy grows up and the couple advance in their respective careers. According to J.D. Reed in *People,* Tanenbaum's novels about Butch and Marlene form a "richly plotted, tough and funny crime series."

Tanenbaum's ability to capture the milieu of the New York City justice system is widely praised. Breen commented: "Throughout the series, Karp's personal and professional relationships and the depiction of the politics of the New York legal system, bolstered by insider details, engage the reader's attention." A *Publishers Weekly* critic explained that, though "Tanenbaum moved to Beverly Hills long ago, his New York is still as fresh as today's police blotter." Reviewing the novel *Corruption of Blood* for *Entertainment Weekly,* Richard North Patterson found that, even if the novel is not set in New York City, "as a portrait of prosecutors at work, it pulses with authenticity."

Immoral Certainty "begins in high gear and remains there," commented Sybil Steinberg in *Publishers Weekly.* A spree of gruesome deaths involves Karp and Ciampi in a complicated whirlwind of investigations. A member of the mob is shot in a restaurant in Little Italy; a woman and her small son are viciously killed in their East Village apartment; and a seven-year-old girl is

found stuffed in a garbage bag, horribly mutilated. Heightening the tension for these two lawyers is the growing complexity of their relationship with each other. When Marlene seems on the brink of solving one of the cases, she disappears, setting the worried Karp off on a determined search to find her. Steinberg concluded: "The elements of the plot converge to form a shocking yet credible conclusion."

Falsely Accused finds Butch, Marlene, and seven-year-old daughter Lucy living in New York. Karp has spent a year in a lucrative position at a downtown law firm, while Marlene has spent the same year being a full-time mom to Lucy. Eager to get back to the work she knows and loves, Marlene starts a private investigation firm with friend and cop Harry Bello. Karp takes on the case of the city's chief medical examiner, who is suing to get his job back after being fired by the major and Karp's nemesis, district attorney Sanford Bloom. Marlene becomes involved in a case helping a young mother stop a stalker, and branches out to help two terrified children in a woman's shelter. In a separate investigation, Marlene's college friend, journalist Ariadne Stupenagel, looks into the deaths of three gypsy cabbies, all of whom committed suicide while in police custody. Amazingly, what Ariadne uncovers seems to have definite connections to Butch and Marlene's current cases. "The links among these three very dissimilar narrative threads strains credulity, but Tanenbaum's talent is large, and so are his characters," commented a *Publishers Weekly* reviewer.

Enemy Within opens with a high-speed chase and shoot-out between two New York City police officers and a wanted snitch. The chase ends with the felon dead. The cop who shot him claims self-defense—the man tried to ram the police car with his SUV. In the highly charged politics of an election year, most everyone is willing to accept that explanation. However, Butch Karp is not so easily convinced. Butch also sees the political elements of two other cases, that of a young black man accused of killing a Jewish diamond seller, and that of a serial killer who preys on the homeless. Butch and Marlene's concern is heightened by the fact that daughter Lucy, who has developed into a genius-level linguist, is doing volunteer work among the homeless, and they are afraid she will encounter the killer. For Marlene's part, she is basking in the financial windfall she has received from technology stocks, but when a female rock star asks for her help, she cannot refuse. *Booklist* reviewer Mary Carroll called *Enemy Within* "vintage Tanenbaum, sure to appeal to fans and likely to increase their number." A

Publishers Weekly contributor concluded that "fans of Tanenbaum's characters, sharp dialogue, and grasp of the intricacies of New York's legal system will not be disappointed."

In the fourteenth Karp and Ciampi novel, *Absolute Rage*, Butch, now Chief Assistant D.A. of New York County, is reeling from thwarted efforts to bring some corrupt politicians to justice. Meanwhile, Marlene's guard dog business is a rousing success. When Marlene spends a summer at the family's farm on Long Island, she strikes up a friendship with Rose Heeney and her family. Rose is married to Red Heeney, a West Virginia union organizer, a job with its own brand of dangers. Marlene offers nineteen-year-old Daniel Heeney a summer job, and the relationship between the families remains warm and friendly. Marlene is later shocked to learn that Daniel's parents and ten-year-old sister Lizzie have been murdered in their home in McCullensburg, WV. When the police arrest Moses Welch, a local mentally impaired man who could not possibly have been involved in the killings, Daniel asks Marlene for her help, which she is happy to give. Coinciding with this request, Karp is hired as a special prosecutor to investigate, and curtail, a rash of violence in West Virginia. In a more personal note, Lucy and Dan find themselves developing a case of young love for each other. "Talk about irresistible—no fan worth his or her salt will miss this earthquake of a thriller," remarked a *Publishers Weekly* critic. Tanenbaum "draws a compelling portrait of the unique and complex relationships between the Karps and their closest friends," commented Jo Ann Vicarel in the *Library Journal*. In reviewing the novel on *BookReporter.com*, Barbara Lipkien Gershenbaum observed that "Tanenbaum's greatest talent lies in his ability to weave several themes into the fabric of a suspenseful and interesting story while at the same time remaining faithful to the personalities of his characters."

In *Hoax*, the Karp and Ciampi family has suffered physically and mentally from the strains of their legal career. Marlene has been injured by a letter bomb, eleven-year-old son Giancarlo has been blinded by an assailant, and Lucy has been kidnapped twice. Still, Butch and Marlene cannot see completely abandoning the work they love. As the story opens, scrupulously honest Butch is considering a run for District Attorney, even though he knows that will put him in contact with dirty politics. Meanwhile, he becomes involved in the investigation of the murder of ML Rex, a prominent West Coast rapper, gunned down in his limousine outside a club where he had just appeared. The prime suspect in the murder is Alejandro Garcia, an ex-convict, aspiring rapper, and ML Rex's rival. As Butch considers his options, Marlene and Lucy attend an art therapy school in Taos, NM, seeking to heal from the traumas of their personal and professional lives. Soon, Marlene is involved in a local case involving a serial killer who preys on children. "In vigorous and full-bodied prose, Tanenbaum gives dimension to a large cast of characters and holds your interest—even when some aspects of his plot veer into implausibility," noted a *Kirkus Reviews* critic. A *Publishers Weekly* contributor assessed the book as "by turns boring, insightful, pedestrian, silly, maudlin, exhausting and exciting."

Fury opens as a decade-old rape case has been reopened. The so-called Coney Island Four were caught and sent to prison for the rape they committed under the Coney Island pier. Now, however, controversial and sleazy lawyer Hugh Lewis, who does not shy from making accusations of racism, has managed to free the four men. Lewis has also filed a 250 dollar million lawsuit against the city on their behalf. District Attorney Butch Karp is suspicious of the entire deal, and suspects corruption and illegal cooperation between the lawyer and a number of Brooklyn politicians. At the mayor's request, he steps up to defend the city against the lawsuit and Lewis's machinations. Marlene, meanwhile, has taken on the case of visiting Russian professor Alexis Michalik, accused of drugging and raping New York University graduate student Sarah Ryder. The story takes a potentially deadly twist when an Iraqi terrorist kidnaps one of Butch and Marlene's children as part of a scheme to blow up Times Square during the New Year's Eve celebrations. Unable to withstand this newest assault on her family, Marlene, with the help of some deadly friends, takes the fight directly to the terrorists. A *Publishers Weekly* critic felt that the book was hindered by too many subplots. "It's too bad Tanenbaum has overstuffed his latest thriller: somewhere beneath the layers of fat there's a svelte, snappy story," the reviewer stated. However, a *Kirkus Reviews* critic concluded that "Tanenbaum writes such a mean page that the faithful will keep turning them anyway."

At their best, the novels featuring Butch and Marlene mix authenticity with a high degree of suspense, witty dialogue, and strong narrative pace. Speaking of *Act of Revenge*, the critic for *Publishers Weekly* found that

"Tanenbaum has crafted a believably twisted gem of a gangster tale with visceral action and smooth comic relief." Reviewing the same novel, the *Kirkus Reviews* writer noted: "As usual, Tanenbaum pulls off a hundred effective scenes in a dozen different tones." A reviewer for *Publishers Weekly* summed up: "For those who prefer their legal thrillers with plenty of spice and a high IQ, Tanenbaum remains an essential addiction."

In 2003, a revelation worthy of one of Tanenbaum's own mystery novels was made about his writing career. For sixteen years, throughout the majority of the Karp/ Ciampi series, the novels had been written by Michael Gruber, an uncredited ghostwriter. Gruber, a former marine biologist who is Tanenbaum's first cousin, got involved with Tanenbaum when the attorney wrote a novel in 1984 and sent it to Gruber for critique, noted Lynn Andriani in *Publishers Weekly*. One of Tanenbaum's high-profile legal cases had become famous, and publisher Franklin Watts was interested in acquiring a legal thriller from Tanenbaum. After reading the hundred pages Tanenbaum sent him, Gruber realized that the book could not be saved. Instead, he proposed a business arrangement to Tanenbaum: for half the advance, Gruber would write an entirely new novel, and they would split the royalties. Tanenbaum's name would be the only one on the book, and the lawyer would provide case reports and background material for Gruber to use to construct the novels. In this way, the highly successful Karp/Ciampi series was launched. Over the years, Gruber began to feel frustrated with his hidden career as a novelist. He realized he could not admit his role as ghostwriter of the Tanenbaum books, but he also could not enjoy all the benefits of being a bestselling author. Friction between Gruber and Tanenbaum increased, Andriani reported, until Gruber concluded he wanted to pursue writing his own books under his own name. Gruber has recently split with Tanenbaum, with *Resolved* being the last book he wrote under their long-term arrangement. He is now forging a career under his own name with novels such as *Tropic of Night* and *Valley of Bones*. Despite the breakup of the pair's lengthy collaborative arrangement, Tanenbaum has continued to publish novels, including *Hoax, Fury,* and *Counterplay.*

BIOGRAPHICAL AND CRITICAL SOURCES:

BOOKS

St. James Guide to Crime and Mystery Writers, 4th edition, St. James Press (Detroit, MI), 1996.

PERIODICALS

Armchair Detective, winter, 1993, review of *Reversible Error,* p. 117; spring, 1995, review of *Justice Denied,* p. 186; summer, 1996, review of *Material Witness,* p. 338; winter, 1997, review of *Falsely Accused,* p. 71.

Booklist, August, 1994, Mary Carroll, review of *Justice Denied,* p. 2029; November 1, 1995, review of *Corruption of Blood,* p. 458; September 1, 1996, review of *Falsely Accused,* p. 69; October 15, 1997, review of *Irresistible Impulse,* p. 392; April 15, 1998, Mary Carroll, review of *Reckless Endangerment,* p. 1395; May 15, 1999, Budd Arthur, review of *Act of Revenge,* p. 1674; June 1, 2001, Mary Carroll, review of *Enemy Within,* p. 1853; June 1, 2003, Stephanie Zvirin, review of *Resolved,* p. 1751; May 1, 2004, Stephanie Zvirin, review of *Hoax,* p. 1524; July, 2005, Stephanie Zvirin, review of *Fury,* p. 1878; August 1, 2006, David Pitt, review of *Counterplay,* p. 9.

Book World, July 12, 1998, review of *Reckless Endangerment,* p. 8.

Entertainment Weekly, July 18, 1997, Richard North Patterson, review of *Corruption of Blood,* p. 76.

Kirkus Reviews, April 1, 1993, review of *Material Witness,* p. 406; June 15, 1994, review of *Justice Denied,* p. 802; September 1, 1995, review of *Corruption of Blood,* p. 1217; July 15, 1996, review of *Falsely Accused,* p. 1001; August 1, 1997, review of *Irresistible Impulse,* p. 1149; May 1, 1999, review of *Act of Revenge,* p. 662; June 15, 2000, review of *True Justice,* pp. 828-829; July 1, 2002, review of *Absolute Rage,* p. 915; July 1, 2003, review of *Resolved,* p. 882; July 15, 2004, review of *Hoax,* p. 658; June 1, 2005, review of *Fury,* p. 608.

Kliatt, April 1, 1993, review of *Material Witness,* p. 16; September, 1993, review of *Reversible Error,* p. 14.

Library Journal, July, 1994, review of *Justice Denied,* p. 130; August, 2000, Craig L. Shufelt, review of *True Justice,* p. 162; October 1, 2001, Theresa Connors, audiobook review of *True Justice,* p. 167; August, 2002, Jo Ann Vicarel, review of *Absolute Rage,* p. 147; May 15, 2004, Theresa Connors, audiobook review of *Resolved,* p. 130.

New York Times Book Review, November 26, 1989, Newgate Callendar, "Spies & Thrillers," review of *Depraved Indifference;* January 28, 1996, review of *Corruption of Blood,* p. 21.

People Weekly, December 8, 1997, William Plummer, review of *Irresistible Impulse,* p. 45; June 22, 1998, J.D. Reed, review of *Reckless Endangerment,* p. 39.

Publishers Weekly, October 26, 1990, Sybil Steinberg, review of *Immoral Certainty,* p. 56; January 20, 1992, review of *Reversible Error;* April 19, 1993, review of *Material Witness,* p. 48; June 20, 1994, p. 103; July 11, 1994, review of *Justice Denied,* p. 62; September 12, 1994, p. 71; July 10, 1995, p. 55; September 25, 1995, p. 42; August 5, 1996, review of *Falsely Accused,* p. 430; September 29, 1997, review of *Irresistible Impulse,* p. 65; April 13, 1998, review of *Reckless Endangerment,* p. 50; April 26, 1999, review of *Act of Revenge,* p. 57; June 12, 2000, review of *True Justice,* p. 50; July 2, 2001, review of *Enemy Within,* p. 50; May 27, 2002, review of *Absolute Rage,* p. 31, and Adam Dunn, "PW Talks with Robert K. Tanenbaum,"p. 32; June 2, 2003, review of *Resolved,* p. 30; August 2, 2004, review of *Hoax,* p. 54; December 13, 2004, Lynn Andriani, "Hook, Line, and Sinker," profile of Michael Gruber; July 11, 2005, review of *Fury,* p. 60; June 26, 2006, review of *Counterplay,* p. 30.

Rapport, Volume 17, number 5, 1993, review of *Material Witness,* p. 30.

School Library Journal, January, 2001, Carol DeAngelo, review of *True Justice,* p. 161.

Trial, September, 2001, Rebecca Porter, review of *Enemy Within,* p. 68.

Tribune Books (Chicago, IL), June 20, 1993, review of *Material Witness,* p. 7; July 24, 1994, p. 2; August 21, 1994, review of *Justice Denied,* p. 7; November 19, 1995, review of *Corruption of Blood,* p. 6.

ONLINE

BookReporter.com, http://www.bookreporter.com/ (December 10, 2007), Barbara Lipkien Gershenbaum, review of *Absolute Rage.*

Brainstorms, http://www.brainstorms.com/ (March 19, 2003), "Michael Gruber at the Mysterious Galaxy," profile of Michael Gruber.

Confessions of an Idiosyncratic Mind Web log, http://www.sarahweinman.com/ (January 10, 2007), "Ghostwriting, Part 1: The Ballad of Michael Gruber," profile of Michael Gruber.

Jackie K. Cooper Home Page, http://www.jackiekcooper.com/ (January 10, 2007), review of *Counterplay.*

MysteryGuide.com, http://www.mysteryguide.com/ (January 10, 2007), review of *No Lesser Plea.**

*   *   *

TARDOS, Anne 1943-

PERSONAL: Born December 1, 1943, in Cannes, France; daughter of Tibor and Berthe Tardos; married Oded Halahmy, November 6, 1976 (divorced, December, 1979); married Jackson Mac Low, January 20, 1990; stepchildren: (second marriage) Mordecai-Mark, Clarinda. *Education:* Attended Akademie fúr Musik und Darstellende Kunst, Vienna, Austria, 1961-63, and Art Students League of New York, 1963-69.

ADDRESSES: E-mail—annetardos@att.net.

CAREER: Poet, artist, and composer. Guest teacher at School of Visual Arts, New York, NY, 1974, 1987, State University of New York at Albany, 1986, University of California, San Diego, 1990, and Schule für Dichtung in Wien, 1992-94. *Exhibitions:* Art work represented in exhibitions at Jack Tilton Gallery, 1989; Museum of Modern Art, Bolzano, Italy, 1989; Venice Biennale, 1990; Galerie 1900, Paris, France, 1990; and Museum of Modern Art, New York, NY, 1993.

WRITINGS:

Cat Licked the Garlic (poetry), Tsunami Editions (Vancouver, British Columbia, Canada), 1992.
Mayg-shem Fish (poetry), Poets & Poets (CT), 1996.
Uxudo (poetry), Tuumba Press (Berkeley, CA), 1999.
The Dik-dik's Solitude: New and Selected Works (poetry), Granary Books (New York, NY), 2003.

Author of the radio plays *Stimmen,* 1986; *Phoneme Dance for John Cage,* 1993; and *Among Men,* 1996. Musical compositions include *Gatherings,* 1980; *Songs and Simultaneities,* 1985; *Museum inside the Telephone Network,* 1991; *Chance Operation: Tribute to John Cage,* 1993; and *Open Secrets,* 1993. Some compositions have been recorded on compact discs.

SIDELIGHTS: Anne Tardos told *CA:* "I write because it gives me pleasure. Some derive pleasure from reading my work. That should be motivation enough."

BIOGRAPHICAL AND CRITICAL SOURCES:

PERIODICALS

Publishers Weekly, October 25, 1999, review of *Uxudo,* p. 76.

ONLINE

Anne Tardos Home Page, http://www.annetardos.com (February 12, 2007).

*   *   *

THOMSON, David 1941-

PERSONAL: Born 1941 in London, England; immigrated to the U.S., 1975; married Lucy Gray (a photographer); children: two. *Education:* Attended Dulwich College, London, and London School of Film Technique.

ADDRESSES: Home—San Francisco, CA.

CAREER: Film critic and biographer. Former teacher of film studies at Dartmouth College.

WRITINGS:

NONFICTION

Movie Man, Stein and Day (New York, NY), 1967.
A Biographical Dictionary of the Cinema, Secker & Warbur (London, England), 1975, third edition, 1994, published as *A Biographical Dictionary of Film,* Morrow (New York, NY), 1975, third edition, Knopf (New York, NY), 1994, revised and expanded fourth edition published as *The New Biographical Dictionary of Film,* Knopf (New York, NY), 2002.
America in the Dark: Hollywood and the Gift of Unreality, Morrow (New York, NY), 1977.
Scott's Men, Viking (New York, NY), 1977, published as *Scott, Shackleton, and Amundsen: Ambition and Tragedy in the Antarctic,* Thunder's Mouth Press (New York, NY), 2002.

Overexposures: The Crisis of American Filmmaking, Morrow (New York, NY), 1981.
Warren Beatty and Desert Eyes: A Life and a Story, Doubleday (Garden City, NY), 1987.
Showman: The Life of David O. Selznick, Knopf (New York, NY), 1992.
Rosebud: The Story of Orson Welles, Knopf (New York, NY), 1996.
Beneath Mulholland: Thoughts on Hollywood and Its Ghosts, Knopf (New York, NY), 1997.
The Big Sleep, British Film Institute (London, England), 1997.
In Nevada: The Land, the People, God, and Chance, Knopf (New York, NY), 1999.
Hollywood: A Celebration, Dorling Kindersley (New York, NY), 2001.
Marlon Brando, Dorling Kindersley (New York, NY), 2003.
The Whole Equation: A History of Hollywood, Knopf (New York, NY), 2004.
Nicole Kidman, Knopf (New York, NY), 2006.

FICTION

A Bowl of Eggs, Macmillan (London, England), 1970.
Hungry as Hunters (novel), Gollancz (London, England), 1972.
Suspects, Knopf (New York, NY), 1985.
Silver Light (western stories), Knopf (New York, NY), 1990.
(With Marlon Brando and Donald Cammell; and editor) *Fan Tan* (novel), Knopf (New York, NY), 2005.

OTHER

Author of screenplay for *The Making of a Legend: Gone with the Wind* a documentary. Contributor to periodicals, including *Vanity Fair, Boston Globe, Film Comment, Movieline, New Republic,* and *Esquire.*

SIDELIGHTS: David Thomson is a renowned film critic, biographer, and fiction writer. Thomson's *A Biographical Dictionary of the Cinema,* published in the United States as *A Biographical Dictionary of Film,* was a compendium of biographical and critical entries on some 1,000 actors, directors, screenwriters, cinematographers, and producers from the film industry. The *Dictionary* was first published in 1975. According to *New Statesman & Society* contributor Sean French, Thomson's work was too selective to be a truly representative overview of the industry, but the work "became addictive. Thomson's passion for the cinema, the ruthless confidence of his judgment, made most critics seem shallow and thoughtless."

Thomson's third edition "at once more brilliant and more cranky than ever," according to Gregg Rickman in *Film Quarterly,* adds an additional 200 entries as well as revisions of original entries. Critics were enthusiastic in their reception of the third edition even if some of Thomson's opinions proved controversial. "Thomson is the Dr. Johnson of film," wrote *New Republic* critic Guillermo Cabrera Infante. "He has compiled a dictionary, he is English, and he knows what he is talking about even when he talks about something else." Infante also praised the book because in addition to being a reference work, it is also "a delight to browse through." The critic concluded: "Had he lived, Dr. Johnson could have said that a dictionary cannot embalm moving pictures. In the same way, Thomson's dictionary is not definitive, it is merely pioneering. But this book is more than a dictionary. It is a toll and a roll and a poll." "Many of us have been waiting for this revision for years," remarked French. The expanded and updated fourth edition of Thomson's work, titled *The New Biographical Dictionary of Film,* appeared in 2002. In an interview on the *New York State Writers Institute* Web site, Thomson stated: "I hope it's a seductive book: once you're in, it's hard to get out. I wanted it to be a book to read—not just somewhere where you look stuff up. One thing leads to another. And I hope that the style takes you over, leads you on. A bedside book. A browsing book. A book that works like a conversation, egging you on, drawing you into your own opinions." Writing in the *Nation,* Lee Siegel called *The New Biographical Dictionary of Film* "a masterpiece of rich insight into the culture of movie-making."

Thomson's essays and reviews have appeared regularly in periodicals, including *Vanity Fair, Film Comment,* and *Esquire.* Many of these have been gathered together in essay collections, including *Overexposures: The Crisis in American Filmmaking.* The collection criticizes, in Thomson's provocative style, the American film industry for using monetary success as the criterion for a successful film (as opposed to an artistic measure of quality). "In framing his indictment," argued Michael Dempsey in *Film Quarterly,* "Thomson ranges over a broad landscape of popular culture: the *Tonight Show,* Jerry Lewis's annual muscular dystrophy telethon, slash'em-up horror movies, the bizarrerie of Los Angeles, personal observation of Rafelson struggling to

prepare his first studio picture *Brubaker* . . . close readings of Alfred Hitchcock and his work . . . But through it all he writhes in furious, liver-gnawing, amazed ambivalence, as an Englishman entranced by movies since childhood, as a literary intellectual who moved here to teach respectably at Dartmouth only to find his senses awash in American garishness, and as a potential moviemaker who shamefacedly wants in on the racket." Richard W. Grefrath in *Library Journal* compared Thomson's writing style to Tom Wolfe's satire, arguing that the "provocative book should be widely read and is highly recommended."

Thomson is also known for his biographies of well known personalities from the film industry. In 1987, Thomson wrote *Warren Beatty and Desert Eyes: A Life and Story.* The biography is "a collage of fact, critical analysis, speculation and pure fiction," according to Gerald Peary in *Maclean's.* The biography also includes, noted Young, a chronological evaluation of Beatty's films and "sophisticated critical reading[s]" of some of his films, including *Splendor in the Grass* and *Reds.* The most unusual feature of the biography, however, is that Thomson juxtaposes the narrative nonfiction biography with a fictional novella, *Desert Eyes,* about a movie star similar to Beatty. This is not to suggest, claimed John Blades in the Chicago *Tribune Books,* "that Thomson, who has solid but quirky credits as a film critic and a novelist . . . has simply fictionalized Beatty's life. His research is sound, if not extensive . . . His book is 'admittedly discursive, playful, speculative,' not to mention intermittently entertaining, windy and provocative. It may also be unique: Just as Hollywood pioneered the screwball comedy, Thomson has invented the screwball biography."

Critics were mixed in their assessment of *Warren Beatty and Desert Eyes: A Life and a Story.* This "heavily playful and relentlessly discursive book makes shameless love to stardom and openly massages its erogenous zones: power, glamour and excitement," remarked David Coward in *Times Literary Supplement.* "It is a pity that Thomson seems to have surrendered to the perverse unreality of the world of movies which he himself analysed very sharply in *America in the Dark.*" Other critics concurred. John Wyver in the *Listener* argued that the approach to biography was intriguing but that the speculative nature of the work was not "securely anchored in substance. . . . [*Warren Beatty*] teases and flirts delightfully with the reader, but then frustrates far more often than it satisfies." Peary concluded: "Some readers may skip the novella inserts simply because the details—real and made-up—of Beatty's own life are fascinating enough. Still, the spicy ingredients of Thomson's biographical stew are delectable reading."

In 1996, Thomson released *Rosebud: The Story of Orson Welles.* Similar to the work on Beatty, *Rosebud* is "a vivid patchwork," according to a *Publishers Weekly* critic—an "almost novelistic examination of" Welles' life. Bonnie Smother in *Booklist* noted that most of Welles' most famous stories have been told many times before. But Thomson, according to Smother, "trots out the myths and reinterprets them in Welles' favor, which he fits into his ingenious conceit of Welles as the antihero Kane." "Thomson gives us the life of Welles," summarized Donald Lyons in *Film Comment,* "complete with humane and knowing portraits of many who crossed Welles's path; he gives us passionate but unblinkered readings of the films; but finally he's after bigger game. He wants to see Welles—the whole of Welles—as telling something about cinema, about America, about life. This is critical biography as poem, as lyric elegy."

Reviewers were also largely positive in their assessment of *Rosebud.* Malcolm Jones, Jr., writing in *Newsweek,* called the work a "superb critical biography." A critic for *Publishers Weekly* recommended the work as not "by any means the only book on Welles to read, but a stimulating and diverting one." Smother ultimately found the book "at once, a brilliant and maddening inquiry." "It is, I hope I've made clear," writes Lyons, "a pleasure to argue with this beautiful book. . . . The book is a meditation, a dialogue—with Welles and with Thomson himself and with his publisher/audience—a questioning full of rue and wonder and love. . . . It's time he [Thomson] be generally recognized not just as one of our sharpest writers on film, but as one of our wisest and best writers, period."

In 1997 Thomson published *The Big Sleep,* a brief critical study of Howard Hawks' epic film. Thomson "is convinced that *The Big Sleep* is 'one of the most formally radical pictures ever made in Hollywood,' because it so recklessly abandons narrative coherence," noted Michael Wood in the *New York Review of Books.* Jeffrey Meyers in the *Virginia Quarterly Review* wrote: "Thomson finds the abandonment of the story a radical triumph that turns the movie into a work about 'movieness.'" Wood disagreed that this is true, and calls the work an "affectionate little book." Meyers concluded that Thomson's study is "clever, eccentric, meandering, and self-indulgent."

In *Beneath Mulholland: Thoughts on Hollywood and Its Ghosts,* a collection of twenty-one essays written between 1980 and 1996, Thomson "delivers an offbeat and often trenchant spin on the culture of Hollywood," a *Publishers Weekly* reviewer observed. In essays like "The Technical Sense of Money," a parody of Hollywood dealmaking; "Not Available for Interview," a profile of legendary film producer David O. Selznick's wayward niece; and the title piece, a hymn to the famous highway that runs above Los Angeles and the San Fernando Valley, Thomson "progressively constructs a Hollywood devoid of artistic integrity and human community," wrote *Booklist* critic Bonnie Smothers. The author "uses the traversing of Mulholland Drive as a metaphor for exploration of the underside—the part hidden from the public and not in the film—of the world of Hollywood films and the people who write, direct, produce, and act in them," wrote Lloyd Eby in the *World & I.* The critic added: "Nearly all the essays in this book have something to do with ghosts, real or imagined, with distinguishing the fictional from the bogus, or with the deformations to life and character that have been wrought through the beguiling and powerful charms of Hollywood and its money." The "search into dark places and dream spaces leads Thomson down some strangely haunting paths," noted Evan Wiener in *Video Age International.* "He studies the topography of Los Angeles (a city famous for having no there there), presupposes that James Dean survived his car wreck and imagines what might have happened to famous screen characters after their film lives ended. The unifying subject is nothing less than life and death in the movies and, conversely, the movies' effect on our lives and deaths."

In 1999, Thomson released *In Nevada: The Land, the People, God, and Chance,* an "entertaining side trip through Hollywood's ultimate back lot: the wide open spaces of the Nevada desert," summarized a *Business Week* critic. The "impressionistic series of sketches," wrote a critic in *Publishers Weekly,* "gives readers the feeling of having a well informed sidekick riding shotgun through sage strewn stretches of Highway 376." The work covers the varied history of Nevada from the mob to the rat pack to the atom bomb to UFOs. "To the crowded gaming tables and the stark mountains that surround them," wrote the critic in *Publishers Weekly,* "Thomson brings an appealingly philosophical frame of mind, an ability to throw sophisticated musings—about transience, history, place—out into the landscape as if waiting to see if they will take root." The *Business Week* critic concluded: "[What] makes Thomson's book so original, and so deeply satisfying, is the way that he pulls all his disparate subjects together in a highly personal and at times lyrical contemplation of close-of-the-century American life."

Since 2001, Thomson has published a pictorial tribute to motion pictures titled *Hollywood: A Celebration*, biographies of Marlon Brando and Nicole Kidman, and *The Whole Equation: A History of Hollywood*, "a philosophical meditation on the myriad ways the movie industry has inspired and influenced L.A. and America, and vice versa," according to *Booklist* contributor Jack Helbig. In *The Whole Equation*, Thomson "explores personalities (Louis B. Mayer, David O. Selznick) and specific films (von Stroheim's *Greed*, Spielberg's *Jaws*) to explain the 20th century's shifting sensibilities." "Strictly speaking, *The Whole Equation* isn't so much a history of Hollywood as a very impressionistic response to Hollywood's unique confluence of art and money, a marriage arranged by the men who ran the studios," remarked Lee Siegel in the *Nation*. Drawing his title from a line in F. Scott Fitzgerald's unfinished novel *The Last Tycoon*, Thomson suggests "that the Hollywood 'equation' includes not just films and directors, but greedy businessmen, stars, artists, and audiences, all of them seeking transformation through celluloid," noted a critic in *Kirkus Reviews*. According to Roy Liebman, writing in the *Library Journal*: "The author has synthesized his longtime fascination with cinema into a most readable but challenging work."

"I have never 'decided' to become a film critic," Thomson stated in his interview on the *New York State Writers Institute* Web site. He added: "I think I'm a writer whose natural subject is film and all the ways it affects us. Thus I like looking at careers, at the history of film, the sociology, what it has done to the world—questions like that. And I love all the ways—and all the new ways—that come along for writing about film."

BIOGRAPHICAL AND CRITICAL SOURCES:

PERIODICALS

Back Stage West, June 26, 2003, Jamie Painter Young, review of *Marlon Brando*, p. 8.

Booklist, May 15, 1996, Bonnie Smothers, review of *Rosebud: The Story of Orson Welles*, p. 1561; September 1, 1997, Bonnie Smothers, review of *Beneath Mulholland: Thoughts on Hollywood and Its Ghosts*, p. 50; August 1, 2002, David Pitt,

review of *Scott, Shackleton and Amundsen: Ambition and Tragedy in the Antarctic*, p. 1914; November 15, 2004, Jack Helbig, review of *The Whole Equation: A History of Hollywood*, p. 543; August 1, 2006, David Pitt, review of *Nicole Kidman*, p. 5.

Business Week, November 8, 1999, "Gamblers, UFOs, and Visionary Mobsters," p. 14.

Commentary, July-August, 2005, Joseph Epstein, "What Happened to the Movies?," review of *The Whole Equation*, p. 52.

Entertainment Weekly, December 17, 2004, Andrew Johnston, review of *The Whole Equation*, p. 91; September 9, 2005, Lisa Schwarzbaum, "Plump Fiction," review of *Fan-Tan*, p. 146.

Film Comment, September-October, 1996, Donald Lyons, review of *Rosebud*, p. 86.

Film Quarterly, spring, 1982, Michael Dempsey, review of *Overexposures: The Crisis in American Filmmaking*, pp. 559; fall, 1995, Gregg Rickman, review of *A Biographical Dictionary of Film*, p. 65.

Hollywood Reporter, December 31, 2004, Gregory McNamee, review of *The Whole Equation*, p. 16.

Kirkus Reviews, October 1, 2004, review of *The Whole Equation*, p. 954.

Library Journal, July, 1981, Richard W. Grefrath, review of *Overexposures*, p. 1440; March 15, 2003, Michael Rogers, review of *Scott, Shackleton and Amundsen*, p. 122; November 15, 2004, Roy Liebman, review of *Scott, Shackleton and Amundsen*, p. 63; September 15, 2006, Jim Collins, review of *The Whole Equation*, p. 62.

Listener, April 23, 1987, John Wyver, "The Charm is in the Imagining," pp. 27-28.

Los Angeles Magazine, January, 2005, "With Regrets," review of *The Whole Equation*, pp. 85.

Los Angeles Times Book Review, March 29, 1987, review of *Warren Beatty and Desert Eyes*, pp. 1, 9.

Maclean's, July 13, 1987, Gerald Peary, "Hollywood Heartbreaker," pp. 50-51.

Nation, June 8, 1998, John B. Anderson, review of *Beneath Mulholland*, p. 42; February 14, 2005, Lee Siegel, "The Moviegoer," review of *The Whole Equation*, p. 29.

New Republic, January 23, 1995, Guillermo Cabrera Infante, review of *A Biographical Dictionary of Film*, p. 40.

New Statesman & Society, November 25, 1994, Sean French, review of *A Biographical Dictionary of Film*, p. 37.

Newsweek, May 27, 1996, Malcolm Jones, Jr., review of *Rosebud*, p. 69.

New York Review of Books, November 20, 1997, Michael Wood, "Looking Good," pp. 27-31.

New York Time Book Review, September 18, 2005, Joe Queenan, "Last Tango," review of *Fan-Tan,* p. 14.

Publishers Weekly, April 22, 1996, review of *Rosebud,* p. 54; September 27, 1997, review of *Beneath Mulholland,* p. 79; September 13, 1999, review of *In Nevada: The Land, the People, God, and Chance,* p. 71; October 29, 2001, "Documenting Two Film Cultures," review of *Hollywood: A Celebration,* p. 56; October 11, 2004, review of *The Whole Equation,* p. 63; July 25, 2005, review of *Fan-Tan* p. 41; August 7, 2006, review of *Nicole Kidman,* p. 49.

Spectator, February 19, 2005, Johann Hari, "The Decline of the West?," review of *The Whole Equation,* p. 41; October 21, 2006, Roger Lewis, "Little and Large," review of *Nicole Kidman.*

Times Educational Supplement, October 17, 1987, David Coward, "Stars Seen Through Cloud," p. 48; August 10, 1990, p. 855.

Times Literary Supplement, July 24, 1987, p. 792.

Tribune Books (Chicago, IL), May 17, 1987, John Blades, "Warren Beatty: The Facts Stranger than Fiction," p. 3.

Variety, October 22, 2001, Dade Hayes, review of *Hollywood,* p. 46.

Video Age International, May, 1998, Evan Wiener, review of *Beneath Mulholland,* p. 14.

Virginia Quarterly Review, spring, 1998, Jeffrey Meyers, "Frozen Eyes," pp. 362-367.

Wilson Quarterly, winter, 2000, David Spanier, "Double Down," p. 125.

World & I, May, 1998, Lloyd Eby, review of *Beneath Mulholland,* p. 276.

ONLINE

Morning News Online, http://www.themorningnews.org/ (March 15, 2005), Robert Birnbaum, "Birnbaum v. David Thomson."

New York State Writers Institute Web site, http://www.albany.edu/ (February 1, 2007), "A Conversation with David Thomson on *The New Biographical Dictionary of Film.*"*

*　　*　　*

THURLO, Aimée
(Aimee Duvall, Aimee Martel)

PERSONAL: Born in Cuba; married David Thurlo (a writer).

ADDRESSES: Home and office—Corrales, NM. *E-mail*—adthurlo@aol.com.

CAREER: Writer and novelist. Full-time writer of romance and mystery novels.

AWARDS, HONORS: RITA Award nomination, best romantic suspense novel, Romance Writers Association, 1989; Career Achievement Award nomination, *Romantic Times Magazine,* 1997; WILLA Award, contemporary fiction, 2003; Career Achievement Award, romantic suspense, 2003.

WRITINGS:

ROMANCE NOVELS; WITH HUSBAND, DAVID THURLO (NOT CREDITED)

The Fires Within, Harlequin (New York, NY), 1984.
Hero at Large, Harlequin (New York, NY), 1984.
Ariel's Desire, Harlequin (New York, NY), 1987.
The Right Combination, Harlequin (New York, NY), 1988.
Expiration Date Harlequin (New York, NY), 1989.
Black Mesa, Harlequin (New York, NY), 1990.
Suitable for Framing, Harlequin (New York, NY), 1990.
Strangers Who Linger, Harlequin (New York, NY), 1991.
Night Wind, Harlequin (New York, NY), 1991.
Breach of Faith, Harlequin (New York, NY), 1992.
Shadow of the Wolf, Harlequin (New York, NY), 1993.
Spirit Warrior, Harlequin (New York, NY), 1993.
Timewalker, Harlequin (New York, NY), 1994.
Bearing Gifts, Harlequin (New York, NY), 1994.
Fatal Charm, Harlequin (New York, NY), 1995.
Cisco's Woman, Harlequin (New York, NY), 1996.
Redhawk's Heart, Harlequin (New York, NY), 1999;
Redhawk's Return, Harlequin (New York, NY), 1999.
Black Raven's Pride, Harlequin (New York, NY), 2000.
Council of Fire, Harlequin (New York, NY), 2007.

ROMANCE NOVELS; "FOUR WINDS" TRILOGY; WITH DAVID THURLO (NOT CREDITED)

Her Destiny, Harlequin (New York, NY), 1997.
Her Hope, Harlequin (New York, NY), 1997.
Her Shadow, Harlequin (New York, NY), 1997.

ROMANCE NOVELS; UNDER PSEUDONYM AIMEE MARTEL; WITH DAVID THURLO (NOT CREDITED)

Secrets Not Shared, Leisure Books (New York, NY), 1981.

ROMANCE NOVELS; UNDER PSEUDONYM AIMEE DUVALL; WITH DAVID THURLO (NOT CREDITED)

Too Near the Sun, Berkley (New York, NY), 1982.
Halfway There, Berkley (New York, NY), 1982.
Lover in Blue, Berkley (New York, NY), 1982.
The Loving Touch, Berkley (New York, NY), 1983.
After the Rain, Berkley (New York, NY), 1984.
One More Tomorrow, Berkley (New York, NY), 1984.
Brief Encounters, Berkley (New York, NY), 1985.
Spring Madness, Berkley (New York, NY), 1985.
Kid at Heart, Berkley (New York, NY), 1986.
Made for Each Other, Berkley (New York, NY), 1987.
To Tame a Heart, Crown (New York, NY), 1988.
Wings of Angels, Crown (New York, NY), 1989.

"ELLA CLAH" MYSTERY SERIES; WITH DAVID THURLO

Blackening Song, Forge (New York, NY), 1995.
Death Walker, Forge (New York, NY), 1996.
Bad Medicine, Forge (New York, NY), 1997.
Enemy Way, Forge (New York, NY), 1998.
Shooting Chant, Forge (New York, NY), 2000.
Red Mesa, Forge (New York, NY), 2001.
Changing Woman, Forge (New York, NY), 2002.
Tracking Bear, Forge (New York, NY), 2003.
Plant Them Deep, Forge (New York, NY), 2003.
Wind Spirit, Forge (New York, NY), 2004.
White Thunder, Forge (New York, NY), 2005.
Mourning Dove, Forge (New York, NY), 2006.
Turqoise Girl, Forge (New York, NY), 2007.

"LEE NEZ" MYSTERY SERIES; WITH DAVID THURLO

(With David Thurlo) *Second Sunrise,* Forge (New York, NY), 2002.
Blood Retribution, Forge (New York, NY), 2004.
Pale Death, Forge (New York, NY), 2005.
Surrogate Evil, Forge (New York, NY), 2006.

"SISTER AGATHA" MYSTERY SERIES; WITH DAVID THURLO

(With David Thurlo) *Bad Faith,* St. Martin's Minotaur (New York, NY), 2002.

Thief in Retreat, St. Martin's Minotaur (New York, NY), 2004.
Prey for a Miracle, St. Martin's Minotaur (New York, NY), 2006.
False Witness, St. Martin's Minotaur (New York, NY), 2007.

OTHER

(With David Thurlo) *Second Shadow* (mystery), Forge (New York, NY), 1993.
The Spirit Line (mystery), Viking (New York, NY), 2004.

Contributor to periodicals, including *National Enquirer, Grit,* and *Popular Mechanics.*

SIDELIGHTS: Aimée Thurlo and her husband, David, have worked as a writing team for decades, although he has often been an uncredited partner in their collaborations. The couple began their writing endeavors with articles for periodicals such as *Grit, Popular Mechanics,* and the *National Enquirer,* but soon branched out into fiction. They produced numerous romance novels before creating their detective heroine Ella Clah, a member of the Navajo Tribal Police. With this mystery series, the Thurlos found a widespread readership.

Born in Cuba, Thurlo has lived in New Mexico for most of her life. Her husband was raised in Shiprock, New Mexico, on the Navajo Indian Reservation, which he left after seventeen years to complete his education at the University of New Mexico. Thurlo and her husband spent years honing their talents, writing romance and romantic intrigue novels under Thurlo's name and the pseudonyms Aimee Martel and Aimee Duvall. Their work from this period includes such books as *Strangers Who Linger, Expiration Date,* and *To Tame a Heart.*

In the early 1990s, the Thurlos took a new direction with their writing. They decided to pool their resources and use their knowledge of genre fiction and Navajo traditions to produce unique mysteries. The Thurlos' first Shiprock novel, *Second Shadow,* combines mystery and romantic elements. Irene Pobikan, a Tewa Indian and an architect, receives her first commission—to renovate the Mendoza hacienda—because of her extensive experience with adobe buildings from the Pueblo. The Mendozas have a history of mistreating the people of her tribe, and tight deadlines force both architect and construction crew to live on the isolated Mendoza property. No sooner does she begin construction, however, than a series of mysterious accidents occurs. When Irene discovers a twenty-year-old corpse on the site and becomes aware of a hostile prowler, she turns to her Tewa beliefs and calls on her guardian spirit, the mountain lion, for protection and help. In the meantime, she finds herself falling for Raul Mendoza despite the fact that his alcoholic brother, Gene, is determined to sabotage her hard work. Also present in the novel is Raul's beautiful but mildly retarded sister, Elena, who has an important secret she cannot share. Although a *Publishers Weekly* reviewer found the novel's "cliffhanger" chapter endings too formulaic, *Library Journal* reviewer Marion F. Gallivan praised the plotting, noting that the suspense "builds effectively to the finale."

Inspired by mystery novelist Tony Hillerman's enthusiasm and buoyed by the initial success of *Second Shadow,* the Thurlos then developed a mystery series set in the Southwest that features Ella Clah, a Navajo FBI agent who combines modern investigative techniques with traditional Native American beliefs to solve mysteries. In the first novel of the series, *Blackening Song,* Ella is called from Los Angeles to return to the Shiprock Reservation, which she had left at age eighteen. Her father, a Christian minister, has been found murdered and mutilated in a way that suggests a ritual killing. Ella's brother Clifford, a *hataali,* or traditional medicine man, has fled and is now a prime suspect. Before the murder, Clifford, a traditionalist, had argued vehemently with his father over the construction of a Christian church on the reservation. With the FBI investigation being conducted by an Anglo who has a troubled history with the Navajo community, Ella finds that she must act as liaison between the bureau, the tribe, and the tribal police.

Teaming up with Wilson Joe, a college professor who is Clifford's closest friend and staunchest defender, Ella finds her brother, who tells her that their father was murdered by Navajo witches called "skinwalkers," members of a religious cult that practices black magic. Rumors about the skinwalkers abound on the reservation, and when ghostly coyotes are spotted before three men are found murdered in a manner similar to that of Ella's father, Ella is forced to reconsider the traditional beliefs she abandoned years ago. A *Publishers Weekly* reviewer commented: "Contrasting the high-tech and hyperrational methods of the FBI with the ritual world of the Navajo . . ., the Thurlos ratchet up a lot of

suspense. Throw away logic and enjoy." A *Library Journal* critic observed that "the action moves swiftly in this well-written mystery."

In *Death Walker,* the second in the Ella Clah series, Ella joins the Navajo tribal police force as a special investigator. The case she faces threatens the cultural traditions of the Navajo people, who revere their elders as "living treasures," those who embody the tribe's heritage and collective wisdom. After tribal historian Kee Dodge is clubbed to death and apparently symbolic religious artifacts are left near his body, one elder after another is similarly slain, and Ella must face the likely possibility that the malignant skinwalkers are preying upon the tribe again. While dealing with a minimal staff, threats directed at her family, and the skewed mind of the psychopathic killer, Ella draws both on her FBI experience and her intuition to solve the crimes. She is aided by her young cousin, Justine Goodluck, who joins the investigation as Ella's assistant. A reviewer for the *Armchair Detective* praised the "grittily convincing atmosphere and landscapes" and noted that the female characters in *Death Walker* are "particularly well drawn." A *School Library Journal* reviewer also praised the Thurlos' use of landscape and description and approved of the way "characters develop into unique individuals with talents, strengths, weaknesses, and idiosyncrasies." This reviewer called *Death Walker* "a fast-paced, intriguing novel."

Bad Medicine, the third novel in the Ella Clah series, begins with two seemingly unrelated homicides. On her way to investigate the fatal clubbing of Navajo-rights activist Stanley Bitah, Ella attends to a report of a drunk-driver fatality. The problem is that Angelina Yellowhair was not drunk at all; she had been fatally poisoned even before her car crashed, and Ella finds herself pulled in many directions as she struggles to focus on both murders. Suspects in Bitah's murder include fellow coal miners who may resent his ties to the Navajo Justice Church, as well as the members of the Brotherhood, a white supremacist group, and the Fierce Ones, composed of residents of the Navajo reservation. However, the suspects must go temporarily uninvestigated because State Senator James Yellowhair, the father of Angelina, is pressuring Ella and tribal medical examiner Carolyn Roanhorse to overlook forensic evidence of drugs in Angelina's body and halt their investigation.

While Ella struggles to balance her cases, Angelina's tissue samples and poisoned organs disappear. Infections soon break out among Dr. Roanhorse's patients, and the medical examiner's credibility, career, and home come under attack. Stories on the reservation suggest that the examiner has been contaminated by the *chindi*, earthbound spirits of the dead, and that Dr. Roanhorse is spreading this contamination to the people. Ella must prove Dr. Roanhorse's innocence before her friend is murdered. A *Kirkus Reviews* critic found *Bad Medicine* "overstuffed" and "too much of a good thing," and added that "trying to sort out the suspects and subplots is like wandering for hours" in a museum "filled with fascinating exhibits."

In *Enemy Way,* the fourth Ella Clah mystery, the Navajo Police force continues to be strained to the limit. Gang violence, drunk driving, and the murder of an old friend's loved one create headaches for Ella as her investigative skills are needed everywhere at once. When her mother is seriously injured in a car accident, Ella takes on family responsibilities that threaten her career just at a time when her old enemies, the skin-walkers, make their presence known once again. A *Publishers Weekly* writer said of *Enemy Way:* "In a world out of balance, Ella strives to find the harmony between work and family, tradition and modernity. She herself remains an intriguing bundle of contrasts."

Shooting Chant finds Ella dealing with increased personal and professional challenges. She is anticipating becoming a single parent, keeping her pregnancy a secret as long as she is able. At the same time, she is working on a case involving LabKote, a medical-supplies company run by outsiders but located on the reservation. It seems LabKote may have contaminated reservation property with some sort of toxin. Then the company's headquarters are broken into, and records pertaining to pregnant women are stolen. Ella feels even more threatened by this development, and by the escalating violence associated with the Fierce Ones, a vigilante group to which her brother belongs. "The Thurlos mix social commentary with plot-twisting suspense in a well-developed and unsentimental tale," remarked a reviewer for *Publishers Weekly. Booklist* reviewer Connie Fletcher also enjoyed "the richly complex Ella and her fight to bring integrity to her work and personal life," and Pam Johnson, writing in the *School Library Journal,* called this "an enticing mystery built on a frighteningly realistic scenario."

Clah's child is a toddler in the next series title, *Red Mesa.* "The moments that single mom Clah steals from her work to spend with her eighteen-month-old daughter,

Dawn, are poignantly rendered," reflected a *Publishers Weekly* reviewer. Yet Ella has her hands full with another mystery. Her cousin and assistant, Justine, has become increasingly wild and unreliable—and then she turns up dead. Ella is targeted as a prime suspect, and she must desperately try to clear her own name as she hunts for the real killer. The result is "an intense, spellbinding family drama," wrote Rex Klett in *Library Journal.*

Tensions between modernist and traditionalist members of the tribe are always a feature in the Clah series, but especially so in *Changing Woman.* In this story, life has become especially hard on the reservation, as unemployment climbs and a drought persists. Some tribe members think that building a casino is the answer, but others, including Ella's mother, Rose, find the idea a threat to many of the traditional values of the Navajo. Although she has never been an outspoken person, Rose begins to change under the pressure of this important issue. The Thurlos "present a good look at the complexities of the gaming issue while maintaining the character-driven essence of the series," stated a *Publishers Weekly* reviewer. Fletcher, in another *Booklist* review, concluded: "Plenty of action, splendid characterizations, and a deep knowledge of contemporary Navajo life makes this a rewarding read."

Plant Them Deep, the next Ella Clah novel, focuses primarily on the activities of Clah's mother, Rose Destea. Rose is a Plant Watcher, and when the Navajo tribe's precious medicinal plants start disappearing, Rose is appointed their guardian. Her investigation soon turns up evidence that the plants are indeed being stolen by persons unknown, but the suspect list includes both tribal and off-reservation suspects. Rose asks the tribal medicine men to reveal the closely guarded location of their ancestral plant beds, but when she receives this information, she finds her safety threatened by someone who will stop at nothing to acquire the valuable herbals. A *Publishers Weekly* reviewer called the novel "the coziest of cozies, long on horticultural detail and short on mystery." However, *Booklist* reviewer Connie Fletcher observed that Rose "remains a fascinating character, and focusing on her life makes a nice twist in a popular series."

Wind Spirit, the ninth novel featuring Clah, concerns conflicts brewing on the Four Corners Navajo reservation between traditionalists and those who want the tribe to adopt new ways; between the tribe and outsiders off the reservation; and in Clah's own mind, as she struggles to reconcile her heritage with her choice of profession. As the novel opens, Clah has suffered a serious accident, falling down an abandoned uranium mineshaft on the reservation. She survives the ordeal, but in doing so, she has raised the suspicions of the reservation residents, who believe that she was saved by evil spirits. To solve her problem, Clah must find an elderly medicine man who will perform a cleansing ritual on her. Arsons and related deaths on the reservation complicate Ella's attempts to redeem herself in the eyes of her people. The authors "hit all the right notes," combining "fast-moving plots and a wealth of fascinating cultural information," commented Fletcher in another *Booklist* review. A *Publishers Weekly* contributor noted that "fans will delve into this one and feel right at home."

When FBI agent Andrew Thomas goes missing on the reservation, Ella Clah is tasked to investigate his disappearance in *White Thunder.* Soon, Clah discovers that Thomas may have interrupted a sacred Navajo ceremony during an unknown investigation of his own, but she doesn't believe that would lead to his murder. If Thomas is still alive, time is a critical factor before he dies of thirst or exposure in the desert. She focuses her questioning on the tribe members who were present at the ceremony, and in the process uncovers a criminal scheme to divert Social Security checks from the Navajo. When Clah discovers a dismembered body bearing Thomas's FBI badge, she still does not believe she has found the man for whom she was searching. As the story progresses, she uncovers FBI involvement in the Social Security scheme, and engages in a dangerous chase to find Thomas before it is too late. *Booklist* critic Wes Lukowsky called the novel "an excellent entry in an underappreciated series."

In recent years, Thurlo has widened her range to include a pair of additional recurring series characters. The first of these, Sister Agatha, is a member of the Sisters of the Blessed Adoration, a cloister in New Mexico. In her first appearance in *Bad Faith,* Sister Agatha is an extern nun, which allows her to interact with the world outside the cloister, running errands, getting the monastery's rattletrap car repaired, and conducting business for the other nuns. Though Sister Agatha has taken her religious vows, she was once an investigative journalist named Mary Naughton who lived a rather wild life and dated local sheriff Tom Green before becoming a nun in her thirties. In the novel, Sister Agatha investigates a death when popular, gentle monastery chaplain Father Anselm

dies an agonizing death during mass, brought on by a virulent poison. Everyone is a suspect for the dutiful cleric, even fellow nuns. With enthusiasm and intelligence, Sister Agatha works her investigation inside and outside the monastery. Fletcher, writing again in *Booklist,* remarked that "Sister Agatha deserves a place with Father Brown in the gallery of canny religious sleuths."

The motorcycle-riding Sister Agatha undertakes the investigation of the disappearance and curious reappearance of a number of religious artifacts in *Thief in Retreat.* The statues and artwork were stolen from the Retreat, a fancy New Mexico resort that was allowed to hold onto the artifacts after the nuns' old monastery was sold. As the curator of the local college museum is called in to consult on the case, Sister Agatha calls on Sheriff Green to assist, even though he is out of his jurisdiction. As the three investigate, they run afoul of the local sheriff, disrupt a mystery writers' conference, and encounter a ghost prowling the halls of the Retreat. "Readers will cheer as Sister Agatha puts God first and follows His lead," commented a reviewer in *Publishers Weekly.*

Prey for a Miracle finds the Sisters providing sanctuary to Natalie Tannen, a little girl who claims that she can see angels. With her mother gravely injured in a suspicious automobile accident, the girl must stay at the monastery until Sister Agatha can unravel the case. Matters are complicated by a tabloid reporter who is looking for the little girl to do a story on her supernatural visions. Natalie is also being sought by earnest pilgrims seeking help from the girl who talks to angels. In a more mundane twist, the Sisters take up the bakery business in order to raise money to fix the monastery's roof. Francisca Goldsmith, writing in the *School Library Journal,* commented that the novel's "pace is sprightly and rides along on the waves of almost-probable events."

Thurlo's second new series character is Lee Nez, a Navajo police officer who works in New Mexico. Nez is not a typical police officer: he is also part vampire, sufficiently cleansed by a Navajo medicine man to allow him a semblance of a modern life. Nez must still subsist on blood—animal blood, not human and an occasional rare steak. His condition gives him physical enhancements, such as supernatural strength and speed, and he ages extremely slowly. In *Second Sunrise,* Thurlo tells Nez's origin story. Near the end of World War II, the still-human Nez ran across a group of Nazis hijacking a U.S. convoy in the desert. In the desperate shootout, Nez's partner is killed and he is gravely wounded, but he is able to locate the Nazis' target—a shipment of weapons-grade plutonium—and conceal it. A vengeful Nazi vampire, Hans Muller, turns Nez into a vampire, hoping to one day find out the location of the plutonium from him. Turning to a Navajo "Hataali," a shamanistic healer, Nez undergoes rituals that preserve his life and blunt the disadvantages of his vampiric state. Six decades later, Nez makes it his mission to rid the world of the evil skinwalkers, even as he discovers that he will once again have to face his progenitor, the vampire Hans Muller. A *Kirkus Reviews* contributor called the book "paced like a hundred-yard dash and yet still somehow a leisurely read. Cross-genre entertainment at the top of its form."

In the second book in the series, *Blood Retribution,* Nez and FBI agent Diane Lopez have managed to come through a confrontation with a violent group of skinwalkers. When they are called away to investigate a jewelry smuggling case that resulted in the deaths of two undercover officers, they discover that the smugglers are skinwalkers, and will not be stopped by anything short of death. Meanwhile, Elka, the sister of Hans Muller, has come to town looking for revenge against Nez, and she has hired a powerful young vampire killer to destroy the undead lawman. The story is "filled with plenty of excitement and intrigue," noted Kristine Huntley in *Booklist.*

Pale Death finds Nez and Lopez on the hunt for a renegade vampire, Stewart Tanner, who was held by the government and subjected to brutal experiments. The torture Tanner received at the hands of the government researchers has driven him mad, and in his deranged state he is causing considerable trouble. When Tanner is finally captured, he is held in jail, but a power outage allows him to escape. He then goes on a vicious killing spree that taxes Nez and Lopez to their limit. Nez must also discover why the vampire population of Four Corners has suddenly started to increase. The authors "smoothly combine action and investigative procedure with insights into Navajo culture," noted a *Publishers Weekly* contributor.

The Spirit Line is a standalone novel again based on Native American lore and tradition. Crystal Manyfeathers is a skilled Navajo weaver who has decided to perpetuate her family's longstanding trade as rug weav-

ers. Disenchanted with life on the reservation and uninterested in the traditions of her native culture, Crystal seeks to earn money for college so she can leave her stifling life behind for good. Still, to please her father, she has agreed to partake in the Kinaalda, the traditional Navajo coming-of-age ceremony, at her upcoming fifteenth birthday. She is steadily working on her first large rug, an important item to be used as part of the ritual. When the rug is nearly finished, however, Crystal elects not to weave in the Spirit Line, a single flawed line of stitches placed into every Navajo rug in respect to Spider Woman. Mysterious illness and visions of Spider Woman plague Crystal, and her situation takes an even more dire turn when the rug is stolen. Asking her friend Junior, a healer in training, for help, the two set out to track down the thieves and recover the important artifact. The novel provides accurate information on "Navajo customs, mostly believable teen dialogue, and a realistic depiction of the conflicts modern Native young people face," commented Cris Reidel in the *School Library Journal.*

BIOGRAPHICAL AND CRITICAL SOURCES:

BOOKS

Heising, Willetta L., editor, *Detecting Women 2,* Purple Moon Press (Dearborn, MI), 1996.
Science Fiction & Fantasy Literature, 1975-1991, Thomson Gale (Detroit, MI), 1992.

PERIODICALS

Armchair Detective, summer, 1996, review of *Death Walker,* p. 361.
Booklist, December 15, 2000, Connie Fletcher, review of *Red Mesa,* p. 792; February 15, 2002, Connie Fletcher, review of *Changing Woman,* p. 996; October 15, 2002, Connie Fletcher, review of *Bad Faith,* p. 392; December 15, 2002, Kristine Huntley, review of *Second Sunrise,* p. 740; February 15, 2003, Connie Fletcher, review of *Tracking Bear,* p. 1054; October 15, 2003, Connie Fletcher, review of *Plant Them Deep,* p. 395; March 15, 2004, Connie Fletcher, review of *Wind Spirit,* p. 1273; May 1, 2004, Gillian Engberg, review of *The Spirit Line,* p. 1497; September 1, 2004, Kristine Huntley, review of *Blood Retribution,* p. 70; March 15, 2005, Wes Lukowsky, review of *White Thunder,* p. 1271; May 1, 2005, Gillian Engberg, "Top Ten Mystery/

Suspense for Youth," review of *The Spirit Line,* p. 1543; October 15, 2005, Kristine Huntley, review of *Pale Death,* p. 34; May 15, 2006, David Pitt, review of *Prey for a Miracle,* p. 28; November 1, 2006, Elliott Swanson, review of *Surrogate Evil,* p. 32.

Drood Review of Mystery, January, 2001, reviews of *Red Mesa* and *Shooting Chant,* p. 23.

Kirkus Reviews, May 1, 1995, review of *Blackening Song,* p. 216; October 1, 1997, review of *Bad Medicine,* p. 1491; February 1, 2002, review of *Changing Woman,* p. 147; October 1, 2002, review of *Bad Faith,* p. 1432; October 15, 2002, review of *Second Sunrise,* p. 1509; February 1, 2003, review of *Tracking Bear,* p. 193; September 15, 2003, review of *Plant Them Deep,* p. 1158; March 15, 2004, review of *The Spirit Line,* p. 278; March 1, 2005, review of *White Thunder,* p. 264; August 1, 2005, review of *Pale Death,* p. 820; March 1, 2006, review of *Mourning Dove,* p. 214; May 15, 2006, review of *Prey for a Miracle,* p. 501; October 1, 2006, review of *Surrogate Evil,* p. 994.

Kliatt, March, 2004, Michele Winship, review of *The Spirit Line,* p. 16.

Library Journal, October 15, 1993, Marion F. Gallivan, review of *Second Shadow,* p. 91; July, 1995, Maria A. Perez-Stable, review of *Blackening Song,* p. 124; April 1, 2000, Susan A. Zappia, review of *Shooting Chant,* p. 135; March 1, 2001, Rex Klett, review of *Red Mesa,* p. 133; November 15, 2002, Patricia Altner, review of *Second Sunrise,* p. 104; March 1, 2003, Rex E. Klett, review of *Tracking Bear,* p. 122; November 1, 2003, Rex E. Klett, review of *Plant Them Deep,* p. 128.

Publishers Weekly, April 5, 1991, Penny Kaganoff, review of *Strangers Who Linger,* p. 140; October 4, 1993, review of *Second Shadow,* p. 65; May 1, 1995, review of *Blackening Song,* p. 46; April 22, 1996, review of *Death Walker,* p. 62; August 25, 1997, review of *Bad Medicine,* p. 48; July 27, 1998, review of *Enemy Way,* p. 57; April 3, 2000, review of *Shooting Chant,* p. 66; January 29, 2001, review of *Red Mesa,* p. 68; February 25, 2002, review of *Changing Woman,* p. 45; October 28, 2002, review of *Bad Faith,* p. 54; November 11, 2002, review of *Second Sunrise,* p. 45; February 17, 2003, review of *Tracking Bear,* p. 60; October 6, 2003, review of *Plant Them Deep,* p. 65; February 9, 2004, review of *Wind Spirit,* p. 60; November 22, 2004, review of *Thief in Retreat,* p. 41; March 14, 2005, "April Publications," review of *White Thunder,* p. 49; August 8, 2005, review of *Pale Death,* p. 216; May 15, 2006, review of *Prey for a Miracle,* p. 51.

School Library Journal, March, 1997, Pam Johnson, review of *Death Walker,* p. 216; January, 1999, review of *Enemy Way,* p. 160; July, 2000, Pam Johnson, review of *Shooting Chant,* p. 128; August, 2003, Pam Johnson, review of *Tracking Bear,* p. 188; June, 2004, Cris Riedel, review of *The Spirit Line,* p. 150; September, 2006, Francisca Goldsmith, review of *Prey for a Miracle,* p. 248.

ONLINE

Aimée and David Thurlo Home Page, http://www. aimeeanddavidthurlo.com (January 10, 2007).

BookBrowser, http://bookbrowser.com/ (January 10, 2007), Harriet Klausner, reviews of *Shooting Chant* and *Changing Woman.*

Fantastic Fiction, http://www.fantasticfiction.co.uk/ (January 10, 2007).

Suite 101, http://www.suite101.com/ (June 20, 2005), Linda Suzane, interview with Aimée and David Thurlo; reviews of *Second Sunrise* and *Blood Retribution.**

*   *   *

TONG, Su
See TONG, Zhong Gui

*   *   *

TONG, Zhong Gui 1963-
(Su Tong)

PERSONAL: Born January 23, 1963, in Su Zhou, China; son of Jin Cai Tong (a cadre) and Wang Feng Ying (a worker); married Wei Hong, September, 1987; children: Tian Mi. *Education:* Beijing Normal University, B.D., 1984.

ADDRESSES: Home—Nanjing, China. *Office*—10 Hu Nan Rd., Sheng Zojia Xie Hui, Nanjing, China.

CAREER: Writer, novelist, and editor. *Zhong Shan,* Jiangsu, China, editor, 1986-92.

MEMBER: Writers' Association of Jiangsu Province.

WRITINGS:

IN ENGLISH; AS SU TONG

Raise the Red Lantern: Three Novellas (contains "Wives and Concubines," "Nineteen Thirty-four Escapes," and *"Opium Family"*), translated by Michael S. Duke, Morrow (New York, NY), 1993.

Short Stories. Selections, Ren min wen xue chu ban she (Beijing, China), 2000.

Rice (novel), Perennial (New York, NY), 2004.

My Life as Emperor (novel), translated by Howard Goldblatt, Hyperion West (New York, NY), 2005.

IN CHINESE; AS SU TONG

Shang Xin De Wu Dao, Yuan-Liou, 1991.

Hong Fen, Yuan-Liou, 1991.

Mi, Yuan-Liou, 1991.

Qi Qie cheng gun, Hua chen chu ban she (Guangzhou Shi), 1991.

Nan Fang De Duo Luo, Yuan-Liou, 1992.

Shi jie liang ce, Jiangsu wen yi chu ban she (Nanjing Shi), 1993.

Shao nian xie, Jiangsu wen yi chu ban she (Nanjing Shi), 1993.

Li hun zhi nan, Hua yi chu ban she (Peking, China), 1993.

Su Tong xiao shuo jing pin (short stories), Xinan shi fan da xue chu ban she (Zhongqing shi), 1993.

Hun yin ji jing, Jiangsu wen yi chu ban she (Nanjing Shi), 1993.

Ci qing shi dai, Changjiang wen yi chu ban she (Wuhan Shi), 1993.

Mo dai ai qing, Jiangsu wen yi chu ban she (Nanjing shi), 1994.

Hou gong, Jiangsu wen yi chu ban she (Nanjing shi), 1994.

Li hun zhi nan, Jin ri Zhongguo chu ban she (Beijing, China), 1995.

Pu sa man, Tian di tu shu you xian gong si (Xianggang), 1999.

Pian duan pin jie, Xi yuan chu ban she (Beijing, China), 2000.

Qi qie cheng qun: Su Tong dai biao zuo, Chun feng wen yi chu ban she (Shenyang, China), 2002.

Ling yi zhong fu nu sheng huo, Jiangsu wen yi chu ban she (Nanjing, China), 2003.

Su Tong Wang Hongtu dui hua lu, Suzhou da xue chu ban she (Suzhou Shi), 2003.

ADAPTATIONS: "Wives and Concubines" was filmed as *Raise the Red Lantern* by director Zhang Yimou in 1992.

SIDELIGHTS: Chinese writer, editor, and novelist Zhong Gui Tong, who writes under the pseudonym Su Tong, is probably best known in America as the author of the source material for director Zhang Yimou's acclaimed film *Raise the Red Lantern,* which received an Academy Award nomination in 1992. The novella "Wives and Concubines," which inspired the film, concerns a young woman who is compelled by circumstance to become the fourth concubine of an old and wealthy merchant. Once situated in the merchant's stronghold, the heroine finds herself embroiled in rivalry with the other concubines. In addition, she uncovers evidence that still another concubine has been imprisoned and, ultimately, executed.

"Wives and Concubines" was included in the English-language volume *Raise the Red Lantern,* which appeared in 1993. Gary Krist, writing in the *New York Times Book Review,* described "Wives and Concubines" as a "subtle, profoundly feminist tale," and he called it "remarkable." Also featured in the book *Raise the Red Lantern* are "Nineteen Thirty-four Escapes," which relates a family's history, and "Opium Family," which re-creates life in a rural village during the time immediately preceding a political revolution.

In Tong's novel *Rice,* "hunger is the unifying trope—hunger for food, sex, the power of life over others (particularly women), and death—all of which may be satisfied by rice," observed Jeffrey C. Kinkley in *World Literature Today.* Tong "employs rice, symbol of Chinese civilization and heaven's bounty, to daring, iconoclastic effect throughout the novel," commented a *Publishers Weekly* reviewer. For the novel's protagonist, Five Dragons, rice becomes not only a source and symbol of power but also a fetish object, which he eats uncooked and which figures prominently in the sexually charged murders of prostitutes he commits. When famine strikes his native village, Five Dragons flees the hardship and heads toward the city, where he manages to find a job with Feng, a rich rice merchant. Working only for the ration of rice he gets to eat, Five Dragons labors and schemes a way to insinuate himself deeper into the merchant's life and family. When the merchant's daughter Cloud Weave finds herself shamed and pregnant by a local gangster, Five Dragons agrees to marry her. Yet he is an abusive husband, and he forces himself on her sister, Cloud Silk. When he sets an arson fire that kills several people, Five Dragons becomes an underworld don. Feng's death sets him up as clan patriarch, and he marries Cloud Silk when Cloud Weave runs away. Later, he fathers a son, known as "Rice Boy," who suffocates his little sister in rice. When the Japanese occupy the area during the war, Five Dragons betrays his former criminal associates. Assuming control of Feng's family rice business, he works to return to his village astride a boxcar of rice, a prodigal hero who has solved the rice shortage forever, if only in his own depraved mind. Tong "depicts a relentlessly ugly world devoid of hope or redemption, where the strong prey on the weak and corruption flourishes unchecked," remarked Scott Veale in the *New York Times Book Review*. *Booklist* reviewer Joanne Wilkinson called Tong's novel a "disturbing tale about the brutality of life" in China of the 1930s, noting that throughout the book, Tong "lovingly fashions many great scenes of intense depravity."

My Life as Emperor recounts the rapid degeneration of the prince of the fictional Chinese Xie empire when he suddenly ascends to the position of emperor. Formerly a shy and wistful lad, fourteen-year-old prince Duanbai becomes a cruel, terrorizing ruler. Besotted with his new power, Duanbai demands instant gratification of his every whim. He uses violence to settle old, petty scores and insults. When he is disturbed by the sound of a group of discarded concubines weeping in the garden, he orders that their tongues be cut out to silence them. Despite his brutality, Duanbai is unprepared for the dangers and deadly intrigues that await him, and he lives in constant fear of attack or assassination. He must particularly guard against the rivalry of other, older brothers, particularly the cunning Duanwen, since they feel they have a greater claim to the throne than Duanbai. For others in his household, including his mother and siblings, connection to the emperor is no reason for fear, but is instead a means to vie for wealth and political power. Despite his less savory characteristics, Duanbai knows friendship, in the form of his closest companion Swallow, a gigantic eunuch, and love, from concubine Lady Hui. In an atmosphere of such raw greed, however, peopled by individuals who seek advancement for themselves at the expense of others, tragedy is inevitable, and Duanbai's immaturity and ineptitude fuels his downfall. Tong's novel "details the coming of age of a boy who succumbs to the seductive influence of ruthless power," commented Sofia A. Tangalos in the *Library Journal*. His "lush prose style . . . provides the perfect counter as well as startling detail and texture, to the perilous court life it recounts," noted a contributor to *Publishers Weekly*. The story, commented a *Kirkus Reviews* critic, "has the energy of white-hot melodrama, and it's a propulsive read."

BIOGRAPHICAL AND CRITICAL SOURCES:

PERIODICALS

Booklist, August, 1995, Joanne Wilkinson, review of *Rice*, p. 1930.
Kirkus Reviews, December 15, 2004, review of *My Life as Emperor*, p. 1163.
Library Journal, February 1, 2005, Sofia A. Tangalos, review of *My Life as Emperor*, p. 71.
New Yorker, May 9, 2005, John Updike, "Bitter Bamboo," review of *My Life as Emperor*.
New York Times Book Review, July 25, 1993, Gary Krist, review of *Raise the Red Lantern*, p. 12; October 22, 1995, Scott Veale, "Books in Brief: Fiction," review of *Rice*.
Publishers Weekly, June 12, 1995, review of *Rice*, p. 44; January 31, 2005, review of *My Life as Emperor*, p. 50.
Sunday Times (London, England), February 20, 2005, Sophie Harrison, review of *My Life as Emperor*.
World Literature Today, spring, 1996, Jeffrey C. Kinkley, review of *Rice*, p. 469.

ONLINE

Curled up with a Good Book, http://www.curledup.com/ (January 10, 2007), Iris Jacobs, review of *Rice*.*

*   *   *

TUCKER, Lisa

PERSONAL: Born in MO; married a jazz pianist; children: Miles. *Education:* University of Pennsylvania, B.A. (summa cum laude), M.A. (English), ABD (American literature); Villanova University, M.A. (mathematics); additional graduate work at Bryn Mawr College (mathematics).

ADDRESSES: Home—NM. *Agent*—(Literary and film) Marly Rusoff, 811 Palmer Rd., Suite AA, Bronxville, NY 10708; (publicity) Megan Underwood or Lynn Goldberg, Goldberg/McDuffie Communications, 444 Madison Ave., Suite 3300, New York, NY 10022.

CAREER: Writer. Member of faculty, Taos Writers' Conference and University of California, Los Angeles; has also taught creative writing at University of Pennsylvania and mathematics at Bryn Mawr College. Has worked variously as a waitress, jazz musician, key-punch operator, and an office cleaner.

AWARDS, HONORS: Fellowships in English and mathematics.

WRITINGS:

The Song Reader (novel), Downtown Press (New York, NY), 2003.
Shout Down the Moon (novel), Downtown Press (New York, NY), 2004.
Once upon a Day (novel), Atria Books (New York, NY), 2006.

Contributor to books, including *Cold Feet* and *Lit Riffs,* and to periodicals, including *Seventeen, Philadelphia Inquirer, St. Louis Post Dispatch, Los Angeles Times, Albuquerque Journal, Publishers Weekly,* and *Pages.*

SIDELIGHTS: Lisa Tucker's novels echo with music, with its ability to uplift as well as bring down, with its meaning, its performance, and its pervasive influence. Tucker's characters also know of life's struggles and how to use their talents and determination to rise above difficult odds. Leeann Norris narrates the story of herself and her sister in *The Song Reader,* Tucker's first novel. The sisters' absentee father walked out seven years before the time the novel begins, and their mother was killed in an automobile accident three years ago. Twenty-three-year-old Mary Beth serves as both sibling and parent to eleven-year-old Leeann, and to Mary Beth's adopted son, two-year-old Tommy, in a small Missouri town in the early 1980s. Mary Beth supports the family by working as a waitress, but her other "job" is her true passion: operating a small business as a song reader. Her clients experience a common phenomenon: sometimes a snippet of song will get stuck in their heads, repeating over and over. Other times, a fragment of lyric would seem suddenly significant, or a tune will trigger powerful emotions. As a song reader, Mary Beth interprets the meaning of the lyrics or music repeating themselves in her clients' heads. She finds the associations between songs and current and past emotional states; she knits together seemingly disparate connections between music and lyric and psychological condition.

At first well-accepted by the community, popular perception of Mary Beth's song-reading concern turns vicious when a client attempts suicide based on Mary Beth's counseling. The near-suicide also exposes a local scandal. Mary Beth's own psyche collapses as a result, and she is hospitalized. It then falls to Leeann to help Mary Beth recover, to locate their father, and to reconstruct the shattered family. "Tucker portrays characters with great depth who will tug at readers' heartstrings," commented Shelley A. Glantz in *Kliatt.* "Tucker's assured debut novel is an achingly tender narrative about grief, love, madness, and crippling family secrets," remarked a *Publishers Weekly* reviewer. And *Booklist* critic Carolyn Kubisz called the book an "engaging and bittersweet story of compassion, forgiveness, and the search for redemption," concluding that "this is a wonderful first novel."

"I think everybody senses that music has something to do with memory," Tucker said in an interview in *Publishers Weekly.* "When you're driving down the street and hear a song from a high school dance on the radio, you find yourself thinking about that dance." Songs often come back to people unbidden, whether triggered by a thought or something in the environment. "I couldn't help wondering: Why that particular song? Why Now?" Tucker remarked. "Could the song have entered your mind at this point in your life because it was telling you something you needed to know?"

Patty Taylor, the protagonist of Tucker's second novel, *Shout Down the Moon,* is also well-attuned to the rigors of struggle. A talented jazz singer, Patty is intent on making a career of music despite her disreputable manager and the band's disdain. She knows that music will make life better for her and her two-year-old son, Willie. After enduring repeated homelessness, the grinding drudgery of dead-end jobs, and devastating personal relationships, snide remarks or sleazy marketing campaigns are trivial obstacles to her career. When Rick, Willie's drug-dealer father, is released from prison, he tracks Willie and Patty down, and she finds herself faced with staying the course toward the dream she has found for herself or being drawn back into the violent, hopeless world that Rick represents and lives in. "Tucker's compulsively readable tale deftly moves over the literary landscape, avoiding genre classification; it succeeds as a subtle romance, an incisive character study, and compelling woman-in-peril noir fiction," observed a *Publishers Weekly* reviewer. "Tucker has stripped Patty's voice of all artifice," wrote Joanne Wilkinson in *Booklist,* "and her straight-from-the-heart narration is instantly gripping."

In the 2006 novel *Once upon a Day,* "the gifted Tucker tells a compelling love story with uncommon empathy and grace," according to *Booklist* contributor Joanne Wilkinson. After her father becomes seriously ill, twenty-three-year-old Dorothea O'Brien leaves their isolated New Mexico ranch, called the Sanctuary, to find her missing older brother, Jimmy. Dorothea, who has never read a newspaper, listened to the radio, or watched television, arrives in St. Louis, where she believes Jimmy has gone in search of answers to the mysteries surrounding the family's past. Dorothea meets grieving cabdriver Stephen Spaulding, who left his medical practice after the tragic deaths of his wife and young daughter, "and as they spend more time together her purity and innocence, not to mention her enthusiastic hunger for sex, draw him back into the world she's just discovering," observed Gregory Cowles in the *New York Times Book Review.* A parallel narrative set in the 1970s centers on singer Lucy Dobbins, her husband, Hollywood director Charles Keenan, and a violent attack on their home by intruders. "The tour de force resolution that ties both stories together is a lyrically poignant reminder of the necessity of hope," wrote a critic in *Publishers Weekly. Library Journal* contributor Andrea Tarr remarked: "Readers will find this captivating, fish-out-of-water fairy tale and mystery-suspense-romance difficult to put down."

BIOGRAPHICAL AND CRITICAL SOURCES:

PERIODICALS

Booklist, April 1, 2003, Carolyn Kubisz, review of *The Song Reader,* pp. 1380-1381; February 15, 2004, Joanne Wilkinson, review of *Shout Down the Moon,* p. 1039; March 1, 2006, Joanne Wilkinson, review of *Once Upon a Day,* p. 68.

Denver Post, May 4, 2003, Robin Vidimos, "Song Stuck in One's Head Holds Meaning," p. EE03.

Kirkus Reviews, February 15, 2003, review of *The Song Reader,* p. 267; February 1, 2004, review of *Shout Down the Moon,* p. 108; January 1, 2006, review of *Once upon a Day,* p. 15.

Kliatt, September, 2003, Shelley A. Glantz, review of *The Song Reader,* p. 22.

Library Journal, April 15, 2003, Patricia Gulian, review of *The Song Reader,* p. 128; March 15, 2006, review of *Once upon a Day,* p. 65; April 1, 2006, Andrea Tarr, "Lisa Tucker: Q&A," p. 84.

New York Times Book Review, April 30, 2006, Gregory Cowles, "Fiction Chronicle," review of *Once upon a Day,* p. 204.

People Weekly, April 12, 2004, Marisa Sandora Carr, review of *Shout Down the Moon,* p. 64.

Philadelphia Inquirer, September 24, 2003, "*Song Reader:* There's More to the Lyrics Than Just the Music"; May 24, 2006, Susan Balee, "Lisa Tucker's *Once upon a Day* Is Sprawling, Short on Humor and Nuance."

Publishers Weekly, March 17, 2003, review of *The Song Reader,* p. 50, and Kevin Howell, "Facing the Music," p. 51; December 22, 2003, review of *Shout Down the Moon,* p. 33; November 28, 2005, review of *Once upon a Day,* p. 20.

Salt Lake Tribune, August 3, 2003, Christy Karras, "Music, Memory Harmonize in Tucker's *The Song Reader,*" p. D4.

School Library Journal, August, 2003, Susan H. Woodcock, review of *The Song Reader,* p. 188; July, 2004, Jackie Gropman, review of *Shout Down the Moon,* p. 132.

Tribune Books (Chicago, IL), May 25, 2003, review of *The Song Reader,* p. 6.

Voice of Youth Advocates, August, 2003, review of *The Song Reader,* p. 232.

ONLINE

BookWeb.org, http://www.bookweb.org/ (May 13, 2003), "*The Song Reader*—Debut Novel Hits the Right Note."

Lisa Tucker Home Page, http://www.lisatucker.com (February 1, 2007).

Pennsylvania Gazette Online, http://www.upenn.edu/ (July-August, 2003), "First Fictions," interview with Lisa Tucker.

V

VAILL, Amanda

PERSONAL: Married; children: two.

ADDRESSES: Home—New York, NY.

CAREER: Writer and critic. Former executive editor for Viking Penguin.

WRITINGS:

Everybody Was So Young: Gerald and Sara Murphy, a Lost Generation Love Story, Houghton (Boston, MA), 1998.
(With Janet Zapata) *Seaman Schepps: A Century of New York Jewelry Design,* Vendome Press (New York, NY), 2004.
Somewhere: The Life of Jerome Robbins, Broadway Books (New York, NY), 2006.

Contributor to periodicals, including *Esquire, New York, Washington Post,* and *Chicago Tribune.*

SIDELIGHTS: Before becoming a full-time writer and critic, Amanda Vaill was executive editor for the distinguished publishing company Viking Penguin. She left that firm so that she could devote all of her time and efforts to her writing projects, which include her critically lauded debut book, *Everybody Was So Young: Gerald and Sara Murphy, a Lost Generation Love Story.* Many critics have proclaimed Vaill's study of the Murphys one of the most complete stories of the couple, who were part of a circle of American writers and art-

ists known as the Expatriates, and were part of a larger circle of artists known as the Lost Generation. As members of this group, which thrived in Paris during the 1920s, the Murphys entertained prominent figures such as the writers Ernest Hemingway and F. Scott Fitzgerald, the artist Pablo Picasso, and the composer Igor Stravinsky. Vaill begins the biography with the couple's courtship and ends with their later years in the United States after they had moved back to New York so Gerald could take over his father's business. According to Vaill, the couple moved to Paris partially as a way to get away from their disapproving parents, as well as to take advantage of a favorable exchange rate, and to tap into the burgeoning cultural movement.

In addition to discussing Gerald's short, but promising, career as an artist, Vaill discusses some of the tragedies that marred the Murphys' seemingly charmed life. Their sons Patrick and Baoth died of severe illnesses in quick succession in the mid-1930s. While Vaill believes the couple had a deep mutual love for one another, she wrote that Gerald had homosexual tendencies, which drove them apart in their later years. Still, Vaill maintains that the Murphys are best remembered as influential members of the Lost Generation that made Paris a cultural center during the period between the great wars. Steve Forbes, a contributor to *Forbes,* called *Everybody Was So Young* a "superbly told tale" that is "riveting." *Booklist* reviewer Donna Seaman felt that the book is a "discerning portrait . . . laced with unforgettable anecdotes." Writing for the *New York Times Book Review,* critic Brooke Allen referred to Vaill as "a skillful and compassionate writer" who has written "a marvelously readable biography."

After coauthoring a book on noted twentieth-century jewelry designer Seaman Schepps, Vaill tackled the complex life of a celebrated choreographer and dancer in *Somewhere: The Life of Jerome Robbins.* As part of her research, Vaill was allowed unique access to Robbins's correspondence and diaries, and was thus able to provide not only a comprehensive critique of his extensive body of work but also an inside view into the insecurities and personal demons that fueled him. Born into a Jewish family in New York City near the end of World War II, Robbins was often treated cruelly by his parents and by the neighborhood kids, and throughout his life he struggled to keep his personal life hidden as his professional career gained momentum. Also included in Vaill's biography are backstage anecdotes from many of Robbins's most successful productions, including *West Side Story* and *Fiddler on the Roof. New York Times Online* contributor Janet Maslin regarded Vaill's writing as "articulate and vivid in describing the particulars of each dance." Other critics also approved of the book. A reviewer for *Publishers Weekly* described the book as "a critically sophisticated biography that's as compulsively readable as a novel," and called it "essential reading for lovers of theater and dance." M.C. Duhig wrote in a review for *Library Journal* that *Somewhere* is a "richly textured portrait of a complex genius," further adding: "This impressive work is thoroughly accessible."

BIOGRAPHICAL AND CRITICAL SOURCES:

PERIODICALS

Booklist, April 15, 1998, Donna Seaman, review of *Everybody Was So Young: Gerald and Sara Murphy, a Lost Generation Love Story,* p. 1409.

Forbes, September 21, 1998, Steve Forbes, review of *Everybody Was So Young,* p. 32.

Library Journal, October 15, 2006, M.C. Duhig, review of *Somewhere: The Life of Jerome Robbins,* p. 66.

New York Times Book Review, May 24, 1998, Brooke Allen, review of *Everybody Was So Young,* p. 12.

Publishers Weekly, September 11, 2006, review of *Somewhere,* p. 45.

ONLINE

New York Times Online, http://www.nytimes.com/ (November 30, 2006), Janet Maslin, review of *Somewhere.**

VAN DRAANEN, Wendelin

PERSONAL: Married; children: two sons. *Hobbies and other interests:* Reading, running, and playing in a rock band.

ADDRESSES: Home—CA.

CAREER: Worked variously as a teacher of high school math and computer science, a forklift driver, a sports coach, and a musician.

AWARDS, HONORS: Edgar Allan Poe Award for Best Children's Mystery, Mystery Writers of America, and Best Book for Young Adults selection, American Library Association, both 1999, both for *Sammy Keyes and the Hotel Thief;* Edgar Allan Poe Award nomination for best juvenile, 2001, for *Sammy Keyes and the Curse of Moustache Mary,* 2003, for *Sammy Keyes and the Search for Snake Eyes,* and 2004, for *Sammy Keyes and the Art of Deception;* Teen's Choice Award, 2004, for *Flipped.*

WRITINGS:

How I Survived Being a Girl, HarperCollins (New York, NY), 1997.

Flipped, Knopf (New York, NY), 2001.

Swear to Howdy, Knopf (New York, NY), 2003.

Runaway, Knopf (New York, NY), 2006.

"SAMMY KEYES" SERIES

Sammy Keyes and the Hotel Thief, illustrated by Dan Yaccarino, Knopf (New York, NY), 1998.

Sammy Keyes and the Skeleton Man, illustrated by Dan Yaccarino, Knopf (New York, NY), 1998.

Sammy Keyes and the Sisters of Mercy, illustrated by Dan Yaccarino, Knopf (New York, NY), 1999.

Sammy Keyes and the Runaway Elf, illustrated by Dan Yaccarino, Knopf (New York, NY), 1999.

Sammy Keyes and the Curse of Moustache Mary, illustrated by Dan Yaccarino, Knopf (New York, NY), 2000.

Sammy Keyes and the Hollywood Mummy, illustrated by Dan Yaccarino, Knopf (New York, NY), 2001.

Sammy Keyes and the Search for Snake Eyes, Knopf (New York, NY), 2002.

Sammy Keyes and the Art of Deception, Knopf (New York, NY), 2003.

Sammy Keyes and the Psycho Kitty Queen, illustrations by Dan Yaccarino, Knopf (New York, NY), 2004.

Sammy Keyes and the Dead Giveaway, illustrations by Dan Yaccarino, Knopf (New York, NY), 2005.

Sammy Keyes and the Wild Things, Knopf (New York, NY), 2007.

"SHREDDERMAN" SERIES

Secret Identity, illustrated by Brian Biggs, Knopf (New York, NY), 2004.

Attack of the Tagger, illustrated by Brian Biggs, Knopf (New York, NY), 2004.

Meet the Gecko, illustrated by Brian Biggs, Knopf (New York, NY), 2005.

Enemy Spy, illustrated by Brian Biggs, Knopf (New York, NY), 2005.

SIDELIGHTS: Wendelin Van Draanen is the author of the popular "Sammy Keyes" mystery series for young readers, featuring an indomitable tomboy with a penchant for landing herself in trouble. The misunderstood heroine, whose formal name is Samantha, often starts out as the primary suspect in some sort of minor crime and finds the real culprit through efforts to clear her own name. The middle schooler also combats some tough family and social situations with the same sense of humor and adventure. Van Draanen's first book in the series—only her second ever published—won the Edgar Award for Best Children's Mystery in 1999.

Until she was in the fourth grade and her sister was born, Van Draanen grew up the sole daughter in a family with three children, having an older and a younger brother. The situation provided the inspiration for the intrepid, tomboy protagonists of her books, though the future author described her own juvenile persona as tentative and shy. Entering adolescence was a time of added uncertainty for Van Draanen. Her coming-of-age adventures formed the basis for the comical problems she later forces Sammy Keyes to suffer.

When Van Draanen was in college, a catastrophe in her family inadvertently opened up a new door for her: their family business was destroyed by arson, and she took time off from school to help out in the aftermath. For a time, they were financially ruined, and Van Draanen was troubled by feelings of anger and helplessness. She

began to have problems sleeping, and to help alleviate some of the stress, she decided to write about the incident with the hope of turning it into a screenplay.

Van Draanen discovered that writing was not only cathartic but enjoyable. What she found most rewarding, she later noted, was the ability to create a happy ending, to have her characters make positive gains through personal difficulties. Van Draanen eventually found her vocation as a high school teacher of computer science, but she also had ten finished novels, each around four hundred pages long, by the mid-1990s. By then she had married and had begun a family of her own in California.

Van Draanen was inspired to try her hand at writing for children as a result of a chance gift from her husband of Ray Bradbury's *Dandelion Wine.* The result was *How I Survived Being a Girl,* published in 1997. It is Van Draanen's first work for young readers before her "Sammy Keyes" series, and the works share a heroine with pointed similarities. Carolyn, the narrator of *How I Survived Being a Girl,* is a tomboy who feels somewhat alienated from the girls in her neighborhood and at school. She much prefers tagging along with her brothers and their friends, especially a neighbor boy named Charlie. During one particular summer, Carolyn spies on neighbors, digs foxholes with Charlie, steals a book, and helps her brother with his paper route.

The setting of *How I Survived Being a Girl* is vague, but reviewers seemed to agree that Van Draanen placed her story at some point in the relatively recent past. Girls still wore dresses to school, for instance, and were strongly discouraged from becoming newspaper carriers—official and unofficial biases that had vanished by the end of the 1970s. Carolyn manages to skirt the skirt issue by wearing shorts under hers; meanwhile, she derides her peers who play with dolls and wear frilly, impractical clothes. Yet, as she begins a new school year in September, Carolyn finds that some of her attitudes are beginning to change. She sees Charlie in a new way, and starts to speak out and become more politically active. She even starts a petition drive to force some changes at her school. When a baby sister arrives in her family, this softens her attitude, too. "I tell her . . . how being a girl is actually all right once you figure out that you should break some of the rules instead of just living with them," says Carolyn at the end of the book.

A *Publishers Weekly* contributor called *How I Survived Being a Girl* an "energetic first novel" and "a sunny, funny look at a girl with a smart mouth and scabby knees." A *Kirkus Reviews* contributor praised Van Draanen's style and the narrative voice of her alter ego, Carolyn. "Her irreverent narration is engaging," stated the reviewer about the book's heroine, "and she's refreshingly astute about family and neighborhood dynamics."

Van Draanen found she liked writing in a child's voice, so she began writing a teen-detective story that later evolved into a popular and much-praised series. The first of these, *Sammy Keyes and the Hotel Thief,* arrived in 1998. Here, readers are introduced to the feisty, intelligent title character who lives with her grandmother in a seniors-only apartment building. Because of this, Sammy is forced to sneak around just to get to school; naturally, her social life is severely curtailed as well. Sammy lives with her grandmother, readers learn, because her mother, whom she refers to as "Lady Lana," has moved to Hollywood.

Sammy has some formidable enemies. One is the nosy Mrs. Graybill, who lives down the hall; another is a girl, Heather, who torments her daily at school. To keep herself amused at home, Sammy often observes the goings-on of the outside world with a pair of binoculars from her fifth-floor window. "Usually you just see people looking out their windows, pointing to stuff on the street or talking on the phone," Sammy states, "but sometimes you can see people yelling at each other, which is really strange because you can't *hear* anything."

Sammy is particularly fascinated by the shady Heavenly Hotel across the street, and one afternoon spots a fourth-floor resident moving about a room rather quickly. She then sees the man rifling through a purse while wearing gloves. As Sammy tells it: "I'm trying to get a better look at his face through all his bushy brown hair and beard, when he stuffs a wad of money from the purse into his jacket pocket and then looks up. Right at me. For a second there I don't think he believed his eyes. He kind of leaned into the window and stared, and I stared right back through the binoculars. Then I did something really, really stupid. I waved."

The man flees the room, and Sammy wonders whether she has just witnessed a crime and if she ought to tell someone about it. Her grandmother is busy making dinner, and getting to a police station is also problematic. Then, her grandmother calls her into the kitchen and reminds her to feed the cat. The doorbell rings, but

Sammy is so agitated that she does not quietly make for the closet, as is her usual drill when an unexpected visitor arrives. "This time, though, I jumped. I jumped and yelped like a puppy. And all of a sudden my heart's pounding because I know who it is," Sammy panics. "It's the guy I saw at the Heavenly Hotel, come to shut me up for good."

Eventually, Sammy manages to tell her story to the police, who fail to take her seriously at first. Meanwhile, Heather is plotting against her at school, but Sammy's cleverness uncovers the plot in time. She also learns that a burglar has indeed been stealing from purses in the neighborhood. Other characters in the book include a pair of comical detectives, a girlfriend named Marissa, a local DJ, and an eccentric astrologer who is also a robbery victim. They all help Sammy bring the thief to justice. "The solution will likely come as a surprise, and the sleuth delights from start to finish," asserted a *Publishers Weekly* contributor in a review of *Sammy Keyes and the Hotel Thief.* A *Horn Book* review by Martha V. Parravano described Van Draanen's protagonist as "one tough, smart, resourceful seventh grader," and compared the heroine and structure of the lighthearted detective novel to those of popular adult mystery writers such as Sue Grafton, who are adept at "making the investigator's character and private life at least as interesting and complex as the plot."

Van Draanen followed the success of the first Sammy Keyes book with a second that same year, *Sammy Keyes and the Skeleton Man.* As it opens around Halloween time, Sammy still lives with her grandmother and is eagerly outfitting herself as the Marsh Monster for the holiday. While trick-or-treating, she and her friends bravely approach the "Bush House," a scary manse with wildly overgrown shrubbery. But then Sammy is nearly knocked down by a man wearing a skeleton costume and carrying a pillowcase. She and her friends advance and discover a fire in the house, and Sammy puts it out. They also find that a burglary has just taken place, and several valuable books are missing from the house.

Sammy, naturally, finds herself drawn into the drama and wants to solve the whodunit. She learns that the Bush House is neglected because its owners, the LeBard brothers, are feuding with one another. Once again, her cleverness helps her find a solution and also helps her keep one step ahead of Heather, who continues to cause her problems. Sammy, for instance, sneaks into Heather's Halloween party and plants a baby monitor in her room—which provides Sammy with evidence that Heather has been making prank phone calls in Sammy's name. Yet Sammy's natural talent for making friends also helps her forge an unusual bond with Chauncy LeBard, and she even gets the two warring brothers to agree to talk. In the end, she unmasks the skeleton man and recovers the missing rarities. Martha V. Parravano, reviewing the story for *Horn Book,* praised it as a "highly readable mystery [that] hits the ground running." Reviewer Lynda Short also offered positive words in *School Library Journal:* "Readers will enjoy the mystery, hijinks, plotting, and adult comeuppance."

Van Draanen's third entry in the series, *Sammy Keyes and the Sisters of Mercy,* was published in 1999. Still walking that fine line between intellectual brilliance and juvenile delinquency, Sammy finds herself sentenced to twenty hours of detention, which she must fulfill by helping out at the local Roman Catholic church. One day, while cleaning the windows of St. Mary's, she sees a girl she does not know and approaches her. The girl vanishes, and Sammy is suddenly alerted to the distress of Father Mayhew, who has just discovered his valuable ivory cross missing. Sammy, of course, is the first suspect in the theft, but other possible culprits surface as well, and in order to clear her own name, she resolves to catch the thief herself. On another day, she again sees the mysterious girl at the church's soup kitchen and eventually learns that she is homeless.

Again, Van Draanen paints Sammy as a typical adolescent. There is more enmity with Heather, and she is determined to beat her foe in the local softball league championships. In the end, it is Sammy's offer to help a group of musical nuns who do missionary work out of an old school bus that helps solve the mystery of Father Mayhew's missing cross. "As always, quirky characters are Van Draanen's strength," remarked Kay Weisman in a *Booklist* review. An assessment from Jennifer Ralston in *School Library Journal* praised the main plot of *Sammy Keyes and the Sisters of Mercy* as well as the other storylines, both recurring and new. Ralston noted the storylines provide "depth and interest to an already engrossing mystery while capturing the angst of junior high school." Beth E. Anderson, reviewing the book for *Voice of Youth Advocates,* commended Van Draanen's heroine. "Sammy is genuine, funny, devoted to her friends and blessed with a strength of character that lets her reach for a peaceful solution," Anderson wrote.

Van Draanen wrote another entry in the series that also appeared in 1999, *Sammy Keyes and the Runaway Elf.*

Set during the Christmas season, this story occurs when Sammy is still in seventh grade and becomes involved in her community's holiday parade. She is assigned to the "Canine Calendar Float" and is charged with babysitting a famous Pomeranian, the calendar cover dog, Marique. Parade chaos ensues, however, when a trio of culprits dressed as the Three Kings throw cats onto the hound-laden float. The prized Marique vanishes, and its owner, wealthy Mrs. Landvogt, blackmails Sammy into finding Marique in order to avoid paying the fifty thousand dollar ransom demanded. An elfin girl, Elyssa, turns out to be a runaway, and Van Draanen weaves her plight and the dognapping together and ties it up, according to critics, with another satisfying conclusion. Once again, however, several suspects must first be eliminated and comical plot twists steered through. This time, Sammy manages to befriend the formidable Mrs. Graybill, too. Remarking on Sammy's penchant for making friends both younger and much older than herself, *School Library Journal* contributor Linda Bindner noted that "Van Draanen handles the relationships with style and sensitivity."

A fifth book in the series, *Sammy Keyes and the Curse of Moustache Mary,* was published in 2000, followed by *Sammy Keyes and the Hollywood Mummy* in 2001. Reviewing the latter title in *School Library Journal,* critic Wanda Meyers-Hines Called it "clever and fast-paced, and . . . filled with cliff-hanger chapter endings and characters with secrets."

The next book in the series, *Sammy Keyes and the Search for Snake Eyes,* finds Sammy being given a "surprise" by a frightened girl in the mall. Sammy understands the girl's fear when she meets the nefarious Snake Eyes. A contributor to the *TeenLit* Web site commented: "The last few sentences of each chapter left me wanting more. At times, I felt I couldn't put down the book."

In *Sammy Keyes and the Art of Deception,* Sammy is at an art gallery for a school project along with Grams and her septuagenarian friend when she sees paintings that fascinate her. Suddenly, a man armed with a squirt gun comes in and steals some paintings. As Sammy and her grandmother try to figure out why the paintings were stolen, several subplots ensue, including Sammy's ongoing feud with Heather, and Sammy's strange feelings for Casey, Heather's brother. Writing on the *KidsReads. com* Web site, Marya Jansen-Gruber noted that the author "has created a wonderfully entertaining story with quirky language and colorful images, one that takes you inside Sammy's thoughts and feelings."

Sammy Keyes and the Psycho Kitty Queen finds Sammy celebrating her birthday when she finds a dead cat. This is only the first sign portending a day of bad luck and puzzles, which include more dead cats turning up in the city dumpsters and the reappearance of her mother, who informs her that her birth certificate is wrong and that she is actually celebrating her thirteenth birthday once again, which Sammy takes as an ominous sign. When Heather's brother Casey gives her a four-leaf clover, however, Sammy's luck begins to turn. Diana Pierce, writing in the *School Library Journal,* called the book "another hit in a solid series." Kathleen Odean wrote in *Booklist* that Sammy's "life [is] believably complicated and imperfect."

In *Sammy Keyes and the Dead Giveaway,* Sammy, for once, is partially guilty of the misdoing, namely the disappearance of her teacher's love bird. When her archenemy Heather becomes a suspect, Sammy starts feeling guilty. Her uneasiness is further heightened when she begins receiving threatening messages. Another mystery arises, however, namely the question of who is throwing rocks through the windows of elderly people's homes. In her review in *Booklist,* Francisca Goldsmith commented that "the clever twist at the end of the story is sure to delight Sammy's fans." *School Library Journal* contributor Elizabeth Fernandez wrote that the story's "final cascade of stunning revelations will have readers on the edge of their seats."

In 2004, the first book in the author's "Shredderman" series appeared on bookshelves. *Secret Identity* introduces readers to Nolan "Nerd" Byrd, a math whiz whose secret identity is Shredderman, a cyber-hero who sets out to expose school bully Bubba Bixby. Bubba not only picks on his classmates but also cheats and steals. With the use of a digital camera, Nolan uncovers the evidence he needs, sets up a Web site to expose the bully, and then tries to figure out how to get people to view the site. Writing on the *KidsReads.com* Web site, Sarah A. Wood called *Secret Identity* "the first book in what promises to be a hilarious, original and action-packed series." In a review for *Booklist,* Jennifer Mattson wrote: "Kudos . . . for delivering a character-driven series that's spot-on for middle-graders and great for reluctant readers."

Attack of the Tagger finds Nolan tracking down a graffiti artist who spray paints everything in sight, including the playground equipment. In the process, however, Nolan becomes a suspect himself and must post photos

and information on his Web site, Shredderman.com, to clear his name. Jennifer Mattson, writing in *Booklist,* called this second installment in the series a "balm for all those dweeby kids who will see themselves in Nolan and cheer him." *School Library Journal* contributor Christine McGinty noted that the story is "packed with plenty of action and humor."

The third book in the "Shredderman"series, *Meet the Gecko,* finds Nolan meeting actor Chase Morton, who plays Nolan's hero, "The Gecko,"on television. When Nolan finds out that Chase is being stalked by an evil reporter, he sets out to use his Shredderman.com Web site to expose the journalist. In his review in *Booklist,* Todd Morning described *Meet the Gecko* as "a light-hearted, fast-moving story." *School Library Journal* contributor Jennifer Cogan wrote: "Reluctant readers will find this book accessible."

In the next book in the series, *Enemy Spy,* Nolan is having difficulty protecting his secret identity from his classmates as he pursues a real-life spy ring and is in danger of being found out by the press as well. Kim Carlson, writing in the *School Library Journal,* commented favorably on the book's "fast-moving plot," and *Booklist* contributor Carolyn Phelan noted: "Writing in first person, Nolan tells his own story in a snappy style."

Van Draanen turns to a more serious theme in her 2006 book titled *Runaway.* Telling her own story through journal entries and poetry, twelve-year-old Holly recounts her experiences as a homeless runaway from evil foster parents. "This is a touching, realistic, beautifully written story that anyone will be able to enjoy," wrote Jocelyn Pearce on the *Curled Up with a Good Kid's Book* Web site. Pam Gelman, writing on the *Common Sense Review* Web site, commented that the author "clearly knows kids this age well." *Booklist*'s GraceAnne A. DeCandido concluded: "The ending of this taut, powerful story seems possible and deeply hopeful."

BIOGRAPHICAL AND CRITICAL SOURCES:

BOOKS

Van Draanen, Wendelin, *How I Survived Being a Girl,* HarperCollins, 1997.

Van Draanen, Wendelin, *Sammy Keyes and the Hotel Thief,* Knopf, 1998.

PERIODICALS

Booklist, September 1, 1998, p. 131; April 1, 1999, Kay Weisman, review of *Sammy Keyes and the Sisters of Mercy,* p. 1415; September 1, 1999, p. 146; March 1, 2001, Gillian Engberg, review of *Sammy Keyes and the Hollywood Mummy,* p. 1272; February 1, 2004, Jennifer Mattson, review of *Secret Identity,* p. 975; September 1, 2004, Jennifer Mattson, review of *Attack of the Tagger,* p. 125; October 1, 2004, Kathleen Odean, review of *Sammy Keyes and the Psycho Kitty Queen,* p. 330; January 1, 2005, review of *Secret Identity,* p. 774; February 1, 2005, Todd Morning, review of *Meet the Gecko,* p. 962; May 1, 2005, Gillian Engberg, review of *Sammy Keyes and the Psycho Kitty Queen,* p. 1543; August, 2005, Carolyn Phelan, review of *Enemy Spy,* p. 2030; September 1, 2005, Francisca Golsmith, review of *Sammy Keyes and the Dead Giveaway,* p. 137; September 1, 2006, GraceAnne A. DeCandido, review of *Runaway,* p. 112.

Children's Bookwatch, February, 2005, review of *Sammy Keyes and the Psycho Kitty Queen;* September, 2005, review of *Enemy Spy;* December, 2005, review of *Sammy Keyes and the Dead Giveaway;* September, 2006, review of *Runaway.*

Horn Book, July-August, 1998, Martha V. Parravano, review of *Sammy Keyes and the Hotel Thief,* pp. 498-499; November-December, 1998, Martha V. Parravano, review of *Sammy Keyes and the Skeleton Man,* p. 743.

Kirkus Reviews, December 1, 1996, review of *How I Survived Being a Girl;* January 1, 2004, review of *Secret Identity,* p. 42; July 15, 2004, review of *Attack of the Tagger,* p. 694; December 15, 2004, review of *Meet the Gecko,* p. 1210; August 15, 2006, review of *Runaway,* p. 853.

Kliatt, September, 2006, Myrna Marler, review of *Runaway,* p. 19.

MBR Bookwatch, June, 2005, review of *Meet the Gecko.*

Publishers Weekly, January 6, 1997, review of *How I Survived Being a Girl,* p. 73; April 27, 1998, review of *Sammy Keyes and the Hotel Thief,* p. 67; February 2, 2004, review of *Secret Identity,* p. 77; January 3, 2005, review of *Meet the Gecko,* p. 57; May 15, 2006, "Fiction Reprints," discusses reprints of author's works, p. 74; October 23, 2006, review of *Runaway,* p. 51.

San Luis Obispo Tribune (San Luis Obispo, California), September 27, 1999.

School Library Journal, February, 1997, Kathleen Odean, review of *How I Survived Being a Girl,* p. 106; July, 1998, p. 100; September, 1998, Lynda Short, review of *Sammy Keyes and the Skeleton Man,* p. 211; July, 1999, Jennifer Ralston, review of *Sammy Keyes and the Sisters of Mercy,* p. 101; September, 1999, Linda Bindner, review of *Sammy Keyes and the Runaway Elf,* p. 229; August, 2000, p. 190; February, 2001, Wanda Meyers-Hines, review of *Sammy Keyes and the Hollywood Mummy,* p. 122; March, 2001, Sarah Flowers, review of *Sammy Keyes and the Hotel Thief,* p. 87; May, 2004, Edward Sullivan, review of *Secret Identity,* p. 158; October, 2004, Diana Pierce, review of *Sammy Keyes and the Psycho Kitty Queen,* p. 180; November, 2004, Christine McGinty, review of *Attack of the Tagger,* p. 156; January 1, 2005, Jennifer Cogan, review of *Meet the Gecko,* p. 774; July, 2005, Kim Carlson, review of *Enemy Spy,* p. 110; November, 2005, Elizabeth Fernandez, review of *Sammy Keyes and the Dead Giveaway,* p. 150; August 15, 2006, Jennifer Ralston, review of *Secret Identity,* p. 853; September, 2006, Faith Brautigam, review of *Runaway,* p. 220.

Time for Kids, September 30, 2005, Brenda Iasevoli, interview with the author, p. 7.

Voice of Youth Advocates, April, 2000, Beth E. Anderson, review of *Sammy Keyes and the Sisters of Mercy,* pp. 40-41.

ONLINE

Common Sense Review, http://www.commonsensemedia.org/ (March 16, 2007), Pam Gelman, review of *Runaway.*

Curled Up with a Good Kid's Book, http://www.curledupkids.com/ (March 16, 2007), Jocelyn Pearce, review of *Runaway.*

KidsReads.com, http://www.kidsreads.com/ (March 16, 2007), Sarah A. Wood, review of *Secret Identity;* Tamara Penny, review of *Sammy Keyes and the Hollywood Mummy;* Marya Jansen-Gruber, review of *Sammy Keyes and the Art of Deception.*

TeenLit, http://www.teenlit.com/ (March 16, 2007), review of *Sammy Keyes and the Search for Snake Eyes.**

W

WALKER, Dale L. 1935-
  (Dale Lee Walker)

PERSONAL: Born August 3, 1935, in Decatur, IL; son of Russell Dale (in the armed forces) and Eileen M. Walker; married Alice McCord, September 30, 1960; children: Dianne, Eric, Christopher, Michael, John. *Education:* Texas Western College (now University of Texas at El Paso), B.A., 1962. *Politics:* Democrat. *Religion:* Protestant.

ADDRESSES: Home—El Paso, TX. *E-mail*—walker dale@prodigy.net.

CAREER: Writer, novelist, historian, and journalist. Freelance writer, 1960—; KTSM-TV, El Paso, TX, reporter, 1962-66; University of Texas at El Paso, director of News-Information Office, 1966-93; Texas Western Press, El Paso, director, 1985-93. *Military service:* U.S. Navy, 1955-59.

MEMBER: Western Writers of America (president, 1992-94), Texas Institute of Letters, Authors Guild.

AWARDS, HONORS: Special Spur Award, Western Writers of America, 1986, for five-year editorship of *The Roundup;* Spur Award, 1988, for best Western short nonfiction; Owen Wister Award, Western Writers of America, 2000; Spur Award, 2001, for Best Western Historical Book (*Pacific Destiny*); Spur Award for best Western short nonfiction, Western Writers of America, 2002, for "Killer of Pain's Transcontinental Journey."

WRITINGS:

(With Richard O'Connor) *The Lost Revolutionary: A Biography of John Reed,* Harcourt (New York, NY), 1967.

C.L. Sonnichsen: Grassroots Historian, Texas Western Press (El Paso, TX), 1972.

The Alien Worlds of Jack London (monograph), Wolf House Books (Minneapolis, MN), 1973.

(Editor) Howard A. Craig, *Sunward I've Climbed,* Texas Western Press (El Paso, TX), 1974.

Jack London, Sherlock Holmes, and Sir Arthur Conan Doyle (monograph), Alvin S. Fick (Amsterdam, NY), 1974.

Death Was the Black Horse: The Story of Rough Rider, Buckey O'Neill, Madrona Press (Austin, TX), 1975, published as *Rough Rider: Buckey O'Neill of Arizona,* University of Nebraska Press (Lincoln, NE), 1997.

(Editor and author of introduction) *Curious Fragments: Jack London's Tales of Fantasy Fiction,* Kennikat (Port Washington, NY), 1975, published as *Fantastic Tales,* University of Nebraska Press (Lincoln, NE), 1998.

(Editor and author of introduction) *No Mentor but Myself: Jack London, the Writer's Writer,* Kennikat (Port Washington, NY), 1979, published with revisions, Stanford University Press (Stanford, CA), 1998, 2nd edition, revised and expanded, Stanford University Press (Stanford, CA), 1999.

Only the Clouds Remain: Ted Parsons of the Lafayette Escadrille, Alandale (Amsterdam, NY), 1980.

Jack London and Conan Doyle: A Literary Kinship, Gaslight (Bloomington, IL), 1981.

(Editor and author of introduction) *Will Henry's West,* Texas Western Press (El Paso, TX), 1984.

(Editor and author of introduction) *In a Far Country: Jack London's Western Tales,* Green Hill (Ottawa, IL), 1986.

Januarius McGahan: The Life and Campaigns of an American War Correspondent, 1844-1878, Ohio University Press (Athens, OH), 1988.

Mavericks: Ten Uncorralled Westerners, Golden West (Phoenix, AZ), 1989.

(Editor and author of introduction) *The Golden Spurs,* Forge Books (New York, NY), 1992.

Legends and Lies: Great Mysteries of the American West, Forge Books (New York, NY), 1997.

(Editor, with Elmore Leonard and Martin Harry Greenberg) *The Western Hall of The Boys of '98: Theodore Roosevelt and the Rough Riders,* Forge Books (New York, NY), 1998.

Bear Flag Rising: The Conquest of California, 1846, Forge Books (New York, NY), 1999.

Pacific Destiny: The Three-Century Journey to the Oregon Country, Forge Books (New York, NY), 2000.

(With Bill O'Neal and James A. Crutchfield) *The Wild West,* Publications International (Lincolnwood, IL), 2001.

(Editor) *Westward: A Fictional History of the American West,* Forge Books (New York, NY), 2003.

Eldorado: The California Gold Rush, Forge Books (New York, NY), 2003.

The Calamity Papers: Western Myths and Cold Cases, Forge Books (New York, NY), 2004.

Mary Edwards Walker: Above and Beyond, Forge Books (New York, NY), 2005.

Contributor to books, including *Wine of Wizardry,* by George Sterling, Pinion Press, 1962; *Passing Through,* edited by W. Burns Taylor and Richard Santelli, Santay Publishers, 1974; *The Reader's Encyclopedia of the American West,* edited by Howard Lamar, Crowell (New York, NY), 1977; *An American for Lafayette: The Diaries of E.C.C. Genet,* University of Virginia Press (Charlottesville, VA), 1981; *Uncommon Men and the Colorado Prairie,* by Nell Brown Propst, Caxton (Caldwell, ID), 1992; *The West That Was,* Wings Books (New York, NY), 1993; *In the Big Country,* by John Jakes, Bantam (New York, NY), 1993; *The Bride Wore Crimson,* by Brian Woolley, Texas Western Press, 1993; *New Trails,* Doubleday (New York, NY), 1994; *The American West,* Grolier (Danbury, CT), 1995; *Legends of the Old West,* Publications International (Chicago, IL), 1995; and *Wild West Show,* Wings Books, 1995.

Contributor to periodicals and newspapers, including *Newsweek, Ellery Queen's Mystery Magazine, Modern Fiction Studies, Soldier of Fortune, Aviation Quarterly, New Mexico Magazine, Montana, Arizona Republic, Louis L'Amour's Western Magazine,* and *Baker Street Journal.* Books editor, *El Paso Times,* 1979-85; editor, *Roundup,* 1980-85; author of column "Out West," *Rocky Mountain News,* 1989-2002.

SIDELIGHTS: Dale L. Walker has written many works on the history of the American West that have earned critical praise for their extensive detail and accessible narrative style. Among his best-received titles are *The Boys of '98: Theodore Roosevelt and the Rough Riders, Bear Flag Rising: The Conquest of California, 1846,* and *Pacific Destiny: The Three-Century Journey to the Oregon Country.*

The Boys of '98 is a history of Theodore Roosevelt's heroic Rough Riders, a volunteer cavalry regiment of the Spanish-American War made famous by their charge up San Juan Hill. While the Rough Riders gained lasting fame for their bravery in battle, they also suffered a high casualty rate—some thirty-seven percent were either killed or wounded. Colonel Roosevelt became a nationally known figure because of his role as their leader, publicity that later led to his running for and winning the presidency of the United States. A critic for *Publishers Weekly* described Walker's *The Boys of '98* as "a human-oriented picture of the regiment, its camp life, battles and struggle with disease." Writing in *Booklist,* John Rowen remarked that "strong research and accessible writing make this study fresh and insightful." Walker first became interested in the topic of the Rough Riders in the early 1970s. At that time he was writing a biography of Arizonan lawman William O. "Buckey" O'Neill, a Rough Rider who was killed in battle. In the course of his research, Walker interviewed several remaining members of the Rough Riders, interviews he later made use of in *The Boys of '98,* published to coincide with the centennial anniversary of the Spanish-American War.

In *Bear Flag Rising* Walker chronicles the events leading up to America's annexation of California in 1846. At the time, California was a province of Mexico, but many Americans had settled there to farm or ranch. When these Americans became disenchanted with Spanish rule, they began to rebel. Walker focuses specifically on the actions and motivations of three key players in the annexation: John Charles Fremont, Commodore Robert Field Stockton, and General Stephen Watts Kearney. Together, these three men maneuvered events in California in such a way as to make the Mexican colony an integral part of the United States. "Utilizing scholarly resources," wrote Terri P. Summey in *Library Journal,* "Walker presents an unbiased account of the conquest." "The author," Margaret Flanagan noted in *Booklist,* "places the key battles and events of the California campaign firmly in historical context."

Pacific Destiny tells the story of how the Oregon territory became a part of America, tracing the region's history from its discovery in the sixteenth century by the Spanish to its settlement in the nineteenth century by Americans following the Oregon Trail. Walker's approach is to highlight the major figures who played parts in Oregon's development. A *Publishers Weekly* critic explained: "Walker constructs a compelling narrative that is a string of unusual profiles rather than an analytic account of a major event in American history." Walker's account is, according to a *Kirkus Reviews* contributor, "a lively, readable history of the exploration and settlement of the Pacific Northwest." Walker told *American Western Magazine* online, "To me, the great 'journey' to the Old Oregon Country is the greatest of Western American sagas."

Januarius McGahan: The Life and Campaigns of an American War Correspondent, 1844-1878, delineates the life and career of Ohio-born journalist McGahan, largely unknown today but whose reporting from Europe and Central Asia was pivotal in developing American attitudes and opinions toward those regions. As a battlefield correspondent, McGahan reported on atrocities committed by Turkish soldiers against native Bulgarian civilians during the Bulgarian uprising in 1876. These dispatches created an international sensation and illustrated how Britain and Prime Minister Disraeli elected to do nothing to stop Turkey's actions. He reported from Brussels and Germany during the Franco-Prussian war; he witnessed the Russian Army's invasion of the walled city of Khiva in Turkestan; and he traveled to the Arctic in search of evidence from the ill-fated expedition of Sir John Franklin. Walker provides considerable material from McGahan's reports and journalistic pieces, showing the reporter's works to be "models of descriptive clarity and narrative power," noted Bruce Allen in *Smithsonian.* "The telling of this irresistible tale gains double impact from Dale Walker's own considerable writing skills," Allen remarked, and concluded that Walker "has done Januarius MacGahan all the honor that has long been due him."

In *Legends and Lies: Great Mysteries of the American West,* Walker sets out to explore some of the enduring legends of the West, considering stories of people, places, and events that may have suffered from elaboration and embellishment through years of telling and retelling. *Wild West* reviewer Leon C. Metz noted that "it isn't Dale Walker's intention to necessarily resolve these mysteries. Instead he separates the reasonable theories from the wacky, the possibilities from the idio-

cies." Walker examines the historical record to find out what happened to the notorious Black Bart, highway robber in California. He notes that Boston Corbett allegedly shot John Wilkes Booth in a barn, but investigates stories that indicate Corbett did not slay Booth after all. He also looks at the stories behind the Lost Dutchman Mine in Phoenix, Arizona; the death of Native American leader Crazy Horse; and the facts of the battle of the Little Big Horn and Custer's fatal failure there. Walker's book "will captivate anyone who loves historical mysteries, the behind-the-scene intrigues that still puzzle and bedevil us today," Metz concluded.

Though most of Walker's works are firmly grounded in the realities of nonfiction, he is also aware of the power of a rousing fictional tale of the Old West. In *Westward: A Fictional History of the American West,* editor Walker presents twenty-eight original western stories, written in commemoration of the fiftieth year of the Western Writers of America. The stories present a rough chronology of the history of the American West, from Don Coldsmith's story about the first horse ever seen by a Native American to Loren Estleman's take on political corruption in the Old West. Other stories cover familiar western staples such as outlaws, gunfighters, grieving widows, and hunters. The collection demonstrates the "vitality and the diversity of the western genre" and also the "enduring appeal of the short story," commented Wes Lukowsky in *Booklist.*

Eldorado: The California Gold Rush contains a broad history of the people, places, and events that made up the frenzied search for gold in the middle of the nineteenth century. Walker looks at the multiple personalities, both well-meaning and nefarious, that streamed into California, looking for easy riches. He notes that prospectors and fortune-seekers came not only from the eastern areas of the United States, but from many other countries as well. He profiles John August Sutter, a German whose infamous mill became the site of the largest gold strike in California in 1848. It includes reports of the arduous journeys and difficult conditions endured by gold-seekers, and how one in five perished within their search. Walker notes the irony of the fact that many of the key figures of the gold rush, including Samuel Brannan, a landowner and tycoon; James Marshall, who first discovered California gold in the American River; and John Sutter himself, died in poverty, without the benefit of the riches they had helped others to find. Walker's "narrative is swift and accurate, and the author does a good job of bringing musty historical figures to life," commented a *Kirkus*

Reviews critic. Throughout the book, Walker is "enthralled with the frontier adventures" that are an integral part of stories of the gold rush, but he "never ignores the toll on humans and nature that exceeded any benefit," commented Tyler D. Johnson in the *New York Times Book Review.*

Mary Edwards Walker: Above and Beyond tells the life story of Civil War-era physician, women's rights activist, and medical reformer Walker, the only woman to have been awarded the Congressional Medal of Honor. An iconoclastic figure in her time, Walker struggled to become a physician and build a practice when female doctors were a rarity and when Union Army officers would not commission a woman to serve. She was a vigorous opponent of what she saw as rampant, indiscriminate amputation by medical practitioners during the Civil War. Little interested in the customs of her day, she was criticized for her actions and behavior, but was a dedicated fighter for the rights of those who could not advocate for themselves. Mary Walker's limited writings, quoted in the book, "melds with Walker's prose in a colorful portrait of an uppity woman" who "inspires and motivates," commented Donna Chavez in *Booklist.*

Walker once told *CA:* "I have been writing professionally since 1960, my freelancing done after hours while holding full-time jobs in news work and university staff positions. I retired in 1993 and now write full time. Most of my work has been periodical nonfiction—magazine articles, reviews, criticism, literary and historical studies, and newspaper work. I have been published in 130 different periodicals, and my books have been, for the most part, outgrowths of the periodical work.

"My best work has been in biography—book-length works on the nineteenth-century war correspondent Januarius MacGahan (which I regard as my best work), Rough Rider William O. 'Buckey' O'Neill, and the American radical writer John Reed (author of *Ten Days That Shook the World*), and hundreds of shorter, biographical pieces for magazines. I have published a great deal about Jack London, a life-long interest of mine and the greatest influence I've had as a writer—a book-length annotated bibliography, three edited collections of his stories, a book-length literary study.

"I write every day, a minimum of four hours, most often longer, and while I have never written much more than my signature in longhand, I began writing on an antique upright Royal, graduated to an IBM Selectric (which I swore was the end of all technology) and presently use, indeed am wedded to, a word processor.

"The writers I admire are a strange mix: I regard the British writers George MacDonald Fraser and Jan Morris as the finest historical stylists in the English language today; I greatly admire the historical novels by the late Will Henry (Henry Wilson Allen); I love the language of certain British military historians—Sir John Fortescue and Alexander Kinglake among them; I am in awe of the work of [Herman] Melville and Cormac McCarthy; I love such mystery-thriller writers as Ed McBain, Lawrence Block, and the late John D. MacDonald, the fantasies of Jack Vance, many Western and other genre writers who are great stylists. I am, and have been most of my working life, absorbed by nineteenth-century military history."

BIOGRAPHICAL AND CRITICAL SOURCES:

PERIODICALS

American Studies International, October, 2001, Matt Weiser, review of *No Mentor but Myself: Jack London on Writers and Writing,* p. 103.

Booklist, April 15, 1998, John Rowen, review of *The Boys of '98: Theodore Roosevelt and the Rough Riders,* p. 1425; June 1, 1999, Margaret Flanagan, review of *Bear Flag Rising: The Conquest of California, 1846,* p. 1780; June 1, 2003, Wes Lukowsky, review of *Westward: A Fictional History of the American West,* p. 1747; November 15, 2004, Gilbert Taylor, review of *The Calamity Papers: Western Myths and Cold Cases,* p. 550; June 1, 2005, Donna Chavez, review of *Mary Edwards Walker: Above and Beyond,* p. 1736.

Kirkus Reviews, October 15, 1997, review of *Legends and Lies: Great Mysteries of the American West;* April 15, 1998, review of *The Boys of '98;* July 1, 2000, review of *Pacific Destiny: The Three-Century Journey to the Oregon Country,* p. 948; November 1, 2002, review of *Eldorado: The California Gold Rush,* p. 1603; April 15, 2003, review of *Westward,* p. 569.

Library Journal, April 15, 1998, Edwin B. Burgess, review of *The Boys of '98,* p. 96; June 15, 1999, Terri P. Summey, review of *Bear Flag Rising,* p. 91; May 15, 2003, Ken St. Andre, review of *Westward,* p. 130.

New York Times Book Review, March 2, 2003, Tyler D. Johnson, "Books in Brief: Nonfiction," review of *Eldorado.*

Publishers Weekly, April 13, 1998, review of *The Boys of '98,* p. 62; May 3, 1999, review of *Bear Flag Rising,* p. 60; July 31, 2000, review of *Pacific Destiny,* p. 86.

Smithsonian, March, 1989, Bruce Allen, review of *Januarius MacGahan: The Life and Campaigns of an American War Correspondent, 1844-1878,* p. 185.

Wild West, April, 1998, Leon C. Metz, review of *Legends and Lies,* p. 62; June, 1998, Candy Mouton, "Many of the Boys of '98 Were Cowboys and Frontiersmen Who Wanted a Piece of the Action," p. 64; August, 2000, Johnny D. Boggs, review of *Bear Flag Rising,* p. 61.

ONLINE

American Western Magazine, http://readthewest.com/ (December 10, 2006), Taylor Fogarty, "An Interview with Dale L. Walker"; "Dale L. Walker Discusses *Pacific Destiny: The Three-Century Journey to the Oregon Country.*"

ReadWest.com, http://www.readwest.com/ (December 10, 2006), Richard S. Wheeler, "An Interview with Dale L. Walker."

*   *   *

WALKER, Dale Lee
  See WALKER, Dale L.

*   *   *

WEATHERFORD, Carole Boston 1956-

PERSONAL: Born February 13, 1956, in Baltimore, MD; daughter of Joseph Alexander and Carolyn Virginia Boston; married Ronald Jeffrey Weatherford (a minister), February 2, 1985; children: one daughter, one son. *Education:* American University, B.A., 1977; University of Baltimore, M.A., 1982; University of North Carolina—Greensboro, M.F.A. *Politics:* Democrat. *Religion:* Methodist.

ADDRESSES: Home and office—High Point, NC. *E-mail*—weathfd@earthlink.net.

CAREER: Writer and educator. English teacher at public schools in Baltimore, MD, 1978; American Red Cross, Baltimore, MD, field representative in Blood Services Department, 1978-79; *Black Arts Review* (radio talk show), creator, producer, and host, 1979; Art Litho Co., Baltimore, MD, account executive, 1981; National Bar Association, Washington, DC, director of communications, 1981-85; B & C Associates, Inc., High Point, NC, creative director, 1985-88 and 1992-95; freelance writer and publicist, 1988—. Fayetteville State University, professor, 2002—.

MEMBER: Society of Children's Book Writers and Illustrators, College Language Association, Associated Writing Programs, North Carolina Writers Network (vice president, 1996-97), Phi Kappa Phi, Delta Sigma Theta.

AWARDS, HONORS: North Carolina Writers Network, winner of Black Writers Speak Competition, 1991, and Harperprints Chapbook Competition, 1995, both for *The Tan Chanteuse;* fellow, North Carolina Arts Council, 1995; Carter G. Woodson Book Award, elementary category, National Council for the Social Studies, 2001, and NAACP Image Award nomination, both for *The Sound that Jazz Makes;* Furious Flower Poetry Prize; North Carolina Juvenile Literature Award, for *Freedom on the Menu* and *Remember the Bridge;* North Carolina Children's Book Award finalist, for *Freedom on the Menu;* shortlist, NCSS Notables, International Reading Association Teachers' Choices, and *Voice of Youth Advocates* Poetry Picks, all for *Remember the Bridge.*

WRITINGS:

FOR CHILDREN

Remember Me, African American Family Press (New York, NY), 1994.

My Favorite Toy, Writers and Readers Publishing (New York, NY), 1994.

The Tan Chanteuse (poetry for adults) North Carolina Writers' Network (Carrboro, NC), 1995.

Juneteenth Jamboree (novel), illustrated by Yvonne Buchanan, Lee & Low Books (New York, NY), 1995.

Me and My Family Tree, illustrated by Michelle Mills, Black Butterfly (New York, NY), 1996.

Grandma and Me, illustrated by Michelle Mills, Black Butterfly (New York, NY), 1996.

Mighty Menfolk, illustrated by Michelle Mills, Black Butterfly (New York, NY), 1996.

Sink or Swim: African-American Lifesavers of the Outer Banks, Coastal Carolina Press (Wilmington, NC), 1999.

The Sound That Jazz Makes (poetry), illustrated by Eric Velasquez, Walker and Co. (New York, NY), 2000.

The African-American Struggle for Legal Equality in American History, Enslow Publishers (Berkeley Heights, NJ), 2000.

Princeville: The 500-Year Flood, illustrated by Douglas Alvord, Coastal Carolina Press (Wilmington, NC), 2001.

Sidewalk Chalk: Poems of the City, illustrated by Dimitrea Tokunbo, Wordsong/Boyds Mills Press (Honesdale, PA), 2001.

Jazz Baby (stories in verse), illustrated by Laura Freeman, Lee & Low Books (New York, NY), 2002.

Remember the Bridge: Poems of a People, Philomel Books (New York, NY), 2002.

Stormy Blues, Xavier Review Press (New Orleans, LA), 2002.

Great African American Lawyers: Raising the Bar of Freedom, Enslow Publishers (Berkeley Heights, NJ), 2003.

Freedom on the Menu: The Greensboro Sit-Ins, paintings by Jerome Lagarrique, Dial Books for Young Readers (New York, NY), 2005.

A Negro League Scrapbook, foreword by Buck O'Neil, Boyds Mills Press (Honesdale, PA), 2005.

Jesse Owens: The Fastest Man Alive, illustrated by Eric Velasquez, Walker & Company (New York, NY), 2006.

Dear Mr. Rosenwald, illustrated by R. Gregory Christie, Scholastic Press (New York, NY), 2006.

Moses: When Harriet Tubman Led Her People to Freedom, illustrated by Kadir Nelson, Jump at the Sun (New York, NY), 2006.

Champions on the Bench: The Story of the Cannon Street YMCA All Stars, illustrated by Leonard Jenkins, Dial Books for Young Readers (New York, NY), 2007.

Birmingham, 1963, Wordsong (Honesdale, PA), 2007.

OTHER

(With husband, Ronald Jeffrey Weatherford) *Somebody's Knocking at Your Door: AIDS and the African-American Church,* Haworth Pastoral Press (Binghamton, NY), 1999.

The Tar Baby on the Soapbox, Longleaf Press at Methodist College, 1999.

The Carolina Parakeet: America's Lost Parrot in Art and Memory, Avian Publications (Minneapolis, MN), 2005.

Contributor of articles and poetry to magazines and newspapers, including *Essence, Christian Science Monitor,* and *Washington Post.*

SIDELIGHTS: The writings of Carole Boston Weatherford, wrote Heather Ross Miller in her review of *Juneteenth Jamboree* for the *African American Review,* "are remarkably forthright celebrations, a colorful assembly of African American tradition, pride, and love." *Juneteenth Jamboree* is the story of a tradition, the celebration of the day in 1865 when Texas slaves learned of their emancipation. It had taken more than two long years for the word to reach them. In Weatherford's novel, young Cassandra has recently moved to Texas and has never heard of "Juneteenth," despite the fact that it became a legal holiday in that state in 1980. She witnesses the elaborate preparations with the eyes of a newcomer and feels the excitement rising in her community without understanding, at first, what it means. Gradually, Cassandra and the reader learn the significance of this historic celebration, its importance amplified by the jubilant crowds, the parades and dances, and the picnic that all bring the community together. "Weatherford does an excellent job," commented Carol Jones Collins in *School Library Journal,* of introducing the reader to this holiday. A *Publishers Weekly* contributor remarked that the "enthusiastic text allows readers to discover—and celebrate—the holiday along with Cassandra."

Sidewalk Chalk: Poems of the City is an expression of pride, according to a reviewer for the *Bulletin of the Center for Children's Books.* Weatherford celebrates the city in twenty vignettes of urban life as a child might experience it. Her poems evoke the spirit of the neighborhood and the daily activities of the people who live there—jumping rope on the sidewalk, getting a haircut, going to the laundromat or to church. "The overall tone of the collection is upbeat and positive," *Booklist* contributor Kathy Broderick remarked. The *Bulletin of the Center for Children's Books* reviewer acknowledged some inconsistency in the quality of the poems but described them as "vivid snapshots of city life."

The Sound That Jazz Makes is a celebration in rhyme of American music and its roots in African-American history. Weatherford's short poems and the paintings of award-winning artist Eric Velasquez depict a musical journey from the drumbeats of Africa to the drumbeats of rap music in the streets of the city. Poet and illustrator lead the reader from the work-chants of the cotton fields to the plaintive laments of the blues echoing through the Mississippi delta, to the celebrations of gospel, the sweet rhythms of the swing era, and the bold harmonies of the nightclubs of Harlem. Weatherford's poems, according to *Booklist* contributor Bill Ott, "possess a flowing rhythm that younger readers [in particular] will respond to eagerly." A *Publishers Weekly* reviewer found the rhymes to be "at odds with" the rhythms of the very music the book is intended to honor, but in *Black Issues Book Review,* critic Khafre Abif described *The Sounds That Jazz Makes* as "a soft poetic journey of rhythm" in which the "words are as seamless as the rhythm's growth" from primitive drumbeats into one of the most far-reaching musical movements of modern times.

Remember the Bridge: Poems of a People is a celebration of the men and women who contributed to African-American history from the earliest times to the present day. Weatherford writes of the great and the not so great: the leaders whose names are familiar and the people whose names were never known. For these latter people she creates fictional profiles, exploring in her poetry how it must have felt to be sold into slavery or showcasing, for example, the diversity of African Americans in a wide array of occupations. A *Publishers Weekly* reviewer appreciated the free-verse poems but was less satisfied with the metered rhymes, and found the chronological narrative somewhat "confusing." A contributor to *Kirkus Reviews,* on the other hand, claimed that Weatherford "brilliantly summarizes . . . a complete timeline" of history. The last poem in *Remember the Bridge* is titled "I Am the Bridge," perhaps an allusion that this book, this poet, and every individual can be a part of what the *Kirkus Reviews* writer called "a bridge toward understanding and acceptance."

Jazz Baby is a collection of story poems designed for toddler and preschool readers. The poems introduce children to the rhythms and sounds of jazz music, the various instruments that jazz musicians play, and the sense of freedom and joy that jazz music can bring. Illustrator Laura Freeman contributes bright, soft-focus, colorful images that complement Weatherford's poetry. Weatherford encourages even the youngest reader to get up and dance and experience the power of jazz. *School Library Journal* reviewer Marge Loch-Wouters called the book a "bouncy celebration of rhythm and music."

Lynda Jones, writing in *Black Issues Book Review,* observed that "parents and children alike will be swept away by *Jazz Baby*'s lyrical celebration of the music."

A number of Weatherford's later books deal with pivotal events and personalities in the civil rights movement and the end of slavery in America. Though these titles deal with complex issues, the occurrences and the forces behind them are portrayed in a manner accessible to young readers. *Freedom on the Menu: The Greensboro Sit-Ins* is told by Connie, an eight-year-old African American girl who experiences, but does not understand, segregation in her North Carolina home, where blacks and whites use separate drinking fountains, swimming pools, bathrooms, and movie theaters. When she and her mother want a refreshing drink from the Woolworth soda fountain, they are forced to stand and sip since no blacks are allowed to sit at the counter. Connie would like nothing more than to be able to sit down and have a big banana split, but she knows that day has not come yet. Connie is on-hand as an eyewitness when a peaceful act of bravery and defiance by four young men sets the stage for the breaking of segregation. The young men stage their sit-in at the Woolworth lunch counter, refusing to leave until they are served. Their act galvanizes the African American community throughout the South, and the citizens engage in protests, pickets, and sit-ins in other southern states. A tumultuous six months later, segregation in the American South has started to retreat in defeat, and a delighted Connie is able to sit at the Woolworth lunch counter and enjoy a longed-for banana split. "Together, author and artist translate a complex issue into terms youngest readers can understand, in a resonant meshing of fact and fiction," commented a *Publishers Weekly* reviewer. Terre Sychters, writing in *Childhood Education,* called the story "a great book to explore a part of history often shortchanged" in school textbooks. A *School Library Journal* reviewer concluded, "these stories bring history to life for today's readers." Weatherford's "quietly moving story pays tribute to the peaceful protesters who did indeed 'overcome,'" commented a *Kirkus Reviews* contributor.

In *A Negro League Scrapbook,* Weatherford tells the sometimes tragic, often inspirational story of baseball's Negro Leagues, teams of African American players that flourished in the late nineteenth and early twentieth centuries. In 1887, the owners of the major league teams declared that black players were no longer welcome in the majors. Because of this segregation, the Negro Leagues were formed to give black players the opportunity to serve on a team and play at a professional level until they were allowed back into the major leagues. Almost fifty years later, trailblazer Jackie Robinson was the first black player to rejoin the major leagues. Weatherford recounts the lengthy history of the Negro Leagues in her book, from inception to demise in 1963, presenting facsimiles of memorabilia such as tickets, banners, equipment, and advertising as though they were affixed in a scrapbook. Though the Negro Leagues were denied access to the major league teams and venues, they still had their own storied history, which Weatherford relates in her book. Throughout, her words and images also evoke the difficult realities of segregation. Even though the leagues were the result of segregation, they were still of considerable significance to the black community, and Weatherford details the cultural importance of the teams. "One doesn't need to be a baseball fan to be fascinated" by the involving story of the Negro Leagues, remarked a *Kirkus Reviews* contributor. Marilyn Taniguchi, writing in *School Library Journal,* noted that Weatherford's book "succeeds as a thoughtful introduction, capturing both the significance of the Negro Leagues and the accomplishments of its great players."

Dear Mr. Rosenwald is set in the rural American South of the 1920s. This "terrific picture book uses evocative free verse to describe the building of a school for black children" using grant money from Sears, Roebuck president and catalog magnate Julius Rosenwald, commented a *Kirkus Reviews* critic. Weatherford describes in detail how Rosenwald was inspired by Booker T. Washington to devote millions of dollars to the construction of schools in black communities, how the targeted communities would receive seed money from Rosenwald for these important construction projects, and how local residents, both black and white, also had to make substantial contributions of cash, land, and other valuable considerations to the projects. The story is told from the point of view of Ovella, daughter of poor sharecroppers, who narrates the process and the difficulties encountered by her friends and neighbors. She also describes their determination to take best advantage of the Rosenwald grant and see the school built. When the White Oak School opened, it used hand-me-down books from the local white school, but there could be no doubt that the students of White Oak had a school of their own, of which they could be proud, and which would give them the educational boost sorely needed to help propel them out of poverty.

Moses: When Harriet Tubman Led Her People to Freedom, recounts the heroic story of Harriet Tubman, her escape from slavery, and her divinely inspired mission to help other blacks flee from slavery through the Underground Railroad. The story is told in three voices; that of the narrator; of Tubman herself; and God, with whom Tubman is in constant communication as she travels dangerous roads at night to avoid detection, as she establishes the structure of the Underground Railroad, and as she constantly risks her own life and safety to help her fellows escape the tyranny and brutality of slavery. Weatherford also includes a foreword that explains the concept of slavery for a child's understanding, and presents a brief biographical sketch of Tubman and her accomplishments. "The migration of African-Americans to the north is rendered breathtakingly by Weatherford in this brilliant picture book," stated a *Kirkus Reviews* critic. "In elegant free verse," Weatherford depicts Tubman's "remarkable escape from slavery and her role in guiding hundreds to freedom," noted another *Kirkus Reviews* contributor. A *Publishers Weekly* reviewer called Weatherford's work a "gorgeous, poetic picture book," while the *Kirkus Reviews* writer summed up the book in a single word: "transcendent."

Weatherford once told *CA:* "As a child, I never aspired to be a writer, although I think I always was one. My first poem—one about the seasons—came to me almost magically. I dictated the poem to my mother on the way home from first grade. She was so amazed that she parked the car and wrote down the poem as I repeated it. She asked my father, a high school printing teacher, to print some of my earliest poems on the letterpress in his classroom. I was thrilled to see my work in print. Having my work published as a child strengthened my belief in my talent so that I could later endure the inevitable rejections of a professional writing career.

"My poetry, nonfiction and historical fiction are inspired by oral traditions and informed by my African-American heritage. My favorite book is an upcoming one—a fictional verse memoir of Billie Holiday—my muse. I grew up listening to my father's jazz collection. So it is no coincidence that my writing often focuses on jazz.

"Of my published books, *Moses* is my proudest accomplishment. My own spiritual and ancestral roots led me to Tubman. One of my grandfathers hailed from Dorchester County, where Tubman was born, and my other grandfather was a Methodist minister. When I sought to address faith in my writing, I found the ideal subject in Tubman, whose conversations with God were her compass on the Underground Railroad.

"I grew up in Baltimore but have roots on a Maryland farm that dates back to the Reconstruction. That land links me to my heritage and inspires my literary mission: to mine the past for family stories, fading traditions and forgotten struggles. I hope that my books, which honor the past and salute unsung heroes, help children understand the freedom struggle, the price of equality, and that our humanity is more important than our differences."

BIOGRAPHICAL AND CRITICAL SOURCES:

PERIODICALS

African American Review, spring, 1998, Heather Ross Miller, reviews of *The Tan Chanteuse* and *Juneteenth Jamboree,* p. 169.

American Visions, December-January, 1995, Yolanda Robinson Coles, review of *Juneteenth Jamboree,* p. 37.

Black Issues Book Review, September, 2000, Khafre Abif, review of *The Sound That Jazz Makes,* p. 81; July-August, 2002, Lynda Jones, review of *Jazz Baby,* p. 77; March-April, 2004, Phebus Etienne, review of *Stormy Blues,* p. 27.

Booklist, December 15, 1999, Carolyn Phelan, review of *Sink or Swim: African-American Lifesavers of the Outer Banks,* pp. 783-784; August, 2000, Bill Ott, review of *The Sound That Jazz Makes,* p. 2133; September 15, 2001, Kathy Broderick, review of *Sidewalk Chalk: Poems of the City,* p. 224; February 15, 2002, Kay Weisman, review of *Princeville: The 500-Year Flood,* p. 1014; February 15, 2003, Gillian Engberg, review of *Great African-American Lawyers,* p. 1080; February 1, 2005, GraceAnne A. DeCandido, review of *A Negro League Scrapbook,* p. 976, and Carolyn Phelan, review of *Freedom on the Menu: The Greensboro Sit-Ins,* p. 980; August 1, 2006, Hazel Rochman, review of *Moses: When Harriet Tubman Led Her People to Freedom,* p. 81; October 1, 2006, Hazel Rochman, review of *Dear Mr. Rosenwald,* p. 61.

Bulletin of the Center for Children's Books, October, 2001, review of *Sidewalk Chalk,* p. 81.

Childhood Education, spring, 2006, Terre Sychters, review of *Freedom on the Menu,* p. 177.

Children's Book & Play Review, March, 2001, AnnMarie Hamar, review of *The Sound that Jazz Makes,* p. 23.

Ebony, September, 2006, review of *Dear Mr. Rosenwald,* p. 31.

Georgia Review, summer, 1997, Ted Kooser, review of *The Tan Chanteuse,* p. 375.

Kirkus Reviews, December 1, 2001, review of *Remember the Bridge: Poems of a People,* p. 1691; December 15, 2004, review of *Freedom on the Menu,* p. 1211; March 1, 2005, review of *A Negro League Scrapbook,* p. 297; May 15, 2006, review of *Moses,* p. S23; August 15, 2006, review of *Dear Mr. Rosenwald,* p. 853; September 1, 2006, review of *Moses,* p. 914.

Publishers Weekly, October 30, 1995, review of *Juneteenth Jamboree,* p. 61; May 15, 2000, review of *The Sound That Jazz Makes,* p. 115; September 17, 2001, review of *Sidewalk Chalk,* p. 82; December 24, 2001, review of *Remember the Bridge,* p. 62; January 3, 2005, review of *Freedom on the Menu,* p. 55; February 7, 2005, "The Roots of Many of Baseball's Greats," review of *A Negro League Scrapbook,* p. 61; July 31, 2006, review of *Moses,* p. 78.

School Library Journal, January, 1996, Carol Jones Collins, review of *Juneteenth Jamboree,* p. 97; July, 2000, Ginny Gustin, review of *The Sound That Jazz Makes,* p. 99; June, 2002, Marge Loch-Wouters, review of *Jazz Baby,* p. 114; March, 2005, Marilyn Taniguchi, review of *A Negro League Scrapbook,* p. 236; April, 2005, Mary N. Oluonye, review of *Freedom on the Menu,* p. 115; August, 2005, Blair Christolon, review of *Freedom on the Menu,* p. 50; October 2005, review of *Freedom on the Menu,* p. S27; October, 2006, Catherine Threadgill, review of *Dear Mr. Rosenwald.*

ONLINE

Carole Boston Weatherford Home Page, http://www.caroleweatherford.com (December 10, 2006).

*　　　*　　　*

WEATHERFORD, Doris 1943-

PERSONAL: Born September 20, 1943, in Jasper, MN; daughter of Harry D. (a mechanic) and Leona (a housewife) Barge; married Roy C. Weatherford (a professor of philosophy), February 8, 1966; children: Margaret Marie. *Ethnicity:* "Scandinavian." *Education:*

Attended Arkansas Technical University, Brandeis University, and Harvard University. *Politics:* Democrat. *Hobbies and other interests:* Flower gardening, volunteer work.

ADDRESSES: *Home*—Seffner, FL. *Agent*—Fran Collin, Collin Literary Agency, P.O. Box 33, Wayne, PA 19087; Valerie Tomaselli, 445 W. 23rd St., Ste. 1-D, New York, NY 10011.

CAREER: University of South Florida, Tampa, adjunct professor, 1995—. Board member, National Women's History Project and National Women's History Museum; Florida Women's Hall of Fame, chair; Florida Commission on the Status of Women, historian; Hillsborough Community College, member of board of trustees.

MEMBER: Authors Guild, Authors League of America, League of Women Voters.

AWARDS, HONORS: Honor Book citation, International Society of School Librarians, 1998, for *A History of the American Suffragist Movement.*

WRITINGS:

Foreign and Female: Immigrant Women in America, 1840-1930, Schocken (New York, NY), 1986, reprinted with new foreword, 1996.
American Women and World War II, Facts on File (New York, NY), 1990.
American Women's History: An A to Z of People, Organizations, Issues and Events, Prentice-Hall (Englewood Cliffs, NJ), 1994.
Milestones: A Chronology of American Women's History, Facts on File (New York, NY), 1997.
A History of the American Suffragist Movement, American Bibliographic Center-Clio Press (Santa Barbara, CA), 1998.
(Editor) *The Women's Almanac,* Oryx Press (Phoenix, AZ), 2000.
(Executive editor and contributor) *A History of Women in the United States: State-by-State Reference,* Grolier Academic Reference (Danbury, CT), 2004.
Real Women: Of Tampa and Hillsborough County from Prehistory to the Millenium, University of Tampa Press (Tampa, FL), 2004.
American Women during World War II: An Encyclopedia, Routledge (New York, NY), 2007.

Author of "Standing on Their Shoulders," a column in *WE—Women's Enterprise.*

SIDELIGHTS: Doris Weatherford ascribes the inspiration for her first book, *Foreign and Female: Immigrant Women in America, 1840-1930* to her discovery during graduate school at Harvard that there were no general books on the experience of female immigrants. Books on the immigrant experience offered only a few mentions of women, and women's history books made very little mention of immigrants. The author's work in general can be characterized by the offering up of heretofore unknown facts and stories about women within historical context.

Weatherford's goal with *Foreign and Female,* as defined in her foreword to a 1996 reprint, is to "provide a glimpse into the lives of these women and to encourage the asking of new questions." Weatherford assembles a topically organized survey of the lives of immigrant women, including their views on life, death, sex, work, family and more. Drawing extensively on journals, letters, and stories of women from almost all the European ethnic groups, Weatherford has the women themselves "speak clearly of their lives," reported Barbara Scotto in the *Wilson Library Bulletin,* "and in doing so, they enrich our knowledge of women's social history."

Continuing her exploration into women's history, Weatherford published *American Women and World War II.* Her focus this time is on the many roles of women during the war, whether on the home front, in the work force, or in the military.

In *American Women's History: An A to Z of People, Organizations, Issues and Events,* Weatherford expands her scope in an encyclopedic effort that includes famous women side by side with the not so famous. This reference, according to James Rettig in *Wilson Library Bulletin,* "compensates for the substantive omissions of standard sources and, thereby, itself becomes a standard source."

The subject of *Milestones: A Chronology of Women's History* is women in history from 1492 to 1995 through brief, chronological entries on women and their achievements as well as events affecting them, all toward placing women in the context of American history in general. Weatherford returns to more specific ground in *A History of the American Suffragist Movement,* in which she "provides a coherent and accessible narrative history as it was viewed by the suffragists themselves," according to J.K. Boles in *Choice.*

Weatherford once told *CA:* "My favorite part of writing is the research and analysis. I love learning new things and putting them into the context of their times. There is so much information available on women that unfortunately has been forgotten, and I enjoy making it available."

BIOGRAPHICAL AND CRITICAL SOURCES:

BOOKS

Weatherford, Doris, *Foreign and Female: Immigrant Women in America, 1840-1930,* Facts on File (New York, NY), 1995.

PERIODICALS

Booklist, June 1, 1994, review of *American Women's History: An A to Z of People, Organizations, Issues, and Events,* p. 1863; June 1, 1997, review of *Milestones: A Chronology of American Women's History,* p. 1763.
Choice, May, 1987, J. Sochen, review of *Foreign and Female,* p. 1479; November, 1998, J.K. Boles, review of *A History of the American Suffragist Movement,* p. 605.
Kliatt, July, 1994, Ruth R. Woodman, review of *American Women's History,* p. 35.
Library Journal, January, 1987, Cynthia Harrison, review of *Foreign and Female,* p. 87; September 1, 1990, Marie Marmo, review of *American Women and World War II,* p. 236; April 1, 1997, Elaine M. Kuhn, review of *Milestones,* p. 86.
School Library Journal, March, 1999, Linda A. Vretos, review of *A History of the American Suffragist Movement,* p. 233.
Wilson Library Bulletin, May, 1987, Barbara Scotto, review of *Foreign and Female,* pp. 70-71; September, 1994, James Rettig, review of *American Women's History,* p. 77.

ONLINE

Doris Weatherford: Biography, http://members.authorsguild.net/dweatherford (February 12, 2007).

WEBER, Ronald 1934-

PERSONAL: Born September 21, 1934, in Mason City, IA; son of Harley George and Anne M. Weber; married Patricia Jean Carroll, December 27, 1955; children: Elizabeth, Andrea, Kathryn. *Education:* University of Notre Dame, B.A., 1957; University of Iowa, M.F.A., 1960; University of Minnesota—Twin Cities, Ph.D., 1967.

ADDRESSES: Home—Valparaiso, IN. *Office*—University of Notre Dame, Department of American Studies, 228 Decio Faculty Hall, Notre Dame, IN 46556. *E-mail*—Weber.2@nd.edu.

CAREER: Writer, lecturer, and educator. Loras College, Dubuque, IA, instructor in English, 1960-62; University of Notre Dame, Notre Dame, IN, assistant professor, 1963-67, associate professor, 1967-76, professor of American studies, 1976—, became professor emeritus; chair of department, 1970-77, chair of Graduate Program in Communication Arts, 1972-79. University of Coimbra, Fulbright lecturer, 1968-69, senior Fulbright lecturer, 1982. Member of executive committee, Catholic Commission on Intellectual and Cultural Affairs, 1993-96.

MEMBER: American Studies Association, Great Lakes American Studies Association (president, 1980-82), Catholic Commission on Intellectual and Cultural Affairs (executive committee, 1993-96).

AWARDS, HONORS: National Endowment for the Humanities fellowship, 1972-73; faculty award, University of Notre Dame, 1976; *The Literature of Fact: Literary Nonfiction in American Writing* was included on *Choice*'s outstanding academic book list, 1981-82; Gannett fellow, Columbia University, 1985-86; bronze medal from Council for the Advancement and Support of Education, 1988.

WRITINGS:

NONFICTION

O Romance Americano, Livraria Almedina (Coimbra, Portugal), 1969.
The Literature of Fact: Literary Nonfiction in American Writing, Ohio University Press (Athens, OH), 1980.

Seeing Earth: Literary Responses to Space Exploration, Ohio University Press (Athens, OH), 1985.

Hemingway's Art of Nonfiction, Macmillan (New York, NY), 1990.

The Midwestern Ascendancy in American Writing, Indiana University Press (Bloomington, IN), 1992.

Hired Pens: Professional Writers in America's Golden Age of Print, Ohio University Press (Athens, OH), 1997.

News of Paris: American Journalists in the City of Light between the Wars, Ivan R. Dee (Chicago, IL), 2006.

EDITOR

America in Change: Reflections on the 60's and 70's, University of Notre Dame Press (Notre Dame, IN), 1972.

(And contributor) *The Reporter as Artist: A Look at the New Journalism Controversy,* Hastings House (New York, NY), 1974.

(With Walter Nicgorski, and contributor) *An Almost Chosen People: The Moral Aspirations of Americans,* University of Notre Dame Press (Notre Dame, IN), 1976.

NOVELS

Company Spook, St. Martin's (New York, NY), 1986.
Troubleshooter, St. Martin's (New York, NY), 1988.
The Aluminum Hatch, Write Way (Aurora, CO), 1998.
Catch and Keep, Write Way (Aurora, CO), 2000.

OTHER

Contributor of numerous articles to periodicals, including *Cimarron Review, Virginia Quarterly Review, Sewanee Review, South Atlantic Quarterly, Journal of Popular Culture,* and *Review of Politics.*

SIDELIGHTS: Ronald Weber is a professor of American Studies whose early writings are dedicated to academic studies of American literature, journalism, and culture. He is particularly interested in how fiction writers produce art and make a living from it. Weber brings an insider's knowledge to his research because he, too, writes novels for the mass market. Only a few months

separate the publication of his scholarly work *Hired Pens: Professional Writers in America's Golden Age of Print* and a "whodunit" fishing novel, *The Aluminum Hatch.*

A *Publishers Weekly* reviewer called Weber "one of the finest writers on writers." This reputation is based primarily on two Weber nonfiction titles, *Hired Pens* and *The Midwestern Ascendancy in American Writing. Hired Pens* profiles authors who attempted—not always successfully—to earn a living on the strength of their journalism and fiction at a time when pulp and higher quality magazines were clamoring for copy. A *Publishers Weekly* reviewer noted that "previous authors have covered the ground he walks in this new book, but no one has covered it better." *St. Louis Post-Dispatch* reviewer Steve Weinberg commented: "Like most authors writing about the freelance life, Weber romanticizes from time to time what is rarely romantic. But he always tempers it with passages explaining the frequently depressing reality of selling second-rate work to pay the bills." *New York Times Book Review* correspondent Brenda Wineapple called *Hired Pens* "a lively, if crowded, survey of commercial writers and editors from the 1830's until 1969," adding that the book "tells of the pain and glamour (with an emphasis on glamour) of the good old days in Grub Street."

The Midwestern Ascendancy in American Writing explores the profusion of Midwestern literary artists in the latter decades of the nineteenth century and the early decades of the twentieth. "*The Midwestern Ascendancy* is very well done," wrote James Hurt in *Studies in American Fiction.* "Weber writes smoothly and lucidly and with an obvious empathy with and affection for the writers he includes."

Weber has also published several detective thrillers, most recently two with fishing themes set in the rural wilds of Michigan. *The Aluminum Hatch* pairs Don Fitzgerald, a lottery-winning journalist and fisherman, with Mercy Virdon, who works for the Michigan Department of Natural Resources (DNR), as an unlikely detective team who together seek to solve the murder of a canoe livery owner on Michigan's Borchard River. *Booklist* reviewer John Rowen observed that "the novel offers a strong mystery, realistic dialogue, well-timed wit," and "vivid descriptions of outdoor life." The novel's setting also reflects Weber's interest in fishing and the outdoors. Virdon and Fitzgerald pair up again in *Catch and Keep,* a novel that combines an assassination-style murder in Detroit with angling adventures in the hinterlands. Rex E. Klett described *Catch and Keep* in *Library Journal* as "a pleasing sequel for fans." While *Mystery Reader* reviewer Jennifer Monahan Winberry found Weber's novel "very strong on atmosphere, but much weaker on characterization," *Booklist* reviewer John Rowan praised the series for its "stylish prose," and "tight plotting," with "a sharp yet affectionate portrait of small-town life."

Weber returned to nonfiction based on the lives and careers of writers in *News of Paris: American Journalists in the City of Light between the Wars.* In the years following World War I, the cost of living was low in Paris, and jobs were plentiful for wordsmiths of various types. Enticed by cheap living and the romance of the city, hopeful journalists and writers thronged to Paris in the years between the two Great Wars. Those interested in "American journalism as practiced abroad in the 1920s and 1930s will enjoy this engaging book," commented Vanessa Bush in *Booklist.* Weber draws on primary documents such as letters, memoirs, and writings of participants to construct his picture of Parisian writers' lives and the practice of international journalism that flourished at the time. The more liberal atmosphere of Paris energized the writers and launched the careers of a number of journalistic and literary icons, including Henry Miller, Gertrude Stein, F. Scott Fitzgerald, Ernest Hemingway, E.E. cummings, and Archibald MacLeish. Weber notes the intrigues and evolutions at major Paris papers, including the *Paris Herald, Paris Tribune,* and the Paris edition of the *New York Herald.* He examines how the rise of the expatriate Parisian journalist was fueled by an American desire to read more about the world and to consider an international perspective on politics and world events. Weber describes both the highs and lows of life in Paris "during the glory years, chronicling everything from deadline desperation to clandestine affairs," remarked a *Publishers Weekly* contributor. A contributor to *Kirkus Reviews* called the book "agreeable, old-fashioned cultural history: heavy on anecdotes, light on analysis." Marc Weingarten, writing in the *New York Times Book Review,* concluded that "Weber's book is an old war chest full of stories about this intoxicating period in journalism."

BIOGRAPHICAL AND CRITICAL SOURCES:

BOOKS

Directory of American Scholars, 10th edition, Thomson Gale (Detroit, MI), 2001.

PERIODICALS

Booklist, March 1, 1998, John Rowen, review of *The Aluminum Hatch,* p. 1098; March 1, 2000, John Rowen, review of *Catch and Keep,* p. 1199; April 1, 2006, Vanessa Bush, review of *News of Paris: American Journalists in the City of Light between the Wars,* p. 7.

California Bookwatch, May, 2006, review of *News of Paris.*

Kirkus Reviews, February 15, 2006, review of *News of Paris,* p. 176.

Library Journal, February 15, 1990, Michael Rogers, *Hemingway's Art of Nonfiction,* p. 186; August, 1992, Charles C. Nash, review of *The Midwestern Ascendancy in American Writing,* p. 102; April 1, 1998, Rex E. Klett, review of *The Aluminum Hatch,* p. 129; April 1, 2000, Rex E. Klett, review of *Catch and Keep,* p. 134; February 15, 2006, Marie Marmo Mullaney, review of *News of Paris,* p. 132.

New York Times Book Review, March 30, 1986, Newgate Callendar, review of *Company Spook,* p. 22; January 18, 1998, Brenda Wineapple, "Grinding It Out," p. 15; April 23, 2006, Marc Weingarten, "Paris Edition," review of *News of Paris.*

Publishers Weekly, January 3, 1986, review of *Company Spook,* p. 44; November 10, 1997, review of *Hired Pens: Professional Writers in America's Golden Age of Print,* p. 63; December 19, 2005, review of *News of Paris,* p. 49.

St. Louis Post-Dispatch, March 29, 1998, Steve Weinberg, "Author Explains History of How Hacks Turned Writing into Careers," review of *Hired Pens: Professional Writers in America's Golden Age of Print,* p. E5.

Studies in American Fiction, autumn, 1995, James Hurt, review of *The Midwestern Ascendancy in American Writing,* p. 248.

Studies in the Novel, summer, 1992, Gerry Brenner, *Hemingway's Art of Nonfiction,* p. 210.

World of Hibernia, spring, 2001, Ronald Weber, "The Loneliness of the Long-Distance Angler," p. 58.

ONLINE

Humanities and Social Sciences Online, http://www.h-net.msu.edu/ (October, 2006), Catherine McKercher, review of *News of Paris.*

Mystery Reader, http://www.themysteryreader.com/ (January 10, 2007), Jennifer Monahan Winberry, review of *Catch and Keep.**

WEIR, Alison

PERSONAL: Married; children: two.

ADDRESSES: Home—Surrey, England.

CAREER: Writer and historian. Ran a school for children unable to cope in mainstream schools.

WRITINGS:

NONFICTION

(With Susan Raven) *Women in History,* Crown (New York, NY), 1981, published as *Women of Achievement: Thirty-five Centuries of History,* Harmony (New York, NY), 1981.

Britain's Royal Families: The Complete Genealogy, Bodley Head (London, England), 1989, new edition, Pimlico (London, England), 2002.

The Six Wives of Henry VIII, Grove Weidenfeld (New York, NY), 1991.

The Princes in the Tower, Bodley Head (London, England), 1992, Ballantine (New York, NY), 1994.

Lancaster and York: The Wars of the Roses, J. Cape (London, England), 1995, published as *The Wars of the Roses,* Ballantine (New York, NY), 1995.

Children of England: The Heirs of King Henry VIII 1547-1558, J. Cape (London, England), 1996, published as *The Children of Henry VIII,* Ballantine (New York, NY), 1996.

Elizabeth the Queen, J. Cape (London, England), 1998, published as *The Life of Elizabeth I,* Ballantine (New York, NY), 1999.

Eleanor of Aquitaine, J. Cape (London, England), 1999, Ballantine (New York, NY), 2000.

Henry VIII: The King and His Court, Ballantine (New York, NY), 2001.

Mary, Queen of Scots, and the Murder of Lord Darnley, Ballantine (New York, NY), 2003.

Isabella: She-Wolf of France, Queen of England, J. Cape (London, England), 2005, published as *Queen Isabella: Treachery, Adultery, and Murder in Medieval England,* Ballantine (New York, NY), 2005.

OTHER

Peter, Good Night, illustrated by Deborah Kogan Ray, Dutton (New York, NY), 1989.

(With Janelle Cherrington) *Bear's Big Blue House: A Book of First Words,* Simon Spotlight (New York, NY), 1999.

Innocent Traitor (novel), Ballantine (New York, NY), 2007.

SIDELIGHTS: Historian Alison Weir has made a career of writing about English royalty, publishing several books for general audiences about famous historical figures and events. Her first biographical work, coauthored with Susan Raven, is the reference book *Women in History*—published in the United States as *Women of Achievement: Thirty-five Centuries of History*—which includes entries on several hundred women of many nationalities and time periods. Her next work, *Britain's Royal Families: The Complete Genealogy,* represents several decades of research on Weir's part, and is a single-volume genealogical record of the royal families of England, Scotland, and Wales beginning in the ninth century and ending with the twentieth-century House of Windsor. It includes family trees and biographical information in what Henrietta Fordham of *Books* described as a "useful and speedy" work.

Two years later, Weir focused specifically on one royal family, that of Henry VIII and his six wives: Catherine of Aragon, Anne Boleyn, Jane Seymour, Anne of Cleves, Catherine Howard, and Catherine Parr. *The Six Wives of Henry VIII* provides information on the spouses and the age in which they lived. It caught the attention of reviewers. Chicago *Tribune Books* critic Lacey Baldwin Smith praised the "gossipy, detailed narrative of sex and pregnancies, births and deaths, dancing and banqueting, mistresses and illicit affairs, and an almost obsessive attention to what men and women wore" during this period in British history. "The resulting panorama of royal family life as it meshed with politics, dynastic needs and history is rich, vivid and generally convincing," added Smith. "The style is simple and direct but gripping, and although the background and cultural atmosphere are occasionally overstated, the composite picture of men and women . . . is enthralling." Although a reviewer for the *Times Literary Supplement* maintained that some parts of *The Six Wives of Henry VIII* are "subjective and unreliable," the reviewer commented that "as a series of impressions of historical characters and events by a nonspecialist, this book is quite entertaining."

The Princes in the Tower deals with the succession to the English throne during the fifteenth century after King Henry VI succumbed to catatonic schizophrenia and was ousted by King Edward IV. After Henry VI was murdered and Edward IV died unexpectedly, Richard of Gloucester made himself king, imprisoning Edward IV's sons in the Tower of London. The boys were never heard from again and Weir delves into this mystery, relating the political machinations that suggest Richard III may have ordered the boys murdered. The story is told in a "highly readable, brisk manner that's at once vivid and scholarly" wrote a *Kirkus Reviews* critic. "Thoughtfully and clearly, she takes the reader step by step through the arguments and issues," commented Patrick T. Reardon in a review for Chicago's *Tribune Books*. "She is no Richard-basher, but neither does she canonize him. And she has no doubt about his guilt." A *Publishers Weekly* reviewer called *The Princes in the Tower* a "carefully researched and absorbing work of scholarship," and a *Kirkus Reviews* critic summed up the work as "a fascinating historical whodunit."

The Wars of the Roses is actually a prequel to *The Princes in the Tower* because it deals with the dynastic struggles prior to the murder of King Henry VI that Weir recounts in the later work. The battles known as the Wars of the Roses involved two dynastic houses: the House of Lancaster, led by Henry VI, and the House of York, led by Richard Plantagenet and then his son who eventually ascended to the throne as Edward IV. While Colin Richmond of the *Times Literary Supplement* commented that Weir broke no new ground with her history, William B. Robison of *Library Journal* praised the work, judging it to be a "well-written, entertaining narrative." A commentator for *Kirkus Reviews* called the work "well researched" and Weir's style "powerful and elegant," yet expressed reservations about the density of the information conveyed being too much for general readers to handle. On the other hand, Debbie Hyman, writing in *School Library Journal*, deemed *The Wars of the Roses* "understandable, interesting, and readable," and a *Publishers Weekly* reviewer called it a "spellbinding chronicle." An *Economist* commentator praised the "little gems of scholarship" and "illuminating asides [that] make Miss Weir's sometimes dauntingly detailed history a joy to read." *The Wars of the Roses* is, in the words of *Booklist* reviewer Brad Hooper, a "perfectly focused and beautifully unfolded account."

In *The Children of Henry VIII* Weir presents biographies of the children of King Henry VIII by his various wives who later reigned over England: Edward VI, Mary I, and Elizabeth I. She also describes the claim to the throne of Lady Jane Grey, the granddaughter of Henry VIII's younger sister. The siblings were diverse in age, experience, and religious convictions and had to each deal with the religious conflicts that played an important role in shaping sixteenth-century England. "That combination of spatial distance and political-religious rivalry could make a narrative bumpy or tedious, but Ms. Weir imparts movement and coherence while recreating the suspense her characters endured and the suffering they inflicted," praised Naomi Bliven in the *New York Times Book Review*. Other reviewers found the work interesting as well. According to a *Kirkus Reviews* critic, Weir's prose moves briskly for the most part and "succeeds not only in bring to life Henry VIII's heirs but also in illuminating the background." Likewise, *Booklist* commentator Brad Hooper remarked on the work's "lush detail and fresh analysis." Wier's "sweeping narrative, based on contemporary chronicles, plays out vividly against the colorful backdrop," maintained a reviewer for *Publishers Weekly*. "Thoroughly enjoyable and well written," praised a *Contemporary Review* critic, while Boyd Tonkin of *New Statesman and Society* deemed the book a "readable and resourceful chronicle."

Weir focuses on one of Henry VIII's heirs to the throne—Elizabeth, the daughter of Anne Boleyn—in *The Life of Elizabeth I* (also published as *Elizabeth the Queen*), which begins with Elizabeth's ascendency to the throne at age twenty-five and tells of the events and issues of her reign as Elizabeth I. Yet, because it is a biography, Weir concentrates on the monarch's personal side, including her relationships with those who knew, served, and loved her. Weir deals, too, with the well-worn question of why Elizabeth never married. The work garnered largely favorable reviews. Although Simon Adams of *History Today* summed up negative criticism about Weir with his comment, "factual accuracy is not her strong point," he commented that "Weir moves briskly and sustains five hundred pages in quite a lively fashion." Weir's "biography is as good as any other for anyone who has not read a life of Elizabeth before," remarked Helen Hackett in the *Times Literary Supplement*. *The Life of Elizabeth I* is a "riveting portrait of the queen and how the private woman won her public role," enthused a *Kirkus Reviews* critic, and "a good read" is how a critic for *Contemporary Review* described the work. A *Publishers Weekly* reviewer asserted: "Weir brings a fine sense of selection and considerable zest to her portrait." Dori DeSpain, writing in *School Library Journal*, called the biography a "fascinating tale that is well told in this engrossing, articulate book," while Elizabeth Mary Mellett, writing in *Library Journal*, described *The Life of Elizabeth I* as a "clearly written and well-researched biography."

For her next historical work Weir moved back in time from her usual time period of fifteenth-and sixteenth-century England to twelfth-century France and England. Her *Eleanor of Aquitaine* tells the story of a powerful, beautiful, and learned duchess who led a long and varied life, becoming the wife of two kings and the mother of ten children, two of whom became kings. Upon the death of her father, fifteen-year-old Eleanor inherited considerable lands in southern France. Her first marriage was to French King Louis VII, whom she accompanied on the Second Crusade. After several years, Eleanor requested an annulment of their marriage, and when it was granted she married the Duke of Anjou, who eventually became the English King Henry II. Because historical records and artifacts from Eleanor are limited, Weir wrote the biography in the life-and-times style. John Jolliffe of *Spectator* called *Eleanor of Aquitaine* a "scholarly as well as fascinating study." Weir "wears her learning lightly," creating a biography that is "exhilarating in its color, ambition, and human warmth," a *Publishers Weekly* critic remarked. Moreover, *British Heritage* reviewer Judy Sopronyi praised Weir's ability to add up the available knowledge into a "rich book" and a "good read," in which "Weir conveys the reality of the beautiful, spoiled, willful, fifteen-year-old Eleanor."

In *Henry VIII: The King and His Court,* Weir offers a narrative account of the life and reign of Henry VIII, who ruled England from 1509 to 1547. Weir "is particularly descriptive about court life, delving into the rise and fall of various political factions led by the Earl of Essex, Thomas Cromwell, and by Cardinal Thomas Wolsey," noted Andrea Ahles, a reviewer for the *Knight-Ridder/Tribune News Service.* Weir also describes the administration of Henry's household, his acquisition of property, and his love affairs. In her author essay on the *Random House Web site,* Weir explained that what caught her attention in writing about Henry VIII "are the fascinating details of everyday life, both descriptive and anecdotal, that bring into sharp focus a world long gone." Some critics, however, found this wealth of detail daunting. "At times," observed a *Library Journal* reviewer, "the weighty detail and numerous characters . . . make the work inaccessible." An *Economist* commentator maintained that "in the end we tire of so many incidental details and long for something more challenging." Other reviewers offered different opinions. *Booklist* contributor Brad Hooper commented that Weir "brings to entertaining light the whole atmosphere of the court of England's great king Henry VIII." A *Publishers Weekly* reviewer maintained that "Weir's fondness for her characters has its difficulties," noting that

Weir is "given to romantic hyperbole." However, this reviewer praised "Weir's nose for detail, her sharpness of eye and her sympathetic touch," which "make this a feast for the senses."

Weir examines "one of the most intriguing murder mysteries in European history" in *Mary, Queen of Scots, and the Murder of Lord Darnley,* remarked *Booklist* reviewer Brad Hooper. Mary, the hereditary queen of Scotland, was married at a young age to the dauphin of France, but when he died, she returned to rule over her Scottish lands. Soon, she married Lord Darnley, a cousin to her and to Elizabeth I of England. Darnley, however, was arrogant, a political liability, and despicable in many ways. His attitude and behavior earned him many enemies, and eventually, when he was involved in the murder of one of her favorite advisors, the enmity of Mary herself. The next year, Darnley himself was killed, the victim of an ill-advised and ineptly conducted murder plot. Queen Mary was implicated in the murder, allegedly so that she could marry her love, the Earl of Bothwell. Though Mary has been accused of involvement in the plot to kill Darnley, Weir does not believe she was part of it, and presents considerable evidence in her book to exculpate Mary. Weir identifies a number of possible suspects, including several conspirators against the queen and Bothwell himself. To this day, there is no definitive answer to the question of who murdered Lord Darnley. Hooper observed, however, that "Weir goes to great lengths to isolate the clues and marshal them into a convincing indictment." Mary "could not hope for a better advocate than Weir, who exhaustively evaluates the evidence against her and finds it lacking," commented a *Publishers Weekly* contributor.

"This is far too long a book—the wretched Darnley can't be worth this much of anyone's time—but as a piece of dogged detective work there is no arguing with it," commented *Spectator* reviewer David Crane, who further remarked favorably on Weir's "monumental scholarship" in the book. *Library Journal* reviewer Isabel Coates stated that Weir "adeptly makes her case," but "her detailed and sometimes dense book will intrigue mainly monarchy buffs." A critic in *Contemporary Review* named it a "well researched and written book" that "must be regarded as the best summation in the defense's case."

Queen Isabella: Treachery, Adultery, and Murder in Medieval England, published in England as *Isabella: She-Wolf of France, Queen of England,* contains Weir's detailed examination of the turbulent life of England's much-maligned Queen Isabella. Dispatched to England by her father, King Philip IV of France, when she was twelve years old, Isabella became the wife of British King Edward II. The marriage was intended to secure peace between England and France, and it succeeded in doing so for a time. However, Isabella's personal and royal life quickly began to unravel. It became clear early on that her husband had little interest in her; the bisexual Edward II was much more enamored of a string of male lovers who came and went from his court. Isabella even found one of Edward's favorites, childhood friend Piers Gaveston, wearing the jewels from her dowry. Though Isabella despised Gaveston, she continued to support the king. When Gaveston was murdered in 1312, she found that she could finally take her place as queen. During this time, however, Isabella was pregnant and spending well beyond even her own luxurious means. Difficulties continued to plague Edward's reign until a new favorite male consort, Hugh le Despenser, arrived and once again created great turmoil in the court and the royal household. Worse for Isabella, when a war with France erupted, her estates were seized and her four children were taken from her. When Edward sent her to France to mediate, Isabella's ire was at a peak. There, she commenced an affair with exiled English traitor Roger Mortimer. When she returned to England, it was not as queen but as part of an invasion from France. Edward was overthrown and Isabella placed her son on the throne. Later, Edward died; some say he was murdered in an especially gruesome fashion, but Weir asserts that Isabella had no role in Edward's death. She carefully constructs a scenario that suggests Edward was not killed at all, but escaped to live out his life as a hermit in Italy.

Weir "puts her exemplary writing skills, as well as her talent for alternative and provocative insight" into history, to the task of reconsidering Isabella's long-suffering reputation, noted Hooper in another *Booklist* review. In her book, Weir "re-examines the evidence, and tries to place the accusations against Isabella into the context of the time and place in which she lived, giving her credit where credit is due, and placing blame perhaps more fairly than ever before," noted reviewer Michelle Heather Pollock on the *Armchair Interviews* Web site. "Isabella has been dead for almost 650 years," commented Alida Becker in the *New York Times,* "but her story has a distinctly modern appeal. Full of violent men with short tempers, conniving politicians and wildly domineering parents—not to mention sumptuous wardrobes, monumental real estate deals and catastrophically strained bank accounts—it's a period-piece

melodrama that doubles as a timeless morality play." Weir "presents a fascinating rewriting of a controversial life that should supersede all previous accounts," commented a contributor to *Publishers Weekly*. Similarly, a *Kirkus Reviews* critic averred that the book is "Sure to reign as the definitive word on Queen Isabella for years to come." *Library Journal* reviewer Robert J. Andrews named the book "a lively work on a colorful period of English history."

Weir takes up a new tool for considering the events of history with *Innocent Traitor,* her debut historical novel. "Weir's erudition in matters royal finds fictional expression in the story of England's briefest reigning sovereign, Lady Jane Grey," commented a *Kirkus Reviews* critic. Young and literate, better educated than most other girls of her time period, Jane Grey suffers constant abuse by her Protestant parents but is nonetheless consistently groomed to be a suitable consort for royalty, specifically Henry VIII's son, Prince Edward. Jane eventually escapes by entering the court of Katherine Parr, Henry's sixth wife. Jane is manipulated into a detested marriage, and when King Edward the VI dies, her parents succeed in placing her upon the throne of England, instead of the rightful heir, the Catholic Princess Mary. Jane rules for only nine days before Mary asserts her power and takes her rightful place as Queen of England, sending Jane to her fate on the executioner's block. The *Kirkus Reviews* contributor called the novel "an affecting portrayal." Hooper, in a *Booklist* review, called the work "a brilliantly vivid and psychologically astute novel." In the details of her novel, Weir "proves herself deft as ever describing Tudor food, manners, clothing, pastimes (including hunting and jousting) and marital politics," noted a *Publishers Weekly* reviewer.

BIOGRAPHICAL AND CRITICAL SOURCES:

PERIODICALS

Atlantic Monthly, March, 1994, Phoebe-Lou Adams, review of *The Princes in the Tower,* p. 130.

Biography, winter, 2006, Alida Becker, "Isabella of England," review of *Queen Isabella: Treachery, Adultery, and Murder in Medieval England,* p. 223.

Booklist, August, 1995, Brad Hooper, review of *The Wars of the Roses,* p. 1928; July, 1996, Brad Hooper, review of *The Children of Henry VIII,* p. 1799; July, 1998, Brad Hooper, review of *The Life* of *Elizabeth I*, p. 1854; January 1, 2000, Brad Hooper, review of *Eleanor of Aquitaine*, p. 871; May 1, 2001, Brad Hooper, review of *Henry VIII: The King and His Court*, p. 1600; January 1, 2003, Brad Hooper, review of *Mary, Queen of Scots, and the Murder of Lord Darnley*, p. 842; September 1, 2005, Brad Hooper, review of *Queen Isabella: Treachery, Adultery, and Murder in Medieval England*, p. 49; November 15, 2006, Brad Hooper, review of *Innocent Traitor*, p. 28.

Books (London, England), November 6, 1989, Henrietta Fordham, review of *Britain's Royal Families: The Complete Genealogy*, p. 24.

Bookseller, June 17, 2005, review of *Isabella: She-Wolf of France, Queen of England*, p. 38.

British Heritage, April, 2000, Judy Sopronyi, review of *Eleanor of Aquitaine*, p. 64.

Choice: Current Reviews for Academic Libraries, November, 2006, C.F. Briggs, review of *Queen Isabella*, p. 551.

Contemporary Review, May, 1996, review of *Britain's Royal Families*, p. 280; September, 1996, review of *Children of England: The Heirs of King Henry VIII 1547-1558*, p. 168; October, 1998, review of *Elizabeth the Queen*, pp. 223-224; October, 2001, review of *Henry VIII: The King and His Court*, p. 251; October, 2003, review of *Mary, Queen of Scots, and the Murder of Lord Darnley*, p. 251.

Economist, July 25, 1981, review of *Women in History*, p. 85; August 26, 1995, review of *The Wars of the Roses*, pp. A73-A74; August 11, 2001, "Hooray Henry; Tudor History."

History Today, July, 1999, Simon Adams, review of *Elizabeth the Queen*, p. 59.

Independent (London, England), February 14, 2007, Marianne Brace, review of *Isabella*.

Independent Sunday (London, England), June 17, 2001, Frank McLynn, "Henry Never Spared a Man in His Anger, or a Woman in His Lust; Prince of Darkness?," p. 19.

Kirkus Reviews, January 15, 1992, review of *The Six Wives of Henry VIII*, p. 106; November 15, 1993, review of *The Princes in the Tower*, p. 1452; June 15, 1995, review of *The Wars of the Roses*, pp. 848-849; June 1, 1996, review of *The Children of Henry VIII*, p. 814; June 15, 1998, review of *The Life of Elizabeth I*, p. 885; January 15, 2003, review of *Mary, Queen of Scots, and the Murder of Lord Darnley*, p. 135; August 1, 2005, review of *Queen Isabella*, p. 840; October 15, 2006, review of *Innocent Traitor*, p. 1045.

Knight-Ridder/Tribune News Service, June 27, 2001, Evie Rapport, review of *Henry VIII: The King and*

His Court, p. K2884; August 22, 2001, Andrea Ahles, review of *Henry VIII: The King and His Court*, p. K0063.

Library Journal, August, 1995, William B. Robison, review of *The Wars of the Roses*, p. 96; July, 1998, Elizabeth Mary Mellett, review of *The Life of Elizabeth I*, p. 104; Mary 1, 2001, review of *Henry VIII: The King and His Court*, p. 100; January, 2003, Isabel Coates, review of *Mary, Queen of Scots, and the Murder of Lord Darnley*, p. 134; October 1, 2005, Robert J. Andrews, review of *Queen Isabella*, p. 90; December 1, 2006, Elizabeth M. Mellett, review of *Innocent Traitor*, p. 116.

Mail on Sunday (London, England), June 10, 2001, Christopher Hibbert, "Henry VIII, the Sixteenth Century's Heart Throb," p. 68.

New Statesman and Society, May 24, 1996, Boyd Tonkin, review of *Children of England*, p. 37.

New York Times, October 16, 2005, Alida Becker, "'Queen Isabella:' Femme Fatale," review of *Queen Isabella*.

New York Times Book Review, August, 4, 1996, Naomi Bliven, "Sibling Rivalry," p. 6.

Observer (London, England), March 9, 1997, review of *Children of England*, p. 18; June 7, 1998, Roy Strong, "Bess Forgotten," p. 18.

Publishers Weekly, May, 29, 1981, Genevieve Stuttaford, review of *Women of Achievement: Thirty-five Centuries of History*, p. 35; January 20, 1992, review of *The Six Wives of Henry VIII*, p. 51; November 29, 1993, review of *The Princes in the Tower*, p. 48; July 3, 1995, review of *The Wars of the Roses*, p. 43; May 27, 1996, review of *The Children of Henry VIII*, p. 56; July 6, 1998, review of *The Life of Elizabeth I*, p. 39; January 17, 2000, review of *Eleanor of Aquitaine*, p. 51; August 23, 2001, review of *Henry VIII: The King and His Court*, p. 57; January 20, 2003, review of *Mary, Queen of Scots, and the Murder of Lord Darnley*, p. 64; August 8, 2005, review of *Queen Isabella*, p. 228; October 2, 2006, review of *Innocent Traitor*, p. 36.

School Library Journal, May, 1996, Debbie Hyman, review of *The Wars of the Roses*, p. 152; April, 1999, Dori DeSpain, review of *The Life of Elizabeth I*, p. 166.

Spectator, October 23, 1999, John Jolliffe, "A Powerful Queen on the Chessboard of Europe," pp. 49-50; May 17, 2003, David Crane, "A Hot Head and a Cool One," review of *Mary, Queen of Scots, and the Murder of Lord Darnley*, p. 61.

Times Literary Supplement, August 16, 1991, review of *The Six Wives of Henry VIII*, p. 28; August 25,

1995, Colin Richmond, "Glossy and Gothic," p. 27; August 7, 1998, Helen Hackett, "How They Got at Gloriana," p. 24.

Tribune Books (Chicago, IL), April 26, 1992, Lacey Baldwin Smith, "England's Henry VIII and His Many Wives," pp. 7-8; February 20, 1994, Patrick T. Reardon, "Did Richard III Do the Deed?," p. 6.

Victoria, August, 2001, Michele Sung, "Portraits of Power," p. 31.

Virginian Pilot, November 11, 2001, Barbara Spigel, "Richly Detailed View of Henry VIII's Court Bound to Be a Success," p. E4.

Wilson Library Bulletin, September, 1981, review of *Women of Achievement: Thirty-five Centuries of Achievement,* p. 63.

ONLINE

Armchair Interviews, http://www.armchairinterviews. com/ (March 10, 2007), Michelle Heather Pollock, review of *Queen Isabella.*

Library Journal.com, http://www.libraryjournal.com/ (January 15, 2007), Wilda Williams, interview with Alison Weir.

Random House Web site, http://www.randomhouse.com/ (April 17, 2002), interview with Alison Weir.*

*   *   *

WEITZMAN, Jacqueline Preiss 1964-

PERSONAL: Born June 19, 1964, in Poughkeepsie, NY; daughter of Ralph J. (an electrical engineer) and Marcia Splaver (an arts presenter) Preiss; married Larry Weitzman (a television producer), September 11, 1994; children: William, Alexander. *Education:* Vassar College, B.A. (with honors), 1986; Parsons School of Design, A.A.S., 1989.

ADDRESSES: Agent—Faith Hornby Hamlin, Sanford J. Greenburger Associates, 55 5th Ave., New York, NY 10003. *E-mail*—jbpweitz@hotmail.com.

CAREER: Bennet-Wallace, New York, NY, design assistant, 1986-88; Charles H. Klein Interiors, New York, NY, designer, 1988-90; Silver & Ziskind Architects, New York, NY designer, 1990-98; writer, 1998—.

AWARDS, HONORS: Notable book citation, American Library Association, 1998, "pick of the lists" citation,

American Booksellers, and inclusion among "100 titles for reading and sharing," New York Public Library, all for *You Can't Take a Balloon into the Metropolitan Museum.*

WRITINGS:

FOR CHILDREN

You Can't Take a Balloon into the Metropolitan Museum, illustrated by sister, Robin Preiss Glasser, Dial (New York, NY), 1998.

You Can't Take a Balloon into the National Gallery, illustrated by Robin Preiss Glasser, Dial (New York, NY), 2000.

You Can't Take a Balloon into the Museum of Fine Arts, illustrated by Robin Preiss Glasser, Dial (New York, NY), 2002.

SIDELIGHTS: Jacqueline Preiss Weitzman's wordless picture book *You Can't Take a Balloon into the Metropolitan Museum* was described by *Booklist* reviewer GraceAnne A. DeCandido as echoing "the style of Eloise and the substance of *The Red Balloon.*" The book was illustrated by Weitzman's sister, Robin Preiss Glasser. DeCandido said the "lively, squiggly ink sketches with characters picked out in watercolor and gouache for accent . . . tell a vivid, happy tale."

A girl and her grandmother are visiting the Metropolitan Museum in New York City. The girl has a big yellow balloon, and the guard stops them at the entrance and tells them the balloon cannot be taken inside. He ties it to a railing for safekeeping, but a pigeon pecks at the string, and it floats away. The guard chases the balloon through the Children's Zoo, the Wollman Ice Skating Rink, and the Palm Court of the Plaza Hotel. Mary M. Burns wrote in *Horn Book* that the chase is "reminiscent of a Marx brothers skit." The action outside the museum is reflected by the art the child and grandmother are simultaneously viewing inside the museum.

When the chaos includes a street musician, they are looking at Seurat's *Invitation to the Sideshow;* when the chase includes a horse, they see chariot races on Greek vases. The group chasing the balloon grows larger and marches into the Metropolitan Opera during a performance of *Aida.* The parallel work of art is the ancient Egyptian *Temple of Dendur.* A mime captures the balloon and returns it to the guard. When the girl leaves the museum and retrieves her balloon, she has no idea of what has transpired.

The book introduces children to some of the treasures to be found in the Met, as well as to other interesting sites in New York City. Burns called *You Can't Take a Balloon into the Metropolitan Museum* "deftly handled, painstakingly executed" and "funny and elegant at the same time. . . . It also celebrates the relationship between art and reality." Walter Goodman wrote in the *New York Times Book Review* that it is a "colorful account." *School Library Journal* reviewer Susan Lissim called it "a fun story with a lovely grandparent/child relationship."

BIOGRAPHICAL AND CRITICAL SOURCES:

PERIODICALS

Booklist, November 15, 1998, GraceAnne A. DeCandido, review of *You Can't Take a Balloon into the Metropolitan Museum;* March 15, 1999, review of *You Can't Take a Balloon into the Metropolitan Museum,* p. 1310.
Horn Book, November, 1998, Mary M. Burns, review of *You Can't Take a Balloon into the Metropolitan Museum,* p. 723.
Kirkus Reviews, October 15, 1998, review of *You Can't Take a Balloon into the Metropolitan Museum,* p. 1539.
New York Times Book Review, November 15, 1998, Walter Goodman, review of *You Can't Take a Balloon into the Metropolitan Museum,* p. 49.
Publishers Weekly, October 26, 1998, review of *You Can't Take a Balloon into the Metropolitan Museum,* p. 66.
School Arts, September, 1999, Ken Marantz, review of *You Can't Take a Balloon into the Metropolitan Museum,* p. 48.
School Library Journal, December, 1998, Susan Lissim, review of *You Can't Take a Balloon into the Metropolitan Museum,* p. 94.

*   *   *

WELLS, Martha 1964-

PERSONAL: Born September 1, 1964, in Fort Worth, TX; daughter of Irvin E. (a contractor) and Mary Wells. *Education:* Texas A&M University, B.A., 1986. *Hobbies and other interests:* History, antiques, folklore.

ADDRESSES: Home—College Station, TX. *Agent*—Matt Bialer, Trident Media Group, 488 Madison Ave., 17th Fl., New York, NY 10022.

CAREER: Writer, novelist, scientist, and computer programmer. Texas A&M University, College Station, systems operator and research assistant for Ocean Drilling Program, beginning 1989; part-time computer programmer.

MEMBER: Science Fiction Writers of America.

AWARDS, HONORS: Compton Crook/Stephen Tall Award nomination and Crawford Award nomination for *The Element of Fire;* Nebula Award nomination, Science Fiction Writers of America, 1998, for *The Death of the Necromancer.*

WRITINGS:

NOVELS

The Element of Fire, Tor Books (New York, NY), 1993.
City of Bones, Tor Books (New York, NY), 1995.
The Death of the Necromancer, Avon Eos (New York, NY), 1998.
Wheel of the Infinite, Avon Eos (New York, NY), 2000.
Stargate Atlantis: Reliquary, Fandemonium Ltd. (Surbiton, England), 2006.

"FALL OF ILE-RIEN" TRILOGY

The Wizard Hunters, Eos (New York, NY), 2003.
The Ships of Air, Eos (New York, NY), 2004.
The Gate of Gods, Eos (New York, NY), 2005.

OTHER

Contributor of short stories to periodicals, including *Realms of Fantasy, Black Gate, Lone Star Stories,* and *Stargate Magazine.*

Contributor to anthologies, including *Mapping the World of Harry Potter,* edited by Mercedes Lackey, Ben-Bella Books (Dallas, TX), 2006, and *Elemental,* edited by Steve Savile and Alethea Kontis, Tor (New York, NY), 2006.

Author's works have been translated into eight languages.

SIDELIGHTS: Fantasy writer Martha Wells has become a popular and critically respected contributor to the genre. Her first novel, *The Element of Fire,* which a reviewer for *Publishers Weekly* called "a rich fantasy debut," was a runner-up for the 1994 Crawford Award and a finalist for the 1993 Compton Crook/Stephen Tall Award. Set in a vaguely medieval time and place, the book tells the story of Thomas Boniface, who must protect the kingdom of Ile-Rien from several threats, including evil sorcerer Urban Grandier and political interloper Denzil, while falling in love with Kade, daughter of the late King Fulstan and Moire, Queen of Air and Darkness. Shira Daemon, in the *St. James Guide to Fantasy Writers,* considered *The Element of Fire* a "really fine first work" despite some minor flaws. Daemon especially admired Wells's skill at creating fully developed characters, her fast pace, and her entertaining approach to sometimes clichéd material.

Wells's next novel, *City of Bones,* was likewise well received; Dorman T. Shindler, in the *Dallas Morning News,* hailed it and its predecessor as "minor classics." Yet Wells's third novel, *The Death of the Necromancer,* is the book that established her critical reputation. Nominated for a prestigious Nebula Award, the novel returns to Ile-Rien two centuries after the events of *The Element of Fire,* making the setting suggestive of nineteenth-century Europe but with distinct elements of magic. Its plot centers on disgraced nobleman and thief Nicholas Valiarde and his conflict with the infamous necromancer of the book's title. To escape the necromancer's clutches, Nicholas must cooperate, however uneasily, with detective extraordinaire Ronsarde. Reviewer Jackie Cassada, in *Library Journal,* hailed the book as an "enchanting blend of detection and sorcery," and Karen Simonetti in *Booklist* deemed it "a chillingly convincing fantasy that will entrap genre readers." A contributor to *Publishers Weekly* observed that "in her third novel, Wells . . . continues to demonstrate an impressive gift for creating finely detailed fantasy worlds rife with many-layered intrigues and immensely personable characters."

In *Wheel of the Infinite,* Wells places her characters and action in a setting reminiscent of India and South Asia. Maskelle, the Voice of the Adversary, has been exiled from the city of Duvalpore but is called back to help defeat the mysterious evil that threatens to destroy the Wheel of the Infinite before the religious rite associated with it can be completed. Roland Green, in *Booklist,* found the novel "an intelligent variation of the standard quest tale," and especially admired Wells's ability to create a convincingly detailed system of religion in the book. A *Publishers Weekly* reviewer considered the novel "fast-paced, witty and inventive," and appreciated its believable characterizations. "There is real reading pleasure here," the critic concluded.

With *The Wizard Hunters,* Wells begins a new trilogy, this one also set in the world of Ile-Rien. At the beginning of the novel, playwright Tremaine Valiarde searches for a way to commit suicide, hoping to kill herself in a way that will cause little notice and the least inconvenience to anyone else. She feels she has nothing to live for. Her homeland of Ile-Rien—where magic, alchemy, and engineering all work—has been invaded by the vicious and mysterious Gardier. Their sleek black airships, impervious to magic spells, have bombed and devastated the landscape and the city of Vienne. Worse, a powerful Gardier spell has caused mechanical and electronic devices on Ile-Rien to explode and become useless. Her father, the influential Nicholas Valiarde, and his colleague, the powerful wizard Arisilde, disappeared some six years ago, presumed dead in a mishap triggered after building a strange magical sphere. Now, Tremaine has found that original sphere. With the help of her wizard guardian Gerard, she activates it, transporting them and several others to another world, a fog-enshrouded island dotted with caves and dominated by the ruins of an enormous city. They also discover a hidden Gardier base on the island. The inhabitants of the new world, the Syprians, have no advanced technology and fear magic, since every wizard on the island is a dangerous psychotic. However, they do want the Gardier off their world. As the novel progresses, Tremaine discovers that the mysterious sphere houses the soul of Arisilde, and that the sphere is their best possible defense against the Gardier and their destructive magic. Fleeing the pursuing Gardier, Tremaine must win the Syprian's trust while also working to find a weakness in the Gardier's seemingly impenetrable defenses. "If you haven't read Wells yet, you've missed one of the more graceful wordsmiths currently writing fantasy, and if you have, you're in for a treat" with *The Wizard Hunters,* remarked Michelle West in the *Magazine of Fantasy and Science Fiction. Library Journal* reviewer Jackie Cassada commented favorably on Wells's "fine storytelling," while Roland Green, writing in *Booklist,* emphasized her "narrative skill and considerably above-average characterization." Tremaine "makes an engaging and resourceful heroine, if a reluctant one, while her well-drawn fellow adventurers add plenty of human interest," remarked a *Publishers Weekly* reviewer. A *Kirkus Reviews* contributor noted that the first book in the new trilogy "wrenches the Valiarde saga into a whole new dimension of wonder, tension, and excitement."

In *The Ships of Air,* Tremaine "emerges as one of the fantasy genre's more distinctive heroines," commented a *Publishers Weekly* reviewer. Tremaine forges an alliance with influential Syprians Gilead, a chosen one of the Syprian gods, and Ilias, a wizard-slayer, to combat the Gardier, sealed by her marriage to Ilias. Using the gargantuan cruise ship Ravenna as a floating base, Tremaine and her allies continue searching for ways to strike at the Gardier while also staying alert for the presence of enemy spies. While leading a raid on the Gardier base, Tremaine and her band are captured and transported to the Gardier homeworld, where their hopes of finding their way back look slim. A *Kirkus Reviews* contributor called the book "agreeably exciting and involving." Wells "has wrought characters and cultures well," commented Frieda Murray in *Booklist.*

The Gate of Gods finds Tremaine and her allies making progress against the Gardier by using the magical spheres created by her father, Nicholas, and the wizard Arisilde. However, the defenders still do not fully understand the forces they are using, and their success against the Gardier invaders is limited. Still trapped inside the magical sphere, Arisilde manages to inform Tremaine about a huge cave that serves as a crossroads among magical gates once traversed by the Gardier. Hundreds of gate circles are carved into the walls of the cave, leading to a myriad unknown destinations. Inside the cave, Tremaine and her allies discover a band of Aelin, residents of the Gardier homeworld from before the time it was transformed by war and evil magic. If Tremaine can discover how the Gardier's world was altered to its present state, she might also uncover the vital clue needed to defeat them and drive them out of Ile-Rien. A *Kirkus Reviews* critic called the book "a yarn borne aloft by its well-above-average characters, including an appealingly brave, flawed heroine." Wells "shows us some very convincing characters in a desperate situation," commented Frieda Murray in *Booklist.*

An anthropology graduate of Texas A&M University, Wells has said that she enjoys the kind of research that makes her fiction distinctive. In an interview on the

Martha Wells Home Page, she tells readers: "I always discover a lot of historical detail that is far stranger than anything you would believe in fiction."

Wells once told *CA*: "*The Element of Fire* is my first professional sale, and my first try at a novel. I was encouraged to consider writing as a serious career by author Steven Gould during a writing workshop he taught in 1984. I work slowly. It took me slightly over a year and a half to write the book, and I have been working on my current novel for over a year.

"Research is very important to me. While the world in *The Element of Fire* is entirely imaginary, it is based heavily on seventeenth-century France. I find that a grounding in the real world, an understanding of how society and culture function and how they are affected by their environment, are essential to the creation of imaginary worlds. Giving attention to the material culture is a serious concern. What level of technology has it attained? What is the effect of literacy? Do the people have printing presses, or are they still struggling to invent the stirrup? These things have an impact on how characters view their world and themselves, and can make the difference between whether those characters seem to the reader like people from another time and place, or like modern Americans in funny clothes. Fantasy novels that reflect this concern are the kind that I most enjoy reading."

BIOGRAPHICAL AND CRITICAL SOURCES:

BOOKS

St. James Guide to Fantasy Writers, St. James Press (Detroit, MI), 1996, pp. 601-602.

PERIODICALS

Booklist, June 1, 1995, Roland Green, review of *City of Bones,* p. 1737; May 15, 1998, Karen Simonetti, review of *The Death of the Necromancer,* p. 1608; June 1, 2000, Roland Green, review of *Wheel of the Infinite,* p. 1866; May 1, 2003, Roland Green, review of *The Wizard Hunters,* p. 1586; July, 2004, Frieda Murray, review of *The Ships of Air,* p. 1830; November 1, 2005, Frieda Murray, review of *The Gate of Gods,* p. 33.

Dallas Morning News, May 21, 2000, Dorman T. Shindler, review of *City of Bones.*

Kirkus Reviews, March 1, 2003, review of *The Wizard Hunters,* p. 352; April 15, 2004, review of *The Ships of Air,* p. 368; September 15, 2005, review of *The Gate of Gods,* p. 1006.

Library Journal, June 15, 1998, Jackie Cassada, review of *The Death of the Necromancer,* p. 100; June 15, 2000, Jackie Cassada, review of *Wheel of the Infinite,* p. 120; April 15, 2003, Jackie Cassada, review of *The Wizard Hunters,* p. 128; May 15, 2004, Jackie Cassada, review of *The Ships of Air,* p. 118; November 15, 2005, Jackie Cassada, review of *The Gate of Gods,* p. 65.

Magazine of Fantasy and Science Fiction, September, 2003, Michelle West, review of *The Wizard Hunters,* p. 42.

Publishers Weekly, June 7, 1993, review of *The Element of Fire,* p. 57; May 15, 1995, review of *City of Bones,* p. 59; May 25, 1998, review of *The Death of the Necromancer,* p. 70; May 22, 2000, review of *Wheel of the Infinite,* p. 78; March 17, 2003, review of *The Wizard Hunters,* p. 58; June 28, 2004, review of *The Ships of Air,* p. 36; September 26, 2005, review of *The Gate of Gods,* p. 67.

ONLINE

Bewildering Stories, http://www.bewilderingstories. com/ (December 10, 2006), Jerry Wright, review of *The Gate of the Gods.*

Blogcritics, http://www.blogcritics.org/ (February 10, 2005), Eoghann Irving, review of *The Wizard Hunters;* (March 10, 2005), Eoghann Irving, review of *The Ships of Air.*

Far Sector SFFH, http://www.farsector.com/ (January 2, 2007), Shaun Farrell, interview with Martha Wells.

Martha Wells Home Page, http://www.marthawells.com (December 10, 2006).

sffworld.com, http://www.sffworld.com/ (May 18, 2003), Rob H. Bedford, review of *The Wizard Hunters.**

*   *   *

WESSON, Marianne 1948-
(Mimi Wesson)

PERSONAL: Born September 14, 1948, in Houston, TX; daughter of Lawrence M. (a certified public accountant) and Julia Lorena (a homemaker) Wesson; married Joel W. Cantrick, June 23, 1973 (divorced, July, 1979); married David Mastbaum, December 27, 1989 (marriage ended); married Ben Herr; children: (first marriage) Benjamin. *Ethnicity:* "Caucasian." *Education:* Vassar College, A.B., 1970; University of Texas, J.D., 1973; passed bar exams: Texas, 1974, Colorado, 1977. *Politics:* Democrat. *Hobbies and other interests:* Running, skiing, raising fish, water gardening, films, motorcycling.

ADDRESSES: Office—University of Colorado School of Law, P.O. Box 401, Boulder, CO 80303. *Agent*—Jed Mattes Literary Agency, Inc., 2095 Broadway, New York, NY 10023. *E-mail*—wesson@colorado.edu.

CAREER: Writer, novelist, educator, radio broadcaster, rancher, and attorney. U.S. District Court, TX, law clerk, 1973-75; admitted to the U.S. Court of Appeals, 5th District, 1976; State of Texas, Austin, TX, assistant attorney general, 1976; University of Colorado, Boulder, associate professor, 1976-80, acting associate vice president for academic affairs, 1989-90, professor of law, 1990—, president's teaching scholar, 1992—, interim dean, 1995-96, Wolf-Nichol Fellow, Senior Scholar, Women's Studies Program; admitted to the U.S. Court of Appeals, 10th District, 1980; Office of the U.S. Attorney, Denver, CO, assistant U.S. Attorney, 1980-82; admitted to the U.S. Supreme Court, 1999. National Conference of Bar Examiners, member of test development committee for multistate bar exam, 1978; Colorado Supreme Court, Denver, member of committee on rules of criminal procedure, 1982-88, member of Colorado Supreme Court grievance committee, 1989-95; legal correspondent, National Public Radio, 1998—. Frequent guest on radio and television networks, including NBC, CBS, ABC, MSNBC, CNN, and Court TV.

MEMBER: American Bar Association, American Law Institute, Association of American Law Schools (chair of section on law and psychiatry, 1987), Society of American Law Teachers, Mystery Writers of America, Sisters in Crime, Authors Guild.

AWARDS, HONORS: Samuel E. Zeigler Foundation fellow, 1978-79; Mary Lathrop Award for outstanding woman lawyer, Colorado Women's Bar Association, 1996; W.H. Smith Fresh Talent Award, 1998.

WRITINGS:

NONFICTION

Crime and Defenses in Colorado, Harrison (Norcross, GA), 1989.

"LUCINDA HAYES" MYSTERY SERIES; NOVELS

Render up the Body: A Novel of Suspense, HarperCollins (New York, NY), 1998.

A Suggestion of Death, Headline Fiction (London, England), 1999, Pocket Books (New York, NY), 2000.

Chilling Effect, University Press of Colorado (Boulder, CO), 2004.

Render up the Body: A Novel of Suspense has been translated into German, Dutch, Norwegian, French, Hebrew and Latvian.

Contributor of articles to feminist and legal publications, including *New Mexico Law Review, DePaul Law Journal, Tulsa Law Journal, Women's Review of Books,* and *University of Colorado Law Journal.*

American Journal of Criminal Law, editor-in-chief, beginning 1972; *Frontiers: Journal of Women's Studies,* board of editors, 1988-90; *Texas Women's Law Journal,* member of board of advisors, 1991—.

SIDELIGHTS: Author and lawyer Marianne Wesson used her legal expertise to create a debut novel that has drawn favorable attention from critics and has been translated into a number of languages. Before serving as a law professor at the University of Colorado, Wesson worked as a federal prosecutor and a trial lawyer. Like her protagonist, Wesson has defended a death-row inmate before a state Supreme Court. *Render up the Body: A Novel of Suspense* (a rough translation of the Latin legal term *habeas corpus*) is the story of Lucinda "Cinda" Hayes, a lawyer who goes from a position in the District Attorney's office to head a rape center in Boulder, Colorado. Cinda's old teacher, now a state Supreme Court Justice, puts pressure on her to represent a death row inmate who is appealing charges of raping and murdering his drug-addicted girlfriend. Cinda has to struggle with her feelings about the death penalty, which she opposes, and her feelings about rape—she does not wish to contribute to what she feels is society's "trivialization" of the crime—before she decides to take the case.

A *Publishers Weekly* reviewer called *Render up the Body* an "intricately layered legal thriller" and looked forward to more fiction from Wesson. While suggesting that Wesson had tried a little too hard to cover all of society's politically correct bases by including gay and lesbian characters and "other good souls trying to buck a sinister white bread establishment," the reviewer remarked that Wesson goes one step beyond the obvious in her treatment of what could be cliche situations. This reviewer termed *Render up the Body* engaging, "strongly plotted," and "told with style," noting that it is a good addition to the legal/thriller genre.

Cinda Hayes returns for a second adventure in *A Suggestion of Death.* While trying to drum up some business for her and law partner Tory Meadows's flagging law firm, Cinda appears on a radio call-in show. There, she receives a call from a frail and timid young woman who, Cinda discovers, is Mariah McKay, the estranged daughter of Harrison McKay, a candidate for state senator. Mariah believes that her father molested her as a child, but her memories of any incidents are vague and nonspecific at best. The woman wants redress for the damage her father caused her, but the statute of limitations is running out on any crimes that might have been committed. Cinda must confront her skepticism on recovered memories. Worse, Cinda must overcome her distaste for the neo-Nazi group that Mariah lives with, even as she ponders the mystery and strange appeal of the group's self-appointed common-law judge, Pike Sayers. Cinda ignores pointed warnings to back off from the case, and by the story's end, tragedy will inevitably enfold the scene. Jenny McLarin, writing in *Booklist,* called the novel a "first-rate character study and a perceptive look at life in Boulder," CO. A *Publishers Weekly* critic named *A Suggestion of Death* a "searingly intelligent legal thriller," remarking that Wesson "writes with a rare blend of fearlessness, insight, and wit." *Library Journal* contributor Michele Leber determined that Wesson's novel stands as a "first-rate legal thriller." The *Publishers Weekly* writer concluded that Wesson is "now clearly on the short list of the best practitioners of the genre."

The third novel in the "Lucinda Hayes" series, *Chilling Effect,* "questions the limits of First Amendment protection," noted a *Publishers Weekly* reviewer. Child murderer Leonard Fitzgerald, who killed a young girl after repeated viewings of a child-porn snuff film, has been declared criminally insane and locked away in an institution. The girl's mother, however, still desires revenge, and decides to sue the snuff film's producers to hold them criminally liable for the behavior incited by their product. Cinda agrees to take the case, suing the producers for compensation for loss. To win, she must prove that Fitzgerald's viewing of the movie caused him to commit murder, and that the film's producers should have known that their movie would cause a death. As Cinda and her law partners descend into the world of pornography, they begin to understand that the first amendment is not so easily challenged.

BIOGRAPHICAL AND CRITICAL SOURCES:

PERIODICALS

Booklist, December 15, 1999, Jenny McLarin, review of *A Suggestion of Death,* p. 760.

Library Journal, December, 1999, Michele Leber, review of *A Suggestion of Death,* p. 189; September 1, 2004, Rex E. Klett, review of *Chilling Effect,* p. 122.

Publishers Weekly, December 8, 1997, review of *Render up the Body: A Novel of Suspense,* p. 56; November 22, 1999, review of *A Suggestion of Death,* p. 41; August 9, 2004, review of *Chilling Effect,* p. 235.

Wichita Eagle, April 5, 2006, "Professors Will Exhume Body to Solve Mystery."

ONLINE

Marianne Wesson Home Page, http://www.wesson books.com (December 10, 2006).

National Public Radio Web site, http://www.npr.org/ (December 10, 2006), biography of Marianne Wesson.

New Mystery Reader, http://www.newmysteryreader. com/ (December 10, 2006), Stephanie Padilla, interview with Marianne Wesson.

Renaissance Online Magazine, http://www. renaissancemag.com/ (January 2, 2007), Graham Brack, "Marianne Wesson Writes Well, but Writes too Much," review of *A Suggestion of Death.*

University of Colorado Law School, http://lawweb. colorado.edu/ (December 10, 2006), bibliography of Marianne Wesson.*

*   *   *

WESSON, Mimi
See WESSON, Marianne

WILLIAMS, Michael 1935-

PERSONAL: Born June 24, 1935, in Swansea, Wales; son of Benjamin (a company salesman) and Ethel (a homemaker) Williams; married Eleanore Lerch (a high school teacher), June 25, 1955; children: Catherine Dilys, Tess Jane. *Ethnicity:* "European." *Education:* University College of Swansea, University of Wales, B.A. (with first class honors), 1956, Ph.D., 1960; St. Catharine's College, Cambridge, diploma in education, 1960; Oxford University, M.A., 1978; University of Wales, D.Litt., 1990.

ADDRESSES: Home—Harcourt Hill, Oxford, England. *Office*—School of Geography, Oxford University, Mansfield Rd., Oxford OX1 3TB, England; fax 01865-271929. *E-mail*—michael.williams@oriel.ox.ac.uk.

CAREER: Writer, geographer, editor, historian, and educator. University of Adelaide, Adelaide, Australia, lecturer, 1960-65, senior lecturer, 1966-72, reader in geography, 1973-78; Oxford University, Oxford, England, lecturer, 1978-90, reader in geography, 1990-96, professor of geography, 1996, director Environmental Change and Management Unit, 1993-98, fellow of Oriel College, 1978—, lecturer in charge at St. Anne's College, 1978-96, vice provost, Oriel College, 2000-02. Part-time lecturer, South Australian Institute of Technology, 1963-70; visitor and lecturer, University College, London, 1966-67 and 1973; visiting fellow, University of Wisconsin—Madison, 1973-74, Flinders University of South Australia, 1984, University of Chicago, 1989, and University of California Los Angeles (UCLA); lecturer at universities in England, Australia, and United States, including University of California, Berkeley, Brandeis University, University of Michigan, Duke University, and North Carolina State University. Expert witness, Australian Federal Commission on Redistribution of Electoral Boundaries and State Commission on Electoral Boundaries, 1968; member of committee for landscape evaluation for the state, National Trust of South Australia, 1974-75.

MEMBER: British Academy (fellow), Royal Geographical Society (member of South Australia council, 1961-70; vice-president, 1974; president, 1975-76; chairman of Historical Geography Research Group, 1983-86), Institute of British Geographers (member of council and chairman of Publications Committee, 1983-88), Australian and New Zealand Association for the

Advancement of Science (honorary editor of publications, 1968-70; member of state organizing committee, 1969-73), Institute of Australian Geographers (member of council, 1968-72), Oriel Society, Forest History Society (judge for Weyerheauser Literary Prize, 1984-86; honorary fellow, 1990).

AWARDS, HONORS: Grants from Australian Research Grant Commission, 1969-73, 1975-78, and 1976-79; John Lewis Gold Medal, Royal Geographical Society, 1974; Biennial Literary Prize, Adelaide Festival of the Arts, 1976, for *The Making of the South Australian Landscape;* grants from British Academy, 1986, 1988, 1995, and 1998; travel grant from Royal Society, 1988, for International Geographical Union; Hidy Award, Forest History Society, 1988; Weyerhauser Prize, American Forest and Conservation Society, 1990, for *Americans and Their Forests,* 2004, for *Deforesting the Earth;* Meridian Prize, Association of American Geographers, for most scholarly work in geography, 2004, and British Academy Book Prize runner-up, both for *Deforesting the Earth.*

WRITINGS:

(Editor) *South Australia from the Air,* Melbourne University Press (Melbourne, Australia), 1969.

The Draining of the Somerset Levels, Cambridge University Press (Cambridge, England), 1970.

The Making of the South Australian Landscape, Academic Press (London, England), 1974.

(With J.M. Powell) *Australian Space, Australian Time: Geographical Perspectives, 1788-1914,* Oxford University Press (Melbourne, Australia), 1977.

The Changing Rural Landscape of South Australia, Heinemann Educational (Melbourne, Australia), 1977, revised edition, State Government Printer (Adelaide, Australia), 1991.

(With B.A. Badcock and D.H. Jaensch) *Adelaide at the Census, 1971* (monograph), Australian Political Studies Association, 1977.

The Americans and Their Forests: An Historical Geography, Cambridge University Press (Cambridge, England), 1989.

Wetlands: A Threatened Landscape, Basil Blackwell (London, England) 1990.

(Editor) *Planet Management,* Oxford University Press (New York, NY), 1993.

(Editor) *Understanding Geographical and Environmental Education: The Role of Research,* Cassell (New York, NY), 1996.

The Landscapes of Lowland Britain, Routledge (New York, NY), 1999.

Deforesting the Earth: From Prehistory to Global Crisis, University of Chicago Press (Chicago, IL), 2002.

(Editor, with Ron Johnston) *A Century of British Geography,* Oxford University Press (Oxford, England), 2003.

(Editor, with Graham Humphrys) *Presenting and Representing Environments,* Springer (Dordrecht, Germany), 2005.

(Editor, with John Chi-Kin Lee) *School Improvement: International Perspectives,* Nova Science Publishers (New York, NY), 2006.

(Editor, with John Chi-Kin Lee) *Environmental and Geographical Education for Sustainability: Cultural Contexts,* Nova Science Publishers (New York, NY), 2006.

Contributor to books, including *Settlement and Encounter: Essays Presented to Sir Grenfell Price,* Oxford University Press (Melbourne, Australia), 1969; *The English Medieval Landscape,* Croom Helm, 1982; *The Earth as Transformed by Human Action,* Cambridge University Press (Cambridge, England), 1991; *Ecology and Empire,* Edinburgh University Press (Edinburgh, Scotland), 1997; *Encyclopedia of American Forest and Conservation History; Methods and Approaches in Forest History,* edited by M. Agnoletti and S. Andersen, CABI Publishing (Wallingford, England), 2000; *The Relations of History and Geography: Studies in England, France, and the United States,* by H.C. Darby, University of Exeter Press, 2002; *Culture, Land, and Legacy: Perspectives on Carl O. Sauer and the Berkeley School of Geography,* Geoscience Publications (Baton Rouge, LA), 2003; *Managing the Forest on Both Sides of the Atlantic: One Hundred Years of the USDA,* edited by A. Sample, 2005; and *World System History and Global Environmental Change,* edited by A. Hornborg, Altamira Press (New York, NY), 2005.

Contributor to academic journals and periodicals, including *Environment and History, History Today, Journal of Historical Geography, Geographical Review,* and *Antipode.*

Editor of *Transactions of the Institute of British Geographers,* 1983-88, *Global Environmental Change,* 1993-96, and *Progress in Human Geography,* 1990—; honorary editor of *Proceedings of the Royal Geographical Society (South Australia),* 1962-70; member of editorial board of *Encyclopedia of American Forest and Conservation History;* member of editorial advisory board of *Journal of Historical Geography,* 1975-79, *Geographical Journal,* 1984—, *Environmental History* (US and UK editions), 2001—; and *Progress in Human Geography,* 2001—.

SIDELIGHTS: Writer, editor, and educator Michael Williams is a British Geographer whose expertise centers around human-applied processes that profoundly change the landscape in which they live, such as wetlands drainage, agricultural clearing, and deforestation. *The Draining of the Somerset Levels* is a "masterly and exhaustive technological study" of the draining and reclamation of the marshlands that once existed in the geographical areas around Britain's Somerset Levels, noted reviewer D.E. Mullins in *Journal of Applied Ecology.* Williams looks at some of the earliest known settlements in the Somerset Levels area, including Iron Age Brythons whose villages had little effect on the regional ecosystem. The first residents to actively participate in drainage and reclamation were early Celts and Anglo-Saxons, which Mullins called "enterprising pioneers of land drainage." Williams describes how ecosystems changed with the draining, how natural resources such as fish, fowl, and peat became more and more scarce, and how other attempts were made at reclamation over long periods of time. "The climate and geology of the Somerset Levels are exceedingly complex, but Dr. Williams guides us unhesitatingly through all their intricacies and makes us understand the practical problems which the men of Somerset had and have to face," observed H.E. Hallam in *Economic History Review.*

The Americans and Their Forests: An Historical Geography provides a historical perspective on the relationship between Americans and the dense forests of America that have provided a considerable bounty of lumber, paper, and other products for centuries. Williams notes that Americans had to shift their attitudes toward forests, from one of "forest as mine," in which resources are stripped away and the remnants abandoned, to "forest as crop," in which forests are renewable resources that must be cultivated, cared for, replanted, and eventually harvested. Williams notes how the use of trees was widespread and largely unchecked during the first three centuries after American colonization, but that concerns about forest supply and sustainability began to arise in the middle of the nineteenth century. "In a synthesis requiring considerable courage, Williams covers this whole vast story," noted Patricia Nelson Limerick in *American Historical Review,* from

Native American uses of timber, to the gigantic lumber mills that harvested vast numbers of trees, to the economic power of the lumber industry, to the timber industry in the Pacific Northwest. He describes techniques, equipment, and procedures used in the timber industry and for transporting logs. Williams also reassesses the reputations of a number of early governmental forest officials as being genuinely concerned with forest depletion and timber usage. In consideration of modern conservation efforts and organizations, Williams also examines changing attitudes towards harvesting of old-growth woodlands, and relates the dissatisfaction many feel with the loss of so many deep, primeval forests. In total, Williams's book "addresses a serious gap in American environmental history: the relationship between one of the most significant biotic features of the American landscape and its human inhabitants over the last four centuries," commented James D. Proctor in *ISIS: Journal of the History of Science in Society.*

Williams turns his attention to Great Britain with *A Century of British Geography,* edited by Williams and Ron Johnston. Williams and his contributors chart the history of geography as an academic discipline in England. He tells how the discipline was established about a century ago, first at Oxford then at the London School of Economics. The authors represented in the collection look at British geography in historical terms and discuss the contributions that geography has made to Britain academically, socially, and culturally. The book "offers detailed—and often lengthy—contributions from leading scholars. It is well edited and nicely produced. It presents British geography in a broadly positive light, while lamenting some of its failures," reported Simon Batterbury in the *Geographical Review.* Topics and themes covered include Environment, Place, Scale, Geography in Action, and the future and development of geography within British universities and educational institutions. "One comes away from reading the book with a sense of just how far British geographical ideas have evolved over the twentieth century," Batterbury observed.

In *Deforesting the Earth: From Prehistory to Global Crisis,* Williams examines the long history of human interaction with forests, and how and where humans felled trees for use in homes, as fuel, to clear land for agriculture, and for other uses geared to ensure human survival. The book is structured in three parts. In the first, Williams looks at forest clearing in the far past and ends his consideration with the state of deforestation in medieval times, when agriculture and rapid expansion led to considerable use of timber and forest products. In this section, Williams "introduces a theme to which he returns time and again throughout the course of his inquiry: the myth of nature as pristine and untouched by human beings before the dawn of the industrial age. This is still a powerful myth today, and Williams devotes many pages of his book to dispel it," noted Judith Tsouvalis in the *Geographical Journal.* The second part of the book covers the use of trees and timber in Europe and other parts of the world from 1500 to 1920. Williams notes how expansion, technology, and economic concerns led to expanded use of forest products during this time. In part three, he concentrates on the period from 1900 to 1995, with a focus on the United States. What Williams "does do admirably well is tell us in great detail about how people did interact with their forests, and how they used trees and the various products they provided," Tsouvalis commented. Tsouvalis concluded that for "those who care about nature in general and forests in particular, and for whom history and geography matter," Williams's thorough study "constitutes essential reading."

Michael Williams once told *CA:* "I have always had a fascination with understanding what we see around us— the visual landscape that more often than not is the product of centuries of human endeavor and transformation. Hence, my earlier work concentrated on specific landscape forming processes, such as draining of wetland environments, forest clearing, and agricultural change. Opportunities to work in Australia and the United States have broadened the range of my work, so that *Americans and Their Forests* is continental in scale and straddles transformations from pre-Indian times to the present. Currently, I write about the global experience in deforestation from antiquity to the current concerns in the tropical rain forests. Too often the mistake is made that environmental change is a product of the present world, when it has been going on since humans inhabited the earth."

Williams added: "Particularly influential in my early work was the writing of H. Clifford Darby and Donald W. Meinig, who taught me a respect for accuracy and clarity of expression."

BIOGRAPHICAL AND CRITICAL SOURCES:

PERIODICALS

American Historical Review, October, 1991, Patricia Nelson Limerick, review of *Americans and Their Forests: A Historical Geography,* p. 1276.

Annals of the Association of American Geographers, March, 1976, J.M. Powell, review of *The Making of the South Australian Landscape,* p. 149; December, 2004, review of *A Century of British Geography,* p. 1006.

Conservation Biology, December, 2004, Donald J. Leopold, "A Seamless Blend of Science and History," review of *Deforesting the Earth: From Prehistory to Global Crisis,* p. 1693.

Economic History Review, August, 1971, H.E. Hallam, review of *The Draining of the Somerset Levels,* p. 485.

Geographical Journal, June, 2006, Judith Tsouvalis, review of *Deforesting the Earth,* p. 173.

Geographical Review, January, 2005, Simon Batterbury, review of *A Century of British Geography,* p. 145.

ISIS: Journal of the History of Science in Society, June, 1991, James D. Proctor, review of *Americans and Their Forests,* p. 352.

Journal of Applied Ecology, August, 1971, D.E. Mullins, review of *The Draining of the Somerset Levels,* p. 623.

Journal of the History of Science in Society, December, 2004, Karen Jones, review of *Deforesting the Earth,* p. 685.

Professional Geographer, November, 1990, Conrad T. Moore, review of *Americans and Their Forests,* p. 518; November, 2005, review of *A Century of British Geography,* p. 617.

ONLINE

Economic History Services, http://www.eh.net/ (August 4, 2003), Gary Libecap, review of *Deforesting the Earth.*

Oxford University School of Geography Web site, http://www.geog.ox.ac.uk/ (December 10, 2006), biography of Michael Williams.*

*   *   *

WINTNER, Robert 1948-

PERSONAL: Born August 14, 1948, in Evansville, IN; son of Leon and Perline Wintner; married, wife's name Anita. *Ethnicity:* "Druid." *Education:* University of Missouri, B.A., 1970. *Religion:* Jewish. *Hobbies and other interests:* Motorcycling, travel, animal welfare.

ADDRESSES: Office—Snorkel Bob's, 6689 Makena Rd., Kihei, HI 96753. *E-mail*—robertw@snorkelbob.com.

CAREER: *Savannah Morning News,* Savannah, GA, writer, 1972-74; Snorkel Bob's (retail snorkel shop), Kihei, HI, founder and owner, 1986—, designer of original equipment, 1999—. Host of Hawaiian radio show *The Real Time Story Hour,* 1980s. Snorkel Bob Foundation, executive director; member of Modern Outreach Management Consortium and North West Hawaiian Island Network.

WRITINGS:

Whirlaway (novel), Smallwood (Tucson, AZ), 1994.
Snorkel Bob's Reality Guide to Hawaii (travel book), Smallwood (Tucson, AZ), 1994.
Hagan's Trial, and Other Stories, Smallwood (Tucson, AZ), 1995.
The Ice King (novel), Smallwood (Tucson, AZ), 1995.
Horndog Blue (novel), Smallwood (Tucson, AZ), 1995.
The Prophet Pasqual (novel), Permanent Press (Sag Harbor, NY), 1999.
Homunculus (novel), Permanent Press (Sag Harbor, NY), 2000.
The Modern Outlaws (novel), ToExcel, 2000.
Lonely Hearts, Changing Worlds (short stories), Permanent Press (Sag Harbor, NY), 2001.
Toucan Whisper, Toucan Sing (novel), Permanent Press (Sag Harbor, NY), 2003.
In a Sweet Magnolia Time (novel), Permanent Press (Sag Harbor, NY), 2006.

Contributor to periodicals, including *Ford Times, Hawaii Review,* and *Sports Illustrated.*

SIDELIGHTS: Robert Wintner has said that he writes fiction based on his own experiences, especially reflecting his flair for travel and adventure. His first novel, *Whirlaway,* follows his exploits sailing from California to Hawaii in 1983. In the novel, two wayward men seek wealth and comfort in an ambitious boating excursion. *Hagan's Trial, and Other Stories* is a collection reflecting the author's affinity for nature and recounting his exploits at racetracks and as a motorcycling traveler in Europe. A *Booklist* reviewer called *Hagan's Trial* "fine" and noted the volume's multiplicity of voices, which were considered "as distinctive as they are entertaining."

The Ice King relates Wintner's early experiences as a girl scout camper, a gambler, and a juvenile delinquent. Subsequent fiction includes *The Prophet Pasqual,* which concerns the efforts of opportunists to exploit an unlikely guru, and *The Modern Outlaws,* a novel about motorcycle aficionados taking to the open road, which prompted praise from *Thunder Press* reviewer Terry Roorda. Wintner "nails the nuances [of the open road-riding experience] with expert prose and paints his imagery with a fine, fresh brush," Roorda observed. "His style and intelligence transcend genre, and with *The Modern Outlaws* he has not so much written an excellent biker novel, as he's written an excellent novel that just happens to be populated with bikers."

Wintner is also the author of *Snorkel Bob's Reality Guide to Hawaii,* wherein he provides vacation information. Patty Campbell, writing in *Wilson Library Bulletin,* described Wintner's literary style as "an easy mix of educated journalese, Hawaiian pidgin, and his own inimitable syntax."

Wintner once told *CA:* "My favorite image of a modern writer is one who must write because she can't not write. She can't just walk away from it. What would be left of her life? Except for right now, because she has a stubborn case of writer's block. Oh, she's tried everything, and she knows it'll go away. She just knows it. She's planning to attend a writer's conference.

"I'm from the experience school of writing. Getting out in the world and mixing it up leaves no room for writer's block. Experience means movement, outdoors, on the road or the open sea, far from home, where the world can be viewed through the eyes of a fresh visitor. Experience is on hold in a classroom or an office or at home. Diesel engines don't have distributors, unless you've never seen one and must make an overeducated guess.

"An author doesn't write because she must fulfill her inner self. She writes to tell a story that is bubbling up to be told. She no more needs to squeeze like hell than she will be able to keep up with the narrative overflowing.

"Style emerges as a function of repetition. Style comes with time over thousands of pages. My narratives are wide-ranging in setting and characterization, yet they share a common thread and a common lament, which is the death of nature. I think my deep personal disappointment over this phenomenon so unique to our time drives my fiction to situations many 'normal' people find troubling. I have little use for prescribed dosage of description, introspection, divorce or the true meaning of love. I favor a radical approach to pesky problems with violence and carnage and always with good manners and good taste. I think this may be what disturbs some of the more fundamentalist reviewers. I often find myself in trouble, just like back in school."

To give Wintner the benefit of the doubt, one might presume that the experiences he credits for his inspiration have more to do with the far-flung places he visits and the varieties of human character he encounters than with actual events he witnesses or acts that he performs. The setting of the novel *Toucan Whisper, Toucan Sing* is a Mexican hotel. The characters include Antonio, an over-endowed pool boy with an active and profitable nightlife, and his mentally impaired brother Baldo, who has a penchant for whacking things with a machete and whose love for helpless animals gets him into big trouble. The plot includes the macabre death of a cruel sport-fisher, a stint in a stereotypical Mexican jail for the pool boy, and, after a wild ride for the reader, a happy ending.

The novel *In a Sweet Magnolia Time* takes place in South Carolina in the turbulent sixties and seems to set itself up as an examination of the effects of desegregation on a deeply entrenched southern culture rooted in racial inequality. The plot revolves around the death of a judge who had transformed himself into an "integrationist" and the effect that his conversion has upon others, particularly the young man who had been groomed to follow in the judge's footsteps. If serious critics approached the novel from this lofty perspective, they may have been disappointed. It isn't long before a theme of revenge and counter-revenge emerges, and the young protege Covingdale embarks on an interracial sexual romp that at least one critic found to be gratuitous in nature and detail. A *Publishers Weekly* contributor commented, however, that "Wintner ends up nicely illuminating a corner of a turbulent era."

Some critics, as Wintner hinted in his remarks to *CA,* may be "disturbed" by his "radical approach" to the workings of human nature, yet other readers seem to enjoy the exotic settings, escapist entertainment, wild plots, and extravagant behavior to be found in his novels. As a *Publishers Weekly* reviewer described *Toucan Whisper, Toucan Sing:* "This book is best suited to being read, cocktail in hand, while a real-life Antonio wanders by."

Wintner later added: "I continue with the good fight on several key conservation issues, focusing on the aquarium industry now extracting eight million reef fish annually from Hawaii reefs."

BIOGRAPHICAL AND CRITICAL SOURCES:

PERIODICALS

Booklist, March 15, 1995, review of *Hagan's Trial, and Other Stories.*

Kirkus Reviews, September 1, 2002, review of *Toucan Whisper, Toucan Sing,* p. 1263; September 15, 2005, review of *In a Sweet Magnolia Time,* p. 1001.

Publishers Weekly, August 29, 1994, review of *Whirlaway,* p. 62; February 20, 1995, review of *Hagan's Trial, and Other Stories,* p. 201; October 21, 2002, review of *Toucan Whisper, Toucan Sing,* p. 55; September 12, 2005, review of *In a Sweet Magnolia Time,* p. 40.

San Francisco Books and Travel, spring, 2000, review of *The Prophet Pasqual,* p. 2.

Thunder Press, July, 2000, Terry Roorda, review of *The Modern Outlaws.*

Wilson Library Bulletin, January, 1995, Patty Campbell, review of *Snorkel Bob's Reality Guide to Hawaii,* pp. 102-103.

ONLINE

Snorkel Bob's: For Discriminating Snorkelers and Divers, http://www.snorkel bob.com (March 10, 2007).

*   *   *

WOODWORTH, Steven E. 1961-
(Steven Edward Woodworth)

PERSONAL: Born January 28, 1961, in Akron, OH; son of Ralph Leon (a pastor and educator) and Erma Jean (a homemaker) Woodworth; married Leah Dawn Bunke (a homemaker), August 13, 1983; children: Nathan William, Jonathan Steven, David Eric, Daniel Timothy, Anna Constance, Elizabeth Grace. *Education:* Southern Illinois University at Carbondale, B.A. (with high honors), 1982; attended University of Hamburg, 1982-83; Rice University, Ph.D., 1987. *Politics:* Republican. *Religion:* Bible Methodist.

ADDRESSES: Office—Department of History, Texas Christian University, P.O. Box 297260, Fort Worth, TX 76129. *E-mail*—S.Woodworth@tcu.edu.

CAREER: Writer, historian, and educator. Teacher at Baptist schools in Houston, TX, 1984-86; Bartlesville Wesleyan College, Bartlesville, OK, instructor in history, 1987-89; Toccoa Falls College, Toccoa Falls, GA, assistant professor, 1989-94, associate professor of history, 1994-97; Texas Christian University, Fort Worth, assistant professor of history, then associate professor of history, 1997—. Houston Community College, adjunct instructor, 1984-87.

MEMBER: American Historical Association, Organization of American Historians, Southern Historical Association.

AWARDS, HONORS: Fletcher Pratt Award, 1991, for *Jefferson Davis and His Generals,* and 1996, for *Davis and Lee at War.*

WRITINGS:

Jefferson Davis and His Generals: The Failure of Confederate Command in the West, University Press of Kansas (Lawrence, KS), 1990.

The Essentials of United States History, 1841 to 1877: Westward Expansion and the Civil War, Research and Education Association (Piscataway, NJ), 1990 revised version edited by Max Fogiel, 2001.

The Essentials of United States History, 1500 to 1789: From Colony to Republic, Research and Education Association (Piscataway, NJ), 1990.

(With Jerome McDuffie and Gary Piggrem) *The Advanced Placement Examination in United States History,* Research and Education Association (Piscataway, NJ), 1990.

Davis and Lee at War, University Press of Kansas (Lawrence, KS), 1995.

(Editor) *The Musick of the Mocking Birds, the Roar of the Cannon: The Civil War Diary and Letters of William Winters,* University of Nebraska Press (Lincoln, NE), 1998.

Six Armies in Tennessee: The Chickamauga and Chattanooga Campaigns, University of Nebraska Press (Lincoln, NE), 1998.

(Editor) *The Art of Command in the Civil War,* University of Nebraska Press (Lincoln, NE), 1998.

(Editor) *Civil War Generals in Defeat,* University Press of Kansas (Lawrence, KS), 1999.

(Editor) *Chickamauga: A Battlefield Guide with a Section on Chattanooga,* cartography by Marcia McLean, University of Nebraska Press (Lincoln, NE), 1999.

No Band of Brothers: Problems in the Rebel High Command, University of Missouri Press (Columbia, MO), 1999.

(Editor) *The Human Tradition in the Civil War and Reconstruction,* SR Books (Wilmington, DE), 2000.

(With Jerome McDuffie and Gary Piggrem) *The Best Test Preparation for the Advanced Placement Examination, United States History,* with CD-ROM, Research and Education Association (Piscataway, NJ), 2000, revised version edited by Max Fogiel, 2001.

Cultures in Conflict: The American Civil War, Greenwood Press (Westport, CT), 2000.

A Scythe of Fire: The Civil War Story of the Eighth Georgia Regiment, HarperCollins, 2001, W. Morrow (New York, NY), 2002.

(Editor) *Grant's Lieutenants,* University Press of Kansas (Lawrence, KS), 2001.

While God Is Marching On: The Religious World of Civil War Soldiers, University Press of Kansas (Lawrence, KS), 2001.

The Loyal, True, and Brave: America's Civil War Soldiers, edited by Steven E. Woodworth, SR Books (Wilmington, DE), 2002.

Beneath a Northern Sky: A Short History of the Gettysburg Campaign, SR Books (Wilmington, DE), 2003.

(With Kenneth J. Winkle) *Oxford Atlas of the Civil War,* foreword by James M. McPherson, Oxford University Press (New York, NY), 2004.

(Author of introduction) *Southern Sons, Northern Soldiers: The Civil War Letters of the Remley Brothers, Twenty-second Iowa Infantry,* edited by Julie Holcomb, Northern Illinois University Press (DeKalb, IL), 2004.

Nothing but Victory: The Army of the Tennessee, 1861-1865, Alfred A. Knopf (New York, NY), 2005.

(With Jerome McDuffie and Gary Piggrem) *United States History,* edited by Paul R. Babbitt, Research & Education Association (Piscataway, NJ), 2005.

(With Mark Grimsley) *Shiloh: A Battlefield Guide,* University of Nebraska Press (Lincoln, NE), 2006.

Also author of (with Gary Piggrem, N.R. Holt, and W.T. Walker) *The Graduate Record Examination in History,* 1993; (editor) *Leadership and Command in the American Civil War,* 1995; *A Deep Steady Thunder: The Battle of Chickamauga,* 1995; and *The American Civil War: A Handbook of Literature and Research,* 1996. Work represented in anthologies, including *The Confederate General,* edited by William C. Davis, Cowles Magazines. Contributor of articles and reviews to history and education journals.

SIDELIGHTS: Writer, educator, and Civil War historian Steven E. Woodworth is a professor of history at Texas Christian University. He is the author or editor of more than two dozen books, most of which concern topics relevant to the American Civil War. His books cover specific regiments, individual generals and campaigns, and overall concepts such as religion as it was practiced by Civil War soldiers. In *Davis and Lee at War,* Woodworth analyzes the strategies two of the Civil War South's most prominent military figures, Jefferson Davis and Robert E. Lee. Woodworth explores how Davis's strategy was not aggressive, but employed endurance and persistence in an attempt to win the war simply by not losing it. Davis believed that Lee would exhaust himself and pave the way for a Northern win. Lee, in contrast, was a bold and aggressive strategist, preferring to fight hard and let his victories accumulate. A succession of quick, decisive victories, Lee believed, would convince the North to give up the war. Woodworth notes how both approaches had merit, but that neither was applied consistently, eroding their effectiveness. It was Lee and Davis's professional relationship, Woodworth argues, that prevented a decision on which strategy to use. Without a strong and consistent strategy, the Confederacy eventually lost. A *Publishers Weekly* contributor called Woodworth's book an "engaging, well-written account" of Davis and Lee's approach to war. "Woodworth has produced a lively and readable narrative account of a topic in need of exploration," commented Kenneth H. Williams in *Civil War History,* though Williams also expressed a desire to see more corroborating evidence. Chris Patsilelis, writing in the *New York Times,* concluded: "This well-written and highly illuminating work is not only an incisive study of military command but a penetrating psychological analysis of Davis, Lee" and other prominent personalities of the Confederacy.

A Scythe of Fire: The Civil War Story of the Eighth Georgia Regiment contains a ground-level history of the Eighth Georgia, a regiment that participated in some of the major battles of the Civil War, including Gettysburg, numerous Shenandoah Valley campaigns, and Appomattox. Woodworth derives his history from a number of primary source documents, such as letters, diaries, newspaper accounts, and other written materials. Woodworth notes that few of the soldiers even mention slavery, nor do they seem to have made any personal decision as to its morality. The narrative demonstrates a strong loyalty among the Eighth's soldiers, both to each other and to the regiment itself. Woodworth relates stories of common experiences, daily hardships, and individual victories, as well as harrowing battle stories. He tells of how even the valiant Eighth Georgia eventually dissolved under the stress of combat and starvation. Jay Freeman, writing in *Booklist,* observed that Woodworth's book illustrated "what war is like at ground level as experienced by common foot soldiers." Woodworth "brings an intensely human Face to this unit, detailing the casualties and human suffering the Civil War entailed," remarked a *Publishers Weekly* reviewer. Woodworth's account chronicles the transformation of the soldiers of the Eight Georgia from "enthusiastic, patriotic boys to war-hardened, weary men who pray for an end to the fighting," noted Robert Flatley in *Library Journal.*

With *While God Is Marching On: The Religious World of Civil War Soldiers,* Woodworth addresses a topic that is often overlooked, downplayed, or ignored in Civil War scholarship: the ways in which Civil War soldiers on both sides of the conflict practiced their religion and managed to justify their religious beliefs with the war they were fighting. Again relying on important primary documents such as diaries and letters, Woodworth describes how most Civil War soldiers, Union and Confederate alike, were Christians, both praying to the same God for guidance and protection, both believing in the righteousness of their struggle and that God would ultimately deliver victory to them. Many of the soldiers found victories in battle to be evidence of God's favor, while defeats were seen as testing and purifying the soldiers. Woodworth explores issues related to the soldiers' views on personal salvation and how both Union and Confederate sides were swept by a "Great Revival" that kept religious observance consistently in the minds of the faithful. Regular prayer meetings and religious services also helped soldiers resist the sins and temptations common to military life. Others, Woodworth notes, believed that their Christianity helped prevent even greater carnage, widespread looting, and violation of the enemy. Soldiers of the Civil War, Woodworth concludes, had a thorough understanding of fundamental Christian concepts and doctrine, and these soldiers continued to practice their religion even in the most difficult periods of the war. In looking at the importance of religion during the Civil War itself, Woodworth "contributes something important to the study of American religious history," commented a *Publishers Weekly* critic. Kathleen M. Conley, writing in *Library Journal,* called Woodworth's book a "much-needed addition to Civil War scholarship." The author "has a fine ear for the telling anecdote, and his narration will satisfy Civil War buffs and American religious historians alike," concluded Dan McKanan in the *Journal of Religion.*

Beneath a Northern Sky: A Short History of the Gettysburg Campaign contains a concise history of what may be the Civil War's best-known battle. In the face of unrelenting volumes of academic and popular scholarship on Gettysburg and the Civil War, "This book is designed to synthesize the voluminous body of literature currently available on the topic into a compelling and concise narrative that will satisfy both novice and logician," noted David Dixon in the *Journal of Southern History.* Woodworth assembles modern scholarship from notable researchers such as Earl J. Hess, David G. Martin, and Richard S. Shue. He "does a masterful job of weaving these complex modern interpretations into a seamless overview" of Gettysburg and the war, Dixon remarked. Woodworth also brings to bear earlier classics and other works. The book includes photographs of the Gettysburg battlefield as well as portraits of significant leaders.

Woodworth and coauthor Kenneth J. Winkle offer a detailed visual resource covering important Civil War places and concepts in *Oxford Atlas of the Civil War.* The book includes "narrative sketches, illustrations, and annotated maps of the major events and battles of the Civil War era," noted Willard Carl Klunder in *History: Review of New Books.* The major portion of the book is divided into five chapters, each of which covers events and activities during a single year from 1861 to 1865. The authors present antebellum topics related to such areas as the spread of slavery, industrial expansion, immigration, and territorial growth. They also provide visual references for post-war subjects such as reconstruction, the spread of Jim Crow legislation, homesteading, sharecropping, and presidential elections to 1892. Maps and illustrations depict not just war-related information, but other data relevant to the world surrounding the war, such as the price of farm land, the spread of railroads, population, and cultural aspects of the Civil War years. Woodworth and Winkle also

include a chronology of the war and a glossary of terms and concepts. Klunder concluded that the book "provides the general reader with a handy reference guide to the Civil War era."

In *Nothing but Victory: The Army of the Tennessee, 1861-1865,* Woodworth examines a largely ignored military division of the North that boasted an impressive string of victories over opponents at Shiloh and elsewhere, that played important roles in decisive battles such as Vicksburg and Atlanta, and that served as a proving ground for many of the Civil War's best generals. The Army of the Tennessee, Woodworth notes, has been neglected while greater attention was paid to hard-fighting units such as the Army of the Potomac and the Army of the Cumberland. He delves into the history and accomplishments of the Army of the Tennessee to show that this unit was just as important as its better-known counterparts, that it served with distinction as great as any other Civil War unit, and that its victories were had through skill and finesse rather than blunt force. He describes how the unit was assembled from volunteers from Illinois, Wisconsin, and Iowa, and how its character and abilities were shaped by commanders such as Ulysses S. Grant and William Sherman. Woodworth notes how the pride of excellence extended through lower-ranked field commanders, company officers, and civilian corps commanders. Woodworth's history of the Army of the Tennessee is "arguably the best one-volume history written to date of a Civil War field army," remarked a *Publishers Weekly* reviewer. "Balanced and readable, Woodworth's work is an exemplary army-level unit history," concluded *Booklist* reviewer Gilbert Taylor.

Woodworth told *CA:* "If I write books, even on topics that are not explicitly Christian, it is for the glory of God. I hope someday to be able to do some writing that will be more explicit in relating history and the Christian world-view."

BIOGRAPHICAL AND CRITICAL SOURCES:

PERIODICALS

American Historical Review, October, 1991, Michael B. Ballard, review of *Jefferson Davis and His Generals: The Failure of Confederate Command in the West,* p. 1296; April, 1997, Richard E. Beringer, review of *Davis and Lee at War,* p. 525.

Booklist, November 15, 1996, review of *The American Civil War: A Handbook of Literature and Research,* p. 607; February 15, 2002, Jay Freeman, review of *A Scythe of Fire: The Civil War Story of the Eighth Georgia Regiment,* p. 989; July, 2005, Abbie Landry, review of *Oxford Atlas of the Civil War,* p. 1938; October 1, 2005, Gilbert Taylor, review of *Nothing but Victory: The Army of the Tennessee, 1861-1865,* p. 21.

Books & Culture, July-August, 2003, David Rolfs, "When Thou Goest out to Battle: The Religious World of Civil War Soldiers," review of *While God Is Marching On: The Religious World of Civil War Soldiers,* p. 19.

Choice, January, 2000, L.E. Babits, review of *Chickamauga: A Battlefield Guide with a Section on Chattanooga,* p. 1000.

Chronicle of Higher Education, October 5, 2001, Nina C. Ayoub, review of *While God Is Marching On.*

Civil War History, March, 1997, Kenneth H. Williams, review of *Davis and Lee at War,* p. 75; December, 1997, Lesley Gordon, review of *The American Civil War: A Handbook of Literature and Research,* p. 335.

First Things: A Monthly Journal of Religion and Public Life, December, 2001, George McKenna, review of *While God Is Marching On,* p. 50.

Historian, spring, 2001, Mark A. Weitz, review of *No Band of Brothers: Problems of the Rebel High Command,* p. 659.

History: Review of New Books, summer, 2005, Willard Carl Klunder, review of *Oxford Atlas of the Civil War,* p. 141.

Journal of American History, December, 1996, Craig L. Symonds, review of *Davis and Lee at War,* p. 1022; September, 1997, Edward Hagerman, review of *The American Civil War: A Handbook of Literature and Research,* p. 666.

Journal of Military History, January, 1999, Judith Lee Hallock, review of *Six Armies in Tennessee: The Chickamauga and Chattanooga Campaigns,* p. 190; April, 2000, Sharon S. MacDonald, review of *No Band of Brothers,* p. 538; July, 2000, Richard M. McMurry, review of *Civil War Generals in Defeat,* p. 846; October, 2001, Herman Hattaway, review of *The Art of Command in the Civil War,* p. 1098; July, 2002, Craig L. Symonds, review of *Grant's Lieutenants: From Cairo to Vicksburg,* p. 853.

Journal of Religion, July, 2002, Dan McKanan, review of *While God Is Marching On,* p. 450.

Journal of Southern History, August, 1999, Kenneth W. Noe, review of *Six Armies in Tennessee,* p. 638; August, 2000, Edward J. Hagerty, review of *The Art of Command in the Civil War,* p. 640; November, 2000, Edward Hagerman, review of *Civil War Generals in Defeat,* p. 877; November, 2001, James M. Beeby, review of *The Human Tradition in the Civil War and Reconstruction,* p. 877; February, 2002, Peter S. Carmichael, review of *Cultures in Conflict: The American Civil War,* p. 193; May, 2003, Anne C. Rose, review of *While God Is Marching On,* p. 441; November, 2003, Dan R. Frost, review of *The Loyal, True, and Brave,* p. 918; November, 2004, David Dixon, review of *Beneath a Northern Sky: A Short History of the Gettysburg Campaign,* p. 934.

Library Journal, March 15, 1999, John Carver Edwards, review of *Civil War Generals in Defeat,* p. 90; August, 2001, Kathleen M. Conley, review of *While God Is Marching On,* p. 134; January, 2002, Robert Flatley, review of *A Scythe of Fire,* p. 126.

Mississippi Quarterly, winter, 1992, William Alan Blair, review of *Jefferson Davis and His Generals,* p. 156.

New York Times, January 28, 1996, Chris Patsilelis, review of *Davis and Lee at War.*

Publishers Weekly, September 25, 1995, review of *Davis and Lee at War,* p. 37; July 23, 2001, "October Publication," review of *While God Is Marching On,* p. 74; January 21, 2002, review of *A Scythe of Fire,* p. 75; September 5, 2005, review of *Nothing but Victory,* p. 46.

Reference & User Services Quarterly, summer, 1998, Hope Yelich, review of *The American Civil War,* p. 307.

Reviews in American History, March, 1994, Brooks D. Simpson, review of *Jefferson Davis and His Generals,* p. 73.

School Library Journal, June, 2005, Patricia Ann Owens, review of *Oxford Atlas of the Civil War,* p. 94; October, 2005, review of *Oxford Atlas of the Civil War,* p. S68.

Teaching History: A Journal of Methods, spring, 2004, Michael E. Long, review of *The Loyal, True, and Brave,* p. 53.*

*   *   *

WOODWORTH, Steven Edward
See WOODWORTH, Steven E.

Y

YARBROUGH, Steve 1956-

PERSONAL: Born August 29, 1956, in Indianola, MS; son of John and Earlene Yarbrough; married, 1987; wife's name Ewa; children: Tosha, Magda. *Education:* University of Mississippi. B.A., 1979, M.A., 1981; University of Arkansas-Fayetteville, M.F.A., 1984.

ADDRESSES: Office—California State University, 5241 N. Maple Ave., Fresno, CA 93749-8027. *E-mail*—stevey@csufresno.edu.

CAREER: Author and educator. Virginia Tech, Blacksburg, VA, teacher, 1984-88; California State University, Fresno, CA, professor of English, 1988—. University of Mississippi, Grisham writer-in-residence, 1999-2000.

MEMBER: Associated Writing Programs, Phi Kappa Phi.

AWARDS, HONORS: National Endowment for the Arts fellowship, 1995-96; Pushcart Prize, 1998, for "Preacher"; California Book Award, Mississippi Institute of Arts and Letters award for fiction, and Mississippi Authors' award for fiction, all 2000; PEN/Faulkner Award nomination, 2005, for *Prisoners of War.*

WRITINGS:

SHORT STORIES

Family Men, Louisiana State University Press (Baton Rouge, LA), 1990.

Mississippi History, University of Missouri Press (Columbia, MO), 1994.
Veneer, University of Missouri Press (Columbia, MO), 1998.

NOVELS

The Oxygen Man, MacMurray & Beck (Denver, CO), 1999.
Visible Spirits, Alfred A. Knopf (New York, NY), 2001.
Prisoners of War, Knopf (New York, NY), 2004.
The End of California, Knopf (New York, NY), 2006.

SIDELIGHTS: Steve Yarbrough's southern roots surface in much of his writing, beginning with the first of his short story collections, *Family Men.* The setting of all the stories is Indianola, Mississippi (Yarbrough's birthplace), and sense of place is of utmost importance in the book. In a *Hudson Review* article, Robert Phillips called Yarbrough's characters "ordinary individuals involved in ordinary relationships which nevertheless perplex and overwhelm them. Yet Yarbrough is an upbeat writer," Phillips concluded, and he "tells his tales in simple language, sometimes spiced with a homely metaphor, as when an old woman feels 'weaker than most folks' faith.'"

Among the stories about fathers and sons is "The Trip," in which a boy compares his father to his grandfather and how their experiences have contributed to their feelings about love. In the title story the narrator considers the influence that his alcoholic father and uncle have had on his life. In "Some Glad Morning," a disabled country singer suspects his wife of cheating. She is (with a former convict who is offered a job in Virginia), and is forced to choose between the two men. The singer attempts suicide, then recovers and begins courting his wife again. Greg Johnson noted in *Georgia Review* that this story "effectively dramatizes one of the book's major concerns, which is not whether you can go home again, but whether you should leave in the first place." Following this theme, the high school football coach in "Between Now and Then" turns down a job coaching a college team because it would mean leaving the woman he loves. "The Full Ride" finds the narrator, who is attending the University of Mississippi on a football scholarship, romantically involved with his high school English teacher. "Yarbrough conveys both the essential innocence of this love affair . . . and the way it preempts the young man's experience of college life," wrote Johnson, who continued by saying that each story in the collection "succeeds on its own terms and displays the author's impressive talent for conveying the lasting effects of home, family, and memory upon his characters." A *Publishers Weekly* contributor called the eleven stories "delights—taut, masterfully executed efforts tracing the growth of character." *Shenandoah* writer Heather Ross Miller said they are "crafted with wit and wisdom and a compelling, indestructible energy."

New York Times Book Review contributor Suzanne Berne said the people of Yarbrough's second collection, *Mississippi History,* are like the Mississippi river: "They willfully keep going, but history—whether personal or collective—chokes off any sort of easy passage." Each of the characters has a connection to Indianola, "where racism is as easy to find as catfish and acts of kindness, and where everybody, somehow, is troubled by the past," commented Berne. In "Stay-Gone Days," Emmie uses her wages from cashiering at a Piggly Wiggly to pay off an old boyfriend who is blackmailing her over her part in a crime they committed years earlier. The title story is about two boys who attend Indianola Academy, an all-white school established during desegregation that Yarbrough himself attended as a student. Kenny's best friend is Chuck Sterne, who is Jewish, and together they laugh at their teacher's racist jokes, but Chuck ignorantly tells an anti-Semitic joke, spoiling their relationship. Berne called the characters of this collection "ungainly, unpoetic, earnest people who work at understanding how the past has snagged their lives; they are grateful to be even partly successful." "Yarbrough's style is crisp and economical, but his stories are deceptively complex," wrote Frank Marquardt in *Review of Contemporary Fiction.* "Yarbrough is writing about dignity as his Mississippians confront the unrelenting struggle to subsist and to love in an often hostile and frequently alienating social environment."

The nine stories of *Veneer* include "The Lady Luck," wherein a movie is being shot in a Mississippi town. Other stories are set further from Mississippi—California and Europe, for example—but they all have a connection to the state. A *Publishers Weekly* contributor said Yarbrough "evokes not the sentimentalized or Gothicized South but one that is warm, engaging, and recognizably human." Randall Curb said in *Southern Review* that Yarbrough, "in addition to owning a sure sense of how to sculpt a story and cadence speech, endows his fiction with a striking particularity. He knows exactly what he can truthfully, pertinently give to his characters that—their origins notwithstanding—will make them solid and distinct."

Yarbrough's first novel, *The Oxygen Man,* is set in 1996, with flashbacks to the early 1970s, and revolves around Ned Rose, who checks the oxygen levels at the stock ponds of a catfish farm near Indianola. The fish farmer is Mack Bell, Ned's former high school football teammate, who is now seeking revenge against underpaid black workers he accuses of vandalizing his ponds, and for whom Ned has long done questionable work. Indeed, Ned and his older sister, Daisy, have spent more than twenty years avoiding each other in the house they share, she because of acts he committed years before. A *Publishers Weekly* contributor wrote that "Yarbrough's bleak and yet extremely tender first novel explores the sad origins of their situation and exposes the sordid complications of small-town small-mindedness." *Booklist* reviewer Frank Caso said that "laden with symbolism, this novel mixes well the classic elements of the family cycle of cause and effect, hidden and imminent violence, and the long gestation before restitution." *Time* contributor John Skow called Daisy "a figure strong enough to have been limned by Faulkner." *Library Journal* contributor Judith Ann Akalaitis said Yarbrough's "intimate descriptions of his characters' lives make them real."

Yarbrough's second novel, *Visible Spirits,* is set in 1902 and is based on fact. Tandy Payne, a gambler and failure, returns to his hometown of Loring, Mississippi, where his older brother, Leighton Payne, serves as both mayor and editor of the newspaper. Tandy wants the job held by Loda Jackson, the town's college-educated black postmistress. Loda, however, unknown to the

Paynes, is also their half sister. The daughter of a slave owned by their once powerful father. Tandy attempts to turn opinion against Loda; he is supported by white planters but opposed by Leighton. Loda, who is married to Seaborn, a successful black insurance company owner, resigns in order to prevent further trouble, but President Theodore Roosevelt, under whose administration Loda had been appointed, refuses her resignation. A *Kirkus Reviews* contributor wrote that "Leighton and Seaborn, the story's moral centers, are repeatedly thwarted in their efforts to keep the peace. . . . Few characters here get what they deserve in life, a characteristically southern insight Yarbrough delivers in fluid prose." Caso, writing again in *Booklist,* called the plot of the book "strong on characterization."

Yarbrough's *Prisoners of War* is a "stark, haunting third novel," noted a *Kirkus Reviews* critic. Set in Mississippi during the early 1940s, the novel follows the young Dan Timms as he waits to become old enough to enlist and join the ranks fighting in World War II. Although Dan is still dealing with the recent suicide of his father, who was traumatized as a soldier during World War I, the death seems to fuel his desire to enlist. The young man's goal is juxtaposed by those of his close friends, Marty and L.C. Having just returned from the war, Marty seems irreparably damaged by the experience, which fuels L.C.'s determination to avoid it at all costs. Writing for *Kliatt,* Heidi Hauser Green noted: "All three youth are haunted by their upbringing; all three are changed by the sacrifices that are being demanded by their country. Steve Yarbrough's account of war is grim and gripping." The story is "philosophically troubling, artistically thrilling, and thoroughly impressive," concluded the *Kirkus Reviews* critic.

The End of California is a novel set in modern-day Mississippi, in the same small town that is home to two of Yarbrough's previous novels. In this case, the town of Loring becomes a refuge for former resident Pete Barrington, who left the town as a high school football star bound for a medical school in California, escaping a messy affair with a classmate's mother in the process. Twenty-five years later, another sex scandal forces his return: his successful medical practice in California is left in shambles after an indiscretion with a patient is revealed. Yet Pete's homecoming is complicated by a long-time grudge held by his former classmate, who blames Pete for breaking up his family. Critiquing *The End of California,* a contributor to *Kirkus Reviews* remarked: "Yarbrough fulfills the novelist's chief task, by giving weight and import to human actions." Jyna

Scheeren also approved of the story, commenting in a *Library Journal* review that the "captivating novel of a prodigal son's return is written with wit, charm, and an obvious affection for the many characters that populate Loring." *Booklist* reviewer Brad Hooper noted: "Small-town ambience, with its conventions and crowdedness, its secrets and suspicions, is evoked with careful detail."

BIOGRAPHICAL AND CRITICAL SOURCES:

PERIODICALS

Booklist, September 15, 1998, Jim O'Laughlin, review of *Veneer,* p. 199; April 15, 1999, Frank Caso, review of *The Oxygen Man,* p. 1514; November 15, 1999, Bonnie Smothers and Brad Hooper, review of *The Oxygen Man,* p. 602; May 15, 2001, Frank Caso, review of *Visible Spirits,* p. 1735; April 15, 2006, Brad Hooper, review of *The End of California,* p. 6.

Georgia Review, winter, 1991, Greg Johnson, "Homecomings," review of *Family Men,* p. 778.

Hudson Review, spring, 1991, Robert Phillips, review of *Family Men,* p. 140.

Kirkus Reviews, March 15, 2001, review of *Visible Spirits,* p. 362; November 15, 2003, review of *Prisoners of War,* p. 1340; May 1, 2006, review of *The End of California,* p. 439.

Kliatt, May, 2005, Heidi Hauser Green, review of *Prisoners of War,* p. 32.

Library Journal, September 15, 1990, Marcia Tager, review of *Family Men,* p. 103; May 1, 1999, Judith Ann Akalaitis, review of *The Oxygen Man,* p. 113; May 15, 2006, Jyna Scheeren, review of *The End of California,* p. 94.

Los Angeles Times Book Review, June 19, 2001, Michael Harris, "Book Review; Book's Strength Lies in Its Silences; *Visible Spirits,*" p. E3.

New York Times Book Review, November 6, 1994, Suzanne Berne, "Southern Discomfort," review of *Mississippi History,* p. 19.

Publishers Weekly, August 3, 1990, review of *Family Men,* p. 64; August 15, 1994, review of *Mississippi History,* p. 91; July 27, 1998, review of *Veneer,* p. 54; March 1, 1999, review of *The Oxygen Man,* p. 58.

Review of Contemporary Fiction, spring, 1995, Frank Marquardt, review of *Mississippi History,* p. 173.

Shenandoah, spring, 1992, Heather Ross Miller, "Storytellers," review of *Family Men,* p. 108.

Southern Review, summer, 1999, Randall Curb, "When Is a Story More Than a Story? A Fiction Chronicle," review of *Veneer,* p. 608.

Time, June 7, 1999, John Skow, review of *The Oxygen Man,* p. 82.

Virginia Quarterly Review, spring, 1995, review of *Mississippi History,* p. 58.*

*   *   *

YEP, Laurence 1948-
(Laurence Michael Yep)

PERSONAL: Born June 14, 1948, in San Francisco, CA; son of Thomas Gim (a postal clerk) and Franche (a homemaker) Yep; married Joanne Ryder. *Education:* Attended Marquette University, 1966-68; University of California, Santa Cruz, B.A., 1970; State University of New York at Buffalo, Ph.D., 1975.

ADDRESSES: Home—Sunnyvale, CA. *Agent*—Maureen Walters, Curtis Brown Agency, 10 Astor Place, New York, NY 10003.

CAREER: Writer. Part-time instructor of English at Foothill College, Mountain View, CA, 1975, and San Jose City College, San Jose, CA, 1975-76; University of California, Berkeley, visiting lecturer in Asian-American studies, 1987-89, University of California, Santa Barbara, writer-in-residence, 1990. Writer of software for Spinnaker, including *Alice in Wonderland,* 1985, and *Jungle Book,* 1986.

MEMBER: Science Fiction Writers of America, Society of Children's Book Writers and Illustrators.

AWARDS, HONORS: Newbery Honor Book award, Children's Book Award from American Library Association, International Reading Association award, and Carter A. Woodson Award from National Council of Social Studies, all 1976, Lewis Carroll Shelf Award, 1979, Friend of Children and Literature award, 1984, and Phoenix Award, 1995, all for *Dragonwings; Boston Globe/Horn Book* award, 1977, for *Child of the Owl,* and 1989, for *The Rainbow People;* Jane Addams Award, Women's International League for Peace and Freedom, 1978, for *Child of the Owl;* Silver Medal, Commonwealth Club of California, 1979, for *Sea Glass;*

National Endowment for the Arts fellowship, 1990; Laura Ingalls Wilder Medal, 2005, for contributions to children's literature.

WRITINGS:

FOR CHILDREN AND YOUNG ADULTS

Sweetwater, illustrated by Julia Noonan, Harper (New York, NY), 1973, reprinted, 2004.

Kind Hearts and Gentle Monsters, Harper (New York, NY), 1982.

The Mark Twain Murders, Four Winds Press (New York, NY), 1982.

Dragon of the Lost Sea, Harper (New York, NY), 1982.

Liar, Liar, Morrow (New York, NY), 1983.

The Tom Sawyer Fires, Morrow (New York, NY), 1984.

Dragon Steel, Harper (New York, NY), 1985.

The Curse of the Squirrel, illustrated by Dirk Zimmer, Random House (New York, NY), 1987.

Age of Wonders (play), produced in San Francisco, 1987.

(Reteller) *The Rainbow People* (folk tales), illustrated by David Wiesner, Harper (New York, NY), 1989.

Dragon Cauldron, HarperCollins (New York, NY), 1991.

The Lost Garden, Messner (Englewood Cliffs, NJ), 1991.

The Star Fisher (also see below), Morrow (New York, NY), 1991.

Tongues of Jade (short stories), HarperCollins (New York, NY), 1991.

Dragon War, HarperCollins (New York, NY), 1992.

(Editor) *American Dragons: A Collection of Asian-American Voices,* HarperCollins (New York, NY), 1992.

Butterfly Boy, Farrar, Strauss (New York, NY), 1993.

The Shell Woman and the King, Dial Books (New York, NY), 1993.

The Man Who Tricked a Ghost, Troll Associates (Mahwah, NJ), 1993.

Ghost Fox, Scholastic (New York, NY), 1994.

The Tiger Woman, Troll Associates (Mahwah, NJ), 1994.

The Boy Who Swallowed Snakes, Scholastic (New York, NY), 1994.

The Junior Thunder Lord, Troll Associates (Mahwah, NJ), 1994.

Hiroshima: A Novella, Scholastic (New York, NY), 1995.

Later, Gator, Hyperion (New York, NY), 1995.

Tree of Dreams: Ten Tales from the Garden of Night, illustrated by Isadore Seltzer, BridgeWater Books (Mahwah, NJ), 1995.

City of Dragons, illustrated by Jean and Mou-Sien Tseng, Scholastic (New York, NY), 1995.

Ribbons, Putnam's (New York, NY), 1996.

The Khan's Daughter: A Mongolian Folktale, illustrated by Jean and Mou-Sien Tseng, Scholastic (New York, NY), 1997.

The Dragon Prince: A Chinese Beauty and the Beast Tale, HarperCollins (New York, NY), 1997.

The Imp That Ate My Homework, illustrated by Benrei Huang, HarperCollins (New York, NY), 1998.

The Cook's Family (also see below), Putnam (New York, NY), 1998.

The Amah, Putnam (New York, NY), 1999.

The Journal of Wong Ming-Chung: A Chinese Miner: California, 1852, Scholastic (New York, NY), 2000.

The Magic Paintbrush, illustrated by Suling Wang, HarperCollins (New York, NY), 2000.

Cockroach Cooties, Hyperion (New York, NY), 2000.

Dream Soul (sequel to *The Star Fisher*), HarperCollins (New York, NY), 2000.

Angelfish (sequel to *The Cook's Family*), Putnam's (New York, NY), 2001.

Lady of Chiao Kuo: Warrior of the South, Scholastic (New York, NY), 2001.

Spring Pear: The Last Flower (in "Girls of Many Lands" series), Pleasant Company (Middleton, WI), 2002.

When the Circus Came to Town, illustrated by Suling Wang, HarperCollins (New York, NY), 2002.

Skunk Scout, Hyperion (New York, NY), 2003.

The Earth Dragon Awakes: The San Francisco Earthquake, HarperCollins (New York, NY), 2006.

Auntie Tiger, illustrated by Insu Lee, HarperCollins (New York, NY), 2008.

"GOLDEN MOUNTAIN CHRONICLES" FOR CHILDREN

Dragonwings, Harper (New York, NY), 1975, twenty-fifth anniversary edition, 2000.

Child of the Owl, Harper (New York, NY), 1977.

Sea Glass, Harper (New York, NY), 1979, reprinted, 2002.

The Serpent's Children, Harper (New York, NY), 1984.

Mountain Light (sequel to *The Serpent's Children*), Harper (New York, NY), 1985.

Dragon's Gate, HarperCollins (New York, NY), 1993.

Thief of Hearts, HarperCollins (New York, NY), 1995.

The Traitor, HarperCollins (New York, NY), 2003.

"CHINATOWN MYSTERY" SERIES; FOR CHILDREN

The Case of the Goblin Pearls, HarperCollins (New York, NY), 1997.

The Case of the Lion Dance, HarperCollins (New York, NY), 1998.

The Case of the Firecrackers, HarperCollins (New York, NY), 1999.

"TIGER'S APPRENTICE" SERIES; FOR CHILDREN

The Tiger's Apprentice, HarperCollins (New York, NY), 2003.

Tiger's Blood, HarperCollins (New York, NY), 2005.

Tiger Magic, HarperCollins (New York, NY), 2006.

FOR ADULTS

Seademons, Harper (New York, NY), 1977.

Shadow Lord, Harper (New York, NY), 1985.

Monster Makers, Inc., Arbor House (New York, NY), 1986.

Pay the Chinaman (one-act play; produced in San Francisco, CA, 1987), published in *Between Worlds,* edited by M. Berson, Theatre Communications Group (New York, NY), 1990.

Fairy Bones (one-act play), produced in San Francisco, CA, 1987.

Work represented in anthologies, including *World's Best Science Fiction of 1969,* edited by Donald A. Wollheim and Terry Carr, Ace, 1969; *Quark #2,* edited by Samuel Delaney and Marilyn Hacker, Paperback Library, 1971; *Protostars,* edited by David Gerrold, Ballantine, 1971; *The Demon Children,* Avon, 1973; *Strange Bedfellows: Sex and Science Fiction,* edited by Thomas N. Scortia, Random House, 1973; *Last Dangerous Visions,* edited by Harlan Ellison, Harper, 1975; and *Between Worlds,* Theater Communication Group, 1990. Contributor of short stories to periodicals, including *Worlds of If* and *Galaxy.* Also author of theatrical adaptation of *Dragonwings,* 1991.

ADAPTATIONS: Dragonwings was adapted as a filmstrip with record or cassette, Miller-Brody, 1979; *The Curse of the Squirrel* was adapted for audiocassette,

Random House, 1989. *Sweetwater* was adapted for audiocassette and produced in Braille. The "Tiger's Apprentice Trilogy" was adapted for film by David Magee and produced by Miramax.

SIDELIGHTS: The author of such award-winning novels as *Dragonwings, Child of the Owl, Sea Glass,* and *Dragon Steel,* as well as of illustrated stories for younger readers, novelist and playwright Laurence Yep is noted for penning fiction that brings the history and culture of Chinese Americans into realistic view. In his books, Yep exchanges the exaggerated, stereotyped images of characters such as Dr. Fu Manchu and Charlie Chan for portraits of the real-life Chinese-American men and women who have enriched North America with both their labor and their willingness to share their cultural heritage. As essayist Joe Stines noted in the *Dictionary of Literary Biography,* "Yep provides the reader with a new way of viewing Chinese-Americans, not as yellow men [and women] living in white society but as ordinary as well as extraordinary people." Best known for his stories featuring children from multicultural backgrounds, Yep claims that writing has aided him in his own search for cultural identity. As he once explained, "In a sense I have no one culture to call my own since I exist peripherally in several. However, in my writing I can create my own."

Born in San Francisco, California, in 1948, Yep was raised in an African-American neighborhood and attended a bilingual school in the city's Chinatown. Despite being of Chinese descent, he fulfilled diverse cultural roles during his childhood. Within his family, he learned both about Chinese culture and about the American society that was now his home. Describing his family's approach to living in a new land, Yep once commented in *Horn Book* that "my mother's family's solution was to juggle elements of both cultures. Though they stayed Chinese in some central core, they also developed a curiosity and open-mindedness about the larger white culture around them." Outside the family home was another story. As Yep once explained in *Literature for Today's Young Adults:* "I was the all-purpose Asian. When [my friends and I] played war, I was the Japanese who got killed; then, when the Korean war came along, I was a North Korean Communist." The fact that Yep did not speak Chinese made it difficult for him to feel totally at home in Chinatown, and he felt equally at sea when he began attending a predominantly white high school.

It was in high school that Yep discovered science fiction, and he began writing stories in the genre and submitting them to magazines. A published sci-fi author by the time he was eighteen years old, Yep would explore the genre further in his later novels. For now, though, it was off to college, first at Marquette University, which Yep attended from 1966 to 1968 and where he became totally immersed in "white" culture. Leaving Marquette, Yep completed his bachelor's degree at the University of California at Santa Cruz in 1970, and went on to earn a Ph.D. at the State University of New York at Buffalo in 1975.

In the midst of his academic studies in New York, Yep took the advice of a friend regarding his writing, and that advice would change his life. "A friend of mine who had gone to work at Harper's asked me to think about writing a science-fiction book for children," Yep recalled to WNYC radio interviewer Barbara Rollock, "and *Sweetwater* was the result."

Sweetwater, published in 1973 while its author was still a student at SUNY Buffalo, focuses on Tyree, a young man who belongs to a group of transplanted colonists called Argans. While among the first groups to settle the planet Harmony, the Argans are now a racial minority within the planet's growing population, and Tyree and his fellow Silkies—half earth-dweller, half amphibian—must scavenge in order to survive. Their struggle for survival in a frequently hostile environment forms the themes of family bonds, individual freedom, cultural traditions, and racism featured in the novel. *Sweetwater* received positive reviews from critics, many of whom concurred with *Vector 78* contributor Brian Stableford that Yep's debut "has one powerful thing going for it, and that is the fact that its writing is, in every sense of the word, beautiful." Praising *Sweetwater* for its concentration upon planetary ecology as well as its discussion of moral choices, Francis J. Molson added in *Twentieth-Century Science-Fiction Writers* that "thematic complexity and verbal richness . . . make *Sweetwater* superior."

In Yep's second novel, *Dragonwings,* he deals directly with his Chinese-American heritage. In preparation for writing the book, he spent six years researching Chinese-American history, uncovering much factual information but little that reflected how immigrant families and individuals actually *felt* upon being confronted by the alien culture of America. His study of immigrant culture included the bachelor societies that provided a social interchange for Chinese men working to provide for families back in China and planning one day to return to Asia. In the course of Yep's research, he discovered two brief newspaper articles from the year 1909, detailing the efforts of a Chinese American bachelor named Fung Joe Guey to build and fly a flying machine. Seeing in Guey's story the basis of a novel, Yep filled in the blanks with his research, creating a rich human story around the newspaper reports.

Published in 1975 and reissued in a twenty-fifth anniversary edition in 2000, *Dragonwings* tells the story of eight-year-old Moon Shadow, a young boy who leaves his mother in China's Middle Kingdom to join his father in the bachelor society of turn-of-the-twentieth-century San Francisco. Moon Shadow's father, Windrider, a kite builder, came to the United States to earn money for his family, but also to explore unknown frontiers. Together father and son fulfill Windrider's dream of flying his own plane. In recounting the adventures and discoveries of father and son, Yep reveals a slice of Chinese-American history. "The story is narrated with humor and detail," Stines summarized in the *Dictionary of Literary Biography,* "blending Chinese folklore, myths, and legends with historical facts, such as the great San Francisco earthquake, the Chinese bachelor community of Chinatown, and the daring biplane flight of Fung Joe Guey." Critics applauded the complexity of Yep's characters and his sensitive portrayal of the prejudice they faced in the United States, Ruth H. Pelmas writing in the *New York Times Book Review* that, "as an exquisitely written poem of praise to the courage and industry of the Chinese-American people, [*Dragonwings*] is a triumph."

Dragonwings is the first volume in the "Gold Mountain Chronicles," a loose-knit novel series following seven generations of the Yep family across one-and-a-half centuries of history that also includes *The Serpent's Children, Mountain Light, Child of the Owl, Sea Glass, Dragon's Gate, Thief of Hearts,* and *The Traitor.* As Claire Rosser noted in *Kliatt,* although each novel can be enjoyed independently, "considering them . . . as a family chronicle that parallels the experiences of many Chinese immigrants to the West Coast adds a great dimension to Yep's work." In his acceptance speech for the 2005 Laura Ingalls Wilder Medal, Yep noted of the series that "America changed the first Chinese who came here as much as they changed their new country; and America has continued transforming their descendants in ways that I'm still trying to comprehend. And along the way, I have encountered true stories buried by time that were real treasures. A cook in a Montana stagecoach station may turn out to be a circus juggler.

A Chinese American grocer may once have been a professional basketball player."

The Serpent's Children, is set in nineteenth-century China amid the Taiping Rebellion. In its pages readers meet Cassia, a young girl who, along with her family, joins a revolutionary brotherhood working to eliminate the corruption brought by the ruling Manchu dynasty and the wealthy landowners in their now-impoverished Kwangtung Province. *Mountain Light* follows Cassia and her father as they return from a trip through China's Middle Kingdom, joined by another traveler, a young man named Squeaky Lau. On the eventful trip, taken on behalf of the revolution, the clownish Squeaky finds that he possesses his own inner strength and is able to bring out good in others. Although he and Cassia fall in love, Squeaky joins the mass migration to the western United States, "land of the Golden Mountain," where he faces the chaos brought about by the California gold rush. *Dragon's Gate* continues the story of the revolutionary family as Otter, Cassia's fourteen-year-old adopted son, also travels to America and works on the Transcontinental Railroad as part of a Chinese work crew carving a tunnel through the Sierra Nevadas during the 1860s. Readers experience firsthand this often-overlooked period in history, as Otter confronts "racial prejudice, cold, starvation, the foreman's whip, and the dangers of frostbite and avalanche while trying to reconcile his ideals and dreams with harsh reality," according to Margaret A. Chang in her appraisal of *Dragon's Gate* for *School Library Journal.* In *Booklist* Ilene Cooper praised *Mountain Light* for its "rich blend of action, moral lessons, and complex characterizations."

A winner of the *Boston Globe-Horn Book* Award, *Child of the Owl* is, like *Dragonwings,* set in San Francisco's Chinatown, but this time the year is 1960, as a young girl raised by a gambling father and then a suburban uncle is confused by her dual American and Chinese heritage. Having been exposed only to American ways and therefore having no means by which to identify with her Chinese background, Casey finds new options for living opened to her when she is sent to live with her grandmother, Paw-Paw, in Chinatown. Paw-Paw tells Casey a lengthy legend about an owl which symbolizes family unity and tradition and provides the young girl a new way of communicating her feelings.

Continuing the "Golden Mountain Chronicles," *Sea Glass* focuses on Craig Chin, a boy whose search for acceptance by both whites and Chinese Americans ends in rejection. Moving from his home in San Francisco's Chinatown to a small town, Craig is dubbed "Buddha Man" by his Anglo schoolmates while also being disparaged by a Chinese neighbor for behaving like "the white demons" he attends school with. Pressures from Craig's sports-minded father to try out for the school team do little to help him assimilate into school culture, but finally an uncle provides the teen with the key to self-acceptance.

In *The Traitor* Yep brings readers to 1885 and the Wyoming Territory, where he introduces Chinese-American Joseph Young—the son of Otter Young of *Dragon's Gate*—and Michael Purdy, a Caucasian who is looked down on in his rustic coal-mining town because he is illegitimate. Because of their outcast status, the boys become friends, and when racial tensions against Chinese mill workers mount and erupt in the event known as the Rock Springs Massacre, the Purdy family helps Joe and his parents escape from the angry mob. While noting that the novel's length may intimidate some readers, Julie Cummins wrote in *Booklist* that "readers will become involved through the first-person voices that capture each boy's feelings of being an outsider and a traitor." Like each volume in the series, *The Traitor* includes an afterword that delves into the historical epoch framing Yep's story, a fact that drew additional praise from a *Kirkus Reviews* writer, who dubbed *The Traitor* "essential reading for all students of America's complex history and culture."

Also with roots in Yep's personal history, *The Star Fisher* and sequel *Dream Soul* are based on the author's parents' life. *The Star Fisher* finds fifteen-year-old Joan Chen moving from the Midwest to a small Southern town in the late 1920s. As the first and only Chinese-American family to arrive in Clarksburg, West Virginia, Joan finds that she must take the first step in building bridges of understanding in her new community, and gradually helps her more traditional parents find a way to assimilate into a community that contains both friends and others whose ignorance makes them bigoted. In *Dream Soul* Joan is now fifteen. The illness of her strict father causes her to rethink the value of her Chinese heritage, as well as its legends, and when her responsibility for the family increases, Joan is able to deal with a family crisis with wisdom and maturity. "Joan's story will appeal to any reader who has ever felt excluded," noted *School Library Journal* contributor Carla Kozak in a review of *The Star Fisher,* the critic adding that the "resilience and humor" of Yep's mother and her family "shine through." Finding the novel an equally praisewor-

thy effort, Alice Phoebe Naylor concluded in her *New York Times Book Review* appraisal that *The Star Fisher* "is a thought-provoking, engaging novel about a fundamental human drama—immigration and cultural isolation." Reviewing *Dream Soul*, *Horn Book* contributor Mary M. Burns wrote that Yep's novel presents an "appealing family story" that mixes "humor with charm in a manner reminiscent of Laura Ingalls Wilder."

Apart from his family's history, Yep also returns readers to the Chinese-American past in books such as *Hiroshima: A Novella, When the Circus Came to Town,* and *The Earth Dragon Awakes: The San Francisco Earthquake of 1906,* as well as installments in several historical fiction series. In *Hiroshima* Yep paints a portrait of the events surrounding the U.S. government's decision to drop an atomic bomb on Hiroshima, Japan, on August 6, 1945, thereby accelerating the end of World War II. Focusing on one of the "Hiroshima Maidens"—girls and women who survived the bombing and who were eventually sent to the United States for reconstructive surgery—Yep describes both the actual bombing and its tragic and devastating long-term aftermath. Praising Yep for composing his factual story using "unadorned prose suiting its somber subject matter," *Washington Post Book World* contributor Elizabeth Hand wrote that Hiroshima "should be required reading in every classroom in [the United States] and beyond."

Through the experiences of nine-year-old Chin and eight-year-old Henry Travis on April 7, 1906, the day their San Francisco community was turned to rubble, in *The Earth Dragon Awakes* Yep shares with readers "a timely reminder of a historical disaster that turned over 2000 acres of city into a wasteland," as a *Kirkus Reviews* contributor explained. Henry is the son of an affluent banker, while Chin, son of the Travis's houseboy, lives with his immigrant family in a lower-class tenement; despite the differences in their family's affluence, the earthquake affected both their lives in dramatic ways. Calling the author's research into the period "exhaustive," Catherine Threadgill also noted in her *School Library Journal* review that because he "peppers the story with interesting true-to-life anecdotes," the novel "should appeal to reluctant readers." While the *Kirkus Reviews* critic praised *The Earth Dragon Awakes* as "solid historical fiction," in *Booklist* Linda Perkins benefits from the boys' dual narration because Yep's text "provides a 'you are there' sense of immediacy" that will attract fans of "action-packed survival stories."

Also based on an actual event—this time taking place at the turn of the twentieth century—*When the Circus*

Came to Town introduces ten-year-old Ursula, an imaginative girl who lives with her family at a Montana stagecoach station. Fortunate to survive a smallpox epidemic, Ursula is left with a face so disfigured that she fears being seen by others, and refuses to leave her room and help her father in the kitchen. When a Chinese cook named Ah Sam is hired to replace the girl, Ursula befriends the man, and the two realize that they share a love for the circus. When a racist traveler breaks Ah Sam's spirit, Ursula braves the stares of the public to reunite him with his relatives. Praising the story as a "moving parable" about the willingness of people to help others through bad times, a *Kirkus Reviews* writer added that Yep successfully uses "believable characterizations to discuss deceptively complex emotions and issues," while Kay Weisman deemed the story "direct, humorous, and poignant" in her *Booklist* review.

In addition to realistic fiction, Yep has also written fantasies and mysteries, as well as a number of novels featuring modern-day children in typical modern-day predicaments. His mystery novels *The Mark Twain Murders* and *The Tom Sawyer Fires* feature nineteenth-century writer Mark Twain as a young reporter in San Francisco who turns sleuth in response to a series of odd occurrences. Mystery again figures in *The Case of the Goblin Pearls,* one of a series of books—"The Chinatown Mysteries"—featuring a group of pre-teens who solve mysteries within their Chinese-American communities while also learning about their varied cultural heritage. In *The Case of the Goblin Pearls,* Lily Lew and her flamboyant actress aunt go in search of a set of priceless pearls stolen from a local sweatshop owner by a masked robber. Praising the novel's "snappy dialogue, realistic characterizations and a plot with lots of action," a *Publishers Weekly* contributor added that Yep's spunky protagonist gains a "growing realization of the complexities of her Chinese heritage." Yep has also reached out to younger audiences in books like *Cockroach Cooties, Skunk Scout* and *Later, Gator,* all which focus on a young boy named Teddy. In *Later Gator* the boy's prank gift of a creepy-looking alligator backfires when he realizes that his younger brother actually takes a shine to his new pet, unaware that it will not live long in captivity, while *Skunk Scout* finds him joining his brother on a camping trip that challenges both the resources and the resilience of the likeable young boys.

The first of several fantasy series penned by the author, Yep's volume "Dragon" novel series was praised by *St. James Guide to Fantasy Writers* essayist Gary Westfahl as "a noteworthy achievement" in the realm of fantasy literature due to the use of Chinese, rather than European, legend as its basis. The series, which begins with *Dragon of the Lost Sea,* introduces readers to Shimmer, a dragon princess who has been exiled from the dragon kingdom of Sambar as punishment for stealing a pearl symbolic of dragon clan leadership. Now disguised as a beggar woman, Shimmer sets out with a young human orphan named Thorn and a monkey wizard called Master of Seventy-two Transformations. Together they attempt to restore the Inland Sea, the dragon clan's ancestral home, which was destroyed when the witch Civet stole the sea's water. In *Dragon Steel,* Shimmer and Thorn are joined by several more companions, including a girl named Indigo, in their attempt to steal a magic cauldron that will allow them to restore the Inland Sea's waters to their proper location. Meanwhile, Shimmer attempts to settle her own accounts to rights when she petitions her uncle, the High King of Sambar, for re-admittance to the kingdom, offering Civet as restitution for Shimmer's own thievery.

The third installment of the "Dragon" series finds Shimmer once again in search of a way to restore the Inland Sea. In *Dragon Cauldron* the magic cauldron has been recovered, but it is cracked, and the only ones able to repair such damage are the Snail Woman and the Smith. Despite numerous obstacles, including an evil magician and a troop of soldiers determined to stop the group, Shimmer and company repair the cauldron, only to lose it again during a flood. It is only in *Dragon War,* the last volume in the series, that the group recovers the cauldron from the hands of the evil Boneless King, who had used it to destroy the dragon clan. Escaping the king's clutches, the group rallies an army of Shimmer's dragon allies and, with the use of shape-changing courtesy of the monkey wizard, defeats the Boneless King and his minions, restoring the Inland Sea in the process.

Reviewers applauded Yep's characters and their comical bantering, his accounts of high adventure, and the ability of each novel in the "Dragon" series to stand independently and be understood by readers unfamiliar with the rest of the saga. Calling the four-volume work "an allegory of perseverance and loyalty," *Voice of Youth Advocates* reviewer Frank Perry added that "the variety of characters, continuity of plot, and incongruence of dragons [disguised] as humans hold fast the reader's attention." In the *Washington Post Book World,* Jane Yolen noted that Yep's "adventures are full of imagination and there is a kind of breezy zestiness . . . that will appeal to younger young adults." In his *Dic-*

tionary of Literary Biography essay, Stines concluded that, "thematically," the "Dragon" series "is characteristic of Yep's writing in its exploration of the ideas of identity, good versus evil, friendship, and loyalty."

The first volume in a trilogy for middle-grade readers that includes *Tiger's Blood* and *Tiger Magic*, *The Tiger's Apprentice* introduces a network of ancient Chinese characters that, inspired by the Chinese zodiac and ancient Chinese legends, secretly exist on Earth. Introduced to this network by his elderly grandmother, Mistress Lee, whose cluttered antique store holds the secrets of the Lore, eighth-grader Tom Lee finds his destiny is woven into this network when he learns that his grandmother is a Guardian. After Mistress Lee is killed by a creature who robs her home of a beautiful artifact, Tom takes her place: he agrees to help retrieve the artifact, which turns out to be an egg. Not just any egg, however: this special egg is that of the phoenix, a magical bird that has will only hatch into a world that has achieved total peace. In his task Tom accepts the guidance of a shapeshifting tiger known as Mr. Hu, another guardian of the egg. Other new friends, who include the dragon Mistral, a golden rat, and a flying monkey, join Tom in his battle against Vatten and his evil Clan of Nine, who hopes, by possessing the egg, to harness its power for apocalyptic purposes. Calling the fantasy novel "enticing," *Booklist* contributor Linda Perkins added that by weaving "elements of Chinese mythology and culture" into his story, Yep imbues his tale with "a distinctively Asian perspective." Enhanced by "nuggets of wisdom. . . . and often elegant prose," *The Tiger's Apprentice* instills in readers "a sense of wonder," according to a *Publishers Weekly* contributor.

The "Tiger's Apprentice" series continues with *Tiger's Blood,* which finds the two guardians of the egg leaving San Francisco for the subterranean safety of the Dragon Kingdom. Recognizing Mr. Hu's failing health, Tom becomes a diligent apprentice, and sets about learning the lore of dragons. When the egg is stolen, Tom fears that Mistral may have been involved, until the dragon proves her loyalty by helping Tom defend his friends from the Clan of Nine. The saga culminates in *Tiger Magic,* as Tom accepts his destiny as both a tiger and "parent" to the recently hatched phoenix. Now he must confront Vatten and his minions. Although he could draw power from the phoenix as well, Tom realizes that such power could ultimately corrupt his good purposes. Noting that *Tiger's Blood* may overwhelm some readers not already familiar with the series, in *School Library Journal* Ginny Collier wrote that "intrigue abounds" in

the second novel of the trilogy, "and the descriptions of the dragons' palace will have readers wishing they could visit it themselves." While a *Kirkus Reviews* writer noted that *Tiger's Blood* lacks the action of *The Tiger's Apprentice,* another reviewer for the same periodical wrote that, with its "factual" battle scenes and philosophical ponderings, *Tiger Magic* is "a nice choice for sensitive readers." In *Booklist* Jennifer Mattson wrote that Yep's "epic dust-ups will thrill action-addicted" fantasy fans.

In addition to full-length fiction, Yep has also compiled several volumes of short stories based on folktales and legends of China. *The Rainbow People* includes twenty stories adapted from the recollections of Chinese immigrants living in Oakland, California's Chinatown that were recorded by a U.S. government-sponsored program during the 1930s. Many of the stories, which Yep divides into sections according to their theme, have their origins in southern China, the birthplace of many of Oakland's immigrant Chinese. Another story collection, *Tongues of Jade,* includes both stories and background information that puts each tale, whether it be a ghost story or a love story, into sociological and historical perspective. Including such titles as "The Little Emperor" and "The Rat in the Wall," Yep's retellings "are liberally dosed with magic, and all praise the qualities . . . necessary to succeed in a foreign and often hostile land," according to a *Publishers Weekly* contributor.

Although Yep worked as a teacher early in his career, with the success of *Dragonwings* he was able to leave academia and pursue his writing full time. Although Yep devotes most of his time to his fiction, he has returned to the college environment on occasion. While at the University of California, he noted the lack of anthologies featuring writing appropriate to the multicultural course he was teaching, and in 1993 he published his own: *American Dragons: Twenty-five Asian American Voices.* Including stories, essays, and verse, the anthology features works by such well-known authors as Maxine Hong Kingston and William F. Wu that are grouped according to themes such as the search for identity, the Japanese experience during World War II, and relationships with Asian-born parents and grandparents. In the book Yep focuses in particular on works relevant to young people attempting to live between two cultures.

While occasionally writing for adult readers, Yep remains an avid proponent of the power of children's literature. "I enjoy writing for children because you can get back to old-fashioned storytelling rather than inflating a text with material about existential crises and whatever are the latest aesthetic and philosophical fads," he once noted in *Twentieth-Century Children's Writers.* "Stories have to be told in concrete, vivid terms and relationships between characters are basic human bonds and therefore more universal." Calling Yep a "bridge builder," Karen Ferris Morgan concluded in her essay for *Twentieth-Century Young-Adult Writers* that, through his novels and short stories, he enables young readers to "look . . . through a window to greater understandings of the worlds of differences and similarities that co-exist in life. Vivid images, complex characters, and well-plotted action" continue to be trademarks of Yep's unique fiction.

BIOGRAPHICAL AND CRITICAL SOURCES:

BOOKS

Children's Literature Review, Thomson Gale (Detroit, MI), Volume 3, 1978, Volume 17, 1989.

Contemporary Literary Criticism, Volume 35, Thomson Gale (Detroit, MI), 1985.

Dictionary of Literary Biography, Volume 52: *American Writers for Children since 1960: Fiction,* Thomson Gale (Detroit, MI), 1986.

Huck, Charlotte S., *Children's Literature in the Elementary School,* 3rd edition, Holt (New York, NY), 1979.

Johnson-Feelings, Dianne, *Presenting Laurence Yep,* Twayne (New York, NY), 1995.

Nilsen, Alleen Pace, and Kenneth L. Donelson, editors, *Literature for Today's Young Adults,* 2nd edition, Scott, Foresman, 1985.

Norton, Donna E., *Through the Eyes of a Child: An Introduction to Children's Literature,* 2nd edition, Merrill, 1987.

St. James Guide to Fantasy Writers, St. James Press (Detroit, MI), 1996, pp. 637-638.

Twentieth-Century Children's Writers, 5th edition, St. James Press (Detroit, MI), 1999.

Twentieth-Century Science-Fiction Writers, 3rd edition, St. James Press (Detroit, MI), 1992, pp. 895-896.

Twentieth-Century Young-Adult Writers, 2nd edition, St. James Press (Detroit, MI), 1999, pp. 724-725.

Yep, Laurence, *Dragonwings,* Harper (New York, NY), 1975.

PERIODICALS

Booklist, September 15, 1985, Ilene Cooper, review of *Mountain Light,* p. 141; April 15, 1992, Candace Smith, review of *Dragon War,* p. 1524; July, 1995, Hazel Rochman, review of *Thief of Hearts,* p. 1880; January 1, 1997, Hazel Rochman, review of *The Case of the Goblin Pearls,* pp. 846-847; February 1, 1997, Karen Morgan, review of *The Khan's Daughter,* p. 940; July, 1997, Karen Morgan, review of *The Dragon Prince: A Chinese Beauty and the Beast Tale,* p. 1817; October 15, 1998, Stephanie Zvirin, review of *The Case of the Lion Dance,* p. 423; May 1, 2000, Stephanie Zvirin, review of *The Case of the Firecrackers,* p. 1606, and Catherine Andronik, review of *Cockroach Cooties,* p. 1671; December 1, 2000, Linda Perkins, review of *Dream Soul,* p. 714; May 15, 2001, Ilene Cooper, review of *Angelfish,* p. 1754; November 15, 2001, Jean Franklin, review of *Lady of Ch'iau Kuo: Warrior of the South,* p. 575; December 15, 2001, Kay Weisman, review of *When the Circus Came to Town,* p. 732; October 15, 2002, Ed Sullivan, review of *Big City Cool: Short Stories about Urban Youth,* p. 401; December 15, 2002, Shelle Rosenfeld, review of *Spring Pear: The Last Flower,* p. 761; January 1, 2003, review of *The Traitor,* p. 894; May 15, 2003, review of *The Traitor: Golden Mountain Chronicles 1885,* p. 1665; June 1, 2003, review of *Skunk Scout,* p. 1779; July, 2003, Linda Perkins, review of *The Tiger's Apprentice,* p. 1893; January 1, 2005, Jennifer Mattson, review of *Tiger's Blood,* p. 865; March 1, 2006, Linda Perkins, review of *The Earth Dragon Awakes: The San Francisco Earthquake of 1906,* p. 94; December 15, 2006, Jennifer Mattson, review of *Tiger Magic,* p. 48.

Bulletin of the Center for Children's Books, April, 1989, p. 211; March, 1991, p. 182; July-August, 1991, p. 279; June, 1995, p. 365; September, 1995, p. 34; December, 2000, review of *Dream Soul,* p. 168; March, 2003, review of *The Traitor,* p. 295; June, 2006, Elizabeth Bush, review of *The Earth Dragon Awakes,* p. 477.

Christian Science Monitor, November 5, 1975, review of *Dragonwings,* p. B7; May 4, 1977, p. 29; October 15, 1979, review of *Sea Glass,* p. B11.

English Journal, March, 1982, pp. 81-82.

Horn Book, April, 1978; May-June, 1989, "The Green Chord," pp. 318-322; March-April, 1994, p. 208; July-August, 1995, Maria B. Salvadore, review of *Later, Gator,* p. 463; March-April, 1997, Maeve Visser Knoth, review of *The Khan's Daughter,* pp. 208-209; September-October, 1997, pp. 594-595; January, 2001, review of *Dream Soul,* p. 99; March-April, 2003, Margaret A. Bush, review of *The Traitor,* p. 219; July-August, 2005, Laurence Yep, "Wilder Medal Acceptance Speech," p. 429;

July-August, 2006, Margaret A. Bush, review of *The Earth Dragon Awakes,* p. 454.

Interracial Books for Children Bulletin, Volume 7, numbers 2-3, 1976, review of *Dragonwings;* Volume 11, number 6, 1980, p. 16.

Junior Bookshelf, February, 1977, p. 48.

Kirkus Reviews, June 15, 1993, p. 794; April 15, 1995, p. 564; May 1, 1995, p. 642; January 15, 1997, p. 148; December 1, 2001, review of *When the Circus Came to Town,* p. 1692; January 1, 2003, review of *The Traitor,* p. 67; March 1, 2003, review of *The Tiger's Apprentice,* p. 402; June 1, 2003, review of *Skunk Scout,* p. 813; December 15, 2004, review of *Tiger's Blood,* p. 1211; March 1, 2006, review of *The Earth Dragon Awakes,* p. 243; October 1, 2006, review of *Tiger Magic,* p. 1027.

Kliatt, March, 2003, Claire Rosser, review of *The Traitor,* p. 18.

Lion and the Unicorn, Volume 5, 1981, pp. 4-18.

Locus, March, 1992, review of *American Dragons,* p. 64.

New York Times Book Review, November 16, 1975, Ruth H. Pelmas, review of *Dragonwings;* May 22, 1977; January 20, 1980, p. 30; May 23, 1982, p. 37; November 6, 1983, p. 44; July 23, 1989, p. 29; October 13, 1991, Alice Phoebe Naylor, review of *The Star Fisher,* p. 31.

Publishers Weekly, September 20, 1991, review of *Tongues of Jade,* p. 135; May 18, 1992, review of *American Dragons,* p. 71; March 4, 1996, review of *Ribbons,* pp. 66-67; December 16, 1996, review of *The Case of the Goblin Pearls,* pp. 59-60; August 25, 1997, review of *The Dragon Prince,* p. 71; March 13, 2000, review of *The Magic Paintbrush,* p. 85; September 25, 2000, Elizabeth Devereaux, review of *Dream Soul,* p. 74; December 24, 2001, review of *When the Circus Came to Town,* p. 64; August 26, 2002, review of *Spring Pearl,* p. 69; April 14, 2003, review of *The Tiger's Apprentice,* p. 71; June 30, 2003, review of *Skunk Scout,* p. 81.

Reading Teacher, January, 1977, pp. 359-363.

School Library Journal, May, 1991, Carla Kozak, review of *The Star Fisher,* p. 113; June, 1991, Margaret A. Chang, review of *Dragon Cauldron,* p. 114; December, 1991, John Philbrook, review of *Tongues of Jade,* p. 132; June, 1992, Margaret A. Chang, review of *Dragon War,* p. 144; January, 1994, Joann Balingit, review of *The Rainbow People,* p. 73, and Margaret Chang, review of

Dragon's Gate, p. 135; March, 1997, Carol A. Edwards, review of *The Case of the Goblin Pearls,* pp. 194-195; October, 1997, Margaret Chang, review of *The Dragon Prince,* p. 125; May, 2000, Elizabeth Maggio, review of *Cockroach Cooties,* p. 159; October, 2000, Cindy Darling Codell, review of *Dream Soul,* p. 175; June, 2001, Marlyn K. Roberts, review of *Angelfish,* p. 160; December, 2001, review of *Lady of Ch'iao Kuo,* p. 149; October, 2002, Be Astengo, review of *Spring Pearl,* p. 178; March, 2003, Barbara Scotto, review of *The Traitor,* p. 244; April, 2003, Eva Mitnick, review of *The Tiger's Apprentice,* p. 170; August, 2003, Linda B. Zeilstra, review of *Skunk Scout,* p. 169; February, 2005, Ginny Collier, review of *Tiger's Blood,* p. 142; May, 2006, Jennifer Ralston, review of *Cockroach Cooties,* p. 50, and Catherine Threadgill, review of *The Earth Dragon Awakes,* p. 94.

Vector 78, November-December, 1976, Brian Stableford, review of *Sweetwater,* p. 30.

Voice of Youth Advocates, August, 1985, Frank Perry, review of *Dragon Steel,* p. 195; December, 1985, p. 323; June, 1991, review of *Dragon Cauldron,* p. 116; December, 1991, p. 320; February, 1996, p. 380; December, 1998, review of *The Case of the Lion Dance,* p. 362; October, 2003, review of *The Traitor,* p. 320; June, 2004, Cynthia Grady, review of *The Tiger's Apprentice,* p. 148; April, 2005, Diane Emge, review of *Tiger's Blood,* p. 65.

Washington Post Book World, May 1, 1977, pp. E1, E8; January 9, 1983, pp. 11, 13; November 6, 1983, pp. 17, 22; May 12, 1985, Jane Yolen, "Fantasy Novels: Of Wizards, Whales, and Worlds Beyond," pp. 13-14; November 10, 1985, p. 20; May 7, 1995, Elizabeth Hand, review of *Hiroshima: A Novella,* p. 14.

Wilson Library Bulletin, June, 1995, p. 120.

OTHER

Yep, Laurence, taped interview with Barbara Rollock, on *The World of Children's Literature,* WNYC Radio, November 1, 1976.*

*   *   *

YEP, Laurence Michael
    See YEP, Laurence

Z

ZIGMAN, Laura 1962-

PERSONAL: Born August 11, 1962, in Boston, MA; daughter of Bernard and Bernice Zigman; married; children: a son. *Education:* University of Massachusetts at Amherst, B.A., 1985; Harvard University, certificate in publishing, 1985.

ADDRESSES: Home and office—Boston, MA. *Agent*—Bill Clegg, Burnes & Clegg, Inc., 1133 Broadway, Suite 1020, New York, NY 10010. *E-mail*—lzigman@aol.com.

CAREER: Writer. Vintage Books, New York, NY, senior publicist, 1986-89; Atlantic Monthly Press, New York, NY, marketing manager, 1989-91; Random House, Inc., New York, NY, publicity director for Turtle Bay Books, 1991-93; Alfred A. Knopf, Inc., New York, NY, promotions manager, 1993-95; writer, 1995—; project manager, Smithsonian Institution, 1996; consultant for Share Our Strength.

WRITINGS:

Animal Husbandry (novel), Dial (New York, NY), 1998.
Dating Big Bird (novel), Dial (New York, NY), 2000.
Her (novel), Knopf (New York, NY), 2002.
Piece of Work (novel), Warner Books (New York, NY), 2006.

Contributor to periodicals, including *USA Weekend, Washington Post, Marie Claire,* and *New York Times.*

ADAPTATIONS: Animal Husbandry was adapted to film as *Someone like You,* 2001; *Piece of Work* has been optioned for film by Playtone Pictures.

SIDELIGHTS: Laura Zigman is an acclaimed novelist whose works chronicle the more amusing aspects of male-female relationships. In 1998 she published her first book, *Animal Husbandry,* which concerns a doomed romance between a television producer and her boss, who ends the relationship as it grows increasingly intimate and domestic. The heroine thereupon formulates the notion that men, like bulls, inevitably desire new mates. Lisa Schwarzbaum, writing in *Entertainment Weekly,* deemed *Animal Husbandry* a "light first novel." Jill Smolowe, however, wrote in *Time* that Zigman's literary debut constitutes "a naughty vivisection of male dating rituals," while a *Publishers Weekly* reviewer described the novel as "a tenaciously observed saga."

Zigman followed *Animal Husbandry* with *Dating Big Bird,* the story of a marketing director who longs for parenthood though her boyfriend, a divorced writer recovering from both alcoholism and the death of his own child, refuses to engage in sexual relations. Faced with a mate unwilling to impregnate her, the heroine eventually considers artificial insemination from a host of individuals, including a Muppet character from public television. *Library Journal* reviewer Jo Manning contended that the finale of the novel is "unbelievable," but she nonetheless described *Dating Big Bird* as "a fast, funny read." Similarly, a *Publishers Weekly* critic decried the novel's ending as "too pat" but deemed the book "a lark of a read." Jane Sicilliano wrote in *Book Reporter.com* that *Dating Big Bird* is "a hilariously human and touching work."

In her third novel, *Her,* Zigman relates the emotional anguish experienced by a graduate school student when her boyfriend's former girlfriend settles nearby. "Envy," Zigman told a *Booklist* interviewer, "compels you to learn things." *Book* reviewer Susan Tekulve called *Her* an "entertaining, fast-paced book," and *Booklist* critic Kristine Huntley found the novel "captivating." In *Publishers Weekly,* a critic acknowledged *Her* as "a wild tale," while the *Borzoi Reader*'s reviewer hailed Zigman's book as a "smart, deeply satisfying romantic comedy."

A stay-at-home mom reenters the working world in *Piece of Work,* Zigman's 2006 novel. Thirty-six-year-old Julia Einstein, a former publicist for A-list celebrities, happily left her career behind to raise her young son, Leo. When Julia's husband, Peter, loses his high-powered job and cannot find another, she is forced to take a position at John Glom Public Relations, a firm which represents the has-beens of the entertainment industry. Julia's first client is actress Mary Ford, a surly seventy-year-old who hopes to jumpstart her fading career by pedaling "Legend," a foul-smelling perfume. While Julia must shake off the years of rust at the office, Peter proves surprisingly adept at managing the household, forming a strong bond with Leo and displaying exceptional culinary skills. "That Julia finds an antidote for Mary's dwindling fame is predictable," noted a critic in *Publishers Weekly,* "but the process generates its share of chuckles." Karen Core, writing in the *Library Journal,* called Zigman's work "humorous and well-written." *Booklist* contributor Carol Haggas praised the handling of her main character, stating: "Vulnerable yet persistent, Zigman's plucky heroine succeeds through an engaging combination of warmth, wit, and wisdom."

Zigman attributes her development as a novelist, at least in part, to her ability to mislead herself with regard to her own talent. "It takes a long time to trust your voice, to talk yourself in to the idea that you know what you are doing," she told an interviewer in the *Borzoi Reader.* "This is best accomplished, I think, by tricking yourself: you tell yourself what a genius you are even though, deep down, you know you're a giant loser."

In a *BookReporter.com* interview, Zigman conceded: "It's very hard not to be your own personal flesh-eating virus—that is, to self-criticize . . . and self-edit everything that comes out on the page or before it even makes it to the page. It's one of the hardest impulses to

stifle." She added: "You get to a point . . . where you fight this internal war as a matter of course . . . and you learn to accept it's presence and simply ignore it."

BIOGRAPHICAL AND CRITICAL SOURCES:

PERIODICALS

Book, May-June, 2002, Susan Tekulve, review of *Her.*
Booklist, September 15, 1998, Whitney Scott, review of *Animal Husbandry,* p. 249; March 1, 2000, Kristine Huntley, review of *Dating Big Bird,* p. 1148; April 1, 2002, Molly McQuade, "Laura Zigman: From Publicist to Novelist," p. 1305; April 15, 2002, Kristine Huntley, review of *Her,* p. 1384; July 1, 2006, Carol Haggas, review of *Piece of Work,* p. 35.
Entertainment Weekly, February 13, 1998, Lisa Schwarzbaum, review of *Animal Husbandry,* p. 66; June 7, 2002, Karen Valby, "*Her* Again," p. 69.
Kirkus Reviews, July 1, 2006, review of *Piece of Work,* p. 655.
Library Journal, March 15, 2000, Jo Manning, review of *Dating Big Bird,* p. 131; August 1, 2006, Karen Core, review of *Piece of Work,* p. 75.
New York Times Book Review, January 25, 1998, Laura Miller, review of *Animal Husbandry,* p. 23; April 9, 2000, Lori Leibovich, "Procreation Anxiety," review of *Dating Big Bird,* p. 23; November 26, 2006, Elsa Dixler, "Fiction Chronicle," review of *Piece of Work,* p. 18.
Publishers Weekly, March 12, 1998, review of *Animal Husbandry,* p. 29; March 13, 2000, review of *Dating Big Bird,* p. 63; April 15, 2002, review of *Her,* p. 41; July 24, 2006, review of *Piece of Work,* p. 31.
Time, January 26, 1998, Jill Smolowe, review of *Animal Husbandry,* p. 73.
Tribune Books (Chicago, IL), May 13, 2001, review of *Dating Big Bird,* p. 6; August 10, 2003, review of *Her,* p. 6.
Washington Post Book World, February 20, 2000, review of *Dating Big Bird,* p. 3; September 3, 2006, Marie Arana, "Laura Zigman: Just like Life," p. 10; September 24, 2006, Sheri Holman, "Adventures in Babysitting," review of *Piece of Work,* p. 6.

ONLINE

BookReporter.com, http://bookreporter.com/ (July 17, 2002), Jane Sicilliano, review of *Dating Big Bird* and interview with Laura Zigman.

Borzoi Reader Web site, http://randomhouse.com/ (July 17, 2002), "A Conversation with Laura Zigman."

Laura Zigman Home Page, http://www.laurazigman. com (February 5, 2007).*

*   *   *

ZUBRO, Mark Richard

PERSONAL: Male.

ADDRESSES: Home—Mokena, IL. *E-mail*—zubrom@ yahoo.com.

CAREER: Novelist and high school teacher.

MEMBER: Mystery Writers of America.

AWARDS, HONORS: Lambda Award for Gay Men's Mystery, Lambda Literary Foundation, for *A Simple Suburban Murder,* 1989.

WRITINGS:

"TOM AND SCOTT" MYSTERY SERIES

A Simple Suburban Murder, St. Martin's Press (New York, NY), 1989.

Why Isn't Becky Twitchell Dead?, St. Martin's Press (New York, NY), 1990.

The Only Good Priest, St. Martin's Press (New York, NY), 1991.

The Principal Cause of Death, St. Martin's Press (New York, NY), 1992.

An Echo of Death, St. Martin's Press (New York, NY), 1994.

Rust on the Razor, St. Martin's Press (New York, NY), 1996.

Are You Nuts?, St. Martin's Press (New York, NY), 1998.

One Dead Drag Queen, St. Martin's Minotaur (New York, NY), 2000.

Here Comes the Corpse, St. Martin's Minotaur (New York, NY), 2002.

File under Dead, St. Martin's Minotaur (New York, NY), 2004.

Everyone's Dead but Us, St. Martin's Minotaur (New York, NY), 2006.

Hook, Line and Homicide, St. Martin's Minotaur (New York, NY), 2007.

"PAUL TURNER" MYSTERY SERIES

Sorry Now?, St. Martin's Press (New York, NY), 1991.

Political Poison, St. Martin's Press (New York, NY), 1993.

Another Dead Teenager, St. Martin's Press (New York, NY), 1995.

The Truth Can Get You Killed, St. Martin's Press (New York, NY), 1997.

Drop Dead, St. Martin's Press (New York, NY), 1999.

Sex and Murder.com, St. Martin's Minotaur (New York, NY), 2001.

Dead Egotistical Morons, St. Martin's Minotaur (New York, NY), 2003.

Nerds Who Kill, St. Martin's Minotaur (New York, NY), 2005.

SIDELIGHTS: As the author of two well-established mystery series, Mark Richard Zubro has made a name for himself as the creator of crime stories centered on gay characters and as a writer who focuses as much on the personal interests of his protagonists as on the crimes being investigated. Zubro draws upon his own experiences as a high school teacher in his series following the amateur sleuthing of Tom Mason, an ex-Marine and Vietnam veteran who is now a teacher. In the series, Tom investigates with his partner, Scott Carpenter, a professional baseball player who is not openly gay. Zubro also writes stories featuring police detective Paul Turner, who is quiet about his sexual orientation on the job, but repeatedly faces challenges to his don't-ask-don't-tell approach. Both series are often set in Chicago.

In the first Tom Mason mystery, *A Simple Suburban Murder,* a murder reveals that Tom's workplace harbors a variety of vile behaviors. The victim is math teacher Jim Evans, who proves to have been a bookie, blackmailer, and child abuser, as well as part of a homosexual child prostitution ring. Tom begins his own investigation when a former student becomes a suspect and then disappears. Enlisting the help of his lover, Scott Carpenter, Tom begins looking for the boy in gay bars. In the end, they succeed in shutting down the prostitution operation as well as the associated production of snuff movies. Zubro's debut earned mixed reviews that warned of the book's sometimes gruesome subject matter. A *Kirkus Reviews* writer deemed it "seamy yet juiceless." However, *Tribune Books* writer Alice Cromie noted that the "gripping story" is full of "sympathetic characters." Similarly, a *Publishers Weekly* reviewer said the book was "surprisingly entertaining."

The murder of a student sends Tom on his second investigation in *Why Isn't Becky Twitchell Dead?* Tom gets involved when a remedial student is arrested for the murder of his girlfriend. In *The Only Good Priest,* Tom and Scott are asked to look into the death of a Catholic priest who was active in the gay community. Father Sebastian's death by poison seems to be getting inadequate attention from both the church and the police department. Tom's interest increases when his nephew Jerry is kidnapped after overhearing a priest talk about being implicated in the death. Reviewers of *The Only Good Priest* felt that Zubro's criticism of the church got in the way of his story. A *Kirkus Reviews* writer said that the book's events "seem to suggest that most lesbians are thugs and most priests are homosexuals and duplicitous."

According to critics, the next mystery in the series, *The Principal Cause of Death,* was more successful than *The Only Good Priest.* In the story, a school principal's death reveals that he was almost universally disliked. *Booklist* reviewer Charles Harmon called the book "delightful" and commended the fast-moving plot and enjoyable characters. "Anyone who's ever worked in a school will relish the faculty infighting and the gossipmongers," he wrote. A *Kirkus Reviews* critic also commented that "the school politics are dead-on."

The story line in *An Echo of Death* shifts the focus away from Tom's workplace to Scott's career in the major leagues. The lovers find Scott's former teammate, Glen Proctor, dead in their apartment. Their sleuthing leads them on a dangerous chase through Chicago. In *Rust on the Razor,* Scott holds a press conference to announce that he is gay. The couple is about to be interviewed on *Nightline* when Scott's father has a heart attack. They travel to Scott's birthplace in rural Georgia, where most of the Carpenter family is less than thrilled with the news about Scott. But things get much worse when the town's homophobic sheriff is found dead in Tom and Scott's rented car. Reviews of *Rust on the Razor* included praise and consideration of the book's appeal to heterosexual readers. In the *Armchair Detective,*

Mark Terry noted that "Tom's observations about his lover and other attractive men . . . may make even the most open-minded of straights uncomfortable. Which is not necessarily a bad thing." A strongly enthusiastic review in the *Lambda Book Report* came from Richard Auton, who described *Rust on the Razor* as "a pulsing mystery which moves so swiftly there is scant time to ponder the outcome."

The novel *Are You Nuts?* opens after Tom and Scott have completed the summer talk-show circuit discussing Scott's coming out. Exhausted, Scott is less than thrilled when Tom's friend Meg is questioned in connection with the murder of a union figure and Tom naturally becomes involved in the case. In *One Dead Drag Queen,* both Tom and Scott are threatened by an anonymous figure, someone who hates both their homosexuality and Tom's volunteer work at an abortion clinic. The clinic and Tom's truck are bombed, putting him in the hospital in a coma. In *Here Comes the Corpse,* longtime lovers Tom and Scott finally decide to solemnize their relationship and marry in a lavish ceremony. The appearance of uninvited guest Ethan Gahain—Tom's very first lover from high school—threatens to disrupt the ceremony, especially after he claims he urgently needs to talk to Tom. Ethan's mission remains unfulfilled, however, as Tom finds him bleeding and dying in the restroom. A *Kirkus Reviews* critic noted that the book is "a touch more sexually explicit" than previous installments in the series, but *Booklist* reviewer Whitney Scott concluded: "Zubro's fans will cheer just about everything in the new Tom and Scott mystery" novel.

Tom and Scott find themselves targeted for murder while vacationing on a remote Aegean island in *Everyone's Dead But Us,* "a gay take on Christie's *Ten Little Indians,*" remarked a critic in *Kirkus Reviews.* After discovering the dead body of a wealthy resort owner, the pair takes off through a blinding rainstorm to seek help, just as a tremendous explosion rips through the compound, killing a number of the resort's staff and leaving the survivors without power or a means to communicate with the mainland. "While no vessel can make it past the roiling waves," observed *Booklist* critic Whitney Scott, "the corpses pile up amid ugly accusations and uglier I'm-so-rich-you-can't-touch-me attitudes." A *Publishers Weekly* reviewer called *Everyone's Dead But Us* a "smoothly written" mystery.

Officer Paul Turner, the protagonist of Zubro's second mystery series, has chosen to be relatively quiet about his sexual orientation, but it is no secret to his straight partner on the force, Buck Fenwick. The real challenge comes when their investigations deal with gays and homophobes. In the first book of the series, *Sorry Now?,* the daughter of a senator is murdered. The investigation reveals that the senator's son is rumored to be gay and suggests that a radical gay group may be responsible for the girl's death. *Sorry Now?* also introduces Paul as the father of two boys, one with spina bifida, and follows his home life as well as the murder case.

Some critics found Turner to be too nice a guy, even when they did not agree on the book's other attributes. In the *Los Angeles Times Book Review,* Charles Solomon stated that "Zubro describes a comic-strip world where the good characters are too good and the bad ones too bad." A *Kirkus Reviews* critic commented that the book's "calculated, middle-class view" and Turner's quiet, fatherly existence resulted in a work that was "sort of dull, even with murder around the edges." A *Mystery Guide* Web site reviewer called the prose "spare and flat," and identified "descriptions of everyday life" as Zubro's strength. A stronger recommendation was voiced in *Publishers Weekly,* where a critic said that Zubro's "blend of personal and political concerns makes this story compelling and even urgent."

The next installment in the series, *Political Poison,* again puts Turner in the middle of political intrigue. When a University of Chicago professor-turned-alderman is poisoned, his powerful political opponents become murder suspects. In *The Truth Can Get You Killed,* a novel about the death of a homophobic federal judge, Turner's investigation is hampered when an important witness, a gay runaway, is found dead on a Chicago street. In a review for *Booklist,* Charles Harmon recommended the novel to Zubro's fans and called it "the year's best gay mystery to date." A *Kirkus Reviews* writer praised the novel, noting that it "adroitly exposes the limits of [Turner's] uneasily semipublic attitude toward his own sexuality." A *Publishers Weekly* critic observed that the book is "a mystery that focuses as much on the difficulties of being gay in a straight world as it does on the murder of a federal judge."

In *Another Dead Teenager* the detectives are given a case in which two teenage boys have been murdered in a warehouse. They come from prominent Chicago families, which puts added pressure on the detectives to quickly solve the case. In *Drop Dead,* the world of fashion proves to be unfamiliar territory for Turner when he investigates the death of a famous underwear model. Reviewers relished the change of scene for the detective team. A *Kirkus Reviews* writer commented: "Zubro expertly keeps up the flow of deliciously catty rumors and counter-rumors," but concluded that "low-level cop humor and satiric lobs at safe fashion targets" minimized the book's impact. A *Publishers Weekly* critic enjoyed the partners' good-cop and bad-cop interactions and noted: "Turner in particular is attractive enough to make this lightweight mystery worth reading." Whitney Scott commented in *Booklist* that Zubro filled the dialogue with "plenty of zingy one-liners."

In *Sex and Murder.com,* Zubro puts his detectives in another business hot spot, the computer industry. Two highly successful software partners are stabbed to death after competing to see who could attract more sexual partners, gay or straight. In *Dead Egotistical Morons,* murder strikes the teenage heartthrobs of the boy band Boys4U. Turner and Fenwick investigate when band frontman Roger Stendar is found dead—perhaps executed—with a bullet to the head. But Stendar apparently was not the only target. The band's stock of bottled water is contaminated, safety equipment used in the band's performances has been rendered useless, and bullet holes appear in the stage. "Slogging, steady police work, mostly by Paul, reveals not only sordid sexual demands made on the boys but betrayal by someone they most trusted," noted a *Kirkus Reviews* critic. *Booklist* reviewer Whitney Scott remarked that the book is "sure to please and to grow Zubro's fandom."

The detectives investigate murder and mayhem at a science fiction convention in *Nerds Who Kill,* the eighth book in Zubro's series. Muriam Devers, a popular author, is found dead in her hotel room, stabbed to death with a broadsword. Turner grows increasingly alarmed when he recalls that his son, Paul, attended the convention in costume, complete with loincloth and broadsword. In *Nerds Who Kill,* the author "takes gleeful aim at venal writers, editors, publishers and agents," remarked a *Kirkus Reviews* critic.

BIOGRAPHICAL AND CRITICAL SOURCES:

PERIODICALS

Armchair Detective, winter, 1994, Bernard A. Drew, review of *Political Poison,* p. 103; winter, 1997, Mark Terry, review of *Rust on the Razor,* p. 93.

Booklist, April 15, 1992, Charles Harmon, review of *The Principal Cause of Death,* p. 1509; October 1, 1994, Charles Harmon, review of *An Echo of Death,* p. 244; July, 1995, Charles Harmon, review of *Another Dead Teenager,* p. 1865; July, 1996, Charles Harmon, review of *Rust on the Razor,* p. 1811; June 1, 1997, Charles Harmon, review of *The Truth Can Get You Killed,* p. 1668; June 1, 1998, Whitney Scott, review of *Are You Nuts?,* p. 1736; June 1, 1999, Whitney Scott, review of *Drop Dead,* p. 1787; July, 2001, Whitney Scott, review of *Sex and Murder.com,* p. 1990; July, 2002, Whitney Scott, review of *Here Comes the Corpse,* p. 1829; August, 2003, Whitney Scott, review of *Dead Egotistical Morons,* p. 1963; May 15, 2006, Whitney Scott, review of *Everyone's Dead but Us,* p. 29.

Kirkus Reviews, January 15, 1989, review of *A Simple Suburban Murder,* p. 91; February 1, 1990, review of *Why Isn't Becky Twitchell Dead?,* p. 145; February 15, 1991, review of *The Only Good Priest,* p. 218; July 15, 1991, review of *Sorry Now?,* p. 895; March 1, 1992, review of *The Principal Cause of Death,* p. 290; May 15, 1993, review of *Political Poison,* p. 628; July 15, 1995, review of *Another Dead Teenager,* p. 989; June 15, 1996, review of *Rust on the Razor,* p. 863; July 1, 1997, review of *The Truth Can Get You Killed,* pp. 989-990; May 15, 1999, review of *Drop Dead,* p. 759; June 1, 2000, review of *One Dead Drag Queen,* pp. 757-758; June 1, 2002, review of *Here Comes the Corpse,* p. 776; July 15, 2003, review of *Dead Egotistical Morons,* p. 943; May 1, 2005, review of *Nerds Who Kill,* p. 442; May 1, 2006, review of *Everyone's Dead but Us,* p. 517.

Lambda Book Report, March-April, 1995, John L. Myers, review of *An Echo of Death,* p. 48; September, 1996, Richard Auton, review of *Rust on the Razor,* p. 31; November, 1999, Kevin Allman, review of *Drop Dead,* p. 14; fall, 2006, Judith A. Markowtiz, review of *Everyone's Dead but Us,* p. 35.

Library Journal, March 1, 1991, Rex E. Klett, review of *The Only Good Priest,* p. 119; June 1, 1995, Thomas L. Kilpatrick, review of *An Echo of Death,* p. 22.

Los Angeles Times Book Review, December 13, 1992, Charles Solomon, review of *Sorry Now?,* p. 8.

Publishers Weekly, December 2, 1988, review of *A Simple Suburban Murder,* pp. 47-48; November 10, 1989, review of *A Simple Suburban Murder,* p. 58; January 12, 1990, Sybil Steinberg, review of *Why Isn't Becky Twitchell Dead?,* p. 50; February 8, 1991, Sybil Steinberg, review of *The Only Good Priest,* p. 50; July 25, 1991, review of *Sorry Now?,* p. 40; May 10, 1993, review of *Political Poison,* p. 55; September 19, 1994, review of *An Echo of Death,* p. 55; July 10, 1995, review of *Another Dead Teenager,* p. 47; June 10, 1996, review of *Rust on the Razor,* p. 89; June 23, 1997, review of *The Truth Can Get You Killed,* p. 75; May 17, 1999, review of *Drop Dead,* p. 60; June 19, 2000, review of *One Dead Drag Queen,* p. 64; July 30, 2001, review of *Sex and Murder.com,* p. 65; May 15, 2006, review of *Everyone's Dead but Us,* p. 52.

Tribune Books (Chicago, IL), June 11, 1989, Alice Cromie, "Chicago Shows Its Ugly Side in Three Novels Full of Crime," review of *A Simple Suburban Murder,* p. 6.

ONLINE

BookBrowser.com, http://www.bookbrowser.com/ (June 8, 2001), Harriet Klausner, review of *Sex and Murder.com.*

Crescent Blues Book Views Web site, http://www.crescentblues.com/ (October 4, 2004), Stephen Metherell-Smith, review of *Drop Dead.*

Holtzbrinck Publishers Web site, http://www.holtbrinckpublishers.com/ (September 22, 2004), profile of Mark Richard Zubro.

Mystery Guide.com, http://www.mysteryguide.com/ (July 6, 1999), review of *Sorry Now?**